PAGES OF HISTORY
1929 to 1945

Troy Record, The Troy Times
and the Times-Record

Developed under agreement with **Historical Briefs, Inc.,**
Box 629, Sixth Street & Madalyn Ave., Verplanck, NY
10596.

Printed by:
Monument Printers & Lithographer, Inc.
Sixth Street & Madalyn Ave., Verplanck, NY   10596

FOREWORD

Daily journalism has been called "the first rough draft of history." In the pages that follow, you can relive some of the most significant days of 20th century history, as well as the recent history of this community, as told in the pages of Troy's daily newspapers.

Many still remember the momentous years recounted in this book, from the stock market crash in 1929 to the end of World War II in 1945. Others, too young to have experienced those days, will learn of these events as many people then did: by reading pages of the Troy Record, the Troy Times and the Times-Record. As the keeper of the tradition of local journalism that began with our paper's founding in 1896, those of us affiliated with The Record today are pleased to bring you this book.

In addition to historic front pages, we have included samples of pages from inside the newspaper, to show you how our newspaper looked in those days and to remind you of the products available -- and those incredible prices.

It was a difficult era in America. During what came to be known as the Great Depression, fully one-fourth of the national workforce was idle. Desperate men sold apples and pencils on street corners. The stability of state employment cushioned the blow of the Depression in this area, but most families suffered in one way or another, as local factory production slowed and retail volume declined.

Many of those who did not lose their jobs took pay cuts. Workers for this newspaper, for example, received 10 percent less in their pay envelopes. President Herbert Hoover's efforts to spur the economy fizzled, but the inauguration of President Franklin D. Roosevelt in 1933 presented new hope. Prohibition was repealed, public works projects were begun, the work week was shortened and Congress passed the Social Security Act. Full recovery, however, did not begin until the late 1930s.

In 1939, Adolph Hitler's panzer divisions roared across Europe. One nation after another fell, until our neutrality appeared no longer justifiable. The national debate was settled December 7, 1941, when Japanese planes showered bombs on Pearl Harbor. The pages of this newspaper recorded the battles, the losses and the victories of the warring countries. On the homefront, women went to work in defense plants: food, gasoline, tires, nylon stockings and many other items were rationed, and no new cars were made.

Yet throughout these years of turmoil, life carried on in the homes and businesses of this community. People still cared about their neighbors. What happened locally -- such tragedies as fires and floods, such joys as weddings and graduations -- also filled the columns of our newspapers.

Some who read this book will find familiar names -- the famous and nortorious, the friends and neighbors who drew notice in this community. Others will find something new in these old pages.

We present this book to you proudly as a tribute to those years -- a time long past, but, because of the historical record provided by this newspaper, an era never to be forgotten.

Rex Smith
Editor
The Record Newspapers

ACKNOWLEDGMENTS

Thanks to joseph Parker, retired copy editor for The Record and president of the Greenbush Historical Society, for editorial guidance in the preparation of this book, and to Gene Baxter, a retired photographer for The Record, for the cover photograph and other photos used in this volume.

COVER DESIGN BY

John Helton

THE WEATHER.
Tonight—Rain.
Tomorrow—Rain.

THE EVENING TROY RECORD

FINAL EDITION

SERIES 1929—NO. 247. WHOLE NUMBER 9305. (Entered as Second Class Matter at the Postoffice at Troy, N. Y., under the Act of Mar. 3, 1879.) TROY, N. Y., MONDAY, OCTOBER 21, 1929. (Published Daily Except Sunday.) PRICE THREE CENTS

NOTABLES GATHER TO HONOR EDISON

Prices Gyrate Wildly in Feverish Trading on Stock Exchange

8,000,000 SHARE DAY SEEN, TICKER 75 MINUTES SLOW

Powerful Support, Thrown Into Market at Opening, Quickly Withdrawn in Flood of Selling.

New York, Oct. 21 (AP).—The stock market was subjected to one of the most overpowering selling movements in its history today. Both the New York Stock and Curb Exchange tickers fell more than 75 minutes behind the breath-taking pace of trading, as leading shares tumbled $5 to $35. The enormous turnover of stock promised to approximate, if not surpass, the March 26 record on the stock Exchange of 8,246,740 shares.

Repeated efforts were made by powerful interests to support the market, but they met with little success until after scores of issues had broken $5 to $35 a share, many to new lows for the year. The selling represented an enormous liquidation of weakened margin accounts, and unloading by discouraged traders who have felt keenly the sharp declines of the past six weeks. Selling orders poured into the market from all parts of the country and from abroad.

Auburn Auto tumbled $35 to a price of $340, which contrasts with its high point of the year of $514. The utilities, many of which are now selling from $20 to $100 or more under their peak prices reached in early September, were conspicuously weak. Such issues as American Water Works, American Power and Light, North American, Electric Investors, Pacific Lighting, Standard Gas and Electric, and Stone and Webster dropped $6 to $14.

General Electric, which opened more than $4 higher, soon showed a net loss of more than $12. U. S. Steel, Youngstown Sheet and Tube, Republic Steel, Atchison, Pere Marquette, Radio, National Biscuit, National Biscuit, National Cash Register and Allied Chemical were among shares dropping from $4 to $10.

Cities Service, which has climbed steadily on the curb during recent months from about $28 to above $68, opened with a block of 80,000 shares, one of the largest transactions in the history of the market, a little above $65, but soon sagged to around $60.

DIVORCEE KILLED IN MYSTERY FALL AT BOAT CLUB HOP

Washington, Oct. 21 (AP).—Edmund J. McBrien of New York City was regarded as the principal witness at a corner's inquest today into the death of Mrs. Aurelia F. Dreyfuss, 29, a New York divorcee, after a mysterious fall from an upper porch of the Potomac Boat Club.

Mrs. Dreyfuss, the former wife of Herbert Dreyfuss, a New York broker, died several hours after the fall and McBrien, who says he is a broker, was held incommunicado by the police for today's inquest.

McBrien's story is that Mrs. Dreyfuss, her brother William, her sister Freda, and himself were chatting on the porch near the end of a dance at the boat club on Saturday night. William and Freda left them and a few minutes later he excused himself to gather up their wraps.

While he was gone, he told the police, some one called that a woman had fallen from the porch and a few minutes later she was identified as Mrs. Dreyfuss. She died some time later at a Washington hospital. McBrien voluntarily gave himself up to the police.

YOUTHFUL LAWYERS "MUST BE ETHICAL"

Memphis, Tenn., Oct. 21 (AP).—The young lawyer, if he accepts the ethics of the profession as set forth by the American Bar Association, must hang out his shingle and while the ink is drying on his sheepskin, sit behind his new desk and wait for his clients to come in. He must not go after them.

If he solicits business, he positively is not ethical, the Committee of Professional Ethics and Grievances of the association says.

Thomas Francis Howe, chairman of the committee, believes "the failure of the leading law schools to make it compulsory for the young student to study ethics with his other class work is regrettable." His committee recommends that the Association of American Law Schools make the question of professional ethics a part of the curriculum.

WIDOW KILLS SELF IN WRITER'S ROOM

Chicago, Oct. 21 (AP).—Mrs. Marguerite C. King, 38, a widow, killed herself early today in the hotel room of Parke Brown, political writer of the Chicago Tribune. She shot herself twice in the breast with a .22 calibre pistol belonging to Brown.

Brown told police that he had known Mrs. King, who came from Grant's Pass, Ore., for about two years and that they had quarreled a fortnight ago.

EX-PREMIER DIES.

Berlin, Oct. 21 (AP).—Vassili Radoslavoff, former Bulgarian premier and Liberal leader, died in a Berlin hospital today after an illness of six months.

Appointed

JOSEPH T. ROBINSON.

PRESIDENT RAPS FLORIDA LEADER'S POLITICAL PLEA

Good Government, Not Patronage, Is Responsible for Success of Republican Party, He Says.

Washington, Oct. 21 (AP).—President Hoover in reply to a protest from Florida over the appointment of a Federal attorney has announced it is the duty of the Chief Executive to make selections on the basis of public service and not for political reasons.

The letter, made public at the White House today, was in reply to a communication from Fred E. Britten, secretary of the Republican party in Florida, on the appointment of Federal District Attorney Hughes. It asserted the Florida secretary and other Republican leaders in that state had overlooked the "primary responsibility" incumbent on the Chief Executive "to appoint men to public office who will execute the laws of the United States with integrity and without fear, favor or political collusion."

letter said olwasta -8o-

"I note your demand," the letter said, "that the organization shall dictate appointments in Florida irrespective of merit or my responsibility and that you appealed to the opponents of the administration to attack me. The success of the Republican party rests upon good government, not on patronage."

AIR MAIL PILOT LEAPS 1,000 FEET

Pittsburg, Oct. 21 (AP).—Tucking his mail bag under his arm, Harry Seivers, pilot of the Pittsburg-Cleveland air mail route, leaped in his parachute 1,000 feet to safety as his plane crashed in a field near Beaver Falls early today.

Sievers was flying from Bettis Field here to Cleveland when his motors stopped. Seizing the lone bag of mail, he leaped. The plane was demolished. Sievers took the mail to the postoffice in Beaver Falls and arrangements were made to transfer it to another plane.

REED, ROBINSON TO REPRESENT U. S. AT ARMS PARLEY

Secretary Stimson Announces Appointment of Two Senators in Behalf of President Hoover.

Washintgon, Oct. 21 (AP).—Secretary Stimson announced today on behalf of President Hoover that Senators Reed of Pennsylvania and Robinson of Arkansas have accepted posts as members of the American delegation to the London Arms parley in January.

The Secretary said Chairman Borah of the Senate Foreign Relations Committee had been asked by President Hoover to serve on the American commission but had found it impossible to accept.

It is possible, the Secretary added, that the selection of the other members of the American delegation, which is expected to comprise five or six delegates, will be deferred until more is known of the general situation to be expected at the discussions.

Commenting on the forthcoming arrival here of the Japanese delegation to the London conference, Stimson said he had informed the Tokyo government he would be glad to confer with its delegation in Washington before they proceed to London.

The Secretary explained the reason for their trip to London by way of the American continent was due to delays on the trans-Siberian Railway on account of the Chinese-Soviet difficulties in Manchuria.

Reed Choice Surprise.

The choice of Senator Reed was looked upon somewhat as a surprise, but it is believed to have been determined upon by the chief executive after conferences with Senate Republican leaders including Chairman Borah of the foreign relations committee, and Senator Watson of Indiana, the party leader.

Senator Robinson has been generally regarded as the logical representative of the minority party. In addition to being the Democratic leader in the Senate he is a member of the foreign relations and naval committees. Also, he was the Democratic vice presidential nominee in the last camaign. Should he be unable to go, Senator Swanson of Virginia, is regarded as an alternative.

In these two senators, Mr. Hoover would have two staunch national defense advocates on his delegation as well as two of the most convincing debaters in the Senate if a treaty of naval limitations is brought before that body for ratification.

Voted Cruiser Bill.

Both senators voted for and advocated the 15 cruiser bill which was passed last session. Senator Reed, who is a veteran of the World War, also is chairman of the military affairs committee.

Moreover, he is a member of the foreign relations committee.

After consulting with Chairman Borah of this committee, Mr. Hoover did not go down the line in rank of Republicans on the foreign relations committee. Reed ranks sixth. Senator Johnson of California, is second.

Both Senators Robinson and Reed voted for and urged the ratification of the Kellogg anti-war treaty last session. As members of the foreign relations committee they have taken an active part in international relations.

Suggested Sinking Ships.

Whether a place on the delegation was offered to Senator Borah is unknown. It is believed, however, that Senator Borah made his position clear to the President along with an intimation that he preferred not to leave America.

The Idahoan did not vote for the 15 cruiser bill and has determinedly advocated that Great Britain go on record for freedom of the seas—a delicate point with that proud maritime nation. At the outset of the negotiations between President Hoover and Prime Minister MacDonald over naval limitations, Senator Borah suggested that Great Britain sink some of her battleships as a means of getting on a parity with this country.

FRENCH FLIERS ARRIVE.

Shanghai, China, Oct. 21 (AP).—The French long distance fliers Dieudonne Coste and Maurice Bellonte arrived here today from Mukden, Manchuria. The aviators went to Mukden after establishing a new long distance record, flying from Le Bourget across Europe and Siberia to Manchuria.

20 Hurt When Church Factions Stage Riot

Evanston, Ill., Oct. 21 (AP).—The internal troubles of the Mount Zion Baptist Church, Negro, reached the razor stage yesterday Three deacons were seriously injured. One, Samuel Sanders, was slashed across the neck and may die. Twenty members of the congregation were cut and bruised.

Three persons were arrested, including the pastor, the Rev. G. A. Long and Simon Matthews and Alex Cob[illegible], deacons. Should the wounded Sanders die, police said charges of murder would be made against the three.

For a year there has been trouble between one faction of the church and the pastor. Yesterday's meeting was under a court order which called upon the church to hold an election before November 4 to determine whether Long should continue as a pastor.

G. W. Gibson, a deacon expelled a year ago, began heckling the pastor and demanding reinstatement. Deacon Matthews pushed forward and told Gibson to sit down. Blows were exchanged and soon the meeting had divided into two sides, one backing Gibson, the others supporting Matthews and the Pastor. Chairs were used as clubs and projectiles. Razors flashed.

Five squads of policemen were required to break up the battle which spread to the church yard and blocked traffic as motorists stopped to watch the fight.

NEWS NUGGETS

BY THE ASSOCIATED PRESS

New York—Following the hounds is second nature to four-year-old Harry Payne Whitney 11. The son of Cornelius Vanderbilt Whitney and grandson of Harry Payne Whitney, both notable horsemen, he already sits his mount like a veteran.

London—British imperturbability perturbs Mme. Aino Kallas, novelist wife of the minister of Estonia. Her greatest ambition she writes, is to see a "really angry Englishman."

New York—Gwendolyn McCormack, attractive daughter of John McCormack, tenor, prefers riding horses and playing golf. She has never sung a note, and furthermore, she doesn't intend to train.

Moscow—A new member in the family of nations, is the Tadjik autonomous republic. Independent for the first time in centuries, about 1,000,000 Tadjiks, living between China and Afghanistan, form the seventh allied republic in the Soviet Union.

New York—A flying ambulance service, to carry invalids and their doctors between New York and any point in the country at any hour, has been established.

Havana—Drenched by torrential rains, this city has not seen the sun for 15 days.

New York—Twenty-one years after she climbed 28,812 feet to the snowclad summit of Mt. Huascara, in Peru, Miss Annie S. Peck plans a plane trip over the Andes. "I am still young and lively," she says.

Mexico City — An artillery shell that didn't explode for Pancho Villa did so when a small boy hit it with a hammer. His father had dug up in the yard. The explosion killed both.

New York—In his floating home, the brigantine Mopelia, Count Felix Von Luckner would like to take a party of good fellows to Africa for an elephant hunt. "One elephant would keep us alive for months," he says. "What do you think the beast grows 40 years for? Why, to make good eating."

Berlin—A new world's glider duration flight record is claimed for Lieutenant Dinort. He kept his glider in the air for 14 hours, 45 minutes at Rossitten, East Prussia.

Washington—There will be lots of turkey for Thanksgiving. Department of Agriculture economists expect a supply nine per cent. larger than last year.

Chicago.—Street cleaners and garbage collectors were on strike today, contending their pay was too small and that they were not given enough work. Realizing the menace to the city's health, efforts were being made at conferences today to effect an immediate settlement.

Chicago.—James Meers has made the startling discovery that golf knickers may look like a balloon, but aren't. Meers, who is 66 years old, put on a pair of plus-fours and went out with the boys early yesterday. The conversation turned to aviation and Meers had an idea. Inflate the knickers, he figured, and the wearer would float through space or upon the surface of waters. With his companions he adjourned to a filling station and the plus fours were pumped full of air. The boys then went to the roof of a small building on the Chicago River bank and Meers jumped. Policemen pulled him out.

London.—A dispatch to the Daily Express from Brussels today said a Roman Catholic priest, flying from Antwerp to Ghent Saturday, pronounced absolution for the dying on behalf of his 11 fellow passengers. The plane's carburetor took fire and the 11, believing they were doomed, besought absolution of the priest; he readily complied. While he recited the solemn words the pilot carried on in growing peril and finally landed his plane safely.

Bellingham, Wash.—Ed Mills, a contractor, was killed yesterday when he jumped from a plane with a parachute which failed to open. It was Mills' first attempt at parachute jumping.

Havana—Senorita Julia Abalo Y Bartlet will be married by proxy on November 7 to John Dorland Y Nieto, chancellor of the Cuban consulate in New York. He will be represented at the religious ceremony in the old Iglesia Parroquia De Vedado by Dr. Miguel Abalo, brother of the bride. The civil ceremony will take place the following day. The bride will then join her husband in New York.

New York—The siege of 429 West 23rd Street has brought Mrs. Tille Hart, the besieged, moral support from hundreds of visitors but it resulted in the ruination of her garden. Several hundred persons, many of them carrying cameras, yesterday visited the Hart home, the only building remaining to prevent the Henry Mandel Associates from constructing a big apartment hotel on the block. They took pictures and greeted every appearance of Mrs. Hart with bursts of applause. But when the day was over and she surveyed her garden it was a wreck. Flowers, benches, shrubs, and almost everything portable had been taken by souvenir hunters.

Roosevelt Field—Pie loving employes of Roosevelt Field were slightly embarrassed yesterday when Col. Charles A. Lindbergh paid a visit and had to be told of the arrival and consumption last week of a gift of mince pie intended for the Colonel. The Colonel expressed his familiarity with customs of flying fields relative to incoming and edible gifts and will make known his enjoyment, by proxy, of the pie by sending an autograph photograph to its maker, Mrs. Elisabeth Gartner, of Lawrence, N. Y.

SENATE TAKES UP RATE SCHEDULES OF TARIFF BILL

Only Proposal of Senator Thomas to Recommit Measure Delays Consideration.

Washington, Oct. 21 (AP)—A motion to return the Tariff Bill to the Finance Committee with instructions to limit revision to farm products was made in the Senate today by Senator Thomas, Democrat, Oklahoma.

The proposal would instruct the committee to strike out all rate changes except those relating to agriculture in general, sugar and tobacco. It would leave the way open, however, for individual senators to offer amendments to the industrial schedules when the measure again came up on the floor.

Discussion started at once.

Washington, Oct. 21 (AP).—Replete with controversies, the rate schedules of the Tariff Bill today absorbed the attention of a Senate already torn by the dissensions of the measure's administrative provisions.

Meanwhile, there was a careful watch for signs of a split in the ranks of the Democratic-Independent Republican coalition which has opposed repeatedly and successfully the legislative meneuvers of the administration Republicans, notably in eliminating the flexible provisions desired by President Hoover and in inserting the export debenture farm relief plan, which the Chief Executive had denounced in no uncertain terms.

Only the proposal of Senator Thomas, Democrat, Oklahoma, to recommit the measure with instructions that it be reported back with a revision upward only for agricultural products remains to be acted upon before the 15 rate schedules and the free list come up for consideration.

Coalition Moves Unknown.

Last reports over the week-end were that the Oklahoma Senator would press his motion despite the lack of organized support for it at this time. A similar move by Senator Borah of Idaho, a leader of the Republican independents opposing the measure in its present form, lost by a single vote last June.

What the Democratic-Western Republican coalition, which eliminated from the bill the flexible provisions desired by President Hoover and inserted the export debenture opposed by the President, expects to accomplish in the rate contest is, generally speaking, the highest protection possible for farm commodities and a lowering of industrial duties.

Say Rates Acceptable.

Republican leaders contend the bill as it now stands on rates is far more acceptable to the President, who recommended a limited revision, than the House measure. They foresee a breaking of the coalition lines on the schedule.

Senator Borah, however, is confident the coalition is strong enough to write the rates it wants and has served notice that if this is not accomplished at the special session it would be at the regular session starting in December, despite the feeling that Mr. Hoover would not recommend tariff revision if the pending bill was deadlocked in conference when the December meeting got under way.

The Senate has a herculean task on its hands to pass the bill on a date that would permit ample time for conferees to adjust differences before the regular session.

While there is a desire on the part of some Democrats and Western Republicans to take up the agriculture schedule first in the Senate, it is believed these sections will be considered in their numerical order with chemicals, oils and paints coming up first. The agriculture schedule is number seven in the bill.

Expect Five Hundred Amendments.

While the sugar discussion is a long way off, the week-end was not without a mention of the subject. Junior Owens, secretary of the American bottlers of carbonated beverages, issued a statement saying the price of Cuban raws at New York had jumped to within five points of the 64 hundredths of a cent increase in tariff proposed by the House since June 13, two weeks after the House bill passed.

On June 13 the price was 1.69 cents, while today it is 2.28, he said.

Approximately five hundred amendments to the House rates have been reported by the finance committee. These must be disposed of before individual amendments are offered. Hundreds of these are in preparation, Senator Brookhart, Republican, Iowa, alone having one hundred to propose to the agriculture schedule.

Six weeks remain in the special session for this work to be completed.

CROWN PRINCE OF ITALY WILL MARRY BELGIAN PRINCESS

Rome, Oct. 21 (AP).—The engagement of Crown Pirnce Humbert of Italy to Princess Marie Jose of Belgium will be officially announced on October 24, the anniversary of the marriage of the King and Queen of Italy.

Brussels, Belgium, Oct. 21 (AP).—Crown Prince Humbert of Italy is expected in Brussels on Wednesday with the object of obtaining the consent of King Albert and Queen Elizabeth to marry Princess Marie Jose.

Honored For His Inventions

(C.) Bachrach

THOMAS ALVAH EDISON.

HUGE FLYING BOAT SETS RECORD WITH 169 PERSONS IN AIR

12-Engined DO-X Makes Amazing One-hour Flight Over Lake Constance in Switzerland.

Altenrhein, Switzerland, Oct. 12 (AP).—DO-X, huge 12-engined flying boat which was launched here last July, today made an amazing one-hour flight with a human load of 169 persons, the first time in the history of aviation that so many persons have been carried into the air on any conveyance.

The giant Dornier plane took off at 11:15 a. m. and landed just one hour later. The machine flew over Lake Constance, her motors working faultlessly, and landed with her 51-ton load at 12:15 p. m. without a hitch.

The DO-X carried 159 passengers and a crew of ten. She had made previous test flights but this was the first time that so great a load was taken up.

The flying boat, which may be used for a trans-Atlantic crossing for the purpose of trying out her capacities, was built in the greatest secrecy. She was designed to carry forty passengers normally but has accommodation for 100 if necessary. Her 12 engines can develop a total of 6,000 horsepower and each can be treated individually without affecting its neighbors.

The DO-X measures 150 feet from tip to tail. Its wings are 10 feet thick and 150 feet from wing top to wing tip. Six great turrets project from each wing and each turret is equipped with two engines of 500 horsepower. The turrets are manned by mechanics who can walk along a passage on the inside of the wings from one turret to another.

$200,000 DAMAGE IN WORCESTER FIRE

Worcester, Mass., Oct. 21 (AP).—One fireman is dead, a dozen others are in a serious condition and several more were less seriously injured in a fire which destroyed a warehouse block in the downtown section this morning. Four alarms were sounded, calling out all available fire fighting apparatus in Worcester.

Lieut. Carl R. Swenson was killed when a wall toppled on a dozen firemen who were within the building.

Damage was estimated at $200,000.

FATHER AND SIX CHILDREN KILLED BY ESCAPING GAS

Pan of Water Believed to Have Boiled Over, Extinguishing Fire Underneath While Family Slept.

New York, Oct. 21 (AP).—A father and six motherless children were asphyxiated by illuminating gas as they slept in their three-room apartment on West 46th Street yesterday.

Police found a pan of water on a kitchen stove which apparently had boiled over, extinguishing the flame and permitting the gas to flow into the rooms.

The bodies were discovered by Samuel Brisnick, a neighbor, when he went to the apartment to tell the father, Walter Cavenagh, a private chauffeur, that his employer had called him on the telephone.

Brisnick found Cavenagh, 42, Ethel, 17; Catherine, 15; Rose, 13; Thomas, 11; George, 9 and Walter, Jr., 8, dead when, unable to arouse the family, he climbed a fire escape and entered through a window.

All were in their beds except Ethel, who was lying on the floor, indicating she had attempted to reach a window or door before she collapsed.

Six prayer books and rosaries were found laid out under the picture of the mother in readiness for the children to attend mass.

Ethel kept house for her father and cared for the younger children. An older daughter, Mary, 20, who lived away from home is the only survivor in the family, the mother died seven years ago.

THREE KILLED WHEN GUARD AT CROSSING LEAVES HIS POST

Penn Yan, Oct. 21 (AP).—Two boys and a girl were instantly killed in a Pennsylvania railroad grade crossing accident here at 1:30 a. m. today. They are Kenneth Parry, 17, and John Entz, 18, both of Seneca Castle, six miles west of Geneva, and Miss Helen Stanhope, 20, of Penn Yan.

The crossing, with gates up, was temporarily unprotected when the light sedan carrying the three ran on the tracks in the path of a fast southbound freight train, according to acting Coroner William G. Halstead, who is holding an inquest.

The coroner said George Hazard, crossing tender, admitted he had left his post for a short time and was away at the time of the accident.

Poincare Undergoes His Second Operation

Paris, Oct. 21 (AP).—Raymond Poincare, former French president and premier, underwent an operation for a pelvic disorder today, the second he has had in recent months for his trouble.

M. Poincare's physicians issued the following bulletin:

"The second operation on President Poincare was performed this morning under good conditions by Dr. Marion, with the assistance of Drs. Gosset, Boivin, and Perard."

The former Premier was in the best of spirits when he was taken to the operating room. He laughed as he told his doctors he did not want all the bedside details of illness broadcast.

"I don't want the newspapers discussing the color of my pajamas, or the form of my bedsocks," he told them.

The first visitor to inquire the result of the operation and inscribe his name in the new visitor's book was Aristide, Briand, who followed M. Poincare as head of the French government. Other members of the government and notables came after him.

At the same time George Clemenceau, former Premier and Minister of War, was under the treatment of his physicians, who found him suffering [illegible] the past few days.

They prescribed an application of ventouses or heated glass cups which have the same effect as mustard plasters.

PRESIDENT HOOVER RECEIVES OVATION IN DETROIT DRIVE

Ford Estimated to Have Spent $2,800,000 for Celebration; 600 To Attend Dinner.

Detroit, Oct. 21 (AP).—In a setting that contrasted early American life with the present, a group of the nation's notables came today to pay tribute to Thomas A. Edison on the fiftieth anniversary of his perfection of the incandescent electric lamp. Most of the ceremonies were held in the early American village reconstructed by Henry Ford at Dearborn, but throughout the city the picture of Edison featured the decorations in honor of the inventor.

Heading the group of notables who came to do honor to Edison was President Hoover, who was to be the guest of Henry Ford, but planning to make a public appearance in Detroit. The president will be the principal speaker at a dinner tonight formally dedicating the new Edison Institute of Technology in the historical village. The President's address as well as the remarks of several others will be broadcast over the largest radio hookup ever attempted.

$2,800,000 Spent for Party.

Although the ceremonies formally celebrated Edison's perfection of the incandescant lamp, the celebration actually was a huge "party" arranged by Mr. Ford for his friend "Tom" Edison. Seemingly no item of expense or effort had been spared by Ford to make the "party" a complete success in every detail. Estimates of the cost of the celebration run as high as $2,800,000 virtually all of which will be met by Mr. Ford.

As an added feature of the ceremonies tonight, Mr. Edison, after returning from the laboratory where he will re-enact the perfection of the lamp, will touch a button that will light a large beacon in East Orange, N. J. The beacon is to stand as a perpetual monument to himself on the original site of his laboratory where the incandescent lamp was born. The beacon is a tribute to Edison by the Edison pioneers who worked with him in the early days.

The beacon is an enormous bulb 17 feet high, inside of which are 600 incandescent lamps.

Receives Ovation.

Through a driving rain and biting wind, President Hoover with the First Lady beside him drove for 12 miles today in an open automobile from Dearborn to this city to greet thousands of people who jammed the plaza in front of the City Hall.

The purpose of the visit was to receive an official welcome from Gov. Fred W. Green and Mayor John C. Lodge but it gave the people of Detroit their opportunity to glimpse a president for the time in more than a decade.

Throughout the long drive the President's car passed through an almost solid lane of humanity lining both sides of beautiful Oakwood Boulevard. Men, women and children were heedless of the elements as they strained to get a view of the President and Mrs. Hoover, nor was the rain sufficient to dampen their enthusiasm.

All along the line the Chief Executive received an ovation, with the crowds cheering and automobile horns, bells and clappers adding to the din. At some places cadets of Detroit high schools with their colors were drawn up at attention and at others little school children waved tiny American flags as they screamed their welcome.

President Hoover Arrives.

The President and Mrs. Hoover were greeted at the River Rouge transfer station on their arrival this morning by Mr. and Mrs. Ford and Mr. and Mrs. Edison. They boarded the Ford train, a reproduction of an old train of the Grand Trunk Railroad, for Smith's Creek Station at the entrance of the early American village, constructed here for Mr. Ford.

The day was one of inspections and greetings, including a motor drive to Detroit for a reception at the City Hall by Governor Green and Mayor Lodge, with a noonday luncheon, an inspection of the Rouge plant of the Ford Company and the Edison buildings, gifts of Mr. Ford in the cause of science.

Distinguished Guests.

At Smith's Creek Station, Mr. and Mrs. Hoover received the distinguished guests who had been invited here by Mr. Ford for the Golden Jubilee Celebration. They included Owen D. Young, chairman of the board of the General Electric Company; John D. Rockefeller, Jr.; Governor Green and several others. They will attend the dinner at which 600 are to be present tonight.

Deferring an inspection until later in the day, the President and

(Continued on Page 20.)

MAN KILLED WHEN REPRIMAND IRKS

New Brunswick, N. J., Oct. 21 (AP).—William Geipel, Jr., 24 years old, was knifed to death in a grocery store at midnight by a man he reprimanded for profanity in the presence of a girl clerk.

Police held Angeles Casttumato, 38, the father of four children, as the slayer. The killing occurred in the store of Edward Fitzgerald.

ZAHAROFF ILL.

Paris, Oct. 21 (AP).—It was learned today [illegible] Zaharoff, international banker, was suffering from a slight illness, but it was denied at his residence his condition was as serious as reported in some Paris newspapers.

THE WEATHER.
Tr... ...r
Tomorrow...F...

THE TROY EVENING RECORD

FINAL EDITION

SERIES 1028—NO. 250.
WHOLE NUMBER 8508.

(Entered as Second Class Matter at the Postoffice
at Troy, N. Y., under the Act of Mar. 3, 1879)

TROY, N. Y., THURSDAY, OCTOBER 24, 1929.

PRICE THREE CENTS

SELLING FLOOD SWAMPS STOCK MART

Albert B. Fall $100,000 Bribery Case Placed in Hands of Jury

PRESIDENT ESCAPES RAILROAD WRECK

New York—The five best dressed men in the country, in the opinion of Dr. Orcella Rexford, woman psychologist, are: Mayor Walker of New York; O. O. McIntyre, writer; Archibald Klumph, Cleveland banker, and Conde Nast, New York publisher.

Philadelphia — George Page, a farmer of Newport, N. J., has got rid of a bullet that lodged in the side of him for 32 years. He was shot by a burglar and since then numerous attempts to remove the bullet failed because of its inaccessible position. It has finally been taken from the anterior portion of the chest. Page is 52 years old.

Stockholm—Most Swedes are good brothes. Several prisons have closed because of lack of patronage. At last tally the total bocescow population of the country was 1,953.

New York—Thea Rasche, aviatrix, has gone abroad without her purse. It dropped into the water while she was leaning over the rail of the liner Resolute waving goodbye to friends.

Paris—Now come oil wells to supply water in a desert. A device of M. Knapen, an engineer, is being tested in Northern Africa. The idea is that air will condense when striking a monster perforated earthenware well shaped like a cup upside and making cooling drafts. M. Knapen says that Theodosia in Crimea, 500 B. C., built air wells that gave the city 2,500 barrels of water a day.

New York—It cost Bob Shawkey $21 to get a telegram informing him that he had been picked as manager of the Yankees. The club sent it collect to the wilds of Canada. Bob had to pay Indian guides, the owner of a sleigh and then some.

Budapest—Because Bessenyei College have worked in vacation and after school hours in order to publish an edition of Bessenyei's poems glorifying the chivalry of Hunyadi Janos, legendary hero of Hungary. They typed out the original manuscript of the unpublished epic in a monastery and worked in the markets and saved from their lunch and carfare allowances in order to pay for the printing of 1,000 copies.

Ossining—Three hundred newspapers are delivered daily to subscribers at Sing Sing, the population of which is 1,953.

New York—Lloyd W. Seamon, who retired from the New York Stock Exchange 21 years ago, was virtually unknown to his expert to brokers and a few friends. In death he has evoked considerable attention by his will, which leaves $5,-000,000, five-sixths of his estate, to charity. Two hospitals receive $1,000,000 each.

New York—A radio broadcasting demonstration with a voice reproduced by an artificial larynx was made yesterday at a luncheon of the Electrical Association of New York. A human broadcast from an airplane flying 2,500 feet above New Brunswick, N. J., related the details of broadcasting development. Serguis P. Grace, assistant vice president of the Bell Laboratories, then communicated with the plane with the artificial larynx. It was said to have been the first time an artificial voice was broadcast.

New York—Six days ago New York was the first direct airmail from Argentina landed in New York completing letters which were posted in Buenos Aires October 15. Heretofore the fastest mail time between the Argentine capital and New York has been 18 days.

Washington—The coming winter may see the United States government, through some one of its many agencies, attracting and supporting the millions of its citizens whose evening pastime is provided by the radio. Commissioner La-Mount, who since he became a member of the Radio Commission has been a strong advocate of better programs, announced today that he intended to sponsor a motion in the commission which if adopted would have the government, preferably through the Radio Commission, broadcast a program on which comment would be asked from listeners.

DANISH FINANCIER COMMITS SUICIDE

Copenhagen, Oct. 24 (AP)—Harald Plum, financier and promoter, was found shot this morning at about the same time the Folkenbanken, with which one of his firms had done business, failed to open its doors. Police said he shot himself. Folkenbanken closed its doors today and suspended payment of several million kroner through engagements with two commercial firms, one of which was said to be the Crown Butter Company, with which Plum was connected.

HEAVY AUTO TAKEN FROM TRACK WITH TRAIN DUE SOON

Negroes Alleged to Have Admitted Plot to Collect Damages for Car's Destruction.

New Albany, Ind., Oct. 24 (AP)—An alleged plot which would have involved President Hoover's special train in a wreck with a heavy sedan five miles north of here was thwarted last night by three men who removed the obstruction from the Baltimore and Ohio tracks about an hour before the train arrived.

The train was halted for 15 minutes while Secret Service men and railroad detectives started an investigation which resulted several hours later in the arrest of two Negros who confessed, according to officers, that they placed the automobile on the tracks in a plot to collect damages for its destruction.

The sedan was placed on the tracks on a steep grade, and was discovered by Enoch Keller, a Negro who had gone to the crossing in the hope of seeing the President as his train passed.

Keller called Edward Hopson, a farmer, and the two, with the assistance of a motorist, George Weir, of Jeffersonville, Ind., removed the machine.

The engineer stopped the train some distance down the track, and the Secret Service men and railroad detectives disembarked. They called in government and local officers from Louisville, New Albany and Jeffersonville.

Through the license plates the automobile was traced to Charles W. Bullock, 19, and John Edward Wright, 43, Negroes. Officers said they admitted that Burdock had placed the car on the tracks and that Wright, who bought it recently for $500, had paid $25 for doing so.

The Negroes were held in jail here, but no charges had been slated against them at noon today.

President Speeding Back to Washington

President's Train, Oct. 24 (AP)—President Hoover was speeding back to Washington today aboard his luxurious special after three (Continued on Page 14)

SARATOGIAN WINS COURT OF APPEALS ACTION FOR $1,000

The Court of Appeals yesterday handed down a decision upholding the action of the Supreme Court and the Appellate Division thereof in awarding $1,000 damages to Tunis R. Thomas against the racing association for the improvement of the Breed of Horses. Mr. Thomas' action against the racing association was a test case and was contested vigorously by the association, as it establishes the liability of the association for injuries to persons attending the races.

Mr. Thomas was kicked by a horse at the race track on September 2, 1927. He was rendered unconscious and was taken to the Saratoga Hospital where he remained five days. He brought suit against the association in Supreme Court and was awarded $1,000 damages. The defendant appealed to the Appellate Division of the Supreme Court, which upheld the action of the trial term. The association then carried the case to the highest court in the state, the Court of Appeals which has now ruled in favor of the plaintiff.

FLIGHT COMPLETED.

Friedrichshafen, Germany, Oct. 24, (AP)—The dirigible Graf Zeppelin, completing a two days' flight to Spain, landed safely at Friedrichshafen this afternoon.

Father Hunted After Gas Wipes Out Five of Family

Hamilton, Ohio, Oct. 24 (AP)—Charles King, Sr., a 36-year-old barber, was sought today to explain the death of his wife, Sarah Ethel, four of his children and the probable fatal illness of another child.

Robert, 14, Leon, 12, and Keith 5, were found dead from inhaling gas by neighbors who broke open the door of the unpretentious two-story home of the King family Thursday. Paul, 10, died in a hospital last night and his mother early today. Paul, 4, would not live.

King disappeared, leaving an enigmatic note which said three Coldwater, Ohio, men "caused me to do this." He did not explain the statement and the only inkling of a motive was the information that the barber sought today or owed money to one of the trio.

King had not returned to his barber shop since Saturday night. Yesterday, neighbors smelled gas coming from his home and forced an entrance. The five children and their mother were placed for many hours in beds. The top had been taken off a gas pipe. Coroner Edward C. Cook said he believed King removed the cap while his family slept.

In the family automobile, the Coroner found the King's auto with clothes and a partly-emptied bottle of liquor.

FIVE KILLED.

Nuremberg, Germany, Oct. 24—Five persons were killed and seven seriously injured in the collision of two passenger trains near Reichelsdorf today.

King will be charged with murder if found, the coroner said.

Escapes Death

PRINCE HUMBERT

ITALIAN PRINCE ESCAPES DEATH FROM ASSASSIN

One of Own Countrymen Fires at Humbert During Ceremony in Brussels Street.

Brussels, Belgium, Oct. 24 (AP)—Crown Prince Humbert of Italy, affianced husband of Princess Marie Jose of Belgium narrowly escaped death today at the hands of an assassin who fired a shot at the royal suitor as the Prince was placing a wreath on the tomb of the Unknown Soldier.

The quick work of one of the Italian Embassy party who knocked down the assassin's arm, seized the gun and overpowered him was believed to have saved the Prince's life.

The assassin, who only escaped lynching through the protection of the police, later told the authorities that he was an Italian named Enrico Diroca, and said that he had only intended to fire in the air as a protest.

The young Prince, whose engagement to the Belgian princess was formally announced today, was on the calmest of those present. He continued the wreath-placing ceremony while hands played Italian anthems, later returning to the Italian Embassy where he is stopping.

Tried Second Shot.

Despite the stringent precautions taken by the police to prevent any unpleasant incident at the ceremony, Diroca succeeded in making his way to a point near the Prince's car, firing the shot when he was about 15 yards away.

As he prepared to fire a second shot his hand was knocked down and he was overpowered. The police succeeded in protecting him from the infuriated crowd and took him to headquarters for questioning. An investigation was proceeding this afternoon and it was thought probable a statement would be issued later.

The couple were formally betrothed today with publication of their engagement in the official gazette Le Moniteur.

Their marriage, in accordance with customs of the house of Savoy,

NEGRO GRID STAR BENCHED FOR GAME

New York, Oct. 23 (AP)—Dave Meyers, N. Y. U. quarterback—Negro—will not play against the University of Georgia November 9, Coach "Chick" Meehan announced today. The Violet team, he added that he never had intended to play the chap who was shifted from a guard position to that of field general immediately before the university's last game.

The announcement of Coach Meehan came at the peak of heated comment upon the possibility of Meyers playing against the Southerners by the newspapers of this section and was the first official statement on the subject.

JURY GETS CASE OF FALL, ACCUSED OF $100,000 BRIBE

Deliberators Recalled to Court Room by Justice Hitz at Request of Counsel.

Washington, Oct. 24 (AP)—After deliberations that had lasted more than two hours and a half today, there was no word from the jury considering the bribery charge against Albert B. Fall. Many spectators, however, were keeping their seats in the court room.

Washington, Oct. 24 (AP)—The jury in the Fall bribery case today began its deliberations on whether the Secretary of the Interior in the Harding administration accepted a bribe of $100,000 from Edward L. Doheny for leasing the Elk Hills Naval Oil Reserve to Doheny's company.

The judge first read instructions agreed to by counsel, thirteen of them being prepared by the government and fifteen by the defense.

The prosecution said it was admitted Fall received $100,000 from E. L. Doheny, oil magnate, and asked that the defendant be found guilty on the bribery charge if it was determined the former cabinet member intended to let his decision in regard to the Elk Hills oil lease be influenced by the money.

The defense asked the instruction that the fact that Fall received the money did not prove the charge; that suspicion or conjecture was not sufficient to establish the charge of bribery or an intent to be influenced; that Fall's failure to take the stand created no presumption against him and that if the jury considers evidence of guilt or innocence equally divided the verdict must be not guilty.

Shortly after the jurors retired, the jury was recalled to the court room by Justice Hitz at the request of counsel that he clear up part of his charges.

Justice Hitz told the jury the action of other government officials in approving the lease of the Elk Hills Reserve was not to be taken as conclusive evidence on either side of the case. He also asserted that nothing he had said was to be accepted as favoring either side, and declared the jurors were the sole judges of the facts.

KIDNAPED DETROIT BOY RETURNED HOME ON $25,000 RANSOM

Detroit, Oct. 24 (AP)—Jackie Thompson, 5, who was kidnaped from in front of his home Sept. 20, was returned unharmed to his parents, Mr. and Mrs. Henry S. Thompson, last night. Police said Thompson paid $25,000 for his son's release.

Two men and two women are being held in connection with the kidnaping. They are James Fernando, 39; his wife, Anna, 23; Emil Suove, 23, and Mary Daggumno, 19. The two men are charged with kidnaping and the women are held for investigation.

Inspector Robert A. MacPherson, a member of the squad which returned Jackie to his home, said Thompson paid $17,000 in $10, $50, and $100 bills to the kidnapers and then gave them four $2,000 notes for the balance.

Jackie was found at the Fernando home, according to police, who said he returned home with $5,000 of the marked money.

REPORTS REQUESTED ON UNMARKED SHOALS.

All residents of Washington, Warren and Essex Counties or elsewhere have been requested by the navigation committee of the Lake George Association to report all unmarked shoals on Lake George which are a menace to navigation.

Before the opening of another season 14 more buoys are to be placed, the association has stated and more will be added as the need arises. The spindles, which the association has placed for many years in use to point out places before May 1 and will remain until November 1 for the benefit of the early trout fishermen.

President Speeding

(Continued on Page 14)

Montana Flier and Plane in Which He Dared Ocean

Wind and weather were in his favor, but lack of fuel and flying experience promised disaster for Urban F. Diteman, who is pictured above with the tiny low-winged monoplane in which he dared a lone hop over the North Atlantic. The 31-year-old cattleman from Billings, Mont., is shown in front of his ship in the close-up at the left. After his unheralded departure from Harbor Grace, Newfoundland, he remained unsighted.

Millions Lost In Hollywood Blast

One Man Killed When Fire Follows Explosion in Film Laboratory; Property Damage Estimated as High as $50,000,000.

Hollywood, Cal., Oct. 24 (AP)—An explosion and fire destroyed the laboratory of the Consolidated Film Industries here early today, causing a loss estimated as high as $50,000,000. Fifty persons in the building fled to safety during intervals between four detonations which wrecked the place. One man was killed.

The only death was that of Albert Lund who was found unconscious near a film polishing machine after firemen had quenched the blaze. He died while being taken to a hospital.

Estimates of loss, pending inventory by Hollywood producing companies, 75 per cent of whom patronize the film laboratory, were tentative. Fire department officials said first estimates compiled by them ran as high as $50,000,000, but fire department and film company officials said initial estimates probably would be greatly reduced, due to the fact that some of the celluloids apparently had not been damaged. The building itself was valued at $400,000.

Included in first reports of master films destroyed was "Hell's Angels," 20,000 feet valued at $60,000; "The Taming of the Shrew," produced by Douglas Fairbanks, value not estimated; "Trespassers," an all-talking production, and "Rio Rita," a talking and singing film.

William Lebarron, vice president and the general manager of Radio-Keith-Orpheum productions, said he believed the first few days' filming of one of his company's most costly productions to have been in the building.

Two women workers, who ran as the first flash of flame spread through the building, said they saw the first explosion occur in a pile of chemicals near one of the polishing machines in an assembly room. They believed to have been knocked unconscious by the blast, and to have lain helpless as the fire swept over him.

C. M. Lockwood, a film company executive working in a projection room, said 35 women and 15 men were in the structure when the first explosion occurred, and that he had accounted for them all except Lund.

The fire spread through the structure rapidly, five minutes after the initial explosion had warned workers of danger, a second occurred, and flames through windows and ignited several automobiles packed in front of the laboratory.

The interior of the building was wrecked, sections were blown down and some sections of the outer portion of the structure fell away, but the four main walls remained standing. Fire fighters succeeded in keeping the flames away from the Famous Players-Lasky studio on one side and the studios of Radio-Keith-Orpheum Pictures on the other.

23 TAKEN OFF VESSEL STRANDED IN GREAT LAKES

Coast Guard Cutter Goes On to Rescue Crew of Another Vessel After Saving Maple Court Men.

Milwaukee, Wis., Oct. 24 (AP)—Capt. H. C. Hubbard of the United States Light House Service reported this afternoon that a wireless message received here said that several bodies with life preservers bearing the name "C. F. Milwaukee" and the pilot house of the ferry had been picked up by a boat 16 miles off Kenosha.

Milwaukee, Wis., Oct. 24 (AP)—Hope that the car ferry Milwaukee of the Grand Trunk fleet with 52 abroad had weathered the 48-hour storm on Lake Michigan, faded today with a report that wreckage from a boat had been picked up ten miles off Wind Point, about four miles south of Racine.

Superior, Wis., Oct. 24 (AP)—The freighter Donaldson, on which two seamen died since Tuesday night, arrived this morning from the Apostle Islands, where it put in to await abatement of the storm which swept the Great Lakes.

Sault Ste. Marie, Mich., Oct. 24 —Twenty-three seamen and officers of the stranded steamer, Maple Court, of the Canada Steamship lines, were rescued by a Coast Guard cutter at 4:30 a. m. today from their vessel, which has been hard aground on Magnetic Reef, Cockburn Island, in Lake Huron, since 4 a. m. Tuesday. The "Maple Court was reported to be in "very bad shape" by members (Continued on Page 14)

SALES BREAK ALL RECORDS; BILLIONS OF DOLLARS LOST

Ticker Two Hours Behind; Bankers Call Hasty Meeting; Rally Checks Decline.

New York, Oct. 24 (AP)—Thomas W. Lamont emerged from the bankers' conference at the office of J. P. Morgan & Co. early this afternoon and announced that he so far as the bankers had been able to learn, no financial houses were in difficulty.

He added that the concensus of the conference had been that many quotations "did not set forth the situation fairly because of the numerous air pockets found in many stocks where there were not many bids."

Chicago, Oct. 24 (AP)—After a wild day of trading in the grain pits during which prices dropped 13c, a sharp rally set in near the close and carried values upward about 7 cents. There was a net loss for the day, however, of about 8 cents with December deliveries quoted at $1.30¾, to ¾.

New York, Oct. 24 (AP)—Wall Street experienced the darkest day in years today as a selling movement approaching panic proportions completely demoralized the stock market and billions of dollars in quoted values disappeared. Such leading stocks as U. S. Steel tumbled $9 a share to $195, Standard of New Jersey $11 to $42.50, American Telephone $22 to $249, and John Manville $40 to $140.

The situation became so acute by early afternoon that a report was sent out over private wires that the Stock Market would be closed at 1 o'clock, but this was later denied by the New York Stock Exchange, which announced just before 1 o'clock that no call had been issued for a meeting of the Board of Governors to take action.

A hasty meeting of leading bankers was convened at the office of J. P. Morgan & Co. shortly after noon, including Charles E. Mitchell, chairman of the National City Bank, and A. H. Wiggin, chairman of the Chase National Bank.

Panic Checked.

The panic appeared to have been checked early this afternoon, as leading bankers issued reassurances, and prices of many leading stocks, after declining $10 to $40 a share, rebounded sharply.

United States Steel common, after dropping $9.50 a share to $194.50, more than regained its loss, selling at 1:30 p. m. at $206, John Manville, which had dropped $40 to $140, jumped to $172. American Telephone, after tumbling $21 to $261, snapped back to $284.

Total sales on the New York Stock Exchange up to 1:30 p. m. were 10,171,900 shares, breaking all records, and comparing with a turnover of 8,246,470 shares for the full session of the previous record day, March 26, last. At 1 p. m. sales were approximately 14,000,000 shares.

Many commission houses reported to have dumped weakened accounts overboard right and left without waiting for response to calls for more margin. Hundreds of leading stocks were swept down to the lowest levels in more than a year. Many issues lost from 5 to 50 per cent. of their quoted values in a few hours.

Customer's rooms of brokerage houses were crowded with pale and harassed faces. In contrast to the shrieking tickers on the exchange floor, these men were ominously silent. A few were confidently placing huge orders to buy, while many more were frantically urging orders to sell.

Swamped.

Wall Street trading facilities again were completely swamped by the deluge of selling. Scenes of wild confusion again prevailed on the floors of the Stock and Curb Exchanges. The quotations on the Stock Exchange ticker fell more than three hours late at the close.

Commodity markets and security markets throughout the country were deluged with selling, in sympathy with the break in security prices. Wheat futures at Chicago and Winnipeg dropped about 2 to 4 cents a bushel reaching new low ground for the current decline.

Selling Orders Four In.

Selling orders poured into the Stock Exchange over telegraph, telephone, and private brokerage wires and by radio from stations throughout the country and specialists were driven frantic in efforts to execute the flood of orders.

Sales on the Stock Exchange from 10 o'clock until noon totaled 9,700,000 shares, a new high record from which 14,000,000 shares it is contracted to the record day's turnover of more than 3,260,000 shares on March 26.

Sales on the curb up to 1:30 also reached a new high level from which 2,585,000 shares was being traded. The curb traded at that time seventy minutes late at the close. A new and wholly unexpected avalanche of selling carried stocks to ever lower levels on the market yesterday carrying prices of stocks down from $10 to $90 a (Continued on Page 14)

HOPE FOR OCEAN FLIER, MISSING 48 HOURS, DWINDLES

Report Black and Orange Wreckage of Airplane Found by Vessel Proves False.

St. John's, N. F., Oct. 24 (By the Canadian Press)—The report from Harbor Grace that the S. S. Kyle had picked up a message was stated by the Newfoundland government to be without foundation. The government has had no message from the Kyle, which is at present on the Northern coast. It is believed the rumor originated from the S. S. Scythia's message last night that no sign of the plane, missing 48 hours, had been seen. The message was in code and the report spread that Diteman had been found.

BY THE ASSOCIATED PRESS

A bit of wave tossed black and orange wreckage reported found in the North Atlantic Ocean brought apparent verification today that another flight had failed.

By ship radio relay from the steamer Kyle came word that an unidentified steamer had found a bit of wreckage floating in the sea along the path that Urban Diteman, Jr., Montana cattleman, had taken toward London in his little monoplane the Golden Hind. The wreckage was painted black and orange. So was Diteman's plane.

New York, Oct. 24 (AP)—A possible landing in Greenland was the only hope airmen held today for the safety of Urban F. Diteman, Jr., Montana cattleman, long overdue on a solo flight from Newfoundland to London.

Nothing has been seen or heard of the flier since he disappeared out over the ocean after taking off from Harbor Grace, N. F., at 10:45 a. m. (Eastern Standard Time) Tuesday. He left a note saying "Am bound for London."

The hope that Diteman might be down somewhere on the coast of Greenland arose from an Exchange (Continued on Page 4)

MRS. McPHERSON TO FACE GRAND JURY

Los Angeles, Oct. 24 (AP)—Aimee Semple McPherson, pastor at Angelus Temple, was under summons to appear before the grand jury today with the books of the Echo Park Evangelistic Association for questioning about an alleged secret bank account, said to exceed $100,-000, which she maintained under the names of "Elizabeth and Ruth Johnson."

Mrs. McPherson and her secretary, Harriet Jordon, were subpoenaed yesterday in connection with an investigation into "charges" filed by the Rev. J. H. Gosen, dismissed assistant pastor of the temple, that there was a secret fund carried to her own use, funds belonging to the church.

CLEMENCEAU PASSES RESTLESS PERIOD

Paris, Oct. 24 (AP)—Georges Clemenceau, former French premier, spent a restless night, with his breathing congested until about 2 a. m. when he went to sleep, his doctors said today. He arose at 7 a. m. breakfasted, and took another nap.

Dr. Degennes said: "Things are not going so badly now. The patient is much better than he was during the night. The threatened lung congestion has been absorbed. But still because of his great age, one must write a report that wreckage from a boat had been picked up ten miles off Wind Point, about four miles south of Racine."

THE WEATHER.
Tonight—Cool.
Tomorrow—Showers.

THE TROY EVENING RECORD

FINAL EDITION

SERIES 1929—NO. 254.
WHOLE NUMBER 9312.

(Entered as Second Class Matter at the Postoffice at Troy, N.Y., under the Act of Mar. 3, 1879.)

TROY, N. Y., TUESDAY, OCTOBER 29, 1929.

PRICE THREE CENTS

RALLY HALTS STOCK MARKET DELUGE

Ten Persons Drown as Steamer Sinks in Storm on Great Lakes

60 SAVED, MANY MADDENED AFTER LONG EXPOSURE

Chief Engineer Dies After Fighting Rescuers Who Tried to Haul Him from Water.

Kenosha, Wis., Oct. 29 (AP).—Between ten and 15 men went down with the lake steamer Wisconsin in a severe storm on Lake Michigan off the Kenosha shore early today.

More than three score were saved, many of them maddened and some near death from the horror and exposure of hours in the wind whipped sea. The three passengers aboard were rescued.

In addition to the nine known dead, four others were missing. They were believed drowned. Nineteen were in hospitals and 49 were rescued safely.

Capt. Dougal Morrison, bound to his duty and true to the tradition of the sea, remained aboard his ship to the last and went down with a score of shipmates. His body was picked up later by Coast Guard crews.

Chief Engineer Judas Buschmann of Manitowoc, Wis., clung to a life raft as the steamer upended, rolled over and sank. Rescuers tried to haul him from the water but, crazed by his plight, he fought them off and died.

Dozen Ships Stand By.

The officers of the Wisconsin's crew stuck to the craft until it sank and were taken from life rafts by rescue boats, a dozen of which rushed to the steamer after the Kenosha Life Guard had taken off most of the crew. One man was reported to have fallen overboard as the rescue was in progress. There were no women aboard.

Elmer Ross of Muskegon, Mich., an oiler, said the crew acted with coolness and obedience throughout the exciting hours preceding the sending of the S O S. The only confusion developed, Ross said, when three lifeboats were launched, the crews having difficulty in handling them in the high seas.

The men in the lifeboats were picked up by the Coast Guard craft and the lifeboats turned adrift.

Boats Seek Survivors.

The two power boats of the Kenosha and Racine Coast Guards pushed out again into the thirty foot waves in the hope that the last remnant of the crew might have escaped on the rafts before the Wisconsin sank.

There was 15 feet of water in the vessel at 3 a. m. when the last of the rescued left the steamer. They had left their shipmates huddled on the deck, clinging to life-rafts, shivering and soaked by the huge waves whipped up by the second violent storm in a week. The Wisconsin had been the only vessel to ride out the gale of a week ago.

Eight life rafts and one of the six lifeboats were still on board when the stern of the ship was seen to sink, the boat rolling heavily on its side and settled beneath the waves.

Chronology Of Disaster.

The Wisconsin, which set out on its regular Milwaukee run from Chicago at 7:25 o'clock last night in the face of a gale, sprang a leak a few hours out.

At 1 a. m. today she wirelessed the Goodrich steamship Illinois, Chicago to Grand Haven, Mich., saying the going was very rough, but that she was proceeding slowly north.

At 1:30 a. m. the Wisconsin wirelessed that a leak had developed, but that she was making some progress.

At 3 a. m. came an SOS and word that the steamer was slowly sinking.

At 4:45 a. m. the Wisconsin's radio operator said the ship was being abandoned by all hands, and that they were being taken aboard Coast Guard boats.

Vessel Sends S O S But Reaches Port

Milwaukee, Oct. 29 (AP).—The freighter Waukegan which early this morning was reported to have issued an S O S, weathered the Lake Michigan storm and arrived here at 4:20 a. m. The Waukegan plys between Chicago and Milwaukee.

OFFICERS ABSENT, TRAFFIC RUNS WILD

Tulsa, Okla., Oct. 29 (AP).—Tulsa motorists for several hours ran through red lights, parked in forbidden spots and in general made merry, with never a traffic cop to say nay. It was Billy Barbee's birthday.

Five years ago Billy was seriously ill and traffic patrolmen were stationed to keep cars quiet in front of his home. He became a favorite of the force and so they gave a birthday party today the entire group rode to his home on motorcycles, two abreast.

WAGGONER FACING LONG PRISON TERM

New York, Oct. 29 (AP).—His sentence reduced by five years, Charles Delos Waggoner, former president of the Bank of Telluride, Col., today faced a ten-year prison term for his $500,000 fraud on New York banks.

The reduction, however, is not expected to affect the actual time Waggoner will spend in jail as Federal Judge Coleman said he would ask the parole board not to free him until at least five years had been served.

Expires

THEODORE E. BURTON.

FOUR MEN LOOM FOR SENATE CHAIR OF T. E. BURTON

Col. Carmi Thompson and Postmaster General Mentioned as Possible Successors.

Washington, Oct. 29 (AP).—The Senate today adopted a resolution expressing its "profound sorrow" over the death of Senator Theodore E. Burton of Ohio and adjourned after a three-minute session out of respect for the dead legislator.

Washington, Oct. 29 (AP).—The White House announced today that President Hoover will attend the public funeral services for the late Senator Burton of Ohio at the Capitol tomorrow. The decision of the President to do this was in keeping with the high respect in which he held the Ohio Senator.

Names of four men were mentioned in political circles here today as possible successors to Sen. Theodore E. Burton, who died in Washington last night.

They were Col. Edward W. Edwards, Cincinnati manufacturer, close personal friend of Governor Cooper; Col. William Cooper Procter, another Cincinnati manufacturer; Col. Carmi E. Thompson, of Cleveland, and Postmaster General Walter F. Brown, of Toledo. The Governor, however, has made no announcement.

Capital Mourns Death of Senator Burton

Washington, Oct. 29 (AP).—The national capital today mourned the death of one of its most loved and respected legislators, Sen. Theodore E. Burton of Ohio.

After a long life, devoted largely to public service and the advance-

(Continued on Page 6.)

CLEMENCEAU FINDS BREATHING DIFFICULT

Paris, Oct. 29 (AP).—Georges Clemenceau, former French premier, who is ill, had some difficulty in breathing last night. Dr. Laubry advanced his visit an hour but found his patient sleeping peacefully. Today M. Clemenceau arose as usual and resumed work on his book.

FIREMAN KILLED, PASSENGERS HURT

Chattanooga, Tenn., Oct. 29 (AP).—Forrest Aderholt, fireman on a passenger train on the Alabama-Great Southern line was killed and several passengers injured when five cars and the engine of the train left the tracks at New England, Ga. 12 miles from here shortly before 7 o'clock this morning.

WINTRY WEATHER SHROUDS FATE OF GIANT AIR LINER

Plane Lost in Storm in Same Region Where Crash Took Lives of Eight Recently.

Albuquerque, N. M., Oct. 29 (AP).—A blinding snowstorm today halted aerial search for the Western Air Express passenger plane missing since yesterday morning in the mountainous New Mexico-Arizona border country with five persons aboard.

Albuquerque, N. M., Oct. 29 (AP).—Winter, closing down over the mountains which form the backbone of the Continental Divide, today concealed beneath a blanket of lowering storm clouds and snow the fate of a Western Air Express liner, lost with five persons aboard.

The giant tri-motored plane, with two passengers and a crew of three, disappeared yesterday morning somewhere along the 180-mile stretch of the Western Air Express route between Navajo, Ariz., and Albuquerque. It is believed to have been forced down by bitter weather which swept the Rocky Mountains yesterday, bringing snow and rain which caused the Western Air Express to order all planes grounded. The order came too late to halt the missing plane at Kingman, Ariz., which it left yesterday at 8:25 a. m. Mountain Time.

Due in Albuquerque at noon, the ship was last sighted over Navajo at 10:30 a. m. at Pinto, Ariz., a few miles east of Navajo, a Santa Fe railroad inspector said he heard a plane in the clouds at 11 a. m. but could not see it.

The plane was bound from Alhambra, a suburb of Los Angeles, to Kansas City.

Those aboard were:

Dr. A. W. Ward, San Francisco, nationally known dental authority, en route to Fort Worth, Tex., to fill a speaking engagement.

W. E. Merz, Mount Vernon, N. Y., en route to his home.

James E. Doles, Los Angeles, chief pilot.

Allan C. Barrie, Burbank, Cal., co-pilot.

R. L. Britton, Los Angeles, formerly of Denver, steward.

The plane was last reported headed for the Mount Taylor region in western New Mexico, where only a few weeks ago a transport air liner was wrecked with the loss of eight lives. A search by scores of airplanes for several days was fruitless, but a passing plane flying on schedule spotted the wreckage.

Some parts of the Mount Taylor region are next to inaccessible. Foot parties only are able to traverse some sections because of deep canyons, precipitous cliffs, heavy underbrush and timber. In other places there are outcroppings of lava, making travel a slow and dangerous undertaking even on foot.

Western Air Express officials were advised by their field manager at Holbrook, Ariz., that the plane passed over Navajo, Ariz., yesterday morning, flying low. A severe storm was raging at the time. Navajo is sixty miles east of Holbrook and 180 miles west of Albuquerque.

ALLEGED ILL FAITH WITH SLAYER SCORED

Colorado Springs, Col., Oct. 29 (AP).—Resentment of police executives of all parts of the United States at what they consider ill faith of the State of Colorado with a criminal has been expressed in scores of telegrams received by H. D. Harper, chief of police here.

Each wire condemns Lamar, Col., prosecuting authorities for not keeping a promise to Ralph Fleagle, condemned bank robber and murderer, that he would be exempted from the death penalty in return for a confession which brought about capture and conviction of two of his companions.

The state did not demand the death penalty for Fleagle but made no effort to obtain a lighter sentence and the jury which convicted him committed him to the noose.

MEXICO TO ADHERE.

Mexico City, Oct. 29 (AP).—The Mexican Senate yesterday voted ratification of Mexican adherence to the Kellogg-Briand pact to outlaw war.

Ex-Cow Puncher Proves He's No Horse Puncher

Evanston, Ill., Oct. 29 (AP).—Policeman Phil Reimen used to be a cow puncher.

Last night a horse roamed at large, nibbling grass from some of the swellest lawns in town. Reimen, the ex-cow puncher, told his companions, Officers Bell and Bussean, that he would capture the horse in no time at all.

Reimen said: "I'll ride that broncho to the station house." Reimen got aboard the beast. In two seconds he was skating across the grass on his ear. The nag continued to nibble the nice grass.

"I am an old time cow puncher," said Officer Reimen. "Leave it to me."

He cut down a clothes line and made a lariat. He whistled it through the air. He pulled in, confidently. He found he had snagged Officer Bell.

People began appearing. There came George Boharas, who sells fruit. He approached the horse.

"Ruth," he said. "She ver' good lady, yes."

He slipped a halter over the willing head and the two started down the street.

"But sometimes," Boharas explained to the officers, "Ruth she eat too many apples."

NUGGETS IN THE NEWS

BY THE ASSOCIATED PRESS

Washington.—If modern inventions are destroying American home life, an exception is seen by Vice President Curtis. "This is not true of radio," he said in a radio address. "It holds a unique place in that it is returning us to our firesides."

London.—Taking full charge for the first time since his illness a year ago made necessary the appointment of six counsellors of state, King George will hold a privy council on November 5 at Buckingham Palace.

New York.—Recovered from the fishes, a gold cigarette case inscribed with names of famous aviators is to be restored to Thea Rasche. It was in the purse she dropped overboard when waving farewell to friends wishing her bon voyage. A diver found it.

New York.—The Leviathan now distributes printed wine lists on westbound trips. Cocktails are 25 cents and highballs 35. On the last trip there was an overstock with the result that jettisoning was necessary when the ship approached New York.

New York.—A poor girl who works in the tobacco fields of North Carolina has realized her dream of becoming a capitalist. She sent her savings of $4 to the Standard Oil Company of New Jersey asking that it be invested in the company's stock. The company returned the money. Other stockholders heard about it and contributed enough to buy her a share. The company found she got the idea from a brother who works in a garage that had just bought a carload of gasoline. The names of the girl and the contributors are not given in the company's magazine.

Berlin.—The first all German sound picture depicts the sinking of the British steamship Titanic by collision with an iceberg.

New York.—Miss Grace Lyon, a young woman of wealth, who has backed swimmers and girl fliers and can fly herself, is having a plane built in which she hopes to fly to Paris next summer with several friends.

London.—A male columnist for the Morning Post writes his delight of women's new "pubbly bonnets," as he calls them, meaning the severe off-the-face hats that have come into vogue replacing those pulled down well over the eyes. Far too many pretty faces, he says, have been concealed by drooping hats.

Boston.—Display of American flags in public schools is regarded by the Right Rev. Paul Jones, acting Episcopal Bishop of Southern Ohio, as "a dangerous fetish worship which promotes thoughts of war among school children." He expressed the opinion in an address criticizing military training in schools and colleges.

Peiping.—Mrs. Woodrow Wilson has ridden a donkey for several hours along the top of the great wall. In a three hour train ride to the scene she rode in a baggage car, the conductor serving tea, rice, cakes and persimmons.

Pittsburg, Pa.—Miss Mary W. Green, dean of women at Carnegie Tech, deplores the existence of a smoking room established by refrenduum of coeds, but bows to recognition of conditions as they exist.

Pittsburg, Pa.—Public school classroom work is to be radiocast via KDKA every Tuesday afternoon next month in an experiment to determine whether radio can become a useful adjunct to teaching.

New York—Selection of architects to draft plans for the development of three city blocks, the site of the proposed new Metropolitan Opera House, has been announced.

LABOR CONGRESS PUT OFF, SOUTHERN TROUBLES BLAMED

A. F. of L. Too Much Engaged in Fight for Life Below Mason-Dixon Line, Says Green.

Washington, Oct. 29 (AP).—The Executive Committee of the Pan American Federation of Labor, headed by William Green, president of the American Federation of Labor, today announced the indefinite postponement of the sixth Pan American Labor Congress on the grounds that "the very existence of the organized labor movement" is threatened by conditions in the Southern states.

"The labor movement in the South," Green's statement said, "finds itself confronted with one of the most gigantic campaigns ever launched by employers to prevent organized labor doing its duty.

"Thus it will be seen that with more than a million members to be called upon, the American Federation of Labor finds it necessary to concentrate all its energies and resources on this titanic struggle in which the very existence of the organized labor movement is at stake."

The Pan American Congress would have opened January 6, in Havana, Cuba.

Its postponement is due, the statement added, to the need for a special organizing campaign which "has been launched and is being carried on among the working people in the South and elsewhere by the American Federation of Labor where over a million members are employed in the different industries of the Southern states and elsewhere."

BAIL BOND BROKER FACES PRISON TERM

Los Angeles, Cal., Oct. 29 (AP).—William W. McGee, bail bond broker, today faced a prison sentence of from one to 14 years because he attempted to bribe a policeman to "forget certain facts" in connection with the trial of Mrs. Lois Pantages on a charge of manslaughter. McGee was tried, convicted and sentenced yesterday by Judge Charles Fricke, who presided at the trial of Alexander Pantages, husband of Mrs. Pantages, on a statutory charge. Both Mr. and Mrs. Pantages were found guilty of the crimes of which they were tried.

ACTRESS' FORMER HUSBAND MARRIED

New York, Oct. 29 (AP).—Hallam Keep Williams, former husband of Ann Murdock, actress, was married to Ruth Anderson, former show girl, at Erie, Pa., on Saturday, it became known today.

Williams, who is wealthy, married Miss Murdock in 1925, shortly after her divorce from her second husband, Harry C. Powers, a New York broker. The marriage ended in a divorce last September.

MISTRIAL DECLARED.

Tampa, Oct. 29 (AP).—A mistrial was declared here today in the case of Sidney J. Catts, former governor of Florida, who had been tried on a charge of aiding and abetting counterfeiting when the jury reported in Federal Court that it had been unable to agree.

GRUNDY STARTLES LOBBY COMMITTEE WITH FRANK IDEAS

Thinks Smaller Western States Have Too Much Voice in Senate on Tariff Legislation.

Washington, Oct. 29 (AP).—Joseph R. Grundy, president of the Pennsylvania Manufacturers' Association, took the breath of the Lobby Committee today when he frankly stated he thought the smaller Western states had too much voice in the Senate on tariff legislation.

Sharply questioned by the Senate investigators, Grundy said it was a "tragedy" that the states contributing negligible amounts in Federal taxes "and with no chips in the game" could help break down a fundamental economic policy.

Senator Walsh, Democrat, Montana, wanted to know how Grundy proposed to silence "Senator Borah and myself for instance," on the Tariff Bill and the witness said "propriety" should dictate that.

Examined by Senator Borah, Republican, Idaho, Grundy persisted that he stood by the Republican platform to give agriculture an equality with industry but he disagreed with the Idahoan that it would be necessary to cut down some industrial tariff rates to obtain this equality.

It was Grundy's second appearance, and he again readily acknowledged tariff increases for which he had worked but denied he had sought any tariff increases on metal materials, saying "I don't play both ends of the game."

Wool was the only farm schedule in which Grundy said he had interested himself.

PARLIAMENT OPENS AS LABOR FACES SERIOUS DANGERS

London, Oct. 29 (AP).—Parliament reassembled today for what was expected to be one of the most important and busy sessions of recent years.

A Labor ministry, in control for the second time in British history, took their seats with the warnings of opposition newspaper editorials thrust at them.

That warning was, substantially, that the virtual truce in party politics, which marked the initial weeks of the Parliamentary session three months ago, is over, and that the Labor government must now prepare to defend their policies.

At convening, Labor's situation undoubtedly was precarious enough, the government polling but 291 members in the Commons, against 260 Conservatives, and 57 Liberals, sufficiently short of a majority that a Liberal-Conservative coalition may at any time give a vote no confidence and bring about its resignation.

Labor's leaders felt they had room for optimism, however, in various developments during the three months Parliament has been in recess, principal among these the popularity of Premier MacDonald's moves toward betterment of American relations, and the promise of David Lloyd George, Liberal leader, that the Liberals would give Labor a chance to work out a constructive program.

REV. DR. STRATON DIES SUDDENLY AT SANITARIUM

Noted Fundamentalist Baptist Pastor Had Been at Clifton Springs Recovering from Breakdown.

Clifton Springs, Oct. 29 (AP).—The Rev. Dr. John Roach Straton, noted militant Fundamentalist Baptist preacher, died at a sanitarium here today. He was 54 years old.

Although seriously ill with a nervous breakdown for the last month, death came unexpectedly at 5:50 a. m. after a heart attack. His wife was at his bedside when he died.

He suffered a slight paralytic stroke last April and immediately after went to a sanitarium at Atlanta, Ga., for a rest. He returned to his home a month ago, but soon suffered from a nervous breakdown and entered the sanitarium here.

He was pastor of Calvary Baptist Church in New York but by his aggressive campaigns against modernism, and especially evolution, he gained nation-wide prominence. During the last presidential campaign he took an active part against the candidacy of Alfred E. Smith, attacking him from his pulpit and campaigning against him in the South.

Modernists vs. Fundamentalist.

Dr. Straton in recent years had clashed repeatedly with proponents of modernistic teachings. He especially was opposed to the theory of evolution and lent his support to the late William Jennings Bryan at the famous Scopes trial at Dayton, Tenn., in 1925.

His campaigns against alleged indecency on the stage date back to 1922 when he engaged in a debate with William A. Brady, Broadway theatrical producer, on a resolution that the modern stage was a menace to public morals. He opposed the study of Darwinism teachings in the public schools and denounced Ku Klux Klan doctrines.

Dr. Straton constantly was in conflict with various members of his congregation at the Calvary Baptist Church, partly through his sermons and because of his other activities.

(Continued on Page 6.)

BLAME DEMOCRATS FOR STOCK MARKET? "AL" SMITH ASKS

Springfield, Mass., Oct. 29 (AP).—"Will they blame the stock market on the Democrats—"Al."

Such was the laconic message sent by Alfred E. Smith to a meeting of the Western Massachusetts Democratic Club last night.

The message was enthusiastically applauded. Coming after Governor Franklin D. Roosevelt of New York, had declared that if such a market debacle ever took place in a Democratic administration it would immediately be hailed as the result of business bungling by the party in power.

FIVE RUSSIANS FACE DEATH FOR MURDER

Moscow, Oct. 29 (AP).—Five Russians, among them one priest, were sentenced to death today in the village of Anfalovo near Moscow for alleged complicity in murder of a government grain collector and wounding of six other village officials.

The public prosecutor charged the priest instigated the murder while one of the four other defendants carried it out. Seventeen shots were said to have been fired by the murderer, alleged to have been a rich peasant's son, who picked off his victims in the middle of the street while his father supplied him with ammunition.

FIRE RAZES MILL.

South Porcupine, Ont., Oct. 29 (AP).—The mill at the Dome Gold Mine, one of the first to be constructed in the Porcupine Field, was destroyed by fire last night with a loss estimated at $1,500,000.

To Wed Soon

Engagement of Miss Bernice Chrysler (above), 21, daughter of Walter P. Chrysler, millionaire automobile manufacturer, and big Ed Garbisch, inset, former All-American football center at West Point and now a cotton broker in New York, is announced.

BANKERS CONFER ON SUPPORT FOR SINKING MARKET

Pool Taking Large Blocks of Stock in Effort to Avert Demoralization of Trading.

New York, Oct. 29 (AP).—Wall Street's most stalwart banking institutions are lending strong support to members of the New York Stock Exchange in order to keep in hand the financial crisis arising from the enormous liquidation of business. It was learned after another conference of leading banking executives at the offices of J. P. Morgan and Co., today.

The conference broke up soon after 1 o'clock this afternoon, planning to convene again after the close of the market. Thomas W. Lamont, senior Morgan partner, received reporters but said there would be no formal statement until perhaps later in the day. In addition to Mr. Lamont, those attending the conference included Charles E. Mitchell, chairman of the National City Bank; Albert H. Wiggin, chairman of the Chase National Bank; Seward Prosser, president of the Bankers Trust Co. and George F. Baker, Jr., of the First National Bank.

It was learned that the so-called banking pool organized last week had been buying hundreds of stock both yesterday and today, and were continuing to take huge blocks at successively lower levels, in order to prevent complete demoralization of trading on the New York Stock Exchange. Without this banking support, it was said that selling orders would so vastly outnumber buying orders that trading would be at a standstill.

16,000,000 SHARE DAY SEEN; TICKER 82 MINUTES LATE

Hundreds of Stocks Touch New Lows for Year in Early Outburst of Selling.

Washington, Oct. 29 (AP).—Senator Brookhart, Republican, Iowa, predicted today that if the severe decline of stock prices in Wall Street continued "banks all over the country" would go into bankruptcy.

Washington, Oct. 29 (AP).—Julius Klein, Assistant Secretary of Commerce, will speak tonight at 10:30 o'clock over a nation-wide radio hook-up of the Columbia Broadcasting Company on business conditions in relation to the stock market.

New York, Oct. 29 (AP).—The crest of the flood of selling, which has wiped out at least 25 billions of dollars in the quoted values of securities in the last five days, appeared to have passed in the New York securities markets early this afternoon when a brisk rally followed another disastrous decline which had carried scores of issue down $7 to $70 a share.

An indicated turnover of 16,000,000 shares was seen in the announcement that total sales to 2:10 p. m. were 13,838,000 shares, with the ticker 82 minutes behind the market.

Total sales in the first half hour were 3,259,800 shares, a record.

Leading New York bankers, who held a long conference at the offices of J. P. Morgan and Co. last evening, apparently stood aside until this necessitous liquidation had been cleaned up, and then placed sufficient supporting orders to assure an orderly market. Prices rallied briskly after the opening decline of selling and then sold off in reflection of the nervousness created by the failure of a New York Curb Exchange firm, which was announced by a general commission business, although the head of the firm handled accounts for personal friends.

Leading bankers again conferred in the offices of J. P. Morgan and Co. in the early afternoon. The conferees included Charles E. Mitchell, chairman of the National City Bank; Albert H. Wiggin, chairman of the Chase National Bank; Seward Prosser, president of the Bankers Trust Co. and George F. Baker, Jr., of the First National Bank.

On the mid-afternoon rebound, the ruling prices of leading stocks rallied $5 to $35 a share, but were still selling well below their closing levels of yesterday. Probably more than half of the 1,000 issues listed on the exchange were selling at new low levels for the year, current quotations in many cases representing less than one-half of the values prevailing less than two weeks ago.

Meanwhile, stocks were being bought on the way down by investment trusts and insurance companies. Albert Conway, Superintendent of Insurance of the State of New York, was quoted on the financial news ticker as stating that in his opinion there had been such a drastic readjustment of prices of leading common stocks in the country that he felt justified in recommending to leading insurance companies to invest substantial amounts of their assets in high grade stocks. A meeting of life insurance company presidents was called in his office for that purpose this afternoon.

Suspension of trading Monday, the day preceding Election Day, is being urged by partners of some of the large commission houses, it was learned today, giving them three days to catch up with the vast accumulation of work that has piled up in the last week, as Tuesday, Election Day, is a holiday. Some action on the proposal may be taken at the meeting of the Board of Governors late this afternoon, although the authorities are understood to be reluctant to take this action for fear that it might be misinterpreted.

Wall Street has never witnessed such a wild opening as today's.

(Continued on Page 6.)

ROCKY MOUNTAINS IN WINTER'S GRIP

Denver, Col., Oct. 29 (AP).—Winter paid a real visit to the Rocky Mountain region last night, leaving a general snow from Montana to New Mexico. Parts of Montana, Wyoming and Colorado and New Mexico reported snow up to five inches.

Airmail transportation on the transcontinental lines was paralyzed when mountains between Salt Lake City and Cheyenne were shut off by fog and snow. Airmail was sent by train through the storm bound region. Highways were reported open and passable, though snow in Wyoming were slightly drifted.

AIR MAIL AVIATOR BURNED TO DEATH

Mount Vernon, O., Oct. 29 (AP).—E. M. Kane, pilot of the Southbound Cleveland-Louisville mail plane of the Universal Line, was burned to death early today when his plane crashed into a grove of trees on a farm eight miles southwest of Mount Vernon.

Chicago Reopens Inquiry In Slaughter of Seven

Chicago, Oct. 29 (AP).—A trail of blood leading to a Detroit policeman's uniform and three 45 caliber pistols in a blood spattered apartment at 910 Dakin Street today had injected new life into the investigation of the St. Valentine's Day slaughter of seven Moran gangsters.

The latest clues developed last night after Alister O'Brien, 28, had been found shot through both jaws in front of the Dakin Street address. Unable to talk at length, he said that he had been wounded by robbers.

Police followed a trail of blood from the entrance to the second floor apartment of Frank McCarthy. Furniture in the apartment was overturned and broken as if a struggle had taken place and the floor was marked with blood. The policeman's uniform, with three gold stars on the shoulders and the number 1691 on the cap, was found on the floor. The pistols were found in a bed.

McCarthy had rented the apartment October 17. He drove a car with Michigan license plates. Mrs. Joseph Clement, manager of the building, said.

Police recalled that in the February gang massacre, which took place less than three miles from the Dakin Street address, men garbed as policemen were among those who manned the machine guns. One of the theories during the investigation was that members of the Detroit "Purple" gang had killed the Moran men in reprisal for a raid.

Mrs. Bernice O'Brien, the wounded man's wife, was taken into custody at the O'Brien apartment, a few blocks away. She asserted she had just returned home from Springfield, Ill., and had not heard of her husband having been wounded. He had recently been engaged, she said, in installing the electric rabbits at a dog racing track and formerly played professional baseball in Portland, Ore.

Further credence to the Detroit gang theory was given by J. C. McMahon, who found O'Brien lying wounded in the street. Just before he found O'Brien, McMahon said, he saw an automobile with Michigan license plates driven away from the front of the place by two men.

LOOKS EASY, BUT ISN'T

HORIZONTAL

1 Behests.
5 Aviators.
7 Notion.
11 Insect.
12 Part of a church.
13 Stringy.
15 Nominal value.
16 Thread.
18 Vapid.
19 Shore.
20 To remove hair.
22 Threadlike.
23 Staples.
24 Meager.
26 Ancient.
29 Static person
36 Female sheep.
40 Tight.
41 Roof's edge.
44 Kiln.
45 Sage.
47 Dyeing apparatus.
48 Contra.

VERTICAL

1 Marvel.
2 Stir.

2 Month.
21 Lubricant.
25 Collection of facts.
27 Lathe device.
28 Constellation.
29 Two fives.
31 Conditions.
30 Round-ups.
32 Full of tidings.
33 Tennis fences.
35 Ocean.
37 To luster.
38 Hall.
41 One and one.
42 To be ill.
43 To insure.

3 Knots of fiber.
4 Twenty-four hours.
6 Faucets.
8 Growing out.
7 Leaner strips.
9 Heavenly.
8 Auto.
10 Night before.
12 To stitch.

YESTERDAY'S ANSWER

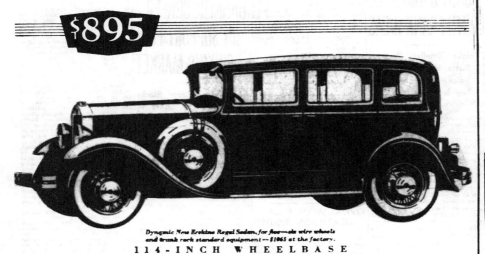

COMMITTEES NAMED TO ARRANGE FOR TROY CAMP SUPPER

Committees were appointed last night to arrange for the chicken supper and entertainment to be held Thursday evening, January 16, at Druids Hall under the auspices of Greater Troy Camp, Modern Woodmen of America. The committees were named at the regular meeting of the camp, presided over by Rasmus Nielsen.

In addition to the supper an entertainment consisting of a musical program and exhibition bouts will be presented. The proceeds of the affair will be for the building fund.

Abraham Harris was appointed general chairman of the committee. James Beale, Van Olinda and R. Kline were named on the refreshment committee; Harry Beattie and K. Connery, floor and sport committee and Henry E. Finkel, door committee. The committees will report January 12, when reservations will close.

At last night's meeting Louis E. Ryan was transferred from the Hartford, Conn. Camp, No. 9708, to the Greater Troy Camp. Mr. Nielsen conducted the ceremonies. The weekly euchre parties will be resumed at Druids Hall next Wednesday evening.

Despite its great height and the large area it encloses, the Eiffel tower in Paris weighs only 8,000 tons.

MILD WEATHER TO HOLD SWAY AFTER WINTER'S WARNING

Moderate temperatures today and tomorrow will relieve Trojans of the state of Winter experienced on Friday and Saturday of last week. According to the U. S. weather man at Albany. Mild and fair weather is forecast for today and is expected to extend over tomorrow and possibly longer.

degrees in Troy has caught many persons unaware and resulted in frozen radiators on automobiles, self unprotected and a general shivering of residents unused to such guard.

Yesterday morning the low mark reached was 40 degrees, but two degrees above the record set in 1921. During the day, however, the mercury showed the influence of the change in weather and rose to above the fifty degree mark. The temperature as low as twenty-four.

PERSHING SPEAKS IN RADIO PROGRAM ON ARMISTICE DAY

American Legion To Conduct Memorial Feature Wednesday Night; Other Radio High Spots.

THIS IS EASTERN STANDARD.

New York, Nov. 9 (P)—The broadcast networks are making ready to observe Armistice day next Wednesday.

In addition to a two-minute period of silence at 11:00 a. m. followed by an address by President Hoover, numerous features are being arranged. Included will be a night program under the auspices of the American Legion at which Gen. J. J. Pershing and Henry L. Stevens, commander of the American Legion, will speak. Music will be provided by the U. S. Army Band. The program will go over WJZ-NBC at 9 o'clock.

TODAY'S RADIO PROGRAMS

TONIGHT.

TOMORROW.

SET NOVEMBER 23 FOR DONATION DAY AT BETHESDA HOME

Donation Day will be held on Monday, November 23, at a meeting Saturday afternoon of the board of managers of Bethesda Home. Mrs. Herbert A. Hunn will have charge of the day's program.

No Blacks

SATURDAY'S ANSWER

STALEY RULES OUT G. O. P. ATTEMPT AT REAPPORTIONMENT

Republican Justice Holds Law Necessary To Secure Change in Congressional Districts.

Albany, Nov. 9 (P)—The Republican party efforts to secure court sanction of its legislative attempt to realign New York state congressional districts without the concurrent action of the Democratic governor tonight met a rebuff from the first court to consider the case.

WORKERS GET $400 IN SALVATION ARMY TAG DAY SATURDAY

The Troy Salvation Army raised $400 in the tag day which they conducted in the city Saturday.

TROY WOMAN ON BOARD MANAGING HEBREW CAMPAIGN

Miss Isabelle R. Hess Elected by Unit Seeking Unity of Judaism; Meeting Held at New York.

(Special to The Troy Record)

New York, Nov. 9.—Miss Isabelle R. Hess of Troy was elected to the Board of Managers of the newly-created northeastern district of the Union of American Hebrew Congregations which yesterday launched its program to stimulate and unify Judaism in the northeastern states.

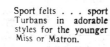

THE WEATHER
Tonight—Fair, cooler
Tomorrow—Fair.

THE EVENING TROY RECORD

Reg. U. S. Pat. Office

FINAL EDITION

Series 1933—No. 202. (Entered as Second Class Matter at the Postoffice at Troy, N. Y., under the Act of March 3, 1879.) TROY, N. Y., TUESDAY, AUGUST 29, 1933. (Published Daily Except Sunday) PRICE THREE CENTS

TRAIN PLUNGES INTO TORRENT; 6 DEAD

"They Say-"

Political Gossip from New York and Washington

WASHINGTON
By Paul Mallon

Re-employment—Even the statue of Freedom on the Capitol dome smiled at the latest NRA yarn from Iowa.

It concerns a young merchant in a small town there. He had to have an NRA emblem and was told that he could not get it unless he hired an additional employe. He had only one boy helping him, and he could not afford another. People coming into the store asked embarrassing questions about the absence of the emblem. He spent several sleepless nights before he hit upon a plan.

He brought his wife into the store and put her to work as the extra employe.

Now his store floats an NRA emblem and he does less work.

• • • •

Moley—The new magazine is "The Personal Political Work" which Prof. Moley was to undertake for Mr. Roosevelt.

The switch was scheduled for September 15, but had to be moved up a week because the story was leaking. The financial backing for the magazine shows how close it is to the President personally.

Those nearest him say the undertaking has been in the making for four months. He has been aware of each step.

The consummation will at least end all those rumors about Roosevelt falling out with his No. 1 brain trustee.

• • • •

Stalling—The government is out of town until after Labor Day

Even the corridors around the NRA are empty. Gone or going are:

The President, Cabineteers Woodin, Hull; Brain Trustees Tugwell, Moley, Sprague; half the under secretaries.

The main idea is to have every one get in a vacation before the hectic winter starts.

The business angle of it is that th cannot do much more than they have done until they see how September goes.

• • • •

Prospects—The signs all indicate the President will give September a full chance before he takes his next step.

Present plans are to conduct a psychology recovery campaign to help the fall upturn along. Mr. Roosevelt's speech Saturday hailing the "upward surge," was only the first step. You will begin to get favorable NRA material shortly by the column full. The open market activities can be made to look like inflation.

Any real inflation (such as dollar revaluation) will be held up the sleeve until needed.

• • • •

Couzens—The idea that Senator Couzens would think for a minute of taking the Treasury secretaryship is considered preposterous by those closest to him.

He told them all before he recently went West that he was not fool enough to bite on anything like that.

The Treasury stories are not sponsored by administration authorities. No one aside from newspapermen ever mentioned the subject to him before he left here.

The current talk seems to center around the fact that he gave anti-Hoover and pro-Roosevelt testimony at the Detroit bank hearing. There is nothing in that.

Couzens' private thoughts about his future have an entirely different slant. He would like to see the Republican Party reorganized. He has no presidential ambitions himself because he is ineligible. He was born in Canada.

However, he would dig down in his jeans to promote a Republican leadership more in keeping with his own political philosophy.

Those old line Republicans who know it are trying to encourage the idea of putting him into the Democratic Cabinet.

Unless the summer heat has warped his judgment, they will be disappointed.

• • • •

Corrections—To keep the record straight, two corrections should be made of recent items in this column.

The C. C. C. boys eat a lot but not

(Continued on Page 3.)

Find Buyers for Live Stock

If you want to sell livestock with the least delay and at the lowest cost, advertise in The Troy Record Classified Section.

You'll find buyers for ... horses, chickens, etc. ... through this ... can ... for prac... you'd like ... your ... will ...

PRESIDENT NAMES SECRETARY ICKES OIL "DICTATOR"

Cabinet Member To Administer New Working Agreement for Petroleum Industry.

Washington, Aug. 29 (A.P.)—Secretary Ickes, in his new role as oil administrator, today told newspapermen he would call together immediately upon appointment by President Roosevelt, the petroleum committee of 15 to discuss price and production control.

President Roosevelt today named Harold L. Ickes, his secretary of the interior, as the administrator of the new working agreement for the oil industry.

The President will name the other 14 members of the oil planning and conservation committee within the next 24 hours, taking under consideration a list of names submitted by Ickes.

As oil administrator Ickes will have the virtual power of dictator over this industry which has been engaged in a war that led to overproduction and a wrecking of prices. Price fixing is possible.

Ickes also is the Roosevelt administrator of the $3,300,000,000 public works program and it is likely he will rely strongly on an immediate assistant, expected to be James A. Moffett, former vice president of the Standard Oil Company of New Jersey.

Naming his cabinet member to this office, the President showed that he intends to keep in close personal touch with the new deal for the disordered oil business as one of the major parts of his recovery program.

Coal Accord Reached.

The NRA worked swiftly today to clinch with a permanent code the basic agreement finally obtained for the coal industry, a victory regarded by Administrator Hugh S. Johnson as one of the most significant advances in the career of the industrial control enterprise.

After skirting the edge of failure for a week, union labor and representatives of the biggest bituminous coal fields of the country, the strictly non-union Appalachian area, last night were brought into a compromise which the administration was ready to approve. Enthusiastic at this outcome, President Roosevelt expressed to Johnson his congratulation in a personal telephone conversation. Today and tomorrow at least were required, in Johnson's estimate, to convert the agreement into a binding code.

Pushes Retailers.

Meanwhile, the administration also was seeking an agreement upon a code for all retailers to bring that mammoth industry within the NRA. Yesterday marked the beginning of the campaign to take the blue eagle into homes to elicit agreements from consumers to buy from establishments that fly the NRA insignia.

Retailers, too, were on notice that the administration was determined this code should go to President Roosevelt before Labor Day, the date Johnson set weeks ago for having the greater portion of the nation's employers under maximum hour-minimum wage agreements.

Textiles, steel, automobiles, lumber, oil and other big industries are aligned already with the NRA program.

Additional significance attached to the coal charter because of the

(Continued on Page 3.)

VISCOUNT GREY SERIOUSLY ILL

Christen Bank, Northumberland, Eng., Aug. 29 (AP). Viscount Grey of Fallodon, one of Great Britain's most distinguished statesmen, was seriously ill today at his home here.

His secretary issued a statement this morning, saying: "Viscount Grey is very ill. His condition is serious."

Viscount Grey is 71 years old. As foreign secretary, he made the famous declaration of war between Great Britain and Germany in 1914.

Mayor Burns Urges President Roosevelt to Back Armor Plate Plant for Breaker Island

New York Guardsmen Reviewed By Commander-in-Chief

This was the scene on the parade grounds at Camp Smith, Peekskill, N. Y., as President Franklin D. Roosevelt, shown standing at attention in his automobile, reviewed troops of the 81st Infantry Brigade, New York National Guard.

BILLIONS READY FOR FUEL IN U. S. RECOVERY DRIVE

Treasury Well Able to Meet Extraordinary Demands for Cash When President Gives Word.

Washington, Aug. 29 (AP).—Dollar by dollar, the billions assembled as fuel for the massive Roosevelt recovery machinery are moving to their task of pumping energy into American trade and agriculture.

Topping the spending list is the $3,300,000,000 public works program, while the least expensive is the broad bulwark of the plan, the NRA, to which went but $225,000 of the $205,000,000 paid out of the treasury since July 1, in emergency outlays.

To meet the extraordinary demands for cash, the Treasury has on hand daily upward of $1,000,000,000 in ready money—the latest balance showing $1,119,000,000 ready for distribution about the country in recovery efforts as well as meeting the government's ordinary operating costs.

Cash Output Delayed.

To date, the public works administration has allocated $1,212,000,000 for construction, including $238,000,000 for battleships, with at least 2,000,000 persons expected to be put back in jobs before its bulging treasure chest is exhausted.

No one knows just how much of the amount allotted actually has been spent, but these figures now are being collected. Estimates range from $100,000,000 to a half-

(Continued on Page 3.)

CHADBOURNE HEADS FUSION COMMITTEE

New York, Aug. 29 (AP).—William M. Chadbourne has been chosen chairman of the Fusion campaign committee which will attempt to unseat Tammany at the city election this fall.

Chadbourne, a lawyer, was an organizer of the Progressive Party and friend of the late Theodore Roosevelt. The Fusion mayoralty candidate is Fiorello H. La Guardia.

MRS. WILSON URGES ALL AMERICANS TO BACK BLUE EAGLE

Washington, Aug. 29 (AP).—Mrs. Woodrow Wilson, widow of the wartime president, today appealed to all Americans to enlist under the Blue Eagle banner in the same spirit which characterized 1917-18.

Recalling the sacrifices made in war days, she said in a statement made public by the NRA:

"In 1933 that same brave spirit is abroad, ready to support the administration in its heroic effort to wage war—one that is less dramatic but even more vital to the life of the country, though there are no flags flying or bands playing for marching troops."

GOVERNOR SIGNS BILLS AIMED AT GANG ELEMENTS

Measures Designed to Protect Legitimate Business, Outlaw Use of Submachine Guns.

Albany, Aug. 29 (AP).—Governor Lehman today signed two bills to curb power of gangsters in New York state, and to outlaw one of their favorite weapons — submachine guns.

The first bill is intended to prevent gang elements from preying upon legitimate business. The other makes possession, transportation or use of a submachine gun by any one other than a police officer a felony.

The "anti-racketeering bill" and the submachine gun measure were passed by the extraordinary session of the Legislature in response to the Governor's demand for drastic new laws to prevent gangsters from interfering with business.

The first measure gives the attorney general sweeping powers to investigate "services" such as the "protection services" by which gangs extort money from business concerns, and to prosecute the promoters in criminal proceedings.

The other bill puts the submachine gun in the same outlawed class as the heavier machine gun. Heretofore there was nothing in the penal law to prevent the use of the submachine gun.

Mr. Lehman also signed a bill to eliminate crime breeding slum districts in cities by permitting the state housing board to borrow from the federal national recovery fund for the construction of low priced dwellings.

The Governor also signed two bills to facilitate the collection of village taxes. One of them permits the village to accept them in installments and the other to issue certificates of deposit in the amount of $10 each for taxes paid in advance. This is similar to the "baby bond" tax plan followed in some cities.

THREE FLIERS DIE AS PLANES COLLIDE

San Antonio, Tex., Aug. 29 (AP).—Two Randolph Field pursuit training planes collided in mid-air four miles northwest of the flying field today, sending three fliers to their deaths while a fourth jumped to safety.

Lieut. Harley R. Grater, flying instructor, and two cadets whose names were not learned immediately, were instantly killed in the spectacular collision.

Young Manchester Girl Swims English Channel

Dover, England, Aug. 29 (AP).—The English Channel was conquered for the first time this year today when Miss Sunny Lowry, 22-year-old Manchester, England, girl, arrived at South Foreland after swimming from Cape Gris Nez, France in about fifteen and three-quarters hours.

She landed, still going strong, at 10:15 a. m. (4:15 a. m., E. S. T.) She started at 6:36 p. m Monday 12:30 p. m., E. S. T.)

Three other swimmers, one of them the American Charles Zimmy, a legless aspirant to channel honors, started across the channel for the Dover Town Gold Challenge Cup.

The others are Mercedes Gleitz, an Englishwoman who first swam the channel in 1927 after eight failures, and E. H. Temme, another Briton, who in 1927 did the distance in 14 hours 29 minutes.

The Dover Cup will be awarded the man or woman who swims from Dover to France in the shortest time this year.

The channel was last negotiated successfully in 1930.

Miss Lowry had made two attempts before succeeding today in becoming the 18th swimmer and the eighth woman to swim the treacherous strip of water.

Miss Lowry's trainer, Jabez Wolfe said she made wonderful time during most of her swim and would have beaten Miss Ederle's record except for conditions encountered in the last mile, which took about five hours to cover.

Miss Ederle's record for the swim, made in 1926, is 14 hours and 31 minutes.

"As we approached shore," he said, "the sea became very choppy, and it was a struggle to get along."

He added he had never trained the girl who finished as fresh as Miss Lowry.

MOVE TO DETAIN INSULL APPROVED BY ATHENS COURT

Former Magnate Loses Point in Fight to Escape Extradition to United States.

Athens, Aug. 29 (AP).—The appeal court approved today the application for formal sanction of the detention of Samuel Insull, former Chicago utilities operator, in connection with American extradition proceedings.

Insull arrived shortly before the beginning of the hearing at 10:15 a. m. escorted by two plainclothes policemen.

After his identity had been established, several questions were put to him regarding himself, his wife, and son.

When asked about his nationality, Insull replied that he was British and was born in London but acquired American citizenship in 1896.

He said he did not know his present status because the American government has cancelled his passport.

The former Chicagoan on Saturday was taken to a private hospital on doctors' orders after a second attempt began to extradite him to the United States on a new indictment charging violation of the bankruptcy act.

A previous attempt to extradite him on mail fraud charges failed.

Insull told the court, composed of five members, that he lived in Chicago as the executive of a utilities cmopany, but that his business extended through several states.

Prosecutor Reganacos formally announced he would issue a writ for Insull's arrest following an American legation note charging him with bankruptcy.

Details of the charge were not known this morning because the indictment had not been submitted.

One of his attorneys requested that Insull be released on bail since there was no fear that he would attempt to escape.

The attorney declared that Insull already had expressed a wish to become a Greek citizen and to establish a permanent home in Greece.

FARM ADJUSTMENT ACT RULED VALID

Washington, Aug. 29 (AP).—Justice Daniel W. O'Donoghue of the District of Columbia Supreme Court today upheld the constitutionality of the agriculture adjustment act.

Dismissing a suit for a temporary injunction which would restrain Secretary Wallace from enforcing the Chicago milkshed agreement, he declared the emergency justified the law.

Attorneys Neil Burkinshaw and Nugent Dodds for the plaintiffs announced they would appeal the decision.

'QUAKE RECORDED.

Washington, Aug. 29 (AP).—A strong earthquake, centered about 7,500 miles from Washington in an unascertained direction, was reported today by Georgetown University seismological observatory. It began at 5:33 p. m., Eastern Standard time yesterday, reached maximum proportions at 6:17 p. m. and ended at 9:30 p. m.

FIVE KILLED AS AIR LINER HITS MESA MOUNTAIN

Big Transport Plane Wrecked in Same Storm That Caused Golden Gate Limited Tragedy.

Amarillo, Tex., Aug. 29 (AP).—Five persons fell to their deaths in a Transcontinental & Western Air Line night mail and passenger tri-motored transport plane when it crashed against the south end of Mesa Mountain near Quay, N. M., early today in the same storm that wrecked a railroad passenger train some 20 miles away.

The dead are Mr. and Mrs. Ralph Gore of Albuquerque, N. M., and their granddaughter, Evelyn Gore, daughter of Mr. and Mrs. Paul Gore of Amarillo; Pilot Howard Morgan and Co-pilot C. W. Barcus, both of Kansas City.

The ill-fated plane was caught in the same terrific storm which washed out a span of the railroad bridge, five miles west of Tucumcari, resulting in the wrecking of the Golden State Limited. The scene of the plane crash is about 20 miles south of Tucumcari.

The plane left here at 11:35 p. m. yesterday to continue the regular night mail and passenger flight westbound when the regular ship was storm-bound in Kansas City.

The last heard from Pilot Morgan was when he reported his position over the emergency field, six miles east of Tucumcari. Radio men here reported they thought they heard him trying to talk one time later. Morgan gave no intimation of a storm or trouble in his last report.

He apparently turned sharply to the left off his course immediately after passing the Tucumcari field, or was forced to turn back somewhere west of there and went to the south off his course.

One report from the scene said the ship caught fire and the two pilots and three passengers were trapped in the blazing wreckage.

Ralph Gore was a railway mail clerk.

CHIEF EXECUTIVE AND PARTY VISIT MENANDS BRIDGE

Site Endorsed by Former Assistant Naval Secretary in 1916 Viewed by Officials.

President Franklin D. Roosevelt heard a suggestion that Breaker Island would be an advantageous site for a governmental armor plate plant as he arrived in the Troy Area this afternoon to inspect the new Troy-Menands and Rensselaer-Albany bridges.

The President was to arrive in Troy late in the day. He reached Rensselaer at press time and was there greeted by Mayor Cornelius F. Burns, Mayor John Boyd Thacher, 2d, of Albany, Mayor John A. Scott of Menands and Mayor James G. Johnstone of Rensselaer.

The presidential party was scheduled to stop at the Troy side of the new bridge. There Mayor Burns will remind the President that when Mr. Roosevelt was assistant secretary of the navy under President Woodrow Wilson he declared, "Of all the places presented as sites for the United States armor plate plant none has advantages superior to Breaker Island.

Plant Never Built.

The statement was made early in 1916 after Congress had appropriated $11,000,000 for construction of the plant and hearings were being held on sites. However, despite this commendation, the plant was never built and the money reverted back to Congress.

Mayor Burns is to suggest to the President that now even as then the site could be used for such a plant and that the need is just as great.

The site where the presidential party was to stop is, by coincidence, an historical one in American naval history. It overlooks the site of the old Rensselaer Iron Works where the plates for the first steel ship, the "Monitor," were built.

Firemen, Police On Hand.

A large crowd assembled at the bridge to greet the President.

(Continued on Page 9.)

MISSING STUDENT FEARED DROWNED

Michigan City, Ind., Aug. 29 (AP).—Rescue squads combed the twenty-mile sandy shore line of Lake Michigan between here and Gary, Ind., today for a youth, who with two others attempted to swim to shore when their 18-foot sailboat capsized during a heavy sea.

The one still missing is Lawrence Carlson, twenty, of Muskegon, Mich., a student in a Michigan college, and owner of the boat. It is feared he may have perished.

His two companions, Glenn Smith, 21, also of Muskegon, a University of Illinois student, and Frank York, 21, of Chicago, reached shore at widely separated points last night after gruelling struggles with the waves. Toray Smith was recuperating in a cottage at Ogden Dunes, west of here and York was in a Gary hospital.

LEAK REPORTED IN EAST RIVER TUNNEL

New York, Aug. 29 (AP).—A report to the transit commission today said that the No. 1 tunnel of the Long Island Railroad, under the East River between Manhattan and Queens "sprang a leak" shortly after 7 a. m.

Trains were proceeding through the tunnel at a speed of ten miles an hour, and heavy congestion in the tube and terminal were reported.

Today's News Flashes

BEEFING AMERICANS.

New York—It is the opinion of Dr. W. Beran Wolfe, psychiatrist, that Americans do not know how to travel.

Back from a cruise in the company of a large number of tourists, he said of his fellow travelers:

"In the venerated buildings of Mediterranean cities, instead of drinking in the beauty and lore of early civilizations, they were beefing about this and that and comparing it to the bank building at home.

TALE OF A FISH.

Wilkes-Barre, Pa.—Here's another fish story.

As told by Motorcycle Officer John Leonard, he gave a goldfish in a bowl to a niece who was visiting him. Playing in the cellar, she put the bowl in a secluded spot.

Recently, Leonard found the bowl in the cellar, with only about an inch of water remaining, but the fish swimming about.

Leonard says he refilled the bowl, and gave the fish its first food in 28 months. The fish died a few hours later.

STATUE DENIED VOTE.

Pittsburg—If James Anderson votes in this fall's elections it will be a miracle.

Investigators sifting fraudulent registrations found at the address given for Anderson, a bronze statue of a James Anderson who loaned books to Andrew Carnegie eighty years ago.

SLOW BUT SURE.

Barry, Ill.—O. E. Marshall, Cedar Vale, Kan., arrived here from his Kansas home in a wheel barrow pushed by Glenn Carter, also of Cedar Vale, en route to the world's fair in Chicago. They expect to arrive Sept. 10.

FLOOD-WEAKENED BRIDGE GIVES WAY UNDER FAST FLIER

Golden State Limited Wrecked in New Mexico; 40 Injured, Many Passengers Missing.

Tucumcari, N. M., Aug. 29 (AP).—At least six persons were killed, 40 injured and many passengers were missing when the Golden State Limited, crack Rock Island train, plunged through a bridge into a waterfilled draw five miles west of Tucumcari at 5 a. m. today.

C. J. Crost of Tucumcari, engineer, and five unidentified passengers were killed. James Randall of Tucumcari, fireman, was missing.

Forty passengers were rushed to a Tucumcari hospital seriously injured and other passengers were missing.

Seven coaches went into the water, along with the locomotive. The draw, ordinarily dry, was a raging torrent fed by heavy rains of the last week, climaxed by a four-inch fall last night.

The Golden State Limited, the fastest train on the Southern Pacific-Rock Island system, was eastbound from the Pacific Coast. It makes the run between Los Angeles and Chicago in 62 hours and was due in Chicago at 9:15 a. m. tomorrow.

Victims Not Identified.

T. F. Wheelock, mail clerk, the only man in the mail car, was among those severely injured.

The coaches plunged into a ditch alongside the earth fill on both the north and south sides, but were only partially in water. Three day coaches carried 43 passengers.

Bodies of five passengers brought to Tucumcari were not identified immediately. It was not known how many of the 43 passengers were dead or missing, but at least forty were brought to hospitals here.

Railroad officials here said the train was running only twenty miles an hour. It had stopped a mile west of the fill to investigate the track for possible damage. The east span of the bridge had been washed out, but the damage could not be seen from the west end.

Locomotive Submerged.

The engine was submerged in the deepest part of the ravine. The mail car rested on top of the engine and the baggage car was at a 45-degree angle to the track beside the mail car. The next car, a coach, was crosswise in the creek bed, partially on top of the baggage car. A pullman tourist sleeper was also across the creek. All these were on the south side of the fill.

On the north side was a club car in the bed of the creek along with a standard coach, which was on its side. The head end of another standard coach was the only other car off the rails, the remaining Pullman coaches remaining on the bridge.

It was not known whether any bodies had been swept away in the torrent, or whether they were lodged in the wreckage. The engine crew runs from Tucumcari to Carrizozo, N. M., and the train crew from Tucumcari to El Paso, Tex.

A special train was being made up at Amarillo to bring survivors to Dalhart, Tex.

The wreck was on the Southern Pacific line, the train being operated over the Southern Pacific tracks west of Tucumcari.

WIDOW GRILLED ON KILLING OF DOCTOR

Spokane, Wash., Aug. 29 (AP).—Two weeks after her wealthy husband, Dr. James I. Gaines, sportsman and drugless physician, was mysteriously shot to death, Mrs. Lily Banka Gaines was held in the city jail today "for questioning."

No charge was filed against her, Prosecutor C. W. Greenough said, emphasizing that she was held "only for questioning."

Mrs. Gaines said she found her husband dying in the driveway of their home early on the morning of August 15 after she had been awakened by three shots. Dr. Gaines had just returned from a boating trip and a late visit to the apartment of Mrs. Harriette Andrews a friend.

PET DOG CAUSES FATAL AUTO CRASH

Montreal, Aug. 29 (AP).—A pet dog was held responsible by police today for the automobile accident near here in which Commander W. F. Newton, 50, of the United States Navy, was killed and his wife injured.

Mrs. Newton was at the wheel with the dog on her lap. The animal jumped suddenly and struck her elbow, causing her to lose control of the machine, and it crashed into a tree.

The Newtons were residents of Washington. He died in an ambulance on the way to a hospital. Mrs. Newton was taken to a hospital for treatment for cuts and bruises.

POST IN ROCHESTER

Rochester, Aug. 8 (AP).—Accompanied by an escort of 16 planes, Wiley Post landed his Winnie Mae at the Rochester airport at 10:15 a. m., E. S. T., today to be greeted by a crowd estimated at 5,000 persons.

The Weather
Tomorrow ... Tonight Cloudy, colder

THE TROY RECORD
EVENING

Series 1935 No. 39. (Entered as Second Class Matter at the Postoffice at Troy, N. Y. under the Act of March 3, 1879) TROY, N. Y., FRIDAY, FEBRUARY 15, 1935.

FINAL EDITION
PRICE THREE CENTS

DENY HAUPTMANN HAD ACCOMPLICE

Legislature Enacts Higher Income, Gasoline Levies

GOVERNORLEHMAN BUDGET AND TAX PROGRAMS VOTED

Senate Speaker and Majority Leader Confident Adjournment by March 15 at Latest.

Albany, Feb. 15 (AP).- With Gov. Herbert H. Lehman's budget and tax programs finally passed after three days of lengthy and bitter debate, New York's legislators today returned to their homes for the week-end confident the present session will end by March 15 at the latest.

Sen. John J. Dunnigan, majority leader, said "we're going to get out of here in the very near future—say early March."

Speaker Irwin Steingut, happy over the swift enactment of the $294,000,000 fiscal program and revenue-producing measures, reiterated "March 15 at the latest."

Reapportionment Congressional and legislative and unemployment insurance, co-ordinated with Federal plans, are the remaining major problems.

Meanwhile, Republicans and motorists alike protested vigorously the passage of the increased gasoline tax bill designed to produce $16,000,000. It is effective April 1.

"The Democratic majority has handed the motorists a $30,000,000 valentine," said Frank J. Smith, chairman of the legislative committee of the State Automobile Association. "Valentines are usually a gift of felicitation this one was a gouge."

Assemblyman Irving M. Ives, Republican minority leader, accused the Dem ratic majority in both houses of ublic-be-damned" methods and uted that Governor Lehman his instance is trying to be dictato."

Not a Vote To Spare.

Smashing down a revolt in party ranks, the Assembly Democratic leadership late yesterday shot the gas tax bill through to approval without a single vote to spare. It passed the Senate.

Its effect is to add one-cent-a-gallon to the present three-cent tax, an increase estimated to produce $16,250,000. The new levy takes effect April 1.

The new income tax rates apply on earnings of $3,000 a year and up, payable next year on 1935 incomes. It is expected to raise $2,000,000.

All of the tax bills slid through the Assembly by the bare passing voote of 76 to 72. In the Senate the vote was 28 to 13, two more "ayes" than necessary. Only one Democratic legislator was missing when the roll was called, Assemblyman Edwin L. Kantowski of Buffalo. All these bills now go to Mr. Lehman for his signature.

Other New Taxes.

The other new Lehman taxes are:

(Continued on Page 2.)

VETERANS PLAN TO MEET SERGT. YORK

All World War veterans and members of veterans' organizations in Troy have been invited to meet Sergt. Alvin C. York, famous soldier, at 7 p. m. tonight in the rooms of Noble Callahan Post, 28 Fourth Street. Sergeant York will speak in Music Hall at 8:15 p. m. tonight under the auspices of Troy Country Day School.

After a welcoming reception at the Post rooms, a large number of Troy veterans will dine with Sergeant York at the Hendrick Hudson, and later will hear him speak.

Commander Samuel T. Ryan of Noble Callahan Post is chairman of the reception committee.

MAN, 85, CUTS TEETH.

Superior, Wis., Feb. 15 (AP). — C. H Wright, who will be 85 on March 15, today was suffering the pain of cutting teeth a third time. A few days ago Wright's gums began t ohurt slightly, and a dentist's examination showed he was getting new teeth.

Work-Relief Measure Nears First Big Test in U. S. Senate

VOTE ON DIRECT AID PROPOSAL TO SHOW OPPOSITION

McCarran To Lead Move for Sending Lump Sum Bill Back To Appropriations Committee.

Washington, Feb. 15 (AP).—The administration's work-relief program today approached its first big Senate test — a motion which would speed passage of the $880,000,000 for direct relief but leave the $4,000,000,000 work-giving fund to a doubtful future.

The outcome was expected by Democratic leaders to provide a major indication of just how rough will prove the huge money bill's journey in the Senate.

Senator McCarran (D-Nev), author of the mandatory "prevailing wage" amendment just barely defeated in committee by administration forces, promised the motion to return the lump-sum measure to the appropriations committee with instructions to split the plan into two parts and rush back the direct relief section.

From Republican ranks was promised a motion to cut one year off the time the huge relief fund would be available for spending. Instead of making the money available until June 30, 1937, Republicans agreed to ask a June 30, 1936 limit.

Favor Wage Clause.

Senator Monary, of Oregon, the minority leader, also announced an "overpowering majority" appeared to favor the McCarran prevailing wage amendment.

He said the Republicans were about evenly divided on the Adams amendment to slice $2,000,000,000 off the appropriation, that they seemed to favor the Metcalf proposal to give preference to war veterans in the relief set-up and also the Hayden amendment to require uniform wages and hours on public roads projects and similar state projects.

Recommital of the bill was only one of a number of proposals before the Republican conference called by Senator McNary, minority leader. Some Republicans are prepared to offer an amendment calling for cash payment of the bonus. Others want to limit the relief fund to $2,880,000,000.

Press Bonus Payment.

The bonus group, which includes some easterners heretofore opposed to cash payment, argued that if $4,880,000,000 was to be spent, it would be better to use some of it to pay the certificates and relieve the government of an obligation which will come due in a few years anyway.

Leaders in Congress said today that if veterans press for immediate payment of the $2,100,000,000 bonds, President Roosevelt plans to insist that they yield all claim to new pension benefits in the future.

The leaders, who declined to be quoted by name at present, said the President remarked that even though such a bargain might not actually be binding in the future it would constitute at least a "moral" deterrent to new demand.

It was emphasized that the President would not willingly see Congress pass a bonus bill even under that agreement. Opinion in Congress as to what will happen to the bonus bills is still divided. Bonus advocates predict victory; some administration leaders say the drive will be beaten, while others foresee a possible compromise.

U. S. NEWSPRINT PRODUCTION JUMPS

New York, Feb. 15 (AP).—Production of newsprint ' the United States and Canada in January totalled 282,625 tons compared with 272,568 in the same month last year and 319,321 in December. Canadian mills turned out 201,959 tons against 239,544 in December and 188,374 in January last year. United States mills during the month produced 80,666 tons compared with 79,777 in December and 84,194 in January last year. The figures are from the newsprint service bureau.

AGED VETERAN OF CIVIL WAR DEAD

Binghamton, Feb. 15 (AP).—Smith Le Baron, 90, commander of Whittlesly Post of the Grand Army of the Republic, at Endicott, died last night in an Endicott Hospital after a brief illness.

Mr. L. E. Baron, who was with Grant's troops when Lee surrendered at Appomatox court house, served with Company G, 15th New York Engineers. His widow and wo daughters survive. The funeral will be held Saturday.

Hauptmann Tense In Cell

This photo of Bruno Richard Hauptmann was taken as he ceased his restless pacing of the floor in his cell at Flemington, N. J. Convicted of kidnaping and murdering the Lindbergh baby, and sentenced to death, Hauptmann still retained some of his composure.

The New Deal Day by Day

Events in Washington Interpreted by Journalist.

BY DAVID LAWRENCE.

Washington, Feb. 15.—The taxi driver who drove me to the Ca· the other day revealed something that is rapidly getting to be a characteristic nowadays of these precincts: Namely, an increasing curiosity about Huey Long and Father Coughlin and their political implications in the passing scene.

"Did you hear Huey Long on the radio when he ripped into Roosevelt?" asked the driver. I regretted that I had not and asked him what the Senator had said.

"Oh, he said that the President hadn't kept his promise to the American people."

"In what way?" I asked.

"Well, he promised everybody a

(Continued on Page 2).

ETHIOPIAN RULER HITS MOBILIZATION OF ITALIAN TROOPS

Mussolini Program "Not Designed To MaintainConndence at Peace Parley," Emperor Says.

Rome, Feb. 15 (AP).—Emperor Haile Selassie declared today in a message to the press of the world that Italian mobilization "is not justified by any military measure on the part of Ethiopia."

The message from the Ethiopian ruler was made public here through his charge d'affaires, Negadras Yesus, who said he also was communicating it to the Italian foreign office.

"The news of the mobilization of

(Continued on Page 2).

Rising Food Prices Seen Crop Program Menace

Washington, Feb. 15 (AP).—Fear that rising food prices may turn the American housewife against the Agriculture Adjustment Administration and its crop reduction programs was expressed today by some AAA officials.

With new crops four months away, they said retail prices are just beginning to feel the full effect of last year's drought and curtailed farm acreage.

Bureau of labor statistics showed increases in the cost of food ranging from 44 per cent for butter to less than one per cent. for wheat cereals. Only potatoes, onions, cabbage and bananas showed decreases.

Average retail figures for the country compared with a year ago showed these increases: Milk 4.5 per cent., cheese 10, beef 17.5, pork chops 34.2, lard 70.5, mutton 18.3, poultry 16.3, eggs 23.4, white bread 5.1, flour 8.5, canned corn 16.4, canned peas 22.5, peaches 10.9.

AAA officials said they believed the public will stand no further increases without vigorous protests.

The possibility of a further rise in retail beef prices was suggested, meanwhile, by the fact that the government purchased and slaughtered millions of head of cattle to keep them from starving in the drought area.

It was recalled that Secretary Wallace anticipated some consumer criticism of his crop restriction plans last summer by asserting that supplies would not be up to normal but that shifts in diet would meet the situation.

COMPLAINTS LINK PUBLIC OFFICERS TO UTILITY FIRMS

Committee Tells Legislature Probe Shows Residential Power Rates "Grossly Excessive."

BY THE ASSOCIATED PRESS.

The New York legislative committee investigating public utilities reported today it had received information "relating to alleged connections between legislators and public officers and the utility companies."

The committee, in its first report to the Legislature, revealed that such information had been "brought to the office."

No details concerning the alleged connections were revealed by the committee, but its members disclosed that private hearings had been held as a result of the information obtained.

"Private hearings have been held and are still in progress, examining the activities and expenditures of all registered lobbyists," the committee also reported.

It said information furnished by legislators a state officials themselves was being tabulated "for the committee's further use."

The report covering the committee's first nine months of work was signed by Senator John J. Dunnigan, Democratic majority leader, its chairman, and by all members.

Power Rates "Excessive."

New York's Legislature appointed the investigating body last April after sensational disclosures by the Federal Trade Commission linking State Senator Warren T. Thayer, Chateaugay Republican, with the Associated Gas and Electric Co. Thayer resigned from the Senate and was found guilty of misconduct.

The Associated and three other holding companies, the committee said, "dominate the electric industry in the state of New York."

The others were listed as Niagara Hudson Power Corp., Consolidated Gas Co., and Long Island Lighting Co.

The committee said in its report that utility stockholders will suffer "loss and grief" unless electric rates are cut sharply.

The committee informed the Legisl that its work had shown reside electric costs to be "grossly excessive."

It noted, however, that "progressive elements" have taken charge of some companies and "relief is now in sight." The committee said some reductions already have been made, and predicted that others would follow.

Protection For Consumers.

"The present rates probably arise from the idea that public utilities are operated by the executives for the sole benefit of the stockholders and without consideration for the consuming public," the committee said.

"A persistence in this belief can only result in loss and grief to the stockholder, unless marked reductions can be had in rates for electrical energy."

The committee said that "no justification exists" for continuing such "trusteeship," and declared that the public "can only be protected by municipal operation or the rates controlled by a municipal yardstick."

"Power, heat and light are now necessities of life, and protection of the consumer is as paramount as protection of the stockholder," said the report.

The committee is charged with investigating lobbying, connections between legislator or state officials and the utilities, rates, financing and all utility practices.

The committee revealed that "certain corporations" sent their records outside of the state, but that later these were brought back and made available for the investigation.

BLASTS DAMAGE HOMES OF MINERS

Wilkes-Barre, Pa., Feb. 15 (AP). Two dynamitings today ushered in the 12th day of a strike of United Anthracite miners of Pennsylvania, after a turbulent 24 hours in which two men were shot dead and two others seriously wounded.

The blasts, both in South Wilkes-Barre, ripped away porches and front doors of homes of miners who are members of a rival union, the United Mine Workers of America, police reported.

No one was injured, police said, but Mrs. James Martin, wife of one of the miners, was treated for shock at her home. The other explosion was at the home of Benjamin Durchrow. Both men are employed by the Glen Alden Coal Company, whose collieries are affected by the strike, police said.

Troy Record Buys Troy Times

The Troy Record has purchased the Troy Times and, beginning tomorrow, The Times will be merged with The Evening Record. The Morning Record will continue as in the past.

The trend in communities the size of Troy in recent years has been steadily toward the consolidation of newspapers. It has long been evident that Troy could not maintain in a territory well cared for by two, one morning and one evening. A reduction in the number could be accomplished only through of the two establishments by purchase. The Record felt that the splendid history of The Times and the high standards which were its tradition warranted negotiations through which its course could continue unbroken.

The Times was established in 1851 by John M. Francis, a young man from the central part of the state who five years before had found a field in Troy worthy of his mettle. With humble beginnings, the daily assumed a leadership among the upstate press with the creation of the Republican Party. Mr. Francis adopted the new organization with enthusiasm; and The Times was known from that time as a party organ. The value the party placed upon Mr. Francis' services was attested by the honors it bestowed upon him. He was minister to Greece, to Portugal and to Austria-Hungary.

Upon his death his son, Charles S. Francis, succeeded him. He maintained the tradition faithfully. He too was interested in diplomacy and served as Minister to Greece and as Ambassador to Austria-Hungary. During his absence from the country William H. Anderson was in charge of the property and thereby became acquainted with the principles upon which the Francis family had founded the paper.

Mr. Francis died in 1911 and five years later a half interest in The Times was sold to Mr. Anderson and he became its publisher. Mr. Anderson entered the employ of The Times when in his teens and has completed more than 50 years of service at the time of its sale to The Record.

The Troy Record was founded in 1896 by a group of Trojans, headed by H. S. Ludlow, who felt a city of the size of Troy ought to have a morning newspaper. At that time there were three evening papers in the field but none in the morning. After three years The Evening Record was founded. The presence of four evening papers in a community of Troy's size was then in no sense unusual; and for a considerable period all of them found ample business to support their publication. But the cost of production has increased immeasurably and one by one they disappeared. The purchase of The Times by The Record is in line with the situation in other communities.

The Record does not propose to end the splendid tradition of The Troy Times. A newspaper which has persisted in this city for 84 years must continue. So The Times will merge with The Evening Record, bringing with it the accumulations of its past history, many of its unique features and much, The Record hopes, of its indomitable spirit. The joint newspaper will begin publication tomorrow night.

HITLER BELIEVES PACT MAY SOLVE GRAVE PROBLEM

Germany Ready To Discuss Proposed Aerial Accord With France and England.

Berlin, Feb. 15 (AP).—Nazi officialdom sees in the Anglo-French proposals for a western European air pact possible solution of the continent's gravest problem.

This attitude was manifest today as Reichsfuehrer Hitler assured the French and British ambassadors he was ready to discuss the proposed pact.

These discussions, official quarters believe, may lead to other agreements of a military and non-aggression character, likely not only to relieve European tension, but also to break down the wall of pacts threatening the reich's borders and answer the long-puzzling question of Germany's armament status.

This view was outlined in Deutsch Diplomatische Korrespondenz,

(Continued on Page 2.)

BOOM IN TRADE GAINING VOLUME, REVIEW REPORTS

Sales in Many Sections Greatly in Excess of Last Year's Figures, Dun and Bradstreet Says.

New York, Feb. 15 (AP).—The advancing tendencies in business and trade that have been prevalent since the first of the year continued in increasing volume during the past week, Dun & Bradstreets Trade Review said today.

Lincoln's birthday was a high spot during the past seven days for the retail trade and sales in many districts were from 30 to 50 per cent. higher than on the same day last year, the survey said.

"The confidence with which retailers view the outlook for spring distribution is accelerating activity in wholesale markets," the Review continued "and while there is a tendency for the recent upswing in some industrial branches to level out, the constant gain in others is lifting the average operating rate higher each week."

Dun & Bradstreet business activ-

(Continued on Page 2.)

Group Urges Laws to Bar Alien Propaganda

Washington, Feb. 15 (AP).—Legislation to protect the United States from foreign "propaganda" and revolutionary activity was recommended to Congress today by a house committee which spent more than a year investigating "un-American" activities.

In its unanimous report to the House, the committee headed by Rep. McCormack (D., Mass.) charged in effect that Soviet Russia has violated its pledge against harboring groups which advocate the overthrow of this government.

It reported that tons of Nazi propaganda have been smuggled into this country, and complimented "twenty-odd-million Americans of German birth or descent" for resisting efforts "to bring them into the Nazi program."

These recommendations for legislation were made:

1. That all publicity, propaganda or public relations agents of foreign governments, foreign political parties or foreign commercial firms be required to register with the Secretary of State.

2. That the Secretary of State be empowered to shorten or end the stay in this country of a temporarily admitted foreigner if he disseminates propaganda or engages in political" work.

3. That the United States negotiate treaties with other nations for the deportation of undesirable aliens to their native lands

4. That it be made unlawful to advise soldiers, sailors or reserves to disobey their laws or regulations

5. That United States attorneys be empowered to prosecute persons who refuse to testify before congressional committees.

6. That it be made unlawful "to advocate changes in a manner that incites to overthrow or destruction by force and violence, of the government of the United States" or any state.

BRUNO ALONE IN KIDNAP-MURDER, OFFICIALS CLAIM

Condemned Man To Be Removed To Death House Tomorrow; "I Am Innocent," He Tells Press.

Flemington, N. J., Feb. 15 (AP). —Bruno Richard Hauptmann, in a statement late today through his attorney, declared: "I feel that a grave miscarriage of justice occurred in connection with my conviction on the charge of kidnaping and murdering the baby of Col. Charles A. Lindbergh and Anne Morrow Lindbergh."

"Before God," Hauptmann said, "I swear I have nothing whatever to do with the kidnaping and the murder of this child and that I know nothing whatever in connection with the crime.

"I also swear that I know nothing in connection with the ransom money other than as I told it on the witness stand at Flemington."

"I sincerely believe," he continued, "that the great admiration of the American people have for the bereaved father, Colonel Charles A. Lindbergh, swayed their judgment against me and I believe it likewise swayed the judgment of the jury which ...ard my cause.

"I am absolutely innocent, and if it be my lot to be obliged to pay the penalty as described by the court, I shall go to my death protesting to the world, my absolute innocence of this crime."

BY THE ASSOCIATED PRESS

Statements that Federal officers and the New York (Bronx County) officials have evidence that Bruno Richard Hauptmann had an accomplice in the Lindbergh kidnaping were termed false today by J. Edgar Hoover, director of the Division of Investigation of the Department of Justice, and Dist. Atty. Samuel J. Foley of the Bronx.

Both officials made their statements in commenting upon reports in the New York Daily News that the authorities, including the Department of Justice, knew Bruno had an accomplice and expected to arrest him.

Hoover said Hauptmann's conviction closed the famous kidnap-murder case so far as his department was concerned. "The evidence clearly showed that Hauptmann was the only suspect and the active perpetrator of the crime," Hoover said.

Foley said that Hauptmann, according to all the evidence, committed the Lindbergh kidnaping and murder alone. He also said the case was closed as far as his office was concerned.

Sheriff John H. Curtiss announced at Flemington this morning that Hauptmann would be removed from the Hunterdon County Jail to the state prison death house at Trenton some time tomorrow.

Will Seek Writ Monday.

Chief of Counsel Edward J. Reilly said that he had never heard that the authorities knew of "an accomplice."

"Eventually, the police may find some truth to my theory that the crime was committed by at least four persons, none of them Hauptmann," Reilly observed, "but I can't recall of the police ever acting on the accomplice angle."

Reilly said that he "will no longer try to solve this crime for the police."

"I'll let them solve their own crimes, henceforth," he remarked. "And I hope they have better luck than they've had with the Lindbergh kidnaping."

Reilly said that the matter of appeal would be worked out by Frederick A. Pope and Egbert Rosecrans, two of his New Jersey associates in the defense of Hauptmann.

"I understand that Rosecrans will seek a writ of error on Monday," he replied, when asked when the defense would start action on the appeal.

"I haven't a dollar," the condemned man told his counsel, "and must depend on the public."

In his only interview during four months in the Hunterdon County Jail, the Bronx carpenter was asked yesterday whether he could not "possibly name persons connected with the kidnaping of the Lindbergh baby."

"As God is my judge," was the reply, "I cannot confess, for there is nothing to confess.

"If I had any confession to make, I would have made it months ago and saved my wife and child all this worry.

"I told everything, on my word of honor. That is, I mean I have not tried to cover up anybody."

Bruno's Accomplice Known.

But the New York Daily News said in a copyright article today that not only were two men involved in the $50,000 ransom fraud Hauptmann was identified as the actual recipient but that police knew the identity of the second and sought to trap him.

This man, the News said, was the one who hid his face with a handkerchief and peered into Colonel Charles A. Lindbergh's automobile while the father of the slain baby awaited his ransom emissary Dr. J. F. Condon. The mystery man moved on and dropped his handkerchief apparent-

(Continued on Page 2).

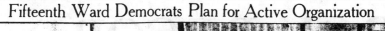

YOUNG PEOPLE TO MEET ON JUNE 7 IN HOOSICK FALLS

Organization Founded in 1889 To Have Semi-Annual Session Afternoon and Evening.

The semi-annual meeting of the Hoosick Young People's Union will be held at the Methodist Church, Hoosick Falls, Sunday, June 7, with afternoon and evening sessions, both of which will be opened with a song service under the leadership of J. Wells Herrington, with his daughter, Miss Evalyn Herrington, as the accompanist. Rev. M. W. Barnard of the White Creek Methodist Church will conduct the devotional service in the afternoon and Rev. Henry Habel of the West Hoosick Baptist Church in the eevning. The benediction will be pronounced in the afternoon by Rev. J. G. Masel of the North Hoosick Methodist Church and in the evening by Rev. Howard Stimel of the Hoosick Falls Methodist Church.

To Extend Welcome.

Words of welcome will be extended by Woodard Hogan, president of the entertaining society and the response will be by Mrs. George MacArthur, president of the Union. During the afternoon program a violin solo will be rendered by Leon Vetal of the Hoosick Falls Methodist Church and a cornet solo by Harold McLucas of the Hoosick Falls Baptist Church. At the afternoon session a double quartet from the Center White Creek Baptist Church will render selections and a one-act play, "The Color Line," will be given by members from the West Hoosick Baptist Church. In the evening Mrs. Ralph Bullock of the Hoosick Falls Baptist Church will render vocal solos.

The address of the meeting will be given during the evening session by Rev. Howard Stimmel, pastor of the Hoosick Falls Methodist Church, who will speak on "This Matter of Growing Up."

The organization is composed of the young people's societies of the Baptist churches at Center White Creek, Hoosick, Hoosick Falls and West Hoosick and the Methodist churches at Eagle Bridge, Hoosick Falls, North Hoosick and White Creek. The officers of the Union are Mrs. George MacArthur, president; Mrs. Harold Andrew, vice president; Miss Ruby Hunt, secretary and Donald White, treasurer. Officers for the ensuing year will be chosen at the evening session of the meeting.

Organized in 1889.

The Hoosick Young People's Union was first organized at a meeting held at the Presbyterian Church, Hoosick Falls, Friday, April 12, 1889, largely through the efforts of George S. McKearin of Hoosick Falls, who had shortly before attended a meeting along those lines at Cleveland, Ohio. The first efforts failed to chrystalize with a permanancy and a renewed attempt at organization was made at a meeting held at the Methodist Church, Eagle Bridge, on August 17, 1894, at which time Mr. McKearin was chosen secretary. The organization has been continued since the latter meeting and has steadily grown in size and popularity. While the attendance at the earlier meetings was about 100 young people there are nearly 500 expected to be present at the coming meeting. The present name of the organization was changed from the Hoosick Christian eEndeavor Union at the meeting held in 1912.

EXPELLED PRIEST RETURNS TO POST

Djibouti, French Somaliland (AP)—Monsignor Andre Jarosseau, French missionary who was expelled by the Italians and then reinstated after Paris made a strong protest to Rome, left here today to return to Harar, second city of Ethiopia.

The prelate, who has devoted fifty years to missionary work among the Ethiopians, particularly among lepers, had been expelled for alleged anti-Italian activities.

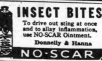

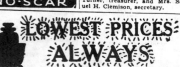

Fifteenth Ward Democrats Plan for Active Organization

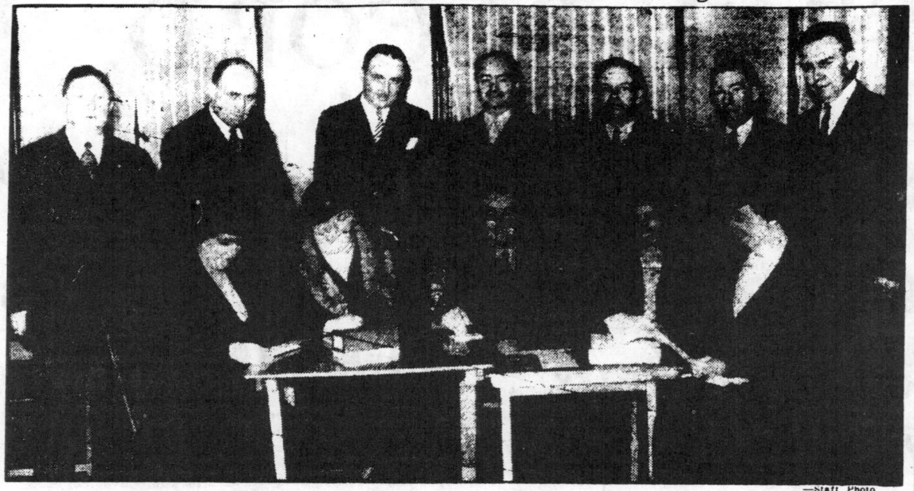

—Staff Photo

Members of the Fifteenth Ward Democratic Club met at Diamond Rock Hall last night and made plans to keep their organization active during the summer months. City Clerk James M. McGrath, member of the club, was made chairman of a clamsteam to be held in September. Common Council President Edward G. Ronan and Mr. McGrath addressed the group. Twenty new members joined the club, bringing the membership to 160. A picnic was also planned for June 20. The club will meet again on June 25. Luke J. Cavanagh, president, is shown seated in center, in photo.

Lansingburg Notes

HIGH SCHOOL HOLDS TAP DAY EXERCISES; STUDENTS HONORED

Seventeen of thirty-nine honor students were "tapped" into the National Honor Society yesterday afternoon at Lansingburg High School. It is the highest award that can be attained by a pupil in the four years of high school study, based on his scholarship, leadership, character and service to the school.

Those admitted to the Lansingburg High School Chapter were Rita Bleibtrey, Edwin Bonesteel, Mette Connor, Helen Day, Betty Duncan, William Fellows, Edna Fuller, Jane Hewes, Betty Jones, Donald MacAuley, Clarence Quinn, Walter Shaw, Jane Smith, Stewart Smith, Donald Stoll, Muriel Taylor and Vinnia Wells. Edwin Bonesteel, son of Mr. and Mrs. Stearns Bonesteel of 387 Fifth Avenue, was elected president for the coming year and William Fellows, son of Mr. and Mrs. James C. Fellows, 569 Seventh Avenue, was elected secretary.

Miss Myrtle Eville, retiring president, welcomed the new members and presented them with their Honor Society pins. Other members who assisted in the "tapping" were the Misses Ruth Murphy, Margaret Bowen, Lucille Paul, Eleanor Beck, Betty Olsen, Eleanor Miller and Gerald Randall and William Babcock.

The speaker of the afternoon was Rev. James A. Perry, Th. D., of the State Street Methodist Church. Following the exercises the honor group was served tea by the Adelphian Society, of which Muriel Taylor is president.

Board Meeting Scheduled.

A meeting of the Board of Education is scheduled for Tuesday evening at the high school.

Junior Club to March.

Members of the Van Arnum Junior Club, No. 17, will meet at 117th Street tomorrow at 8:30 a. m. to take their place in the Memorial Day Parade. The members will be attired in white, with white sailor hats, red and blue capes and will carry flags.

Hear Convention Report.

A report of the eastern district convention at Newark, N. J., early in the month was given to the members of the Haabets Fremtid, Danish Sisterhood, at their meeting in their 112th Street rooms last evening by Miss Abelone Smith who was the delegate. There will be only one meeting a month in June, July, and August instead of the usual two during the other months of the year.

Eastern Star Meets.

A memorial service for deceased members was conducted by Palestine Chapter, O. E. S., at the Lansingburg Masonic Temple last evening with the officers under the direction of Worthy Matron Mrs. Aura T. Webster and Worthy Patron William Groesbeck in charge. The officers also conferred the initiatory degree upon a class of candidates. A social hour followed the meeting with Miss Harriett Darby as chairman of the committee in charge.

Card Club Entertained.

Mrs. Clarence M. Twamley entertained the G. C. G. Bridge Club yesterday afternoon at her home, 908 Third Avenue, marking the last meeting of the group for the year. The club has completed nine years of existence. The prizes for the play went to Mrs. Harry H. Seiffert, Mrs. Jack Harney and Mrs. Robert VanSteenburg. Officers elected at the meeting for the ensuing year were Mrs. Earl T. Lawrence, president; Mrs. Harold Turner, treasurer, and Mrs. Samuel H. Clemison, secretary.

CHANGES LISTED IN MEMORIAL DAY PLANS FOR THIS VICINITY

Samuel J. Kirkpatrick, chairman in charge of Memorial Day exercises in this section tomorrow, has announced several changes in the program.

At St. John's Cemetery Rev. James R. Simpson, O. S. A., will give the principal address and Alson Spain of St. Augustine's School will deliver Lincoln's Gettysburg Address. "Taps" will be sounded by a group from Troop 8, Boy Scouts of America of St. Augustine's School, under direction of Troop Committeeman William J. Higgins.

The principal address at the river bank and at the old village cemetery will be given by Rev. Thomas T. Base of the Third Avenue Church of Christ.

The parade will start promptly at 8:45 a. m. from G. A. R. headquarters in Second Avenue at 117th Street.

MORE THAN 2,000 TICKETS SOLD FOR JUNE NIGHT FESTIVAL

A committee meeting was held in the chapel hall at St. Augustine's Church, Lansingburg, last evening to make further plans for the June Night Festival sponsored by the combined societies in the parish on the city lawn at 123rd Street and Second Avenue on Tuesday evening, June 9, to raise funds for the building fund of the church.

Joseph B. Nial, chairman, presided. Reports of the progress of the ticket sale were made. More than 2,500 tickets have been sold to date, it was reported. Edward Kennedy said he needed additional men to serve on his grounds committee and a call was made for volunteers. Mrs. Edward Broderick and Mrs. John O'Neil reported on the card party they held this week to raise money for the festival fund.

BIG BILL THOMPSON THREATENS TO RUN AS AN INDEPENDENT

Chicago (AP)—The bulky form of William Hale "Big Bill" Thompson, former mayor of Chicago, cast a shadow on Republican unity in Illinois today.

Thompson hinted he intended to run in the fall as an independent candidate for governor.

This would bring him in competition with Wayland Brooks, Republican nominee, and Gov. Henry Horner, a Democrat, making it a three-sided quarrel.

The former mayor charged bluntly, in confirming reports he was circulating "Thompson for Governor" pledge cards, that he had been "double crossed" in the April 14 primaries.

He had a one-man ticket in the race, T. V. Sullivan for attorney general. Sullivan lost. Thompson asserted it was because a Republican order went out to "slaughter Sullivan" two days before the voting.

ERIE G. O. P. CHIEF ASSUMES LEAD IN ANTI-HILLES MOVE

Buffalo (UP)—Erie County G. O. P. Chairman Edwin F. Jaeckle today asserted that a secret meeting of powerful Republicans has been called for this afternoon in New York City to pave the way for re-election of Charles D. Hilles as the party's national committeeman for New York State.

Jaeckle dispatched a telegram to Melvin C. Eaton, Republican State Chairman and ally of Hillies, demanding that the secret meeting be abandoned.

The Erie County leader yesterday assumed the lead in a long smouldering rebellion against the rule of Hilles. He, with other local party leaders, demanded that Hilles retire for the benefit of the party.

Hilles, in New York City, has remained silent, refusing to answer Jaeckle's demand for his retirement.

MORE TOWNSEND AIDS MAY FACE CONTEMPT ACTION

Reluctance of Additional Witnesses to Testify in Old Age Pension Probe Presents Problem.

Washington (AP)—With its knotty problem of what to do with Dr. F. E. Townsend solved by the House's shouted approval of a resolution citing him and two aides for contempt, a House investigating committee today faced new troubles.

The possibility arose that additional contempt citations may be forthcoming as the result of the reluctance of certain witnesses to testify in the inquiry into the old age pension plan.

While the committee mulled over developments, Speaker Byrns prepared to certify to the United States district attorney today all documents in the contempt citation against Dr. Townsend, the Rev. Clinton Wunder and John B. Kiefer.

Chairman Bell (D-Mo.) said he planned to confer with Leslie A. Garnett, federal attorney, and would co-operate with him in moving against Townsend, Kiefer and Wunder.

Bell believes that Dr. Townsend's walk-out on the committee a week ago, his subsequent defiant statements and the failure of Wunder and Kiefer to appear for examination were sufficient for a grand jury indictment.

Garnett said he believed he could obtain an indictment next week but was doubtful whether the case could be brought to trial before fall.

Conviction on a contempt charge carries a maximum penalty of twelve months in jail or a $1,000 fine or both.

The investigating committee planned to resume hearings Monday with Charles M. Hawkes, of Boston, Townsend manager for Massachusetts, the witness.

FOUR TROJANS GET DIPLOMAS MONDAY AT UNION COLLEGE

Four Trojans, one of whom has attained the honor of membership in Phi Beta Kappa, national honor society, will be graduated at the 141st Commencement exercises Monday, June 8, at Union College. They are John D. Hall, son of Mr. and Mrs. Albert E. Hall of 612 Fifth Avenue; Robert S. Langer, son of Samuel J. Langer of 37 Collins Avenue; Harry O. Lee, son of Mr. and Mrs. Henry Lee of Winter Street, and Raymond F. Robinson, son of Mr. and Mrs. Edwin H. Robinson of 835 Eighth Avenue.

Hall, a graduate of Lansingburg High School, was recently awarded a graduate scholarship in political science at Syracuse University. He has been a four year honor nma.

Besides being a member of Phi Beta Kappa, Langer is editor of the literary quarterly and took highest honors at the recent prize day exercises. Lee assisted in organizing the Social Problems Forum. He is a graduate of Catholic Central High School.

Robinson, also a graduate of Lansinburg High School, has been awarded his varsity letter in lacrosse and has attained mention on the Dean's List for high scholarship.

TEMPLE BETH EL SERVICE.

Rabbi Joel S. Geffen will speak on "The Ethics of the Fathers" at the Temple Beth El service at 8 p. m. today. Services will be held at 9 a. m. tomorrow for adults and at 10:30 a. m. for children. The religious school will meet Sunday at 10 a. m.

LINER QUEEN MARY MAY SET NEW MARK FOR OCEAN CROSSING

Aboard the S. S. Queen Mary en route to New York (AP)—Maintaining her high pace for the second day at sea, the Queen Mary jockeyed clearly today for a position to set a new transatlantic speed record and return the blue ribbon to Britain.

Apparently well-founded reports were current aboard the great ship that on the fast first day's run from the Cherbourg breakwater, the world's second largest liner bettered 32 knots an hour.

The average speed for the first leg of this maiden voyage to the United States was 28.73 knots.

The Queen Mary's bigger French rival, the Normandie, made her record westward crossing of four days, three hours, 13 minutes from Bishop's Rock to Ambrose Lightship at an average speed of 29.94 knots.

The British contender continued her high speed, and while officials still disclaimed at this stage any purpose of trying to break the record, it was emphasized the ship was traveling at a rate which placed her in a strategic position to displace the Normandie.

PLAN MEMORIAL TO FAMED ACTOR

Chicago (AP)—A memorial to "De Lawd" will be unveiled tomorrow at Lincoln Cemetery.

A life-size statue of the late Richard B. Harrison, who enacted the role of "De Lawd" in more than 1,659 performances of "Green Pastures," will be dedicated with ceremony. Participants include the Harrison Memorial Foundation, the White Rose League, the Harrison Dramatic Players and George Giles Post of the American Legion.

Men's Club to Offer Magician

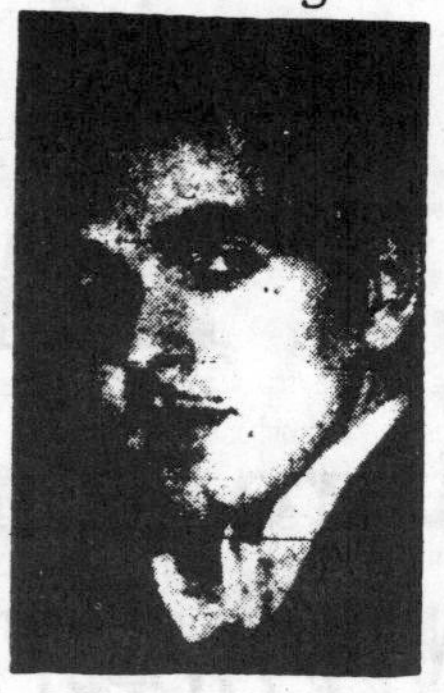

PIERCE THE MAGICIAN

A program of legerdemain will be presented Tuesday at 8 p. m. in the assembly room of the Fifth Avenue-State Street Methodist Church under the auspices of the Men's Club by Pierce the magician.

Pierce is one of the youngest professional magicians on the American stage. He was affiliated with the late Howard Thurston. His program is arranged for entertainment of both young and old. He is assisted by Miss Lois Lake.

Ralph M. Sheldon, president of the Men's Club, is general chairman of the committee arranging the presentation, while Miss Clementine Switzer has charge of the ticket sale.

"DUST BOWL" AREA DRENCHED BY RAIN

Lamar, Col. (AP) They patched their rubber boots and long unused mud chains today in the Southwest's drought and dust sector.

Bankful streams, some constituting flood threats, coursed through the area after six successive days of rain. Highway and railroad bridges were washed out.

Motorists, used to being stranded on the highways by blinding clouds of dust, revel in an almost forgotten experience—getting stuck in the mud.

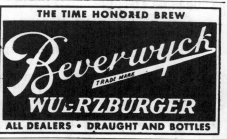

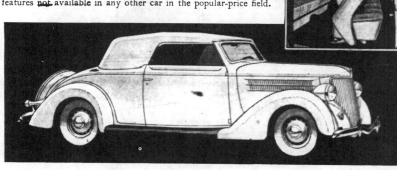

SIGNALS CROSSED.

Minneapolis — When Detective James Connolly was "planted" in a harness shop to lie in wait for burglars who had been busy in the neighborhood, his superiors neglected to tell Patrolman Donald A. West about it. As West walked his beat, Connolly, mistaking him for a prowler, fired a shot. West was slightly wounded. The burglars didn't show up.

BYGONE FASHIONS PROVES SUCCESS TO LARGE CROWD

Woman's Benevolent Society of Presbyterian Church Sponsors Affair; To Give Show at Hoosick

HOOSICK FALLS

Hoosick Falls—The style show, "Fashions of Bygone Days," presented last evening in the Presbyterian Church parlors, under the auspices of the Woman's Benevolent Society, was well attended and proved to be a very enjoyable affair. Besides those from Cambridge in the cast there was a vocal quartet composed of Mr. and Mrs. John Nicol, Miss Cretta Benway and Robert Dewar, with Mrs. James Coghill as accompanist, and two juvenile models—Virginia Bentley and Nancy Jones, both 7, all of this village.

Academy Reunion.

The Alumni Association of St. Mary's Academy has decided to hold its annual reunion and reception to the graduating class of the academy Thursday evening, June 25, at Riley's at Saratoga Lake.

To Make Official Visit.

Mrs. Grace Reiss of Brooklyn, Grand Associate Matron of the Order of Amaranth State of New York will make an official visit to Hoosick Falls Court of Amaranth at its "step-up" night meeting this evening.

To Present Minstrel Show.

A minstrel show and dance will be presented Thursday and Friday evenings at the new parish hall in Hoosick under the auspices of All Saints' Church of that place by a cast of about 50. The program will be in three parts. The first part will consist of solos, choruses and endmen jokes; part two will be a one-act play while the last part will include specialties. Following the program each evening there will be two hours of dancing to the music of Hynick's Musicmakers. The entertainment will be under the charge of Warren Bovie who has directed the rehearsals. Soloists in Part 1 are Jean Paddock, Lillian McNeilly, Vera Cipperly, Rudolph Marshall, George Rifenburg, Ethel Cipperly. The cast of the play is composed of Misses Edith and Martha Enquist, Warren Bovie and Mrs. Owen Paddock. Those presenting specialties are Mrs. Almon Hewitt, Jean Paddock, Vera Cipperly, Blanche Cipperly and Ellsworth Stevens. The music will be by Mrs. Charles Breer, Leon Wilcox and Harold McLucas. Warren Bovie will be interlocutor and the endmen are Charles Williams, George W. Bovie, Harold Prebble, Marshall Rudd, George Rifenburg, Ellsworth Stevens, Ira Stevens and George Enquist. Members of the chorus are Vera Cipperly, Doris Cipperly, Eleanor Cipperly, Blanche Cipperly, Ethel Cipperly, Caroline Colehamer, Florence Bell, Jessie Surdam, Lillian McNeilly, Annette Paddock, Mary Ellen Fowler, Hazel Slade, Genevieve Kjelgaard, Jean Paddock, Mrs. Harry Bratt, Mrs. George Rifenburg, Mrs. Walter Colehamer, Mrs. Owen Paddock, Mrs. George W. Bovie, Mrs. William Gardner, Mrs. Ellsworth Stevens, Mrs. Harry Webster, Charles Breer, Raymond Colehamer, Robert Bovie, Arthur Burdick, Frank Pierce, Lyman Rudd, Rudolph Marshall, James Lohnes and Harry Webster.

Brevities.

First and Second Wards will play a baseball game tomorrow evening on the Athletic field.

A free chest clinic will be held from 2 to 4 p. m. tomorrow at the Municipal Building under the direction of Dr. John J. Randall of Pawling Sanitarium.

A public card party will be sponsored by the Parent-Teacher Association tomorrow at 8 p. m. in the high school auditorium for the benefit of the high school's Washington in 1937 Club.

COMMITTEE MEETS TO PLAN PARISH FETE

Committees in charge of the annual June festival of St. Peter's Church Sunday evening, June 22, at Frear Park, conducted an enthusiastic meeting last evening at St. Peter's Lyceum.

The meeting was in charge of William R. Conroy, general chairman, and Mrs. Edmund M. Sullivan, co-chairman. There was a large attendance. Edward Clossen and Mrs. W. Leo McCarthy will be chairman and co-chairman respectively, in charge of the list of patrons and patronesses. Mrs. Michael J. Hubbard will be in charge of awards. The committees will meet next Monday evening at the lyceum.

Striking View of Ship Christening

Miss Mai Duane, descendant of William J. Duane, Secretary of the Treasury in President Jackson's cabinet, took no chances on fizzling the christening of the new U. S. Coast Guard Cutter at Philadelphia Navy Yard. She gritted her teeth, grasped the baptismal bottle of champagne firmly and used both hands to smash the flagon against the Duane's prow. Then look what happened.

Fiftieth Anniversary Of R. P. I. Class of '86 To Be Marked June 12

The fiftieth anniversary of the class of '86 at Rensselaer Polytechnic Institute will be observed with a gathering Friday night, June 12, at the Hendrick Hudson.

A committee of Troy members of the class including John Knickerbacker, Frederic M. Cummings and Albert F. Demers have been planning for several months for the half-century observance. Mr. Knickerbacker is permanent vice president of the class.

The class had hoped to have a gathering which would equal that of the 45th anniversary when 25 members were present. However, the five years have taken their toll in death and sickness. Fifteen of the class have assured the committee of their attendance at the reunion and several others hope to be here.

Among those who have promised to come here at commencement time is Tracy C. Drake of Chicago, prominent alumni and founder of the Polytechnic. He also will attend a dinner of the Polytechnic Board June 11 when he will be honored as the original editor of the publication.

Professors to Attend.

President William Otis Hotchkiss of the Institute and Assistant Director Ray Palmer Baker will be among the guests. Three professors, one of whom was an instructor and the other two students when the class of '86 graduated, will be present. They are Charles W. Crockett, professor emeritus, Edward R. Carey and Edward F. Chilman.

One guest who had attended every reunion dinner of the class and who was a young instructor when the students of '86 graduated from the Institute, will be missing this year. The late Director Palmer C. Ricketts was a firm friend of the class and never failed to attend their gatherings.

Members of the class who have promised to attend the reunion include Henry B. Davenport of Charleston, W. Va., and Ezekiel C. Davenport of Charles Town, W. Va., brothers; Henry V. Macksey of Brookline, Mass., Tracy C. Drake of Chicago, organizer of the Drake Hotel Company of that city and builder of the Blackstone Hotel and the Blackstone Theater.

Also Thomas F. Lawlor of Poughkeepsie, Superintendent of Public Works there for many years; Commodore Vincent B. Ward of Palm Beach, Fla., retired oil man and engineer; Albert L. Hauck, prominent engineer, Norport, Ohio.

The three Trojans who will be present are Mr. Knickerbacker, best know for his philanthropies, Mr. Cummings, architect for many buildings in this city, and Mr. Demers, associate editor of The Record Newspapers.

Hope To Be Present.

Among those who hope to be present is George R. Sikes of Buffalo, consulting engineer.

Those who are unable to come due to pressure of business or ill health are Henry M. Fairchild of New York, Octavius A. Zayas, engineer and diplomat, Havana, Cuba; Edward B. Ashby, grand marshal of the class of '86; James E. Larowe, of Detroit; Enrique Tonceda, R. P. I. distinguished chemist; Stewart K. Smith, St. Louis, Mo. engineer and inventor; Major C. B. Eckels, World War veteran, Long Beach, Cal.; George C. Spafford of Rockville, Ill., bank president; John Chambers of Louisville, Ky., State Engineer of Kentucky; James Morrison Colwell of Santa Barbara, Calif.; George Roberts of Harrisburg, Pa., member of the Trojan Hook and Ladder Company during his school days here; Walter B. Price of Jefferson City, Mo.; Edward W. Scott, Jr., of New York City, Theodore R. Hinsdale of Seattle, Wash., and Robert J. Evans of Denver, Col.

Necrological Roll.

Also Charles E. Barthell of Arbor, Mich.; George A. Dar of Orange, N. J.; M. Ward Easby of Philadelphia; Enrique de Garay of Mexico City; Thomas T. H. Harwood of Detroit; Paul W. Horbach of Omaha, Neb.; Edward C. Justh of New York; Frederic M. Kimball of Cana, Colombia, S. A.; Mario de Mendoza of Rio de Janiero; James I. Plumb of Islip; John Raum of Washington, and Ben A. Stribling of San Antonio, Tex.

Those who have died since the 45th reunion have been listed by Mr. Demers, who is acting secretary of the class. They are: Walter Jermyn of Oswego; Elisha K. Camp of Atlantic Highlands, N. J.; James H. Caldwell of Troy; Dwight A. Hitchcock of Detroit; Edwin N. Sanderson of New York; Morris R. Sherrerd of Newark, N. J., and Howard H. Shields of Bennington, Vt.

HOLD THREE MEN AFTER ATTACK ON ROAD JOB WORKER

Two Saratoga Residents and West Milton Man Arrested; John Covel, 28 Died Yesterday From Injuries.

Police at Saratoga Springs state that charges of first degree murder would probably be preferred against John Deuel, 21, his brother, Joseph Deuel, 24, of Saratoga and Oscar Fitzgerald, 35, of West Milton, as the result of the death of John Covel, 28, of Saratoga, in the Saratoga Hospital at noon yesterday. The trio will be arraigned before City Judge Anthony J. LaBelle of Saratoga Springs late this afternoon.

Covell, according to coroner's physician Dr. F. Scott Towne, died of a fractured skull and a hemorrhage of the brain. He was the victim of an assault Saturday evening while acting as a flagman on a Saratoga-Springs-Albany Road construction job, and was taken to the hospital by Trooper J. J. Finn and Sergt. John McNamee of the State Police. The Sergeant later said that Covell, before his death, had signed complaints against the men to be arraigned today, charging them with kicking him unconscious.

Salvi Salvato, 22, of Ballston Spa, also was arrested by police, as was Mrs. John Deuel, and both are being held as material witnesses. Police said that two Greenwich girls were also available as witnesses but refused to reveal their names.

Investigations by state and local police have revealed that a car containing seven or eight persons, including those named in the charges, was stopped by Covell and an argument developed, allegedly because the flagman made disparaging remarks about the female occupants of the car. Passing motorists called the State Police upon finding the unconscious man. District Attorney John B. Smith and police officials made the arrests immediately after Covell's death, nabbing the men in the vicinity of Saratoga.

Coroner Dr. Robert B. Castree of Saratoga County said that an inquest will be conducted immediately after the arraignment today.

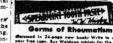

CHURCHES DECIDE VACATION SCHOOL TO START JUNE 23

Registration of Pupils Completed by Mrs. James Van Vrankin and Her Assistants.

STILLWATER.

Registration for the Vacation Church School, to be conducted in Stillwater June 23-July 4, has been completed under the direction of Mrs. James Van Vrankin, assisted by Misses Lorraine Carey and Dorothy Rogers of the Presbyterian Church, Misses Sara Finger and Mildred Hayner of the Baptist Church, and Misses Florence Lee and Mary Darrow of the Methodist Church.

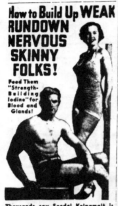

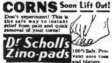

Personal.

Miss Mary Rancourt and Miss Lena Albertene of Hoosick Falls were recent guests of friends in town.

Mrs. Lawrence Lane of Elizabeth, N. J., is spending several days with her mother, Mrs. Nellie Baldwin of South Main Street.

Mr. and Mrs. Claude Cooke and family of Carteret, N. J., and Mrs. N. J. Cooke of Clarion, Pa., have been recent guests of Mrs. Nellie Baldwin.

Mrs. Albert Wagner has been confined to the house by illness.

Mrs. Philip Powell was called to Hemstreet Park yesterday by the serious illness of her mother, Mrs. Emma Lane.

Allen Gifford of the East Side was graduated from the Albany Medical College Monday. He is a graduate of the Stillwater High School in the class of 1927 and Union College. He will serve his interneship at the Leonard Hospital in Troy.

Church Notes.

Rev. Dayton L. Jones and Mrs. Earl Ward motored to Salem yesterday to attend a district stewards conference.

The members of the Senior Baraca Class of the Baptist Sunday School, of which Harvey Van Vrankin is president, enjoyed a hot dog roast Monday evening at the home of A. S. Hannay. Frederick Hayner had charge of the roast. This took the place of the monthly class meeting and social.

Rev. Dayton L. Jones will lead the weekly prayer service at the Methodist Church tomorrow evening. Rev. Arthur H. Landmesser of the Pawling Avenue Methodist Church of Troy will conduct the prayer service at the Baptist Church. The Board of Education will meet at the close of the service.

The members of the Junior Philathea Class of the Presbyterian Sunday School were entertained Monday evening at the home of Miss Marguerite Stephens. In the absence of the president, Mrs. Edward Gilgallon, Mrs. Walter Curtis presided over a short business session. A social time was enjoyed, delicious refreshments being served by the hostess. Next month the class will enjoy a picnic supper at the Ryan camp across the river.

NORTONVILLE

Albert Reed of Melrose called at the Reed homestead Monday.

Miss Bernice Barber passed a few days with Mrs. Guy Barber at Hoosick.

Mrs. Barbara Doyle visited her parents, Mr. and Mrs. Richard Holbritter, Sunday.

Mrs. Clarence Mason called on Mrs. John Ford Sunday at the Samaritan Hospital, Troy.

James Holbritter has sold his farm, farming implements and stock to James Brown of Troy.

Mr. and Mrs. Ernest Darrow of Valley Falls were recent callers at the home of S. W. Humphrey.

Mr. and Mrs. Fred Bolander called on Mrs. Etta Smith and daughter at Boyntonville Sunday.

Mrs. Nathan Herrington visited her mother, Mrs. Ellen Sherman, and sister, Mrs. Ellen Stiles, recently.

Mrs. Willard Bell and nephew, Albert Brown, of Easton, called Sunday on Mr. and Mrs. Fred Bolander.

Mrs. George Yates of New London, Conn., is passing the summer with her daughter, Mrs. Joseph Ashcroft.

Mr. and Mrs. Clifford Rogers and son Richard of Troy were week-end guests at the home of Richard Holbritter.

Mr. and Mrs. Frank Humphrey and daughter of Pittstown were Sunday evening guests at the home of S. W. Humphrey.

Mr. and Mrs. Harry Duran, Mrs. Addie Snyder and children and Mrs. Marcia Heger and daughter Florence called at the home of Leighton Banker Sunday.

Mr. and Mrs. Burton Barber attended the wedding of Mrs. Barber's brother, Gustav Requat, in New York recently. Mrs. Milford Strait of Hoosick accompanied them.

Landon Boom Is No 'Accident'; It's Masterpiece Of Planning

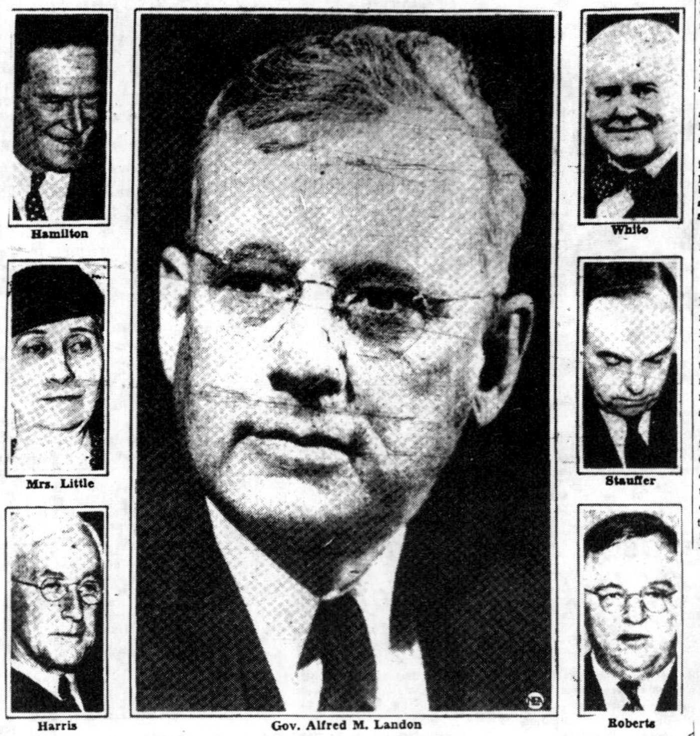

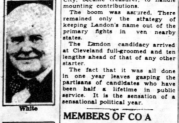

Hamilton — Mrs. Little — Harris — Gov. Alfred M. Landon — White — Stauffer — Roberts

Clustering around the rising Landon star are a set of faces mostly new to the national political heavens. If the unequaled boom they have engineered for the Kansas governor bears the expected fruit, Hamilton will be the new chairman of the national committee. All the others would be very close to the ear of the Republican nominee.

Candidacy Built With Care By Friends of Kansas Governor.

By WILLIS THORNTON.
NEA Service Staff Correspondent.

Cleveland From a little known prairie state politician to a front seat on one of the gaudiest convention band-wagons of recent times, all in one year.

That's the success story of Alf Landon of Kansas, and the details of how it all happened are the awe of delegates as wave after wave of rumor of "Landon on the first ballot" sweep the convention city.

Like many things which seem to have "just happened," the Landon boom didn't "just happen" at all. There was good, solid powder in it, but don't think the priming wasn't carefully adjusted, the fuse nicely set, and the match assiduously applied.

Two years ago, newspaper readers noted a small paragraph in the political news, to the effect that Kansas had re-elected a Republican govenor. H'm! Not only elected in 1932, but the only Republican governor to be re-elected amid the 1934 Democratic landslide! H'm! Oh, well, Kansas always was naturally Republican, wasn't it?

Who Is This Landon?

The modest suggestion by a Kansas City paper at that time, that this made Landon a Republican presidential possibility, caused practically not even a mild ripple. Landon? Landon?

So the winter of 1934-5 slid by, with never a further mention of Landon except by an occasional correspondent, desperate for a "political dope story," who noted that Landon was the only Republican governor who looked like campaign material at all. The country let Landon lapse back into what Grover Cleveland became famous for calling innocuous desuetude.

But a certain group of Kansas City friends of the governor, mostly newspapermen, did not forget. The Kansas City Star's managing editor, Roy Roberts, a college chum of Landon, and Lacy Haynes, Star political expert, were prominent among them.

They never quite let the Landon idea die in their own paper. They had friends throughout the country. Roberts had been a widely known Washington correspondent.

Landon Acquires Manager.

In the meantime, Landon had pulled off a little coup of his own which strengthened his home defenses. When Landon was breaking into politics as campaign manager for the liberal Clyde Reed, the opposing manager for the conservative group was one John Hamilton of Topeka, a good-looking young law teacher and legislator.

This rivalry between Landon and Hamilton continued after Reed's election as governor, and Hamilton even prevented Landon's election as precinct committeeman in one contest. But shortly after Landon's first election as governor, David Mulvane, veteran national committeeman, died. And Landon was big enough, or foxy enough, as you choose, to name his old rival Hamilton as national committeeman. The breach was healed, and Kansas Republicanism became a unit instead of a divided camp of old Bull Moose and conservative, with highly individualistic wings adhering to Senator Arthur Capper and to Publisher William Allen White. Landon had closed up his home front, and also provided himself with a very astute campaign manager.

Came the end of the fiscal year. Kansas had balanced her budget. So had several other states. But something about Kansas and budget-balancing seemed to go together, and Landon was chosen to

How Boom Began.

Almost immediately Landon and balanced budget, Landon and economy in government became synonymous. This was midsummer of 1935.

All this was right down the alley of Publisher William Randolph Hearst, who had been bitter in denunciation of government spending. He sent investigators to Kansas and combed the Landon record. Finding it clean, he threw all his publicity resources, newspaper, magazine, newsreel, and radio, into the now mounting Landon boom.

William Allen White, "the sage of Emporia," whose political judgments are known and respected in the prairie states and nationally, now endorsed Landon as the Republican "white hope."

Keep Ball Rolling.

By this time, magazine and newspaper special writers were beginning to hit the Kansas trail. All the inner Landon council will deny that they were directly solicited, but there undoubtedly were a few personal strings pulled.

It was still all talk. Not a shadow of organization beyond this personal but incessant activity of friends. They had never stopped writing, to everyone they could think of, inside and outside the state.

On Oct. 1, 1935, Oscar Stauffer, publisher of a chain of Kansas and Missouri papers called a meeting in a Kansas City club of Kansas publishers, 90 per cent. of whom are Republican. Prominent were Fred Harris, an Ottawa lawyer; Jack Harris and Fred Brinkerhoff of Hutchinson and Pittsburg; Roberts, Haynes, and others.

Stauffer was chosen to head an active committee for Landon. It started work Oct. 15, sending out letters and literature, mostly reprints of newspaper articles, in response to inquiries.

No contributions of more than $500 were accepted at first, and Stauffer for months used the letterhead of his own paper, the Arkansas City Traveler. A booklet "Kansas, Example of Good Government," was printed.

"Wait For the Breaks."

The Landon backers wrote letters incessantly to friends in other states, former Kansans in positions of influence in far cities. The bandwagon began to roll of its own momentum.

Thus Stauffer and his fellow Landon backers were able to devise a strategy that fitted nicely with the governor's own inclinations. It was "sit back, say as little as possible, and wait for the breaks."

An ostentatious visitation by Hearst and a party of allies to meet Landon at Topeka was considered "a mixed blessing" by the Landon friends, but it did add to the Landon publicity.

A women's dvision of the Landon committee under Mrs. E. C. Little, widow of a congressman, later to appear at the convention as delegate-at-large, was chosen. W. T. Grant, head of the Businessmen's Assurance Co. of Kansas City, became treasurer, to handle mounting contributions.

The boom was assured. There remained only the strategy of keeping Landon's name out of the primary fights in ven nearby states.

The Landon candidacy arrived at Cleveland full-groomed and ten lengths ahead of that of any other starter.

The fact that it was all done in one year leaves gasping the partisans of candidates who have been half a lifetime in public service. It is the sensation of a sensational political year.

MEMBERS OF CO A PRACTICE ON RANGE

Members of Company A, 105th Infantry, participated in rifle marksmanship practice on the Rensselaerwyck range at Rensselaer early last night. Those on the range, numbering approximately thirty men, were in command of Capt. W. Frank Leversee and Lieut. John B. Prout.

The remainder of the company, in charge of Lieut. William J. O'Brien received instructions in extended order drill, combat practice and use of concealment and cover. Packing of equipment for the annual two weeks' field training period at Camp Smith was supervised by Supply Sergt. William J. Dinan.

Lieut. John B. Prout and Sergt. Anthony Willetts left early this morning for Camp Smith where they will fire on the regimental rifle team in the brigade championship match today.

A non-commissioned officers' school will be conducted at the Troy Armory Sunday morning, June 21 at 10 o'clock. All non-commissioned officers of the company have been ordered to attend this meeting.

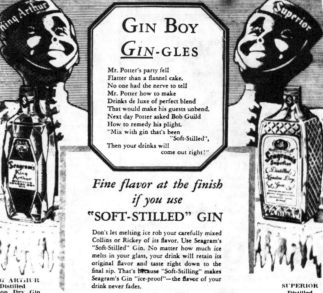

THE WEATHER
Tonight—Cloudy, cooler.
Tomorrow Fair.

THE TIMES RECORD

FINAL EDITION

Series 1936—No. 142.

TROY, N. Y., MONDAY EVENING, JUNE 15, 1936.

PRICE THREE CENTS

BONUS BONDS FLOOD INTO TROY AREA

Congress Must Break Tax Jam to Adjourn Saturday

The New Deal Day By Day

Events in Washington As Interpreted by David Lawrence.

Washington — The campaign ahead looks as if it may develop both a sense of proportion and a sense of humor.

Ever since the Republican convention at Cleveland adjourned, it has been a matter of considerable curiosity among political folk to know just what Chairman Jim Farley and the Democratic National Committee's publicity experts would say about the nomination of Governor Landon and the platform.

Now that Mr. Farley has spoken,

(Continued on Page 9.)

NEW PARKING SITE PLANNED BY CITY

Plot on Front Street, Near Fulton, Being Sought for Public Use.

The Troy Common Council probably will be asked to approve the lease of a large plot of ground on Front Street between Fulton Street and Broadway, for use as free public parking space, at its meeting Thursday night. Negotiations between the city and the Union Home Furnishers, Inc., and the Charles H. Dauchy Company, joint owners, have been under way several days.

Acquisition of the site, through long term lease, will answer a part of the city's problem to provide sufficient parking space and yet leave city streets clear for shoppers and general traffic. The spot is declared large enough to hold 150 cars without overcrowding.

During the last eight years the place has been operated under private lease as a paid parking area. It was stated last night that the operator has been given notice that the city will take charge some time this week.

ONTARIO DOBBINS, LURED BY SCENT OF NEW HAY, QUIT WORK

Hamilton, Ont. (UP)—Jack Watt, salesman for a local milk company, claimed a new record for his team or horses today when he reported they traced the scent of new hay, carried to them on a breeze, for two miles to a hay-field where he finally discovered them munching happily.

Watt said he left the team to deliver milk to a customer's house, and on returning saw his team racing down the street. He followed them two miles before finding them standing in the hayfield, eating hard. The wagon-tongue was broken in the dash, but no further damage resulted.

GRIM UNDERTAKER JOKE COMES TRUE

Boonton, N. J. (UP)—"How's business?" Frank Althoff, 63, asked his undertaker friend, Thomas Lewis.

"Bad," Lewis said.

"That's tough," said Althoff with a grin. "I'll try to hustle some up for you."

An hour later Althoff was injured fatally by a fall into an automobile service station grease pit. Lewis will direct his funeral.

CUTTING TEETH AT 74.

Nebraska City, Neb. (UP)—Mrs. Isabelle Thomas, 74, of Palmyra, is cutting teeth again. A dentist extracted her teeth some months ago. Recurring pain caused Mrs. Thomas to investigate. She discovered two new teeth.

RENTED ROOM TO THE FIRST MAN

EAST Side—527 Pawling Ave.; near bus, garage, nice room, all conveniences; $2.50. Gentleman preferred. Inq. evenings only.

The first man to answer this Classified Ad decided to rent the room.

The way for you to get a lodger for that cool, comfortable spare room of yours is to use a Classified Ad. When persons seek a furnished room they look in the Classified Ads first.

TROY 317

GOVERNOR LANDON OUTLINES VIEWS ON U. S. PROBLEMS

G. O. P. Nominee Approves Objectives but Not Methods of Many New Deal Experiments.

After finishing his Cleveland assignment, Lyle C. Wilson, chief political reporter of the United Press, hastened to Topeka to interview Alf M. Landon, the Republican choice for President. His dispatch follows.

BY LYLE C. WILSON

(Copyright, 1936, by United Press)

Topeka, Kan. (UP)—Gov. Alf M. Landon today prescribed "the American way" as the proper approach to the problems of a nation harried by unemployment and business uncertainty.

"The American way," he told the United Press in the course of a two-hour interview, "means education and debate in Congress and out of it. We all get impatient when we are not getting things done. There are interminable delays. But that is the American way and that is the path we must follow."

Governor Landon explained his views on the use of professional brains by the Federal Government, and on currency, social security and minimum wages.

Seeks Expert Advice.

You come away from the 1880 model governor's mansion here convinced that you have been listening to a man who is doing some of the hardest thinking of his lifetime. And you bring away with you the memory of a man who is looking for expert knowledge.

You go in seeking an interview with a presidential candidate, or an outline of a politician's plans for winning a national election. Your host rumples his gray hair and smiles. He meets each question promptly. More often than not, he meets it with another question.

The Governor's quest for cold and accurate information led to mention of the so-called brain trust recently assembled in Washington by the G. O. P.

What would happen to the professional brains department now that the G.O.P. leadership has moved West with curly-haired John D. M. Hamilton in charge?

No Professors on Bridge.

Governor Landon disposed of that in 15 words.

"I believe," he said, "in research men. But I do not believe in making research men administrators."

Professors, it appears, would have no place on the bridge if Governor Landon were the skipper in Washington.

But brain trusts are not worrying the man who was nominated last week to be the Republican candidate for President. Social security, the problems of laboring men and women and monetary control are more directly before him. It is in attacking those problems that he emphasizes the American way.

"Look Before You Leap," is a copybook maxim that might properly be set down as a Landon motto. But that caution does not apply to campaign methods. The strategy established last week when Gov. Landon telegraphed his own interpretation of the Republican platform, in three vital planks, to the Republican National Convention in Cleveland will be carried into the presidential campaign.

Few Subtleties Expected.

Once in December and again today the writer has been a guest in the cupaloed and corniced home in which the state of Kansas houses its governors. He has read Landon's speeches and from a combination of public and private utterance, draws the conclusion that there will be few subtleties in the sunflower campaign for the White House.

"What the hell do we mean?" was Sen. William E. Borah's question upon reading Gov. Landon's interpretation and extension of the money plank of the Republican platform. The plank pledged a stable currency, balanced budget and restoration to Congress of authority to regulate the value of the dollar an authority now lodged with the President, who may still reduce the gold content of the dollar by almost ten cents. Lashed by Borah and other silver men from the West, the Republican platform makers avoided mention of the gold standard. Gov. Landon's telegram, read to the convention before he was nominated, said that a requisite of sound and stable currency "is a currency expressed in terms of gold and convertible into gold."

But the Governor explained that the gold standard could not be restored until and unless it can be done without penalizing our Democratic economy and without in-

(Continued on Page 22.)

Auto Victim

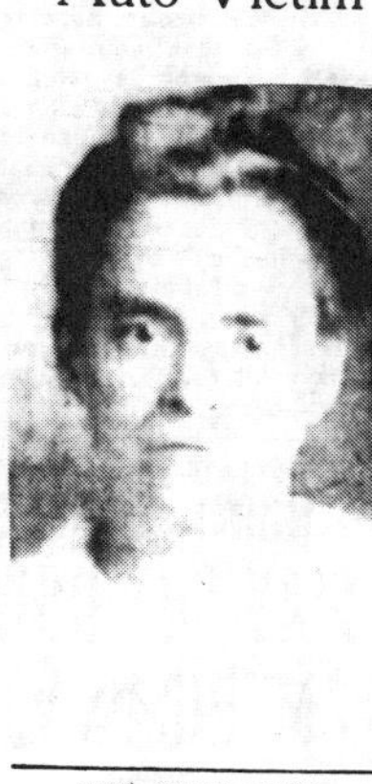

MRS. MARY NASH.

MRS. MARY NASH, STRUCK BY AUTO, DIES AT HOSPITAL

Accident Occurred Last Night in Hoosick Street; Auto Operated by Ralph Germain.

Mrs. Mary A. Nash, 62, of 2356 Seventh Ave., died at 2:10 a. m. today in the Troy Hospital of injuries suffered late last night when she was struck by an automobile in Hoosick Street, between Sixth and Seventh Avenues.

Coroner John H. Clinton is continuing his investigation into the accident. An autopsy was performed this morning by Dr. J. P. Jaffarian and Dr. J. J. Keenan at the Leonard Hospital. The autopsy disclosed that Mrs. Nash died of internal hemorrhages, multiple fractures of the ribs and a compound fracture of the right leg.

The machine, it is said, was driven by Ralph Germain of 455 Tenth Street. He was driving east in Hoosick Street on his way home when the accident occurred. Germain hurried the woman to the hospital where she was under the care of Dr. R. P. Doody.

The accident occurred about 11:10 o'clock. Sergt. George F. Preston, of Central Police Station, investigated the accident.

Mrs. Nash was a native of Watervliet but had lived in Troy many years. She was the widow of Richard L. Nash. Surviving are two daughters, Miss Gertrude M. Nash, and Mrs. Thomas J. Brady; four sons, William C., Raymond A., Richard L. and Edward F. Nash, all of Troy, and sister, Mrs. William J. Shaughnessy of Watervliet. Mrs. Nash was a member of St. Peter's Church.

The funeral will be held Wednesday at 9 a. m. from the residence and at 9:30 a. m. from St. Peter's Church where a solemn requiem mass will be celebrated. Burial will take place in St. Peter's Cemetery.

NEW FRENCH STRIKE LOOMS AS LIVING EXPENSES INCREASE

Paris (AP)—Prospects of living cost increases brought warnings of a new French strike today.

Workers, returning to their jobs assured of more pay and shorter hours, may ask additional wages if prices of necessities go "too high," labor officials asserted.

A new walkout might be called, they declared, regardless of the fact higher costs of food and other commodities could be traced directly to the fattened pay envelopes and forty-hour week demanded and received by the strikers.

Only a small percentage of the workers who have failed to negotiate the difference with employers continued their "folded arms" strike by occupying their factories.

MOTHER RECEIVES CORNELL DIPLOMA

Ithaca (AP)—Among the 1,300 Cornell seniors to receive diplomas here today was Mrs. Callie Simpson Smith, widow and mother of two children.

Mrs. Smith came to Cornell College of Home Economics 28 years after she had left a small finishing school which long ago had been merged with another institution. Not having credits from an accredited school she was refused at first, but finally was admitted "on trial."

Mrs. Smith was forced to take early classes, that necessitated her rising at 6 o'clock each morning to care for two fatherless children, aged ten and 13 years. Her day usually ended at midnight.

CONFEREES MAKE LITTLE PROGRESS ON COMPROMISE

Relief Bill, Chain Store Regulatory Measure, Coal Control Also Up for Action.

Washington (AP)—Amid expressions of hope but doubt for Saturday night adjournment, Congress assembled today after a week's respite to tackle anew its knotty legislative problems.

Leaders of the House and Senate launched an intensive drive to wind up the work of the 74th Congress before the Democratic National Convention next week, but there were several barriers to be hurdled before they may reach their goal.

One of the most stubborn obstacles in the path of adjournment is the strife-torn tax bill on which conferees worked throughout last week with little material progress toward a compromise on controversial points.

When Congress recessed a week ago today for the Republican convention it was the hope of leaders that conference reports on the revenue bill and other measures would be ready for final action today.

Other Obstacles Loom.

Conferees on the $2,430,829,000 deficiency-relief bill did not meet last week and still have several knotty problems to solve before they make their report.

In addition to the tax and relief bills, Congress has yet to act on conference reports on the Treasury-Postoffice, the Interior Department and the District of Columbia appropriation bills as well as the Robinson-Patman chain store regulatory measure, the anti-lobby bill and a number of minor bills.

The Vinson-Guffey coal bill, designed to replace the Guffey coal act invalidated by the Supreme Court has not yet come up in either House or Senate and some members seemed determined to stay here until it is passed.

May Extend Into July.

Senate Majority Leader Robinson, of Arkansas, said "It all depends upon the bills now in conference between the House and Senate," when asked regarding the chances for adjournment by Saturday night. He said conferees would have to work fast on the revenue and deficiency bills.

The same view was expressed by Speaker Bankhead although he said the House could very quickly clean up its important unfinished business.

The possibility existed that if Congress does not finish its work this week, it will be in session through the first of July since it was understood a week's recess would be taken for the Democratic National Convention in the event adjournment sine die can not be reached by Saturday night.

POPE CREATES TWO NEW CARDINALS

Vatican City (AP)—Pope Pius XI raised two old friends to the princely rank of cardinal today behind the guarded doors of a secret consistory. The two new princes of the church are Monsignors Giovanni Mercati and Eugenio Tisserant, "bookworm" friends of the Holy Father.

Both of the new cardinals were closely associated with the Pontiff for years before his election. Mercati came with him to Rome to take up his duties in the Vatican library. Tisserant has been associated with the library for thirty years.

Mail Sacks To Groan 'Neath Bonus Bonds

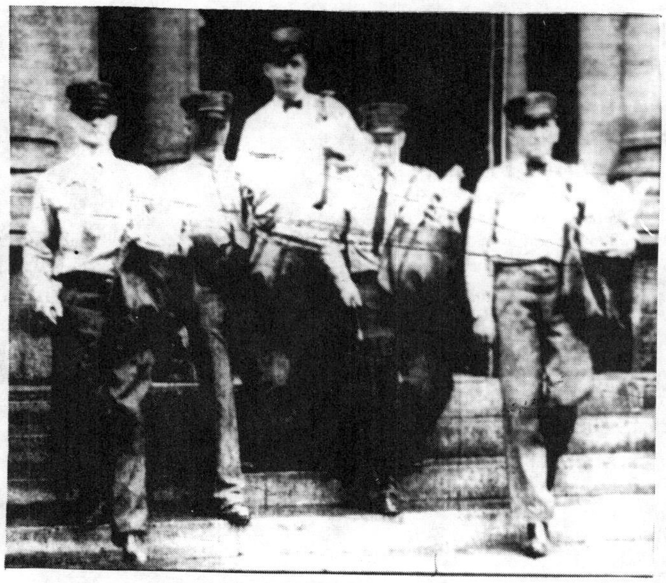

Carriers from the Troy Postoffice with their mail sacks loaded as they will be at 6 p. m. today when they start out to deliver Bonus Bonds to Troy's 3,500 World War veterans. Left to right, C. Elmer Doring, William H. Hilton, Jr., Charles S. Carroll, Jacob H. Coons and John L. Wortz.

WHITEHALL NATIVE DIES IN NEW YORK OF AUTO INJURIES

Ernest J. Harris Injured on Saturday Night; Funeral Services Were Held This Afternoon.

Ernest J. Harris, 34, a native of Whitehall, died yesterday morning in a New York City hospital of injuries suffered Saturday night in an automobile accident in New York.

The body was taken to Whitehall yesterday and the funeral was held this afternoon at 2 o'clock from the home of his father, John Harris, on the Whitehall-Comstock road. Rev. William A. Frazer of the First Presbyterian Church, Whitehall officiated. Interment was in the North Granville Cemetery.

The survivors are his widow and three children, his father, one brother, Henry Harris of Whitehall, and one sister, Mrs. Lena Slight of Plattsburg.

FATHER COUGHLIN DIRECTS BLAST AT ROOSEVELT, LANDON

Boston (AP)—The Rev. Father Charles E. Coughlin, of Detroit, planned today to make a speech in New York next Friday that "would startle the nation."

The head of the Union for Social Justice did not say what would be the subject of his speech when he made the statement after a radio interview last night, but only a few minutes before he had said that "neither of the presidential candidates is worth a nickel"—not even "a plugged nickel."

In the radio interview Father Coughlin charged the Roosevelt administration with going "off the gold standard and on to the dole system."

He added that it did not follow that those on the dole would vote to uphold such a system.

Cluett-Peabody Employment Up 77 Per Cent. From '32-'33

Employment today in the three plants of Cluett, Peabody & Company, Inc., is 77 per cent. higher than in the period 1932-1933, according to R. Oakley Kennedy, vice president of the shirt and collar concern.

A steady and material increase in weekly earnings of Cluett, Peabody & Company employes also is noted by Mr. Kennedy. The three plants of the concern are located here, at Atlanta and at Leominster.

"Aggregate employment in our three plants has increased steadily during the past five years," Mr. Kennedy said. His statement was included in reports from leaders in 12 diversified industries to the effect that "industry is maintaining improved wage and hour standards and employment is approaching and in some cases exceeding 1929 levels."

PRESIDENT WILL WAGE BATTLE ON NEW DEAL RECORD

High Administration Circles Say Landon Challenge Will Be Accepted; Backs "Little Fellow."

Washington (UP)—President Roosevelt will accept Gov. Alf Landon's challenge to fight the presidential campaign on the New Deal's record, Democratic leaders indicated today.

The President returns today from a 4,000-mile southwestern speaking trip to remain until Congress adjourns, probably Saturday. His renomination at the Democratic National Convention next week is regarded as certain.

He plans to follow the precedent he set four years ago at Chicago and address the Philadelphia convention in accepting the nomination. His speech probably will be the Democratic campaign keynote.

Immediately after the convention Mr. Roosevelt probably will go to his Hyde Park, N. Y., home for a brief rest and for work on the opening speech of his re-election campaign to be made July at Monticello, Va.

A huge gathering is expected to hear him there at the home of Thomas Jefferson, just outside Charlottesville. Party leaders expect the address to be one of the major speeches of a campaign that will take him into many states.

The Monticello address may be the occasion of a defense of constitutionality of New Deal aims.

In the minds of political observers, definitely cast his lot with the "little fellow" in the half dozen major and minor speeches he made in as many states in the last week.

He promised attainment of declared administration objectives, lashed out against monopolies as the economic stranglers of the small man, struck at so-called chiselers and declared for continuation of the government's war on "exploitation of the many by the few."

He wound up by remarking at the birthplace of Abraham Lincoln at Hodgenville, Ky.: "Here we can renew our pledge of fidelity to the faith which Lincoln held—in the common man—the faith, so simply expressed when he said: 'As I would not be a slave, so I would not be a master.' This expresses my idea of democracy. Whatever differs from this, to the extent that difference is no democracy."

The President's trip, which produced at least three addresses of first page calibre in contrast to oft-repeated White House declarations before he started out that his talks would be historical and only for local consumption, has convinced administration friends that he has taken the offensive in his bid for re-election and that he is ready for a busy summer and fall.

FLORIDA BEACH RESIDENTS FLEE PATH OF STORM

Peninsula Lashed by High Winds, Heavy Rainfall; Streets Flooded; Some Towns Isolated.

Fort Myers, Fla., (AP)—A tropical storm swept in from the Gulf of Mexico today, isolated one town south of here and drove hundreds of persons from beach-front homes.

The center of the disturbance apparently passed over Naples, forty miles south of here, shortly after midnight. Forty-mile-an-hour winds were accompanied by torrential rains which raised a flood menace all over extreme southwestern Florida.

Residents of Bonita Springs, twenty miles to the south, reported by telephone that the Imperial River had gone out of its banks and forced them into the second floors of their homes. A few minutes later all means of communication with the town failed.

Veritable cloud bursts preceded the storm in this sector for the past three days with Naples reporting a fall of 16 inches in the past 72 hours. Rain still fell early today all along the coast.

The storm highway department closed the Tamiami Trail—only direct cross-state link between Fort Myers and Miami—after river waters submerged the pavement at many points.

Southwest winds bringing high tides aggravated flood conditions at coastal points.

The storm—unusually early for disturbances of its type—originated somewhere in the neighborhood of the Yucatan Peninsula and moved in a northeasterly direction across the gulf.

The Miami Weather Bureau reported at 10 a. m. that the center of the storm had passed over the city and was moving out into the Atlantic Ocean in a southeasterly direction.

The Coast Guard air station at Miami reported a thirty mile wind. Skies seemed to be clearing a bit and the steady rain that had been falling since Friday eased slightly. The wind caused no damage in Miami but many streets were flooded.

Friends Fear For Quins' Mother As Stork Nears

Copyright, 1936, by United Press.

Callendar, Ont. Fear was expressed today that a child birth expected this week or next might prove fatal to Mrs. Elzire Dionne, mother of the quintuplets.

M. Legros, father of Mrs. Dionne, who revealed to the United Press that the child, or perhaps children, is expected "this month," revealed today that he and Oliva Dionne, the quints' father, had discussed the danger to the young mother and that both were worried.

Friends of the Dionnes who had kept silent because they knew the family wanted to avoid publicity, talked freely today in the "I-knew-it-all-the-time vein." Many of them share the fears as Dionne and Legros.

Dr. M. G. Ranney, who is treating Rose and Herbert, two of the elder brothers and sisters of the quintuplets for measles, and who has had recent opportunity to see, if not to examine the mother, things danger is present but not great.

He sees no change that another birth could imperil the mother's life "unless the excitement of publicity and visitors crowding around brought on some complications."

"Papa" Dionne still disclaims any knowledge of the coming birth and has not even discussed it with Ranney. But the doctor explained that "that's nothing new in this district."

"The people here always wait until the last minute," he said, "and then perhaps call you in the last day or night and tell you that a baby is expected."

The mother no longer receives visitors, and she never leaves the house during the day. It is known that she turned down yesterday afternoon a contract offer to appear at a club anniversary celebration before the end of the month.

No matter what physician the parents chose to assist at the next birth, it will not be Dr. Allan Dafoe, who delivered the quintuplets. The Dionnes broke finally with him when he supported the Ontario government in making the "quins" wards of the state.

WATERVLIET MAN REPORTED FIRST TO RECEIVE PAPER

James E. Gillon, Special Clerk in Postoffice in Arsenal City, Gets Document at 8:30 A. M.

Bonus bonds began to flood into the Troy Area today with James E. Gillon of 1216 Sixth Avenue, Watervliet, special clerk in the Postoffice there, believed to be first local veteran to receive his bonds. He received his bonus payment from Acting Postmaster William F. Parker, Jr., of Watervliet at 8:30 a. m. with ceremony.

Payments running close to $2,500,000 were awaited in Troy alone. Distribution of the bonds in this city will start at 6 p. m. tonight. Approximately 3,500 Trojans are eligible to receive bonus bonds. In Watervliet 600 veterans will receive bonds, the average amount being approximately $500.

Troy Area veterans form part of a vast national army of three million who will receive a total of nearly $1,850,000,000.

In preparation for the gigantic job of distributing the bonds preparatory to immediate cash redemption, if desired, the vaults of 12 Federal Reserve bank centers in the country were opened last night to permit the shipment of the bonds to strategic distribution centers. The Troy consignment arrived today.

Delivery Here Today.

Locally, plans have been made by Postmaster Edward J. Fitzgerald for a 6 p. m. delivery today. Veterans expecting the bonds should remain at their homes to receive the bonds and sign necessary receipts. Veterans must be identified. No persons, other than the veterans, will be given the package.

Tomorrow, veterans seeking an immediate redemption of bonds, may call at the postoffice where, on the second floor, a special office has been outfitted to take care of veterans' wants. At that place the veterans may leave the bonds, receiving in return a receipt. The cashable check may be expected within 36 hours and will be sent from Troy. Veterans not in need of immediate cash have been urged to wait a few days before

(Continued on Page 11.)

Disabled War Veteran Gets Certificate No. 1

Washington (UP)—Patrick J. Luby, wearing a hospital bathrobe, a broad smile and carrying a heavy cane today received veterans service certificate No. 1 for $780.

The presentation ceremony at Walter Reed Hospital formally started the gigantic task of distributing bonus certificates to ex-soldiers throughout the country.

Pat, who is 44 and a native of Ireland, was a wagoner in the World War, serving two years and four months at the front with the First Engineers. He was wounded by shrapnel.

Postmaster Vincent C. Burke handed Pat his certificate while the movie cameras ground and Representative Wright Patman, father of the bonus law, stood by triumphantly. Asked what he planned to do with his money Luby said:

"I'll put a little in the bank, and spend the rest for clothes."

PENN YAN NATIVE LANDS HUGE TROUT

Penn Yan (AP) Fish stories were supported by evidence this week-end in the Finger Lakes. Walter Wren of this village fishing in Lake Keuka, caught a trout weighing 15 pounds, four ounces, and measuring 34 inches from tip to tail. It was the largest catch in ten years, though under the record of a 22-pounder caught two decades ago.

In Seneca Lake trout also are biting, according to reports from Geneva. Several catches above ten pounds were reported.

LITHUANIA DEFAULTS.

Kaunas, Lithuania (AP)—Lithuania is in no position to pay her war debt installment of $942,760 to the United States, officials announced today. Lithuania owes the United States a debt installment of $166,441 plus an additional $776,319 in default.

The Index

THE WEATHER
Tonight—Rain, colder.
Tomorrow—Much colder.

THE TIMES RECORD

FINAL EDITION

Series 1936—No. 261. (Entered as Second Class Matter at the Postoffice at Troy, N. Y., under the Act of March 3, 1879.) TROY, N. Y., TUESDAY EVENING, NOVEMBER 3, 1936. (Published Daily Except Sunday) PRICE THREE CENTS

TROOPERS ASKED IN ALBANY ELECTION

Slight Gains For Roosevelt Noted In Early Election Returns

The New Deal Day By Day

Events in Washington As Interpreted by Frank R. Kent

One of the things which the recent campaign demonstrated again is the complete futility of the third party movements launched within one year of a presidential election. None with that little background ever has amounted to much and none is likely to.

True, the Bull Moose Party of Theodore Roosevelt in 1912 carried six states—with a total electoral vote of 87, but it had no effect upon

(Continued on Page 2.)

MILLSFIELD, N. H., FIRST TO REPORT, GOES FOR LANDON

Somerset, Vt., and New Ashford, Mass., Also Back G. O. P., but Roosevelt Leads in Kansas.

BY THE ASSOCIATED PRESS.

The tiny northeastern New Hampshire community of Millsfield, voting as a town for the first time, today snatched the title of "first in the nation" from New Ashford, Mass.

By lamplight, in a small tar-paper roofed building used as temporary town hall, five votes were cast for Governor Alf M. Landon for president while President Roosevelt received two.

The Millsfield voters gathered in the polling place to begin balloting at 12:01 a. m.

Five hours later and only a few minutes before the New Ashford vote was announced Somerset, Vt., in the lumber region of former President Calvin Colidge's native state, cast its seven votes for the Kansas governor. No Democratic vote was cast.

New Ashford for Landon.

New Ashford, preparing weeks in advance to maintain a record first established in 1916, announced it had given the Republican standard bearer 26 votes and President Roosevelt 19.

In the last presidential election of the 33 ballots cast former President Hoover received 24. President Roosevelt 8 and one was blank.

Tolland in the western part of Massachusetts completed its voting at 6:30, giving Governor Landon 44 votes and President Roosevelt 21.

Other Early Returns.

Other early election returns:

State of Kansas, 115 precincts: Roosevelt 2,342, Landon 1,641.

Five Houston, Texas, precincts: Roosevelt 126, Landon 21.

Pointe Aux Barques, Mich.: Roosevelt 6, Landon 8.

Birmingham, Alabama. One precinct and absentee ballots: Roosevelt 903, Landon 29.

Kansas City, Kan. Five precincts: Roosevelt 42, Landon 20.

Carrollton, Ga. One precinct: Roosevelt 500, Landon 40.

Martin Station, Ala.: Roosevelt 11, Landon 0.

Nutbush, N. C.: Roosevelt 31, Landon 0.

Browns Farms, Fla.: Roosevelt 8, Landon 0.

Livermore, N. H.: Roosevelt 7, Landon 1.

Waterville, N. H.: Landon 4, Roosevelt 1.

Fairmount, W. Va. Five precincts: Roosevelt 399, Landon 300.

Huntington, W. Va. Nine precincts: Roosevelt 447, Landon 303

Mount Washington, Mass.: Landon 26, Roosevelt 15.

NATION'S VOTERS SURGE TO POLLS IN MIGHTY TIDE

Figures from Solid South Show Democratic Ranks Unbroken; Neighbors Wildly Acclaim Landon.

BY THE ASSOCIATED PRESS.

Amid increasing portents of a record shattering vote, the nation today scanned the mixed trends of early returns from a hard-fought Roosevelt vs. Landon election contest.

Running according to pre-ballot forecasts, Franklin D. Roosevelt piled up a mounting lead in the solid South. In New England, Alf M. Landon held onto a margin of two score votes, all of them cast and counted before breakfast time.

In other sections there was seesawing, with the Democratic nominee most frequently ahead on the basis of scattered returns that totaled only a pin-point fraction of the 45,000,000 figure predicted by some as the possible 1936 vote total.

Roosevelt Leads in Kansas.

In Landon's home state of Kansas, an incomplete vote from 126 precincts out of 2,690 gave Roosevelt 2,715 to 2,133 for the Republican nominee. Fifteen Topeka precincts gave Landon a 675 to 515 advantage.

In West Virginia, incomplete returns from thirty of Huntington's precincts gave the Democratic standard bearer 1,926 votes as against 1,176 for Landon.

From the metropolitan centers of New York, Chicago and elsewhere came reports that heavy voting promised to shatter all records. The presidential and vice presidential nominees of both major parties all had voted well before noon, and even the weatherman held out an encouraging hand.

Although the voting started shortly after midnight, the fact that many polls will remain open until 11 p. m. eastern time dimmed hope of anything conclusive until long after nightfall.

The first fragments from New England showed that President Roosevelt had made tiny gains over the early bird votes cast for him in 1932. In New Ashford, Mass., the count was 26 to 19 for Landon today, as against 24 to 8 for Herbert Hoover in 1932. In Tolland, Mass., Landon led 44 to 21, as against 39 to 22 in 1932.

Neighbors Welcome Landon.

Governor Landon himself lost little time in voting. At 9:10 a. m.

(Continued on Page 2.)

Vital States To Watch For Victory Hint

By the Associated Press.

Straws in the election winds to watch tonight:

NEW YORK—This state usually votes for the winner. Its loss by Landon would be almost fatal. Roosevelt might lose it and win.

PENNSYLVANIA — Another state Landon cannot easily afford to lose. If it leans Democratic, a topheavy Democratic victory is indicated.

MASSACHUSETTS - Rhode Island—Democratic majorities here, or in Landon's home state of Kansas, would point to a major Republican disaster.

CALIFORNIA—Its loss by Roosevelt would badly upset Democratic expectations and strongly suggest a Landon victory.

OHIO, INDIANA, ILLINOIS — If these states and the East swing Republican, a close election is certain. If Democratic, Roosevelt would look the winner.

'Twas Day Before Election

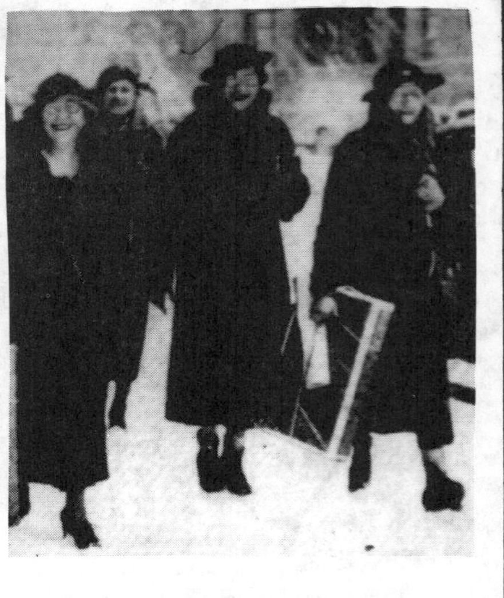

Denver upheld its tradition for early snows when storms from the Rocky Mountains blew down on the city and dusted it with wintry white. These smiling shoppers give a Christmas air to the scene, but it was only the day before Election Day. (A. P. Photo).

OLD GUN BURSTS, GRAFTON YOUTH'S ARM BADLY HURT

Raymond Moon, 22, in Hospital After Muzzle-Loader Explodes on His First Shot.

One arm badly torn when he fired an old muzzle-loading shotgun for which he had traded another gun Raymond Moon, 22, son of Joel Moon, proprietor of the Mountain Top House at Grafton was in Samaritan Hospital today.

Dr. Peter L. Harvie, who is attending him, said that Moon's left arm is seriously lacerated but that the extent of injury to the arm has not been determined. Hospital authorities said that his condition was considered "good."

Young Moon was injured shortly after midnight in the yard at the rear of the hotel. The Moon family were entertaining guests and their son was showing off the old gun. He and some of the others went into the hotel yard to try the gun. Moon, his family said, put a charge in the gun and fired it.

The gun blew to pieces as Moon fired and bits of wood and metal littered the yard. The young man, bleeding profusely, was carried into his home and later removed to the hospital.

The gun, it is said, had not been discharged in the last 14 years. Moon is employed by his father at the Mountain Top House. He was formerly in the army and was stationed for three years at the Plattsburg barracks.

TORNADO STRIKES CAPE GIRARDEAU

Cape Girardeau, Mo., (AP)—A tornado struck Cape Girardeau shortly before midnight last night and in a minute of destructive fury, did more than $50,000 damages to 150 homes and store buildings.

Only one injury, a woman who was struck by flying timber while she was seated in an automobile, was reported.

REBELS PLANNING MADRID ASSAULT WITHIN FOUR DAYS

Fascists Plant Big Guns Only Seven Miles from Capital; Report Loyalists Retreating.

BY THE ASSOCIATED PRESS.

Fascists planted their guns today almost in the shadow of Madrid.

Insurgents under Gen. Jose Varela, sweeping toward the capital from the South, entered the village of Fuenlabrada, seven miles away and less than three miles from a government military airport at Getafe, a Madrid suburb.

They also occupied the village of Pinto, about ten miles south of Madrid at the opposite end of a contracting fascist semi-circle of men, artillery, tanks and warplanes.

Prepartions were speeded for an attack on Madrid which insurgent officers said they were confident could be taken in no more than four days.

Three fascist fliers were killed near Talavera de La Reina when their tri-motored Martin bomber was shot down by government warplanes. They bailed out from a low altitude but crashed to earth under half-opened parachutes.

Fascist officers, literally within sight of the towers in the center of Madrid, said the government defense line was melting. They declared the Madrid militiamen were abandoning the fight and running back to Madrid.

Government armored trains were forced out of action when insurgent bombers cut railroad lines from Madrid to Toledo and Aranjuez.

On the west of Madrid government tanks and artillery backed up the defense line against another insurgent thrust which aimed at Villa Viciosa, about ten miles from the besieged city of Brunete-El Escorial sector.

The Madrid air ministry said government planes had bombed fascista bases at Talavera de La Reina and north of Toledo.

Alcala de Henares, about 15 miles northeast of Madrid on the Guadalajara road, was shelled by insurgent air raiders who also raked Getafe with machine gun fire.

Missouri Man Faints As Wife Bears Quadruplets

Senath, Mo., (AP)—Two of the quadruplets born last night to Mr. and Mrs. James Bridges died today in their isolated two-room river valley cabin.

Dr. F. W. Speidel, a physician here for 36 years, said the Bridges' quadruplets—one boy and three girls—cannot live unless they get care this community cannot provide. He labored far into the night on arrangements to transfer them to the nearest hospital at Jonesboro, Ark., and carefully planned ways of overcoming hazards involved in the move.

The boy was born first at 6:30 p. m. and the third girl was born at 6:36 p. m. Dr. Speidel said they were nine-month babies, normal except in size and number.

"I guess they're about two and one-half to three and one-half pounders," the white-haired physician stated. "We had no scales, and besides, I didn't have time to weigh them."

The father, a share cropper, fainted when told the news.

"I don't know what we're going to do," Bridges said when he recovered. "I have no money to take care of them, but I sure want 'em to live."

Word was received that an ambulance carrying a trained nurse and medical supplies had been sent from Memphis, Tenn. The informant said hospitals donated the supplies and Miss Ruth Treadway, the nurse, offered her services when informed of the family's poverty.

Aid from the American Red Cross was promised by F. A. Winfrey, assistant midwestern manager in St. Louis, who said he was authorizing the Duncan County chairman, Elmer Blakemore at Kennett, Mo., to "take whatever steps are necessary."

Mrs. Bridges is 35, her husband 44. They have had five other children but only one, a four-year-old girl, is living.

STUDENT FOUND IN ADIRONDACK WOODS

Lake Placid, (AP)—James Patnode, 16-year-old Lake Placid high school football player, told a searching party who found him after he had been lost for more than 24 hours in the Adirondack Woods near here, that he'd "had better times."

Patnode said he was on his way back to camp when he met the searching party. He told of wandering into the tent of Neil Moody at noon yesterday. Moody, he said gave him his first food since Sunday morning when he lost his way in the Little Coldbrook section of the woods.

MOTORIST KILLED.

Schroon Lake (U.P.)—Lawrence W. King of Chateaugay was killed last night in a crash involving a truck and trailer and another truck of the State Highway Department.

TROY VOTES FAST, HEAVILY, POLITICAL LEADERS DECLARE

Balloting at Rate of One Per Minute Reported from Several Sections of This City.

"Voting heavy and fast" summed up the steady stream of reports pouring into Democratic and Republican headquarters today as Troy, with the rest of the nation, awaited the outcome of the presidential and lesser campaigns.

At Republican headquarters leaders said:

"We have no specific reports, but from all districts in the city we hear that the vote is fast and heavy. In several districts two-thirds of the vote was in by 1 p. m. In other districts half of the vote was in."

At Democratic headquarters leaders said:

"Rate of One a Minute."

"We have no definite word yet, but the people are certainly voting early. In many places they were voting at the rate of one a minute."

Little word was received concerning the vote throughout the county.

As is the case each year, rumors were circulating this morning of "a big fight" in this or that ward. This newspaper was asked whether it was true that "a special squad of police" had been sent to this or that district to quell a disorder. Queries at police headquarters revealed that there had been no disorder warranting police action.

At the offices of the county Board of Elections in the Court House, Commissioners Edward T. Nehill and George T. Morris were on duty early. In contrast to other general elections, there were no reports of broken or defective voting machines although outside in Second Street stood an automobile truck with two voting machines ready to speed to any district where a voting machine might become inoperative.

Quiet, Declares Morris.

"As far as we are concerned, this election thus far has been a mighty quiet one," Commissioner Morris told The Record Newspapers. "Everything appears to be proceeding smoothly."

The offices of the Board of Election were the only offices open today in the Court House. The City Hall was also virtually closed.

At the various polling places throughout the city special police were on guard but the bluecoats found little out of the ordinary to do; it was just stand around and watch the crowds of voters going in and out of the polling places. The busiest persons about the polling places were the Republican and Democratic workers. Automobiles kept departing from the voting places and then hurrying back with voters, the largest number of those carried in the cars being women and elderly or infirm men.

EASTERN JAPAN AROUSED TODAY BY EARTHQUAKE

Tokyo (AP)—All Eastern Japan was shaken today by an earthquake which aroused the capital from sleep just before dawn and sent city residents scurrying to the streets in night clothes.

The Central Meteorological Observatory said "No serious damage has been reported so far but aftershocks may continue." There were no known casualties.

"Fortunately the center of the earthquake was the sea bed," the observatory declared. "If it had occurred on land it would have been a disastrous earthquake."

The shocks were felt over more than half the mainland. Seismographs recorded the duration of the tremors at ten minutes and individuals in the earthquake region could feel them for at least six minutes.

Times Record Readers To Get Election News At Breakfast

Likelihood of a close contest and the fact that New York State's polls do not close until 9 p. m. this year mean that the victor in the presidential race may not be known until early Wednesday morning.

So that you will know Wednesday at the breakfast table who has won, a copy of The Troy Record will be left at the door of all readers of The Times Record getting home delivery through carrier or newsdealer.

The Troy Record's final edition will be published after 5:30 a. m. and thus will contain later and more complete election and general news than any other newspaper offered for sale in the Troy Area.

We believe that for the convenience of having the latest facts about national, state and local contests the first thing Wednesday morning, you will be only too pleased to include payment for this extra service to your respective carrier or newsdealer.

STORMY WEATHER MAY CUT DOWN AMERICA'S VOTE

Midwest States Deluged with Rain; Blizzard Rages in South Dakota; Farmers May Stay at Home.

BY THE UNITED PRESS

Rain, snow, cold or overcast skies prevailed over a large part of the United States today, threatening to influence the course of the national election.

Particularly bad was the weather in the Mid-West, where some political observers believe the election may be settled. Rain and snow may keep hundreds of farmers on their farms, to the loss of whichever party (both claim the rural vote) their votes were destined for.

A blizzard raged in the north and west of Iowa and elsewhere in the state there was rain. In Northern Illinois there was snow, with rain in the southern part of the state. There was snow in Wisconsin and Northern Michigan, and rain prevailed generally through Indiana, and snow fell generally in Minnesota, with eight inches at Fergus Falls.

In South Dakota a terrific blizzard was piling up drifts on highways, threatening to close them altogether. Officials could not order out snow ploys until the blizzard had halted, which may not be until late today. South Dakota's population is scattered and this probably will cut down its vote drastically.

It was raining and cold in parts of Ohio, Tenne ssee, Kentucky, Western Pennsylvania and New York. Rain but mild temperatures were predicted for Pennsylvania and New York, whose large electoral votes are claimed by both parties.

Overcast skies and occasional showers were forecast for New England.

Only the Pacific Coast and the deep South had promise of ideal election weather—fair skies and high temperatures.. The Rocky Mountain States were crusted with snow and had below freezing temperatures from the blizzard moving through South Dakota and Western and Northern Iowa.

STATE OFFICIALS BET DONKEY RIDE ON DEMOCRAT VOTE

Columbia, S. C. (AP)—Upon the Roosevelt votes of South Carolina and Mississippi depended today an election bet of the states' lieutenant governors which called for the loser to ride a donkey to Washington.

If South Carolina has fewer Roosevelt votes than Missippi, J. E. Harley has promised to make the ride and if the order is reversed the excursion goes to J. B. Snyder.

DRUNKS IN FRACAS AT ANTI-NEW DEAL PRAYER MEETING

Hartford Band Carries on After Police Reserves Eject Hecklers, Egg Thrower.

Hartford, Conn. (U.P.) — Having lasted out a group of drunken hecklers, the Hartford praying band went home today with a final, "oh, God, hear our cause," after a night of prayer for the defeat of President Roosevelt.

The band—four men, four women, and a child—gathered at Sister Cora Bogue's rooming-house apartment under the leadership of Brother George W. Smith.

His walrus moustache quivering, Brother Smith, public stenographer and evangelist, intoned:

"I'm sure the Good Lord will not let us down. If He should decide against us, the Lord's will be done—but we will go right on praying."

Nearly forty persons, not members of the band and many of them drunk, crowded into Sister Cora's apartment when the prayer meeting started at 10 p. m. One carried a bag of eggs. Others had plastered New Deal posters on the door of the house.

One of the hecklers pretended to faint. Sister Cora, a registered nurse, quickly brought him out of it. There were snickers. Three men became embroiled in a drunken row. A reporter called police. One heckler complained before he was ejected that he didn't want to leave the "Republican rally."

"This is not a political gathering," said Brother Smith. "It is a prayer meeting.

"Could we realize what the passing of human liberty means," Smith said, "we would be shocked beyond the power of endurance."

The egg-carrier went into action. His missle, however, struck a fellow inebriant. "You ought to be ashamed," said Sister Cora.

At midnight the last of the interlopers staggered out.

"Some great blessing may come out of this meeting," Brother Smith sighed. Then he locked the doors and the little band began to pray.

SALINAS LETTUCE STRIKE CALLED OFF

Salinas, Calif. (AP)—Salinas' violence-marred lettuce workers strike was ended by a vote of union workers announced here early today. It lasted two months.

The vote by members of the Fruit and Vegetable Workers' Union here and at Watsonville was 613 for returning to work immediately and 342 against.

Several outbreaks in which police, highway patrolmen and special deputies drove back pickets with tear gas, occurred during the strike.

COLONEL MUNDY GIVEN PROMOTION

Albany (AP)—Maj. Gen. William N. Haskell, commanding general of the 27th Division, New York National Guard, announced the promotion of Lieut. Col. Joseph A. S. Mundy to a full colonel and his appointment as chief of staff of the division.

Colonel Mundy succeeds the late Col. William R. Wright. He enlisted in the old 23rd Infantry 35 years ago and served on the Mexican border and in the World War.

WASHINGTON QUIET CITY ELECTION DAY

Washington (AP)—Life in the nation's capital today was unique among communities of the land.

Six hundred thousand people and not a local vote.

Seventy square miles and not a ballot box.

The promised land of politicians and not a candidate's free cigar.

Incidentally, the capital is about the only place in the country where you can buy a drink today.

Record Newspapers Prepared To Screen Election Returns

Election returns in the exciting national, state and county contests today will be provided for the public again this year by The Record Newspapers on a screen placed opposite the newspaper building on Broadway. **Although the New York State polling places will not close until 9 p. m., reports will be available earlier from some other states and information from these sources will be flashed to the screen beginning at 7 p. m.** The service will continue through the night as long as public interest warrants.

Two election night extras will be published by The Times Record, the first as quickly as returns are received indicating a national trend; the second after New York State polls have closed and carrying complete tables on local contests and the latest available reports from other fronts in the election battle.

The Troy Record's final edition tomorrow will be published after 5:30 a. m, and thus will contain the latest and most complete election and general news.

G.O.P. CANDIDATE'S WIFE NABBED FOR 'DELAYING VOTING'

Republican Chairman Charges Election Machinery Breakdown "Due to Failure of Police to Enforce Law."

Election Day troubles in Albany, climaxing a long investigation into alleged false registrations there, began early today with the arrest of Mrs. Colin D. MacRae, wife of the Republican candidate for Congress in the 28th District, and brought forth a demand from the Albany County Republican Committee that State Police be called out.

Conditions approaching the riot stage were reported in Albany where the voting from an early hour was heavy.

"Election law machinery broken down due to failure of police to enforce election law," Charles C. Wing, Albany County Republican chairman, telegraphed Governor Herbert H. Lehman. "Even officials of county board of elections are prevented from repairing curtains on machines. Wife of Republican candidate for Congress and accredited watcher at polls arrested for attempting to prevent wholesale law violations. Demand police protection."

Mrs. Colin MacRae Arrested.

The Republican chairman said that reference to "repairing curtains" referred to a complaint from the Second District in the Seventh Ward that the custodian of the voting machine had been prevented from repairing a torn curtain and that reports from ten other districts indicated that curtains had been "torn and not repaired."

Mrs. MacRae was arrested on a charge of "obstructing, delaying and hindering voting" at St. Sophia's Church, polling place of the First District, 14th Ward, where she was an accredited Republican watcher. She spent twenty minutes in a Second Precinct cell, then was released in $200 bail for hearing later.

The arrest followed Mrs. MacRae's protest against assistance being provided a voter whose name, she charges, was not marked for assistance on the registration books. The complaint against her was signed by Frank Schermerhorn, who charges she stood in front of the voting machine and declared, "This man cannot vote if he has assistance."

Meanwhile, warrants in two other election cases were sworn out before Police Justice Edward S. Kampf. One was obtained by Edward Wagner, Republican poll worker, who accused William Quinn, Board of Elections chairman of third degree assault. Wagner said Quinn tried to cut a hole in an election booth curtain and struck at him when he attempted to remonstrate.

Jacob M. Olshansky, another Republican worker, made a similar charge against Joseph Judoski. Neither defendant was arrested.

Governor Declines Request.

The Republican County Committee sent a telegram to Police Chief David Smurl asking the "immediate removal" of Policeman Delehanty who arrested Mrs. MacRae. Smurl replied, "The officer has his time in court before a judge and there is not a thing I can do about it."

Mrs. MacRae, interviewed after her arrest, told newspapermen: "I didn't believe such conditions existed. I had heard a lot of stories but I didn't believe them. I wanted to see for myself. I wish other citizens could see the same thing. I went to the polling place at 5:45 a. m. today and went in. We went over to the voting machine, the Democratic inspectors and I. There was a patch on one side of the curtain but above the patch the curtain was very flimsy, rubbed thin so you could see right through it. I protested. I insisted that the voting should not go on until it was repaired."

Mrs. MacRae said that she was "thrown out twice before she was arrested."

Governor Lehman, in New York, told reporters, "I have not seen the telegram sent me by Mr. Wing but State Police never are called out for election trouble. We have 9,000 election districts in the state and 600 state troopers."

The Index

THE WEATHER
Tonight: Cloudy, warmer.
Tomorrow: Cloudy.

THE TIMES RECORD

FINAL EDITION

Series 1936—No. 269. (Entered as Second Class Matter at the Postoffice at Troy, N. Y., under the Act of March 3, 1879) TROY, N. Y., THURSDAY EVENING, NOVEMBER 12, 1936. PRICE THREE CENTS

$25,000 BLAZES DAMAGE 10 BOATS HERE

CITY PREPARING SPECIFICATIONS ON NEW HIGH SCHOOL

Board of Contract Expected to Start Negotiations for Receipt of Contracts Tomorrow.

To assure completion of Troy's new $1,200,000 PWA high school within the required 18-month period, the Board of Contract and Supply at its meeting tomorrow is expected to start negotiations for receipt of contracts.

Specifications are expected to be prepared for the building of foundations for the school, structural steel and roofing materials.

When the Troy Common Council last week accepted provisions for the project, officials announced that ground would be broken as quickly as possible and that actual work had to begin not later than January 11.

Will Hasten Bids.

Although the foundation work will naturally be the first undertaken by contractors, the Board of Contract and Supply is planning to receive bids for the roofing and steel girders as soon as possible to assure no delay in the work. The building must be complete and ready for occupancy by January 11, 1938.

While it is imperative that only the foundation contracts be completed now, officials are making certain that there will be no hitch that will cause the city to fail in keeping its part in the PWA provisions. Consequently other bids will be received as soon as possible as well.

Corporation Counsel Frank S. Parmenter is scheduled to go to New York within a few days to confer with PWA officials concerning legal technicalities involving the transfer of the $643,090 grant from the PWA fund to the city of Troy.

Certificates of Indebtedness.

Officials have explained that Troy will pay its share of the cost of the school on the pay-as-you-go basis. It is understood that 25 per cent. of the grant will be turned over to Troy at the outset. This will relieve Troy of any hardship in placing money for the contracts as the city's fiscal agents will be able to use the government's 25 per cent. first. When this is expended the city will provide a portion of its share. Troy's share of the entire cost is 55 per cent.

Although city officials have made no announcement concerning the method of providing its share, it is believed that the city will not issue bonds at the start, but will issue certificates of indebtedness for its costs. At the completion of the work the certificates will be refunded through the issuance of bonds for the total amount.

TREASURY WILL ASK CONTINUATION OF MONETARY POWERS

Washington (AP).—Treasury officials hinted today that the administration will ask Congress to continue indefinitely its present far-reaching monetary powers.

A bill will be offered in the first few days of the session, one high authority said, extending the government's authority to maintain the $2,000,000,000 stabilization fund and the President's special powers to vary the gold content of the dollar. Both are scheduled to expire January 30 under present law.

The official asserted it had not been finally determined whether the extension would be asked for some fixed period or indefinitely, but added that the prevailing opinion of treasury experts favored unlimited continuance.

This was desirable, it was said, because of this country's participation in the new monetary agreement with France and England.

Loyalists Hold Madrid In All-Night Battle

INSURGENTS OPEN DRIVE ON CAPITAL FROM NORTHWEST

University City Section Scene of Bloody Clash; Rain Grounds Planes; Climax App... ..es.

Madrid (AP).—Insurgent armies struck viciously at Madrid's most vulnerable approahc in a driving rain today.

They attacked University City on the northwest, apparently the key to their whole advanc . This section, on the city's outskirts, is not defended by the Manzanares River, which has so far been a barrier to Madrid from the southwest.

Moving up through Casa Del Campo, the former game preserve across the river on the west, the insurgents met a violent artillery barrage.

Cannon roared throughout the night. Machine gun and rifle fire broke the sudden silence when the big guns ceased.

The bitter struggle for the easiest road into the capital was rapidly approaching a climax.

Rain Quenches Fires.

The rain and the low ceiling kept war planes out of action, but the rival guns kept pounding positions spotted by lightning flashes during the night.

Several fires, set off by the artillery bombardment in the city, were put out by the rain.

The clatter of horses' hoofs and the tramp of thousands of feet gave evidence the government was pouring reinforcements into strategic points as rapidly as possible.

Among many unconfirmed reports was one that a thousand insurgents had been trapped in Casa Del Campo. Official sources did not bear out the report.

Heavy Fighting Reported.

A close observation of the sector, moreover, showed heavy fighting in progress, with no indication the insurgents' rear lines had been cut.

University City itself was under heavy shellfire, preparatory to the intended penetration.

The defense council, however, took heart as successive enemy thrusts failed to open a way across the Manzanares. Officials also were pleased with the account which a column of 1,000 volunteer anti-fascists from several foreign nations gave of themselves in a night of desperate fighting.

Pressure of government troops attempting to flank the insurgents from the southeast is increasing, defense leaders said, creating a precarious situation for the attackers.

Shells Crash In City.

The onslaught started shortly before midnight but died down a few hours later although Fascist and Socialist guns diminished fire there the roar of insurgent cannon still sounded from the southwest.

As shells crashed into Madrid from some batteries, other gun emplacements were vacated and the cannon moved forward.

Socialist troops in the front line trenches around the Manzanares River bridge on the Madrid-Toledo highway could see the death-dealing gun muzzles 200 or 300 yards in front of them.

Government gunners labored feverishly to return the vengeful fire. White hot shells from the Socialist guns streaked across the dark sky while red glares from unceasing fires illuminated the Rosales district north of the northern railroad station.

MANY WOULD ADOPT WAIF FOUND WITH DOG IN LOUISIANA

Nesw Orleans (AP)—There were many would-be foster parents today for the blue-eyed, blond baby boy mysteriously brought out of the Piney Woods of St. Tammany Parish by a dog.

Doctors at Charity Hospital said the infant apparently was about eight days old and in good health. It weighed six pounds and three ounces.

Most insistent of those seeking the child was Mrs. Louis E. Crawford, wife of a Works Progress Administration employee making $26.25 a month.

Mrs. Crawford said she stepped from the porch of her one-room cabin home near Pearl River late yesterday to take the infant from "a great, big, brindle dog." She said the animal was carrying it through the woods in his mouth and that the child was wrapped in a coarse swaddling colth.

Welfare workers brought the baby to the hospital here over the protests of Mrs. Crawford.

The mystery surrounding the baby was as deep as ever. It was thought hitchhikers had abandoned it but the sheriff said a number of them he had detained had been released.

Nobel Winner

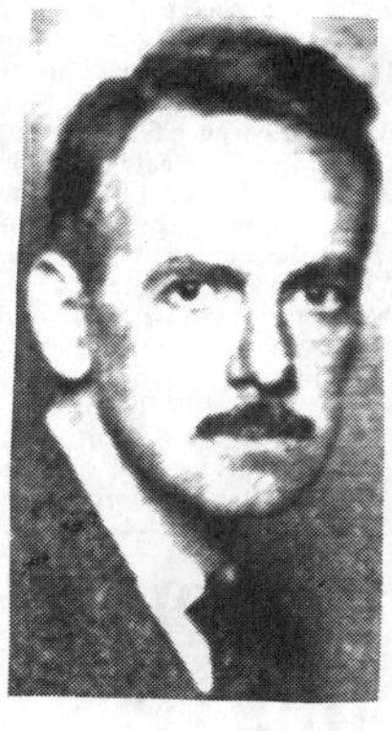

EUGENE O'NEILL

MAN KILLED WHILE CHANGING TIRE ON PITTSFIELD ROAD

Wilfred Madore, 27, of Pittsfield Fatally Hurt at 6 P. M. Yesterday; Companion Injured.

One man was killed and another seriously injured when they were struck by a truck on the Pittsfield road about two miles from the Route 9 intersection while changing a tire on their car at about 6 o'clock last night.

The dead man was Wilfred Madore, 27, of 102 Lincoln Street, Pittsfield, Mass.

The injured man is Raymond Beaulieu, 30, of 3 Oatman Terrace, Pittsfield, Mass., compound fracture of the right leg and other injuries.

Madore was pronounced dead upon arrival at Memorial Hospital, Albany. Emil Unruh, 44, of 269 Swinton Avenue, New York, driver of the truck, which is owned by the Pine Hill Crystal Spring Water Company, of 517 East 132nd Street, New York City, was arrested by state police on a charge of operating a motor vehicle in a culpably negligent manner and was committed to the Rensselaer County Jail in default of $5,000 bail when arraigned before Justice of the Peace George K. Irish, town of East Greenbush. Hearing was set for November 18.

According to state police, Madore and Beaulieu with the latter's wife and his brother, Leon Beaulieu, and the Misses Lorette Martin and May Malloy, all of Pittsfield, were driving toward Albany when a tire on their car went flat.

Madore and Raymond Beaulieu were standing in the rear of the auto removing a spare tire when the truck struck them, troopers said. Madore and Raymond Beaulieu were taken to Memorial Hospital by George Pappalau who lives near the scene of the accident.

Leon Beaulieu, the three women and Unruh were taken to the East Greenbush state police outpost for questioning by Asst. Dist. Atty. Charles G. Maloy. Coroner John H. Clinton of Troy was summoned and participated in the investigation, but, owing to the fact that the victim was pronounced dead in Albany, turned the investigation over to Coroner Ernest A. Hein of that city.

Madore died from a broken neck, ruptured spleen, punctured liver and broken right leg.

Sergt. Ralph Fitch and Troopers F. C. Knight and J. E. Falle of the East Greenbush outpost, conducted the state police investigation.

HUNTER KILLED BY BUCKSHOT CHARGE IN NORTH WOODS

Lowville (AP)—Claude Davoy, 48, of Croghan, died after his windpipe was shattered by buckshot rebounding from a rock.

Davoy, hunting north of here yesterday with his wife and two other members of a party of 11, stepped back and to one side after wounding a buck in order to give the other two a shot.

They fired and with Davoy's wife started in pursuit of the deer. Part of the charge rebounded from the rock and struck Davoy.

He was taken to Lowville Hospital where he died shortly after an emergency operation.

Five sons and six daughters, ranging in ages from 18 months to 18 years survive.

EUGENE O'NEILL WINS NOBEL PRIZE FOR LITERATURE

Noted Playwright Second American to Be So Honored; Nation's Outstanding Dramatist.

Stockholm, Sweden (UP)—Eugene O'Neill, American playwright, has been awarded the 1936 Nobel prize for literature, it was announced today.

The Nobel prize for literature is worth about $40,000. The 1935 prize will not be awarded.

The Nobel prizes are awarded for general literary merit, and not for any specific work.

O'Neill has been recognized for years as America's outstanding dramatist. His playwrighting career began in 1919 when he wrote the "Moon of the Caribbees" and "Beyond the Horizon."

There soon followed "Emperor Jones," "Anna Christie," "Desire Under the Elms," "All God's Chillun's Got Wings," "Ah, Wilderness," and others, all successes.

O'Neill successfully defied convention when he wrote "Strange Interlude," requiring five and a half hours to perform. "Mourning Becomes Electra," which was produced in 1931, was another extraordinary production.

Second American Honored.

The outstanding recognition of the Nobel prize went to O'Neill in his 48th year. He was the second American to be honored with the Nobel prize for literature, Sinclair Lewis, novelist, having been given it in 1931.

O'Neill's personality is as extraordinary as his writing. He remains aloof from social contact.

His career in the world started when he was ousted from Princeton University during his freshman year for tossing a beer bottle through the window of Woodrow Wilson, then president of the institution. He went to work thereafter in a mail order house.

O'Neill married first when he was 21, was divorced, and went off to Central America looking for gold and adventure. Later he became a sailor. After wandering about the world he obtained a job as a cub reporter on the New London, Conn., Telegraph.

In 1914 he began writing plays and went to Harvard for a year to study dramatic writing. He made a contact with the Provinceton Players which brought him fame in the 1920-21 season when "Emperor Jones" immediately won the widest recognition.

Working on "Masterpiece."

O'Neill married a second time in 1918, and, following a divorce, again in 1929. His third wife was Carlotta Monterey, actress.

O'Neill, who has lived most of the time in recent years at Sea Island, Georgia, arranged recently to sell his home there and go to the Pacific Coast. He left New York Nov. 1. Telling his publishers that he intended to make a leisurely trip to California and then live in Seattle, Wash., for about a year.

He is working now on a series of seven to nine plays that will portray the development of an American family from revolutionary days to the present. He informed his publishers he wanted to obtain some of the material in the Northwest.

PONTIFF ILL WITH BRIGHT'S DISEASE

Vatican City (UP)—Members of the Papal household today admitted that Pope Pius XI. is suffering from Bright's disease or dropsy.

They indicated that the condition of the Pope's kidneys was a cause of concern. His face as well as his legs have been slightly swollen, it was stated. The Pope is 79 and his condition is constantly watched closely. It was learned yesterday that the Pope experienced difficulty in walking.

"An American Soldier, Known But To God"

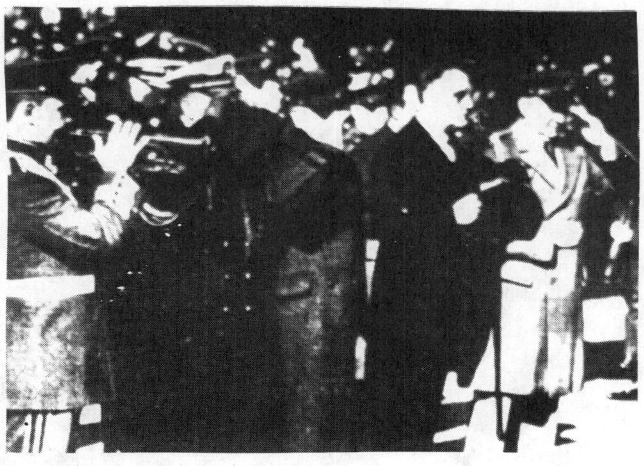

In simple, poignant ceremonies at Arlington National Cemetery, the American Unknown Soldier received the nation's homage from those of high and low rank alike. Here, uncovered before the tomb, President Roosevelt paid his respects on the 18th anniversary of the signing of the Armistice. With him (left to right) are Admiral William H. Standley, General John J. Pershing and Col. Edwin M. Watson, the President's military aide. (A. P. Photo.)

MRS. SIMPSON TO LEAVE SOON FOR FRENCH RIVIERA

Former Baltimore Girl and King Edward "Remain Closest of Friends," London Hears.

London (UP)—Mrs. Wallis Simpson intends soon to leave for the continent, perhaps to remain there until her decree of divorce becomes absolute next spring, it was learned today.

She will stay on the Riviera with her friends Mr. and Mrs. Herman Rogers of New York, who were members of the party which, including Mrs. Simpson, the King entertained at Balmoral Castle, Scotland, several weeks ago.

The plan of Mrs. Simpson to go abroad has been forming in her mind ever since she obtained a decree nisi of divorce from Ernest Simpson October 27. But it was a surprise that she might remain on the continent until the six months' period had expired next April 27—when she may obtain an absolute divorce decree. The absolute decree is necessary before she can remarry.

Mrs. Simpson's consideration of the possibility of a long stay coincides with an increasing crowded engagement list for the King. He was at Portland today to inspect the fleet. He must go next week-end to visit distressed areas—in which, as in housing and slum clearance, he is deeply interested. Further, from now until his coronation next May he will be increasingly busy with details of arrangements for the ceremony, which he personally must approve.

Gossips seized at once on the intention of Mrs. Simpson to go abroad as a possible indication that her friendship with the King was waning. It was believed this gossip was inspired by persons who desire to end the friendship.

The King and Mrs. Simpson remain the closest of friends, and the King continues to say it with flowers. Loads of gardenias, carnations and shaggy chrysanthemums as big as one's head are delivered at Mrs. Simpson's house daily.

The New Deal Day By Day

Events in Washington As Interpreted By Frank R. Kent

It is hardly likely that analysis of the recent election returns, which, despite their one-sided nature, still goes on among the political statisticians and observers in all parts of the country, will soon grow tiresome, but the book should not be closed completely without a record being made of

(Continued on Page 6.)

ROCKEFELLER, JR., VOICES PRAISE OF FARLEY'S ADDRESS

Democratic Chairman's Election Night Plea for National Unity Lauded by Oil Magnate.

New York (UP)—Democratic National Chairman James A. Farley's radio address after midnight on Election Night was, in the opinion of John D. Rockefeller, Jr., one of the "most statesmanlike utterances made on either side during the entire campaign."

Rockefeller, who contributed to Gov. Alfred M. Landon's campaign, made this known in a letter to Farley, written as "one citizen to another," and made public today at National Democratic Headquarters.

The letter, dated November 7, follows:

"As one citizen to another I want to give myself the satisfaction of telling you that I think the radio talk which you made after midnight on Election Night, as reported in 'The Sun,' was one of the most statesmanlike utterances made on either side during the entire campaign.

"Such words as these—'we may look forward to four years of uninterrupted effort to accomplish the completion of economic recovery, of industrial welfare and of permanent establishment of real liberty in the United States,' and 'no American need have any fear of the future. Franklin D. Roosevelt's mission is to see that all of us have a square deal,' and 'I know that all who hear these words will join me in the hope the scars of this great political battle will soon be healed.' Such words as these, I say, coming from you, will go a long way towards inspiring confidence and bringing about the cooperation of all citizens, irrespective of party, in dealing with the many problems so vital to our national life that confront us as a people. Your statement exemplifies the finest kind of sportsmanship. I congratulate you on it."

'FRISCO-OAKLAND BRIDGE OPENED BY MR. ROOSEVELT

World's Largest Span Fulfills Century-old Dream; Crowded Peninsula Linked to Mainland.

San Francisco (UP)—Dignitaries and 300,000 visitors came here today to celebrate the opening of the San Francisco-Oakland Bay bridge—dream of bay residents for 100 years and largest span in the world.

At 12:30 p. m. (3:30 p. m. EST.) President Roosevelt will press a button in the White House, lighting two green lamps on the span and officially opening the world's largest bridge to traffic.

Gov. Frank F. Merriam, preceding the presidential flash, will make two speeches, one at the Oakland end of the bridge and the other at the San Francisco end. He will cut a ribbon and announce the bridge formally open.

Then a 100-year-old dream will be realized San Francisco's crowded peninsula will be linked with California's inland valley empire and her sister cities on the eastern shore of the bay, Oakland, Berkeley, Alameda, Richmond and Albany.

World's Greatest Bridge.

Opening of the bridge replaces the intricate system of ferry service which has served the bay cities since the pioneer days of the old West. The ferries which have served as an outlet for San Franciscoans will continue to operate but at greatly reduced schedules. Next year street car service will start across the bridge.

The gigantic eight and one-fourth mile long bridge dwarfs other spans the world over. The George Washington Bridge, the Queensboro Bridge and the Brooklyn Bridge of New York; the Delaware River Bridge, the Quebec Bridge and the Ambassador Bridge in Detroit all could be placed end to end and the San Francisco-Oakland Bridge still would out-measure them.

Construction began July 9, 1933 and was finished yesterday. Test borings first were taken in the bay in 1920.

Features Two Decks.

Engineers believe the San Francisco-Oakland Bridge will stand unsurpassed for the next 1,000 years. Not that improved engineering methods will not make a larger bridge possible, but because there remains no larger body of unspanned water where traffic is apt to justify the cost of building such a bridge.

There are two decks on the bridge—which combines the suspension and cantilever type. The upper deck will be devoted to passenger vehicles on a six-lane highway.

The lower deck will be used for suburban trains, used principally by commuters between Oakland and San Francisco. These trains will begin service early next year.

Disabled Veteran Ends Life As Buddies Parade

Philadelphia (UP).—The sight of his World War buddies marching by in an Armistice Day parade was too much for Sergt. Frank Koenig, who had lived for 18 years in agony from war wounds. He killed himself.

Koenig was riddled with machine gun bullets at Soissons. At a base hospital, surgeons found he also had been gassed. After he returned home, his wounds still tortured him, and gas-poisoned tissues in his stomach and throat wracked him with pain.

He found a job, and tried to support his wife. But he had to take long periods off from work for treatments. And eventually Koenig found himself drifting precariously from one small job to another. A week ago the pain grew worse. He could eat nothing but broth.

When the sound of marching bands reached his room yesterday, Koenig looked out a window. He stared for a while, then went to the cellar. His body was found at the end of a rope.

SPECTACULAR FIRE DESTROYS ONE TUG AND SEARS OTHERS

Man Narrowly Escapes; Troy, Lansingburg and Cohoes Departments Called to Fight Flames.

Spectacular fires causing damage estimated at $25,000 to four tugs and six barges lighted up the Troy and Cohoes waterfronts early today, threatening the Matton drydocks and calling out Troy, Lansingburg and Cohoes fire equipment. One boatman, known only as "Nick" narrowly escaped with his life. Cause of the fire is undetermined.

The boats damaged include:

The Irving G. Keller, tug owned by the McCarren Towing Lines of 19 State Street, New York City, destroyed.

The Triton, tug owned by the Lake Champlain Dispatch Company, port side seriously damaged.

The Helen V. Murray, tug owned by the Murray Towing Company, scorched.

The Madeline Murray, tug owned by the Murray Towing Company, slight damage.

Six barges, owned by the Hedges Transportation Company, Murray Transportation Company and Matton Towing Corporation, all seriously scorched.

Boatman Loses Belongings.

The boatman "Nick" Wall, who discovered the fire on the Keller, lost all his belongings, even to his false teeth. At first it was feared he had been burned to death, but later in the morning officials discovered that he had left for New York to report the loss of the barge Irving G. Keller, to the concern owning it.

The Irving G. Keller, Triton and Helen V. Murray were moored together at the Lake Champlain Dispatch Company terminal at the foot of 120th Street, the first named being on the outside and the other two against the dock.

About 4 a. m., "Nick," asleep in the stern cabin, was awakened by dense, choking smoke. Partly overcome, he staggered on deck and found the boat on fire from bow to stern. The fire, he said, seemed to have started around the smokestack. He jumped on board the Helen V. Murray and began blowing the whistle. A full crew were asleep on the Helen V. Murray and several men on the Triton. Soon the whistles of both tugs were screeching.

An alarm was turned in from Box 613. George Godfrey, dispatcher of the Lake Champlain company, said that when he reached the waterfront he found the Triton still untouched and made a frantic attempt to cut her loose from the Irving G. Keller. The deck of the latter boat was abandoned when the line between the two boats began to burn.

As the line broke, fire hoses playing on the boats drove the Keller out into the river and she drifted blazing across the river and against the six barges tied up at the Matton docks. Whistles on that side of the river began to screech and sirens to sound as the Cohoes fire department responded to a general alarm. In the meantime the port side of the Triton was burning merrily on the Troy side of the river, the Murray was scorching and the Troy fire department had been called.

Just as it seemed the six barges and the Matton dry dock were doomed to destruction, the Madeleine Murray which yesterday pumped water all day on the Hannah Newell, burning barge beached below Madison Street, came down the river from Waterford and towed away the Irving G. Keller.

Blaze Easily Extinguished.

The Madeleine Murray caught fire but the blaze was easily extinguished by members of the crew. The Irving G. Keller was beached just north of the 112th Street bridge and on the west side of the river. The tug is considered a total loss.

Police of the Fourth Precinct began an investigation of the fire on this side of the river with Patrolmen John C. Christiansen and Enoch Eaton in charge. Cohoes police investigated the fire on their side of the river.

Officials of the Matton concern said their damage would be small.

The Index

NEW SERIAL BEGINS TODAY!

Romance features an intriguing mystery leading up to that

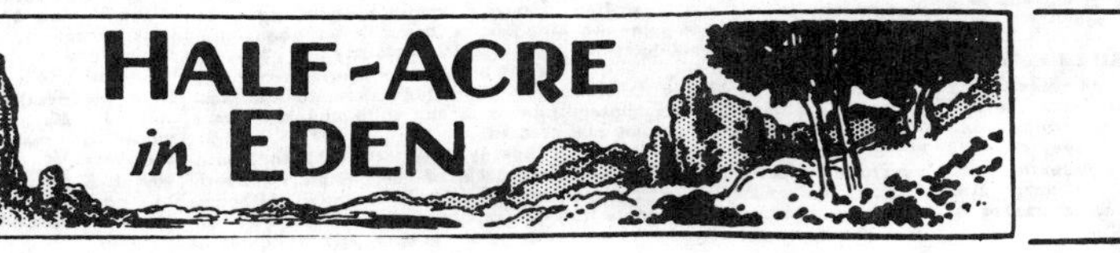

and a jealous woman learns nothing can keep true love apart

TURN TO PAGE 10

THE WEATHER
Tonight—Fair.
Tomorrow—Fair.

THE TIMES RECORD

FINAL
EDITION

Series 1937—No. 122.　(Entered as second class Matter at the Postoffice at Troy, N. Y., under the Act of March 3, 1879.)　TROY, N. Y., MONDAY EVENING, MAY 24, 1937.　(Published Daily Except Sunday)　PRICE THREE CENTS

SOCIAL SECURITY ACT HELD VALID

John D. Rockefeller, Sr., Founder Of Great Oil Fortune, Dies At Age Of 97

AGED CAPITALIST EXPIRES IN SLEEP AT FLORIDA HOME

Pioneer Petroleum Magnate Rose from $4.50-a-Week Clerk to Master of Legendary Wealth.

Ormond Beach, Fla. (AP).—John D. Rockefeller, Sr., the founder of the world's greatest "dollar dynasty," lay stilled in death today—just 26 months short of his cherished desire to live to be 100.

He would have been 98 years old July 8.

The aged capitalist died Sunday morning at 4:05 o'clock, E. S. T., at his winter home, "The Casements," drifting peacefully off to his final sleep after complaining that he felt "very tired."

His physician, Dr. Harry L. Merryday, attributed death to sclerotic myocarditis, a hardening of the heart muscles.

The nonagenarian Croesus, who rose from a $4.50 a week clerk to mastership of a fortune estimated as high as $2,400,000,000, died a comparatively "poor man."

A family spokesman said he left a "relatively small, very liquid" estate.

Long ago, since his retirement from active business at the age of 57, he had turned the bulk of his fabulous riches over to his only son, John D. Rockefeller, Jr., or spread-eagled it in philanthropic endowments to the far ends of the earth.

In his lifetime, out of the golden torrent that gained him the sobriquet of the greatest "Money Titan" in all history, he had given away the amazing sum of $530,830,000. Other gifts by his son raised

(Continued on Page 13).

DUKE OF WINDSOR DENIES KNITTING WALLIE'S SWEATER

Monts, France (INS) — Anger overcame the Duke of Windsor today after a long siege of baseless reports published abroad.

The former British King, it was learned, was particularly annoyed by a story that he was knitting a pull-over sweater for Mrs. Wallis Warfield, whom he is marrying June 3.

Herman L. Rogers of New York, the Duke's spokesman, reflected the former King's pique at his latest press conference, when he warned that his chats with reporters might have to be suspended if untrue stories were dispatched.

He completely blasted reports that the Duke knits to soothe his nerves.

"The Duke never knits," Rogers said emphatically. "The story is utterly ridiculous—false—stupid. So far as jangled nerves are concerned, the Duke sleeps well and keeps himself in good shape by golf and other exercise."

Rogers also said the Duke and his future Duchess are not now contemplating any trip to America, or buying any property there.

MURDER MYSTERY STORY BRINGS OUT POLICE RESERVES

Boston (INS)—The footsteps of the "phantom" came ever closer, closer.... .

Capt. James R. Hawkes, 41, retired Army officer, let his pulse move from the detective story magazine murder mystery he was reading. He listened.

He leaped to his feet, drew a service pistol and began firing. He continued firing, bullets shattering windows and imbedding in an apartment house across the street.

Ten policemen, answering frenzied calls of a score of terrified occupants of a Back Bay apartment house, found Captain Hawkes in the bathroom. He told of his fears of a prowler, but admitted he may have been upset by the murder mystery.

He was ordered to the psychopathic hospital for observation today.

The Index

Rockefeller—An Eminent American From Youth to Old Age

This group of photos shows John D. Rockefeller, Sr., who died at Ormond Beach, Fla., at various stages of his long life. 1—A young man. 2—In middle thirties, early in his career as president of the Standard Oil Company. 3—About peak of his active career, 1911. 4—When oil trust was dissolved in 1911, leading to his retirement. 5—On his 97th birthday in 1936 at his Lakewood, N. J., home. 6—Believed to be last picture of Rockefeller showing him arriving at Ormond Beach October 9, 1936. (Copyright by Englebrecht from Associated Press.)

FORMER OFFICIAL, SISTER STRICKEN WITHIN 5 HOURS

Brother Dies Playing Golf and Anna Quillinan, Court Stenographer, Succumbs to Shock.

A double funeral for former Dist. Atty. Timothy J. Quillinan, and his sister, Miss Anna R. Quillinan, for many years stenographer in Rensselaer County Surrogate's Court, both of whom died suddenly within a period of five hours Saturday, will be conducted privately from their respective residences tomorrow morning and thence to St. Patrick's Church, where at 10 o'clock, a solemn requiem mass will be celebrated. Friends are invited to attend services at the church.

Mr. Quillinan, who was in his 67th year, died at the Troy Country Club at about 4 o'clock Saturday afternoon, shortly after being taken ill at the sixth hole of the Country Club golf course. He resided at 195 Fifth avenue, Lansingburg.

With Two Sons.

The former district attorney, long prominent in the legal profession in Troy, had been with his two sons, Francis and Walter Quillinan, and Thomas W. Rourke and Homer Lasher, when he complained of feeling ill on the golf links. His automobile was brought to

(Continued on Page 10).

102 CRAFT UNIONS LAUNCH CAMPAIGN AGAINST LEWIS' CIO

Cincinnati, O., (AP)—Representatives of 102 craft unions affiliated with the American Federation of Labor meet today to declare war against John L. Lewis' Committee for Industrial Organization.

The delegates will pass upon recommendations drafted yesterday by the Federation's executive council, chief of which called for an assessment against members to raise funds for an intensive organization campaign.

"The primary purpose of this meeting," said Federation President William Green, "is to make provision for the great wave of organization spirit which is sweeping the country."

He said the Federation was not disturbed by Lewis' activities, and that there was no connection between his call for today's meeting and Lewis' announcement last month that the CIO issue local charters to local unions, central and state bodies.

However, he had been assured that the Federation was ready to purge completely all state federations of labor and all city central labor bodies of CIO affiliates.

Memorial Day Proclamation

Calling upon the citizens of Troy to participate in memorial services scheduled, Mayor Chester J. Atkinson issued a proclamation today for Memorial Week, as follows:

"Memorial Day is dedicated to patriotism and consecrated to those who sacrificed and died for our country. Memorial Week has become one of the most significant of our national anniversaries. On this day the nation pauses to remember and to take stock in its spiritual resources. It is an appropriate time for quickening our national pride, for recalling our debt to the past, for renewing our love and reverence for ancestors and for departed relatives and friends, a season of pilgrimages to national shrines and visits to graves of our cherished dead.

"Because the thoughts and emotions fostered by Memorial Day observance enhance our national life and character and in the belief that one day is too short for full expression of these sentiments, I, Chester J. Atkinson, Mayor of the City of Troy, do hereby call upon the citizens of Troy and all organizations interested in memorializing the dead and honoring our country, both military and civic, to observe the seven days concluding May 30 as Memorial Week, in the City of Troy, to be dedicated to memorial ceremonies of every kind."

GLADYS MAC KNIGHT SAYS CONFESSION RESULT OF DURESS

Jersey City, N. J. (AP)—Gladys MacKnight flatly repudiated today her alleged confession that she killed her mother with a hatchet.

The 17-year-old girl, on trial for murder with her former sweetheart, Donald Wightman, 18, declared the incriminating statement was obtained by Bayonne police through duress. She stuck to her story that Wightman struck the fatal hatchet blows.

On the stand at the opening of the second week of her trial, Gladys asserted she was "shocked" when detectives first told her she was charged with the murder of her mother. It was then, she said, that she sent her father, Edgar Mac Knight, this message:

"Tell my father I had nothing to do with it. I loved my mother and couldn't do that to her."

Gladys testified that a Bayonne detective sat with his face a couple of inches from her face and "kept telling me I had killed my mother and to come clean or he'd make me come clean."

"You're going to get the third degree and get it good,' she said the detective told her.

HIGHWAY SAFETY PATROL STARTED IN TROOP G AREA

Lieut. H. A. Keator Placed in Command of New Unit; Will Work from Newtonville Outpost.

A new highway safety patrol in command of Lieut. Harvey A. Keator, supervising officer, was inaugurated within the area served by Troop G, New York State Police, by an official act this morning.

The supervising officer will have exclusive jurisdiction over the men assigned to him, being responsible only to the commanding officer, Capt. John M. Keck, for the enforcement of traffic regulations, highway safety and education and engineering in the Troop G territory.

The new unit will be stationed at the Newtonville outpost and its personnel includes all men assigned to motorcycle duty and the new White safety patrol car. Assisting Lieutenant Keator will be Sergeant Peter Fitzpatrick and Corp. Edward F. Markle.

The Only Exceptions.

The only exception to the present system is that the men will be used exclusively for traffic regulation and only in extreme emergency and with the consent of the Commanding Officer will they be removed from their assigned duty. Assignments, and changes in the traffic detail will be made by the supervising officer with the approval of Captain Keeley.

At headquarters in Newtonville, a "spot" map will be employed to keep track of accidents. Various color markers, each indicating a particular type of accident, will be used to mark scenes of mishaps, the exact location to be marked on the map for the information of the Commanding Officer and to assist in the selective enforcement and assignment of the patrols. The map will also serve as a visible accident record.

Plan Careful Study.

A careful study will be made by Lieutenant Keator of the territory to determine the particular places and scenes of frequent highway accidents and when such information has been gathered and compiled the program of selective enforcement will be officially begun.

Concentration of traffic patrols will be made at points that have been known to be dangerous and as the situation in that respect changes the patrols will be shifted to take up their duties in some other place, where accidents have become frequent.

The patrol is the first of its kind in the state and follows closely upon the heels of the use of the White Safety patrol which has accomplished great good in the short time of its existence in cutting down the number of accidents in this immediate vicinity.

FIVE RECOVERING FROM EFFECTS OF FOOD POISONING

Prompt Medical Attention Believed to Have Averted Tragedy in Ross Home; Son Summons Aid.

Five members of one family, stricken by food poisoning yesterday, are well on their way to recovery at the Samaritan Hospital. Early discovery and prompt medical attention are believed to have saved them from more serious results.

The victims are:

Mrs. Pauline Ross, 50, of 2315 Fifth Avenue, recovered consciousness.

Mrs. Joseph Hayes, 22, of 32 Thirteenth Street, her daughter, condition good, having been the next most seriously affected.

Fred Ross, 20, a son, not serious.

George Ross, 13, another son, also not serious.

Joseph Hayes, Jr., a grandson, only slightly ill.

The entire family, with the Rosses at their home, and Mrs. Hayes and her son at her Thirteenth Street residence, apparently was stricken about the same time. Police rushed the Rosses to the hospital and only an odd chance brought speedy treatment to Mrs. Hayes and her child.

Staggers Into Station.

Police had their first inkling of the case a few minutes after midnight when Fred Ross staggered into the Central Station, retching severely, to tell Sergt. Timothy J. Mahoney of the family's plight and appeal for aid.

His mother and younger brother, he groaned, were lying at home unconscious and although he had tried to contact several physicians he had been unsuccessful.

Police managed to reach Dr. Leo S. Weinstein who rushed to the home. Sergt. Mahoney, with Patrol Driver Joseph F. Markham meanwhile hurried to the Fifth Avenue address with Fred Ross.

There they were directed by the physician to take Mrs. Ross who was unconscious and apparently in a serious condition, to the hospital. Meanwhile the boys became worse and were taken to the hospital in Dr. Weinstein's car.

Treatment was given the three immediately and the boys told that their sister and her baby had been present for dinner and might be affected.

Trying to Aid Child.

"Patroldriver Markham sped to the Hayes home, where he found Mrs. Hayes, seriously ill herself, vainly striving to administer to her son. She was taken to the hospital with the child and both were treated.

Speedy treatment of the family was declared responsible for averting a wholesale tragedy. Although all responded favorably, the condition of mother and daughter is

Third Son Born To Lindberghs May 12 At Their English Home

Cleveland (UP)—Mrs. Charles Long Cutter, aunt of Mrs. Charles Lindbergh, told the United Press today that Colonel and Mrs. Lindbergh were parents of another son.

Mrs. Cutter's housekeeper said Mrs. Cutter received news of the birth Friday.

The baby was said to have been born on May 12, Coronation Day. It was not known here what it has been named.

London (UP)—No confirmation could be obtained at Weald, Kent, where Col. and Mrs. Charles A. Lindbergh live, that Mrs. Lindbergh gave birth to a son on May 13.

Residents of Weald said, however, that last Wednesday they saw Colonel Lindbergh "tearing down the road in his car accompanied by Mrs. Lindbergh." He appeared to be in a terrific hurry.

The Lindberghs were married May 27, 1929, and their first son, Charles A., Jr., was born June 22, 1930. He was kidnaped from his Hopewell, N. J., home March 1, 1932, and later his body was found in the woods. Bruno Hauptmann died in the electric chair for his murder. The second son of the flying couple, Jon Morrow Lindbergh, was born August 16, 1932. Threats against the life of their second son caused the Lindberghs to take refuge in England in 1935.

President Urges Congress To Pass Wage, Hour Laws

Special Message Outlines Chief Executive's Plans for "Extending Social Progress" in U. S.

Washington (INS)—In one of the most important proposals of his White House incumbency, President Roosevelt today called upon this session of Congress to enact legislation giving the government "some control over maximum hours, minimum wages, the evil of child labor and the exploitation of child labor."

A special message to Congress outlined his philosophy, which followed the essence of the outlawed NRA.

The President did not specify the maximum hours or minimum wages he desires, Congress, he said, should have little trouble in arriving at a basic formula.

Legislation will establish it on a flexible basis of a 35-to-40 hour week and a 40-cent an hour minimum wage.

Of prime interest to industry, Mr. Roosevelt further proposed:

"That only goods which have been produced under conditions which meet the minimum standards of free labor shall be admitted to interstate commerce."

Possibly anticipating constitutional objections the President advised Congress:

"The time has arrived for us to take further action to extend the frontiers of social progress. Such further action initiated by the legislative branch of the government, administered by the executive, and sustained by the judicial, is within the common sense framework and purpose of our constitution and receives beyond doubt the approval of our electorate. xxxx

"Enlightened business is learning that competition ought not to cause bad social consequences which inevitably react upon the profits of business itself.

"All but the hopelessly reactionary will agree that to conserve our primary resources of man power, government must have some control over maximum hours, minimum wages, the evil of child labor and the exploitation of child labor."

The President said there should be little dispute with his proposal to rule out of interstate commerce the products of manufacturers who employ child labor, who deny workers the right of self-organization and collective bargaining and who fail to meet minimum working standards.

In connection with the right of the worker to organize, the President by the LaFollette committee, declared that abuses disclosed as "fear of labor spies, the hair of company unions, or the use of strikebreakers," must "be promptly curbed."

Mr. Roosevelt, in effect challenging the courts, said his plan was "within the common sense framework and purpose" of the Constitution.

Selected

DR. F. M. SULZMAN NAMED TO OFFICE IN TRUST COMPANY

Physician Selected Today as Vice President to Succeed Former Supreme Court Justice Coffey.

Dr. Frank M. Sulzman was named vice president of the Troy Trust Company today by the Board of Directors. He succeeds former Supreme Court Justice James V. Coffey, who died recently.

Dr. Sulzman has been a director of the bank since 1932.

He was graduated from Waterford High School in 1892 and received his Master of Arts degree from Villanova University. He was graduated from Albany Medical College in 1902.

Dr. Sulzman is a member and past president of Rensselaer County Medical Association. He is a member of the American Medical Association, the American Academy of Ophthalmology and Otolaryngology, the American Laryngological, Rhinological and Otological Society and the American College of Surgeons.

Dr. Sulzman is a member of the staff of the Troy Hospital and has served as secretary, treasurer and president. He also is a member of the staff of the Cohoes Hospital. He is president of the Board of Directors of the Community Hotel Association and a member of the Troy Country Club, Troy Council, K. of C.; Father Van Rensselaer Assembly, Fourth Degree, K. of C., and Troy Lodge of Elks.

'AVIATORS' LIVES MAY BE SPARED

Paris (UP)—Two German aviators, under sentence of death at Bilbao for aiding the Spanish nationalists, may be exchanged for two Russian aviators who are prisoners of the nationalists, according to word from diplomatic sources at the frontier today.

Dr. Weinstein said the upset condition of the systems of the victims apparently was caused by partaking of the pie.

The case following by less than ten days the death, by ptomaine poisoning resulting from what was described as "bad food," of John H. Mackle, 75, of ptomaine poisoning resulting from what was described as the family declared was bad food. Mackle died May 14, after a short illness. Mackle, also made seriously ill, re-covered.

COURT BACKS JOB INSURANCE AND OLD AGE PENSIONS

New Deal Scores Smashing Victory in 5 to 4 and 7 to 2 Decisions on Welfare Legislation.

Washington (AP)—The Supreme Court today approved the constitutionality of the twin keystones of the New Deal social security act—old age pensions and unemployment insurance legislation.

The decisions, coming as the climax of a Supreme Court term in which no New Deal legislation has been disapproved, established the validity of two of the most sweeping projects undertaken by the Roosevelt administration.

The court upheld Federal unemployment insurance provisions by a 5 to 4 vote. The old age pensions verdict was by a 7 to 2 vote. In a third verdict, the court approved by a 5 to 4 vote the provisions of the Alabama state unemployment act a state law enacted to carry out by local co-operation the general terms of the Federal unemployment act.

The decisions thus upheld the entire comprehensive federal-state unemployment alleviation scheme contemplated by framers of the Social Security Act.

Cardozo Writes Opinions.

The series of opinions virtually completed the court's work for the year, a year marked by outbreak of one of the most intense controversies ever to involve the high tribunal, as a result of President Roosevelt's judiciary reorganization proposal.

Justice Benjamin N. Cardozo, liberal jurist and youngest member of the high bench in point of service, wrote both of the important majority opinions upholding old age pensions and unemployment insurance.

The terms of the decisions were broad, affirming in the unemployment insurance case the right of the Federal Government to launch a program for the general welfare of the nation in concert with the states.

Close scrutiny was expected to be given the opinions for indications as to whether they carried the legal basis for achievement of other administration goals through the medium of legislation drafted along the general lines of the security act.

Closer Agreement.

The unemployment decision revealed a split among the court jurists following generally the lines of previous five to four decisions.

Three separate dissenting opinions were presented—written by Justices George Sutherland, Pierce Butler and James C. McReynolds. Justice Willis Van DeVanter, who retires from the bench June 2—the day after the court's last session of the present term—joined in the Sutherland dissent.

The court achieved closer agreement in the old age pensions verdict, although Justices Butler and McReynolds dissented. In the majority ruling they presented no formal opinion in support of their position.

In the decision on Alabama's state unemployment insurance law, the division returned to the now familiar five to four count. Justice Harlan F. Stone wrote the majority opinion while Sutherland presented a minority opinion in which he was joined by Van Devanter and Butler. McReynolds dissented without formal opinion.

The Federal law was drawn to encourage states to pass their own unemployment insurance laws, a method adopted because of the fear of constitutional objections to outright unemployment insurance by the federal government.

Five Major Questions.

There were four opinions. Justices George Sutherland, Pierce Butler and James C. McReynolds wrote separate dissents. Justice Willis Van Devanter joined Sutherland's opinion.

The majority opinion passed on five major questions.

It held that the tax was an excise tax and approved it.

It held the tax not invalid in spite of the exemption of employers of fewer than eight persons.

The court held that the statute does not call on the states to surrender essential powers.

It held that the tax was not coercive on the states.

It found that Title 9, the tax provision, alone was at stake in the present court test and that it was separable from Title 3, which set up the unemployment compensation provisions.

Alabama Case Involved.

The unemployment insurance provisions of the Social Security Act constituted one of the major phases of the law. Other involved old age pensions, also before the court.

The unemployment insurance phase of the law is provided in two separate titles of the act. Title III provides for grants to the states for the administration of state unemployment insurance funds. Title IX provides for a tax on payrolls starting at one per cent. The latter title was more directly involved in today's decision.

The case on which the test acted was brought by the Charles C. Steward Machine Company of Birmingham, Ala., which sued to recover $46 in Federal taxes paid on its payrolls to Collector of Internal Revenue Harwell G. Davis.

THE WEATHER

Tonight—Cloudy, cooler.
Tomorrow—Rain.

THE TIMES RECORD

FINAL EDITION

(Entered as second Class Matter at the Postoffice at Troy, N. Y., under the Act of March 3, 1879.)

Series 1938—No. 230.

TROY, N. Y., THURSDAY EVENING, SEPTEMBER 29, 1938.

(Published Daily Except Sunday)

PRICE THREE CENTS

DEWEY NAMED FOR GOVERNOR
PEACE RUMORED NEAR AT MUNICH

HITLER REPORTED READY TO ACCEPT BRITISH PROGRAM

"Symbolic Occupation" of Sudeten Towns by German, British, French, Italian Troops One Feature.

Munich (AP)—A German government spokesman said tonight that the four-power Munich conference, seeking a new basis for European peace, had practically reached an agreement for a "token occupation" of the Sudetenland by the German army.

While the German chancellor and the premiers of Britain, France and Italy still were negotiating in the glistening Fuehrerhaus—at 8:10 p.m. (3:10 p.m., E. S. T.)—the spokesman said only one difficulty remained:

"The question of just how quickly and from what point men of the hour at Munich must be withdrawn to permit Adolf Hitler's troops to march into the Sudetenland.

Castel Gandolfo, Italy (UP)—Pope Pius XI broadcast throughout the world tonight a prayer for peace in Europe.

"We pray to God for the successful conclusion of negotiations," (at Munich) the Pope said, his voice breaking with emotion.

"We pray that the good God will give us a little more life in which to see the re-establishment of good will in the world."

BY THE ASSOCIATED PRESS

Europe's hopes of escaping war rose today, buoyed by British and German optimism that the four men of the hour at Munich could agree on a peaceful solution of Germany's demands on Czechoslovakia.

Twice today British Prime Minister Chamberlain and French Premier Daladier, spokesmen for Europe's democracies, sat across a fateful conference table from Reichsfuehrer Hitler and Premier Mussolini of Italy, powerful partners of the Rome-Berlin axis.

After an interlude of almost two hours following a two-hour meeting in the resplendent Nazi Fuehrerhaus, the conferees returned.

They were believed to be discussing a compromise plan striking a balance between Hitler's threat to march into Czechoslovakia with booming guns, if necessary—unless the Sudetenland were ceded to Germany by Saturday and a British-French proposal designed to forestall German use of force.

Peace Hopes Brighter.

Hopes for an early settlement assuring Europe of peace for the moment were expressed by British and German officials alike as the four statesmen went into another conference late this afternoon.

It was indicated Reichsfuehrer Hitler might be permitted a peaceful march into Czechoslovakia's Sudetenland Oct. 1—Saturday—for at least a symbolic occupation.

Informed German sources at Munich said tonight that Hitler had agreed that the German army would make only a "parade occupation" of the Eger and Asch regions of extreme western Czechoslovakia on Oct. 1 and 2.

Other sections of the Sudetenland are to be occupied only gradually, these informants said, under the plan said to have been accepted by the fuehrer in place of his original intention of having his armies march in Saturday with flags waving.

Allied Troops to March.

Under the occupation plan, it was said that detachments of the British, French and Italian armies would march with the German troops to make it look less like a German invasion.

This token occupation, however, would show sympathizing that Germany had become the master of the regions of Czechoslovakia whose population is predominantly German.

In "doubtful areas," where the non-Germanic proportion is larger, it was believed French, British and Italian army contingents would safeguard a plebiscite from which there would be no appeal.

Czechoslovakia, meanwhile, accepted the British compromise "in principle" and with some reservations and sent an envoy to Munich to inform the conferees.

Nations Still Arming.

Still, however, many countries took no optimistic chances while unending streams of motorized German forces were arriving at the edge of Czechoslovakia and border clashes still were occurring in Sudetenland.

A decree empowered the French government to mobilize the entire nation should the four-statesman conference prove a barren.

Great Britain went ahead with defense measures—digging park trenches, dugouts and shelters, evacuating cities, recruiting men. The British press and London Stock Exchange were generally optimistic over the relaxed international tension.

Peace Or War Up To Them

NEVILLE CHAMBERLAIN.

ADOLF HITLER.

EDOUARD DALADIER.

BENITO MUSSOLINI.

TORNADO STRIKES CHARLESTON, S. C.; 25 KNOWN DEAD

More Than 100 Persons Injured; Waterfront and Residential Sections Suffer Heavy Damage.

Charleston, S. C. (UP)—A tornado ripped across the Charleston industrial and residential and waterfront today, taking a heavy toll of dead and injured and causing heavy property damage.

Digging into debris in heavy rains which followed the tornado, authorities predicted the death toll would be high.

At least 25 were known dead and more than 100 injured.

Many of the victims were Negroes.

The twister struck along the water front, mowing down frame structures and unroofing many buildings. It was reported that the mill of the Charleston Paper & Pulp Co. was wrecked and some employees trapped in the debris. Firemen were summoned to the mill and asked to bring acetylene torches to cut through the wreckage.

The storm swirled around the waterfront, skipped the business section, and then headed toward Sullivan's Island.

It was reported the roof of the Trimod Hotel crashed in, trapping several guests. Fifteen houses were demolished and the roof of City Hall ripped off.

Police found the body of one man in the wrecked annex of Sacred Heart Catholic Church.

The city was without outside communication. One telephone line was in operation between here and Columbia. Power failed.

A heavy rain followed the twister, flooding the city.

Roofs lay in the streets. Automobiles were injured since the storm struck before schools opened. Signs on buildings were blown away.

The roof of one school was torn off. Officials said that no school children were injured since the storm struck before schools opened. Physicians and nurses were mobilized for emergency work. Many injured were reported in hospitals.

The storm struck hardest in the old slave market section along the waterfront. The wind cut a semicircle through the city and headed toward Sullivan's Island.

First reports from Sullivan's Island said that several persons had been injured and were being brought to Charleston hospitals for treatment.

Former Trojans In Storm-Stricken City

A number of Trojans anxiously awaited word this afternoon of friends and relatives living in tornado stricken Charleston.

Mrs. George W. Moore and Miss Winifred Podmore of Roosevelt avenue, R. F. D. No. 1, Troy, are awaiting word from their brother Joseph Podmore and family who reside in the stricken city. Mr. Podmore is a former Trojan.

ARRAIGN WOMAN IN ALCOHOL CASE IN POLICE COURT

Mrs. Mary Marvillo of Earl Street Pleads Not Guilty to Charge of Selling Untaxed Fluid.

A 70-year-old Troy woman, charged with selling alcohol illegally, faced Judge James F. Byron in Police Court this morning.

She is Mrs. Mary Marvillo of 113 Earl street. She was taken before the court on the arm of her son, who also served as interpreter for her. She speaks only Italian.

She was charged with violation of Section 100 of the Alcoholic Beverage Control Law.

She pleaded not guilty through her son and her case was adjourned two weeks. She had been arrested on a warrant served by Detective Edmund Sullivan and Plainclothesman John Buehler. The warrant was served a week ago but the woman was unable to appear because of illness.

It is alleged that officers investigating the sale of untaxed alcohol in the city, made illegal "buys" in her place.

REV. M. E. PEABODY BECOMES BISHOP OF EPISCOPAL CHURCH

Syracuse (UP)—Rev. Malcolm E. Peabody of Chestnut Hill, Pa., was consecrated Bishop-Coadjutor of the Protestant Episcopal Church Diocese of Central New York today at impressive rites attended by twenty bishops and 800 other church notables.

Rev. Mr. Peabody eventually is to succeed Rt. Rev. Edward H. Coley of Utica as bishop of the diocese.

Consecration rituals which at noon climaxed the three-hour ceremony were performed by Most Rev. Dr. Henry St. George Tucker of Richmond, Va., presiding bishop of the church. Bishop Coley and Rt. Rev. Dr. Henry Knox Sherrill, Bishop of Massachusetts, were co-consecrators.

Other bishops participating were Rt. Rev. Drs. Francis M. Taitt of Pennsylvania, Julius W. Atwood, retired, Missionary District of Arizona; Arthur W. Moulton of Utah, Cameron J. Davis of Western New York, William Appleton Lawrence of Western Massachusetts and Wallace John Gardner of New Jersey.

LETTERS GRANTED ON BOLTON ESTATE

Letters of administration on the estate of Katherine E. Bolton, who died in this city Sept. 22, were granted today by Judge Bertram P. Kavanagh in Rensselaer County Surrogate's Court.

There is an estate of not to exceed $5,000 personal and $3,500 real. Beneficiaries of the estate are two sisters, Bessie A. MacDougall and Susan J. McManus, both at 85 Fourth street. Harry F. Whiton is attorney for the estate.

$110,000 DAMAGE CAUSED BY STORM TO COUNTY ROADS

Superintendent Hansen Seeks WPA Grant to Repair Highways Hard Hit by Recent Disaster.

Rensselaer County today through John W. Hansen, County Superintendent of Highways and John E. Armstrong, County WPA Administrator speeded plans toward the application for WPA funds for repair of damage estimated at $110,000 caused to the highways by last week's storm. Superintendent Hansen and Administrator Armstrong conferred today at the court house and it was indicated that the Federal authorities are ready to approve the application. Under the plan, $74,000 would be expended for labor, $6,000 by the Federal authorities for materials and $30,000 by the county highway department for materials and equipment.

Superintendent Hansen said the estimate of $110,000 damage was based on his personal inspection of the damage and from reports submitted to his office by town superintendents of highways. Temporary repairs have been made in many places but where bridges have been washed out the task has been more difficult.

Final Approval of Funds.

Formal approval of the application for WPA funds, the Highway Department superintendent said, must be made by the Board of Supervisors and that board will meet on Sept. 11. At a conference between Superintendent Hansen and representatives of the Building and Supply, Highway and Finance committees of the Board of Supervisors, Mr. Hansen was instructed to proceed with negotiations for the WPA funds.

According to Mr. Hansen ten bridges of 25 feet span or longer were washed out or badly damaged by flood water throughout Rensselaer County. A number of smaller bridges on the lesser used roads were also damaged, he said, adding that the total number of destroyed or damaged bridges in the whole county on all the roads would probably be more than twenty. The bridges of more than 25 feet span must be replaced or repaired by the County Highway Department; the smaller structures on town roads will be fixed by the town highway departments, it was said.

It was stated that as soon as WPA funds are made available the task of repairing the bridges will be started and this, it is expected, will be in the very near future, probably next week.

Photographs Taken.

As a result of his personal inspection of the highways throughout the county, Superintendent Hansen had photographs taken of the places of major damage. Today nearly a score of these photographs were mounted on large boards in the office of the Highway Department superintendent, where they attracted much interest.

Superintendent Hansen told the observers that one could not appreciate the extensive damage unless he had personally seen it or saw the pictures. At one point on the Poestenkill-Berlin road, as one of the photographs shows, the entire roadway was washed away, and a temporary new road had to be provided by cutting into the woods and removing some of the trees.

How Europe Escaped War By Two Hours

(Copyright, 1938, by United Press)

Rome—A trustworthy diplomatic source informed the United Press today that Europe was just two hours away from war at noon yesterday when Premier Benito Mussolini telephoned Adolf Hitler and urged him to postpone his planned invasion of Czechoslovakia.

The United Press was given what was purported to be the true facts of yesterday's events which temporarily saved Europe from disaster, together with a time-table of them.

Hitler, it was said, had planned to enter Sudetenland at exactly 2 p.m. with sixty divisions of troops supported by 3,000 airplanes.

Lord Perth, British Ambassador, paid two hasty visits to Count Galeazzo Ciano, Italian foreign minister—the first at 10:15 a.m., the second at 11:30.

Named

REV. JOHN J. FEARY.

REV. J. J. FEARY ST. MARY'S CHURCH ADMINISTRATOR

Native of Watervliet Will Have Charge of Parish Pending Permanent Appointment.

Rev. John J. Feary, assistant pastor of St. Mary's Church, has been named administrator of the parish by Most Rev. Edmund F. Gibbons, D. D., Bishop of Albany.

Father Feary, who has been an assistant pastor at St. Mary's for the last 11 years, has been acting in charge of the parish activities for several months during the illness and death of Rt. Rev. Mgr. William P. Fitzgerald, D. D, V. F., LL.D., whose funeral took place Tuesday following his death last week after a long illness.

The administrator is a native of Watervliet where he was graduated from St. Patrick's School. He later was graduated from Niagara University and from St. Bernard's Seminary in Rochester.

Father Feary went first to the Church of the Blessed Sacrament at Hague-on-Lake George for the summer of 1927 following his ordination in June, that year, at the Cathedral of the Immaculate Conception in Albany by Bishop Gibbons. That fall he came to St. Mary's Church.

He has been director of the Confraternity and the Rosary Society and at present is director of the Holy Name Society.

He is one of the best known and most popular Catholic clergymen in the city, having a host of friends among all denominations. Before his labors became so arduous, he was a familiar figure on the golf course and tennis court, pleasures he has been compelled to forego during the last few months.

WATER WAGON BURNS

Anderson, S. C. (AP)—The city water truck here—loaded with 300 gallons of water—caught fire and burned today. Faulty ignition caused the blaze as the new street flusher began its daily tour. Firemen extinguished the flames. The damage—$300.

WAGNER LASHES G.O.P. CHIEFTAINS IN KEYNOTE TALK

Senator Charges People's Mandate Was Ignored at Albany Session; Move to Draft Lehman Gains.

Rochester (UP)—Delegates staged a wild demonstration on the floor of the Democratic State Convention today in an effort to "draft" Gov. Herbert H. Lehman for a fourth term.

Rochester (AP)—Republican leaders of New York's recent constitutional convention were flayed as "deaf to the people's mandate and blind to the people's need" by United States Senator Robert F. Wagner, in keynoting the Democratic state convention here today.

"Never was there a finer opportunity and a clearer mandate to embrace the liberalism to which the people of New York are so firmly dedicated," the veteran senator declared.

"* * * But they scuttled our proposals for public ownership and development of the water power of the St. Lawrence and Niagara Rivers. By supporting a radical departure from our traditional method of judicial review, they sought to paralyze our administrative agencies and overload the courts."

Lauds Democratic Party.

"On legislative reapportionment, they forced a political monstrosity which destroys every principle of representation in a democracy."

Wagner declared that some Republicans deserted their leaders and united with the progressive Democratic minority will the people have a chance in November to adopt proposals for housing, for health insurance and a bill of rights for labor.

The state political campaign is expected to center on numerous issues stemming from the constitutional convention.

Lauding the Democratic Party as "leading the American people to progress up the middle way—and the middle way in America means constitutional government," Wagner asserted that "from Jefferson to Roosevelt, the Democratic Party has insisted that our fundamental law was broad enough and wise enough to meet the changing needs of a progressive people. * * *"

"Court Has Decided."

"Two years ago," he continued, "when reaction sought to cloak itself in the charge that we were violating the Constitution, we submitted the controversy for decision by our highest tribunal. The Supreme Court has decided. Let the Liberty League lawyers who sought to write advisory opinions for the judges note this fact: Every one of the main constitutional questions underlying the New Deal program has been decided by the Supreme Court in favor of the views proclaimed by the Democratic Party.

Speaking on the accomplishments of the Democratic administration in the state and nation, Senator Wagner declared that "any proposal to strengthen and improve the basic purposes" of his national labor relations act "merit and receive the consideration of every member of Congress."

"The national labor relations act was never intended to cover the whole field of industrial relations but only to establish the rights of self-organization and collective bargaining," he pointed out. "I have always maintained that, like all

LEAGUE OF NATIONS RAISES ITS VOICE IN APPEAL FOR PEACE

Geneva (UP)—The League of Nations Assembly associated itself today with President Roosevelt's appeal to Adolf Hitler and Eduard Benes for peace.

The assembly passed this resolution:

"The representatives of 49 nations meeting as delegates to the assembly of the League of Nations have watched with deep and growing anxiety the development of the present grave situation in Europe. The Assembly is convinced that existing differences are capable of being solved by peaceful means.

"It knows that recourse to war whatever the outcome is no guarantee of a just settlement and must inevitably bring untold suffering to millions of individuals and overthrow the whole structure of civilization in Europe.

"The assembly is voicing the prayer of the peoples of all countries when it expresses the earnest hope that no government will attempt to impose a settlement by force. It welcomes and fully associates itself with the messages of the President of the United States in this regard."

For Governor

THOMAS E. DEWEY.

G. O. P. PLATFORM HITS ALLIANCE OF CRIME, POLITICS

Saratoga Convention Also Denounces Misuse of Relief Funds; Urges Congress to Keep Peace.

Saratoga Springs (AP)—A tentative campaign platform condemning "alliance between the underworld and politics," protesting the use of federal relief funds for "political purposes" and urging Congress to keep America at peace was submitted today to New York's Republican Convention.

The 19-plank platform, was the shortest in the party's history, was drafted after a dogged all-night battle described by one member of the conclave's rules committee as "chaotic."

The declaration of state Republican policy contained a pledge for law enforcement and for use of "the full power of the state" to eliminate the "menace" of "crime in politics"—a principle designed to accentuate the prosecuting record of the party's apparent choice for governor, District Attorney Thomas E. Dewey.

One Amendment Hit.

Bitter debate in drafting the platform ended in approval of all but one of the 57 proposed amendments.

REPUBLICANS PICK "RACKET" BUSTER TO HEAD TICKET

Saratoga Convention Hall Scene of Wild Demonstration; Offered as Man 'Known by Performances'

Convention Hall, Saratoga Springs (UP)—Thomas E. Dewey, 36-year-old "racket" buster and district attorney of New York County, was nominated by acclamation today as the Republican candidate for governor of New York.

The Republican state convention, the most enthusiastic in many years, nominated the youthful prosecutor with utmost confidence that he would be elected in November and return politically important New York to the Republican fold.

Dewey was nominated by William F. Bleakley, the 1936 Republican candidate for governor. Earlier the convention, amidst wild cheering, adopted a platform assailing the New Deal and pledging the party to an intensive drive to restore business recovery.

Wild Demonstration.

Not in many years had a Republican convention nominated its standard-bearer with such a demonstration.

"Dewey, Dewey, Dewey," the marching delegates chanted during the parade of the counties.

Every delegation in convention hall joined the parade, which stopped all proceedings of the convention. Two bands led the demonstration.

The platform, the party's most liberal in years, was dictated by the Dewey forces.

Even as Dewey was nominated, the remainder of the ticket still was to be completed. A behind-the-scenes controversy over the nomination for lieutenant-governor was going on.

Dewey's nomination, which had been expected for more than a month despite his silence on whether he would accept, came on the first order for a call and by acclamation.

"Party Drafts Mr. Dewey."

Permanent Chairman Oswald D. Heck, Schenectady, declared Dewey the "unanimous choice of the convention for the office of governor" after the delegates shouted down plans to complete the ticket.

"Is there any opposition to Mr. Dewey's nomination?" Heck asked.

"No," the delegates shouted in unison.

"The Republican Party hereby drafts Mr. Dewey in the interest of greater service for the state," Heck said, amidst a din of cheering.

The Republican leaders were certain that in Dewey and the liberal platform, which also attacked any alliances between gangland and office holders, they had a powerful weapon for the November campaigns.

Heck declared that Dewey would arrive in Saratoga Springs tonight to deliver his acceptance speech. He simply told the convention:

"It is imperative that every delegate be in his seat tonight at 7:30 when the convention will reconvene," the convention recessed at 12:15 p.m. until 7:30 p.m.

Heck and George E. Medalie, Dewey's unofficial "manager," drafted a telegram to Dewey notifying him of his nomination.

Seek Balance of Ticket.

The telegram:

"You are hereby notified that the Republican Party has drafted you as its nominee for the office of governor of the State of New York in the interest of service for the entire state."

It was signed by Heck and Katherine Kennedy, secretary of the convention.

Immediately after the convention recessed, a group of Republican leaders met in a downtown hotel to attempt to complete the rest of the ticket.

Sen. Frederic H. Bontecou of Dutchess and Thomas Broderick of Rochester still were being mentioned for lieutenant-governor.

A statement was circulated on

CHAMBERLAIN IN OPTIMISTIC MOOD LEAVING ENGLAND

London (INS)—Prime Minister Neville Chamberlain of Britain uttered a heart-felt expression of hope that European peace can be rescued today as he departed for Munich to attend the momentous four-power conference there.

The prime minister, who was given a rousing send-off by members of his cabinet, took off from Heston Airport at 8:35 a.m.

Before stepping into his plane, he voiced in a few poignant words the hopes for peace—the cause to which he has devoted all his energies in the past few weeks.

"When I was a little boy," he said, "I used to repeat:

"'If at first you don't succeed, try, try again.'

"That is what I am doing. When I come back I hope I may be able to say, as Hotspur says in Henry IV:

"'Out of this nettle of danger we have plucked this flower safely.'"

MUNICH CONFERENCE DRAWS SUSPICION OF SOVIET RUSSIA

Moscow (AP)—The Munich four-power conference aroused suspicion today in Moscow, which always is alert against any attempt to exclude Soviet Russia from the councils of Europe.

In Soviet circles there was a tendency to regard the conference of the heads of German, French, British and Italian governments as an intensification of efforts by "bourgeois imperialist statesmanship" to strike a bargain with aggressors at the expense of small countries.

The Soviet press has been that the conference should be for the purpose of uniting peaceful nations against aggressors—not attempting to bargain with aggressors.

In conformity with this policy the Soviet government last night cordially welcomed President Roosevelt's suggestion of an international conference to unravel the Czechoslovak crisis and offered "to take an active part in such a conference."

(Continued on Page 15.)
(Continued on Page 6.)
(Continued on Page 3.)

BEMAN PARK.

The Women's Missionary Society of the Church of Christ, Disciples, will meet today at 8 p.m. at the home of Mrs. Nelson H. Schmay, 2179 Fourteenth Street. Mrs. Clarence Lewis, president, will conduct the meeting and the program will be in charge of Mrs. John Hubbell.

Tomorrow, the Ladies' Aid Society will meet at the church at 2:30 p.m. for an afternoon session, followed by supper at 6 p.m. The weekday school of religious education will resume sessions tomorrow at 3 p.m. after the holiday recess and the midweek church service will be held at 8 p.m. in charge of the pastor, Rev. George H. Brown.

Choir rehearsal will be held at the church Thursday at 7 p.m.

A social and reception in honor of Mr. and Mrs. Herbert Read of Savannah will be given by the Christian Endeavor Society Saturday at 7:30 p.m. in the church parlors. Mr. Read is a former president of the society. Edward Welch, present head of the group, will be master of ceremonies.

Turn to Page 16 for a full page of pictures of Gov. Herbert H. Lehman's fourth inaugural ceremonies at the State Capitol.

Albany (AP) — Gov. Herbert H. Lehman, yesterday inaugurated into office for his fourth term, denounced dictatorships—"Communist, Fascist, or Nazi"—and pleaded for continued economic and social reforms to make it impossible for them "to happen here."

The 60-year-old executive appealed in his inaugural address for combined efforts of labor, industry, agriculture and government "to solve the economic and social problems that now confront us."

He called on the nation to present an "unyielding defense of the civil and religious liberties vouchsafed to us by the Constitution and statute."

Politics Almost Ignored.

Victor over Thomas E. Dewey, New York City's Republican district attorney, in one of the state's closest gubernatorial battles last November, the Democratic Governor almost completely ignored politics in his denunciation of dictatorships.

Only once did he indicate the nature of his legislative program to an overflow crowd of approximately 2,500 persons in the Assembly chamber. Citing seven "concrete examples" of what "the people through their government must continue to do" lest democracy fail before dictatorship he listed:

"The removal of glaring social and economic inequalities, the assurance of decent wages and fair conditions for labor, an equitable distribution of national income, equal bargaining rights for labor and capital, the provision of recent housing with public assistance, protection of the savings of the people, establishment within the economic resources of the country of social security in old age and during periods of enforced unemployment."

National Figures Present.

A nineteen-gun salute marked the administration of the gubernatorial oath by Secretary of State Edward J. Flynn. Dignitaries of state and nation attended the ceremonies including Postmaster Gen. James A. Farley, Secretary of Labor Frances Perkins and U. S. Senators James M. Mead and Robert F. Wagner.

At private ceremonies after the inaugural, other elected state officials were sworn. They included Lieut. Gov. Charles Poletti, Atty. Gen. John J. Bennett, Jr., and Comptroller Morris S. Tramaine.

In his plea for the safeguarding of democracy, Lehman urged "a militant defense" of civil and religious liberties, "continued concern" in the social and economic well-being of every citizen, and "an awakened national spirituality."

Urges Dedication To Task.

"Our immediate task and responsibility," he said, "is so to order our public affairs that such things cannot happen here. To that task and to that responsibility, let us again dedicate ourselves, not merely in hopes and wishes but in actions and objectives.

"I am convinced," the Governor said, "that the greatest safeguard to democracy is a sincere recognition by its people of the eternal truths on which all true religion is based.

"An attack on one religion weakens all religious faiths since the basis of all true religion is charity, justice and tolerance." x x x If man will live up to all those simple concepts of all religion, democracy will be safe."

COYOTE MAKES GOOD.

Providence, R. I. (UP)—Instead of an alarm clock, Mrs. Josephine Nelson has a pet coyote named Cowboy that wakes her each morning by licking her face. A gift from her brother, an Oklahoma Teachers' College student, the coyote plays around the house with her two cats and is tied to the bedpost each night.

WASHINGTON COUNTY SURROGATE'S COURT

The following are among the proceedings in the Surrogate's Court for the week ending Dec. 31:

Estate of Martha J. Ashton, White Creek; compulsory accounting adjourned to Jan. 17, at Salem.

Estate of D. Warren Dunn, Granville; last will admitted to probate; letters testamentary issued to Lorene E. Dunn.

Estate of Mary Allen, Jackson; last will admitted to probate; letters testamentary issued to Martha J. Jordan and Libbie D. Luke.

Estate of Sarah E. Main, White Creek, decree entered in judicial settlement of the account of executor.

Estate of Stephen B. Sweet, Granville; compulsory accounting adjourned to Jan. 17, at Salem.

Estate of Caroline La Point, Kingsbury; citation issued on probate of last will, returnable Jan. 11, at Hudson Falls.

Estate of G. Myron Allen, Granville; citation issued in probate of last will, returnable Jan. 24, at Salem.

Estate of Charlotte O. Gates, Greenwich; citation issued in probate of last will, returnable Jan. 3, at Salem.

Estate of Elizabeth H. Jones, Granville; last will admitted to probate; letters testamentary issued to Anna J. Griffith and Catherine J. Jones.

Estate of Hannah D. Langdon, Kingsbury; instrument settling estate filed and recorded.

Orders entered in the following estates exempting said estate from tax under the Estate Tax Law: Estate of Hosannah L. Gardner, Fort Ann; estate of J. Edward Tefft, Greenwich; estate of Maroeline Gardner, Kingsbury; estate of Elizabeth L. Maxwell, Cambridge.

Orders entered in the following estates determining the tax under the Estate Tax Law: Estate of Mary H. Arnott, Cambridge; estate of Anna Cornell, Easton; estate of Anna L. Douglass, Hampton; estate of Orson D. Griffin, Kingsbury; estate of Sarah E. Main, White Creek; estate of Ella C. Shields, Salem;.

Guardianship of William T. Munson, Granville; annual account filed.

Estates of Tom Gitsham and Sarah Jane Gitsham, Kingsbury; compulsory accounting adjourned to Jan. 11, at Hudson Falls.

Estate of Seymour Bartholomew, Whitehall; letters of administration issued to Henry Bartholomew.

Estate of William Mullen, White Creek; citation issued in judicial settlement of the account of administration, returnable Jan. 17, at Salem.

Estate of Oron D. Griffin, Kingsbury; release filed.

Estate of Louise Chandler, Granville; letters of administration issued to H. Gray Haskins.

Estate of George MacOmber, Fort Edward; order entered authorizing compromise of action; restriction on letters of administration removed.

BACON HILL.

Winifred Brown recently visited Verna Beagle at Schuylerville.

Mrs. Augustus Deyoe and daughter, Shelia, were Tuesday dinner guests of Mrs. Hazel Sparling.

The children of this section are enjoying skating on Beans pond this week.

Russell Coffin of Easton was a Thursday caller on relatives in Bacon Hill.

Ethel Coffin has returned from a few days visit with her cousin, Betty Farnum, at Menands.

A special meeting of the Bacon Hill Start and Finish 4-H Club was held at the home of the leader, Mrs. Westley Coffin, Tuesday to plan for a holiday party.

Ethel Coffin spent an afternoon with her cousin, Jane Vanderwerken, who is visiting her grandmother, Mrs. Walter McClaren.

Mrs. Border Morris and daughters and Mrs. Dorothy Vanderwerker were Thursday callers at J. B. Vanderwerker.

Elaine and Esther Coffin are spending the week-end with grandparents, Mr. and Mrs. Fred Vanderwerker at Saratoga Springs.

Mr. and Mrs. Westley Coffin and family attended the family dinner party on Christmas at the home of Mrs. Coffin's parents, Mr. and Mrs. Fred Vanderwerker at Saratoga Springs.

An enjoyable time was had on Thursday evening when the girls of the Bacon Hill Start and Finish 4-H Club entertained the Bacon Hill billies, the boys 4-H Club. Games were enjoyed and there were gifts for all from the Christmas tree. Refreshments were prepared by the girls.

Sportsman Urges Freeing Of Captured Swordfish

Sydney, Australia (UP)—Sportsman Dr. Bruce Hittman has proposed to the New South Wales Game Fishing Association that hereafter marlin and swordfish be released after being caught.

"Any real fisherman hates to see swordfish killed after a game fight," he said. "The real thrill is merely in the fight and not in the obsequies."

He proposes slipping a noose over the tail, instead of gaffing them, extracting the hook and then tagging them for future checking if they are again caught.

CRANIUM CRACKERS

Some of the following statements are true. Some are false. Which are which?

1. A sadist is the high priest of a Hindu cult.
2. Camels used to inhabit parts of what is now the United States.
3. The Louvre is the name of a department store in Paris, France.
4. Mona Lisa is the name of a river in Hawaii.
5. A drachma is a camel driver.

Answers on Page 12.

MRS. A. E. SAMUELS INSTALLED HEAD OF WATERVLIET O. E. S.

Willetta Chapter Inducts Entire Officers' Slate at Ceremony Conducted by Past District Officer.

Mrs. Alice E. Samuels was installed worthy matron of Willetta Chapter, Order of the Eastern Star, of Watervliet, last night by Rt. Worthy William Groesbeck of Troy, of the Second Albany-Rensselaer past district deptly grand lecturer District, to succeed Mrs. Bernice Meneely.

Rt. Worthy Mrs. Ann Bristol of Schenectady, associate grand marshal of the State of New York, was an official visitor. Degrees were worked on both incoming and outgoing matrons, both of whom received many gifts and flowers. Rt. Worthy Mrs. Ouida Willis, rendered solos. Refreshments were served after the ceremony and the next meting was announced for Jan. 18.

Other officers installed are: Jared S. Horton, worthy patron, reelected; Miss Olive McBain, associate matron; Worthy Mrs. Amy Leitzell, treasurer; Worthy Mrs. Bertha Bortle, secretary; Mrs. Virginia Hoffman, conductress; Mrs. Dorothy Poole, associate conductress; Mrs. Meneely, chaplain; Miss Jane Hart, Marshal; Mrs. Louise Helwig, associate marshal; Mrs. Helen Robinson, historian; Mrs. Florence Rousseau, musician; Mrs. Mary Thorns, warder; Jurene Stelle, sentinel.

Star points are: Mrs. Ruth Hill, Ada; Mrs. Christine Balfort, Ruth; Mrs. Florence Kemp, Esther; Miss Ruth Bart, Martha, and Mrs. Louise Carr, Electa. Mrs. Emily Dickson is color bearer and Worthy Mrs. Gertrude Kittell is trustee for thre years.

ONLY BONDS WERE BURNING.

Florence, Col., (AP)—Firemen discovered that the fire at City Hall was a "pleasant" one. City councilmen reported they merely had decided to have a bonfire at their regular meeting to burn $7,000 worth of redeemed bonds, to cancel city indebtedness.

Still Coughing?
Even if other medicine has failed, don't be discouraged, try Creomulsion. Your druggist is authorized to refund your money if you are not thoroughly satisfied with the benefits obtained. Creomulsion is one word, ask for it plainly, see that the name on the bottle is Creomulsion, and you'll get the genuine product and the relief you want. (Adv.)
CREOMULSION
For Coughs or Chest Colds

ROLLER SKATING
ST. JOSEPH'S CLUB
Fourth and Jackson
Skating, Tuesday, Thursday, Saturday and Sunday Nites
Matinee Every Sat. and Sun.
Bargain Nite for Ladies Every Saturday Nite, 25c

At Willetta Chapter Installation

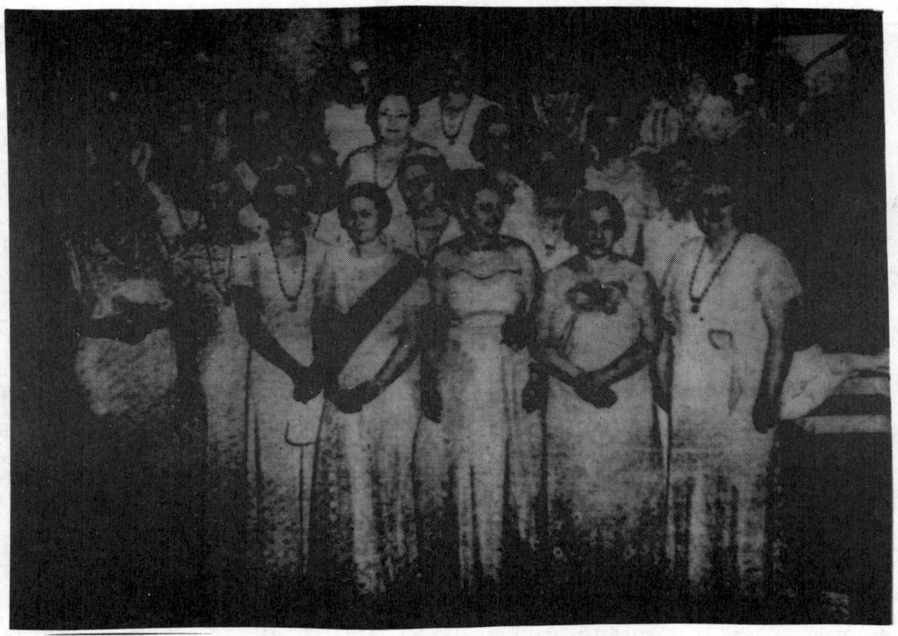

Officers of Willetta Chapter, Order of the Eastern Star of Watervliet, who were installed last night in Masonic Temple, that city. Left to right they are: Front row, Bernice Meneely, Ruth Burt, Virginia Hoffman, Alice Samuels, Olive E. MacBain, Gertrude B. Kittell and Emily Dixon; second row, Louisa Hellwig, Florence Croker, Bertha M. Bortle, Christina Balfoort and Lida Flanigan; third row, Ethel Graham, Nellie Beverage, Elva Hart, Mary Thorns and Ruth Hill; rear row, Jean Hart, Florence Rousseau, Dorothy Poole, Amy Leitzell, Louise Carr, Florence Kemp, Helen Robinson and Jurene Stelle.

MELROSE.

Miss Ida Doty was a New Year's guest of Mr. and Mrs. Charles H. Wetsel.

The Epworth League joined with the league at Schaghticoke Sunday evening when a special service was held.

Mr. and Mrs. Luther Moon had as holiday guests Mr. and Mrs. Wilbur Simon and family and Miss Ethel Reed.

Mrs. Harry Wing of Raymertown was New Year's guest of her brother, Chauncey Douglas, and daughters, Sibyl and Arlene.

Mr. and Mrs. Arnold Nible were New Year's guests at the home of her parents, Mr. and Mrs. Clarence Eycleshymer, of Johnsonville.

Mr. and Mrs. Bert Boice were holiday guests at a family party at Schoharie last week-end. Mr. and Mrs. Boice entertained the family group New Year's.

The cottage prayer meeting will be held this evening at the home of C. D. Viall. The service will be in charge of the Sunday School Board under the direction of Mr. Viall.

A meeting of the Melrose Home Bureau will be held Monday at the home of Mrs. Clarence Derrick. The meeting will begin at 10 a.m. and continue throughout the day. Miss Doris Brigdon of Cornell, instructor, assisted by Mrs. Ralph Button, food leader, will prepare the luncheon. Reports will be given on the visit to Schenectady and on the music conference held in Troy recently which was conducted by John Jones of New York City.

Linked in Love
She had him first
He wanted her
But then came Janet
What happens when two women love the same man? Cynthia thought she knew. So did Janet. But they discovered that neither knew—for the outcome was something they had not even dreamed. You'll follow their heart-touching experience in the thrilling new serial of modern youth looking for love and home and a place in the world.
No Time to Marry
Beginning Monday In
THE TIMES RECORD

● SERIAL STORY

SKI'S THE LIMIT

BY ADELAIDE HUMPHRIES

COPYRIGHT, 1938 NEA SERVICE, INC.

CAST OF CHARACTERS.
SALLY BLAIR—Heroine. She had everything that popularity could win her, except
DAN REYNOLDS — Hero. He might have had Sally but while he was king on skis
COREY PORTER was king of the social whirl. So . . . But go on with the story.
Yesterday: At Lake Placid Sally sees Dan again, talks with him in the belief she may be able thus to forget him forever.

CHAPTER XXIII

There had been nothing for Corey to do but to follow Sally. Corey never refused a dare, which was practically what Sally's remark, "You're not afraid to go, are you?" had meant.

If Dan was surprised when they approached him, he did not betray it. His color, underneath the smooth deep tan, might have deepened a bit, but his gray eyes were grave and steady.

"We came to congratulate you on winning," Sally said, holding out her hand. "How are you, Dan?" There was no need to ask, this was the Dan of old, sturdy and strong as the mountains he set out to conquer.

"I'm very well, thank you," he returned, taking her hand, but only for a brief moment. "And how are you, Sally?" he added, though there seemed no need to ask that, either. Sally's dark eyes had never been brighter, she had never looked more lovely.

Was that all he had to say to her? Sally wondered. Didn't he know what just seeing him did to her? Wasn't his heart hammering painfully, too?

"I'm fine," Sally said. "Never better, thank you." She tossed her dark curls. He must see how gay she was, how right her world. "Well, you've got what you wanted — at last," she said. "You've made the Olympics this time, Dan."

"I guess that's right," Dan said. His glance went to her left hand. She had taken off her heavy mittens, on her third finger Corey's diamond sparkled in the bright sun. "I see you've got what you wanted, too," Dan added.

"Yes," Corey spoke up, he could not keep the smug satisfaction out of his tone, "congratulations are in order again. Since Sally's what I want."

"I wish you both all the happiness in the world," Dan returned.

• • •

Which world do you mean? Sally wanted to ask. Mine, or yours, Dan? But she knew the answer to that question. She knew now that Dan would never come back. He had not belonged in her world. He had been right in going away.

She knew the answer to a lot of other questions too. This meeting, instead of convincing her that she could put Dan out of her heart, had shown her that she still believed in him, whether he ever believed in her again or not, that she could never forget him.

How could she go on pretending now? How could she be the glamour girl, always laughing and gay? How could she live through these next days knowing Dan was so near, yet lost to her forever, knowing she must go on being the Sally Blair who wore Corey's ring on her engagement finger?

That next day Corey and Sally had planned to climb to the top of one of the highest trails. The sky was so serene, as azure as the day before. But far to the north was one slate-colored patch. The air hung too heavy and charged.

"Do you think there's any chance of a storm?" Corey asked, a bit dubiously. "Maybe we'd better not try it today, Sally."

"Why not?" Sally's dark eyes challenged the sky. She wasn't afraid of danger. She wanted, if anything, to force it, to lose herself in a new fight.

"Check," Corey said, using their old phrase for agreement. He wouldn't refuse to go just because of one gray cloud.

On their way they met Dan. He saw their skis and poles, walked over to them. He said, "Hello. You're not really going up today, are you? Don't you know the air's not right? There's going to be a blizzard." Dan could tell without looking at the slate sky what the weather promised. He was mountain-bred, mountain-trained.

• • •

"Blizzard!" Sally laughed. "Why, the sky's as clear as a bell. We don't mind a little snow, Dan! Even though we don't belong in this world." There was bitterness as well as irony in her tone.

"You don't know what you're talking about" Dan returned roughly. He turned on Corey, "You're not going to let her go, are you?" he asked.

"Why not?" Corey said, as Sally had to him. "We're going up into the divide, above timber . . ."

"You're crazy, if you do that!" Dan spoke earnestly now. His grave eyes pleaded with Sally. "Don't try that trail today," he warned.

Sally shrugged her shoulders beneath her plaid jacket. Why should Dan ask her not to go? It did not matter to him what she did. She would show him that she would not run away from his world. "We'll be all right," she said briefly. "I can't really see what concern it is of yours, Dan." She knew that was a cruel thing to say. But she wanted to hurt him. If only she could make him suffer, as he had made her, make his heart ache.

"Perhaps you're right," Dan said. He flinched, a tiny white line drawn around the stern set of his nice mouth. He knew Sally again thought him a coward. He knew she meant he had forfeited the right to make what she did any concern of his.

• • •

Corey never had known Sally to be gayer than she was that day, full of fun and laughter, the way he liked her to be. The skiing was perfect what with the sharp wind against their faces, the blood racing through their bodies, the music of swift flight, the poetry of pure motion.

When they had had their fill, gloriously tired with the good weariness of clean physical effort, they stopped for time to rest. Corey built a fire beneath an icy waterfall; they had brought along steaks to broil, buns, a thermos of hot coffee.

"I guess our friend Reynolds is the one who is slightly crazy," Corey chuckled. "It's been a perfect day. I wouldn't have missed it for anything, would you, my sweet?"

"No," Sally returned. But somewhat absently. She had been watching that leaden patch in the north. While they picnicked it had spread to alarming proportion, like thick gray felt. She called Corey's attention to it now, adding that perhaps they had better pack up and start down trail.

"They're just night clouds beginning to gather." Corey refused to be alarmed. But even as he spoke a snokflake drifted down. Another followed, and then another. They scrambled to their feet. "I guess we had better get going," Corey agreed. Now the snow fell with a smothering, soft persistency. The world was being blotted out before their eyes. They could not even see the waterfall that had looked like frozen rain.

"We'd better not use our skis," Sally said. They would carry them over a cliff too swiftly! It would be safer to walk. She thought of the divide, if they missed the trail, that sheer drop of more than 5,000 feet. No one could manage that jump and stop himself with a christie, not even Dan.

They plowed ahead, heads bent, shoulders touching, not wasting breath in speech. The wind had come up. It flung itself against them, lashing their eyes, tearing the breath from their nostrils. The snow struck in sharp pellets with terrific force.

It seemed to Sally they had endured this torture for hours. The sky was almost black, the tangled underbrush weighted with deep snow, the tall pines bent in the wind's fury.

Suddenly Corey stopped; he sank down on a log. "Sally," he said. "I think we're lost. We've missed the trail

(To Be Continued)

IN NEW YORK YOU'LL LIKE
THE DIXIE HOTEL
250 WEST 43rd STREET
TIMES SQUARE, N. Y. C.
DAILY RATES
$2.50 SINGLE
$3.50 DOUBLE

BEER SALES HALTED DURING SESSIONS OF SUNDAY SCHOOL

Sacramento, Cal. (INS) — Now they're holding Sunday School in beer parlors.

Because church construction at Redding, in northern California, has not kept pace with the incoming population at the nearby site of the $170,000,000 Central Valley Project, a Community Sunday School has been meeting in the open.

Recently, however, rain was feared so Chester Barger invited teachers and children into his tavern where classes proceeded with their programs.

Barger suspended sales of beer acros the counter until classes adjourned.

PARIS AND LONDON HAIL ROOSEVELT'S SANCTIONS HINT

First Berlin Newspaper Comment Views President's Message "In Tracks of Wilson."

London (AP)—Great Britain and France last night officially welcomed what they considered President Roosevelt's veiled threat of economic sanctions against aggressors.

Britain quickly rebroadcast in German and Italian pointed passages of his address to Congress.

The speech was heard clearly in England from semi-official British Broadcasting Corporation facilities. Thousands stopped in the rain to listen at open shop doors. Newspapers displayed the address prominently.

Study Advance Copies.

Prime Minister Chamberlain and Foreign Secretary Viscount Halifax studied advance copies of the message to Congress in a conference at the Premier's residence.

In Germany and Italy, where contents of the speech were not known until the dinner hour, there was no immediate official reaction.

The Italian press, however, said the new congressional session opened in an atmosphere of "scandal" and charged United States officials with using relief money for political purposes.

The first Berlin reaction to the address came in the Lokal Anzeiger, which commented under the heading "in the tracks of Wilson" that the address was "what was expected."

Though there was general agreement on all of the President's observations about aggressors, both Britain and France gratefully noted these two passages:

Seen As Definite Threat.

"We have learned that when we deliberately try to legislate neutrality, our neutrality laws may operate unevenly and unfairly—may actually give aid to an aggressor and deny it to the victim," and "war is not the only means of commanding a decent respect for the opinions of mankind."

The first of these statements was accepted here as a prelude to a modified, new neutrality act. The second was taken as a threat of economic sanctions against first, Japan, then perhaps insurgent Spain and finally against any major aggressor in Europe.

TOMHANNOCK.

Mrs. Bolt of Poestenkill is visiting her daughter, Mrs. Clayton Rifenburgh.

Mrs. Vera Shephard and Mrs. James Hammond of North Bennington, Vt., called on Viola Brundige Monday.

George Brenerstuhl and Frank Burdick have returned to school at Cobleskill after spending the holiday vacation at their homes here.

An all-day meeting of the Ladies' Aid Society of the Methodist Church was held at the home of Viola Brundige one day this week. Election of officers for the current year was held. A covered dish luncheon was served at noon.

STATE
Last Times Today
"ILLEGAL TRAFFIC"
with J. Carroll Naish and Mary Carlisle
—Co-Feature—
"RENFREW ON THE WHITE TRAIL"
with James Newill and Carol Hughes
5TH AVE. LAST TIMES TONIGHT
"TOO HOT TO HANDLE"
with Clark Gable and Myrna Loy
Also March of Time and Short Subjects

THE SCREEN'S SWEETHEARTS OF SONG . . .
In a Pageant of Melodious Splendors!
More magnificent than "The Great Ziegfeld"... more romantic than "Maytime"... more tuneful and funnier than "Naughty Marietta"!
VICTOR HERBERT'S Love Songs! "Pretty As A Picture" "Sweethearts" ...many, many more!
Jeanette MacDONALD NELSON EDDY
in VICTOR HERBERT'S SWEETHEARTS
In Magnificent TECHNICOLOR
with FRANK MORGAN · RAY BOLGER
FLORENCE RICE · MISCHA AUER
HERMAN BING · REGINALD GARDINER
Screen Play by Dorothy Parker and Alan Campbell
Directed by W. S. VAN DYKE II
Produced by HUNT STROMBERG
A Metro-Goldwyn-Mayer PICTURE
ADDED UNITS
PETE SMITH "HOT ON THE ICE"
TROY NEWS EVENTS
TROY STARTS TODAY

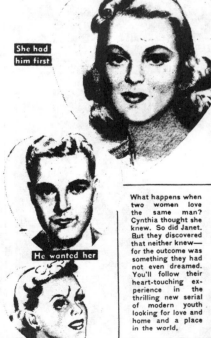

SHUSHAN.

Mrs. Harry Peck is ill.

Little Richard McCauley is ill.

Mr. and Mrs. John Doane spent Thursday in Troy.

Emerson McLenithan and Nelma Keiski were in Troy Saturday.

Mrs. Leonard Russell and daughter Betty were in Troy Thursday.

Mr. and Mrs. Clifford Ellis entertained 14 guests at dinner New Year's Day.

Miss Evelyn Ellis of Granville spent last week with Mr. and Mrs. Clifford Ellis.

Mr. and Mrs. Edgar Watkins entertained the bridge club at dinner Friday evening.

Mr. and Mrs. Edward Hayes visited his mother, Mrs. Mae Hayes, in Pawlet Sunday.

Mr. and Mrs. Fred Knapp spent Sunday with Mr. and Mrs. John Reilly at Mechanicville.

Miss Helen Stevenson has gone to Cambridge to spend some time with Mrs. Henry Skellie.

Lester Walters has returned to New York after spending two weeks with Mrs. Walters.

Mr. and Mrs. Harold Campbell and sons of Salem visited Mr. and Mrs. Thomas Stanton Sunday.

Miss Margaret Stimpson was a dinner guest of Mr. and Mrs. Edgar McDonald in Cambridge Sunday.

Mrs. Charles Hutchen, who had spent a few days with Mrs. E. C. Clark has returned to her home at Cossayuna.

Mrs. Anna Armstrong entertained Mrs. Jennie Foster, Isaac Shields and Mrs. Samantha Orcutt at dinner Monday.

The infant son of Mr. and Mrs. Kenneth Rich is at the McClellan Hospital for treatment for an abscess in his ear.

Mr. and Mrs. Frank Santus and Mr. and Mrs. Julius Moller and son Donald of Cambridge took dinner New Year's evening with Mr. and Mrs. Sam Reid in Greenwich.

The Ladies' Aid Society of the Methodist Church met last Wednesday with Mrs. Clifford Eagle and decided to hold a roast pork supper when Rev. Ernest Tripp makes his annual visit on Feb. 2.

At the Grange card party last week, the first prize, a rooster, was won by Mrs. Thomas Stanton, second prize went to John McCarty and the consolation to Mrs. John Deane. Another card party will be held on Tuesday evening.

Harry Peck had an accident near White Creek Monday. The car he was driving skidded on the icy road and crashed into a telephone pole. The car was badly damaged but Mr. Peck fortunately escaped injury. The car belonged to Charles Peck.

Mrs. Charles Anton entertained at dessert bridge and five hundred Friday afternoon. Mrs. Clarence Randall of Ossining won the first prize, Mrs. Harry Harrington of Cambridge second and Miss Florence Hurd of Cambridge had high score at five hundred.

The following books have been presented to the library: "The Cape Cod Mystery," by Taylor; "The Dim Lantern" and "The Blue Window," by Temple Bailey; "If I Were You," by Woodhouse; "For Goodness Sake,' by Carolyn Wells; "The Ex-Detective," by Oppenheim; "How Good a Detective," by R. A. Ripley; "The American Manners," by George Mellon. "The State vs. Edna Jepson," by Marity.

WRITES NEWS RELEASE.

San Francisco (U.P.)—Pretty blonde Mrs. Kathleen Walker believes in handling her own press relations. When she was handed down an interlocutory divorce decree, she immediately handed to reporters a typewritten statement of the whole affair. Her principal complaint was that her husband, as a service station attendant, had too much beautiful women in the world.

AMERICAN
STARTING TODAY
EVER BEEN IN LOVE? ARE YOU STILL IN LOVE? THEN SEE
There Goes My Heart
Featuring
FREDRIC MARCH
VIRGINIA BRUCE
PATSY KELLY
WIVES, BRING HUBBY! GIRLS, BRING THE BOY FRIEND!
HIT 2
Edmund Lowe · Helen Mack in "Secrets of a Nurse"

LINCOLN Now
MICKEY ROONEY and Hardy Family
OUT WEST WITH THE HARDYS
LEWIS STONE · MICKEY ROONEY
and MGM's Famous Family
"I DEMAND PAYMENT"
Starts SAT. "I AM A CRIMINAL"

BIJOU
Last Times Tonight
Jean Arthur, Lionel Barrymore, James Stewart, Mischa Auer and Edward Arnold in
YOU CAN'T TAKE IT WITH YOU
Also ADDISON RICHARD in
"ROMANCE OF LOUISIANA"

LANSING
Last Times Tonight
JOE PENNER and JUNE TRAVIS in
Mr. Doodle Kicks Off
—Also—
JACKIE COOPER, ROBERT WARWICK, LUCY GILMAN in
"GANGSTER BOY"

CASINO WATERFORD TODAY Double Feature
JOHN BARRYMORE in
"HOLD THAT CO-ED"
ALSO GLENDA FARRELL in
"TORCHY GETS HER MAN"

Last Day "GIRL DOWNSTAIRS" "LITTLE TOUGH GUYS IN SOCIETY"
PROCTOR'S
GIANT TWIN BILL!
UP! WAY GOES
AMERICA'S LAUGH AVERAGE
...with 'Misser Average Man' what the fun's all about!
Thanks for Everything
ADOLPHE MENJOU · JACK OAKIE · JACK HALEY
ARLEEN WHELAN · TONY MARTIN · BINNIE BARNES
GEORGE BARBIER · WARREN HYMER
Plus the Most Sensational Expose of Hell on Earth!
56,000 DOOMED MEN HAVE WRITTEN ITS SHAMEFUL STORY!
And Warner Bros. Have Filmed It At Last!
DEVIL'S ISLAND
With BORIS KARLOFF

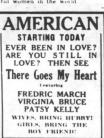

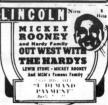

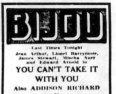

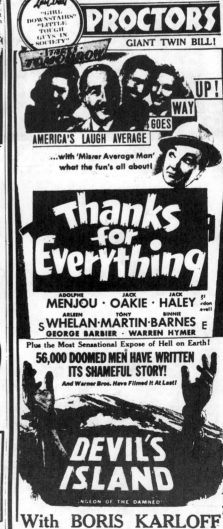

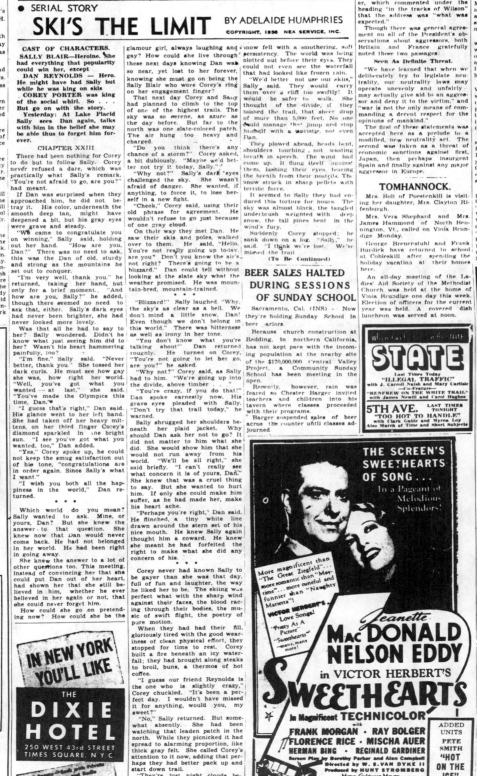

PRESENTING THE WIDE WORLD IN PICTURES

Wide World Photos, Inc.

THE COASTGUARD ATTEMPTS TO RESCUE SHIPPING FROZEN IN THE HUDSON RIVER: Sailors on the ice-breaking cutter Comanche making tow lines fast to an oil barge and a tug which were caught in the ice jam near West Point, N. Y., after a cold wave of near-zero temperature which swept the Hudson Valley bringing waterway traffic to a standstill.

BRITAIN'S NEW DEFENSE CHIEF: Admiral of the Fleet Lord Chatfield, who built up the British Navy to its present peak of efficiency and power, who was appointed to the Cabinet post of Minister for Coordination of Defense, succeeding Sir Thomas Inskip. Premier Chamberlain has named the latter Secretary of State for the Dominions.

FEDERAL JURIST RESIGNS AFTER DEWEY MAKES CHARGES: Judge Martin T. Manton of the U. S. Circuit Court of Appeals, who resigned shortly after the New York prosecutor sent to Chairman Sumners of the House Judiciary Committee, charges that the jurist or corporations owned or controlled by him, received over $400,000 from litigants.

"THE REIGN OF THE DICTATOR IS UPON US": Richard B. Bennett, former prime Minister of Canada, declares that "no longer is it possible to say with authority that democracy is the supreme form of government through the world," as he speaks at a farewell dinner given in his honor in St. John by citizens of his native province of New Brunswick on the eve of his departure for England, where he will make his future home.

WHEN ONE HEN SAW THE LIGHT: Miss Gretchen McGowan of the Rural Electrification Administration in Washington, compares an egg (right) laid by a hen owned by a farmer of Russellville, Ky., with an electric bulb similar to one at which the hen continuously stared while in the henhouse.

ACCUSER OF HINES COMMITS SUICIDE: George Weinberg, one of the State's witnesses in the New York City trial of Tammany Leader Jimmy Hines, who died soon after shooting himself with a guard's gun in the house in White Plains, N. Y., where he had been kept with other witnesses. Weinberg was one of the leaders in the Dutch Schultz policy racket in New York.

POST-MUNICH ARCHITECTURE IN ENGLAND: One of the iron air-raid shelters, similar to those used near the Front during the World War, which are being manufactured in large numbers at a Hoddesden plant. When the hut has been placed on its site, the owner covers it with sandbags and earth.

FIRST U. S. AMBASSADOR TO COLOMBIA LEAVES FOR POST: Spruille Braden, who has been American Minister to the Republic since last April, sails from New York for Bogota as Ambassador after the legation was elevated to embassy rank as a result of increasing relations between the nations. Mr. Braden's appointment was confirmed by the Senate Jan. 16.

GERMANY'S ONE-TIME "ALL-HIGHEST" ON THE EVE OF HIS 80TH BIRTHDAY: Former Kaiser Wilhelm II, from a photograph made at Doorn, The Netherlands, shortly before he celebrated his anniversary with a gala dinner at which thirty members of Germany's former royal families were guests of honor.

LEADERS AT INDIA'S "INDEPENDENCE" MEETING HELD IN DELHI: Rani Laxmibai Rajawde, president of the All-India Women's Conference, photographed with other officials at a recent session of the conference which adopted a resolution demanding complete independence and separation from Great Britain.

NEW YORK FINANCIER QUITS HOSPITAL AFTER MYSTERIOUS SHOOTING: Jules E. Brulatour, who was wounded by a bullet on Jan. 22 in his Park Avenue residence, leaves for home with his wife, the former Hope Hampton. He faces Sullivan law prosecution for ownership of the pistol which figured in the shooting and which he said accidentally discharged while he was cleaning it.

WHERE THE BARGES OF PHARAOHS USED TO TRAVEL IN CENTURIES PAST: Accompanied by one of his guests, King Farouk, nineteen-year-old ruler of Egypt, is rowed through the reeds on the Nile near El Manzuria, while on the duck-hunting expedition at which he was the host to a group of fellow-sportsmen.

POINTING TOWARD THE 1940 U. S. OLYMPIC SWIMMING TEAM: Mary Hoerger, fifteen-year-old aquatic marvel of Miami Beach, soaring through the air into the Roney Plaza pool, during a recent exhibition at the Florida resort. Mary won the senior diving championship of the United States at the age of eleven.

AN AIRPLANE MAKE A CLOSE-UP OF THE WORLD'S TALLEST BUILDING: An aerial view of Midtown Manhattan, New York City, showing in the foreground the tower of the Empire State Building, with the new television sending apparatus on its top. Behind the tower stretching northward, is Central Park. In the distance at the upper left is the George Washington Bridge which spans the Hudson River.

THE FORMER CHAMPION STEPS BACK INTO THE RING: Jess Willard, once the world's heavyweight titleholder, refereeing a bout between Buster Carroll of Lowell, Mass., and Mickey Serrian of Syracuse, N. Y., in the American Legion Arena at West Palm Beach, Fla., proclaims Carroll the winner.

PICTORIAL NEWS OF THE WORLD

Watervliet Arsenal Starts Making Nation's Big Guns Again

PREPARE FOR WAR TO INSURE PEACE GOVERNMENT PLAN

Sixteen-Inch Steel Monsters To Be Used in Coastal Defense Being Turned Out.

(Continued From Page 1.)

inch, 14 inch and 16 inch guns here under construction. A 16 inch gun is 70 feet long and a huge crane is required to lift it. The biggest lathes in the world are used here, lathes that are 208 feet long.

Head whirling from a look upwards to the ceiling, the visitor is led out on the grating over the shrink pit and the world falls from under him as he looks down 104 feet into the depths. The shrink pit is as awful to the average mortal as a quarry hole and yet there has never been an accident in the pit, Major King says. The foreman of the pit has held that job for many years.

In the Shrink Pit.

Into the pit the sleeve of these 16 inch guns is lowered and the heat of electric ovens expands the steel so that the harder inner cylinder of steel, already bored, can be forced into the sleeve. When the sleeve cools and contracts, the two are bound tightly together.

One of the monsters is on a lathe and the visitor comments that he would like to see some of the steel shavings from such a big gun.

"Shall I take a little piece off the outside for you," a workman asks and grins at Major King.

The breech mechanism on these 16-inch guns opens by air compression. The combined strength of two men hanging on it cannot force that door open any faster. The visitor is boosted up and peers down the barrel which seems so large that he could easily crawl inside and live there comfortably.

Along comes the crane, picks up the barrel of a 10-inch gun, swings it around and lowers it to trestles. The whole move takes about five minutes and is accomplished without a sound from any of the five men helping guide the gun into place.

The first 16-inch gun manufactured in the United States was made at the Watervliet Arsenal. When President McKinley visited the arsenal in 1898 he saw this gun under construction and according to his own words was "bewildered and almost stunned" by the immensity of it. His reaction is echoed by any non-military visitor.

Prepare for Peace.

All these preparations at the arsenal are not reassuring to a peace loving citizen but the arsenal staff takes a different viewpoint. They are preparing against war—not for war.

At the close of the World War the late Francis K. Kyle, who later was a member of the staff of The Record Newspapers, compiled a history of the Watervliet Arsenal under the direction of Col. J. W. Benet. This history, consisting of hundreds of pages, is the only one of its kind in existence. The information given hereafter was obtained from it.

The Watervliet Arsenal was founded in 1813 as an appropriate equipping point for artillery trains, the need for it arising from conditions incident to the War of 1812. A tract of 12 acres and a few modest buldings formed the nucleus of the present plant of about 142 acres, 70 buildings and costly machinery.

The arsenal was first known as "a supply depot near Albany" or "the arsenal at Gibbonsville," the site being referred to by that name.

It was not until 1817 that the term, Watervliet Arsenal, was formally applied. Maj. James A. Dalliba, first commanding officer, was then in charge.

Fixed amunition, small articles of equipment and gun carriages were first made at the arsenal. In 1887 it was chosen as a location for the Army gun factory.

Construction work at the arsenal is divided into six periods. The original arsenal of 20 buildings was erected from 1813-1817. A stone arsenal and a magazine were built and additional shops constructed from 1826-1830. In 1839, commanding officers' quarters, quarters for other officers, a barracks, a magazine and a wall along the river were constructed. Shops and storehouses were extended to meet Civil War needs from 1864-1867. Twenty years later when the Army gun factory was established, the north and south wings of the cannon shop were built.

Millions Are Spent.

Then in the 19 months between the declaration of war and the signing of the Armistice the plant was enlarged and equipped for the manufacture of light and heavy mobile artillery in quantities and the immense shop erected for the manufacture of liners for cannons. There was expended for construction, equipment and maintenance from April 7, 1917 to June 30, 1919 the sum of $12,206,300.

On April 6, 1917 there were 568 employed at the arsenal and in November 1919, a total of 5,024. At one period during the World War 87 officers and a detachment of nearly 800 soldiers were stationed at the post. Expenditures of the war period totaled $17,000,000 while the expenses of the remainder of the fiscal year 1919 brought war figures to $25,367,777.

By 1918 the Watervliet Arsenal was ready for occupancy by and employment of a force of from 10,000 to 12,000, but signing of the Armistice stopped the expansion.

Payroll figures during the war are highly significant. In April, 1917, with 568 employed, the payroll was $42,218; November, 1917, 1,195 employed, payroll $113,859; March, 1918, 2,566 employed, payroll $195,400; November, 1918, 5,024 employed, payroll $547,769; June, 1919, 4,406 employed, payroll $430,059. Then came the gradual slacking.

During the last year of the war the arsenal manufactured 578 guns of calibers from 1.457 inches to 16 inches and relined or modified 160 guns and manufactured 21,246 spare parts.

In March, 1920, an electric furnace 71 feet in depth was installed in the big gun shop with a capacity for the requirements of a 16-inch gun. The first "shrink" in this pit was that of a tube into a 6-inch army gun. A few days later the successful "shrink" on a 12-inch gun satisfied officials that the oven was a success. Two months later a second electric furnace 27.6 feet in depth was installed.

First Arsenal Cost $15,000.

Costs of construction in the early days of the arsenal as compared with the great development during the World War are interesting. The first brick arsenal, built in 1813, cost $15,000. The commissioned officers' quarters cost $5,000; the office and commissary shop, $5,000; barracks, $3,600; two buildings for the enlisted men, $1,000 each; two stables, $200 each, and a timber shed, $500.

The stone arsenal built in 1826 cost $30,000 and the east magazine, $15,000.

None of these buildings are standing today.

Commissioned officers' quarters built in 1840 cost $28,000 and the west magazine $15,000. The storehouse, built in 1859, totaled $55,000; officers' double quarters in 1867, $18,000, and officers' single quarters, $10,000.

The north and south wings of the gun shop built in 1891 cost $586,519, the water tower, $13,000 and the hospital annex in 1902, $20,674.

Then came the great war and in 1918 the mobile artillery shop was constructed at a cost of $483,000; the cafeteria, $55,000; non-commissioned officers' quarters, $13,760; main office extension, $90,000; enlarged storehouse, $7,079; steel stockroom, $22,150; storehouse, $66,167; pump house, $44,500; concrete storehouse, $58,500.

U. S. Points With Pride.

The boiler house was built at a cost of $97,500. The new gun shop cost $812,000, the brass foundry, $29,800; liner shop, $554,000; forge shop, $44,500; wood reamer building, $9,500; carpenter shop, $52,250; new tool room, $65,750, a fire house, $7,335 and cantonment buildings, $62,257.

In 1920 an oil storehouse was built at a cost of $15,000 and an extension to the south wing of the cannon shop, $185,000. The roof also was raised at this time.

The gun shop then was built costing $2,763,677, liner tools included. The breech mechanism building totaled $675,749; eight cantonment buildings, $34,065, another oil storehouse, $11,267; a new tank in the water tower, $19,425 and raising the roof on the heavy field cannon shop, $92,000.

The government built $35,000 of roads through the grounds, laying two miles of pavement, and was done with wartime improvements.

Is it any wonder that the United States points to the Watervliet Arsenal as the very center of its new national defense program?

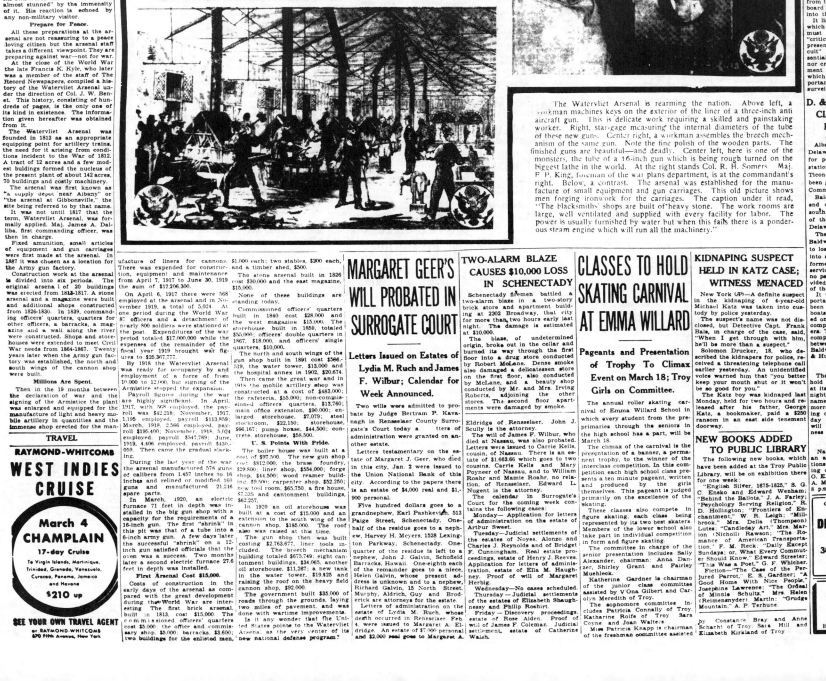

Watervliet Arsenal Rearming Nation to Insure Peace

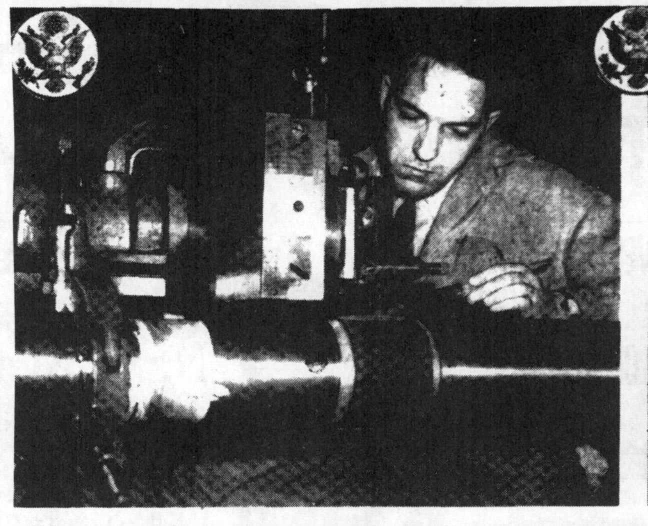

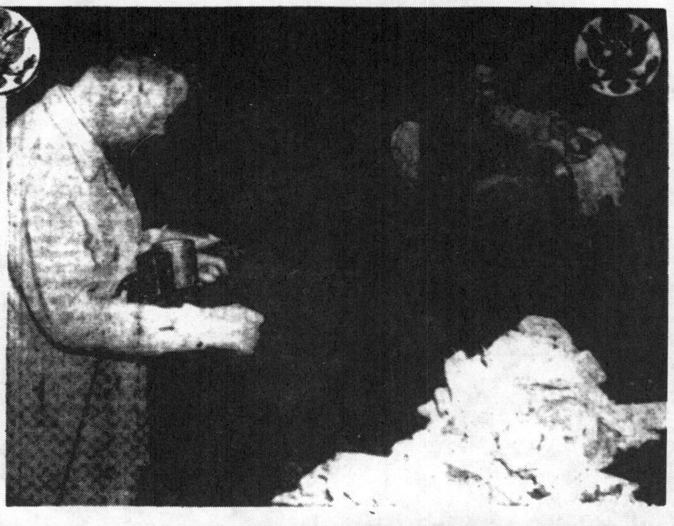

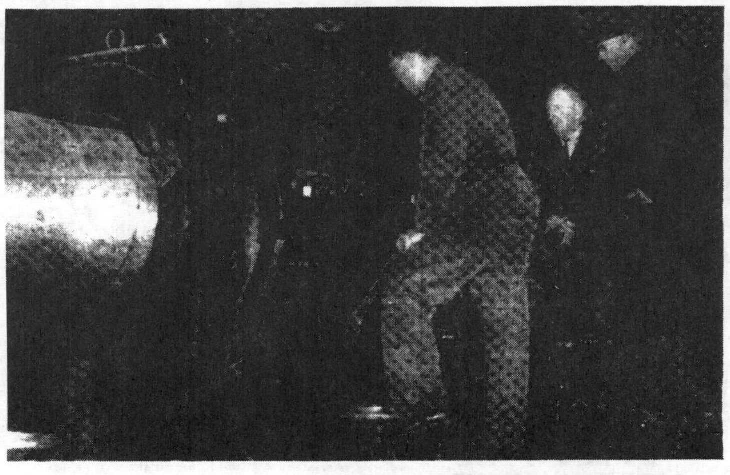

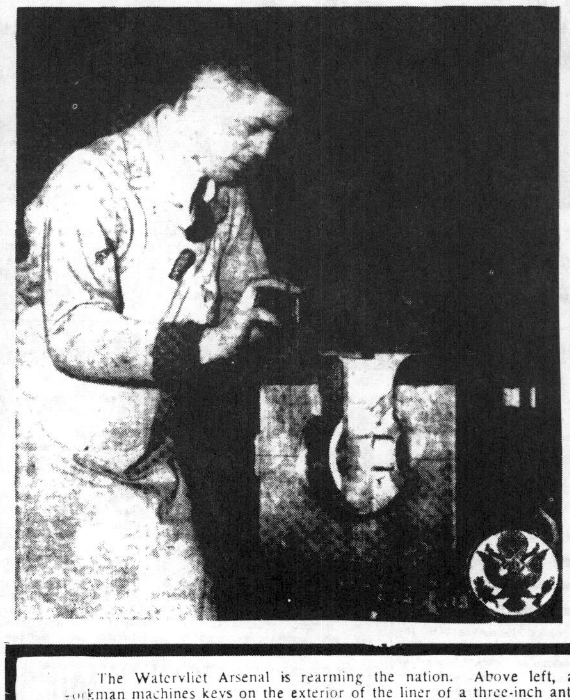

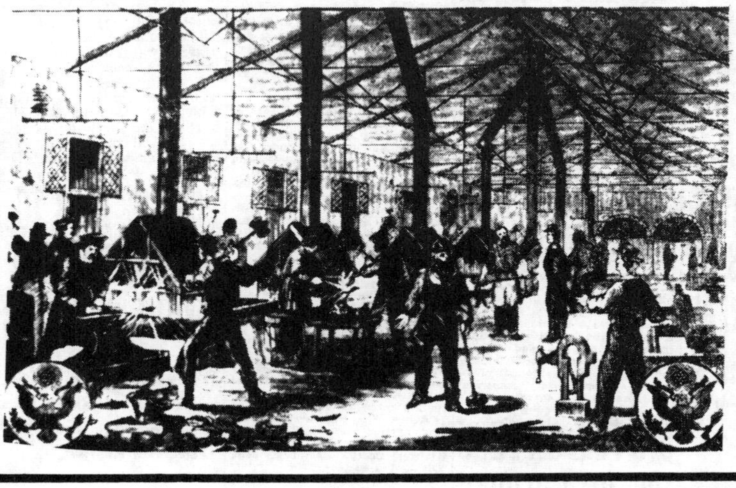

The Watervliet Arsenal is rearming the nation. Above left, a workman machines keys on the exterior of the liner of a three-inch anti aircraft gun. This is delicate work requiring a skilled and painstaking worker. Right, star-gage measuring the internal diameters of the tube of these new guns. Center right, a workman assembles the breech mechanism of the same gun. Note the fine polish of the wooden parts. The finished guns are beautiful—and deadly. Center left, here is one of the monsters, the tube of a 16-inch gun which is being rough turned on the biggest lathe in the world. At the right stands Col. R. H. Somers. Maj. F. P. King, foreman of the war plans department, is at the commandant's right. Below, a contrast. The arsenal was established for the manufacture of small equipment and gun carriages. This old picture shows men forging ironwork for the carriages. The caption under it read, "The blacksmiths' shops are built of heavy stone. The work rooms are large, well ventilated and supplied with every facility for labor. The power is usually furnished by water but when this fails there is a ponderous steam engine which will run all the machinery."

PROPOSAL TO BUY RAW MATERIALS FOR WAR FAVORED

Senate Committee Approves $100,000,000 Plan as Preparedness Measure; Not in Defense Program.

Washington (AP)—A program to buy and store up $100,000,000 worth of raw materials necessary in time of war was approved unanimously by the Senate Military Committee.

"World conditions make this bill very, very timely," said its sponsor, Senator Thomas (D.-Utah).

A government board to be set up would decide just what materials would be bought, but the committee compiled a long list of things which might possibly be purchased. These included aluminum, rubber, silk, tin, wool, tungsten, ferrograde manganese, sugar, iron and steel, copper and chlorine. The purchases would be made over the next four years. Some of the materials in the list have to be imported.

The bill is not part of the administration's defense program, but Senator Thomas declared that it was closely in line with the program.

He said, concerning his bill, that "the committee and the Army and Navy have been studying this problem intensively" for several years.

The money would be used "to provide for the common defense by acquiring stocks of strategic and critical materials essential to the needs of industry for the manufacture of supplies for the armed forces and the civilian population in time of national emergency, and to encourage as far as possible, the further development of strategic and critical materials within the United States."

"We think," Thomas said, "that we have worked out a general bill that will take care of national defense, which will help in the development of some things we are backward in and make us more self-sufficient, and which will keep this problem of strategic materials constantly in the mind of the government."

Much study must be devoted to the subject, he said, before purchases of supplies can be begun. However, as indicative of what might be purchased, a committee report included a memorandum from the Army and Navy munitions board dividing such raw materials into three categories.

It listed "strategic materials" for which dependance, partial or entire, must be placed upon imports; "critical materials," or materials presenting "serious" but "less difficult" procurement problems; "essential materials, neither strategic nor critical," for which no procurement problem was expected but which are nevertheless of such importance as "to require constant surveillance."

D. & H. REQUEST TO CLOSE STATION AT BALDWIN GRANTED

(Staff Correspondence.)

Albany—An application of the Delaware & Hudson Railroad Corp. for permission to discontinue the station at Baldwin in the Town of Ticonderoga, Essex County, has been granted by the Public Service Commission.

Baldwin is located at the north end of Lake George and at the south end of the Baldwin branch of the Champlain Division of the Delaware & Hudson Railroad.

There is no station building at Baldwin and it has been the custom to load and unload freight directly into and out of cars on track. In former years there was passenger service on the Baldwin Branch but no passenger service has been provided on the branch since the close of the 1932 boating season.

It was testified that boat transportation on Lake Champlain has been discontinued and that the boats which were formerly operated on Lake George by the railroad company have been leased to others. There is at present no freight company or passenger connection between Lake George boats and the Baldwin Branch of the Delaware & Hudson Railroad.

MARGARET GEER'S WILL PROBATED IN SURROGATE COURT

Letters Issued on Estates of Lydia M. Ruch and James F. Wilbur; Calendar for Week Announced.

Two wills were admitted to probate by Judge Bertram P. Kavanagh in Rensselaer County Surrogate's Court today a tters of administration were granted on another estate.

Letters testamentary on the estate of Margaret J. Geer, who died in this city, Jan. 2 were issued to the Union National Bank of this city. According to the papers there is an estate of $4,000 real and $1,900 personal.

Five hundred dollars goes to a grandnephew, Earl Pashkevich, 513 Paige Street, Schenectady. One-half of the residue goes to a nephew, Harvey H. Meyers, 1528 Lexington Parkway, Schenectady. One-quarter of the residue is left to a nephew, John J. Galvin, Schofield Barracks, Hawaii. One-eighth each of the remainder goes to a niece, Helen Galvin, whose present address is unknown and to a nephew, Richard Galvin, 15 North Street. Murphy, Aldrich, Guy and Broderick are attorneys for the estate.

Letters of administration on the estate of Lydia M. Ruch, whose death occurred in Rensselaer Feb. 4, were issued to Margaret A. Eldridge. An estate of $7,000 personal and $2,000 real goes to Margaret A. Eldridge of Rensselaer. John J. Scully is the attorney.

The will of James F. Wilbur, who died at Nassau, was also probated. Letters were issued to Carrie Kells, cousin, of Nassau. There is an estate of $1,663.66 which goes to two cousins, Carrie Kells and Mary Poyneer of Nassau, and to William Roahr and Mamie Roahr, no relation, of Rensselaer. Edward L. Nugent is the attorney.

The calendar in Surrogate's Court for the coming week contains the following cases:

Monday— Application for letters of administration on the estate of Arthur Sweet.

Tuesday—Judicial settlements of the estates of Noyes, Alonzo and Charles J. Reynolds and of Bridget F. Cunningham. Real estate proceedings, estate of Henry J. Reeves. Application for letters of administration, estate of Ella M. Haughney. Proof of will of Margaret Herbig.

Wednesday—No cases scheduled.

Thursday — Judicial settlements of the estates of Elizabeth Shaughnessy and Philip Roshirt.

Friday — Discovery proceedings, estate of Rose Alden. Proof of will of James F. Coleman. Judicial settlement, estate of Catherine Walsh.

TWO-ALARM BLAZE CAUSES $10,000 LOSS IN SCHENECTADY

Schenectady firemen battled a two-alarm blaze in a two-story brick store and apartment building at 2202 Broadway, that city for more than two hours early last night. The damage is estimated at $10,000.

The blaze, of undetermined origin, broke out in the cellar and burned its way through the first floor into a drug store conducted by Robert McLane. Dense smoke also damaged a delicatessen store on the first floor, also conducted by McLane, and a beauty shop conducted by Mr. and Mrs. Irving Roberts, adjoining the other stores. The second floor apartments were damaged by smoke.

CLASSES TO HOLD SKATING CARNIVAL AT EMMA WILLARD

Pageants and Presentation of Trophy To Climax Event on March 18; Troy Girls on Committee.

The annual roller skating carnival of Emma Willard School in which every student from the preprimaries through the seniors in the high school has a part, will be March 18.

The climax of the carnival is the presentation of a banner, a permanent trophy, to the winner of the interclass competition. In this competition each high school class presents a ten minute pageant, written and produced by the girls themselves. This pageant is judged primarily on the excellence of the skating.

These classes also compete in figure skating, each class being represented by its two best skaters. Members of the lower school also take part in individual competition in form and figure skating.

The committee in charge of the senior presentation includes Sally Alexander, chairman; Anna Danzer, Shirley Grant and Fairley Muehleck.

Katherine Gardner is chairman of the junior class committee assisted by V'Ona Gilbert and Carolyn Meredith of Troy.

The sophomore committee includes Patricia Connally of Troy, Katharine Rolfe of Troy Sara Coyne and Joan Walters.

Miss Patricia Knapp is chairman of the freshman committee assisted by Constance Bray and Anne Schacht of Troy; Sara Hill and Elizabeth Kirkland of Troy

KIDNAPING SUSPECT HELD IN KATZ CASE; WITNESS MENACED

New York (AP)—A definite suspect in the kidnaping of 4-year-old Michael Katz was taken into custody by police yesterday.

The suspect's name was not disclosed, but Detective Capt. Frank Bals, in charge of the case, said, "When I get through with him, he'll be more than a suspect."

Solomon Drucker, 18, who described the kidnapers for police, received a threatening telephone call earlier yesterday. An unidentified voice warned him that "you better keep your mouth shut or it won't be so good for you."

The Katz boy was kidnaped last Monday, held for two hours and released after his father, George Katz, a bookmaker, paid a $250 ransom in an east side tenement doorway.

NEW BOOKS ADDED TO PUBLIC LIBRARY

The following new books, which have been added at the Troy Public Library, will be on exhibition there for one week:

"English Silver, 1675-1825," S. G. C. Ensko and Edward Wenham; "Behind the Ballots," J. A. Farley; "Psychology Serving Religion," R. D. Hollington; "Frontiers of Enchantment," W. R. Leigh; "Millbrook," Mrs. Della (Thompson) Lutes; "Candleday Art," Mrs. Marion (Nicholl) Rawson; "The Romance of American Transportation," F. M. Reck; "Daily Except Sundays; or, What Every Commuter Should Know," Edward Streeter; "This Was a Poet," G. F. Whicher.

Fiction—"The Case of the Perjured Parrot," E. S. Gardner; "A Good Home With Nice People," Josephine Lawrence; "The Ordeal of Minnie Schultz," Mrs. Helen (Reimensnyder) Martin; "Grudge Mountain," A. P. Terhune.

AT ALL-TROY CLUB.

The All-Troy Athletic Club will hold its weekly social and dance at its clubhouse on Second Avenue night at 8:30. Play in the dart tournament at the club will continue tomorrow afternoon. A special meeting of the club will be held Monday at 8:30 p.m. A buffet lunch will be served following the business session.

SPEAKS TOMORROW.

Nathan Pollard, Albany, will give an address on the housing conditions of Negroes in Troy at a meeting of Collar City Lodge, I. B. P. O. E. of W., at the Seventh Avenue A. M. E. Zion Church tomorrow at 8 p.m.

THE WEATHER
Tonight—Cloudy.
Tomorrow—Cloudy.

THE TIMES RECORD

FINAL EDITION

Series 1939—No. 76. (Entered as Second Class Matter at the Postoffice at Troy, N. Y., under the Act of March 3, 1879.) TROY, N. Y., FRIDAY EVENING, MARCH 31, 1939. (Published Daily Except Sunday) PRICE THREE CENTS

BRITAIN AND FRANCE TO FIGHT IF GERMANY ATTACKS POLAND

PUBLICITY GROUP FROM TWO STATES CONVENES IN TROY

College News Directors Meet at The Hendrick Hudson; Floyd Tifft, R. P. I., Speaks at Session.

Publicity directors from colleges in New York State and New Jersey belonging to the American College Publicity Association met today in Troy for a two-day conference. Two college presidents, Dr. Dixon Ryan Fox of Union, and Dr. William Otis Hotchkiss of R. P. I. will address the meeting tomorrow

"Racoon coats, petting co-eds and gin bottles have been largely driven out of the public's picture of colleges," Floyd Tifft, publicity director of Rensselaer Polytechnic Institute and chairman of the meeting, told the first session this afternoon in The Hendrick Hudson.

He continued:

Many still think of colleges as swanky clubs, as havens for boondogglers, finishing schools, degree bill, or, worse still, just groups of buildings. To many 'college education' means mostly a way of learning how to make money; or it means a costly thing, claiming more than it delivers; or a breeding period for dangerous contemps; or just a conglameration of superficialities.

Of late, we have succeeded, however, in giving the public enough real news of colleges to create a growing consciousness that colleges are places where earnest young people learn how to live and be of greatest service; that they are fountainheads of science and discovery and strongholds of culture.

But the fact remains that there are almost as many definitions of higher education as there are college presidents, and to date we have no one dominant goal to symbolize collectively. The public thinks in terms of symbols, but higher education has not yet settled upon a common conception of its objectives, out of which one dominant symbol would emerge. Our biggest job is to find a powerful universal symbol as truly representative of higher education as the raccoon coat, the petting co-ed, the gin bottle, and the galloping gellapie have been falsely representative.

Franklin Dunham, educational director of the National Broadcasting Co.; Harold Wynne of Burrelle's Clipping Bureau; W. N. Paxton, chief of the Albany Bureau of the Associated Press; Donald Coe of the Albany Bureau of the United Press, and Clyde D. Wagoner, manager of the General Electric Co.'s News Bureau were on today's program.

Wilson L. Fairbanks, telegraph news editor of the New York Times, will speak tomorrow.

Colleges and schools represented at the meeting included: New York State College of Home Economics, Cornell, Hobart, Keuka, Niagara University, Packer Collegiate Institute, Pingrey School, Manhattanville College of the Sacred Heart, Rutgers, Sarah Lawrence College, Skidmore, Union, University of Rochester, Alfred, Manhattan, the College of St. Elizabeth Convent, Vassar, Springfield College, Bard College, and in this immediate area, R. P. I., Russell Sage College, Emma Willard, Siena College, and the College of St. Rose.

U. S. NATIONAL BANK CALL ISSUED TODAY

Washington (UP)—The comptroller of the currency issued a call today for the condition of all national banks at the close of business Wednesday, March 29.

A similar call was issued by the Federal Reserve Board to the state banks belonging to its system. Altogether, 5,220 national and 1,113 state banks were asked to report.

The Federal Deposit Insurance Corp., which sometimes issues simultaneous calls to insured state banks not belonging to the Federal Reserve, did not participate in today's call.

The Index

Early Arrivals At Publicity Directors Event

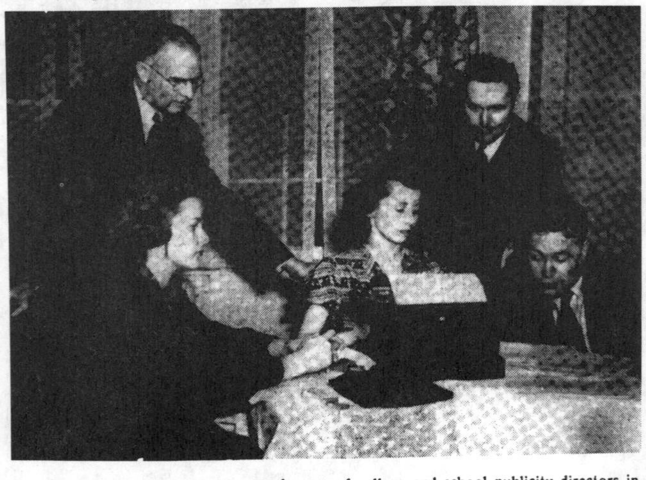

Early arrivals at the two-day conference of college and school publicity directors in this state and New Jersey included the past president of the American College Publicity Association, Ralph S. Clark of New York City, who is standing at the left. At the right, standing, is Floyd Tifft, chairman of the conference. Seated are, left to right, Mrs. Harold E. Wynne, Miss Louise Sutherland and Harold E. Wynne of a New York City press clipping service who is one of the speakers.

SEVERAL TO LOSE WELFARE JOBS AS RESULT OF TESTS

Department Applies for Sixty-day Extension Before Naming Stenographers and Clerks.

With some incumbents in the Troy Welfare Department failing in the exams and others being "far down" on the lists, several will lose their jobs as the result of qualifying examinations for clerks and stenographers, the results of which were announced today.

Incumbents probably will not be dismissed immediately, however, as the Troy department has applied for an extension of sixty days before naming stenographers and clerks. This will permit the training of newcomers for the positions so that department functions will not be disrupted.

Frank J. Hayden, R. D. 2, Oakwood Avenue, by virtue of his veteran's preference rating, is No. 1 on the general clerk's list. Neil W. Humphrey, 160 Third Street, is No. 2 and Simon Van Eck, 54 109th Street, is No. 3. Mr. Hayden is an incumbent.

Names Heading List.

Josephine A. Heffernan, 2161 Twelfth Street, is No. 1 on the stenographers' list; Evelyn D. Harrigan, 318 Second Street, No. 2, and Lillian A. Lansing, 300 Third Street, No. 3. Miss Lansing is an incumbent.

Notices of the results of the examinations were mailed out yester-

(Continued on Page 21.)

SAYS CANADA WILL NO CONSCRIPT FOR ANY WAR OVERSEAS

Ottawa, Ont. (INS)—Prime Minister W. L. Mackenzie King today was on record with a pledge that his government will never conscript Canadian citizens for war service overseas.

The prime minister's unexpected declaration was made before a packed chamber and gallery in the Dominion House of Commons in the face of a strongly growing nationalistic movement in Quebec.

Dr. R. J. Manion, leader of the conservative party once characterized by strong imperial attachments, joined the prime minister in expressing belief that there was no necessity for conscription.

King's statement, devoted to a review of what Britain could and could not expect from Canada in the event of war, contained an assertion that in no event could Canada be depended upon for automatic aid. In the event of war, the prime minister told Commons, his government would propose a course of action and Parliament would be the final judge of its wisdom.

NATURE CAUSED 181 DEATHS DURING '38

Washington (AP) — Weather Bureau preliminary reports showed today that tornadoes caused 181 deaths, 1,321 injuries and property losses exceeding $8,045,000 in the United States last year.

The toll from similar storms in 1937 was 29 deaths and property damage of $3,152,875. The number of tornadoes last year was 200 compared with 123 in 1937.

Lady Peel, Revolts At Son's Moustache

New York (UP)—Sir Robert Peel stepped off the liner Aquitania today proudly displaying his new moustache, and ran smack into his mother, Beatrice Lillie, and an ultimatum.

The moustache, said the stage star, had to go.

"What do you think I am,' she groaned before an interested audience of ship news reporters. "An old woman? I'll kill you if you don't take that thing off."

Sir Robert, who is 18, six feet two inches tall, and a student at Harrow, looked highly embarrassed as his mother added:

"I'm going to break his neck."

Miss Lillie—Lady Peel off stage—said she went to bed early last night in order to meet the boat this morning. She indicated the shock of the moustache was a poor reward for her pains.

"Son," she said to Sir Robert, "I want to talk to you like a mother. We are going over to the apartment. Right now. And off comes that thing."

LINGERING WINTER CAUSES DELAY IN CANAL OPENING

No Traffic Looked For on Waterway Before April 17; River Level Slowly Dropping.

Opening of the Barge Canal will be postponed for several weeks, Harvey O. Schermerhorn, commissioner of canals, announced today, because of the unusually cold spring and large amounts of snow on the watersheds of the Hudson and Mohawk Rivers.

The Federal lock at Bond Street will be open in about a week, James Whalen, superintendent, has stated. The lock usually opens at least a week before the Barge Canal opens.

"It is impossible to anticipate the opening of the canal for the season before April 17," Commissioner Schermerhorn said, "The unusually cold spring has prevented any appreciable run-off of the winter precipitation and until at least a portion of the snow now in the watersheds has disappeared it is in everybody's interest not to attempt navigation on the system prior to the date indicated."

Commissioner Schermerhorn said that the "specified date for official opening of the canal will be announced later."

Quantities of debris went down the river past Troy today following the high water of the last few days. The river level is slowly dropping, engineers at the Federal dam said, and is now about two feet above normal above the dam.

GOVERNOR LEHMAN URGES ABOLITION OF MORTGAGE BODY

Albany (UP)—Governor Lehman today recommended abolition of the mortgage commission this year.

In a letter to the state Legislature, the governor said:

"I recommend the passage, at this session, of legislation to abolish the mortgage commission of the state of New York as of Sept 30 this year."

Lehman said in his statement to the Legislature that he had recommended creation of the commission to "meet a most distressing emergency situation" but that now "the commission has rendered splendid service, and its task will soon be completed."

ESTIMATE BOARD SETS SALARIES IN WELFARE BUREAU

Majority Reported to Be Virtually Unchanged; Accountant Tops List With Pay of $2,400.

Troy's Board of Estimate and Apportionment today fixed salaries for Department of Welfare personnel in connection with the placing of the department on a permanent basis as required by the public welfare law.

Welfare officials said that "virtually all the salaries are the same as before."

Classifications of the office and positions in the department is now being reestablished by the Municipal Civil Service Commission.

The salaries were fixed by the board today as follows:

Accountant, $2,400.
Assistant case supervisor, $1,500.
Administrative assistant, $2,000.
Resource assistant, $1,500.
Store manager, $1,800.
Investigator, $1,040 to $1,300.
Account clerk, $1,200 to $1,300.
Resource clerk, $1,140.
Distribution clerk, $1,020.
Clerk, $900.
Stenographers, $900 and class su-
Clerk, $900.

SPRATLY ISLAND OFF FRENCH INDO-CHINA ANNEXED BY JAPAN

Tokyo (UP)—The foreign office announced today that it had advised France that Japan was annexing the Spratly Island group off the southeast coast of French Indo-China.

Charles-Arsene Henry, the French ambassador, was notified of Japan's decision today, it was said.

France in 1933 announced the annexation of the Spratly, Amboina Cay, Itu-Abut, Deux Iles, Loaita and Thi-Tu groups of tiny islands, hardly more than dots on the map, which spread eastward from a point about 300 miles southeast of Indo-China.

The groups—of which only Spratly was mentioned—lie between 7:52 and 11:29 north latitude, 111:55 and 114:25 east longitude.

They are about midway between Indo-China and Palawan Island, the westermost of the Philippine Islands.

Explaining its action, the foreign office said that Japanese nationals had been active in the Spratly group since 1917.

GOVERNOR SIGNS BILL EXTENDING FLOOD AID BOARD

Col. Ogden J. Ross Heads Commission, Which Will Continue to Function Until at Least April 30.

(Staff Correspondence.)

Albany—Extension of the life of the State Flood Control Commission, headed by Col. Ogden J. Ross of Troy, is provided for in the Hollowell Bill signed today by Gov. Herbert H. Lehman.

Under the measure the commission's life is extended to April 30 but other pending legislation is expected to make provision for its continuance for at least another year.

The commission has many important projects pending, serving as a liason with federal authorities in flood control measures, among them being projects on the Hoosac River and in the Saratoga Lake territory.

To date Governor Lehman has signed 178 new laws for the present session of the Legislature.

Legislation Awaits Agreement.

Little legislation of any general importance can be expected until the Legislature has agreed upon its action on the Governor's recommendations for appropriations and new taxes.

Such an agreement is expected as the result of a recess which has been taken until April 10.

So far fiscal experts in the respective houses of the Legislature have not been able to find a common ground as to just what cut in expenditures must be made and as to what taxes should be substituted for those proposed by Governor Lehman.

The Governor vetoed today a bill to permit officers and employees covered by State Civil Service to withdraw their contributions from the state retirement system instead of taking an annual pension.

Governor Lehman's Comment.

"This bill by giving the option to all members, regardless of length of service, would defeat the primary purpose of the retirement system," Lehman said, after explaining that persons with five years service or less are permitted to withdraw their contributions.

He also vetoed a bill permitting payment of fees to directors and committee members of credit unions, explaining:

"Credit union should not be operated for the benefit of directors, committee members and officers. All of the proposed amendments in this bill are for the benefit of directors and committee members at the expense of the shareholders."

BIG FIRE SWEEPS TWO CITY BLOCKS AT SANDUSKY, OHIO

Two-Million-Dollar Blaze Devastates Downtown Business District; Scores Driven from Homes.

Sandusky, O. (AP)—Fire starting in the M. R. Herb department store destroyed buildings in two city blocks in the downtown business district today with damage estimated by Fire Chief Wilson McLaughlin at "over two million dollars."

More than 100 persons living in apartments over the stores were driven to the street. No one was injured.

The fire spread from the Herb department store on East Market Street eastward to Wayne Street and north to East Water Street.

Most of the buildings were destroyed and only parts of crumbling walls remained.

It was the worst fire in Sandusky's history.

In addition to destruction of buildings in the two blocks, plate glass windows in seven stores on the south side of East Market Street were broken by the intense heat. Water ruined window stocks.

Thirty men from the local Ohio National Guard unit diverted traffic and spectators from the district. The American Legion also was ready if needed.

The fire, discovered at 4 a.m. by a night patrolman, was not brought under control until 8 a.m. Its origin has not been ascertained.

FESTIVAL TONIGHT.

Washington (AP)—The capital will hold its annual festival tonight to celebrate the blooming of the Japanese cherry trees along the Potomac River. Thousands of tourists will be here during the week-end to see the blossoms.

Warns of War

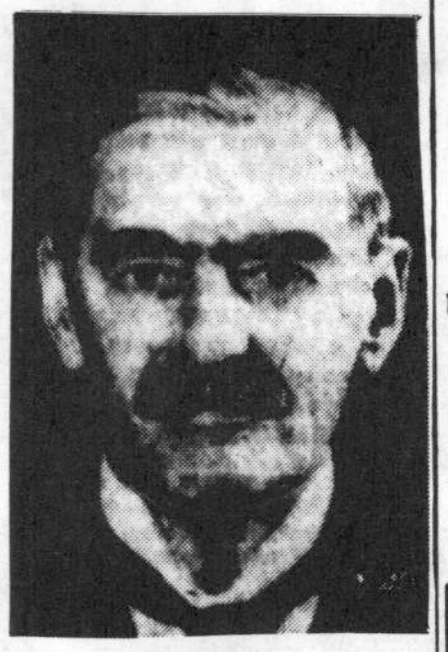

NEVILLE CHAMBERLAIN

NAZI NEWSPAPERS UNITE IN BITTER BLAST AT BRITAIN

Berlin Press Charges "Campaign of English Lies" in Polish Question; Troop Movements Denied.

Berlin (UP)—The Nazi press—as if at a pre-arranged signal—united today in a bitter attack on Great Britain.

Immediately after announcement of British and French military pledges to Poland, the state-controlled Nazi newspapers marked a sharp increase in tension between the two nations by a campaign which apparently had been arranged by the propaganda ministry.

"English lying agitation regarding Poland," screamed the headline in the Lokalanzeiger, denouncing as "lies" the London rumors of German troop movements toward the Polish corridor.

"Fake English report from the Polish frontier," said another typical headline, charging Britain with falsely building up a crisis on the basis of rumor in order to further her program of encirclement of the Reich.

Adolf Hitler's next move may be dependent on Britain's action regarding military aid to Poland.

Diplomatic quarters made no effort to conceal their fears that the international situation was becoming grave again.

"Impudent English lies about a German ultimatum to Poland," read the newspaper Nachtausgabe headline, "invented reports of troop movements."

"A new lying maneuver by England against Germany," the Angriff, newspaper of Propaganda Minister Joseph Goebbels, said. "Old tactics of May, 1938."

The Angriff charged Britain with attempting to further its policy of encirclement of Germany by spreading false reports of German troop movements toward Poland.

"They are obviously preparing for political action and making it palatable to the English public by scaring it in advance," the newspaper said. Such methods can only damage England's reputation."

SWITZERLAND READY FOR ANY SURPRISE ATTACK ON FRONTIER

Zurich, Switzerland (UP)—Switzerland has taken emergency precautions within the last few days to guard all frontiers against surprise attack, it was learned today.

All frontier residents liable for army service are ready to fight within two or three hours after an alarm and they possess emergency ammunition whose exact nature is secret.

The federal government has ordered all mines along the frontier loaded ready for use, and roads and bridges specially guarded.

Measures taken in view of alarming reports are more extensive even than those taken in September during the Czechoslovak crisis, it was understood.

In taking them the government denied that its measures were the result of concentrations of German troops in southern Germany, and warned the public not to be alarmed at rumors that the country was in danger.

BANK PROMISES NOT TO EVICT FROHMAN

New York (INS)—Daniel Frohman, 87, the "grand old man" of the theater, can keep his apartment atop the Lyceum Theater where he has entertained many famous persons.

The bank which is foreclosing on the property instructed its agent to spend as much money as is necessary to provide Frohman, a retired theatrical producer, with all necessary comforts and assured his friends that no matter what final disposition is made Frohman will not be evicted.

Chamberlain Gives Solemn Warning To Nazis Against Grab

Unprecedented Declaration Causes Excitement In Commons As Prime Minister "Tosses Away Umbrella for Gun;" Poles Will Have Military Aid If They Resist Nazi Aggression; Aroused Democracies Determined to Halt Hitler's March to The East; Russia May Also Take Part.

Warsaw (UP)—Sources close to the government said tonight that "if Germany fails to respect our frontiers we will fight."

The repeated expressions of determination to resist any thrust directed at Poland assumed special significance as official circles enthusiastically greeted the British government's announcement of military aid in event Poles are compelled to fight a defense war.

Poland has no intention of asking Germany to give any pledges regarding the Polish frontiers, officials said, because the Nazis understand that they will have to fight if they make any move toward this country.

BY THE UNITED PRESS.

Great Britain forcefully warned Adolf Hitler today against another grab in Europe, declaring that Britain and France will fight if Poland's independence is menaced during the present European security consultations and Poland fights back.

In a declaration unprecedented since the World War and one representing a complete change in British policy, Prime Minister Neville Chamberlain told a cheering House of Commons that Britain will go to the aid of Poland if that nation is attacked and that France, known to have the finest troops in all Europe, will do likewise. He revealed that Britain is in close consultation with Soviet Russia on the matter.

Never before has the British government committed itself to armed aid in defense of a nation east of the Rhine. Some observers saw Britain shifting her military frontier from the Rhine to the Vistula River in Poland.

Thus an aroused democratic bloc put military teeth into Europe's faltering "Halt Hitler" movement and sought—without abandoning the hope that the great powers can yet live peacefully together—to end the Nazi method of expansion by threat of armed force.

Chamberlain's statement was acclaimed in Paris, where it was viewed a great blow to Germany because it officially creates a bloc of nations mutually pledged to smash Nazism if it tries to repeat the Czechoslovak coup.

Typical comment of the man in the Paris street was:
"Chamberlain's umbrella has given place to a gun."

Chamberlain, who suffered humiliation after humiliation in his campaign of "appeasement" starting with the Munich conference, astonished Commons by his complete change of attitude. It was emphasized the government still held all its horror of war but was represented a feeling that Germany must stop short, and that the sooner Britain said so, the greater hope there would be that Germany would stop this side of war.

After Chamberlain's speech, a British government spokesman indicated that the military pledge given to Poland may apply to the Polish Corridor and even to Danzig.

Asked whether German action affecting the corridor would bring British aid, the spokesman pointed out that the statement clearly guarantees British assistance in event of "any action." Regarding Danzig, he said the pledge would apply if Poland resisted action against Danzig with its national forces.

Denounces Threat of Force.

The spokesman, asked about the possibility of a similar pledge to Rumania, emphasized that the statement was merely a "preliminary" announcement. He said the United States had been informed of the government's deliberations. He indicated that the British decision eliminates the possibility of Polish-German negotiations on Danzig and the Corridor.

In his speech Chamberlain revealed the solidarity of France and Britain, saying the French government had authorized him to make it plain that it stood in the same position as the British government.

Chamberlain made the specific statement that in the event of any action which clearly threatened Polish independence during the present consultations and which the Polish government considered it vital to resist, His Majesty's government would feel bound at once to lend the Poles all the support in their power.

Chamberlain began by saying that the government had no official confirmation of rumors of a projected attack on Poland and that the government must be considered as accepting such rumors as true.

He said that His Majesty's government had constantly advocated adjustment by the means of free negotiation of the differences arising among the peoples of Europe.

In the opinion of the government, there should be no ques-

(Continued on Page 16.)

POWERS LOOK TO POLAND FOR NEXT MOVE IN CRISIS

Warsaw Must Decide Whether to Resist Nazi Aggression; Rumania's Decision Recalled.

BY J. C. OESTREICHER
(International News Service Foreign Editor.)—

After months of jockeying and striving for "appeasement," Great Britain cast the die today for armed resistance against the imperialistic expansion of Nazi Germany.

It was a historic decision announced by Prime Minister Neville Chamberlain to the House of Commons today, and represented the first real fruits of the "stop Hitler" movement begun when the chancellor seized by threat of force the rump state of Czechoslovakia.

The British commitment, decided upon in full cooperation and collaboration of France, is peculiarly contingent upon one factor.

Namely, that it is up to Poland to decide whether it wants military assistance from Britain and France or not.

In his brief but intensely important statement to the house, Chamberlain emphasized that Britain and France had taken this step on their own initiative, ostensibly for the sole purpose of scaring Hitler out of further aggrandizement. Before the armies of Britain and France are mobilized, Poland must first

(Continued on Page 5.)

FIRST LADY PLANS "BLUEBIRD BLUE" EASTER ENSEMBLE

New York (INS)—A dressmaker's ensemble in "bluebird blue" has been chosen by Mrs. Eleanor Roosevelt, wife of the President, for her Easter outfit, it was revealed today by Miss Lucille Mahoney of a New York department store.

The coat of navy wool, semi-fitted and with open cut embroidery, will be worn over the dress of "bluebird blue" sheer crepe. The dress has a flair skirt and bracelet-length sleeves with fan tucks along both edges of the belt.

The "First Lady" has selected a navy blue straw sailor hat with a tailored bow at the back and matching gloves and handbag.

481 CASES LISTED FOR COMING TERM IN SUPREME COURT

A total of 481 cases are listed in the calendar for the April term of Supreme Court for Rensselaer County which will open Monday with Supreme Court Justice Sydney F. Foster of Monticello presiding.

Of this number 56 are listed as preferred causes and 425 as general causes.

A grand jury is sitting with this term of court.

THE WEATHER
Tonight—Cloudy, cool.
Tomorrow—Fair, warmer.

THE TIMES RECORD

FINAL EDITION

Series 1939—No. 100. (Entered as Second Class Matter at the Postoffice at Troy, N. Y., under the Act of March 3, 1879) TROY, N. Y., FRIDAY EVENING, APRIL 28, 1939. (Published Daily Except Sunday) PRICE THREE CENTS

HITLER REJECTS ROOSEVELT'S APPEAL FOR PEACE GUARANTEE

LANSINGBURG BOY NAMED TO ACT AS CITY'S EXECUTIVE

Other Appointments Announced for Boys' and Girls' Week; Will Be Guests of Rotary Club.

James R. Reid, 18, son of Mr. and Mrs. Robert H. Reid of 666 Third Avenue, has been selected to be "boy mayor" during the observance of Boys and Girls' Week which commences tomorrow.

This announcement was made today by Edward A. Kane, chairman of the boys' work committee of the Troy Rotary Club.

Reid is a senior at Lansingburg High School.

In addition to the appointment of a "boy mayor" the committee through Mr. Kane revealed the appointments of the other city officials who will take office next Tuesday and will be the guests of the Troy Rotary Club at its regular weekly luncheon that day.

Other Appointments.

Seven students from Troy High School will fill the posts of president of the Common Council, Commissioner of Public Works, Corporation Counsel, Police Magistrate, Commissioner of Welfare, Superintendent of Recreation and Commissioner of Taxation and Assessment. Two students from LaSalle Institute will fill the posts of Fire Chief and City Comptroller while four seniors from Lansingburg High School will act as Mayor, City Engineer, Superintendent of the airport and City Treasurer. Two Camp Fire Girls will act as secretary to the mayor and secretary to the recreation commissioner. Five students of Catholic Central High School will take office as City Clerk, Superintendent of Schools, Chief of Police, Commissioner of Health and Commissioner of Public Safety.

A total of twenty students from the four Troy high schools and the Camp Fire Girls' unit will take part in the one day administration of high school students. During the day the students will meet the officials they will replace for the day and will learn the work of their offices.

Guests of Rotary Club.

At 12:15 p.m. the "officials" will be the guests of the Rotary Club at which time a special program will be given. "Mayor" James Reid will be the guest speaker. Mayor Frank J. Hogan and his secretary, James Blake, will also be present at the dinner as guests.

An entertainment program will be enjoyed with selections by the Troy Boys' Club Harmonica Band. John Potenze, member of the band, will render several vocal solos and John Romeo, also with the unit, will give a number of accordion

(Continued On Page 13)

BOY ACCIDENTALLY LOCKED IN RUMBLE SEAT FOR 2 DAYS

Riverside, N. J., (AP)—Eight-year-old Robert Perry was recovering today from a two-day accidental imprisonment in the locked rumble seat of a parked automobile.

Pale and weak from hunger, Robert climbed from his cramped quarters Tuesday after a guard at the Frankford Arsenal, Philadelphia, told the car's owner, Miss Louise Presbrey "a kitten's crying in your car."

Miss Presbrey, manager of the Arsenal Cafeteria, said the car had been parked at the Central Airport in Camden from Sunday until Tuesday while she visited Washington. Robert told her he climbed into the seat Sunday night and it snapped shut.

Robert's parents had notified the police he was missing Sunday night. The youngster told police he had "just run away."

THREE PLEAD GUILTY TO MURDER CHARGES

White Cloud, Mich., (AP)—Three members of a family who confessed plotting the death of 20-year-old Helen Cassidy to gain custody of her four children, pleaded guilty today to charges of first degree murder, making sentences of life imprisonment mandatory.

Elton Cassidy, 24, brother-in-law of the victim, admitted he choked her to death last Feb. 26 at her farm home and hanged her body in a stairwell to simulate suicide. The others who entered pleas of guilty in circuit court are Charles Cassidy, 23, estranged husband of Helen, and Mrs. Matilda Cassidy, 46-year-old mother of Charles and Elton.

VASSAR CHOIR TO SING.

Hyde Park (UP)—The Vassar College Choir will entertain tonight at the home of President Roosevelt's mother, for the President and Mrs. Roosevelt and their royal guests, Crown Prince Olaf and Crown Princess Martha of Norway.

LaGuardia Greets Royalty

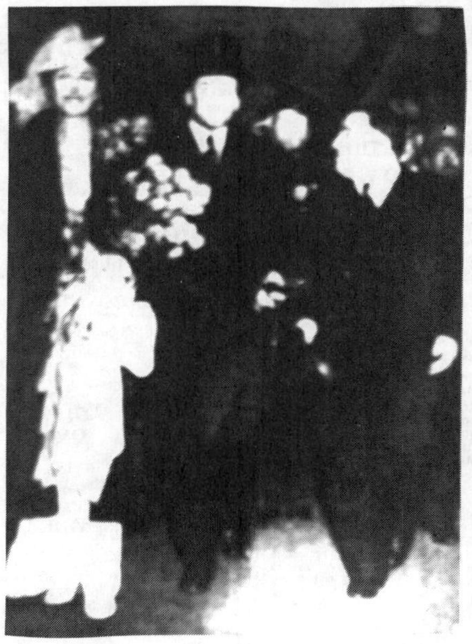

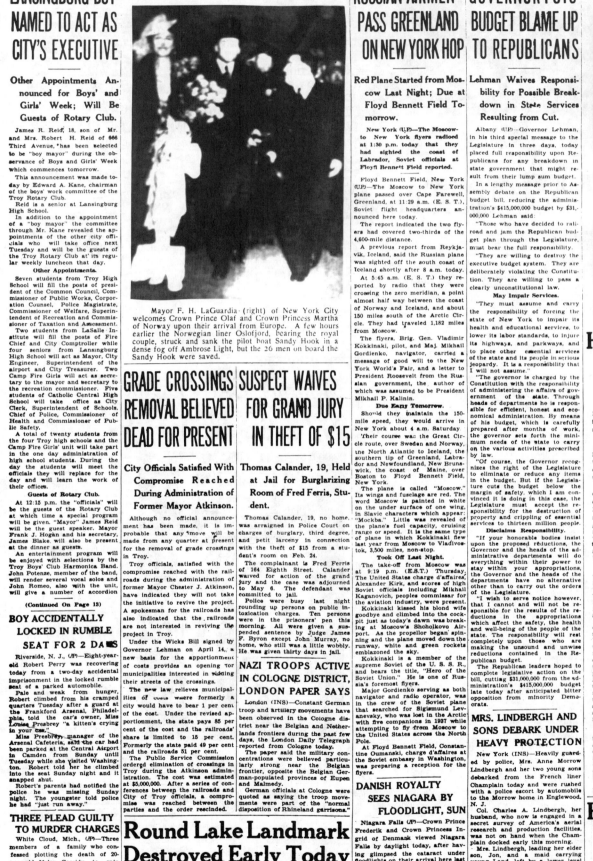

Mayor F. H. LaGuardia (right) of New York City welcomes Crown Prince Olaf and Crown Princess Martha of Norway upon their arrival from Europe. A few hours earlier the Norwegian liner Oslofjord, bearing the royal couple, struck and sank the pilot boat Sandy Hook in a dense fog off Ambrose Light, but the 26 men on board the Sandy Hook were saved.

GRADE CROSSINGS REMOVAL BELIEVED DEAD FOR PRESENT

City Officials Satisfied With Compromise Reached During Administration of Former Mayor Atkinson.

Although no official announcement has been made, it is improbable that any move will be made from any quarter at present for the removal of grade crossings in Troy.

Troy officials, satisfied with the compromise reached with the railroads during the administration of former Mayor Chester J. Atkinson, have indicated they will not take the initiative to revive the project. A spokesman for the railroads has also indicated that the railroads are not interested in reviving the project in Troy.

Under the Wicks Bill signed by Governor Lehman on April 14, a new basis for the apportionment of costs provides an opening for municipalities interested in ridding their streets of the crossings.

The new law relieves municipalities of costs where formerly a city would have to bear 1 per cent of the cost. Under the revised apportionment, the state pays 85 per cent of the cost and the railroads' share is limited to 15 per cent. Formerly the state paid 49 per cent and the railroads 51 per cent.

The Public Service Commission ordered elimination of crossings in Troy during the Atkinson administration. The cost was estimated at $5,000,000. After a series of conferences between the railroads and City of Troy officials, a compromise was reached between the parties and the order rescinded.

SUSPECT WAIVES FOR GRAND JURY IN THEFT OF $15

Thomas Calander, 19, Held at Jail for Burglarizing Room of Fred Ferris, Student.

Thomas Calander, 19, no home, was arraigned in Police Court on charges of burglary, third degree, and petit larceny in connection with the theft of $15 from a student's room on Feb. 24.

The complainant is Fred Ferris of 164 Eighth Street. Calander waived for action of the grand jury and the case was adjourned to May 6. The defendant was committed to jail.

Police were busy last night rounding up persons on public intoxication charges. Ten persons were in the prisoners' pen this morning. All were given a suspended sentence by Judge James F. Byron except John Murray, no home, who still was a little wobbly. He was given thirty days in jail.

NAZI TROOPS ACTIVE IN COLOGNE DISTRICT, LONDON PAPER SAYS

London (INS)—Constant German troop and artillery movements have been observed in the Cologne district near the Belgian and Netherlands frontiers during the past few days, the London Daily Telegraph reported from Cologne today.

The paper said the military concentrations were believed particularly strong near the Belgian frontier, opposite the Belgian German-populated provinces of Eupen and Malmedy.

German officials at Cologne were quoted as saying the troop movements were part of the "normal disposition of Rhineland garrisons."

Round Lake Landmark Destroyed Early Today

An old landmark at Round Lake was destroyed by fire early today when flames, believed to have originated in a defective chimney, razed the old former Dunning house on the highest point in the village.

This house was built by the Dunning family which once owned most of what is now Round Lake. For many years it was occupied by "Pop" Williams, a Civil War veteran and was the home for several years of the late Jacob VanStone Jacobs, former county clerk of Rensselaer County and the place where he died.

It was owned by Earl Manderville and occupied by him with his wife, Beatrice. About 2:15 a.m. today John Bond, an employee on the place which is a garden and poultry farm, crawled down the stairs from his room on the second floor almost overcome by smoke. He aroused the Mandervilles and Mrs. Manderville drove the farm truck to the fire alarm box on the Municipal Building nearly a half mile from the home and sounded an alarm.

Because the house was so far from a hydrant that a line could not be laid no effort was made to quench the flames but firemen concentrated their efforts on rescuing furniture.

The loss is about $5,000, partly covered by insurance.

This is the third fire on the property within the last few years, a tenant house having burned in the summer of 1937 and a large barn about two years previous to that.

RUSSIAN AIRMEN PASS GREENLAND ON NEW YORK HOP

Red Plane Started from Moscow Last Night; Due at Floyd Bennett Field Tomorrow.

New York (UP)—The Moscow-to New York flyers radioed at 1:30 p.m. today that they had sighted the coast of Labrador, Soviet officials at Floyd Bennett Field reported.

Floyd Bennett Field, New York (UP)—The Moscow to New York plane passed over Cape Farewell, Greenland, at 11:29 a.m. (E. S. T.), Soviet flight headquarters announced here today.

The report indicated the two flyers had covered two-thirds of the 4,600-mile distance.

A previous report from Reykjavik, Iceland, said the Russian plane was sighted off the south coast of Iceland shortly after 8 a.m. today.

At 5:45 a.m. (E. S. T.) they reported by radio that they were crossing the zero meridian, a point almost half way between the coast of Norway and Iceland, and about 150 miles south of the Arctic Circle. They had traveled 1,182 miles from Moscow.

The flyers, Brig. Gen. Vladimir Kokkinaki, pilot, and Maj. Mikhail Gordienko, navigator, carried a message of good will to the New York World's Fair, and a letter to President Roosevelt from the Russian government, the author of which was assumed to be President Mikhail P. Kalinin.

Due Early Tomorrow.

Should they maintain the 150-mile speed, they would arrive in New York about 4 a.m. Saturday.

Their course was the Great Circle route, over Sweden and Norway, the North Atlantic to Iceland, the southern tip of Greenland, Labrador and Newfoundland, New Brunswick, the coast of Maine, over Boston to Floyd Bennett Field, New York.

The plane is called "Moscow." Its wings and fuselage are red. The word Moscow is painted in white on the under surface of one wing, in Slavic characters which appear: "Mockba." Little was revealed of the plane's fuel capacity, cruising range or speed. It is the same type of plane in which Kokkinaki flew last year from Moscow to Vladivostok, 3,500 miles, non-stop.

Took Off Last Night.

The take-off from Moscow was at 9:19 p.m. (E.S.T.) Thursday. The United States charge d'affaires, Alexander Kirk, and scores of high Soviet officials including Mikhail Kaganovich, peoples commissar for the aviation industry, were present.

Kokkinaki kissed his blond wife goodbye and climbed into the cockpit just as today's dawn was breaking at Moscow's Shcholkovo Airport. As the propellor began spinning and the plane moved down the runway, white and green rockets emblazoned the sky.

Kokkinaki is a member of the supreme Soviet of the U. S. S. R., and bears the title, "Hero of the Soviet Union." He is one of Russia's foremost flyers.

Major Gordienko serving as both navigator and radio operator, was in the crew of the Soviet plane that searched for Sigismund Levanevsky, who was lost in the Arctic with five companions in 1937 while attempting to fly from Moscow to the United States across the North Pole.

At Floyd Bennett Field, Constantine Oumanski, charge d'affaires at the Soviet embassy in Washington, was preparing a reception for the flyers.

DANISH ROYALTY SEES NIAGARA BY FLOODLIGHT, SUN

Niagara Falls (AP)—Crown Prince Frederik and Crown Princess Ingrid of Denmark viewed Niagara Falls by daylight today, after having glimpsed the cataract under floodlights on their arrival here last night.

The royal couple included Canada in their American tour when they crossed the Niagara gorge for a scenic drive.

Joined here by Otto Waldsted, Danish minister to the United States, the prince and princess were scheduled late today to return to Buffalo, where they disembarked from their special railroad car last night.

Among the 1,000 who greeted them in Buffalo was Eric Carstensen, Buffalo municipal engineer, who had been Prince Frederik's classmate in the Danish naval college.

65 SLAIN IN RIOT.

Bombay (AP)—An estimated 65 persons were killed today in Gangpur, a small native state in Eastern India, when police fired on a mob of rioting natives.

GOVERNOR PUTS BUDGET BLAME UP TO REPUBLICANS

Lehman Waives Responsibility for Possible Breakdown in State Services Resulting from Cut.

Albany (UP)—Governor Lehman, in his third special message to the Legislature in three days, today placed full responsibility upon Republicans for any breakdown in state government that might result from their lump sum budget.

In a lengthy message prior to Assembly debate on the Republican budget bill, reducing the administration's $415,000,000 budget by $31,000,000 Lehman said:

"Those who have decided to railroad and jam the Republican budget plan through the Legislature, must bear the full responsibility.

"They are willing to destroy the executive budget system. They are deliberately violating the Constitution. They are willing to pass a clearly unconstitutional law.

May Impair Services.

"They must assume and carry the responsibility of forcing the state of New York to impair its health and educational services, to lower its labor standards, to injure its highways, and parkways, and to place other essential services of the state and its people in serious jeopardy. It is a responsibility that I will not assume."

"The governor is charged by the Constitution with the responsibility of administering the affairs of government of the state. Through heads of departments he is responsible for efficient, honest and economical administration. By means of his budget, which is carefully prepared after months of work, the governor sets forth the minimum needs of the state to carry on the various activities prescribed by law.

"Of course, the Governor recognizes the right of the Legislature to eliminate or reduce any items in the budget. But if the Legislature cuts the budget below the margin of safety, which I am convinced it is doing in this case, the Legislature must accept the responsibility for the destruction of property and crippling of essential services to thirteen million people.

Disclaims Responsibility.

"If your honorable bodies insist upon the proposed reductions, the Governor and the heads of the administrative departments will do everything within their power to stay within your appropriations, the Governor and the heads of the departments have no alternative other than to carry out the orders of the Legislature.

"I wish to serve notice however, that I cannot and will not be responsible for the results of the reductions in the appropriations which affect the safety, the health and well-being of the people of the state. The responsibility will rest completely upon those who are making the unsound and unwise reductions contained in the Republican budget.

The Republican leaders hoped to complete legislative action on the bill, cutting $31,000,000 from the administration's $415,000,000 budget late today after anticipated bitter opposition from minority Democrats.

MRS. LINDBERGH AND SONS DEBARK UNDER HEAVY PROTECTION

New York (INS)—Heavily guarded by police, Mrs. Anne Morrow Lindbergh and her two young sons debarked from the French liner Champlain today and were rushed with a police escort by automobile to the Morrow home in Englewood, N. J.

Col. Charles A. Lindbergh, her husband, who now is engaged in a secret survey of America's aerial research and production facilities, was not on hand when the Champlain docked early this morning.

Mrs. Lindbergh, leading her elder son, Jon, and a maid carrying young Land, left by a lower level and were hustled into a car which drove them to the tunnel connecting New York and New Jersey. At the New Jersey exit of the tunnel they were met by a police escort.

GANDHI PLANS DEATH FAST IF WAR COMES

London (AP)—Mohandas K. Gandhi was quoted by Exchange Telegraph, a British news agency, today as threatening to fast unto death in the event of European war.

The wizened Indian spiritual leader said in a message to the world, the agency reported:

"I shall die for peace xxx I am quite capable of fasting unto death to prevent western humanity from embarking on suicide on a scale hitherto unknown in the history of the world."

Says Germany Wants Peace

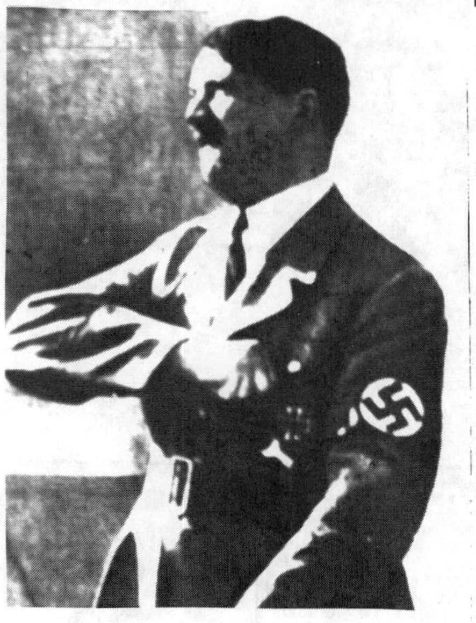

Although rejecting President Roosevelt's appeal for a ten-year European peace guarantee, Adolf Hitler, shown above in a characteristic oratorical pose, insisted that Germany wants only peace.

Hitler's Replies To Points Made In Roosevelt Appeal

Berlin (UP)—Here are Adolf Hitler's replies to points made in President Roosevelt's peace message of April 15.

Mr. Roosevelt—You have repeatedly asserted that you and the German people have no desire for war. If this is true there need be no war.

Herr Hitler—I wish to point out that I have not conducted any war; that for the past year I have expressed my abhorrence of war and of war mongers; and that I am unaware for what purpose I should wage war at all. I should be thankful if Mr. Roosevelt would give me some explanation in this connection.

Mr. Roosevelt—I am convinced that the cause of world peace would be greatly advanced if the nations of the world were able to obtain a frank statement relating to the present and future policy of governments.

Herr Hitler—I have already done this, Mr. Roosevelt, in innumerable public speeches and I am doing it in the course of this meeting of the German reichstag. I must however decline to give such explanation to any one other than the people for whose existence and life I am responsible and who on the other hand have alone the right to demand that I account them. However, I give the aimes of German policy openly so the entire world can hear in any case.

Mr. Roosevelt—Are you willing to give assurance that your armed forces will not attack or invade the territory or possessions of the following independent nations. (The President then named 31 nations in Europe and the Near East.)

Herr Hitler—All the states bordering Germany have received much more binding assurances than the suggestion Mr. Roosevelt makes to me in his peculiar telegram. But should there be any doubt as to the value of these general, direct statements which I have so often made then any further statement of this kind, even if addressed to the American President, would be equally worthless. (Hitler then named the states that had been asked by the reich if they feared attack. All had replied in the negative, he said.)

Mr. Roosevelt—You realize I am sure that throughout the world hundreds of millions of human beings are living today in constant fear of a new war. . . . The tide of events seems to have reverted to the threat of arms.

Herr Hitler—As far as Germany is concerned, I know nothing about this kind of threat against other nations, although every day I read in democratic newspapers lies about such a threat.

Mr. Roosevelt—The leaders of the great nations have it in their power to liberate their peoples from the threat of disaster that impends.

Herr Hitler—If that is true, then it is punishable neglect, to use no worse words, if the leaders of the nations who have corresponding powers are not capable of controlling newspapers which are agitating for war and so to save the world from the threatening calamity. I am unable to understand further why these responsible leaders instead of cultivating diplomatic relations between nations, make them more difficult—indeed, disturb them, by recalling their ambassadors without any reason.

Mr. Roosevelt—Any major war . . . . must bear heavily on (all nations) for generations to come. Victor nations, van-

(Continued on Page 14.)

How World Capitals View Hitler's Reply

European and American reaction to Fuehrer Adolf Hitler's reply to President Roosevelt's appeal for peace guarantees, as summed up in Associated Press, United Press and International News dispatches received by The Times Record follows:

Washington: Congressional opinion divided. Some believe Hitler's words mean more trouble for Europe. Others believe dictator left "an opening for conciliatory action."

Hyde Park—"No comment," President Roosevelt says.

London—Great Britain steps up preparedness program. Denunciation of Anglo-German naval treaty by Hitler regarded empty political gesture but junking of friendship treaty with Poland viewed as grave move holding possibilities of trouble. Stock market prices advance, reflecting "constructive" interpretation on Hitler's words.

Paris—French circles feel world is entering a period of increasing tension. Fear possible Nazi move against Poland may cause trouble. Britain and France pledged to aid Poland if latter resists any invasion.

Warsaw—Poland is ready to accept joint Polish-German control of Danzig but rejects cession of port to Reich. Officials believe door still open to negotiations for friendly settlement of questions between Germany and Poland.

Berlin — German Reichstag and entire German people support Hitler's stand, Marshal Herman Goering tells Fuehrer after address.

Rome — Mussolini endorses Hitler's speech as "setting out facts in accordance with historic and present-day truth."

FUEHRER DENIES ANY INTENTION OF STARTING BIG WAR

Denounces Anglo-German Naval Treaty and Pact With Poland but Stresses Peace Desire.

Berlin (INS) In a bristling speech denouncing the Anglo-German naval treaty and his non-aggression pact with Poland, Reichsfuehrer Adolf Hitler today sarcastically rejected President Roosevelt's demand for a European peace guarantee but at the same time disclaimed any intention of war.

Addressing the Reichstag on the twentieth anniversary of the day that German delegates left Berlin to sign their names to the "shameful" Treaty of Versailles, the Fuehrer insisted he had no territorial designs upon France or any other non-German nation, but once again voiced his demand for return of the Reich's war lost colonies.

In the course of his long speech to his Nazi deputies, which held the entire civilized world under unprecedented tension for more than two hours, the Fuehrer time and again expressed his unequivocal wish for peace but served notice upon the world that these are the tenets of Germany policy.

Demands Return of Danzig.

1. Danzig must be allowed to return to the Reich.

2. The German-Polish non-agression treaty has been rendered invalid by Poland's rejection of Germany's offer for a peaceful settlement of the corridor problem and by her participation in Britain's program of "encirclement."

3. The Anglo-German naval treaty, restricting the Reich to 35 per cent of England's naval power, has ceased to exist because of Britain's insistence upon regarding Germany as a potential enemy.

4. Germany will make known her policy toward any individual countries that ask for it, but the Reich's only answer to Mr. Roosevelt is that there is now a "Monroe Doctrine" for Central Europe just as in the Americas.

5. Germany never again will enter a conference room unarmed.

"Germany Wants Peace."

The German nation is dedicated to peace, the Fuehrer said, but should war come "German resistance will be such that 1914 would be as nothing compared to it.

The Saar plebiscite, Hitler said, solved for all time all territorial problems between France and Germany and there are no German claims upon England save those regarding colonies. He emphasized the desirability of continued collaboration with the British Empire, but threw the onus for present strained relations upon London.

"I have never made any demands that would interfere with Great Britain's interests," the Fuehrer declared, but a moment later stated that he considered the German-

(Continued on Page 14.)

PARIS GOVERNMENT SEES "IMPLICATIONS" IN HITLER'S SPEECH

Paris (UP)—French government circles feared today that Adolf Hitler's denunciation of the German friendship treaty with Poland and his references to Danzig were "dangerous implications."

Speculation on whether the Hitler remarks would be followed by some move against Poland in the near future was raised in well-informed quarters. If Poland resisted such a move, it was pointed out, Britain and France are pledged to assist the Warsaw government immediately.

Small significance was attached to Hitler's denunciation of the British-German naval treaty because official sources said that Germany already was believed to have exceeded the naval limitations in some categories and the denunciation was foreshadowed some time ago. Acceleration of negotiations to bring Soviet Russia into the British-French anti-aggression front was foreseen as a result of the Hitler speech.

The Index

NEW YORK FACING CURTAILMENT OF LIGHT, GAS SERVICE

Metropolitan Area Suffers as Coal Deadlock Continues; Railway Service Affected.

New York (AP)—A curtailment of light and gas service in the metropolitan area—where subway service already has been materially reduced because of coal shortages resulting from the bituminous shutdown—was predicted last night by Chairman Milo Maltbie of the State Public Service Commission "unless coal production at the normal rate is immediately resumed."

At the same time he announced that the commission had called a hearing for today to ascertain the exact situation in the metropolitan area. Six utilities systems will appear.

"Generally speaking," Maltbie said, "conditions throughout the state have not reached such a critical stage (as here) but it is probable that unless conditions improve hearings regarding the coal supplies of upstate companies will promptly follow.

"The situation has been discussed with Governor Lehman and the action now taken by the commission meets with his complete approval."

Meanwhile, the New York Central railroad announced that the shortage had necessitated more than 30 adjustments in local train schedules for New York State, effective today.

Trains affected are on the Harlem, Hudson and West Shore divisions, the Buffalo division between Buffalo and Suspension Bridge, on the St. Lawrence division, on the Auburn road and two trains between Syracuse and Rochester.

The revised schedule, mostly affecting non-rush-hour service, was announced as effective until further notice.

Class Day Officers For Lansingburg High

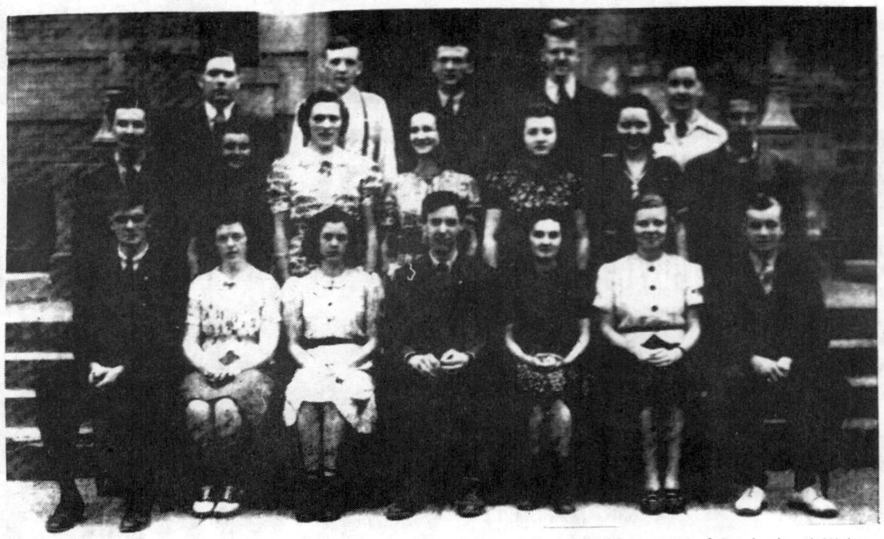

Officers who will preside at the annual Class Day exercises of the Lansingburg High School Tuesday, June 27, are shown here. Left to right they are, front row, Edward Cooney, Betty Jones, Muriel Marcou, John Dougrey, Marian Williams, Mildred Rowland and Walter Neals; middle row, Ned Curran, Jean Ibbott, Peggy Shields, Barbara O'Bryan, Barbara Olcott, Barbara Bowker and James Reid; rear row, Richard Flagler, Andrew Bryce, Leonard Bleecker, Robert Anderson and Norman Mealy.

Fall From Street Car Kills Aviatrix

London (AP)—Mrs. G. A. R. Williams, who as Lady Mary Heath was internationally known as an aviatrix, died yesterday of head injuries suffered in a fall down the stairs of a double-deck street car.

The 43-year-old flyer, whose name was bracketed with Charles A. Lindbergh's by the International League of Aviators as an outstanding flyer of 1927, was unidentified when taken to a hospital. Relatives established her identity after death.

Mrs. Williams, who was reported to have been the first woman in the world to be licensed as a regular commercial pilot, had been out of the public eye in recent years because of poor health.

In 1929, at the height of her career, Lady Heath was nearly killed in the crash of her plane at the Cleveland air races. She lingered near death for several days. Ten months later her nurse and constant companion, Miss Florence Madden, filed a petition in Cleveland for a guardian for Lady Heath, stating the flyer was "incompetent by reason of mental disorders" resulting from the accident.

In 1936, a London magistrate sentenced her to 28 days in jail for disorderly conduct. She was charged with being intoxicated in a central London subway station.

The flyer was married three times. After her third marriage, in 1931, to Williams, also a well-known British flyer, she said "This is the first time I have married a young man." He was 33.

Her first husband, Major Elliott Lynn, was 76 when they were married, and her second, Sir James Heath, was 75 at their marriage in 1927.

In the three years from 1926 through 1928 she flew more than 100,000 miles and in her lifetime flew 2,750 hours as a pilot in 77 different types of airplanes and gliders. She flew solo from Cape Town to London in 1928.

EAST SIDE.

The annual meeting of the Parent-Teacher Association of School 14 was held yesterday. Miss Catherine Coyne's 4A class presented a playlet entitled, "The Elves and the Shoemaker." Mrs. Michael Fazioli, president, was in charge of the business meeting and spoke on the highlights of the Cornell Institute meeting at Ithaca in April, to which she was a representative. Motion pictures were shown by Mr. Sweeney of the Troy Boys' Club entitled "On the Firing Line." Mrs. Bessie Paige Hansen, director of the Rensselaer County Public Health and Tuberculosis Association, explained the pictures as they were shown. Mrs. Hanson urged the public to attend the clinics that are free if one has the slightest doubt about an illness.

The business session followed with yearly reports. Announcement was made of the Spring Conference of Parent-Teacher Associations to be held Thursday, May 18, at Lake George. Those wishing to attend must make reservations with Mrs. George Patterson before Monday, May 15. The following delegates will represent the school at the meeting of the Troy Council at School 14 Wednesday, May 24: Mrs. James Beals, Mrs. Robert Howes, Mrs. T. J. Donovan, Mrs. Dennis Drislane, Mrs. William Phillip, Miss Grace Bauer, Mrs. Floyd Carlock, Mrs. Agnes Reid, Mrs. Nicholas Zaccaro and Mrs. John Osganian. A Flag Day celebration will be conducted at the school May 28. Mrs. P. H. McKeon, official of the state association, installed the newly elected officers. All officers were reelected with the exception of Mrs. James Bryans, membership and Mrs. Philip White, program. Mrs. George Patterson was presented a past president's pin and responded with a few remarks of appreciation. Mrs. D. A. Gillespie will be hostess for the council meeting May 24. A social followed yesterday's meeting and refreshments were served in charge of Mrs. Clarence Milanese, assisted by Mrs. Nicholas Zaccare, Mrs. August Lemke, Mrs. Chester Bagraw, Mrs. Lynn Merrill and Mrs. William Philip.

Association Meets.

The East Side Association postponed its meeting scheduled for last night and will meet next Tuesday night at School 16. At that time captains in the financial drive now being conducted by the association are expected to make reports to the executive committee.

Birthday Surprise.

Miss Mary C. Snyder, daughter of Mr. and Mrs. Stephen J. Snyder of 527 Pawling Avenue, was surprised pleasantly yesterday at her home with a party in honor of her seventh birthday. Playmates and neighbors attended. The table decorations were in pink and white with a birthday cake with seven pink candles as a centerpiece. The guest of honor's sister, Miss Louise Snyder, favored with piano selections. Those present included Mrs. Henry Rowekamp and daughter, Betty Rowekamp; Mrs. William Dowd, Kenneth and Nancy Finnegan and Miss Betty Swarthout. Miss Snyder received many lovely gifts.

Trinity Methodist.

The Ladies' Aid Society of Trinity Methodist Church will meet tomorrow at 2 p.m. with Mrs. Ernest F. Tripp at her home, 97 Twenty-third Street. A meeting of the Kilogne No. 1 Group of the Camp Fire Girls will be held tomorrow at 7:30 p.m. in the church annex in charge of Miss Dorothy Rudd, guardian. The Tanda Group also meets tomorrow at 7:30 p.m. in charge of Miss Ruth Locke. Her group will work on the trail seeker rank. Plans will also be made for a Camp Fire social. The Kilogne Group No. 2 will meet Friday at 7:30 in the church annex with Miss Ethel Locke in charge. The young married couples and young adults will conduct an informal gathering tomorrow at 8 p.m. in the church recreation rooms. Games, motion pictures and refreshments will be included in the evening's program. The teachers will be in charge of arrangements.

School 15 P.-T. A Elects.

Mrs. George L. Carrier was re-elected president of the Parent-Teacher Association of School 15 at its annual meeting yesterday. Others elected were: Mrs. Edward Buckley, first vice president; Mrs. Walter Allen, second vice president; Mrs. Anko Prins, secretary, and Mrs. Millard Blood, treasurer. Mrs. John Walthers was named corresponding secretary. Miss Eugenia Van Arnum, principal of the school, was chairman of the nominating committee. Mention was made of the card party and food sale to be held at the school Friday from 2 until 4 p.m. with the following in charge: Miss Van Arnum, Mrs. Carrier, Mrs. Walthers, Mrs. Allen, Mrs. Daniel Cowley, Mrs. Blood and Mrs. Clifford Cooper. Miss Esther Waterbury, kindergarten teacher, was chosen to make a summer round-up of children who will be ready for school in fall. The social hour following yesterday's meeting was in charge of Mrs. James MacAllister, Mrs. Chester Ott and Mrs. George Dearstyne.

Brevities.

Mrs. David Snover of Kinloch Avenue will entertain the Women's Missionary Society of the Third Presbyterian Church tomorrow at 7:30 p.m. at her home.

The Church School officers and teachers of Memorial Presbyterian Church will conduct a supper meeting tomorrow at 6:30 p.m. W. A. Bird, superintendent, will be in charge of the business session.

A tea will be held tomorrow at 2:30 p.m. at the home of Mrs. Ernest Ruether on Highland Avenue by the Women's Auxiliary of the Church of the Ascension. Troop 5, Boy Scouts, will meet tomorrow at 7:30 p.m. in the parish house in charge of scoutmaster, Walter Wells.

The Women's Guild of the Second Baptist Church will conduct a business meeting tomorrow at 2:30 p.m. in the church parlors. Mrs. A. P. Phillips will preside. Plans will be made for a strawberry festival. Tomorrow at 7:30 p.m., the World Wide Guild will meet with Miss Evelyn Roeck on the Brunswick Road. Miss Lois Hakes will preside.

PLAN RECEPTION FOR NEW TROY PASTOR TONIGHT AT CHURCH

Elders and their wives will form the receiving line at the reception which will take place tonight at the Church of Christ, Disciples, in honor of the new pastor, Rev. Cyrus M. Gonigam, and Mrs. Gonigam. The reception will be followed by the annual congregational meeting.

Those greeting visitors, in addition to Mr. and Mrs. Gonigam will be Mr. and Mrs. Howard Coonley, Mr. and Mrs. Louis A. Rochford, Mr. and Mrs. August H. Schmay and Mr. and Mrs. John Curtis. A committee of deacons, headed by John R. Jones, will act as ushers.

Mr. Rochford will preside at the business meeting when officers will be elected and reports received.

Refreshments and an entertainment will conclude the evening. There will be readings by Miss Mary Bass and solos by Donald Glossner. The Tri-City Little Theater will present a skit. Refreshments will be supervised by Mrs. Harold McChesney and Mrs. Nelson H. Schmay.

In the tarin of the construction of long-range bombers ordered in Canada last year, members of a British official mission have left England for Australia and New Zealand to explore air defense plans.

CRANIUM CRACKERS

Occupy Yourself With Occupations

Here are five occupations: palaeontologist, joiner, ophthalmologist, cooper, voyageur.

From the list of descriptive phrases below, can you select the proper one to fit each occupation?

Treats diseases of the eye.
Travels about world to make surveys.
Finishes house woodwork.
Studies antiquity.
Studies plants and herbs.
Makes barrels and casks.
A policeman.
A boatman.
Performs operations on the abdomen.

Answers on Page 16.

BALDWIN INDICTED FOR TAKING BRIBE

New York (AP)—Asst. Dist. Atty. Alexander R. Baldwin of Brooklyn was indicted yesterday on a charge of accepting an $800 bribe from Isidore Juffe, an accused fur racketeer, to neglect his duty in the prosecution of that case.

He was the third aide of Dist. Atty. William F. X. Geoghan to be indicted in the investigation of alleged official corruption in that borough being conducted by Special Asst. Atty. Gen. John Harlan Amen.

Amen's appointment by Governor Lehman followed a statement attributed to Juffe that he had "paid plenty" to escape prosecution. Juffe himself was indicted some weeks ago, with nine others, on charges of grand larceny and bribery.

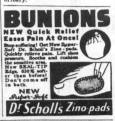

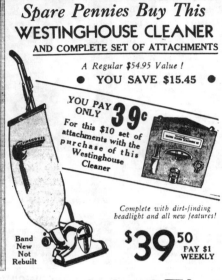

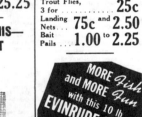

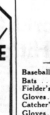

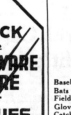

Tony Takes Terrific Trimming But Earns Crowd's Plaudits For Game Stand

REFEREE DONOVAN HALTS TITLE FIGHT IN FOURTH ROUND

Challenger, Helpless and Groping, Gives Greatest Performance of Career; Joe Says He Was Tough.

New York (AP)—The roof finally fell in on Tony Galento last night and nearly killed him, but before it happened the bold New Jersey barkeep gave a great fight crowd in Yankee Stadium a succession of thrills it will not soon forget.

Yes, Champion Joe Louis butchered the poor galoot, sent him falling to his knees bleeding and helpless so that Referee Arthur Donocan had to stop it in 2:29 of the fourth round. That was almost the preordained result. But Tony gave an account of himself that will enshrine him in the minds of those who saw.

Tony, the round-man, never took a backward step. In the third round, when his face already was cut to ribbons and the heart would long since have been beaten out of a less brave fighter, he swung a left to Louis' jaw that sent the champion bouncing on the canvas.

In the opening minutes, when the fight was young, he rocked the big bronze champion to his heels with another terrific left and for a fleeting instant held the championship in the chubby fists that have drawn ten thousand beers. He did everything he said he would do —except knock out "dat bum." Tony, the man they've all been laughing at, climaxed his career with his greatest performance.

Louis, who had knocked out his three previous challengers in less than a round each, said it was the toughest fight he ever had. In that terrible last round, when Galento was defenseless, Joe said he had to hit him a dozen times as hard as he ever hit a man before Tony finally fell into the referee's arms, groping for the ropes in a desperate effort to keep his feet.

Referee Arthur Donovan finally had to stop the proceedings at 2:29 of that heat.

Face Beaten To Pulp.

He intervened as Galento, no longer the shouting, boasting barkeeper, fell to his knees and wrapped his arms around the referees' knees, his face beaten to a pulp, with blood streaming from eyes and mouth.

But while it lasted, it was one of the wildest slugging battles the champion has had since he won the title from old Jim Braddock two years ago this month. Unafraid of the vaunted dynamite thrown by the Dusky Destroyer, the short, squat Galento rushed in with his tree-like left arm flailing, and actually had the champion hanging on from two fearful smashes to the chin in the first round.

In the second, Louis, who seemed to be extremely cautious of Galento's famed portside fist in the early going, opened up momentarily, and Galento went down from a left and right, delivered as Galento charged.

But Tony turned the tables in the third, charged in, and shot a short right uppercut to the chin and a left to the mid-section which suddenly and amazingly dropped Louis to the seat of his pants in mid-ring. The champion got up and managed to stave off the Galento rush the rest of the round, and with that, Tony's hopes came to an end.

Within Punch of Title.

At that point, Galento was within one punch of the World Heavyweight Championship. Had he been able to land one solid smash when the Tan Terror came up off the floor, had be been able to charge in and connect with Louis in his dazed condition, he would have climaxed one of the most amazing rises Fistiana has ever seen. But he just didn't have it.

So Joe came out in the fourth round, ready to toss his thunder. For a few seconds, they fought on even terms. Then Louis' ring greatness was proved. He moved in with the grace and rhythm of a perfect machine, and opened up. In just a moment, he had Galento back against the ropes and he smashed over left, right, left and right again to the jaw and head. Each punch seemed to open a new stream of blood from Tony's face.

Momentarily Referee Donovan separated them, but forward again charged the champion. This time he backed the challenger against the ropes on another side of the ring, but still near the Galento corner. Joe pumped both death-dealing fists into Tony's face more times than an adding machine could tally them. This blood-and-thunder assault proved too much for the game Galento, who weighed 233¾ to Joe's 200¾.

PANTHERS HOST TO MONITORS TONIGHT

Lou Maslan's Panthers will play host to the Green Island Monitors at 6:30 p.m. today at Prospect Park as the Islanders seek their first win in more than a season over the Panthers.

Al (Lefty) Bosko or Clayton Whitney will pitch for the Panthers with Roy Woolsey catching. Doug Rivett or Harold Kuentzel will hurl for the Monitors and Jim McMeel will catch.

Wrestling Results

By the Associated Press.

St. Louis—Ali Baba, 206, Kurdistan, threw Daniel Savage, 240, Kentucky, 5:56.

San Antonio—Everett Marshall, 226, La Junta, Col., defeated Rudy Dusek, 220, Omaha, straight falls.

Tony Galento Goes Down In Blaze of Glory

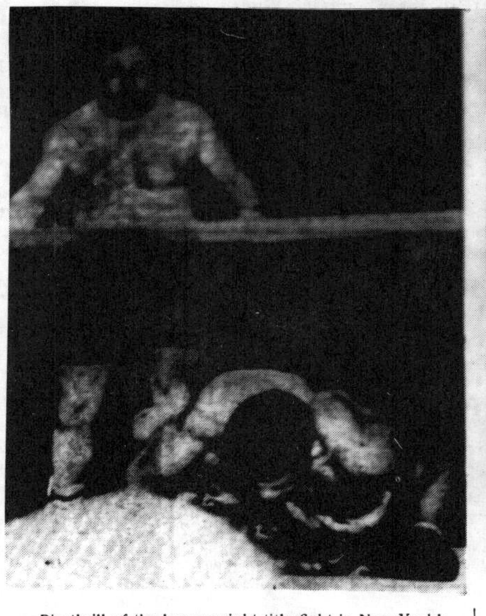

Big thrill of the heavyweight title fight in New York's Yankee Stadium was the third round scene in which Tony Galento dropped Joe Louis for a count of two. Champion Louis came back to win by a technical knockout in the next round.

Joe Louis' rapier-like blows finally told in the fourth round and the expected happened—exit Tony Galento by the technical k. o. route! Here the open-mouthed Galento is on the floor as Referee Donovan motions Louis away.

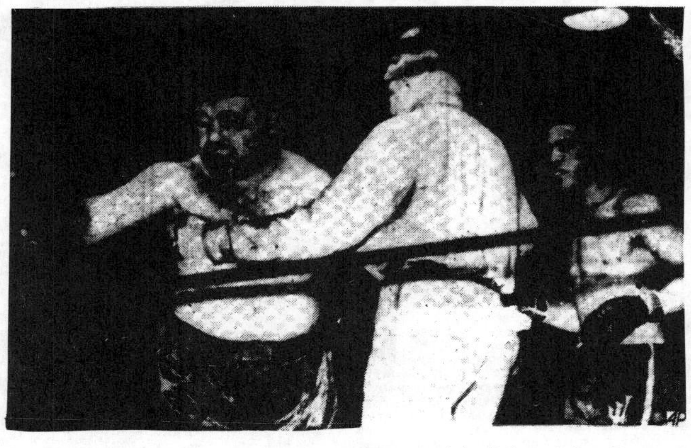

Bloody, beaten Tony Galento is shown the way out by Referee Arthur Donovan just after the latter had declared Joe Louis the winner on a technical knockout. This, the end, came in 2:29 of the fourth round, before an estimated crowd of 40,000 in New York's Yankee Stadium.

Tony Claims Never Threw Sunday Punch

New York (INS)—It may surprise you today to learn:—

(1) That it was a light left from Tony Galento that drove Joe Louis cowering into a corner in the first round last night.

(2) That it was a light left that caused the champion to waver, back water and then hold on more than once.

(3) And that it was a light left to the jaw that set Joe down in the third round.

You may be surprised, too, to know:—

(1) That the champion honestly admits he was badly hurt when Galento dropped him.

(2) That he was still groggy when he arose.

(3) And that he never unleashed more terrific punishment within so short a time as he did against Galento.

For further interesting details follow me into the dressing rooms of the champion and challenger just after the battle.

We're in the Louis dressing room where the visiting clubs dress to meet those other great hitters, the Yankees.

The writer opens up the barrage of questions. Was he really hurt when Tony dumped him.

"Sure was." Groggy when he got up? "Yes, I was." Can Tony punch as hard as Max Baer or Max Schmeling? "I think so."

How come Tony tagged him so often? "Well, I was falling in with my punches and he just tagged me, that's all."

Did he ever hit anybody harder than he hit Tony?

"I don't think so. Guess I hit Baer more but not as hard. I had to punch down at Galento."

Now into Galento's room where the Yanks don their monkey suits. Place is packed. Photographers, sports writers, and "yes" men fighting to get in. Tony sits on a rubbing table. He's wearing a bath robe, two gorgeous "shiners" and a rubber eye bag is being applied to his puffed features by Whitey Bimstein, his second.

"I just got careless," Tony keeps repeating. "I was afraid he might open up these old scar tissues on my eyes and that's just what happened. When I got cut I got careless. Then he tagged me.

"But, say, the guy can't take a punch and I'll knock him out next time sure. I clipped him with a light left and down he goes. I hit him with a light left in the first and he backs up like a scared rabbit."

Tony repeate dthis light left so often that I thought it must be something he had read, so I said: "Do you mean to say you could have hit Joe harder than you did?"

"Sure thing," our hero replied. "I never landed my Sunday punch. If I had, I'd be champion. Gee I wish I could see you guys. Something's running into my eyes."

Outside the sweating dressing room we saw Mrs. Galento standing in a corner, dressed very neatly and looking plumply pretty.

"Well," she answered our sympathy, "Tony certainly didn't let anybody down. He must have given everybody a real thrill. And I'm still proud of him and I love him."

And I imagine that's just about how all the fight fans feel about him.

RED WINGS GIVE UP ON CONACHER

New York (AP)—Manager Jack Adams of the Detroit Red Wings of the National Hockey League announced yesterday the club would not renew its option on Charley Conacher, 29-year-old right winger. Conacher went to Detroit last year from the Toronto Maple Leafs on a three-year option and purchase plan.

Connie Smythe, Toronto manager, said Conacher automatically would revert to the Leafs. He hinted several other teams were interested in acquiring him.

The N. H. L.'s board of governors vetoed a list of changes proposed by the International-American League in the five-year working agreement between the two circuits, which still has two years to run. A committee composed of N. H. L. President Frank Calder, Smythe and Art Ross of Boston was appointed to continue discussions with International-American delegates.

POLISH A. C. WINS FROM HOMESTEADS

The Polish A. C. defeated the Homestead nine last night at Geer Field, 13 to 3. It was the eleventh win of the season for the South Enders.

Chick Dwyer on the mound for the winners, allowed nine hits and fanned ten. The Polish A. C. made 15 hits off Grimes.

Witkowski, Edwards and Galusky led the attack for the winners while Grimes and Goldsberry were outsanding for the losers.

ALBIA NINE WINS FROM 4-H TOSSERS

The Albia nine defeated the Kiwanis 4-H Club last night at Wynantskill, 13 to 8.

Smith with two hits and Nuttall and Dundon with a double each led the attack for the winners. Powell with two hits was best for the losers.

Seemaker, Nuttall and Henningson formed the battery for the Albia nine. Bielas, Brust and Finkle worked for the 4-H team.

JONES NINE WILL PLAY INSULARS

The Jones A. C. will clash with the Cohoes Insulars tonight at 6:15 o'clock at the Laureate grounds. Both teams will present strong lineups.

Fermosca, Mattarazzo and Decker and Jacobsen will work for the Jones A. C.

Louis, Pastor Next, Smart Money Says

BY EDDIE BRIETZ.

New York (AP)—The betting is it will be Louis vs. Bob Pastor in Detroit in September . . . Louis said he'll fight Nova next, but Mike Jacobs wants the Detroit match and will go to work on Joe's handlers today . . . The Pastor end has been closed for days . . . This might mean Nova and Galento will go in Philadelphia in the late summer or fall, with the winner fighting the Louis-Pastor winner in the Yankee Stadium next June . . . Nova was around crying "bring on Louis!" but it looks like they'll decide to send him to school a little more first.

What surprised the boys was not that Galento hit and hurt Louis—everybody knew he could hit—but that he stood up so well under Louis' murderous punches . . . Nobody can question Old Tony's gameness . . . He was in there slugging when a lot of other guys we could name would have been on the deck and glad to be there . . . General Phelan said: "It was a good fight and on the level." . . . Nobody hollered gimmick . . . A couple of Bronx process servers charged into Louis' dressing room after the fight, but got the old heave-ho . . . Pete Herman, the old bantamweight champ, is blind, but he came all the way from New Orleans to be present.

Mr. Westbrook Pegler, one of our favorite authors, wants a niche in the hall of fame reserved for sports writers who have contributed a lot to baseball . . . If there are any minor league angles we want to nominate Cy Sherman of the Lincoln (Neb.) Star . . . He's been boosting baseball and all sports for 40 years—amost as long as Bill Klem has been calling 'em right . . . He's a unique character in that he always buys—that's what we said—his own tickets for the home games . . . Several years ago U. of Nebraska gave him an honorary "N" monogram . . . If minor league baseball owes any writer a little debt of gratitude, Cy Sherman is the guy.

SIDELIGHTS FROM THE TITLE FIGHT

Orange, N. J. (UP)—At 2:12 a.m. today pudgy Tony Galento pushed through the milling mob in his saloon and ordered drinks on the house. He didn't act like a man who had just taken the beating of his life, but his face was swathed in enough bandage to wrap a mummy.

"Yea, Tony," the crowd yelled. "We want Tony. Win, lose or draw you're our Tony. You fought him too clean."

Tony didn't linger long to listen to their adulation. He retired to the kitchen to talk with his manager, Joe Jacobs.

The crowd kept screaming about the unfairness of Referee Artie Donovan in stopping the fight while Tony was still on his feet. They didn't know that Tony had just come from the doctor. They didn't know that under those bandages 23 surgical clamps were holding Tony's battered features together.

Then the police came and cleared all but about 200 out of the saloon. Galento came out of the kitchen with his manager, and little "Sir Echo" Jacobs began challenging Louis for another chance to win the heavyweight title next September. He said if necessary Tony would fight Lou Nova to prove he rated another chance.

New York (INS)—All Harlem wore a grin today.

But there was praise for Tony Galento, the Orange, N. J., barkeep-boxer who crossed the Hudson with a song in his heart only to have both the song and his heart broken by the hammering blows hurled by a maddened Joe Louis in Yankee Stadium.

Up in the ebony belt they called Louis the "royal high executioner of the heavies" but admitted they couldn't understand how the roly-poly one managed to stay over three rounds and also send the champion to the canvas for a short count.

"That Galento—he's got a heart if nothing else," said one rabid follower of the devastating Detroiter.

"The butcher put another ham in storage," declared another as his teeth flashed in the dim lighted Lenox Avenue sector.

An ambulance went clanging down the street.

"Just going to get Galento," he added and emphasized his statement with a hearty, toothy laugh.

New York (INS)—Joe Louis can be taken! The smoothest, coldest fighting machine that has held the heavyweight championship in many years can be beaten. If it was a secret, it isn't today.

Galento—the beer barrel fighter, the guy who trains on thick black cigars, almost took Louis. He wasn't the man to do it but he almost did it and if the wrong man almost did it, the right man can do it.

Galento carried into the ring what other fighters have left in the dressing room—courage. Just as the Galento supporters expected, Tony threw his heart at the champion when he didn't have anything stouter left to throw.

New York (INS)—For 11 minutes 29 seconds of brawling Joe Louis will receive about $100,000, it was estimated today. It is the toughest hundred grand he has earned since becoming champion.

Gross receipts were announced as $283,303.68. The bout was seen by 34,852.

Including radio rights, which were sold for about $25,000, it was a $300,000 fight. Louis' share of the purse will be 40 per cent, with Tony Galento getting 17½ per cent. His end will come close to $45,000, which probably will be much easier to take than the fourth round with the Brown Meatchopper.

ALBANY SENATORS DEFEAT GRAYS, 5-3, TO SQUARE SERIES

Williamsport, Pa. A sparkling relief pitching job by Kenny Weafer after Paul Gehrman had been removed for a pinch hitter last night gave the Albany Senators a 5-3 win over the Grays to even their current series at one game apiece.

The teams clash tonight in the rubber game with Glenn Spencer probable pitcher for the Grays against either Bill Gilvary, who mopped up for the last out last night, or Lefty Jack Cannon.

Gehrman got away to a poor start in the first frame when Mule Haas doubled after a walk and a single to drive in two runs.

Albany got them back in the fifth, when Burman singled with the bases loaded. In the eighth Burman drove in another tally and with two on, Barath followed with a double for two more tallies.

Haas drove in the last Williamsport run in the eighth. After Weafer retired the first two batters in the ninth, Gilvary, a southpaw, went in to pitch to Alta Cohen, portsided pinch hitter.

The Scranton miners made it two in a row last night over the Springfield Nationals, but they had to battle through 12 innings.

The Miners triumphed 7 to 6 only after Penrose Miller blasted out a triple in the twelfth, scoring Tony Fiarito and Jack Baer. A homer by Gus Brittain earlier in the inning had given Springfield a one-run lead.

Scranton's performance shared attention with that of the Elmira Pioneers, who won their second straight victory against Binghamton, 8 to 5. Elmira came from behind in the sixth with a five-run rally, which sewed up the contest.

A series between Wilkes-Barre and Hartford was deadlocked at one game each when the Senators came through with a 7 to 6 triumph. Rowell drove in the winning run in the ninth with a single after the score had been tied.

Rabbit Maranville is back in the ranks. The 48-year-old manager of the Albany Senators yesterday announced that he had put his name on the eligibility list in order to play with the A's Friday night in a series opener at Elmira.

That game is "Rabbit Maranville Night" in honor of the former major leaguer who led the Pioneers to the second half N. Y.-Penn League pennant in 1936.

It is believed Maranville will replace Harold Blackstock, young shortstop who has been playing despite a badly bruised finger on his throwing hand.

Though 48, Rabbit is in good condition and has been working out daily with the team.

ALBANY.

	AB.	R.	H.	O.	A.
Burman, 2b	4	1	2	2	1
Barath, 3b	5	0	1	3	3
Jorgensen, lf.	4	0	0	3	0
Lewis, lf.	2	0	0	0	0
Weaver, p.	2	0	1	0	1
Gilvary, p.	0	0	0	0	0
Greene, 1b	4	0	0	7	1
Blackstock, ss.	4	1	2	2	1
Whitehead, cf.	4	1	2	2	0
Chozen, c.	4	1	2	5	0
Gehrman, p.	0	0	0	1	1
xJackson, rf.	3	1	0	2	0
Totals	36	5	10	27	8

WILLIAMSPORT.

	AB.	R.	H.	O.	A.
Rhein, ss.-2b	3	1	0	1	4
Hankins, rf.	4	1	1	1	1
McQuillen, lf.	4	1	1	2	0
Haas, 1b	4	0	3	8	0
Richardson, 2b	2	0	0	0	0
McNamara, ss.	2	0	0	0	0
Brancato, 3b	3	0	0	6	1
Fuchs, cf.	4	0	0	7	0
Gray, c.	4	0	2	2	0
McCrabb, p.	3	0	0	0	4
zCohen	1	0	0	0	0
Totals	34	3	7	27	10

x-Batted for Gehrman in 5th.
z-Batted for McCrabb in 9th.

Albany	000 020 030	—5
Williamsport	200 000 010	—3

Errors—McNamara 2. Runs batted in—Haas 3, Burman 3, Barath 2. Two base hit—Haas 2, Gray, Barath, Blackstock. Sacrifice—Gehrman. Left on bases—Albany 6, Williamsport 6. Bases on balls—Gehrman 2, McCrabb 1. Struck out—Gehrman 2, Weafer 1, McCrabb. Hits—Off Gehrman 2 in 4 innings, Weafer 5 in 4 2-3; Gilvary 0 in 1-3. Winning pitcher—Weafer. Umpires—Parker, Winters and Williams. Time—1:57.

TRIPLE 7 WINS.

The Triple 7 softball nine defeated the Manufacturers' National Bank, 13 to 12, last night at Knickerbacker Playgrounds. Blanchette, Palso and D. Wilson featured for the winners and Keegan and Evers for the losers. For games with the Triple 7 write A. Burkhardt, 39 Northern Drive.

THE STANDINGS

National League

YESTERDAY'S RESULTS.

New York 7, Philadelphia 1.
Brooklyn 6, Boston 1.
Chicago 8, St. Louis 4.
Pittsburg at Cincinnati, postponed, rain.

GAMES TODAY.

Boston at New York.
Philadelphia at Brooklyn (night game).
Chicago at St. Louis.
(Only games scheduled).

STANDINGS.

	Won	Lost	Pct.
Cincinnati	38	22	.633
New York	35	27	.567
St. Louis	33	26	.559
Chicago	32	31	.508
Brooklyn	29	29	.500
Pittsburg	27	31	.466
Boston	24	35	.407
Philadelphia	19	38	.333

American League

YESTERDAY'S RESULTS.

1—New York 23, Philadelphia 2.
2—New York 10, Philadelphia 0.
Detroit-Cleveland, not scheduled.
Other games postponed, rain.

GAMES TODAY.

New York at Washington, 2 games.
Philadelphia at Boston, 2 games.
St. Louis at Chicago, 2 games.
Detroit at Cleveland.

STANDINGS.

	Won	Lost	Pct.
New York	48	13	.787
Boston	33	23	.589
Cleveland	33	29	.532
Detroit	33	30	.524
Chicago	30	28	.517
Philadelphia	25	37	.403
Washington	24	40	.375
St. Louis	17	43	.283

Eastern League

YESTERDAY'S RESULTS.

ALBANY 5, Williamsport 3.
Hartford 7, Wilkes-Barre 6 (10 innings).
Elmira 8, Binghamton 5.
Scranton 7, Springfield 6 (12 innings).

GAMES TODAY.

ALBANY at Williamsport.
Springfield at Scranton.
Hartford at Wilkes-Barre.
Binghamton at Elmira.

STANDINGS.

	Won	Lost	Pct.
Springfield	39	21	.650
Williamsport	34	27	.557
Scranton	31	30	.508
Elmira	31	30	.508
ALBANY	31	32	.492
Binghamton	31	32	.492
Wilkes-Barre	28	37	.431
Hartford	21	38	.356

International League

YESTERDAY'S RESULTS.

Rochester 8, Toronto 6.
Newark 4, Syracuse 2.
Buffalo 9, Montreal 3 (8 innings, called by agreement).
Jersey City at Baltimore, postponed, rain.

GAMES TODAY.

Syracuse at Jersey City.
Newark at Baltimore.
Rochester at Montreal.
Buffalo at Toronto.

STANDINGS.

	Won	Lost	Pct.
Jersey City	41	28	.594
Rochester	39	29	.574
Syracuse	39	34	.534
Newark	37	34	.521
Buffalo	33	35	.485
Baltimore	31	35	.470
Montreal	29	38	.433
Toronto	25	40	.385

KNICKERBACKER LEAGUE.

The Knickerbacker Softball League opened its season last night with the following results: Wagars 11, Trylons 7; Fifth Avenue Merchants 4, DuBois A. C. 3; Gophers, 15, Twin Maples 8. The league will play its next games tomorrow night.

CROONQUIST SETS NEW RECORD IN COLLEGE TOURNEY

Des Moines (AP) Two kings of college golf were shaken off their thrones yesterday, but the joint downfall was scarcely noticed as Neil Croonquist, a pint-sized swinger from Minnesota, took the Wakonda Club course to a cleaning here with a sensational 69, three strokes under par.

Croonquist, on the light side of 150 pounds, blasted Billy Cordingley of Harvard out of the running with a 4 and 2 second round victory in National Collegiate golf tournament here.

Among other things, Croonquist toured the first nine in 31 strokes, five under par and a competitive record for the course.

Cordingley, a Des Moines native, had the dubious distinction of losing by the sizable 4 and 2 margin after shooting a one-under par 35 on the first nine and a 70 for the full 18.

The boys played out the second round even though the match ended on the 16th green.

Meanwhile Sid Richardson of Northwestern, medalist, and John P. Burke of Georgetown, defending champion, both were knocked off in a day of rain and upsets.

Richardson, whose 144 led the qualifying field by three strokes, took it on the chin from Art Floberg of Beloit, 5 and 3, in a first round battle.

Burke, title winner at Louisville last year, was eliminated, 2 and 1, by John Hayes of Marquette in the second round.

The day's casualties included all three qualifiers from the Northwestern team, which won the Big Ten title this year.

KINGSTON PLANS TO SIGN NEW MEN

Kingston, which returns to Troy for a Fourth of July game, may present new faces on that appearance. With Kingston's new park about due to be opened, Owner Matt Davies intends to strengthen his club.

He had two Troy boys in the lineup last night, Al Jacobsen and Jimmy Halligan. Jacobsen got one of the five hits off Filley, a lusty single to left. He caught a good game and his peg in the second, attempting to nip Yanni stealing, was true but no one covered the bag. Later he broke up a double steal by catching Willie Kane going into third.

Davies said he may use Jacobsen in games upstate.

In Troy's big seventh, "Shine" Kane hit a hard ball to left that ordinarily would have been good for a triple. He slipped and fell rounding first and was held to two bases.

Many favorable comments were heard concerning the new screen along third base which gives the bleacherites full protection.

With Jackie Lyons missing, Yanni went back to his old position at shortstop and Leo Ploski played second. Leo played a good second base. He went into short right for two fly balls and came up with all seven ground balls hit at him. All in all he had a busy time with nine chances.

Since the city removed the cobbles from the infield, Troy hasn't had a fielding error in the infield.

Charley Neff, strikeout king of the Colonials, was on the bench but Davies decided his club wasn't going to do anything with Filley so let Brown go the route.

Next game for the Troy club is Sunday afternoon at Bennington at 2 p.m. Don Steffins will pitch. This is a first half game and the final one of the half for Troy. Filley will get the mound assignment when the Bearcats return to play Scotia here Sunday night at 6.

An important announcement concerning assignment of umpires for future Troy-Cohoes games is expected soon. The teams meet at 116th Street Wednesday night.

Leonard's Work Against Yankees Tops Holiday Feats

A BIT OF THIS AND A BIT OF THAT

By JACK (Peerless) McGRATH

There is a faint suspicion that Joe Jacobs is writing the scripts for Larry MacPhail, peppy prexy of the Dodgers.

"We wuz robbed!" wailed Larry in a tremulous tenor that put even Joe Jacobs in the shade.

It all grew out of a fist fight between Leo Durocher, middleweight manager of the Dodgers, and Zeke Bonura, superheavyweight first sacker of the Giants.

But it wasn't the discrepancy in weights that vexed MacPhail. No sir. He was yelling because Bill Terry, Giants' manager, "runs the league."

The Durocher-Bonura fight, to rehash history, went like this: Durocher, running out a double play ball, stepped on Bonura's dainty foot and ole Zeke fired the ball—and his glove—at Lippy Leo, thereupon starting a fist fight on the right field line.

Again we emphasize it was not the injustice of the weights at which the fighters entered the arena that MacPhail wailed about. He "wuz robbed" because Lippy Leo was fined $25 for fighting back at Bonura, who drew a $50 assessment for starting the affair.

Putting his best pout forward, MacPhail shouted that Terry (1) was trying to run the league, (2) he was trying to intimidate the umpires, (3) he was always crabbing and (4) he didn't like the Dodgers.

And wasn't this wail to League Prexy Ford Frick will avail is uncertain. But the suspicion grows that Terry got the best of the wordy battle.

When someone remarked that the Bonura-Durocher main event wasn't much of a fight, Bill remarked:

"How could it be with Durocher in it?"

*   *   *

Harry Hesse, former outfielder for Albany in the old Eastern League, is now an instructor in the Eastern Baseball School at Woodhaven, N. Y. Gene Sheridan, another instructor connected with the school, played with Pittsfield in the old Eastern at the same time Hesse was starring for the Senators. Sheridan was a third baseman.

*   *   *

You're asking me I'm telling you: Basketball is the only major sport played in the United States which is purely of American origin. All other games either are direct importations from foreign lands, or are hybrids.

Dr. James Naismith created basketball while he was a physical director at the Y.M.C.A. in Springfield, Mass., late in 1891, but the first real game was not played until Jan. 20, 1892.

Basketball first was played with seven men on a side, then nine, then eight and now five. At one time the game consisted of three periods of 20 minutes each. Now it is two of 20 for college teams and three of 15 for the American Professional League.

*   *   *

Charles Benjamin (Babe) Adams, pitcher for the Pirates for 18 years, was born in Tipton, Ind., in 1888. He threw and batted right-handed.

Adams first gained recognition in 1908 when he pitched for Louisville, a club to which he had been farmed by the Pirates. He returned to the Pirates in 1909 to win 12 and lose three games during the championship season. That autumn the Pirates played Detroit in the World Series. The Tigers lost principally because Adams pitched three games all of which he won. He was in 27 innings, allowing only 18 hits and five runs.

At that time such sluggers as Sam Crawford and Ty Cobb were in their prime.

Adams remained with the Pirates until 1917, when he was sent back to the Western League. He advanced the next year to Kansas City, where he won 14 and lost three games, allowing only 1.67 earned runs per inning. This brought another recall by the Pirates.

In 1919, ten years after he had starred as a juvenile in the World Series, the "Babe" won 17 and lost ten for Pittsburg and gave only 1.98 earned runs. For a second time in his long career he was a pitching sensation, but now the fans marveled at the skill of a man of his long years of service.

"Babe" was one of the most powerful pitchers in the history of the game. His winning record in the National League shows 204 victories as against 104 defeats. He had blinding speed and a sharp curve. Adams allowed only 2.11 earned runs per game throughout his minor career.

KNUCKLE BALLER STOPS CHAMPIONS FOR THIRD TIME

Dutch's Work Gives Nats Even Break in Twin Bill; Tabor Hits Three Homers to Tie Mark.

By The Associated Press.

It seems that Emil (Dutch) Leonard, the Washington Senators' "old man with the knuckle ball," was just about the biggest firecracker in baseball's whole Fourth of July package.

And what a stirring triumph his 3-2 conquest of the New York Yankees was! It came in the first game of the double-header to their pal and one-time first baseman, Lou Gehrig.

With the season's biggest crowd there to honor the "iron horse," with the Yankees determined to make it a gala occasion, Old Dutch stood up there and mowed the Yanks down allowing only six hits in what certainly must rank as one of the most courageous pitching performances of the year.

And just superlative job must take precedence over some other magnificent baseball doings in a day when 249,541 holiday noisemakers watched their favorites in bargain bills.

Such doings, for instance, as Jim Tabor's three homers for Boston's Red Sox—two of them with the bases loaded—to tie the major league mark; or superb elbowing by Danny MacFayden and Milt Shoffner of the Bees in stopping the Giants twice; or Buck Newsom's shutout of the Cleveland Indians—or any one of a dozen other feats.

But overshadowing them all stands Old Dutch, coolly winning his third game 'from the fearsome champions, holding them to four measly runs in the thirty innings he has toiled against them this season as his knuckleball has done everything but laugh in their faces.

Dutch won, 3-2, but the champs won the second game for Lou by 11-1 as Steve Sundra shelled the Senators with a six-hit job that was no slouch itself.

Tabor's homerun feat was only part of the show as the second place Redsox slammed the Athletics all'oved the lot in their twin engagement, by 17-7 and 18-12. His act of homerun company but he stood out like Durante's nose.

The Cincinnati Reds stayed in first place though they howed to Mace Brown of the Pirates 4-3 in the second game. It was his first full game and he made the most of it. The Reds combined seven hit and Lee Grissom's shutout relief hurling in the first game to win, 7-4.

Especially Strong In Backs.

Early reports on 1939 football leaders are to the effect that Notre Dame, Fordham and Cornell will be especially strong in backs.

JONES A. C. WINS AT ROUND LAKE

The Jones A.C. nine turned back the Round Lake A.C. by a 5-1 score yesterday at the latter's grounds. Durivage pitched three-hit ball for the locals.

The Jones nine collected eight hits off two home twirlers, Reynolds and J. Mulligan collecting a pair of safeties apiece.

UNSEEDED PLAYERS WIN RIDGE OPEN

Glen Ridge, N. J. (P)—Two unseeded players, Jonn H. Curtiss of Ithaca, N. Y., and George Dunklin of the University of Virginia, reached the quarter-final rounds of the Ridge open men's singles and doubles play yesterday.

In the singles, Curtiss outplayed George McCall of the Arlington Players' Club, 6-8, 6-2, and Dunklin defeated David Hooperk of Maplewood, 6-2, 6-3.

Dunklin and Landon Buchanan of the University of Virginia beat Arnold La Force and Richard Hoover of Elizabeth, 8-6, 6-3, in doubles play; while Curtiss and Charles Allen of Charleston, S. C., reached the quarter-finals by a default.

Babe Ruth, (right) cheers up his pal, Lou Gehrig, who broke down when thundering cheers swept Yankee Stadium in his honor and the band played "I Love You Truly." Flanked by former teammates and present mates of the current world champion Yankees, all gathered to do him honor, Gehrig's shoulders bent and tears rolled down his cheeks.

Babe Cheers Up His Pal

Dempsey Gets Well Wishes From World

BY EDDIE BRIETZ.

New York (P)—Jack Dempsey has received nearly 2,000 wires from all over the world since he became ill . . . What other sports figure—Babe Ruth excepted—could tie that? . . . Don Budge, who was guaranteed $75,000 for 18 months as a pro, has passed the $55,000 mark . . . Lou Nova and family, take off for the coast Sunday . . . One way to save dough: Don't let the Giants and Yanks will renew broadcast rights next season . . . (Both are pretty well fed up) . . . The bankers who own the Hippodrome will tear the joint down when the 20th Century moves out this month.

Jimmy Grippe always shouts instructions to Melio Bettina, his light-heavyweight champ (in New York State) in Italian . . . If Johnstown and Technician ever get together again, you may be surprised . . . Lawson Little appears to be coming into his own as a medal play golfer . . . Another famous invalid who is doing all right, thank you, is Bill Klem, the "old arbitrator." . . . Billy Conn, who fights Melio Bettina in the Garden July 13th, starts training in Joe Louis' old spot at Pompton Lakes this week . . . Remember the $800,000 Roosevelt Raceway? . . . It's now a two-bit parking lot.

Shirley Povich, Washington Post says: "The suspicion is that the Nats can spot the Brooklyn Dodgers four brain concussions, a strong streak of inherent lunacy and a complete misunderstanding of right and wrong and out-daffy 'em . . . Brooklyn baseball is safe, sane and r a n k reactionary compared to the 1939 performances of the never - a - dull-moment Nats." . . . Lou Nova is picking up a few kopecks by making personal appearances with the Bar-Nova fight films in nearby small towns . . . He gets 25 bucks per appearance and averages three or four a day . . . Nat Fleisher in flying to Venezuela to referee Joey Archibald vs. Simon Chavez Sunday afternoon . . . Nat says it's the longest trip—3,700 miles—any guy ever made to referee a fight . . . Add horses to watch: Ken's Pop, the 2-year-old which romped home in its last two starts . . . Quite a few of the boys who bet the Yanks would be leading by 15 games on July 4 spent yesterday paying off.

Lou Gehrig Honored At Yankee Stadium

New York (P)—A bunch of the boys whooped it up at the Yankee Stadium yesterday for the guy who's known as Lou.

In the most amazing and heartfelt demonstration ever staged on a baseball diamond, they crammed into one hour all the appreciation and honor Lou Gehrig earned—but neither asked nor received—in his 15 years of service with the New York Yankees.

In the end it was too much for Lou, this "Lou Gehrig Appreciation Day" put on for the "Iron Horse" that infantile paralysis has put in the roundhouse to end the greatest endurance record the game has ever known.

Flanked by former team-mates of the great 1927 team and present mates of the current World Champions, all gathered to do him honor, Gehrig's shoulders bent, and tears rolled down his dimpled cheeks.

There were in addition to the current Yankees and their rivals of the day, the Washington Senators, 14 old-time Yankee players.

There was the one and only Babe Ruth, who, with Lou, made up the greatest "one-two" batting punch ever to give a pitcher the willies. There was old "Poosh 'Em Up" Tony Lazzeri, second-baseman on the '27 club, and Jumping Joe Dugan, a third base magician in those days, and Outfielders Bob Meusel and Earl Combs, Shortstop Mark Koenig, Pitchers Herb Pennock, Waite Hoyt, Bob Shawkey and George Pipgras and Catchers Wally Shang and Benny Bengough.

Then there were Wallington, whose first base job Gehrig took 'way back from in '25, and Everett (Deacon) Scott, whose old "iron man" record of 1,307 consecutive games Lou sent far into eclipse with his own all-time high of 2,130 consecutive games played from June 1, 1925 until last April 30, when he told Manager Joe McCarthy he thought his continued appearance in the line-up was hindering the team.

At the end Ruth and Gehrig posed together for the cameramen. And that was the picture you took with you—the Babe hugging Gehrig, the band playing "I Love You Truly," and far out in center field, the pennant of the 1927 World Champions fluttering as a solid roar of cheers cascaded down on one of the greatest ball players of all time.

Scores In American

Scores In National

THE WEATHER
Tonight—Fair.
Tomorrow—Fair.
Monday—Showers, cooler.

THE TIMES RECORD

FINAL EDITION

Series 1939—No. 196. (Entered as Second Class Matter at the Postoffice at Troy, N. Y., under the Act of March 3, 1879.) TROY, N. Y., SATURDAY EVENING, SEPTEMBER 2, 1939. (Published Daily Except Sunday) PRICE THREE CENTS

BRITAIN AND FRANCE READY TO DECLARE WAR ON NAZI GERMANY

Flying Back to England

The Duke and Duchess of Windsor, shown above in their most recent photo, were reported flying back to England today in the face of the war crisis. The Duke, it was said, will take an "important job" in the nation's defense forces.

DUKE OF WINDSOR AND WIFE TO FLY BACK TO ENGLAND

Former British Monarch and American Bride To End Exile in View of Grave War Crisis.

Paris (AP)—British sources close to the royal family said the Duke of Windsor was flying back to England today for the first sight of his homeland since his abdication from the throne Dec. 10, 1936.

It was believed the Duchess, the former Wallis Warfield, his American-born wife, would go with him.

These sources said the former British King sent for his private pilot, who left Farnborough, England, this morning for the Riviera, where the Duke and Duchess have been living.

The plane's departure time for England was not disclosed. Thus, the imminent threat of war has ended a voluntary exile of nearly three years into which Windsor plunged for "the woman I love." He abdicated as King on Dec. 10,

(Continued on Page 2.)

The Index

CANADA TAKES ON MILITARY ASPECT AS FORCES RALLY

Uniformed Men Placed on Guard at Many Points; Parliament Will Meet Thursday.

Toronto (Canadian Press)—Marching soldiers, uniformed men on guard at bridges, public works and utilities, the refusal of grocers to sell more than a few pounds of sugar at a time, brought to Canada the reality of war abroad today.

The Dominion's defense forces, rallied to service yesterday by proclamation of Prime Minister Mackenzie King, neared war-time strength. Parliament members headed for Ottawa and the special session next Thursday which will decide the extent of Canada's co-operation "at the side of Great Britain."

Provincial cabinets mapped plans for guarding power and industrial plants. Recruiting offices were opened. The defense purchasing board asked bids for manufacture of 28,000 pairs of ankle boots for the Canadian military forces. The German exhibit at the Canadian National Exhibition was closed.

Premier Mitchell Hepburn of Ontario offered his services in any capacity in a message to the prime minister.

Pending the meeting of Parliament, the government prepared to meet any emergency that might arise "in the event of the United Kingdom becoming engaged in war in the effort to resist aggression"—in the prime minister's words.

King's proclamation of the war measures act of 1914 put the militia, air and naval services on an active-service footing. Defense Minister Ian Mackenzie said the permanent naval services already are on active duty and the reserve forces will be called up as required.

POLISH TROOPS RESIST INVASION ON THREE FRONTS

German Envoy Handed Passports; Many Cities Bombed By Nazis; 16 Raiders Shot Down.

Warsaw (AP) — President Ignace Moscicki declared Poland under a "state of war" today as official reports said Polish forces were resisting German invasion on three fronts.

The "state of war" supersedes the "state of national emergency" decreed yesterday.

An extraordinary session of parliament assembled to enact emergency war measures, and the German charge d'affaires was handed his passports with a request that he leave Poland.

Under instructions from his government, the Netherlands minister assumed charge of German affairs.

A general staff communique reported heavy fighting through the night in the border area but there were no details. Fighting also was reported in Danzig.

Sirens wailed two air raid warnings in Warsaw but German planes failed to appear. There was a heavy mist.

The government announced it had answered President Roosevelt's appeal for nations to refrain from bombing civilians by issuing Army orders not to bomb open cities or expose civilians to direct or indirect danger.

It proclaimed, however, that Germans were making unprovoked attacks and Polish civilian losses already made Germany's compliance with the humanitarian request doubtful.

Warsaw awakened to air raid sirens at 5:45 a.m. But no planes appeared and no firing was heard. The all clear signal was given in twenty minutes.

Marshal Edward Smigly-Rydz addressed a message to Poland's Army, declaring:

"The time has come to fulfill our duty as soldiers. You are fighting

(Continued on Page 4.)

Polish Agency Reports 130 Killed In Air Raids

London (AP) — (By radio) — The British Broadcasting Co., in a news summary today, said that a Polish telegraph agency report declared 130 persons had been killed, 12 of them soldiers, in 94 German air raids on Polish territory.

The number of seriously wounded, the report added, "is large."

The broadcast also quoted an official Polish communique signed by Marshal Smigly-Rydz as saying the Polish army had generally repulsed the German attack, had destroyed seven German tanks and taken several prisoners in one section.

BRITISH CRUISER REPORTED TRAILING NAZI LINER BREMEN

New York (UP)—North German Lloyd Line officials were hopeful today that the continued silence of the $20,000,000 luxury liner Bremen was evidence that all was well and that it had not been stopped at sea by a British war vessel.

The Bremen left here Wednesday night ostensibly for Europe although it was reported that once out to sea it changed its course for the greater safety of a neutral port in South America.

One unconfirmed report that followed the Bremen out of the harbor was that the British cruiser Berwick, which earlier had slipped away from Newport, R. I., had been assigned to trail the great ship and take it captive if Britain declared war on Germany.

North German Lloyd Line officials said they felt the Bremen would have communicated with its headquarters had it been menaced. They assumed it was refraining from wireless communication to conceal its position.

JAPANESE ENVOY TO ROME QUITS POST

Tokyo (AP) — Recall of Toshio Shiratori, ambassador to Italy and long an advocate of a military alliance among Japan, Germany and Italy, was reported today by Domei, Japanese news agency. Poor health was given as reason for his orders to return to Japan.

(However, the Japanese government, since signature of the German-Russian nonaggression pact, has turned its back on the policy of close cooperation with the Rome-Berlin axis for which Shiratori had fought.)

Germans Open Attack On Westerplatte

First pictures of the German invasion of Poland are shown above. In the upper view Nazi troops are advancing on Westerplatte, adjacent to Danzig. Polish sources reported that this attack was repulsed. The lower photo shows smoke rising from Westerplatte after the German cruiser Schleiswig-Holstein (on left) loosed a salvo from its big guns.

PRESIDENT WILL OUTLINE POLICY IN "WAR" ADDRESS

American People, Meanwhile, Are Advises To "Keep Cool" in Face of European Emergency.

Washington (UP)—The administration awaited word today that Great Britain and France had gone to war against Germany.

President Roosevelt will address the nation tomorrow night to allay national anxiety.

The capital was convinced that Great Britain and France would be at war with Germany within 24 or 48 hours. Mr. Roosevelt's peace-protective policy for the United States was expected to unfold quickly when European hostilities became general.

A highly placed informant said it probably would be determined by Monday whether the neutrality law would be invoked and Congress summoned in special session to revise it.

Having pledged his every effort to keep the United States out of war, Mr. Roosevelt adopted a cautious policy of awaiting developments. So far he is committed to nothing beyond a general peace-protective program.

Officials were gratified by mar-

(Continued on Page 2.)

Say Hitler Carries Gun For Self Destruction

New York (INS)—Since his dramatic war address to the Reichstag, Chancellor Adolf Hitler of Germany has been carrying a gun on his person with which to end his life should the tide of battle turn against Germany, according to a story in the London Daily Express as read early today on an NBC broadcast from London.

In his Reichstag address announcing hostilities against Poland, the Fuehrer declared: "I will lead you to victory and if not to victory to my own death for I shall not live in defeat."

DUBLIN PARLIAMENT ASKED TO PASS LAWS FOR WAR EMERGENCY

Dublin (AP) — Prime Minist Eamon De Valera today called on the Dail (Parliament) to pass emergency laws for control of food, currency, transport and shipping.

Compulsory blackouts were ordered, beginning tonight, following a first, partial blackout last night.

An emergency powers bill before the Dail provides for censorship of the press, the right to regulate and control all essential services and "acquisition by agreement or compulsion on behalf of the state of any currency other than Irish."

The measure also would permit arrests without warrants.

SHIPPING NEWS CENSORED.

Paris (AP)—All shipping news in Paris newspapers was censored today. The papers were reduced to four pages to conserve newsprint.

Hitler To Respect Undefended Cities

Berlin (UP) — Fuehrer Adolf Hitler agreed unconditionally to President Roosevelt's proposal that the nations refrain from bombing undefended cities or anything but military objectives, it was announced today.

Hitler's message said:

"The opinion expressed in President Roosevelt's message that it is the law of humanity to refrain under all conditions of military activity from bombing non-military objectives is fully in accordance with my own viewpoint and in accordance with what I have always represented.

"Therefore I agree unconditionally to the proposal that governments participating in current hostilities give a public declaration to this effect.

"For my part, I already announced publicly in my Reichstag speech on Friday that the German air force has received orders to restrict their action to military objectives.

"It is self-evident that the pre-requisite for continuance of this order that the same rule be imposed on the air force of our opponent.

(Signed) "Adolf Hitler."

TOTAL BLACKOUT BRINGS NIGHT OF GLOOM IN LONDON

Trains Run Without Headlights, Street Traffic Crawls; Windows Heavily Curtained.

London (UP)—London and southern England emerged at dawn today from a night of such darkness that the glow of a cigarette on a street or road was startling, and the flash of a match dazzled the eyes.

An emergency blackout, which the country thought would be the first of many, was an almost complete success.

Music and laughter could be heard from behind black curtained windows. Automobiles were either without lights or showed faint purple and blue tinted bulbs. They were guided by tiny cross slits in covered traffic lights, or by prescience. Busses ran without lights inside. There was one serious accident. A bus and a private car collided at Twickenham and one man was killed. At such hotels as the Savoy here doormen used flashlights to guide arriving and departing guests.

Trains Dim Lights.

Not a vestige of light showed in the vicinity of Buckingham Palace, where King George and Queen Elizabeth slept.

On occasion the pedestrian came on a gang of workmen or volunteers piling up sand bags in front of buildings.

Trains had no headlights. They carried only small tail lights. Passenger coaches were unlighted. Locomotive fire boxes were screened.

Women Pray At Tomb.

People thought that it had come. There was no excitement, but there was a new spirt of comradeship. People who usually remain silent and reserved talked to each other in busses, street cars, subways and trains.

A new spirt was evident, too, in churches and in the vicinity of Westminster Abbey, where the Unknown Solider lies, and at the cenotaph to the war dead in Whitehall, near the prime minister's residence in Downing Street.

Many people, chiefly women, went to the Abbey and stood before the tomb with their heads bowed in prayer.

ALLIES AWAIT HITLER'S REPLY TO ULTIMATUM

France Will Fight Unless Germany Halts Present Aggression In Poland, Daladier Says; Polish Troops Resist Nazi Invaders; British Cabinet Placed On War Footing; Italy to Take No military Initiative.

BY THE ASSOCIATED PRESS

A tense world looked toward Paris and London today awaiting decisions by Britain and France on whether they would declare war on Germany.

A sober Chamber of Deputies granted Premier Daladier implied authority to declare war in a unanimous adoption of a war-budget bill of 69 billion francs (approximately $1,656,000,000).

While statesmen fought desperately for an eleventh hour peace in Europe, the Polish embassy reported that Warsaw had been bombed six times during the day by German warplanes.

The German radio announced that two German columns which had entered Pomorze (the Polish Corridor) from the east and west had effected a junction, thus bottling up Polish forces on the northern part of the Corridor.

The Berlin radio broadcast a warning that an air raid was expected on Berlin, shortly before Alexander Shkvartzeff, new Soviet ambassador to Germany, and seven members of a Soviet military mission landed at Tempelhof Airdrome.

Premier Daladier already had made France's position clear in a statement to the Chamber of Deputies that France was ready to participate in any eleventh hour peace efforts, but at the same time stood ready to fight for Poland if German "aggression" was not halted.

"There is no Frenchman marching toward the lines who marches with hatred of the Germans, but he marches knowing the very existence of his country is at stake," Daladier told the cheering Chamber of Deputies.

CHAMBERLAIN DEFERS STATEMENT

Prime Minister Chamberlain deferred his vital statement on Britain's stand until later in the day. It was presumed he still awaited an answer from Germany to Britain's and France's "last warning" to halt the Reich's armies.

Parliament was called for another emergency session tomorrow.

Without formally declaring war, Daladier bound France's fate to that of Poland by declaring:

"Is there a German-Polish war? No! There is a step in Hitlerian Germany's effort to dominate the world."

However, Daladier left a slight hope for peace.

"Even at this moment, if the Germans leave Poland, if they stop their aggression, France will not refuse efforts for negotiation."

"If representations are tried again we again are ready to associate in them," Daladies continued.

The Premier left no doubt, however, that France is determined to carry out her pledge of aid to Poland if war persists rather than to permit a dismemberment like that which befell Czecho-Slovakia at Munich last September.

"Gentlemen, today it is France that commands!" he said, concluding among the cheers of the Chamber.

POLAND VICTIM OF AGGRESSION

"Poland is the victim of aggression and is assured the support of nations of free men," Daladier declared.

Daladier took pains to pay tribute to Italy—France's ally in the World War and now Germany's axis partner.

"I am happy to render homage to the noble efforts of the Italian Government," the Premier said, referring to Rome's proposal for a peace conference.

"Efforts for peace, even though they remain futile, will at least show responsibilities."

Herriot told the Chamber: "In this moving moment many words are not necessary to consecrate the will for union which arises from every French heart.

"After twenty years' labor, which was not enough to repair the disasters of the last Germanic aggression, we are now in the presence of a new defiance.

DALADIER DENOUNCES HITLER

"The man who made Austria disappear, who martyrized the Czechs, who peopled the whole world with exiles, is using force once more with a mixture of brutality and deceit with cynical procedure which the Prime Minister of Britain already denounced yesterday."

Herriot said Poland—"This nation of fineness and culture

(Continued on Page 2.)

STATE AUTO BUREAU MAKES APPEAL FOR CARE OVER WEEK-END

Albany (AP)—New York's Motor Vehicle Department appealed today for "safe driving" over the Labor Day week-end as transportation agents forecast a record week-end for travel.

State Motor Vehicle Commissioner Carroll E. Mealey asked motorists to drive with "care and patience" in their travels to and from week-end resort.

"If each person who drives a car during the week-end and on Labor Day will remember to blend a little patience with common sense rules of safety," he said, "the holiday traffic accident toll will be materially reduced."

FRENCH AIR MINISTRY TAKES NOTED HOTEL

Paris (INS)—The Hotel George V., on the Champs Elysees, one of the most fashionable hostelries in Paris and a favorite of American tourists, was taken over in its entirety by the French Air Ministry today.

Air Minister Guy Lachambre and his assistants prepared to move in immediately.

SLOVAKIA PROTESTS USE BY GERMANS OF NATION AS WAR BASE

Warsaw (INS)—The Polish News Agency stated today that the Slovak minister to Warsaw had protested to Foreign Minister Josef Beck against German troop occupation of Slovakia.

The minister protested against the use of Slovakia as a base for warlike action against Poland and the "brutal disarmament of the Slovak army," the News Agency declared.

The minister was quoted as saying that the Slovak people at home and abroad "would never submit to violence of the third Reich."

NEW ZEALAND GIVES SUPPORT TO BRITAIN

Auckland, New Zealand (UP)—New Zealand will give her full support to Great Britain and has advised the British government of its entire approval of its course Acting Prime Minister P. Fraser announced today.

Ordinary and special reservists have been called up and arrangements made to inspect all ships entering defended ports.

Marketing·Cooking·Service

Chinese Really Know How To Cook Rice Properly

"Rice, the staff of life in the Orient, is not sufficiently appreciated in western countries," says Dr. Victor Heiser, prominent physician. "It is scorned as a dull and uninteresting dish, at least above the Mason and Dixon line. That's because it is not cooked properly, and usually appears in the form of a soggy horror, against which the little girl in Milne's famous poem very reasonably rebelled.

"It is an excellent food and we should learn to prepare it as the Chinese do, every kernel moist and thoroughly cooked, but separate from the mass. In the South, where rice is so frequently combined with chicken, many housewives know the trick. Properly cooked, rice is as flavorful as our baked potato, and the unpolished grains are much richer in vitamin B than that potato is.

The Department of Agriculture reports large crops during recent years have resulted in increased stocks carried over each year. So there's plenty of rice now on hand.

Here's a genuine Chinese recipe for cooking rice. Try it and you'll understand how good a bowl of rice really can be.

Chinese Rice.

One cup rice, one and a half cups water.

Wash rice thoroughly in several changes of water, until the water comes clear. Put rice in pot, add the one and a half cups water and boil five minutes with lid off; turn flame lower and let the water boil off. Turn flame to lowest point, put on lid and heat for twenty minutes. A crust should form at the bottom, but it should not burn.

Try Novelty Cake To Please Gang After Game

A novelty cake with a chocolate, a maple sugar cream pie and a mound of rich ice cream—three sure-fire successes when your young sons and daughters ask the gang in. A football cake, with a gridiron decoration in frosting will bring "whoops" from the lusty visitors. It's simple enough. Use a plain and easy-to-make frosting and give it a surprise note by a dash of peppermint flavor.

Chocolate Peppermint Icing.

Two squares unsweetened chocolate, 1 can sweetened condensed milk, 1 tablespoon water, few drops oil of peppermint or peppermint extract.

Melt chocolate in top of double boiler. Add sweetened condensed milk and stir over rapidly-boiling water 5 minutes, until mixture thickens. Remove from heat. Add water and peppermint. Cool. Spread on cold cake. When the chocolate frosting has set, trace white lines of gridiron, using plain sugar and water icing. To make your own children swell with pride.

Maple Cream Pie.

This maple cream pie will cause your youthful guests to tell their mothers that you are the best cook in the neighborhood. Watch your own children swell with pride.

One and one-quarter cups shaved maple sugar, packed tight in cup, 1 pint milk, 3 tablespoons cornstarch, 1-3 cup milk, 2 eggs, 1/2 teaspoon salt, 1 1-4 tablespoons butter, 1 teaspoon vanilla, whipped cream.

Place maple sugar and scalded milk in top of double boiler over boiling water. When sugar is entirely dissolved, add the cornstarch which has been smoothed to thin paste in the cold milk. Stir well and cook for about 30 minutes. Beat eggs well in large bowl, then pour the sugar mixture over the eggs. Return all to the double boiler and cook one minute. Remove from heat. Add butter, salt and vanilla. Cool. Pour into baked pie shell. To serve, cover evenly with thin layer of whipped cream.

Soup Satisfies When Days Are Cold

The chilly days are here when soup becomes a welcome addition to any meal. You'll dip and lift your spoon again and again and hunger will be pleasantly quieted when you serve good old-fashioned potato soup.

Here's a potato soup recipe that will become a favorite. Try it.

Cream of Potato Soup.

Boil together until tender four medium potatoes, sliced, two sweet Spanish onions, using a small amount of water. Drain. Save the water and rub the vegetables through a coarse strainer.

Cook together two tablespoons flour, two tablespoons butter, salt and pepper, one cup potato water, three cups rich scalded milk. Combine with the onion and potato pulp. Beat with an egg beater, add one tablespoon chopped parsley and serve topped with toasted bread cubes, if desired.

Hot Stuff — These Mexican Recipes

Enchiladas are hot stuff. When the American Dietetic Association met in Los Angeles for their annual convention, they went in for Mexican and Southern California specialties. This is the enchiladas recipe they used.

Enchiladas.
(About 10)

Four tablespoons fat, 1 cup black ripe olives, 1/2 pound white cheese, 1 large onion, 1 teaspoon salt, 1 tablespoon olive oil, 12 dried red chiles, 2 tablespoons fat, 3 tablespoons toasted breadcrumbs, 1 clove garlic, 1 tablespoon vinegar, 1 teaspoon salt.

Filling: Mince onion, salt and wilt in olive oil. Grate cheese. Pit olive.

Chili drench: Wipe chilis clean, stem, slit, remove seed veins and seeds. Cover with boiling water, cook until pulp separates from hulls. This should be a light puree. Heat fat in skillet. Brown flour or toasted breadcrumbs slightly. Add well-mashed garlic and vinegar. Simmer for twenty minutes. Assemble all ingredients and place a large, warmed platter on small table near stove. Keep chili sauce on stove, simmering very slowly.

In another skillet, heat fat and fry tortillas, one at a time. Do not fry crisp. Then immerse in chili and lift to warm platter. On half the chili-drenched tortilla place one level tablespoon grated cheese, one level tablespoon minced onion, and one tablespoon pitted olives. Fold as turnover. Repeat process until platter is filled. Then pour over all the chili that is left, sprinkle freely with grated cheese and minced onion. Garnish with balance of pitted olives. Place on warming shelf to keep hot, but not dry out.

Sunday's Menu.

Breakfast: Orange juice, fried ham, scrambled eggs, toasted raisin bread, coffee, milk.

Dinner: Chopped eggs and green pepper canapes, roast chicken, chestnut stuffing, giblet gravy, stuffed baked potatoes, buttered cauliflower, lettuce and grapefruit salad, steamed cherry pudding, foamy sauce, coffee, milk.

Supper: Tortillas, fruit bowl, tea or coffee, milk.

Tortillas.
(About 10)

One 15-ounce can of hominy, 1 tablespoon cornmeal, 2 tablespoons cold water.

Drain hominy, put through fine food chopper twice. Add cornmeal and water. Mix well. Roll dough with hands into small biscuits about 1 1/2 inch in diameter and 1/4 inch thick. Place moist napkin on bread board. Place "biscuit" on napkin and cover with another moist napkin. Place a second bread board on top of upper napkin, and exert an even pressure upon board until biscuit has wafer-like thinness. When the napkins are carefully removed, the biscuit will have become perfectly round with a smooth edge. Bake on extremely hot, slightly greased iron griddle. After two or three minutes turn with pancake turner. When tortilla is slightly browned remove and place in recepticle between cloths to keep warm.

Old-fashioned Doughnuts

FOR homey eating enjoyment, fresh doughnuts win first place this month. Old-fashioned yeast doughnuts fried to a rich golden brown are irresistible with a pot of hot coffee on nippy fall mornings.

Old-fashioned Yeast Doughnuts.

1/2 cup milk
1/2 cup lukewarm water
1 cake compressed yeast
2 tablespoons melted shortening
4 tablespoons sugar
2 teaspoons salt
1 egg or 2 egg yolks
3 1/2 to 4 cups sifted flour

Scald milk. Pour lukewarm water over crumbled yeast. Add milk to shortening, sugar and salt. Cool to lukewarm and add yeast and beaten egg. Stir in flour to make a soft dough. Turn out on well-floured (about 1/2 cup flour) board and knead until satiny and smooth (8 to 10 minutes). Place in greased bowl, cover and let rise until doubled in bulk. Let rise again until doubled. Punch down and allow dough to "rest" 10 minutes. Roll out 1/4 inch thick. Cut with doughnut cutter or in strips 3" by 1 1/2", cover and let rise until double in bulk. Place raised side of doughnut in hot fat first (375°F.) and fry, turning over only once. Drain on absorbent paper and sprinkle with sugar. Yield: About 2 dozen doughnuts.

APPLE COFFEE CAKE.

1/2 cup milk.
1 cake compressed yeast.
1/4 cup melted shortening.
1/4 cup sugar.
1 egg or 2 egg yolks.
1/2 cup raisins.
1 1/2 cups sifted flour.
3 to 4 medium apples.
4 tablespoons sugar.
1 teaspoon cinnamon.

Soften yeast in milk which has been scalded and then cooled to lukewarm. Add shortening, sugar, and fill greased cake pan one-half and sprinkle over apples. Let rise eggs, salt, raisins and enough flour to three fourths full. Arrange until puffy. Bake in moderately to make a stiff drop batter. Beat apple slices overlapping in rows hot oven 400 degrees F. 25 to 30 until smooth. Cover and let rise over top. Mix 4 tablespoons of minutes. Yield 1 coffee cake 8 until double in bulk. Stir down sugar with 1 teaspoon cinnamon inches by 8 inches by 2 inches.

ROLLED LAMB POT ROAST

4 1/2 lb boneless lamb roast (rolled shoulder or breast of lamb)
1 bud garlic
1 teaspoon salt
1/8 teaspoon pepper
3 tablespoons fat
6 small onions
6 small carrots
6 potatoes

Turn fire very low, slip a rack under der the meat, add the water and seasonings, laying thin slices of the garlic on top of the meat. Cover closely and let simmer for 2 1/2 hours. Remove meat to hot platter and thicken gravy with flour and water. Serve with boiled rice or plain boiled potatoes. Serves 12.

On this page appear 16 representative pictures from more than 4,500 local news photographs published by The Record Newspapers in 1939. How many do you remember?

POLITICS—An Eighth Ward voting machine in the spotlight.

COSTUMES—Formal, left, for Catholic Central High graduates, and ancient, above, for Bethlehem Rebekahs.

YOUTH AND AGE—A guest gets a drink at a children's party and Mrs. Nettie Root, below, is 101 at Valley Falls.

CURRENT EVENTS—The "Queen Mary" pays a visit to Troy.

HOT NEWS—An Averill Park guest leaves a fire in a hurry.

FUN AND FROLIC—Two women "Roosevelts" charm Poestenkill.

RELIGION—Bishop Edmund F. Gibbons mourns for his Pope at Albany cathedral.

PERSONALITIES—The Comerford triplets hear brother sound off on their third birthday.

DISASTER—A building collapse buries ten automobiles in Troy garage, above. Center, a truck driver meets sudden death at Waterford.

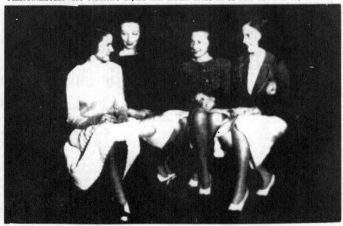

FASHIONS—Campus style show, the latest in spring hosiery a la Russell Sage College.

SPORTS—"How'm I doin'?" as seen at the Y. W. C. A. swimming pool, above. "Butch" Gilleron goes through the ropes at Waterford, center. Far right, a Troy High vaulter clears the bars.

THE WEATHER
Tonight—Cloudy, warmer.
Tomorrow—Light snow.

THE TIMES RECORD

FINAL EDITION

Series 1940—No. 24. (Entered as Second Class Matter at the Postoffice, Troy, N. Y., under the Act of March 3, 1879) TROY, N. Y., MONDAY EVENING, JANUARY 29, 1940. PRICE THREE CENTS

ADIE HITS PROPOSED RELIEF CUT

St. Patrick's Pupils to Return to School Studies Wednesday

LOSS OF $30,000 CAUSED BY FIRE IN CHURCH BUILDINGS

Temporary Quarters Secured Pending Decision to Build, Buy or Lease New Structure.

Plans were made this morning to care for the 434 children who formerly attended St. Patrick's School, swept by fire Saturday night, until a new school is built or a building purchased or leased in which to conduct classes. The fire caused damage to the school and rectory estimated at $30,000.

Beginning Wednesday morning the first, second and third classes of St. Patrick's School will be housed in School 1 and the fourth, fifth and sixth grades in School 3. The seventh and eighth grades will attend classes in the music room of St. Patrick's which was not damaged by the fire. All classes will be kept intact with the Sisters of St. Joseph to teach them.

Rev. Matthew K. Merns, 80-year-old pastor of St. Patrick's was out at 6 a.m. today visiting the fire-wrecked school building to see what could be salvaged from the rectory and helping with plans for caring for the children.

The two assistant priests, Rev. Thomas J. Quinn and Rev. Theodore D. Black, William A. Dunne of the Troy School Board, and John A. Bond, city building superintendent, visited Schools 1 and 3 this morning.

The young priests then turned their attention to the rectory and saved what they could of clothing, books, papers and personal belongings.

Father Merns' Statement.

Father Merns, who is now living at Troy Hospital, said this morning:

"First we must care for the children. Then we will decide what to do about the rectory and school. The insurance adjusters are at the building today and the trustees plan to meet as soon as the adjusters finish."

The board of trustees of the parochial school of which Father Quinn is chairman, will hold their first meeting late today.

Mayor Frank J. Hogan, himself a graduate of St. Patrick's School, was helping the assistant priests this morning with their plans for the future. A building near the church may be rented within a few

(Continued on Page 6.)

(A page of pictures of the fire will be found on Page 10).

CHILDREN SLAIN BY FATHER, WHO FIRES HOUSE, KILLS SELF

Tragedy Near Middlefield, Conn.; Despondent Man Binds and Gags Wife Outside Home.

Middlefield, Conn. (INS)—Despondent over financial difficulties a salesman for a Waterbury firm today killed his two small daughters and himself and destroyed his home by fire after carefully insuring the safety of his wife.

The victims were Alden G. Schlosser, 35, a ginger ale salesman, and his daughters, Alice, 5, and Jeannette, 3.

Armed with a small bore rifle, Schlosser early this morning trussed up his wife with a clothesline, taped her mouth to prevent her screaming, then carried her outside the couple's home at nearby Lake Beseck. His last words to her were:

"When you hear the first shot, it will be the oldest child."

Schlosser reentered the house and severed the telephone wires. Outside, shivering in the cold, his wife saw Schlosser going from room to room, setting small cottage afire. Then she heard thre shots in rapid succession, the first two snuffing out the lives of her children, the last marking the suicide of her husband.

Aroused by the flames shooting skyward, neighbors ran to the Schlosser home where they found Mrs. Schlosser struggling helplessly in her bonds. Charred bodies of the three victims were recovered by firemen.

GERMAN SOLDIERS ADOPT ALLIED SONG

Berlin (UP)—German soldiers now are singing the favorite song of Allied soldiers of the World war, "Pack Up Your Troubles In Your Old Kit Bag." However, the lyrics have been changed to "It's A Long Way Back to the Homeland."

Salvage Work Underway At St. Patrick's Rectory

Workmen carry personal possessions of the three priests of St. Patrick's Church from the smoke and water damaged rectory in River Street between Douw Street and Ingalls Avenue. On Saturday evening fire ruined St. Patrick's School, above the rectory, causing damage estimated at $30,000. This morning the priests salvaged what they could of books, clothing and papers from the rectory. The steps to the rectory made precarious going since they, like the rest of the building and a corner of the church, were encrusted with ice.

COLD TO CONTINUE IN TROY AREA FOR ANOTHER 24 HOURS

Forecaster Notes Deficiency in January of 222 Degrees; Below Zero Prevails Again.

Predicting no real break in the long cold spell for another 24 hours, Gustave S. Lindgren, head of the U. S. Weather Bureau, pointed out a strange coincidence today. War years are cold years.

In January, so far, there has been a deficiency of 222 degrees, or that many degrees below the normal average temperature. In 1917 and 1918, World War years, the winters were the coldest on record.

Cloudy Tonight.

The U. S. weather bureau predicts increasing cloudiness tonight and "not quite so cold" with a minimum of 5 degrees above zero. There will be light snow tomorrow.

Sub-zero weather struck the area again this morning.

The official low mark was 2 below zero, the weather bureau reported.

The Troy Area had lower temperature readings than that, Poestenkill reported 8 below zero, the town of Sand Lake from 8 to 10 below, Grafton and Berlin 10 to 12 below, Taborton 13 below.

Troop G barracks' thermometer showed 4 below at 7 a.m. The East Side reported 2 below.

Cold Continued Steady.

Mr. Lindgren said today that although there has been no really extreme weather this month, the cold has been markedly steady. The ice is thicker than it has been in years averaging from 12 to 14 inches on the ponds of the area. Second crops of ice have been harvested by the ice companies and most ice houses are filled.

On only four days this month, Mr. Lindgren said, has the temperature maximum been at 32 degrees or above. The maximum Jan. 12 was 32, Jan. 13, 36, Jan. 14, 38 and Jan. 15, forty degrees. All other days this month have had maximum temperatures below 32.

The number of degrees below the normal average temperature recorded this month becomes more startling when compared with other months and years.

In December there was a deficiency of 44 degrees. In January, 1939, the Weather Bureau marked up a deficiency of only 34 degrees.

MORE THAN $300,000 RAISED FOR FINLAND

New York (INS)—More than $300,000 already has been raised for the Finnish Relief Fund by newspapers of the United States, it was reported today by former President Herbert Hoover, director of the campaign. California led with contributions of $73,501. Pennsylvania was second with $39,074.

Arizona Bill, Famed Indian Fighter, Dead

San Antonio, Tex. (AP)—Arizona Bill, who hated a bed worse than a rattlesnake, died in one yesterday.

The 96-year-old Army veteran had fought Indians from the Rio Grande to the Rockies. Always he had insisted on sleeping outdoors.

Born Raymond Hatfield Gardner at Logansport, Ind., he was captured by Comanches who raided his father's wagon train in East Texas. At 8 he was traded to the Sioux for nine ponies and five blankets. He stayed with the Sioux until he was 13, then ran away. At 15 he was in the United States Army and later was a courier for Gen. Ulysses S. Grant. Wounded three times he was transferred to the command of General Custer as an advance scout.

Arizona Bill left the Army to ride for Wells Fargo's pony express out of St. Joseph, Mo., but that life palled. He went back to the Army as a scout in the Arizona Indian campaign.

Eventually he joined Buffalo Bill's Wild West show and traveled abroad.

Arizona Bill spent most of his last years in border Army camps.

POESTENKILL MAN HELD BY TROOPERS FOLLOWING FIGHT

Noel Sourier Alleged to Have Wielded Butcher Knife After Quarrel Last Night.

Corp. L. G. Egleston of the Averill Park Patrol, Troop G, New York State Police, last midnight fought and overcame barehanded a man much larger than he, armed with a long butcher knife with which he is alleged to have attempted to kill the trooper.

Corporal Egleston received a call from Mrs. Noel Sourier of Poestenkill calling from a neighbor's house, that her husband had put her out of the house and locked the door in her face.

The corporal, slight of build, went to the home and called for Sourier who is 64 years of age, to open up and let his wife come in. The man replied that he would kill the Trooper if he entered the house but Egleston pushed the door in with his shoulder and the larger man retreated toward a stairway.

Egleston thought he was going for a gun and started in pursuit but the man turned, armed with a butcher knife said to be at least a foot long and lunged at the pursuing officer.

The trooper dodged the descending blade and struck Sourier with his fist. Even then, with the man in a half-stunned condition, Egleston had difficulty in placing handcuffs on his prisoner.

He was committed to the Rensselaer County Jail by Justice of the Peace Garrett Ives and all the way to the jail struggled against the handcuffs until his wrists were severely lacerated.

Today his condition prohibited his being arraigned on the disorderly conduct charge under which he was committed. It is possible more serious charges will be laid because of his attack on the trooper.

PONTIFF TOLD OF NAZI TERRORISM IN POLISH AREAS

Priests and Thousands of Civilians Shot, Families Broken Up and Churches Closed.

Rome (INS)—A report charging a German campaign against the Catholic Church and the Polish people in sections of German-occupied former Poland, where 15 priests and thousands of other persons are said to have been shot, has been presented to Pope Pius XII with authorization of Auguste Cardinal Hlond, primate of Poland, it was revealed today.

Submitted to the Pontiff last week and detailing events up to Dec. 30, the report asserted that the German authorities in the archdioceses of Gneizno and Poznan are conducting a program of "real extermination, conceived with diabolical malice and unequalled cruelty."

In addition to breaking up families and jailing scores of thousands of persons, the memorandum claimed, the Germans have closed churches in various districts and have sent Poles to concentration camps in the Reich.

The report added that "this extermination... all too often is motivated by a perverse sadism."

Shipped Like Cattle.

Stating boys under 14 years of age and young girls—"especially the good-looking ones"—are being sent to Germany for a "Hitlerian education," the report added:

"The others, women and babies, sick and aged, after days or weeks

(Continued on Page 6.)

WOMAN DEAD AT 101.

Mohawk, N. Y. (UP)—Death of Helen H. Burill, a direct descendant of Col. Nathaniel Green, aide to George Washington, was reported today at a home for aged women. She died Saturday at the age of 101.

NEW YORK SALES TAX UPHELD BY SUPREME COURT

Highest Bench Rules City's 2 Per Cent Levy Constitional as Applied in Interstate Commerce.

Washington (UP)—The Supreme Court today handed down a series of important tax decisions, including a ruling that New York City's 2 per cent sales levy is constitutional as applied to goods moving in interstate commerce.

The tax cases produced a sharp division among the Supreme Court justices, resulting in dissents and split decisions in each case.

On the New York Sales tax issue—presented to the court in a series of three cases Chief Justice Charles Evans Hughes and Justices James C. McReynolds and Owen J. Roberts dissented from the majority view.

The other tax decisions:

Upheld the applicability of the Federal inheritance tax to irrevocable trust funds designed to revert to their maker in case of the prior death of the beneficiary.

Upheld constitutionality of a Kentucky state tax on bank deposits which taxes out-of-state bank deposits at a higher rate than those held in Kentucky banks.

The majority opinion in the important New York sales tax case, was written by Justice Harlan F. Stone. It held that New York City was constitutionally entitled to levy its sales tax on such materials as coal shipped into the city from out-of-state mines and other articles of interstate commerce.

Companies involved in the New York City cases were the Berwind-White Coal Mining Co., Philadelphia, the Compagnie Generale Transatlantique (French Line); Felt & Tarrant Manufacturing Co., a Chicago comptometer firm; and A. H. Dugrenier, Inc., Haverhill, Mass., vending machine makers.

MRS. LINDA C. ODELL, WIDOW OF FORMER GOVERNOR, EXPIRES

Newburg (AP)—Mrs. Linda Crist Odell, 81, widow of Benjamin Barker Odell who served as New York's Governor from 1901 to 1904, died yesterday.

A native of nearby Pine Bush, Mrs. Odell was first married to Van Rensselaer Traphagen, and her sister, Estelle Crist, was Odell's first wife. After the deaths of Traphagen and the sister, Mrs. Traphagen married Odell in 1891.

Odell, a Republican, was a member of Congress from 1894 to 1898, and in 1900, while chairman of the Republican state committee, was nominated for Governor.

Funeral services will be held tomorrow in the First Presbyterian Church at 2:30 p.m. with burial in Woodlawn Cemetery.

LABOR SECRETARY "WOOZY IN HEAD," LEWIS DECLARES

C. I. O. Chief Makes Blistering Attack on Miss Perkins in Demand for Relief of Jobless.

Columbus, O. (AP)—John L. Lewis, describing Secretary of Labor Perkins as "woozy in the head," today expressed contempt for persons "who refuse to raise their hands to relieve the distress of the jobless."

The U. M. W. president, addressing the United Mine Workers' convention, recalled that he had made repeated efforts to get Secretary Perkins and President Roosevelt to call a conference of labor, business and government officials to study unemployment problems.

Two weeks ago, Lewis said, he sent four labor men to discuss the situation with Miss Perkins, but she told them she did not think the problem was serious and to give the Democratic Party time and everything would be worked out.

"After three hours they went away woozy in the head just like the good woman who is Secretary of Labor," Lewis asserted.

"I have only contempt for the opposition of those who refuse to raise their hands to relieve the distress of the jobless," he continued.

Lewis said President Roosevelt four years ago told him and business leaders unemployment problem was "interesting" and asked them for a memorandum on it. Nothing further has been done, Lewis declared.

Concerning Miss Perkins, Lewis said:

"I like her a lot. I think she would make a good housekeeper, but I don't think she knows any more about the economic problems of this country than a Hottentot does about the moral law."

Lewis and his first assistant, Philip Murray, who said that unless unemployment was solved "uprisings might develop from people seeking a right to live," spoke for a resolution urging a government-sponsored conference on the problem.

Delegates adopted the resolution unanimously after giving Lewis a tremendous ovation. He concluded with the assertion that "I'm not going to take these things lying down as long as you're with me."

Lewis asked why the politicians had not answered his demands for a conference.

"Some gentleman may tell you that his favorite politician is a great friend of labor and is lying awake nights worrying about the problems of Europe and Asia.

"But," he shouted, "that doesn't put my men to work in the coal mines."

JOB QUITTERS MAY LOSE ALL BENEFITS FOR UNEMPLOYMENT

New York (INS)—Voluntary job quitters would lose their unemployment insurance benefits under a revision of the law being considered by the State Labor Department, it was learned here today.

New York at present is the only state granting these benefits to persons who leave their jobs voluntarily.

Employers have contended that such benefits are unfair because they go mostly to persons who leave jobs for vacations, to retire, marry or because of approaching motherhood. Labor leaders contend, however, that without voluntary quit benefits many persons would cling to substandard jobs.

Other changes being considered are a reduction in the non-compensible waiting period from three weeks to two weeks and a reduction in the basic tax rate of from 2 per cent to 2.7 per cent. Employers who pay the federal unemployment insurance tax at present receive a rebate of three-tenths of one per cent but this exclues employers with four or seven workers who are not included in the federal law.

BALD HEAD SAVES MAN FROM DEATH

New York (AP)—Cap. Ellef Tellefsn doesn't care if friends tease him about his bald spot. It saved his life.

The captain was crossing from a tug to his construction company barge last night when he slipped and fell into the ice-choked East River.

Two men heard him but could not locate him in the darkness. They were about to give up the search when they saw his bald head bobbing in the shadows.

They tossed him a rope and hauled him to safety.

KILLED AT CROSSING.

Tillsonburg, Ont. (UP)—Mrs. Ignatz Braun, 44, wife of a Tillsonburg tobacco farmer, was instantly killed yesterday when the car driven by her son Carl was hit by a train at a level crossing one mile east of here. Carl Braun, 18, suffered concussion but will recover. Eleanor Braun, 11, third member of the party escaped with shock.

Throne Waits?

Next ruler of Sarawak, British colony in North Borneo, may be the widowed Countess of Inchcape, above, daughter of the land's white rajah. This announcement by her mother, the ranee, followed ousting by the rajah of his 27-year-old nephew as crown prince and heir-presumptive to the Sarawak throne.

FINNS CAPTURE RED POSITIONS IN COUNTER ATTACKS

Defenders Smash Nine-day Drive of Russians, Who Leave 1,500 Dead; Soviet Bomber Shot Down.

Helsinki (UP)—An official communique today said that Finnish counter-attacks had captured Russian positions northeast of Lake Ladoga after smashing a nine-day Red Army flanking attack on the Mannerheim Line and turning back thrusts in the Aittojoki sector.

A total of 1,250 Russian dead were left on the fields of battle northeast of the lake at Aittojoki, on the south central front, in Sunday's fighting, the communique said. Another 160 were taken prisoner.

The communique disclosed that the weakening Russian offensive which had failed in nine days of hammering at Finnish lines was broken up sufficiently on Sunday to permit the Finns to make their first counter-attacks.

"Our troops . . . captured a few enemy strong points," the communique said.

Red Bomber Shot Down.

Finnish aircraft shot down a Red Army bomber at Pasila, on the immediate outskirts of Helsinki, during the fourth air raid alarm of today, which was at 4:57 p.m.

The air alarms which sounded in Helsinki today caused Finns to expect a new Red Army bombing campaign in revenge for what appeared to be Russian failure to break through the Finnish lines northeast of Lake Ladoga.

The Russians were estimated at Helsinki to have lost about 15,000 men, including perhaps 5,000 dead, in the nine days of assault designed to flank the Mannerheim Line on the Karelian Isthmus.

Over the week-end, they continued to attack but each thrust was weaker, according to the Finnish reports from the front, and it was believed that the offensive in which more than 40,000 men participated had been halted for the time being.

Profit by Mistakes.

The unsuccessful Russian drive to encircle the lake, however, demonstrated to neutral observers the difficulties which the Finns will face in coming months. The Red Army command appeared to have functioned more efficiently than in earlier thrusts farther north of the lake, where the Finns had destroyed whole divisions that fell into traps.

This time the Red Army profited by earlier mistakes and avoided traps set for them late last week by the Finns. The blasting fire of Finnish artillery against their rear communication lines failed to cut the advancing units off from their base or to pave the way for panic-stricken retreat.

Furthermore, fresh Russian troops were moving into the lines northeast of Lake Ladoga, where the quality of Soviet units appeared to be greatly improved and where the famous Marshal Simion M. Budenny, Russian Vice Commissar of Defense, was reported by Helsinki newspapers to have been put in command.

REDUCTION TALK LIKELY TO START FURTHER PROTEST

Slashes of Millions Among Suggestions to Be Taken Up at State Conferences During Week.

BY EDWARD McDONALD

Albany—An outcry against deferment of or a reduction in relief authorizations for the next fiscal year was made today by State Commissioner of Welfare David C. Adie.

Aroused by talk the Legislature might cut the $60,000,000 relief allowance in the Executive Budget by 25 per cent to avoid a tax increase, Commissioner Adie issued a warning of consequences.

Adie's blast may be the signal for a repetition of declarations from governmental departments a year ago that slashes in appropriations would be ruinous.

These would be evidence of an increasing opinion the Legislature may, despite pre-session bi-partisan conferences, be compelled to attempt a downward revision of Gov. Herbert H. Lehman's $396,000,000 budget.

Among the suggestions which will be taken up in conferences this week are.

1. That the $60,000,000 budget appropriation for relief be cut 25 per cent, with an agreement that the 1941 Legislature will make up any deficit.
2. A request that Governor Lehman revise upwards by $15,000,000 his estimate of revenue from existing taxes.
3. A reduction in state aid for education.
4. Cuts elsewhere in the proposed $396,000,000 budget for 1940-41.

Considering Relief Cut.

The suggested reduction in the relief appropriation is receiving chief consideration at the present time. Its advocates point out that December home relief costs dropped more than $1,100,000 and that the anticipated upswing in business may make $45,000,000 sufficient for 1940 relief reimbursements.

They also emphasized that the relief cut would not mean less aid for the needy or financial loss to the localities because they would retain on the books the statute requiring the state to reimburse the

(Continued on Page 20.)

HAROLD WALTERS GETS THIRTY DAYS FOR FALSE ALARM

Grant Avenue Man Pleads Guilty in Police Court; Investigate Another Needless Call.

Harold Walters, 25, 42 Grant Avenue, who admitted that he was the man who pulled a false alarm at 12:52 a.m. yesterday as Troy firemen were having a breathing spell from one of their busiest week-ends, will serve a thirty-day jail sentence for his act.

Capt. Michael B. Shea of the First Precinct, after spending the night investigating the case, brought Walters before Judge James F. Byron in Police Court this morning.

The police captain told the court that Walters had sounded Box 178, Campbell's and Sherman Avenues, early Sunday morning.

At first Walters pleaded not guilty to the charge but he later changed his plea.

Police are also investigating another false alarm received later in the morning. This false call was sounded from Box 448, Hoosick Street and Lake Avenue, at 4:45 a.m.

The Index

Society News

Mrs. Schuyler Guest At Two Parties

Miss Anna Nolan and Miss Elaine Foley entertained today at a cocktail party at the Foley home in Cohoes in honor of Mrs. J. Bradford Schuyler, the former Miss Mary L. Boland of Troy. Assisting the hostesses were Mrs. Leo F. Boland and the Misses Mildred Foley, Eleanor Dooley and Theora Marshall.

Thursday evening Mrs. Joseph A. Niles entertained at her home in Gale Place for Mrs. Schuyler at a supper party. The table was centered with gardenias and decorations were in blue and white. Guests were Mrs. Boland and the Misses Francis Daley, Margaret Leary, Marie Kerwin, Winifred Riley, Marion Miller and Teresa Conway.

Y. W. Program For Month Announced

February activities of the Health Education Department of the Y. W. C. A. will continue Monday at 7:30 p.m. when the regular monthly family relations program will present junior and senior students from the Russell Sage College Home Economics Department in the fashion clinic, "Clothes for the Occasion." Miss Dorothy Gordinier, chairman of city and county activities for the clothing students, has announced that the girls, wearing some garments that they have made, will explain and demonstrate "the philosophy of dress."

"The philosophy of dress is art," says Miss Gardiner. "It's using your mind. First you use it consciously through the help, advice, information and experience of others; then, through the assimilation of this knowledge you use it unconsciously, for it has become a part of you. To look well is to feel well, to feel well is to be poised, and to be poised is to be happy." Commentator for the fashion show will be Miss Bette Standish, senior, from Bridgeport, Conn. All girls are invited to attend.

Other February activities include a meeting of the All-Association Council, Wednesday at 7:30 p.m. On Thursday all association groups which meet regularly on this night of next week, are being urged to attend the Community Cavalcade at Music Hall.

Mrs. Lewis Rose will give her two final lectures on Current History this month, Wednesdays, the 14th and 28th at 11 a.m.

The council will sponsor the annual Hot Cross Bun sale Wednesday, Feb. 21, to raise money for departmental conference funds which are used for girl delegates to summer meetings.

Tuesday Club To Hear Talk on Armenia

The Tuesday Club will meet Tuesday at 2 p.m. at the home of Mrs. Seth N. Genung, 702 Third Avenue. The club usually meets at 2:30 p.m. but a business meeting has been planned for the earlier time.

The guest speaker will be Rev. Ephraim Jernazian, who will talk on Armenia.

Mrs. Genung will have as assistant hostesses Mrs. William H. Shumway, Mrs. Leland Smith and Miss Sarah Ide.

To Be Wed In June

Mr. and Mrs. Joseph Brassard of 79 Adams Avenue, Cohoes, announce the engagement of their daughter, Aline Brassard, to Arthur J. Peat, son of Mr. and Mrs. Nelson Peat of 17 Edward Street, that city. The wedding is scheduled to take place in June.

400 Couples Dance at Successful La Salle Military Ball

Among the La Salle Institute students attending the annual ball given by the Ladies' Auxiliary last evening at The Hendrick Hudson were: Col. Walter H. Dugan, commanding officer of the La Salle regiment, pictured at left, with his guest, Miss Mary Cooley. They led the grand march at midnight to the marches played by Jack Lanny and his Imperial Collegians. At top, from left to right, are Miss Joan Cannon, John and Thomas Thomas and Miss Doris Molloy. In the center picture are, left to right, Walter Duffy, Miss Jeannette Wilson, Joseph Rosamilia, Miss Mary Buckley, Anthony Colaneri and Rosemary Morse.

To Take Part

Miss Eleanor Holland of Saratoga Springs will take part in the annual winter carnival at Hamilton College this week-end as a member of the queen's court. Miss Sylvia Elliman of Scarsdale is to be the queen.

Bridge Tournament

The fifth annual contract bridge tournament conducted by the American Contract Bridge League for this district will be held at Wolfoerts Roost Country Club, Feb. 16 and 17. The women's pair event is scheduled for 1:30 p.m., Feb. 16 and team-of-four event, Feb. 16 at 8 p.m. Open pair events will be held at 2 and 8 p.m., Feb. 17.

Reservations may be made through the Troy representatives, Mrs. Thomas J. Duffy, Mrs. James F. Lucey, Mrs. Milton M. Wiener, Miss Sally Elizabeth Luby and Maurice I. Isenbergh.

Bridal Couple of This Morning

Mr. and Mrs. James L. Roark, above, are shown coming down the aisle of St. Joseph's Church following their marriage this morning. Also in the picture is George Roark, who was best man. Rev. James E. O'Neill officiated at the ceremony. Mrs. Roark was formerly Miss Mary Hill, daughter of Mr. and Mrs. Andrew Hill and she was attended by her sister, Miss Alice Hill. Mr. Roark is a resident of Albany.

Miss Schlegel Wed To H. G. Bovee

Miss Elizabeth Schlegel, daughter of Mr. and Mrs. John Schlegel of 465 Tenth Street, became the bride of Harry G. Bovee, son of Mrs. Margaret Bovee of Eagle Mills, this afternoon at St. Paul's Evangelical and Reform Church. Rev. H. P. Vieth officiated at the ceremony.

John Kienle of Eagle Mills played a program of organ music and Mrs. Albert Steinhilber sang. The church was decorated with bouquets of white carnations, white snapdragons and cyclamen and palms.

Mrs. Louis Paytrie of Eagle Mills, sister of the bridegroom, was matron of honor and John J. Schegel, brother of the bride, was best man. The ushers were John Bovee and Frederick and William Schlegel.

The bride wore a gown of ivory slipper satin, princess style, with a train and full length veil held on by a cap of orange blossoms. She carried calla lilies. Mrs. Paytrie was in blue velvet with matching accessories and she had a bouquet of snapdragons.

Following the ceremony there was a reception at The Hendrick Hudson. Mr. and Mrs. Schlegel and Mrs. Bovee received with the wedding party. Mrs. Schlegel and Mrs. Bovee were both in blue with shoulder bouquets of gardenias.

Later Mr. and Mrs. Bovee left on a wedding trip to Florida and upon their return will reside in Eagle Mills. Mrs. Bovee traveled in a royal blue utfit with brown accessories.

Mr. and Mrs. Bovee were graduated from Troy High School and she is with the Troy office of the New York Telephone Co. Mr. Bovee is with the Troy Buick Co., Inc.

Troy Women Officiate At Service

Delegates from two Troy auxiliaries to the Sons of Union Veterans of the Civil War were present last night at the installations of officers of the Elmer Elsworth Auxiliary, No. 14, of Waterford, and acted as installing officers. The ceremonies were held in the G. A. R. Hall in Cohoes.

Attending were Mrs. Mabel M. Bailey, Mrs. Florence H. Brown, Mrs. Sarah Wescott and Miss Mina Wescott, Col. A. D. McConihe Auxiliary; Mrs. Mary Mericel, Mrs. Frances Sloat, Mrs. Elizabeth McGarry, Miss Grace Cummings and Mrs. Harriet LeBeau, William B. Tibbits Auxiliary.

Miss Alice Morissey is the new president and Mrs. Dorothy Devoe, the outgoing president.

Sage Chapter Entertains College Faculty

The Troy Chapter of the Russell Sage College Alumnae Association gave a tea party today at Caldwell-Ide House for the members of the college faculty.

The reception rooms and the tea table were decorated with bouquets of flowers and the guests were received by alumnae officers and the chairman of the tea, Miss Marion O'Hanlon.

Miss Eileen Coffey headed the serving committee which was made up of Mrs. W. Van Kirk Brownell, Mrs. Edward M. Hutton, Mrs. Wray Jordan, Mrs. Prentice J. Rodgers and Misses Florence Beebe, Eleanor Brearton, Jean Cohen, Carol Flack, Frances and Helen Neary, Anita Rioux and Shirley Sager.

Bride of Today Honored At Recent Shower

Miss Betty C. O'Brien, daughter of Mrs. Elizabeth O'Brien of 9 Albia Avenue, was married to Thomas Riley, son of Mrs. Mary Riley of 1511 Fifteenth Street, this afternoon in a ceremony at the Sacred Heart Church. Rev. Edward T. Reilley officiated.

Mrs. Catherine Sullivan sang and the church was decorated with palms and bouquets of flowers.

Miss Helen Perry attended the bride and Peter Magneito was best man. The bride wore a wine velvet outfit and she carried an arm bouquet of Talisman roses. Miss Perry was in royal blue velvet with yellow roses.

A reception was then held at the O'Brien home and Mrs. O'Brien and Mrs. Riley received with the bridal party. Later Mr. and Mrs. Riley left on a wedding trip to New York and upon their return will reside at 554 Second Avenue. Mrs. Riley traveled in an aquamarine outfit.

Mrs. Riley was guest of honor at a personal shower Thursday evening given by the Misses Mildred Sheridan and Betty Maloney, at the latter's home at 7 Albia Avenue.

Games were played and Mrs. Rosalia McGrath rendered vocal selections assisted by Miss Maloney at the piano. Miss Perry and Miss Sheridan gave dance exhibitions. After the presentation of gifts, refreshments were served from a table decorated in pink and white, with a wedding cake as a centerpiece.

Other guests included Mrs. O'Brien, mother of the bride-to-be, Mrs. John Maloney, Mrs. Rosalia McGrath, and the Misses Peggy Kelly, Helen Wilson, Ann Kaperka, Louise Purcell, Loretta Langton, Marion Barber, Dorothy Page, Rita McLoughlin, and Grace Ryan.

ABOUT TOWN

VACATIONING IN FLORIDA

Mrs Mary E. Grimm and her brother, Frederick Grimm, left today for Florida where they will spend the remainder of the winter season.

ON CRUISE

Mr. and Mrs. Ralph Gallagher of Brunswick Hills left yesterday on a cruise to Bermuda.

IN NEW YORK

Duncan B. Kaye of North Lake Avenue is in New York City.

ARE AWAY

Mr. and Mrs. C. W. Frear of 65 Second Street are visiting in New York City.

BOARD TO MEET

The Board of the Junior League will meet Tuesday afternoon at the home of Mrs. William Mackay Peckham on Collins Avenue. The league will meet the following Tuesday.

Betrothed

Mr. and Mrs. Harry J. Ridgway of Crescent Terrace, Crescent, announce the engagement of their daughter, Miss Virginia Ridgway, to Carrol I. Anderson, son of Mr. and Mrs. Irving Anderson of 142 Third Street, Waterford. No date has been set for the wedding.

To Have Easter Wedding

—Lloyd Photo.

Mr. and Mrs. James F. Egan of 351 Third Street have announced the engagement and forthcoming marriage of their daughter, Miss Dorothy Ann Egan, to Howard R. Spratt, son of Mr. and Mrs. Patrick J. Spratt of 435 Third Street. The wedding will take place Easter Monday morning in St. Joseph's Church.

Lawyer Discusses Women's Place In Indian Nationalist Movement

Bhicoo Batlivala, native of India and a member of the English bar, spoke yesterday afternoon to the members of the Ilium Club on the part being played by Indian women in the government of India and its attempt to gain dominion status in the imperial system of the British Empire.

Miss Batlivala opened her lecture with a resume of the history of the women of India and in this refuted the general impression that they have always been mere chattels. Miss Batlivala said that until the coming of the industrial revolution and political unrest in the 19th Century Indian women were culturally equal to their menfolk and worked side by side with them in the economic field. Of course, she also said, there is much poverty which has kept even this equality at a low level.

Miss Batlivala strongly supported the Indian National Congress led by Mahatma Ghandi with the adoption of non-violent resistence as the means to attaining social and economic reforms.

As for India's place in the world she stated that India would cooperate with the democracies against naziism and fascism but that India demanded that the principles of democracy applied to itself. She said that India does not oppose any country in this feeling but that it is an "uncompromising issue of principal," that there is no hatred and ill will as in South Africa and in Ireland and that as soon as the system goes "we will offer our friendship."

In 1936, the speaker said, a constitution offering provincial autonomy was offered to the country and the great movement of the Congress was under way with 205 million out of the 280 million people there upholding the position of that body. Economic and social reforms were begun and a National Economic Planning committee started. However, the finance of the country was, and still is, she said in the hands of the imperial government as is shown in the fact that although India has to some degree free education under the Congress it was voluntary on the part of the workers and teachers. Since the opening of the war the Congress has become powerless and government is by proclamation.

Miss Batlivala also spoke against the situation of taxation without representation and the fact that a large portion of Indian wealth leaves the country either in the form of taxes and tariffs or as the salaries of the imperial officials.

In conclusion Miss Batlivala stated that a democracy in India would prove a "boomerang" to nazism and fascism for, she said, she has spoken with many leaders of these movements on the continent and in Japan and they have pointed out India to her as a model for their aggressions. On the idea that India cannot govern itself because of the racial differences she called this a "red herring" and that such a problem as does exist could be overcome if all religious faiths were considered equal. However, she said that so far in elections Christians may only vote for Christians, Hindus for Hindus and so on.

Following the lecture tea was served by Mrs. Raymond P. Neitzel and her committee. Two guests were present at the meeting, Mrs. G. Brooks Kafka and Mrs. Seth N. Genung.

Dinner Speaker

Miss Elsie M. Frost, instructor in home economics at Russell Sage College, spoke last night at a dinner meeting at Mildred Elley School in Albany. Her topic was "Color, Its Place in the Business Girl's Wardrobe." The latter part of the program was given over to an informal discussion on the clothing selection problems of the girls.

Guest of Choir

—Lloyd Photo.

Mrs. John J. Cairns of 21 Park View Court was given a surprise party at her home recently by the members of the former adult choir of the Sacred Heart Church. The occasion was to note their years of association at the church to which Mrs. Cairns came as organist in 1918. With the exception of three years, 1933 to 1936, she held that position until Oct. 1939 at which time she went as organist to St. Lawrence's Church. The party included the choir members, their husbands, wives and friends. Mrs. Cairns was presented a wardrobe traveling bag by the adult choir, and the children's choir gave her a black leather hand bag.

Form Newman Club At Business College

Students at the Troy Business College have recently formed a Newman Club. Election of officers was held this week with the following results: Miss Regina Kenny, president; Robert Conway, vice president; Miss Helen Purcell, secretary and Miss June Szumowski, treasurer. Rev. John J. Collins of Rensselaer, active in Newman Club work in this vicinity, spoke to the club at a recent meeting.

PREVENTION SEEN AS CHIEF AIM FOR WELFARE GROUPS

Methodist Union Hears Talk by Eric W. Gibberd; Complex Development Causes Problems.

Prevention of future social welfare problems rather than just efforts to alleviate those with us at present should be the objective of social welfare minded and Christian people, Eric W. Gibberd, executive secretary of Troy Council of Social Agencies, told members of the Methodist Social Union at their quarterly dinner meeting in Fifth Avenue-State Street Methodist Church parish house last night.

An interest in, and responsibility for what happens to human beings is not merely a desirable attribute of Christianity, Mr. Gibberd declared. This interest and responsibility are the essential qualities which mark Christianity as different from other religions.

Contributing Factors.

Depression has not been the only source of social problems, Mr. Gibberd emphasized as he outlined the major problem created by the millions of unemployed, with whole families in need of assistance. The complex development of city and industrial life has been one of the heavy contributing factors, he said.

"It is not enough that we continue the welfare work and institutions of another generation. We must strive, also to eliminate the basic causes in the future. Prevention must be our watchword," Mr. Gibberd said. "We must establish fences at the top of the hill as well as keep ambulances at the bottom.

"In the face of social problems, the Christian religion cannot remain impassive. The social responsibility of the Christian Church is not denied. It needs expression of its social gospel and social welfare needs the dynamic uplift and power of the Christian religion."

Avenues for Service.

To each person, the speaker pointed out, there are two opportunities for service the one a personal contribution and the other personal service. Last week's Community Cavalcade, he said, showed the effectiveness of organization made possible by unstinted personal service.

Through contribution and service, he declared, it is possible to give the help needed and to continue the humanitarian works of the past and, at the same time, provide the necessary support for the social engineering which, properly applied, will one day eliminate nearly all of the problem confronting the world today.

Lowell H. Bryce presided at the meeting and introduced Mr. Gibberd. The invocation was offered by Rev. James A. Perry, Th.D., pastor of the host church.

Methodist Social Union Has Quarterly Dinner

Enjoying the dinner of the Methodist Social Union at the Fifth Avenue-State Street Methodist Church last night are, left to right, Lowell H. Bryce, Eric W. Gibberd, speaker, and Mr. and Mrs. Frank P. Himes.

St. Joseph ASPIRIN
NONE SURER
NONE MORE DEPENDABLE
NONE FASTER
WORLD'S LARGEST SELLER AT 10¢

TWO YOUTHS FROM VALLEY FALLS SIGN WITH COMPANY A

Committee Named to Work on Outdoor Range Plans; Discuss 1940 Easter Dance of Corps.

Two more Valley Falls youths signed up for service with Company A, 105th Infantry, at the Company's weekly drill at the Armory last night, raising the total number of Valley Falls men on the company rolls to more than a dozen.

Bernard LaBarge, who had enlisted several months ago and then transferred to the inactive National Guard due to his having taken employment in the central part of the state, applied last night to be transferred back to active duty with the company and another Valley Falls man, Daniel Boone, made application for enlistment for a three-year period. Pvt. James Hennessy was honorably discharged upon the expiration of the second year of his current enlistment.

Several members of the Valley Falls group called on Capt. William J. O'Brien, company commander, last night and offered to arrange range facilities in the Valley Falls area for outdoor firing. It was decided to appoint a committee from the group next week to work in conjunction with non-commissioned officers in investigating the possibilities of the plan.

The drill was preceded by the first of the weekly non-commissioned officers' meetings to be conducted prior to the regular drills. Lieut. John B. Prout was in command of the group. Announcement was made that a written quiz will be required from each non-commissioned officer to be submitted next Tuesday night with full answers. The work for the drill and that of next week was outlined during the non-coms' meeting.

The company was in command of Captain O'Brien, assisted by Lieutenant Prout, and included a 15-minute company inspection; a 10-minute period of close order drill by squads; 10 minutes of close order for platoons, followed by thirty minutes of rifle and preliminary rifle marksmanship. This was divided into three groups in charge of the following: Sergt. Robert Beaudoin, sighting and aiming; Sergt. Anthony Willett, sling adjustment and firing positions, and Sergt. Felix N. Champitto, rapid fire exercises. The instruction period was concluded with a company close order drill.

A non-commissioned officers' meeting was conducted following the drill when it was decided to conduct a meeting of the company next Tuesday evening to prepare initial plans for the 1940 Easter dance of the Junior Company, Troy Citizens' Corps. Following the preliminary meeting next Tuesday evening, the Senior Company members will be invited to participate in the next session when plans will be discussed along the lines of reviving the Corps ball along the lines of its original form.

Supply Sergt. William J. Dinan began preparations last night of the Corps dress uniforms together with refitting of the uniforms to the present company members.

STEPHENTOWN.

Schools of the town were closed Monday in observance of Lincoln's Birthday.

Miss Mary Atwater spent the week-end in Dobbs Ferry with her friend, Miss Eva Shaw.

Chauncey Bateman left Saturday for Florida. He was accompanied by Charles Bloodgood of Albany.

Theo, youngest child of Mr. and Mrs. William Molt, jr., is convalescing from pneumonia following whooping cough.

Mr. and Mrs. Edward Evans of East Nassau are visiting their brother and sister-in-law, Mr. and Mrs. Elmer Evans.

Mrs. Marie Fitzgerald was a guest over the week-end and holiday of her sister, Mother Anna Laurentia, in Hoosick Falls.

Mrs. Addie Orcutt returned to her home in Fort Ann Sunday after spending some time with her sister, Mrs. Burt Bullion, and family.

Mrs. Mary Ward, teacher in the Goold district, is ill. Her daughter, Miss Mary Ward, student in St. Rose's College in Albany, is home.

On account of the regular meeting of the United Stephentown District Parent-Teachers' Association falling on Feb. 22, the next meeting will be Feb. 29.

Rev. and Mrs. Homer B. Silvernail recently attended the fifth annual study conference of the Congregational Christian Ministers, which was held in Springfield, Mass.

Miss Phyllis Reynolds entertained a former classmate in Albany State College, Miss Katherine Rectenwald, of Long Island, who is now teaching near Watertown, over the week-end.

Arthur Pease is among the group of Rensselaer County Farm Bureau members attending the 32nd annual Farm and Home Week of the New York State College of Agriculture, Home Economics and Veterinary Medicine at Ithaca.

Fourteen relatives and friends of George Fitzgerald, who is in the third year class of the Christian Brothers' Academy in Albany, attended the winter review and drill at the State Armory in Albany last week. George is now a member of the band.

Mr. and Mrs. Edwin Lawless entertained over the week-end and holiday Mr. Lawless' mother, Mrs. M. Fowler, and granddaughters, the Misses Lois and Myrle Swisher of Brooklyn, Mr. and Mrs. Carl Degs and daughter, Miss Evelyn, of East Orange, N. J.

The congregation of the Garfield Methodist Church united with the Berlin church Sunday for their annual meeting and fourth quarterly conference. The meeting was held in the Berlin Church. Rev. Ernest E. Tripp, district superintendent, preached the sermon and presided at the sessions.

BUSKIRK.

Harry Bailey who has been ill for two weeks is slightly better.

Miss Amy Bailey was a recent guest of Miss Mabel Hodge at Cambridge.

William J. Spink has returned from a visit with James Cummings in Watervliet.

Mr. and Mrs. Fred Buckley called Sunday on Mr. and Mrs. David Ryan at Beach Hill.

Mr. and Mrs. E. C. Rogers, Mr. and Mrs. Francis Rogers were called to Colonie by the death of the two-months-old son of Mr. and Mrs. Harold Rogers.

Mr. and Mrs. Stanley Wallace and daughter, Marcia Jean, of Glens Falls, Mr. and Mrs. Earle Sutherland of Cambridge and Mr. and Mrs. Kenneth Wallace and children of Valley Falls were recent guests of Mr. and Mrs. Clarence S. Wallace.

Lemon Juice Recipe Checks Rheumatic Pain Quickly

If you suffer from rheumatic, arthritis or neuritis pain, try this simple inexpensive home recipe that thousands are using. Get a package of Ru-Ex Compound today. Mix it with a quart of water, add the juice of 4 lemons. It's easy. No trouble at all and pleasant. You need only 2 tablespoonsful two times a day. Often within 48 hours—sometimes overnight—splendid results are obtained. If the pains do not quickly leave and if you do not feel better, Ru-Ex will cost you nothing to try as it is sold by your druggist under an absolute money-back guarantee. Ru-Ex Compound is for sale and recommended by Boxer's Drugs and good drug stores everywhere. Adv.

"They Say-"

Political Gossip from Our National Capital.

By HUGH S. JOHNSON.

New York City—There is no earthly reason why Mr. Roosevelt should not send Sumner Welles abroad as ambassador-at-large to Europe. There is nothing new in the idea. For several years we had Norman Davis abroad on a similar job. There is an ugly precedent in Mr. Wilson's "twin soul," Colonel House. But the very ugliness of it tends to avoid its danger.

Mr. Wilson finally came to feel that Colonel House's secret commitments had foreclosed and embarrassed his plans for world peace. That feeling became so bitter that in parts of Mr. Wilson's inner circle, they ran the Colonel's name and title together in pronouncing and forgot the "H" in his surname.

No Danger From Welles.

There is no danger of that kind of result here. Mr. Roosevelt has no "twin soul." Mr. Sumner Welles, in spite of a rather snooty Groton-Harvard exterior and his apparent authorship of the absurd "safety zone" around the Americas, is a good listener and a man not likely to exceed his authority in committing his country to anything not authorized by his boss. If we get mired in European mud beyond our depth, it will be by no over-reaching or indiscretion of Mr. Welles. It will be because our own All-Highest willed it so.

That the Boss has reached such a conclusion now is not likely. He couldn't as yet carry the country with him. But there is no doubt whatever that, like Woodrow Wilson, Mr. Roosevelt feels a heavenly call to make right the wrongs of the whole world. It is one of the strongest of the incentives that are leading him so to draw all lines as to make his reelection inevitable.

Argument for Third Term.

Whether intended or not, this and all his recent actions and expressions, tend to be, first, an argument for a third term and second, if he gets it, a mandate to go farther in mixing us in European affairs.

The argument will be that, by this increasingly close contact with the interior stresses and strains of the European vortex, no new administration would be as well fitted to deal with it. If he is overwhelmingly elected, the "mandate" will be that his pre-election actions sufficiently revealed his purpose to take a dominant part in the reconstruction of the world and that his election would indicate a vote of confidence in that policy and a popular command to carry it further.

The effect, if not the purpose of sending Mr. Welles on this mission when neither belligerent seems to have requested it, or even especially to welcome it, is the cleverest kind of both personal and political strategy.

Berle Seen Great 'Thinker.'

Mr. Welles has a colleague and Mr. Roosevelt an international adviser in Assistant Secretary of State, Adolf Berle, the ex-infant prodigy or—if you like an alternative phrasing—the infant ex-prodigy. Mr. Berle has recently uttered very expansive thoughts on our coming reenactment of our 1919 role as saviour of the world. We would again bail out its battered hulk financially by the use of the gold we have purchased from it at nearly double its value—giving it back if necessary.

The generosity of some great "thinkers" with other people's money is almost divine. In addition to generosity, Mr. Berle has the supreme self-confidence of a really brilliant intellect. Without a misgiving, he would undertake the financial reorganization of Heaven without a retainer, or charge Hell with a bucket of water. So, also, it is to be feared, would the President.

None of these are dangers to be very much feared if they are clearly and promptly recognized. Our people are a long way from being ready again to be the world's boob fat boy with the bag of candy. We won't be, if we just don't go to sleep with the national thumb in the mouth of any aspiring international messiah.

ITCHING OF ECZEMA
To subdue the desire to scratch and relieve the burning irritation rely on the soothing medication of
RESINOL

REG. $4
VONETTE Permanent WAVE
2 for $4.01
MON., TUES., WED.
SHAMPOO and WAVE 50c
CHARM BEAUTY SALON
5 THIRD ST.
TROY 6943
OPEN EVENINGS

DE SOTO
_PRICED THIS YEAR
$20 to $48 Lower
Yet Whole Car is Bigger... Packed With New Value!

Car illustrated is De Soto De Luxe Sedan, $905 at Detroit

Here's the Biggest Buy in Its Field! High Quality Workmanship . . . 100 Horsepower Performance . . . 122½" Wheelbase . . . All at a Sensationally Low Price!

HERE'S STYLE, POWER AND BIGNESS, all at a lower price! Think of it! . . . all this big-car luxury . . . yet, this year, De Soto's prices are actually $20 to $48 lower!

There's brilliant, new performance in De Soto's big, Super Economy Engine . . . unbelievable comfort in De Soto's new, wider seats, new Floating Ride! But find out about these thrills for yourself! Drive a De Soto before you buy any car!

Remember, you'll get a *good* deal from your De Soto dealer. See him today. DE SOTO DIVISION OF CHRYSLER CORPORATION, Detroit.

MAJOR BOWES, C.B.S. NETWORK, THURS., 9-10 P. M., E. S. T.

THIS YEAR'S PRICES $20 — $48 LOWER!
De Luxe Coupe $845 | De Luxe Sedan $905
Delivered at Detroit, Michigan, Federal taxes included. Transportation, state and local taxes, if any, extra.

LOOK AT THIS VALUE!
Advanced Styling • 100 Horsepower Engine • 122½" Wheelbase • New Floating Ride • Perfected Handy Shift Sealed Beam Headlights • Bigger Windows • Rear Doors Full Width at Bottom • Wider Seats • Warning Signals on All Dash Gauges • Larger Rear Window Non-slam Doors Sealed Against Dust, Drafts.
LOOK — RIDE — THEN DECIDE!

★ ★ DE SOTO ★ ★
THE GREAT AMERICAN FAMILY CAR
DE SOTO AND PLYMOUTH DEALERS
FRANK A. RICHTER, Inc.
Second and Division Sts. Troy 6710-6711
ASSOCIATE DEALERS
WALTON MOTORS, WATERVLIET
H. E. HULL & SONS, COHOES

SHARLETS SHOP

3-THIRD ST. OPPOSITE FREARS-TROY
QUITTING BUSINESS FOREVER
$15,000 STOCK and FIXTURES
ORDERED SOLD BY STOCK ADJUSTER IN 8 DAYS TIME

COME AND BUY AS YOU NEVER HAVE BEFORE! THIS GROUP OF ARTICLES VALUES $1.00 $1.50 $2.00 WILL ALL GO FOR 15c
25 AND 50c

AS FOLLOWS SILK and SATIN SLIPS, GOWNS, BLOUSES, SKIRTS, SWEATERS, DANCE SETS, GLOVES, etc. YOUR CHOICE 15c 25c
ALL SALES FINAL
EXTRA SALES GIRLS Wanted
After years of honorable and successful business, Sharlets, 3 Third St. and 294 River St., Troy, is forced to sell out to the bare walls and take a terrific loss on stock and fixtures. It will pay you to wait in line when sale opens Thursday at 9:35 A. M.
SALE OPENS THURS. 9:35 A. M.

Silk DRESSES
A GROUP OF 200 DRESSES REGULAR $3.00 $5.00 WILL SELL FAST FOR 70c AND $1.30
NOTICE! NO MATTER WHERE YOU LIVE OR HOW FAR YOU HAVE TO TRAVEL, COME TO THIS GOING OUT OF BUSINESS SALE AND YOU WILL NOT BE DISAPPOINTED.
Value $4.95
SILK and FLANNEL HOUSE COATS SPORT JACKET, Etc. $1.00 Value $4.95
All Sales Final
ALL WOOL SKIRTS Value $1.98 50c

POGGI INDICTED FOR LOCAL ASSAULT

New York (AP)—John Poggi, 43, financial district newsstand operator, was indicted yesterday on a charge of first degree assault with intent to kill in connection with the mysterious attack on Milton B. Logan, former president of the American Art Association-Anderson Galleries.

The charge grew out of an alleged "murder for insurance" conspiracy laid to Logan's former business associate, John T. Geery, who subsequently committed suicide.

BLAME YOUR LIVER IF—

If your liver doesn't secrete 20 to 30 ounces of bile every day into your intestines—constipation with its headaches, mental dullness and that "half-alive" feeling often result. So you see how important it is to keep bile flowing freely! And what finer aid could one desire than Dr. Edwards' Olive Tablets, used so successfully for years by Dr. F. M. Edwards for treating his patients for constipation and sluggish liver bile.

Olive Tablets are unsurpassed in effectiveness because they stimulate liver bile to help digest fatty foods, they tone up muscular intestinal action, at the same time help elimination. Being purely vegetable, Olive Tablets are wonderful! Test their supreme goodness TONIGHT! 15¢, 30¢, 60¢. All drugstores.

IN RACE WITHOUT RESERVATIONS, FARLEY DECLARES

Postmaster General Says His Name Will Be Presented Before Democratic Convention.

Boston (AP)—Postmaster General James A. Farley planted himself solidly in the fight for the Democratic presidential nomination yesterday, asserting without any reservations whatsoever that his name would be presented to the Democratic national convention at Chicago.

The very positiveness of his statement magnified its political significance in view of his previous silence over his official entrance in the Massachusetts presidential primary and because of the widespread speculation as to whether President Roosevelt would seek a third term.

Farley's statement was made in Springfield, where he conferred with Massachusetts party leaders before motoring to the suburbs of Boston to deliver an address to Wellesley College students on the subject, "Behind the Ballots."

The Postmaster General first was asked about his purpose in granting William Burke, chairman of the Massachusetts state Democratic committee, his power of attorney—as required under this state's laws —to enter a slate of delegates in the Bay State presidential primary pledged to him.

Subsequently Shadowed in Doubt.

That move—initially interpreted as meaning that he was in the field "on his own"—subsequently was shadowed in doubt by Burke's announcement that he was entering the slate pledged to the Postmaster General in the belief that the President would not seek a third term, and with the assumption that, if he did, he would receive the support of "Mr. Farley and the Democratic party as a whole."

Until yesterday, neither the President, nor Burke, nor Farley himself had said anything to clarify even partially the situation which many of Massachusetts' politicians and political observers found perplexing.

Even with that doubt, however, little opposition to the Farley slate has developed. With the deadline having passed for additional entrances, in only five of Massachusetts' 15 congressional districts do the Farley candidates face a contest from "independents."

At the same time, in response to questions, Farley said flatly that he was "in no combination with anyone." Close associates of Vice President Garner said in Washington earlier this week that he was seeking a political alliance with Farley in an effort to prevent a third term nomination.

The Democratic national committee chairman expressed belief, also, that the "accomplishments of the Democratic administration will be the platform upon which the Democratic nominee for President, whoever he may be, will campaign this fall."

pearance of deciding to make a statement on the spur of the moment.

"To clear up any misunderstanding," the Democratic national committee chairman told newspapermen, "let me say that my name will be presented to the Democratic national convention at Chicago, and that's that."

"Frankly, Without Reservation."

"I am sure that anyone who has known me during my political career will know that I make that statement frankly and without reservation."

Immediately, Farley was asked whether this meant the President had decided against seeking a third term, or whether he meant to convey that he was in the fight to the finish regardless of Mr. Roosevelt's intentions. Smiling, he evaded every inquiry. He also met with the same diplomatic "silence" a question as to whether he would accept the second place on the Democratic ticket in the event that he could not get the presidential nomination.

Character Building Agencies of the Community Chest

Marie Nikles, Julie Nugent and Mary Peterson, left to right, practice typing and general stenography at the Troy Y. W. C. A. classes for girls in various subjects is one of the many forms of service to the community by the Y. W. C. A.

Vocational Project Helps Y.W.C.A. Girls

The Young Women's Christian Association is conducting a program of vocational guidance for unemployed women, especially girls just out of high school who have never had a job, in a new project which leaders of the association planned to meet a new community need.

With the cooperation of the school authorities, a special committee of the association last fall circulated a questionnaire among the girl graduates of the various high schools in this city and vicinity in 1937, 1938 and 1939 in an attempt to learn what special vocational help any of the girls might need. More than 12 per cent of the girls questioned responded to the questionnaire and the association

decided on the basis of the information obtained, to expand its program to include assistance for the community's unemployed young women.

Because the girls feared they would lose their skill in the various techniques they had learned in school unless they obtained the work for which they were trained at once, the association opened classes in typewriting, shorthand, sewing and the like, a total of 17 classes in all, to help the girls brush up on their work and 100 enrolled in the classes. In these classes, the girls are taught nothing new, merely given the opportunity to practice the business skills they know until such time as they can find work.

The girls are also being given a course in personality development in a further effort to help them get jobs. The course includes a

review of business English, public speaking and dramatics.

The work of the association with the unemployed young women of this section is only another demonstration of the type of community service which the Y. W. C. A. provides here. The association is not self-centered, serving only a small group of girls and young women in its building on First Street. This program reaches out to many parts of the community.

The association has clubs and special activities for the grade school girls, high school girls, young women employed in the factories, and the business and professional women and cooperates with other institutions for girls and young women in the city. The association conducts a weekly swimming class for the girls of the Day Home and a class in social dancing for young people employed by the National Youth Administration.

The Y. W. C. A. served a total of 9,110 different persons in this area in 1939. This figure includes the people served by the dormitory and cafeteria of the association and the members of the various organizations not directly connected with the Y. W. C. A., who met in the association building for one type of function or another during the year.

As one of the character building agencies of the Troy Community Chest, the Y. W. C. A. is dependent for a considerable portion of its support upon the Chest. All persons interested in helping the association in its work are being asked to contribute to the general fund of the Chest during its third annual appeal for funds March 29 to April 5.

GERMANY OUSTS ALL CONSULATES IN POLISH AREAS

American Envoy Withdrawn at Request of Berlin but State Department Reserves All Rights.

Washington (AP)—Germany forced the United States to withdraw its Consulate General from Poland, where 532 American citizens live.

The State Department announced that it had acceded to the German demand but "reserve all of its rights in the matter."

No reason was given for Germany's action, which affected other countries as well. It was understood that Germany was dissatisfied with the activities of some other consulates and ousted them all.

Leave For Berlin.

The three Americans comprising the staff of the Consulate General left yesterday for Berlin. All matters in connection with American citizens in Poland will be handled through the American Embassy in Berlin.

The State Department said that "representations were made to the German government stressing the difficulty of rendering assistance and protection to American citizens without consular representation in Warsaw."

Secretary Hull said he was making distinct progress in Berlin, however, toward obtaining permission for a number of American relief workers to enter German-occupied Poland to supervise relief distribution.

Germany, according to dispatches received here, is refusing to permit American and other foreign newspapermen to go to Poland.

The consular officers who left were George J. Haering, consul; Carl Birkeland, vice consul, and William R. Morton, vice consul. It is understood they will remain in the American Embassy in Berlin.

When the German armies invaded Poland in September, 1939, the Polish government retired from Warsaw and finally crossed the border into Rumania. The American embassy, headed by Ambassador Anthony J. Drexel-Biddle, accompanied the government.

Still in Drexel-Biddle's Charge.

When the Polish government traveled to France and set up a provisional capital at Angers, the American Embassy was established here provisionally, and is still in charge of Ambassador Drexel-Biddle.

The American Consulate General, however, not being accredited to the Polish government, remained behind and endured the siege of Warsaw. Consul General John K. Davis was in charge, with two consuls and five vice consuls under him. Finally, just before the fall of Warsaw, the German army commander permitted foreign representatives to go out by a special train and by automobile. Consul General Davis and all but one vice consul left for Koenigsberg.

CONSULATE PICKETS AGAIN DISPERSED

New York (AP)—In a fast-swinging melee before thousands of people on Fifth Avenue, police late yesterday broke up a demonstration by several hundred pickets be-

fore the French Consulate in Rockefeller Center.

Twenty-two of the demonstrators—protesting what they described as a French decree ordering Spanish refugees in France back to Spain—were arrested, and as the patrol wagons moved off some of them sang "The Star Spangled Banner."

No one was seriously injured, but several women shoppers fainted in the excitement.

An attempt to picket the consulate was similarly halted last Friday.

(The French Embassy last week issued a statement denying any intention by that government to repatriate Spaniards against their will.)

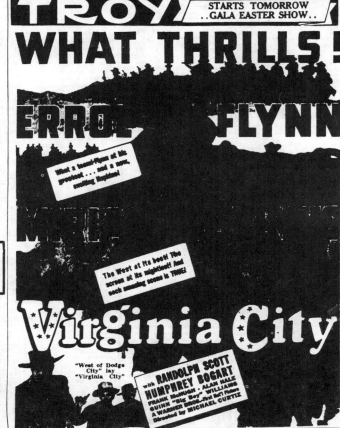

Troy Haymakers Accept Invitation To Participate In Saratoga Tourney

LONG ISLAND U. TO DEFEND CROWN WON LAST YEAR

Local Club Honored After Hanging Up Record of 19 Straight; Three College Clubs Listed.

The Troy Haymakers, winners of 19 straight before their sudden demise in the Gold Medal tournament at the Y. M. C. A., were today extended an invitation which they accepted to participate in the second annual Saratoga A. A. U. basketball tournament at Saratoga Springs Friday, Saturday and Sunday nights, March 29, 30, 31.

There they will compete with some of the strongest clubs in the East. Long Island University is the defending champ.

The Haymakers supplant the state A. A. U. champions of Connecticut whose finals won't be finished until Thursday night of next week and who can't therefore compete.

Three of the entrants are college clubs. Besides Long Island University, they are Canisius College of Buffalo, coholder of the Little Three crown and Bay Path Institute of Springfield, Mass., only undefeated entry in the tournament and winner of 20 straight games.

Other entrants are:

New York Ohrbachs, who have won championship of the Metropolitan A. A. U. district two years running and, according to New York sports writers, excel the big city's college clubs.

Amsterdam Textiles, Adirondack A. A. U. titleholders, who will no doubt present the tallest team in the tourney with five men over six feet.

Saratoga Kaysees, who have defeated club teams from all over eastern New York, New York City, Rochester, and include in their lineup a collection of the district's topnotch basketball players coached by the ultra-successful Sig Makofski of Schenectady.

Corinth EMBA, which has won 23 of its 27 games.

Four games, starting at 7 p.m. will be played Friday, March 29; two on Saturday, March 30, and championship and consolation contests on Sunday night, March 31.

The tourney draw will be announced early next week.

EXPERTS CHOOSE ALL-HOCKEY TEAM

Toronto (AP)—The Boston Bruins and New York Rangers, the one-two teams in the National Hockey League, dominated the all-league team selected by 28 writers in N. H. L. cities.

Each placed two men on the first team while three of the Bruins and two of the Rangers were named to the alternate sextet. Rangers selected for the first team were Dave Kerr, winner of the Georges Vezina trophy as the goal tender with the fewest goals scored against him, and Bryan Hextall, the league's leading goal-scorer.

Milt Schmidt, center on Boston's terrific "kraut" line, and Aubrey (Dit) Clapper, a power on the defense, were the Bruins chosen. Ebbie Goodfellow of Detroit and Hector (Toe) Blake of the Montreal Canadiens complete the first team with Paul Thompson of Chicago awarded the coach position for his great first year job.

Only Clapper and Blake were members of last year's all-star sextet. Eddie Shore, traded to the New York Americans in mid-season by Boston, was missed for the second time in the ten years the teams have been chosen.

16 Year Between Championships For These Two Teams

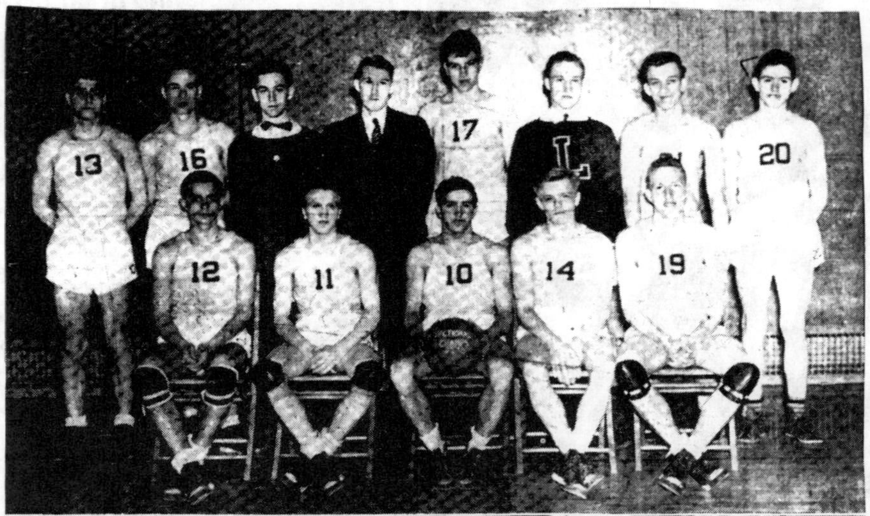

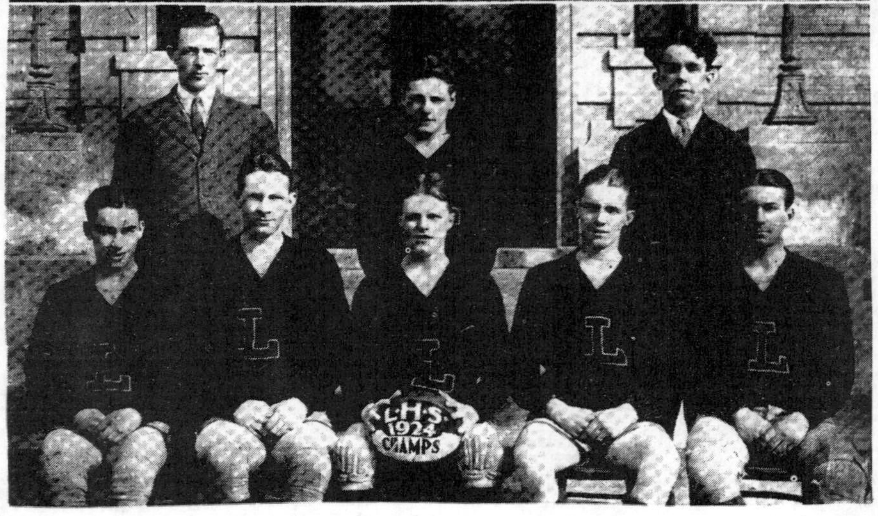

Lansingburg High School's basketball quintet won the Northeastern New York Public High School championship in "B" class at Rensselaer Polytechnic Institute last week. It was the first sectional title for the uptown school in 16 years. And above you see the two teams that turned the trick during that period. At the top is the present crack quintet representing the 'Burg. In the front row are, left to right, Nick Lennek, Irwin Bentzen, Capt. Roy Blair, Joe Hoffman and John Wallace; rear, Dewey LaSalle, Jim Conboy, Assistant Manager Charles Fake, Coach Walter S. Eckerson, George Hall, Manager William Howland, Walt Girwin and Chuck Boland. The boys will be feted by the Lansingburg P.-T. A. faculty members and interested alumni at the school next Wednesday night. And probably they'll at that time reminisce about the last championship 'Burg club that you see in the second photo above. Boys in that shot are: Front row, left to right, the late Artie Gronau, "Red" Thompson, Phil Draper, Tom Whalen and Fred Bartholomew. Rear, Coach Howard Hughes, Bert Copeland and Manager Kellogg Kyle.

HOPPE REGISTERS SEVENTH STRAIGHT IN BILLIARD EVENT

Chicago (AP)—Willie Hoppe of New York certainly is ruling the world three cushion billiard tournament in kingly fashion.

The present world 18.1 balkline and cushion caroms champion and former holder of the 18.2 balkline and three cushion titles scored his seventh straight triumph last night to remain the only undefeated player in a field of 11.

Hoppe's seventh victim was Jay Bozeman of Vallejo, Cal., The 50-41 defeat in 40 innings dropped Bozeman from the runner up spot to fourth place with five victories and three losses and lifted Allen Hall of Chicago into the No. 2 position.

Hall takes on Joe Chamaco of Mexico City, tied with Welker Cochran of San Francisco for fifth place, in tonight's feature match. Hoppe will be idle.

Hall advanced yesterday by thumping Art Thurnblad of Kenosha, Wis., 50 to 34 in 34 innings, the third lowest game of the tournament. Young Jake Schaefer of Cleveland climbed into third place with a 47 innings, 50 to 41 decision over Chamaco. Art Rubin of New York whipped Otto Reiselt of Philadelphia, 50 to 40, in 39 innings in the other match.

MEDWICK LEAVES FOR CARDS' CAMP

St. Louis (AP) — Slugging Joe Medwick, the St. Louis Cardinals' lone holdout, made hurried preparations last night to leave for St. Petersburg, Fla., to confer with Vice President Branch Rickey in a belated effort to reach a salary agreement and join his teammates.

The hard-hitting outfielder said Rickey had invited him to the Redbirds' training camp for a conference.

Medwick's decision to return to St. Petersburg came just a day after the Cards' other holdout, Catcher Don Padgett, signed his 1940 contract.

It is understood the club has offered Medwick $18,000, the same as he received last year, while the outfielder wants either $20,000—his 1938 pay—or $22,000.

Fights Last Night

By The Associated Press.

San Francisco—Lloyd Delucchi, 163, San Francisco, knocked out Bobby Murphy, 157, Long Beach, (7).

New Haven, Conn.—George Pepe, 148, Meriden, Conn., and Frank Young, 149, New Haven, drew (6).

RACING NOTES

By the Associated Press.

Distance racing to assist in developing stamina in thoroughbreds will be emphasized at the 30-day Arlington Park meeting opening June 24.

The long-distance program as outlined at present calls for a race at a mile and a quarter over the main course for $1,200; one at a mile and five-eighths for $1,500; one at a mile and a half for $1,500, and the two-mile handicap.

Arlington's midweek racing will be bolstered by a $2,000 feature each Wednesday.

Timber Lady is back on starter "Buddy" Winfield's schooling list to hold the dubious distinction of being the only thoroughbred so censured.

The mare, which had a bad habit of wheeling at the start, schooled in perfect fashion before she was permitted to go to the post at Tropical last Monday, and it had been thought her barrier antics had been corrected. At the start, however, she again went sideways and is back on the "dunce list" once more.

Nutty has been ordered destroyed, following her fall on Saturday in three-horse pileup near the head of the Tropical Park stretch. The three-year-old daughter of Peanuts-Pretty Play suffered a fractured jaw in the spill.

Jockey Eddie Robart will leave Tropical Sunday for his home in Pawtucket, R. I., for several weeks rest before joining the stable of G. Megill in New York. Megill is preparing 25 head for campaigning over the metropolitan tracks, and Robart will assist in the exercising duties as well as doing much of the riding for the stable.

During the first 14 days of racing at Tropical 36 claims were recorded by the racing secretary's office. The claims totaled $59,350. The largest claim was for $3,500 as Mrs. W. Hodson took Go home from the Maemere farm. Three claims for $3,000 apiece found Cerisse 3rd, Maetran and the Thrush all going to new homes.

Mrs. W. T. Anderson's Gay American, a four-year-old gelding, has found the Tropical Park track much to his liking, as evidenced by his second straight victory, scored yesterday in the featured Stuart purse.

He finished half a length in front of A. J. Brown's The Thrush, racing the distance in 1:44 2-5.

NEGRO FIVE WINS PRO CAGE EVENT; BREWERS THIRD

Chicago (INS)—The Harlem Globe Trotters, great Negro aggregation whose players hail mostly from the midwest cities and play all their games on the road, today held the championship of the National Professional Basketball tournament.

The Globe Trotters, in a closing rally, last night beat the Chicago Bruins, 31 to 29, in the finals of the annual tournament. Fourteen of the nation's best quintets entered the tourney.

With only five minutes to play, the Globe Trotters had trailed 29-21. The Globe Trotters came up to the finals the hard way. They eliminated the New York Renaissance, last year's titleholder, and scored victories over flashy outfits from Ft. Wayne, Ind., Oshkosh, Wis., and Washington, D. C.

The Washington Brewers last night won the consolation or third-place honors by defeating the Syracuse Reds, 34-30.

RANGERS TO FACE BRUINS AT BOSTON

BY UNITED PRESS.

Two National Hockey League teams will be idle as play in the Stanley Cup eliminations continues on two fronts tonight. The New York Americans, who have to win to remain in the playoffs, meet the Detroit Red Wings tomorrow night at Madison Square Garden.

In tonight's contests, the New York Rangers, winners of a 4-0 decision in the first game, meet the Boston Bruins at the latter's rink in a best four-out-of-seven series.

The Toronto Maple Leafs, winners of a 3-2 overtime contest in their series C, best two-out-of-three inaugural, play the Chicago Black Haws at Chicago in the other game.

MIKE JACOBS LOOKS FOR $80,000 GATE

New York (INS) Beset by lawsuits and bedeviled by postponements, Uncle Mike Jacobs today breathed a sigh of relief as he pocketed the signed contracts of Champion Lou Ambers and challenger Lew Jenkins for a lightweight title battle in Madison Square Garden May 10.

"Theres' one that won't get away from me and it should draw at least $80,000," said Mike.

What he didn't say, but which is nonetheless a fact, is that he had to promise Al Weill, manager of Ambers, to give Arturo Godoy another shot at Joe Louis this summer before Al would consent to let Ambers go with Jenkins.

Gold Medal Tourney Reaches Semi-Finals

The ninth annual Gold Medal tournament for district amateur basketball teams reached the half-way mark last night at the Y. M. C. A. with the Castleton Recreation five winning over the Moore-Chevrolets of Scotia, 36 to 33; American-Lithuanians of Amsterdam defeating the Troy Hebrews, 41 to 32; Behr-Manning beating Waterford Owls, 42 to 38 and the All-Troy triumphing over the Y Eagles by a score of 44 to 29.

The semi-finals tonight will pit Behr-Manning against Castleton in the second game and the Lithuanians against the All-Troys in the curtain raiser.

There will be no games tomorrow, Good Friday, and the tournament will end Saturday night.

MOORE CHEVROLET.

	F.G.	F.B.	T.P.
Givens, rf.	2	0	4
George, lf.	2	2	6
Smith, c.	2	3	7
J. Mabee, rg.	4	4	12
Bain, lg.	1	0	2
O. Mabee, rf.	0	2	2
Lehman, lg.	0	0	0
Totals	11	11	33

CASTLETON.

	F.G.	F.B.	T.P.
Murray, rf.	3	0	6
Lock, lf.	2	1	5
Ryan, lf.	0	0	0
Mangin, c.	0	0	0
Wasko, rg.	1	1	3
Price, rg.	2	1	5
Flynn, lg.	6	5	17
Totals	14	8	36

Referee, Champagne. Umpire, Purcell. Scorer, Topping. Timer, Ruff. Score at half time, 19-17, Moore Chevrolet. Team fouls called, 18-13, Castleton.

TROY HEBREWS.

	F.G.	F.B.	T.P.
Jaffee, rf.	4	4	12
Uberlin, lf.	4	1	9
Fares, c.	2	2	6
Kloud, rg.	0	0	0
Gordon, lg.	2	0	4
Feldman, rg.	0	1	1
Cohen, lf.	0	0	0
Totals	12	8	32

AMERICAN LITHUANIAN CLUB.

	F.G.	F.B.	T.P.
Kristie, rf.	2	0	4
Dargus, lf.	5	2	12
Mateunas, c.	4	0	8
Alexander, rg.	4	0	8
Liberis, lg.	0	1	1
Zoal, rf.	3	0	6
Togaila, lg.	1	0	2
Totals	19	3	41

Referee, Champagne. Umpire, Purcell. Scorer, Topping. Timer, Ruff. Score at half time, 21-11, American Lithuanian Club. Team fouls called, 14-12, Troy.

BEHR-MANNING.

	F.G.	F.B.	T.P.
Kennedy, rf.	0	2	2
Devine, lf.	3	0	6
Krambuhl, c.	6	2	14
Anslow, rg.	4	1	9
Bentzen, lg.	3	2	8
Bartnick, rf.	1	1	3
Totals	17	8	42

WATERFORD OWLS.

	F.G.	F.B.	T.P.
Bartnick, rf.	3	0	6
Church, lf.	3	0	6
Geiger, c.	2	2	6
Kidwell, rg.	4	1	9
Brown, lg.	1	0	2
Scofield, lg.	4	1	9
Cerqua, rf.	0	0	0
Totals	17	4	38

Referee, Cahill; umpire, Cole; score at half time, 23-16 Behr-Manning; fouls called, 14-8, Waterford Owls.

"Y" EAGLES.

	F.G.	F.B.	T.P.
E. Fennell, rf.	3	0	6
Turino, lf.	1	4	6
Frawley, c.	3	0	6
Kennedy, rg.	1	0	2
McLaughlin, lg.	1	3	5
T. Andrews	1	0	2
W. Andrews	1	0	2
Totals	11	7	29

ALL TROYS.

	F.G.	F.B.	T.P.
Gray, rf.	1	4	6
Kerwin, lf.	2	1	5
Miller, c.	5	1	11
Daus, rg.	0	0	0
Powers, lg.	1	2	4
Degnan, rf.	5	1	11
Lewis	3	1	7
Totals	17	10	44

Referee, Cahill; umpire, Cole; score at half time, 14-11, All-Troys; fouls called, 12-10, "Y" Eagles.

"Y" QUINT DIVIDES IN PAIR OF GAMES

The "Y" Juniors won over the Up-to-Date five by a score of 32 to 29 and the "Y" Squirts dropped a 23 to 21 decision to Maplewood at the Y. M. C. A. last night.

Mirch with 11 was high for the jayvees while Kaplan paced the Up-to-Date quintet with 16. Tonia's ten were high for Maplewood while McCumber with eight was top man for the Squirts.

COMPANY C WINS OVER ALBANY FIVE

Company C, 105th Infantry, played host to the Company C unit of the 10th Infantry last night at the local armory and emerged with a 37 to 26 victory over the Albany cagers.

CHUCKTA LEADS 'VLIET HI CAGERS

Metro Chuckta, Watervliet High School flashy forward, led the Arsenal City quint to one of its most successful seasons in recent years by scoring 182 points in 18 games for an average of 10.12 points per game, the team won 11 and lost seven.

Manager Joseph Fanning of the Watervliet basketball team announced that the team compiled a tofal of 566 points and lost most of their decisions by two or four-point margins. Chuckta, it was announced, also led the school for individual team scoring in the Tri-City League, Public High School Legaue and in three independent contests.

Tom Jones, Watervliet coach, announced the following tabulations:

Name	Games Played	F.G.	F.B.	Total	Ave.
Metro Chuckta	18	71	40	182	10.12
James LeCuyer	18	46	16	108	6.00
P. Kowalchyk	17	33	17	83	4.86
William DiBacco	17	19	6	44	2.56
George Stewart	8	17	5	39	4.87
Joseph DeCarlo	18	13	9	35	1.94
Paul Fedorchak	14	9	3	21	1.50
Louis Huban	15	6	4	16	1.06
Robert Gray	14	5	1	11	.78
Raymond Manny	10	4	1	9	.90
James McMahon	9	4	0	8	.88
John Kapela	12	2	2	6	.50
John Vosburgh	4	2	0	4	1.00
Totals		231	104	566	

MAY BUY TEAM.

Montreal (INS)—Leo Dandurand, of Montreal, former part owner of Montreal Les Canadiens, yesterday offered to purchase the National Hockey League tail-enders to prevent their dropping out of the circuit next season.

Nurmi Says Finns To Stage Olympics

Detroit (INS)—In sipte of the the European war, the 1940 Olympics will be held in Helsinki, Paavo Nurmi, the Flying Finn of the twenties asserted today.

"I know what I'm talking about," Nurmi insisted. "They're already talking about the Olympic meeting and making plans for it at home. It will be held and you can bet every penny you have on it."

Nurmi, touring the United States with his protege, Taisto Maki, for the benefit of their war torn homeland, predicted Maki would "crack a lot more records at the Olympic meeting."

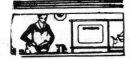

Round Table Talk about Food

Daily Dinner Menus Help You Plan Interesting Dinners

Sunday Dinner.
Cranberry juice
Chicken fricasse with boiled broad noodles
Fresh peas and carrots
Fruit salad
Pecan cookies
Tea coffee or milk

Monday Dinner.
Savory meat loaf
Escalloped potatoes
Buttered string beans
Lettuce and watercress salad
Fruit gelatine
Coffee, tea or milk

Tuesday Dinner.
Lamb ragout, French style
Parsley potatoes
Spring salad
Apricot shortcake
Coffee, tea or milk

Wednesday Dinner.
Onion soup
Salmon and corn loaf with egg sauce
Spinach
Celery and radishes
Strawberry charlotte
Coffee, tea or milk

Thursday Dinner.
Veal cutlet with mushroom sauce
Parsley potatoes
Red cabbage, German style
Endive salad
Cream puffs, butterscotch sauce
Coffee, tea or milk

Friday Dinner.
Fresh pineapple fruit cup
Baked haddock
Creamed new potatoes
Broccoli
Lemon chiffon pie
Coffee, tea or milk

Saturday Dinner.
Baked ham with apricots and
Sweet potatoes
Creamed celery
Jellied tomato salad
Cottage pudding with fruit or rum sauce
Coffee, tea or milk

BROWN AND WHITE.

One and a half cups of dark brown sugar are equivalent to a cupful of granulated sugar.

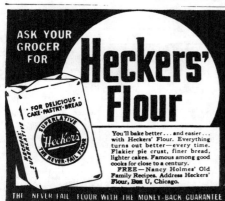

Honey Rhubarb Pie Will Give Desserts New Slant

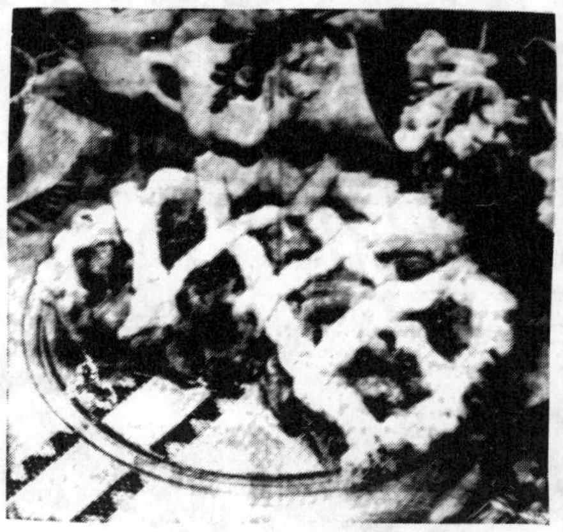

Honey rhubarb pie for spring dessert.

Combine honey with spring rhubarb, bake in your flakiest pastry and you'll feel as frisky as a young lamb.

Honey Rhubarb Pie.
(Serves Six.)

Pastry for shell and lattice top—4 cups fresh rhubarb, ½ cup honey, ½ cup sugar, 2½ tablespoons quick cooking tapioca, ¼ teaspoon salt.

Line a glass pie plate with pastry. Mix rhubarb cut up in small pieces, honey, sugar, tapioca, and salt together and pour into pie plate. Place lattice crust over the top and bake in a moderately hot oven (400 degrees F.) for 45 minutes or until rhubarb is done. Serve from the attractive glass pie plate at the table.

To a simple dinner add this bountiful dessert and you'll have a feast:

Apple Pan Dowdy.
(Serves Six.)

Six tart apples, 2-3 cup sugar, 1 teaspoon cinnamon, 2 tablespoons butter, 1 recipe baking powder biscuits (using 2 cups flour).

Pare and slice apples and arrange them in a well-greased one quart utility dish, about 10x6x2 inches. Mix sugar and cinnamon together and sprinkle over apples and dot with butter. Roll the baking powder biscuit dough out to one-half inch thickness and cover apples. Gash in several places to allow escape of steam. Bake in a moderate oven (350 degrees F.) for about thirty minutes. Serve hot with nutmeg cream.

Nutmeg Cream.

Two tablespoons finely granulated sugar, ¼ teaspoon nutmeg, 1 cup light cream. Mix sugar and nutmeg together. Pour cream over sugar and stir until dissolved.

Include Fresh Vegetables In Menus For Early Spring

This is the time of year when we particularly crave fresh fruits and vegetables, the season that used to be dedicated to the sulphur and molasses bottle and to other concoctions similarly designed for the prevention or cure of that mysterious malady known as "spring fever!" Today we know we can accomplish much the same purpose by eating the right kind of foods during the winter months and by increasing our supplies of vegetables, salads and fruits for the next six weeks or so. General food supplies are so much less restricted than they were forty or fifty years ago so that it is only in very isolated sections of the country that a well balanced, varied diet cannot be secured all year round.

Fresh vegetables and fruits are speedily transported in refrigerated cars from the south, the southwest, from California, Mexico, Puerto Rico, Cuba and reach us during those months when local crops are not available; canned vegetables and fruits in a bewildering array are stocked by grocery stores everywhere, and more recently we have an increasing variety of the quick-frozen foods. Early spring however, is always made more thrilling by the appearance of the first pink stalks of rhubarb in the markets, and the first mess of turnip greens, dandelion greens, field salad or beet tops from the home garden! These with green peas, early asparagus, radishes, spring onions, and the already mentioned available vegetables add a liberal supply of vitamins and minerals to the diet. Use them as generously as possible in your meal plans for the next few weeks.

Protective Foods.

Keep these seasonal requirements in mind in the meals you plan for this week; for instance, greens, either raw or cooked, should be liberally used, fruits also have a large place in the food list for the week: milk, eggs, butter and fish join the group of health providing foods so necessary in building strong bodies and in establishing resistance to colds. The wise housekeeper knows she can do more to keep her family well with good food, and do it more pleasantly, than she can with medicine from the drug store.

Simple meals can be most effective and attractive. Try for new flavor combinations, or variations in flavor combinations whenever possible. For example, the addition of chopped chives and crisp bits of fried sausage to scrambled eggs; a little sherry in the salad dressing for the fruit salad the use of sliced dates with stewed rhubarb; celery and a bit of garlic to lamb stew.

For Sunday's dinner a chicken fricassee is a good choice for the main course. Serve boiled broad noodles with liberal amounts of chicken gravy instead of mashed potatoes. Buy a stewing chicken for the fricassee—selecting one that weighs about five pounds. If the family is small, serve the breast and second joints for one meal, saving the drum sticks, back, and wings to cream or turn into chicken hash or chicken creole for another meal. A chicken of this weight is a better buy than a smaller one and it has more flesh in proportion to the amount of bone than one weighing 3 or 3¼ pounds. When chicken fricassee is made, there is always chicken stock leftover which we have utilized this week in making the cream of chicken soup served on Monday. Add to the stock any vegetables left over from Sunday, dilute with a little water if necessary and simmer for thirty minutes or more to blend the chicken and vegetable flavors. Before serving add 1 to 2 cups milk and thicken with flour to the consistency of any other cream soup.

A savory meat loaf can take care of the meat problem for one night's dinner, and does it inexpensively. Such recipes make a small amount of inexpensive meat do extra good service—one pound of chopped flank or bottom round will make a meat loaf for six persons. Lamb ragout is also a comparatively inexpensive, and a very delicious, meat dish. Buy two pounds of lean lamb shoulder or meat from the shank for this, cutting it in small even shaped pieces.

This Recipe May Be Used In Individual Dishes

4 tablespoons butter
4 tablespoons flour
2 cups light cream or top milk
½ teaspoon salt
Dash of pepper
Dash of cayenne
Dash of paprika
½ teaspoon Worcestershire sauce
2 tablespoons parsley, chopped
2 cups crab, shrimp, or lobster, cut in ½-inch pieces
¼ cup soft buttered crumbs

Melt butter in saucepan, add flour, and stir to a smooth paste. Add cream and cook until thickened, stirring constantly. Add seasonings, Worcestershire sauce, ½ of parsley, and fish. Pour into well-greased casserole. Sprinkle crumbs and remaining parsley over top. Bake in moderate oven (350 degrees F.) twenty minutes, or until crumbs are browned. Makes six small servings. May also be baked in individual ramekins.

MOLASSES LAYER CAKE.

Cream together 1-3 cup shortening and 1 cup soft brown sugar. When well blended add 1 egg and beat hard until smooth. Then stir in 1 cup dark molasses and ½ cup thick sour milk. Sift together 2¼ cups flour, ¾ teaspoon salt, 1 teaspoon baking soda, 1 teaspoon each cinnamon and ginger, ½ teaspoon cloves. Add this to the molasses mixture and beat just enough to make a smooth batter. Pour into two well greased layer cake pans and bake in a moderate oven 350 degrees—for twenty to 25 minutes, depending on the depth of the pans. Cool slightly, remove from the pans and when cold spread raisin filling between the layers and orange icing on top.

Buttered Crumbs Make Novel Vegetable Sauce

Looking for a new wrinkle to dress up vegetables? Here it is: Fine dry bread crumbs browned in butter, and served as a sauce. Melt 2 tablespoons of butter in a saucepan, add ½ cup dry bread crumbs, and stir over a low fire until the crumbs are browned. Serve on any cooked vegetable.

Broccoli is especially delicious with buttered crumbs flavored with lemon juice. For broccoli at its best, undercook rather than overcook it. Begin by selecting firm, deep green heads—stalks with yellow flowers are old. Remove the outside leaves from the main stalks. Peel off the thick, woody skin at the bottom, and split the stalk in half lengthwise, o rin quarters if it is too thick. Keep the stalk in half lengthwise, or in quar-attached.

Place in a deep enough pan to allow the stalks to stand upright so that the flowers will be steamed. Pour in enough boiling salted water nearly to cover the stalks but not the flowers. Place a lid on the pan and allow to boil furiously about ten minutes, or until stalks are just tender enough to pierce with a fork, and before the color has changed from bright green to brown. Remove lid at once. Drain and serve with buttered crumb sauce, prepared as above and blended with 1 tablespoon of lemon juice.

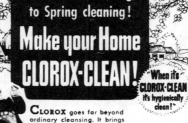

THE WEATHER
Tonight—Rain.
Tomorrow—Rain.

THE TIMES RECORD

FINAL EDITION

Series 1940—No. 95. (Entered as Second Class Matter at the Postoffice at Troy, N. Y., under the Act of March 3, 1879.) TROY, N. Y., SATURDAY EVENING, APRIL 20, 1940. (Published Daily Except Sunday) PRICE THREE CENTS

DEATH TOLL IN LITTLE FALLS RAILWAY CRASH EXCEEDS THIRTY

Governor Lehman Vetoes Two Bills On Troy Election Case

EXECUTIVE GIVES NEW REASONS FOR REFUSAL TO SIGN

Official Points Out That Quo Warranto Proceedings Should Be Invoked for Speedy Determination

(Staff Correspondence.)

Albany—Gov. Herbert H. Lehman today closed the door to a settlement of Troy's five-month-old mayoralty dispute, other than by a jury trial in Supreme Court, by disapproving the Hastings-Whitney bills which would have permitted a recasting of ballots in the Second District of the Eighth Ward in that city.

Republicans, who contend County Commissioner of Welfare John J. Ahern won from Mayor Frank J. Hogan last November but that a defective machine in the Eighth Ward left the returns incomplete, sought legislation to permit a recast so there could be a settlement of the controversy by a secret ballot.

More than a month ago Governor Lehman rejected another bill applying to the Troy situation on the ground it might set a dangerous precedent in precipitating future controversies as well as that it would permit citizens of a district to have a second choice in the selection of the head of the municipal government.

To meet these executive objections the measures vetoed today were drafted, approved by the Legislature, then sent to Governor Lehman.

Governor Issues Memorandum.

In a memorandum of disapproval of the proposals today, Governor Lehman said:

These bills are equally as objectionable as a previous bill which I disapproved as "unjust and unfair." These bills contain several seriously unsound provisions apart from the fact that the bills are made retroactive so as to care for a situation in the City of Troy. That situation is before the courts in quo warranto proceedings.

In my earlier memorandum I said: "In a quo warranto proceeding the court, with the aid of a jury, may determine from the evidence presented the number of votes actually cast. By so doing the court and the jury decide the only issue—how the voter voted on Election Day—on the facts and not by conjecture." These bills are disapproved.

One bill, sponsored by Sen. Clifford C. Hastings, would have stipulated citizens permitted to recast a ballot would be required to swear to an intention to support the same person for the office of Mayor they intended to support in the original election. The other, by Assemblyman Maurice Whitney, would have limited settlement by recast to disputes created last fall.

May Start Next Week.

Atty. Gen. John J. Bennett, jr., on the petition of Commissioner Ahern, has directed the institution of quo warranto proceedings through which Ahern desires to show that more than 309 citizens of the Eighth Ward voted for him against Hogan but that a defective machine was unable to register more than 11 votes for Ahern.

Former Asst. Dist. Atty. John J. Kelly of Rensselaer County has been appointed by the attorney general to prosecute the proceedings. Associated with Kelly is former Supreme Court Justice Ellis J. Staley of Albany, former Mayor

(Continued on Page 9.)

TROJAN BELIEVED TO HAVE LOST LIFE AS TRAIN CRASHED

Humphrey A. See, jr., Railroad Policeman Aboard Limited; C. Stewart Ferguson Escapes.

One Trojan, a New York Central policeman, is believed to be dead and another, C. Stewart Ferguson of 36 Bouton Road escaped from an overturned club car without injury in the wreck of the crack New York Central train, the Lake Shore Limited, last night at Little Falls. Prof. H. W. Thompson of New York State College for Teachers, author of a recent book containing folk lore of Rensselaer County, was among the injured. He was on his way to lecture at Hamilton College.

Railroad Policeman.

Humphrey A. See, jr., of 461 Second Avenue, policeman with the New York Central since 1925, boarded the train at Albany. New York Central police headquarters said that although no positive identification of his body has been made, he is believed to have died in the wreck.

Several bodies can be seen trapped in an overturned car. They have not yet been removed. Tentative identification of one of these bodies as See is understood to have been made.

The office of Capt. Joseph P. Boyle at Albany, after communicating with the officer at the scene of the accident, said that it has been positively established that See was on the train and is unreported and that tentative identification of a body in the wrekage has been made.

See, a yard policeman at Utica, had Thursday night off and spent the time at home with his wife and four children. He was to report for work on the midnight shift at Utica last night.

See is a cousin of LeGrand Wagar, division chief of the New York Central Police.

Telephoned to Wife.

Mr. Ferguson, an employee of the General Electric Co. left last night for a month's business trip to California. He was accompanied by an official of the plant, Edward Feiniger of Schenectady.

He telephoned his wife early today that he had escaped without injury and had found some of his luggage. The General Electric Co. sent a car to Little Falls to return him later today to Troy.

Four members of the Rensselaer County Democratic delegation to the Farley dinner in New York City left the train at Albany last night. City Treasurer John F. Shannon, Comptroller Edward J. Ronan, George Curley, deputy assistant corporation counsel, and Joseph M. Mesnig, assistant attorney general, and Eli Koplovitz, Troy attorney, returned home ahead of the rest of the delegation.

News of the wreck of the train on which they had traveled to Albany reached them only a few hours after their return home.

Every available New York Central policemen in the area was sent to Little Falls this morning to assist with work of removing bodies from the wreckage.

SECOND OF SIX I.R.A. PRISONERS DIES AS HUNGER STRIKE ENDS

Dublin (U.P.)—The second of six Irish Republican Army hunger strikers was dead today but the other four, who had called off their strike, apparently were recovering.

Only a few hours after the government had announced that the five hunger strikers surviving after the death last Tuesday of Anthony Darcy had started taking nourishment, one of them, John McNeela, died at St. Bricin's military hospital where he was serving a two-year term for possession of a wireless transmitter and belonging to an illegal organization.

The prisoners had been fasting 57 days. At Darcy's funeral at Headford yesterday, police and I. R. A. members battled with sticks and truncheons. Two lorries full of soldiers in full war kit were sent to Headford from Galway to restore order.

The other four prisoners were John Plunkett, Michael Traynor, Thomas Grogan and Thomas McCurtain.

WOMAN DIES OF BURNS.

Buffalo (U.P.) — Mrs. Madeline Vastello, 22, critically burned Monday when her clothing was ignited by a hot water heater in her home here, died at Emergency Hospital today.

Where Lake Shore Limited Met With Disaster

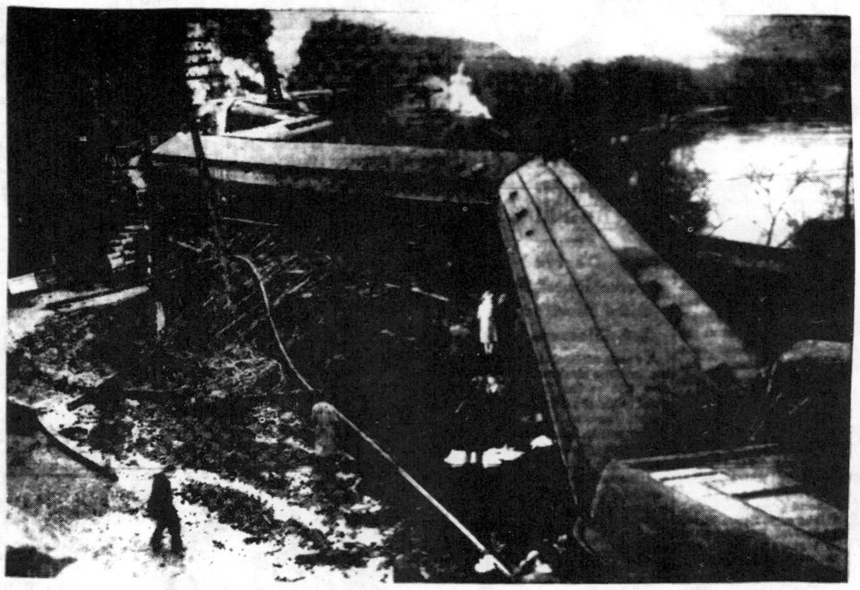

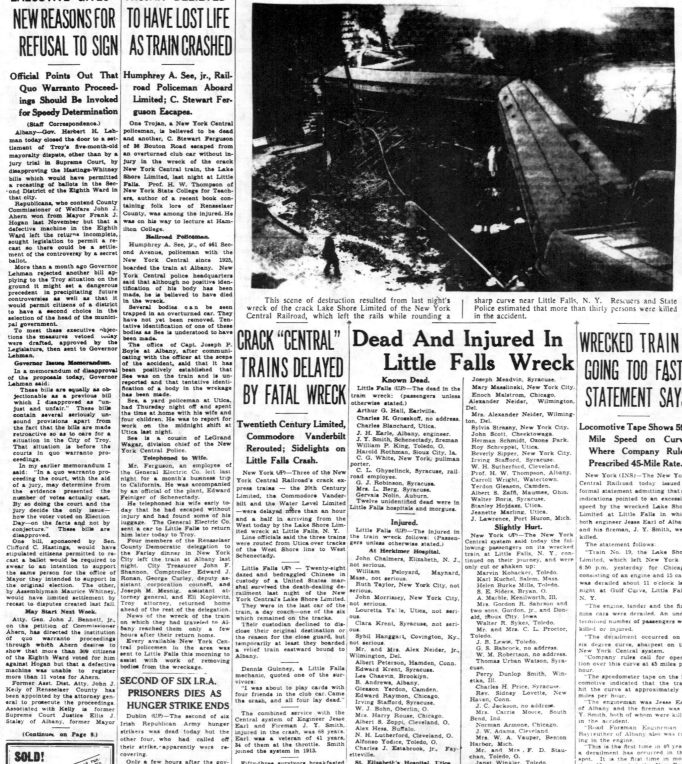

This scene of destruction resulted from last night's wreck of the crack Lake Shore Limited of the New York Central Railroad, which left the rails while rounding a sharp curve near Little Falls, N. Y. Rescuers and State Police estimated that more than thirty persons were killed in the accident.

CRACK "CENTRAL" TRAINS DELAYED BY FATAL WRECK

Twentieth Century Limited, Commodore Vanderbilt Rerouted; Sidelights on Little Falls Crash.

New York (AP)—Three of the New York Central Railroad's crack express trains — the 20th Century Limited, the Commodore Vanderbilt and the Water Level Limited —were delayed more than an hour and a half in arriving from the West today by the Lake Shore Limited wreck at Little Falls, N. Y.

Line officials said the three trains were routed from Utica over tracks of the West Shore line to West Schenectady.

Little Falls (AP) — Twenty-eight dazed and bedraggled Chinese in custody of a United States marshal survived the death-dealing derailment last night of the New York Central's Lake Shore Limited.

They were in the last car of the train, a day coach—one of the six which remained on the tracks.

Their custodian declined to disclose their original destination or the reason for the close guard, but temporarily at least they boarded a relief train eastward bound to Albany.

Dennis Guinney, a Little Falls mechanic, quoted one of the survivors:

"I was about to play cards with four friends in the club car. Came the crash, and all four lay dead."

The combined service with the Central system of Engineer Jesse Earl and Fireman J. Y. Smith, injured in the crash, was 68 years. Earl was a veteran of 41 years, 34 of them at the throttle. Smith joined the system in 1913.

Fifty-three survivors breakfasted as guests of the railroad at Utica, 30 miles west of the crash. Others left in taxicabs and automobiles offered by area residents for nearby hotels, eager to leave the scene without attempting to recover personal belongings.

Rep. Fred J. Douglas (R.-N. Y.), 71-year-old Utica physician, gave medical aid. His Son, Dr. James Douglas, arriving 17 minutes after the crash, crawled into the locomotive car to administer aid to the dying engineer.

State Police estimated approximately 4,000 persons, some with nightclothing under hastily donned coats, were attracted to the scene. A drizzling rain which began soon after dawn hampered rescue work.

"COW THIEF" ENUMERATED.

Waco, Tex. (AP)—The census will list one cow thief. "His folks said he had been sent to the penitentiary twice for stealing cows, so they guessed that was his profession," explained the enumerator to his boss.

Dead And Injured In Little Falls Wreck

Known Dead.

Little Falls (U.P.)—The dead in the train wreck: (passengers unless otherwise stated.)

Arthur G. Hall, Earlville.
Charles H. Grosskoff, no address.
Charles Blanchard, Utica.
J. H. Earle, Albany, engineer.
J. Y. Smith, Schenectady, fireman
William P. King, Toledo, O.
Harold Rothman, Sioux City, Ia.
C. G. White, New York, pullman porter.
C. L. Ghyselinck, Syracuse, railroad employee.
G. J. Robinson, Syracuse.
Mrs. L. Berg, Syracuse.
Gervais Nolin, Auburn.

Twelve unidentified dead were in Little Falls hospitals and morgues.

Injured.

Little Falls (U.P.)—The injured in the train wreck follows: (Passengers unless otherwise stated.)

At Herkimer Hospital.

John Chalmers, Elizabeth, N. J., not serious.
William Peloyard, Maynard, Mass., not serious.
Ruth Taylor, New York City, not serious.
John Morrissey, New York City, not serious.
Louretta Yalle, Utica, not serious.
Clara Krent, Syracuse, not serious.
Sybil Hanggart, Covington, Ky., not serious.
Mr. and Mrs. Alex Neider, jr., Wilmington, Del.
Albert Peterson, Hamden, Conn.
Edward Krent, Syracuse.
Lee Chaevin, Brooklyn.
B. Andrews, Albany.
Gleason Yerdon, Camden.
Edward Raymon, Chicago.
Irving Stafford, Syracuse.
W. J. Bohn, Oberlin, O.
Mrs. Harry Rouse, Chicago.
Albert S. Zoppi, Cleveland, O.
Alex Hess, Buffalo.
N. H. Lutherford, Cleveland, O.
Alfonso Yodice, Toledo, O.
Charles J. Estabrook, jr., Fayetteville.

St. Elizabeth's Hospital, Utica.

Roy Schreppel, Utica.

At Faxton Hospital, Utica.

Harold H. Farnam, Baldwin, L. I.

At Little Falls Hospital.

William Braski, New York City.
Hyman Blits, Toledo, Ohio.
Jean Berta, New York City.
Dr. Carlyle Baatian, New York City.
Louis R. Chreist, South Bend, Ind.
J. A. Chrisman, South Bend, Ind.
June Donovan, West Brookline, Mass.
Inga Dahlhaug, Minneapolis, Minn.
Lucille Gregor, Chicago.
Mary Gabso, Schenectady.
Louise Gifford, Syracuse.
Sterling Haggard, Covington, Ky.
C. A. Haley, Marshfield, Wis.
Thomas L. Jones, West Englewood, N. J.
Ray Jennings, (address unknown).
Bridge Lo Giudice, Utica.
Robert W. Muessle, South Bend.
Merrill Morehouse, Bronx.
Richard Muhs, Chicago.
Joseph Meadvin, Syracuse.
Mary Maslinski, New York City.
Enoch Malstrom, Chicago.
Alexander Neider, Wilmington, Del.
Mrs. Alexander Neider, Wilmington, Del.
Sylvia Strasny, New York City.
John Scott, Cheektowaga.
Herman Schmidt, Ozone Park.
Roy Schreppel, Utica.
Beverly Sipper, New York City.
Irving Stafford, Syracuse.
W. H. Sutherford, Cleveland.
Prof. H. W. Thompson, Albany.
Carroll Wright, Watertown.
Yerdon Gleason, Camden.
Albert S. Zaffi, Maumee, Ohio.
Walter Boris, Syracuse.
Stanley Hojdasz, Utica.
Jeanette Marling, Utica.
J. Lawrence, Port Huron, Mich.

Slightly Hurt.

New York (AP)—The New York Central system said today the following passengers on its wrecked train at Little Falls, N. Y., continued on their journey, and were only cut or shaken up:

Marvin Kobacker, Toledo.
Karl Kuchel, Salem, Mass.
Helen Burke Mills, Toledo.
S. E. Siders, Bryan, O.
A. Marble, Kenilworth, Ill.
Mrs. Gordon R. Sahrson and two sons, Gordon, jr., and Donald, Sioux City, Iowa
Walter R. Sykes, Toledo.
Mr. and Mrs. C. L. Proctor, Toledo.
J. B. Lewis, Toledo.
G. S. Babcock, no address.
W. M. Robertson, no address.
Thomas Urban Watson, Syracuse.
Perry Dunlop Smith, Winetka, Ill.
Charles H. Price, Syracuse.
Rev. Sidney Lovette, New Haven, Conn.
J. C. Jackson, no address.
Mrs. Carrie Moore, South Bend, Ind.
Norman Armone, Chicago.
J. W. Adams, Cleveland.
Mrs. W. A. Vauper, Benton Harbor, Mich.
Mr. and Mrs. F. D. Stauchan, Toledo, O.
Janet Winkler, Toledo.
L. P. Spare, Sandusky, O.
W. M. Fanning, Larchmont.
D. H. Hurlburt, Adrian, Mich.
Miss Inga Balhaug, Minneapolis, Minn.
Alec B. Hess, Hackensack, N. J.
Miss Isabella Palmer, Albany Hospital, Albany.
Charles Gratten, conductor of train.
Timothy J. O'Hara, 72 Bloomingdale Avenue, Saranac Lake.
Douglas Brown, Rochelle.
Henry Proppogen, attorney, Toledo, O.
Mrs. Allan Brantingham Rockford, Ill.
Mr. and Mrs. W. C. Lehman, Bryan, O., (or Carmelton, Ind.).
J. C. Acklein, Perrysburg, O.
C. Bruice, Kew Gardens.
J. S. Irwin, Toledo.
Mr. and Mrs. Roy Pade, Yonkers.
Mrs. William Lehman, Carmelton, Ind.
B. J. Axling, Chicago.
Paul Doyle, jr., Chicago.
Emery Wilson, Buffalo, believed to be a dining car waiter.
Mrs. Harry L. Mahoney and infant daughter, Cuyahoga Falls, O.
W. C. Friedlay, New York.
Herman Adams, Buffalo.
Clarence Nettig, San Diego, Cal.
M. H. Chutley, Auburn.
R. M. L. Carson, Glens Falls.
William Taylor, Brighton, Mass.
G. W. Patton, Kansas City, Mo.
H. S. Wandling, Toledo.
Mrs. J. Reed Saue, Rye.

WRECKED TRAIN GOING TOO FAST, STATEMENT SAYS

Locomotive Tape Shows 59-Mile Speed on Curve Where Company Rules Prescribed 45-Mile Rate.

New York (INS)—The New York Central Railroad today issued a formal statement admitting that all indications pointed to an excessive speed by the wrecked Lake Shore Limited at Little Falls in which both engineer Jesse Earl of Albany and his fireman, J. Y. Smith, were killed.

The statement follows:

"Train No. 19, the Lake Shore Limited, which left New York at 6:50 p.m. yesterday for Chicago, consisting of an engine and 15 cars, was derailed about 11 o'clock last night at Gulf Curve, Little Falls, N. Y.

"The engine, tender and the first nine cars were derailed. An undetermined number of passengers was killed or injured.

"The derailment occurred on a six degree curve, sharpest on the New York Central system.

"Company rules call for operation over this curve at 45 miles per hour.

"The speedometer tape on the locomotive indicated that the train hit the curve at approximately 59 miles per hour.

"The engineman was Jesse Earl of Albany and the fireman was J. Y. Smith, both of whom were killed in the accident.

"Road Foreman Engineman A. Bayreuther of Albany also was riding in the engine.

"This is the first time in 40 years a derailment has occurred in this spot. It is the first time in more than 13 years that the New York Central has had a passenger fatality in a train accident."

PAYROLLS INCREASE.

Albany (UP) Employment and payrolls in the construction industry showed marked increases from mid-February to mid-March, signifying a belated spring recovery, the State Labor Department announced today. Employment rose 1.6 per cent, payrolls 10.7 per cent and man-hours 8.6 per cent.

Fast New York Central Train Jumped Track On Sharp Curve; 75 Injured

Twenty-four bodies Recovered from Wreckage But More Victims Are Buried Under Overturned Cars; Many Passengers Killed in Sleepers As Pullmans Are Telescoped; Locomotive Exploded, Killing Engineer and Fireman; Crash Awakens Entire City.

BY PAUL H. KING.

Little Falls (UP)—The Lake Shore Limited, luxury express train which jumped the track and piled into a cliff here last night, was running 14 miles an hour faster than regulations permitted, the New York Central Railroad said today.

The State Police said that at least 33 persons were killed as Pullman coaches piled atop each other and the charging locomotive exploded. At least 75 persons were injured.

Coroner Fred C. Sabin announced officially that 24 bodies have been recovered, of which 12 were identified. He said four to six bodies could be seen still in the wreckage. The bodies were under two cars, which must be moved before they can be recovered. He said it was possible more bodies were concealed in the wreckage.

In a violent snowstorm hundreds of rescue workers continued digging into the wreckage for additional bodies of dead and injured. The snow piled up rapidly and hampered the work.

At Albany, Governor Lehman directed state police and public works employees to give all possible aid at the scene of the wreck.

Officials attempting to determine the cause of the accident indicated that the train, one of the New York Central's flyers competing for the passenger business between New York and Chicago, roared into Little Falls at high speed. The train was running behind time. The engineer's watch stopped at 11:33 o'clock. The train was due in Utica, twenty miles west, at 11:28 o'clock.

(In New York, company officials said: "Company rules call for a speed of 45 miles an hour for a curve at that (Little Falls) point. The speedometer tape in the engine cab registered 59 miles an hour. Engineer Jesse Earl and fireman J. Y. Smith were both killed.)

Train Chicago-Bound.

The Lake Shore Limited, one of the crack trains of the New York Central operating between New York and Chicago, left New York City at 6:61 p.m. Friday and had been due in Chicago at 1:10 p.m., E.S.T., today.

Railroad officials at Albany would not say whether the limited was late at Albany, its last station stop before the accident. The train, however, was due in Utica at 11:28, at almost the same time the accident occurred, 73 miles west of Albany and twenty miles east of Utica.

Trainmaster J. D. Carkuff of Albany, who said he originally understood the train was composed of both heavy and lightweight cars, announced later that he had been informed by Assistant Superintendent B. H. Dayton at the wreck scene that all cars were standard weight, heavy type Pullmans and coaches.

Locomotive Jumped Track.

Rounding a sharp curve at high speed while entering the outskirts of Little Falls, the locomotive leaped its track, careened over the other tree tracks of the right-of-way, and crashed into the side of a 200-foot rock embankment. Its boiler exploded, shooting up a huge cloud of live steam.

By a strange freak, the baggage car immediately behind was broken free and rolled on down the tracks, halting 200 yards away. But the mail car, directly behind the baggage car, piled into the locomotive and was telescoped into a fourth of its length. The following Pullman smashed into this wreckage, the next Pullman piled on top of the first Pullman, and a third Pullman piled into this mountain of wreckage.

This third Pullman was smashed. The Pullman behind it was telescoped and its roof was partly torn off, the heavy steel torn as though it was paper. The seven Pullman coaches next following were flopped on their sides, their windows were broken, their wheels torn off or loose, but otherwise they did not appear severely damaged. Five coaches—all Pullmans except one—behind them remained upright on the tracks. The last coach was a day coach which contained 36 Chinese prisoners of the immigration service en route to San Francisco for deportation.

Victims Mangled.

The engineer and his fireman were killed. The two mail clerks were believed to have been killed. The remainder of the dead were from the first two Pullman

(Continued on Page 4.)

The Index

LONDON REPORTS SAFE LANDING OF 50,000 SOLDIERS

Allied Forces Now Ready for Major Operations, Government Spokesman Reports.

London (INS)—British and French forces totaling more than three divisions or 50,000 men have been safely landed in Norway without the loss of a single soldier, according to information in London today.

In keeping with its policy of secrecy, described as "essential to success of the undertaking," the British war office would furnish no figures on the exact size of the allied expeditionary force.

But dispatches from Stockholm estimated the number at 50,000 men and there was no attempt to deny this figure.

"Not One Man Lost."

British officials were more ready to discuss the success with which the operations have been carried out. Stating that not a single man had been lost, informed quarters said:

"This achievement proves above everything the complete control exercised by the allied fleets over Europe's sea routes."

The allied army, the spokesman declared, "is now in a position and is ready for major operations."

Just what these operations will be and where they will take place was a matter of speculation, although all information continued to point to Trondheim as the most likely battlefield of a major clash.

Large-Scale Landing.

British officialdom virtually confirmed a large-scale British landing at Molde, [illegible] miles southwest of Trondheim, close to a strategic railway spur leading to Trondheim and to Oslo. They took exception to publication of Stockholm dispatches disclosing that information to this effect had reached Mrs. J. Borden Harriman, United States Minister to Norway, holding that premature revelation of British movements was "harmful."

There was abounding confidence, [illegible] the British undertaking would succeed. Informed quarters dismissed the possibility [illegible] "blitzkrieg" in the Far North, giving the impression that the present landings are part of a long range campaign designed ultimately to cut off Reichsfuehrer Adolf Hitler's forces in Norway and nullify the gains he has already made in Scandinavia.

THE WEATHER
Tonight—Cloudy, cool.
Tomorrow—Fair, warmer.

THE TIMES RECORD

FINAL EDITION

Series 1940—No. 113. (Entered as second Class Matter at the Postoffice at Troy, N. Y., under the Act of March 3, 1879.) TROY, N. Y., SATURDAY EVENING, MAY 11, 1940. (Published Daily Except Sunday) PRICE THREE CENTS

NAZIS BLASTED FROM AIRPORTS IN ROTTERDAM AND THE HAGUE

GERMAN BOMBERS TAKE HEAVY TOLL IN FRENCH TOWNS

More Than 100 Persons Killed or Wounded in Raids; Nazis Repulsed in Luxembourg.

Paris (U.P.)—German airplanes attacked at dawn today along the whole length of the Belgium-Netherlands front while German land forces, covering the left flank of the entire operation, attacked the new allied positions in Luxembourg.

Fighting was continuous from the North Sea to the Moselle River at Sierck, on the French-Luxembourg border.

It followed the general line extending from the Zuyder Zee in Holland, along the Yssel and Meuse Rivers, then along the German frontier past Aix-La-Chapelle, through Luxembourg.

The French high command said that more than 100 persons, mostly women and children, had been killed or wounded in German air raids on France yesterday and that the French air force had counter-attacked, bombing German air fields all last night, apparently in reprisal.

Air raid sirens and anti-aircraft guns had awakened Paris at dawn again today.

The 501st French war communique said: "Our movements continued all night in Belgium. Violent attacks by the enemy could not achieve new progress in southern Luxembourg. There was nothing to report in Lorraine-Alsace (the French-German front.)"

French Retain Gains.

Military authorities said that at the end of yesterday's action French columns held all ground gained in Luxembourg despite bitter German attacks.

At the same time it was said that a German division attacked in the sector east of the Moselle River in an attempt to force the French to retreat from Luxembourg, but the maneuver failed. authorities said that French advance posts, conforming to plan, had withdrawn to a fortified line and artillery checked the Germans.

Air force authorities asserted that the Germans lost 150 planes in Holland, Belgium and France yesterday. Another plane was said to have been downed in Switzerland. The planes included heavy bombers which had been converted into troop transports. The French claimed to have suffered no plane losses or equipment damaged in yesterday's German bombing of the Percy and Noel airfields.

Many Civilians Killed.

Although no bombs had been dropped on Paris, the government was swamped with reports of the bombings of open French towns yesterday. Casualties were heavy. They included:

Henin-Leitard — One woman killed, three injured:

Bruay—One man killed, four injured.

Lens—A family of Polish miners killed.

LaFere and vicinity—Ten killed, thirty injured.

Loan—Four killed, ten injured.

Nancy and vicinity—16 killed, 13 injured.

Colmar—The prefecture bombed.

Pontoise, 24 miles from Paris—Two killed.

Lambersart—Four killed, eight injured including a 73-year-old man and a 13-year-old girl.

At Lyons, incendiary bombs set workers' homes afire in the Deeimes suburb.

Nancy was bombed three times. There were alarms from 4 a.m to 7:30 a.m.; 1 p.m. to 4:30 p.m., and 5:30 p.m. to 6:30 p.m. An empty school was destroyed by a bomb.

In northern France, Bouai, Hazebrouck, Doullens, Abbeville and Lambersart were bombed.

North Troy Flat Speedily Rented

NORTH, 896 3rd Ave. — Corner house, first flat, all improvements, reasonable. Ready June 1st. Inquire J. J. Perkins, 872 3rd Ave.

"I'm mighty pleased with the results," says the North Troy woman who ordered this Classified Ad in The Record Newspapers. To get tenants for your property tell prospective renters what you have by describing it in the Classified Section.

Phone Troy 6100

England Gets New Leader

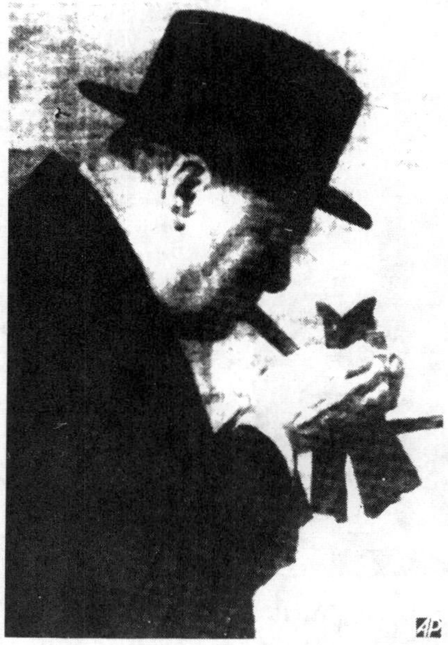

Winston Churchill, hated by Hitler and noted for aggressiveness, is shown as he put a match to his cigar after a cabinet meeting in London—scarcely an hour or two before he replaced Neville Chamberlain as prime minister. Photo was radioed from London.

BARGE CANAL TO REMAIN FREE OF FEDERAL CONTROL

Local Congressmen Aided Defeat of Wheeler-Lea Bill Relating to Interstate Commerce Body.

The Record Newspapers Bureau, Washington, D. C.

By Rep. E. Harold Cluett of Troy and Rep. William T. Byrne of Loudonville, joining with 207 other Democrats and Republicans in administering a general shellacking to the Wheeler-Lea transportation bill, it means that the New York State Barge Canal and the Hudson River will not be placed under control of the Interstate Commerce commission as transportation agencies.

The vote on the motion of Rep. James W. Wadsworth of New York to recommit the bill was carried by a vote of 209 to 182, thus pigeonholing for this Congress, and perhaps for all time, a measure which was advocated by President Roosevelt in his first race for president.

Under the provisions of the proposed legislation, coastwise, inland, Great Lakes common and contract carriers by water engaged in interstate commerce (transporting goods that enter interstate commerce) would be placed under jurisdiction of the Interstate Commerce Commission.

Vote On Recommittal.

Practically all upstate members of the House were included in the 209 who voted to recommit the bill to the House Committee on Interstate Commerce for further consideration. The instructions to the committee carried, under the motion of Representative Wadsworth, are that a bill be reported that would not permit any railroad man to lose his job due to probable consolidation of railroads, that a carrier in water transportation might lower rates to a level of a compensatory return, and that all farm products handled by rail should have the same consideration as to rates by the Interstate Commerce Commission as those for export.

The motion to recommit was so cleverly phrased that the farm,

(Continued on Page 7.)

MRS O'DAY GIVES UP DELEGATE'S POST TO SENATOR WAGNER

Albany (AP)—Rep. Caroline O'Day of Rye, was withdrawn as a delegate-at-large to the Democratic National Convention in Chicago to provide a place for U. S. Senator Robert F. Wagner, whose name was inadvertently omitted from the Democratic State Committee's designating resolution.

This was disclosed today with release by Secretary of State Michael J. Walsh of official lists of the major parties' delegates.

The Democrats listed 204 names, including 18 delegates-at-large who will have only half a vote each, and the Republicans, 186 names, including eight delegates at large who will have full votes.

SWISS FRONTIER TENSE AS PLANES ROAR OVERHEAD

Army Mobilized, Bringing 300,000 Fresh Troops To Colors; Bombing Probe Continued.

Berne (AP)—Switzerland's frontier population, told by Generalissimo Henri Guisan that the fully mobolized Swiss army "is ready to do its duty on each of our frontiers," was tense today after a night in which foreign planes several times flew over Swiss cities.

For the first time since the war began a Swiss air patrol flew over Basel, at the junction of the Swiss, French and German borders, to protect the city last night.

German planes passed over Basel en route to France, but were seen returning to Germany later in the night after they had been met by heavy French anti-aircraft fire.

Over Schaffhausen, near the German frontier in the north, six foreign war planes of unknown nationality were seen flying from east to west through a heavy fog yesterday afternoon.

The Swiss made no protest over 27 bombs which dropped on Swiss territory yesterday. An inquiry still is going on. It is believed they were released by a German pilot seeking to escape from a French pursuit squadron.

General Guisan issued an order of the day which declared the army's determination to defend Switzerland "with its last drop of energy" against "all aggressors who ever they may be."

The general mobilization order of yesterday went into effect at dawn today, bringing to the colors 300,000 to 400,000 fresh troops, it was estimated. It was reported that 300,000 men for some time had been in the Winkelried Line facing Germany and in small fortifications facing France.

The order of the day said that general mobilization had been imposed "by the gravity of the international situation."

RUMANIAN PREMIER QUITS, CAROL SEEKS UNITED GOVERNMENT

Bucharest (AP)—The government of Premier Gheorghe Tatarescu resigned today and King Carol immediately requested the outgoing premier to form a new national-union government.

Quarters close to the government said King Carol wanted representatives of all political thought, from Extreme left to the extreme right, represented in the new government because of belief that Rumania must be united in the face of a possible extension of the war throughout Europe.

The monarch was understood to be alarmed at the manner in which dissatisfied factions opened the way in other countries for Nazi penetration.

NAZI JUGGERNAUT HITS UNEXPECTED SNAG IN HOLLAND

Rotterdam Recaptured By Dutch at Cost of 1,000 Men; German Parachute Troops Annihilated.

Amsterdam (INS)—Nazi Germany's attempted blitzkrieg occupation of The Netherlands ended in failure today when Dutch troops aided by the British Royal Air Force recaptured the Rotterdam airport, Holland's last base remaining in German hands.

At the same time, a swift and effective Dutch counter-attack completely annihilated the Germans who had landed by plane, parachute and flat-bottomed boat on the Island of Dordrecht southeast of Rotterdam.

The Dutch themselves lost 1,000 men in this battle, probably the bloodiest of the war to date, but emerged completely victorious, with Rotterdam again safe and Germany's foothold in western Holland loosened.

News of Holland's latest successes in holding off and even successfully counteracting the Nazi juggernaut reached Amsterdam coincident with a terrific new German air attack upon the Amsterdam airport in which cargoes of heavy caliber bombs were dropped upon the flying field and surrounding buildings.

Dutch Hold Hague.

Together with the stirring news from Rotterdam, it was ascertained definitely that Queen Wilhelmina's capital, The Hague, remains in Dutch hands.

Its airport changed possession three separate times in terrific fighting between Dutch soldiers and German parachute troops but has now been consolidated by the Dutch.

The Rotterdam airport was retaken after stubborn fighting, an official announcement said, which was preceded by a heavy British air force attack. "Great loss of life" was reported.

All magnetic mines sown by the Germans in Dutch harbors have been mopped up, it was announced. Two-thirds of Holland's gold was sent abroad before the invasion and the remainder is being sent out today.

The official statement did not minimize the losses sustained by the Dutch infantry at the hands of German parachute troops. As a result of losses sustained by the First Army Corps in these operations in north and south Holland, reinforcements are needed to keep the situation in hand.

Enemy Wiped Out.

"The German plan makes it necessary for us to scatter our forces, which in normal events would be kept together," the announcement said.

"The Dutch navy played a great part in the Dordrecht attack, and accounted for a lot of Germans. The enemy there was wiped out completely, including men, airplanes and stores.

"It was a bitter fight.

"We now have to be constantly vigilant, since fresh parachutists are arriving constantly."

At the Rotterdam airport, known as Waalhaven, the Dutch had to contend not only with parachute troops but men landed from air transport planes which came down in Rotterdam harbor.

"The parachutists established themselves at Waalhaven proper as well as behind dykes and in the fields, causing a lot of obstruction and a great deal of difficulty in dislodging them," the military spokesman said.

"Fairly strong parties had to be detailed to mop them up."

Holland's success in ejecting the Germans at such short notice was hailed by neutral observers, who believed the German plan called for complete occupation of The Netherlands in 24 hours.

Nazis Poorly Equipped.

Military instructions found on captured German parachutists revealed that Germany hoped to occupy all of Holland within 24 hours, the high command announced today.

The Germans vastly underestimated the resistance Nazi troops would have to face, it was said.

In addition, the communique described the Germans as low in morale and poorly equipped.

Latest ward in Amsterdam indicated that the Dutch forces were holding the Nazis in check all along a 250-mile eastern front.

Queen Wilhelmina today telegraphed King Victor Emmanuel of Italy appealing to the "noble sentiments and humanitarian feelings" of the House of Savoy in the conflict thrust upon Holland.

LINER CLAIMS RECORD.

New York (AP)—The Argentina, of the American Republic Line, docked today with 284 passengers, claiming a record passage of ten days and ten hours from Rio de Janeiro to New York. Her master, Capt. Thomas M. Simmons, said his ship's average of 19 knots per hour for the 4,748-mile voyage set a new merchant ship mark.

Nazis Meet Strong Resistance

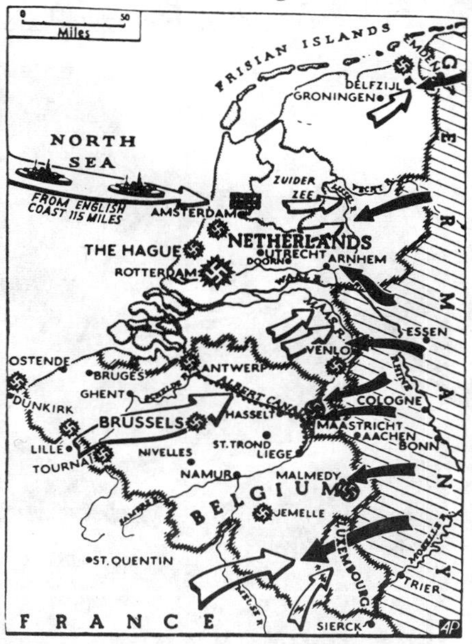

Germany's blitzkrieg thrusts (black arrows) into Holland, Belgium and Luxembourg, met determined resistance by Allied forces moving up to battle (white arrows). Nazi symbols show cities bombed—or where Hitler parachuted troops to the ground. First major battle was at Rotterdam, where parachuted Nazis fought Dutch troops. Dutch reports said British had landed at several coastal points, with British detachments passing through Amsterdam. Germans claimed to have taken Maastricht and Malmedy.

BERLIN REPORTS NAZI VICTORIES IN NEW INVASION

Germans Claim Allied Troops Repulsed, More Than 300 Planes Destroyed; Warships Sunk.

Berlin (AP)—Lightning successes were reported today by the German high command on land and sea and in the air as Adolf Hitler's personally-directed warriors relentlessly pressed their total-warfare against the Allies on a front extending from the Arctic to mid-Europe.

A high command communique from Hitler's headquarters at the front reported these successes:

1. The destruction of between 300 and 400 enemy airplanes on the ground and the shooting down of 23 more in airfights during operations in France, Holland and Belgium.

2. The repulse of enemy border troops in The Netherlands and Belgium by the German western army with the aid of the air force and parachute troops.

3. The sinking of an enemy destroyer, one enemy submarine and two merchantships.

4. Bomb hits on one British battleship and a cruiser off Narvik, Norway, where the situation is unchanged with the German garrison still besieged by the Allies.

In the air, the Germans acknowledged the loss of eleven of their own planes and said 15 others were missing.

Mass air attacks were carried out yesterday on air bases in Belgium, France and Holland.

Airports Raided.

Seventy-two airports were raided, the report said, and numerous airport buildings and hangers were destroyed by fire and explosions.

"Especially hard hit were the French air bases at Metz, Nancy, Rheims, Romilly, Dijon and Lyon," the communique added.

A charge that the Allies had killed two civilians during air raids on the Ruhr was made in the communique, which added that several civilians were injured and slight material damage caused.

(Continued On Page 2)

FARMHAND DIES IN BLAZE HE STARTED

Binghamton (U.P.) — Benjamin Stout, 70-year-old farmhand, lost a race with fire yesterday and burned to death.

Stout was trapped by a brush fire which he started on the Elizabeth Johnson farm near Glen Castle, where he was employed. As the blaze swept out of control, he attempted to flee but was overcome by smoke. More than 40 acres of timber were destroyed before Chenango firemen and volunteers extinguished the blaze. Stout's body was found later by Fire Warden Carl Hendrickson.

POPE PIUS PRAYS FOR TRIUMPH OF BELGIUM, HOLLAND

Pontiff Throws Moral Support to Catholic and Protestant Lands Invaded by Germans.

Vatican City (AP)—Pope Piux XII today threw his moral force in support not only of Catholic Belgium but also the Duchy of Luxembourg and Protestant Holland in messages to their rulers saying he was praying for thei rtriumph.

Vatican officials disclosed the Pope had anticipated an appeal for support from King Leopold, one of the most devoutly Catholic of present-day sovereigns, by sending his message last night before receiving one from the King. Leopold's message arrived this morning.

The Pontiff told King Leopold he was praying for the restoration of Belgium's "full liberty and independence."

The Pope's message was made public a short time after he had received Myron C. Taylor, President Roosevelt's personal envoy to the Vatican, in a separate private audience.

Pope's Message.

Similar messages also were sent by the Pope to Queen Wilhelmina of The Netherlands and Grand Duchess Charlotte of Luxembourg.

The message to King Leopold said:

"In a moment when, for the second time against its will and right, the Belgian people sees its territory exposed to the cruelties of war, we, being profoundly moved, send Your Majesty and to the entire nation so beloved by us, assurance of our paternal affection and, while praying to the all-powerful God that this stern trial may end with the restoration of full liberty and independence of Belgium, we send your majesty and your people our apostolic blessing with all our heart."

The Pope's message to Queen Wilhelmina said:

"Having learned with deep emotion that your majesty's efforts in

(Continued On Page 2)

GRAND DUCHESS OF LUXEMBOURG SAFE

London (AP)—It is understood that Grand Duchess Charlotte, ruler of German-invaded Luxembourg, has arrived safely on French soil, Reuters (British News Agency) announced today.

Many citizens of the tiny principality escaped by automobile into France this morning, according to the agency.

The Grand Duchess Charlotte, now 44 years old, has ruled the Duchy of Luxembourg since Jan. 15, 1919, succeeding her elder sister, Marie Adelaide, who relinquished her title to enter a convent in Italy. The sister died in 1924.

Their father, Grand Duke William, IV, who preceded them on the throne, died in 1912.

Dutch And Belgian Defenses "Smear" Hitler Blitzkrieg

Twenty Killed As German Air Raiders Bomb Amsterdam; Berlin Reports Fort Captured Near Liege; French Army Advancing Against Foe in Luxembourg; Allies Pour Troops Into Invaded Countries; Nazis Drop Parachute Troops Into Belgium and Bomb Brussels; Conflicting Claims of Successes.

BY THE ASSOCIATED PRESS.

Warfare in the German-invaded lowlands centered in The Netherlands today.

The Nazis were reported to have been blasted from footholds in Rotterdam and The Hague. A bombing attack on Amsterdam led to a death toll estimated at twenty.

Dutch and Belgian defenses apparently held Adolf Hitler's legions at bay in border regions as defenders fought for time to enable Allied troops to get into position and, in the case of The Netherlands, for flood waters to cut the country in half.

At the lower end of the 200-mile front from the North Sea to the juncture of the French, Luxembourg and Belgian borders, French reported they had repulsed a large scale German attack while their forces advanced against the Germans in Luxembourg.

The Netherlands foreign minister announced from London that all airdromes which the Germans had seized yesterday in their lightning attacks by land and air had been recaptured.

Authorized Germans in Berlin, however, had disputed this. They said their troops still held the airdromes both in The Netherlands and in Belgium which they seized yesterday. They admitted, however, that fighting was going on there.

Nazis Report Fort Captured.

DNB, official German news agency, identified as a strong fort before Liege, 25 miles within Belgium, the fort which the Germans announced yesterday they had captured.

Nearly 26 years ago the grey-clad legions of Kaiser Wilhelm in the drive on Paris beat at the forts of Liege for more than a week before they fell—precious time of vast importance to the Allies.

In the new conflict DNB boasted "one of the strongest forts in the area before Liege proved completely defenseless against surprise attack by German planes."

In the widely conflicting claims of success against their rivals' air power, the Germans reported the greatest results—300 to 400 destroyed on the ground and 23 more in the air. The British said their fliers yesterday destroyed at least 50 German planes, while some 20 British craft were missing.

Anti-British posters in Rome and an alleged attack on two British diplomats were marked out for a protest by the British ambassador to Rome, while students in Milan staged a pro-German demonstration. Premier Mussolini applauded a statement of displeasure over Allied contraband control.

French Report Advance.

As the forces of western Europe surged over the historic battleground of the lowlands, Pope Pius XII expressed in messages to King Leopold, Queen Wilhelmina and Grand Duchess Charlotte a prayer that "this stern trial" of their countries would end with restoration of liberty and independence.

While warplanes operated behind the front lines, with German flyers dropping more parachute troops in Belgium and bombing Brussels twice, indecisive fighting swept over a 200-mile front.

The French general staff said French troops were "maintaining our advance" in Luxembourg and reoccupied outposts deserted yesterday in the Moselle region when the Germans hurled against them a full division (from 12,000 to 15,000 troops).

The German high command, from Adolf Hitler's secret headquarters, declared its forces were "on a swift forward attack" after the penetration of The Netherlands, Belgium and Luxembourg.

While the French reported 100 French civilians were killed or wounded yesterday in German air raids over France, the Germans charged that two civilians were killed during the night in Allied attacks in the Ruhr region.

Picture On War Fronts.

The European war, plunging into a critical and possibly decisive phase, today shaped up like this:

Britain and France—The Allies hurried land, sea and air forces to aid Belgium and Holland, counting the Nazi invasion of the low countries a grave threat to the Maginot Line and England's insular security. The Allied powers said at least 180 German planes had been downed, damaged or captured.

Germany—Terming this "the decisive hour," Germany poured more contingents across the Belgian and Dutch frontiers and hurled her air forces behind the battle lines seeking a lightning conquest before effective Allied aid arrives. The blitzkrieg was launched, Germans declared, to forestall a similar Allied invasion. Thus far 100 Allied planes have been destroyed, they said.

Belgium—Invaded by land and air, the Belgians said their stubbornly resisting troops, fortifications and tank traps had held up the German advance while 200,000 British soldiers swept in from the west to give assistance.

Blitzkrieg Called Failure.

The Netherlands — Germany's blitzkrieg was called a failure although more parachute troops were raining down on Dutch soil. All airports were recaptured. British sources said the maximum German advance was 13 miles.

Luxembourg—The tiny grand duchy was largely overrun by Germany before French troops made contact for battle.

Switzerland—Anxious over their neutrality, the Swiss put through complete mobilization.

Italy—Some fascists cheered for a German victory in the low countries but Italy still remained on the sidelines apparently waiting to see which side would win before jumping into the fray.

Japan—Domei news agency dispatches reported Japan had decided to state again her concern over any change in the status of The Netherlands East Indies.

All the world watched the swiftly developing conflict which presaged the greatest blood-letting of the war. Still stalemated on the concrete-and-steel frontier between Germany and France, the war seemed destined to run its bitterest course on the lowland soil which for centuries has been a European battleground.

The Dutch and Belgians reported

(Continued On Page 2)

Dutch Women Break Shoes On Nazi Skulls

Amsterdam (INS) — Some Dutch women in their cloppety wooden shoes and their starched white aprons met some German parachute troops in their white parachutes in a downtown Amsterdam street—and now there are a lot of broken wooden shoes and a lot of broken German heads.

The parachute troops landed in a suburban market place.

There was not very much of anything left of the Nazis after they were finally rescued by Dutch soldiers, the Nazis having been subjected to what some people might call a lady-like blitzkrieg, carried out with rolling pins, wooden shoes and heavy frying pans.

The Index

THE WEATHER
Tonight—Light rain.
Tomorrow—Cloudy, warmer.

THE TIMES RECORD

FINAL EDITION

Series 1940—No. 137. (Entered as second Class Matter at the Postoffice at Troy, N. Y., under the Act of March 3, 1879.) TROY, N. Y., MONDAY EVENING, JUNE 10, 1940. (Published Daily Except Sunday) PRICE THREE CENTS

ITALY DECLARES WAR ON BRITAIN AND FRANCE

Britain Lands New Army In France To Aid Paris Defense

Germans Push Advance Wedge to Within 35 Miles of French Capital; Weygand's Army Fights Back Furiously Inflicting Tremendous Casualties on Enemy for Every Mile Gained; Titanic Batle Line Extends from Channel to Argonne Forest.

Berlin (AP).—Italian forces marched into French territory through the Riviera at approximately 6:30 p.m. tonight (11:30 a.m., E.S.T.).

This information was given reporters by authorized sources at a conference at the Berlin Foreign Office called by Foreign Minister Joachim Von Ribbentrop.

BY THE ASSOCIATED PRESS.

Britain rushed fresh troops to France in her darkening 11th hour today as 1,800,000 tank-led German troops plunged forward to new successes on the 200-mile western front and reached two points within 35 miles of Paris.

Hitler's high command said German troops were moving toward the lower Seine—apparently in a sharp circling movement in the Rouen-Gisors sector on the western road to Paris—and toward the historic Marne in the Soissons-Reims area, northeast of Paris.

"Operations are proceeding on schedule," the high command asserted, while Berlin declared the seven-day-old battle for the French capital was now "entering the decisive stage."

In the heightening emergency, Prime Minister Churchill informed Premier Reynaud of France that an unspecified number of British troops have already been landed in France and that "further extensive reinforcements will shortly be available."

With the French reported sacrificing ground only "when covered with German dead," Generalissimo Maxime Weygand sounded a heartening note with this declaration:

"The enemy has suffered heavy losses. Soon he will come to the end of his effort."

"From the sea to the Argonne the battle continued more and more violently," said the French high command's morning communique. The French were resisting powerfully as the battle went through its sixth day. The question today was whether the Germans could continue, despite frightful losses, the offensive that had forced the French lines back.

Removal of at least part of the French government departments from Paris was indicated strongly in advices reaching New York, although there was no official announcement in the French capital.

In the last war, the government moved to Bordeaux for a few months late in 1914 when the Germans threatened Paris.

Trading on the Paris Bourse (Stock Exchange) was suspended this morning an hour after the session opened.

The Germans Sunday extended the fighting front to the Argonne forest, throwing 3,500 new tanks and 600,000 fresh troops into that sector and dropping parachute soldiers behind the lines.

"Hold Tight," Weygand's Order.

The French, however, said the parachutists were encircled and were being cleaned out while the defense lines held firm and even counter-attacked at one point.

Soon after Generalissimo Maxime Weygand of the French forces predicted that the battle soon would extend clear to the Swiss frontier, the mighty guns of France's Maginot Line opened up against the German West Wall.

They blasted away for an hour and 25 minutes, drawing German replies in kind, and then both sides suddenly fell silent. Fires blazed on both sides.

General Weygand predicted that the end of the Nazi effort must come soon, and told his men to "hold tight" in what he called "the last quarter of an hour."

Paris Has New Air Raid.

The Paris region was subjected to renewed German aerial bombardment, while the British said their planes ranged over Germany Sunday to destroy ammunition dumps and oil stocks and French aviation drew active combat in attacks on German troop columns.

In the titanic struggle to save their homeland against the biggest German offensive of the war, the French dropped back yesterday to a main line along the heavily wooded Bresle River, which empties into the sea at Eu,—a line line extending through the Oise Valley to the Marne plains south of the Aisne.

Today the center of the Weygand line was still falling back to meet the threat to its left flank from the mighty German tank column which broke through to the Seine.

But the right flank was reported striking back around the Argonne.

The Germans were using not only masses of infantry and their force of armored vehicles, but were drawing on their strength to the full with big guns and dive bombers and parachute troops trying to smash the French lines with all the ferocity and skill at their command.

The order to suspend trading on the Bourse was issued by the Board of Governors, and it could not be learned immediately whether the exchange would be moved outside the city.

The order annulled the latest quotations established in heavy trading.

Hurling what military experts considered their full force into a gigantic battle of men and machines, the Nazis battered ahead with planes, tanks and guns and followed up with waves of fresh infantry along a meandering front over 200 miles long from the English Channel east to the Maginot Line.

Titanic Battle Rages.

With the Allied defenders reported sacrificing ground only "when it was covered with German dead" under Generalissimo Maxime Weygand's order to "hold tight' 'in "the last quarter of an hour," the titanic battle of France blazed most fiercely in three major sectors:

1. On the Allies' western flank,

(Continued On Page 3)

ARMY OF 400,000 IN U. S. APPROVED BY HOUSE GROUP

Washington (U.P.)—The House Military Affairs Committee was reported authoritatively today to have approved a bill increasing the authorized strength of the Regular Army to 400,000 men.

This new action today on the defense program was reported as President Roosevelt prepared to deliver a "very important pronouncement" on the international situation at Charlottesville, Va., this evening. It was reported the President's address at the University of Virginia might deal with proposals for compulsory military training

The House committee action came on a bill by Rep. Overton Brooks, D., La., which called for an increase from the authorized strength of 280,000 to 375,000. The committee changed the bill to make the Army strength 400,000 and then voted to approve it, it was said.

Furnished Place Rented To Reader

EAST SIDE—Completely furnished apartment, all modern equipment including heat, electric, gas; adults. J. H. Sipperley, 3 Gregory Court, 4 to 8.

A reader of The Record Newspapers, deciding that was just what he wanted, answered the above Classified Ad and rented the furnished apartment. Someone will be looking over the Classified columns tomorrow for another furnished place. Have you one for rent?

Phone Troy 6100

Liner Roosevelt Refugees Greeted On Arrival In New York

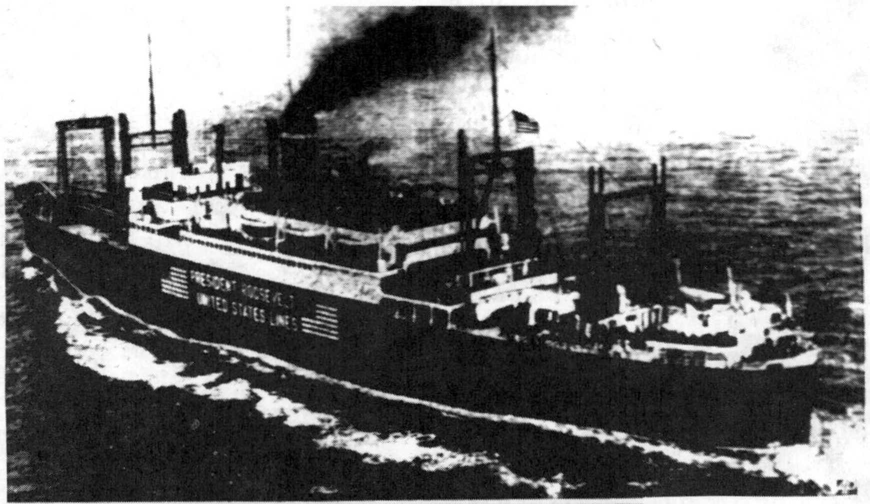

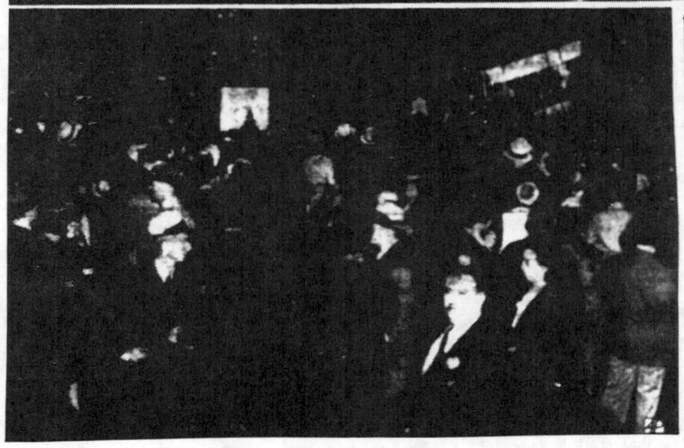

The United States liner President Roosevelt is shown in this airview (upper) as she neared her New York port with approximately 700 American refugees aboard. Lower view shows scene on the pier as friends were on hand to greet the refugees when they arrived in New York from Galway, Ireland, aboard the liner. Making up the ship's human cargo fleeing the terrors of the European war were Rhodes scholars, students who had been studying for the priesthood in Italy, relatives of consular officials and American businessmen who had been seeking contracts from the Allies.

FORD INSPECTING ARMY PLANE AT DEARBORN TODAY

Motor Magnate To Decide Whether Ships Are Adaptable for Mass Production at River Rouge.

Dearborn, Mich., (U.P.) — Henry Ford and his engineers inspect one of the Army's best fighting planes today to see if its parts are adaptable to mass production in his vast River Rouge plant.

If the ship, a Curtiss P-40 pursuit model, is found to be of a design suitable to the Ford assembly lines, the automotive genius may inaugurate a new era of airplane manufacture in the interests of national defense. Ford has said he could build 1,000 standardized planes daily if the government did not interfere with his operations.

The government's desire to cooperate with Ford was seen in the War Department's immediate offer to send one of its latest models to the Ford airport for inspection, accompanied by a technician to answer questions about it.

All Metal Plane.

The Curtiss P-40 is a single-seated, all-metal monoplane, powered with an Allison liquid-cooled engine, equipped with supercharger, and reportedly is capable of 400 miles an hour. It has retractable landing gear and machine guns mounted in the wings.

In addition to the two wing machine guns, the P-40 has two machine guns synchronized to fire through the propellor. It carries oxygen tanks and a heater to permit flying six miles up. The motor is of 1,000 horse power.

Blue prints of the model were expected to arrive tomorrow, although the principal study will center on the component parts in relationship to one another, as they would be thrown together in actual assemblage.

5,000 Planes Daily.

Ford's interest in mass production of aircraft was stimulated by President Roosevelt's proposal for a 50-000-plane-a-year program. Ford had asked to see a standard type plane "as soon as possible," and had added that "if there is anything I can do to further the national defense program, please do not hesitate to call on me."

If an emergency required the full production facilities of the River Rouge plant, it probably could pour out planes at a rate far greater than that estimated by Ford. Some production experts said the factory—the largest industrial unit in the world would be able to turn 5,000 ships a day off its essembly lines once they were geared up. Its daily automobile capacity is 10,000 cars and 25,000 engines.

The Dearborn plant alone could exceed the production of airplane factories in Germany, which has been estimated as high as 10,000-per-month. Aircraft factories on the West Coast have been filling orders by the Allied armies and would not be able immediately, unless a crisis occurred to play a major part in the proposed 50,000 planes-a-year program.

KILLED BY LIGHTNING.

Syracuse (U.P.)—A bolt of lightning killed Edward Polly, 17, yesterday as he dug for fishing worms in a Syracuse park. His brother, Michael, 12, was seriously injured.

ALLIES WITHDRAW ALL FORCES FROM NORTHERN NORWAY

Troops Transferred To Western Front, Leaving Narvik To Nazis; Haakon in England.

Stockholm, Sweden (U.P.)—Capitulation of the Norwegian army and withdrawal of Allied forces from Narvik, the great iron ore port, left Germany unchallenged today along the entire Norwegian coast and put her in position to dominate Russia's Arctic trade route.

It was made known that Gen. C. G. Fleischer, commander in chief of the Norwegian forces in the north, had ordered his men to surrender after King Haakon, Crown Prince Olav and members of the Norwegian government had been embarked in Allied warships.

Diplomatic sources here asserted that the king, the crown prince and others had embarked several days ago.

(The British ministry of information in London, announcing the Allied withdrawal from northern Norway, said today that King

(Continued on Page 22.)

HOME SALVATION OF LIFE, LEHMAN SAYS

Albany (U.P.)—Governor Lehman said today that one of the "really great needs" of modern life is a "strengthening of home life and family ties."

Lehman made the statement in connection with observance of Father's Day, June 16.

"In the perlexing and troublesome times that lie ahead the salvation of our democratic way of life may be found in the home," he said.

HEADS CLARKSON TECH.

Potsdam (U.P.)—Dr. John A. Ross has been named acting president of Clarkson Tech succeeding Dr. James S. Thomas, resigned.

Flash of Distant Artillery Lights Up Sky Over Paris

BY KENNETH DOWNS.

Paris (INS) — The battle of France roared towards its grim climax today as the Germans hurled every ounce of their might into a gigantic drive to encircle and capture Paris.

The steady pounding of artillery and the thud of bombs was heard clearly in the capital—as they have been for the past 12 hours—and a thin layer of smoke blanketed the city, rising from bomb-ignited fires.

It was impossible to say how many million men are fighting but the bulk of the entire French and German forces are engaged along the 185-mile front from the sea to Montmedy, with German tanks hammering at the Rouen-Gisors area only 35 miles northwest of Paris.

No details of the fighting were contained in this morning's French

(Continued on Page 22.)

SEEK SABOTEURS IN ATTEMPTED SINKING OF OLD U. S. VESSEL

Portland, Ore. (INS)—Saboteurs who attempted to sink the 44-year-old battleship Oregon, now a museum piece of the Spanish-American war, were hunted by police today under special orders of Mayor Joseph K. Carson.

The inglorious effort was discovered by custodians after the venerable warship, famous in American history for its race around Cape Horn in 1898, had taken on about 600 tons of water and was slowly settling into the Williamette River at a Portland marine park. The water was let in through a seacock in the port shaft alley.

In ordering the investigation, the Mayor declared: "There is no question in my mind that it was sabotage."

Nazis Near End Of Effort, French Say

Paris (INS) — In line with Gen. Maxime Weygand's order of the day to "hold fast," all French positions are being maintained despite redoubled German attacks along the entire front, a French military spokesman declared today.

The spokesman admitted there had been some infiltration by German tanks.

General Weygand's order said:

"The German offensive is now launched on the whole front, from the sea to Montmedy . . . the order still is for each man to fight without thought of falling back, eyes fixed right ahead, in the place where the high command has placed him.

"The commander-in-chief is fully aware of the magnificent example of unflinching effort and valor that the armies engaged, as well as the air force, have shown.

"He thanks them for this.

"France asks still more

"Officers, non-commissioned officers and men, the salvation of the country demands not only your courage but all the stubbornness, initiative and fighting spirit of which I know you are capable.

"The enemy has suffered considerable losses. Soon he will reach the end of his effort.

"This is the last quarter-hour. Hold fast."

Mussolini Sends Nation On March "To Break Chains"

Allied Ambassadors Handed Passports at Rome As Il Duce Salutes Hitler and Tells 80,000 Romans Conflict Is Struggle Between Poor and Rich; Denounces Decrepit Democracies" and Says Hour of Destiny Has Arrived for Fatherland; Allied Capitals Calm.

BY THE UNITED PRESS.

Premier Benito Mussolini threw Italy's armed strength into the war on the Mediterranean front today as German armies hammered closer and closer to Paris.

Striking at an hour when Adolf Hitler's legions were rolling with crushing weight into the heart of France, the Fascist premier declared that Italy would "break the chains" of the British and French in the Mediterranean.

Even as he spoke to a madly cheering throng from the balcony of Venice Palace, the forces of fascism were on the march and the British and French ambassadors had been given their passports.

"The hour of destiny has arrived for our fatherland," Mussolini said. "We are going to war against the decrepit democracies. . . to break the chains that tie us in the Mediterranean."

The news of Italy's entrance into the war was received calmly in London and Paris where this eventuality had long been expected and prepared for.

More than a week ago the Allies had completed all precautions on land and sea and in the air to meet Italy's blow.

Some of these measures, such as the concentration of French and British fleets in the eastern Mediterranean, already had been announced.

Others have been kept secret, but it is known that the Allies will not remain merely on the defensive, either on land or sea or in the air.

Mussolini, speaking in a strained, powerful voice to perhaps 80,000 persons in the Venice Palace Square and side streets and the millions throughout Italy and the world, said that there is but one watchword for the Fascists:

"It is to win!"

"We salute the fuehrer of Germany," he added. "Fascist Italy is on her feet and prepared to strike."

The premier, who once said that Italy had 10,000,000 bayonets ready for action, declared that "this gigantic struggle is a logical part in our revolution."

"The revolution," he continued, "asserts itself against those who control the riches of the earth.

"It is a struggle of one century against another."

"We will take up arms to solve the problems of our continental frontiers and our maritime frontiers," the premier said.

"We shall win and we shall give a long period of peace and prosperity to Italy and the world.

"People of Italy: To arms!

"Your tenacity, bravery and courage will prevail."

Says King Agrees.

The premier announced that the ambassadors of Britain and France had been informed of the declaration of war.

"In this hour, we turn our thoughts to the King-Emperor," Mussolini said of King Victor Emmanuel.

"As always, the King has interpreted the soul of the Fatherland."

The premier said that the King had correctly viewed the attitude of Italy as sympathetic toward Germany and that "for the third time Fascist Italy enters war as one man."

Italy wanted to keep the conflict from spreading to other countries, he said, but a great people cannot permit others to hamper its development.

Britain and France, he said, had tried to halt the progress of the Italian people and Italy has decided to accept the sacrifices and hardships of war together with the Germans.

"The Dies Are Cast."

"The dies are now cast." Mussolini said. "It is a struggle of a young progressive people against decadent nations. This gigantic struggle is only a phase in the development of our revolution."

The Allies, he asserted should not have rebuffed "the peace offers of Hitler" but all this "is a fact of the past."

"The entire world," he said, "is witness to the fact that Fascist Italy has done everything possible to avoid the storm the world is now witnessing."

"Italy is striking to solve first the problem of continental frontiers—Savoy and Nice in France—and then the problem of sea frontiers—Corsica, Malta, Cyprus, Suez and other Allied possessions—by military force, the premier said.

"Poor Against Rich."

"This gigantic battle is the battle of the poor peoples against the rich and fierce holders of the world's gold," Mussolini shouted.

But, he said, Italy does not desire to bring other countries into the war—naming Switzerland and the Balkans, Turkey and Egypt. His reference to Egypt and Turkey appeared to be a bid to persuade those two allies of Britain to remain neutral.

Mussolini has said that he could put 10,000,000 bayonets in the field, but reliable sources have estimated the strength of the Italian army at from 2,000,000 to 3,000,000, in addition to a first line air force of possibly 3,000 and a navy which is short on capital ships but strong in small torpedo boats.

Italy's air force is considered by most experts as top-notch, but under normal conditions the important northern industrial areas of Italy would be vulnerable to swift and devastating attack by Allied airplanes. Whether Germany's hammer blows in the north had changed that situation remained to be seen.

Italy's Military Strength.

Italy can bring to Germany's side an army of probably 2,000,000 men, a first line air force of 2,500 and 3,500 planes and a navy of six dreadnaughts, 21 cruisers, 110 submarines and 200 to 300 minor warships.

Italian forces are deployed in three principal theaters:

The northern frontier along the chain of Alps between France and Italy.

At key points in the Mediterranean.

In Africa.

The largest concentration of Italian troops, possibly a million men, is believed to be in position along

(Continued On Page 3)

O'CONNOR CALLS ON VOTERS TO SPURN BROWDER PETITION

Albany (U.P.)—Former Rep. John J. O'Connor, New York Democrat who was "purged" in the 1938 primaries, appealed to upstate voters today to refuse to sign petitions to place the name of Earl Browder on the November election ballot as the communist candidate for president.

O'Connor, who has offered himself as a candidate for vice president on the Republican ticket explained that at least fifty signatures were required in each county and added that [illegible] 1938.

"Unless the voters are on guard it will be easy for the communists to obtain signatures from those who are kept in ignorance that they are signing a Communist Party petition" O'Connor said, in a prepared statement.

The Index

THE WEATHER
Tonight: Fair, cool.
Tomorrow: Fair, [illegible]

THE TIMES RECORD

FINAL EDITION

Series 1940—No. 157.

(Entered as second Class Matter at the Postoffice at Troy, N. Y., under the Act of March 3, 1879.)

TROY, N. Y., WEDNESDAY EVENING, JULY 3, 1940.

(Published Daily Except Sunday)

PRICE THREE CENTS

TROY BEGINS DEFENSE PROGRAM

Knox Denies G. O. P. Appointments Mean Coalition Government

NAZI AIRMEN BOMB ENGLAND

GERMANS STAGE DARING DAYLIGHT ATTACK ON COAST

Balkan Situation Easier but Anti-Semitic Riots Are Spreading Throughout Rumania.

BY THE ASSOCIATED PRESS.

German U-boats and bombing planes attacked Britain with new fury today, while the official Nazi agency, DNB, published alleged Allied "win the war" plans for dragging most of Europe into the ten-months-old conflict.

DNB asserted documents captured in France disclosed an Allied program for entangling Rumania, Turkey, Greece, Yugoslavia and Scandinavia to gain wide-spread new battlefronts against Germany.

The Nazi high command said German planes attacked a convoy off the English Channel coast and sank 18,000 tons of British shipping. German submarines, the high command reported, torpedoed another 39,000 tons.

German sky raiders, displaying new boldness in a daylight sortie instead of their usual night-masked attacks, bombed the south coast of England today after an earlier assault that killed 12 and wounded 123.

Troops Attacked.

One Nazi plane machine-gunned soldiers near the beach. Incendiary bombs also were dropped.

British R. A. F. fighters shot down a Nazi bomber off the east coast.

An official air ministry communique issued shortly after noon said anti-aircraft guns were still in action.

With apparent easing of the Balkan crisis, permitting Hitler to divert attention from southeast Europe, Britons wondered if the intensified Nazi air raids signalled the opening of the long-awaited "Battle for Britain."

Things were far from quiet, however, in southeast Europe.

Bloody anti-semitic riots spread through Rumania, and King Carol's hostile neighbor, Hungary, was mobilizing its army to the greatest peacetime strength.

Carol Near Abdication.

Carol himself was reported on the verge of abdicating several days ago after sharp criticism over his surrender of Bessarabia and North Bucovina to Russia. He was said to have been dismissed by his cabinet.

Hungarian army reinforcements streamed toward the border with Rumania but the latter based hopes for peace on Carol's bid for

(Continued On Page 13)

PERSHING APPROVES MILITARY TRAINING

Washington (U.P.)—Gen. John J. Pershing said today in a letter to the Senate Military Affairs Committee that a system of compulsory military training "might well be a determining factor in keeping us out of war."

Chairman Morris Sheppard read Pershing's letter as the committee opened hearings on the Burke-Wadsworth compulsory military training bill which requires the registration of all males from 18 to 65 years of age for some form of defense training.

Pershing said that had a training system been in effect prior to the last World Yar it would not have been necessary for the United States to send "untrained" troops to Europe. It probably would have saved thousands of lives, he added.

Stimson and Knox Quizzed

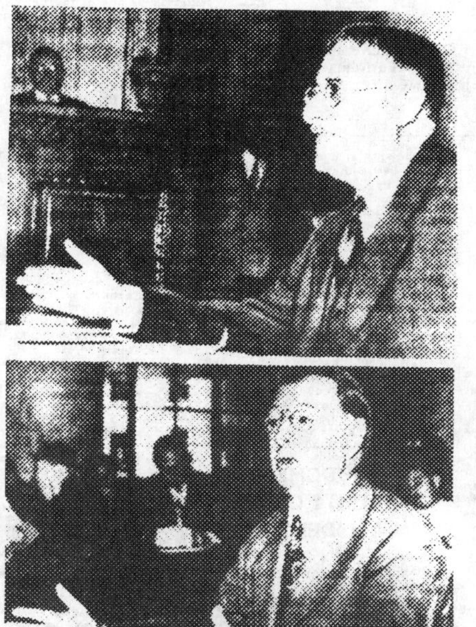

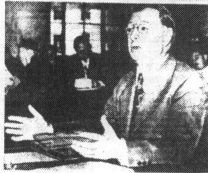

Henry L. Stimson, above, and Col. Frank Knox, below, President Roosevelt's Republican nominees for the posts of Secretary of the Army and Navy respectively, are pictured as they appeared before Senate committees for questioning on their attitudes in foreign affairs. Both declared U. S. should give Great Britain every aid "short of war."

PACKARD COMPANY AGREES TO MAKE AIRPLANE ENGINES

President Discusses New Defense Measures; Navy Awards Contracts for More Warships.

Washington (AP)—The National Defense Commission announced today that the Packard Motor Co. had agreed tentatively to undertake a contract for 9,000 aircraft engines—3,000 for the United States and 6,000 for Great Britain.

William S. Knudsen, in charge of defense production, said the agreement was subject to approval of the Packard directors. Henry Ford refused the order, saying he would work only for the United States.

Meanwhile, a supplementary defense program which may run into additional billions of dollars was talked over at a conference between President Roosevelt and key men in the defense setup.

White House officials were unable to suggest what amount the program might reach or in what manner or when it would be submitted to Congress.

There have been indications that the supplementary program was intended to build up the Army in such equipment as guns, tanks and planes.

The Navy awarded contracts today to the Newport News, Va., Shipbuilding and Drydock Co. for three aircraft carriers to cost $43,662,000 each and two cruisers to cost $19,272,500 each. They are the last of the 92 combatant vessels for which Congress had provided funds.

The airplane motors in the Packard transaction are of Rolls Royce design, hitherto made only for Britain.

M. M. Gilman, Packard president said his company's Detroit plant would be tooled and prepared to begin actual production ten months from the date the contract is actually signed.

Knudsen said the production, as estimated, would start at the rate of twenty engines a month and reach a total of 840 monthly after 15 months.

The Packard Co. manufactured aircraft motors for the United States and Allies in the World War and several years ago experimented with a diesel aircraft motor.

TONY DENIES HE'S DEAD.

Newark, N. J., (AP)—Rumors that Tony Galento was dead spread rapidly today. Awakened from a sound sleep, he denied them with: "I'm all right. I'm asleep. Goodbye."

U. S. ENVOYS WILL LEAVE POSTS IN CONQUERED LANDS

German Request for Withdrawal of Diplomatic Missions Will Probably Be Granted.

Washington (INS)—While no official announcement has been made on the subject, it was learned today that the administration sees no other course than to yield to Germany's request that all American diplomatic missions be withdrawn from the conquered territories of Norway, Belgium, Holland and Luxembourg.

Whether these envoys will be sent to join the exiled governments of these countries in London, or whether they will be recalled to the United States, has not yet been decided. It is considered most likely that they will return to this country, as the regular London embassy can keep in contact with the various governments now functioning in Great Britain.

Those affected by the German or-

(Continued on Page 20.)

WILLKIE PREDICTS NEW DEAL WILL BE OUTSTANDING ISSUE

New York (U.P.)—Party labels will mean less in this campaign than an attitude of acceptance or rejection of the New Deal philosophy, Republican presidential candidate Wendell L. Willkie told press conference questioners today.

"We have certain basic beliefs in this country on which people divide," Willkie said. "There are those who have the New Deal philosophy and those whose philosophy is contrary to the New Deal. That is the fundamental domestic issue this year."

Willkie smilingly informed questioners that he agreed with the statement made in St. Louis yesterday by John L. Lewis of the Congress of Industrial Organizations that if President Roosevelt were renominated the Republican candidate would beat him.

"I don't feel," he continued, "that it make any difference who the Democrats nominate. I think we are going to win and I haye already expressed my preference as to the Democratic nominee."

Willkie repeatedly has said he wants Mr. Roosevelt renominated so that he may have an opportunity to meet and beat "the champ."

SEES ACCEPTANCE OF CABINET POST DUTY AS CITIZEN

Publisher Pictures Himself and Stimson "Two Private Individuals Trying to Do Job."

Washington (AP)—The Senate Naval Affairs Committee approved, 9 to 5, today the nomination of Col. Frank Knox, Chicago Republican, to be secretary of the Navy.

This action cleared the way for Senate consideration, probably early next week, of the Knox appointment and of the nomination of Henry L. Stimson, also a Republican, to be secretary of war.

Washington (AP) — Col. Frank Knox, one of two Republican leaders called to cabinet positions by President Roosevelt, told a Senate committee today that despite inclusion of political opponents in the Democratic administration "you haven't got a coalition government."

Knox, Chicago newspaper publisher and 1936 vice presidential nominee of his party, appeared before the naval committee for the second day in connection with his nomination to be Navy Secretary. Henry L. Stimson, cabinet member in two Republican administrations, won approval of the military committee yesterday for his nomination by President Roosevelt to be Secretary of War.

Knox reiterated, as Stimson and he had testified yesterday, that both men accepted the cabinet positions out of a sense of duty.

Senator Holt (D., W. Va.) asked whether Knox thought there was any "danger" in the formation of a coalition government.

"You haven't got a coalition government," the witness replied. He said it was his idea that a "coalition" implied official party action on both sides.

"We are not representing the Republican Party at all," he added of Stimson and himself.

"Two Private Individuals."

"We are just two private individuals trying to do a job," he continued. "For a long time I have been a reserve officer and if I had been called to duty by a Democratic administration I would have gone as quickly as if it had been a Republican administration that issued the call. I regard this position in the same light."

Knox repeated today the denial he made yesterday that he ever had urged that American soldiers be sent to Europe to aid the Allies.

He re-emphasized his advocacy of strong defenses also, saying he thought there was still danger that the United States might be drawn into war, if any of the aggressors attempted to seize American possessions.

Mrs. Helen Essary, columnist for a Washington newspaper, had been invited to testify today about an article she wrote June 22, asserting Knox had told her that he favored sending not only cash, credit and supplies, but also men to fight for the Allies.

She did not appear, and Chairman Walsh (D., Wash.) said he had communicated with her husband, Fred Essary, a Washington correspondent for a Baltimore newspaper.

Against Sending Troops.

Essary told him, Walsh said, that Mrs. Essary's recollection of her Knox interview was substantially what she had written. Walsh added that Mrs. Essary was reported to be in Rehoboth Beach, Del.

Knox said he had spoken to Mrs. Essary at a party in Washington on Jan. 30, but had had so many conversations then that he could not remember all of them in detail. He insisted, however, that sending men to Europe was not his position and never had been.

Walsh also reported that a committee member had told him that a constituent said he could produce affidavits of a movement to permit the British fleet to use American harbors.

Knox said he had not heard of any such a proposal and expressed the opinion that if any British fighting ships put into American harbors they would have to be interned.

The nomination of Stimson, secretary of war in President Taft's cabinet and secretary of state under President Hoover, was approved by the military committee 14 to 3, after he testified that he did not want to send men to Europe.

Hitler--Where France Thought He'd Never Be

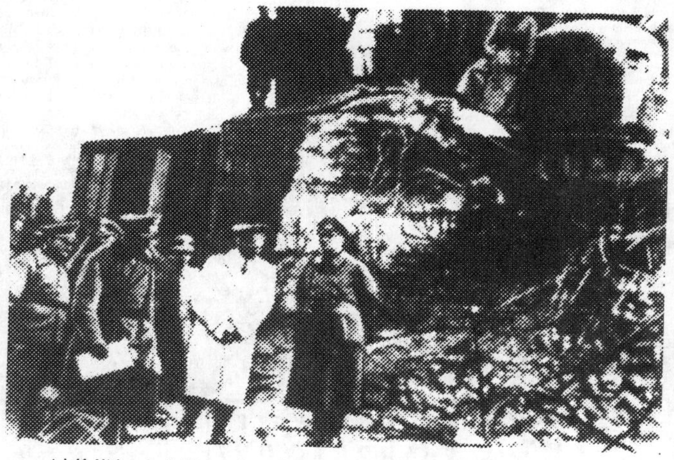

Adolf Hitler, in light trench coat, walks in triumph through the Maginot Line in the Vosges Mountain district. Accompanied by staff officers, he inspected destroyed fortifications. In the party were Col. Gen. Wilhelm Keitel (holding map) and Gen. Dollmann, right. Photo flown to Berlin and flashed to New York by radio.

A. F. Of L. "Neutral" In Presidential Race

Washington (U.P.)—The American Federation of Labor today declared itself a neutral in the 1940 presidential campaign, amid increasing signs that President John L. Lewis of the Congress of Industrial Organizations might form a third party with Sen. Burton K. Wheeler, D., Mont., as its candidate.

The announcement was made by the A. F. L.'s Publicity Director Philip Pearl in his "Facing the Facts" column of the federation's official weekly news service.

Pearl said the A. F. of L. regarded President Roosevelt and the Republican presidential nominee Wendell L. Willkie as "patriotic Americans" and that the United States would have nothing to fear "if either the Democratic or Republican candidates win."

The A. F. of L. would "certainly have nothing to do" with a third party threatened by Lewis and Wheeler, Pearl said, because such a movement is "inimical to the best interests of the country."

He accused Wheeler of seeking to "appropriate the 'peace' issue for himself and to accuse others of trying to force this country into war." He said the A. F. of L. "does not believe that President Roosevelt or Mr. Willkie have any such intentions."

"If he (Wheeler) persists in what is apparently his present intention of running for president on a third-party ticket . . . he will thereby sever friendly relations with the A. F. of L.," he said.

NAZI WHITE BOOK CHARGES PLOT TO SPREAD WARFARE

Berlin Says Allies Sought to Line Up Scandinavia and Balkans Against Germany.

Berlin (AP)—Alleged allied "win the war" plans for creating wide-spread new battlefronts against Germany—purportedly by entangling Scandinavia, Rumania, Turkey, Greece and Yugoslavia in the European struggle—were repulsed today by DNB, the official German news agency.

DNB asserted allied documents seized by Hitler's conquering German armies in France constituted "the greatest of sensations . . . intrigue such as the world never yet has seen."

One of the documents, DNB said, was signed by Generalissimo Maurice Gamelin, former allied commander-in-chief, dated last March 16, just three weeks before Germany marched into Denmark and Norway.

The five documents published today, a spokesman said, are only the first in a series in an official Nazi foreign office white book.

A second group, to be published tomorrow, deals with asserted allied machinations to involve Turkey.

A third group, the spokesman said, concerns allied preparations for the Flanders campaign.

The Gamelin document, as quoted by DNB, was entitled "conduct of war" and called for action described as "wear and tear of German forces x . x in order to strike perceptible if not decisive blows against Germany."

DNB further quoted Gamelin:

"At the moment, it appears very difficult to achieve good results on land outside the unoccupied areas. Therefore, Germany must be forced to come out of its present waiting position."

TRAFFIC ACROSS CANADIAN BORDER SLOWS TO TRICKLE

New Wartime Passport Requirements Cause; Many Aliens Reported Stranded in Canada.

Albany (AP) The flood of travel between Canada and New York has slowed to a trickle in the wake of new war-imposed United States passport requirements.

Immigation officials on the American side of the peace bridge at Buffalo also say many alien residents, of inestimable number, are stranded in Canada.

Canadian officials warned certain of them they would have difficulty in returning; some replied they would "take a chance." One estimate said it would take at least a month to obtain re-entry permits.

July 2, 1939, 24,870 automobiles crossed the peace bridge; yesterday, fewer than 3,000 passed.

At Ogdensburg, fewer than 100 persons entered from Canada Dominion Day (Monday) in contrast with 3,000 on the Canadian holiday a year ago. Most of those passing through immigration inspection there were Americans and Canadians who commute and thus are exempt from the new passport regulation.

Ogdensburg immigration inspectors said the travel slump was due to new United States requirements of passports from all aliens entering this country, effective last Monday.

A single Canadian passport was presented the first day, and the shrinkage of Dominion Day Canadian visitors was "without precedent," they asserted. Border traffic was exceptionally heavy at Ogdensburg Sunday.

At Watertown, W. Grant Mitchell executive secretary of the Thousand Islands Bridge Authority, reported no Canadian automobiles came over the international bridge the first day and a half. About 1,200 cars crossed last Saturday and 1,800 Sunday.

ENVOYS PREDICT DEADLOCK IN WAR, THEN PEACE MOVE

Diplomats Feel Germany Will Fail in Attempted Conquest of Britain by Invasion.

London (U.P.) Key foreign diplomats in London believe that the war will be deadlocked after an unsuccessful attempt by Germany to invade Britain and that peace discussions will then be started, a survey indicated today.

Diplomats have been reporting to their governments that Britain shows no inclination of wanting peace talks now.

They have been expressing the conviction that Germany will fail to conquer Britain by invasion.

See Raids Indecisive.

They hold also that a formidable British invasion of Germany or of German-occupied regions appears most improbable.

They expect big air raids in which grave damage will be inflicted on both countries, but they believe that these raids will be indecisive.

One prominent foreign ambassador asserted to the United Press that German agents had recently presented peace suggestions to a group of private citizens here and that the private citizens were rebuffed when they sounded official quarters on them.

Bases of the German proposals were reported to be:

1 British recognition of a new Pan-Europe under German leadership.

2 Britain to cede to Germany some colonies, which ones could not be learned.

3—French, Belgian and Dutch colonies to become "European colonies," for exploitation under some arranged plan.

4 Germany to conclude an alliance with the British Empire.

Spain Mentioned.

According to one version, the area which Germany would organize politically and economically under Pan-European program would include part of European Russia.

British authorities and the Spanish embassy (Spain has been mentioned in some reports as a possible peace intermediary) said that they were unaware of any such plan.

Some doubt was expressed in well-informed quarters regarding the third point of the reported German suggestions, on the ground that Germany would avoid risking Japan's enmity by embracing the Dutch East Indies in a new category of "European" colonies.

Asked whether this reported German plan was authentic, the ambassadorial informant said: "One hundred per cent."

CUNARD LINE HAS 100TH ANNIVERSARY

London (AP)—The Cunard Line, its many wartime activities shrouded in secrecy, reached its centenary today, but the date was not marked by any celebration.

The line already has lost two of its ships—the Carinthia and the Bosnia—in the war with Germany, and is believed to have given many of its liners to the government for use as armed merchant cruisers.

EDUCATION BOARD TO TRAIN WORKERS AT LOCAL SCHOOL

Vocational Classes To Be Held for 200 Men Under $9,000 Allotment from Government.

In order to provide an improved and increased supply of industrial workers for the Troy Area in connection with the expanded natonal defense program, the Troy Board of Education today set up vocational school facilities at Troy High School for two hundred men under a $9,000 allotment received from the government.

Although the vocational school connected with the High School usually closes during the summer, George H. Krug, Troy superintendent of schools, announced today that classes will start as soon as possible after next Monday and continue for eight weeks until Saturday, Aug. 31.

Joseph E. Sproule, director of vocational education in the school, was appointed by the Board to direct the school. He will be assisted by a corps of ten teachers.

Courses Free.

The courses at the High School, at the corner of State Street and Seventh Avenue, are being sponsored by the local board and the New York State Education Department for the United States Government.

The courses are tuition free open to men who are employed or employable in industries essential to national defense. Only those men who will profit by the instruction to be given will be admitted to the courses.

As the local board established the school but seven days after President Roosevelt approved the national defense program, officials recalled that twenty-two years ago, a similar defense training school was conducted at Troy High.

List of Courses.

The courses to be offered will include:

Machine shop practice, flat metal work, house construction and cabinet making, elementary electricity, advance electricity, mechanical drafting and blue print reading.

The following persons will be admitted to the classes:

1—Persons regularly employed in industries and occupations essential to the rational defense. These people will receive advanced instruction and shop practice. The aim will be to "step-up" their skill.

2 Persons selected from the public employment office registers who have had appropriate indus-

(Continued on Page 11.)

THREE GIRLS AND BOY COMPANIONS KILLED INSTANTLY BY TRAIN

Chicago (AP)—Three girls and their three boy companions were killed instantly by a train at a grade crossing near suburban Maywood last night as they sped to a hospital for medical assistance.

The six young victims were attending a roadhouse party when one of the girls complained of an attack of appendicitis. Her companions decided to take her to a hospital in an automobile.

Witnesses said the driver ignored signal lights and bells and swerved around a line of cars stopped for the uncoming Soo Line passenger train. The body of one boy was thrown clear but the other victims were crushed in the wreckage as the locomotive carried the car 1,800 feet.

The victims were Lorraine O'Leary, 19, Lorraine Norris, 17, and Catherine Clark, 19, all of Oak Park, Ill., and Francis Frehe, 19, the driver, Joseph Santo, 19, and John Brennan, 18, all of Chicago.

The Index

ADOPTED SLANG.

The United States contributes so largely and amusingly to slang in the English language that many words, once slang, now are an inseparable part of the language.

M'KEON ELECTED BY POLICE GROUP POLLING 116 VOTES

Motorcycle Officer Defeats Minehan, Eaton in Three-cornered Contest; Conference Delegates Named

Motorcycle Officer Harold J. McKeon was elected president of the Troy Police Benevolent and Protective Association yesterday to succeed Plainclothesman Daniel H. Sheehan, Detective Bureau.

Officer McKeon emerged the victor in a three-cornered contest. The candidate on the regular ticket, he obtained 116 votes, defeating Patrolman Michael Minehan, First Precinct, who received 27 votes, and Patrolman Enoch Eaton, Central Station, who received 21 votes. One hundred and sixty-three votes were cast.

Four Other Contests.

Four other contests were decided. Plainclothesman Michael J. Kane, Detective Bureau, was re-elected recording secretary, defeating Patrolman Coleman J. Lyons, Central Station, by a vote of 101 to 61. Patrolman John T. Switzer, Central Station, was re-elected treasurer, defeating Patrolman Edward Kirkpatrick, First Precinct, by a vote of 120 to 43. Kane and Switzer were regular ticket candidates and Lyons and Kirkpatrick were on the opposition ticket.

Patrolman Raymond O'Bryan, First Precinct, defeated Patrolman James Flynn, same station, for the office of delegate from that precinct to the State Police Conference at New York City Aug. 13, 14, 15 and 16, by a vote of 14 to 8. In the remaining contest, fo. delegate to the conference from Central Police Station, Patrolman Charles Hayner defeated Plainclothesman William R. Conroy by a vote of 41 to 23.

Only Independent Candiate.

Officer Eaton was the only candidate on the independent ticket. Others chosen, without opposition, include: Patrolman John B. Dwyer, Central Station, first vice president; Patrolman Edmund Burke, Central Station, second vice president; Plainclothesman Kyran J. Devery, Central Station, financial secretary; Traffic Officer David J. Hutchinson, sergeant-at-arms, and Fingerprint Expert Daniel J. McCarthy, Detective Bureau, Patrolman Joseph Derkowsky, Central Station, Patrolman John Christensen, Fourth Precinct, Motorcycle Officer William Ryan, Traffic Bureau, and Patrolman William J. Ryan, First Precinct, directors.

Others chosen as delegates to the State Police Conference, without opposition, include: Motorcycle Officer Martin Burke, Traffic Bureau; Patrolman John Christensen, Fourth Precinct, and Capt. Frank J. Connery, above the rank of patrolman.

The tellers of election were Patrolman William H. Walsh, Central Station, and Motorcycle Officer Martin Burke. The election polls were open from 2 p.m. to 9 p.m.

ROTATION CHANGES TIME.

The earth's eastward rotation on its axis causes the celestial scenery to circle westward. Each night a star rises nearly four minutes earlier than on the previous night.

Police Association Elects Officers

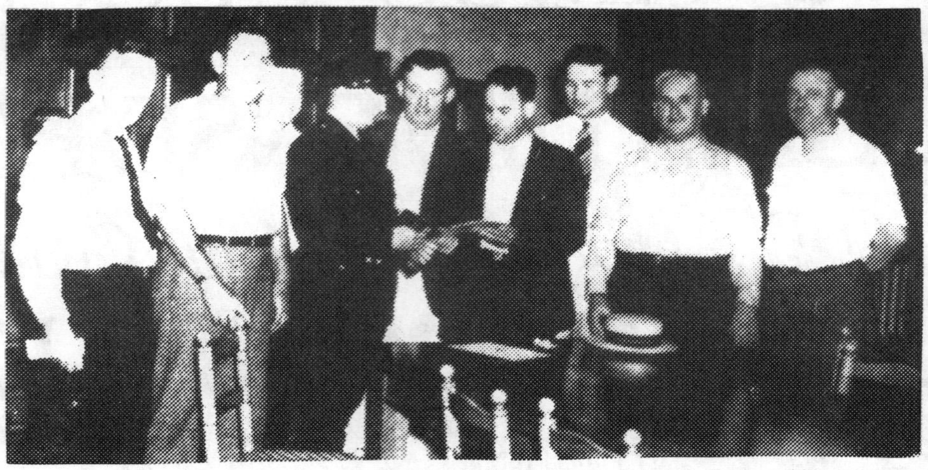

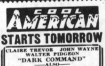

The Troy Police Benevolent and Protective Association held its annual election yesterday. In a three-cornered contest for president, Motorcycle Officer Harold J. McKeon, fourth from left, won the office. Others in the group above include, left to right, Patrolman Edmund Burke, second vice president; Patrolman Raymond O'Bryan,, delegate; Patrolman Charles Hayner, delegate, Plainclothesman Michael J. Kane, recording secretary; Plainclothesman Daniel H. Sheehan, retiring president, who is turning over the gavel to Officer McKeon; Patrolman John Dwyer, first vice president; Patrolman John T. Switzer, treasurer, and Mortocycle Officer Martin Burke, delegate.

"They Say-"

Political Gossip from Our National Capital.

By HUGH S. JOHNSON.

Washington—An editorial in the Washington Post asserts what this column has long emphasized—that the Monroe Doctrine is a two-way street. The part nobody knows, or few seem to remember, is as clearly stated as the parts about Europe keeping out of the Americas. Indeed, it is the justification for them. "In wars of European powers relating to themselves, we have never taken any part nor does it comport with our policy to do so * * * Our policy in regard to Europe * * * remains the same, which is not to interfere in the internal concerns of any of its powers: to consider the government de facto as the legitimate government to us."

The editorial approves the part of Secretary Hull's current statement: "The Government of the United States pursues a policy of non-participation and non-involvement in the purely political affairs of Europe." But the editorial says also: "If we should refuse, for instance, to recognize in due course the Russian seizure of Bessarabia, it would be appropriate for Moscow to point out that thereby we would violate an expressed provision of the Monroe Doctrine."

Long Way from Part of Doctrine.

Indeed it would be appropriate, but the remark only goes to show how far we have already kicked the stuffing out of that part of the Monroe Doctrine. Maybe we didn't do it by declaring war on Germany in 1917 for interference with our commerce, but we certainly did at the end of that war. At least the President tried to do it by sitting in at Versailles to remake the map of Europe. There was no "policy of non-participation and non-involvement," to requote Mr. Hull. It was no policy "to consider the government de facto as the legitimate government to us." Nothing could make this clearer than the Post's remark about what Russia could say to us if we do not recognize her seizure of Bessarabia.

There is an element of curious error there, but it doesn't affect the argument. The error, from what I can learn, is that we have never recognized the Rumanian seizure of Bessarabia from Russia. For a long time our State Department maps designated the province as Russian territory under Rumanian military occupation. But either way you look at it, it wasn't the Monroe Doctrine "to consider the government de facto as the legitimate government to us."

The constant pulsing of the pump of publicity designed to drag us into this war on such distortions of the Monroe Doctrine and much other sloganeering never misses a beat. The "military expert" Major Elliot, has now joined our "military expert" Secretary of War, in insisting that we make our harbors bases for the British fleet. He goes further than Wrong Horse Harry and wants us to occupy stations in the Cape Verde or Azores Islands and the West Coast of Africa.

Why Rush Into War.

Of course, this would be war. To excuse it as "undeclared war" or "undercover war" is to adopt the very poisonous deceit we so lately condemned in Spain and China.

Why should we rush to war with many of the controlling strategic developments still unknown? The tide of battle may turn eastward. Russia may collide with either Japan or Germany. The British Navy is still so superior that it doesn't need ours—we have no army or equipment to send. This war has been going on ten months. Britain has had plenty of money here. Our production facilities have been wide open to her. If she hasn't had many deliveries — and she hasn't—it is exclusively her own fault, her delays and indecision.

There is no important effective thing we could have done to help her that we have not done. Let's not go off half-cocked where we have nothing to gain and everything to lose. Let's see all the cards in this game. Let's get the true facts and use some sense.

APPEAL JUDGMENT OF COUNTY COURT IN ACCIDENT CASE

An appeal from three verdicts totaling $13,454, awarded in Washington County Court as the result of an automobile accident, was filed yesterday with the county clerk in behalf of Lewis R. Koller, an employee of the General Electric Co. at Schenectady.

The verdicts were given Mr. and Mrs. Albert Armstrong and their daughter Marion, of Argyle, after trial of a damage suit arising from the accident Oct. 29, 1939, near the Schaghticoke Fair Grounds. All the plaintiffs were injured.

105TH INFANTRY REPAIRS 14 TRUCKS

Members of Service Company, 105th Infantry, devoted their weekly drill period at the Troy Armory last night to work on the reconditioning of 14 motor trucks in preparation for the first Army maneuvers in northern New York during August.

At present there is a total of 27 trucks in the regiment, 14 of these being at Troy. Seven more trucks and additional station wagons, bringing the total number of vehicles in the regiment to 46, are expected t arrive in the next few days.

During last night's drill of Service Company, Col. Floyd D. Garlock, Regular Army instructor attached to the 105th Infantry, inspected the tires on the trucks and provision was made for replacements for the coming maneuvers.

Cranium Crackers

Some Famous Buildings.

How is your store of knowledge of the world's famous buildings and monuments? Here are five questions; you should be able to answer three of them.

1. Locate the following buildings and monuments: (a) Taj Mahal; (b) Arc de Triomphe; (c) Sphinx; (d) Trajan Column; (e) Parthenon.

2. When was the Washington Monument built?

3. What famous Italian painter and sculptor was also architect on St. Peter's Church in Rome?

4. What building, known as the "Cradle of Liberty" because it was a meeting place for revolutionists prior to the War of Independence, is still in use as a public market place?

5. What was the first public building erected in Washington, D. C.?

Answers on Page 12.

NEWCOMER TOPS RIFLEMEN LIST IN COMPANY C MATCH

Private Peter Eaton of 105th Infantry Scores 98 Out of 100 in Practice Session.

Pvt. Peter Eaton, of Company C, 105th Infantry, topped the list of scorers in the company at the outdoor rifle practice at the new New York State range at Guilderland Sunday with a score of 98 out of a possible 100.

During the firing, Private Eaton was permitted to fire the new Garand semi-automatic rifle and once again demonstrated his marksmanship ability by scoring a perfect score of fifty out of fifty on the 200-yard range. Eaton, a newcomer in the ranks of Company C riflemen, is one of the newer members of the company, having enlisted on May 15 of this year.

Approximately fifty members of the company attended the practice which was in charge of Capt. William A. Fletcher, assisted by Lieut. William C. Preston. Dinner was served on the range under the supervision of First Sergt. Edward M. Smith, Supply Se[illegible] John J. Sheehy and First [illegible] Charles Gillett. A return trip to the range will be made in the near future. The trip was made by truck convoy under the supervision of Sergt. Arthur Teal.

Individual scores included:

Private Eaton, 98; Sergt. Edward McGlynn, 96; Pvt. First Class Rutherford Kendall, 94; Corp. Thomas Carhart, 92; Corp. Francis Souto, 92; Pvt. Timothy Shaughnessy, 92; Pvt. Henry Nolal, 92; Pvt. Philip Gongolesky, 92; Sergt. Thomas Donnelly, 92; Pvt. Alfred Cote, 92; Pvt. Nicholas Rinaldo, 90; Corp. James Denenny, 90; Pvt. Joseph Foster, 88; Pvt. Edwin Lacey, 88; Pvt. Joseph Reigert, 88; Pvt. James Poleski, 88; Pvt. John Lucky, 86; Pvt. Michael Shaughnessy, 86; Pvt. William Shaughnessy, 86; Pvt. First Class William A. Fletcher, 86; Pvt. Howard Manny, 84; Corp. Joseph Cardany, 84; Pvt. Harry Scheel, 84; Corp. Michael Centrella, 84; Pvt. James Alderamian, 82; Pvt. John Knox, 80; Pvt. Rocco DeCarlo, 80; Corp. William Luby, 80; Pvt. Oscar Gilbert, 78; Pvt. Lawrence Foulkes, 78; Pvt. Edward Zambelli, 70; Pvt. Andrew Abbott, 70 and Pvt. Donald Belcher, 66.

TWO MEN KILLED BY RAILROAD TRAINS

Completing his first day's work as a Delaware and Hudson Railroad section hand, Herman Tobben, 35, Whitehall, was instantly killed yesterday afternoon when he was struck by a northbound passenger train at Schenevus.

Michael Janis, 68, Fort Johnson, was instantly killed early last night near his home when he was struck by an eastbound New York Central railroad freight engine. Officials termed the fatality accidental after an investigation. Janis is survived by his wife and six children.

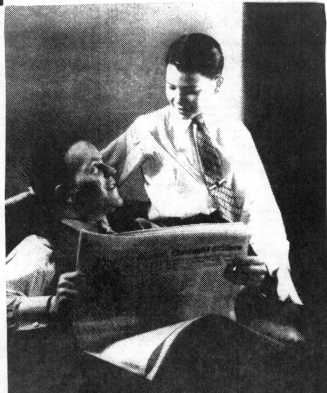

ARREST THREE MEN FOR GAMBLING ON PASSENGER TRAIN

Charged with gambling on a railroad train, three New York residents, after a losing day at the Saratoga race track, found themselves in additional difficulty Saturday night.

They were arrested on a New York Central Railroad train by Railroad Patrolman George Brehm, Cohoes. Brought to the Central Station when the train stopped at Troy, they gave their names as George Carlafter, 24, Andrew Blasko, 36, and Harold Kessler, 22.

Following a conference between Charles Grosberg, Troy attorney engaged by the trio, and Police Judge James F. Byron, the three were released in $25 bond for appearance in Police Court Thursday

MRS. LUCY HARRISON, SCHAGHTICOKE, HURT IN AUTO COLLISION

A Schaghticoke woman, Mrs. Lucy Harrison, of Main Street, was treated at Saratoga Hospital Saturday for injuries suffered when the car in which she was riding and driven by her husband, Frank T. Harrison, figured in a collision with a truck in Union Avenue, Saratoga Springs. The truck, police said, was owned by the Saratoga Racing Association and operated by Edward C. Hanehan of Saratoga Springs.

Mrs. Harrison was given treatment for bruises and lacerations about the right leg and arm and later discharged.

MOHAWK DRAMA FESTIVAL
CHARLES COBURN, Director
Opening Tues., Aug. 13, 8:45
SALLY EILERS
IN
"Smilin' Through"
with Glen Langan, Mary Hutchinson, Ralph Clanton, Philip Huston.
All Seats Reserved 800 at $1 Orch. $1.50—$2
Phone Schenectady 6-1241
In Troy: Cluett's, 7 Broadway
In Albany: Van Curler's, 120 State St.

We are writing a lot of Automobile Liability and other forms of Insurance. Why? Because we have what you need at the lowest price and first class service.
Stock and Mutual Companies.
Talk to us. Please. No obligations.
Chas. H. Gardner
15 First St., Troy, N. Y.

C. W. LARMON DIES, FORMER OFFICIAL OF NEARBY COUNTY

Served as State and Village Official Aiso; Known as Leader of Republican Party.

Charles W. Larmon, former assemblyman from Washington County, and onetime member of that county's Board of Supervisors as well as past village president of Salem, died Saturday at his home in East Broadway, Salem, after a short illness. He was 83 years of age.

Mr. Larmon's public career started in 1886 when he was elected supervisor from the Town of Salem. At the organization meeting of the board he was elected chairman.

In 1888, after expiration of his county term, he was elected assemblyman, serving for two terms. At the turn of the century he was elected president of Salem Village, an office he held several years until he joined the staff of the State Department of Agriculture as a statistician.

After a few years he returned to Salem where he opened a combination coal office and feed supply store, a business he operated until a few years ago.

In 1936, in answer to his party's call, he again sought office as county supervisor and was elected. He retired from public life after the one term.

From his earliest days he was an active member of the Republican Party and for years was recognized as one of the county leaders. At the time of his death he still held membership in the Republican County committee.

He was active in Masonic circles, and was a 32nd degree Mason. Two years ago he was granted an honorary life membership by Salem Lodge, F. and A.M.

Mr. Larmon was a member of the United Presbyterian Church at Salem, and also was an honorary member of Salem Union Grange.

The only survivors are his wife and a daughter, Miss Frances Larmon of Mamaroneck. Funeral services will be conducted from the United Presbyterian Church tomorrow at 2:30 p.m., with Rev. S. Lloyd Hibbert officiating. Interment will be in Evergreen Cemetery, Salem.

NOTE ANNIVERSARY.

The 110th anniversary of the North Argyle United Presbyterian Church at Argyle, was observed yesterday with a communion service. Rev. Milton Scott of Weehawk, N. J., was guest preacher, and assisted the pastor, Rev. Paul L. Reynolds.

Attend ALTAMONT FAIR
THE ALBANY-SCHENECTADY COUNTY FAIR
MERCHANT AND FARM IMPLEMENT DISPLAYS
6 DAYS AUGUST 12-13-14 15-16-17 6 NIGHTS
3 DAYS HARNESS RACING—TUES.-WED.-THURS.
2 DAYS A.A.A. SANCTIONED AUTO RACING FRIDAY AND SATURDAY
GRANGE EXHIBITS—4H CLUB AGRICULTURE
ADMISSION
GENERAL . . . 25c——GRANDSTAND . . . 40c
DAY PRICES—TUES.-WED.-THUR.
AUTO RACES FRI. and SAT. General Admission $1

Eightieth Taborton Picnic Draws Crowd

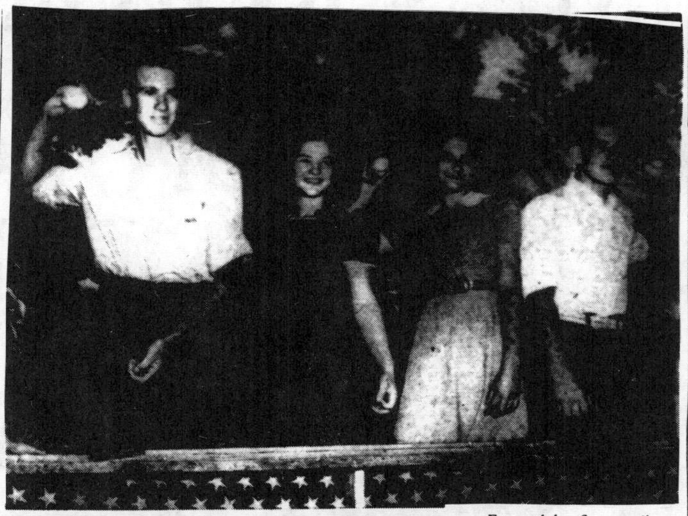

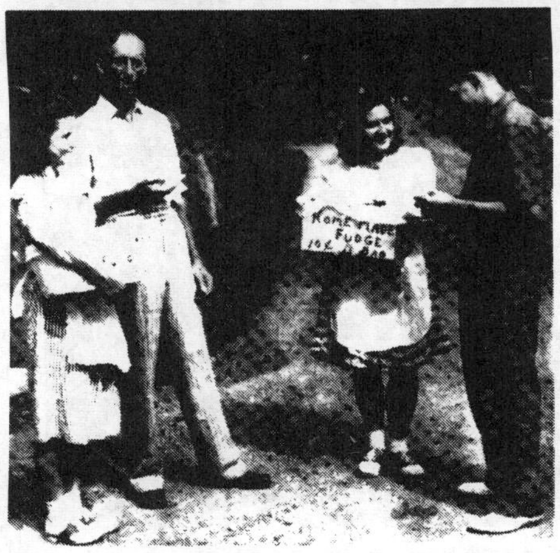

Favored by fine weather, the eightieth annual Taborton picnic of the Zion Evangelical and Reformed Church there Saturday, brought out a large crowd. Knocking down milk bottles at a picnic booth, above, are Raymond Teal, Misses Martha Sullivan, Evelyn Dobert and Marshall Hoffman, left to right. Selling candy below are Misses Dorothy Dobert, left, and Helen Lindman, and the prospective customers are Walter Momrow and Willard Gundrum, right.

ON THE AIR

Radio Programs from Local Stations.

TONIGHT

216—WTRY—TROY—950.
P. M.

5:00—Dance Time.
5:15—Evelyn Johnson, pianist.
5:30—Buddies.
5:45—Interlude.
5:50—Biography.
5:55—News.
6:00—Dinner Music.
6:15—Sports Review.
6:30—Evening Varieties.
6:55—News.
7:00—The Answer Man.
7:05—Interlude.
7:15—B. S. Bercovioi, News Comments.
7:30—Gypsy Melodies.
7:45—Joshua Spaulding's Scrapbook.
7:55—News.

230—WHAZ—TROY—1300.
P. M.

6:00—Dinning Sisters.
6:15—Gordon Gifford, barytone.
6:30—Bethincourt's Band.
6:45—Transcribed Program.
7:00—Masters' Orchestra.
7:15—Rev. Robert E. Van Deusen, talk.
7:30—Concert Music.
7:45—Health Hunters.
8:00—Studio Trio.
8:15—American Family Robinson.
8:30—R. P. I. String Trio.
8:45—Lest We Forget.
9:00—Green Hornet.
9:30—Paul Martin's Music.
10:00—News.
10:15—Hudson Orchestra.
10:30—Adventure in Reading.
11:00—Heatherton's Orchestra.
11:30—Morgan's Band.
12:00—Barnett's Orchestra.

379—WGY—SCHENECTADY—790.
P. M.

5:00—Girl Alone.
5:15—Life Can Be Beautiful.
5:30—Jack Armstrong.
5:45—The O'Neills.
6:00—News.
6:05—Varieties.
6:15—Superman.
6:30—National Defense Opportunities.
6:45—Bolley's Sports Review.
7:00—Pleasure Time; Waring's Orchestra.
7:15—European News with John B. Kennedy.
7:30—Healey, Current Events Commentator.
7:45—Your Neighbor.
8:00—The Telephone Hour.
8:30—Concert.
9:00—Dr. "I. Q."
9:30—Showboat.
10:00—Contented Hour
10:30—George Burns and Gracie Allen.
11:00—News.
11:05—On with the Dance.
11:15—Jack Little's Orchestra.
11:30—Dorsey's Orchestra.
12:00—News.

219—WOKO—ALBANY—1430.
P. M.

5:00—By Kathleen Norris.
5:15—Beyond These Valleys.
5:30—Concert Orchestra.
5:45—Scattergood Baines.
6:00—News.
6:15—Hedda Hopper's Hollywood.
6:30—Paul Sullivan.
6:45—Edwin C. Hill.
7:00—Amos 'n' Andy.
7:15—Kearns Orchestra.
7:30—Blondie.
8:00—So You Think You Know Music.
8:30—Pipe Smoking Time.
8:55—Elmer Davis.
9:00—Forecast.
10:00—Lombardo's Orchestra.
10:30—News.
10:45—Genevieve Rowe, soprano.
11:00—Bob Trout, News.
11:05—State Police News.
11:15—Alexander Orchestra.
11:30—Clinton Orchestra.
12:00—Kemp Orchestra.

TOMORROW

216—WTRY—TROY—950.
A. M.

6:00—Morning Round-up.
6:45—Produce Market Report.
6:55—News.
7:00—Rio Grande Serenaders.
7:15—Songs of the West.
7:30—Timekeeper.
7:55—News.
8:00—Timekeeper Continued.
8:30—Good Morning Newspaper.
8:35—Timekeeper Continued.
8:55—News.
9:00—Gaslight Harmonies.
9:15—Hill Billies.
9:30—The Green Joker.
9:45—Interlude; Weather Report.
9:55—News.
10:00—Morning Varieties.
10:15—Organ Melodies.
10:30—Concert Orchestra.
10:55—News.
11:00—Evelyn Johnson, pianist.
11:15—Time Out.
11:30—Happy Jim Parsons.
11:45—Troy Chapel Service.
11:55—News.
12:00—Songs of the West.
P. M.
12:15—Hits and Encores.
12:30—Farm Program.
12:45—The Bandsmen; Weather Report.
12:55—News.
1:00—The Bands Play On.
1:30—Program Prevue.
2:00—Kay Moser's Matinee.
2:55—News.
3:00—Potpouri.
3:30—News.
3:40—Stock Market Report; Weather Report.
3:45—Dance Time.
3:55—News.
4:00—Rhythm and Romance.
4:15—The Little Concert.
4:30—Lest We Forget.
4:45—U. S. Navy.
4:55—News.
5:00—Rendevous with Romance.
5:15—Evelyn Johnson, pianist.
5:30—Birds of a Feather.
5:45—Interlude.
5:55—News.
6:00—Dinner Music.
6:15—Sports Review.
6:30—Hollywood Chatter.
6:45—Quartet.
6:55—News.
7:00—For Men Only.
7:05—Interlude.
7:15—B. S. Bercovici, News.
7:30—Black Friars.
7:55—News.

379—WGY— SCHENECTADY—790
A. M.

6:30—Jake and Carl.
6:45—Rural Reporter.
6:50—Musical Clock.
7:00—Church in the Wildwood.
7:15—Time to Shine.
7:25—Marc Williams, songs.
7:30—News.
7:35—Musical Clock.
7:45—Gene and Syracuse.
8:00—Musical Clock.
8:30—Tune Topics.
8:45—Market Basket—Martha
9:00—Landt Trio.
Brooks.
9:15—Woman in White.
9:30—Houseboat Hannah.
9:45—The Right to Happiness.
10:00—The Man I Married.
10:15—Midstream.
10:30—Ellen Randolph.
10:45—By Kathleen Norris.
11:15—The Road of Life.
11:30—Against the Storm.
11:45—The Guiding Light.
12:00—Liebert, Organist.
P. M.
12:10—News.
12:15—The O'Neills.
12:30—Farm Paper of the Air.
1:00—Household Chats—Betty Lennox,
1:15—The Ross Sisters.
1:30—Master's Orchestra.
1:45—News.
1:50—Masters' Orchestra.
2:00—The Light of the World.
2:15—Arnold Grimm's Daughter.
2:30—Valiant Lady.
2:45—Hymns of All Churches.
3:00—Story of Mary Marlin.
3:15—Ma Perkins.
3:30—Pepper Young's Family.
3:45—Vic and Sade.
4:00—Backstage Wife.
4:15—Stella Dallas.
4:30—Lorenzo Jones.
4:45—Young Widder Brown.
5:00—Girl Alone.
5:15—Life Can Be Beautiful.
5:30—Jack Armstrong
5:45—The O'Neills.
6:00—News.
6:05—Varieties.
6:30—"Industry and National Defense"—Leo A. Stebbins.
6:45—Youth in the Toils.
7:00—Pleasure Time; Waring's Orchestra.
7:15—Round Robin Coverage of News from Europe, with John B. Kennedy.
7:30—Hotel America.
8:00—Johnny.
8:30—Musical Treasure Chest.
9:00—Battle of the Sexes.
9:30—Meredith Wilson Musical Review.
10:00—Summer Pastime.
10:30—Uncle Walter's Doghouse.
11:00—News.
11:05—On with the Dance.
11:15—Garr's Orchestra.
11:30—Gordon's Orchestra.
12:00—News.

219—WOKO—ALBANY—1430.
A. M.

6:00—Farmer's Almanac.
7:00—News.
7:05—Music of Tomorrow.
7:15—Saratoga Association.
7:30—Musical Train.
7:45—News.
8:00—Musical Clock.
9:00—Woman of Courage.
9:15—Interlude.
9:25—Eleanor Walter.
9:30—Dancing Through the Years.
9:45—Opportunity Knocks.
10:00—Newsflash.
10:05—In Our Time.
10:15—Myrt and Marge.
10:30—Hilltop House.
10:45—Stepmother.
11:00—Mary Lee Taylor.
11:15—Short Short Story.
11:30—Big Sister.
11:45—Aunt Jenny.
12:00—News.
P. M.
12:05—Quik Quiz.
12:15—When a Girl Marries.
12:30—Romance of Helen Trent.
12:45—Our Gal Sunday.
1:00—Musical Menus.
1:30—Forrest Willis.
1:45—Opinions Wanted.
2:00—Young Dr. Malone.
2:15—Joyce Jordan, Girl Interne.
2:30—Fletcher Wiley.
2:45—My Son and I.
3:00—Society Girl.
3:15—The Fair.
3:30—Interlude for Strings.
3:45—"A Friend in Deed."
4:00—Of Men and Books.
4:15—Tunes from the Tropics.
4:30—Music from the Gold Coast.
5:00—By Kathleen Norris.
5:15—Program.
5:30—Answer for Cash.
5:45—Scattergood Baines.
6:00—News.
6:15—Program.
6:30—Paul Sullivan.
6:45—Edwin C. Hill.
7:00—Amos 'n' Andy.
7:15—Kearns' Orchestra.
7:30—Helen Menken.
8:00—Court of Missing Heirs.
8:30—Gluskin Orchestra.
8:55—Elmer Davis, News.
9:00—We, the People.
9:30—Prof. Quiz.
10:00—Miller Orchestra.
10:15—Public Affairs.
10:30—News.
10:45—Four Clubmen.
11:00—Interlude.
11:05—State Police News.
11:15—Kavelin Orchestra.
11:30—Garber Orchestra.
12:00—Elliott Orchestra.

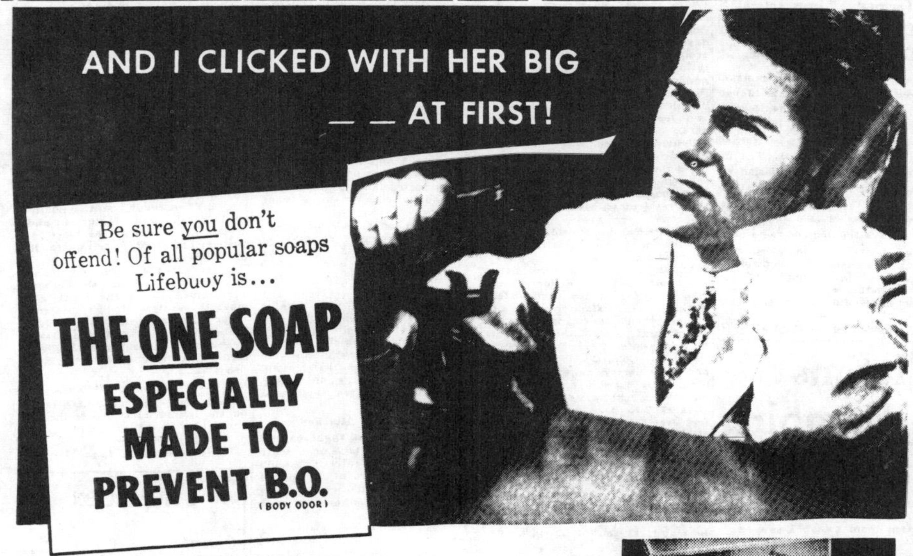

NATURALLY, YOU WANT TO BE PROTECTED FROM "B.O." THEN ISN'T IT SENSIBLE TO USE A SOAP ESPECIALLY MADE TO PREVENT IT? THAT SOAP IS LIFEBUOY. NO OTHER POPULAR SOAP HAS LIFEBUOY'S *DEODORIZING* INGREDIENT.

Lifebuoy has always been the soap for fastidious people. So clean—so wholesome—the big coral cake that looks different—smells different—acts different! Protects you longer!

ALL-OVER protection is vital—to avoid offending. Lifebuoy in your daily bath is the answer. Gets after all perspiration—whether due to heat, exercise, or nervousness.

For a rousing, pep-up bath . . . Lifebuoy again. Such soft, creamy handfuls of purifying lather. Feels mint-fresh! Makes you glow! More folks bathe with Lifebuoy than any other soap. Get Lifebuoy today!

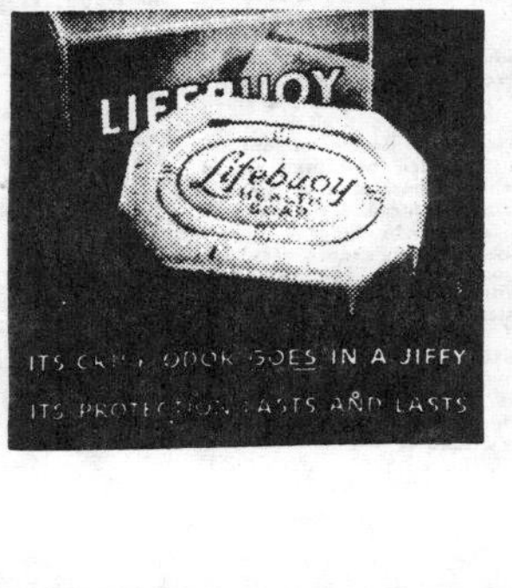

LIFEBUOY HEALTH SOAP

EAST GREENBUSH PLANS EXPANSION OF FIRE DISTRICT

Petitions Will Be Given Public Hearing Thursday August 22 at Club Edgewood.

Petitions for the enlargement of Fire District No. 3 of the Town of East Greenbush, now comprising virtually all of the village of East Greenbush, will be given a public hearing Thursday, Aug. 22, at 7 p.m. in the Club Edgewood.

The petitions, circulated and signed by property owners in the southern section of the town, ask that the district be enlarged several times over its present area. The Town Board will conduct the hearing.

To meet requests, a large area centering upon the junction of the Troy Road with the Albany-New York road, must be taken into the present district. The new territory, extending from village limits to a point below the highway junction, would include territory reaching back nearly four miles on both sides of the main highway. In the direction of Troy, that line would be almost to Couse Corners.

If the new territory is taken into the district, the recently purchased fire equipment will be adequate to fulfill all demands, it is said. Several hundred private homes, farms and restaurants and public stopping places are in the area which seeks the fire protection.

REPORT 4,678 USED POOL DURING WEEK

The continued warm spell and classes of the Learn-to-Swim Campaign of The Record Newspapers and the Troy Recreation Department were responsible in part for a heavy attendance at the municipal pool at Prospect Park in the week ending last night.

During the week, 4,678 made use of the pool. The attendance last Monday was 618 persons; Tuesday, 566; Wednesday 809; Thursday, 820; Friday, 828; Saturday, 574 and yesterday, 463.

SERGEANT HYATT WILL BE HONORED BY 105TH FRIENDS

Whitehall Man Well Known Here, Rounds Out 25 Years of Service With Regiment.

BY DONALD S. MacNAUGHTON.

DeKalb Junction—Sergt. Wilbert "Boots" Hyatt, of the anti-tank platoon of Regimental Headquarters Company, 105th Infantry, of Whitehall, completed 25 years of service with the regiment yesterday and will be honored at a reception attended by friends throughout the 105th during one of the rest periods in the First Army maneuvers this week.

Though his service has always been with the Whitehall unit, "Boots" is probably the most familiar character among the enlisted personnel of the entire regiment, and throughout his quarter century of service has made hundreds of friends in every community in the regimental area.

His service record has been outstanding. During the World War, he received a British distinguished conduct award as well as a citation from Gen. John J. Pershing, commander of the A. E. F. and conspicious service cross from the State of New York.

He first enlisted in Company I of the Old Second Regiment, at Whitehall Aug. 11, 1915. He served four months on the Mexican Border in 1916 and had ten months of foreign service in France and Belgium during the World War. Shortly after his discharge from war service, he reenlisted in Company I in 1919 as a private and was appointed corporal three months later.

Sergeant Hyatt reenlisted in the Howitzer Company and was appointed first sergeant of that unit in 1924. He served in this capacity until the Howitzer Company was abolished last year and its personnel incorporated into the anti-tank platooon of Regimental Headquarters Company of Troy. He then became platoon sergeant of the Whitehall outfit.

He is receiving the warm congratulations of hundreds of members of the regiment upon rounding out 25 years of service, and it is expected practically every unit in the regiment will be represented at the reception. "Boots" was presented to Lieut. Gen. Hugh A. Drum, commander of the First Army maneuvers on the occasion of a recent visit by General Drum to the 105th camp area.

STEAL WATCH AFTER SMASHING WINDOW IN JEWELRY STORE

Covering a brick with a handkerchief, an unidentified thief tossed a brick through a window of Myers' jewelry store at 415 Fulton Street yesterday morning and stole a wrist watch, valued at $15, from the window. Detectives are investigating the theft.

Thieves entered the garage of James McNamee of 482 Tenth Street Saturday night or early yesterday and stole a set of socket wrenches, three screw drivers, a fog light, an extension auto wrench, eight gallons of gasoline, an automobile jack and two pairs of sun glasses. The loot was valued at $17, a report filed at the Detective Bureau claims.

Mrs. Mollie Casale of 1316 Fifth Avenue reported her son's bicycle, valued at $20, stolen from in front of her home yesterday.

THREE HUNDRED AT ANNUAL OUTING OF TRAVELERS' COUNCIL

Marked by entertainment and sports for afternoon and night, Troy Council, United Commercial Travelers, Saturday conducted their annual outing and clambake at Brookside Park. Approximately 300 members, wives, families and friends attended.

The sports included several baseball games for men, races and other competitive events for children, and special games for women. Approximately 100 prizes, presented by merchants of the vicinity, were awarded.

Special guests were Thomas King, Buffalo, past grand councilor, and A. J. Snyder, Troy, grand page of the state organization.

Guy Bull was general chairman.

fith Otto J. Swensson serving as chairman of the ticket committee.

PROCTORS
NOW! 2 Big Hits!
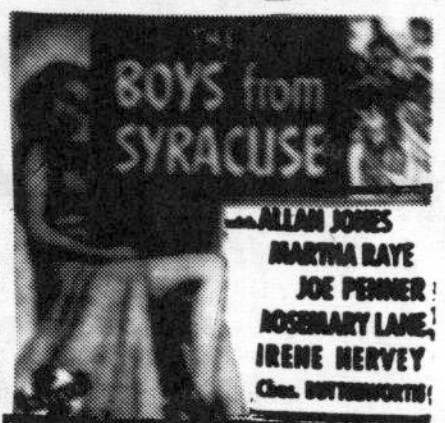

PLUS HIT NO. 2
The Man I Married
BENNETT LEDERER NOLAN STEN KRUGER

NOW COOL AMERICAN NOW
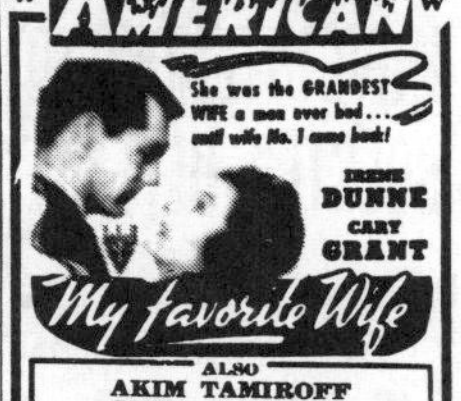

ALSO
AKIM TAMIROFF
GLADYS GEORGE
The Way of All Flesh

COOL LINCOLN NOW 2 First Runs
Gene Autry
Carolina Moon
2nd Hit • FRANKIE DARRO "CHASING TROUBLE"

BIJOU LAST TIMES TODAY
BONITA GRANVILLE and WILLIAM HOLDEN in
"THOSE WERE THE DAYS"
—Also—
Florence Rice and Kent Taylor in
"THE GIRL IN 313"
LATEST NEWS
Scientifically Air Conditioned
COMFORTABLY COOLED

LANSING TONIGHT
John Wayne • Claire Trevor • Walter Pidgeon
"DARK COMMAND"
—PLUS—
"BAD BOY"
with JOHNNY DOWNS
CARTOON

PALACE Free to the Ladies Royal Ruby Tableware
LAST TIMES TONIGHT
"BROTHER ORCHID"
Ed. Robinson • Ann Sothern
"FLIGHT ANGELS"
Virginia Bruce • Wayne Morris
Tomorrow
"Typhoon" "Opened By Mistake"
MATINEE 10c To All Until 5 P.M.

COOL STATE LAST TIMES TODAY
EDWARD G. ROBINSON
"BROTHER ORCHID"
Lee Powell and Chief Thunder-Cloud
"HI-YO SILVER"
LADIES! Tomorrow and Wed. 7-inch Gray Rose Plate and Tickets BIG SOUP PLATE!

AUTO VISION ROUTES 9 AND 20
JOHNSON & EDGEWOOD
NOW PLAYING
SPENCER TRACY
"MAN'S CASTLE"
— INDIVIDUAL SPEAKERS —

CASINO WATERFORD TODAY
Anna Neagle and Ray Milland in
"IRENE"
Also 3 Stooges "Nutty But Nice"
And "Pardon My Berthmarks"
And Shorts

TROY Tomorrow
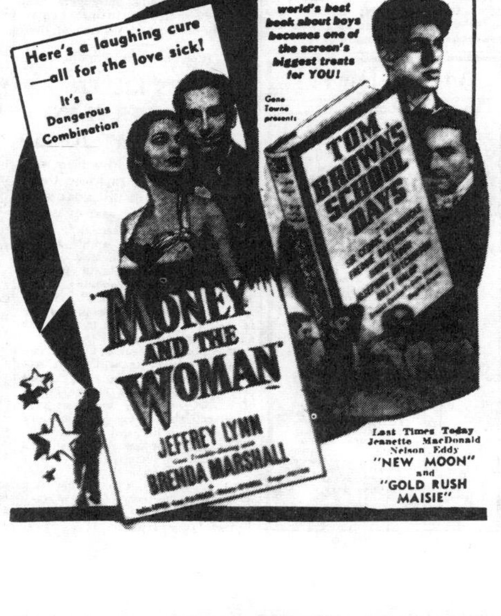

Last Times Today
Jeanette MacDonald
Nelson Eddy
"NEW MOON"
and
"GOLD RUSH MAISIE"

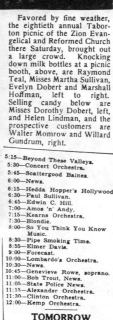

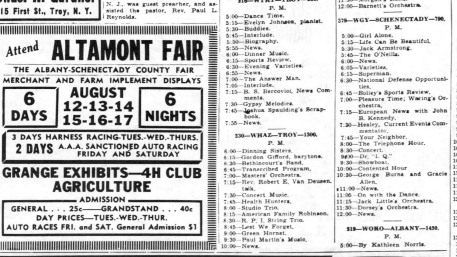

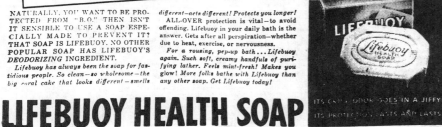

THE WEATHER
Tonight—Cloudy.
Tomorrow—Showers, warmer.

THE TIMES RECORD

FINAL EDITION

Series 1940—No. 194. (Entered as Second Class Matter at the Postoffice at Troy, N. Y., under the Act of March 3, 1879.) TROY, N. Y., FRIDAY EVENING, AUGUST 16, 1940. (Published Daily Except Sunday) PRICE THREE CENTS

NAZIS RAIN BOMBS ON LONDON AS 2,500 PLANES RAID BRITAIN

U. S. Negotiating With Britain For Western Hemisphere Bases

ROOSEVELT SAYS MOVE INTENDED TO BOLSTER DEFENSE

President Insists Deal Has No Relation To Proposal To Sell Destroyers To British.

Washington, (U.P.)—President Roosevelt revealed today that the United States is negotiating with the British Empire for acquisition of naval and air bases to bolster western hemisphere defenses.

"The United States government is holding conversations with the government of the British Empire with regard to acquisition of naval and air bases for the defense of the western hemisphere and especially the Panama Canal," Mr. Roosevelt said.

"The United States government is carrying on conversations with the Canadian government on the defense of the western hemisphere."

The negotiations with Canada are separate from those being conducted with London, the President explained.

He also disclosed that the U. S. Army and Navy have high officers in Great Britain at the invitation of the British government to act as observers of hostilities there.

The Army observers are Maj. Gen. Delos Emmons, commander of the general headquarters air force, and Brig. Gen. George B. Strong, assistant chief of staff in charge of the war plans division.

No Relation to Destroyers.

The naval observers are Rear Admiral Robert L. Ghormley, assistant chief of naval operations, and his staff.

This was the first word that these high officers have been sent abroad.

Mr. Roosevelt insisted that the negotiations for acquisition of British naval bases have no relation to increasing discussion of proposals for this country to sell fifty or more destroyers to Britain. He said merely that the conversations are in progress on a quid pro quo basis, and are proceeding.

Beyond that the President would not go. He refused firmly to dis-

(Continued on Page 2)

EUROPE'S '40 CROPS AVERAGE GOOD, SAY GERMAN EXPERTS

Berlin (AP)—Europe's 1940 crop prospects were described as "average good" today by German agricultural experts, who said the Reich's food situation was excellent with record root crops (potatoes, beets, etc.) in the offing.

These experts said the rationing system had greatly helped Germany to reduce cereal consumption, and declared there was absolutely no cause for worry since the Reich's grain supplies were still plentiful.

Figures were unavailable, it was said, because statistics on Germany's food supplies are regarded as a military secret.

The German experts declared that Britainwould be to blame if her blockade caused grain shortages in countries formerly allied with her—France, Norway and the lowlands, for instance.

These sources said that the Balkans would produce smaller grain surpluses than heretofore. Norway, Denmark, Sweden, Holland and Belgium will need imports of cereals as they always have. France, it was asserted, must look after her own needs; normally she is self-sufficing as far as grains are concerned, the Germans said.

London Raids Seen As Sign of Greater Blows

By The Associated Press.

Military experts saw the Nazis' double-barrelled raid on London yesterday—at Croydon airport, eight miles from Piccadilly Circus, and London's Tilbury docks—as an ominous signal of far greater blows to come.

It was recalled that the bombing of Paris airports June 3 signalled the opening of the full-blast offensive against France that ended a forthnight later in France's surrender.

Paris itself capitulated on June 13, ten days after the raid.

Still another "storm warning" was seen in a Berlin radio broadcast saying that all French owners of sea-going craft of any size were requested to report immediately to French naval authorities—possibly for use in Hitler's threatened cross-channel invasion of England.

START DRIVE IN SENATE TO DEFER ACTION ON DRAFT

Move Comes After House Approval of Bill Empowering President To Call Out National Guard.

Washington (U.P.) — Anti-conscription leaders in the Senate started a drive today to postpone consideration of the Burke-Wadsworth civilian draft bill until the 77th Congress convenes next January.

Several members opposing a peace-time draft said they expected strong support for the move. Sen. Alva B. Adams, D., Colo., said he believed the conscription issue should be avoided until senators and representatives return home, talk it over with their constituents, and get fresh viewpoints.

Both the Senate and the House were in recess today to enable Republicans to go to Elwood, Ind., to hear their presidential candidate, Wendell L. Willkie, deliver his acceptance address tomorrow.

Indications were that Willkie's stand on the conscription issue in that speech may have a vital influence on congressional action. Most Republicans in both chambers have remained silent and efforts to obtain the nominee's views in advance of his speech were said to have been fruitless.

Announce Opposition.

Sens. Arthur H. Vandenberg of Michigan, Robert A. Taft of Ohio and John Thomas of Idaho appear to be the only Senate Republicans who have announced views irrevocably opposed to a peace-time draft. Vandenberg would neither confirm nor deny reports that a telegram he sent Willkie on the draft was not answered.

News of the deferment drive came after the House approved, 342 to 33, the bill empowering President Roosevelt to mobilize 360,000 members of the National Guard and organize reserves for 12 months of service with the regular army anywhere in the western hemisphere.

The bill now goes back to the Senate for concurrence in House amendments, some of which may be disputed in the upper chamber.

In approving the bill, an important segment of President's Roosevelt's "total defense" program, the House made five major changes in the Senate version.

1—It deleted a section which would have made employers who refuse to rehire guardsmen and reservists at the termination of their

(Continued on Page 2)

FIVE MEN KILLED IN POWDER PLANT BLAST AT JOPLIN

Joplin, Mo., (AP)—Five men were killed today in an explosion which wrecked a unit of the Atlas Powder plant six miles east of Joplin in Southwestern Missouri.

The plant, which employs approximately 400 men and is one of three powder plants in this vicinity, has been producing nearly 2,000,000 pounds of TNT monthly. Over half of the production is being purchased by British agents, officials said.

The blast demolished the "No. 2 punch house" in which the five victims were working. Each unit of the plant is built in the center of a dirt retaining wall designed to direct the force of explosions away from other units.

The blast, of undetermined origin, occurred shortly after 8 a.m.

The dead: Joe Bates, Joplin; Leroy Crampton, Carterville; Sidney Dietz, Carthage; Harold Gallagher, Webb City; and George Brown, Prosperity.

BRITAIN ACCUSED OF SINKING GREEK SHIP BY FASCIST

Virginio Gayda Claims Move an Attempt To Precipitate Crisis Between Italy and Greece.

Rome (AP)—Virginio Gayda, authoritative Fascist editor, today accused the British admiralty of sinking the Greek light cruiser Helle yesterday and called it an attempt to precipitate a crisis between Italy and Greece.

Gayda, editor of Il Giornale D'Italia, denied British suggestions that an Italian submarine had torpedoed the Helle in Tinos Island Harbor yesterday and declared it was evident this was "a new plot."

The sinking of the cruiser, he wrote, was "obviously a new blow struck by the British admiralty which, in perfect agreement with the propaganda services, thought it could surely lay the responsibility on Italy. profiting from the present diplomatic phase of the Italian-Greek conflict with the obvious aim of provoking Greek reaction."

Other authoritative Italians also charged Britain with attempting to perpetuate a "second Athenia" case on the world in the sinking of the Helle.

Meanwhile, Italian communiques announced that British planes had soared for the second time in three days over the Alps divide and bombed northern Italy, and that the Italian offensive in Africa still was in full swing.

Two Killed in Raid.

Today's British air raid did only slight damage, Italians said, in two villages of Merate and Olgiate near Turin. Only two persons were killed and five hurt in contrast to the 22 killed and fifty injured in last Wednesday's Milan and Turin attacks, they declared.

Turin anti-aircraft batteries were reported to have shot down a British plane in today's raid.

Announcing that no Italian submarine was in the vicinity of Tinos Island, Greece, when the Greek cruiser was sunk in that harbor yesterday, Italian authorities said none of their commanders had reported such an attack, and high Fascist said Britain was responsible.

These Fascist sources alleged that the British ordered the Greek warship sunk in order to stir up trouble between Greece and Italy. repeating the Athenia case.

Throughout the war the Italian press has supported German contentions that the British liner Athenia. torpedoed with a loss of 113 lives on the first day of the war was sunk by the British themselves to cast blame on the Germans.

Fascists said there was no connection between the sinking of the Helle and the decapitation of Daut Hoggia. Albanian "patriot" near the Greek border, and that Italy would persist in her demands for "justice" for Albania and Albanians despite the newest British "maneuver."

Italy's Course Clear.

Gayda wrote that "the problem of Italo-Greek-Albania relations which shows itself acute after the assassination of Hoggia, "awaits its necessary satisfactory solution."

Italy, he declared, intends its limitation of the dispute and its course towards a solution "to be quite clear and separate from all criminal speculations of England which would like to profit from the present Greek complications after having largely created them."

(The Greek government announced the 2,115-ton, American-built Helle was sunk by an unidentified submarine which remained submerged during the attack. Two of the three torpedoes the submarine fired were said to have injured a number of civilians on the quay of Tinos Harbor.

(The Greek government promptly ordered all Greek ships to remain in port).

STATE DENIES GIVING OUT-OF-STATE FIRMS $125,000 CONTRACTS

Albany (AP)—Director Joseph V. O'Leary of the State Division of Standards and Purchase has denied award by his office of $125,000 in printing contracts to out-of-state firms the last six weeks.

His statement yesterday was in reply to one by William Talbot, label director of New York Typographical Union, Local 6, claiming the division had awarded $300,000 worth of contracts over the period, $125,000 to out-of-state shops.

O'Leary placed the total of awards at nearly $600,000 but asserted only about three of them about $18,000 worth—went out of the state.

Wreckage of Air Attack On British Midlands

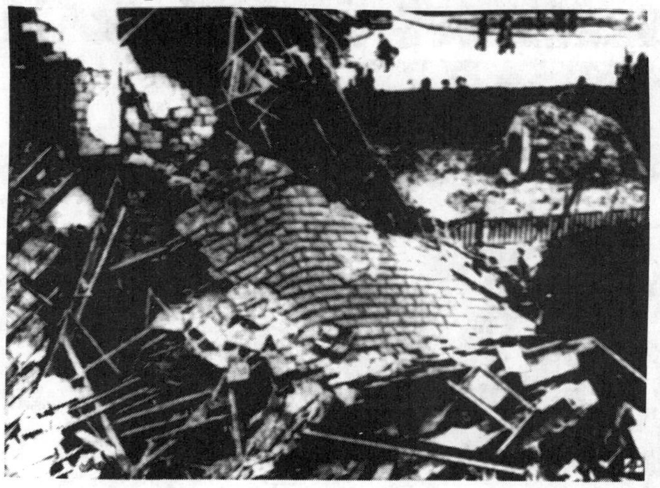

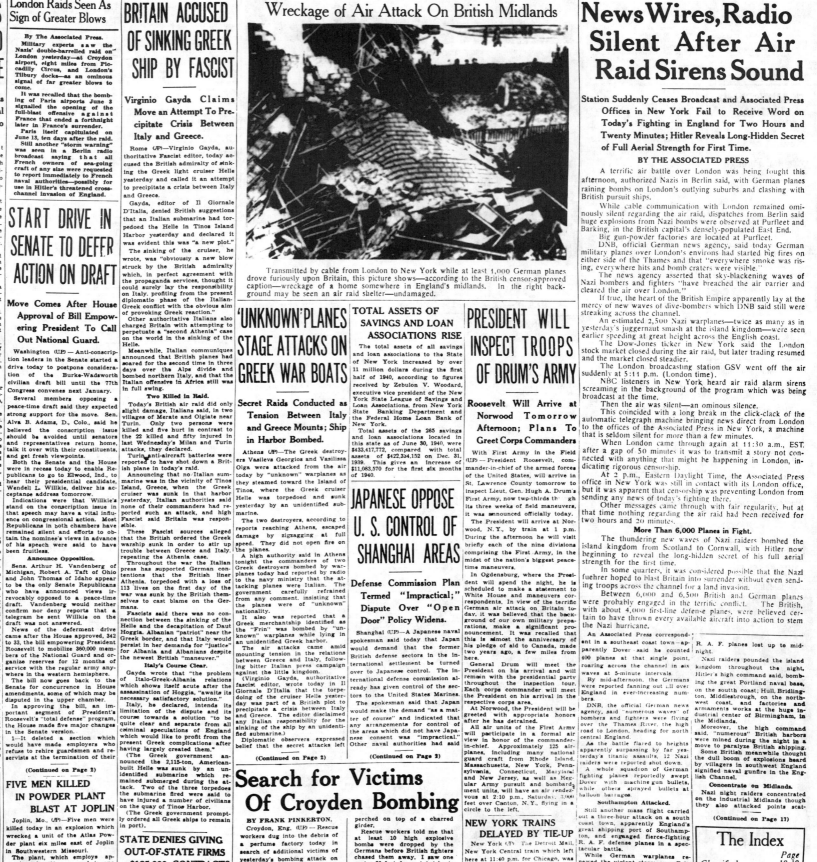

Transmitted by cable from London to New York while at least 1,000 German planes drove furiously upon Britain, this picture shows—according to the British censor-approved caption—wreckage of a home somewhere in England's midlands. In the right background may be seen an air raid shelter—undamaged.

'UNKNOWN' PLANES STAGE ATTACKS ON GREEK WAR BOATS

Secret Raids Conducted as Tension Between Italy and Greece Mounts; Ship in Harbor Bombed.

Athens (AP)—The Greek destroyers Vasilevs Georgios and Vasilissa Olga were attacked from the air today by "unknown" warplanes as they steamed toward the Island of Tinos, where the Greek cruiser Helle was torpedoed and sunk yesterday by an unidentified submarine.

The two destroyers, according to reports reaching Athens, escaped damage by zigzagging at full speed. They did not open fire on the planes.

A high authority said in Athens tonight the commanders of two Greek destroyers bombed by warplanes today had reported by radio to the navy ministry that the attacking planes were Italian. The government carefully refrained from any comment. insisting that the planes were of "unknown" nationality.

It also was reported that a Greek merchantship identified as the "Frin" was bombed by "unknown" warplanes while lying in an unidentified Greek harbor.

The air attacks came amid mounting tension in the relations between Greece and Italy, following bitter Italian press campaign against the little kingdom.

(Virginio Gayda, authoritative fascist editor, wrote today in Il Giornale D'Italia that the torpedoing of the cruiser Helle yesterday was part of a British plot to precipitate a crisis between Italy and Greece. The editor disclaimed any Italian responsibility for the sinking of the ship by an unidentified submarine.)

Diplomatic observers expressed belief that the secret attacks left

(Continued on Page 2)

TOTAL ASSETS OF SAVINGS AND LOAN ASSOCIATIONS RISE

The total assets of all savings and loan associations to the State of New York increased by over 11 million dollars during the first half of 1940, according to figures received by Zebulon V. Woodard, executive vice president of the New York State League of Savings and Loan Associations. from New York State Banking Department and the Federal Home Loan Bank of New York.

Total assets of the 265 savings and loan associations located in this state as of June 30, 1940, were $433,417,772, compared with total assets of $422,334,152 on Dec. 31, 1939. This gives an increase of $11,083,570 for the first six months of 1940.

JAPANESE OPPOSE U. S. CONTROL OF SHANGHAI AREAS

Defense Commission Plan Termed "Impractical;" Dispute Over "Open Door" Policy Widens.

Shanghai (U.P.)—A Japanese naval spokesman said today that Japan would demand that the former British defense sectors in the international settlement be turned over to Japanese control. The international defense commission already has given control of the sectors to the United States Marines.

The spokesman said that Japan would make the demand "as a matter of course" and indicated that any arrangements for control of the areas which did not have Japanese consent was "impractical." Other naval authorities had said

(Continued on Page 2)

Search for Victims Of Croyden Bombing

BY FRANK PINKERTON.

Croydon, Eng. (U.P.) — Rescue workers dug into the debris of a perfume factory today in search of additional victims of yesterday's bombing attack on this airport suburb of London.

A row of unclaimed bicycles in a shed next to the factory was mute evidence of the possible fate of their owners. The bicycles, protected by a brick wall. escaped damage.

I tramped through Croydon in the early hours along roads flanked by four-foot mounds of debris which had been shoveled off the highway. Office equipment and furniture from damaged buildings lay on the sidewalks where they had been spewed by bombs.

The only note of cheerfulness which assailed my ears came from an uncaged canary, perched on top of a charred girder.

Rescue workers told me that at least 10 high explosive bombs were dropped by the Germans before British fighters chased them away. I saw one crater 30 feet deep. A brick air raid shelter beside a public swimming pool had been reduced to rubble by a direct hit, but its only occupant, a small boy, was dug out alive.

From the debris of one of the damaged buildings rescue workers removed a 17-year-old youth uninjured. He celebrated his escape by joining cheerfully in the search for his comrades.

The rescue work had been continued until after midnight and was resumed at dawn.

Except for the rescue work, Croydon went about its business as usual. Many early shift workers had no idea of the extent of the damage.

PRESIDENT WILL INSPECT TROOPS OF DRUM'S ARMY

Roosevelt Will Arrive at Norwood Tomorrow Afternoon; Plans To Greet Corps Commanders

With First Army in the Field (U.P.) — President Roosevelt, commander-in-chief of the armed forces of the United States, will arrive in St. Lawrence County tomorrow to inspect Lieut. Gen. Hugh A. Drum's First Army, now two-thirds through its three weeks of field maneuvers, it was announced officially today.

The President will arrive at Norwood, N.Y., by train at 1 p.m. During the afternoon he will visit briefly each of the nine divisions comprising the First Army, in the midst of the nation's biggest peace-time maneuvers.

In Ogdensburg, where the President will spend the night, he is scheduled to make a statement to White House and maneuvers correspondents. In view of the terrific German air attack on Britain today, it was believed that the background of our own military preparations, make a significant pronouncement. It was recalled that this is almost the anniversary of his pledge of aid to Canada, made two years ago, a few miles from here.

General Drum will meet the President on his arrival and will remain with the presidential party throughout the inspection tour. Each corps commander will meet the President on his arrival in the respective corps area.

At Norwood, the President will be greeted with appropriate honors after he has detrained.

All air units of the First Army will participate in a formal air view in honor of the commander-in-chief. Approximately 125 airplanes, including many national guard craft from Rhode Island, Massachusetts, New York, Pennsylvania, Connecticut, Maryland and New Jersey, as well as Regular Army pursuit and bombardment units, will have an air rendezvous at 2:10 p.m., Saturday, 3,000 feet over Canton, N.Y., flying in a circle to the left.

NEW YORK TRAINS DELAYED BY TIE-UP

New York (UP) The Detroit Mail, New York Central train which left here at 11:40 p.m. for Chicago, was delayed about four hours early today when a tire on an engine wheel broke at Tivoli, 98 miles from New York. No one was injured.

New York-bound trains were delayed up to two hours and outgoing trains to three hours by the tie-up, which occurred at a place where the road has only two tracks.

FIND MASSENA SUICIDE.

Fish Creek (UP)—The body of James Borgese, 29, of Massena, N. Y., was found in a parked automobile near here yesterday. A piece of garden hose was found running from the exhaust pipe to the interior of the car. Coroner William Wardner of Saranac Lake issued a verdict of suicide.

News Wires, Radio Silent After Air Raid Sirens Sound

Station Suddenly Ceases Broadcast and Associated Press Offices in New York Fail to Receive Word on Today's Fighting in England for Two Hours and Twenty Minutes; Hitler Reveals Long-Hidden Secret of Full Aerial Strength for First Time.

BY THE ASSOCIATED PRESS

A terrific air battle over London was being fought this afternoon, authorized Nazis in Berlin said, with German planes raining bombs on London's outlying suburbs and clashing with British pursuit ships.

While cable communication with London remained ominously silent regarding the air raid, dispatches from Berlin said huge explosions from Nazi bombs were observed at Purfleet and Barking, in the British capital's densely-populated East End.

Big gun-powder factories are located at Purfleet.

DNB, official German news agency, said today German military planes over London's environs had started big fires on either side of the Thames and that "everywhere smoke was rising, everywhere hits and bomb craters were visible."

The news agency asserted that sky-blackening waves of Nazi bombers and fighters "have breached the air barrier and cleared the air over London."

If true, the heart of the British Empire apparently lay at the mercy of new waves of dive-bombers which DNB said still were streaking across the channel.

An estimated 2,500 Nazi warplanes—twice as many as in yesterday's juggernaut smash at the island kingdom—were seen earlier speeding at great height across the English coast.

The Dow-Jones ticker in New York said the London stock market closed during the air raid, but later trading resumed and the market closed steadier.

The London broadcasting station GSV went off the air suddenly at 5:11 p.m. (London time).

NBC listeners in New York heard air raid alarm sirens screaming in the background of the program which was being broadcast at the time.

Then the air was silent—an ominous silence.

This coincided with a long break in the click-clack of the automatic telegraph machine bringing news direct from London to the offices of the Associated Press in New York, a machine that is seldom silent for more than a few minutes.

When London came through again at 11:30 a.m., EST, after a gap of 50 minutes it was to transmit a story not connected with anything that might be happening in London, indicating rigorous censorship.

At 2 p.m., Eastern Daylight Time, the Associated Press office in New York was still in contact with its London office, but it was apparent that censorship was preventing London from sending any news of today's fighting there.

Other messages came through with fair regularity, but at that time nothing regarding the air raid had been received for two hours and 20 minutes.

More Than 6,000 Planes in Fight.

The thundering new waves of Nazi raiders bombed the island kingdom from Scotland to Cornwall, with Hitler now beginning to reveal the long-hidden secret of his full aerial strength for the first time.

In some quarters, it was considered possible that the Nazi fuehrer hoped to blast Britain into surrender without even sending troops across the channel for a land invasion.

Between 6,000 and 6,500 British and German planes were probably engaged in the terrific conflict. The British, with about 4,000 first-line defense planes, were believed certain to have thrown every available aircraft into action to stem the Nazi hurricane.

An Associated Press correspondent in a southeast coast town—apparently Dover said he counted 400 planes at that single point, roaring across the channel in six waves at 5-minute intervals.

By mid-afternoon, the Germans were reported fanning out all over England in ever-increasing numbers.

DNB, the official German news agency, said "numerous waves" of bombers and fighters were flying over the Thames River, the high road to London, heading for north central England.

As the battle flared to heights apparently surpassing by far yesterday's titanic assaults, 12 Nazi raiders were reported shot down.

A whole squadron of German fighting planes reportedly swept Dover with machine gun bullets, while others sprayed bullets at balloon barrages.

Southampton Attacked.

Still another mass flight carried out a three-hour attack on a south coast town, apparently England's great shipping port of Southampton, and engaaged fierce-fighting R. A. F. defense planes in a spectacular battle.

While German warplanes renewed the violent storm over Britain in heavy pre-dawn raids, British R. A. F. bombers winged across the snow-capped Alps today to attack cities in northern Italy for the second time in three days.

Fascist authorities in Rome reported two killed, five wounded. In Wednesday's raid, 22 were killed and fifty injured.

The German high command, in the wake of the greatest aerial assault in war annals against Britain yesterday, reported 143 R.A.F planes destroyed in raids against armament factories, harbors, airdromes and balloon barrages. Only 29 Nazi planes were listed as missing.

The British said 169 German planes were shot down to 27 R. A. F. planes lost up to midnight.

Nazi raiders pounded the island kingdom throughout the night, Hitler's high command said, bombing the great Portland naval base, on the soutth coast; Hull, Bridlington. Middlesbrough, on the northwest coast. and factories and armaments works at the huge industrial center of Birmingham, in the Midlands.

Moreover. the high command said. "numerous" British harbors were mined during the night in a move to paralyze British shipping.

Some British meanwhile thought the dull boom of explosions heard by villagers in southwest England signified naval gunfire in the English Channel.

Concentrate on Midlands.

Nazi night raiders concentrated on the industrial Midlands though they also attacked points scat-

(Continued on Page 17)

The Index

THE TIMES RECORD

COHOES BRANCH OFFICE, 298 ONTARIO STREET | TROY, N. Y., MONDAY EVENING, SEPTEMBER 9, 1940. | PHONE COHOES 511

Cohoes Youth Taken To Safety After Climbing Side Of Building

SAVE YOUTH FROM DEATH PLUNGE OFF NINE-STORY LEDGE

Lawrence Perry of 188 Main Street, Cohoes, Scales Side of Envelope Company's Plant.

After a nerve-wracking hour and one-quarter during which a tense crowd watched from below, Lawrence Perry, 17, of 188 Main Street, Cohoes, was rescued from the narrow brick ledge outside the ninth floor of the building at 60 Olmstead Street, Cohoes, last night.

Apparently the victim of a nervous upset induced by a youthful love affair gone awry, Perry had climbed up to the outside of the building in "human-fly" fashion to the ninth floor ledge and there clung tenaciously to the two-inch-deep crevices formed by raised brickwork on the building's face, treacherous handholds that meant difference between life and death on the pavement below.

Spurns Rope.

Repeatedly he refused to grasp a rope which firemen lowered from the roof of the 12-story building, shifting it as Perry shifted his position. The structure houses the Cohoes Envelope Co., Inc.

The youth finally was persuaded to approach closely enough to one of the few ninth floor windows to permit him to be pulled to safety by Patrolman Harry Donahue of the Cohoes Police Department and Joseph A. Cooley, 30 Chestnut Street, a reporter for The Record Newspapers who had gone to the scene to "cover" the story.

With Donahue, Cooley spent more than an hour leaning out of the window, talking quietly, coaxingly to Perry in the hope of having him come close enough to the window to enable them to grab him and haul him inside.

Visibly weakening as the long ordeal progressed, the youth finally inched his body within reach of the waiting pair.

Drops In Faint.

When they yanked him in young Perry was in a state of nervous collapse. He stood for a moment and then dropped in a faint from which police and firemen revived him. It was necessary to carry him from the building on a stretcher.

He was taken to Cohoes Hospital where, it was said, his condition was reported "improved" today. A police detail remained at his bedside throughout the night.

Perry was discharged from the Cohoes Hospital about a month ago where he had been ill with pneumonia.

Police found several letters in the youth's pockets. The majority were signed "Mary," and one was signed by Perry. This read as follows:

"Mary thinks Albert is better than I. Well, if I'm not good enough for her, I don't want to live. I love her too much to go on without her."

The boy was first seen working his way up the side of the building at 9 p.m. by Earl Carroll, 159 Bridge Avenue, Cohoes, an employee of the Abso-Fresh Bakeries, Inc., across the street. He told his superior, Harold Huffman, 121 Columbia Street, who called police.

Beyond Reach Then.

Perry was only about twenty feet from the ground when first seen by Carroll but, by the time police arrived, he was beyond reach and above the windows which broke through the walls on the lower floors.

Police sent a call to fire headquarters and a hook and ladder company responded. By the time they raised an extension ladder, Perry had climbed so high that the ladder was a full forty feet too short.

Tense drama was enacted in the eyes of the growing crowd which jammed the street below.

From floor to floor police followed the youth in his death-defying "human fly" act. From each convenient window Donahue and Cooley repeated their arguments, cajolingly and calmly.

At the sixth floor the boy paused and wiped his apparently perspiring hands upon his thighs.

He asked Cooley's identity and, hearing it, said:

"I don't want any publicity. I'm not up here for a show."

Cooley and Donahue told him that if he wanted to avoid publicity, the time to come in was then, before the crowd below grew.

The same argument was repeated from floor to floor but Perry's desperately taut face refused to soften.

Hear Him Muttering.

Occasionally, the watching pair in the window could hear him mutter:

"He made a fool out of me. He made a fool out of me."

From the sixth floor onward, the rope lowered by firemen brushed closely alongside. The boy shifted his location repeatedly, ignoring the rope and pushing it aside. He continued up.

Between the ninth and tenth floors it was evident that the desperate strength that had carried him upward in the almost superhuman climb was failing.

He stopped to rest—to wipe his hands more frequently—to talk with Donahue and Cooley.

Finally he began to weaken and then slowly to inch his way across the building face to the window where the two talked unceasingly and waited.

Perry's whole body trembled from the effort. When he had to cross a corner jutting out in his path it seemed that death was tapping his shoulder, so weakened had he become.

Close To Window.

A final, all-consuming move overshadowed by a desperate, perspiration-seamed face, and he was close to the window.

Without a word Donahue and Cooley acted together. Their hands shot out and dug into Perry's clothing. With a single heave they had him across the sill and then inside. They stood the boy on his feet.

He wavered—then collapsed.

As his wriggling body disappeared from view there was an audible expression of pent-up emotion from the crowd below. It could be heard a block away.

For 75 minutes they had watched drama—a boy clinging to brick handholds far above the street, his white shirted, flannel-trousered figure outlined in the glare of two powerful searchlights from the fire department.

They had watched the dangling rope hanging from the roof like a serpent, only it meant life when death was evident.

Down on the street a group of firemen, aided by volunteers from the crowd, had stood those 75 minutes holding a lifenet. Necks twisted as they looked upward, they shifted their position a foot at a time, trying always to keep the net directly under the boy in hopes of catching him should he plunge.

Summons Priests.

Fire Chief James H. Golden, recalling a case in New York wherein a priest had coaxed a youth to safety under similar circumstances, sent a call to St. Joseph's Church, Perry's parish, but just before the priests arrived, Perry had been pulled to safety.

The police were in charge of Night Chief James S. Collins and included Patrolmen Donahue, James Lahey, and Albert Marios who were in the building, and Joseph Garrett, Charles O'Rourke and John Lis of the street detail.

Chief Golden's fire department crew included John Barron, Sylvester Maloney, William Chabot, Harry Green, William Whalen and Harold Grogan. Maloney and Green assisted in reviving Perry.

The building, a huge brick factory, has a main height of seven stories. In the center there juts upward a wide, tower-like addition. Perry had started from the ground and made his way halfway up the tower section before his determined will weakened.

Collapses After Being Rescued

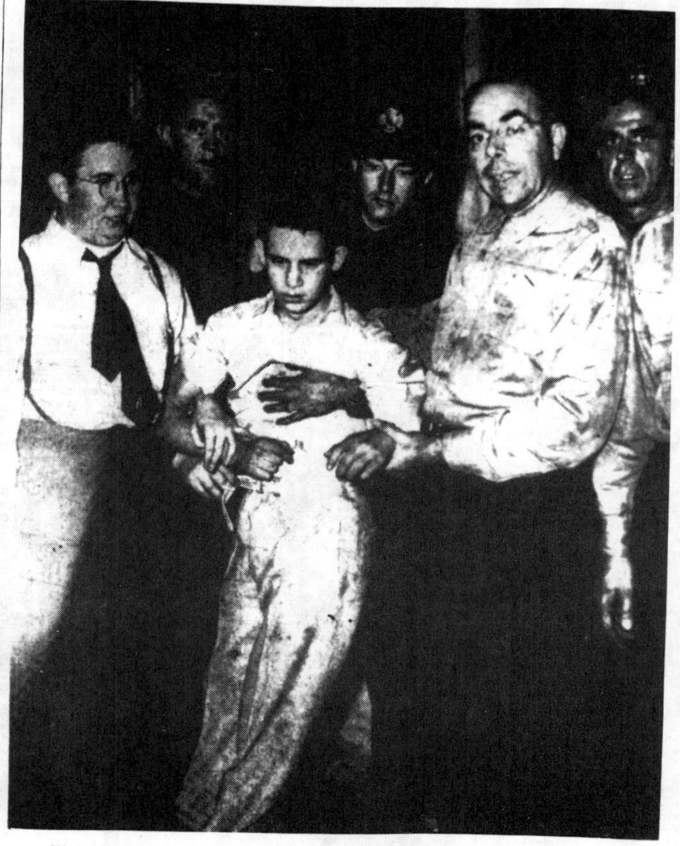

His feet once more on the ground, Lawrence Perry, 17-year-old Cohoes youth who defied death last night on a ledge outside the ninth floor of a Cohoes factory building, is shown with the two men who snatched him from his perch, Joseph A. Cooley, left, a reporter for The Record Newspapers, and Patrolman Harry Donohue, right. In the rear are three Cohoes firemen involved in the drama.

ADJOURN CASE OF HOTEL PROPRIETOR

Adjournment was taken until tomorrow morning today in Police Court in the three separate jury trials scheduled in the cases of Alexander Chatko and two others.

Chatko, proprietor of the Mohawk Hotel, is charged with breaking the Sabbath and violation of Section 5, Local Law No. 2, in operating a grill without a city license.

Fred Anselment of 37 Mohawk Street and Hardy Mayott of 106 Johnston Avenue are charged with disorderly conduct. The three were arrested about two weeks ago and are out on bail.

RANGERS RECEIVE CONTEST AWARD AT ADAMS, MASS.

Drum and Bugle Corps Finishes Season With Four First Place Awards and Two Second.

Finishing the season with a record of four first place awards, two second prizes and one third, the Bugle and Drum Corps of the Cohoes Boy Rangers yesterday participated in the final drill of the series conducted by members of the Interstate Junior Bugle and Drum Corps Alliance.

Receiving a rating of 93.60, the Rangers won third place at yesterday's drill held in Adams, Mass., under the sponsorship of the Z. N. P. Corps, Polish National Alliance.

The Junior American Legion Corps of Fort Edward took first honors with a mark of 94.825. Rated at 94.45, the Junior Corps of the Hoosick Falls American Legion was awarded second place.

In seven competitions under the alliance direction, the Rangers never failed to attain a mark over ninety for their performances.

At the state junior championships held recently in Schenectady the Rangers were tied for second place with the Grand Street Boys of New York City.

Church Unit To Meet.

Plans for fall activities will be discussed at a meeting of the Church Work Society of St. John's Episcopal Church to be conducted in the parish house Wednesday at 2:30 p.m.

Among the events to be discussed will be a social to be held in the near future at the home of Mrs. William Strang, president of the group.

COHOES CHURCHES OPEN ACTIVITIES OF FALL SCHEDULE

Initial Sessions of Numerous Organizations To Be Held During This Week.

A full calendar of church activities is scheduled this week at Cohoes as numerous organizations affiliated with the various congregations conduct their initial fall sessions.

The Silliman Club of Silliman Memorial Presbyterian Church will meet in the church house today at 8 p.m. Following the business session a social period will be conducted under the direction of Mrs. J. Nelson Hayner's Group. Rev. Francis L. McCauley will officiate at the mid-week prayer service Thursday at 7:45 p.m. The church will be represented at the fall meeting of the Troy Presbytery and Spiritual Life Conference Monday and Tuesday, Sept. 23, and 24, at Wilmington, Vt., Dr. Peter K. Emmons of Scranton, Pa., will lead the gathering.

A meeting of the consistory of the Reformed Church will be held in the church study today at 8 p.m. On Thursday at 7:45 p.m. a service will be conducted preparatory to the Lord's Supper. Holy Communion will be observed Sunday morning.

The Board of Education of the First Methodist Church will meet in the church parlors Thursday at 7:45 p.m. to discuss plans for the fall and winter. The group was formed in accordance with the regulations of the United Methodist Church. Autumn activities of the church school, Epworth League and organized classes will be outlined. Regular mid-week gatherings will be resumed after Rally Sunday.

Rev. George F. McElvein will officiate at the mid-week prayer service Thursday at 7:45 p.m. at the First Baptist Church. Members of the Women's Missionary Society will meet at the parsonage Friday at 7:45 p.m. Mrs. Harry Hardenburgh, president of the unit, will preside. Members of the Mr. and Mrs. Club will stage a clamsteam Saturday afternoon at the Hardenburgh camp at Babcock Lake.

The Servio Circle of St. James' Methodist Church will meet today at 7:30 p.m. at the residence of Mrs. Charles Spengler, 163 Simmons Avenue. A session of the Ladies' Aid Society will be conducted at Mrs. Goldsworthy's home on Central Avenue Wednesday at 2 p.m.

Welfare Clinic Slated.

A child welfare clinic under the auspices of the Health Department will be conducted at the City Hall tomorrow beginning at 10 a.m. Dr. M. J. Keough, health commissioner, will be in charge, assisted by Mrs. Helen McKee and Mrs. Velma Flurl, city nurses.

MISS KASPAR WED TO JOHN CHIPLOCK AT ST. MICHAEL'S

Rev. V. W. Gierlacki,, Pastor, Officiates in Ceremony; Reception Held at Home of Bride's Parents.

Miss Stella J. Kaspar, daughter of Mr. and Mrs. Peter P. Kaspar, 65 Cohoes Road, and John G. Chiplock, son of Mrs. Michael Chiplock, R. D. 2, Watervliet, were married at 2 p.m. yesterday at St. Michael's Church, Cohoes. The pastor, Rev. Valentine W. Gierlacki, officiated.

The wedding marches were played by Anthony V. Berdar, church organist, with Miss Helen Cermuga playing violin accompaniment. Miss Cermuga also sang "Ave Maria."

Miss Rita E. Kaspar, sister of the bride, was maid of honor, and Andrew Vetoich was the best man. The bridesmaids were Miss Margaret Ryan, Albany; Miss Helen Chiplock, Watervliet; Miss Christine Skau, Troy; Miss Arlene Chiplock, sister of the bridegroom, and Miss Irene Charcynski, Watervliet.

The bride wore white slipper satin trimmed with Chantilly lace with long train. Her veil was of tulle with lace coronet and edged with lace and held with orange blossoms. She carried bridal roses, lilies of the valley and baby breath in shower form.

Her maid of honor wore a gown of yellow moire with a tiara of flowers and a short veil. She carried tailisman roses.

The gowns of the bridesmaids were of similar pattern. Miss Ryan wore peach ta ta with tiara of flowers and short veil and carried red roses. Miss Helen Chiplock's gown was sky blue with matching tiara and veil. She carried pink roses. Miss Skau's gown was of orange taffeta with tiara of flowers and matching veil and yellow roses.

The dress worn by Miss Arlene Chiplock was rose pink taffeta with tiara and veil to match and red roses. Miss Charcynski wore aqua with matching tiara and veil and pink roses.

The ushers were Anthony Whitney and William Chiplock of Watervliet, Frank Vojcheck of Green Island, Benedict Puipas of Schenectady, Joseph Bojanowsky, Amsterdam, Emmett Catlin, Troy, and Thomas Carhart, Watervliet.

After the ceremony, a reception was conducted at the home of the bride's parents, following which a wedding dinner for 125 relatives and friends was served at the Circle Inn, Latham.

In the receiving line with the bride and groom were the bride's parents and the bridegroom's mother. Mrs. Kaspar wore a dress of soldier blue and carried a corsage of talisman roses. Mrs. Chiplock wore a dark blue dress and had a corsage of pink roses.

The couple left on a wedding trip to Washington, D. C., and Virginia Beach. The bride's traveling outfit was of soldier blue with wine accessories.

Upon their return they will reside at 65 Cohoes Road.

Lions' Club Session.

A luncheon meeting of the Cohoes Lion's Club will be conducted tomorrow at Santspree's on White Street. Gilbert H. Robert, president of the unit, will preside.

Lodge Meets Tonight.

Spartana Rebekah Lodge will hold its first fall meeting today at 8 p.m., at the rooms in the Rialto Theater Building on Remsen Street. Mrs. Ovela Bertrand, noble grand, will preside during the business session which is to be followed by a social period.

Post Will Meet.

Members of Cohoes Post, Veterans of Foreign Wars, will meet Thursday at 8 p.m. at the group's quarters on Remsen Street. Commander David Mayeroff will preside during the business session, which will be followed by a social period.

Club to Meet.

The first meeting of the Fellowcraft Club of Cohoes Lodge, No. 116, F. and A. M., is scheduled to be conducted today at 8 p.m., at the Masonic Temple. William K. Powers, president of the group, will preside during the business session, which will be followed by a social period.

Meetings of Cohoes Chapter, No. 168, R. A. M., will be resumed at the temple Wednesday night. The business session will be presided over by Edward Carpenter, high priest.

Obituary.

Israel Shepard, jr., (Chabot) of 47 White Street died yesterday afternoon in St. Peter's Hospital, Albany, following a brief illness. A lifelong resident of Cohoes, he was a member of St. Joseph's Church. Survivors include his mother, Mrs. Alida Shepard; wife, Catherine Elliott Shepard; one daughter, Mrs. Neils Jensen of Cohoes; three sons, Raymond of Cohoes; Frank of White Plains, and William of Dalton, Mass; five sisters, Sister Mary Paul Eugene, stationed at St. Joseph's Convent, Cohoes; Mrs. Alfred Audet of Schenectady; Mrs. George Crapo, Mrs. Harold Sickles and Miss Irene Shepard, all of Cohoes; four brothers, Wilfred, William, Augustus and Alfred Shepard, all of Cohoes; four grandchildren and several nieces and nephews. The funeral will be held Wednesday morning from the residence and from St. Joseph's Church at 8:30 a.m. Burial will be in St. Joseph's Cemetery, Waterford.

Couple Married Yesterday at St. Michael's

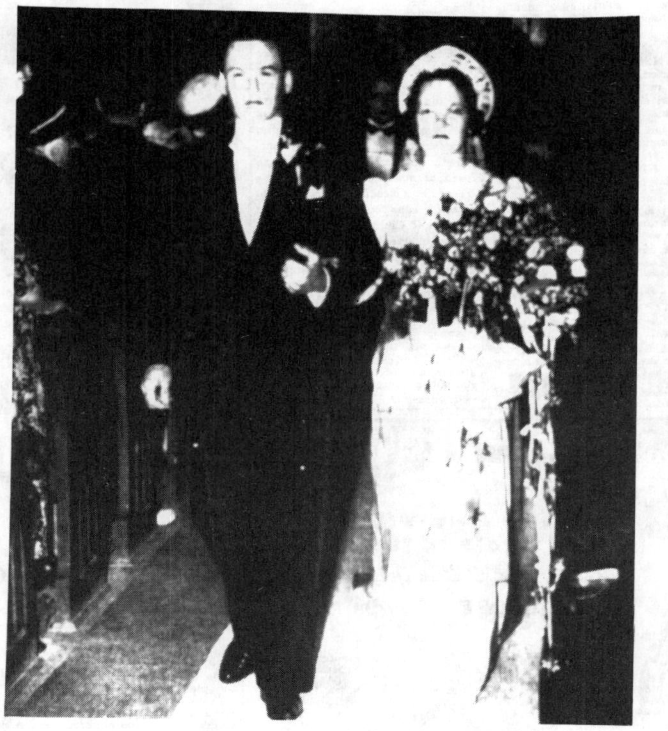

Miss Stella J. Kaspar, daughter of Mr. and Mrs. Peter P. Kaspar of Cohoes Road, and John G. Chiplock, son of Mrs. Michael Chiplock of Watervliet, were married yesterday afternoon in St. Michael's Church. Mr. and Mrs. Chiplock are shown leaving the church following the ceremony.

KRYSKOWSKI-GUZY CEREMONY HELD IN CHURCH AT COHOES

Mangum Street Woman Becomes Bride in Service Conducted at St. Michdel's Church.

At 2:30 p.m. yesterday in St. Michael's Church, Cohoes, Miss Mildred Guzy, daughter of Mr. and Mrs. George Guzy of 21 Mangam Street, Cohoes, became the bride of Walter Kryskowski, son of Mr. and Mrs. John Kryskowski of 9 Van Vechten Street. The ceremony was performed by Rev. Valentine Gierlacki, pastor.

The bride's dress was modeled on princess lines, of ivory white faille taffeta with pearl clips outlining the sweetheart neckline and long court train. Her long bridal illusion veil was caught with a halo of orange blossoms and she carried a bouquet of bridal roses and orange blossoms.

Her sister, Miss Sophie Guzy, was maid of honor, with the bridegroom's sister, Miss Anna Kryskowski, acting as bridesmaid.

Mr. Kryskowski had Joseph Sebonia as his best man, Naster Celeniski was usher.

Both the maid of honor and the bridesmaid wore gowns of velveray taffeta, princess style, with matching halo of flowers and shoulder veils. The maid's dress was rose, the bridesmaid's, powder blue. Miss Guzy carried Queen Mary roses and gypsophilia. Miss Kryskowski's bouquet contained rapture roses and gypsophilia.

During the church ceremony Anthony V. Berdar, church organist presided at the organ and John Kelly sang "Ave Marie."

Following the service a reception was held in P. N. A. Hall in Mohawk Street. When the couple left for a wedding trip to New York, Mrs. Kryskowski was attired in black with black suede accessories. Upon their return they will reside at 2627 Third Avenue, Watervliet.

Out-of-town guests at the affair included Mr. and Mrs. Andrew Busosky of Pennsylvania; Mr. and Mrs. Frank Kowski, Jersey City, N. J.; Mr. and Mrs. J. Kryskowski, and daughter, Mary, of Jersey City and Mr. and Mrs. Leon Kowalski of Greenwich, Conn.

HOME BUREAU TO MEET WEDNESDAY

The first fall meeting of the Cohoes Home Bureau will be conducted Wednesday at 2 p.m. at the Young Women's Christian Association building on Mohawk Street.

Mrs. James J. Carroll, chairman of the group, will preside during the business session, following which a home-made rolls demonstration will be given by Mrs. James B. Cundiff, who is a member of the Rensselaer unit.

COHOES HIGH CLASS WILL HOLD REUNION

Members of the 1937 graduating class of Cohoes High School will hold an informal get-together at 8 p.m. today at the Circle Inn at Latham.

Arrangements for the affair are under the direction of Everett Fairfield, a member of the class. About fifty members of the class are expected to attend the gathering, which is being held instead of a formal reunion planned some time ago.

'CYCLE DEATH OF COHOES RESIDENT CALLED ACCIDENT

A decision of accidental death was announced today by Coroner Philip Morrissey of Albany County in connection in the case of Charles Frament, jr., of 113 Maple Avenue, Cohoes, who was fatally injured Aug. 29 when the motorcycle he was operating was involved in a collision with a train at the Delaware Avenue crossing.

The decision followed an investigation into the mishap conducted by the coroner in cooperation with the Cohoes Police Department and the District Attorney's Office.

To Elect Staff.

Officers of the Ladies' Auxiliary of E. T. Ruane Post, American Legion, are scheduled to be elected at the group's annual meeting tonight at the quarters on Oneida Street. Mrs. Anna Mae Patnode, president, will preside during the business session, which will be followed by a social period.

Change Party Site.

The card party to be conducted tomorrow afternoon under the auspices of the Board of Managers of the Home for Aged Women, originally scheduled to take place at the home, will be held instead at the Masonic Temple, it was announced today by the arrangements committee. The change was decided upon because of the serious illness of one of the women at the institution.

COUNCIL DEFERS INSTALLATION TO THURSDAY, OCT. 3

Knights of Columbus Ceremony Postponed; Originally Scheduled to Be Held Sept. 19.

Originally scheduled for Thursday, Sept. 19, the annual installation of officers of the Cohoes Council, No. 192 Knights of Columbus, has been postponed until Thursday, Oct. 3, according to Hugh McKee, who will be reinstalled as grand knight at the ceremony.

District officials will be in charge of the program which will be held in the rooms on Remsen Street. Other officers who will be seated at the time are John Roberts, deputy grand knight; John F. Looby, chancellor; Paul Bourgeois, warden; George W. Maloney, recorder; Emmett R. Ryan, treasurer; Gerald Havern, advocate; Harry Dickey, inside guard; John W. O'Connor, outside guard; William Briere, organist; Desmond Havern, council trustee and Milton McKinney, building trustee.

Plans are being made by the local group to join in the annual pilgrimage of the New York State Council and the Order of Alhambra to the Shrine of the North American Martyrs at Auriesville, to be conducted on Sunday, Sept. 29.

Members desiring to join the group are requested to call at the council rooms. If enough reservations are made a bus will be secured to carry members to the train at Albany.

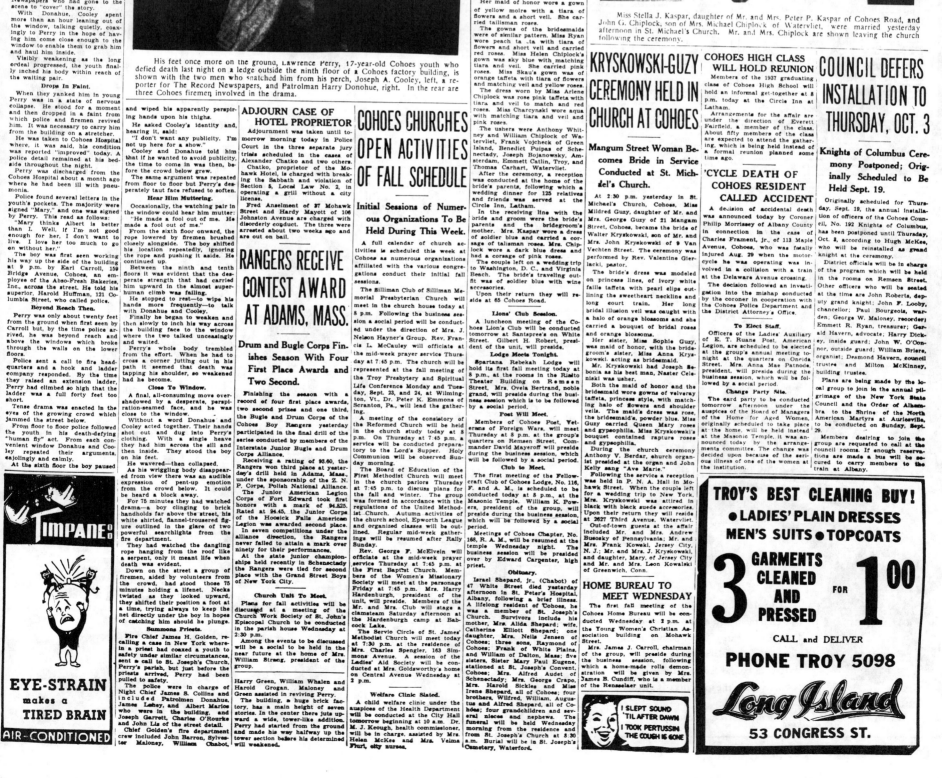

SYCAWAY.

The Queen Esther Standard Bearers' Circle had its first fall meeting at Memorial Methodist parsonage, South Lake Avenue, last night. Miss Marilyn Hayward presided and received reports from the secretary, Miss Janet Wallis, and the treasurer, Miss Virginia Diehl. The program was devoted to the summer missionary institute at Poultney, which took the form of a house party at Green Mountain Junior College. Miss Hayward, the Misses Martha Wallis, Irene Cook and Betty Cipperly gave papers on various high lights of the five days of the sessions. The annual election will be held at the October meeting. A social hour included refreshments, served buffet style.

Personal.

Mrs. Milton Morrill has returned to Trenton, N. J., after a two weeks' vacation. Mr. Morrill, who came for a short stay, accompanied her home.

Mr. and Mrs. Andrew Patterson of Hoosick Road have had as guests Mr. and Mrs. Thomas Patterson of New York City, who left yesterday for a tour of Canada.

Mrs. Herbert Bacheller and son, Herbert Edward, have returned to Huntington, W. Va., after a stay of several weeks with Mrs. Bacheller's parents, Mr. and Mrs. Edward Haber, 17 Lee Avenue.

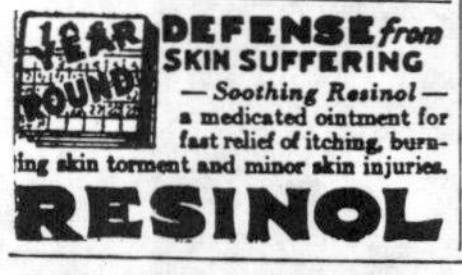
YEAR ROUND
DEFENSE from SKIN SUFFERING
— Soothing Resinol —
a medicated ointment for fast relief of itching, burning skin torment and minor skin injuries.
RESINOL

CHRISTIAN SERVICE GROUP FORMED BY WOMEN OF CHURCH

Long-standing Organization at State Street Methodist Consolidated Under New Name.

Women's organizations which have functioned for scores of years in Fifth Avenue-State Street Methodist Church went out of existence last night when their members formed the charter group of the new Woman's Society of Christian Service. That step is a direct outgrowth of last year's union of the three branches of Methodism, the Methodist Episcopal Church, Methodist Church, South, and Methodist Protestant Church.

The charter session was conducted in the parlors of Fifth Avenue-State Street Church with 58 women present to sign the new rolls. They came from the Woman's Foreign Missionary Society, Woman's Home Missionary Society, younger groups affiliated with these two, the Woman's Church Society, and such other church groups as may wish to join the single organization. The Christian Service group will perform all the services of these separate societies under one head, but by means of a series of sub-divisions.

Mrs. A. R. Joy was elected president of the new society, with Mrs. William H. Dolan, vice president in charge of program; Mrs. Charles Downs, vice president in charge of missions; Mrs. J. Harold Hirst, vice president in charge of local service; Mrs. William J. Armstrong, treasurer; Mrs. Arthur E. Xander, corresponding secretary; Mrs. Thurman A. Hull, recording secretary;

The charter rolls will be kept open until Oct. 15.

Rev. James A. Perry, Th.D., pastor, opened the meeting and presided until the officers were elected. He lead in prayer and then made a statement of the purposes and plans of the society.

These purposes include: Help develop and support Christian work among women and children around the world; develop spiritual life; study the needs of the world; take part in such services as will strengthen the local church, improve civic, community and world conditions; to enlist others in this Christian fellowship, and secure funds for the activities in the local church and the support of the work undertaken at home and abroad for the establishment of a World Christian Community."

Acting for the women of the church, Mrs. Merton I. Roy presented corsages to Mrs. William Herbert, retiring mission society president; Mrs. Henry Kreiss, retiring president of the Woman's Church Society, and Mrs. Joy, the new Christian Service president.

Mrs. Belle Judd presided at the piano during the enrollment ceremony and also for the general program. Decorations, consisting of fall flowers, were arranged by Mrs. James A. Perry, and refreshments were supervised by Mrs. Dennie B. Riggs.

New Officers of Christian Service Group

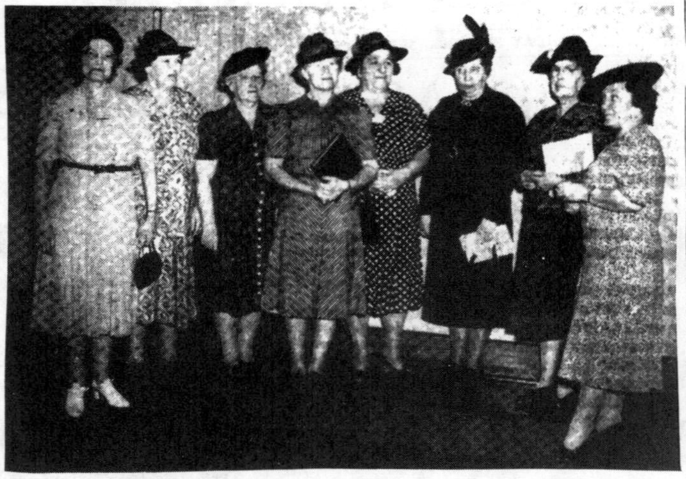

Officers of the new Women's Society of Christian Service, organized at a meeting last night at the Fifth Avenue-State Street Methodist Church, are shown above. Left to right are Mrs. Charles Downs, second vice president; Mrs. Arthur E. Xander, corresponding secretary; Mrs. William J. Armstrong, treasurer; Mrs. Thurman A. Hull, recording secretary; Mrs. T. Edward Burnap, group leader; Mrs. William H. Dolan, first vice president; Mrs. Archie R. Joy, president, and Mrs. J. Harold Hirst, third vice president.

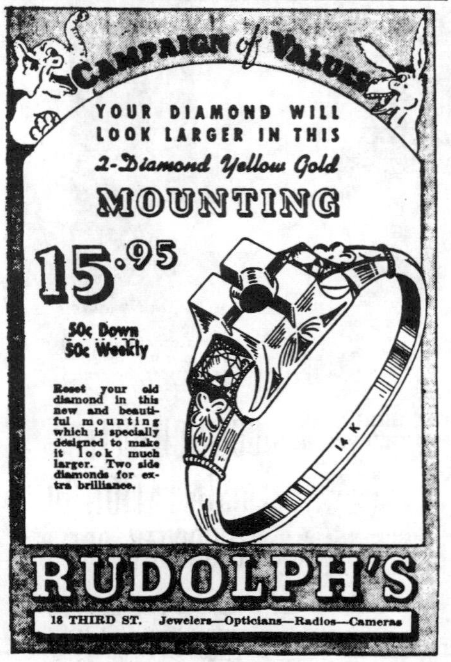
CAMPAIGN of VALUES
YOUR DIAMOND WILL LOOK LARGER IN THIS
2-Diamond Yellow Gold
MOUNTING
15.95
50c Down
50c Weekly
Reset your old diamond in this new and beautiful mounting which is specially designed to make it look much larger. Two side diamonds for extra brilliance.
14 K
RUDOLPH'S
18 THIRD ST. Jewelers—Opticians—Radios—Cameras

NEW GAINS SEEN FOR ROOSEVELT IN THREE BIG STATES

Gallup Poll in Ney York, Pennsylvania and New Jersey Shows Decided New Deal Trend.

BY DR. GEORGE GALLUP
Director, American Institute of Public Opinion.

Copyright, 1940, by American Institute of Public Opinion. All rights reserved. Reproduction strictly prohibited except with written consent of the copyright holders.

Princeton, N. J.—Dramatic new gains for President Roosevelt in a month which saw a fierce flare-up of the German onslaught on Great Britain, as well as the President's transfer of 50 destroyers in exchange for naval bases, are revealed in the American Institute of Public Opinion's latest returns from three pivotal eastern states—New York, Pennsylvania and New Jersey.

Gaining four percentage points on Wendell Willkie in New York state, three in Pennsylvania and five in New Jersey, President Roosevelt has taken the lead away from the Republican candidate in these three states and buttressed his national position at this stage of the race, the survey shows.

Tabulating Returns.

Whether or not President Roosevelt's gains in these states have been duplicated in other parts of the country remains to be seen. Returns from the Institute's third, state-by-state survey of Roosevelt-Willkie sentiment are being tabulated and will be reported Friday in the The Record Newspapers.

What has happened in these three eastern states since the previous Institute survey, Aug. 25, is sufficient to show the problem that faces Mr. Willkie on his present trip through the far West, however. As in the past, the intensification of the war in Europe has been followed by a rise in Roosevelt support. Mr. Willkie, whose active campaign is just beginning, must now attempt to overhaul President Roosevelt in states like New York, Pennsylvania and New Jersey, which the Republican candidate held during the first weeks of the campaign and which are probably necessary for his election.

Race Still Close.

The race in these three states is still close—as close as it was a month ago—but the advantage lies today with President Roosevelt instead of with Mr. Willkie, the survey shows.

The state-by-state vote of those with definite choices at this time, with the net change for Roosevelt since Aug. 25, is as follows:

Electoral Votes	Today % Roos'vlt	% Wilke	Points of change for Roos'v'lt
47 New York	52%	48%	+4
36 Penns'lvania	52	48	+3
16 New Jersey	54	46	+5

In each of these states the Institute survey found a substantial number of voters "undecided" or without definite choices at this time—12 per cent of New York, 11 per cent in Pennsylvania and 13 per cent in New Jersey. Many of them still say, "We don't know very much about Willkie yet; we're waiting to hear what he has to say."

99 Electoral Votes.

The importance of New York, Pennsylvania and New Jersey lies in the fact that together they account for 99 electoral votes, or almost one-fifth of the 531 in the electoral college.

In New York City, where President Roosevelt registered 75% of vote in 1936, he now leads by 67 per cent. In Philadelphia where Roosevelt received 62 per cent of the vote four years ago, his strength today is at 60 per cent.

The trend since the Aug. 25 survey is shown in the following figures:

	% FDR	% Wil'ke	Gain for FDR
New York City	67%	33%	+4
Upstate New York	38	62	+4
Philadelphia	60	40	+3
Rest of State, including Pittsburg	49	51	+4

NOTED DIARIST

HORIZONTAL
1, 7 Author of the most famous diary.
11 Betimes.
12 Herb.
13 Area measure.
14 Remote.
15 Ream (abbr.).
16 Pound (abbr.)
18 To immerse.
20 North America (abbr.).
21 Rubber tree.
22 Meadow.
24 Bones.
25 He lived in the —— century.
31 Indian weight.
33 Eye.
34 Newspaper paragraphs.
36 Endures.
37 To pilfer.
38 Antitoxin.
39 Corded fabric.
41 Mink.
42 Three.
45 Term in logic.
48 Beast of burden.
50 Long since.
52 Not widespread.
53 Snaky fish.
54 Weight.
55 Form of "be."
56 Nay.
57 Constellation.
58 He wrote with frankness or ——.
59 He was a —— of England.

Answer to Previous Puzzle

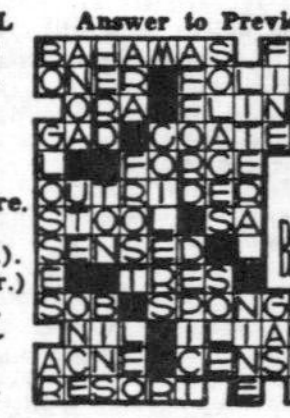

VERTICAL
2 Eagle's home.
3 Mother.
4 Stunted child.
5 Enthusiasm.
6 Shaped like a lyre.
7 Recreation tract.
8 Tree.
9 Italian river.
10 Screams.
13 He was secretary to the —— or navy.
17 Species of yucca.
19 Meat pie.
21 Theater guide.
23 To turn aside.
24 Fish-eating beast.
26 Holding devices.
27 Neither.
28 Earth circle.
29 To recede.
30 An effort.
32 The heart.
35 Chinese measure.
40 Pertaining to the poles.
41 Malefactor.
43 Instrument.
44 Pressing tool.
46 Gypsy.
47 To sunburn.
48 Pertaining to air.
49 Slovak.
51 Completion.
53 To sup.

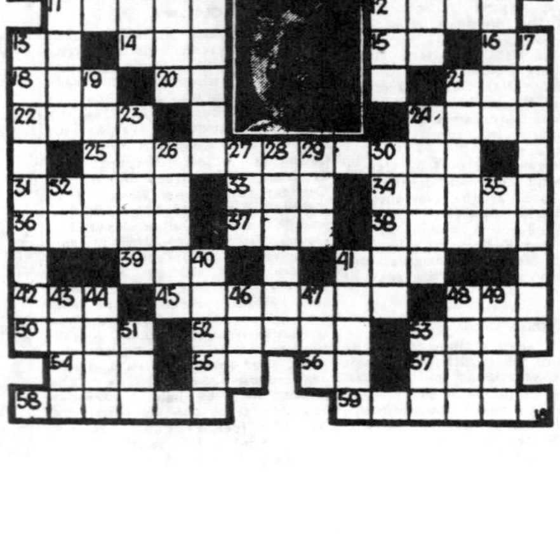

SUSPENDED STATE ARCHITECTS SEEK $25,000 BACK PAY

Cohoes Man and 26 Others Bring Suit Alleging Salaries Were Changed by Officials.

Roy W. Legg of Cohoes and 26 other former assistant architects in the State Department of Public Works have brougth suit to recover $25,000 in back pay. The application will be argued before Supreme Court Justice Harry E. Schirick Sept. 27 at a special term in Albany.

Arthur W. Brandt, superintendent of public works, Miss Grace A Reavy, Howard G. E. Smith and Howard P. Jones, Civil Service Commissioners, and Morris S. Tremaine, comptroller, are respondents.

Harry W. Williams, attorney for the petitioners, claims the architects are entitled to the amounts sought under a section of the Civil Service law which provides an employee reinstated from a preferred list to the same or to a similar position shall receive at least the same salary such employee was receiving at time of separation from service."

The petitioners, Williams claims, were suspended for lack of funds July 31. They had been in service up to that time after having been reinstated following suspension for lack of funds on prior dates. The architects contend they did not receive the same salaries when reinstated as they had received at the time of the original separation from service. Wage claims range [illegible] $1,425.

REACH SETTLEMENT IN ACCIDENT CASE

A settlement has been reached in a lawsuit brought by John Conway of this city in behalf of his daughter, Helen Conway, 9, against Edward H. Howe, 419 Fifth Avenue. Papers noting the settlement were filed today at the county clerk's office. The amount was not disclosed.

The girl was struck by a car operated by Howe on July 1 at Tyler and First Streets. Henry S. Bayley was attorney for Mr. Conway.

Athlete's Foot Stopped Quick!

Don't suffer with cracked, bleeding irritated Athlete's Foot any longer—KRYSO, a new, quick action liquid checks Athlete's Foot quick—Get your bottle of KRYSO now—Only 49c—Rapid action—Sure relief. On sale at Donnelly & Hanna and all good drug stores.—Adv.

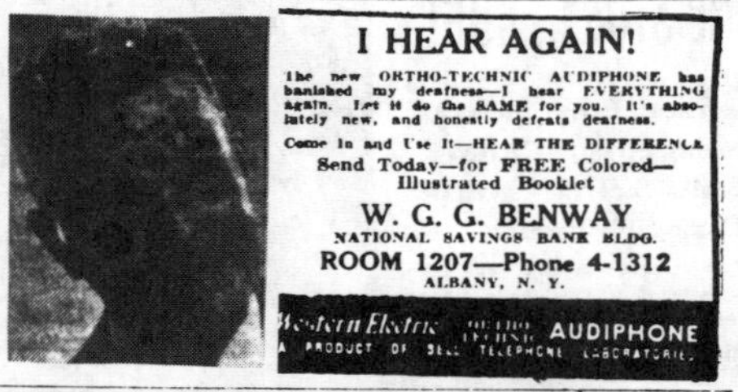
I HEAR AGAIN!
The new ORTHO-TECHNIC AUDIPHONE has banished my deafness—I hear EVERYTHING again. Let it do the SAME for you. It's absolutely new, and honestly defeats deafness.
Come In and Use It—HEAR THE DIFFERENCE
Send Today—for FREE Colored—Illustrated Booklet
W. G. G. BENWAY
NATIONAL SAVINGS BANK BLDG.
ROOM 1207—Phone 4-1312
ALBANY, N. Y.
Western Electric AUDIPHONE

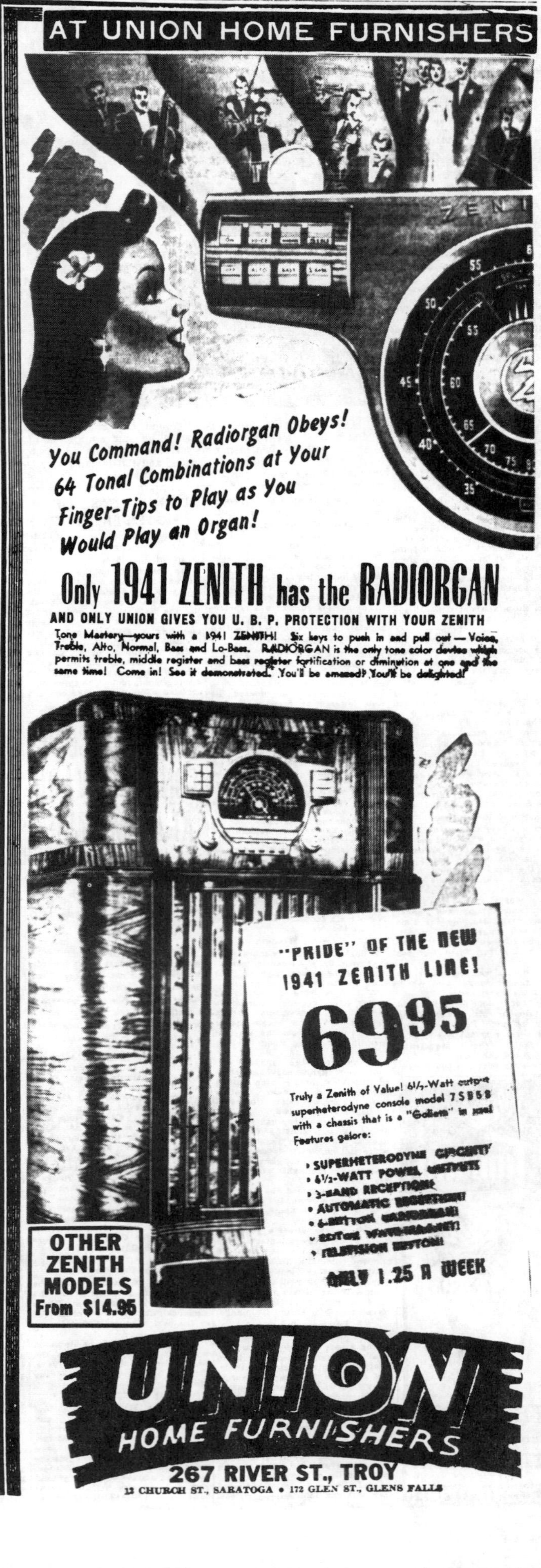
AT UNION HOME FURNISHERS
You Command! Radiorgan Obeys!
64 Tonal Combinations at Your Finger-Tips to Play as You Would Play an Organ!
Only 1941 ZENITH has the RADIORGAN
AND ONLY UNION GIVES YOU U. B. P. PROTECTION WITH YOUR ZENITH
Tone Mastery—yours with a 1941 ZENITH! Six keys to push in and pull out—Voice, Treble, Alto, Normal, Bass and Lo-Bass. RADIORGAN is the only tone color device which permits treble, middle register and bass register fortification or diminution at one and the same time! Come in! See it demonstrated. You'll be amazed! You'll be delighted!
"PRIDE" OF THE NEW 1941 ZENITH LINE!
69.95
Truly a Zenith of Value! 6½-Watt output superheterodyne console model
with a chassis that is a "Goliath" in
Features galore:
SUPERHETERODYNE CIRCUIT
6½-WATT POWER OUTPUT
3-BAND RECEPTION
ONLY 1.25 A WEEK
OTHER ZENITH MODELS From $14.95
UNION HOME FURNISHERS
267 RIVER ST., TROY
13 CHURCH ST., SARATOGA • 172 GLEN ST., GLENS FALLS

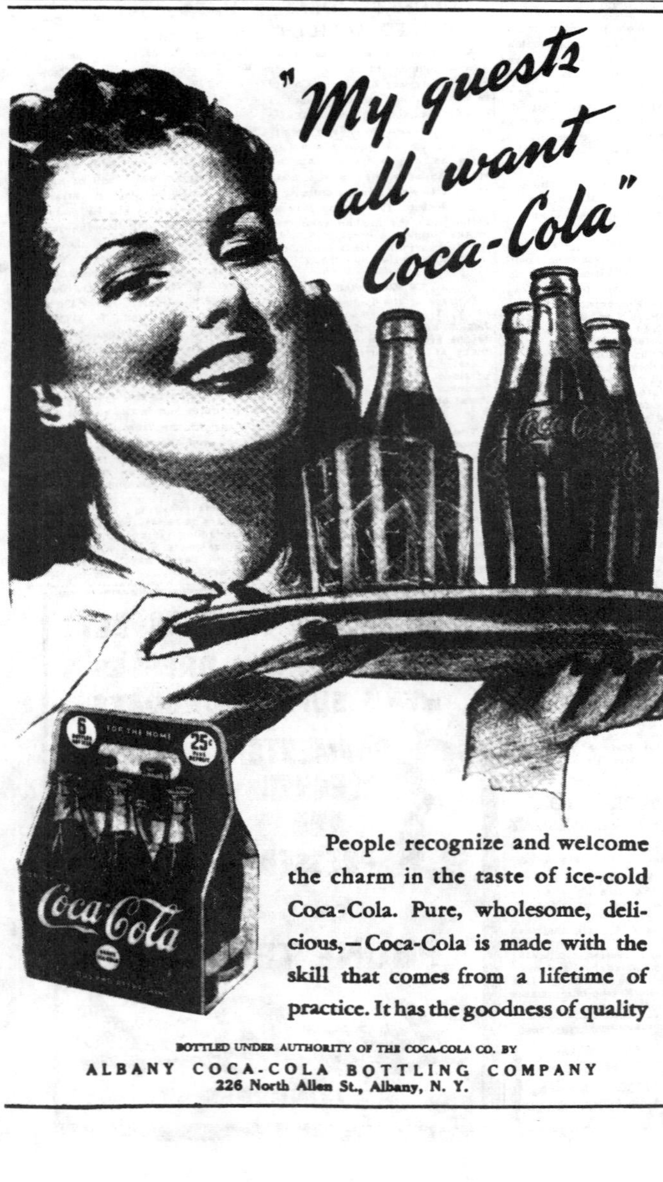
"My guests all want Coca-Cola"
People recognize and welcome the charm in the taste of ice-cold Coca-Cola. Pure, wholesome, delicious,—Coca-Cola is made with the skill that comes from a lifetime of practice. It has the goodness of quality
BOTTLED UNDER AUTHORITY OF THE COCA-COLA CO. BY
ALBANY COCA-COLA BOTTLING COMPANY
226 North Allen St., Albany, N. Y.

MEETING DATE CHANGED.

The Troy High School Parent-Teacher Association will meet tomorrow night in School 5 instead of tonight as previously announced. George H. Krug, superintendent of schools, will be the speaker.

APOLLO LODGE OF MASONS CONFERS DEGREE ON CLASS

Senior Warden Presides Over Work; Body To Exemplify Ritual Later for Schenectady Unit.

The second degree was conferred on a class of candidates at a communication of Apollo Lodge, No. 13, F. and A. M., at the Masonic Temple last night. The work was in charge of Andrew G. Short, senior warden of the lodge, with Worshipful Norman F. Coons presiding in the west and Worshipful Clarence J. Ryan in the south. The acting master was assisted by Worshipful Walter M. Douglas and Worshipful J. W. Fraser, present master.

Refreshments were served in the cafeteria of the temple at the close of the meeting, under the direction of Alton R. Holmes.

The lodge will endeavor to sell sixty boxes of Christmas cards this fall for the benefit of the Masonic Home at Utica. The card sale is in charge of Wallace Bethem.

At the next communication of the lodge Tuesday evening, October 15, the first degree will be conferred under the direction of Kenneth Herrington, junior deacon. Andrew G. Short will be in charge of the refreshments.

Apollo Lodge will confer the first degree at Schenectady for St. George's Lodge, No. 6 of that city on October 24. It is expected that two or three bus loads of Apollo members will attend the Schenectady meeting. Transportation is being arranged without charge.

The third degree will be conferred for Apollo Lodge by Christopher Yates Lodge, No. 971, of Schenectady at the Troy temple Tuesday evening, October 29. Refreshments will be served by the Apollo Fellowcraft Club under the direction of George Reed, president.

Honored On Golden Wedding Day

Shown above with some of the flowers they received on their fiftieth wedding anniversary from friends and relatives are Mr. and Mrs. Abram Herman of Taborton. The couple was entertained at a dinner party at Glass Lake Hotel last night.

● SERIAL STORY

THIS COULD BE YOUR STORY

BY MARGUERITE GAHAGAN

COPYRIGHT, 1940, NEA SERVICE, INC.

All characters, organizations and incidents of this serial are entirely fictitious.

* * *

Yesterday: Sue Mary goes to Ross Clark's home to help him with some important work. The old man is worried about his son, questions her about Vera. But Sue Mary knows he doesn't realize what his son may do under Vera's persuasion.

Joe Is Hurt

CHAPTER XXI.

The cleaning women had left only one dim light burning in the office and the rows of desks and filing cabinets stretched out endlessly in the shadowy darkness. Sue Mary stopped to feel the unfamiliar stillness.

She was terribly tired and she hoped she could concentrate enough on the work to get it out quickly. She went down the hall into a side office where she could get the full sweep of the breeze and turned on the dim desk lamp. Her notes seemed inches thick and she turned the pages, thinking of the time it would take to get them in order.

She was deep in concentration when she heard the voices from old Ross Clark's private office, down the hall. She listened, and then quietly went over to the small file room that opened between the rooms. The voices could be heard distinctly in the stillness.

"We've had some wonderful evenings, darling." Vera's voice came to her, and Sue Mary detected a note of tenseness. "Is your head aching? Here, let me put a cold cloth on it."

"Just want to be quiet. Kiss me and stop talking." Young Ross Clark's voice was thick.

"Kiss me and then I'm going to sleep. Got a big business meeting tomorrow. Airport stuff. The old man is hipped on my being there."

"Family prestige—" His voice trailed off and after a moment Sue Mary heard Vera laugh.

She stood there listening to her own breathing in the silence. It seemed ages before Vera left the room and went to a phone in the outer office. Sue Mary felt she must be discovered as she edged her way into the outer hall to stand behind a door and strain to hear every word...

"Well, he's handled it more cleverly than I thought he would," Vera said softly into the phone. "But there are loopholes big enough for us to blow the story wide open. I mean his gambling debts and the fact that he's using this guy ... as a cover-up on the real estate deal.

"I know that there are papers here we should have. No, I haven't got them. Tomorrow would be the time to break the news.

"Yes, I know—but Nick—listen. This isn't the time to try and find them. He'll have the signed papers, deeds, figures—all that stuff here tomorrow. We can get it. Then. Or get a camera and take copies. That wouldn't be stealing.

"No—I'm not afraid. Well, listen, Nick. Tomorrow is the time. No, I can't talk any longer. I'll explain in detail when I see you. I want to get out of here. 'Bye, darling."

* * *

Time passed. Long after Vera's heels had had a tatoo out of the office and she had heard the elevator door clang shut, Sue Mary went back to her work. Somehow she finished it, somehow she had courage enough to look in on Ross Clark, jr. sleeping on his father's old black, leather-covered couch. And then she left.

The air was cool and the streets silent and deserted. A paper truck went by and someone threw a bundle of morning editions to a sleepy-eyed boy on the corner. Sue Mary brought one and read it on the late bus going to the apartment.

She skimmed the unpleasant bulletins from Europe and then looked at a picture on the front page. More trouble at Smithson. The picket line continued to parade although strike notice hadn't been posted by the union.

There would be a showdown, though, within the next two days, the story read. The thing was getting out of hand, for late that afternoon when the day shift had quit, fights had started—again no one knew how—and three factory workers had been injured.

In the hospital was Joe Stefanski, 24, employed in the research department.

Stefanski, according to fellow workers and plant officials, had had no part in the recent difficulties, but had been struck by a flying missile. It was not known if he suffered a skull fracture but X-rays had been taken.

Sue Mary went by her stop and walked back the two blocks in a state of terror. She stopped under another street light to reread the story. The words "Joe Stefanski, 24," stared at her from the white paper.

Her eyes finally focused on the picture. And from the blurred faces in the group standing behind the picket line she recognized one: Nick.

There could be no mistaking her hair, with that one unruly lock falling across the forehead; the line of his lips as he talked to another man, and the frozen gesture there on the page, that he always used when involved in excited conversation.

The night was endless. She had wanted to go to Joe, but a frantic call she made to the hospital made it pointless. Mr. Stefanski was unconscious. He was doing well as could be expected. He could see no one; would recognize no one in his present condition.

So she went to the apartment.

climbing the steps wearily and trying to get to bed without awakening Natalie.

So much had happened in the past few hours that Sue Mary's mind refused to function normally.

Vera and Nick were slowly tightening the net around her. Stupid Ross Clark, jr., so that their political strategy would work to the benefit of the party. Nick and the YP gang were stirring up trouble at the Smithson factory so that production at Gull Plane would be halted all in the name of their type of Americanism.

All to keep the United States safe from war mongers, capitalists, munition makers. That was their cry.

And "Joe in the hospital. Joe, who was typical of young America. She thought of him working his way through college; working side by side with common laborers in the factory, retaining his safe, sane philosophy, winning a place in the research department and anticipating his future of usefulness.

Now Joe was an innocent victim of those who cried that they were fighting to help the underprivileged worker, and tried to undermine the government.

Tomorrow night no, tonight, for the sky was already turning a faint gray Vera and Nick would try to get evidence enough on young Ross Clark to forge a weapon that would insure old Gov. Russell Miller's defeat.

And soon, Sue Mary repeated over and over against her pillow, the X-rays would tell Joe's fate.

(To Be Continued.)

TITCOMB AUXILIARY WILL CONDUCT SALE

Names of new members were presented last night at a meeting of Mollie E. Titcomb Auxiliary, Army and Navy Union, in Young's Hall on State Street. Mrs. Bertha L. Coiteux, president.

Plans were discussed for a rummage sale Oct. 24 and 25. Mrs. Maude Van Tassel was named chairman of the committee and will be assisted by Mrs. Elizabeth McGarry, Miss Agnes Coiteux, Mrs. Helena Hopper, Mrs. Hattie LaBeau and Mrs. Agnes McGarry.

An inspection will be conducted at the first meeting in November with Mrs. Margaret Miller, past department president, as inspector. It was also announced members of the auxiliary will attend a testimonial dinner in honor of Mrs. Albina Aschet of Cohoes, department chaplain, to be given Monday night at G. A. R. Hall in Cohoes.

Mrs. Amy McFee was appointed historian of the auxiliary. One member, Miss Mary I. Weaver, was reported ill. A social hour at the close of the meeting was in charge of Mrs. Elizabeth McGarry, committee chairman.

FIREMEN CALLED FOR SLIGHT FIRES

Two minor fires resulted in calls for fire apparatus early last night.

At 6:34 p.m. Pumper 3 was summoned to a bonfire in the street between Ida and Jefferson Streets and Second and Third Streets. No damage resulted.

Pumper 7 was called to a fire blaze in Spring Avenue near Central Avenue at 7:23 p.m. The firemen used a booster line There was no damage.

TO NOTE BIRTHDAY.

Doris Egli, daughter of Rev. Oscar Egli, pastor of Zion Evangelical and Reformed Church at Taborton, and Mrs. Egli, will entertain 15 guests this afternoon at the manse with a party in honor of her ninth birthday. Decorations will be in pink.

TABORTON COUPLE, WED FIFTY YEARS, GUESTS AT DINNER

Mr. and Mrs. Abram Herman Honored by Relatives, Friends on Golden Wedding Date.

Mr. and Mrs. Abram Herman, lifelong residents of Taborton, celebrated their fiftieth wedding anniversary with a dinner last night at Glass Lake Hotel. Seventy-five guests, including the couple's six children and nine grandchildren, were present.

Among the guests was Mrs. Lena Timber who on Oct. 1, 1890, was bridesmaid for the couple when they were married by the late Rev. F. Ewald at the old Leffler homestead at Taborton. The best man was the late George Herman, died several years ago.

The hotel dining room was decorated in a gold color scheme set off by clusters of cut flowers. A large wedding cake formed the table centerpiece. Rev. Oscar Egli, pastor of Zion Evangelical and Reformed Church, Taborton, offered the invocation. He served also as toastmaster.

Acting in behalf of the other children and relatives, Clarence Herman, Hammonton, N. J., a son, addressed the jubilarians thanking them for the care they had given their children and for their goodness throughout life. He presented them a purse. The nine grandchildren tendered a basket of fifty yellow roses.

Another basket of flowers came from the congregation and the Ladies Aid Society of the Taborton Church. Mrs. Herman is a life member of the Ladies Aid, and the couple are lifelong members of the church. At services Sunday, Mr. Egli extended the congregation's congratulations to the couple.

Other speakers included Mrs. Charles Hoffman, Menands, an old friend, and Mr. Egli.

At services Sunday, Mr. Egli extended the congregation's congratulations to the couple. Music for dancing was played by Fisher's orchestra.

CROWDS ATTEND MASONIC TEMPLE FASHION PREVUE

The spacious ballroom of the Masonic Temple was jammed to overflow last night for the annual fall and winter fashion prevue of furs and women's apparel presented by Lord & Tann.

Tailored suits and coats, wool and silk dresses, afternoon dresses, dinner and evening gowns, fur trimmed cloth coats, evening wraps and a complete showing of furs were featured. The program opened at 8 p.m. with music and the prevue began at 8:30.

The colorful fashion parade was climaxed by the showing of a complete bridal party. Millinery for the prevue was by Seeley's and shoes by Philpot & Thomas.

Models who displayed the apparel included Jean Tann, Sally Sise, Martha DeSilva, Carolyn Boxley, Carolyn Bussey, Rita Frank, Margaret Deveny, Dorothea Hughes, Julia O'Connor, Sally Carpenter, Mary Swinnerton, Marie Shimkitis and Mrs. George B. Boxley.

PARISH UNITS TO BE FORMED IN KNIGHTS

The Knights of Columbus unit of St. Francis de Sales parish will meet tomorrow evening at 8:15 o'clock in St. Francis Hall to select permanent officers. Charles A. Cassidy, temporary chairman, and William G. Hayes, temporary secretary, will be in charge of the gathering.

Knights of Columbus of Sacred Heart parish will meet at the K. of C. rooms tomorrow evening at 8:30 o'clock to form a unit.

Reelected By Emerald Club

CHARLES E. DUNCAN.

Charles E. Duncan was reelected president of the Emerald Athletic Club at the annual meeting last night at the clubrooms on Congress Street.

Other officers are: Michael J. DeBonis, vice president; James J. O'Brien, renamed recording secretary; William Caven, financial secretary; Leo C. Mullin, reelected treasurer; Rollin J. Hurd, trustee for three years.

After the business session, a turkey dinner was served for 120. Music was furnished by Porter Potts' orchestra. The dinner was under the direction of Charles Schermerhorn, aided by the house committee, Thomas J. Noonan, Frank J. Farina and William C. Hoy.

NEWSWRITERS ELECT AND SET DEC. 14 AS ANNUAL SHOW DATE

The Troy Newswriters conducted their annual meeting yesterday afternoon at the Rensselaer County Court House to make preliminary plans for the annual show and to elect officers.

The show, lampooning politics and politicians locally as well as nationally, will be presented Saturday, Dec. 14 in The Hendrick Hudson and, in accordance with custom, will be preceded by a reception and dinner.

Officers, reelected are: Norman F. Bowen, president; Joseph J. Horan, vice president; Joseph R. Snyder, secretary, and Julius J. Heller, treasurer. Two applications for membership were received from Donald C. Schneider and Joseph Cooley, and accepted.

GRANT LETTERS ON WATERVLIET ESTATE

Miss Catherine M. Cavanaugh of Watervliet yesterday was granted letters of administration on the estate of her mother, Mrs. Catherine Cavanaugh, who died Aug. 15 in Watervliet. The letters, given by Surrogate Edward G. Rogan of Albany County showed an estate of $5,000 personal and less than $5,000 real property.

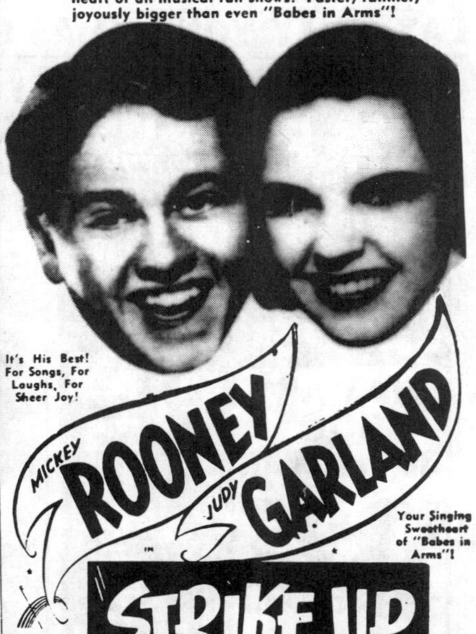

Two sons, Joseph T. and Thomas F. Cavanaugh, of Watervliet and two other daughters, Elizabeth F. Cavanaugh of Watervliet and Rose B. Shanley of Troy, also share the estate.

OSBORNE NAMED TO ANDERSON POST ON WHITEFACE BOARD

State Commissioner of Conservation Litgow Osborne was today named by Gov. Herbert H. Lehman to succeed the late William H. Anderson of Troy as a member of the Whiteface Mountain Memorial Highway Commission.

Other members of the commission are J. Hubert Stevens of Lake Placid and Roger B. Prescott of Keeseville. C. F. Anderson of Troy is secretary of the commission which looks after the operation of the toll highway, one of the most picturesque in the country.

William H. Anderson served as chairman of the commission since its creation in 1929. It constructed the highway which is a memorial to World War veterans.

The road was opened in 1935 and dedicated the same year.

TAX RETURNS ON GASOLINE INCREASE

Albany (UP)—Automobiles consumed 1,294,507,048 gallons of gasoline in the first eight months of 1940, a gain of 42,987,708 gallons over the corresponding period last year, the State Tax Department reported today.

August taxable sales of 200,000,491 gallons provided $7,923,866 in revenue, a gain of $739,093 over August, 1939.

UNION OF BARBERS HEARS REPORT ON MEMBERS DRIVE

Only 37 Out of 158 Shops Not Affiliated, Survey Shows; Plan Meeting October 29.

Local 150, Journeymen Barbers International Union, A. F. of L., meeting at the Troy Labor Temple last evening, made plans for a meeting Tuesday evening, Oct. 29, also at the Troy Labor Temple, to complete its drive to unionize all barber shops in the city.

The union commenced its unionization campaign two weeks ago and hopes to have 100 per cent success by the time of the Oct. 29 meeting. Of 158 barber shops employing a total of 172 barbers in the city, only 37 shops are not unionized, union officers pointed out last evening. Two barbers joined the union last night. Anthony Merlino, third vice president of the International Union with headquarters at Indianapolis, Ind., is in charge of the drive, assisted by a committee of local barbers including Charles J. LaHait, chairman, and Frank L. Walsh, secretary-treasurer.

A special committee was also named to communicate with other unions affiliated with the Troy Federation of Labor to enlist their support in the drive and to invite them to attend the Oct. 29 meeting. Placed on this special committee were Mr. LaHait, Michael B. Hughes, William Quinn, Charles Moak, Patrick Donnelly and Frank Milanese.

Speakers at the Oct. 29 meeting will include Ralph W. Eyclesheimer of the musicians' union; Christopher W. Gilhooley of the coke workers' union and I. Seymour Scott, president of the Troy Federation of Labor.

SOCIAL AGENCIES MEMBERS STUDY VALUE OF INDEX

The first of a series of special meetings to help acquaint member agencies of the Troy Council of Social Agencies with ways in which the Central Index may assist them in their work was held yesterday afternoon in the office of the Troy Catholic Charities. Rev. John G. Hart, director of the Troy Catholic Charities, is also head of the newly-formed Advisory Committee of the Central Index. Both he and Eric W. Gibberd, executive secretary of the Troy Council of Social Agencies which operates the Central Index led the discussion.

Representatives of child welfare agencies here which make use of the Index attended the session. The subject of discussion was "Methods by Which the Central Index Can Improve the Service of the Dependent and Neglected Children of This Area."

A meeting for representatives of the local health agencies will be held at the Troy Catholic Charities office next Wednesday at 3 p.m. A second meeting for representatives of child welfare agencies will be conducted the next day in the office of the Troy Council of Social Agencies.

There will be a meeting next Monday, Oct. 28, for representatives of the family welfare agencies at the Troy Catholic Charities office and there will be a meeting for representatives of the recreational agencies of the city the following day at the Y. M. C. A.

Present at the meeting yesterday were Miss Marjorie R. Nail, student counselor at the Knickerbacker Junior High School; John T. Fagan, secretary of the Rensselaer County Child Welfare Board; Miss Eileen N. Kinsella, case consultant for the Rensselaer County Children's Service Bureau; Miss Abbie Brady of the Troy Catholic Charities.

Also Miss Catherine Doyle of the Mohawk and Hudson Valley Humane Society; Herbert J. Hunn, superintendent of the Troy Orphan Asylum; Mrs. Rachel S. Newlin, superintendent of the Day Home, and Miss Elizabeth T. Flynn of the Central Index office.

Barbers' Local Conducting Campaign

Among those who attended the meeting of the local Barbers' Union and heard reports on the membership campaign being conducted were, left to right, front row, Clem Zoto, Charles Perazzini, Charles LaHait, John Palladino, Patrick Donnelly, Albert Carlson and Theodore Mertens. In the rear, left to right, Albert B. Catone, Rocco Boyce, Theodore R. Kori, Charles Moak, Patrick Mulcahy, William Mertens and Joseph Baisch.

THE WEATHER
U. S. Weather Bureau.
Tonight—Snow flurries, colder
Tomorrow—Cloudy, cold

THE TIMES RECORD

FINAL EDITION

Series 1940—No. 263. | Entered as Second Class Matter at the Postoffice at Troy, N. Y., under the Act of March 3, 1879 | TROY, N. Y., WEDNESDAY EVENING, NOVEMBER 6, 1940. | (Published Daily Except Sunday) | PRICE THREE CENTS

President Roosevelt Reelected; Willkie Calls for United Nation

LEADERS SEEK TO ANALYZE RESULT OF ELECTION HERE

Democratic Defeat Creates Political Speculation; Republican Chairman Has No Comment.

Rensselaer County political leaders this afternoon were attempting to make an analysis of the returns which showed that the unprecedented registration in the county at large has created a crossword puzzle.

Wendell L. Willkie carried Rensselaer County by a margin of 8,513, overcoming Roosevelt's plurality in the City of Troy of 2,381. Roosevelt had carried Troy four years ago by more than 5,000. Previously Roosevelt had knocked down all political lines to roll up unprecedented pluralities.

Dean P. Taylor, militant young Rensselaer County Republican leader had no comment to make today other than to say, "The people of Rensselaer County have supported the principles of the Republican Party, in seeking service from officials in contrast to political self-perpetuation."

Rensselaer County Democratic headquarters in the absence of Cornelius A. Casey, county leader, had no comment to make on the returns. One of the party lieutennats stated that the results spoke for themselves.

Decline To Speculate.

Informed political quarters declined to speculate on the persistent rumor of a change in Democratic leadership which might place the reins of party direction in the hands of persons who have long protested against the retirement of Joseph J. Murphy.

Republicans swent through the county, capturing every office at stake including the seat in the lower house of the Legislature from the strong Democratic first district.

In that district J. Eugene Zimmer of Troy, young American Laborite, who had Republican endorsement, won by 1,006 from the veteran Democrat, Assemblyman Philip J. Casey.

Republican control of the upper house of the Legislature was insured when the Democratic drive against Sen. Clifford C. Hastings, Republican failed.

Hastings won by 4,498 from John L. Fleming, jr., Democrat although Fleming carried the City of Troy by 3,623.

Democratic state leaders made a special fight against Hastings but the Republican was returned for a third term by a margin far above

(Continued On Page 11.)

SEN. TOWNSEND OF DELAWARE BEATEN; GOP WINS GOVERNOR

Wilmington, Del (AP)—Marching back into power Democrats carried Delaware for President Roosevelt, won every major state office except the governorschip and defeated U. S. Senator John J. Townsend, jr., and Rep. George S. Williams.

With only 32 of the 249 precincts unreported, President Roosevelt's lead over Wendell Willkie stood at 57,233 to 45,404.

James M. Tunnell, sr., Democrat, piled up a surprisingly large vote defeating Senator Townsend. In 217 districts. he was out in front 31,756 to 26,673.

Mayor Walter W. Bacon of Wilmington, Republican nominee for governor, received 48,923 votes to 40,872 for Josiah Marvel, jr., Democratic state chairman, in 203 districts.

A "Liberal" Democratic ticket, placed in the field a month before the election, ran third in all contests.

He Came From Syracuse ....!

WATERFORD, 143 Saratoga Ave.—4-room completely furnished, heated apartment, shower, continuous hot water. Call Waterford 318-J.

Says the party who ordered the above Classified Ad in The Record Newspapers, "We had several inquiries. The man who rented our furnished apartment came from Syracuse to work in the arsenal." How about getting your furnished accommodations rented?

Phone Troy 6100

"Signs Up" For Third Term

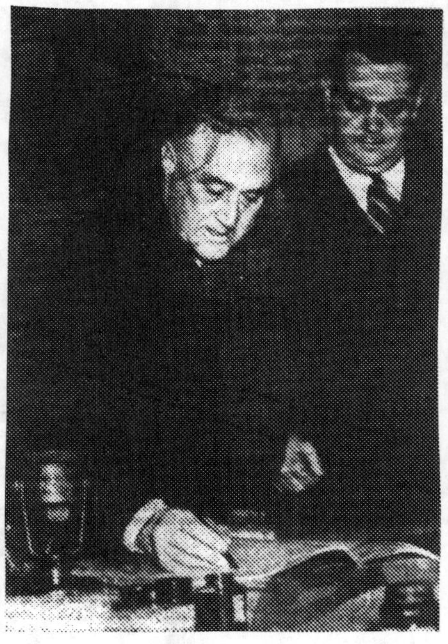

President Franklin Delano Roosevelt ended his now historic campaign for a third term as he signed the register preparatory to registering a Democratic vote at Hyde Park yesterday. With him is Presidential Bodyguard Thomas Qualters.

LEWIS LIKELY TO RETIRE AS C. I. O. CHIEF ON NOV. 18

Labor Leader Refuses to Comment on Election of President Roosevelt; Successors Discussed.

Washington (UP)—Chairman John L. Lewis of the Congress of Industrial Organizations withheld comment today on the election which probably will end his reign as C.I.O. chieftain.

Lewis ten days ago denounced President Roosevelt's candidacy, described him as an "erratic, warmongering politician" and staked his C.I.O. leadership on the election of Wendell L. Willkie.

Appealing to labor to support this stand, he said that Mr. Roosevelt's reelection would "mean that the members of the Congress of Industrial Organizations have rejected my advice and recommendation.

"I will accept the result as being the equivalent of a vote of no confidence," he continued, "and will retire as president of the Congress of Industrial Organizations at its annual convention."

The convention will be held in Atlantic City Nov. 18. Lewis' aides thought he would abide by his promise, though remaining president of the United Mine Workers' Union, one of the C.I.O.'s largest affiliates.

An early renewal of negotiations to heal the four-year-old breach in organised labor appeared likely as a result.

Three men, all considered more friendly than Lewis toward an agreement to end the rift, have been mentioned as his successor. They are Sidney Hillman, Philip Murray and R. J. Thomas.

Hillman, labor representative on the national defense commission, and head of the Garment Workers' Union in the C.I.O., has been a leader in peace negotiations with the A. F. of L.

Murray, soft-spoken chairman of the C.I.O.'s steel workers' organizing committee, announced his support of President Roosevelt a week before Lewis urged his followers to vote for Willkie.

Thomas is the young, dynamic head of the C.I.O. faction of the United Automobile Workers. He, also, was active in support of President Roosevelt. Many labor officials consider him the logical man to succeed Lewis.

LEIBOWITZ ELECTED KINGS COUNTY JUDGE

New York (AP)—Samuel S. Leibowitz, noted lawyer and chief defense counsel in the Scottsboro case, was elected judge of Kings County (Brooklyn) today.

Running on the Democratic-American Labor Party ticket, Leibowitz polled a 2 to 1 majority over his Republican opponent, Orrin G. Judd.

ROOSEVELT WINS NEW YORK STATE BY 250,000 VOTES

Republicans Score Gains in Legislative Contests, However; Mead Reelected U. S. Senator.

Albany (UP)—President Roosevelt has won the 47 electoral votes of his home state by a plurality of 250,000 votes, returns from all but 17 of New York's 9,322 electric districts showed today.

In the closest presidential election in 12 years, unofficial tabulations of 9,305 districts gave the President 3,274,934 votes and Wendell L. Willkie, 3,020.664.

U. S. Senator James M. Mead, Buffalo Democrat, was reelected, defeating Rep. Bruce Barton, New York City Republican, by a substantial margin.

Returns from 9,200 districts gave Mead 3,261,413 and Barton 2.808,-175.

Unreported districts were in rural areas and the number of registered voters in those sections were not sufficient to overcome the leads piled up by the President and Mead.

Mr. Roosevelt and the entire Democratic state ticket were assured victory.

Roosevelt Strong Upstate.

Mrs. Caroline O'Day and Matthew Merritt, Democrats seeking reelection as congressmen-at-large, held commanding leads over their opponents, Mary Donlon and Messmore Kendall.

But because of close vote for President, Republicans were able to strengthen their hold on the Assembly and Senate. The G. O. P. gained three seats in the upper house and a like amount in the Assembly.

Mr. Roosevelt showed unexpected strength in many Republican strongholds. He was only slightly behind in Schenectady County and captured Erie, home of Republican State Chairman Edwin F. Jaeckle.

Willkie's upstate ote, which Republican leaders had hoped would go to a 750,000 majority, was well behind the 650,000 obtained by Dist. Atty. Thomas E. Dewey in his unsuccessful bid for governor two years ago.

Congressmen Defeated.

With Mr. Roosevelt the remainder of the state ticket was virtually assured victory. At least three incumbent congressmen were defeated.

William T. Pheiffer, Republican, defeated Rep. James H. Fay, Democratic incumbent in the Sixteenth New York District, according to unofficial tabulations. Fay, a strong supporter of the New Deal, succeeded John J. O'Connor to the House of Representatives in 1938. O'Connor, outspoken critic of Mr. Roosevelt, was beaten for reelection in the so-called "purge."

In the Fifth District, Brooklyn, James J. Heffernan, Democrat, defeated Marcellus H. Evans, Republican, by a vote of 63,105 to 51,546.

Former Congressman Alfred L. Beiter, Buffalo Democrat, made a come back in the 41st District, defeating incumbent J. Francis Harter, Republican.

Republican Gains.

The G. O. P. won eight lower House seats, making a net gain of three. New Republicans elected included Henry Latham, Queens; J. E. Zimmer, Rensselaer; Robert Doscher, Rockland; L. W. Oliffe, Kings; Francis E. Dorn, Kings; Paul McAvoy, Kings, H. E. Miller, Kings, and G. Archinal, Queens.

The President ran ahead of Willkie in several upstate cities including Buffalo, Albany, Troy, Amsterdam, Hudson, Oswego and Rochester.

Rep. Hamilton Fish, who has vigorously opposed many of the President's policies, was re-elected by a small majority. He defeated Hardy Steelholm, Dutchess County Democrat.

Opposition to Fish spread across party ranks after he sponsored the so-called 60-day delay clause to the Burke - Wardsworth conscription bill.

Mr. Roosevelt carried Erie County with the aid of A. L. P. votes. Willkie received more votes than the President, 132,430 to 172,[illegible], on the straight party ticket, but the Labor Party added 17,128 votes to give him the lead for the county.

G.O.P. CANDIDATE ACCEPTS DEFEAT WITH GOOD WILL

Calls on Followers to Work for Unity of American People; Feels No Bitterness.

New York (UP)—Conceding his defeat by President Roosevelt, Wendell L. Willkie today called upon his millions of followers to "continue as I shall to work for the unity of our people, in the completion of our defense effort, in sending aid to Britain and in insistance upon removal of antagonisms in America—all to the end that government of free men may continue and may spread again upon the earth."

Speaking over all major radio networks after he had dispatched a telegram of congratulations to Mr. Roosevelt on his reelection, Willkie said that he accepted the voting results "with complete good will."

"The popular vote shows the vitality of our Democratic principles and adherence of our people to the two-party system," Willkie said.

"I extend my thanks to the thousands who so zealously and wholeheartedly worked for my election in various organizations, and to the added millions who supported me.

"Work For Unity."

"I know that they will continue as I shall to work for the unity of our people, in the completion of our defense effort, in sending aid to Britain and in insistence upon removal of antagonisms in America—all to the end that government of free men may continue and may spread upon the earth," he said.

His telegram of congratulation to Mr. Roosevelt, in which he wished the Chief Executive "all personal health and happiness," was dictated by Willkie shortly before 10:30 a.m. E.S.T. He went on the air at 11:45 a.m., E.S.T., from a small room on the ballroom floor of the Hotel Commodore to amplify his concession telegram.

Motion picture kleig lights beat down on Willkie as he stood before a battery of microphones to tell the people that he accepted defeat after one of the most arduous campaigns ever waged by any man for the presidency.

Holds No Ill Will.

Willkie told newspaper reporters after the broadcast that he "never felt better" and was "proud to have led this crusade."

"I believe deeply, if anything more deeply than ever, in the principles I preached," he said. "I think that their ultimate adoption in America is indispensable to the preservation of this free way to life."

"I end the campaign as I entered it—without any ill will or bitterness toward anybody," Willkie added.

Willkie said he would spend the next "two, three or four days here."

"Then," he said, "I'm going somewhere for a vacation and some rest. My personal plans are not complete beyond that."

Willkie chatted amiably, smiled for photographers and asked newspaper reporters who had been with him on his campaign special if they had "got any sleep last night."

Popular And Electoral Vote Returns By States

AT 2 P. M. (EASTERN TIME)
BY THE ASSOCIATED PRESS.

State	Voting Units	Units Reporting	Popular Vote: Roosevelt	Popular Vote: Willkie	Indicated Electoral Vote: Roosevelt	Indicated Electoral Vote: Willkie
Ala.	2,300	1,248	159,441	23,907	11	
Ariz.	430	311	45,362	24,903	3	
Ark.	2,169	857	63,006	14,027	9	
Cal.	13,692	11,020	1,262,738	896,259	22	
Col.	1,610	725	93,992	104,043		6
Conn.	169	169	417,858	361,869	8	
Del.	249	217	57,233	45,404	3	
Fla.	1,428	985	263,090	102,063	7	
Ga.	1,720	1,410	196,657	29,046	12	
Ida.	792	502	68,383	56,830	4	
Ill.	8,378	7,722	1,964,381	1,837,500	29	
Ind.	3,898	3,198	739,631	759,338		14
Iowa	2,453	1,891	450,787	480,149		11
Kans.	2,734	1,997	228,752	322,956		9
Ky.	4,343	2,292	304,477	198,705	11	
La.	1,712	537	146,977	24,412	10	
Me.	629	623	154,732	163,782		5
Md.	1,331	1,246	364,168	250,362	8	
Mass	1,810	1,698	981,571	869,248	17	
Mich.	3,632	2,679	744,217	739,148	19	
Minn.	3,696	1,410	333,351	296,117	11	
Miss.	1,668	635	87,190	4,179	9	
Mo.	4,479	3,964	819,683	723,994	15	
Mont.	1,195	638	85,143	55,674	4	
Neb.	2,043	1,543	181,283	253,999		7
Nev.	260	203	19,396	14,096	3	
N. H.	294	294	125,625	109,992	4	
N. J.	3,631	3,488	973,031	915,915	16	
N. M.	919	442	61,598	41,795	3	
N. Y.	1,319	9,293	3,256,726	3,021,421	47	
N. C.	1,916	1,688	562,213	176,171	13	
N. D.	2,261	840	54,946	63,513		4
Ohio	8,675	8,059	1,561,903	1,441,962	26	
Okla.	3,613	3,054	408,584	297,527	11	
Ore.	1,693	1,120	111,679	106,328	5	
Pa.	8,118	7,751	2,076,378	1,822,496	36	
R. I.	259	259	181,881	138,432	4	
S. C.	1,277	953	81,867	4,144	8	
S. D.	1,963	1,414	85,047	119,401		4
Tenn.	2,300	2,125	323,710	150,531	11	
Texas	254	224	504,433	118,198	23	
Utah	831	457	84,511	52,100	4	
Vt.	246	246	64,244	78,335		3
Va.	1,716	1,675	233,676	107,419	11	
Wash.	3,018	1,558	212,278	137,842	8	
W. Va.	2,389	1,426	313,257	226,780	8	
Wis.	3,038	2,802	641,301	626,724	12	
Wyo.	697	575	46,403	42,113	3	
Totals	127,245	99,463	22,198,790	18,451,138	468	63

PLAN UNITY RALLY TONIGHT TO HEAL ELECTION WOUNDS

Supporters of Both Presidential Candidates Appeal for Harmony; Would Burn Campaign Materials

New York (UP)—Out of the bitterness of a fiercely fought presidential battle, came pleas for national unity today from the supporters of both candidates.

The people were told that it is their first duty now to foster and promote a national unity and present to the totalitarian powers a solid, undivided front.

Chairman William Allen White, of the committee to defend America by aiding the Allies announced that "unity mass meetings" would be held throughout the nation within the next few days.

"The mass meetings," White said, "should plead for unity of national spirit in support of a foreign policy to defend America by aiding the Allies. This is appropriate inasmuch as both presidential candidates pledged all aid to the Allies."

White proposed that all Democratic and Republican campaign literature and buttons be burned at public "unity" bon fires.

"Forget Bitterness."

In Chicago, Frank Knox, secretary of the Navy, asserted that it now "becomes the ty of every good American to foster and promote a national unity.

"It has been the undisguised hope of Berlin, Rome and Tokyo," he said, "that the election would leave

(Continued on Page 24.)

SULTAN OF JOHORE WEDS RUMANIAN GIRL

London (AP) — The fabulously wealthy Sultan Ibrahim of Johore, 67, married Marcella Mendl, blonde Rumanian beauty, today. The bride will be 25 years old tomorrow.

The Sultan, who has ruled his Indian state for 45 years, recently mourned the death of Lydia Cecily King, 27-year-old dancer friend. She was killed Oct. 11 in a Canterbury air raid.

DEMOCRATS KEEP CONTROL OF BOTH HOUSE AND SENATE

Forenoon Tabulation Shows Election of 222 Party Members in Lower Branch of Congress.

Washington (AP)—The Democrats, riding a tide of votes with President Roosevelt, kept control of Both House and Senate in Tuesday's election.

An official tabulation this forenoon showed they had won 222 House seats, for more than a majority, to 107 for the Republicans. In addition, one incumbent American laborite was re-elected. A majority is 218.

Contrary to Republican predictions that they would gain from 50 to 80 seats, the returns indicated that the Democrats might win a few more than their present house strength of 258.

The Democrats have held control of the House since John N. Garner, now vice president, was chosen speaker in 1931, and of the Senate since victors in the first Roosevelt landslide of 1932 took office on March 4, 1933.

Their majority in the new Senate, convening next Jan. 3, was hardly in danger but any vestige of doubt was eliminated when the tabula-

(Continued on Page 4.)

BARTON PUZZLED BY RETURNS FROM REPUBLICAN AREAS

New York (UP)—Representative Bruce Barton, Republican, conceded today that he had been defeated for the Senate but consoled himself with the thought that he held a seat in the House of Representatives until Jan. 3.

The advertising executive sent a telegram of congratulations to the victorious incumbent, Senator James Mead but he accepted the verdict philosophically.

"We tried hard," he said, "but we couldn't get enough votes."

Some of the returns puzzled Barton and at times he remarked, "it can't be so," as messages told of large blocks going to his opponent in normal Republican territory.

Third Term Sweep Near Total of 468 Electoral Votes

Roosevelt Leads In 39 States, Willkie Holding Margin Only In Nine With Total of 63 Electoral Votes; Defeated Candidate Congratulates Winner; Democrats Score Gains In Congressional and Gubernatorial Contests.

BY THE ASSOCIATED PRESS.

The picture of yesterday's national election, as it shaped up at 2 o'clock this afternoon, follows:

Presidential: President Roosevelt led in 39 states with 468 electoral votes; Willkie 9 with 63.

Popular vote at that hour: With 99,463 of the nation's precincts counted the total vote was 40,649,938 with Roosevelt having 22,198,790 and Willkie 18,451,-148.

House: Democrats elected 239; Republicans 118; American Labor 1. The Democrats picked up 17 seats in Connecticut, Pennsylvania, Rhode Island, New York, West Virginia, Ohio and Delaware. Republicans gained 8 seats in Illinois, Oklahoma, New York, California and Missouri.

Senate: 18 Democrats and 8 Republicans elected. Harold H. Burton, Republican, defeated John McSweeney, Democrat, in Ohio; Hugh A. Butler, Republican, defeated Robert Leroy Cochran, Democrat, in Nebraska, and James H. Tunnell, sr., Democrat, defeated John G. Townsend, jr., Republican. Henrik Shipstead, formerly Farmer-Labor, was reelected as a Republican, making a net turnover of two for the Republicans.

Governors: 14 Democrats elected, 7 Republicans. Five turnovers—in Connecticut, Michigan and Rhode Island where incumbent Republicans lost to Democrats and in Nebraska and Illinois where Republicans ousted Democrats.

BY THE ASSOCIATED PRESS.

President Roosevelt, the precedent-breaker, smashed one of America's most ancient traditions today with a dramatic and sweeping victory in his battle for a third term.

His election was conceded in mid-morning by Wendell L. Willkie, his dogged, hard-hitting Republican opponent, who had made the third term question one of the two outstanding issues of a slambang campaign.

Congratulates President.

At 10:30 a.m., EST., in New York, Willkie's press secretary, Lem Jones, gave out the text of this congratulatory telegram:

"Franklin D. Roosevelt,
"President of the United States,
"Hyde Park, New York.

"Congratulations on your reelection as President of the United States. I know that we are both gratified that so many American citizens participated in the election. I wish you all personal health and happiness. Cordially,

"WENDELL L. WILLKIE."

At Hyde Park, the President accepted "with sincere thanks," Mr. Willkie's message of congratulation.

"Please accept my sincere thanks for your message of congratulations," Mr. Roosevelt replied. "I greatly appreciate the assurance of your good wishes for my health and happiness which I heartily reciprocate."

Throughout last evening Willkie sat in his hotel room, analyzing the returns and watching the President amass commanding leads in virtually all the key states having big blocks of electoral votes. But grimly, he clung to a dwindling hope of victory, and finally he retired with the announcement that not until today would he have anything to say on the election's outcome.

The President spent last evening at his Hyde Park home, where in 1932 and 1936 he saw himself elected to the presidency, and where, just as in both those years, his happy neighbors thronged the spreading lawns and serenaded him with bugles and drums.

"Same Franklin Roosevelt."

Promptly at midnight, Mr. Roosevelt greeted the sernaders from the portico. "Full returns" were lacking, he said, but the situation looked "all right."

"We, of course, face difficult days," he said. "But I think you will find me in the future just the same Franklin Roosevelt you have known for years."

The full extent of the President's victory could not be measured finally in advance of a more complete tabulation of the votes of several states.

Nevertheless, it appeared this afternoon that his election had been accomplished with 468 of the country's 531 electoral votes. The number required for election is 266. Indications were that his

(Continued on Page 4.)

STATE'S DELEGATION IN CONGRESS LIKELY TO STAY UNCHANGED

New York (INS)—With one district still listed as doubtful, the political makeup of New York State's Congressional delegation was unchanged today at 26 Democrats and 19 Republicans.

The Democrats gained an upstate seat when Alfred L. Beiter (D) defeated incumbent J. Francis Harter (R) in the 41st district, Erie County. They lost that advantage, however, when incumbent James H. Fay (D) was defeated by William T. Pfeiffer (R) in the 16th district, Manhattan.

Incumbent Pius L. Schwert (D) was believed to have been reelected over Edward F. Moss (R) in a close race in the 42nd district, Erie.

GOV. LEHMAN URGES RIVAL PARTIES TO FORGET DIFFERENCES

New York (UP)—Gov. Herbert H. Lehman today urged members of opposing political parties to forget their differences and join in the defense of democracy.

"I'm very happy indeed at the results," the Governor said.

And in a statement issued before he retired, added:

"This is no time for triumph or gloating. Let us forget the election. Let us wipe out all hard feelings and join together to make our country so strong that no one will dare to attack us.

"We must forget all differences and divisions and concentrate on working as a united people in the defense of a democracy we all hold so dear."

The Index

SOCIAL WORKERS SEMINAR ELECTS STAFF FOR YEAR

Miss Grace E. Allison, Superintendent of Samaritan Hospital, Chosen for Executive Position.

Miss Grace E. Allison, superintendent of the Samaritan Hospital, was elected president of the Social Work Executives Seminar at a luncheon meeting at the Troy Y. W. C. A. Monday noon.

Rev. John Hart, director of the local Catholic Charities was chosen vice president and Miss Mary Elizabeth Hess, executive secretary of the local Camp Fire Girls, was named secretary-treasurer.

Named to the executive committee were Herbert J. Hunn, superintendent of the Troy Orphan Asylum; Verne C. Braddon, general secretary of the Troy Y. M. C. A.; Eric W. Gibberd, executive secretary of the Troy Council of Social Agencies and Community Chest, Inc., and Mrs. Rachel S. Newlin, superintendent of the Day Home and retiring president of the seminar.

Talks were given on the work of the Rensselaer County Tuberculosis and Public Health Association in the schools, of the Catholic Charities and of the Mohawk & Hudson River Humane Society.

Arrangements were made for a Christmas party at the next meeting Friday evening, Dec. 20, at the Day Home. Mrs. Newlin will have charge of arrangements.

Announcement

WALT BARNES

Is Now Conducting the Socony Station AT

679 Burden Ave., Troy

Your Patronage Appreciated

Dinner Held For Arsenal Veterans

World War veterans of the Watervliet Arsenal were guests at a dinner Saturday night sponsored by Trojan Post, V. F. W. In photo, left to right, seated are: John M. Cusick, Mrs. Thomas Conroy, Mrs. Thomas McGovern and Charles McCumber; standing, James P. Broderick, James Boyle, Mrs. James Broderick and Thomas Conroy. Others on the committee were John Nagle, Andrew McDermott, Edward Wood, Leo Tromble and Thomas McGovern. Mr. and Mrs. Thomas Shaughnessy entertained with vocal numbers. Norman Leicht was elected president of the group. Thirty couples danced to music by Nolan's Orchestra.

ON THE AIR

Radio Programs from Local Stations.

TONIGHT.

379—WGY—SCHENECTADY—790.
P. M.

5:00—Girl Alone.
5:15—Lone Journey.
5:30—Jack Armstrong.
5:45—Life Can Be Beautiful.
6:00—News.
6:05—Varieties.
6:30—The Serenaders.
6:45—Lowell Thomas, Commentator.
7:00—Pleasure Time; Waring's Orchestra.
7:15—Newsroom of the Air with John W. Vandercook.
7:30—Crosby's Dixieland Music Shop.
8:00—Good News.
8:30—The Aldrich Family.
9:00—Music Hall With Bob Burns.
10:00—Rudy Vallee Program.
10:30—Musical Americana.
11:00—News.
11:05—On With The Dance.
11:15—National Defense Opportunities.
11:30—Dreamin' Time.
12:00—News.

219—WOKO—ALBANY—1430.
P. M.

5:00—Four Smart Boys.
5:15—Dancetime.
5:30—Concert.
6:00—News.
6:15—Outdoors with Bob Edge.
6:30—Paul Sullivan.
6:45—Edwin C. Hill.
7:00—Amos 'n' Andy.
7:15—Lanny Ross.
7:30—Vox Pop.
8:00—Ask-It Basket.
8:30—Strange As It Seems.
8:55—Elmer Davis.

9:00—Bowes' Amateur Hour.
10:00—Miller Orchestra.
10:15—Selective Service Program.
10:30—News.
10:45—State Police News.
11:00—Interlude.
11:05—Bowling Program.
11:15—Masters.
11:45—Program.
12:00—Kearns Orchestra.

TOMORROW.

216—WTRY—TROY—950.
A. M.

6:00—Morning Roundup.
6:45—Produce Market Report.
6:55—News.
7:00—Rio Grande Serenaders.
7:15—Timekeeper.
7:55—News.
8:00—Timekeeper Continued.
8:30—Good Morning Newspaper.
8:33—Timekeeper Continued.
8:55—News.
9:00—Number Please.
9:15—Dusty Miller and his Colorado Wranglers.
9:30—Timely Events.
9:45—Interlude.
9:55—Record News.
10:00—Dearest Mother.
10:15—Organ Melodies.
10:30—Masters of Music.
10:45—Interlude.
10:55—News.
11:00—Joshua Spaulding.
11:15—Evelyn Johnson, pianist.
11:30—Troy Chapel Service.
11:45—Interlude.
11:55—News.

P. M.

12:00—U. S. Army Program.
12:15—Checkerboard Time.
12:30—Noonday Frolic.
12:55—News.
1:00—Col. Jim Healey.
1:15—The Bands Play On.
1:30—Farm Program.
1:45—Kay Moser's Matinee.
1:55—News.
2:00—Kay Moser's Matinee Continued.
2:55—News.
3:00—From the Concert Hall.
3:30—Monitor News.
3:40—Stock Market Report.
3:45—Organ Swing.
3:55—News.
4:00—George Marriner, tenor.
4:15—Episcopal Church on the Air.
4:30—Sign Off.

379—WGY—SCHENECTADY—790.
A. M.

6:30—Musical Clock.
6:40—Rural Reporter.
6:45—Church in the Wildwood.
7:00—Ed McConnell.
7:15—Time to Shine.
7:25—Musical Clock.
7:30—News.
7:55—Sports and Music.
7:45—Gene and Syracuse.
8:00—Musical Clock.
8:30—Playhouse.
8:45—Market Basket—Martha Brooks.
9:00—Musical Clock.
9:15—Your Treat.
9:30—Housebeat Hannah.
9:45—The Right to Happiness.
10:00—This Small Town.
10:15—By Kathleen Norris.
10:30—Ellen Randolph.

10:45—The Guiding Light.
11:00—The Man I Married.
11:15—Against the Storm.
11:30—The Road of Life.
11:45—"David Harum."
12:00—News.

P. M.

12:10—Mid-Day Serenaders.
12:15—The O'Neills.
12:30—Farm Paper of the Air.
1:00—Produce Market Reports.
1:05—Household Chats—Betty Lennox.
1:30—The Landt Trio.
1:45—Songs of a Dreamer.
2:00—Betty Crocker.
2:15—Arnold Grimm's Daughter.
2:30—Valiant Lady.
2:45—The Light of the World.
3:00—Story of Mary Marlin.
3:15—Ma Perkins.
3:30—Pepper Young's Family.
3:45—Vic and Sade.
4:00—Backstage Wife.
4:15—Stella Dallas.
4:30—Lorenzo Jones.
4:45—Young Widder Brown.
5:00—Girl Alone.
5:15—Lone Journey.
5:30—Jack Armstrong.
5:45—Life Can Be Beautiful.
6:00—News.
6:05—Superman.
6:30—Tunes and Topics.
6:45—Bolley's Sports Review.
7:00—Pleasure Time; Waring's Orchestra.
7:15—Newsroom of the Air With John W. Vandercook.
7:30—Alec Templeton Time.
8:00—Lucille Manners, Soprano; Black's Orchestra.
8:30—Farm Forum.
9:00—Waltz Time With Frank Munn, Tenor.
9:30—Everyman's Theater.
10:00—Wings of Destiny.
10:30—Electric City Almanac.
11:00—News.
11:05—On With the Dance.
11:15—The Story Behind the Headlines.
11:30—U. S. Antarctic Service Expedition Salute From Seattle, Wash.
12:00—News.

219—WOKO—ALBANY—1430.
A. M.

6:00—Reveille.
7:00—News.
7:05—Melody Moments.
7:15—Musical Train.
7:45—News.
8:00—Musical Clock.
9:00—Newsflash.
9:05—Interludes.
9:15—American School of the Air.
9:45—Opportunity Knocks.
10:00—By Kathleen Norris.
10:15—Myrt and Marge.
10:30—Stepmother.
10:45—Woman of Courage.
11:00—Short Short Story.
11:30—Martha Webster.
11:45—Aunt Jenny.
12:00—News.

P. M.

12:00—Quiz Quiz.
12:15—When a Girl Marries.
12:30—Romance of Helen Trent.
12:45—Our Gal Sunday.
1:00—Musical Menus.
1:30—Forrest Willis.
1:45—Kate Smith Speaks.
2:00—Young Dr. Malone.
2:15—Joyce Jordan, Girl Interne.
2:30—Fletcher Wiley.
2:45—My Son and I.
3:00—Mary Margaret McBride.

CHILDREN'S ROOM AT LIBRARY WILL OPEN NEXT WEEK

New Department in Lansingburg Branch Prepared by NYA; Book Week To Be Observed.

The Troy Public Library will begin its observance of National Book Week next week by opening a children's room at the Lansingburg Branch Library in the old Vocational School Building, 114th Street at Fourth Avenue, with special exercises Monday afternoon.

The new room is across the hall from the present first floor room occupied by the library. Young men employed by the NYA have constructed bookshelves and redecorated the room in preparation for its library use.

Monday's exercises will include the cutting of a ribbon at the door of the new room and a tea to be served by a committee of Lansingburg women interested in the branch library, headed by Mrs. J. Philip Reimherr.

All library borrowers and friends of the Troy and Lansingburg libraries are invited to attend.

At the main library on Second Street, National Book Week will be observed all next week with a special display of new books, including books on child psychology and picture books for pre-school children.

A book quiz for children will be conducted Tuesday at 4 p. m. in the Art Gallery of the main library.

A picturebook hour will be conducted for the small children Friday at 4 p. m. and a story hour for all children will be conducted in the Art Gallery Saturday at 11 p. m.

National Book Week traditionally centers around the interest in children and children's books.

Children have been heavy borrowers from the Lansingburg branch library and the new children's room is designed to help meet the increasing demand for children's service there.

3:15—Golden Treasury of Song.
3:30—A Friend in Deed.
3:45—Exploring Space.
4:00—Portia Blake.
4:15—We, the Abetts.
4:30—Hilltop House.
4:45—U. S. Recruiting.
5:00—Four Smart Boys.
5:15—It's Dancetime.
5:45—Scattergood Baines.
6:00—News.
6:15—Hedda Hopper's Hollywood.
6:30—Paul Sullivan.
6:45—Edwin C. Hill.
7:00—Amos 'n' Andy.
7:15—Lanny Ross.
7:30—Al Pearce's Gang.
8:00—Kate Smith Variety Show.
8:55—Elmer Davis.
9:00—Johnny.
9:30—Program.
10:00—Believe It Or Not.
10:30—News.
10:45—State Police News.
11:00—Bob Trout, News.
11:05—Bowling Program.
11:15—Masters.
11:45—Murphy Orchestra.
12:00—Harbeck Orchestra.

Boston College Gains Three Berths On Associated Press All-Eastern 11

BACKS INCLUDE O'ROURKE KRACUM REAGAN. MATUSZK'

Cornell Gains Two Spots, Harvard, Georgetown, Penn, Pitt, Yale, Fordham One Each.

BY HERB BARKER

New York (AP)—Boston College, unofficial champion of the East, places three men on the all-Eastern football team compiled today by The Associated Press.

Drawn from the Boston array which will face Tennessee in the Sugar Bowl New Year's Day are Charley O'Rourke, brilliant back; Chet Gladchuk, huge center, and George Kerr, scholarly guard.

Cornell, although it dropped its last two games and with them the Ivy League title to Penn, gains two places on the all-star team. The other places are shared by Harvard, Penn, Pitt, Georgetown, Yale and Fordham.

O'Rourke's backfield mates on the mythical team are Walt Matuszczak, Cornell quarterback; Francis Xavier Reagan, sensational Penn star, and line-cracking George Kracum of Pitt.

With Gladchuk and Kerr in the line are Loren Mackinney of Harvard and Alan Bartholemy of Yale at the ends; Nick Drahos of Cornell and Joe Ungerer of Fordham at the tackles, and Agostino Lio, Georgetown veteran, teaming up with Kerr at guard.

Of these, all are seniors except Mackinney and Bartholemy, who are juniors. Drahos and Lio are the only repeaters from the all-star team of 1939. The 1940 team averages 202 pounds in the line and 185 in the backfield, where O'Rourke's 158 pounds cut sharply into the average.

Reagan's place on the team was secure beyond any challenge for the great Penn triple threat stood out head and shoulders beyond any Eastern rival for all-around value. Only in the Michigan game was he stopped cold, and in that test Penn's line was clearly outplayed.

But the other three backfield nominees all had to withstand real competition. Matuszczak, husky blocker and play-caller for Cornell, barely beat out another blocker, Boston College's Henry Tocsylowski. O'Rourke, a standout in Boston's vital game with Georgetown when Georgetown's 26-game unbeaten streak was broken, found a half dozen serious challengers on his heels, among them Andy Tomasic of Temple, Hal McCullough of Cornell, Dave Allerdice of Princeton, Len Eshmont of Fordham, Bill Busik of Navy and Henry Mazur of Army.

Kracum beat out such other fullback aces as Steve Filipowicz, Fordham sophomore, Mort Landsberg or Cornell, Jim Castiglia of Georgetown and Walter Zirinsky of Lafayette.

Competition over the whole way was sharp all the way. Bartholemy, a fine pass catcher and great defensive player, was Yale's most consistent player all season. Mackinney, who did most of Harvard's kicking, performed brilliantly, particularly in the closing stages of the season when Harvard began to move. But their edge was small over such rivals as Alva Kelley of Cornell, Hugh Barber and Joe Siegal of Columbia, Vince Dennery and Jim Lansing of Fordham and Len Warner of Penn.

One of the season's finest wingmen, Gene Goodreault of Boston College, drops back among the honorable mentions because his injuries suffered in the Georgetown game kept him out of the Eagle's important games with Auburn and Holy Cross.

The toughest choice of the lot was at center, where the east had a banner crop including the 245-pound Gladchuk, Len Gajecki of Penn State, Don Snavely of Columbia, Lou De Filippo of Fordham, Ray Frick of Penn and Frank Finneran of Cornell.

Few could challenge Kerr and Lio at the guard position, and Drahos and Ungerer were equal standouts at the tackles, where

the field was limited to an extraordinary degree.

(Other Sports on Page 29.)

Associated Press All-Eastern

THE ALL-EASTERN TEAM

Position	Player and College	Class	Age	Height	Wt.	Home Town
End	Loren MacKinney, Harvard	JR.	20	6:01	180	Chapel Hill, N. C.
Tackle	Nick Drahos, Cornell	SR.	21	6:03	213	Cedarhurst, N. Y.
Guard	George Kerr, Boston College	SR.	21	5:10	191	Brookline, Mass.
Center	Chet Gladchuk, Boston College	SR.	21	6:00	245	Bridgeport, Conn.
Guard	Agostino Lio, Georgetown (x)	SR.	21	6:00	215	Passaic, N. J.
Tackle	Joe Ungerer, Fordham	SR.	22	6:00	202	Bethlehem, Pa.
End	Alan Bartholemy, Yale	JR.	20	6:11	188	Portland, Ore.
Back	Walter Matuszczak, Cornell	SR.	22	5:10	176	Lowville, N. Y.
Back	Francis Reagan, Penn.	SR.	22	6:00	185	Philadelphia
Back	Charles O'Rourke, Boston Col.	SR.	21	5:11	158	Malden, Mass.
Back	George Kracum, Pitt.	SR.	22	6:01	196	Hazleton, Pa.

(x) Choosed for second year in succession.

SECOND TEAM

Ends, Hugh Barber, Columbia, and Alva Kelley, Cornell; tackles, Gene Flathmann, Navy, and Bill Collins, Lafayette; guards, Lou Young, Dartmouth, and Joe weidner, Army; center, Leon Gajecki, Penn State; backs, Henry Toczylowski, Boston College, Andy Tomasic, Temple; Dave Allerdice, Princeton, and Steve Filipowicz, Fordham.

Honorable Mention.

ENDS—Berthold, Syracuse; Davis, Colgate; Dennery, Fordham; Farabaugh, Navy, and Bill Collins, Lafayette; Goodreault, Boston College; Hershey, Cornell; Kelly, Dartmouth; Kopcik, Georgetown; Krieger, Dartmouth; Kucrynaki, Penn; Lansing, Fordham; Mahalic, Temple; Maroufes, Brown; Piro, Syracuse; Schmuck, Cornell; Shonk, West Virginia; Siegal, Columbia; Stanley, Princeton; Tanasey, New York University; Varga, Penn State; Warner, Penn; Zoeller, Navy.

TACKLES: Beola, Georgetown; Brooks, Bucknell; Buck, Colgate; DeFilippo, Bucknell; Pribish, New York University; Pinerras, Cornell; Prick, Penn; Gillie, Tech; Eissr, Harvard; Engler, Penn; Garvey, Quigley; Kellar, Holy Cross; Kowalsky, Pitt; Kusman, Fordham; Levy, Columbia; Mazek, Columbia; Mazzo, Boston College; Peterett, New York University; Platt, Penn State; Rigan, Syracuse; Stasica, Villanova.

GUARDS—Burnham, Yale; Collins, Villanova; Conti, Cornell; Dern, Yale; Drutsa, Temple; Dunbar, Cornell; Fitt, Pitt; Pallikova, Georgetown; Gallagher, Columbia; Hauserman, Lehigh; Marone, Manhattan; McIntyre, Columbia; Mendelson, Penn; Mott, Penn State; Nopper, Duquesne; Peabody, Harvard; Pierce, Fordham; Plaweck, Duquesne; Arnort, Fordham; Vincek, Navy; Zabicki, Boston College.

CENTERS—Abram, Harvard; Bessel, Bucknell; Buck, Colgate; DeFilippo, Fordham; Falbish, New York University; Finneran, Cornell; Frick, Penn; Gillis, Army; Mattura, Georgetown; Moseley, Yale; Simms, Navy; Simco, Pitt; Snavely, Columbia; Warmuth, Lafayette.

BACKS—Abram, Harvard; Duquesne; Allen, Penn; Anderson, Yale; Arico, Dartmouth; Bason, Villanova; Bass, New York University; Blumenstock, Fordham; Butefino, Cornell; Busik, Navy; Canais, Syracuse; Hiami; Piwecki, Manhattan; Castiglia, Georgetown; Cassady, Boston College; Davis, Cornell; Detwiler, Brown; Donelli, Duquesne; Dutcher, Penn; Eshmont, Fordham; Farrell, Lafayette; Fedora, Georgetown; Frank, New York University; Gardella, Harvard; Gebert, Navy; Germass, Columbia; Geyer, Colgate; Ghecas, Georgetown; Goversali, Columbia; Hall, Dartmouth; Harrell, Navy; Harrison, Yale; High, Brown; Hoague, Colgate; Holovak, Boston College; Jones, Pitt; Koehling, Georgetown; Landsberg, Cornell; Lee, Harvard; Lutry Sowell, Army; Mazur, Army; McCullough, Cornell; McNally, Manhattan; Mirabito, Syracuse; Morris, Syracuse; Moyer, Lafayette; Muha, Carnegie Tech; Natowich, Holy Cross; O'Leary, Brown; Oumanski, Holy Cross; Patrick, Penn State; Peters, Princeton; Peters, Penn State; Petrella, Penn State; Raeton, Catholic; Savignano, Brown; Schmidt, Rutgers; Sobolt, Cornell; Seymour, Yale; Smalts, Penn State; Spraysr, Harvard; Sullivan, Holy Cross; Supulski, Manhattan; Utz, Rutgers; Will, Colum; bai; Willoughby, Yale; Whiteking, New York University; Wolfe, Dartmouth; Wood, Columbia; Zirinsky, Lafayette.

HAWKS FIRE 1455 IN PISTOL LEAGUE

Taconic Hawks last night defeated the Rangers, 1455 to 1392 in one of three matches of the Troy Pistol League on the River Street range.

The Skiparee Majors defeated the Taconic Eagles, 1403 to 1385 in the second match and the Hendrick Hudson Stars beat the Fitzgeralds, 1443 to 1342 in the third and concluding match.

Tonight the 44 Club fires against Troy Savings Bank, Arsenal Women meet Palma Club and Arsenal Owls complete against Arsenal Police.

Last night's results:

Rangers.

G. G. Wells	272
R. Pattison	291
M. VanAlstyne	280
H. Seight	287
R. S. Johnson	273
Total	1392

Taconic Hawks.

J. Chlipock	291
J. Nihl	291
H. Petrushka	292
N. Hare	284
A. Vetoich	293
Totals	1455

Taconic Eagles.

M. Petruska	285
M. VanDervoort	275
V. Dorfner	270
F. Prout	292
F. Gordon	264
Totals	1385

Skiparee Majors.

J. Case	270
J. McLean	279
W. Cronin	283
J. Torpey	292
L. O'Hearn	289
Totals	1403

Fitzgeralds.

F. Tanner	255
O. Demarest	275
D. Callahan	292
D. Gardiner	260
F. Watson	260
Totals	1342

Hendrick Hudson Stars.

F. Schaaf	283
S. Adolf	292
A. Bouchey	286
D. Lindgren	291
R. Petrik	291
Totals	1443

THREE RANGERS ON INJURED LIST

New York (AP)—The hospital chart on the injured members of the New York Rangers showed yesterday that:

Art Coulter's shoulder will be in a cast for another week but that when it is removed he will be able to leave the hospital.

It will take at least that long before it can be determined if it will be necessary to operate on Alex Shibicky's shoulder.

Coulter suffered a fractured shoulder bone in a game with the Americans, Nov. 19, and Shibicky a separation of the right shoulder in last week's game with the same club.

Dutch Heller, who has been playing with a cut achilles tendon, also may be forced to remain in Montreal for additional treatment.

LAMBERT TROPHY AWARDED TO B. C.

New York (AP)—Boston College's unbeaten, untied Eagles yesterday were named winners of the August V. Lambert memorial trophy, awarded annually to the outstanding Eastern college football team.

The Eagles, who will play Tennessee in the Sugar Bowl New Year's Day, were the unanimous choice of 56 writers and radio commentators. Cornell, winner of the trophy last year, was seventh.

Once-beaten Fordham, headed for the Cotton Bowl, was the second choice and Georgetown, defeated only once and that by one point by Boston College, was ranked third. The Hoyas, who will play Mississippi State in the Orange Bowl, were trailed by Pennsylvania, Lafayette, Penn State and Cornell.

SPORTS MIRROR

By The Associated Press.

Today, a Year Ago — Russ Bauers, Pittsburgh pitcher, hurt in auto accident at Lakewood, N.J.

Three Years Ago — Jack Doyle, veteran betting commissioner, retired from billiard business in Broadway, after 31 years.

Five Years Ago—Catholic University selected to compete in Orange Bowl at Miami New Year's Day.

Jacobs Starts More Fights Than Blonde

New York (AP)—Mike Jacobs, in the busiest winter of his seven-year promotional career, is starting more fights than a tricky-eyed blonde at a stevedores' ball.

Before the flowers thrust up their little noggins in May, the Maestro of maul will have staged more than twenty bouts during the Madison Square Garden season, and several more outside of New York. Which shapes up as a record of some sort.

Mr. Jacobs and his disobedient store teeth arrived today at Detroit where he will have a finger in the pie Friday night when big Abe Simon tries to clinch a title shot at Joe Louis by beating another Detroit Negro, Roscoe Toles.

After the Detroit show, "uncle" Mike returns to Manhattan for Monday's signing of Billy Conn to defend his light heavyweight title against Tommy Tucker of New York at an undisclosed site and date. It seems that Billy-The-Kid's six-month time allowance has expired, and he must defend the 175-pound crown shortly or give it up, even though this defense interrupts his ambitious campaign among the heavies.

Mr. Jacobs must drum up three more title matches for Bomber Louis, who already is slated for two: Against Al McCoy at Boston, Dec. 16, and against Red Burman at New York, Jan. 31. Jacobs is putting "Playboy" Louis on a fight-a-month schedule to be certain that the somewhat leggy champion will be in good shape when he begins May training for his outdoor June defense against Billy Conn or Maxie Baer—If Louis still has the title then. Bomber Joe's three additional defenses probably will be made at Philadelphia, Detroit and Chicago.

Jacobs, who already has staged seven bouts this season at the Garden and one in Boston, will be busy meanwhile ballyhooing five other shows already set for the Garden:

(1) Ken Overlin defends his middleweight crown on Dec. 13 against young Steve Belloise who almost kayoed Overlin in a previous non-title engagement; (2) Lew Jenkins, lightweight king, and Fritzie Zivic, welterweight champ, tangle in a non-title 12-rounder on Dec. 20; (3) Billy Soose, who has registered non-title victories over both middleweight champions—Overlin and Tony Zale—fights 10-rounds with undefeated young Tami Mauriello of New York on Jan. 3; (4) on Jan. 10, two heavyweight 10-rounders match Pat Comiskey against Lou Nova, and Lee Savold against Bill Poland, and (5) Henry Armstrong

tries to recapture the welterweight title from Fritzie Zivic on Jan. 17.

During the next couple of weeks get league will be announced because matches still has about eight Garden dates to fill before April, when the rodeo moves into the house that Rickard built. He also has other out-of-town commitments.

Yes, cholmondeley, old Uncle Michael is certainly startin' a lot of fights.

COLONIE HOST TO AMSTERDAM FIVE AT MAPLEWOOD

Victorious in the season's inaugural last week against the strong Castleton American Legion squad, the Colonie A. A. basketeers will seek their second win when they entertain the Mount Carmel five from Amsterdam tonight at the Maplewood School gym.

The visitors have a sharp shooting and fast breaking quintet. Composed of former scholastic stars and college ball players, the invaders have the distinction of holding three city titles. It is the only team to win three championships, A, B and C, in city league competition. The Carpet City aggregation comprises a roster of highly rated players. In the lineup will be found a trio of sharp shooting forwards who carry on the offense, namely Elmy, Gaetano and Romano; a pair of scholastic stars, Cooley and Mercadante set up the defense while the towering Lanzi is stationed in the pivot position. G. Sandy, E. Sandy and Quattrochi round out the squad.

Scheduled to meet the toughest available, the Colonie A. A. quintet is considered stronger this season than last and is composed of the area's outstanding players. Nazarko, Pettigrew, Patti, Kapitula, Brown, Bloomer, Christie, Buckley, Tanner and Fedorchak compiled 45 points in subduing Castleton last week. When Jim Butler, the area's towering center and the mainstay of the Mustangs last season, ready to join the team, Colonie definitely is more formidable than before. Coach Tom Couch hasn't announced his starting lineup but it is expected that Pettigrew and Patti will team up at forward with Bloomer and Brown at the guard position while Butler handles the pivot position.

The Colonie Ponies, who also won their opening encounter, will engage the Troy Boys' Club Americans at 7:30 in a preliminary to the main attraction which is scheduled to get under way at 9 p.m.

SHEPHERD QUINT TRIUMPHS, 39-33

The Shepherd A. C. trimmed the Silver Aces last night at St. Peter's Lyceum, 39 to 33.

Gardner with 14 points and Jordon with nine were outstanding for the winners. Welch with 12 was best for the losers.

DARTMOUTH GRID CAPTAIN.

Hanover, N. H. (AP)—Charles M. Pearson, of Madison, Minn., was elected captain of the 1941 Dartmouth varsity football team by the Indians' lettermen.

"Y" TO PROMOTE 3 CAGE LEAGUES

The boys' physical department of the Troy Y. M. C. A. will promote three basketball leagues for young boys in the Troy Area. The midget league will be for boys 9 to 12 years of age; junior, 12 to 14 years and intermediate, 15 to 17 years of age.

The leagues are tentatively scheduled to open the week of Jan. 6 and individual trophies will be given the winning and runner-up teams.

The midget and junior teams will play Saturday afternoons and the intermediates will play Monday nights.

Information and entry blanks can be obtained from Robert G. Ayers, director of the boys' division, at the Troy Y. M. C. A.

EAGLES TURN BACK COEYMANS, 48 TO 42

The Eagle A. C. trimmed the Coeymans Alumni last night at St. Peter's Lyceum, 48 to 42. Caswell with 25 points and Wilcox with 13 starred for the winners. Conrad had 16 for the losers.

EAGLES A. C.

	F.G.	F.B.	T.P.
Caswell, rf.	11	3	25
Grimes, lf.	0	0	0
Brown, c.	0	0	0
Wilcox, rg.	6	1	13
Conrad, lf.	4	0	8
Lewis, lg	1	0	2
Totals	22	4	48

COEYMAN ALUMNI

	F.G.	F.B.	T.P.
Clinton, rf.	7	2	16
Reynolds, lf	0	0	0
Perisco, c.	2	1	5
Rangello, lg	1	0	2
Tiberco, lg.	2	0	4
Wagoner, rf.	3	1	7
Page, lg.	0	0	0
Romano, rf.	1	4	6
Stephans, rg.	1	0	2
Totals	17	8	42

Referee—McLoughlin. Timekeeper—Reigert. Score at half time—21-16, Eagles. Fouls called—10-9, Eagles.

AMATEURS QUALIFY FOR BOSTON BOUTS

Eight youthful amateur boxers punched and pummeled their opponents in the Capitol arena at Albany last night to win trips to Boston for the all-Eastern diamond belt finals Dec. 23.

Al Reed of Albany won the heavyweight championship when Howard Singleton of Rome, who entered the finals by knocking out Ed Galliard of Albany in the second round.

The winners:

112 pounds: Doug McDonald, Glens Falls, over Warren Parker of Albany; 118 pounds, Joe Mario, Albany, over William Johnson of Albany; 126 pounds, Tom Rotolo, Rome, over Archie Gooday of Albany; 135 pounds, Fred Baia, Amsterdam, over Tony Barone of Albany; 147 pounds, Jim Rouse, Albany, over Lester Brown of Albany; 160 pounds, Joe Carter, Rome, over Hod Dockett of Hoosick Falls; 175 pounds, Don Ladue Rensselaer, over Connie Mahar of Rensselaer; heavyweight, Al Reed, Albany, over Howard Singleton of Rome.

Illegal Killers Threatens Maine Game

Game wardens in Maine are fighting an uphill battle to keep illegal killers from slaying whitetail deer, the state's last real big game animal. Above Maine wardens are shown exhibiting a pile of illegally shot deer seized in raids on hide-outs.

School 16 Children Entertain Mothers

AMERICANS CAST 49,808,624 VOTES AT NATION'S POLLS

Final Returns Show Roosevelt Total 27,241,939, Willkie's 22,327,226; New G. O. P. Record.

Copyright, 1940, by the Associated Press

Washington—The American electorate cast a new record vote of 49,808,624 last Nov. 5 and chose Franklin D. Roosevelt as the nation's first third term president by a plurality of 4,914,713.

Final returns as compiled by the Associated Press—official in 46 states and unofficial in Nebraska and Rhode Island—show the popular vote to have been divided this way:

Franklin D. Roosevelt, Democrat, 27,141,939.

Wendell L. Willkie, Republican, 22,327,226.

Norman Thomas, Socialist, 116,796.

Roger W. Babson, Prohibition, 58,600.

Earl R. Browder, Communist, 48,789.

John W. Aiken, Socialist-Labor, 14,861.

Others, 413.

Nebraska and Rhode Island hoped to complete their official canvasses before Monday, when the presidential electors meet in the 48 states for the formality of casting their electoral votes, which were divided 449 for Roosevelt and 82 for Willkie. Nebraska's unofficial total was complete except for two precincts.

Willkie Vote G. O. P. Record.

The President's total popular vote, including 417,418 American Labor Party votes in New York State, was 509,558 less than the previous high of 27,751,597 which the Chief Executive himself established four years agow ith the aid of 274,924 American Labor votes. His 192 total was 22,821,857.

Willkie's popular vote was the largest ever given a Republican nominee, winner or loser. It included 22,428 independent Democrat votes in Georgia and 2,496 Jeffersonian Democrat votes in South Carolina. The previous record Republican vote was 21,392,190 for Herbert Hoover over Alfred E. Smith in 1928.

Only 239,459 votes were cast this year for minor party candidates. This was their smallest showing since 1924, when they polled 121,587, not counting the vote cast for the LaFollette third party ticket. There was no so-called "third party" in the field this year.

Roosevelt Plurality Shrinks.

The total popular vote was 4,161,507 above the previous record of 45,647,117 in 1936 and 9,992,102 more than the 1932 total of 39,816,522. It was within one-fifth of 1 per cent of the 49,719,200 estimated by the Associated Press on Oct. 24 as the probable vote this year. The AP's pre-election estimate four years ago was 45,473,000, which was within two-fifths of 1 per cent of the actual vote.

President Roosevelt's plurality was the smallest since Woodrow Wilson's 591,385 in 1916, and represented a recession from his 11,072,014 and 7,060,016 margins in 1936 and 1932, respectively. But his electoral vote of 449 to 82 for Willkie was exceeded only by his own 523 to 8 and 472 to 59 victories in his two previous elections. Otherwise this closest approach was Hoover's 444 to 87. in 1928.

Roosevelt carried 38 states. Willkie's pluralities weer in Colorado, Indiana, Iowa, Kansas, Maine, Michigan, Nebraska, North Dakota, South Dakota and Vermont.

New York oVte Close.

The President's percentage of the total vote was 54.7; Willkie's 44.8, and minor party candidates 0.5. Roosevelt's 1936 percentage was 60.8; 1932, 57.3.

Texas gave Roosevelt the largest plurality of any state—640,099. Wyoming gave him the smallest—6,654. Willkie's biggest plurality was in Kansas—124,435; his smallest in Michigan—6,926.

Roosevelt's New York vote was cut from 1,112,552 four years ago to 224,440 this year. The 1940 American Labor Party vote was nearly twice as large as Roosevelt's plurality in eNw York. Democratic leaders, however, contend that Roosevelt would have received all of the A. L. P. vote as Democrats if the separatep arty had not been organized in 1936. Without the A. L. P. votes, Roosevelt's total would have been 192,978 less than Willkie's in New York.

SOCIETY NEWS

Final Arrangements Made for Parish Party

Final arrangements have been made for the Christmas card party to be held tonight by the Woman's Auxiliary of the Italian Community Center. Proceeds will be used as a fund to fill Christmas baskets for needy families.

Mrs. Nicholas F. Brignola and Mrs. Xavier Capuano are co-chairmen.

Committees have been selected as follows: Mrs. James Testo and Mrs. Ben Marsicano, tickets; Mrs. John Rea and Mrs. Humbert Grande, prizes; Mrs. Frank Pisanello and Mrs. Ambrose Perrotta, tables; Mrs. William Tedesco and Mrs. John D'Alessandro, chairs; Mrs. Patriok Zucaro and Mrs. Angelo Valenti, refreshments; Mrs. Philip Cirillo and Mrs. Lois Argera, tallies and pencils.

Jewish Juniors To Hold Dance

The Troy Section of the National Council of Jewish Juniors met Tuesday evening in the vestry rooms of the Third Street Temple. A Dutch supper was served at 6 P.m. to 35 members.

Further plans were discussed for the Christmas dance to be held at the Colonie Country Club Christmas Eve. Miss Lilyan Cohen is general chairman with Miss Jeanne Lesnick in charge of publicity.

Plans were also made for the sleighride with Miss Ethel Raufman in charge.

Daughters Hold Meeting

The Kings' Daughters of the United Presbyterian Church met Wednesday at the manse with Mrs. Clarence F. Anderson as hostess. Mrs. Fred Greenwood, president, led the opening devotions, assisted by Mrs. Robert A. Bills. Mrs. Margaret Turcotte, secretary, and Mrs. John C. O'Melia, treasurer, presented reports.

A Christmas program was given with Mrs. O'Melia as leader. Mrs. Robert L. Trotter gave a story on "The King's Gift." Plans were completed for the annual Christmas cheer work for shutins and needy. During the social hour Mrs. Anderson, assisted by Miss Margaret Simpson, served refreshments with holiday decorations in keeping with the Christmas spirit.

Choral Union Rehearses

A meeting and rehearsal of the Troy Choral Union was held Wednesday evening at the home of Mr. and Mrs. Harry Quinn, 166 Ninth Avenue. A rehearsal of Christmas music was conducted by Raymond Campbell who also was acting accompanist on the piano. Mrs. Harry Strunk announced she had procured the Lansingburg High School for next Wednesday night's rehearsal. The Union members are preparing to present a public program in January.

Mrs. Quinn served buffet refreshments at the social hour following the two hours' rehearsal.

Dinner Plans Complete

Mrs. Florence H. Brown has completed plans for the turkey dinner being tendered by her Red team to the Blue team, winners in the summer contest of the Rensselaer County Woman's Republican Club, Inc., to be served at Odd Fellows' Hall, Lansingburg, tomorrow at 6:30 p.m. under the direction of Mrs. John C. Neal. Mrs. Minnie Armitage, captain of the winners, will head her table, with covers for the 27 members.

The Red team table will also have covers for 27 with Mrs. Brown as hostess for her group.

Hostess to Class

A Christmas party for members of the Amicitia Class of the First Baptist Church was held Wednesday evening at the home of Mrs. Ray Smith in Eagle Mills. Dinner was served for 12. The hostess was assisted by Mrs. Henry Closson and Mrs. William F. Haase.

Miss Marion Franklin presided at a short business meeting. The next meeting will be in January at the home of Mrs. Paul Snyder on the Pinewoods Avenue Road.

Christmas Party Held

The Corvinare Club held its annual Christmas party last night at Dom's Tavern. Supper was served followed by an evening of entertainment and games. The members also participated in a grabbag.

Club Hostess

Members of the Mecotam Club met last evening at the home of Mrs. John Rogers. Plans were made for a Christmas party and grabbag next week at the home of Mrs. Henry Breault.

MONOGRAM GLOVES.

When the party is over, do you find yourself the not too happy possessor of somebody else's black gloves that don't fit, while some unspecified guest has meanwhile made off with your own pets? If this problem rings a familiar bell, then

Savory Cream Sauce.
(One Cup)

Two tablespoons butter, 2 tablespoons flour, one-half teaspoon salt, one tablespoon minced fresh parsley, one teaspoon minced celery leaves, pinch dry mustard, one teaspoon Worcestershire sauce, one-eighth teaspoon pepper, one-half cup vegetable or meat stock, one-half cup rich milk.

Melt butter in saucepan, stir in flour and seasonings. Slowly add milk, stirring over low heat until mixture thickens. Then slowly stir in stock and stir until mixture is smooth and has boiled once. Serve very hot with two cups cubed turnips or other winter vegetables.

Children of the primary grades of School 16 entertained their mothers yesterday afternoon at the monthly meeting of the Parent-Teacher Association with the presentation of the Christmas play, "The Sign of the Shoe." The play was given under the direction of Miss Frances Dwyer, teacher of the third grade.

THE WEATHER
U. S. Weather Bureau.
Tonight—Fair, cold.
Tomorrow—Fair, warmer.

THE TIMES RECORD

FINAL EDITION

Series 1941—No. 16. (Entered as Second Class Matter at the Postoffice at Troy, N. Y., under the Act of March 3, 1879.) TROY, N. Y., MONDAY EVENING, JANUARY 20, 1941. (Published Daily Except Sunday) PRICE THREE CENTS

Roosevelt Pledges Third Term To Preservation Of Democracy

Hitler, Mussolini Hold Conference On War Situation

Aid for Italy in Africa and Albania, Attitude Toward U. S. Believed Under Discussion.

BY THE ASSOCIATED PRESS.

Adolf Hitler and his sorely-pressed axis partner, Benito Mussolini, met at an undisclosed spot today amid fascist assertions that a vast new German-Italian offensive was brewing against Britain in the Mediterranean war theater.

A German communique said that the conference exemplified "the close fighting alliance existing between the German and Italian people" and that the two leaders were "in complete accord."

With official details lacking, it was assumed in well-informed quarters that the discussion touched upon these subjects:

Subjects Discussed.

1. The Greek and North African campaigns, and how Hitler can rescue Italy's battered legions.

2. The battle of Britain, with probable emphasis on the question of delivering a knockout blow before American aid becomes effective.

3. Axis policy toward the United States as a result of President Roosevelt's program of help for Britain.

In Rome, fascist editor Virginio Gayda, frequently known as Mussolini's mouthpiece, declared:

"The axis in the Mediterranean is assured that the war will continue to develop in this area with increased forces capable of facing and beating down increased enemy forces."

While the axis leaders conferred, the British reported still another success in the drive to "tear Italy's African eempire to tatters and shreds"—as promised by Prime Minister Winston Churchill.

Rout Fascist Troops.

British troops were reported to have driven into Italian Eritrea at two points after routing two fascist divisions (about 24,000 men) and inflicting 2,000 casualties in fierece actions around Kassala, in the Anglo-Egyptian Sundan, East Africa.

Sweeping across the border into Eritrea, the British said they were "now operating" eastward of Tesenei and Sabderat "in contact with the retreating enemy."

Tessenei, several miles inside Eritrea, is an important rail head and center of a cotton growing region. Sabderat is on the frontier, twenty miles east of Kassala.

London military quarters said the capture of Kassala, held by the Italians since last July, was carried out by "numerically inferior British forces against an enemy very well armed and equipped."

Supported by Ethiopian tribesmen, the British were reported to be pursuing Fascist legions fleeing eastward all along the 200-mile Sudanese border front.

Nazis Bomb Suez Zone.

British light tanks and armored cars led the pursuit, it was said, knifing at Premier Mussolini's east African domain in a drive keyed with the British counter-invasion against the Italians in the Libyan desert of North Africa.

With the African theater assuming front-rank imoprtance, Hitler's high command disclosed briefly that Nazi bombers attacked "militarily important objectives" in the Suez Canal zone—vital link in Britain's lifeline to her Far East possessions—apparently flying from the new German dive-bomber base at Catania, Sicily, 1,000 miles away.

Thick weather over the English Channel kept R.A.F. bombers grounded during the night, but Hitler's high command reported Nazi raids on London, Southampton and other ports on the southeast English coast.

For once, official German and British tallies of Nazi planes shot down agreed—an overnight total of five.

Greeks Advance.

German planes droned high over the empire capital for seven hours until the all-clear signal sounded at 2 a.m., but few bombs were reported dropped.

British bombers continued their attacks on Tobruk where British siege forces are waiting to strike when the garrison and defenses of the Libyan base are weakened.

Snowstorms hampered armies on the Albanian front, but reports from the Yugoslav frontier last night indicated large forces were concentrating for a decisive battle in the Tepeleni-Klisura sector. These reports said the Greeks had advanced along the Albanian coast to Dukati, 15 miles north of Chimara and almost half way from Chimara to the port of Valona. There, it was said, the Greek advance was checked by Italian counter attacks.

The Greeks reported ambushing counter attacking Italians north of Klisura and hurling them back with heavy losses.

ACCIDENTS COST 1,354 LIVES.

Albany (UP)—Industrial accidents took 1,354 lives during 1940, the state labor department reported today. December mishaps caused 109 deaths.

QUADRUPLETS ARE BORN TO 98-POUND INDIANA MOTHER

Girl Baby Dies Shortly After Birth; Two Girls and Boy Live; Mother Rallies After Ordeal.

Michigan City, Ind. (INS)—Quadruplets, three girls and a boy, were born today to 35-year-old Mrs. Eva Swanson, but one of the girls, weakened by respiratory troubles upon delivery, died.

Dr. R. A. Gilmore, who delivered the children, announced that the girl died in an incubator. The infant who succumbed was the last to be born and had already been designated as "Linda" by the parents.

The other two girls and the boy were "all right," Dr. Gilmore said, and are expected to survive. Mrs. Swanson likewise was getting along favorably, the physician said.

The parents said they would name the boy either Philip or Stephen, and the first of the four to be born will be named Jennifer. Phoebe was the name chosen for the other surviving girl, who was the third child to be delivered.

Caesarian Operation.

Quadruplets occur about once in 750,000 births.

The children were born in a Caesarian operation that was completed in half an hour by Dr. Gilmore and the seven physicians he called in to help him. Nine nurses also were on hand to help in the delivery.

Dr. Gilmore said there was only a five-second lapse between the birth of the first baby and that of the fourth.

The babies weighed between 36 and 41 ounces "with blankets," Dr. Gilmore said. Born at 9:30 a.m., they were not weighed without blankets immediately.

The mother went through the operation under a local anaesthetic. They were her first children.

Dr. Gilmore praised the attitude of both the mother and father, Melbert O. Swanson, an office worker in a furniture factory.

Blood Transfusion.

He said they were both told last November that quadruplets were expected, and that both were "extraordinarily happy" about the impending births.

Helping the physician in the operating room were two physicians to give transfusions, two to take care of the babies, one to administer the anaesthetic and two to assist Dr. Gilmore.

The blood transfusion was necessary to boost the strength of Mrs. Gilmore, who weighs only 98 pounds and is 4 feet 11 inches tall.

The babies were put in an incubator immediately after birth and will remain there for about two months, or when they reach a weight of five pounds.

DR. H. E. CRUTTENDEN, COOPERSTOWN, DIES

Cooperstown (UP) — Dr. Harry Lee Cruttenden, 64, prominent physician and baseball enthusiast, died yesterday. He was instrumental in obtaining the original Doubleday Field, where Abner Doubleday is believed to have organized the first baseball game, as a municipal memorial to the national sport.

GARNER RETIRES TO PRIVATE LIFE AFTER 40 YEARS

Rejects All Business Offers, Telling One Firm Reputation for Honesty "Not for Sale."

Washington (AP)—The gavel fell today for bluff, hearty John Nance Garner after almost two score crowded years in the nation's capital.

His last official duty was to administer the oath of office to his successor—Henry Agard Wallace—as the 32nd vice president of the United States. Then it was home to Texas and the quiet role of private citizen.

It was the tenth inauguration for "Cactus Jack" since he started his career as a member of the House in 1903—the year the Wright brothers made the first successful airplane flight at Kitty Hawk. Those were the days of bicycles built for two and that very new fangled invention—Marconi's wireless. New York was yet to open its first subway, and the Panama Canal was a distant dream.

Want Private Life.

Today the 72-year-old Garner was full of smiles and jests, as he bade goodbye to the many colleagues of his 38 years in Congress—thirty years as a member and Speaker of the House and eight as vice president.

He confided to reporters that what he had in mind now was to get home to Uvalde, Tex., as quickly as possible. Once there, he intends to look over some rental houses he has had built, go over his fishing tackle, oil up his gun, and settle down to live to 93 at a leisurely pace.

Teh outgoing vice president explained that he had selected 93 as his goal because he wanted to say before he died that he had spent more than half his years in private life. He spent eight years in office in Texas before he came here.

Besieged with offers to go into private business, Garner has turned them all down.

Reputation Not "For Sale."

One particularly attractive overture, involving a five-year contract at $50,000 annually, was said to have been made by an insurance company.

The insurance official was reported to have told Garner that his firm was willing to pay such a salary because it wanted his reputation for honesty associated with the company.

Garner, who has said he wanted to become a plain citizen, without any connections of that kind, was understood to have replied that his reputation for honesty was not for sale.

President Roosevelt—"The Boss" to Garner for the last eight years—was said to have told the Texan during a recent White House chat that he ought to devote another ten years of his life to public service. Garner's reported answer was that he thought his services were not indispensable and that he hoped he would never again be required to hold any office.

COLONEL DONOVAN WARMLY RECEIVED AT SOFIA. BULGARIA

Sofia, Bulgaria (UP)—Col. William J. (Wild Bill) Donovan, who is touring the war fronts in a semi-official capacity for the United States, arrived today from Greece.

He was met by United States Ambassador George H. Earle. Well informed quarters said Donovan had come to explain the American viewpoint on the war and to sound out the Bulgarian attitude.

Bulgarian officials said Donovan, World War commander of the 165th (Fighting Irish) Regiment of New York, was "exceptionally welcome." They expected him to confer with Bulgarian cabinet ministers and to be received by King Boris.

Donovan has been in Britain, Egypt and on the Libyan and Greek fronts.

German Air Blitz Cost 21,579 Lives in England

London (INS)—Since Germany's aerial blitz against England began last September, 21,579 persons have been killed, including 2,351 children under 16 years of age, it was announced officially today.

In that same period, German air raids have injured 30,556 persons so seriously that they required hospital treatment, the announcement said. Among the wounded were 2,457 children.

During the month of September civilian air raid casualties totaled 3,793 killed and 5,604 injured, the statement added. These figures covered casualties throughout the United Kingdom.

First Third Term President

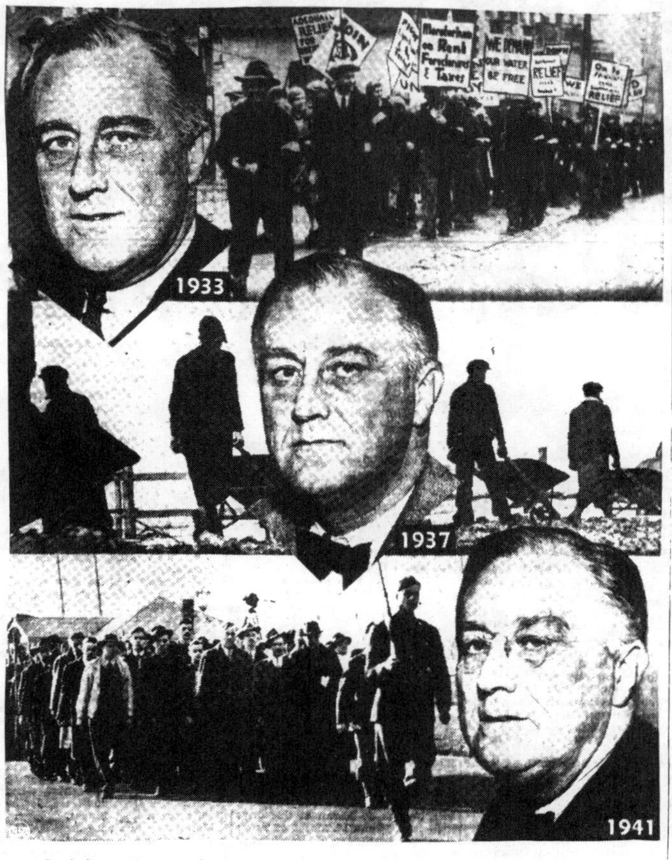

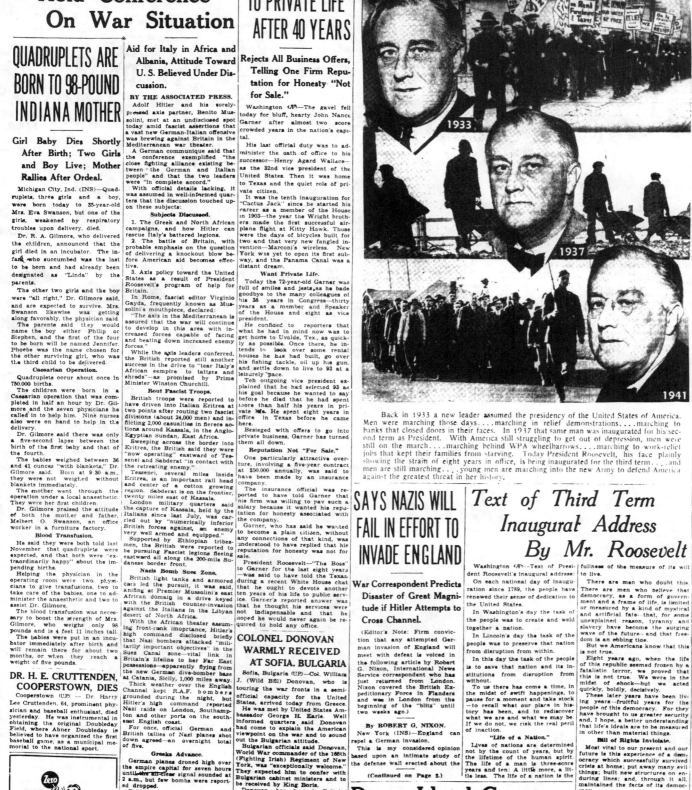

Back in 1933 a new leader assumed the presidency of the United States of America. Men were marching those days....marching in relief demonstrations....marching to banks that closed doors in their faces. In 1937 that same man was inaugurated for his second term as President. With America still struggling to get out of depression, men were still on the march....marching behind WPA wheelbarrows....marching to work-relief jobs that kept their families from starving. Today President Roosevelt, his face plainly showing the strain of eight years in office, is being inaugurated for the third term...and men are still marching....young men are marching into the new Army to defend America against the greatest threat in her history.

SAYS NAZIS WILL FAIL IN EFFORT TO INVADE ENGLAND

War Correspondent Predicts Disaster of Great Magnitude if Hitler Attempts to Cross Channel.

(Editor's Note: Firm conviction that any attempted German invasion of England will meet with defeat is voiced in the following article by Robert G. Nixon, International News Service correspondent who has just returned from London. Nixon covered the British Expeditionary Force in Flanders and was in London from the beginning of the "blitz" until two weeks ago.)

By ROBERT G. NIXON.

New York (INS)—England can repel a German invasion.

This is my considered opinion based upon an intimate study of the defense wall erected about the

(Continued on Page 2.)

Text of Third Term Inaugural Address By Mr. Roosevelt

Washington (AP)—Text of President Roosevelt's inaugural address:

On each national day of inauguration since 1789, the people have renewed their sense of dedication to the United States.

In Washington's day the task of the people was to create and weld together a nation.

In Lincoln's day the task of the people was to preserve that nation from disruption from within.

In this day the task of the people is to save that nation and its institutions from disruption from without.

To us there has come a time, in the midst of swift happenings, to pause for a moment and take stock—to recall what our place in history has been, and to rediscover what we are and what we may be. If we do not, we risk the real peril of inaction.

"Life of a Nation."

Lives of nations are determined not by the count of years, but by the lifetime of the human spirit. The life of a man is three-score years and ten: A little more, a little less. The life of a nation is the fullness of the measure of its will to live.

There are men who doubt this. There are men who believe that democracy, as a form of government and a frame of life, is limited or measured by a kind of mystical and artificial fate—that, for some unexplained reason, tyranny and slavery have become the surging wave of the future—and that freedom is an ebbing tide.

But we Americans know that this is not true.

Eight years ago, when the life of this republic seemed frozen by a fatalistic terror, we proved that this is not true. We were in the midst of shock—but we acted quickly, boldly, decisively.

These later years have been living years—fruitful years for the people of this democracy. For they have brought to us greater security and, I hope, a better understanding that life's ideals are to be measured in other than material things.

Bill of Rights Inviolate.

Most vital to our present and our future is this experience of a democracy which successfully survived crisis at home; put away many evil things; built new structures on enduring lines; and, through it all, maintained the facts of its democracy.

For action has been taken within the three-way framework of the Constitution of the United States. The coordinate branches of the government continue freely to function. The Bill of Rights remains inviolate. The freedom of elections is wholly maintained. Prophets of the downfall of American democracy have seen their dire predictions come to naught.

Democracy is not dying.

We know it because we have seen it revive—and grow.

We know it cannot die—because

(Continued on Page 2.)

Dame Lloyd George Dies In Wales Home

Criccieth, Wales (UP) —Dame Margaret Lloyd George, wife of Britain's World War prime minister, died today before her husband, rushing to her bedside from the midlands, could reach here.

The white-haired little Welchman, who was on his way here from Churt, Surrey, by automobile, ran into a snowdrift early Sunday. Physicians advised him to remain at Currugydruidon and it was believed he might not be able to attend the funeral.

Mrs. Lloyd George was a dame of the British Empire and was formally addressed as "Dame Margaret." The title of dame is the feminine equivalent of knight.

The Lloyd Georges were married in 1888, and celebrated their golden wedding anniversary three years ago. She was 75; Lloyd George was 78 Friday.

They have two sons and two daughters.

Dame Margaret's fatal illness followed a fall seven weeks ago when she injured her ankle.

Lloyd George, who had been at his model farm at Churt left immediately when he learned of her relapse.

She was made a dame of the British Empire in 1919, at the same time that she was appointed justice of the peace.

At the time of their golden wedding anniversary, Lloyd George said: "We have lived in perfect harmony for over fifty years."

ROCHESTER FATHER ENDS LIFE WITH GAS

Rochester (UP)—Suicide of Raymond Levey, 31, father of two children, was attributed today to despondency over his inability to find employment. Levey was found dead by his wife, Anna, in the gas-filled kitchen of their second floor apartment here.

President Calls On United America To Battle Tyranny

Chief Executive Urges People to Act "Quickly, Boldly And Decisively" to Preserve the "Sacred Fire of Liberty and the Destiny of the Republican Form of Government;" Vast Throng of Nearly 1,000,000 Persons Views Inauguration Spectacle; Garner Administers Oath to Henry A. Wallace As Vice President.

Washington (INS).—Franklin Delano Roosevelt entered American history today as the nation's first third-term President and immediately dedicated his future to perpetuating the "integrity of democracy" and to preserving its institutions against tyranny and slavery.

With representatives of the axis powers sitting behind him, amid an inaugural crowd of 100,000 on the Capitol Plaza, the President called on the American people to act "quickly, boldly and decisively" to preserve the "sacred fire of liberty and the destiny of the republican form of government."

Clear but sub-freezing weather bathed his third term inauguration in sunshine—a happy augur to New Dealers, after his blustery, rainswept inaugurations of 1933 and 1937.

The President rode to the capitol down historic Pennsylvania Avenue, through shivering crowds of nearly 1,000,000 persons, who stood in curbstone lines for hours to cheer his passage. The crowds were still there an hour later as he returned to the White House, sworn to faithfully execute the office of President for another four years.

Mr. Roosevelt keynoted his third term with a simple inaugural speech, after Chief Justice Charles Evans Hughes administered the presidential oath to him for the third term. His chief appeal was to the American people to "muster the spirit of America and the faith of America" to uphold their sacred democracy.

The President departed from his text once and then perhaps inadvertently. In the text, he asked his countrymen to "take stock" in order to "rediscover what we are and what we may be" and added:

"If we do not, we risk the real peril of inaction."

To the cheering crowd and his words were broadcast throughout the world to invisible multitudes he said:

"If we do not, we risk the real peril of isolation the real peril of inaction."

"We Do Not Retreat."

His peroration was his pledge to preserve the integrity of democracy in the midst of a war torn world. And of this high resolve, he said triumphantly:

"We do not retreat. We are not content to stand still. As Americans, we go forward, in the service of our country, by the will of God."

The President began his precedent-shattering third term a moment after Vice President Henry A. Wallace was sworn in by the retiring Vice President John Nance Garner. With Wallace inaugurated, Chief Justice Hughes administered the 152-year-old oath to Mr. Roosevelt, the President touching his hand to the 200-year-old Roosevelt family bible at a passage, ending:

"And now abideth faith, hope, charity; these three; but the greatest of these is charity."

Then the President dedicated his inaugural address to "democracy." He reviewed the place democracy has taken in the development of mankind, remarked that it was "still spreading on every continent" and told the American people its preservation furnished "highest justification for every sacrifice that we may make in the name of national defense."

Huge Crowd Cheers.

A huge crowd, swarming across the Capitol plaza and shivering in intensely cold clear weather, cheered the President repeatedly.

The President's message was broadcast to the nation by short wave radio to the ends of the earth. Millions upon millions of human beings heard him but of them all, the proudest probably was his 86-year-old mother, Mrs. James Roosevelt, who had the great privilege of watching her son take the presidential oath for the third time in eight years. A score of other Roosevelts were in the thronged stands.

Mr. Roosevelt began by comparing the tasks of his third term administration to those of Washington and Lincoln. He said:

"On each national day of inauguration since 1789, the people have renewed their sense of dedication to the United States.

"In Washington's day the task of the people was to create and weld together a nation.

"In Lincoln's day the task of the people was to preserve that nation from disruption from within.

Our Chief Task Today.

"In this day the task of the people is to save that nation and its institutions from disruption from without."

"To us there has come a time, in the midst of swift happenings, to pause for a moment and take stock—to recall what our place in history has been, and to rediscover what we are and what may be. If we do not, we risk the real peril of inaction.

"Lives of nations are determined not by the count of years, but by the lifetime of the human spirit. The life of a man is three-score years and ten: A little more, a little less. The life of a nation is the fullness of the measure of its will to live.

"There are men who doubt this. There are men who believe that democracy, as a form of government and a frame of life, is limited or measured by a kind of mystical and artifical fate—that, for some unexplained reason, tyranny and slavery have become the surging wave of the future—and that freedom is an ebbing tide.

"But we Americans know this is not true."

"Freedom Maintained."

The President touched briefly on the eight years of his first two administrations in 1933 when "the life of this republic seemed frozen by a fatalistic terror," and the later years "that have brought to us greater security and, I hope, a better understanding that life's ideals are to be measured in other than material things."

Then he proudly pointed to preserving democracy during the eight years, asserting:

"The bill of rights remains inviolate. The freedom of elections is wholly maintained. Prophets of the downfall of American democracy have seen their dire predictions come to naught.

"Democracy is not dying."

The President said a nation, like a person, has a body, a mind and "something deeper the spirit, the

(Continued on Page 2.)

TWO WOMEN KEPT DEAD SISTER'S BODY IN HOME SINCE JULY

Camden, N. J. (INS)—Two elderly sisters who had kept the body of a third in their home since last July were to be examined by psychiatrists today.

The two sistres, Miss Rebecca Miller and Mrs. Margaret Deane, were found living in indescribable filth and shabbiness here by a curious policeman who befriended the former when she became lost while taking a walk.

The three sisters had lived for years with virtually no contact with the outside world and when Jennie, about 70, died last July they just kept on living as formerly. The dead woman was buried by city authorities.

The Index

JUNIOR CHAMBER AT RENSSELAER TO CONDUCT DINNER

Annual Event of Business Men's Group Will Be Held on Tuesday, February 25.

Tuesday, Feb. 25, is the date for the annual dinner of the Rensselaer Junior Chamber of Commerce, it was announced yesterday.

Frank J. Polsinello, chairman of the dinner committee, said that Charles Harvey of Niagara Falls, president of the state organization, will be guest of honor at the event. In connection with the program, the chamber's choice of the city's most distinguished younger citizen for 1940 will be announced.

Pinboys Make Contribution.

Largest contribution to date toward the Rensselaer March of Dimes for infantile paralysis sufferers was made by pinboys at the Rensselaer Recreation Bowling, according to Joseph Feily, chairman of the drive in Rensselaer. Five boys, Richard Sillery, John Betage, Lois Cross, Peter Tagliento and Charles Motta, added $7.50 to the fund.

Mr. Feily has called a meeting of all workers for 7:30 p.m. today at the city building to receive reports on the progress of the drive.

Funeral of Mrs. Mann.

The funeral of Mrs. Lewis F. Mann, wife of L. F. Mann, Rensselaer funeral director, was held yesterday afternoon from the residence, 1601 Broadway. Delegations were present representing Hilltop Lodge of Rebekahs and Philippine Chapter, Order of the Eastern Star. Rev. Jasper E. McIntyre, pastor of Broadway Methodist Church, officiated and bearers were Clarence Thompson, Police Chief Richard S. Goode, Henry Bonacker, Chester Teeling, Charles Leverance and Roy Winne. Interment was in Albany Rural Cemetery.

Reception Planned.

A reception is being planned for Monday night at the Rensselaer Masonic Temple in connection with the official visit of Walter J. Allard, district deputy grand master, to Greenbush Lodge, F. & A. M. The district Past Masters Association will also meet at the temple the same night.

Supper to End Contest.

A supper for the congregation and Sunday school, with members of the victorious red team as guests of the blues, will mark the close of the attendance contest at the Broadway Methodist Church tonight in the church parlors. Arrangements are in charge of Mrs. C. F. Tefft, Mrs. J. E. McIntyre and Miss Jane Dow.

To Have Skating Party.

Young people of St. Paul's Lutheran Church will meet at 7 p.m. today to go to Crooked Lake for a skating party. Refreshments will be served at the lake.

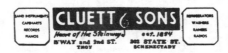

Introducing Another Police School Class To Tear Gas

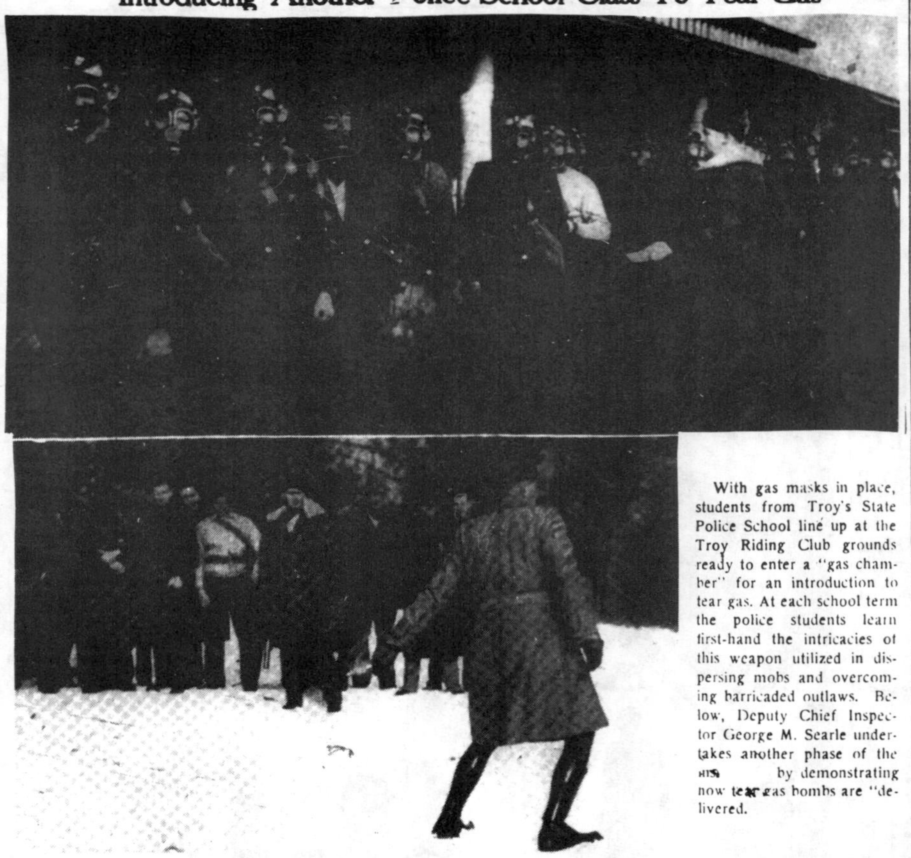

With gas masks in place, students from Troy's State Police School line up at the Troy Riding Club grounds ready to enter a "gas chamber" for an introduction to tear gas. At each school term the police students learn first-hand the intricacies of this weapon utilized in dispersing mobs and overcoming barricaded outlaws. Below, Deputy Chief Inspector George M. Searle undertakes another phase of the HIS by demonstrating now tear gas bombs are "delivered.

MILK PRICES FIRM IN STATE DESPITE ADVERSE DECISION

Injunction Against Referendum on Amendment Has Little Effect on Cost, Survey Discloses.

The Record Newspapers Bureau, Washington.

The Milk Marketing Agreement in Michigan has been declared unconstitutional, and a chaotic situation prevails there as to fluid milk prices, much as is expected in New York State, following issuance of an injunction against a referendum on amendments to the New York Milk Shed agreement.

Regardless of the adverse decision against the Government as to the referendum, the Department of Agriculture reports that throughout New York State thus far, prices have showed a firm tone. Price changes for fluid milk, though not extremely numerous, were all higher. With butter prices declining materially during December, prices for surplus milk, which are based on those for butter, in many markets were definitely weaker.

In the East, where the major portion of the fluid milk of the country is consumed, changes in price were confined to one market—Manchester, N. H. Class 1 prices on this market were 12 cents higher per hundredweight, although there was no change reported in retail prices.

Markets in southeastern Wisconsin exhibited strength. At both Kenosha and Racine, Class 1 prices rose 21 cents per hundredweight, with an accompanying increase of one cent per quart in retail prices. At Milwaukee a 23-cent increase per hundredweight was shown along with a one-cent increase per quart in retail prices.

Two-quart containers are reported as being used in 16 different cities widely scattered throughout the country, while 11 cities report prices of four-quart containers. Prices for milk delivered to homes in two-quart containers range from ½ cent to three cents less than those delivered in single-quart containers, while in four-quart containers, savings are from 1¼ to 3¼ cents per quart. Prices at stores for two-quart containers ranged from ½ to two cents per quart less than those for single quarts. In four-quart containers, the reduction per quart was from ½ to 2½ cents in the markets reporting their use. Though a number of cities have reported discounts for certain quantities of milk delivered per month or at one delivery during the day, it was impossible to show such discounts in the present issue of this report.

RAYMERTOWN.

Mr. and Mrs. Charles Bulson were recent guests of Mr. and Mrs. John Dixon of Brunswick.

Mrs. Earl Cushman spent Wednesday with Mrs. Henry Hovran ton and family of Brunswick.

The Misses Mae, Elaine and Billie Tschumi spent a day recently with their sister, Mrs. Hayner Bornt.

Mr. and Mrs. Bernard Weiss recently entertained at supper the Misses Mae, Elaine and Billie Tschumi.

Chauncey Smith has returned home after spending a few days with his sister, Mrs. Grace Frier, of North Hoosick.

Mr. and Mrs. Leighton Holbritter daughter Rita and son Carl and Miss Barbara Jeanne Humphrey of Nortonville were recent dinner guests at the home of Mrs. M. C. Snyder.

PETERSBURG.

Albert White is ill.

Lawrence Carr is ill.

Mrs. Edna Stewart is improving.

Mrs. Cora Smith is convalescing.

Leyton Reynolds is able to be out.

Mrs. John J. Moon is convalescing.

Lucien Price of Boston was a recent visitor of Miss Lydia McKown.

Mrs. Nellie Merrihew of Troy called Tuesday on her grandmother, Mrs. John J. Moon, at the home of Mr. and Mrs. John H. Moon.

The Petersburg branch of the Home Bureau will hold a supper at the Methodist Hall Thursday evening. Serving will begin at 5:30. Price 35c.

Miss Rosalie Smith of Williamstown and Dr. Florence Bascom, professor emeritus of geology at Bryn Mawr and now of Williamstown, visited Miss Lydia McKown recently.

Berkshire Star Chapter, No. 500, O. E. S., will hold a card party this evening at Masonic Hall. The committee is Miss Irma Maxon and Mrs. Nellie Hull of Berlin. Refreshments will be served and prizes awarded.

Mr. and Mrs. Jay Spencer gave a dinner Sunday in honor of Miss Stella Spencer who was celebrating her birthday. Guests besides the guest of honor included Mrs. Roy Warren of Albany, Mr. and Mrs. Lawrence Carr and Miss Elizabeth Carr of Petersburg.

The United Petersburg Parent-Teacher Association will hold a food sale at Jones and Jones store tomorrow morning for the benefit of the dental clinic. The next meeting of the Parent-Teacher Association will be held Tuesday evening, Feb. 11, at the auditorium of Public School No. 4.

"They Say-"

Political Gossip from Our National Capital.

By HUGH S. JOHNSON.

Washington—The President says that any suggestion that, under the "lease-lend" bill he might transfer part of our Navy to another nation is a "cow-jumped-over-the-moon" idea—meaning, we may suppose, Mother Goose nonsense or a palpable impossibility. "Hi-diddle-diddle, the cat and the fiddle, the cow jumped over the moon." He also says that he never even considered using the Navy to convoy American shipments to Britain.

A great deal of confusion is creeping into this debate. There is nothing in the "lease-lend" bill about convoying ships. Providing they are not violating the Neutrality Act and the President's own proclamations thereunder, by entering proclaimed war zones, or otherwise, American ships can still sail the sea. If there is danger of illegal interference with them by another nation while they are in pursuit of their lawful business, the President doesn't need any additional authority to protect them with naval convoys. Therefore the convoy argument is not properly in the debate on the "lease-lend" bill.

Something Else Again.

But this "cow-over-the-moon" business is something else again. There is no authentic record of any cow jumping over any moon, but there is a very recent and rather startling record of a President transferring a very substantial part of our Navy, to wit, fifty destroyers, to a belligerent nation. It was done without any specific authority. There is also a considerable record of diddling public opinion just before election or during the debate on hotly contested legislation by promises that were quickly forgotten—for example, the 1932 promise not to violate the gold covenants in our bonds and money. That was the highest diddle-diddle in all our economic history. But there was no remedy. All that happened was that "the little dog laughed to see such sport and the dish ran away with the spoon."

If there is no intention to transfer any part of our sorely needed armament, why is it necessary to grant unlimited authority to do so? With a little paraphrasing and transposition, which does no violence to its intent, the 1776 bill authorizes the President "to sell, transfer, lease, lend or otherwise dispose of * * * any weapon, munition, aircraft, vessel or boat * * * any component material * * * any other commodity or article for defense."

President Can Give Anything.

This "includes any (such defense) article * * * manufactured or processed * * * or to which the United States * * * has or hereafter acquires title, possession or control." This transfer may be made to the "government of any country whose defense the President deems vital to the defense of the United States." The terms of transfer "shall be those which the President deems satisfactory and the benefit to the United States may be payment or repayment in kind or property, or any other direct or indirect benefit which the President deems satisfactory"—for example, a few kind words or, under the common law of consideration in England and our country, so slight a thing as "a peppercorn, a nut or a bunch of hay."

There is no doubt about it, the bill in its present form includes outright donations to the President of the power of gift of any or all of the defense resources of the United States, the power to wage all-out economic war and a very substantial part of the power to wage undeclared military and naval war for any cause or without cause and for or against any nation anywhere in the world.

There has been no showing of necessity for any such drastic delegation of power, any such abdication of Congress. The argument is not against that assertion—not that such powers are not granted by the bill but only that such extreme powers will not be used "Hi-diddle-diddle."

WYNANTSKILL.

Mrs. Joseph Thiell entertained her bridge club Wednesday afternoon. Winners were Mrs. Isaac Film and Mrs. Thiell.

Mr. and Mrs. William Graham have returned to Waterloo, Iowa, where they were called by the death of Mrs. Pascal Fonda.

Mrs. Gerrie Austin was tendered a surprise party Wednesday evening in honor of her birthday anniversary. Cards were played after which refreshments were served to more than twenty relatives and friends. The honor guest received a variety of gifts. Mrs. Carl Austin and Mrs. Milton Austin were hostesses.

Cranium Crackers

Famous Women—

Until the 20th century, the woman's place was generally considered to be in the home, but before that time there were many who played important parts in world events. How many of these famous women can you identify?

1. Name the Indian girl who reportedly saved an early American colonist from death.

2. What archduchess of Austria, born in Vienna, married a French king and was later beheaded in Paris?

3. Who was the woman that offered to pawn her jewels to aid an Italian navigator in his business of exploration?

4. What Egyptian woman was wooed by two well-known Romans?

5. Who was the 19-year-old girl that was burned at the stake after leading French troops into battle against the English?

Answers on Page 20.

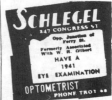

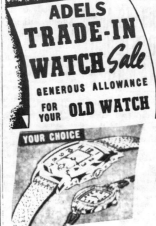

Holdouts Evaporate As Lombardi, DiMaggio, Other Stars Sign

SCHNOZ COMES TO TERMS WITH REDS AFTER PHONE TALK

Report Big Catcher Will Get $18,000; Yankee Outfielder's Salary Placed at $35,000.

BY JUDSON BAILEY.

New York (AP)—The holdout mist that shrouded the start of baseball's spring training has lifted like a fog under a bright sun.

The evaporation that has been going on quietly but steadily for several days swooped up Joe DiMaggio of the New York Yankees, Ernie Lombardi of the Cincinnati Reds, Don Padgett of the St. Louis Cardinals and Burgess Whitehead of the New York Giants yesterday.

That's a lot of high priced talent to bring to terms in one day and virtually denuded the ranks of the holdouts.

DiMaggio, especially, had been expected to make a determined stand for a big boost in salary but was believed to have compromised at $35,000, a raise of $2,500 and half of the increase he had sought.

Even so this was sufficient to keep him the second highest paid player in baseball and maintain his record of not having reported to camp on time since he joined the Bombers as an $8,500 outfield hand in 1936. He planned to leave his San Francisco home today and arrive in Florida Monday or Tuesday.

Greenberg Still Unsigned.

Hank Greenberg of the Detroit Tigers, reputed the top salaried star of the major leagues, is one of the half dozen important players who hasn't yet signed. However, he is not considered a holdout.

He received $39,000 or $40,000 from the American League champions last year in addition to bonuses and his cut in the World Series. He arrived home from a Hawaiian vacation a few days ago to find a contract that will provide a raise of two or three thousand dollars.

He says he will sign when he goes to the Tigers' camp this week-end. It may be that he wants to talk over some adjustment of his contract to meet his expected draft into the Army in June.

Of the grade-A holdouts left, Johnny Mize of the St. Louis Cardinals is the Kingpin. The slugging first baseman is understood to be asking $17,500, which would put him up in the salary bracket left vacant when the club traded Joe Medwick to Brooklyn last year.

The Chicago Cubs are carrying on a bitter battle with Outfielder Hank Leiber, a chronic late signer, and with Pitcher Bill Lee, who was paid $21,000 in 1939 and $18,000 last year, but was reported cut to $10,000 this spring.

Wants Two-Year Contract.

Roy Weatherly, fleet centerfielder of the Cleveland Indians, has a little different plaint. He and his club have agreed on the amount of his salary, but he wants a two-year contract and Owner Alva Bradley says he isn't giving any.

With the exception of a few scattered rookies or secondary performers, every other club in the big leagues has satisfied its squad.

Lombardi settled for about $18,000 in a telephone talk last night with Warren Giles, general manager of the world champions. It was understood the agreement included the promise of a bonus if the big backstop hit over .300 this year. He was to leave Oakland, Cal., today for camp.

Earlier this week the Boston Red Sox apparently tamed the turbulent Ted Williams, who agreed to $18,500 and was to bring his signed contract to camp Wednesday. Up until today he still hadn't arrived, however.

Harry Danning of the New York Giants, outstanding catcher of last season, signed for $17,000 and the promise of a bonus Wednesday and immediately was converted into an outfielder.

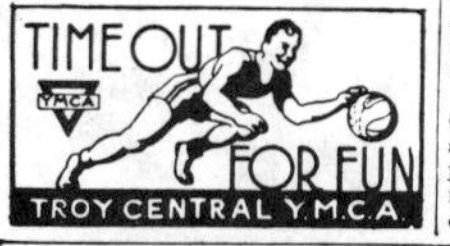

They're Rensselaer's Opponents Tomorrow

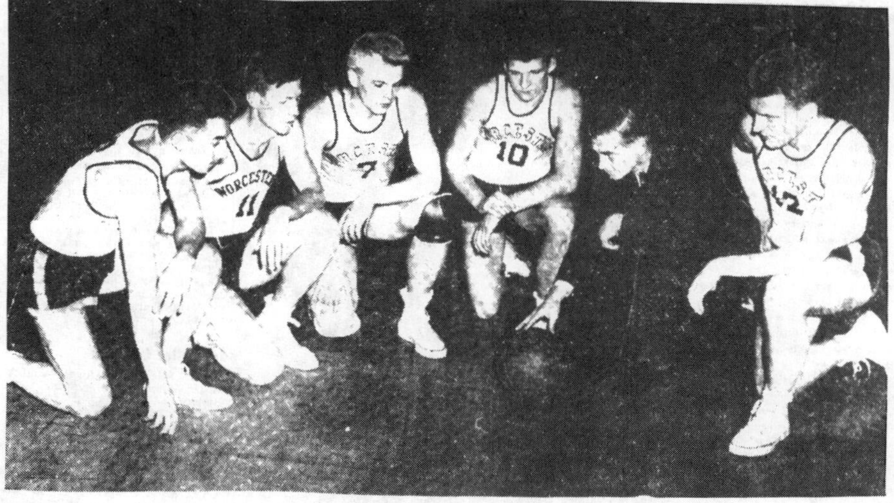

Coach Ivan "Pete" Bigler explains a play to his Worcester Poly quintet which he expects them to use when they face R. P. I. at the '87 gym here tomorrow night.

The game will be the final on the schedule of each team. From left to right are Franny Ongelia, George Knauff, Al Bellos, Bill Stone, Coach Bigler and Bob Lotz.

LA SALLE SEXTET BLANKS BURG HIGH

Scoring heavily in the final two periods, La Salle Institute's varsity hockey squad chalked up its seventh win of the season, defeating Lansingburg High, 4 to 0, yesterday at Knickerbacker rink.

La Salle's first score came when Quinlan came out of a scrimmage in front of the nets to bang home the puck, and early in the third period Pemrick outraced the 'Burg defenses to score twice in rapid succession.

Quinlan closed out the scoring midway through the third session with a goal from far out.

Wednesday the Cadets shaded Cohoes High, 1 to 0, at the Spindle City school's rink.

Don Buckley scored unassisted in the first period to give the Cadets the edge. Stellar defensive work by Ned Dougherty and Pete Doyle and the work of Bud Sanvidge around the nets checked several Cohoes rallies.

BEARS SIGN CATCHERS.

Newark, N. J. (AP)—The Newark baseball Bears of the International League announced yesterday the signing of catchers Charlie Fallon and Dallas Warren. Warren was with the club last year. Fallon played with Knoxville.

Worcester Seeking 9th Victory Here

Worcester, Mass. Worcester Tech, once more on the victory trail after trouncing Massachusetts State last Saturday night, Worcester, 51 to 42, will wind up its season against Rensselaer Saturday at Troy, N. Y.

The Engineers, with less of the height advantage that for three successive seasons made them one of the outstanding court combinations of New England, this year have been in and outers. But they have managed to corral eight wins of the 14 games played so far. Their win over Massachusetts State last week-end was the first since mid-February, but none the less impressive as Tech led from whistle to gun and outspurted every State drive.

Worcester has won from Bates, Northwestern, Assumption, Tufts, Trinity, St. Anselm, Coast Guard and Massachusetts State. On the other side of the ledger are losses to Boston University, Springfield, Brown, Rhode Island State, Clark and Connecticut University. Coach Pete Bigler's charges dropped a few close ones, but were expected to do no better when Co-captain Johnny Wells became ineligible for more than the first half of the schedule. Since his return at mid-year, he has failed to show last year's form, which ranked him as one of the highest scoring centers in New England.

Because of Wells' lapse, Coach Bigler has been using another senior, George Knauff, at center. Knauff's play has been so much faster than Wells', that he has won first call in the last three games and is now considered the first string center.

Coach Ed Donald of R. P. I. put his basketball squad through its paces last night in the final practice session of the season. The boys have been working this week on an offense that can be counted on to click against giant Worcester Tech at '86 gym tomorrow night.

One important factor in tomorrow's game that undoubtedly will spur the Donaldmen to their best effort is the presence of three seniors in the starting lineup and three more in reserve as first-string subs. These men, Coleman, Carman, Knuebel, Mueller, Zirkuly and Madden, with the exception of the latter, have been playing together since their freshmen days and can be counted upon to fight their hardest in their final court appearance for Old Rensselaer.

Another factor apt to play a part in the contest is the loss to Drexel last week which sacrificed all chances for the best basketball year on the Hill since 1923.

A plausible explanation of that defeat is not overconfidence, as has been stated by many, but over-anxiety at keeping alive that chance for a record season. This may account for the many shots last Saturday which almost, but quite, went in.

Incidentally, the Drexel defeat is currently being referred to on the campus as "The Philadelphia Story" in which the unexpected man won.

ROOKIE STARS AS CANADIENS SCORE

By the Associated Press.

The beleaguered New York Americans finally have been mathematically eliminated from their already remote chance at the Stanley Cup playoffs, but the rights of the downtrodden are being preserved by the Montreal Canadiens.

Les Canadiens came up to their final game with the strong Toronto Maple Leafs last night without a single victory and only one tie to show for seven previous matches this season.

They had a rookie goal-tender, Paul Bibeault, who had been signed out of the amateur ranks just a few hours earlier. But they thrilled 9,533 Montreal fans with a 4-3 triumph to show that it could be done.

Bibeault was nervous at the start and let the Leafs whip away to a 3-1 lead in the first period, but once he settled down the youngster shut Toronto out. Late in the second period he was nothing less than brilliant in rebuffing the Leafs while his team was two men short because of successive penalties, and this performance was justly rewarded.

WIN COVETED TITLE.

Toronto, Ont. (UP)- Skip "How" Palmer and his Alberta rink were on their way back to Calgary, Alta., today with the coveted MacDonald's Brier Tankard and the 1941 Dominion curling championship title. The Alberta four captured the granite crown after a decisive 11-8 victory over A. H. Wakefield's Manitobans in the final round of the Dominion bonspiel at the Granite Club here last night.

Wrestling Results

By The Associated Press.

Reading, Pa. Jim Londos, 202, Greece, defeated Max Krauser, 235, Poland, (43:00).

BOYS' CLUB WILL SPONSOR TOURNEY

The 14th annual amateur basketball tournament sponsored by the Troy Boys' Club will be held March 24 to 29, George Ray, physical director at the State Street club announced alst night.

The tournament will be open to teams of high school age and 16 are expected to enter. Entry blanks may be secured at the Boys' Club and must be returned not later than 9 p.m. Wednesday, March 19. Complete details can be obtained from Mr. Ray at the Boys' Club.

Last year's winner was the Lansingburg Boys' Club and the champs are expected to defend their title. Runner-up was the Unique squad composed of former Troy High School stars.

Teams entered in last year's tournament, some of which are expected to compete in this event, include the Stillwater Clowns, Watervliet Garnets, Cohoes Potshots, Rowe Cleaners, Cohoes Independents, St. Mary's of Waterford, Service Company, Showmuts, Panthers, Clipper Crafts, Shamrocks, McGowans, F. L. V. of Mechanicville, Coleman Clippers and Marras.

Junior and intermediate tournaments sponsored by the Troy Boys' Club in recent years have been very successful, drawing outstanding young clubs from all sections of Northeastern New York.

This year's event is expected to attract all of the district's outstanding high school stars and competition should be keen.

Pairings for the opening round of play will be announced in the near future.

CONN LANDS KAYO ON DANNY HASSETT

Washington, D. C., (UP) Light Heavyweight Champion Billy Conn of Pittsburg scored a fifth-round knockout victory over Danny Hassett of Philadelphia last night.

Conn, who meets Joe Louis for the heavyweight title in June, had little trouble with Hassett during the first four rounds and ended the bout after 35 seconds of the fifth with a stinging left to the head.

Hassett tried to rise at the count of eight but his handlers pulled him to his corner.

(Other Sports on Page 30.)

Getting Ready For ABC Tourney

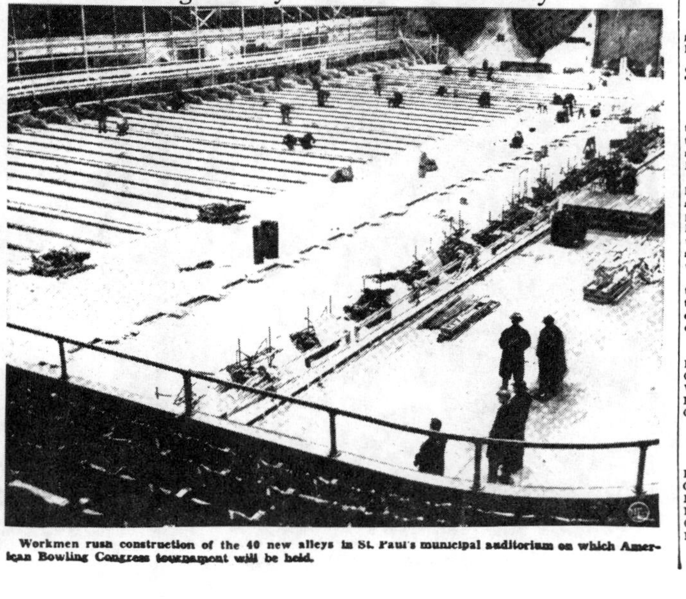

Workmen rush construction of the 40 new alleys in St. Paul's municipal auditorium on which American Bowling Congress tournament will be held.

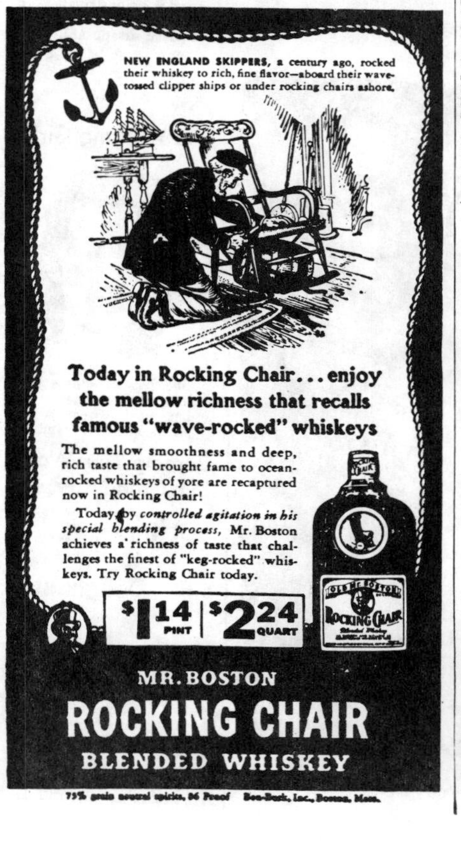

STENGEL CLAIMS BOSTON INFIELD BEST DEFENSIVELY

San Antonio, Tex. (AP) Old Casey Stengel's weather-beaten face wrinkled into a smile for the first time since the rains came.

"Nope, they won't be knocking anything through our infield this season not through those kids."

Old Casey, the keeper of the Boston Bees, was speaking of what most baseball wise men insist will be the greatest defensive infield in the major leagues, come summer.

"Youth, speed, great arms and hustle that's my infield," quoth the mighty Casey. "Defensively, they'll be as good as anything in either league.

"Now you take Eddie Miller out on shortstop. Ground balls just run into his glove. He's a sure shot fielder got that class on every play. He's the kind of kid who attracts your attention the minute you walk into the park.

"Second Base Now there's a boy, Carvel Rowell. He hit .305 last season and batted in 58 runs besides doing a good job out there around second base. Hits into a double play like Hornsb, back in his prime. You know sweeps that throw to first across the letters on his shirt. Miller and Rowell knocked off more double plays than any combination in the league last year.

"Our boy Sebastian Sisti on third looks good. He's a smart boy out there and he didn't hit so badly.

"Of course we feel like there isn't a better fielding first baseman in either league than Babe Dahlgren. I haven't seen him play too much, but they tell me he is smooth. He should round out a pretty tough defensive infield."

The old warrior's happiness over getting Dahlgren wasn't concealed. He figured the Bees came up with quite a prize when they bagged the New York Yankee's successor to Lou Gehrig the other day.

Rain has kept Dahlgren from showing too much in workouts, but Stengel commented:

"He's had a chance to get in a couple of days infield work and I like him. He's class."

Dahlgren is the oldster of the combination at 29 years. Miller is 24 (he's the chatterbox who amazed the critics last season by popping 13 home runs in the Boston park, a difficult feat because of the depth of the fields and the wind currents); Sisti, 20, and Rowell, 26.

Doughty little Miller banged in 79 runs last season with his .276 average. The combination of Miller, Rowell and Sisti accounted for 171 runs batted in.

Old Casey isn't so sure but what maybe that tight infield will make his Bees a little rowdier than the seventh place club of last year.

VULTURES WIN IN PLAYOFF AT YMCA

The Vultures came from behind in the closing moments of the game to nip the Eagles, 40-39 in the first playoff game in the senior house league last night at the Y. M. C. A.

Trailing by two points at intermission, the Vultures came back strong in the third period to knot the count and finally won out as the game was drawing to a close.

Burke and Riley with 12 and nine points respectively, were high for the winners while Turino was outstanding for the Eagles with 21.

Monday the Celtics play the Clan Lads and the winner of that contest meets the Vultures. The first game Monday will be at 7:30 p.m.

VULTURES.

	F.G.	F.B.	T.P.
Burke, rf.	5	2	12
Kreegan, lf.	2	1	5
J. O'Brien, c.	2	0	4
M. O'Brien, rg.	1	0	2
Malone, lg.	2	4	8
Riley, lg.	4	1	9
Totals	16	8	40

EAGLES.

	F.G.	F.B.	T.P.
Turino, rf.	8	5	21
McLaughlin, lf.	3	1	7
Frawley, c.	4	0	8
Andrews, rg.	1	0	2
Fennell, lg.	0	0	0
Murphy, rg.	0	1	1
Totals	16	7	39

Referee, Cahill. Scorer, Montgomery. Score at half time, 21-19, Eagles.

ST. PETER'S UPSETS EAGLES A. C., 33-23

St. Peter's Juniors, preliminary team all season to the Eagles A. C., turned the tables on the latter in a special game last night at St. Peter's Lyceum, 33 to 23.

The Juniors built up a six point lead in the first half and kept a safe distance in front by the simple expedient of silencing the Eagles' two biggest guns, Don Caswell and Jackie LeMay. Caswell scored only two points and LeMay was blanked.

Jim Graham was the big gun in the upset, scoring ten points for the Juniors. "Ap" O'Connell had eight. Coonrad and Wilcox scored eight each for the Eagles.

EAGLE A. C.

	F.G.	F.B.	T.P.
D. Caswell, rf.	0	2	2
Coonrad, lf.	4	0	8
Wilcox, c.	4	0	8
LeMay, rg.	0	0	0
Graves, lg.	2	1	5
Totals	10	3	23

ST. PETER'S JUNIORS.

	F.G.	F.B.	T.P.
K. Caswell, rf.	2	2	6
O'Connell, lf.	3	1	7
McGrath, c.	3	0	6
Healey, lg.	2	0	4
Graham, rg.	5	0	10
Marcil, lg.	0	0	0
Totals	15	3	33

Today's Sport Parade

BY HENRY McLEMORE.

Daytona Beach, Fla (UP) Sir Thomas More must have had a grudge against sports writers when he conceived Utopia because no where on that blessed and imaginary island does he have a place for Gene Sarazen.

What would sports writing be without a Sarazen?

Talk about a baby without a mother, a ship without a rudder, or an owl in the land of the midnight sun, let's talk about a real tragedy. What if Sarazen had not been gifted with his fantastic imagination, his willingness to let it run wild at any time, and his ability to perform the spectacular at just the right moment for himself and the sports writers?

Let the head lines on the sports pages get a little dull and the sawed-off, psuedo farmer from Connecticut moves in with his vocal chords and golf sticks to remedy matters. It was to oblige a sports writing pal who needed a story that Sarazen sprung his celebrated demand for larger golf cups. He swears he scored his famed double eagle in the masters' tournament to give needed publicity to the tournament sponsored by his friend, Bobby Jones.

And consider the national open tournament last year. What would Lawson Little's victory have been worth if Sarazen hadn't tied him and prevented him from scoring a walk over over the disqualified Oliver? He gave Little the satisfaction of winning it the hard way in an 18-hole playoff. Only a couple of days ago Sarazen took a hitch in his knickers, which he bought in England in the days of the feather ball and which simply won't wear out, and caused most of the excitement in the Miami four ball tournament. He didn't play half as well throughout the tournament as did his partner, Benny Hogan, but at the crucial moment he rolled in a putt from just this side of Pittsburg for an eagle. It was the most spectacular shot of the tournament, and he would make it.

Heaven only knows the number of things he has praised and condemned in golf during the past 15 years to make stories for newspapermen and publicity for himself.

With the same tongue with which he advocated larger cups because putting was too difficult, he suggested to me the planting of flowers and shrubbery on the greens to make putting, which he said had become entirely too simple, more complicated.

One month he was attacking the Ryder cup team matches with England as pure nonsense, and the next month he was posing alongside the rail of the Aquitania as he sailed to play on the Ryder cup team.

What he has said about his own organization, the P. G. A., would fill two books. One book would be devoted to praise for that organization and its works, and the other to condemning it down to its fifth assistant corresponding secretary.

He has openly urged his fellow golfing professionals to boycott the United States open until the first prize money was raised to some more substantial sum. While carrying on this fight he was also waging a battle to force the U. S. G. A. to pass a law which would make all former open champions automatic qualifiers in the U. S. open, such a law would save Sarazen the trouble and, as he admits, the risk, of having to qualify each year.

Sarazen's lovely inconsistency of mind, coupled with his consistent brilliancy of performance on the golf course, are two of the things that keeps us sports writers hoping that he will outlast even those brown knickers of his.

MICHIGAN DEFENDS BIG 10 TRACK TITLE

Lafayette, Ind., (INS) The University of Michigan's seven-year stranglehold on the Western Conference indoor track crown will be at stake tonight and tomorrow in the 31st Big Ten indoor meet at the University of Purdue's new fieldhouse.

For the first time since they began their championship parade in 1934, the Wolverines this year are given little chance to win the team title, with Indiana's star-studded squad considered the top-heavy favorite.

MOVE UP TO THIRD.

Buffalo (UP) The Buffalo Bisons lifted themselves into a third place tie in the Western Division of the American Hockey League last night by vanquishing the New Haven Eagles, 4-3, in Memorial Auditorium.

14 THE TIMES RECORD, TROY, N. Y., MONDAY EVENING, MARCH 10, 1941.

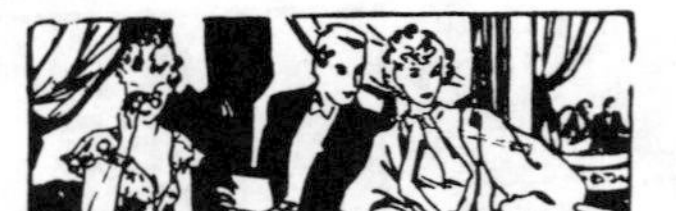

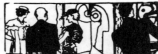

Society News

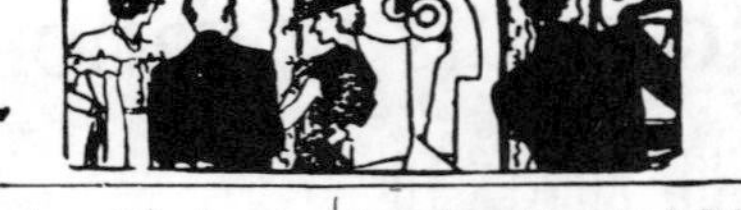

Second Lenten Luncheon To be Conducted

The parish women of St. Paul's Episcopal Church will hold the second in a series of Lenten sewing sessions and luncheons tomorrow at the Martha Memorial Guild House. The women will meet in the morning to sew for the Instructive District Nursing Association.

The guest preacher for the noonday Lenten service will be Rt. Rev. Theodore R. Ludlow, D.D., Suffragen Bishop, Diocese of Newark, who will also be a guest at the luncheon.

The chairman is Mrs. Donald A. Douglas, who will be assisted by Mrs. David W. Houston, jr., Mrs. R. Stanley Thomson, Mrs. Leslie W. Rolfe, Mrs. Arthur Willink, Mrs. James L. Thompson, Mrs. John P. Ramsey, Miss Alice King Potter, Mrs. L. H. Baker, Mrs. Charles P. Ferguson, Mrs. Charles M. Connolly, Miss Charlotte C. Battin and Mrs. Harold E. Blashfield.

Mrs. Hanley Honored by Sister

Mrs. Charles B. Meeson of Melrose was hostess recently at a surprise miscellaneous shower in honor of her sister, Mrs. William Hanley, the former Miss Ina Boyne. Refreshments were served from a table decorated in pink and white and centered with a bouquet of sweet peas.

The guests were Mrs. Bessie P. Amyot, Mrs. Edgar F. Gebhardt, Mrs. Preston K. Jones, Mrs. Robert J. Hayes, Mrs. Mae Joy, Mrs. Samuel J. Stewart, Mrs. Lancelot Dearborn and Miss Marion Stewart of this city, Mrs. Arnold Nible and the Misses June and Joan Meeson of Melrose.

Miss Abrams' Wedding

Miss Betty Bradley Abrams, daughter of Mrs. Elizabeth S. Bradley of Arlington, Vt., a former resident of Cambridge, and John T. Cleghorn of Mount Vernon were married Saturday at 4 p.m. in St. Luke's Episcopal Church at Cambridge. Mr. Cleghorn is the son of Mrs. Susan Embury Cleghorn and the late Dr. Carl Cleghorn of Manchester, Vt., and Miami, Fla.

Rev. Frank H. Frisbie, rector of St. Luke's, performed the ceremony. Miss Lucille Ferguson of Cambridge was maid of honor and John Clark of Manchester best man. Theodore Bradley of Boston, a cousin, gave the bride away.

The couple will live in Mount Vernon where Mr. Cleghorn is in business.

Guest at Luncheon

Miss Kathleen M. Ahearn of Watervliet, a bride of the near future, was recently entertained at a luncheon at the Aquarium restaurant by the office force of the Prudential Insurance Co.

On Southern Wedding Trip

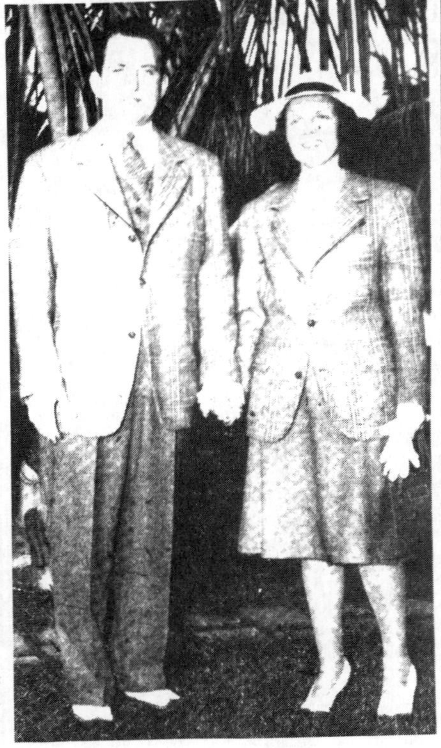

Mr. and Mrs. Ralph F. Passonno are pictured at Fort Lauderdale, Fla., where they are spending part of their wedding trip. Mr. and Mrs. Passonno were married Saturday, Feb. 22, at St. Francis' Church in this city. Upon their return north this spring they will make their home in Buffalo. Mrs. Passonno is the former Miss Dorothy J. Shannon, daughter of City Treasurer John F. Shannon and Mrs. Shannon. Mr. Passonne is the son of Mrs. Fred J. Passonno of Cleveland Heights, Ohio.

Student Here To Wed Indiana Girl

Mr. and Mrs. Trygve Storm of Fort Wayne, Ind., announce the engagement of their daughter, Miss Harriet Marie Storm, to Rudolph Chauncey of this city, son of Mr. Chauncey Kurz of this city son of Mr. and Mrs. Harry Kurz of Youngstown, O. No date has been set for the wedding.

Miss Storm attended Wittenberg College, Springfield, O., where she became a member of Gamma Phi Beta Sorority. She is active in her sorority alumnae affairs and in the College Club, Fort Wayne branch of the American Association of University Women.

Mr. Kurz also attended Wittenberg College and is now a student at Rensselaer Polytechnic Institute, where he is a member of Beta Theta Pi fraternity.

Three Groups To Hold Joint Session

Members of the Troy Chapters of Junior and Senior Hadassah and the Business and Professional Group of that organization will hold a joint meeting at 8:30 p.m. Wednesday at the Jewish Community Center. Mrs. David G. Weisberg will preside.

The Business and Professional Group and Junior Hadassah will present a program including a group of Purim songs and dances and a skit.

A ceremony has also been planned to celebrate the 29th birthday anniversary of Hadassah, woman's Zionist organization, founded by Henrietta Zold for the purpose of carrying on medical and child welfare work in Palestine. A request has been made for donations of yarn to be used for Red Cross work carried on in Palestine by Hadassah.

A social hour will follow and Mrs. Samuel Levy will act as hostess.

PERSONAL

Joseph R. Feeney, jr., of 179 Ninth Street is ill at the Troy Hospital.

Mr. and Mrs. Herman Grethen have returned home after spending two months at Hollywood, Fla.

Mrs. Louis E. Kolo of 2421 Lavin court has just returned from a four weeks' trip to Miami, Fla., and Havana, Cuba.

Mrs. Helen A. Kaperka and daughter, Miss Anne C. Kaperka, have left for Johnstown, Pa., to spend two weeks visiting relatives.

Mr. and Mrs. Walter J. Shannon of 426 First Street are home from a motor trip to Miami, Fla. They also spent a week in Havana, Cuba.

Miss Elaine L. Harrison or 574 Sixth Avenue, this city, attended the formal dinner-dance of the Omicron Gamma Omega fraternity of Moravian Colleg, Bethlehem, Pa., Saturday evening at ... Common Manor, Wind Gap, Pa. She was the guest of Morrell E. Grigg, of Bangor, Pa., a senior at Moravian College, president of the fraternity, and captain of Moravian's championship football team. Miss Harrison is a student nurse at St. Luke's Hospital, Bethlehem, and is the daughter of Mr. and Mrs. Fred Harrison.

To Appear Here

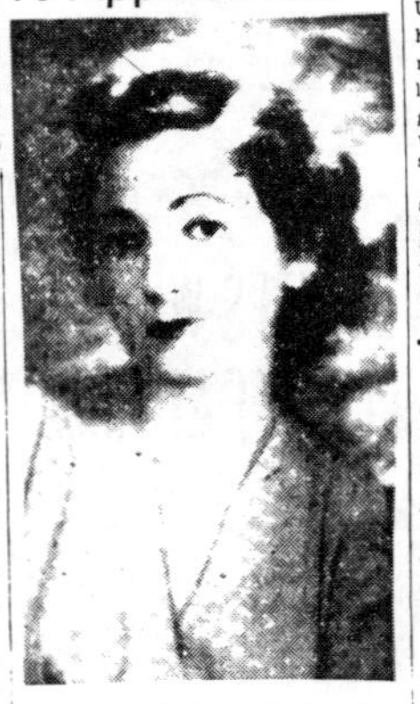

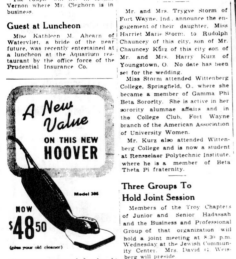

Pictured above is Anastasia Kirby, well-known Boston writer and monologuist, who will be presented at the Troy Woman's Club Wednesday afternoon in a program of "Character Sketchings of Her Own Creation." In addition to children's books and sketches Miss Kirby has written articles and stories for several magazines and newspapers. She founded "Young New England" in Boston, which she now directs as a cultural, educational and entertainment center for boys and girls

DELAWARE'S ANCIENT BLUE LAWS IGNORED

Wilmington, Del. (AP) Although still in effect Delaware's ancient Sunday blue laws under which 498 persons were arrested a week ago were disregarded yesterday.

Four bowling alleys and one dance hall in the Wilmington Area and other business whose operators were arrested last week were open as usual.

The State Legislature passed a bill Friday repealing the old colonial law permitting only work of "necessity" on the sabbath and Atty. Gen. James Morford had announced no one would be molested.

The bill, which Gov. Walter W. Bacon is expected to sign today, provides for local option whereby each incorporated city or town will decide for itself what Sunday activities will be permitted.

CATHOLICS TO BEGIN WAR RELIEF DRIVE

Washington (AP)—A nationwide campaign among American Catholics for funds for relief of suffering and distress abroad was announced yesterday by the Bishops' Relief Committee.

The announcement, made through the National Catholic Welfare Conference, said a special appeal would be made in most dioceses on Sunday, March 30.

"The decision to have a single fund-raising campaign was made," it added, "in the interest of efficiency and economy, as well as for the avoidance of the multiple appeals to church members."

In some parts of Australia ... of cattle are shipped to market in huge freight planes.

Troy Y.W.C.A. Clubs Join In Observance

When the Business and Professional Girls' Clubs of the Troy Young Women's Christian Association of which Miss Marion Way and Miss Florence Lawler are presidents, join with the clubs of Albany and Schenectady tomorrow in Albany, the event will be one of 500 programs held for "Nation-Wide Observance" throughout the United States, with more than 60,000 young women participating. The theme will be "Vitalize Democracy."

This will be the 14th annual nation-wide observance and will emphasize the world-wide affiliation of these business groups. Messages have been received already from clubs which send greetings out of China, Canada, South America, New Zealand and Australia, while others which have sent them in former years are now hindered by the war.

Members of the local clubs going to the Albany meeting will participate in the discussion following the main address of the evening by Glen Jackson of the State Department of Welfare, using the theme of the meeting for his subject. This theme was selected by the National Council of the organization, as the first step in a three-year program, adopted last April in the assembly of several hundred delegates who met in Atlantic City at the same time the National Board of the Y. W. C. A. held its biennial meeting there. In addition to the social and recreational activities which the Troy clubs take part in at the "Y," they are attempting to equip themselves for leadership through the democratic processes of the United States.

This agency is a member of the Community Chest and Council of Social Agencies in Troy.

Social Plans Complete

The Women's Auxiliary of Beth Israel Synagogue has completed plans for the mah jong social to be held tomorrow evening.

Daughters Plan Supper

The King's Daughters of the United Presbyterian Church will have a covered dish supper tomorrow at 6:30 p.m. in the church lecture room for members and guests. Mrs. Frederick L. Greenwood will preside at the business sessions.

Thurday at 2:30 p.m. the Woman's Missionary Society will have its annual election of officers at the home of Mrs. J. B. McIsaac, 27 Lansing Avenue. Mrs. Henry C. Martin will preside.

To Have Meeting

The Woman's Auxiliary of Noble-Callahan Post will have its monthly business meeting today at 8 p.m. at the Hall-Rand Building. Mrs. Thelma Warren will preside.

ABOUT TOWN

LEAVE TODAY

Mr. and Mrs. R. Oakley Kennedy, jr., left today for Atlanta, Ga.

ENTERTAIN AT TEA

Dr. James H. Donnelly and Mrs. Donnelly entertained yesterday afternoon at a small tea for Mr. and Mrs. Robert E. Coburn.

AT PALM BEACH

Mrs. Chester I. Warren and Miss Anna T. Shields are vacationing at Palm Beach, Fla.

Bride-Elect Of April

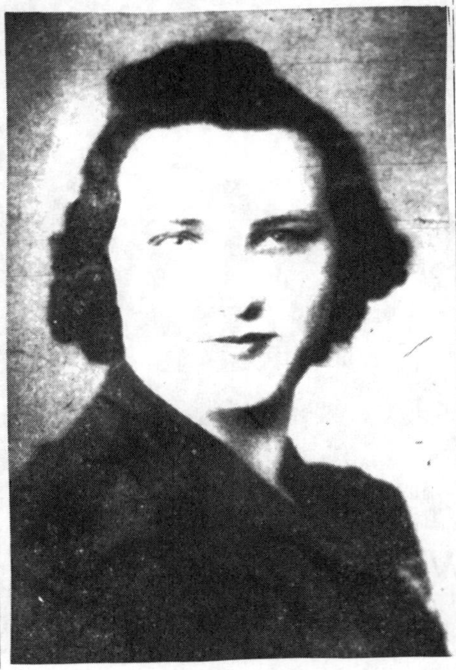

—Louis Kurz Photo.

Mr. and Mrs. William E. Yaiser of 40 Ferry Street, announce the engagement of their daughter, Miss Mary Virginia Yaiser, to James Sheridan Allen, son of Mr. and Mrs. James H. Allen of 3245 Sixth Avenue. The wedding will take place Sunday, April 27, at St. Mary's Church.

Engaged

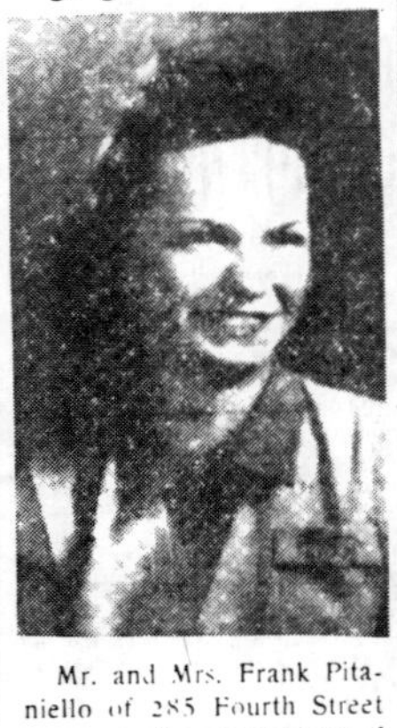

Mr. and Mrs. Frank Pitaniello of 285 Fourth Street announce the engagement of their daughter, Miss Dorothy Pitaniello, to Thomas Patregnani, son of Mr. and Mrs. Amedeo Patregnani of Waterford. The wedding will take place April 20.

Division To Meet

The Red Cross Division of the Troy Woman's Club will meet Wednesday at 10 a.m. in the auditorium of the Manufacturers National Bank. Mrs. W. H. Jarvis is in charge of the work.

COMMITTEES NAMED TO MAKE PLANS FOR TRI-CLUB DANCE

Miss Elaine Schroder, general chairman, and Miss Mildred Geddis, cochairman of the St. Patrick's Shamrock Shindig Dance, being sponsored by the Tri-Y Club of Lansingburg High School to be presented Friday at the school gymnasium, have appointed the remainder of their committees.

Decorations will be in charge of Marjorie Aston and Nancy Romp. Their assistants will be June Bohrer, Esther Roberts, Dorothy Hicks, Helen Larkins, Jean Whitman and Dorothy Roux.

The music committee includes Miss Lois Lallman, chairman; Miss Betty Mower, cochairman, and the Misses Gloria Phillips and Dorothy Wakely, assistants.

They have secured Dick Shannon's orchestra and are arranging their selected dance numbers. Dance programs will be selected by Miss Lois Hutchinson, Miss Ethel Johnson, Miss Gertrude Beattie and Miss Helen Conboy. Refreshments are being arranged by the Misses Joyce McLean, Joan Lewis and Eleanor Fitzgerald.

Miss Sallie Brennan has charge of tables for games.

Celebrate Birthday

Mr. and Mrs. Robert R. Tamm of 2422 Lavin Court entertained Saturday evening in celebration of Mr. Tamm's birthday anniversary. The guests were Mr. and Mrs. George L. Wallace, Mr. and Mrs. Walter A. Bonesteel, Mr. and Mrs. Clifford Bonesteel, Mr. and Mrs. George S. Finkle, Miss Margaret J. Finkle and Arthur Bulius.

The evening was spent at games followed by refreshments with a birthday cake forming the table centerpiece along with cut flowers and candles.

Vicinity Club To Hear Health Officer

The Woman's Club of Valley Falls and Vicinity will meet Wednesday at 2:30 p.m. at the home of Mrs. Jeanne Beecroft in Schaghticoke. Dr. Frank E. Coughlin, district state health officer, will be the speaker. His topic will be "Cancer Control."

Mrs. Beecroft is program chairman and has arranged a musical entertainment of Irish melodies.

The refreshment committee is made up of Mrs. Sadie Foster, Mrs. Margaret Crink, Mrs. Lovette Button, Mrs. Flora Hill and Mrs. Margaret Coleman.

In Ballet Concert

Miss Alice K. Rainey, daughter of Dr. John J. Rainey and Mrs. Rainey, a student at Georgian Court College, Lakewood, N. J., presented a ballet solo yesterday afternoon in a ballet drama concert given by students at the college.

SYCAWAY.

The annual meeting of the women's organizations of Memorial Methodist Church will be held Wednesday at 6:15 p.m. Yearly reports will be received from treasurers of all societies, following a covered dish supper.

Mrs. Wallace Bryce will preside at Christian Service for Women's session. Mrs. Denton R. Bryce has arranged a program of entertainment. Mrs. Fred J. Schoonmaker, president of the Philosophians, and Miss Lillian Miller, president of the Excelsior group, will have charge of the supper.

Wednesday at 7:45 p.m. a midweek church service for men will be held in the Brotherhood room. Wednesday at 8:30 a meeting of the church finance committee is scheduled.

Friday at 5:30 p.m. Group 2 will serve a fish supper at the Church House with Mrs. William B. Patton and Mrs. Albert E. Bleckner as cochairmen. Friday at 7:15 p.m. the Business Grils' Group will meet at 7 p.m. Miss Lois Bryce will have a party in the Brotherhood room for her class.

Lenten Devotions.

Religious instruction for school children of the Church of Our Lady of Victory will be held Wednesday at 3 p.m. At 7:30 p.m. Wednesday Lenten devotions will include recitation of the Rosary, benediction of the Most Blessed Sacrament and a sermon by Rev. Thomas Barrett of Haines Falls. Friday at 7:30 p.m. Lenten devotions will include the Stations of the Cross and benediction of the Most Blessed Sacrament.

Personal.

Mrs. Alec Gailey of Genessee Street underwent an operation at the Samaritan Hospital Saturday.

Thomas, James and William Azer of Utica, former residents of this section, were week-end guests of Mr. and Mrs. Ashley and family of Lee Avenue.

Mr. and Mrs. John Duncan and sons, John and Kellar, of North Lake Avenue have returned from a three weeks' stay at Killarney, Fla., where they were guests of Mr. Duncan's parents, Mr. and Mrs. Robert Duncan.

Plan Food Sale.

The Ladies' Auxiliary of the Church of Our Lady of Victory has planned to hold a food sale and New England dinner Saturday at the Catholic Club House on North Lake Avenue. The food sale will open at 10 a.m. and the dinner from 11:30 a.m. to 2 p.m. Mrs. Clark Partell is general chairman. Mrs. George R. Weber will have charge of the dinner and will be assisted by Mrs. George T. Ahern and Mrs. Harry Culkins. The proceeds are for the church building fund. The following will canvass the parish: Mrs. John J. Rainey, Mrs. Bertram P. Kavanagh, Mrs. John T. McNamee, Mrs. James J. Sheedy, Mrs. William E. Cashin, Mrs. Paul W. Hook, Mrs. Stephen J. Johnson, Mrs. Joseph Trank, Mrs. Daniel Carhart, Mrs. James McKiernan, Mrs. James O'Brien, Mrs. August Frank and Mrs. James J. Sheedy.

A variety of home baked pastries, bread, beans and salads will be solicited for the patrons.

Russell Sage Students Hold Annual Upperclass Prom

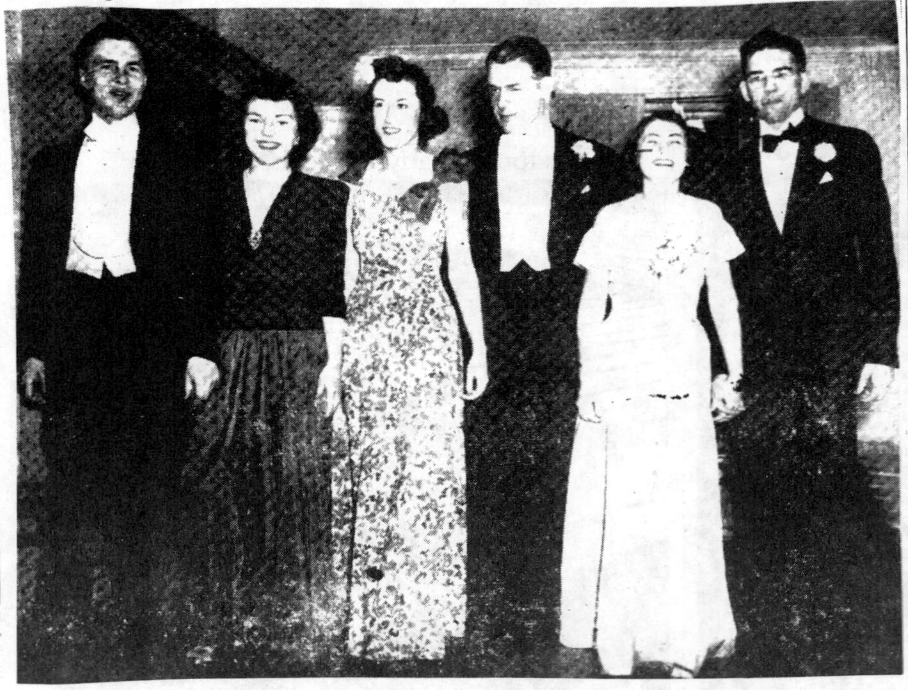

MacGregor Tuttle, Betty Kingsbury, Helen Himes, Paul H. Jones, jr., Lorraine Mershone and Edward Freiburghouse, left to right, are shown entering The Hendrick Hudson ballroom where the Upperclass Prom of Russell Sage College was staged Saturday night.

Here's the Cast of The Times Record's Swell New Serial

The Heiress

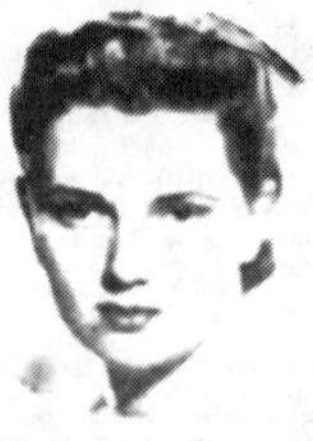

She runs away from millions to seek love and adventure as a salesgirl in the store she owns.

The Business Man

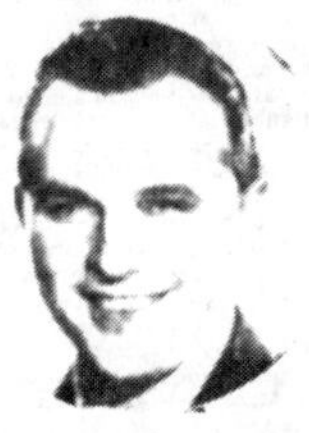

He hates wealthy glamor girls, thinks they should be chloroformed —until he falls in love.

The Count

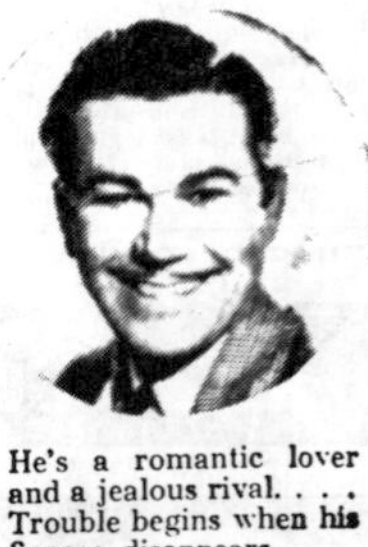

He's a romantic lover and a jealous rival. . . . Trouble begins when his fiancee disappears.

The Working Girl

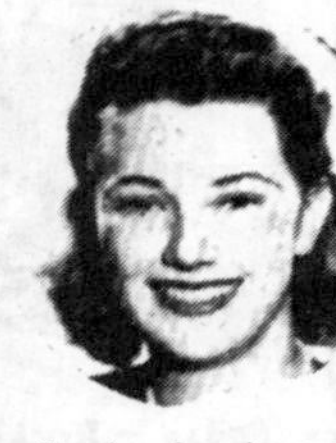

She has happiness and love until the secret of her past threatens to wreck all her dreams.

Coming Your Way In a Grand Romance

Dollars to Doughnuts

Beginning Tomorrow in The Times Record

A New Value ON THIS NEW HOOVER

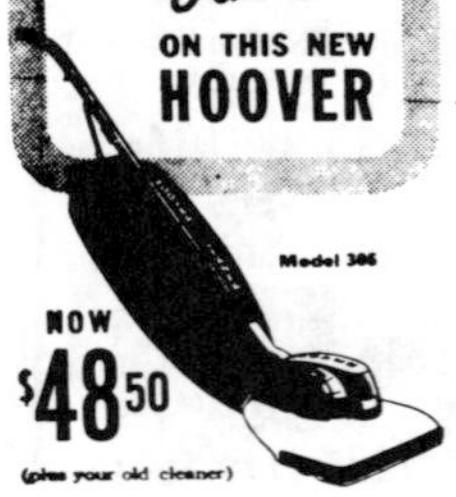

NOW $48.50 (plus your old cleaner)

Cleaner money never before bought as much cleaner value as we are offering in this late-model Hoover with ultra-modern design and ultra-modern conveniences. Call or phone for immediate delivery or pre-purchase trial. Cleaning tools for small additional sum.

FREARS

WET BLANKET A COLD'S ATTACK

And as sure as you breathe you'll give head cold miseries the air.

Just 2 drops Penetro Nose Drops instantly start you on the open-nose way out of cold-stuffiness. This famous 2-drop way of heading off head colds' misery often prevents many colds from developing.

And remember, free and easy breathing takes the kick out of head colds—helps cut down the time these colds' miseries hang on and on. Use Penetro Nose Drops. Generous supply, 25c.

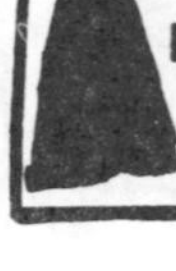

TO-HIRE
Evening Gowns
Dinner Gowns
Wraps
Bridal Gowns
Veils, Etc.

Bride & Gown
RENTAL SHOP
462 BROADWAY
ALBANY, N. Y.
Opposite Postoffice
Tel. 4-6555

Marketing·Cooking·Service

Economical Meal Makes Tasty Dinner For Two

This week's dinner is not especially one that can be prepared in the wink of an eye, but is for the day you feel like puttering around the kitchen and filling the house with savory smells of cooking. However, it is an economical meal, economical in cost that is, and appetizing in appearance and taste.

The main course is Stuffed Cabbage Rolls, served along with mashed potatoes and shredded green beans. As an appetizer you might serve a fruit cup made of little apple balls, cubed pineapple and halved red grapes and for dessert a deep dish cherry pie. Like the sound of these things? Complicated? Not at all—it only looks that way.

For the main course you need cabbage, of course. Buy a small firm head—you will need very little of it for this meal, but the rest will do for slaw or for cabbage soup or scalloped cabbage another day—or two or three days. Chopped meat, good old hamburger is also needed—one-half pound. Buy also one-half pound fresh string beans, a can of sour pitted cherries and a small can of cubed pineapple. If no apples are on hand buy one large red one—a Delicious or Jonathan and half a pound of red grapes. You will have some of these left over, however.

About an hour and a half before dinner, peel potatoes and drop them into cold water. Shred the beans and drop them in cold water also. Make the pie crust and put it in the refrigerator to chill. Halve and pit the grapes and mix the other fruits for the fruit cup which also goes into the refrigerator to chill.

Stuffed Cabbage Roll.

Separate 5 large cabbage leaves from the head of cabbage leaving them whole. Cover these leaves with boiling water and boil for 3 to 5 minutes, then drain them and let them cool while mixing the filling. Mix ½ pound finely chopped beef with ¾ teaspoon salt, 1 tablespoon minced onion, 1 large slice bread squeezed through cold water, a little pepper, ½ teaspoon grated lemon rind and ½ teaspoon poultry seasoning, 1 well beaten egg yolk (save the white to mix with mayonnaise or use as a meringue for a dessert the next day). Blend thoroughly. Spread out the cabbage leaves and put a large spoonful of the filling in each one. Fold over the ends and then roll up like a jelly roll. Fasten the ends with two toothpicks. Sprinkle the rolls with a little flour. Melt 1½ tablespoons butter or shortening in a saucepan, put in the rolls and brown them slightly. When browned, add hot water to barely cover them and drop in a bouillion cube. Cover and cook slowly for 45 minutes.

Deep Dish Cherry Pie.

Sift ¾ cup flour with ½ teaspoon each salt and baking powder. Rub

Chicken Mousse Loaf Has Colorful Garnish

in ¼ cup shortening and when blended, add 2 tablespoons very cold water or just enough to make a stiff dough. Chill before using. Put 1½ cups canned sour cherries with ¾ cup juice in a small deep baking dish, add 1-3 cup sugar and mix lightly. Roll out the pie crust to fit the top of the baking dish—or use individual casseroles. Cut two slits in the crust and bake the pie in a moderate oven for 25 to 30 minutes or until the crust is well browned. Serve warm plain or with hard sauce.

Cook the shredded beans in boiling salted water for 15 to 20 minutes, then drain and season with salt, pepper and butter.

Potatoes will be more fluffy when mashed if you use hot milk instead of cold with them.

Dinner For Two Features Fillet Of Flounder

Here is a dinner menu using fish that should win you words of high praise! Like the menus we have given in this column for the past few weeks, this may be prepared without much effort, and even if you do not have much skill —forty minutes should be about enough, or fifty minutes at the most.

Fillet of flounder forms the main course, and you will need in addition a small can of mushrooms, a sprig or two of parsley and some fine, stale breadcrumbs. The menu:

Tomato Juice With Hot Cheese Canape
Fillet of Baked Flounder
New Potatoes Au Natural
Chopped Spinach With Egg Garnish
Honeydew Melon   Coffee

Mashed potatoes may be substituted for the boiled new potatoes if the latter are too expensive, and sliced oranges or a mixture of grapefruit and oranges, or any preferred canned fruit instead of the melon. Fresh, canned or frozen spinach will require 1 pound of the fresh vegetable, a package — frozen spinach or 1 can. If frozen or canned spinach is used, there will probably be enough left over for cream of spinach soup for another day. Frozen spinach will cook in 8 minutes—canned needs 5 minutes cooking in the juice in the can. Put an egg in to boil with the potatoes.

New Potatoes

New potatoes, well scrubbed and cooked for 15 minutes without peeling, are delicious just now and go well with the fish. Of course they may be scraped or peeled before serving if you wish. The order of preparation for the menu given is as follows:

Put tomato juice in coldest part of refrigerator to chill.
Wash spinach if fresh vegetable is used.
Put water on to boil for vegetables
Scrub potatoes.
Light oven for the fish.
Prepare fish according to recipe below.
Put potatoes on to boil.
Prepare four canapes ready to toast.
Prepare spinach on to cook.
Prepare melon ready to serve.
Toast canapes.
Serve dinner.

Spinach Timbales.

1 cup cooked spinach
¼ teaspoon salt
1 teaspoon onion juice
2 eggs, well beaten
2 tablespoons butter
Dash of pepper
1 1-4 cups milk.

Chop spinach, force it through a coarse sieve. Add seasonings, onion juice, well -beaten eggs, milk, and melted butter. Stir just enough to blend. Turn into greased molds or custard cups, set in a pan of hot water which has been lined with several thicknesses of brown paper, and bake at 350 degrees for 30 minutes, or until a clean, dry knife inserted into the timbale comes out clean. Unmold and serve at once.

◆ Chicken Mousse With Deviled Eggs.

2 cups boiling chicken broth
¼ cup cold broth
4 tablespoons gelatine
2 cups finely chopped or ground, cooked chicken.
1 cup finely diced celery
1-4 cup finely diced sweet pickle
1-4 cup finely diced green pepper
1 pimiento chopped
1 cup salad dressing
¾ teaspoon salt
1-4 teaspoon white pepper
Dash of cayenne
3 to 4 tablespoons lemon juice
1 cup heavy cream, whipped
Deviled egg halves
Parsley, or celery leaves
Cucumber slices, tomato slices.

Soften gelatine in the cold broth. Dissolve thoroughly in boiling stock. Chill until syrupy or almost jelly-like in consistency. Combine chicken, celery, pickles, pepper and pimiento. Add mayonnaise, seasonings and lemon juice. Add thickened gelatine mixture. Fold in the whipped cream. Taste and add more seasonings if necessary. Mixture should be rather highly seasoned since it is served quite cold. Pour into a mold rinsed with cold water. Chill. Unmold. Garnish with greens and deviled eggs. Slice to serve. Yield: Five to six cup mold.

Deviled Eggs.

1 tablespoon cream or mayonnaise
½ tablespoon vinegar or lemon juice
½ teaspoon mustard
¾ teaspoon Worcestershire
3-8 teaspoon salt
¼ teaspoon pepper.

Cut hard cooked eggs in half crosswise or lengthwise. Remove yolk and put through a sieve. Add seasonings and beat until smooth and fluffy. Refill shells. Garnish top with chopped chives, parsley, paprika, caviar. Add other seasonings such as onion juice, caviar, anchovies, ham, sardine, cheese to the yolk mixture is desired. Yield: Six eggs.

New Tricks Go Well With Old Favorites

Make 2 cups white sauce and add to it 1 cup grated American cheese, 1 teaspoon dry mustard or 1 tablespoon prepared mustard, ½ teaspoon paprika, 1½ teaspoons Worcestershire sauce and salt to season. Pour this over boiled macaroni just before serving and serve very hot with sweet pickles and crisp cabbage salad. Bake tart shells in very small muffin tins and when done fill with strawberry jam. A combination of salmon and oysters served as a deep dish pie is "news" for dinner. This is one of the nicest fish recipes we have used in a long while so I hope you will try it. The salad is made by arranging sections of grapefruit and wedge-shaped pieces of firm sweet apples in rows on a bed of watercress, escarole, lettuce or endive. Use a few of those little fed colored preserved grapes for garnish and serve the salad with a thin cream mayonnaise it takes the place of dessert. Soak 1 cup dried white beans for next day's soup.

Cook finely cut cabbage, the beans, a slice of bacon and an onion in 2 quarts of water for several hours. Add any other vegetables if they are handy and thicken with a little barley, fine noodles or rice added half an hour or more before the soup is done . . . Broil thin slices of liver that has been dipped in salad oil and serve very hot with a gravy that contains lots of sauted onions . . . Make rich pie crust and roll it quite thin. Cut in squares and roll half a ripe banana up in each square, leaving the ends open—roll the banana first in a mixture of powdered sugar and cinnamon. Bake in a hot oven and serve hot with lemon sauce.

Crab Salad.

1 cup crabmeat (fresh or canned)
¼ cup diced celery

ECONOMICAL!

1 spoonful of IVANHOE goes as far as 2 spoonsful of ORDINARY DRESSING IN FLAVOR AND APPEARANCE

2 hard-cooked eggs, diced
2 tablespoons chopped sweet pickles
1 tablespoon lemon juice
¼ teaspoon salt
¼ teaspoon paprika
½ cup mayonnaise

Mix half of mayonnaise with other ingredients. Chill, serve on squares of jellied tomato juice and top with rest of mayonnaise. Garnish with sliced pimiento stuffed olives.

FIREMEN PUT OUT FLAMES IN GRASS IN HOUSE GARDEN

Seventieth Anniversary of Women's Foreign Missionary Society of Baptist Church Observed.

HOOSICK FALLS

A telephone call to the Seth Parsons Steamer House yesterday shortly after 1 p.m. brought the fire truck and the call-men of the Fire Department to Mechanic and White Streets, where a grass fire had broken out in the garden back of the house occupied by Mr. and Mrs. Joseph McGarvin and family. The fast-spreading blaze was extinguished in about 15 minutes by the use of the truck's storage water tank and booster pump.

Anniversary Party.

Peggy Leonard observed the sixth anniversary of her birthday at her home, 15 Mechanic Street, with a party. She received many gifts. The birthday cake was made by her aunt, Mrs. Edward Riel of Bennington, Vt. Mrs. Riel was a guest this week of her mother, Mrs. Rose Ward, in this village.

Philathea Meet.

The Philathea Class of the First Baptist Church Wednesday made plans for the sending of Easter gifts to the shut-ins and older members of the church. It was announced that the next meeting, April 16, will be of the social variety with a supper served at 6:30 p.m. by a committee composed of Mrs. Paul Stewart, Mrs. John Howland, Mrs. James Waddell, Mrs. Edmond L. Worden, Mrs. Harold Baker, Miss Ophie Wilson and Mrs. Tibbits Sweet.

Gleaners' Society.

Mrs. Charles Piritz, the new president of the Gleaners Society at West Hoosick, presided at her first meeting Wednesday afternoon at the home of Mrs. Forrest Sherman with 23 members of the society in attendance. Mrs. Piritz gave an outline of the group's work for the ensuing year including missionary and White Cross activities, also a hobby exhibit. A program in observance of the seventieth anniversary of the Woman's American Baptist Foreign Missionary Society, the theme of which was "A New Lease on Life," was presented by Mrs. Ernest Habel, Mrs. Henry Street, Mrs. Robert Abbott, Mrs. Piritz, Mrs. Lester Pine, Mrs. Harold Pine and Mrs. Charles Eddy. Refreshments were served by Mrs. Ralph Griswold and Mrs. Edgar Hunt.

70th Anniversary Noted.

The seventieth anniversary of the Woman's Foreign Missionary Society of the Baptist Church was observed by the Baptist Woman's Society yesterday in the Philathea room in the First Baptist Church with a special program that was presented under the direction of Mrs. B. Legus Hunt in the form of an historical sketch by a cast composed of Mrs. Edward Nolt, Mrs. Ira Cornell, Mrs. James Tuttle, Mrs. Clayton Sherman, Mrs. Osmund Eldredge, Miss Ophie Wilson, Miss Ethel Van Wert and Mrs. James Smith. The program also included a vocal solo by Mrs. Frank S. Stevens accompanied at the piano by Miss Lucina Herrington. During the business session plans were launched for the society's annual turkey dinner which, as in the past, will be served the public in the fall; also for a rummage sale to be conducted later this spring.

Brevities.

The Mapletown Happy Helpers' 4-H Club will continue on the tools and fabrics project tomorrow afternoon at the home of its leader, Mrs. Edward Emmons, East Hoosick.

The meeting of the new club in the Baptist Sunday School scheduled for Wednesday, was postponed to the same day next week at 7:30 p.m. in the church hall.

The annual spring rummage sale of St. Mark's branch of the Girls' Friendly Society will be conducted tomorrow at 2 p.m. in St. Mark's parish house. It will include clothing, household goods, rugs and chintz curtains.

A public card party will be sponsored by Clan MacIntosh, Order of Scottish Clans, tomorrow evening in the Clan's rooms in the Leary Block. Five hundred, pitch and pinochle will be played and there will be prizes and refreshments.

Nine members of the Hoosick Falls Home Bureau met yesterday afternoon in the American Legion rooms in the Municipal Building with Miss Mabel A. Milhan of Troy, Rensselaer County Home Bureau agent, and discussed with her the tentative project program of the unit for the coming year. Plans were started for a food lesson April 23 at 11 a.m. in the Legion rooms, also for a talk May 14 at 2 p.m. by a state health nutritionist.

STARTING THE HUGE ARCH OF STEEL OVER THE NIAGARA RIVER: View taken from the Canadian side showing the present stage of construction of the new Rainbow Bridge near the Niagara Falls Gorge. The 950-foot arch of the structure, the longest hingeless arch span in the world, will be completed next August.

Y.M.C.A. GROUPS HAVE REGIONAL SESSION TO PLAN ANNIVERSARY

The Troy Y. M. C. A. was represented yesterday at a conference meeting in the Schenectady Y. M. C. A. of two groups formed by associations in northeastern New York to participate in the centennial advance program which will mark the 100th anniversary of the founding of the Y. M. C. A. movement.

Trojans attending were Stephen H. Sampson, member of the board of directors; Verne C. Braddon, general secretary; and John C. O'Melia, membership secretary.

The conferring groups discussed Y. M. C. A. finances and general agencies and dealt with problems of inter-relationship between local, state and national associations and the finances involved in these sections.

John E. Long, safety superintendent for the Delaware and Hudson Railroad, served as conference chairman, with Mr. O'Melia as secretary. Victor Larsen, representing the national Y. M. C. A. program, was the speaker.

SMITH PROPOSES SINKING FUND FOR STREET REPAIRING

Seventeenth Ward Alderman Seeks to Have Portion of Parking Meter Revenue for Work.

A proposal for creation of a sinking fund to build up reserves for street improvement expenses was placed before the Troy Common Council last night by Alderman Henry E. Smith, Seventeenth Ward, with the announcement that if his plan is legal it will be followed by the necessary legislative steps.

The sinking fund would be created, Alderman Smith proposes, with a percentage of the moneys collected in Troy's parking meters.

The arrival of spring, he told the council, finds the city again faced by the same problem where streets are concerned.

"Each year," he declared, "We put a specified sum in the budget for street repairs but we know it is never enough. All the time our streets are getting worse. They are wearing thin and it is only a question of time when they must be resurfaced."

He spoke of the condition of alleys, especially, which at this time of the year are hub-deep in mud. These conditions would be eliminated, he declared, if a fixed sum was set aside, in addition to budget appropriations, to carry out a comprehensive repair program.

"I intend to press for legislation to care for this situation," Alderman Smith said. "I intend to ask that a share of the money from parking meters be put aside for street repairs and replacements. I don't speak just for my own ward but for the entire city.

"The money in those meters comes from the motorists. Surely they are entitled to consideration. I think this is a good way to get our streets fixed."

His plan received the immediate approval of Alderman Jesse J. Smith, Sixteenth Ward, whose pleas for street improvements have enlivened meetings for several years.

Answers to Cranium Crackers

Questions on Page 8.

1. True. The White, Black and Red Seas all touch the 35th and 40th meridians.
2. False. Sofia is capital of Bulgaria; Sollum is a city in Egypt; Salonika is the second city of Greece.
3. True. Troops from Union of South Africa (British) are now advancing in Italian East Africa.
4. True. Southernmost point of British Isles is on 50th parallel, but all of U. S. lies below this line.
5. False. The Aral Sea is in Russia. The Aegian lies between Greece and Turkey.

Joins the Army

Veteran luxury liner, the S. S. Washington, formerly owned by United States Lines, arrives at Brooklyn army base to enter service as a troop transport. Sentry stands guard.

U. S. Weather Bureau.
Tonight—Rain, cooler.
Tomorrow—Fair, cool.

THE TIMES RECORD

FINAL EDITION

Series 1941—No. 110. (Entered as Second Class Matter at the Postoffice at Troy, N. Y., under the Act of March 3, 1879.) TROY, N. Y., FRIDAY EVENING, MAY 9, 1941. (Published Daily Except Sunday) PRICE THREE CENTS

Workman Dies As Flames Sweep Through Vacant Troy Warehouse

BRITISH BOMBERS BLAST GERMANY IN TERRIFIC RAID

More Than 300 R. A. F. Planes Drop 1,000 Tons of Bombs on Berlin, Hamburg, Bremen and Emden

BY THE UNITED PRESS.

Great Britain's growing air force seized the offensive today in the largest bombing attack of the war against Germany while Royal Air Force night fighters again took a heavy toll of Luftwaffe bombers over England.

The battering British attack in which more than three hundred planes dumped about 1,000 tons of bombs on Hamburg, Bremen, Emden and Berlin coincided with new blows and counter-blows on the warfront in the Middle East, with the British reporting rapid progress against pro-axis troops in Iraq.

The Iraqi were cleared off the plateau from which they had shelled the R. A. F. air base at Habbaniyah and were pursued by British imperials toward Baghdad.

German Raider Sunk.

In the Indian Ocean, the British reported that they had sunk a German armed merchant raider, believed to have been the speedy former transatlantic liner Hansa, 21,131 tons, rescuing 27 British prisoners and capturing 53 German seamen.

The British cruiser Cornwall, a 10,000-ton vessel, suffered slight damage in its encounter with the Nazi raider but its fighting ability was not impaired.

It was believed that the raider was armed with six 5.9-inch guns and torpedo-tubes and that she was fitted for mine-laying. The speed of the raider was thought to be about 19 knots and it was believed the vessel may have carried an extra size crew of about three hundred men to enable it to put prize crews on seized ships.

The scanty reports given out by the admiralty indicated that the German ship gave battle when intercepted by the British cruiser.

Suez Canal Bombed.

German and Italian planes bombed the Suez Canal, reporting that an attack of several hours had done heavy damage to installations and railroads in the area toward which the axis campaign in the Mediterranean is aimed.

Rome reported that British airplanes had bombed the big axis base at Benghazi, on the Libyan coast, but that Italian torpedo-carrying planes had scored hits on a British battleship, an aircraft carrier, two cruisers, a destroyer and three large merchant ships in three attacks on a Mediterranean convoy that appeared to be carrying reinforcements to the Middle East.

The R. A. F. bombardment of Germany, including minor thrusts at Berlin, appeared to be a result of the long uphill fight toward aerial parity with the luftwaffe American-built airplanes were understood to have figured prominently in the attack, which extended 600 miles from British bases to Posen, Poland, and was admitted in Berlin to have been a strong bombardment as far as Hamburg and Bremen were concerned.

Shipping Bases Ablaze.

Tens of thousands of incendiary bombs and tons of Britain's dread new high explosive bombs were showered upon Bremen, Hamburg and Emden, causing devastation comparable to the heaviest Nazi attacks on Britain, the air ministry reported.

New-type American craft partici-

(Continued on Page 6)

BOMB WIPES OUT FAMILY.

London (AP)—Three generations of one family—three children, their father and mother and their grandfather—were wiped out during the night in London by a bomb which demolished their home.

10 Calls About Station Wagon

PLYMOUTH, 1939 station wagon, fully equipped, in very good condition. Will sell reasonably. Telephone North 323.

The North Troy man who ordered this Classified Ad in The Record Newspapers reports that he received ten inquiries and got a buyer for the station wagon. You can sell your car, truck, trailer or motorcycle the same easy way.

Phone Troy 6100

Where One Man Burned To Death And Two Others Were Rescued Today

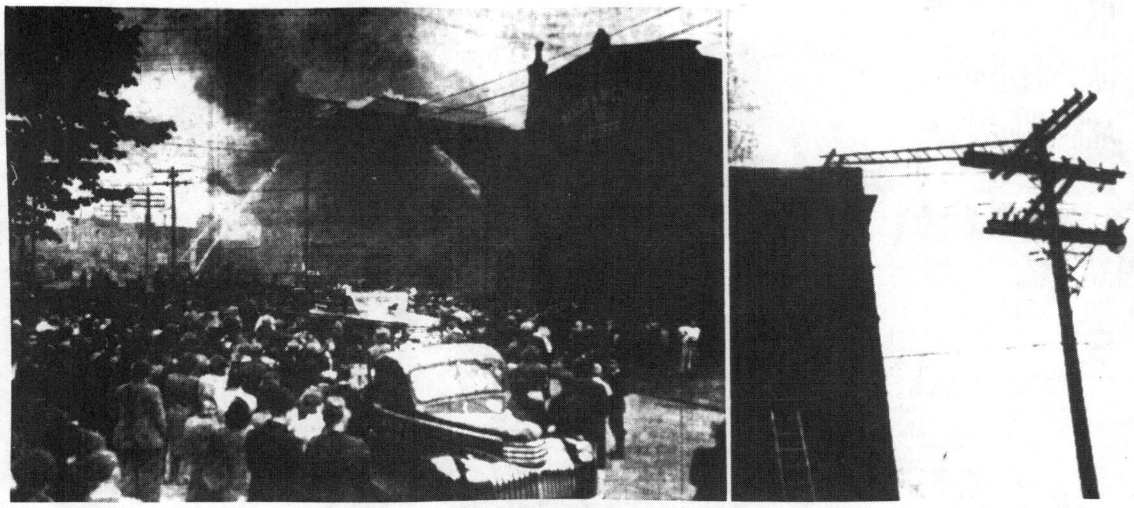

Above, at left, is a general scene of the fire which destroyed the interior of a former paint factory at Liberty and River Streets this morning, taking the life of one workman and threatening the lives of others. High up from the corner of the roof to the power pole can be seen the ladder over which two workmen climbed to safety. The window, second from the corner through which a stream of water is being poured, is the one through which the victim tried to escape and through which his body was taken. At the right is a close-up view of the frail ladder of escape which saved the lives of the two who crept over it to the pole and then climbed down through power wires to safety.

JAPANESE LOSING HOPE OF CRUSHING CHINESE BY FORCE

Tokyo Paper Hints Government May Curtail Hostilities, Adopt More Peaceful Policy.

Tokyo (U.P.)—Government leaders, abandoning hope of crushing China by armed force, are considering a revision of policy under which the scale of hostilities would be reduced and every effort made to promote peaceful conditions and improved trade in Chinese areas now under Japanese control, it was indicated today.

Intimation that the government might soon alter its Chinese policy was given by the Japan Times and Advertiser, a mouthpiece of the foreign office, from which it receives a subsidy.

"Ideas of overcoming this mastodon of nations (China) must have little more appeal, even to the most sanguine of soldierly minds," it said.

Soon after the publication of this editorial, it became known that Kumataro Honda, ambassador to the Japanese-sponsored Nanking regime in China, was coming here next week for conferences on China policy.

"Two-Fold Policy."

The Nanking regime was set up by Japan in an attempt to undermine the Chinese government. It purports to administer Japanese-occupied territory in the name of the Chinese people.

The Times and Advertiser was the medium by which, on April 30, a world "peace plan" was published here which would have given Germany complete domination of Europe and Japan complete domination of the Far East.

Today the Times and Advertiser said that Japan's policy in China was two-fold—to restore peace throughout the country and to develop China as a partner on Japan's Greater Asia "co-prosperity sphere."

"A peaceful China must necessarily mean the termination of hostilities," it said. "Hostilities would cease either by elimination of the cause of friction or the provision of conditions which would assure a basis for orderly living . . .

"The effect of a Japanese conquest over the Chinese government

(Continued on Page 38.)

PARKING PROBLEMS HIT CITY BUSINESS, EXECUTIVE DECLARES

Albany (U.P.)—Disintegration of city business centers unless greater provision is made for parking automobiles was forecast today by Roy Hofford, executive vice president of the State Real Estate Association.

Hofford said that what is needed in every city is "some serious thought to city re-planning that will match the automobile economy."

As business moves to the suburbs, he said, it leaves "depreciated values, tax delinquency and blighted areas in the central district."

"The automobile which has brought about parking problems and congestion is largely responsible for this shift," he said.

Russia Recalls Envoys From Norway, Belgium

Moscow (U.P.)—The Soviet foreign commissariat notified the Norwegian and Belgian legations today that since their German-occupied countries no longer are sovereign states their ministers in Moscow have no official standing.

Norwegian Minister Einar Maseng and First Secretary Ivar Lunde and Belgian Minister Guy Heyndrix and Counsellor Harold Heyman prepared to leave as soon as their affairs are put in order.

FEDERAL RESERVE BOARD MAY CURB "BUYING ON TIME"

Installment Purchases To Be Regulated in Order to Prevent Inflation, Conserve Resources.

Washington (AP)—The Federal Reserve Board disclosed today that it is prepared to curb instalment selling of automobiles and other consumer goods in order to prevent inflation and to conserve industrial resources for the defense program.

The board and a staff of experts, headed by Dr. Carl Parry, has made a study of the problems of "buying on time" and are waiting for President Roosevelt and Price Administrator Leon Henderson to authorize them to seek congressional powers to regulate the business.

The proposed powers would permit the board to say how much should be paid down on articles and how much time consumers should get to pay off the remainder.

If the powers are voted, plans call for applying them immediately to the new and used car financing business. Experts believe that down payments should be boosted above one-third of total price and that the payment time for the balance should be cut down from the present average of 18 months to about a year.

The automobile business was ticketed for initial action, first because it is responsible for about half of the instalment financing in the country, and secondly because automobile plants, labor and materials are needed for the defense program.

Refrigerators, radios, furniture and other expensive consumer items would be next on the list, officials said.

The experts view financing of new houses as the biggest problem after automobiles, but said it was one which might be sidestepped. Although home construction may compete with defense needs for labor and materials, the experts credit it with important social benefits and not that in some areas the defense program, itself, is responsible for large new housing demands.

DENY GREEKS INTERNED.

Sofia (INS)—The official Bulgarian agency today flatly denied reports that distinguished Greek personalities have been sent to concentration camps in Bulgaria by the Germans.

U. S. AIMS TO OUST AXIS AIR SERVICES IN LATIN AMERICA

Sumner Welles and Jesse Jones Directing Drive as Part of Western Hemisphere Defense Program.

Washington (INS)—As a major part of the western hemisphere defense program, the United States government, it was learned today, has embarked upon a far-reaching campaign to wipe out every German and Italian air line in Latin America.

American dollars and diplomacy are being utilized to break the Axis aeronautical hold on South America.

Undersecretary of State Sumner Welles is directing the diplomatic end of the drive. Secretary of Commerce Jesse Jones is providing the dollars to help finance replacement of the Axis air services.

The State Department already has succeeded in talking the governments of Columbia and Peru into ousting the Nazi airlines in those countries.

Efforts now are being made to persuade Brazil, Bolivia and Ecuador to do likewise.

Grave Threat To Defense.

The American government hopes to replace the Axis airlines with services operated and controlled by the nations of this hemisphere. The plan is to have American-made planes piloted by South American aviators fly most of the commercial routes in Latin America. Arrangements are being made to train Latin American aviators in this country.

Existence of the rapidly expanding Axis air services was considered a grave threat to western hemisphere defense, and especially the defense of the Panama Canal.

At one time, German commercial aviators in Columbia were operating within 150 miles of the canal. The German aviators were known to have flown over the canal in recent years and to have photographed the Canal Zone as well as the entire Columbian terrain stretching along both the Pacific Coast and the Caribbean Sea.

German planes being operated in Peru until late last month were Lufthansa machines with a cruising range that could enable them to fly non-stop to the Panama Canal with a load of bombs.

Nazi Planes In Brazil.

Two Junkers JU-58 planes are now operating in Ecuador, within a few hours flight of the canal. There are eight German aviators and four radio mechanics there who are known to be thoroughly familiar with flying conditions in the northern part of South America.

In Brazil, the Germans have more than twenty three-motored Junkers as well as several four-motored Fockewulfs.

In addition to wiping out the Axis airplanes in Latin America, the United States government also is seeking to persuade Brazil to cancel the Italian airline that now operates regularly between Italy and that country.

This Axis air service across the South Atlantic is regarded as a vitally important source of information for Germany and Italy. Mail carried by the line is uncensored and American officials fear it constitutes a regular channel for military and diplomatic secrets concerning the western hemisphere defense program.

Hamilton Complaint Against Burr Found

New York (INS)—A complaint signed by Alexander Hamilton, and naming Aaron Burr among a group of defendants, was found on file in the storeroom of the Federal Court building here today.

The document, written in long hand on heavy parchment and demanding the execution of a deed conveying a huge tract in the Ontario country, was filed Aug. 14, 1799, just five years before Hamilton died of a wound received in a duel with Burr.

SECOND GIRL DIES AS POSSE HUNTS MANIAC SLAYER

Former Convict, Who Shot Sister-in-Law and Companion, Believed Hiding in Desert.

San Bernardino, Calif. (AP)—The second woman victim of a desert shooting, Rose Destree, 17, died today while a posse searched Cable Canyon for the gunman, a reputed ex-convict, in the belief he is hiding there with a man as hostage.

Miss Destree was shot and Mrs. Jean Wells, 20, was killed in El Cajon Desert yesterday by a gunman who first placed the baby of Mrs. Wells in the dead mother's arms before fleeing.

The leader of the searching posse of forty, Undersheriff James W. Stocker, broadcast a statewide order for the arrest of Mrs. Wells' brother-in-law, Alfred Wells, 30, after quoting Miss Destree as saying he was the gunman.

Wells' brother, David Raymond Wells, 24, the husband of the slain woman, has been missing since the desert shooting. Stocker said the Cable Canyon search was prompted by reports that Alfred Wells was hiding in a cabin there with his brother as hostage.

Stocker quoted Miss Destree, a friend of Mrs. Wells, as saying Alfred Wells was angry because his half-sister, Violet Davis left his home and that Wells believed Mrs. Jean Wells helped Violet leave. Violet later was found at her mother's home in Escondido. Stocker identified Alfred Wells as a former San Quentin convict.

NAZIS MAKE SECOND PROTEST TO U. S. OVER SHIP SEIZURES

Washington (INS) — The State Department today received a second and stronger protest from Germany over seizure of two Nazi cargo ships by the U. S. Coast Guard March 30 along with 26 Italian vessels.

The new protest, handed the department by the German Embassy on instructions from Berlin, protested the seizure and also declared that the German government "reserves all rights" in behalf of the ship owners.

It was understood that this reservation, not made in the previous protest, was stated to enable owners of the boats to claim compensation.

HOUSE ECONOMY GROUP PLANS BIG CUT IN SPENDING

Congressional Block Aims at $2,000,000,000 Reduction in Non-defense Expenditures.

Washington (INS)—Details of a program to cut almost $2,000,000,000 from non-defense spending were disclosed today by members of the congressional economy bloc.

The group, moribund during recent defense outlays, has come to life because the administration has made no moves to follow up Secretary of the Treasury Morgenthau's plea for non-defense saving, members declared.

Its program has been worked out by Rep. Taber (R.-N.Y.) ranking minority member of the House appropriations committee, after conferences with both Republican and Democratic leaders.

Proposed Reductions.

It contemplates a drive for the following cuts in non-defense activities:

From relief $800,000,000; from the Civilian Conservation Corps, $250,000,000; from the National Youth Administration, $75,000,000; from farm tenancy, $60,000,000; Surplus Commodities Corporation, $100,000,000; civilian pilot training program, $20,000,000; and miscellaneous small cuts "from many agencies like the Federal Communications Commission, the Securities and Exchange Commission, the Federal Power Commission, etc., $500,000,000.

While some of these funds already have been voted by the House in approving previous appropriation bills, Taber promised that his group "will find ways of getting them back before the members."

Justifies Relief Cut.

Taber said that his group will justify the huge relief cut from an estimated $1,000,000,000 down to only $200,000,000 -"because at the present time they report a shortage of labor and yet go on spending money on the WPA."

On other proposed cuts, the New Yorker said:

"The CCC wouldn't have 75,000 members (it estimates it will have 259,000) if it didn't put on a campaign to get them when men are needed elsewhere.

"The NYA is demoralizing our young folks by soliciting members for private boarding schools and certainly should be cut. The farm tenancy is an absolute racket, setting up new people in business.

"The surplus commodities outfit is going out and buying things at bottom prices and giving them to people who should pay for them. The FSA is a poorly managed and wasteful racket.

"The Army won't recognize civilian air training anyway so that can be cut. For the rest you will find that a good $500,000,000 can be saved by eliminating waste and inefficiency."

LEHMAN SETS HOSPITAL DAY.

Albany (U.P.) — Governor Lehman today recommended observance of the birthday of Florence Nightingale on Monday as National Hospital Day. He called for support of hospitals and interest in their operation.

Clyde Man Killed, Firemen Injured At Two-Alarm Blaze

Trapped Man Beat Frantically on Screened Window in Attempt to Escape, Says Eyewitness.

"I know I will dream of that sight for nights to come," said Miss Minnie Lee Stephens who saw the victim of the River Street fire today beat frantically on the screened window through which his body later was drawn from the inferno of the burning building at Liberty and River Street early this morning.

Miss Stephens in her quiet, Mississippi drawl she came north to be near her brother who is employed at the Watervliet Arsenal told of her horrible experience.

She is employed as bookkeeper for Bernard G. Smith, wholesale meat dealer, in his office at 72 River Street, in full view of one corner of the burned building.

"I was working at my desk," Miss Stephens said, "when I heard the shouts of several men and distinguished the word 'Fire.'

Saw Fire Pierce Roof.

"I thought it might be this building so I ran to the door just in time to see the flames break through the roof of the big building. Two men had laid a ladder out from the corner of the roof to the arms of the electric light line pole on the street corner and were climbing over this on their hands and knees. They slid down the pole to safety."

Miss Lee shuddered as she went on, "Then I saw the third man in the window on the upper floor, second back from River Street, beating at the screen placed over there apparently to prevent the windows from being broken by thrown stones.

"He knocked the screen out, looked down toward the ground and then ran screaming back into the building.

"That's the last I saw of him until the firement hoisted his burned body up from within the burning building and lowered it to the ground.'

The girl's grey eyes showed the effect of that sight as she repeated that she was afraid she never could wipe from her mind's eye the terror on the victim's face nor erase from memory the sound of his screams.

Wants To Forget Sight.

Miss Marion J. Clifford of 10 Larch Avenue, bookkeeper for the Bayer and McConihe Co. in the office of their lumber yard across a sixty-foot lane from the burning building, declared she never had seen a fire spread so quickly.

She, also, heard the shouts of the workmen next door and ran to the window of the office looking out on the burning building and said that the entire rear portion already was a mass of flames

Impregnated, apparently, with amalgamated gum, a paint ingredient, formerly ground in the building before it was abandoned as a factory about ten years ago, the walls and ceiling carried the fire like wicks, she stated, and in a moment the flames were leaping through the roof.

"I could hear the men on the roof call to the one who went down to his death to stay up and those on the ground shouted the same advice but he disappeared from the roof and when I next saw him they were lifting him out the window. Then I turned away.

"The place was an inferno and the smoke billowing from the windows hung heavy in the air until there was a huge cloud over that and this building.

"It was thrilling, at first, but I never want to see such a sight again"

$6,000 Damage When Fire, Caused by Burning Tar, Races Through Building at Liberty Street.

Anthony Ciavonia, about 52 Clyde laborer, was burned to death and three firemen sustained minor injuries as a $6,000, two-alarm fire originating in an overheated asphalt pot heater, swept through an empty three story brick warehouse owned by the R. & E. Feed Co. at Liberty and River Streets, shortly after 10 a.m. today.

While Ciavonia was trapped on the third floor of what is better known as the old Connors Paint Co. gum mixing plant, four Trojans escaped from the building, two of them risking contact with a 2,300-volt high tension wire as they placed a ladder from the top of the building to a street corner power pole and crawled fifty feet to the ground.

Firemen Injured.

The firemen injured are:

Patrick J. Byrne, Central Headquarters, hoseman, treated at his home for slight injuries and exhaustion.

Carl E. Larkin, Central Headquarters, hoseman, treated for minor injuries to one hand.

John Slattery, Central Headquarters, injuries to one hand. He was treated at the Troy Hospital.

The men who escaped from the roof are:

Samuel Clevitz, 377 Second Street.

Martin Miller, 45, R. D. 1, Rensselaer.

Two others working on the first floor over the asphalt pot and who escaped are:

Antoni Villa, 45, rear 1459 Fifth Avenue.

John Alaway, Negro, 146 River Street.

Recently Purchased.

Raymond Ellenbogen, 161 Second Street, who operates the R. & E. Co., distributor of poultry feeds, told police that he had purchased the building on Jan. 1, this year. He said he had hired the five men as laborers to assist in renovating the building in preparation for using it as a warehouse.

Residents of the neighborhood said the old Connors' plant had not been in use for many years.

Ellenbogen, giving a statement to Capt. Michael B. Shea and Capt. Frank J. Connery at the First Precinct, described the circumstances that led to the accident as follows:

Villa was tending an improvised heater, heating asphalt, in the rear of the first floor of the building. Alaway was busy at other work nearby.

Ciavonia was on the third floor. Clevitz and Miller were on the roof where they were "tarring" the roof with the hot asphalt. Villa would hoist the hot pot of asphalt up to Ciavonia on the third floor, with a block and tackle. Then Ciavonia would take the pot of asphalt up a ladder, from the third floor to the roof, to give it to the two men working there.

Out of Control.

Suddenly the fire got out of control and Villa yelled to Alaway to come to his aid.

"It was getting too hot, I could not shut it off, so I yelled over to the other fellow for help,' Villa told police.

Alaway then shoveled sand and dirt on the out-of-control fire, but the flames increased in intensity. In a few minutes the flames leaped skyward, fanned by a draft, and caught hold of the upper timbers

(Continued on Page 19)

MME. CHIANG KAI-SHEK GIVEN CHINESE DRESS BY MRS. ROOSEVELT

New York (U.P.)—A Chinese dress made in American was en route to Mme. Chiang Kai-Shek in China today, the gift of Mrs. Eleanor Roosevelt.

The President's wife visited a preview of Chinese legendary print dresses to be sold here for Chinese relief, picked out one for the Chinese generalissimo's wife, and bought two for herself.

Mrs. Roosevelt enclosed a gift card in the package thanking Mme. Chiang for her kindness to James Roosevelt, who recently visited Chunking.

The note read:

"I hope you will enjoy this dress made here from the material being sold for Chinese relief. You were so kind to my son and we deeply appreciate it.

"With every good wish for this good cause and to you and Mr. Generalissimo. Believe me,

"Cordially yours,
"ELEANOR ROOSEVELT."

"SMALL BOYS BEWARE!"

North Bellmore, (INS) — After washing his neck so vigorously that he sprained it, 14-year-old Paul Bauer was in Meadowbrook Hospital today.

ESPOSITOS REFUSE TO EAT OR SPEAK

Ossining (INS)—The "mad dog" Esposito brothers, William and Anthony, who are doomed to die in the electric chair next month for a New York City payroll slaying, today were reported by Sing Sing Prison officials to be on a "speech-and-hunger" strike.

Authorities were undecided whether the brothers plan to try to cheat the chair by starving themselves—a scheme which would be met by forced feeding—or are putting on another "act" in keeping with the insanity pose they kept up throughout their trial.

The Index

THE WEATHER
U. S. Weather Bureau.
Tonight—Fair, frost.
Tomorrow—Fair, warmer.

THE TIMES RECORD

FINAL EDITION

Series 1941—No. 113. (Entered as Second Class Matter at the Postoffice at Troy, N. Y., under the Act of March 3, 1879.) TROY, N. Y., TUESDAY EVENING, MAY 13, 1941. (Published Daily Except Sunday) PRICE THREE CENT

Hess Fled Reich After Break With Hitler Over Russia, British Report

FLIGHT OF HESS VIEWED BLOW TO GERMAN MORALE

Diplomats Believe Desertion of Hitler's Closest Friend Must Lead to Uneasiness in Reich.

Washington (A.P.)—Diplomatic circles seemed agreed today that the melodramatic flight of Rudolf Hess to Britain would be a great blow to the morale of the German people, no matter what explanation they accept.

Both the official German and the British accounts of the war's strangest episode, it was said, contain elements that can hardly be reassuring to the average man in the third reich.

These sources reasoned as follows:

The German version speaks of Hess's "failing health for years" and raises doubts as to his sanity, at least at the time he decamped. Inasmuch as Hess continued active in important government and Nazi Party affairs almost to the end, the inevitable question arises as to Hess' mental condition for some time past.

In short, the German people may well wonder how long important affairs have been in the hands of a man of dubious mental stability.

"Why This Turnabout?"

The British account shows different seeds of doubt. It represents Hess, long one of Hitler's closest associates, as deserting der fuehrer at the high tide of victory to surrender voluntarily in Great Britain. And it stresses his complete sanity.

Accepted in this light, Hess' flight can only dumbfound the average German, it was said. There never had been any question of Hess' loyalty to Hitler in the past. He had stuck to der fuehrer during the most discouraging days of the Nazi movement. Why this amazing turnabout? Did it mean he saw defeat ahead for the reich? Had he lost faith in Hitler?

Diplomatic quarters here were frankly bewildered as to the complete significance of the entire matter. Apparently authoritative reports reaching the capital, however, agreed on three points: That Hess' identity had been established beyond doubt; that he was perfectly sane, and that he fled Germany for fear of his life.

Information has been reaching London for some time past, it was said, that relations in inner Nazi councils were strained, and Hess' flight was looked on as confirmation of such reports.

Reason For Breach.

A likely reason for the breach, one informed source said, was disagreement over Germany's future military moves, but this makes for a strange denoument. Hess, it was explained, had been usually identified with the so-called left wing of Nazi officials who advocated a knock-out invasion of Britain, whereas the generals and right wing officials favored the Mediterranean and Middle East theater of operations for the present.

If that caused the break, then Hess did the amazing thing of seeking refuge in a country whose conquest he had been urging. However, it was pointed out that England probably was the only place in the Old World where he would be out of Germany's reach.

Whatever the complicated background, the belief here was that British authorities were alive to the possibility of an audacious Nazi trap, or "plant," and would be exceedingly wary in making use of any information he might offer.

But should his good faith be established beyond doubt, it was pointed out, the British would have a wealth of highly reliable and valuable information at their disposal. The only comparable situation would be for one of Churchill's war cabinet to go over to Hitler, it was said.

YOUNG MOTORIST KILLED.

Elmira (AP)—Robert Dubois, 20, Elmira, died yesterday of injuries received when the car in which he was riding crashed into a house at Webb Mills.

These Little Pigs Went To Market!

PIGS—Six weeks old pigs of all kinds for sale. Apply Mrs. P. Fields, Pleasantdale, North Troy. North 443-R.

Yes, a Pleasantdale woman used the Farmers' Market of The Record Newspaper' Classified Section to describe the pigs she had for sale. Of course, she soon had a buyer for them! Sell your surplus stock this same practical way.

Phone Troy 6100
Or Mail Your Ad

King's Friend

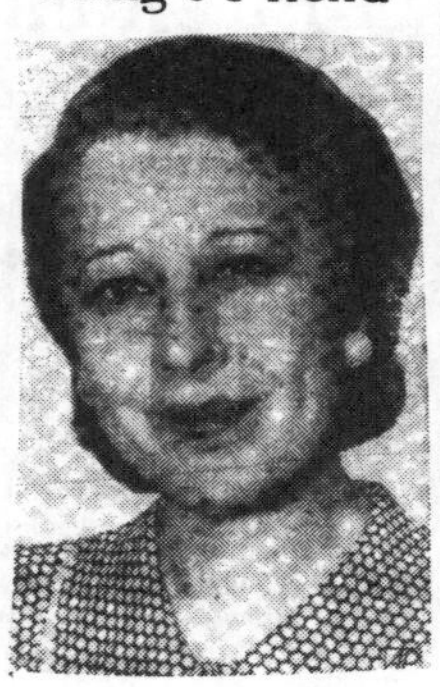

Madame Elena Lupescu, rarely photographed in recent years, smiles at the Belmont Manor Hotel, Hamilton, Bermuda, after arriving there with former King Carol of Rumania aboard the liner Excambion.

BRITISH SHIPPING TOLL IN ATLANTIC HITS RECENT LOW

Sharply Reduced Sinkings in April Reflect Effectiveness of New Defensive Measures, London Says.

London (AP)—British merchant shipping losses in the battle of the Atlantic in April—301,070 tons out of a total of 488,124 tons sunk in all theaters of the war during the month—were the lowest in 11 months, it was announced today.

The month's total previously was included in an announcement Saturday, which placed losses in the year since the Nazi invasion of the low countries at 1,098 ships, totaling 4,734,407 tons.

The sharply reduced sinkings in the Atlantic, authoritative quarters asserted, indicated the effectiveness of counter-measures against Adolf Hitler's air, surface and undersea weapons.

"There are no signs that the results of the great efforts the enemy is making will enable him to attain the quick victory he needs," one highly-placed informant said.

The losses in the battle of the Atlantic, plus 187,054 tons of ships lost in the removal of troops from Greece and in other areas of the Mediterranean, made up the April total.

British, allied and neutral vessels in British service were included in the figures.

Since the war's start the admiralty announced that losses were 1,508 British, allied and neutral ships totalling 6,127,673 tons for a monthly average of 306,354 tons.

Before the April figures were announced, the previous month's low total was in January, when the British announced 306,002 tons were lost.

Asked whether Britain could stand these losses for another year, an authoritative source said: "We are facing the situation with anxiety, tempered with confidence."

COURT DENIES BAIL TO NAZI NEWSMEN

New York (INS)—Manfred Zapp and Guenther Tonn, American managers of Transocean, German propaganda news service, remained at Ellis Island today after U. S. District Court Judge Samuel Mandelbaum dismissed a writ of habeas corpus, and refused a plea for release on bail.

The two men will now be detained at the immigration center on the island until their deportation hearing begins or until they are taken to Washington to be tried on an indictment there charging them with failure to register as alien agents with the State Department.

NAZIS THINK HESS HAD 'DELUSIONS' OF ARRANGING PEACE

Berlin Also Hints Hitler's Associate May Have Been "Trapped" by British; His Family Not Molested.

Berlin (AP)—Rudolf Hess, number three man in the Nazi hierarchy, made his fantastic flight to England because "he appears to have lived under the hallucination that he was still able to bring about an understanding between Germany and England with old English acquaintances," the Nazi Party announced officially today.

A party communique said Hess, second only to Reichsmarshal Hermann Wilhelm Goering as Adolf Hitler's personally-chosen heir apparent, had suffered serious physical disability for years "and recently resorted increasingly to various aids, mesmerizers, astrologers and so forth."

"It, however," the statement added, "also is imaginable that, in the last analysis Hess intentionally was lured into a trap by the British.

Hitler Takes Over Office.

"The National Socialist Party regrets that his idealism fell victim to such fateful delusion," it went on. "This will not interfere with the continuation of the war against England forced upon the German people."

A qualified spokesman said that "the assumption that his curious conduct, which is a deep personal tragedy, was due to mental disorder is the most charitable view to be taken, and that view is to be held in view of the present knowledge."

Hitler, meanwhile, personally took over Hess' party office, formerly known as the "office of the deputy of the fuehrer" and changed the title to "party chancellery."

Germans in responsible position took sharp issue with the British interpretation of events, which challenged the soundness of Hitler's action in designating a man pronounced mentally incompetent as successor to the party leadership after Goering.

"Demoted," Nazis Say.

"What happened 18 months ago (when he was made Hitler's deputy) was that Hess was not promoted to third ranking Nazi," a spokesman said, "but was demoted from second place."

"As deputy to Hitler he would normally have succeeded the fuehrer. But in view of the abilities and temperaments of the available men, Hitler by formal act chose Goering as his immediate successor.

"From the de jure point of view this was an incongruous arrangement, but one now shown to have been fully justified. The fact is that Hess was removed from the position which could have made him immediate successor to the fuehrer."

Hess was described as a man, who in the vigor of his powers, performed great service for the party but was retiring by nature and suffering increasingly from physi-

(Continued on Page 8.)

SYRACUSE JUDGE FORFEITS BAIL OF BARON VON WERRA

Syracuse (AP)—Federal Judge Frederick H. Bryant ordered forfeiture of Baron Franz Von Werra's $5,000 bail today when the German war flier's counsel failed to produce him in answer to illegal entry charges.

"We do not know where he is," Attorney James H. Davies told the court.

Judge Bryant denied Davies' motion to dismiss the complaint against Von Werra, who escaped to the United States from a train en route to a Canadian prison camp.

The flyer, held under $15,000 bond pending deportation proceedings in New York has disappeared and is reported to have fled to Peru.

Hess' Flight To Scotland Causes World Sensation

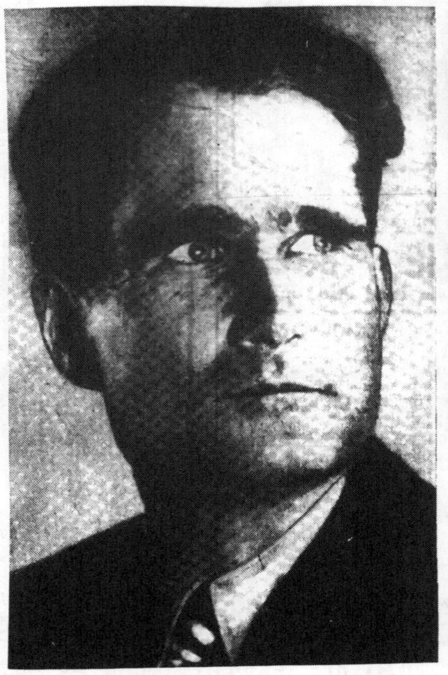

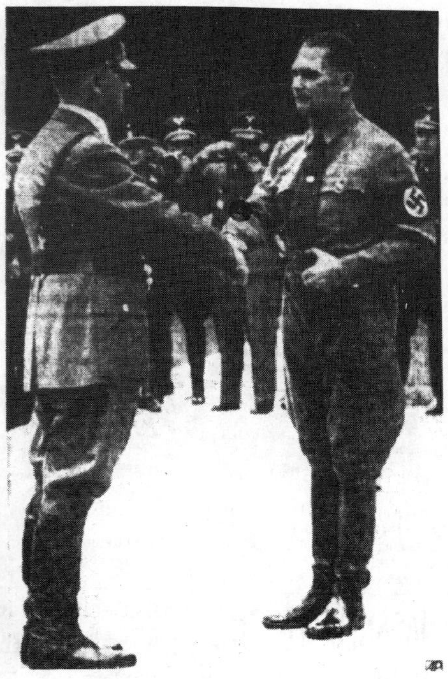

The world today was speculating on the reason for the fantastic flight of Rudolf Hess, above, third most powerful man in all Germany, who parachuted to earth on a Scotland farm after fleeing from the Reich in a German Messerschmidt fighter plane. Hess was one of Adolf Hitler's closest friends and most trusted advisers since the Munich beer hall days when the Nazi party was a fledgling in Germany. Hess is shown in the photo at upper right as he greeted Hitler on the occasion of a Nazi Party rally at Nuremberg, Germany.

J. W. T. MASON, U. P. WAR EXPERT AND AUTHOR, EXPIRES

Noted Writer Suffered Heart Attack After Filing Column Yesterday; Died This Morning.

New York (UP) J. W. T. Mason, United Press war expert and author of books on philosophy, died of a heart attack today at Doctors' Hospital. He was 62 years old.

After writing and filing his famous column "Today's War Moves" at the offices of the United Press yesterday morning Mason returned to his hotel in Manhattan. There he suffered a heart attack. His wife called a physician and Mason was taken at once to the hospital where he died at 3 a.m.

Mason was born in Newburg, Jan. 3, 1879, the son of John A. and Georgiana L. Mason. He was married to Edith Hannah Halbert, daughter of Capt. Frederick Halbert of the British mercantile marine on Feb. 24, 1903. They had one child, Margaret E. H. Mason.

Mason started his journalistic career as a reporter for the Harlem Local Reporter in 1898. Eventually he became European manager of the Scripps-McRae and Publishers' Press Associations and served as European manager of the United Press in 1907-08.

In 1914-18 he was the United Press' war expert. After the World War he wrote on foreign affairs for La Prensa of Buenos Aires and other newspapers and traveled extensively on foreign assignments.

He made a special study of western and far eastern philosophies and religions, lectured widely, and was made an officer of the Order of the British Empire and a member of the Order of the Rising Sun, fourth class, of Japan.

He was associated with many societies and clubs in India, Japan, New York, Washington and London.

He was author of Commercial Progress in the Philippine Islands, Creative Freedom, the Creative East, Kami Nagara No Michi and Sozono Nihon, both written in Japanese. The meaning of Shinto, Shintogan Mita Obei, and the Spirit of Shinto Mythology.

PLAN CONSTRUCTION WORK AT PINE CAMP

Washington (AP)—Two New York State Army posts are among those allocated $3,942,670 by the Army construction of administration buildings, Red Cross recreation buildings, barracks for medical, personnel and ambulance garages.

For Pine Camp, N. Y., $4,750 was designated for an administration building; $39,300 recreation building; $16,600, barracks, and $1,400, garages.

Camp Upton, N. Y., will receive $26,500 for a recreation building.

Scottish Plowman Hero of Moors for "Capture" of Hess

M'Lean Family Says Parachute Visitor Was Cultured Gentleman; Glad to Be Out of Germany.

BY GEORGE H. MILNE.

Glasgow, Scotland (UP)—David McLean, Scottish plowman who "captured" Rudolf Hess with a hay fork, was a hero of the war today and his cottage on the moors a few miles from Glasgow became a center of wide interest.

It was only last night that the McLeans—David, his mother and his sister—knew the identity of the man who came down by parachute near their cottage.

I had heard of the landing of a mysterious German aviator at the McLean farm and I hastened there with pictures of Hess. I put them before a score of people who had talked with him. They identified him long before the London announcement that Hess was the flying visitor.

They also emphasized that he seemed completely in his right mind and that he was glad to be out of Germany.

"Sure, that's the man," McLean said when I showed him Hess' picture.

"No doubt about it," said his mother. "So we had a distinguished visitor after all."

Orderlies at the military hospital to which Hess was taken for a time said that his toenails had been carefully manicured.

The McLeans and others at the farm were thrilled and excited at being the center of a world story.

"We knew when he came into the

(Continued On Page 13)

TOLL CALL SLIPS USED BY STATE IN GRAFT PROBE CASE

Trial of Solomon and Mullens Continued at New York in Burland Printing Action.

The state continued laying the groud-work of its case against William Solomon, Tammany district leader, and Charles H. Mullens, former assistant state comptroller, today, at New York with the identification of numerous telephone toll slips designed to show constant contact between the two defendants, the Associated Press stated this afternoon.

Solomon and Mullens are being tried on charges of accepting $28,000 in bribes and illegal fees in obtaining $750,000 in state printing contracts for the Burland Printing Co., in 1935, 1936 and 1937.

The toll slips, identified by Harrison C. Price, chief file clerk of the bureau of audit and control of the state comptroller's office, showed a sharp increase in the number of calls made by Mullens from his private telephone in Albany, to Solomon and to Charles C. Walsey, president of the Burland Company, before and after July 23, 1935.

It was on this date, the state alleges, that Walsey paid $8,000 to Mullens and Solomon.

Similarly, the toll slips indicated Mullens made numerous calls to Solomon in June, 1936 and June, 1937. Assistant Dist. Atty. Murray Gurfein asserted that $10,000 was paid in each of those months to the defendants by the Burland Company.

Price testified there were 15 calls from Mullens to Solomon between June 17, 1935 and July 31, 1935, in contrast to the remaining five months of that year when there were only 17 calls from Mullens to Solomon.

The witness said there were seven calls from Mullens to Walsey between July 2 and July 22, 1935, and only three calls during the remainder of the year.

BUFALO WOMAN SUICIDE.

Buffalo (UP)—A suicide certificate was issued today in the death of Mrs. Grace Roberta Lens, 24, found shot to death in her suburban home yesterday. Mrs. Lens was chief clerk of the Amherst-Clarence Selective Service Board.

U. S. PLANS TRADE CONCESSIONS TO LATIN AMERICAS

Lowering of Duties on Argentine and Uruguayan Canned Meats Initial Move Considered.

Washington (UP) The United States Government, it was learned today, has decided that substantial economic concessions must be granted the Latin American republics in the interests of western hemisphere defense.

As an initial move in this direction, the government intends to call upon the American people, and especially the armed forces of the nation, to eat Argentine and Uruguayan canned meats, especially corned beef.

A considerable reduction in the tariff duties on these meats is planned under the trade agreements which the State Department has announced will be negotiated with those two countries.

Tariff reductions on nearly twenty other Argentine and Uruguayan products also are contemplated, but the meat concession is considered the most important.

It was this government's refusal to grant concessions on canned beef which led to the breakdown of the trade negotiations with Argentine and Uruguay in January, 1940.

The government now takes the position that the solution of Latin America's economic problems, and especially a lessening of its economic dependency on Europe, can be found only by the creation of new markets for its products in this country.

Tokyo Shocked By Desertion of Hess

Tokyo (INS)—Japanese officialdom was frankly stunned and bewildered today by the strange flight to Britain of deputy Nazi leader Rudolf Hess.

The semi-official newspaper Asahi and the Tokyo Nichi Nichi made no attempt to disguise their shock and surprise. The diplomatic repercussions felt in Tokyo represented the first reaction to the Hess affair among Nazi Germany's axis partners.

Attaches of the German embassy likewise were visibly disturbed. All day long there was an indescribable hustle and bustle in and about the swastika-draped structure.

Although obviously distressed, Japanese circles expressed belief that Hess' flight would not connote a serious internal crisis in the Reich so long as victories continue and Adolf Hitler remains "hale and strong."

Saburo Kurusu, former Japanese ambassador to Berlin who last saw Hess when Germany staged a huge festival in honor of Japan's 2600th anniversary, was considerably shaken.

"Frankly, I felt a greater attachment for Hess than for any other German except Hitler," he said.

"Hess was a different type of man from Goering, Goebbels or Von Ribbentrop. There was something about him that reminded me of an Oriental fighter.

"Hess had a great desire to visit Japan and I sometimes wonder how greatly Hitler allowed himself to be influenced by Hess in reposing trust in Japan."

All Japanese newspapers gave wide prominence to stories of Hess' amazing venture.

U. S. Marines Quell Shanghai Outbreak

Shanghai (UP)—United States Marines were called out to restore order today after a battle between international settlement police and pro-Japanese Chinese police in which an American and nine other persons were wounded.

The fight started when settlement police halted an automobile containing Mrs. Ho Sze-Pao, wife of the chief of a special police branch office in the Shanghai "badlands," for a routine search as the car arrived at the barricade separating the "badlands" and the settlement.

Jurisdiction over the "badlands" at the edge of the settlement is disputed and Chinese followers of Wang Ching Wei, head of the Japanese-sponsored Nanking regime, have set up a special police force to dominate the area.

Mrs. Ho's bodyguards fired on the settlement police at the barricade without explanation. Police returned the fire. Reinforcements rushed up from both sides of the barricade and settlement police arrested 16 Wang Ching Wei men, but not until A. Wickdahl, an American probationary sergeant of the settlement police, Mrs. Ho, two of her bodyguards, a Chinese municipal policeman and five others had been wounded.

GERMAN LEADER SEES MISSION TO "SAVE HUMANITY"

No. 3. Nazi Chieftain Suffers Ankle Fracture in Parachute Landing; Bitter Foe of Communists.

BY THE UNITED PRESS

A split with Adolf Hitler over increasing German collaboration with Soviet Russia was advanced by British sources today as an explanation of the war's weirdest melodrama—the flight of Rudolf Hess by warplane from Germany to Scotland.

The No. 3 Nazi leader, dropping by parachute from a Messerschmidt fighting plane over Scotland Saturday night, was known to be a bitter foe of Communism and British sources reported that his first words to a Scottish farmer after he parachuted to earth ten miles from Glasgow were:

"I have come to save humanity."

British quarters reported that Hess' intense hatred of the Communist regime and his belief that Hitler had embarked the Third Reich along a path of increasing collaboration with Russia well might prove to have motivated the Nazi leader's strange flight to Britain.

Hess, responsible British sources said, appears "to have got religion."

Bullet Holes in Plane.

Hess, it was reported in Glasgow, narrowly escaped being shot down by British Spitfire fighters and the tail of his plane was found to be punctured by many bullet holes when it crashed on the estate of the Duke of Hamilton, a few miles from Glasgow.

Prime Minister Winston Churchill told the House of Commons that he did not desire to speak today regarding the arrival in Britain of Rudolf Hess but he promised a full statement in the near future.

"This is one of those cases in which the imagination is somewhat baffled by the facts," Churchill said.

Some members of Commons warned Churchill to bear in mind—in his handling of Hess—"this gentleman's record of devotion to the evil genius of Europe."

Hess was reported in bed in a hospital "and writing a great deal."

His only injury was a small fracture of a bone in his ankle. The ankle was encased in splints and bandages.

Hess was resting comfortable and was being attended by a British officer, London reports said.

Hitler Takes Over Duties.

In Berlin, Hitler took over personal command of the Nazi Party and unexpectedly addressed a conference of party leaders, who demonstrated what was described officially as "an overwhelming resolution and will to victory." Nazi spokesmen, apparently anticipating a public declaration by Hess, said that his words could not be accepted because of his mental condition and possibility that he would speak under duress. Nazi sources said that "we know that British rulers will make every crude misuse of this situation."

"Who knows," the spokesman added, "by what ugly means some sort of a confession may be extracted from him. We cannot even know if he actually makes any statements which may be credited to him."

Only Slightly Injured.

The first official to recognize the mysterious airman as Hess was a young detective officer in the Renfrewshire police.

"I should know you," the detec-

(Continued on Page 8.)

HUDSON BOY KILLED BY NEW YORK TRAIN

Hudson (UP)—Joseph Lesson, 7, died accidentally when he was struck by a projecting part of the New York Central's crack Twentieth Century Limited and hurled against a signal post, authorities ruled today.

Lesson was standing on the right-of-way with a companion watching a freight train when the train sped by at 70 miles an hour. The companion was not injured.

The Index

37075 HBL TROY N.Y. "THE WAR YEARS"

THE WEATHER
U. S. Weather Bureau.
Tonight—Rain, cooler.
Tomorrow—Rain.

THE TIMES RECORD

FINAL EDITION

Series 1941—No. 131. (Entered as Second Class Matter at the Postoffice at Troy, N. Y., under the Act of March 3, 1879.) TROY, N. Y., WEDNESDAY EVENING, JUNE 4, 1941. (Published Daily Except Sunday) PRICE THREE CENTS

FORMER KAISER WILHELM DEAD

Aid Appointed To Work On Revaluation Of Property In Troy

ALL REAL ESTATE TO BE REVALUED FOR TAX PURPOSES

Former R. P. I. Assistant Professor Engaged; Expect to Complete Project During July, 1942.

Rather than engage a professional firm to scientifically revalue Troy real estate for the purpose of future assessment, one of the chief objectives announced by Mayor Frank J. Hogan at the start of the preesnt term of office, the city Bureau of Engineering will do the work and has engaged G. Saxton Thompson, Northern Drive consulting engineer and former R. P. I. assistant professor, to assist in the project.

Mayor Hogan made the announcement today as Mr. Thompson, designer of several well-known Troy buildings, was appointed assistant engineer in the Bureau of Engineering.

Special Account.

The revaluation plan, which Mayor Hogan hopes to have completed by July, 1942, is being financed by a special $25,000 account placed in the current budget.

The Mayor had planned to engage a firm of professional real estate appraisers to do the work, having since the first of the year interviewed representatives of firms located in Cleveland, New Haven and Philadelphia.

Instead Mr. Thompson and City Engineer Charles F. Crowley will supervise the project. Regular employees of the Bureau of Engineering and other persons to be appointed to conduct a field survey will complete the work.

From time to time municipal officials have pointed out the need for revaluing Troy real estate in order that all tax assessments in the city be placed on an equitable basis. For example, officials pointed out today, some property in the city of Troy is assessed at the same figure at which it was assessed years ago before the village of Lansingburg became part of the city of Troy. The original assessment figure, in such cases, is used as a basis for the levying of the real estate tax, no allowance being made for improvements to property or for depreciation to property.

No Taxing Discrepancy.

With all city property revalued scientifically, the assessments will be equitable and there will be no taxing discrepancy, officials have pointed out.

After the whole revaluation job has been completed it is the intention of the administration to submit the matter to the general public before action is taken. The matter will be discussed at a public meeting.

Regard the decision to have the Bureau of Engineering do the work, the Mayor said, "We have found that there are many revaluation plans in use today. There is the Cleveland plan and the Pittsburg plan, for instance. There are good and bad sides to all these plans. We have decided to do the revaluation work by our own plan, incorporating some of the features of all of them. Because we know the property and the people involved better than an out-of-town

(Continued on Page 2.)

Appointed

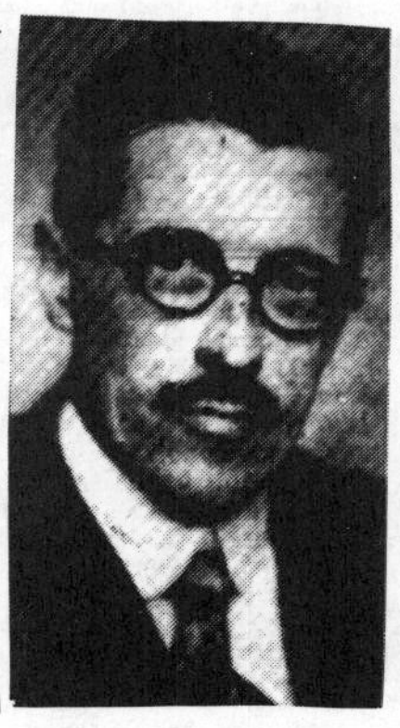

G. SAXTON THOMPSON

MEDIATION BOARD OFFERS PLAN FOR COAL SETTLEMENT

Operators and Miners Meet in Washington to Hear Proposals; Other Major Cases Considered.

BY THE ASSOCIATED PRESS.

The Defense Mediation Board called together in Washington today representatives of northern and southern soft coal operators and the United Mine Workers (C. I. O.) to hear board recommendations for settlement of their wage contract controversy.

Hinging upon acceptance or refusal of the terms was a threatened new strike of 400,000 coal miners in the seven-state Appalachian bituminous industry. The walkout was postponed by President John L. Lewis of the U. M. W. pending the board's report.

The recommendations were to be made public after they had been submitted to participants in the three-way controversy, but board officials said the closed parleys might last until tomorrow.

A board panel headed by W. H. Davis, vice chairman, began drafting the recommendations ten days ago after efforts to mediate the dispute failed. The board has no power to enforce its recommendations, but following President Roosevelt's proclamation of an unlimited national emergency, Davis said:

"The President said that the recommendations of the Mediation Board should be followed. I assume he meant what he said."

Crux of the controversy is the historic wage differential between northern and southern mines. The northern operators have met union demands for a wage increase of $1 a day to $7. The southerners have raised their rate to $6.60. The U. M. W. demands a uniform $7 scale, and its contract with the northern group provides that a strike may be called if a lesser wage is paid elsewhere.

Two other major cases engaged board members.

A panel considered the threatened strike of United Auto Workers (C. I. O.) at the Inglewood, Cal., plant of North American Aviation Corp., while another group continued its efforts to induce 12,000 C. I. O. lumberworkers in 52 Puget Sound logging camps and mills to return to work pending settlement of the dispute.

Day-long discussion yesterday

(Continued On Page 13)

EASTERN STATES FACE SHORTAGE OF GASOLINE AND OIL

Rigid Restrictions May Bring "Gasless Sundays" Next Month; Transportation Chief Difficulty.

Washington (AP)—Secretary Ickes said today "all of us" would have "to make some kind of adjustments" to meet the prospective oil shortage under which industry representatives have suggested might lead to "gasless Sundays" and less heat from oil burners.

"We face a set of hard facts," the Interior Department chief declared in his first formal statement since President Roosevelt made him petroleum coordinator for defense. He added briefly:

"I am sure that American industry, as well as individual citizens, can help to meet the situation. Conservation of petroleum products is certainly one way."

As another conservation measure, Ickes has recommended establishment of nationwide daylight saving time, and it was learned today this probably will be recommended soon by the Office of Production Management.

Shortage Feared In July.

The recommendation, to save electricity, probably will be made to governors, one official said, and it is unlikely that any legislation will be requested to put the change into effect.

The oil shortage, petroleum experts said, will begin in the East in July and become progressively more acute during the autumn months.

To combat the approaching scarcity and to keep it from curtailing defense production, they recommended that rigid restrictions be imposed on the use of oil. Specifically, it was suggested that "Gasless Sundays" be started, and that the temperature in oil-heated homes be kept five degrees lower this winter. No federal program has yet been formulated, however.

A full report on the situaton was submitted yesterday to Secretary Ickes, defense petroleum coordinator, by a committee of the petroleum industry. The industry pledged its support "to any extent" in helping to meet the anticipated emergency.

"Gasless Sunday" Loom.

Only last week Ickes, himself, mentioned the possibility of "Gas-

(Continued On Page 24)

CONGRESSMAN FROM NEW YORK DIES AT SESSION OF HOUSE

Washington (AP) — Representative Edelstein (D.-N. Y.) dropped dead outside the House chamber today a few minutes after making a speech on the floor.

Dr. George W. Calver, capitol physician, said heart failure was the cause of the death of the 53-year-old bachelor congressman.

Shocked colleagues gathered around the stricken member as Calver made his examination.

1,408,600 DEFENSE WORKERS NEEDED

Washington (AP) The Labor Department estimated today that 1,408,600 additional workers would be required in certain key defense industries by April, 1942.

Its estimates indicated that the labor force would have to be expanded to provide 323,900 additional workers for shipbuilding; 408,400 for aircraft; 291,000 for machine tools and ordnance, and 384,700 in other metal working defense industries.

Keene Youth Missing In Adirondack Woods

Keene (AP)—Hundreds of searchers, by land and air, today scoured the heavily forested Adirondacks near Hurricane Mountain for 19-year-old Charles Quinett, Keene, missing since Sunday.

Quinett took his gun into the woodlands "to do some shooting," his family told Conservation Department forest rangers, and when he failed to return last night his disappearance was reported to State Police.

The Conservation Department's airplane, a dozen forest rangers, 75 Civilian Conservation Corps workers and scores of volunteers are in the search.

Quinett is of slender build, about 5 feet 10 inches in height, and has light brown hair.

TROY INDUSTRIAL AREA CALLED KEY IN DEFENSE PLANS

Mayor F. H. LaGuardia Comments on Lack of Equipment to Protect Coastal Cities from Raids

(Staff Correspondence.)

Albany—Evidence that Troy's industrial area must be used as a key point in all plans for New York State defense in the event of declarehd war is seen in a statement today in Boston by Mayor F. H. LaGuardia of New York, U. S. director of civilian defense.

Commenting on the present lack of equipment to protect coastal cities from air raids, Mayor LaGuardia said "all the coastal cities would be tempting targets to any enemy air raiders in the event of war" and named New York and Boston particularly. Then he added:

"When I say Boston, I mean Troy of the Watervliet Arsenal. When I say New York, I mean Albany or Schenectady. When I say Philadelphia, I mean Pittsburg too. When we say coastal cities we mean a fairly wide area."

Many Establishments.

In the Troy Area, in addition to the Watervliet Arsenal, are many industries closely identified with defense work. In addition to mills, clothing manufacturing establishments, etc., there are the Republic Steel plant, the Hudson Valley Coke Products Corp. and several heavy industry establishments in the Watervliet-Colonie sector.

Schenectady, with the General Electric and American Locomotive plants in particular, looms large in the defense picture. In the same section or many important rail and water transportation routes extending to all points of the compass. State defense authorities have long had their proximity to the coast in mind.

Referring to the lack of air defense equipment, Mayor LaGuardia said:

"We know what equipment we need but let's not kid ourselves. The equipment does not exist. If it did exist, not a city in America could afford to buy it."

Auxiliary Fire Fighting.

Auxiliary fire fighting equipment is most needed. Mayor LaGuardia estimated that it would cost between $75,000,000 and $100,000,000 to fit out the auxiliary fire departments needed. He said civilian defense equipment would have to take its turn—in the hope that the production of more urgently needed war material would make air raid protection unnecessary.

The Mayor expressed the belief that Congress would have to provide the supplementary fire equipment needed for municipal areas. Declaring that "we can plan to meet any situation that may arise," he explained that plans already have been prepared for the design of equipment needed.

Major Gen. John F. O'Ryan is in direct charge of this work in New York State, including air raid defenses for civilian and industrial security.

SOCIAL STATUS OF MME. LUPESCU HAS HAVANA PUZZLED

Havana (INS)—Not the war, not questions of state or high finance, but the social status of titian-haired Mme. Magda Lupescu was the burning question bandied about in Havana today.

The question took this form: Is La Lupescu going to be snubbed by Cuban society?

Just what the answer will be is not yet clear. But society folk thought they saw a trend after former King Carol of Rumania lunched yesterday with British Minister Sir George Ogilvie-Forbes.

Mme. Lupescu did not accompany the ex-king to lunch.

What's more, gossip over Havana's teacups indicates a split between the elder conservatives and the more liberal members of Havana society over the future status of the new rivals.

ROYAL AIR FORCE PLANES BOMB OIL DEPOT AT BEIRUT

London Reports "Precautions" Taken to Meet Threat of War in Syria; Mosul Occupied.

BY THE ASSOCIATED PRESS

With the British public clamoring for action, R. A. F. warplanes today bombed the oil depot at Beirut, French-ruled Lebanon, in what may have been the opening blow in the next great campaign of the war.

Simultaneously, authoritative quarters in London said Britan had now taken "necessary precautions in regard to Syria" neighboring French colony in the Middle East and imperial headquarters at Cairo announced that British troops had occupied Mosul, the center of Iraq's rich oil fields

As the war momentarily threatened to boil over into this new theater in the Eastern Mediterranean, the Syrian high command declared that the army of the Levant was ready to defend its territory against any attacks.

British Attack Beirut.

In Berlin, a Nazi spokesman said France had taken "certain protective measures" along the borders of some of her colonial possessions an evident reference to Syria and Lebanon.

Reports reaching Vichy, the French capital, said British planes this morning attacked Beirut, blowing up reservoirs and bombing the oil depot there.

Reports from Vichy said, without official confirmation, that France had sent 150 warplanes to Syria

In the background of the war, Germany's former Kaiser Wilhelm II died in his Dutch exile at Doorn even as Germans under the swastika regime of Adolf Hitler declared that Britain was "bleeding to death" from wounds in her lifelines across the sea.

The ex-emperor, whose fierce bristling moustache and gleaming death's head war helmet symbolized German military might when Hitler was an unknown corporal on the western front, will be given a simple burial at Doorn, it was announced.

Crown Prince Friedrich Wilhelm, the oldest living son, succeeds as head of the Hohenzollern dynasty.

Familiar Claim.

The Nazi claim that England was "bleeding to death" based on an assertion that half Britain's prewar merchant fleet has been destroyed would have rung familiarly in the old Kaiser's ears. He would have recalled an hour of false hope in his own heydey, in April, 1917, when the British were declared to have been "beaten to their knees" by the Kaiser's sink-on-sight U-boat campaign. Less then 17 months later, Wilhelm fled a beaten Germany to take refuge in Holland. He never went back.

Recapitulating the 12-day battle of Crete, the Germans asserted that 12,000 more British and Greek troops had been captured on the blitz-ravaged Mediterranean island, making a total of 25,000.

The latest group of captives, it was said, included 8,000 British and 4,000 Greeks.

Previous British reports said 15,000 troops had been safely withdrawn from Crete, out of an original contingent of some 30,000.

Amid official silence, Britons waited for word that the war may already have flamed into action in France's Middle East colonies of Syria and Lebanon.

Cabinet Minister Lord Beaverbrook's newspaper, the London Evening Standard, declared British troops should occupy Syria at once—if necessary for the defense of Palestine and Cyprus and demanded

Demand Drastic Action.

"Are we afraid of war with France? It would be better if we saw the issue as clearly as Admiral Darlan (French vice premier.)"

The newspaper asserted that Darlan, bitter foe of England, had offered Syria to Germany as payment in his "betrayal on the instalment plan."

The British press and public alike demanded that Britain "act boldly and stop placating Vichy."

In the still raging "battle of the lakes" in Ethiopie, the British announced the capture of 17,000 more prisoners, including 5,872 Italians, along with 14 tanks, 700 cars and 85 guns.

The lake region is in south central Ethiopie, where scattered remnants of the Duke of Aosta's Fascist armies have been holding out for several weeks.

NAZI SHIP FINALLY REACHES ARGENTINA

Buenos Aires (AP) The 5,522-ton German freighter Frankfurt arrived here today from Talcahuano, Chile, where she had been tied up since the start of the war.

The Frankfurt sailed May 18, thus completing in 17 days a 3,000-mile voyage around Cape Horn to this Argentine port in American coastal waters

Former War Lord Dead

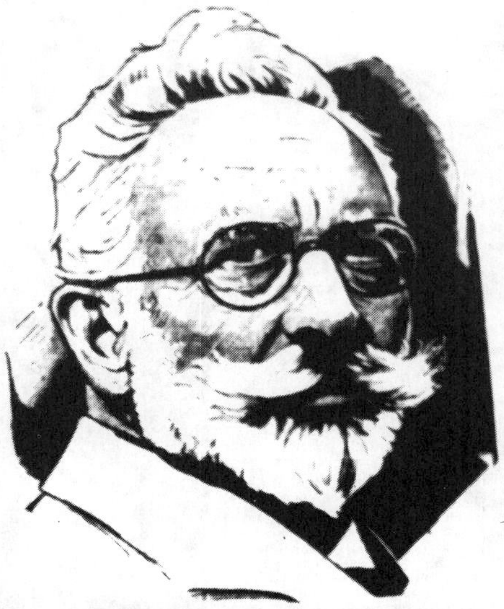

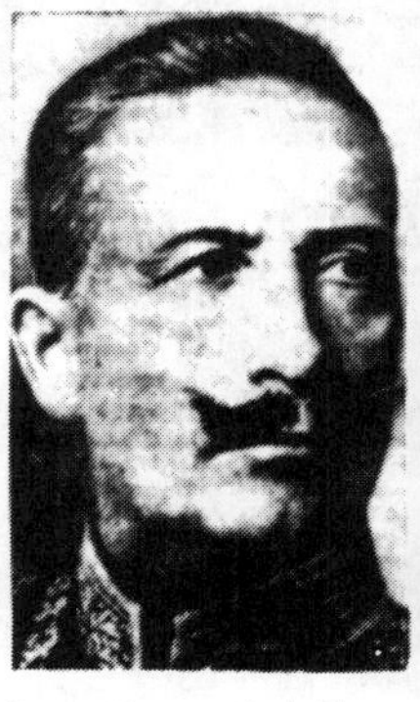

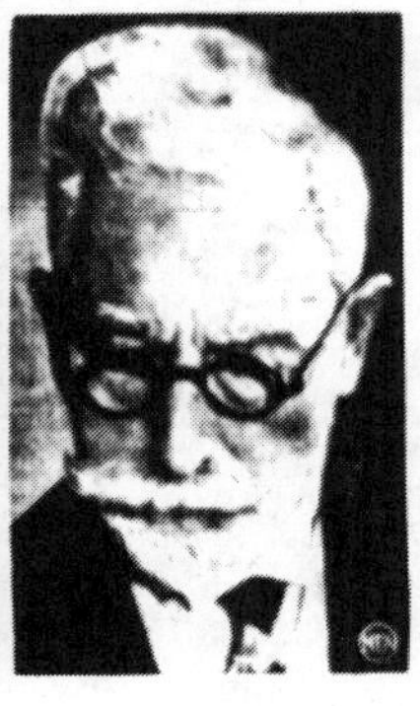

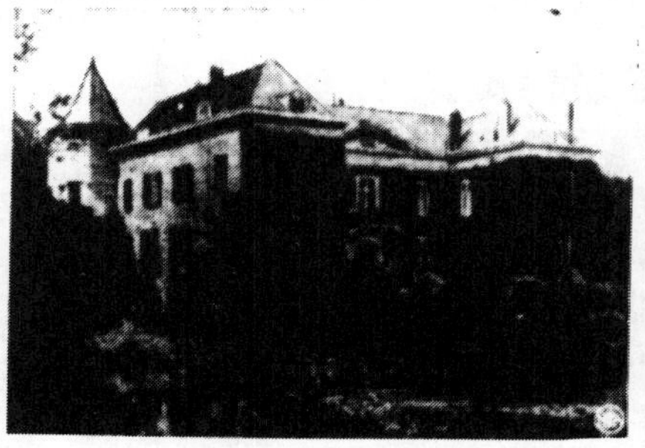

Wilhelm II, former war lord of Germany, died in exile at Doorn, Holland, this morning. The upper NEA sketch of Wilhelm was drawn by an artist three years ago on a visit to Doorn. Just below, the former kaiser is shown, left, in a wartime photograph back in 1918, and at right, in one of his last photos. Below is shown the ancient castle at Doorn, where Wilhelm passed his last years.

Former Kaiser's Chronology

BY THE ASSOCIATED PRESS.

Jan. 27, 1859—Born, Friedrich Wilhelm Victor Albert Hohenzollern.

Feb. 27, 1881—Married to Augusta Victoria, daughter of Duke Friedrich of Schleswig-Holstein.

May 6, 1882—First son born; five other sons and a daughter born of this union.

June 15, 1888—Became Emperor Wilhelm II of Germany on death of his father, Emperor Friedrich, who had reigned but 99 days.

1890—Breaks with "Iron Chancellor" Bismarck, taking over personal charge of government.

Aug. 1, 1914—Germany declares war on Russia as outgrowth of Sarajevo assassination of Archduke Franz Ferdinand of Austria-Hungary. Allies line up against Germany and central powers.

Nov. 9, 1918—Advised by his generals of imminent defeat, Kaiser signs abdication and speeds by car to Amerongen, The Netherlands, moving to Doorn a year later.

Jan. 20, 1920—Holland refuses allied demand for Wilhelm's surrender.

April 11, 1921—Former Kaiserin dies.

Nov. 5, 1922—Wilhelm married to widowed Princess Hermine of Reuss over objections of family and monarchists.

June 4, 1941—Death ends quiet life of exile at age of 82.

Britons Learned To Pity Former Kaiser

London (UP)—Twenty-five years ago Britons hated Kaiser Wilhelm like they do Adolf Hitler today. In after years they learned to pity the Kaiser.

The Press Association recalled that the British Ambassador to Berlin, Sir Frank Lascelles, reported in 1896 that Wilhelm had assured the German Ambassador to Paris that "I am not a bad sort of fellow." The agency also cited the book, "Peace Patrol," by Lieut. Col. Stewart Rodie, a member of the Disarmament Commission.

"Rodie subscribes to the theory that the Kaiser was not responsible for the actions of his statesmen," the Press Association said. "They kept unpleasant things from him and flattered him. They made up his mind for him. They would put a question and all unperceived would slip the answer into it."

Dealing with events leading up to the first World War the Press Association said of the Kaiser:

"As his importance increased the Kaiser himself appears more and more to have lost his sense of values.

"He was genuinely surprised when at last he was brought face to face with the facts and realized that the tragedy at Sarajevo was to be the signal for the breaking of the storm. In the last days of 1914 he signed fateful documents with a trembling hand. He was convinced, nevertheless, that he possessed an invincible army. Before long the actual control of the troops passed from him."

LAST OF GERMAN EMPERORS DIES AT DOORN HOUSE

War Lord of Europe's Last Conflict Succumbs to Lung Embolism; In Exile Since 1918.

Doorn, Holland (UP)—Former Kaiser Wilhelm II, 82, last of Germany's Hohenzollern emperors, died at 11:30 a.m. today (5:30 a.m., E. D. T.) at Doorn House.

The once mightiest ruler of the Eastern Hemisphere, war lord of the last war and a figure of world power for thirty years, had suffered an embolism of the lung during the night.

His end was sudden but peaceful. He had suffered a cold and an internal ailment which sapped his strength and kept him indoors at his estate, where he had spent most of the more than twenty years since, on Nov. 10, 1918, he fled across the Netherlands frontier from Germany with a few faithful officers and, over his vigorous protest, surrendered his sword to a young Dutch sergeant

Members of the Hohenzollern family were summoned from Germany to join the Princess Hermine of Schoenaich-Carolath, his second wife, at his bedside. But after spending the Whitsun week-end holiday with Wilhelm, most of them returned to Germany yesterday and there was not time to call them back.

By Wilhelm's death the former Crown Prince Wilhelm, 49, who had remained in Germany quietly during the rise of the Nazis, became head of the house of Hohenzollern, founded by Burchardus of Zolorin who died about 1061.

Fought Fatal Illness.

Wilhelm, once the symbol of Prussian militarism, had remained in exile, embittered for years because of charges that it was he and his little group of confidantes who had precipitated the last war.

He fought hard against his illness, and at 7 30 last night his household said that he had shown such improvement that he was believed out of danger.

Prince August Wilhelm, his fourth son, and his only daughter, the Duchess of Braunschweig, among others, had returned to Germany in the belief that the danger was passed.

Funeral arrangements awaited instructions from the Hohenzollern family. Usually well informed German sources had said, however, that Wilhelm probably would be buried in Holland.

Wilhelm had lived here for 23 years in faded grandeur surrounded by mementoes of his pompous days.

He could have spent his last days on German soil, but declined an invitation from Adolf Hitler, preferring to die here since he could not go back to Germany as emperor.

Once the mightiest military ruler in the world, he died a stooped, lonely, white-haired old man, isolated from nearly all human contacts because of a fear of crowds and of "microbes."

Resigned To Exile.

Wilhelm in the morning usually took a short walk in the park. But even this activity had to be curtailed for he would go indoors

(Continued on Page 2.)

MORTON DOWNEY GRANTED DIVORCE

Bridgeport, Conn., (UP)—Morton Downey, the silver voiced tenor who introduced a song called "I'll Always Be In Love With You," in one of his early pictures, won an uncontested divorce today from screen actress, Barbara Bennett.

Downey charged intolerable cruelty at the hearing held in chambers before Judge Robert L. Munger.

He received custody of their five children, Michael, 11, an adopted son; Sean Morton, 9; Lorelle Ann, 7; Anthony Patrick, 6, and Kevin, 3.

The Index

MAN ARRESTED FOR BREAKING SON'S LEG

Rochester (UP)—A second degree assault charge was placed against Joseph F. Pencola, 27, today after he allegedly beat his 5-year-old son Robert with a broom handle, braeking his right leg.

Pencola told police he found Robert and a second son, Ronald, 2, starting a fire in their bedroom.

"I only hit him a couple of times," the father said. "I didn't think I hit him hard."

Brief Funeral Rites Held For Lou Gehrig

New York (AP) — In a service marked by the same simplicity that characterized his life, final tribute was paid Lou Gehrig this morning at Christ Episcopal Church, the Bronx.

Gehrig, baseball's iron man, died Monday night after an illness of two years during which he courageously fought the inroads of an apparently incurable malady.

The tiny church, seating about 200, was less than half filled. The family had requested a private service and only relatives, close friends, baseball and civic officials and a few newspapermen were present.

"The service was read by the Rev. Gerald Barry from the Episcopal prayer book, and was completed in less than ten minutes. Mr. Barry, after finishing the ritual, remarked simply

"It is customary to deliver an address at funerals, and it is permissible in this church. However, it is the wish of the bereaved that this be not done. I am requested to say simply there will be no eulogy because you all knew him so well."

Gehrig's body lay in a mahogany casket covered with a spray of roses. The front of the church was banked solidly with floral pieces, and car after car at the curb was filled with other offerings. A crowd of 250 persons waited patiently in the rain for the service to end.

The body, accompanied by the pallbearers and family, was taken immediately to a crematory.

Included among those present at the final service were Will Harridge, American League president; Leslie O'Connor, secretary to Commissioner Landis; Eddie Collins, Red Sox general manager; Tom Richardson, Eastern League president; Ford Frick, National League president; Bill Terry and Eddie Brannick of the New York Giants, and Deputy Mayor Rufus E. McGahen, representing Mayor Fiorello H. LaGuardia, who was out of the city.

Manager Joe McCarthy and catcher, Bill Dickey, of the Yankees, were among the pallbearers, as was dancer Bill Robinson. The Yankee front office was present almost intact.

Last night they stood for hours receiving the condolences of hun-

(Continued on Page 19)

CHARACTER KEY TO CURE OF WORLD'S ILLS, BISHOP SAYS

Emma Willard Graduating Class Told "Education Dangerous Thing" at Baccalaureate.

"We can get along better with second class brains than with second class character," Rt. Rev. G. Ashton Oldham, D.D., S.T.D. Bishop of the Episcopal Diocese of Albany, told the graduating class at Emma Willard School in a baccalaureate sermon last night in the school chapel.

"The world is full of people with plans and schemes, economic and otherwise, for remedying the evils from which we are suffering," the baccalaureate speaker declared. "But so far nearly all of them have failed, not because the plans were wrong in themselves, but for lack of sufficient individual virtue.

"No structure is better than the materials that enter into it; no nation or community is better than the individuals who compose it. The best of organizations can be perverted to bad ends by evil men, while a very inadequate organization may serve in the hands of righteous people.

Character Is The Key.

"If the world is to be saved from war, and if our cities are to be saved from vice and political corruption, it depends, in the long run, entirely on the character of our citizens."

The Bishop declared that "education is a very dangerous thing—the training of the intellect alone may destroy our civilization," and held that "most of the present evils facing our world are the work of clever but unscrupulous men."

"Thus education may be either our salvation or our ruin, depending upon the purpose for which it is used, and these in turn depend upon the character of the individual. We can get along with second class brains better than with second class character.

"Every school, therefore, that includes in its educational program stress on character-building is rendering a high service to our country and to the world. We are happy that Emma Willard, without neglecting the intellectual, has always laid great stress on character.

"In the ultimate, character is dependent upon religion. As said the Duke of Wellington: 'Education without religion will surround us with clever devils.' This is a truth some educators need to learn.

World Needs High Standards.

"The crying need of the day is young men and women who have high standards of purity and honor, whose word is as good as their bond, whose desire is to serve and to give and not merely to get. And these and many other virtues are dependent ultimately on belief in a holy and righteous God. A free civilization and Christianity belong together."

As part of commencement weekend at Emma Willard, "Prunella" or "Love in a Garden," was given Saturday at the school as the Senior Class play, with Miss Patricia McCarthy of Maple Avenue in the leading role of "Patricia."

June Queen Rules Over Emma Willard Exercises

Attended by the senior class, Julia Lusk of Peoria, Ill., Emma Willard School's June Queen, arrives in her chariot, above, for the June Day exercises. While the junior, sophomore and freshmen classes stage their Maypole dance, right the June Queen looks on from her throne in the background. A hoop held by two students, below, frames another view of the colorful campus program.

BLAIR GRADUATE.

Robert B. Payne, son of Mr. and Mrs. R. Smith Payne of 40 Pinewoods Avenue, will be graduated today from Blair Academy at Blairstown, N. J. During the last school year Payne was a member of the Scientific Club and the golf, tennis and swimming teams.

Dance and Pantomime.

Fair" set the atmosphere for the play. The prologue consisted of songs and dances by strolling players. Among them were Gloria Robinson, Jane Reynolds and Trent Cluett who appeared in the Pierrot and Pierette dance.

Others in the dance were Sue Kruidenier, Eloise Rogers and Jean VanDerwerke. A clown dance was given by Louise Ashworth, Anne de Windt, Annalee Eggaton and Barbara Rigbie. Taking part in a pantomime "Who Laughs Last" were: Pierrot, Jean Skerry; Pierette, Camilla Adams; Harlequin, Betsey Copp, and Columbine, Marie Fulmer.

Strolling singers were Betsey Barrett of Granville, Claire Bryant and Joan Walters. They were accompanied by a flutist, Margaret Keck. Townspeople watching the dancers were Barbara Gibson, Margaret Simonson, Lucy Whitbeck, Marjiou Wieboldt and Patience Wilbur.

In the play itself Miss McCarthy appeared as Prunella, Priscilla Rubb as Pierrot, Rita Ninsley as Scaramel, Winifred Reudemann as Hawk, Elizabeth Whitman as Callow, June Willard as Mouth, Audrey Howland as Doll, Marilay Kelly as Romp, Suzanne Masten as Tawdry, Betsy Young as Coquette, Jane Seddon as Prude, Ann Seacrest as Privacy, Barbara Magnard of Troy as Prim, Louise Bull and Julia Lusk as gardeners and Dorothy Ward as the statue of Love.

Mrs. Mary Hare Thompson, head of dramatics at the school, directed the play. Miss Margaret Page, head of the art department, was in charge of art work. Miss Virginia Cramer directed the music. Miss Louise Leland had charge of the dancers assisted at the piano by Miss Grace Bartholomew. Edward A. Rice played the violin.

Ushers were Misses Betty Bienneister, Marion Curtis, Marjane Hunter, Dorothy McShane, Margaret Morris, Jean Orth. Mary Sheary and Ingrid Sieving of Troy, June Haggerty of Cohoes and Sula Coyne, Jean Atkinson, Audrey Dennett, Pauline Hurff.

Art and Stage Crews.

Priscilla Baker headed the art crew and All-chaire Medlicott, the stage setting crew assisted by Jane Blish, Sylvia Ann Hayes, Jeanne Skerry, Annette Freiberger, Barbara Gibson, Barnare Robison, Anne Remsen, Elizabeth Chapman, Kathleen Driscoll and Louise Coolidge. Betsy Barrett was in charge of properties assisted by Martha Ellis, Marilyn Kaye, Jean Weed and Patience Wilbur.

The costume committee was headed by Mary Louise Davison assisted by Caroline Hill, Margaret Simonson and Ann Thom. Susanne Landis was student director, Mary Haskell, stage manager and Emma Soper, assistant, house business manager.

Step singing took place last evening. The seniors stood on the school gymnasium steps. Familiar hymns which were sung included "For the Beauty of the Earth," "Ancient of Days," "Love Divine" and "O Comrade of the Human Heart." The step songs, in which the seniors sang to the juniors and the juniors to the seniors, followed "The Star Spangled Banner."

Emma Soper of Bloomington, Ill. president of the senior class, "presented the steps" to Ruth Scherm of Bronxville, president of the junior class. The seniors then marched to the center of the triangle, the juniors took their place on the steps and the Alma Mater and benediction hymn were sung. Singing was under the direction of Miss Virginia Cramer.

Lemon Juice Recipe Quickly Checks Pain Due to Neuritis

PROGRAMS GIVEN ON CHILDREN'S DAY IN TWO CHURCHES

Junior Catholic Daughters' Troops Attend Communion Breakfast in Mechanicville K. of C. Hall.

STILLWATER

Children's Day was observed in the Methodist and Schoonmaker Memorial Presbyterian Church yesterday morning with appropriate exercises.

Songs were sung by the Presbyterian Sunday School groups, salutes to the American and Christian Flags were given and baptism administered.

The program included: "A Little Girl's Message," Florence Ryan; "An Original Greeting," Earl Wilbur; "A Good Excuse," Priscilla Sanders; "Do Your Bit," Bobby Brown; song, Joan Travis; "No Doubt About It," Ellen Sanders; "An Important Item, Lenetta Aldrich; "A Happy Thought," Marion Alice Tomkinson.

Primary department: Pantomime, junior girls; "Jack's Sermon," Elting Doughty; "A Smile," Dorothy Stephens; "If I Were a Rose," Arlene Tomkinson; "What He Thought," John Travis; "What Twill Do," Clara Anna Gilgallon; "Learn A Lesson," Priscilla Aldrich; "Heaven's Postman," Ann Case; "A Message of Jesus," Mary Jane Friendship. Junior department: "Be What You Think You Are," Nancy Doughty; "Keep Sunny," Betty Brown; piano solo, Nancy Schreiber; exercise, "The Bravest One," Philip Case, Baxter Collin, Patrick Gilgallon, Richard Sherman and Billy Talmadge.

The Sunday School program follows: Processional; salute to American and Christian Flags; welcome to all by Sunday School group; song, "This Is My Father's World"; recitation, "If I Were Big," Martha Humphrey; exercise, "God's Word Is in the Garden," Marilyn Cowin, John Ford, Eleanor Gailor, Harold Bryan and Donnalie Robinson; song, "Thy Word Is Like A Garden, Lord;" recitation, "His Lamb," Nancy Hinkley; exercise, "Children's Day," Zelma Bryan, Sylvia Knibbs; recitation, "A Girl's Speech," Beverly Coons; song, "A Happy Day," Donnalie Robinson and Marilyn Cowin, Donald Coons and Bobby Hanna; recitation, "A Tiny Tot." Annetta Smith; recitation, "Why?", Charles Peacock; reading, "The Bell of the Angels." Lois Coons; vocal duet, "God's Care," Ruth Ford and Frances Peacock; exercise, "The Clock," Eugene Smith, Phyllia DeWein,

Lorraine Lowell, Donald Coons reading, "A Fair Proposition," Edward Bryan, closing song, "Joy, Joy, Joy."

Class To Be Entertained.

The Presbyterian Guild will be the guests of Mrs. Walter Curtis in Schenectady tomorrow evening.

Attend Communion Breakfast.

The members of Troops 13 and 14, Junior Catholic Daughters, attended a communion breakfast at the K. of C. Hall in Mechanicville yesterday. The members of Troop 13 attending were the Misses Frances Tanner, Anna Mae Reddy, Betty Brown, Betty Perrino, Betty Sheridan, Mary Stewart and Margaret Walker. Troop 14 included the Misses Jean Bull, Barbara Bull, Dorothy Britt, Betty Nelson and Joan McClements.

Personal.

Mrs. Walter Church is visiting her husband in Boston.

Jackie Crawford of Hoosick Falls spent the week-end with his grandparents.

Miss Catherine Tanner has returned to Schenectady after spending the past few days with her parents.

Herbert Cossey, Arthur Wagoner and Edward Britt who are stationed at Fort Totten, N. J., spent the week-end here.

Miss Catherine Finnegan has returned to Washington, D. C., where she is employed, after spending the week-end with her parents.

Mrs. Stuart Carson and daughter have returned home after spending the past week with Mrs. Carson's parents in New York.

TRAFFIC DISRUPTED ON ERIE MAIN LINE

Tuxedo (AP)—An oil tank car, buckling in a heavily-loaded freight train, ripped up 100 feet of track yesterday and blocked all traffic on the main line of the Erie Railroad.

The train, bound for the Erie's Jersey City terminal where a $10,-000,000 fire destroyed the Mid-Hudson warehouse May 31, was approaching the Orange-Rockland County boundary at 6:20 a.m. (E.D.T.) when the drawhead coupling the tank car suddenly pulled loose. The tanker careened across both the north and southbound tracks, turning over three of the freight seventy cars and tearing out large sections of trackage. No one was injured.

Passengers of Erie trains tied up by the break were relayed between Tuxedo and Suffern by bus.

U. S. MAY OPEN ICELAND LEGATION

Washington (AP)—Informed quarters predicted yesterday that President Roosevelt would seek indirect congressional sanction for the establishment of diplomatic relations with Iceland by asking an appropriation to open a legation in Reykjavik, the Icelandic capital.

TROY ELKS' LODGE SELECTS DATE FOR ANNUAL CLAMBAKE

John F. Jackson Appointed Chairman of Event Scheduled for Sunday, September 14.

The annual clambake of Troy Lodge of Elks will be conducted Sunday, Sept. 14, it was voted last night at a meeting of the membership at the clubhouse.

John F. Jackson was appointed chairman for the event. David S. Barry and Charles L. Moore will act as assistant chairmen.

T. M. Guerin, jr., exalted ruler, presided at the session and heard preliminary reports on the success of the Fourth of July picnic at the Troy Riding Club grounds. The holiday feature attracted approximately 10,000 persons, the committee reported.

The annual budget was discussed and copies are to be distributed to members.

A lodge of sorrow was conducted for Lee J. Goshorn, Henry J. Downs and Rollin J. Hurd, members who died during the last month, and eulogies were delivered by the exalted ruler.

The session last night was the only one scheduled for this month, the next meeting being slated for Aug. 14.

Mayor Frank J. Hogan, Mr. Guerin, several past exalted rulers and a delegation of members of the lodge will leave Sunday and Monday for Philadelphia to attend the convention of the Grand Lodge.

PILOT'S ESTATE.

Letters of administration in the estate of Aaron O. Allan, Albany pilot killed in a plane crash near Defreestville July 2, were issued yesterday. Mrs. Margaret Allan, his mother, is administratrix. Mr. Allan left personal property amounting to $1,000.

Doll And Pet Shows Staged At Troy Playgrounds

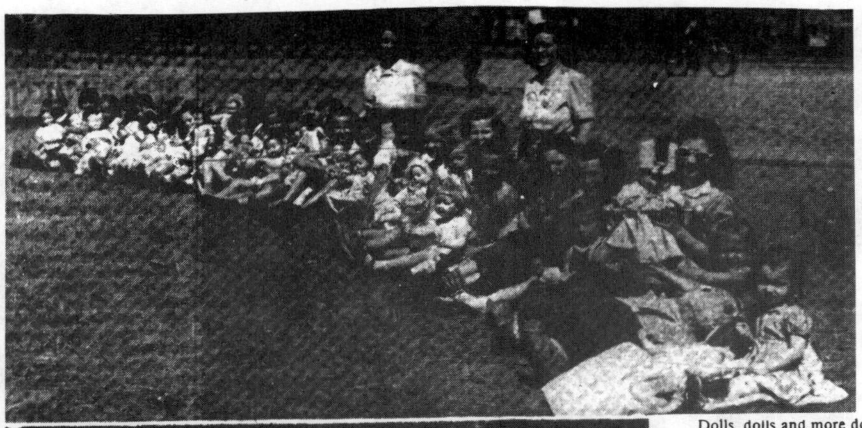

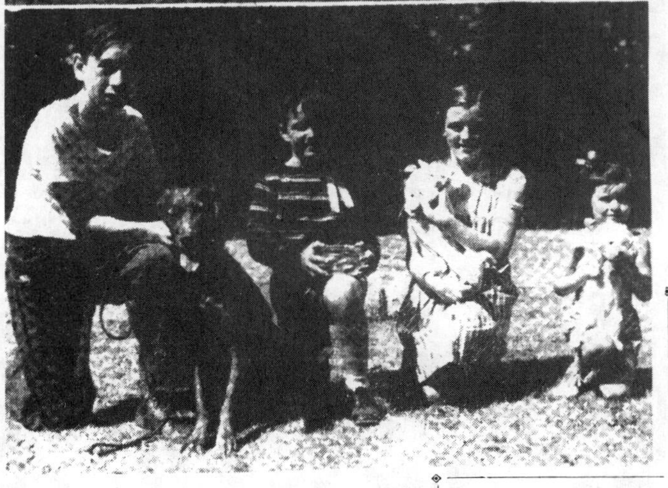

Dolls, dolls and more dolls are displayed above for the doll show staged yesterday at the 112th Street Playground. With the children are the playground directors, Misses Marge Geer, left, and Mary Cooley. Winners in the Prospect Park pet show proudly display their entries below. Left to right are Tom Naples with his first prize dog; Ned Tamus, second smallest pet—a turtle; Grace Woolsey, third most handsome kittens, and Janet Walkinshaw, with the cutest dog.

Boy's Setter Wins At Park Pet Show

A handsome Irish setter owned by Tom Naples captured three first prizes to monopolize the laurels at the first pet show of the season conducted at Prospect Park playground yesterday. Tommy's setter, "Lady," won first prizes for being the largest pet, the most handsome and the most clever.

Other winners included:

Largest—second prize, Marguerite Murray and third, Grace Brehm; smallest pet—Bill McBride's honey bee; second prize, Ned Tamus, with a turtle, and Bill Love, who entered a tiny kitten; most handsome, Roger Ryan, Marjorie Blair and Joan Brehm, tied for second, and Marguerite Murray and Grace Woolsey, tied for third; cleverest pet—Nancy Poland, second prize and Mary Blair, third; most unusual, Bill McBride took first with his bee; Ned Camus, second and Grace Woolsey, third; cutest—Janet Walkinshaw first, Nancy Poland, second, Anthony Stewart.

EAGLE MILLS.

Rev. Paul E. Diehl, pastor of the Eagle Mills Church of Christ, will bring a series of three sermons on the Disciples of Christ. The first will be "Our Plea, the Unity of all Christians"; the second, "Our Plan, the Restoration of the New Testament Church," the third, "Our Purpose, to Make Known to the World that Jesus is the Christ, the Son of the Living God." The pastor will deliver the first of the series Sunday at 11 a.m. Bible School will be held at 10 a.m. under the leadership of Miss Lillian French.

The Women's Missionary Society of the Church of Christ held its July meeting at the home of Mrs. Frank Ferguson of Brunswick Road Wednesday afternoon. Miss Audna Coonrad led the society in the study of Japan. The devotions centered on the theme, "The Word of God." Mrs. Henry Cranston and Mrs. Frank Ferguson used scripture relating to the theme, and Mrs. Lester Coonrad and Miss Audna Coonrad continued with the development of the theme. Mrs. Thomas Miller gave a report on "A Decisive Hour of Christian Missions." Mrs. Paul Diehl gave a report on "The Farmers of Japan," by Kagawa; Miss Frances Band also reported on "Children of Calamity." Mrs. Leslie Clum reported and commented on "Christianity and World Crisis." Rev. Paul E. Diehl gave a review of Kawaga's message to the International Convention of the Disciples of Christ. Mrs. Leslie Clum closed the meeting by prayer after which the business of the society was transacted. The treasurer reported that the society had met its goal for the Missionary year to the United Cristian Missionary Society. The hostess, following the business meeting, served a tasty lunch to the society. The next meeting will be in September, as in August the society will have its annual picnic.

DR. PERRY TO SPEAK AT EAST WHITEHALL

The 115th anniversary of the East Whitehall Brick Church will be commemorated Sunday at 2:30 p.m. at exercises at which Rev. James A. Perry, Th.D., pastor of the Fifth Avenue-State Street Methodist Church of Troy, will be a speaker. Dr. Perry is a former pastor of the East Whitehall Brick Church. Rev. Fred W. Vogel, D.D., Middleburg, another former pastor, will also speak.

There will be special music and a homecoming celebration after the service, according to Rev. Edgar F. Redfern, pastor of the Whitehall and East Whitehall Methodist Churches.

SPANISH TROOPS HEAD FOR RUSSIA

San Sebastian, Spain (AP)—The first contingent of Blue Legion volunteers crossed into occupied France yesterday en route to fight beside the German army against Russia.

POWNAL.

Leo King and Amie Lassard have returned from a motor trip to Sherbrooke, Canada.

Mr. and Mrs. John Patterson, jr., and small son have returned to Milford, Conn., after spending a few days with local relatives.

Mr. and Mrs. Herbert Fink of Wilston Park, Nassau, are at their summer cabin on the Pownal slopes of Mt. Anthony.

Floyd Mattison of this town has returned from Watchung, N. J., with his bride, the former Miss Lila M. Wilday of that place. The marriage was solemnized in the garden of the home of Mr. and Mrs. Henry Wilday, parents of the bride, Saturday. A number of relatives of the bridegroom attended from this town, his brother-in-law, Fred Towslee, serving as best man.

There was a reunion Tuesday afternoon at the Bushnell school attended by a number of former pupils, their families, and friends. Seven who were in school there 55 years ago when Miss Eva Rockwood of Bennington was the teacher, were present. They were Mr. and Mrs. Walter Niles, Mr. and Mrs. James Hathaway, Mrs. Loren Fowler, Mrs. Benjamin Amadon, Mrs. Eva Howard Estes. Mrs. Fowler was the former Jennie Hicks; Mrs. Amadon is her sister Julia; Mrs. Niles was then Laura Safford; Mrs. Hathaway was Carrie Wood; Mrs. Perkins of Brunswick, Me., was Freda Heinrich. The outside of the school seemed much the same to these who knew it long ago, but changes and improvements had made a great difference in the interior.

DEFENSE STUDY TO BE CONDUCTED BY WPA ORGANIZATION

Civilian Groups in Troy Will Be Surveyed as to Part They Will Play in Emergencies.

The Record Newspapers Bureau, Washington.

Civilian organizations in Troy and other communities in upstate New York will be surveyed within the next sixty days to determine the part that they may play in home defense.

The WPA has announced the plan for the nationwide survey which will reach more than 200,000 national, state and local civilian organizations with memberships of 50,000,000 individuals.

The project will provide basic information for programs of the Office of Civilian Defense, under the direction of Fiorello H. LaGuardia and other agencies. The survey will be conducted by the WPA Historical Records Survey under the general supervision of Mrs. Florence Kerr, assistant WPA commissioner and assistant to Mr. LaGuardia in the Office of Civilian Defense.

With information available for county seats and towns of more than 2,500 poulation, Mrs. Kerr said, civilian emergencies can be handled with dispatch by the appropriate organizations in all large cities and more than 5,000 towns. Information regarding all civilian organizations will be obtained on special forms by project workers of the Historical Records Survey. These records will become a national master directory in punch card form. When the OCD is about to inaugurate a particular activity—from consumer protection to air raid warden services—the punch cards of suitable organizations can be assembled automatically for any or all states. Similar lists will be retained in each state.

"It is imperative that this survey be completed within the next sixty days as one of the important steps for the work of the Office of Civilian Defense said Mrs. Kerr. "It is our hope that all organizations approached by the Historical Records Survey will offer their full and prompt cooperation."

The index will include civic organizations, service organizations, welfare and charitable groups auxiliary religious groups engaged in service work, chambers of commerce, national and state headquarters of labor unions and citywide trade councils, Parent Teacher Associations, patriotic societies, professional associations, home demonstration clubs and farm organizations, alumni groups, motorists' clubs, youth organizations and historical societies.

Purely social clubs will be omitted. While churches will not be listed, indexes of such organizations have already been compiled by the Historical Records Survey and are available.

CANADIAN OFFICIAL

HORIZONTAL
1 English official in Canada, Earl of ——.
7 He is governor ——.
12 Fish eggs.
13 Brinks.
15 To pilfer.
16 Pealed.
17 To trim.
18 Night.
20 Organ of sight
21 Assassin.
23 Male sheep.
24 Italian river.
25 To soften leather.
27 Antagonist.
30 Okra soup.
33 To eject.
34 Acid.
35 Celerity.
37 To intone.
38 Measure of length.
39 Egyptian deity.
40 Bashful.
41 African tribe.
42 Negative.
44 To graze.
49 Food container.
50 To canter.
52 To stop.
53 Young horse.
54 Epoch.
55 Stormed.
56 Stir.
57 He is Queen Mary's —— (pl.).
58 His official residence is in ——, Canada.

Answer to Previous Puzzle

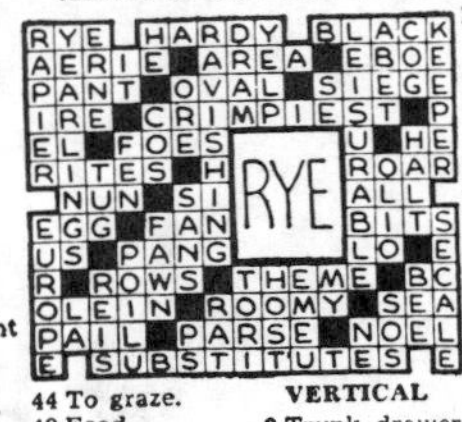

VERTICAL
2 Trunk drawer
3 Whetstone.
4 Limb.
5 Tidy.
6 Norse mythology.
7 Sheaf of wheat.
8 Domestic slaves.
9 Unit of work.
10 Bellow.
11 Father.
14 Lump.
16 He ——s the British crown.
19 His is a most —— post.
21 Sun.
22 Shred.
24 Father.
26 Weakly sentimental.
28 Supplicant.
29 To contend.
31 Ratite bird.
32 House of one story.
36 To fish.
37 Mine shaft hut.
40 Professed creed.
43 Bull.
45 160 square rods.
46 To scorch.
47 Labels.
48 To consume.
49 Musical term.
51 To make lace.
53 Kitty.

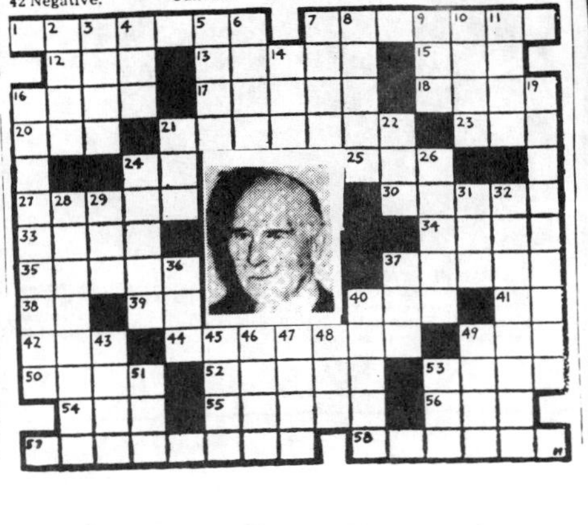

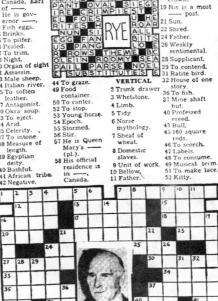

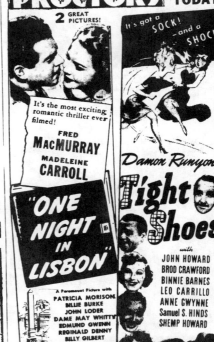

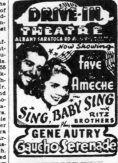

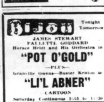

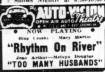

PRESENTING THE WIDE WORLD IN PICTURES

Wide World Photos, Inc.

WOMEN VOLUNTEERS IN NATIONAL DEFENSE: Girls waiting in line at Fort Benning, Ga., to register for special services under the nation-wide program of the Women's Volunteer Service Committee. They are classified according to the special kind of training they have had. Special training courses will be offered the girls who are 15 years of age or older.

AFTER CONFERRING WITH PRESIDENT ON ARMY PROBLEMS: Representative Andrew J. May (left) and Senator Robert Reynolds, chairmen respectively of the House and Senate Military Affairs Committees, on the White House porch after the discussion on extending draftees' period of service and the removal of the prohibition against sending selectees and guardsmen abroad.

THE BRITISH AND THEIR ALLIES ARRIVE IN DAMASCUS: The local inhabitants crowd the streets to see the first of the Imperial soldiers and the Free French forces of General de Gaulle, drive through the city after the Vichy government troops had moved out.

DETROIT VETERAN SURRENDERS TO YOUTH: Charley Gehringer, of the Tigers, one of the greatest second basemen of all times, greets Lambert (Dutch) Meyer, his replacement who was recalled from Buffalo. Meyer is a former football star of Texas Christian University, where he was coached by his uncle and namesake, "Dutch" Meyer.

CALLS LINDBERGH A NAZI TOOL: Secretary of the Interior Ickes, speaking at the Bastile Day meeting held in New York under the sponsorship of the France Forever organization, declares Charles A. Lindbergh is a mouthpiece of the Nazi party in the U. S. The speech was one of the most bitter attacks ever made on Mr. Lindbergh by any member of the Roosevelt Administration.

PREPARING FOR THE SECOND DRAFTEE LOTTERY: Girls in Washington filling the 800 colored capsules which will be used for the numbered sequence calling the 750,000 young men who registered for selective service on July 1 for classification in the second drawing for the draft army.

"DIPLOMAT" RETURNS, A SCHOOLBOY AGAIN: Bobby Gallagher of New York, 16 years old, as he arrived from Rio de Janeiro where he was sent as one of the youthful good-will "ambassadors" sponsored by business and industrial leaders of the U. S. and Brazil. Now that he's home, he must start cramming for Regents' examinations that he missed because of his 3-week trip.

IN FASHION'S SPOTLIGHT: Josephine red, the purplish tone worn by Napoleon's empress, appears in the feathers on this black velvet sailor. The feathers are quill tips specially cut and dyed.

NEW REGENTS OUST GEORGIA EDUCATOR: Dr. W. D. Cocking, dean of the University of Georgia's School of Education, who was accused by Governor Talmadge (right) of advocating racial equality in the State's higher education system, testifying at the Atlanta hearing at which the Regents Board, reorganized by the Governor, voted his dismissal by a 10 to 5 vote.

SPONSOR USES BEER AT NAMING OF BRITISH TANK: Lieut. Peter Gill breaks a bottle of beer on the gun of the "Waltzing Matilda," a new heavy-infantry tank placed in service at a camp on the southwest coast of England.

A PROTEST AGAINST GOVERNMENT "DICTATION": Marion Hatt, a farmer of Jackson, Mich., burning his 17-acre wheat crop because of "too much government dictatorship on crops." He destroyed the grain when a Federal Conservation Service official refused to give him a wheat-marketing permit because he exceeded the government quota by two acres.

A LORRY THAT WILL NEVER CARRY GERMAN TROOPS AGAIN: Twisted metal is all that remains of a Nazi army machine which was hit by a bomb dropped by a Royal Air Force flier in an attack on an Axis convoy crossing a North African desert.

AIR RAID WARNING IN CHUNGKING: Balloons strung on poles in various sections of the capital serve as a warning that Japanese planes are headed for the capital area. When enemy planes are sighted flying directly toward the city, the balloons are dropped and sirens are sounded.

GERMAN SHIPPING IN A FRENCH PORT: Nazi soldiers stand guard along the waterfront of a seacoast town in occupied France, where vessels of all kinds are being assembled for what may be an invasion attempt against Britain.

PICTORIAL NEWS OF THE WORLD

THE WEATHER
U. S. Weather Bureau.
Tonight—Showers, warmer.
Tomorrow—Fair, cooler.

THE TIMES RECORD

FINAL EDITION

Series 1941—No. 192. (Entered as Second Class Matter at the Postoffice at Troy, N. Y., under the Act of March 3, 1879.) TROY, N. Y., FRIDAY EVENING, AUGUST 15, 1941. (Published Daily Except Sunday) PRICE THREE CENTS

Roosevelt-Churchill Hint At Swift Aid For Russia In War With Nazis

Twelve American Flyers Among 22 Dead In British Air Crash

R.A.F. FERRY UNIT REPORTS SECOND TRAGEDY OF WEEK

Arthur Purvis, Chairman of British Supply Council, Among Men Who Died In Flaming Wreckage.

London (AP)—Twelve American flyers enlisted in the transatlantic bomber ferry service were killed yesterday in a take-off crash in which 22 persons in all died, including the Rt. Hon. Arthur Purvis, chairman of the British Supply Council in North America.

The crash, announced by the R. A. F. ferry command today, followed an almost identical ferry service accident Sunday in which another 22 were killed, making the week's toll 44 lives, including those of 19 Americans.

Not a man escaped yesterday's accident. The big plane, which was taking the Americans back to America in a group so that they could fly more new bombers back to Britain, burst into flame immediately on crashing.

Among the American victims was Capt. Joseph Creighton Mackey, 31, of Kansas City, who was the lone survivor of a crash in Newfoundland last February in which Sir Frederick Banting, codiscoverer of insulin, and two others were killed.

The dead included nine Canadians, among them Purvis, and one Englishman. Eleven of the Americans were pilots, and one was a radio operator. Seven of the Canadians were radio operators, one was a pilot.

Victims Listed.

The victims were listed as follows:

Capt. J. C. Mackey, Kansas City.
Capt. A. C. Earl, Huntington, W. Va.
Capt. M. D. Dilley, Kansas City.
Capt. J. J. Kerwin, Oakland, Calif.
Capt. E. B. Anding, Merrick, N. Y.
Capt. M. J. Wetzel, Jamesburg, N. J.
Capt. Gerald Hull, Royal Oak, Mich.
Capt. E. Hamel, Braintree, Mass.
Capt. P. F. Lee, jr., Frederick, Md.
Flying Officer W. L. Trimble, Fort Worth, Tex.
Flying Officer E. W. Watson, Torrence, Calif.
Flight Engineer R. F. Davis, Seattle, Wash.
Rt. Hon. Arthur P. Purvis, Montreal.
Capt. J. J Moffat, Toronto.
Radio Operator R. Coates, Yarmouth, N. S.
Radio Operator W. F. J. Goddard, Toronto.
Radio Operator R. A. Duncan, Port Arthur, Ont.
Radio Operator A. Tamblin, Port Arthur, Ont.
Radio Operator D. N. Hannant, Victoria, B. C.
Radio Operator J. P. Culbert, Montreal.
Capt. R. C. Stafford, Maidenhead, Berks, Eng.

Crashed at Take-off.

Officer Watson was the only man taken out of the plane alive, and he died in a hospital during the night.

The 22 were killed in a take-off accident, the second such accident to befall the ferry command within a week. Seven American officers died in the other crash, which occurred Sunday, making a total

(Continued on Page 2)

CIGARETTE TAX INCREASES.

Albany (UP)—State cigarette tax collections for July totaled $2,309,828.04, an increase of more than $100,000 over July 1940's $2,207,826.49, the State Tax Department announced today.

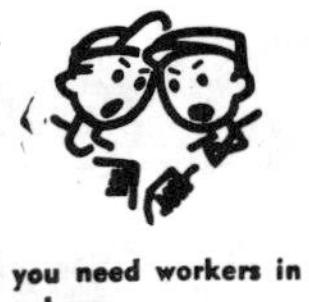

If you need workers in a hurry
A little ad will end your worry!

CARPENTERS (2) non-union wanted. Apply 1523 5th Ave., Watervliet, at 7:30 A.M.

Here's a Classified Ad from The Record Newspapers that brought good results in solving a Watervliet man's employment problem. Classified Ads are fast and inexpensive.

PHONE TROY 6100

Village Correspondent Airs Woes With Verse

Waterbury, Conn. (AP)—The sympathies of rural news gatherers the nation over are with the Oakville correspondent who sent the following report to the Waterbury American yesterday as his daily stint:

"Oakville—There can be a heap of grieving, while the hair is growing gray, for a lot of suffering sinners that one passes on the way, but the heartfelt sigh is deepest and the saddest tear is shed, for the village correspondent when the village news is dead.

"When no one throws a party and no one wrecks a bus; and no one gets arrested for stirring up a fuss; when no one starts a fire, and no one weds or woos—ah! the village correspondent when there isn't any news."

SARATOGA BOARD INSISTS ON NEW SITE FOR BRIDGE

Deadlock on Location of Hemstreet Park Span Continues; Supervisors Meet Here Monday.

Attempts to end, by conference, a potential deadlock over selection of a site for a proposed $200,000 bridge across the Hudson River, from Hemstreet Park in the Town of Schaghticoke to Mechanicville, have failed, according to a statement today by LeRoy H. Nible, head of the Rensselaer County Board of Supervisors.

Nible said that requests for conferences of Hemstreet Park representatives with Saratoga County officials had been rejected by County Superintendent of Highways Roy Williams, as well as by Mayor Homer Eckerson of Mechanicville, on the ground there has already been sufficient talk.

Saratoga County's Board of Supervisors is scheduled to meet late this afternoon to act on a pending resolution authorizing the expenditure of that county's share of the proposed project. Williams may also recommend that the county approve plans for location of the new bridge about 500 feet north of the present structure.

Old Bridge Condemned.

Hemstreet Park residents have been urging the construction of the new bridge at the site of the structure, condemned as unsafe for normal traffic, which it is to replace. They have asked this as a convenience and as a stimulant for the revival of oil and brick business in that section.

Saratoga County representatives, as well as those of the City of Mechanicville, demand the new location. Nible, as a representative of the Town of Schaghticoke, sought

(Continued on Page 18.)

SECOND C. I. O. STRIKE HALTS PRODUCTION AT BRIGGS PLANT

Detroit (UP)—The second strike within thirty hours at the Briggs Manufacturing Co.'s Mack body plant today idled approximately 9,500 workers in the automotive industry.

Company spokesmen asserted that C. I. O. United Automobile Workers in the body-in-white and the press shop "pulled another unauthorized strike and refused to work."

Lack of manpower, they said, forced the closing of the entire plant—affecting an early shift of 4,500 men.

Two U. A. W. shop stewards were dismissed yesterday for what the company called insubordination in provoking a slowdown of production. Union officials charged, however, that the men were discharged for refusing to force workers to "work under speedup conditions without adequate manpower."

REDS FALL BACK TO NEW DEFENSE LINE IN UKRAINE

Russians Also Battle Against New Drive on Leningrad In North; German Cities Bombed Again.

BY THE ASSOCIATED PRESS.

Russia's armies were apparently falling back beyond the Dnieper River, the next great defense line in the Ukraine, authoritative London quarters said today, while on the north, other Soviet troops battled fiercely to check a three-way German onslaught against Leningrad.

Soviet officials acknowledged that Marshal Semeon Budyenny's army of the southwest had abandoned the Bug River town of Pervomaisk, 115 miles northwest of Nikolaev, and Bevo, 100 miles northeast of Nikalaev.

There was no indication, however, that Nazi columns storming into the rich grain, iron and industrial province had yet captured either Odessa, Russia's big Black Sea port, or the manufacturing city of Nikolaev, 65 miles east.

London advices said there was some danger that Russian forces defending Odessa and Nikolaev might be cut off by German troops advancing toward the industrial center of Dnepropetrovsk, at the great bend of the Dnieper River.

Report Heavy Fighting.

A Red army war bulletin, silent on the bloody struggle in the Ukraine, mentioned only that fierce all-night fighting raged in the sectors of Kakisalmi, 75 miles north of Leningrad; Staraya Russa, about 140 miles south of Leningrad, and in Estonia, southwest of the old-time capital of the czars.

Italian military dispatches said Fascist troops entering the fight on the southern front had made their first contact with the Russians, encountering furious resistance.

The Germans claimed that all crossings of the Dnieper River for several hundred miles south of Kiev were already in Nazi hands, but there was no detailed report of any crossing.

British observers estimated that the area reported over-run by German, Hungarian, Rumanian and Italian troops contained about 50 per cent of the Ukraine's heavy industries.

German Cities Bombed.

Adolf Hitler's high command reiterated yesterday's claims of big gains in the Ukraine and declared briefly that "on other parts of the east front, fighting continued to be successful."

In the war in the air, the British reported that more than 300 R. A. F. bombers blasted overnight at Hanover, Brunswick, Magdeburg, Rotterdam and Boulogne. The Germans said an attempt was also made to attack Berlin, but claimed that Nazi defenses repulsed the raiders.

The British said yesterday's score was 14 German planes downed to five British craft missing.

The largest convoy to reach Malaya since the European war began landed thousands of Australian soldiers at Singapore, where they were dispatched immediately to defense posts. A British spokesman said the Far Eastern army was now considered sufficiently numerous and powerful to make any potential invader think ten times before attempting to strike at British interests in the area.

AUTOMOBILE UNION DELAYS ELECTION

Buffalo (UP)—The United Automobile, Aircraft and Agriculture Implement Workers' Union (C. I. O.) delayed its election of officers today at the request of Philip Murray, C. I. O. president.

Leaders of both right and left wing factions agreed on the action, which put off until late today a decision as to whether the union will retain its "liberal" secretary-treasurer, George F. Addes, or replace him with Richard T. Leonard, a conservative.

Lehman Asks Women On Defense Councils

Albany (UP)—Governor Lehman believes that women have "abundantly demonstrated that they can play an important role in the defense program."

Before leaving for a week's vacation on Nantucket Island, the governor sent letters to local defense councils urging the appointment of women to defense councils and special defense committees.

Lehman recalled that he had created the division of women's activities of the state council of defense, headed by Mrs. Winthrop Pennock of Syracuse. The governor added:

"Mrs. Pennock is at present developing plans for a volunteer participation program to be recommended by the state council of defense to each local defense council. In many places volunteers are already organized.

"A plan for enlistment of volunteers will have to be undertaken by the local defense council as part of its machinery. Mrs. Pennock's division will shortly be prepared to offer such a plan in complete detail and also will be able to come into a community, when requested, to help the local defense council put the plan in operation."

Roosevelt And Churchill Meet On Atlantic

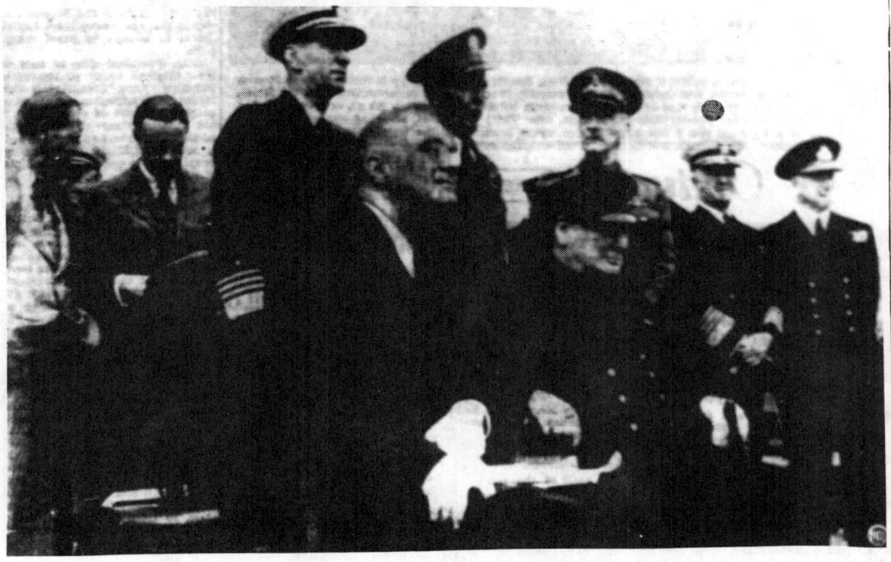

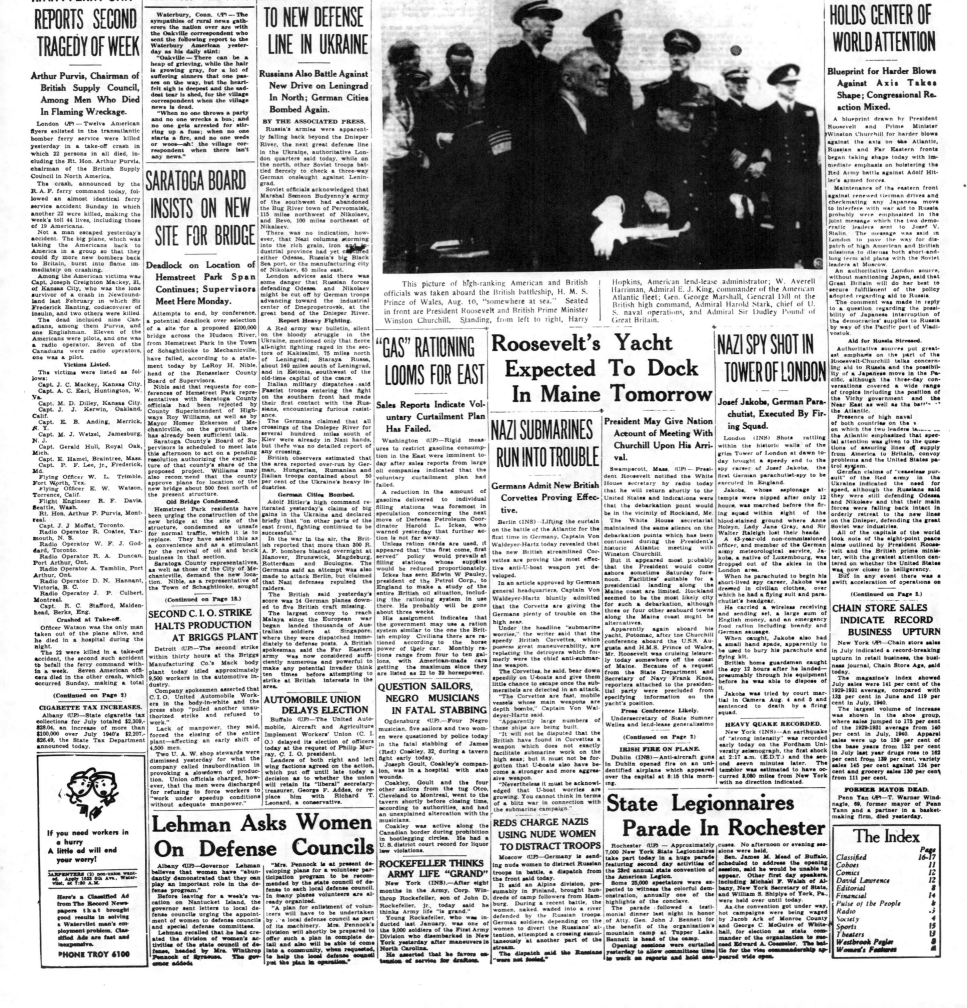

This picture of high-ranking American and British officials was taken aboard the British battleship, H. M. S. Prince of Wales, Aug. 10, "somewhere at sea." Seated in front are President Roosevelt and British Prime Minister Winston Churchill. Standing, from left to right, Harry Hopkins, American lend-lease administrator; W. Averell Harriman, Admiral E. J. King, commander of the American Atlantic fleet; Gen. George Marshall, General Dill of the British high command, Admiral Harold Stark, chief of U. S. naval operations, and Admiral Sir Dudley Pound of Great Britain.

"GAS" RATIONING LOOMS FOR EAST

Sales Reports Indicate Voluntary Curtailment Plan Has Failed.

Washington (UP)—Rigid measures to restrict gasoline consumption in the East were imminent today after sales reports from large oil companies indicated that the voluntary curtailment plan had failed.

A reduction in the amount of gasoline delivered to individual filling stations was foremost in speculation concerning the next move of Defense Petroleum Coordinator Harold L. Ickes, who warned yesterday that further action is not far away.

Unless ration cards are used, it appeared that "the first come, first served" policy would prevail at filling stations whose supplies would be reduced proportionately.

Ickes has sent Edwin W Pauley, president of the Petrol Corp., to England to make a study of the entire British oil situation, including the rationing system in use there. He probably will be gone about three weeks.

His assignment indicates that the government may use a ration system similar to the one the British employ Civilians there are rationed according to the horse power of their car. Monthly rations range from four to ten gallons, with American-made cars getting the maximum since they are listed as 22 to 39 horsepower.

QUESTION SAILORS, NEGRO MUSICIANS IN FATAL STABBING

Ogdensburg (UP).—Four Negro musician, five sailors and two women were questioned by police today in the fatal stabbing of James (Red) Coakley, 32, during a tavern fight early today.

Joseph Goult, Coakley's companion, was in a hospital with stab wounds.

Coakley, Goult and the four other sailors from the tug Otco, Cleveland to Montreal, went to the tavern shortly before closing time, according to authorities, and had an unexplained altercation with the musicians.

Coakley was active along the Canadian border during prohibition in bootlegging circles. He had a U. S. district court record for liquor law violations.

ROCKEFELLER THINKS ARMY LIFE "GRAND"

New York (INS).—After eight months in the Army, Corp. Winthrop Rockefeller, son of John D. Rockefeller, jr., today said he thinks Army life "is grand."

Young Rockefeller, who was inducted last January, was one of the 9,000 soldiers of the First Army Division who disembarked in New York yesterday after maneuvers in North Carolina.

He asserted that he favors extension of service for draftees.

Roosevelt's Yacht Expected To Dock In Maine Tomorrow

NAZI SUBMARINES RUN INTO TROUBLE

Germans Admit New British Corvettes Proving Effective.

Berlin (INS)—Lifting the curtain on the battle of the Atlantic for the first time in Germany, Captain Von Waldeyer-Hartz today revealed that the new British streamlined Corvettes are proving the most effective anti-U-boat weapon yet developed.

In an article approved by German general headquarters, Captain Von Waldeyer-Hartz bluntly admitted that the Corvetts are giving the Germans plenty of trouble on the high seas.

Under the headline "submarine worries," the writer said that the speedy British Corvettes, which possess great maneuverability, are replacing the detroyers which formerly were the chief anti-submarine weapon.

The Corvettes, he said, bear down speedily on U-boats and give them little chance to escape once the submersibels are detected in an attack.

"The Corvettes are fast, mobile vessels whose main weapons are depth bombs," Captain Von Waldeyer-Hartz said.

"Apparently large numbers of these ships are being built.

"It will not be disputed that the British have found in Corvettes a weapon which does not exactly facilitate submarine work on the high seas; but it must not be forgotten that U-boats also have become a stronger and more aggressive weapon.

"Nevertheless it must be acknowledged that U-boat worries are growing. You cannot think in terms of a blitz war in connection with the submarine campaign."

REDS CHARGE NAZIS USING NUDE WOMEN TO DISTRACT TROOPS

Moscow (UP)—Germany is sending nude women to distract Russian troops in battle, a dispatch from the front said today.

It said an Alpine division, presumably in Finland, brought hundreds of camp followers from Hamburg. During a recent battle, the women, naked. waded into a river defended by the Russian troops. German soldiers, depending on the women to divert the Russians' attention, attempted a crossing simultaneously at another part of the stream.

The dispatch said the Russians "were not fooled."

President May Give Nation Account of Meeting With Churchill Upon His Arrival.

Swampscott, Mass. (UP)—President Roosevelt notified the White House secretary by radio today that he will return shortly to the United States and indications were that the debarkation point would be in the vicinity of Rockland, Me.

The White House secretariat maintained the same silence on the debarkation points which has been continued during the President's historic Atlantic meeting with Winston Churchill.

But it appeared most probably that the President would come ashore sometime Saturday forenoon. Facilities suitable for a presidential landing along the Maine coast are limited. Rockland seemed to be the most likely city for such a debarkation, although three or four other seaboard towns along the Maine coast might be alternatives.

Apparently again aboard his yacht, Potomac, after the Churchill conference aboard the U.S.S. Augusta and H.M.S. Prince of Wales, Mr. Roosevelt was cruising leisurely today somewhere off the coast of Maine. Because of a request from the State Department and Secretary of Navy Frank Knox, reporters attached to the presidential party were precluded from specifying information on the yacht's position.

Press Conference Likely.

Undersecretary of State Sumner Welles and lend-lease generalissimo

(Continued on Page 2)

IRISH FIRE ON PLANE.

Dublin (INS)—Anti-aircraft guns in Dublin opened fire on an unidentified airplane which appeared over the capital at 8:15 this morning.

NAZI SPY SHOT IN TOWER OF LONDON

Josef Jakobs, German Parachutist, Executed By Firing Squad.

London (INS) Shots rattling within the historic walls of the grim Tower of London at dawn today brought a speedy end to the spy career of Josef Jakobs, the first German parachutist-spy to be executed in England.

Jakobs, whose espionage attempts were nipped after only 12 hours, was marched before the firing squad within sight of the blood-stained ground where Anne Boleyn, Lady Jane Gray, and Sir Walter Raleigh lost their heads.

A 43-year-old non-commissioned officer, and member of the German army meteorological service, Jakobs, a native of Luxembourg, was dropped out of the skies in the London area.

When he parachuted to begin his short-lived spy career, Jakobs was dressed in civilian clothes, over which he had a flying suit and parachutist's headgear.

He carried a wireless receiving and sending set, a large sum of English money, and an emergency food ration including brandy and German sausage.

When caught, Jakobs also had a small hand spade, apparently to be used to bury his parachute and flying kit.

British home guardsmen caught the spy 12 hours after he landed—presumably through his equipment before he was able to dispose of it.

Jakobs was tried by court martial in Camera Aug. 4 and 5 and sentenced to death by a firing squad.

HEAVY QUAKE RECORDED.

New York (INS)—An earthquake of "strong intensity" was recorded early today on the Fordham University seismograph, the first shock at 2:17 a.m. (E.D.T.) and the second seevn minutes later. The temblor was estimated to have occurred 3,080 miles from New York with no direction indicated.

State Legionnaires Parade In Rochester

Rochester (UP)—Approximately 7,000 New York State Legionnaires take part today in a huge parade featuring second day activities of the 23rd annual state convention of the American Legion.

Some 25,000 spectators were expected to witness the colorful demonstration, annually one of the highlights of the conclave.

The parade followed a testimonial dinner last night in honor of Atty. Gen. John J. Bennett for the benefit of the organization's mountain camp at Tupper Lake. Bennett is head of the camp.

Opening sessions were curtailed yesterday to allow committees time to work on reports and hold caucuses. No afternoon or evening sessions were held.

Sen. James M. Mead of Buffalo, scheduled to address the opening session, said he would be unable to appear. Other first day speakers, including Michael F. Walsh of Albany, New York Secretary of State, and William S. Shiplye of York, Pa., were held over until today.

As the convention got under way, hot campaigns were being waged by Jacob Ark of Monroe County and George C. McGuire of Whitehall, for election as state commander of the organization to succeed Edward A. Coeseler. The battle for the vice commandership appeared wide open.

SEA CONFERENCE HOLDS CENTER OF WORLD ATTENTION

Blueprint for Harder Blows Against Axis Takes Shape; Congressional Reaction Mixed.

A blueprint drawn by President Roosevelt and Prime Minister Winston Churchill for harder blows against the axis on the Atlantic, Russian and Far Eastern fronts began taking shape today with immediate emphasis on bolstering the Red Army battle against Adolf Hitler's armed forces.

Maintenance of the eastern front against renewed German drives and checkmating any Japanese move to interfere with war aid to Russia probably were emphasized in the joint message which the two democratic leaders sent to Josef V. Stalin. The message was said in London to pave the way for dispatch of high American and British missions to discuss both short-and-long term aid plans with the Soviet leaders at Moscow.

An authoritative London source, without mentioning Japan, said that Great Britain will do her best to secure fulfillment of the policy adopted regarding aid to Russia.

The comment was made in reply to a question regarding the possibility of Japanese interruption of the democracies' supplies to Russia by way of the Pacific port of Vladivostok.

Aid for Russia Stressed.

Authoritative sources put greatest emphasis on the part of the Roosevelt-Churchill talks concerning aid to Russia and the possibility of a Japanese move in the Pacific, although the three-day conversations covered a wide range of tropics including the position of the Vichy government and the Near East as well as the battle of the Atlantic.

Presence of high naval of both countries on the v on which the two leaders ta... the Atlantic emphasized that special attention was given to the questions of assuring lines of supply from America to Britain, convoy problems and the United States patrol system.

German claims of "ceaseless pursuit" of the Red army in the Ukraine indicated the need for speed, although the Russians said they were still defending Odessa and Nikolaev and that their main forces were falling back intact in orderly retreat to the new lines on the Dnieper, defending the great Soviet war industries.

All of the capitals of the world took note of the eight-point peace aims outlined by President Roosevelt and the British prime minister, with the greatest attention centered on whether the United States was now closer to belligerency.

But in any event there was a swift acceleration of operations on

(Continued on Page 2.)

CHAIN STORE SALES INDICATE RECORD BUSINESS UPTURN

New York (AP)—Chain store sales in July indicated a record-breaking upturn in retail business, the business journal, Chain Store Age, said today.

The magazine's index showed July sales were 141 per cent of the 1929-1931 average, compared with 133 per cent in June and 119 per cent in July, 1940.

The largest volume of increase was shown in the shoe group, where sales jumped to 175 per cent of the 1929-1931 average from 140 per cent in July, 1940. Apparel sales were up to 159 per cent of the base years from 132 per cent in July last year drugs rose to 162 per cent from 139 per cent, variety sales 145 per cent against 124 per cent and grocery sales 130 per cent from 111 per cent.

FORMER MAYOR DEAD.

Penn Yan (AP)—T. Warner Windnagle, 69, former mayor of Penn Yann and a partner in a basket-making firm, died yesterday.

The Index

COMMON COUNCIL TO FIX POLLING PLACES

Polling places for the November elections and next year's primaries will be designated tonight by the Common Council. The Troy aldermen are to resume semi-monthly meetings tonight after a summer recess and the approval of the polling places is one of the principal matters scheduled for the meeting.

NEW DIRECTOR FOR DRAMA AT JEWISH CENTER ARRIVES

Sol Schwarz of New York Introduced to Junior Board Members at Meeting Last Night.

Sol Schwarz of New York, who has had experience in the motion picture production studios in Hollywood, has been engaged as director of the drama for the Jewish Community Center.

He has already assumed his new duties, and was introduced to the members of the junior board of directors who confirmed his appointment at a meeting at the Center last night.

For seven years he was dramatic director at the Jewish Community House in Bensonhurst at Brooklyn.

He will direct the theatrical productions at the Center here and has announced plans for the presentation of a three-act play, "See My Lawyer," a hit on Broadway last season, at the Center Nov. 16, try-outs for which will be held next Wednesday.

Charles Cohen, recently named by the Senior Board to act as chairman of the Advisory Committee of the Junior Board, was introduced by Fred A. Glass, executive director of the center, to the Junior Board last night.

"Peace, On Earth," "Let Freedom Ring" and other plays.

He was also actor and stage manager for the Group Theater of New York.

In Hollywood he worked in make-up for both Warner Bros. and Metro-Goldwyn-Mayer, assisting in the production of such well known motion pictures as "Marie Antoinette," "Adventures of Marco Polo," "Test Pilot" and "Buccaneer."

The Junior Board of Directors of the Center met last evening to outline its program for the coming year.

The members decided to conduct two types of cultural activities this year. They planned to conduct cultural programs once a month for all junior members of the Center and their friends and also to sponsor a forum series of lectures and the like for junior members and the general public.

The board also voted to hold several social events, such as dances, during the year, the first of which will be an open house dance Sunday, Sept. 14, to which all younger members of the Jewish community will be invited. A committee consisting of Boris Paul, Miss Frances Novick and Miss Paula Goodman, was designated to take charge of the first event.

The group decided to sponsor three dramatic productions this year. Arrangements were made also to sponsor hobby clubs and holiday parties.

The board made arrangements to hold a party for boys and girls at the center Saturday evening, Sept. 13, as part of the open house program planned by the Center for that time.

POWNAL.

Thomas Haley of Hennington is spending this week with his sister, Mrs. W. F. Galusha, and other relatives.

Mrs. George Wilson and children have returned from two weeks spent with her parents, Mr. and Mrs. Amos Duval, at Chautauqua.

Kenneth Wells and children, Kenneth, jr., and Robert have returned to Manchester, Conn., after a week-end visit at the home of Charles Leonard.

Edgar Rathbun and Mrs. Frank L. Haley have received word of the death of a relative in Pittsfield Ward Brown, a resident of this village about 25 years ago. The funeral was held in Pittsfield Tuesday afternoon.

Harold Pratt returned yesterday, bringing Mr. and Mrs. James de Fuente after being their week-end guest in New York. The de Fuente family will spend two weeks more in the village before the opening of the fall concert season.

Mrs. Carolyn Prezzi was badly shaken up and bruised last week as she was driving to her work in Williamstown. The door of her car came open on the downgrade near the Kawee gift shop and as she tried to close it without stopping she lost control of the car which left the road, went down a bank and landed on its side.

Mr. and Mrs. George Heggie and children have returned to North Adams after an extended vacation at the home of Mrs. Heggie's parents, Mr. and Mrs. M. B. Bates. On Labor Day they were hosts to the following out-of-town relatives: Mr. and Mrs. George Hong of Bladwinsville, Mass.; Mr. and Mrs. Andrew Heggie of North Adams and Miss Julia Bates of Bennington.

Mr. and Mrs. William A. Mason were pleasantly surprised yesterday by their sons and daughter at a family dinner which al lthe immediate families attended at the home of the parents in celebration of their 33rd wedding anniversary. William A. Mason and Minnie Goodrich were married at the Methodist parsonage in this village by Rev. Mr. Mitchell, then pastor here. Both have spent their entire lives in Pownal except for a few years in Williamstown when Mr. Mason was employed at Mount Hope farms.

WHITEHALL.

Mr. and Mrs. Joseph Santora of Woodstock are visiting Mrs. Santora's parents, Mr. and Mrs. Joseph Bettini.

Mr. and Mrs. Charles Carswell spent the week-end with Mrs. Carswell's parents, Mr. and Mrs. Frank Kelly, Rutland.

The Whitehall Republican Club has completed plans for a clam-steam at Huletts Landing, Lake George, Sunday.

Changes in canal personnel have brought Benjamin Rock from Lock 13 at Utica to Lock 12, this village and James McCarthy from local lock to Syracuse.

INJURED AT WORK.

Joseph Pechette of Schuylerville, an employee at the United Paper Board mill at Victory Falls, was severely cut on the right hand yesterday when he caught his hand in a paper machine. Dr. James English attended Pechette and ordered him to the Saratoga Springs Hospital.

Students Register At City Schools On Opening Day

What subjects and what teachers were the main themes of conversation among hundreds of young people yesterday as schools reopened for another year. Above, Thomas O. Treharne, principal of Lansingburg High School, registers a group of girls. Below, at left W. Kenneth Doyle, principal of Troy High School, addresses an assembly of old students who returned yesterday. Freshmen, transfers and graduate students registered in the afternoon. At LaSalle Institute, right, below, Brother A. Patrick, new director and principal, receives the registrations of Alfred Collins and Frank Varone.

EDWARD J. RYAN, 53, DIES OF INJURIES IN UPSTATE CRASH

Crushed Chest and Fractured Skull Results in Troy Man's Death at Glens Falls Hospital.

A crushed chest and a fractured skull received in a Labor Day automobile accident resulted in the death yesterday afternoon of Edward J. Ryan, 53, of 450 Eighth Street, Troy, in the Glens Falls Hospital.

Ryan was driving alone Monday on the Hudson Falls-Fort Edward highway when his car and one driven by Ralph A. Haakin, 41, of Fort Edward, collided. Five persons were admitted to the Glens Falls Hospital as a result of the accident. One of them, James Quinn, 20, of 178 Sixth Avenue, Troy, is still in the hospital with a broken nose and a cut face.

A native of Troy, Mr. Ryan was a son of the late Joseph and Mary Agnes Winters Ryan. He was educated in the Troy schools, and for the last 25 years has been employed by the Manning Paper Co. He was a member of the International Brotherhood of Paper Makers, Local 17, and of St. Patrick's Church.

Surviving are his wife, Mrs. Mary Wall Ryan, a son, Edward W. Ryan and a daughter, Betty Ryan, all of Troy, and two sisters, Mrs. James Connelly and Miss Katherine Ryan of Glens Falls.

Funeral services will be held Saturday at 9 from the George F. McLoughlin & Son Funeral Home, 3258 Sixth Avenue, and at 9.30 a.m. from St. Patrick's Church, where a requiem mass will be sung. Burial will be in St. Peter's Cemetery.

JOINS SCHOOL STAFF.

Miss Georgeanna Jaynes of Treadwell has assumed her new duties as cafeteria manager at the Averill Park Central School. She recently graduated from the New York Technical Institute at Delhi.

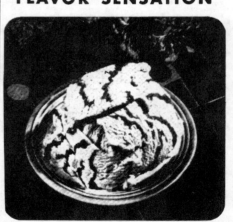

MOVIE STAR

HORIZONTAL
1 Dream.
5 Brag.
9 Tag.
10 Green spot on desert.
12 Conducted.
14 Mistake.
16 Small rug.
17 Dark brown.
19 Trimmed with balls.
21 Horses.
22 Make evident.
23 A state (abbr.).
25 Rest.
26 Nova Scotia (abbr.).
27 Symbol for tellurium.
28 Bark.
30 Compass point.
31 Used in baseball.
32 He portrayed "Pasteur."
33 His first name.
34 Wooden pin.
35 Steamship (abbr.).
37 Spanish gentleman.
39 Aerial railway (abbr.).
40 Perform.
41 Exists.
43 Symbol for nickel.
44 Superiority.
48 Forgive.
50 Bodies at rest.
52 To check growth.
53 Wager.
55 Roofing stone.
56 Wine cup.
57 Irked.
59 Prefix (pl.).
60 Theme.
61 Stir to action.

VERTICAL
1 Unit of electrical capacity.
2 Homes.
3 Company (abbr.).
4 Sweet potato.
5 A small amount.
6 Bone (Latin).
7 Rains and hails.
8 Wigwam.
9 Three (Italian prefix).
11 Dips in the middle.
13 Performed.
14 Black wood.
15 Having recollection.
17 Vantage places.
18 Not a liability.
20 Love.
21 Senior (abbr.).
24 Desert animal.
27 Claw.
29 Bulldog (slang).
31 Young flower.
34 Fruit (pl.).
36 Let it stand.
38 A relative.
40 Fields.
42 Found on a fish.
44 Feather.
45 Genus of wild goats.
46 Plural suffix.
47 Warehouse.
49 Greek letter.
51 It is.
53 Turkish title.
54 Terrace (abbr.).
57 Southern state (abbr.).
58 Perform.

BOOSTER NIGHT TO BE OBSERVED BY COUNTY GRANGES

Program on September 30 Designed to Acquaint Public With Work of Organization.

All subordinate units of the Grange in Rensselaer County will observe "Booster Night" Sept. 30, with meetings in their own halls.

"Booster Night" is observed by the Grange nationally each year and is intended to help the public become acquainted with its work. As elsewhere in the country, each subordinate unit in this section will invite their friends and all other persons interested in agriculture to attend their meetings that night.

Programs are being arranged by the various groups to demonstrate in one way or another the types of work which they do through the entire year.

Elton K. Hanks, agricultural agent in charge of the Rensselaer County Farm Bureau, will deliver an address at the "Booster Night" meeting of Hoosick Grange at Thorpe's Hall in Hoosick Falls.

Spelling Bee Planned.

A spelling bee will be conducted between six former teachers and six present teachers of schools in the Town of Hoosick at the meeting of Hoosick Grange at Hoosick Falls tonight. Elton J. Hakes, district superintendent of schools, will referee the bout. Mrs. Burton Pine will head the team of former teachers and Eugene Avery is selecting the personnel of their opponents.

Stiff competition is expected in three matches to be conducted at the meeting of Pomona Grange, West Sand Lake Grange Hall, next Wednesday. The contests will be log-sawing, with the log-sawing match between teams of women, and a yeast roll contest, all in the afternoon. The meeting will get under way at 10.30 a.m.

Compositions entered by children of the juvenile Granges of the county in the national essay contest on the general subject of "What America Means to Me," are being submitted to the state juvenile superintendent for judging. A publicity contest for lecturers of the various Granges in the county will close at the end of this month. The best book of clippings of Grange activities submitted in the competition will be entered in a state contest.

Brunswick to Work Degrees.

Brunswick Grange, meeting at Center Brunswick tomorrow, will work the third and fourth degrees on six candidates, Ralph Bonesteel, Miss Eleanor Krogh, Miss Esther Herrington, Albert Thomas, George Calhoun and Russell Peetz. Plans will be completed for the annual clambakeam to be held by the group Sept. 20, at 6 p.m. at the hall. Johnsonville Grange will pay off its mortgage with $500 it made conducting a restaurant at the Schaghticoke Fair this year. The Johnsonville Grange has been running a restaurant at the fair for eight years, to raise the money.

East Greenbush Grange Monday elected its delegates and alternate to the meeting of the State Grange at Rochester in December. Mrs. Edwin Newkirk was named delegate and Mr. Newkirk associate delegate with Mrs. Cornelius VanKampen as alternate and Mr. VanKampen as associate alternate.

The lecturer's program included community singing, recitation of poems by Mrs. George Reed and Miss Jennie Juretta, a reading by Miss Catherine Kemp, an outline of current events by Cornelius VanKampen and the reading of an article on farm labor as affected by the draft by Robert Newkirk.

Reading Club Children Get Awards

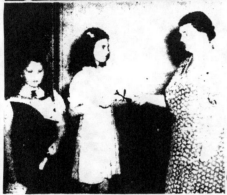

The Summer Reading Club of the Troy Public Library Children's Department closes with a party and awards to readers of ten or more books this season. Helen Cullitz, center below, who read thirty books, and Dolores Houghton, who read 27, receive certificates from Miss Fanny C. Howe. Pictured at the party yesterday, above, are Vernon Zuckerman, Martin Smith, Ann Singsheimer, Helen Cullitz, Anna Mae Conroy, Elizabeth Kasparian, Rita Stanger and Margaret Ann Thomas.

WYNANTSKILL

Mr. and Mrs. Fred Sturges are enjoying a motor trip through the Adirondack Mountains.

Mr. and Mrs. Terjian and family are recent visitors in Canada, making the trip by motor.

James Kelley of Ashcroft Street underwent an operation for appendicitis at the hospital in Troy recently.

Mrs. Cora Hidley underwent an operation at the Troy Hospital for the removal of a tumor. Dr. O. P. Smith performed the operation.

Dr. and Mrs. John Kazuton of New York were recent guests of Mr. and Mrs. Charles Moore. Mrs. Kazuton was formerly Miss Lama Moore, R. N.

A turkey supper will be served at the Reformed Church Thursday evening, Sept. 18, under the auspices of the Ladies' Aid Society from 6 p.m. on.

Milton Kenneth Austin celebrated his tenth birthday at his home Monday afternoon. Games were played and refreshments served to ten guests from a table centered by a cake with ten candles. Milton received a number of gifts.

A Townsend Club was organized last evening at Firemen's Hall with an enrollment of 26 members. The following officers were elected: President, Russell Vanderzee; first vice president, Henry Lutz; second vice president, Samuel Williams; secretary and treasurer, Mrs. George Film. Rev. Lewis Moody of Eagle Mills presided at the election and Fred G. Brooks was the speaker and showed interesting movies. The next meeting will be held Tuesday evening, Sept. 23, at George Film's gas station. The members were invited to attend a meeting and entertainment of Club No. 2 in observance of Founders Week at the Y. W. C. A. Friday evening, Sept. 19. Music was furnished by Mrs. Hans Lund, pianist, after which refreshments were served.

JOHNSONVILLE.

Miss Arline Depew of Defreestville was a recent guest of Mrs. Kenneth Heald.

The Woman's Society of Christian Service will meet with Mrs. E. I. Van Doren at 2 p.m. tomorrow.

The Woman's Society of the Presbyterian Church will meet in the church parlors tomorrow afternoon.

Mrs. Franklin Losaw and daughter of Hyde Park were week-end guests of Mr. and Mrs. A. J. Losaw.

Mr. and Mrs. Charles Conquest and son Leon were week-end guests of Mr. and Mrs. Charles O'Donnell and sons at Glens Falls.

Edward Powers has returned to Newport, R. I., after spending a nine-day furlough at the home of his parents, Mr. and Mrs. John Powers.

Miss Ruth Dunham is at Vassar College, Poughkeepsie, where she is taking three weeks of practice work before entering Morrisville College for the fall term.

GRAFTON.

The tax books are now at the Town Clerk's office.

Mr. and Mrs. C. W. Ellett spent the week-end in the north.

Rev. and Mrs. V. Vanderlinder and son are enjoying a two weeks' vacation.

Priv. Raymond Moore, stationed at Plattsburg, is home on a short furlough.

Mrs. Catherine Coffey of Troy spent the week-end with Miss Gertrude Magill.

Mr. and Mrs. Fred Stanley and son have returned to Utica after a few weeks' visit with Mr. and Mrs. Jay Smith.

Mr. and Mrs. Charles Moore and daughter, Nancy Jane, are spending some time with Mr. and Mrs. C. Simmons.

Cranium Crackers

Imperiled Iran

War struck for the third time in another continent when Iran followed Iraq and Syria as an Asiatic battleground where the British were getting the jump on the Germans. Here's your chance to take a penpoint tour of this fabled land.

1. By what name was Iran formerly known and what are its inhabitants called?
2. What is Iran's capital, and by what title is the ruler, Riza Kahn Pahlavi, known?
3. Which of these resources are not found in Iran: Iron, oil, borax, bauxite, cobalt, rubber.
4. For what wool product is Iran especially famous?
5. What famous king of ancient Iran invaded Greece in 480 B. C. after defeat at Marathon and was checked at now famous Thermopylae Pass?

Answers on Page 12.

CAMBRIDGE.

Mrs. George Ridler and son Theodore have been spending a few days in New York.

Miss K. Frances Cleave, superintendent of the Mary McClellan Hospital, will attend the 43rd annual convention of the American Hospital Association in Atlantic City, N. J., next week.

Maj. Robert R. Raymond, jr., son of Col. and Mrs. R. R. Raymond, stationed at Fort Bragg, N. C., is under orders to go to Puerto Rico and expects to leave Sept. 26. Robert Burlingame of New York City, a grandson, has enlisted in the U. S. Navy.

THE WEATHER
U. S. Weather Bureau.
Tonight—Cloudy, warmer.
Tomorrow—Cloudy.

THE TIMES RECORD

INTER-AMERICAN EDITION

Series 1941—No. 236. (Entered as Second Class Matter at the Postoffice at Troy, N. Y., under the Act of March 3, 1879.) TROY, N. Y., TUESDAY EVENING, OCTOBER 7, 1941. (Published Daily Except Sunday) PRICE THREE CENTS

Sage College To Confer Six Degrees As Part Of Inter-American Week

Nazis Suffer Huge Losses In Ukraine, London Informed

Invaders Being Pounded by Heavy Guns of Red Fleet; Revolt Spreading on Continent.

By THE ASSOCIATED PRESS

Adolf Hitler's high command claimed victory over the Russians today in a great new battle in the Ukraine, north of the Sea of Azov, but London military quarters reported that the Germans had been checked with severe losses and that guns of the Soviet Black Sea fleet were heavily pounding the invaders.

Front-line dispatches to Red Star, the Soviet Army newspaper, reported a violent battle was raging on the central (Moscow) front, with Marshal Timoshenko's troops striking fierce blows against German armored wedges driven into the Russian lines.

Soviet infantry, supported by tanks and aviation, were reported to have attacked heavy German troop concentrations immediately after a long march, destroying 198 tanks and killing more than 1,000 Nazis in three sectors.

German Losses Heavy.

Red Star said a Soviet tank battalion ambushed a Nazi tank column southeast of Kiev, the German-held Ukraine capital, and smashed seven tanks. Bloody German losses were reported here, as well.

On the northern front, the Red Army announced that Leningrad's defense guns had smashed 19 German earth-and-timber forts on the approaches to the old czarist capital, silenced two artillery batteries and put other Nazi siege weapons out of action.

Masses of German troops were said to have been dispersed by Soviet fire.

Germany's bitter war to stamp out revolt in the conquered nations by firing-squad, hangman and guillotine brought six more executions—and one suspended death sentence.

But rebellion continued to spread.

Serb Rebels Attack Town.

German press dispatches acknowledged that Nazi troops and two companies of Croatian Ustachas had been required to smash a putsch led by an attorney's daughter in the west Serbian town of Sabac, in old Yugoslavia.

Serb rebels had stormed the town, these dispatches said, far outnumbering the German garrison which "offered heroic resistance" until rescued by Nazi reinforcements.

Bands of Chetniks (guerrilla fighters) and armed farmers took part in the attack on the town, which lies only forty miles west of Belgrade, the former Yugoslav capital, the Germans said.

Simultaneously, the British government announced it was collecting evidence against Germans responsible for murder, oppression and cruelty to hostages and others in Nazi-occupied territories.

In Paris, the body of a woman with ankles bound and a paving-stone tied to the neck, was taken from the River Seine. Police identified it as that of Madame Tonia Masse, secretary of the anti-Bolshevist League of Paris.

Report Reds Retreating.

A bulletin from Hitler's field headquarters indicated that the battle north of the Azov Sea was part of the "gigantic new developments" which the fuehrer himself declared had begun last Wednesday.

"German troops, shoulder to shoulder with troops of the Allied countries, are pursuing the defeated enemy," the Nazi communique said.

"Motorized and tank units thrust deep into the enemy retreating columns."

The Russians, acknowledging that the Germans had "wedged into our lines" at an unspecified sector of the western (Moscow) front, reported that Soviet tanks and bombers had destroyed 34 Nazi tanks in fierce counter-blows.

BOY DIES OF INJURIES.

Leroy (AP)—Francis D. Carli, 5, died yesterday of injuries suffered Sunday when the automobile in which he was riding with his parents collided with a trailer truck.

Study South America, Advice of AP Editor

Syracuse (AP)—The American public, already the best informed in the world, is due to learn more of its neighbors to the south in the next few months, says the foreign news editor of the Associated Press.

"The time has arrived for a better understanding of South America and to accomplish this newspapers here probably will print more and more news from those countries," J. M. Roberts told the New York State Society of Newspaper Editors yesterday.

WOODLAND BABE FOUND ALIVE, SAFE AFTER EIGHT DAYS

Pamela Hollingworth, Aged 5, Found in New Hampshire Wilderness by CCC Searchers.

Conway, N. H. (AP)—Pretty little Pamela Hollingworth sat up in a hospital bed today and ate her first meal in eight days — the amazing survivor of more than a week of wandering and waiting in the freezing cold of the heavy forests that blanket Mount Chocorua.

Chipper and apparently little affected by her long stay in the open, the 5-year-old youngster's first thoughts were of scrambled eggs.

Hospital authorities were astounded at her conditon. Dr. Albert Williams at Memorial Hospital said she probably could go home in two or three days, that her lungs were clear and that her tiny toes—frostbitten by temperatures which sank to nearly twenty degrees above zero were responding to treatment.

Slept Beside Road.

Recalling that she wore only overalls and sneakers and was without shelter night after night, the doctor said Pamela showed more than normal stamina and was "amazingly rational" when she was found just as darkness fell last night after hope for her had been abandoned. She had wandered away from a family picnic on Sept. 28.

Her father, Joseph Hollingworth, Lowell, Mass., business man, reiterating that he knew he would "find her alive," said Pamela told him she had slept "side of a road until one day I crawled to a brook."

The girl was found near a tiny mountain stream, and the father said he believed she had not wandered far from it during the entire week. This, doctors believed, enabled her to conserve her strength.

Search of the wilderness near a road where Mrs. Thelma Knight, an Augusta, Me., school teacher, reported seeing a small girl a week ago Sunday, led to the finding of "Pammy."

Authorities telephoned to Mrs. Knight last week and she returned to Conway on Sunday and pointed out the spot where she had seen the girl. It was at the end of a day's search in that region yesterday that Pamela was found.

The curly-haired child, weighing 45 pounds when she vanished from a family picnic Sept. 28, was eight pounds lighter when amazed searchers heard her shout "hi" just before dusk fell last night.

Veteran Woodsmen Amazed.

Veteran woodsmen and medical men termed her survival even more

(Continued on Page 6)

Several Girls Wanted Bicycle

BICYCLE—Girl's Cadillac, size 26. In perfect condition. Will sel reasonably. Tel. Troy 6136-W for further details.

Is there a girl's bicycle stored away around your home because it's no longer used? There's a market for it now, because this Classified Ad in The Record Newspapers recently brought several inquiries about the bike.

Phone Your Ads To
TROY 6100

Send Greetings On Troy's Unity Program

Among scores of well-wishers for the success of Troy's Inter-American celebration were the above, top (left to right), are shown Dr. J. M. Troncoso, minister to the U. S. from the Dominican Republic; Capt. C. E. Alfaro, ambassador from Ecuador; Gen. Anastazio Samozo, president of Nicaragua; below, (left to right), Dr. C. A. Arroyo del Rio, president of Ecuador; Gov. Herbert H. Lehman, Gen. Fulgencio Batista, president of Cuba; bottom (left to right), Gen. Isaias Medina, president of Venezuela; Dr. Julian R. Caceres, minister from Honduras, and Dr. Aurelio F. Concheso, ambassador from Cuba.

Hemisphere Leaders Acclaim Troy's Inter-American Week

Leading a host of well-wishers for the success of Troy's Inter-American Week celebration, Governor Herbert H. Lehman, in a letter to The Record Newspapers, has sent greetings to the representatives of the 21 American republics who will be in attendance and expressing gratification at this effort of the people of Troy toward promoting closer hemisphere relations.

"I think this plan is a splendid one," wrote the Governor, "and should do much to cement friendly relations with other American republics. I would be very pleased indeed if through the columns of your papers you would convey hearty greetings to the representatives of the South American republics. I hope it will be possible for me to welcome some of them in person during their stay in Troy.

"I hope the celebration will be most successful in every way.

If my official duties permit, Mrs. Lehman and I hope to attend one or more of the sessions."

Leaders from all parts of the hemisphere have hailed the event as a notable step in furthering the national effort as a friendlier spirit and understanding among all the American nations. Diplomats, statesmen, business and professional men and writers have written commending the event. Excerpts from their letters follow:

Comments of Ambassadors.

ARNO KONDER, minister plenipotentiary counselor of the embassy of Brazil:

It is with great pleasure that I express my great appreciation for the interesting and important initiative of Russell Sage College which contributes so much for the development of closer ties be-

(Continued on Page 6)

FLAG RAISING TO MARK OPENING OF EVENT TOMORROW

Wife of President Roosevelt To Lead Music Hall Panel Discussion on Friday Afternoon.

One of the outstanding features of Inter-American Week will be the conferring of honorary degrees on six distinguished women representing six republics to the south, the executive committee announced today.

The program opens formally at 11 a.m. tomorrow with a flag-raising ceremony in Sage Park.

Mrs. Franklin Delano Roosevelt will present the candidates for the degrees. The colorful ceremony will take place Friday night when Russell Sage College sponsors a convocation in Music Hall.

Mrs. Roosevelt was made a Doctor of Humane Letters by Russell Sage in 1929 and is one of the first persons to receive an honorary degree from the college.

On 25th Anniversary.

The women to be honored by Russell Sage College, which is marking its 25th anniversary in connection with the Inter-American program, are as follows

Senorita Maria Josephina Rabello Albano of Brazil

Senora Ester Neira de Calvo of Panama

Senorita Marina Nunez del Prado of Bolivia.

Senora Ana Rosa de Martinez Guerrero of Argentina

Senorita Graciela Mandujano of Chile.

Mrs. Concha Romero James of Mexico.

This group of national leaders will come to Troy primarily for a panel discussion Friday afternoon in Music Hall on the subject, "The Women of the Americas: Their Part in Promoting Inter-American Understanding and Good Will."

They will participate in the discussion under Mrs. Roosevelt's leadership.

Also to be present will be Miss Mary N. Winslow of Washington, adviser for civic projects on the staff of the Coordinator of Inter-American Affairs.

For Inter-American Week.

The group is being brought together especially for Inter-American Week of Troy by the Office of the Corordinator of Inter-American Affairs.

It is expected that the role which women can play in helping to achieve hemispheric solidarity will be discussed from many points of view, and that an important contribution to good will among the Americas may result from the exchange. The afternoon panel discussion under Mrs. Roosevelt's aegis and the international slate of speakers will be among the first of its kind in the United States. "This fact, and indeed the whole program of Inter-American Week, is a mark of the growing internationalism and broader thinking of the people of the United States," said Miss Gertrude Norton, chairman of the women's committee in charge of the roundtable discussion.

All of the women taking part in the panel discussion are distinguished in their own countries,

(Continued on Page 18.)

Churchmen Advocate 'Angelus Hour' in U. S.

New York (INS) — The Federal Council of Churches today proposed that a modern "Angelus Hour"—a daily minute of prayer—be instituted by various church congregations throughout the United States.

Delegates to a council-sponsored meeting, representing 16 different denominations, agreed that such a daily minute of silence, marked by the ringing of church bells, would be a significant expression of Christian unity and faith in the future.

America Rediscovered—An Editorial

Historians of the future undoubtedly will record the fact that the continent of America was rediscovered—by Americans—some time about 1939, coincidental with the formal opening of the second World War.

Rumors of the opening up of an entirely new hemisphere in 1492 by an obscure Italian idea-man named Christopher Columbus had gradually leaked out to the great mass of Americans during the 450 years following that discovery, but as far as any feeling of relationship of solidarity of interests was concerned, the land which Columbus discovered might just as well have been far across the China Sea.

It is a sad fact that throughout its history the United States has felt itself infinitely more closely related to the culture, history and commerce of various European nations than to the Republics to the South. The average North American child can reel off the date of the Norman Conquest in England, the glories of the Renaissance in Italy, the salient causes and effects of the French Revolution, but the average North American adult is abysmally ignorant, for example, of the causes and effects of the Mexican Revolution, or the great names of America: Bolivar, San Martin, Sucre, O'Higgins, Hidalgo.

Similarly, the people of Latin America have never considered their destinies tied to the strange rude people to the North, but rather to the decayed grandeur of an ancient empire across the sea, to what the Liberator, Bolivar, was pleased to call "the decadent philosophies" of the Old World.

What relations have existed between the two Americas have not always been felicitous, or conducive to better understanding. Generations of myopic North American diplomats and professional politicians addicted to shaking the "big stick" at the slightest provocation, or even without any provocation, haven't helped. Nor has a loud and truculent press, whose attitude toward Latin America has often been dictated by an impassioned defense of large commercial interests in the United States which periodically seem to be involved with the very unreasonable, very backward Hispano-American governments, been of much service. The average literal-minded Latin American didn't have to believe in fairy tales. The "Ogre of the North" was a very real and very terrifying old gentleman with a high hat, white goatee, striped pantaloons, and a voracious appetite who lurked across the Rio Bravo just achin

(Continued on Page 22)

The Index

Need For More Trade Between Americas Stressed At Meeting

(Continued From Page 11.)

problems the United States will face when the national defense effort shall be required no more, and when the 15,000,000 workers who will be employed in that effort in the next one or two years shall return to the industries of peace.

"A better and wider economic co-ordination between the United States and the rest of the nations of the continent may be enormously profitable to this country as well as to the rest of America. It will strengthen the bonds of every order which ties us to this great republic. But in searching for the solution of these problems it is paramount to keep always present the same good will and good neighbor doctrine which, are materializing the political unity of the continent."

Must Buy, Too.

Mr. Watson, summarizing the three addresses, declared that "we have learned, if we will sell our products, we must buy Latin-American goods."

Commenting on a statement of one of the speakers that "We would like very much to be your best customer, but we beg of you to consider our economic problems for other nations will compete with you which have no time to consider idealistic relations before business," he declared that "every Latin-American country can look to us not only as a good neighbor in conversation but also in every

way, not forgetting the protection of the lives and property of your people." In conclusion he called for complete application of the Golden Rule in the solution of all difficulties.

Samuel W. McCochrane, president of the Troy Chamber of Commerce, acted as chairman of the meeting. Flags of the 21 republics were on standards across the stage.

A program of Latin-American music by the Troy Vocal Society opened the meeting. The chorus was directed by Dr. Elmer T. Tidmarsh with H. Townsend Heister at the piano.

The meeting was sponsored by the Troy Chamber of Commerce, the Troy Business and Professional Women's Club and the Junior Chamber of Commerce.

Frank Callahan of Schenectady, chairman of the Inter-American committee of the United States Junior Chamber of Commerce, was among the guests seated on the platform.

Gifts To College.

The flags of Venezuela, Mexico and Nicaragua, a painting of Simon Bolivar — South America's greatest hero–the gift also of Venezuela, and an age-old silver necklace and headpiece—the gift of the republic of Chile, were presented to the college yesterday as tokens commemorating the first citywide endeavor in this North American republic to promote understanding and good will, peace, friendship and solidarity, throughout the New World.

Later in the day, in the presence of eminent visitors from Latin-America, a city street was formally designated Bolivar Avenue as Troy's expression of Inter-American good will.

The ceremony took place in the Highland Avenue extension with Mayor Frank J. Hogan and Dr. James Laurence Meader, president of Russell Sage College, participating. As the new street sign was erected, City Clerk James M. McGrath read the ordinance adopted by the Common Council giving the new name to the street.

Latin-American Culture and Economics Discussed

Angel Ortega of Cuba, R. P. I. graduate, above left, presided at yesterday afternoon's Music Hall Inter-American meeting on the culture and art of Latin-American countries, at which Dr. Robert F. Pattee, below, right, of the State Department and Dr. Robert C. Smith, below, left, of the Library of Congress were principal speakers. At the evening meeting on economic relations, also in Music Hall, Thomas J. Watson, International Business Machines Corp. president, above right, is shown presiding.

The Political Stage Today

By David Lawrence

Washington — "Equal justice under law" is the motto which is engraved on the building which houses the Supreme Court of the United States and it is salutary to ask every now and then whether that guarantee is more honored nowadays in the breach than in the observance.

For several months now high officials of the Roosevelt administration and many senators have been carrying on a campaign of persecution against the Aluminum Company of America, calling it a monopoly and a trust and an octopus and what not. The country has been asked to believe that this so-called monopoly was responsible for the aluminum shortage or for lack of expanded facilities.

This week Judge Francis G. Caffey of the United States District Court has cleared the aluminum company of such charges after a trial which lasted nearly three years and after one of the most exhaustive inquiries and evidence-taking processes in the which history of federal court legislation.

Will the high officials of the administration and the senators who have been so loose in their charges now acknowledge they have been in error? Will they seek to undo the wrong they have done? Will they endeavor to erase the innuendoes and suspicions they have levelled against an innocent company? It will provide an interesting test of "equal justice under law."

Final Judgment To Come.

It is true the final judgment has not been rendered and that the case will be appealed to the Supreme Court where it is often the technical difference between Tweedle Dee and Tweedle Dum that decides many a charge especially in these days of a court chosen largely from a class conscious clique. But the decision by Judge Caffey at least reveals that the question of monopoly was not so clearly resolved as Secretary Ickes seems to have thought it to be. Mr. Ickes has insisted that he was asked to deal with a monopoly and refused to grant the Aluminum Company of America the power it wanted in the northwest which with to make aluminum. His constant defense has been that the law forbids him to grant power to a monopoly. So he prejudiced the case and withheld the power.

Now Mr. Ickes has gone so far as to criticize Jesse Jones, Federal Loan Administrator, because he went ahead and made a contract with the aluminum company for the operation of an aluminum plant for the government. The company gave its services gratis in building the plant but Mr. Ickes seems to think the contract is a bad one because it doesn't tie the aluminum company in knots and presuppose bad faith and eventual non performance before operations start. In such an atmosphere of suspicion no good contract could be written

Implies Officials Best Judges.

Mr. Ickes speaks of freedom "for the press" and not "of the press" and he implies that administration officials with political axes to grind are the best judges of what is fair

or unfair for the newspapers to print. But the eminent Secretary of the Interior omits to say a word about the freedom or license permitted to government officials to use their offices to smear any company, institution or individual they please and they cannot be held accountable for their rampages.

Oddly enough, democracy doesn't want even reckless talking officials to be curbed. It's one of the aspects of give and take which lend zest to the democratic process and it would be a dull world indeed if the Secretary of the Interior or some of his friends on Capitol Hill were not permitted to spread their accusations against the aluminum company on the record from time to time. Unfortunately, however, it isn't the way to get aluminum manufactured and over in Germany, Herr Hitler doesn't have to worry about aluminum production or the petty prejudices of the members of his official entourage. He gets aluminum produced because he gives the task to those who know how to make it. It would be wonderful if all the aluminum needed for defense could be produced in America right now leaving such adventures as lambasting the alleged monopolies to the post war days when there may be time

for these things and when tempers may be a lot more judicial than they appear to be in government circles today.

Society News

Engagement of Sage Student Announced

Mr. and Mrs. John Allen Van Wie of 492 Pawling Avenue announce the engagement of their daughter, Miss Elinor F. Van Wie to Douglas H. Moreton, son of Mr. and Mrs. Harry H. Moreton of Los Angeles, Cal., and East Orange, N. J.

Miss Van Wie is a graduate of Emma Willard School and a member of the senior class at Russell Sage College.

Mr. Moreton was graduated from Menlo Junior College and the Rensselaer Polytechnic Institute, Class of 1941, where he was a member of the Rensselaer Society of Engineers.

The announcement was made at an informal party held this afternoon at the home of the future bride's parents.

No date has been set for the wedding.

Sage Alumnae Hold Party At Hotel

Approximately 75 tables of bridge were in play this afternoon at the card party and fashion show given by Troy Chapter of Russell Sage College Alumnae at The Hendrick Hudson.

Mrs. A. Kendall Roberts was general chairman, assisted by the following committee chairmen; Refreshments, Miss Jane Smith; prizes, Mrs. David E. Hunt; fashion show, Mrs. E. Stewart Ferguson; tickets, Mrs. Edward M. Hutton, jr.; music; Mrs. Edward Schnurr; candy, Miss Bettina Ellis; tallies, Miss Dorothy C. White; waitresses, Miss Catherine Carrigan; reservations, Mrs. James E. Covert; posters, Mrs. Eric W. Barnes; door prize, Miss Carolyn Boxley, and publicity, Miss Sally Sise.

A fashion show was a feature of the afternoon, with the fashions furnished by William P. Herbert and Co.

Individual table prizes were packages of assorted Christmas wrappings.

Dance Pupils Enjoy Costume Party

The annual Halloween costume party of the juvenile dance pupils of Miss Irma J. MacNaughton was conducted this afternoon at her studio, 71 Fourth Street.

The program included entertainment in the form of novelty dances, solos and group numbers, and a variety of Halloween games for the children. Prizes were awarded for the prettiest and funniest costumes and refreshments were served.

Given Party

Miss Florence Schmidt of Brunswick gave a farewell party in honor of Miss Dorothy Nixson of Eagle Mills last night. Miss Nixson will make her future home in Troy. The color scheme was in keeping with the Halloween season. Games were played and vocal selections were rendered.

Wed Recently in Church Ceremony

—Lloyd Photo.

Mr. and Mrs. Charles Bulson are pictured above after their marriage. Mrs. Bulson was Miss Lillian Gutbrod of Eagle Mills, daughter of Mr. and Mrs. D. C. Gutbrod, before her marriage to the son of Morris Bulson of ...

Engagement Announced

MISS ELINOR F. VAN WIE

PERSONAL

Miss Rita L. Glasheen of 218 Hoosick Street is spending the week-end in Philadelphia.

Clarence Derrick of Melrose is convalescing from a recent operation in the Samaritan Hospital.

Pvt. First Class Walter M. Gorman, son of Mr. and Mrs. Walter M. Gorman, 45 Glen Avenue, is home on a 15-day furlough from Fort Sheridan, Ill.

Mr. and Mrs. Michael Fazioli and daughter, Miss Theresa Mary Fazioli, of 2235 Fourteenth Street are in New York for the week-end. They attended the Army-Notre Dame game.

Miss Kay Wilson of Central Avenue is spending the week-end with her mother, Mrs. Harriet Wilson. Miss Wilson is a student at Edgewood Park Junior College. She has as house guests two fellow students, Miss Pat Benyam of Porto Rico and Miss Minna Shaw of Worcester, Mass.

Miss Louise M. Cutler, daughter of Mr. and Mrs. S. Oley Cutler of 131 First Street, a junior at Good Counsel College, White Plains, attended the Army-Notre Dame game today in New York. Following the game, Miss Cutler was among those present at the military ball, an annual dance held each year at the Hotel Astor.

New Chaplain Of Newman Club.

Rev. Edward O'Malley of St. Mary's Church will succeed Rev. Aloysius Bernhard as chaplain of the Russell Sage chapter of Newman Club. Father Bernhard has been transferred to Little Falls.

Sage-R. P. I. Discussions To Open Soon

The Rensselaer Polytechnic Institute-Russell Sage Student Relations Committee has announced the first of a series of discussions between the two colleges will be held next Thursday night.

Dr. Isabelle Wagner of the Russell Sage faculty will speak on "Courtship and Marriage Problems in this Defense World."

The program for the future will be the discussion of two different groups. The first discussion group will be open to all students of both colleges; the second will be restricted to members of the R. P. I. Debating Club and the members of the Russell Sage forum groups.

Junior-Freshman Banquet.

Russell Sage Juniors entertained their Freshman sisters at a banquet at The Hendrick Hudson Thursday night.

The invited guests included Miss Mary T. Scudder, Miss Bernice Smith, Miss Doris L. Crockett and Miss Gertrude E. Hodgman.

Committee chairmen who arranged the banquet included: Misses Sumi Yamaguchi, Susanne Reynolds, Lorraine Rothdard and Barbara Brown.

E. W. Graduate Wed in Home Ceremony

The marriage of Miss Suzanne Whidden, daughter of Mrs. William B. Whidden, of Hingham, Mass., and Livingston, Mont., formerly of Hewlett, L. I., to Homer Cook, son of Mr. and Mrs. Willis Cook, of Laurel, Mont., was solemnized Thursday at Hingham, Mass., at the home of the bride's maternal grandparents, Mr. and Mrs. Roger Dix.

The ceremony was performed by Rev. Daniel R. Magruder in the presence of the families and a few intimate friends.

The bride attended the Lawrence School, Hewlett, L. I., and the Emma Willard School.

This year she entered Montana University, where her brother, Roger Whidden, is a student. The family's Montana home is the J.N. ranch near Livingston. The late Mr. Whidden was identified with the celanese industry in its early years.

Mr. Cook rode his own saddle horses in the rodeo recently held in Madison Square Garden, New York, and has been riding in the rodeo in Boston this week. The couple will reside near Livingston.

Cooksboro Unit Given Lesson in Hygiene

Mrs. John D. Fogarty was hostess to the Cooksboro Unit of the Rensselaer County Home Bureau in her home on the Speigletown Road yesterday.

Mrs. Harold O'Brien, chairman, presided at the business meeting, opened with the "Star Spangled Banner."

Following the business session, Mrs. Lester B. Campbell, food leader, gave the first lesson in "Intestinal Hygiene and Proper Foods." There were 16 members present and three guests. The next meeting will be at the home of Mrs. George I. Yearsley on Wednesday, Nov. 26.

Miss Martha Helen DeSilva Bride of Robert V. Gray

Miss Martha Helen DeSilva, daughter of Mr. and Mrs. ElRoy DeSilva of 253 Sixth Avenue, became the bride of Robert V. Gray, son of Mr. and Mrs. Milton V. Gray of 262 Fourth Avenue, today at 3:30 p.m. The ceremony was performed at the home of the bride's parents by Rev. A. Abbott Hastings, D.D.

The house was attractively decorated with palms and white chrysanthemums. The marriage took place before an improvised altar banked with white flowers and ferns. Mrs. Betty Christensen Minor provided the appropriate wedding music.

Miss Jane Faith Kraeger of New York, cousin of the bride, was maid of honor. The bridesmaids were Miss Alice Fay and Mrs. Herman Ludwig. Milton F. Gray, jr., was best man for his brother. Thomas E. Farnam and Edward V. Masterson acted as ushers.

Given in marriage by her father the bride was gowned in ivory satin fashioned on princess lines. Her long veil of tulle was fastened with orange blossoms. She carried white chrysanthemums.

The attendants were dressed alike in gowns of orchid taffeta and amethyst velvet made on basque style. They wore amethyst velvet Juliet caps and carried old fashioned bouquets.

A small reception followed the ceremony at the home of the bride's parents. The bridal party was assisted in receiving the guests by the mothers of the bride and bridegroom. Mrs. DeSilva was attired in beige with brown accessories. Mrs. Gray wore a soldier blue ensemble with matching accessories. Both had shoulder bouquets of orchids.

Mr. and Mrs. Gray left on a wedding trip to New York. The bride traveled in a beaver brown and beige ensemble with matching accessories. On their return they will reside at 336 Third Avenue after Nov. 15.

Mr. Gray is associated with the Ludlow Valve Co.

The out-of-town guests at the wedding included Mr. and Mrs. Warren Ellard Kraeger and E. C. Petty, all of New York, Dr. and Mrs. Frederick N. Tate of Albany, Mr. and Mrs. John Kirchner of Montreal, Can., and Mr. and Mrs. Karl DeSilva of Lake Placid.

MRS. ROBERT V. GRAY

—Conklin Photo.

Business and Professional Group of Hadassah Meets

The members of the Business and Professional Group of Senior Hadassah met Thursday night at the home of Miss Esther Gordon, 167 First Street. Miss Ida Goldstein, president, presided at the meeting.

The meeting opened with a tribute to the late Supreme Court Justice Louis D. Brandeis, an ardent Zionist.

A membership campaign is being launched. Plans were made for a membership tea to be held Nov. 30. A representative of the National Speaker's Bureau will talk to the new members at this tea about the aim and work of Hadassah. Miss Florence Newman was appointed chairman.

Following the business meeting Miss Gordan presented a travelogue on her recent trip to Alaska. The next meeting will be Nov. 13.

Home Bureau Is Given Food Lesson

The Melrose Home Bureau held a food lesson accompanied by a talk on intestinal hygiene yesterday afternoon at the home of Mrs. John Ryan, unit chairman, in Valley Falls.

Luncheon was served by the following committee: Mrs. Edward Nicoll, food leader, Mrs. John Russell and Mrs. Harold McMahon.

Mrs. Nicoll gave a talk on nutrition and hygiene. Mrs. Wyatt Doremus and her daughter, Miss Jean Doremus of Schaghticoke, two new members, were welcomed by the unit chairman. This brings the total membership to forty.

The next meeting will be held at the home of Mrs. Harold McMahon in Valley Falls, Nov. 27.

Guests at Gay Halloween Party

Enjoying themselves as they attended the harvest home dinner and barn dance held last night at the Troy Country Club are, pictured from left to right, Dana Miller, Mrs. John Mitchell, Lieut. Mitchell and Miss Julie Jones.

Betrothal Made Known to Friends

Announcement is made of the engagement of Miss Ruth H. Kalbfleish, above, daughter of Mr. and Mrs. Henry J. Kalbfleish and granddaughter of Mrs. Louise Kalbfleish of Latham, to Pvt. Carl Henry Robinson, son of Mr. and Mrs. R. H. Robinson of Watervliet. The wedding will take place Christmas Day at the Newtonville Methodist Church.

ABOUT TOWN

WEEK-END GUEST.

Miss Kathryn Schacht, a student at Smith College, is spending the week-end with her parents, Mr. and Mrs. Elmer C. Schacht of Hawthorne Avenue.

ATTENDING PLAY.

Dr. and Mrs. Harry Wygant, Dr. and Mrs. G. Elmer Martin and Mrs. Richard Bolton of Cohoes are spending the week-end at Hanover, N. H. They will attend the Dartmouth Players' production of "Mr. and Mrs. North."

IN ATLANTIC CITY.

Misses Anna and Kate Mahoney are spending a few days in Atlantic City, N. J.

RETURN HOME.

Mrs. Leslie W. Rolfe and her mother, Mrs. John K. Drake of 1715 Fifth Avenue have returned from Fairfield, Conn., where they spent the summer and early fall months.

VISIT PARENTS.

Mrs. Albert Edmund Cluett, jr., of East Lansing Mich., and children Albert E. Cluett 3rd and Sandra Louise, are the guests of Mrs. Cluett's parents, Mr. and Mrs. James E. MacChesney.

GUEST AT HOUSE PARTIES

Miss Marion Wygant is in Hanover, N. H., attending the fall house parties at Dartmouth College as the guest of Richard Bolton of Cohoes.

Mrs. Nims Opens Weekly Contract Series

Mrs. H. Miles Nims has opened a weekly series of afternoon contract bridge games at the Hotel Troy. This week's winners were North-South, Mrs. W. J. Fagan and Mrs. T. C. Farnan; second, Mrs. S. B. Persian and Mrs. H. T. McGowan; third, Mrs. Milton Wiener and Mrs. Thomas J. Duffy. East-West, first, Mrs. A. C. Young and Mrs. James Mahoney; second, Mrs. John Degan and Mrs. Louis K. Moore; third, Mrs. John Paine and Mrs. Charles S. Ehrlich. Games begin promptly at 1:30 p.m.

Decker, Quinn Nuptials Solemnized

Miss Mary F. Quinn, daughter of Mr. and Mrs. William H. Quinn of 1321 Fifteenth Street, was married to Carl L. Decker Thursday morning in the rectory of St. Francis de Sales' Church. The ceremony was performed by Rev. Joseph Greissmer.

Mrs. Thomas E. O'Brien, cousin of the bride, was matron of honor. The best man was Joseph A. Dippold.

The bride was attired in a light blue dress trimmed with squirrel. She wore brown accessories and a shoulder bouquet of American Beauty roses. Mrs. O'Brien wore a print dress, beige coat trimmed with lynx and ginger brown accessories. Her shoulder bouquet was of pink roses.

After a wedding trip South the couple will reside at Whiteview. Mr. Decker is associated with McLeod & Henry Co.

La Salle Auxiliary Holds Halloween Dance

The Ladies' Auxiliary of LaSalle Institute conducted its annual Halloween party and dance last night in the school gymnasium.

The hall was decorated in the spirit of Halloween, with more than 200 attending the affair. Refreshments were served. Miss James W. Fitzgerald was general chairman of the event and was assisted by Mrs. John M. McNulty.

Miss Higbee Married to Lieut. Schongar

Miss Carolyn Parks Higbee, daughter of Col. and Mrs. Lester C. Higbee of 500 First Avenue, was married this afternoon to Lieut. George Philip Schongar, jr., son of Mr. and Mrs. George Philip Schongar of 36 Glen Avenue. The ceremony was performed at 3 o'clock in the First Presbyterian Church, Lansingburg, by Rev. Seth N. Genung.

Church decorations were of palms and white chrysanthemums. Miss Margaret Jane Gary presided at the organ and played the appropriate wedding music.

Miss Sharlotte Parks Higbee was maid of honor and her sister's only attendant. George Kuns was best man for Lieutenant Schongar. The ushers were Lawrence C. Day, Carl R. Scriven, Kenneth R. Levanway and Everett J. Higbee, jr., of Atlantic City, N. J., cousin of the bride.

Given in marriage by her father, the bride wore a gown of white satin fashioned with a square neckline, long tight sleeves and train. Her three-quarter length veil of tulle fell from clusters of orange blossoms. She carried a shower bouquet of Star-light roses and white orchids.

Her attendant was gowned in Iceland blue satin fashioned with a square neckline and three-quarter length sleeves. She carried an arm bouquet of yellow chrysanthemums and wore yellow flowers in her hair.

Immediately after the ceremony a reception was held at the home of the bride's parents. Mrs. Higbee was attired in royal blue with black accessories and a shoulder bouquet of pink roses. The mother of the bridegroom wore a black ensemble trimmed with gold with matching accessories and a shoulder bouquet of Talisman roses.

Lieutenant and Mrs. Schongar left on a wedding trip through New England. The bride traveled in an infantry blue plaid suit with brown accessories and a shoulder bouquet of white orchids. They will be at home in Anniston, Ala., after Dec. 1.

The bride is a graduate of Russell Sage College and attended Marshall College in Huntington, W. Va. Lieutenant Schongar is a graduate of Troy High School and is stationed with the 105th Infantry at Fort McClellan.

Among the out of town guests were Mr. and Mrs. Josiah Bowen Higbee of Absecon, N. J.; Mr. and Mrs. Everett J. Higbee of Atlantic City, N. J.; Mr. and Mrs. Clarence W. Higbee, Misses Barbara and Priscilla Higbee, all of Scarsdale; Mr. and Mrs. Fred Snyder of Tarrytown; Miss Katherine Masterson of Yonkers; Mr. and Mrs. Myron Bates of Pittsfield, Mass.; Mr. and Mrs. Leslie Goodell, Misses Betty and Dorothy and Robert Goodell, all of Philadelphia, Pa.; Mr. and Mrs. Thomas Shade of Scotia, Mrs. Truman Preston and Miss Joan Preston of Syracuse; Mrs. Fred Hodgson of Verona, N. J.; Mr. and Mrs. C. C. Covert of Staten Island; Lieut. Col. Edwin B. Gore and Lieut. and Mrs. Harry B. Murch, all of Albany; Miss Elizabeth MacMillan, Sylvan Thompson and Miss Mildred Thompson, all of Schenectady.

MONTANA TO HAVE TWO THANKSGIVINGS

Helena, Mont. (AP)—Montana will celebrate Thanksgiving Day twice this year.

Atty. Gen. John W. Bonner ruled that both Nov. 20, proclaimed Thanksgiving Day by President Roosevelt, and Nov. 27, favored for the traditional observance by Gov. Sam C. Ford, will be legal holidays.

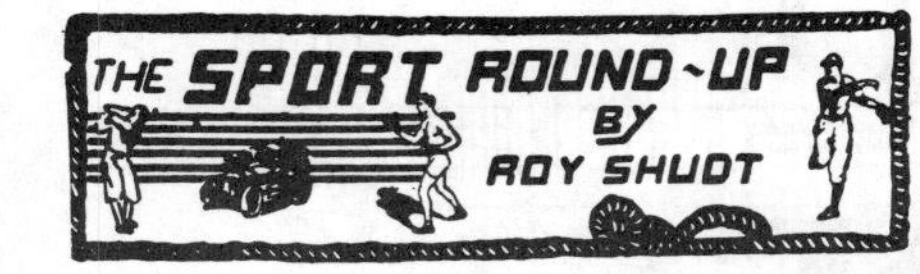
THE SPORT ROUND-UP
BY
ROY SHUDT

Putting one word after another . . . And our athletes continue to get around. Marty Gallagher, who played end and played it well for Lansingburg High School's eleven for two years, is in the Navy . . . and stationed on the other side of the country . . . Marty's with the Flying Squadron at North Island, San Diego, Cal. . . . Remember when Jimmy Golden was cutting capers for the basketball squad at Catholic High? Well, right now he's at Fort Benning, Ga., and I'm glad to report he's well again after being laid up four months with an appendectomy and sinus . . . Jimmy's with Company G, 22nd Infantry . . . The nation's urging its youth to get in shape with more track meets and cross country runs. They don't have to pass that word along to sophomore Bob Scarry at Waterford High. He cracked the course record the other day as Waterford bowed to Nott Terrace seconds, 28-27. . . . Bob went the route in 12:29 to lower the old mark of 12:45. . . . Sorenson was beaten half a step for fifth, otherwise Waterford'd have won, 28-27. . . . Unable to schedule a suitable opponent, the Bearcats will be idle tomorrow, but will resume Nov. 9th at Notre Dame Field with the Brown Bombers as opponents . . . That's the only club to beat them this year.

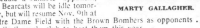

MARTY GALLAGHER.

Just a thought . . . Why not a repeat of the Army-Navy game for the West Coast, same's they do in radio? . . . With the country hepped up over defense, might be well to send the service outfits, and their corps, to the Rose Bowl. . . . 'Twould break tradition, not having a Pacific Coast team, but then changing the date of Thanksgiving has set the tempo for such things . . . Note to a booster of an L. H. S. player: If you'll send along your name and address as evidence of good faith, I'll be glad to publish your letter . . . This sounds logical: Since no one else seems able to handle him, the story is that Roy Weatherley will go from Cleveland to Cincinnati where the master diplomat, Bill McKechnie, hangs out. . . . If the weatherman is kind that'll be a great show tomorrow at Notre Dame Field . . . Between halves, the mounted troop of Cadets and girls from Catholic High, who also ride, will put on an exhibition of jumping . . . They say the gals do mighty well, too . . . And I suppose the bands of both schools will be out in full force . . . So tell ma to get the dinner on early . . . Game time's 2:15 . . . And here's a tip to the band. . . Don't get hurt . . . The other day when Sedan High in Kansas played and lost, 12-0, not a gridder was injured . . but . . . one bandsman blew a face ligament . . . another had a baritone horn rammed down his throat and lost a tooth.

For you lefties who play first base—Charley Grimm, the ex-guardian of the initial sack, prefers a southpaw for the position because they're flashier than the right-handed kind . . . Talk is that Jimmy Dykes, seeking power for the White Sox, will offer Cleveland the aging Joe Kuhel, for Jeff Heath, the gardener with the bulging muscles and .330 batting average . . . Buddy Myer, released by Washington, may land the managing job at Chattanooga . . . Pretty bleak looking place these days —Hawkins Stadium . . . Remember all the fun you had there last summer . . . or did you? . . . The kid on our street who recently moved here from Pittsburg: "I can remember way back when I used to go out of town and brag about Pitt's great football teams. Now I'm glad to speak of the Russians chances of holding out this winter against the Nutzies." . . . Now that Ralph Semerad has issued first cage call at Union, one of the chaps he must replace is Al Turchick, the Watervliet lad who was co-càptain of last season's quintet . . . I'd like to see Ralph, a fine lad, have a good year . . . Wish him victories in every game . . . 'cept against R. P. I.

California's Boxing Commission is talking of creating a trust fund for every boxer and wrestler under its jurisdiction, extracting a percentage from the athlete's earnings and holding it until he retires . . . Evidence indicates the crew that put over Rapid Bone is the same one which foisted Laddie Boy on the poor, unsuspecting bookies in '38 . . . It wouldn't be Larry MacPhail if somebody wasn't getting peeved at him . . . Now, it's the Brooklyn Dodger footballers who resent being forced to wear sneakers when they practice at Ebbets Field . . . Owner Dan Topping claims he will lease an adjoining parking lot and re-sod it . . . Compared to MacPhail, Jock Sutherland, Dodger boss, says the folks he feuded with back in Pittsburg were mere babe in arms . . . Warren, O. High's football tea mand its coach, drew razzberries from Sam Otis, Cleveland Plain-Dealer sports editor, after the coach, Pierre Hill refused to allow pictures of the team to be taken before the game with Massilon. Commenting on the fact that his cameraman had driven 100 miles for the pictures, Otis wrote: "A choice slice of bologna to Coach Pierre Hill and his Warren High team. Why bring up a bunch of school boys along the lines of superstition? That's not the kind of stuff to beat Massilon.

Mickey Kupperberg and all the lads are back with the Celtics who open their season tomorrow night in an exhibition against the Newark, N. J., Hebrews . . . Obie Slingerland was in the starting backfield for Amherst against Mass. State today . . . Glad to hear that Dick Mooradian is going in there to start for Lafayette . . . Talk is that the colleges that go in for football don't look to Troy because the lads can't last the four years . . . Hmm . . . A certain lad had no less than five offers last year . . . Now that the Bearcats are on top of the football heap, why don't they bring one of those North Adams teams over here? . . . Zylonites, Stonebreakers or whatever their name was . . . or is . . . They used to ride roughshod over some Bearcat teams . . But I doubt that they would the 1941 edition . . . Back from the basketball officials meeting, Johnny Cassidy says the major change in amateur play is giving permission for the pivot player to stay in the outer circle (back of the free throw line) as long as he wishes, with or without the ball . . . fan-shaped backboards now are legal and recommended with others still legal . . . moulded ball also is recommended . . . otherwise the rules are the same . . . Back from Watertown where they lost, the Hudson Falls Greenjackets report they tasted the height of rough play there. "No wonder they win so many games. Why they were so bad their own fans even booed them," one of the boys remarked.

BUD WARD GAINS QUARTER FINALS

Mexico City, (U.P.)—Marvin (Bud) Ward, Spokane, Wash., U. S. amateur champion, meets Spec Stewart of New Mexico today in the third-round of the Mexican amateur golf championship.

Ward advanced to the quarter finals yesterday, defeating P. J. M. Walker and William Kennedy in the first two rounds. Ward went six up on both his opponents.

Stewart defeated C. L. Somers, Mexico City, 4 and 3, in his second round match.

COURT MANAGERS WILL MEET AT SPA

Saratoga Springs—Managers of teams in the Saratoga County Basketball League will meet Monday at 8 p.m. in this city.

The Waterford Knights of Columbus won the 1940-41 title. Saratoga led the league the year previous, while the Stillwater Collegians captured the crown on several earlier occasions.

FOOTBALL RESULTS.

Penn State, 42, N. Y. U. 0.
Clemson 19, G. Washington 0.
Case 27, Carnegie Tech 0.
Miami 6, Texas Tech. 0.

Troy Pro Cagers Will Play At St. Patrick's Gym

SAHAGIAN SEEKS MAC KINSBRUNNER AND MOE GOLDMAN

Season Opens November 26th With Saratoga Springs; Owner in New York After Players.

Troy's professional basketball team will play its home games in the New York State League at the spacious new St. Patrick's Hall on Sixth Avenue, between Ingalls and Douw Street, it was announced last night by Paul Sahagian, head of the local organization.

Negotiations for the use of the hall were completed yesterday and Sahagian will go to work next week on plans for seating arrangements.

Sahagian was enthusiastic about the new home site of the club.

"The layout is the finest in the city for basketball and I am confident the fans will go for it in a big way. It is clean, roomy and well lighted and will provide a splendid setting for the league games," Paul declared.

Sahagian left last night on a weekend talent hunt in New York. Tonight he will meet with Eddie Gottlieb, owner of the Philadelphia Sphas of the American League, and Turk Karam, pilot of the Glens Falls entry in the state circuit.

The trio will watch a group of last year's metropolitan college stars perform in a New York gym and when Sahagian returns he expects to be able to announce the signing of several players.

Among the players Sahagian is particularly interested in are Bob Lewis, former New York U. star; Jim Norton, with St. Francis College last year and Lou Lubin, Brooklyn College captain of last season. Paul also will look over several former Long Island U. stars.

Two American League stars who may be seen in Troy uniforms this season are Moe Goldman, flashy center of the Philadelphia Sphas, and Mac Kinsbrunner, playing-pilot of the New York Jewels.

Both have been favorites in Troy since American League days and Goldman is rated as one of the fastest centers in pro ball. Kinsbrunner, a member of the famous St. John's College "Wonder Five" of some years back, is recognized as one of the smartest field generals and ball handlers in the history of the American League.

Troy will play its first home league game against Saratoga Springs on Wednesday, Nov. 26, but Sahagian is planning to arrange an exhibition game for the week previous against some first class attraction.

Today's Sport Parade

By HARRY FERGUSON.

New York (U.P.)—Scattered paragraphs containing scattered thoughts:

Take one last look at the magic dozen of unbeaten, untied major teams, because the list is going to shrink this afternoon: Notre Dame, Minnesota, Army, Penn, Fordham, Texas, Texas A. & M., Duquesne, Temple, Vanderbilt, Texas Tech and Duke.

Notre Dame and Army are the only ones in the select circle who lock horns with one another, but plenty of others are in for a tough afternoon, to wit: Minnesota, Penn, Temple, Vanderbilt and Fordham. If there are nine unbeaten, untied major teams left by tonight your agent is prepared to eat a football if somebody will furnish the catsup.

The scene was the living room of F. J. Hassett in Parkersburg, W. Va. Two radios were going – one carrying the Notre Dame-Illinois game, the other Parkersburg High School against Huntington High. Hassett was interested in the Earley boys, one of whom was right halfback for Notre Dame and the other right halfback for Parkersburg High. Suddenly both radios blared at once: "Earley has scored." It was true, too. Simultaneously Bill Earley scored for Notre Dame and Fred Earley for Parkersburg.

Larry MacPhail, emerging from the north woods after a hunting trip, was in excellent voice, denying the following in behalf of Brooklyn's beloved bums (remember them?): (1) That he was going to cut Leo Durocher's salary because The Lip was going to become bench manager instead of a player manager; (2) That he had opened negotiations with the Pittsburg Pirates for infielder Arky Vaughan; (3) That Coach Chuck Dressen was going to get the gate because he created trouble on the club; (4) That there is a big deal cooking with the Phillies.

This is a tough day for Elmer Oliphant, the great back of yesteryear. He first became prominent in football as a star for Purdue and then went to West Point where he gathered more laurels. Oliphant's problem is what game to see. Purdue is playing Fordham at the Polo Grounds and Army is meeting Notre Dame at the Yankee Stadium. He'll probably settle for half of each game.

Picking the pros tomorrow:
New York Giants over Chicago Cardinals.
Washington Redskins over Pittsburg Steelers.
Cleveland Rams over Detroit Lions.
Philadelphia Eagles over Brooklyn Dodgers.
Chicago Bears over Green Bay Packers.

They're Ready For Tomorrow's Big Game

RED McLOUGHLIN

JAMES MAHONEY

Three boys who figure to occupy prominent roles in tomorrow's Catholic High-La Salle grid game at Notre Dame Field are shown here. Mahoney is the boy who carries the mail once he hits the open field. Kenna can run that ball and he can pass. McLoughlin is a power on the Catholic High line.

Troy High Shellacks Hudson Falls, 19 to 0

Troy High's gridders, held scoreless in the first half, put touchdowns across in the third and fourth quarters to defeat Hudson Falls High School, 19-0, last night at R. P. I.'s North Field.

The Upstaters battled evenly with the Trojans during the first two periods and Coach Eddie Picken's boys went without a tally. In the first period an inspired Hudson Falls line held for downs after Troy High moved to the Hudson Falls eight on a drive of forty yards.

Troy opened the scoring in the third period when Bill Everton tallied on an end run from the 15 yard line. Willetts' kick was wide.

Lou Cioffi scored Troy's second six-pointer early in the fourth period on a center plunge, climaxing a drive of fifty yards. Willetts' kick was true. Troy took possession at the mid-field stripe and moved the ball into scoring territory on runs by Cioffi, Everton and Muscatello and a 15-yard pass from Cioffi to Purcell.

Frank Manetti, substitute end, closed out Troy's scoring when he took Cioffi's pass on the three and tallied standing up.

Troy started its final drive on its own forty when Uzewitz intercepted a Hudson Falls pass and moved it to the visitors' 35. Koshgarian took it to the thirty and Everton took it through center to the twent. Everton moved it to the ten and on the next play Cioffi tossed the touchdown pass to Manetti. Willetts' kick was blocked.

Troy scored first downs almost at will while Hudson Falls succeeded in scoring only one first down.

TROY.		HUDSON.
Willetts	Left End	DePalo
Wimney	Left Tackle	Simons
Baumback	Left Guard	Dickinson
Usewitz	Center	Barrett
O'Brien	Right Guard	LeRoy
Testo	Right Tackle	J. Murray
Carelli	Right End	Winslow
Jacobs	Quarterback	Smith
Everton	Left Halfback	Webb
Cioffi	Right Halfback	R. Murray
Muscatello	Fullback	Gilbert

Score by periods

Troy	0	0	6	13	—19
Hudson Falls	0	0	0	0	— 0

Touchdowns — Everton, Cioffi, Manetti. Goals from touchdowns—Willetts (place kick). Referee—Whittner. Umpire—DeBois. Head linesman—Graham. Time of periods —8 minutes. Substitutions—Hudson Falls: Cornell, LaPointe, Mazaver, S. DePalo. Troy: Purcell, Schultz, Crowley, Berger. Koshgarian, Howser, Foster, Manetti.

'VLIET GARNETS TO PLAY MERRIMACS

The Watervliet Garnets will play the Schenectady Merrimacs tomorrow at 2:30 p.m. at Brotherhood Park, Watervliet.

On the Garnet squad are Molocco, Maderosian, Cyhowski, Sandy, Salkis, Valastro, Burnstein, Pratt, Sacco, B. Wido G. Wido, Galonka, Koneski, Thomas, Pinicchi, Tatomas, DeCatis and Curtis.

Expect CCHS-LSI To Fill Air With Passes

Passes and more passes will be the order of the day tomorrow afternoon when La Salle and Catholic High clash in their annual grid contest at Notre Dame Field.

The kickoff is scheduled for 2:15 p.m.

The game may develop into a passing duel between Mike Furdyna of LaSalle and Tom Kenna, Catholic High's ace flinger.

Both boys are better than average passers and both teams use passing attacks extensively. Kenna holds a slight edge over Furdyna in the passing department and if End Tom Quinn can get his hands on one of Kenna's long passes it may spell victory for the Eighth Streeters.

The teams will take the field with mediocre records. La Salle has defeated St. Mary's of Glens Falls and has dropped consecutive games to Vincentian, C. B. A., Troy High and Nott Terrace.

Catholic High holds wins over C. B. A. and Cathedral Academy of Albany but has lost its last two games to Lansingburg and Vincentian. It will be the final game of the season for both schools and both will be out to close the year with a victory.

Despite earlier season form both schools will put determined teams on the field tomorrow. The annual battle has always been an outstanding date on the local scholastic schedule and the famous inter-city rivalry between the two schools will probably attract a large turnout.

Jim Mahoney is the speahead of La Salle's running attack.

Red McLoughlin, all-city guard last year, is Catholic High's kicker par excellence.

Fights Last Night

By The Associated Press.

Augusta, Maine—Jackie Fisher, 167, Waterville, outpointed Tiger Lambett, 161, Biddeford, Maine (8).

Fair or Foul

BY LAWTON CARVER

New York (INS)—On opposite sides of a gridiron marked off in Yankee Stadium two young men sit today with their thoughts, their hopes and their jitters, while 75,000 people go wild.

The two young men know more about what is going on out there on the gridiron than anybody else on the premises, and the game means more to them than to anybody else, for this is the highlight of the year for them and for their teams. One is Frank Leahy of Notre Dame, the other Red Blaik of Army, personable gentleman of the mad sports whirl who follow the strange profession of coaching football teams.

Either might have been a big man, even a rich man, in business. They have the education, the background, the vision and the courage to be standouts in any company, but like so many of their ilk and brood have never been able to tear themselves away from the typically American game that means so much to so many people for a couple of months every year.

There will be some humor perhaps and undoubtedly some heartaches down there on the benches before today's sun sets, for the lives of football coaches are strangely built on the surge of success and the setbacks of failure. They win or they lose, but they still are not far different from the fuller brush man, your meat cutter or the glib gent who rented you your apartment or sold you your house, or that silly looking hat your wife is wearing—perhaps to a football game.

The big difference is that the football coach's success and failure come to him out there under a spotlight which grows brighter in ratio to his position in the football world.

Hence Frank Leahy and Red Blaik at the moment are in the position of a couple of gentlemen on a stage that can be seen all over the nation, for the game in which their teams clashed today approaches most closely to a spectacle designed of and for the people.

Somehow Notre Dame has been adopted by the man in the street, and Army, of course, like Navy, has its special niche because it is a service school. Then, too, there is all that tradition and fanfare behind the tussle to make it a perennial sellout and one of the highlights of the year even when the records of the two elevens are not so hot.

This time they are undefeated, and Army is about to become the miracle team of the year with any luck at all. The football gents from up the Hudson won just one game last season and that by a single point. They are banging away this time.

So you can imagine the thoughts of the Cadets' coach today, as he views this great spectacle in his first year at the helm of his own school, where he played football, got his Second Looie's commission upon graduation, then resigned from the Army to follow the gridiron's white stripes as a professional tutor of football teams.

Leahy, too, as everybody knows, is back at his Alma Mammy, successor to Elmer Layden and in his first year there quite in keeping with the predictions Knute Rockne is alleged to have made in the dim nd distant past. Briefly, Rockne said Leahy would come to be known as one of the greatest coaches of all time. This was when Leahy was an undersized tackle with a bunged up knee.

So they sit out there today at Yankee Stadium watching their handiwork and playing every play themselves to the point of exhaustion. They groan at a mistake by their own men, thrill to their better plays and hope quite humanly for a victory.

But actually what they hope for is nothing more nor less than your eagerness to make that sale, or to get that contract for putting in the new sewers over on Main Street or to build a better mouse trap than the next guy. Coaches are human, too. The only strange thing about them is the profession they follow.

FLORIDA GATORS SHOULD CAPTURE HARD LUCK TITLE

New York (AP) — (The Record Newspapers Special News Service) —A tourist bureau would tell you that the best way to take in Florida would be my automobile or bicycle, but developments this fall indicate an even better way is to complete a forward pass or boot a placekick in the last couple of minutes of play.

Practically everybody has been taking in those Gators, and they usually wait until everybody is ready to go home before getting in the dirty work. The folks down there are beginning to suspect they don't live right.

This is no attempt to alibi for a beaten team or to build Coach Tom Lieb as a martyr. But there's no harm in feeling sorry for a fellow who would be caught without a hot dog if it were raining mustard, is there?

The tragic facts are these:

The Gators lost to Mississippi State on a 42-yard punt return; they lost to Villanova on a 53-yard pass; they lost, 13-2, to Maryland, with Maryland scoring on a 57-yard pass in the last two minutes after a penalty on a fourth-down incomplete pass had enabled Maryland to retain possession of the ball; they lost to L. S. U., 10-7, on a field goal in the last eight seconds (there was a little grumbling on that one, some of the Floridans charging the kick was something of a P. S. to the regular game, and that the clock stuttered).

And if that weren't enough, the Gator Pups, or whatever the freshmen are called, lost 16-3 to the Georgia Tech freshmen on a field goal in the last second of play on the same night the varsity was losing to L. S. U.

Lieb has put together a fine team down in the land of the sunshine (California papers please copy). The draft and defense work made big inroads in his squad, and he has only 15 or 16 men he can use without weakening the team more than a little.

About the only consolation the team has so far is that, with the exception of the Mississippi State game, it has "won the statistics." The Gators have piled up forty first downs to 26 for opponents, gained 488 yards from rushing Towoi, and 281 from passing to 272.

Naturally if you started a personal diary of every team which has been the victim of tough luck this fall you'd soon run out of ink, but we doubt if there is any team which can match the Gators' feat of losing four games on as many plays. Take away those four plays and Florida's record would list three wins and three ties instead of two wins and four defeats.

Twenty years from now the Florida fans probably will look back through the records and, coming upon 1941, will remark: "What a punk team the Gators had that year."

That's the way it is. Nothing is remembered but the final score as the years pass, which probably is as it should be inasmuch as the idea of the game still is to win.

But the Gator fans right now can tell you that they have a good country ball club which would have a respectable record were it not for a jinx. And they don't mean high jinx. The boys are taking their football seriously.

The only break they ask is that the games be shortened to 58 minutes. Or, the skeptical add, 60 minutes against L. SU.

When Football Aces Finish Their Chores, They Turn Insurance Men

BY PAT ROBINSON.

New York—(INS)—If there are any football upsets today . . . you might find one or two of the following teams scoring them . . . Army . . . W. & M . . . Purdue . . . Holy Cross . . . Manhattan . . . Villanova . . . Michigan State . . . Syracuse . . . Northwestern . . . Columbia . . . Vanderbilt . . . Santa Clara . . . Baylor . . . Louisiana State . . . N. Y. U. and even hopeless Princeton . . . But don't bet anything on that last one . . .

Notre Dame-Army parties going on all over town last night . . . and now we know what happens to old football aces . . . They become insurance salesmen . . . Frinstance . . . Ran into George Vergara . . . one of the Seven Mules . . . the great line that played in front of the Four Horsemen of Notre Dame . . . back in '24 . . .

George was a roomie of Jim Crowley . . . one of the Horsemen . . . and now coach for Fordham . . . George is selling insurance . . . Soo Too is big Bill Edwards of Princeton . . . Also Red Cagle of the Army . . . Big Bill is now down to a trifling 245 pounds . . .

Cagle and Vergara officiate every Saturday at football games . . . and both say . . . they not only do not see the games . . . but don't even know what the score is . . . when the game is over . . .

Cagle says the smartest, most care-free games are those played by the 150-pound teams . . . "Those kids," he says, "make up plays as they go along and you are liable to see them passing from behind their own goal lines any time . . ."

Vergara . . . recalling Knute Rockne . . . tells of Max Hauser . . . sub for Jim Crowley . . . Max couldn't swim a stroke . . . but he lost his life trying to save a girl swimmer on the coast.

And the distinguished looking party with the silver hair and black moustache is Col. Jack Jouett . . . who played end on the first Army-Notre Dame game back in 1913 . . . He played opposite Rockne that day . . . "but the guy who really slaughtered me that day," he says, "was a tackle named Jones . . . Every time Jones hit me . . . and he never missed . . . I would up somewhere over by the sidelines . . . And that darned Rockne kept telling me not to worry . . . he'd seen Jones hit other fellows harder than me and he hadn't killed one of them! . . ." Jouett now is a big shot in the aeronautical end down in Washington . . .

By the way . . . you can get choice seats for that Army-Notre Dame affair . . . from the speculators . . . for $25 a pair . . . Notre Damers are going to go Hollywood today . . . with gold pants . . . made of nylon . . . and remind ex-Governor Hoffman of New Jersey . . . to recite the football scream . . . he wowed them with last night . . .

Oldtimers were commenting on sad state of Pitt . . . whose tub thumper boasts about the impending duel . . . between the Pitt and Ohio State bands . . . bands, mind you, not football teams . . .

And Frank Leahy . . . N. D. coach tells us that Angelo Bertelli . . . his star forward passer . . . also is a great catcher . . . And Dr. T. H. Henry . . . father of sports writer John Henry . . . here rooting for the Irish . . . tells us he roots more for his home state team . . . Mississippi State . . . because he brought several of that great team into the world . . .

Which reminds us that we hope Wisconsin's Badgers aren't too rough on Syracuse's end . . . Paul Berthold . . . today . . . because Paul became a daddy just before his team entrained for the West.

THE WEATHER
U. S. Weather Bureau.
Tonight—Snow, warmer.
Tomorrow—Snow flurries.

THE TIMES RECORD

FINAL EDITION

Series 1941—No. 288. (Entered as Second Class Matter at the Postoffice at Troy, N. Y., under the Act of March 3, 1879.) TROY, N. Y., MONDAY EVENING, DECEMBER 8, 1941. (Published Daily Except Sunday) PRICE THREE CENTS

CONGRESS DECLARES WAR AGAINST JAPAN

American Warships Battle Japs In Pacific

An Editorial.

AMERICA FOLLOWS THE PRESIDENT.

Confronted with the true scope of the infamy of Japan's attack upon Hawaii and other American Pacific outposts, as revealed by the President in his address to Congress asking a declaration of a state of war, there can be no question of divided policy in America today.

The time for argument has ended, the period of debate has passed. There is only one course of action open to the people and that is to follow the President to the end that this war will be won with a finality that will make it impossible for us ever again to be faced with such a danger.

The degree of the treachery that animated the Japanese in their onslaught upon us is revealed in the very vastness of their operations. While seeking to lull us into a sense of security under the guise of carrying on conversations designed to settle our differences peacefully, they were secretly preparing for this surprise attack.

If they sought by these means to terrify us into submission, they reckoned wrongly the American temperament. Stunned though we were by the suddenness and ferocity of the attack, caught off guard, we are not awed. We are, rather, moved by calm determination and confidence that this war shall be won and our assailants punished. And we are—to a degree that we have not been in eight long years—a united people.

America's safety is at stake; our country is threatened. And before this danger and this threat, America will rise as one man and strike back with all its vast might.

There is no room here longer for divided policies; there can be no blind seeking for partisan or group advantage. American lives have been lost and American property destroyed by an unwarranted and unprovoked attack by a treacherous and venal nation, a nation whose treachery becomes the more monstrous in the light of the many benefactions America as a nation has showered upon her.

In asking for a declaration of a state of war President Roosevelt has taken the only course open to him. They were the words the people were waiting to hear. They will follow him to one man to victory!

LOCAL RESIDENTS RALLY TO CALL OF NATIONAL DEFENSE

Trojans Asked to Enroll in Civilian Effort; Office Opens Tomorrow; City and County Acts.

Defense machinery of city, county and state was thrown into action today as President Roosevelt called on Congress to declare war.

At the very moment the President spoke in Washington, the Committee for Organization of Civilian Defense Volunteers in Troy announced that an office will be opened at 7 State Street tomorrow morning for the enrollment of every man and woman in this city to do protective and other civilian defense work.

All through the city defense groups made their plans.

The Rensselaer County Defense Council met to prepare a civil defense program for the 14 towns of the county.

The Second Regiment, State Guard, was standing by to await further orders. Col. Lester C. Higbee had informed the guard to be ready for the call which will come from Governor Lehman.

Rensselaer County Chapter, Red Cross, executive officers met with the chairman of the Disaster Committee, Colonel Higbee. All day long offers to assist the Red Cross had been pouring in at headquarters.

School children pledged their allegiance to their country. Patriotic organizations were prepared to work swiftly.

Spirit of Unity.

A feeling of unity pervaded the community and the state. Republicans pledged their complete cooperation with Governor Lehman. Mayor Frank J. Hogan met with different civilian defense groups and patriotic organizations all day long.

The world situation affected the community in another way. Guards were stationed at plants now working on defense orders.

At Watervliet Arsenal additional guards were on duty this morning and Brig. Gen. Alexander G. Gillespie, commanding officer, said "We're on the alert."

The civil defense program for the 14 towns of the county in relation to the present emergency was out-

(Continued on Page 5.)

BRITISH GUNBOAT SUNK AT SHANGHAI; U.S.S. WAKE SEIZED

Japanese Take Over International Settlement Waterfront in Surprise Attack.

Shanghai (U.P.)—The British gunboat Peteral sank in the Whangpoo River off the Shanghai waterfront under blasting of Japanese fire today and the United States communications ship Wake, its crew overwhelmed as it lay at anchor, was captured.

Lieut. Commdr. John Polkinhorne, 63, British naval reservist, and a former Tientsin River pilot who commander the Peterel, was believed, with most of his crew, to have gone down with his ship.

The Peterel opened fire, under odds it knew were hopeless, when the Japanese orderd it to surrender.

Wake Had No Chance.

The Wake had no chance to fire. The Japanese, in a sudden attack as they took over the water front of the international settlement off which the two tiny gunboats were anchored, boarded it and forced its surrender.

At 6 a.m. the Wake's lights were ablaze, as debris from the furiously burning Peterel floated by.

Japanese gunboats had opened direct fire on the Peterel, which had very light armament and only half its crew aboard.

The Japanese flag was raised over the Wake.

Believe Liner Sunk.

American service officers here expressed belief that the Japanese probably had sunk or seized the American liner President Harrison, which was believed to have been somewhere off the mouth of the Yangtze River in the Shanghai area, on its way to Chingwangtao in the north to pick up 203 marines, awaiting evacuation Dec. 10.

It was forecast that the marines would be disarmed and interned, first American prisoners of the Pacific war.

Japanese marine debouched along the international settlement water front, the control of which Japan had long sought, as the Japanese gunboats opened fire on the Peterel.

LEGION PLEDGES DEFENSE SUPPORT

Beacon (U.P.)—The unstinted effort of 100,000 New York State Legionnaires for national defense was pledged today by State Commander Jacob Ark of Rochetser.

Ark, emphasized that Legionnaires maintained more than 1,000 air raid warning posts throughout the state.

Heavy Loss Of Life And Naval Damage Reported In Hawaii

Japanese Claim Battleships Oklahoma and West Virginia Sunk; White House Reports 3,000 Casualties In Oahu Attack; Britain Declares War on Japan; Thailand Capitulates After Brief Attack; British Battle Landing Forces At Singapore; Philippine Key Points Attacked.

BY THE UNITED PRESS.

The United States and Britain smashed back at Japan today on a 6,000-mile Pacific war front that flamed from Hawaii's coral beaches to the jungle shores of Malay and Thailand.

The American battle fleet was reported challenging the Japanese striking force which raided Hawaii with heavy loss of life and naval damage. A great naval engagement was rumored in the waters west of America's Pacific Gibraltar.

Here is the picture:

London: Prime Minister Winston Churchill carries Britain into war against Japan with a formal declaration before parliament.

Tokyo: Japanese naval command claims sinking of U. S. battleships Oklahoma and West Virginia; damage to four other battleships; damage to four heavy cruisers; heavy destruction of U. S. planes; probable sinking of U. S. aircraft carrier (rumored to be the Langley); capture of "many" enemy ships; sinking of U. S. minesweeper Penguin at Guam.

Hawaii: White House reports 3,000 casualties, including 1,500 fatalities, in Japanese air attack; loss of "old" American battleship and destroyer.

Japanese Ships Destroyed.

Washington: American battle fleet carrying out sweeping operations and has destroyed "a number of" Japanese submarines and planes.

The White House statement on the Oahu attack said:

"American operations against the Japanese attacking force in the neighborhood of the Hawaiian islands are still continuing. A number of Japanese planes and submarines have been destroyed.

"The damage caused to our forces in Oahu in yesterday's attack appear more serious than at first believed.

"In Pearl Harbor itself one old battleship has capsized and several other ships have been seriously damaged.

"One destroyer was blown up. Several other small ships were seriously hurt. Army and Navy fields were bombed with the resulting destruction of several hangars. A large number of planes were put out of commission.

3,000 Casualties In Oahu.

"A number of bombers arrived safely from San Francisco during the engagement—while it was underway. Reinforcements of planes are being rushed and repair work is underway on the ships, planes and ground facilities.

"Guam, Wake and Midway Islands and Hongkong have been attacked. Details of these attacks are lacking.

"Two hundred Marines—all that remain in China—have been interned by the Japanese near Tientsin.

"The total number of casualties on the Island Oahu are not definitely known but, in all probability, will mount to about 3,000. Nearly half of these are fatalities, the others being wounded. It seems clear from the report that many bombs were dropped in the city of Honolulu, resulting in a small number of casualties."

Philippines Attacked.

Thailand: Apparently caving in to the Japanese with little or no fight; Tokyo claims Japanese troops moving into the country under "Agreement" reached with Bangkok government, Japanese reported storming into southern Thailand in preparation for drive on Singapore.

Singapore: British battling Japanese landing forces which have established series of beachheads along eastern coast; Royal Air Force heavily engaged.

Manila: Waves of Japanese bombers attack key points in Philippines, including U. S. Army base at Fort Stotsenburg, Davao and the vicinity of Bagiuo. Japanese landings rumored but not confirmed.

Chungking: China moves to declare war on Germany and Italy as well as to formalize the long existing state of war with Japan.

China: Japanese attack Hongkong twice by air; take over Shanghai international settlement; occupy Tientsin British concession and intern 200 American Marines.

Pacific Isles: Japanese attack American islands of Guam and probably Wake; attack British island of Nauru; Japanese naval squadron reported off Cocos Islands in Indian Ocean.

Australia and Dutch East Indies: All armed forces on the alert; no Japanese attacks yet reported.

Berlin and Rome: Indicate Germany and Italy will join their Axis partner in war against the United States but no tangible action yet.

Naval Battle Rages.

The Japanese imperial forces said to have suffered severe losses of airplanes and several warships, were in action on these fronts:

A major naval battle was reported west of Hawaii, with the American fleet attempting to destroy enemy warships and airplanes that blasted Pearl Harbor naval base and Honolulu.

The American fleet steamed out of Pearl Harbor naval base yesterday shortly after Japanese planes, attacking without a declaration of war or any warning whatever, had bombed the great Pearl Harbor base, Honolulu City, and scattered Army and Navy bases on Oahu Island.

Naval gun flashes were seen from the coast, and the roar of the guns

(Continued on Page 22.)

Families Told Two U. S. Soldiers Slain By Japs

Arnold, Pa. (U.P.)—The War Department today notified the family of Pvt. George G. Leslie, 20, an enlisted man in the United States Air Corps, that their son was killed yesterday in the Japanese attack on the Hawaiian Islands.

News of their son's death from gunshot wounds was received by Mr. and Mrs. George S. Leslie at their home here. He was stationed at Wheeler Field, in Hawaii. He enlisted last April.

Woodland, Cal. (U.P.)—Mr. and Mrs. Peter Christiansen of Woodland, were notified by the Navy Department today that their son, 1st Lieut. Hans Christiansen, 21, was killed in action at Pearl Harbor yesterday. Christiansen was in the aviation branch of the U. S. Marines.

FORFEITS BAIL.

Bail of $5 was forefeited by Kenneth C. Wardell, 22 of 297 Fourth Street, Troy yesterday in Schetady Police Court after he was arrested on a charge of passing a stop sign.

WAR MESSAGE

Washington (UP)—The text of President Roosevelt's war message to the Congress of the United States:

Yesterday, Dec. 7, 1941—a date which will live in infamy—the United States of America was suddenly and deliberately attacked by naval and air forces of the empire of Japan.

The United States was at peace with that nation and, at the solicitation of Japan, was still in conversation with its government and its emperor looking toward the maintenance of peace in the Pacific. Indeed, one hour after Japanese air squadrons had commenced bombing in Oahu, the Japanese ambassador to the United States and his colleague delivered to the Secretary of State a formal reply to a recent American message. While this reply stated that it seemed useless to continue the existing diplomatic negotiations, it contained no threat or hint of war or armed attack.

Attack Deliberately Planned.

It will be recorded that the distance of Hawaii from Japan makes it obvious that the attack was deliberately planned many days or even weeks ago. During the intervening time the Japanese government has deliberately sought to deceive the United States by false statements and expressions of hope for continued peace.

The attack yesterday on the Hawaiian Islands has caused severe damage to American naval and military forces. Very many American lives have been lost. In addition, American ships have been reported torpedoed on the high seas between San Francisco and Honolulu.

Yesterday the Japanese government also launched an attack against Malaya.

Last night Japanese forces attacked Hongkonk.

Last night Japanese forces attacked Guam.

Last night Japanese forces attacked the Philippine Islands.

Last night the Japanese attacked Wake Island.

This morning the Japanese attacked Midway Island.

Japan has, therefore, undertaken a surprise offensive extending throughout the Pacific area. The facts of yesterday speak for themselves. The people of the United States have already formed their opinions and well understand the implications to the very life and safety of our nation.

Asks War Declaration.

As Commander-in-Chief of the Army and Navy I have decided that all measures be taken for our defense.

Always will we remember the character of the onslaught against us.

No matter how long it may take us to overcome this premediated invasion, the American people in their righteous might will win through to absolute victory.

I believe I interpret the will of the Congress and of the people when I assert that we will not only defend ourselves to the uttermost but will make very certain that this form of treachery shall never endanger us again.

Hostilities exist. There is no blinking at the fact that our people, our territory and our interests are in grave danger.

With confidence in our armed forces—with the unbounding determination of our people—we will gain the inevitable triumph—so help us God.

I ask that the Congress declare that since the unprovoked and dastardly attack by Japan on Sunday, Dec. 7, a state of war has existed between the United States and the Japanese empire.

FRANKLIN D. ROOSEVELT.

The White House,
Dec. 8, 1941.

MANILA REPORTED UNDER ATTACK BY JAPANESE PLANES

Fort McKinley and Nichols Airfield Objectives of Raid; Large Fires Are Raging.

New York (U.P.)—The National Broadcasting Co. correspondent at Manila reported today that Japanese planes carried out a heavy attack on Ft. McKinley and Nichols airfield at Manila at 3:09 a.m. Tuesday (2:09 p.m. E. S. T. Monday), and started large fires.

The broadcaster, described the attack which was in progress as he broadcast, as carried out with "fiendish accuracy."

The Japanese bombers, despite a terrific curtain of American anti-aircraft fire, touched off a huge fire, apparently in a gasoline dump.

Another objective of the Japanese raid was the big transmitter of the Radio Corp. of America, Manila's chief communication link with the outside world.

The broadcaster said it was reported an American destroyer was damaged in the raid.

Manila, P. I. (U.P.)—Press dispatches reported that 100 to 200 troops, sixty of them Americans, were killed tonight when Japanese warplanes raided Iba, on the west coast of the Island of Luzon, north of the Olangapo naval base.

The Manila Tribune, a Filipino newspaper, said 200 troops were killed or injured at Iba and it said that sixty of the casualties were Americans. The American-owned Manila Daily Bulletin placed the casualties in the Iba raid at 100 killed or injured.

WESTERN COAST STATES PUT ON WARTIME "ALERT"

Vital Harbors, Arsenals and Manufacturing Plants Guarded Against Possible Attack.

San Francisco (U.P.)—All military and civilian defense organizations on the West Coast were organized today on a wartime basis.

Possibility that the West Coast with its vital harbors, arsenals, shipbuilding yards and airplane manufacturing centers might be the next target of the Japanese bombers was reflected in the speed with which defense plans were put into operations.

A contingent of anti-aircraft units, here from Camp Haan in what had been planned as practice maneuvers, were shifted from various points in the San Francisco Bay area to Vallejo and Benicia to guard the Mare Island Navy Yard and the Benicia Arsenal.

Navy censors moved into the offices of all radio and cable communications companies, checking all messages before transmission to Honolulu or the Orient. Similar censorship was in effect at the other end of the circuits.

Recruiting of Naval, Army and Marine forces was put on an "unlimited" wartime basis.

Local members of the Federal Bureau of Investigation were ready for any possible order to round-up Japanese nationals or suspected Japanese sympathizers.

U. S. Will Triumph "So Help Us, God" President Pledges

Senate Approves War Resolution By 82 To 0; House Votes 388 to 1, Lone Dissenter Being Rep. Jeannette Rankin, R., Mont., Who Also Voted Against World War; Chief Executive Denounces Japanese Attack On Hawaii As Dastardly"; Declares Negotiations By Tokyo Envoys Were False And Deceptive.

Washington (UP)—Congress today proclaimed existence of a state of war between the United States and the Japanese empire 33 minutes after the dramatic moment when President Roosevelt stood before a joint session to pledge that we will triumph—"so help us, God."

Democracy was proving its right to a place in the sun with a split-second shiftover from peace to all-out war.

The Senate acted first, adopting the resolution by a unanimous roll call vote of 82 to 0, within 21 minutes after the President had concluded his speech.

The final House vote was announced as 388 to 1. The lone negative vote was cast by Rep. Jeannette Rankin, R., Mont., who also voted against entry into World War 1.

The resolution now has to be signed by Speaker Sam Rayburn and Vice President Henry A. Wallace before it is sent to the President at the White House. His signature will place the United States formally at war against the Japanese empire, already an accomplished fact.

Haiti and Honduras both declared war on Japan this afternoon.

The resolutions were before both houses within 15 minutes of the time Mr. Roosevelt ended his seven-minute, 500-word extraordinary message.

There was a half second of uncertainty in the House when Rep. Jeannette Rankin, R., Mont., objected to unanimous consent for immediate consideration of the war resolution.

Jeannette Rankin Hissed.

Speaker Sam Rayburn brushed the objection aside. It was she who in the small hours of April 6, 1917, faltered, wept and finally voted "no" against a similar resolution aimed at Germany.

When the clerk came to her name on the roll call today, she voted no again.

A chorus of hisses and boos greeted her vote, the first cast against the war resolution.

Rep. Harold Knutson, R., Minn., who also voted against American entry into the World War in 1917, said today this nation "has no choice but to declare war on Japan."

"I do not see that we have any other choice," Knutson told reporters. "They declared war on us."

Miss Rankin and Knutson are the only present members of the Houes who voted against war in 1917.

Only Miss Rankin and Rep. Clare Hoffman, R., Mich., had remained seated when the House gave a standing ovation in response to Roosevelt's solemn statement:

"I ask that the Congress declare that since the unprovoked and dastardly attack by Japan on Sunday, Dec. 7, a state of war has existed between the United States and the Japanese empire."

President Denounces Japan.

In a staccato of short sentences, the President told where the Japanese had hit yesterday throughout the Pacific area and how their representatives here had at the same time been continuing deceptive and false negotiations for maintenance of peace. And he said, simply, that he had ordered "all measures be taken for our defense."

"Always will we remember the character of the onslaught against us," the President said grimly.

"No matter how long it may take us to overcome this premeditated invasion, the American people in their righteous might will win through to absolute victory."

Chairman Tom Connally, D., Tex., of the Senate foreign relations committee introduced the war resolution in the Senate at 12:50 p.m. He asked for its immediate consideration but Sen. Arthur H. Vandenberg, R., Mich., asked him to suspend the request so he could comment upon the resolution.

Vandenberg Backs President.

Vandenberg told the Senate that "when war comes to us . . . I stand with the commander-in-chief, notwithstanding past differences on foreign policy."

He said "there can be no shadow of doubt as to our answer to Japan," and added that "you (Japan) have unsheathed the sword and by it you shall die."

When Vandenberg [illegible] Senate roll call on [illegible] resolution was taken.

Democratic Leader [illegible]

(Continued on Page [illegible])

AIR RAID WARDENS ON ATLANTIC COAST ORDERED ON ALERT

New York (U.P.)—The air raid precaution service in 13 eastern coast states and the District of Columbia was ordered on the alert by the Army Air Corps today.

The first interceptor command at Mitchel Feld, near here, charged with protecting northeastern United States from air raids, ordered all personnel of the ground observation system to duty at 6 a.m. The personnel is made up largely of civilian volunteers.

"All planes are to be reported," the command instructed the observers in a broadcast.

The order applies to the ground observers in Maine, New Hampshire, Vermont, Massachusetts, Rhode Island, Connecticut, New York, Pennsylvania, New Jersey, Delaware, Maryland, Virginia, North Carolina and District of Columbia.

CAPITAL RESIDENTS PUT ON THE ALERT

Washington (AP)—Residents of the nation's capital and vicinity were put on the alert today against any possible violence.

J. Russell Young, commissioner of the District of Columbia and coordinator of the metropolitan area of civilian defense, asked all air raid wardens to arrange for a "constant watch" and suggested that "citizens not attending to necessary business should remain indoors and off the streets."

The Index

THE WEATHER
U. S. Weather Bureau.
Tonight—Continued cold.
Tomorrow—Fair and cold.

THE TIMES RECORD

FINAL EDITION

Series 1941—No. 291. (Entered as Second Class Matter at the Postoffice at Troy, N. Y., under the Act of March 3, 1879.) TROY, N. Y., THURSDAY EVENING, DECEMBER 11, 1941. (Published Daily Except Sunday) PRICE THREE CENTS

UNITED STATES AT WAR WITH GERMANY, ITALY

U. S. Army Bombers Sink 29,000-Ton Japanese Battleship

Claim Airport On Luzon Seized By Jap Parachutists

United States and Philippine Troops Battle to Drive Nippon Landing Forces Into Sea Along Northern And Western Coasts of Island; Tokyo Reports Guam Occupied and 350 Americans Captured.

BY THE ASSOCIATED PRESS.

The sinking of the 29,000-ton Japanese battleship Haruna by U. S. Army bombers off the northern coast of Luzon in the Philippines was announced today in Washington by Secretary of War Stimson, confirming earlier reports from Manila.

Japanese parachutists were reported to have seized an airport six miles from Iligan in eastern Luzon today while United States and Philippine troops battled to drive Japanese landing forces into the sea along the northern and western coasts of the island.

A United States Army spokesman declared a short time before the parachute landing was reported by the Philippine constabulary that "the situation is completely in hand" and that Japanese forces along the coast were being mopped up.

He disclosed that a United States Army bomber had struck a heavy blow at Japanese naval forces which supported the landings, blasting a 29,000-ton capital ship with three direct bomb hits and two close alongside, and leaving her "blazing fiercely."

(He identified the ship as a battleship of the Haruna class. These were battleships completed from 1913 to 1915 and later rebuilt with increased armor).

Drive To Check Fifth Column Activities.

Iligan, scene of the reported parachutist landing, is in the province of Isabela, some seventy miles south of the port of Aparri and 180 miles northeast of Manila.

Throughout the islands, authorities sped the roundup of suspects in a drive to check fifth columnist activities. Several former followers of Benigno Ramos, leader of the Sakdalista uprising of 1935, were taken into custody. Ramos for years was an exile in Japan.

An air raid warden said the special telephone line linking his office with Nichols air depot had been cut and thus the Army Signal Corps had been unable to notify civilian officials in time for an alarm before the start of an air attack yesterday.

A spokesman said President Manuel Quezon received a message from President Roosevelt praising the Philippines for their "magnificent defense against wanton invasion." The President also sent congratulations to General Douglas MacArthur, Army commander in the Philippines.

Simultaneously, a Tokyo radio broadcast said Japanese landing forces had occupied the capital of U. S.-owned Guam Island in mid-Pacific, capturing 350 Americans including Gov. George McMillin and other officers.

Domei, the Japanese news agency, said Japanese troops also landed on Wake Island, another American outpost.

Domei said the Japanese landing on Wake Island followed violent aerial attacks in which warehouses were smashed and set ablaze and seven U. S. Army planes shot down in a single day's dogfights over the island.

Airmen "Human Torpedoes."

Reports that Japanese airmen were making themselves "human torpedoes" found apparent substantiation in a bulletin from Tokyo imperial headquarters which said two Japanese planes in an attack on an airport near Manila "dived headlong into enemy positions."

In disclosing that American troops had won round No. 1 in the battle of the Philippines, a spokesman at Gen. Douglas MacArthur's headquarters declared:

"The situation is completely in hand.

"Enemy detachments that landed on the Luzon coast are being dis-

(Continued on Page 10.)

DIES IN FIRE AT HOME.

Albion (AP)—Mrs. John Sutton, 77, died today during a fire which damaged the kitchen and interior of her home.

These Nations Now Officially at War

BY THE ASSOCIATED PRESS

Here are the 36 nations officially in the second World War:

The United States vs Germany, Italy, Japan, Manchukuo.

Britain, Canada, Union of South Africa, Australia, New Zealand, Netherlands, Free French and China vs Germany, Italy, Japan, Manchukuo, Finland, Rumania, Croatia, Hungary.

Russia, Norway, Luxembourg, Belgium, Czechoslovakia, Poland, Yugoslavia, Greece, Ethiopia vs Germany, Italy, Finland, Rumania, Croatia, Hungary.

Costa Rica, Cuba, Haiti, El Salvador, Honduras, Dominican Republic, Nicaragua, Guatemala, Panama, Bolivia vs Japan and Manchukuo.

The most important neutrals include:

Argentina, Brazil, Bulgaria, Chile, Colombia, Ecuador, Mexico, Paraguay, Peru, Portugal, Spain, Sweden, Switzerland, Turkey, Uruguay and Venezuela.

JAPAN, THAILAND CONCLUDE ACCORD

Tokyo (By official Japanese wireless) (INS)—The Japanese information bureau announced today that Japan and Thailand had concluded an "offensive-defensive alliance."

Thailand capitulated to Japan on the opening day of the Far Eastern war. Thereafter an agreement was reached permitting Japanese troops to move across Thai territory.

RUSSIANS CLAIM NEW SUCCESSES ON THREE FRONTS

Nazis Retreating With Bloody Losses in Rout from Rostov-on-Don, Reds Report.

BY THE ASSOCIATED PRESS.

Russian armies claimed smashing new successes on the Ukraine, Moscow and Leningrad fronts today even as Germany and Italy declared war against the United States, merging the wars of the east and west in a gigantic world conflict.

Soviet dispatches from the southern front pictured Field Marshal Ewald Von Kleist's armies as retreating with new bloody losses in the rout from Rostov-on-Don.

"Pursuit of the enemy continues. Roads are littered with enemy dead," the Russians said.

On the central front, the Moscow radio reported 12,000 Germans killed and wounded as Russian troops in four days of fierce fighting recaptured the town of Olets, in the Orel sector 200 miles south of the U. S. S. R. capital.

Other Soviet troops operating in the Stalinogorsk sector, 120 miles southeast of Moscow, were credited with driving the Germans from six populated centers.

On the Leningrad front, the Soviet radio said Russian soldiers who dislodged the Germans from Tikhvin, 110 miles east of the old Czarist capital, were "successfully pursuing the Germans, retreating in disorder, and have occupied 15 villages."

In his address to the Reichstag, declaring war on the United States, Hitler gave another expansive recital of Russian losses, asserting that the Germans had taken 3,806,865 Soviet prisoners and captured or destroyed 21,391 tanks, 32,541 guns and 17,325 aircraft.

The Nazi high command said only "local actions" were occuring on the Russian front.

In North Africa, British mobile columns were reported striking sharply at Axis forces retreating westward across the Libyan desert from the El Adem area, 15 miles south of Tobruk.

British patrols operating along the Libyan coast between Tobruk and the Egyptian frontier were said to have destroyed 38 tanks in workshops in addition to 27 reported captured yesterday.

Premier Mussolini's high command acknowledged that British pressure on the Italian stronghold at Salum was continuing and reported 35 British tanks destroyed in fighting south and southwest of Tobruk.

GENERAL PERSHING, WORLD WAR LEADER, OFFERS SERVICES

Washington (AP)—"Black Jack" Pershing, who won his spurs and his nickname in the now embattled Philippines, wants to do his bit this time, too.

But his World War chauffeur, John W. Smallwood, has a better chance to do it in the armed forces.

Gen. John J. Pershing, the A. E. F.'s commander who is now 81 and ailing, offered his services to the nation once more yesterday to the "last ounce" of his strength.

By coincidence, Smallwood chose the same day to volunteer at Cumberland, Md., for another hitch as doughboy after two decades of civilian life.

President Roosevelt thanked General Pershing warmly for his offer. "I am deeply grateful," he wrote, ". . . You have never been placed on the retired list. You are very much on the active list and your services will be of great value."

As for Smallwood, he passed the Army's physical examination. However he is 44 and the present maximum age is 35, but a waiver of this regulation will be sought in his case.

WAR BULLETINS

Washington (INS).—The Senate and House today passed a resolution amending the draft law to allow American troops to be used anywhere in the world while National Selective Service Headquarters announced it was considering raising an army of 4,000,000 men immediately. The Senate vote was 86 to 0. The House vote was by voice without a roll call. The bill now goes to the White House. At the same time, Senator Walsh, D.-Mass., chairman of the Senate naval affairs committee, announced from the floor of the Senate that a bill will be introduced soon to extend the draft act to the Navy. Walsh added that the Navy expects to take 50,000 selectees "in the near future."

Tokyo (Official Radio Received by AP).—The navy section of Japan's imperial headquarters declared today a United States destroyer and submarine were sunk and a transport ship was damaged heavily in the Japanese bombing attack yesterday on Cavite and Manila Bay. The war bulletin said at least 81 United States planes had been destroyed in the attack—45 in the air combat and 36 on the ground.

New York (AP).—The United States Marine garrison at Peiping was disarmed today by Japanese troops, the German wireless said. There were no incidents and the Americans were told to remain in their barracks until further orders. The garrison, about seventy men, was under orders to leave China when the war broke.

Batavia, Java (AP).—A Netherlands East Indies army communique declared today that Australian bombers based in the Nei raided a Japanese air base on the little island of Pobra between the Celebes and the Japanese-mandated islands southeast of the Philippines.

La Paz, Bolivia (Delayed) (AP).—Bolivia declared war upon Japan today, becoming No. 10 in the list of Latin American republics to take such action.

MOVE TO PREVENT WORK SHUTDOWNS DURING AIR ALERTS

Four Aircraft Plants Closed During Three-hour Alarm Last Night on West Coast.

Los Angeles (U.P.)—Southern California's defense industries, including aircraft plants building $1,000,000,000 worth of airplanes, strengthened defense precautions today in order to prevent costly shutdowns during air raid alarms.

Four aircraft plants were closed last night, halting production of vital planes and parts because of a three-hour air raid alarm. The Army said an unidentified plane was overhead.

Consolidated Aircraft, building $750,000,000 worth of heavy bombers. Ryan Aeronautical and Solar Aircraft, building training planes, and Rohr Aircraft, manufacturer of equipment were told by the Army to order their 17,000 night shift workers home because their plants could not be completely blacked out.

Shipyards, where most of the activity is out of doors, also were hampered by the blackouts and production was delayed.

The Army said it would cooperate to prevent delays when possible and ordered elimination of all practice blackouts. The alert signal will also be dispended with and henceforth warnings will be flashed only when aircraft is approaching and immediate full blackouts are necessitated.

The alarm last night was spread throughout Southern California from Baker's Field to the bomber town of Tijuana, Mexico, and the southern tip of Nevada where Boulder Dam is located, when the Army heard an unidentified plane "over and south of Los Angeles."

Planes of interceptor command were sent up, searchlights switched on, anti-aircraft units ordered to blast the plane, and the entire area blacked out.

Col. Harry S. Fuller, air raid warning official here, said that "by a process of elimination" the Army had concluded the plane was an enemy.

CITIZENS TO GET ADVANCE NOTICE OF ANY BLACKOUT

Mayor Makes Announcement Before Going to Albany to Attend Conference With Gen. O'Ryan.

Troy will not have a blackout demonstration until residents have had plenty of advance notice about it, Mayor Frank J. Hogan said today.

Meanwhile Mayor Hogan and other area mayors were in Albany conferring with Maj. Gen. John F. O'Ryan, state civilian defense director, relative to blackout procedure and other defense matters.

Joseph F. Purcell, secretary to the Mayor, accompanied him.

Governor Lehman yesterday instructed major defense cities of the state to hold practice blackouts immediately.

Hospitals and other public institutions in Troy began taking blackout precautions today. Windows not equipped with heavy dark green curtains will be covered with black material or painted black.

The sale of black flannelette and sateen, flashlights and candles mounted today as many householders prepared for any emergency. Authorities say that no main switches will be pulled for a complete blackout but people are taking no chances.

In Schenectady one newspaper office already has covered its windows with black paint.

Several industrial plants in this area are taking similar precautions and others held meetings today to decide what steps shall be taken to darken large buildings in which work goes on all night.

STEUBEN DEER KILL REPORTED NEAR 400

Bath (AP)—Chief Game Warden Andrew Vromwald of Oleon said today he believed the take of antlerless deer during Steuben County's three-day special season ended last evening would probably total 400.

Vromwald said the staff of 25 deputies assembled for the season reported checking 54 kills in the field and added "undoubtedly many more hunters will report direct to the State Conservation Department in Albany as required. Probably the total take will be 400."

NEW WEAPONS NOT USED TO SINK SHIPS

London (AP)—Repeated attacks by Japanese bombers and torpedo planes sank the British battleship Prince of Wales and the battle cruiser Repulse yesterday off Malaya, it was announced officially today.

An official spokesman said "there is no reason to suppose any new weapons or explosives were employed."

He added:

"There is reason to believe the loss of life in the Prince of Wales and the Repulse has been less heavy than at first feared."

British Rescue More Than 2,000 Men Aboard Ships Sunk By Japs

Singapore, Straits Settlements (UP)—More than 2,000 survivors of the battleship Prince of Wales and battle cruiser Repulse, arriving in Singapore today, told how the great British battle craft had gone down fighting under perhaps the most ferocious airplane attack in naval history.

Survivors said more than sixty Japanese planes attacked the 35,000 ton Prince of Wales, pride of the Royal Navy, for three hours before it went down.

The guns of both ships, they said, were still in action as the crippled ships, hit several times in vital parts, were on the verge of sinking.

It was announced officially that more than 2,000 men had been saved.

(The normal complement of the Prince of Wales is about 1,500 and the normal complement of the Repulse is about 1,200.)

The survivors indicated that the Japanese had paid heavily in planes for their attack. A single anti-aircraft gun was credited with shooting down several planes, but the ordeal was such that an accurate count of enemy losses could not be made.

Repulse's guns were blazing fiercely as it listed to port.

Survivors said that Repulse's crew scrambled on the decks when ordered to abandon ship and slid down the side to drop into the sea.

They were picked up by destroyers from life rafts and brought to Singapore.

Cecil Brown, correspondent for Columbia Broadcasting System, was among those rescued from Repulse.

Capt. William G. Tennant, commanding officer of the Repulse, was rescued.

HITLER BLUNDERED IN SOVIET ATTACK, CHURCHILL STATES

Prime Minister Speaks Gravely of U. S. and British Naval Losses; Sees African Victory.

London (AP) — Prime Minister Churchill spoke gravely today of United States and British naval losses in the Pacific and the Far East, declared Adolf Hitler committed a colossal blunder in attacking Soviet Russia, and predicted ultimate British victory in North Africa despite unexpected reverses.

"It may well be," he declared in a sweeping review of the broadened war, "that we shall have to suffer considerable punishment, but we shall defend ourselves with the utmost vigor and in close cooperation with the United States and Netherlands Navy.

"No one can underate the gravity of losses inflicted on the United States nor underrate the length of time it will take to marsha. the great forces necessary in the Far East for absolute victory."

Speaking seriously and appearing tired, Churchill nevertheless declared confidently that the naval might of Britain and the United States "was very greatly superior and still is largely superior to the combined forces of the three Axis powers."

He said bluntly that because of American naval losses Britain must expect that United States naval aid in the Atlantic and the volume of American supplies for Britain to be reduced, but added:

"I cannot doubt now that the 130,000,000 people of the United States have bound themselves to this war and once they get settled down to it... That the flow of munitions and aid of every kind will vastly exceed anything that could have been expected up to the present."

Tells of Libyan Campaign.

Of the sinking of Britain's battleship Prince of Wales and battlecruiser Repulse by Japanese air attack off Malaya, the Prime Minister said he understood they were without support of their own land-based fighter planes "because of an attack which had been made on the airdromes."

He told the House of Commons the ships were sunk by Japanese aerial torpedoes.

Churchill described the British campaign in Libya as the only place the British could open a field of fighting that would aid Russia.

"The Libyan offensive," he said "did not take the course its authors expected, although it will reach the end at which they aimed."

He said Hitler had made one of the "outstanding blunders of history" in attacking Russia, pictured the Germans as in retreat on the Russian front after suffering enormous losses and said Britain was now bent on annihilation of retreating German forces in Libya with good prospects of success.

Speaking shortly before Mussolini announced the Axis declaration of

(Continued on Page 9.)

Congress Action Counters Earlier Axis Declarations

Not A Single "No" Vote Registered in Either Senate or House After President Requests Move Against "the Forces Endeavoring to Enslave the Entire World"; Hitler and Mussolini Acted Earlier.

BY THE ASSOCIATED PRESS.

The Congress of the United States without dissent voted war against both Germany and Italy today, swiftly countering Axis declarations of war against this country.

Not a single "no" vote was registered in either Senate or House.

The Senate voted 88-0 for war against Germany, 90-0 for war against Italy.

Mr. Roosevelt signed the German war resolution at 3:05 p.m., E. S. T. and the Italian resolution at 3:06 p.m.

The House vote for war with Germany was 393, with one member, Montana's Republican woman representative Jeanette Rankin, who cast the lone vote against war with Japan and who voted against the war with Germany in 1917, recorded as "present."

Congress' lightning speed in passing both resolutions—even more rapidly than in voting war against Japan—came after a message from President Roosevelt urging a "rapid and united effort" for victory "over the forces of savagery and barbarism."

"The long-known and long-expected has taken place," Mr. Roosevelt said, in a noon message to Congress.

"The forces endeavoring to enslave the entire world now are moving toward this hemisphere. Never before has there been a greater challenge to life, liberty and civilization . . .

"I therefore request the Congress to recognize a state of war between the United States and Germany, and between the United States and Italy."

Hitler Reiterates Familiar Theme.

Only a few hours earlier, the Axis dictators had invoked war against the United States, with Premier Mussolini exhorting crowds in Rome that "it is an honor to fight together with the Japanese."

Reichsfuehrer Adolf Hitler, lengthily addressing a wildly cheering Reichstag, reiterated his familiar theme that the war would determine the history of the entire world for the next 500 to 1,000 years.

"Italian men and women, once again I tell you in this great hour: We shall be victorious!" Il Duce shouted from the balcony of the Palazzo Venezia in Rome.

Washington had already discounted both declarations by the Axis powers with the official comment "So What?" and it appeared the European dictators were offering Japan moral support rather than any possibility of actual fighting aid.

In Berlin, Hitler told the Reichstag:

"This has become the greatest year of decision by the German people—and your greatest decision stands before us."

The two dictators began their addresses almost simultaneously, at about 8 a.m., E.S.T.

Both had been foreshadowed, a Japanese spokesman having declared yesterday that "Japan expected Germany and Italy to declare war on the United States" in fulfillment of the Rome-Berlin-Tokyo alliance of totalitarianism against democracy.

Galleries Partly Filled.

Senate galleries were only partly filled during the momentous action. Lord Halifax, the British Ambassador, and Lady Halifax, sat in the diplomatic galleries with other representatives of the diplomatic corps.

Minority Leader McNary (R.-Ore.) submitted a unanimous resolution of Republican members pledging support to the President in prosecuting the war to a successful conclusion.

At the other end of the capitol, jammed galleries and a crowded floor waited for the representatives to follow the lead of their senatorial colleagues.

Rev. James Shera Montgomery, the House chaplain, opened the session with an appeal for divine aid for the nation.

Archduke Otto of Austria, whose country was aligned against the United States in the World War, was one of those who occupied a seat in the diplomatic gallery.

In a brief, six-paragraph message to Congress, which [illegible] declarations of war on this [illegible]try by the two Axis partners, [illegible] Roosevelt asserted that "the [illegible]

(Continued on [illegible])

Hitler's Speech Twists Announcer's Tongue

New York (AP)—Berlin's announcer in English, solemnly reading a translation of Hitler's speech today, got his tongue twisted, N. B. C. reported.

"When the attack . . ." he stopped and began stammering.

"By . . .

"Upon . . .

"Against . . ."

Then he started over again.

"When the war with Greece and Yugoslavia began, that war was really nothing compared to the beginning of the larger struggle in which we are still at present engaged."

DIES OF INJURIES.

Utica (AP)—Robert Hammond, 50, Poland, died today of injuries suffered when struck by a boom while loading logs for a lumber company near Noblesboro yesterday.

Disloyal Americans Next On F. B. I. List

Washington (AP)—The Department of Justice turned its attention today to disloyal Americans—potential Benedict Arnolds.

The Federal Bureau of Investigation was understood to be scrutinizing particularly persons suspected to be fifth columnists, those who have been propagandizing, on Axis behalf, and those whose loyalty is questionable.

In an initial sweep against alien enemies, Attorney General Biddle announced yesterday, 2,303 Japanese, Germans and Italians have been arrested. Biddel said the total eventually might reach 2,500; other officials estimated the number at 3,000.

Estimates on the number of Americans listed as probable aides or dupes of the enemy were unavailable. Officials took a cautious attitude toward that phase of the government's work because of numerous legal complexities involved.

It was explained that while any German, Italian or Japanese citizen could be picked up under the designation of "enemy alien," and without further procedure, no American citizen may be arrested except on a charge of violating the law. For this reason, the F. B. I. will perforce move more slowly in the later phases of its program. Some activities which are illegal for aliens are permissible for Americans. For every United States citizen seized, the government must have prepared a case for presentation in court, while in the case of an alien only informal procedure is necessary.

Biddle said that the aliens seized would be given hearings before civilian boards which will make recommendations to him. The Army will have custody of those aliens ordered held for the duration of the war. The immigration service will handle parolees.

A number of United States citizens including correspondents, were arrested in Germany today in reprisal for the arrest in the United States of German and Italian nationals, DNB said in a report heard in London by Reuters.

"As a reprisal for President Roosevelt's order, which is against international law, for the arrest of German press correspondents and German and Italian nationals in the United States, North American journalists and a number of North American nationals were arrested in Germany today," the report said.

The Index

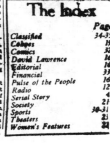

LABOR PEACE SEEN LIKELY, RESULT OF LEWIS' OVERTURES

Washington (AP) — Labor circles appeared convinced yesterday that mechanical difficulties in the way of union of the A. F. of L. and C. I. O. could be overcome in new peace negotiations proposed by John L. Lewis.

Privately, some labor men said the biggest barriers in the past had been psychological ones or "mental attitudes" and expressed belief that these had been largely swept away by the war and the fact that Lewis took the initiative in the new efforts at union.

Within the A. F. of L., the failure of past negotiations had been attributed to Lewis personally. William Green, A. F. of L. president, asserted once that a peace formula was worked out in 1937 by A. F. of L. and C. I. O. representatives but was vetoed by Lewis, then president of the C. I. O.

It was taken for granted that the negotiations would be reopened soon, although there was no indication yesterday that any steps had yet been taken toward setting a date.

BURGLARS STEAL U. S. FOOD STAMPS

Buffalo (AP) — Cracksmen yesterday battered open a safe in the Erie County Welfare Department and stole $190,680 worth of negotiable federal food stamps.

Assistant Detective Chief Michael J. Scanlon said the burglars apparently gained entrance to the office, located in the county office building, with a duplicate key and drilled the safe. Police fixed the time of the burglary at about noon, when employees in the building reported hearing hammering.

TO HELP relieve COLDS

FATHER JOHN'S MEDICINE

Registered in U. S. Pat Office

WORKS 2 WAYS

While helping your cold, it also aids in building strong, sturdy bodies.

It is rich in the essential vitamins A and D which are needed to fight colds.

Its use for 85 years is convincing—it must have merit.

VON REICHENAU'S DEATH BLAMED ON ARMY INTRIGUE

British Press Skeptical of Announcement Nazi Field Marshal Sucaumbed to Apoplexy.

London (AP)—Sinister intrigue behind the back of Adolf Hitler caused the death of Field Marshal Gen. Walter von Reichenau, the British press reasoned yesterday with unanimous skepticism of the official announcement that he died of apoplexy.

(The British radio late last night reported that Gen. Heinrich von Stuelpnagel had been relieved of his post as leader of the 17th German army now fighting in the Ukraine. The broadcast was heard by CBS.)

Its evidence, of course, was circumstantial, but newspapers offered three principal arguments to support their contention that von Reichenau died at the hands of his fellow officers, probably in a violent outburst of dissension between the Nazi Fuehrer and his war command.

They were:

1. Von Reichenau's reputation as Hitler's most pro-Nazi general;
2. The background of dismissal and sudden illness among the Germans' top generals;
3. Von Reichenau's singular physical fitness, a matter he made almost a fetish.

The apoplexy diagnosis put forward Saturday in the official Berlin announcement of the death was looked on with particular suspicion by many British writers because von Reichenau was known to have kept himself always in peak condition, even working out at the front with Walter Neusel, the former German heavyweight boxer.

Some took the view that von Reichenau was eliminated as an open challenge by the army to Hitler. This supposition was based on the report that he was being considered by the Nazis as commander-in-chief of the army despite the opposition of strong, influential elements in it.

Finally, his death following the death of Gen. Ernst Udet, the dismissal of Field Marshal Gen. Walther von Brauchitsch, whose place Hitler himself took as commander-in-chief of the army, and a harvest of rumors that other general had been ousted from their commands or had begged off further service, the press contended, should leave no doubt of heat between the Nazis and the army leaders.

WAKE PRISONERS REACH YOKOHAMA

Tokyo, (Official broadcast recorded by (AP))—The second group of U. S. prisoners of war, 1,235 men from the garrison of Wake Island, reached Yokohama yesterday.

Showing little signs of ordeal except overgrown beards and soiled uniforms, the men all indicated they were more worried about the concern of their families back home than about themselves.

Four Victims Of Airliner Crash In Nevada

CAPT. WAYNE WILLIAMS. (PILOT)

MORGAN A. GILLETTE. (CO-PILOT)

Screen Actress Carole Lombard (right), her mother, Mrs. Elizabeth K. Peters (left), and twenty other occupants of a luxurious TWA plane crashed to flaming death on 8,500-foot Table Mountain, 35 miles southwest of Las Vegas, Nev. They're shown with film star Clark Gable, husband of Miss Lombard, who was dissuaded yesterday from joining the party which went to the wreck scene.

Carole Lombard's Body Brought To Las Vegas, Nevada

Las Vegas, Nev. (AP)—The bodies of nine persons, including that of actress Carole Lombard, among the 22 who were killed Friday night in the crash of a giant airliner against a cliff 35 miles southwest of here, were brought to Las Vegas last night.

A coroner's jury held that Miss Lombard had died of injuries received in the "crash of a TWA liner en route from Las Vegas to Los Angeles, near Double or Nothing Mountain."

Deputy Coroner Jack Larry earlier had said that the body of Miss Lombard's mother, Mrs. Elizabeth Peters, had been identified and brought here, but a check just before the inquest with dental records from Hollywood, proved the identification erroneous.

Dental Records Used.

Identification of stewardess Alice Getz was described as positive. This would indicate that the unidentified body was that of Mrs. Lois Hamilton of Lincoln Park, Mich., the only other woman aboard the plane.

A wisp of blond hair and dental records identified Miss Lombard. The inquest was held so her body could be sent to Glendale, Cal., for burial, but officials indicated this action now would be delayed until her mother's body is identified.

Fifty persons were able to reach the scene of the crash over steep and rocky trails, to find wreckage strewn over a wide area.

Bits of the plane and personal belongings of the passengers lay in the snow, some clinging to pine trees.

Twenty enlisted men under command of Lieuts. W. B. Hunt and S. R. Keddington of the Army Air Corps prepared for at least a two-day effort to remove the bodies.

Bodies Lifted Up Cliff.

The bodies were wrapped in Army blankets and lifted with ropes to the top of a 200-yard cliff. From there they will be carried on horses eight miles over trails to motor vehicles below.

The actress' grief-stricken husband, film actor Clark Gable, who flew here immediately upon learning of the tragedy, attempted to join the rescue party, but was dissuaded by friends. When advised of the accident, he was waiting at a Los Angeles airport to greet Miss Lombard, who was en route home from a government defense bond-selling campaign in Indianapolis, where sales for one day totaled nearly $2,500,000.

The accident, the country's most tragic involving a film celebrity since actor Will Rogers and pilot Wiley Post perished in the crash of their plane in Alaska in 1935, had a fateful touch in that Miss Lombard's press representative, Otto Winkler, had tried unsuccessfully to discourage her from making the trip by plane. They flipped a coin and the actress won over Winkler's proposal that they return by train.

Four persons, who had been passengers aboard the plane, narrowly escaped a similar fate because they were asked to vacate their seats at Albuquerque so that the Army fliers could get aboard. They are Joseph S. Szigeti, Hungarain violinist; Miss Mary Anna Johnson of Benicia, Cal.; Mrs. Florence Sawyer of Portland, Me., and Mrs. Carl Brandener of Holton, Kans.

Besides the 15 Army flyers who were ferry pilots en route to California for new assignments, the dead included the plane's pilot and co-pilot, Capt Wayne Williams of Reseda, Cal., and Morgan A. Gillette of Los Angeles, and Stewardess Alice Getz of Glendale, Cal.

EIGHTY FIREMEN ARE OVERCOME AT MALDEN, MASS., BLAZE

Malden, Mass. (AP)—Eighty firemen were overcome by smoke and escaping illuminating gas yesterday in a furious fire that swept a downtown business block.

The fire was controlled by relief crews of firemen summoned from a half dozen neighboring cities, and at one time direction of their work was left to visiting fire officials when all three Malden deputy chiefs were overcome.

The nearby police station and fire station were turned into emergency hospitals, and a dozen doctors and nurses directed the work of rescue crews sent by the Boston Fire Department and the gas company.

The fire was discovered about 2 a.m. (E.S.T.) and firemen who first reached the scene soon sounded a second, and then a general alarm, as smoke and fumes from broken gas mains overcome whole crews of fire fighters.

A number of the firemen were overcome twice and even three times, returning to their tasks after being revived. Only three were affected seriously enough to require hospitalization, but later many showed more serious after affects.

Firemen said damage would amount to between $40,000 and $50,000. The building housed five stores on the street level and six offices on the second floor.

The fire department of this industrial city of 57,000 persons was left crippled and the stations last night were manned by a half hundred volunteers from neighboring communities.

According to estimates, the average American worker worked 37.6 hours and earned an average of $24.44 a week, in 1939.

SETS BILLION QUOTA FOR DEFENSE BONDS

Washington (AP)—A $1,000,000,000 quota for purchase of defense bonds by its members and affiliated unions during the coming year has been set by the American Federation of Labor.

Announcing the quota yesterday, President William Green said an intergrated drive to get every A. F. of L. worker to invest in defense bonds would be inaugurated Feb. 22 with a joint appeal by Green and Treasury Secretary Morgenthau.

POSTMEN TO FETE RETIRED CARRIERS AT DINNER EVENT

Robert A. Warnock, Jacob H. Coons and Elmer E. Howe Will Be Honor Guests Tonight.

Three recently retired Troy mail carriers will be honored tonight at the annual meeting of Trojan Branch of the National Letter Carriers Association in Dania Hall. Special honors will be paid Robert A. Warnock, Jacob H. Coons and Elmer E. Howe.

In addition to paying honor to the veteran members of the association new officers will be installed and a musical program and social hour enjoyed. A meeting of the Credit Union of Postal Employees, featured by the payment of a dividend, will follow the association meeting. Ralph J. Germain will preside at the credit union meeting at which two directors, two committeemen and one supervisory committeeman will be named.

To be installed as officers of th Letter Carriers Association are Albert H. Snover, president; William P. Wansbury, vice president; Thomas J. Bailey, recording secretary; Albert J. Thoun, financial secreatry; J. Lawrence Munson, treasurer; Francis J. Thompson, collector for Mutual Benefit Association; Arthur J. Gummer, collector for S. B. A.; James A. Smith, station clerk; Thomas Conally, sergeant-at-arms; Ralph J. Germain, trustee for three years; and William J. Burke, trustee for two years. Installing officers will be Oliver Lee, past president, and Elmer L. Howe, also a past president.

A musical program will be presented under supervision of the Letter Carriers Association members headed by Harry P. Cheney, Ernest Sharp, William P. Wansbury, Otto G. A. Krause and Clyde Meighan.

The social hour committee representing Credit Union members comprises Jacob H. Coons, Ralph J. Germain, Albert C. Goerold, Frank LeMay, Hugh F. McNamara and R. A. Warnock.

BURMA PREMIER ARRESTED IN PLOT TO AID JAPANESE

London Indicates Move Thwarted Coup to Hand Over "Kipling Country" to Nipponese.

London (AP)—Bland, skirt-wearing Premier U Saw of Burma, the southeast Asiatic British possession vital to Singapore's defense has been arrested by the British for conspiring with the Japanese.

An announcement early today from No. 10 Downing Street, Prime Minister Churchill's official residence, indicated the arrest thwarted an attempted coup by the disgruntled U Saw to hand over to the Japanese the storied "Kipling country" of 14,000,000 people.

Since quitting London in a huff last November after failing to obtain dominion status for Burma the little Oriental has been breathing defiance at the British government.

Used As British Base.

Burma is being used as a base for British aerial assaults on Japanese forces driving down Malaya toward Singapore and is expected to be jumping-off place for a flank attack against the invaders from the east. It also is vital as a port of entry for American aid moving to China over the Burma Road.

"From reports received about U Saw's movements after his good will mission to this country it has come to the knowledge of His Majesty's Government that he has been in contact with Japanese authorities since the outbreak of the Japanese war," the British announcement said.

"This fact has been confirmed by his own adimission," the statement added. "His Majesty's Government accordingly has been compelled to detain him and it will not be possible to permit him to return to Burma."

Colorful Diplomatic Figure.

The statement did not say where U Saw was arrested or where his contact with the Japanese took place.

He went from London to Washington and last was reported in Hawaii, having gone there by clipper plane, when the Japanese started the war.

With his polished manners and picturesque dress, U Saw was regarded as one of the most colorful figures in the diplomatic world.

After conferring here with Churchill and L. S. Amery, Secretary for India, the Burmese premier broke his long silence with the curt announcement that his trip "was not satisfactory and not commensurate with the amount of risk I have taken in coming to England."

"We would rather trust the devil we know that the devil we don't," he added.

U Saw, whose exact age is unknown, brought presents for Churchill on his London visit but upon departing said with a shrug of his oriental shoulders:

"Britain Has Nothing to Give."

"When I get back to Burma I shall have to say that Britain has nothing to give you, in which case . . . ."

Burma, formerly a province of the India Empire, as constituted since the annexation of Upper Burma in 1886, comprises the British territory of Upper and Lower Burma, the extensive native states known as the Federated Shan States, and Karenni, as well as several tracts of unadministered territory in the more remote parts.

The extreme length from north to south is almost 1,200 miles and the broadest part is 575 miles east to west.

Its importance in the present war lies chiefly in its position as a possible starting place for a flank attack upon the Japanese beating down through Malaya and as the starting point for the Burma Road, supply lifeline for the central Chinese forces of Generalissimo Chiang kai-Shek.

LEFT FROM WORLD WAR.

Assets totaling $144.78, a balance left over from its activity during the World War and kept intact through the intervening years, has been given by the Home Defense Committee of Columbia County to the Red Cross chapter of that county. The committee was active during the last war.

Could Nero Have Fiddled With Stomach Ulcer Pains?

The historic fiddling of Nero after his feasting could hardly have been possible if he suffered after-eating pains. Don't neglect your suffering. Try a 25c box of Udga for relief of ulcer and stomach pains, indigestion, gas pains, heartburn, burning sensation, bloat and other conditions caused by excess acid. Udga Tablets must help or money refunded. At drug stores everywhere.—Adv.

Answers to Cranium Crackers

Questions on Page 3.

1. —Alaska was purchased from Russia in 1867 for $7,200,000; Virgin Islands from Denmark in 1916 for $25,000,000.

2. No. Hawaiian Islands were annexed to U. S. at their own request in 1898 after their queen had been deposed and a republic formed in 1893. U. S. used Hawaii as a naval base in War with Spain.

3. Midway Island was annexed by U. S. in 1867; Guam in 1898, ceded by Spain after the war; Wake in 1899, taken possession of in the name of the U. S. by American seamen landing there.

4 Swains Island, just north of Samoa Islands in the Pacific, was claimed in 1925. Samoa Islands (Tutuila and Manua) were acquired in 1899 through treaty with Britain and Germany.

5. U. S. holds Canal Zone in perpetuity by treaty of Nov. 18, 1903, with Panama.

U. S. ARMY CORPS

HORIZONTAL

1 U. S. Army Corps wearing pictured insignia, —— ——.
12 Pacify.
13 Wharves.
15 Rhode Island (abbr.).
17 Sidewise.
18 Music note.
19 Hotel.
21 Tone E (music).
22 Bright color.
23 Prohibit.
25 South African tribesman.
27 Come back.
28 Head cover.
29 Russian (abbr.).
30 Iniquity.
33 Music note.
34 Implement.
35 Springy.
39 Indications.
42 Chum.
43 Separate from others.
45 Place.
47 Advertisement (abbr.).
48 Attorney (abbr.).
49 Beverage.
51 Therefore.
52 Upper part of head.
54 Assists.
56 Imagine.
57 Malicious burning.

VERTICAL

1 Samarium (abbr.).
2 Sick.
3 Charm.
4 Pertaining to a nationalist.
5 Affirmative.
6 Certified public accountant (abbr.).
7 Lubricant.
8 Condiment.
9 Inspect closely
10 Steamship (abbr.).
11 Silkworm.
14 Field —— sets are used in its equipment.
16 Bury.
18 Turkish cap.
20 Not artificial.
22 Allowances of provisions.
24 Passenger vehicles.
26 Lose bulk.
31 Organs of smell.
32 Pay back.
36 Boy.
37 Giant (myth.).
38 Company (abbr.).
39 Symbol for tantalum.
40 Animal.
41 Parts of boats.
44 Music note.
46 2000 pounds.
48 Constellation.
50 Away from (prefix).
52 Brought forward (abbr.).
53 New York (abbr.).
54 Exclamation.
55 Tin (symbol).

Answer to Previous Puzzle

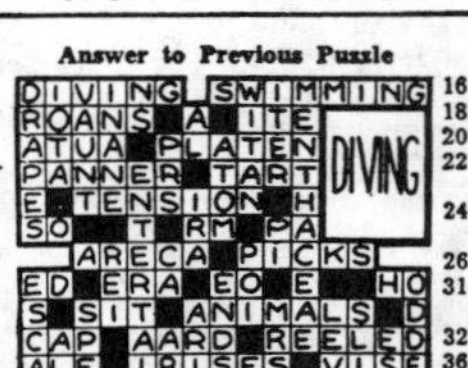

HOW YOU CAN GET A $100 LOAN FOR $8.90 (TOTAL COST)

Repay in six monthly instalments of $18.15 each, a total of $108.90—No endorsers or guarantors required

NEED EXTRA CASH? If you have a job, you can get a Household Finance loan at very reasonable cost. Suppose you borrow $25 and repay in four monthly instalments of $6.65 each, a total of $26.60. The cost of your loan is only $1.60. Or take a $50 loan repaid in four monthly instalments of $13.29 each, totaling $53.16. You pay just $3.16 for your loan. A $100 loan, repaid in six monthly instalments of $18.15 each, costs only $8.90.

All you do

You may apply for any loan shown in the table. And you may choose the payment plan which best fits your own income. So why not phone or visit us now? All you do to apply for a Household loan is to tell us how much you need and how you wish to repay. You need no endorsers or guarantors—just the ability to repay in small monthly instalments. This saves you the embarrassment of asking friends or fellow-workers to sign the loan papers with you. And at no time do we question friends or relatives about your credit.

You get your loan simply and privately.

Household Finance loans are made in three ways. First way: On your personal note. No security required. Note loans are made, under proper conditions, to both single persons and married couples. Second way: On your car. This plan may suit you best. Third way: On your furniture. Many people prefer this plan. When making car and furniture loans, we consider character and income far more important than the value of your security. Your loan will be made the way which is best for you.

Let us help you

Payments in the table include all charges at the rate of 2½% per month on that part of a balance not exceeding $100 and 2% per month on that part of a balance in excess of $100. You pay nothing more.

If you need money, see us at once. Or just phone and tell us how much you wish to borrow. We are always ready to make helpful loans. Phone or visit us without obligation.

FIND HERE THE CASH LOAN YOU NEED

CHOOSE YOUR MONTHLY PAYMENT HERE

	2 payments	4 payments	6 payments	8 payments	10 payments	12 payments	15 payments	18 payments
$ 25	$12.97	$ 6.65	$ 4.54	$ 3.49	$ 2.86	$ 2.44		
50	25.94	13.29	9.08	6.97	5.71	4.87		
75	38.91	19.94	13.62	10.46	8.57	7.31	$ 6.06	$ 5.23
100	51.88	26.58	18.15	13.95	11.43	9.75	8.08	6.97
125	64.79	33.20	22.67	17.41	14.26	12.16	10.07	8.69
150	77.70	39.79	27.16	20.85	17.07	14.56	12.05	10.39
200	103.51	52.97	36.13	27.72	22.68	19.33	15.98	13.76
250	129.26	66.11	45.08	34.57	28.27	24.08	19.89	17.11
300	155.02	79.26	54.02	41.41	33.85	28.82	23.80	20.46

WE GUARANTEE the total amount figured by using this table to be the full amount you will pay, when payments are made on schedule. You will pay less if you pay your loan ahead of time since you pay charges only for the actual time you have the money. Payments include charges at the rate of 2½% per month on that part of a balance not exceeding $100 and 2% per month on that part of a balance in excess of $100.

B. E. HENDERSON, PRESIDENT

Other loans also made in multiples of $5.00

HOUSEHOLD FINANCE Corporation

ESTABLISHED 1878

Burdett Bldg., Suite 20, Second Floor, 251 River St.
N. W. Trew, Mgr. Phone: Troy 5122
TROY, NEW YORK
6th Fl., The Nat'l Savings Bank Building, 90 State St., Albany
A. B. Brittain, Mgr. Phone: 5-2326

HALF SOLES Leather or Composition

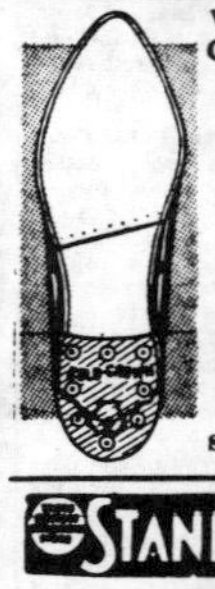

WOMEN'S & CHILDREN'S 64c Pair Attached

MEN'S & BOYS' 69c Pair Attached

SHOE REPAIR BASEMENT

STANLEYS

JANUARY SALE!

1/2 Off On All Machine PERMANENTS

Modern . . . . Reg.	$3.00	$1.50
French Oil . . Reg.	3.50	1.75
Silver . . . . . Reg.	4.00	2.00
Triumph . . . Reg.	4.50	2.25
Duart . . . . . Reg.	5.00	2.50
DeLuxe . . . . Reg.	6.00	3.00

For Your Appointment Call Troy 1910

These Great Values Are Offered Only Once-A-Year!

BEAUTY SHOP SECOND FLOOR

STANLEYS

TROY'S BUSIEST DEPARTMENT STORE STANLEYS CORNER THIRD AND STATE STREET

PROVING TROY'S BUSIEST STORE COMES THRU AGAIN WITH THE VALUE OF THE TOWN!

3 PIECE CUSTOM MADE

SLIP COVER SET

$17.95 2 CHAIRS AND DAVENPORT

FIT AND WORKMANSHIP FULLY GUARANTEED!

At this low price you can afford to keep your upholstered living room furniture looking colorfully smart and new looking. Compare the price. Stanley's Third Floor Curtain Department.

AND THEN TOO YOU HAVE YOUR CHOICE OF MANY ATTRACTIVE PATTERNS IN QUALITY FABRICS!

The material is measured and cut in your home . . . and for your convenience, our slip cover expert will complete the set here at Stanleys. Re-Do Your Furniture Now!

YOU DON'T NEED CASH!

SO HURRY IN TODAY AND TAKE ADVANTAGE . . . . A VALUE WE MAY NOT BE ABLE TO OFFER AGAIN!

CREDIT COUPON PLAN

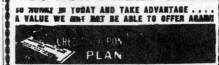

THE WEATHER
U. S. Weather Bureau.
Tonight—Light snow.

THE TIMES RECORD

FINAL EDITION

Series 1942—No. 21. (Entered as Second Class Matter at the Postoffice at Troy, N. Y., under the Act of March 3, 1879.) TROY, N. Y., MONDAY EVENING, JANUARY 26, 1942 (Published Daily Except Sunday) PRICE THREE CENTS

U. S. TROOPS IN NORTH IRELAND

AMERICAN FLYERS BOMB JAPS

Submarine Sinks Seventh Vessel Off Atlantic Coast

Tar Loses Teeth But Woman Gets Respect

New York (AP)—More respect for the womanhood of the Brooklyn waterfront is what Mrs. Arthur Lindsay wants, and from now on she'll probably get it.

The women of Third Avenue, Brooklyn, she said in court, are sick and tired of being annoyed by some seamen who accost them on the street and go around ringing doorbells at all hours of the night.

Nevertheless, Mrs. Lindsay accepted a mumbled apology from sailor Stephen Anderson, whom she had had arrested for disorderly conduct.

The husky mariner could barely make himself understood for the simple reason that Mrs. Lindsay had knocked out four of his front teeth when he spoke to her on the street.

HOUSE RECEIVES BIGGEST U. S. NAVY BILL IN HISTORY

Appropriations Measure Totals Nearly 18 Billions; "Supremacy on Seas" Described Goal.

Washington, (UP)—A $17,722,565,474 naval appropriations bill—the largest in history and designed to give the United States "unquestioned supremacy" of the seas—was approved by the House appropriation committee today and sent to the House floor.

The bill, carrying more than $8,000,000,000 or 46 per cent of its total, for increases in the Navy's tonnage—from battleships to tugs—includes grants for fiscal 1943 and supplemental funds for 1942—$13,430,339,974 for 1943, and $4,292,225,500 for the present fiscal year.

The committee commenting on its first wartime naval supply bill, termed the program "stupendous," but said "it can be accomplished with unbelievable dispatch."

The measure follows by three days unanimous House approval of a $12,525,872,474 grant for 33,000 Army airplanes. That measure until today ranked as the largest appropriation in history.

Heavy Spending Planned.

The committee, although censoring its wartime report, observed that "complete details, which have been painstakingly examined," were made available to the committee by the Navy Department.

The Navy's Bureau of Aeronau-

(Continued on Page 20.)

NEW TAXES NEEDED, CHAIRMAN GEORGE TELLS REPORTERS

Washington (AP)—A month's intensive study has convinced most congressional fiscal experts that the bulk of a proposed $9,000,000,000 addition to federal revenues will have to be raised by some new form of taxation, Chairman George (D., Ga.) of the Senate Finance Committee said today.

"The great problem," he declared, "is to determine whether this should be a sales tax, a withholding tax on payrolls or some other system. There has been no definite decision made on that point."

George told reporters, howeevr, that "satisfactory progress" toward the formation of a new tax program was being made in daily conferences between treaty officials and representatives of the joint congressional committee on internal revenue.

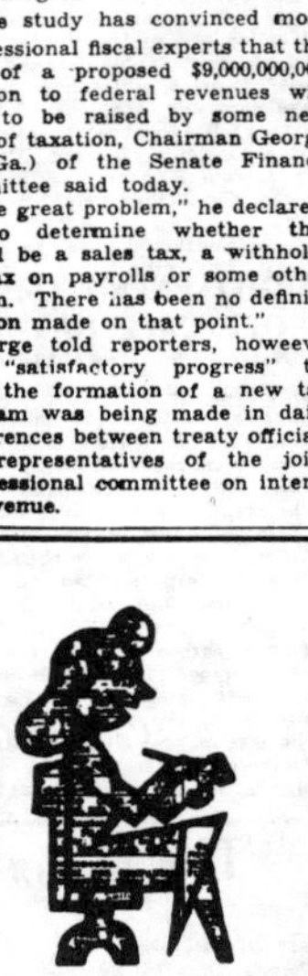

SPEAKING OF "DICTATORS"—

If you need someone to take your dictation, do other office work, phone a "Help Wanted" ad to Troy 6100 for a good selection of competent applicants.

SHIP TORPEDOED SATURDAY; FEAR 22 SEAMEN LOST

Twenty-one Survivors of S. S. Venore Landed at Norfolk, Va.; Captain Among Missing.

Norfolk, Va. (UP)—The Navy today disclosed sinking of the SS. Venore off the Atlantic coast with the apparent loss of 22 lives—the seventh ship known to have been sunk off the United States east coast since Axis submarines began intensive operations near shore Jan. 14.

Twenty-one survivors were brought here from the Venore, an 9,016-ton ore carrier owned by the Ore Steamship Co. of New York. The vessel was sunk early Saturday by a submarine which first fired two shells at it and then sent it to the bottom with a torpedo.

The indicated loss of life in the seven sinkings—and in an eighth attack that damaged but did not sink the SS. Malay—stands at 97.

Survivors of the Venore said the first indication they had that a submarine was nearby was when the first shell landed amidships on the port side as they were steaming at full speed. The second shell hit ten minutes later, with the torpedo following in about a half hour.

Captain Believed Lost.

Some men were washed overboard by a wave which swept over the deck after the torpedo landed, some jumped overboard, and some were lost when one of the Venore's two lifeboats capsized. All 21 survivors were in the second lifeboat, which was launched safely immediately after the torpedo hit.

All of the ship's officers were saved except two. One of the missing was Capt. Albert Tyler, of Santumas Island in the West Indies. Survivors believed he went down with his ship.

William Newton, Baltimore, an engineer, said the submarine made no attempt to capture the one lifeboat which got away, nor was there any attempt to shell the lifeboat.

"I was on watch in the engine room," he said. "We were shelled twice and torpedoed once. Nobody was killed aboard the ship.

Sub 300 Yards Away.

"The force of the torpedo sent a shower of water which knocked several men overboard. Others jumped into the lifeboats and abandoned ship because it then was sinking rapidly."

He said the submarine was about 300 yards away and that men in the one lifeboat which was launched successfully lay down in the bottom and allowed it to drift after pulling a short distance away. He said they did this because they did not wish to attract the submarine's attention.

He said the lifeboat was picked up Sunday morning after being afloat for about 36 hours. All the men were suffering from exposure and exhaustion, he said.

E. F. Driver, of Macogdoches, Tex., a fireman, said the survivors saw some ships during the 36 hours they were adrift "but they didn't see us or didn't want to see us for fear we had a sub on our trail."

Distress Call Heard.

"There was no fire," he said, "We started to abandon ship after the second shell because we were positive a torpedo would follow. It did follow shortly afterward.

"Most of the crew in the engine room did not come up above deck until after the torpedo. After the torpedo, the water was coming in every where, even down the ventilators."

The Navy partment at Washington disclosed that the first word of the attack on the Venore— a 550-foot ship built at the Sparrows Point, Md., plant of the Bethlehem Shipbuilding Co., in 1921—came in the form of a distress call heard at 12:47 a.m., E. S. T., Saturday.

A second message, asking for immediate assistance, was heard two minutes later, and at 1:22 a.m. the Venore's radio announced, "cannot stay afloat much longer."

List of Missing Men.

The fifth naval district public relations office released this list of crewmen unaccounted for after the sinking of the Venore:

F. Uuurloo, master; Vernon W. Minzey, radio operator; J. Batulis, boatswain; Oswald Wassland, quartermaster; Walter G. Walker, able bodied seaman; William Johnson, able bodied seaman; Johnny Austin, ordinary seaman; John E. Mahoney, ordinary seaman; Charles H. Newton, third assistant engineer; Claudi Figueras, deck engineer; Alexander Toon, oiler; Carmela Dejesus, oiler; Carmelo J. Brand, oiler; George C. Roby, wiper; William L. Davis, wiper; Edward Williams, wiper; Lorenzo Gardner, steward; William E. Oliver, chief cook; E. Chisholm, mess boy; Courtland Verdel Aikens, mess boy; S. J. Nevette, mess boy.

Addresses of the missing men were not available here.

Tanker Sunk Off Jersey

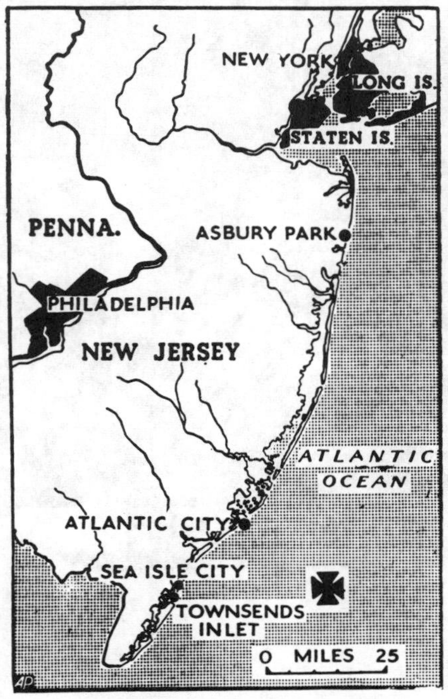

A cross marks the approximate location where three torpedoes from an enemy submarine sank the Norwegian motor tanker Varanger off Sea Isle City, N. J. The ship's entire crew of forty was saved and were landed at the nearby Townsend's inlet Coast Guard station.

RED ARMY MOPS UP NAZI INVADERS OVER WIDE FRONT

Hitler Reported to Have Moved from Smolensk as Russian Advance Threatens City.

BY THE ASSOCIATED PRESS.

Russian soldiers fighting their way forward in the coldest weather in decades were reported mopping up vast areas of the Russian front after virtually wiping out the winter line established by Adolf Hitler.

Russian reports said clean-up operations were in full swing in the section east of a 270-mile line running from the vicinity of Smolensk, 230 miles west of Moscow, to Orei and Kursk.

Hitler Moves Again.

There was no information just how far the Russians were from Smolensk but the British radio broadcast a Stockholm report that Hitler had moved his headquarters from Smolensk 200 miles west to Minsk, capital of White Russia.

The Russians said the Moscow region and that around Tula, 200 miles south of the capital, were "completely free of Germans." The Kalinin sector ninety miles northwest of Moscow is being cleared, it was said.

The Russians announced the recapture of Nelidovo, on the Moscow-Riga Railroad 170 miles northeast of Moscow and fifty miles west of Rzhev, northern anchor of the crushed German front before Moscow.

At sea, the Russians said, their forces sank a 5,000-ton German transport in the Barents Sea.

300,000 German Dead.

In the Donets Basin, Russian armies were said to have advanced 12 miles in twenty hours and recaptured 13 villages.

A Soviet communique supplement said Soviet planes yesterday destroyed five German troop trains, three infantry battalions and a cavalry squadron, 280 truckloads of troops and ammunition and four tanks.

The Soviet information bureau, denying a Berlin radio broadcast that the Russians had lost 1,000,000 men during the past six weeks, declared the Red Army in reality lost about 30,000 dead while the Germans between Dec. 6 and Jan. 15 lost 300,000 soldiers and officers killed.

FORMER ACTRESS DEAD.

New York (AP)—Mrs. Harriet E. B. Flanning, 60, a former vaudeville actress known as Harriet Ward, died last night of a heart attack.

TANKER SUNK OFF JERSEY COAST BY ENEMY SUBMARINE

Norwegian Tanker Crew Saved; Torpedo Explosion Shook Houses in Many Communities.

Sea Isle City, N. J. (AP)—Striking without warning, an enemy submarine sunk the Norwegian tanker Varanger in a pre-dawn attack only 35 miles off the Atlantic coast yesterday but the crew of 42 was saved.

Three torpedoes rammed the 9,305-ton motor ship within 12 minutes in the closest to United States shore enemy attack on shipping but for the first time no lives were lost. The explosions shook houses in several South Jersey communities, including Atlantic City, twenty miles north of here.

The survivors escaped in two lifeboats which were taken in tow by two fishing smacks that came upon the oil-drenched seamen five hours after the ship went down about 3:30 a.m. (E. S. T.) 35 miles southeast of here.

Landed at nearby Townsend's Inlet Coast Guard Station, seven of the crew were treated for exposure and injuries received in getting off their doomed ship.

Submarines Sighted.

Fourth Naval District headquarters at Philadelphia said apparently two enemy undersea craft engaged in the attack but added this was not confirmed. Dr. Alexander Stuart of Sea Isle City, who treated the injured, said practically all

(Continued on Page 20.)

Nelson "Outlaws" Alibis Or Excuses

Washington, (INS)—War production czar Donald M. Nelson today issued orders to his entire organization that President Roosevelt's far reaching war production goals must be accomplished and that he will not stand for any "alibis or excuses."

"We don't want any alibis or excuses," Nelson said. "I don't want them, the President doesn't want them, the people of the United States are not interested in them."

Nelson told hundreds of war production board executives that, "these goals can be met, they will be met, even if it means doing the impossible.

"If any of you have felt that they are impossible, I can only say that from now on we must do the impossible."

Nelson warned his staff members that the job they do in 1942 will be "all-important"—that it is "no use for us to talk about the great production we are going to have in 1943, 1944 or 1945 if we don't first meet the goals set for 1942."

Nelson bluntly told employees of the War Production Management that "neither past achievements nor personal relationships count."

"Nothing counts but getting the job done, and performance is the only test," the production czar continued. "Every one of us here is going to be judged in just one way—'by their fruits ye shall know them.'"

NIPPONESE LOSE WARSHIPS, PLANES IN STRAITS BATTLE

Americans Sink Eight to Ten Vessels; Japs Nearer to Singapore; Menace to Australia Grows.

BY THE UNITED PRESS

The armed forces of the United Nations, sparked by slashing American air and sea attacks, crippled Japan's powerful far eastern offensive today and battled deeper enemy thrusts toward key bases and supply lines along a 4,000-mile front.

A total of 26 fatal or damaging hits on Japanese warships and transports and the destruction of a dozen enemy planes was reported in allied communiques giving a sketchy picture of a four-day battle in the Macassar Straits, where American flying fortress bombers and naval units scored outstanding triumphs over the Japanese.

The American forces sank eight or ten enemy ships, boosting their total for the war to at least fifty Japanese vessels, while Dutch bombers and submarines accounted for the remainder.

The communiques failed to give an exact total of enemy ships sunk or damaged in the battle of Macassar Straits and a series of announcements may have contained some duplications or the same ship may have been attacked more than once by allied forces.

But it was emphasized that the Japanese invasion forces were battered when they landed at the East Borneo oil port of Balik Papan and where engaged by Dutch forces. A landing also was made in southwestern Celebes.

Japs Taking Heavy Blows.

In general, the Japanese offensive was taking heavy punishment but making some progress on the Malaya, East Indies and Australian fronts. In Burma, Tokyo broadcasts claimed some gains but the British said they were holding firmly before Moulmein.

New Japanese landings were made in the islands north of Australia where Allied planes bombed an invasion force estimated at 10,000 men; British bombers started big fires in Bangkok; Chinese squadrons bombed the Japanese base at Hanoi and British defense forces exacted a heavy toll from the enemy as they pulled back about ten miles on important sectors of the Malaya front, some fifty miles north of Singapore.

The important town of Batu Pahat, on the west coast of Malaya, sixty miles north of Singapore Island, was abandoned to the Japanese after a fierce battle and Tokyo broadcasts claimed that they had advanced 12 miles southeastward and were fighting near Kluang, fifty miles from the big naval base of Singapore.

A Japanese convoy of warships and several transports was sighted off the east Malaya coast, north of Mersing, as the Japanese apparently attempted new landings about fifty miles north of the naval base on that sector.

British Pushed Back.

British reinforcements reached the central Malaya sector and in-

(Continued on Page 2.)

NEGRO WOMEN DIE IN HORNELL BLAZE

Hornell (AP)—A Negro woman and her mother burned to death early today in a fire of undetermined origin which damaged two midcity buildings containing stores and apartments.

Steuben County Coroner Milton G. Burch identified the dead as Mrs. Mary Aikens, 39, and her mother, Mrs. Cora Dunn, about 65.

Their bodies were found about four hours after the fire was discovered at 4 a.m.

To Be White House Guest

This smiling lad looking at a "Fight Infantile Paralysis" poster in New York is 4-year-old Gerry King, who has been invited by Mrs. Eleanor Roosevelt to have luncheon at the White House on Jan. 30. Young Gerry, a New Yorker, has spent more than three years of his brief life in hospitals for infantile paralysis treatment and has been aiding in the "March of Dimes" campaign by making personal appearances.

CONGRESS BLASTS 'INCOMPETENTS' IN ARMED SERVICES

Pearl Harbor Report Brings Demands for Drastic Action; Kimmel and Short May Face Trial.

Washington (AP) Angry demands came from Congress members today for the expulsion of any "incompetents" holding responsible positions in the war effort and for courts martial to mete out punishment on those responsible for the debacle of Pearl Harbor.

A furore of rare bitterness on both sides of Capitol Hill followed the week-end report of a presidential investigating commission, blaming non-cooperation and "dereliction of duty" by Hawaii area commanders of the Army and Navy for success of the Japanese sneak attack on the great Pacific naval base.

Many senators and representatives asserted that the commission's conclusions pointed to a pressing need for a super-command with control over the operations of both armed services.

Although the investigating commission decided that the Secretaries of State, War and Navy as well as the Army Chief of Staff and Chief of Naval Operations had "fulfilled their obligations," some Congress members professed to find fault with provisions made here for Hawaii's defense.

Two Officers Blamed.

The five-man commission, headed by Associate Justice Owen J. Roberts of the Supreme Court, reported to President Roosevelt that

(Continued on Page 2.)

The Index

PUNCHBOARDS AND MACHINES IN TROY SENT INTO HIDING

No Comment from Either Chief of Police or District Attorney on Latest Crusade Move.

Dist. Atty. Earle J. Wiley and Chief of Police John B. Conroy reiterated blunt statements of "no comment" today when asked if they had taken steps which accounted for the sudden disappearance of pin-ball machines and punch boards from many stores throughout the city Saturday afternoon and evening.

Neither official would commit himself to a statement that he had not taken action, both simply insisting they had "no comment."

The recent seizure of more than 3,000 of the pin-ball machines in New York City, following a court decision that their operation is illegal, apparently had much to do with their disappearance here.

Questioned in regard to the matter, Dist. Atty. Earle J. Wiley said he had taken notice of the fact they had been declared illegal in New York and that Mayor LaGuardia had instituted a campaign against them.

During the last few weeks the county prosecutor has closed Troy's red light district by the padlocking of several places of alleged prostitution and has ordered the closing of alleged horserooms operated in Troy.

CONFISCATION OF BISHOP'S ESTATES BY NAZIS CLAIMED

New York (INS)—German repression of religion in captive Luxembourg has been climaxed with confiscation of the estates of the Bishop of Luxerbourg, according to the assertion of the secret "Freedom Radio Station" of Belgium in a broadcast today. The program was heard by CBS and NBS.

"Priests and monks in the grand duchy have been forcibly defrocked and many have been thrown into concentration camps," the broadcast said. "More than 200 priests were deported to Germany on made-up accusations."

A policy of "systematic starvation" is in operation in Belgium, the station added While the German ministry of public health has set a minimum of 3,000 calories daily as the normal food requirement, it was said that no more than 1,500 calories is obtainable by the average citizen in Belgium.

GENERAL HARTLE CHIEF OF SECOND A. E. F. TO EUROPE

Stimson Reveals Arrival of Doughboys in Erin; Base Under Construction for Several Months.

Washington (UP)—An American expeditionary force has landed in Northern Ireland, where a powerful military base has been under construction by American technicians for many months, the War Department revealed today.

A dispatch from Belfast indicated the U. S. forces may already have been in action against German airplanes.

The size of the American force, the date of its arrival in Ireland or of its departure from the United States, was not revealed by Secretary of War Henry L. Stimson who made the announcement.

The move sent organized units of American fighting men the closest they have yet been stationed to the European battle front. Previously forces were sent to Iceland.

Hartle In Command.

The American force in Ireland is commanded by Maj. Gen. Russell P. Hartle.

The Belfast dispatch reported "slight enemy air activity over Northern Ireland this afternoon." The ministry of security for Northern Ireland said "our air defenses were in action."

The war department did not reveal whether the arrival of the American expeditionary force means that they will take over the northern Ireland base or whether the move merely is the initial stage of sending U. S. fighting men into action in Europe.

However, the selection of Hartle to lead the U. S. force seemed to indicate that the Americans would be ready for any sort of action. Hartle has served as the commander of the mobile army force in Puerto Rico, a capacity in which he carried on active training maneuvers with light, fast-moving American Army units.

Important Base.

Hartle returned to the United States for duty with the Sixth Division at Fort Leonard Wood in June, 1941, and in August he was assigned to the 34th Infantry Division at Camp Claiborne, La., participating in the extensive Army southern maneuvers.

The exact nature of the Northern Ireland base never had been revealed. However, it has been under construction by American engineers and American labor forces for a year or more. Many reports from Ireland have emphasized the size and extent of the base, presumably adapted to provide for not only land and air but also for sea forces.

The American forces were sent to Northern Ireland which is part of the United Kingdom, not to be confused with independent Eire, which is neutral and has re-emphasized its neutrality since the entry of the United States into the war.

Strength of Force Secret.

Stimson made the announcement in the first extraordinary communique issued by the War Department since the outset of the war.

Stimson did not make public the designation of the units, their makeup or strength.

Similarly, he did not disclose the "ports of embarkation, dates of sailing, or other details" of the troop movements from the United States.

It was the first known movement of American troops as such to Europe during the current war, although some technicians have accompanied Canadian units to Britain for training and have gone to Libya and elsewhere for similar purposes.

General Hartle, commander of the troops, is a native of Cheweville, Md. He is 52. He served in the Philippines, on the Mexican border and is a World War veteran.

JAPANESE ATTEMPT UNSUCCESSFULLY TO TRICK U. S. SOLDIERS

With the U. S. Army, Batan Front—The Japanese are trying every form of trickery against Gen. Douglas MacArthur's defenders of Batan Peninsula—but the Americans refuse to be fooled.

Take, for example, the Japanese attempt to pass American sentries by dressing soldiers in American or Filipino uniforms.

The Americans discovered an infallible way to detect them due to the inability of the Japanese to pronounce the letter L, which they say as R. They simply pick a password with numerous Ls, such as lollapalooza.

Sentries challenge approaching figures and if the first two syllables of lollapalooza, for instance, should come back as "rorra" they open fire without waiting to hear the remainder.

THE WEATHER
U. S. Weather Bureau.
Tonight—Continued cold.

THE TIMES RECORD

FINAL EDITION

Series 1942—No. 28. (Entered as Second Class Matter at the Postoffice at Troy, N. Y., under the Act of March 3, 1879.) TROY, N. Y., TUESDAY EVENING, FEBRUARY 3, 1942. (Published Daily Except Sunday) PRICE THREE CENTS

American Bombers Sink Two More Jap Transports Off Borneo Coast

ARMY STANDARDS TO BE LOWERED, HERSHEY ASSERTS

Selective Service Director Predicts Need for Manpower Will Bring Revision.

Washington, (AP) — Brig. Gen. Lewis B. Hershey, selective service director, said today that army entrance standards inevitably would be lowered as the need for manpower developed, and predicted that men with minor defects would be taken in for limited service "by the hundred thousands.'

He appeared before a special House committee investigating migration of defense workers and concentrating now on methods of mustering all available manpower for prosecution of war effort.

A prepared statement Hershey brought with him said:

"Allowance and allotment legislation has been proposed, and if enacted in proper form, it will release for induction many registrants, now deferred on the grounds of dependency."

Dependency Rule Stands.

He noted at one point however, that dependency still would remain "an outstanding condition of deferment."

Hershey asserted flatly that competition among the various employers of manpower "must be controlled or eliminated," adding:

"Although war industrial production must be maintained it should not be permitted to draw unnecessarily upon the supply of potential 1-A men or upon men engaged in war or agricultural production."

Saying that he was "frightened" at the American "philosophy of abundance," Hershey said "we haven't enough manpower for everything.

Survey Shows Shortage.

"A survey of our manpower," he said, "reveals that there are not enough young, 100 per cent perfect men to fill the total manpower requirements of all users of manpower, if we contemplate the possibility of having an armed force of 7,000,000 or 8,000,000 men,' and materials to equip it.

"In the near future, Hershey told the committee, "the Army will be inducting through selective service men from all groups between 20 and 45. He added:

"There is no question but that some of the older men will be assigned to jobs requiring less physical strain than those to which the younger men will be assigned.

FRENCH INDUSTRY DECLARED TO BE IN SERIOUS SITUATION

Vichy, Unoccupied France (AP).—Vichy newspapers today quoted Francois Lehideux, secretary of public works, as saying that shortages of materials and fuel had created a grave situation for French industry from which "only strict discipline can save us."

"We have no more coal, no more gasoline, no more cement, no more steel, even no more water to feed our turbines," Lehideux was quoted as saying in a speech at Marseille.

He declared that the monthly supply of gasoline available in France had dropped from 213,000 tons in 1938 to 8,000 tons at present, and that coal supplies had dropped from 4,500,000 to 2,800,000 tons in the same period.

The lack of non-ferrous metals—except aluminum, which France still is exporting—constitute another major problem, he said.

DESTROYER COMMISSIONED.

Boston (UP)—The destroyer Fitch was commissioned at Boston Navy Yard today. Launched last June 14, the Fitch was named for a civil war officer and was sponsored by Mrs. H. Walter Thomas of Salt Lake City, Utah.

"I'll Be Back In A Flash With Some Cash!"

Yes, that's practically what your Classified Ad says to you when you phone Troy 6100 and order a "For Sale" ad in The Record Newspapers. Every day folks raise cash by means of Classified Ads.

Lower Temperature Seen Before Morning

It is going to be cold tonight. The U. S. Weather Bureau has predicted temperatures from 6 to 1° below zero before morning.

Sub-zero temperatures prevailed all through the area today with an official low mark of 5 below zero.

In the hill sections of Troy the mercury dropped to 14 below. In the rural areas readings from 15 to 20 below were reported.

RUSSIANS IGNORE "40-BELOW" COLD IN NEW OFFENSIVE

German Generals Demand More Troops from Hitler; British Attacking Enemy in Libya.

BY THE ASSOCIATED PRESS.

Russian troops dragging machine guns and cannon on sledges at 40 degrees Fahrenheit below zero were reported surging forward at several points today in a drive aimed against Smolensk, 210 miles west of Moscow.

At the same time, the British radio said German generals had demanded that Hitler send twenty fresh, picked divisions to the Soviet front immediately, threatening that otherwise it would be "very difficult if not impossible to prevent a general Russian break-through."

Soviet dispatches said German air and tank reinforcements arriving on the southern (Ukraine) front were being more than matched by Red army weapons.

Testifying to Red air force superiority, dispatches from the front credited one Russian air unit with destroying 17 Nazi planes in a week and long-range bombers with deepening their offensives far into the German rear.

Nazis Admit Pressure.

Dragging machine guns and cannon on sledges over the same roads used against Napoleon, the Russians were pressing forward on several fronts, all pointed toward Smolensk, 210 miles west of Moscow, and keeping up their fast pace despite determined German resistance.

Russian forces were reported to have killed some 1,400 Germans in three different sectors of the front and to have thrown back Nazi counter attacks launched in a vain effort to stem the retreat.

In the Ukraine, the German high command acknowledged fresh Soviet pressure northeast of Nazi-held Taganrog, on the Sea of Azov, but asserted that elsewhere on the 1,200-mile battlefront German troops scored local successes despite "stubborn enemy resistance."

British Attack in Africa.

In North Africa, British troops, thrown back 225 miles in less than two weeks, were reported attacking Field Marshal Erwin Rommel's armies "wherever found" in western Libya in an attempt to check the Axis counter-offensive.

A British spokesman, emphasizing the prime necessity of destroying the enemy's forces in desert warfare, declared:

"Area is not important. Tanks, men and trucks are."

Cairo headquarters indicated that Gen. Rommel's vanguards had reached the vicinity of Slonta, 105 miles northeast of Bengasi and 225 miles northeast of El Agheila, high-water mark of the British January offensive.

While the British said they now were taking the initiative, the German high command gave this version:

"In Cirenaica (Libya), the retreating enemy again was brought to battle and dislodged."

Premier Mussolini's high command also asserted that German and Italian motorized columns continue to advance eastward "despite enem yresistance," and indicated that Axis spearheads had knifed more than 110 miles beyond newly-recaptured Bengasi.

NIMITZ REPORTS AMERICAN FLEET "BUSY" IN PACIFIC

"Every Ship, Every Man and Every Plane" Engaged in Safeguarding America, Admiral Says.

Honolulu (UP).—Admiral Chester W. Nimitz, commander in chief of the Pacific fleet, said today in a message to America that every ship, every plane and every man in the fleet was in action over the vast Pacific war zone to safeguard the country and take the war to Japan's front door.

Following up the communique in which he announced that the fleet had done extensive damage in a bold raid on the Marshall and Gilbert Islands with little loss to itself, Nimitz said:

Fleet Busy Every Moment.

"...Your fleet is busy every moment of every day and night across the vast reaches of the Pacific; especially in those areas where we can most effectively harass the enemy and contribute to our own security."

He recalled that he had said when he assumed his command on Dec. 31 in a brief war time ceremony at Pearl Harbor: "I have just assumed a great responsibility and obligation which I shall do my utmost to discharge."

Pointing out the vastness of the war zone entrusted to him, stretching nearly half way around the world and extending from Arctic to Antarctic, Nimitz said he knew the people wanted to know "where's the fleet?"

Safeguarding America.

"This question was answered in part Sunday by the splendid achievements of our ships and planes in attacks on enemy concentrations in the Marsball and Gilbert Islands," he said.

"...I can attest that every ship, every man, every plane, every officer and man of the Pacific fleet afloat, aloft and ashore is being utilized to the fullest extent both to safeguard America and bring the war to the enemy's doorstep."

Nimitz, a submarine expert whose naval career has extended over forty of his 56 years, was called Dec. 17 from his post as chief of naval operations to take charge in the Pacific ten days after the Japanese sneak attack.

He had said little while he prepared his plans to carry out the Navy's tradition of offensive warfare.

AGRICULTURE DEPT. TO MOVE WORKERS FROM WASHINGTON

Washington (AP)—Budget Director Harold D. Smith announced today that the Agriculture Department had agreed to move 3,848 employees out of Washington to make room for defense workers.

Approved by President Roosevelt, the transfers will send 1,140 farm credit administration employees to Kansas City, 700 agriculture adjustment administration employees to various cities where the agency now has field offices, 1,155 rural electrification administration employees to St. Louis, 633 Farm Security administration employees to Cincinnati, and 220 Agriculture Department, solicitor's office workers to various cities.

The Farm Security administration previously had been scheduled to move to St. Louis.

INCREASE EXPECTED IN UNEMPLOYMENT

Los Angeles (AP).—Industrial switchover to war projects will cause an increase of 2,000,000 unemployed, to a total of 6,000,000, within a few months, WPA Chief Howard O. Hunter predicted in an interview.

"But when war industries get into full production they will call for about 15,000,000 workers as compared to the present 5,000,000," he added. Hunter is here on an inspection trip.

He said unemployment should be negligible by the end of the year.

Official Navy Pictures Reveal Pearl Harbor Horror

These official U. S. Navy pictures, among the most dramatic of all time, were taken during the Japanese sneak attack on Pearl Harbor, Hawaii, on Dec. 7. The upper photo shows the U. S. S. Destroyer Shaw blowing up at the height of the raid. A sheet of fire gushes from the magazine of the vessel, one of three destroyers lost in the attack. Below the spectacular death of the 26-year-old battleship Arizona is shown a few moments after a Japanese bomb dropped down the smokestack of the vessel, causing the magazine to explode.

GEN. MACARTHUR'S BATAN DEFENDERS VICTORIOUS AGAIN

Enemy Landing Attempts in Philippines Broken Up; Nipponese Bombers Attack Singapore.

BY THE ASSOCIATED PRESS.

Australian Army Minister Francis M. Forde declared today that "a big movement by the Allies is under way" to counter Japan's sweep in the Far Pacific.

In a broadcast to the Australian imperial force at Singapore, Forde declared that each hour Japan's siege armies were held at bay permitted the massing and deployment of more reinforcements and the accumulation of more weapons.

"It does not need my words to impel you, therefore, to hold on," he said.

Forde did not specify the nature or direction of the big new Allied movement.

BY THE UNITED PRESS.

American and British bombers struck today at Japanese thrusts toward the Burma Road, Singapore and vital allied bases in the Dutch East Indies

United States Army battle planes sank two and probably three more enemy transports in the Macassar Straits off the east coast of Borneo and half dozen more Japanese planes were destroyed during raids of a pre-invasion character on the Island of Java, site of United Nation supreme headquarters. The operations brought the toll of Japanese ships to 35 and of planes to about thirty but the big Dutch naval base of Soerabaya was damaged by air attack.

In the Philippines, the men of Gen. Douglas MacArthur broke up two new Japanese attempts to land shock troops on Batan Peninsula in a drive toward the island fortress of Corregidor. American planes aided land and beach fighters in wiping out enemy landing parties and pushing back flanking attacks.

MacArthur reported that the Japanese had lost a large number of men and boats in their vain landing attempts and that his men had "over run three lines of enemy trenches and captured much equipment in breaking up an attack on his right flank.

Jap Barges Shattered.

The defense forces, however, had been pushed back to a line about 15 miles from the tip of the Batan Peninsula and the enemy attacks obviously were becoming more intense.

The latest Japanese attacks on Batan occurred last night.

At dawn a number of shattered Japanese barges, some ablaze and others bullet-riddled and adrift, were seen along the beach.

It was evident that the Japanese, using their best troops including the "tatori," which correspond to the famous British commandos, were making a desperate and costly attempt to drive MacArthur's American and Filipino forces from their last foothold on the Philippine mainland.

A War Department communique Monday told of the shattering of a "desperate" double-barreled Japanese offensive, unleashed on both the east and west coast of mountainous Batan about 17 miles north of stubbornly resisting Corregidor in Manila Bay.

On Mac Arthur's right flank, pre-

(Continued on Page 2.)

SIGHT ENEMY U-BOAT OFF CAPE HATTERAS

New York, (INS)—Sighting of an enemy submarine off Cape Hatteras by officers and men of the American freighter S.S. Bellingham, was revealed today by the Third Naval District headquarters. The Navy announcement said:

"On the night of Jan. 27 the S.S Bellingham while northbound off Cape Hatters, sighted an enemy submarine. Capt. H. C. Willis immediately changed course and shortly thereafter the submarine was dropped from sight. No attack was apparent to the ship's officers on the bridge. A fireman who was on the after deck thought afterward that he had seen a torpedo cut across their wake."

Nazi Seaman Tells How Sub Met Doom

Horta, The Azores, (UP)—The only known survivor of the German submarine destroyed by two destroyers off the Azores yesterday told his story today.

A sub-lieutenant, he said the submarine was on the surface about four miles off Pico Island when dawn broke. Two destroyers sighted it. As it dived one destroyer opened fire. Hit, the submarine had to return to the surface.

Approximately 15 men of the submarine's crew had climbed through the conning tower to the deck when the destroyer scored a direct hit which practically cut the submarine in two, the sub-lieutenant said.

All of the Germans dived into the sea and the sub-lieutenant, a strong swimmer, struck out for shore where he was taken into custody for interment by Portuguese authorities. As he swam ashore, he heard explosions like those of depth charges. He assumed that some of his shipmates had been picked up by the destroyers.

(The Horta dispatch which passed through the Portuguese censorship, did not identify the nationality of the destroyers. They could have been British or American.)

YOU NEED AN HOUR OF PEACE
In these bewildering times. Where can a man turn to replenish the wells of his courage . repair the walls of his faith, except with a glass of fine Utica Club Pilsner Lager or XXX Cream Ale.—Adv.

HARVARD CAMERAS SNAP NEW COMET

Solar Visitor To Reach Nearest Point to Earth Next Month.

Cambridge, Mass., (AP)—A new comet, which will become almost visible to the unaided eye early in March, was announced by the Harvard College Observatory today.

The discovery, by Dr. Fred L. Whipple, was made on photographic plates recorded by Harvard patrol cameras. A fairly small object— now a hundred million miles distant, according to computations by R. N. Thomas of the Harvard astronomical staff—the comet is expected to come within 60,000,000 miles of the earth at its closest approach in March. By comparison, the sun is 93,000,000 miles distant.

Dr. Whipple said that it now appears in the morning sky, just before dawn, almost overhead in the constellation Coma berenices Its motion in the sky will bring it farther southward and westward each night, and it will move south of the equator in March. Dr. Whipple said that after the middle of February, the comet, now of the tenth magnitude, should be visible to amateur observers using small telescopes.

Note Date Of First U. S.-German Break

BY THE ASSOCIATED PRESS.

Twenty-five years ago today the United States severed diplomatic relations with Germany after she had reverted to a policy of unrestricted submarine warefare.

A formal declaration of war, however, did not come until April 6, 1917.

When the breach in relations occurred, the warring nations were Germany, Austria-Hungary, Bulgaria and Turkey ranged against Great Britain, France, Belgium, Russia, Montenegro, Serbia, Rumania, San Marino, Italy, Portugal, Greece and Japan.

President Wilson was in the midst of peace sounding when, on Jan. 31, 1917, Germany announced she would resume unrestricted submarine warfare effective the following day. She had given a pledge against such a policy in 1915.

She issued instructions on how American vessels should be marked to avoid being torpedoed and announced the United States would be permitted to send only one steamer a week to England and that to the single port of Falmouth, with arrival and departure days stipulated by Germany.

President Wilson's answer was to recall Ambassador James W. Gerard from Berlin and to hand the German envoy in Washington, Count Von Bernstorff his passport.

PHILADELPHIA AREA TO BE BLACKED OUT

Philadelphia, (INS)—Philadelphia and seven adjoining counties will be plunged into complete darkness for 15 minutes tonight in the most extensive and one of the most important blackouts ever attempted in America.

From 10:30 to 10:45 p.m. the blackout will cover a 3,500-square mile area involving 3,000,000 persons in Philadelphian Bucks, Chester, Delaware and Montgomery counties in Eastern Pennsylvania, and Camden, Burlington and Gloucester counties in Southern New Jersey.

BIG LEAGUES VOTE 14 NIGHT GAMES

New York (AP).—The major league baseball clubs today voted to increase the night-game limit from seven to 14 games at the home park of each club with the exception of the Washington Senators, who were granted 21 night games.

APPROVE CHINA LOAN.

Washington (UP).—The House Foreign Affairs Committee today unanimously approved a joint resolution to grant China a $500,000,000 loan to help prosecute her war against Japan.

HATFIELD-M'COY CLANS DROP FEUD

Instructor and Girl Student Descendants of Ancient Foes.

Chicago, (INS) — The historic Hatfield-McCoy feud which erupted many years ago in West Virginia showed no signs whatever of reviving today at nearby Fort Sheridan where thousands of Uncle Sam's soldiers are putting in their best training licks.

James A. McCoy, a descendant of the original feudin' McCoys, is chief instructor at the 6th Corps Area motor transport training school there. So they may have been some concern when it was noised about that a Hatfield was en route to the school.

But there was no cause for anxiety. A car drew up and out stepped the Hatfield. It was not one of the old-time gun-totin' Hatfields, but pretty Miss Helen Ryan Hatfield. Although her great-great grandfather was a brother of the original Hatfield who started the feud, she allowed she wasn't looking for trouble, but merely wanted instruction in being a Red Cross driver.

She and McCoy agreed to dispense with the feud, at least for the duration.

The Index

Requested Favored In Bahamas With Alsab Out

BY HUGH FULLERTON, Jr.

New York (Wide World)—Suggestions noted: Jesse A. Linthicum, sports ed. of the Baltimore Sun, would like to see something more done about getting basketball referees off the court . . . It was tried out in Oregon a few days ago with reported success . . . Linthicum advanced the idea five years ago and still thinks it would help a game that needs help in some sections . . . On the other side, Herb (N. Y. Post) Allen suggests that if New York referees were put in coops above the backboards, Pat Kennedy would drop through the hoop oftener than the ball . . . Dan Parks of the Olean, (N. Y.) Times Herald votes for the extension of his plan of having every basketball team devote one game to national defense with admission payable only in defense stamps.

Yesterday's crack from Tuscaloosa, Ala., at Vanderbilt athletics resulted in some smoking rejoinders—and this corner apparently helped warm things up by neglecting to mention that the six games in which the Commodores were accused of getting rough were the Bama-Vandy clashes . . . Chancellor O. C. Carmichael points out that Vandy's foreign language requirements were dropped only as a war measure for "superior students," and Court Coach Norman Cooper says Jack Jenkins was his only player to get the bounce for roughness. That was in the Alabama game and he hasn't even fouled out of any other . . . Seems certain, though, that any future roughness won't be regarded as unnecessary.

Banjo Smith, Columbia, (S. C.), Record: "Elizabeth Ryan, the veteran red-head who won 19 Wimbledon championships, says women tennis players would be fine if they'd just learn to use their heads. This probably makes the first time you've ever heard tennis compared to automobile driving."

Harry Hurst, Montreal lightweight, has applied for enlistment in the R. C. A. F. His manager says he hasn't been fighting well because he was worrying about not being in uniform . . . Lift a stein for dear old C. C. N. Y.—The Beavers have three steins in the service. Jerry, 1938 grid captain, is in the Army Air Corps; his brother Harry, 1939 leader, has joined the Navy and Stan, track and cross country manager, is in the Army . . . The aerial game apparently had its attractions for Ken Kavanaugh of L. S. U. and Buddy Elrod of Mississippi State, who used to catch passes in football. Both are in the Air Corps now . . . Headline: "Harp on Ft. Riley squad" . . . Well, Ben Sheridan is one old Notre Dame boy plae e there.

Spencer Murphy, pro at New York's Glen Oaks Golf Club, got word the other day that he was pappy of a baby girl. A short time later he heard that 2,000 steel club heads, held in England, had been released for shipment. Murphy still is trying to decide which was the better news . . . The Chicago Cubs are set for the season in one respect. They have enough baseballs on hand to last through 1942 . . . The Green Bay Packers' Corp has tapped its reserve fund to purchase all the defense bonds the law allows . . . Joe Kirkwood, the trick-shot golfer, will dodge the winter tournaments and appear in sportsmen's shows in Boston, New York, Detroit and Indianapolis . . . Danny MacFayden's Hebron Academy hockey team is doing so well that fans suggest a trial against a crack Canadian schoolboy outfit.

POLICE WIN TWO IN PISTOL LEAGUE

The Police team in the Troy Pistol League won two matches last night defeating the Wild Life team 1,470 to 1,465 and the Hawks by the close score of 1,467 to 1,463. In the other two matches last night the Hendrick Hudson Aces outshot the Rensselaer Valve five, 1,411 to 1,403 and the Arsenal Owls routed the Watervliet Cubs 1,403 to 1,324.

Scheduled for tonight are matches between the Arsenal Owls and the Manufacturers' Bank at 8 o'clock and the Padua team and the Mount Royals at 9 o'clock.

Last night's scores:

POLICE.	
A. Watson	297
Capt. Hammett	296
C. Rafferty	294
E. Bradshaw	293
F. Meagher	290
Total	1,470

WILD LIFE.	
W. Maxwell	288
F. Lotz	293
A. Jones	294
J. Spain	298
N. Jones	292
Total	1,465

POLICE.	
A. Watson	296
Lieut. Bradshaw	291
Capt. Hammett	294
C. Rafferty	289
F. Meagher	297
Totals	1,467

HAWKS.	
J. Petruska	293
E. Collins	296
J. Nial	295
L. Hare	288
J. Prout	291
Total	1,463

HENDRICK HUDSON ACES.	
J. Gardner	288
G. Kotz	278
M. Bress	281
A. Latterick	283
N. Zeitler	281
Total	1,411

RENSSELAER VALVE.	
W. Felt	275
C. Pollay	281
C. Canova	290
W. Nead	284
F. Loeble	273
Total	1,403

ARSENAL OWLS.	
F. French	274
R. Cobb	282
V. Oliver	284
A. Buttleman	286
J. Weisenhoffer	277
Total	1,403

WATERVLIET CUBS.	
J. Leffler	245
T. Henebury	267
J. Sawyer	253
B. VanAlstyne	285
E. Hogan	274
Total	1,324

AUKER IMPROVING.

Detroit (AP)—Elden Auker, St. Louis Browns pitcher who was injured in a traffic accident yesterday, was described in "excellent condition" last night at Henry Ford Hospital.

BEN HOGAN PAID $3.85 PER STROKE

Atlanta (AP)—It's nice work if you can get it—and golfer Ben Hogan is getting it, at $3.85 a stroke.

That's little Ben's take—if you want to be as inquisitive as an income tax collector—since the start of his winter tournament tour, and the long-hitting Hershey professional has nine more stops before he shoots for Craig Wood's crown in the Masters' Tourney climaxing the winter tour at Augusta April 9.

He has won $7,207 with 632 holes of competitive golf since Dec. 11, counting an 18-hole playoff with Jimmy Thomson for $3,500 first money in the Los Angeles Open—just 1,885 strokes at that little white ball.

He closed out 1941 with the Miami Open and two Texas tournaments at Harlingen and Beaumont, winning $2,275 to bring the year's total to $18,358. In January, he won another $4,932, including first place at Los Angeles, $375 for fifth at Oakland, and $1,000 for winning the San Francisco Open. He slacked off at Rancho Santa Fe, in the Bing Crosby Amateur-Pro, tying with Horton Smith and Byron Nelson for 14th place and a check for coffee money, $57.

Oddly enough, four strokes blown along the way have cost Nelson perhaps $2,400.

The former open champion, second to Hogan in winter tour winnings, shot his way over the same tournament courses for $4,782, including first money at Miami and Oakland. Excluding Hogan's playoff, Nelson finished just four strokes back of little Ben—1,817 to 1,813.

Sam Snead, who blew himself out of $3,500 top money at Los Angeles, is third in tourney winnings at $2,785. He won $1,000 at Miami to become runner-up in 1941 winnings, and the rest in January's four California tournaments.

CHICAGO ATTORNEY WITHDRAWS STAR; IMPOST TOO HIGH

Ben Whitaker's Hopeful To Carry 121 Pounds; Beat Track Record in Early Workout This Week.

Miami, Fla. (UP)—Requested became favorite today for the $5,000-added Bahamas Handicap at Hialeah Park Saturday after withdrawal of Alsab, racing's "million dollar baby," because of the heavy 128-pound impost assigned him.

Albert Sabath, owner of Alsab, announced that he would withdraw the brown colt after learning yesterday that Racing Secretary Charles J. McLellan gave him top weight in a field of 19.

Alsab set the turf world agog last year by winning 15 of his 22 starts to earn $110,000. The $700 wonder horse of 1941—a leading Kentucky Derby contender — was to have made his 3-year-old debut in the Bahamas.

Owned by Texan.

Requested, arch-rival of the Sabath entry, is owned by Ben F. Whitaker of Texas. Beating the track record in a workout early this week, he now becomes the favorite with second impost of 121 pounds.

The Bahamas is for seven furlongs and Requested ran the mile in 1:38.4 in a workout Tuesday morning. This clipped one-fith second from the track record established last Saturday by Eternal Peace, Requested's stablemate weighted at 111 for the race. Alsab tied the mark in a Monday workout.

Alsab traveled the fastest mile ever recorded for a 2-year-old to defeat Requested in the Champagne Stakes at Belmont last October.

The Bahamas was slated as a homecoming for the Sabath colt as well as a renewal of his rivalry with Requested. Starting his campaign here last year, Alsab ran his poorest race. He finished last in a field of 14 at Hialeah last February, a race in which Requested romped off with show money.

Explains Withdrawal.

Explaining Alsab's withdrawal, Sabath said he felt the heavy impost was too much for the young horse to carry. The colt would continue training, he said, for the rich $25,000-added Flamingo Stakes Feb. 28—the winter test for Kentucky eligibles.

Alsab also is entered in the $50,000-added Widener Cup Classic, feature winter season money event. He may be entered in some smaller race as a tune-up for the Flamingo.

Other imposts for the Bahamas included: Eternal Bull, 120; Bright Willie, 117; First Fiddle, 115; American Wolf, Figgeritout and Sir War, 114; Rodney, 113; Bold Question and Tomochichi, 112; Alohort, 110; Sweep Swinger, 109; Eire, 108; Incoming, Sergeant Bill and Aletern, 105, and Automaton, 103.

ANGOTT BOUT OFF UNTIL MARCH 6TH

New York (AP)—The 12-round non-title bout between Lightweight Champion Sammy Angott and Bob Montgomery of Philadelphia, scheduled for tomorrow night at Madison Square Garden, was postponed until March 6 yesterday when the titleholder turned up with a rib injury.

Angott said he first felt the pain during a workout yesterday. An examination showed he had a dislocation of the 12th rib on the left side. Promoter Mike Jacobs said he would not put on a substitute bout.

RIGGS TO REJOIN TENNIS TROUPE

Minneapolis, Minn (INS)—Bobby Riggs, laid up by the flu and a fever of 102½, was expected to rejoin the professional tennis safari tonight at Naperville, Ill. The round robin stars made a three-man appearance in Minneapois, last night, with Fred Perry defeating Lester Stoefen, 6-3, 4-6, 8-6, and Donald Budge defeating Perry 8-6, 6-1. The victory put Budge in top place in the standings.

Won't Talk About '42 Terms

JOE DI MAGGIO.

Joe DiMaggio Mum On Yanks' 1942 Offer

New York (AP)—Joe DiMaggio received his 1942 contract from the New York Yankees in yesterday's mail and this year's biggest baseball salary struggle immediately swung into motion.

The Yankees payroll is a zealously protected secret, but most writers believed the club had offered its centerfielder close to $40,000 for the coming season, an increase of about $4,000 over the sum he was thought to have received in 1941.

"This is just the start of negotiations," said DiMaggio, and added that he and his wife and baby were not going to let the salary discussion hold up their Florida vacation. They will leave today or tomorrow for St. Petersburg and wait for the Yankees to open their training camp there the last of this month.

DiMaggio was guarded in his talk about a contract.

"You know that letter the boss (President E. G. Barrow) sends with every contract about not settling this thing in the newspapers," explained DiMaggio. Consequently he would not say whether there was much of a difference between his desires and the club's offer, or whether he thought a long dispute might result.

"I haven't made any plans to see Mr. Barrow personally," he added. "I had this trip to Florida planned for three weeks and I think we can reach an agreement in correspondence. I want to get down there where I can get some exercise and get loosened up before we start training."

DiMaggio has been with the Yanks six years and won the American League batting championship twice. He hit .375 last year, finishing behind Boston's Ted Williams and Cecil Travis of Washington. But he broke a 44-year-old record by hitting safely in 56 consecutive games and this power propelled New York to its fifth world championship in six years and helped swell the club's attendance both at home and away.

He has been a persistent holdout in previous years, usually waiting until training has started before signing, and in 1938 did not come to an agreement until the season was a week old.

Then the club made him get into condition at his own expense and did not start his pay until he made his debut April 30.

However, the money amounting to about $1,500 was made up to him in his contract the following year.

Today's Sport Parade

BY JACK GUENTHER.

New York (UP)—Something has been added to a famous indoor sport and a substantial number of career pessimists are blinking their eyes in amazement at the result. The sport is hockey and the added ingredient is an epochal victory streak which surpasses anything that has happened on ice since the bloodhounds first started chasing little Eva.

Hockey has been a pretty sick kid for the last couple of seasons. The cash customers stayed away from the rinks in impressive numbers. When the war brought along military conscription the sport was written off as incurable. But the year 1941-42, which was expected to be the worst, is proving itself one of the most successful in a decade.

Credit for the amazing revival goes to the New York Rangers, who are to hockey what Joe DiMaggio was to baseball last summer. The Rangers haven't been held scoreless in 85 matches, or since April 9, 1940; they have lost but one of their last 14 matches; and they are pumping along toward a second all-time National League record with much enthusiasm.

This enthusiasm has been matched only by that of the patrons, who are storming the box-office with all their old-time vigor and proving again that in any sport there is no substitute for a winner. Since the Rangers broke the old consecutive scoring mark of 77 games they have drawn better than any championship boxing contests.

A few nights ago 16,121 persons paid to watch them smack around the Toronto Leafs. This is a remarkable turn-out for a sport which was punch-drunk just 12 months ago, but the customers paid not just to watch the streak extended but also to see three Rangers who are rapidly becoming legends. These are Bryan Hextall, Lynn Patrick and Phil Watson.

When hockey old timers get together they always argue the merits of the great forward lines. There was the old Ranger trio of Bun and Bill Cook and Frank Boucher. There was the Boston combination which set the modern record of 179 goals in a single season, the second record at which the Rangers now are skating. Today there is also the Hextall-Patrick, Watson line.

These three boys the racking an the greatest number of Ranger goals of which 128 have been scored to date—with a full third of the season yet to play. Hextall is the league's leading individual scorer with 35 points while his two mates are tied for second with 34 each. These figures are pretty fair evidence of the boys' potency.

But the three of them don't compose the whole team. Owner Lester Patrick has put together a squad which is three deep at the forward positions. There are two other lines only a shade less efficient than the first and all the boys are offensive wizards who can be subbed for a few minutes without the loss of too much effectiveness.

Offense is the one-word hockey philosophy of the Rangers. The players are smashing, slashing fellows who leave Goalie Jim Hendy to fend for himself while they carry the puck and the battle into enemy territory and never stop sharp-shooting at the cage. This is the reason they are a poor third in league defense but still top the standings.

New York apparently has only one serious rival to contend with during the remainder of the season. That is Toronto. The famed "Kraut" line of the Boston Bruins has enlisted en masse in the Royal Canadian Air Force—leaving the Rangers to carry the league at the gate in addition to carrying their fight for the league championship.

They are the only glamor figures left now, but as long as their streak continues they will pack in the crowds. Once it is halted, attendance may drop. This is a situation which is keeping the rival managers walking the floor at night—every night. For if the rival teams kill off the Ranger streak they may find they've also killed the goose who lays golden box office receipts.

Bits Of Sports Reported Briefly

New York (AP)—Camp Upton, the present home of Heavyweight Champion Joe Louis, is going to have facilities for its own boxing matches, thanks to Promoter Mike Jacobs.

Jacobs disclosed today he is sending the camp all equipment necessary for boxing bouts, including a ring, lights and 800 chairs.

New York (AP)—Babe Ruth, former home run king of the New York Yankees, leaves today for Hollywood to begin work on the movie based on the life of Lou Gehrig.

At the same time, Bill Dickey, the veteran Yankee catcher, was expected to arrive in the film city. Both men will play themselves in the picture.

Hot Springs, Ark. (AP)—The question of whether Yankee Joe DiMaggio or Ted Williams of the Red Sox is the best hitter isn't even debatable as far as little Frankie Pytlak, Boston's veteran catcher, is concerned.

"Ted Williams is a better hitter than Joe DiMaggio," argued Pytlak, one of the first arrivals at this growing baseball colony. "If they had pitched right to Williams last year, he'd have hit .420 or better."

Los Angeles (AP)—Fight Promoter Joe Lynch will hand Commander Richard Bolton of the U. S. Navy a check for $3,898 today, the proceeds from the Chalky Wright-Richie Lemos boxing show Tuesday night.

The Naval Relief show grossed $9,199, Lynch said. Wright, who won a sixth round KO, and Lemos each received $1,748. Wright gave the rest of his winner's purse, $874, to the relief fund.

Los Angeles (AP)—A horse trading deal which ended unhappily for C. W. Stratton, California turfman, landed in court today with a $15,000 damage suit against Alfred Gwynne Vanderbilt.

Stratton asserted he paid Vanderbilt $10,000 for Atavistic and spent $5,000 more training the glossy chestnut which ran last at Santa Anita a year ago.

Stratton charged he was misled concerning the animal's physical condition. It won two out of five starts while runnin gas a 3-year-old under Vanderbilt colors.

Philadelphia (AP)—Mrs. Jane Vaughan Sullivan has decided to defend her United States senior women's figure skating title at Chicago during the championship meet Feb. 19, 20 and 21.

Jane, wife of Lieut. Riggs Sullivan of West Point, won her title last winter at Boston.

Chicago (AP)—Elmer Layden, commissioner of professional football, was confined to his home today, suffering from a seriously wrenched knee caused by falling on an icy street.

Layden injured his left knee—his good one, having injured his right during his Notre Dame athletic career.

Chicago (AP)—Northwestern University's annual Southern baseball trip was cancelled today in favor of a schedule with Army camps and Naval stations.

Kenneth L. Wilson, director of athletics, said that in scheduling the service games the university was following its plan of cooperating in every way possible with the war effort.

For ten years the Wildcat nine has traveled South for games with Louisiana State, Tulane and Alabama.

CATHOLIC HIGH TO FACE VINCENTIAN ON ALBANY COURT

Catholic High basketeers will start the second round of the 1942 Catholic League season tomorrow night meeting the Vincentian Institute five at Albany. The locals are odds-on favorites to repeat their early season performance in which they handed the Albany tossers a decisive trouncing.

C. C. H. S. now holds first place in the Catholic League with Vincentian holding the second notch. The locals have won five games, including wins over Vincentian and La Salle, while the Vincentian five has dropped games to both Catholic High and La Salle. In recent games, C. C. H. S. has been handed two defeats, losing to Lansingburg and Watervliet, but hope to get back into the win column when they open the second round of league competition.

Coach O'Kane's starting lineup will likely include Bill Murray in the pivot post, Jim Ryan and Jack Kelly in the forward positions, with Bob Trombly and Dan Quinn in guard positions. The preliminary contest will bring together the Junior Varsity quints of the two school.

HAS NARROW ESCAPE.

Lafayette, Ind. (INS) — Ward ("Piggy") Lambert was back drilling his Purdue basketball five today following a narrow escape when his automobile plunged down a 40-foot embankment and overturned on the outskirts of Indianapolis. Lambert's wife suffered a slight knee injury.

SPORTS MIRROR

By the Associated Press.

Today a year ago—Clarence (Ace) Parker signed two-year contract with football Dodgers, virtually ending all hopes of baseball career as contract called for him to report Aug. 15.

Three years ago—Sydney Wooderson elected to run in Princeton meet June 17 and A.A.U. called off projected all-star meet between United States and Britain.

Five years ago—National League mid-winter meeting scouted reports of plan to organize players for "collective bargaining" under "C. I. O."

BOYS' CLUB CLIPS ST. LAWRENCE'S 5

A field goal by Bill Mulligan in the closing 30 seconds of play gave the Troy Boys' Club varsity a 45 to 44 win over St. Lawrence Five last night in the Greater Troy League contest at the Larries gym. The victory put the Boys' Club in first place in the league standing.

Bernie Malacco with 17 points topped the winners. Mike Gully and Ted Majer had 14 points each for the vanquished.

In the preliminary the Boys' Club Jayvees beat St. Lawrence Jayvees, 25 to 13. It was the 23rd win of the season for the Boys' Club.

The Boys' Club will meet Beaunit Mills Five at Van Schaick tomorrow night at Cohoes.

TROY BOYS' CLUB VARSITY.	F.G.	F.B.	T.P.
Bradley, f.	2	1	5
Fletcher, f.	0	0	0
Macharra, f.	0	0	0
Malacco, f.	6	5	17
Keville, c.	2	4	8
Lemke, g.	3	1	7
DeBonis, g.	1	0	2
Mulligan, g.	2	2	6
Totals	16	13	45

ST. LAWRENCE VARSITY.	F.G.	F.B.	T.P.
Gully, f.	4	6	14
Comerford, f.	0	0	0
Colaruso, f.	2	0	4
Agars, f.	0	0	0
Biette, c.	1	1	3
Alvey, g.	4	1	9
Majer, g.	4	6	14
Totals	15	14	44

UNDEFEATED TROY QUINTET POINTS FOR COHOES TILT

Troy High's undefeated basketball team will be pointing for its seventh consecutive win of the current season tomorrow night when it stacks up against the Cohoes High five on the local court.

With one of the outstanding scholastic teams in the Troy Area, Coach Eddie Pickens has brought his charges undefeated through six games, having registered wins over Hudson, Lansingburg, Watervliet, LaSalle, Amsterdam and Albany. Only in the Watervliet game were the locals really challenged and in this encounter they emerged on the long end of a 36 to 31 count.

Scheduled to start tomorrow's contest are "Tee" Grimes, captain, and Lou Cioffi in the forward berths; Walt Willetts in the pivot position, and George Collins and Bob Coonradt at the guard posts. Reserves include Bill Deegan, Irwin Berger, Bob Purcell, Walt Winney, Al O'Brien and Joe Muscatello.

The Junior Varsity teams of the two schools will meet in the preliminary go with Troy Jayvees comprising "Zip" Gordon, Dan Pafundi, Doug Carey, Frank Hoenigsbaum and Ed Verillo.

BENNY McCOY JOINS U. S. ARMED FORCES

Chicago (INS)—Benny McCoy, 26-year-old infielder of the Philadelphia Athletics, joined the ranks today of the high-priced athletes in the American armed forces.

He was sworn in as a coxswain in the Naval Reserve at the Great Lakes Naval Training Station. McCoy, whose home is in Grand Rapids, Mich., would have been subject to early call for the Army had he not signed up with the Naval Reserve.

GREENBERG AGAIN HONORED.

New York (INS)—Sergt. Henry (Hank) Greenberg, former Detroit Tiger baseball star and Ambassador Laurence A. Steinhardt, American ambassador to Turkey today held the annual citations of honor awarded by the Young Men's Hebrew Association.

Larry MacPhail Declares War No Excuse For Cutting Baseball Salaries

STATES DODGERS WHO EARN RAISES TO BE GIVEN THEM

Continues Policy of Paying Men on Basis of Last Season's Work; Talks With Own Men.

Miami Beach, Fla. (AP)—Free-handed Larry MacPhail, whose spending gave the Brooklyn Dodgers a National League pennant, can't see the war as an excuse for cutting baseball salaries.

While other clubs are reported tightening their purse strings in the face of the national emergency, MacPhail said Brooklyn players who earned salary raises will get them.

"When a ball player comes to me and starts talking about a contract," the executive continued, "He usually says he expects to have a big year.

"I always tell him 'brother, I put out on the basis of what you did last year.' I've said that all my life. The player knows it.

"I may expect him to have a good year, but I point out that if he does he'll benefit the following season.

"We had a good year. We won the pennant and we brought a lot of people into the ball park.

"We'd better get hurt now before we start crying too hard. It's up to us to give the players what they are due, and take a shot on taking in the money to pay them.

"What right have we to get panicky and start talking war in discussing terms?"

As the Dodger players gathered at Miami for a flight today to the Havana training camp, eight still had not signed contracts—but MacPhail declared the club was "in pretty good shape."

"The only one essential difference," he said, "is in the case of Pitcher Whitlow Wyatt.

"Wyatt is the only fellow I expect to have any trouble with," MacPhail continued. "I've talk to him once but we couldn't get together then.

"He had a whale of a season, and he's entitled to more money.

"But it was Wyatt's first big year, and he can't expect to jump over the heads of fellows who have been up there for a long time."

MacPhail said he would hold talks at Havana with the players who haven't signed.

TROY HIGH MEETS RIVALS FRIDAY

The oldest of Troy's intra-city basketball rivalries will be continued Friday night when Troy High's undefeated basketeers take on the Lansingburg quint in a Public High School League tilt on the Knickerbacker Junior High court.

Records of past performances usually mean little when these two teams clash, but Troy High's string of nine consecutive victories certainly gives them an edge. Hailed as the best balanced quintet in many years at Troy High, the outfit stars its two sharpshooting forwards, Ted Grimes and Lou Cioffi.

The 'Burg five have a record to be proud of themselves, six straight, with a total of nine victories to two losses. In the first encounter of these two squads, Troy trounced the 'Burg, 35-19, and the North Enders are looking for a chance to redeem themselves. On that occasion, the 'Burg five failed to solve Troy's defense, but they have worked out the problem to their own satisfaction since then and expect Chuck Boland, Nick Lennek and Jack Fisher to pepper the hoop.

Saturday evening LaSalle Institute meets Troy High in a try to bounce back on the winning trail after being swamped under a deluge of points last week by Cathedral Academy. For the Cadets it will be a chance to redeem themselves and keep them in the running for city championship honors. Last week's setback at the hand of the Albanians terminated a three-game winning streak that had brought them up to second place in the Catholic League pennant race.

A LaSalle court squad has not stopped a Troy High team since the 1939-40 edition did it at the State Armory in the Principal's tournament, by a 21-20 count. Since then the Pickenmen have captured four in a row, with their most recent victory coming earlier this year by a 31-16 score.

In order to break the losing streak the Cadets will throw everything into the fray to try to come out on top. It will be an all-out effort to halt the onsurging Troy High quintet and will be quite a feather in the caps of the Fourth Streeters should they win.

Strenuous drills have been the order so far this week and no definite starting lineup has been named by Coach Tom Farnam, who is very much displeased with the way his boys showed up against Cathedral. All members of the varsity are fighting for a berth on the starting five in order to avenge the previous setback handed them by their opponents.

Student interest in the game has reached a very high pitch with both student bodies going behind their respective teams 100 per cent. In view of this fact the school authorities have made preparations to accommodate the largest crowd of the season. Many new bleachers have been added to make room for all spectators.

HOCKEY SCORES.

Montreal Canadiens 2, New York Rangers 1 (overtime).

Giants' New Pilot Takes Over

Mel Ott (center), new manager of the Giants, talks things over with Pitchers Carl Hubbell (left) and Hal Schumacher during the New Yorkers first 1942 baseball workout at their Miami, Fla., training camp.

CONSIDER ENDING CADETS' HOCKEY PLAY THIS SEASON

The remainder of La Salle Institute's hockey schedule probably will be cancelled as a result of the automobile accident Monday night in which five of the players received injuries, was announced last night. The accident occurred as the team was returning from a game in which they trimmed Hoosac School, 3-0.

The victory marked the fourth win for the Cadet sextet and extended their string of official triumphs to five, since the tie with Cohoes is recorded as a win for both contestants. Jim Donnelly and Jack Horton starred for the Cadets, the former with a goal and two assists and the latter with two goals and an assist. Don Kruse shared the assist on one goal.

Including the last game, top scoring honors for the team go to Donnelly with six goals and three assists for nine points, while Horton is runner-up with five and two for seven points. John Quinlan with five points and Kruse with two complete the season's scoring for La Salle.

The shut out was the first recorded in scholastic competition in this area for the season. The Cadets netted their first tally in the opening period with Donnelly sinking it on assists by Horton and Kruse. The second period was scoreless, but Horton and Donnelly alternately assisted and tallied for the other two goals in the last period.

FRNKA MAY GET YALE GRID POST

Philadelphia (AP)—The Record said last night it had learned Henry Frnka, head coach at Tulsa University, will be sounded out within a few days on a proposal to become head football coach at Yale University.

The newspaper said a prominent Yale alumnus close to the football advisory committee, declared that Ray Morrison, Temple football coach, had suggested Frnka be interviewed.

The alumnus, who declined the use of his name, added that the advisory committee also intends to confer with Maurice 'Clipper" Smith, Villanova coach, and E. E. "Hooks" Mylin, Lafayette coach.

Frnka, a native of Greenville, Tex., went to Tulsa a year ago after serving as assistant to Morrison at Temple.

"The Yale matter came up so suddenly I haven't really considered it. I haven't been contacted officially by the Yale folks but I feel that it's a fine compliment to be mentioned."

Business Men Plan Dinner For Hornsby

By HUGH FULLERTON, JR.

New York (Wide World)—Look for the first robin of spring any day now, folks . . . The first of the new crop of football heroes has arrived . . . Ed Danforth of the Atlanta Journal says that Charley Tripp, the Wilkes-Barre, Pa., boy at Georgia, can heave a thirty-yard forward pass and by the time the receiver has straightened out to run, there is Charley alongside him yelling for a lateral . . . Holdover story from last season also deals with Georgia . . . It seems that when Quinton Lumpkin, the Bulldogs' 225-pound frosh coach, was heading for the Orange Bowl, he stopped in a Florida town for a shave . . . "Hurry up," he told the barber, "I've got to work out this afternoon." . . . Came the reply: "Yes, sir. Where are you wrestling tonight?"

One-Minute Sport Page.

The Fort Worth (Tex.) Junior Chamber of Commerce will throw a luncheon for Rogers Hornsby Feb. 25 and is inviting baseball men and sports writers from throughout the nation . . . Tommy Hitchcock, former ten-goal polo player, took up skiing this winter and hasn't broken any bones yet . . . An all Chinese hockey team is playing in Canada and making out pretty well . . . The National Semi-Pro Baseball Congress is planning a national registration day for all prospective players March 30 . . . Looks like Uncle Sam was about six weeks ahead on that one . . . The sandlotters' idea is that anyone who'd like to play can sign up at the nearest sporting goods store and an effort will be made to find teams for all of them . . . Bob Harmon, who has kept Columbia sports in the papers for several years, has been granted leave of absence to go into service with the Naval Reserve.

Today's Guest Star.

R. G. Lynch, Milwaukee Journal: "Ski jumping is the only sport in which the athletes are at the mercy of kibitzers. All sports have wiseacres who tell competitors, 'You would do better if you did it thus or so.' In skiing they make judges out of the kibitzers and the 'judges' make the sport ridiculous."

Quote, Unquote.

Oscar Vitt: "If Ty Cobb were playing today, he would steal 150 bases a season. The pitchers don't bother to develop a fake movement to first or second any more. Runners are seldom picked off the bags."

Hot Stove Warmup.

Jess Danna, the 22-year-old pitcher Mel Ott took with him to the Giants' camp, used to be a medical student at Louisiana State. But the first day at Miami he worked too hard under the hot sun and had to accept a treatment and lecture from Trainer Willie Schaefer . . . Billy (Sonny) Skiff, jr., whose pop caught for Newark 15 years ago, will get a tryout with the Bears this spring. He's a catcher, too . . . The Knoxville Smokies shouldn't worry about night life at their Tallahassee, Fla., training base. The town is blacked out because of the naval air base there . . . Dan Taylor, veteran Cleveland newspaperman, is the Indians' new publicity man . . . The Tigers have booked seven Ladies' Days for the season . . . The Texas League will contribute $200 to the State High School Baseball Tournament . . . Eddie Froelich, trainer for Chicago's Blackhawks and White Sox, isn't worried about the prospect of 14 night games. He was at Kansas City last summer and claims he only saw the sun on Sundays.

Cleaning the Cuff.

The Australia-New Zealand hockey match, involving teams of soldiers who never were on skates until they reached Canada last year, will supply the comedy for Montreal's "Victory Loan" clash between the old Maroons and old Canadiens . . . The Arkansas Athletic Association is considering awarding a Neil Martin trophy in memory of the former Razorback football and cage star who was killed in a plane crash in Burma . . . When Mrs. Ed Weiner, wife of the old-time N. Y. U. footballer, heard about a West Point appointment being reserved for Colin Kelly, Jr., she wrote to George Halas to save a spot on the Chicago Bears 15 years from now for "Hoss" Weiner, jr.

Catholic Central Beats Amsterdam

Catholic High's basketeers last night nosed out St. Mary's of Amsterdam, 35-33, in the third overtime period, when Ned Conway sank a long shot with less than a minute to go. At the conclusion of the regulation time, the teams were deadlocked at 31-all.

Langley tallied first in the overtime with a field for St. Mary's, but Bob Trombley came back with a hoop for Catholic High. In the closing seconds, Jim Ryan looped another one in, but Referee Cassidy ruled that the gun went off before the ball was shot, disallowing the score.

No points were tallied in the second period, despite the fast play of both outfits. In the final chapter, Conway tallied and Catholic High went on the defense for the remaining minutes to protect their slim lead successfully. Catholic High set the early pace, leading 18-13 at the half, but St. Mary's tied the score by the end of the third period and the contest seesawed until the regulation time was up with the score still deadlocked.

Kelly and Trombley were high for C. C. H. S. with 12 points each and Ryan had seven, while Oldrych paced the home team with 14. St. Mary's Jayvees won the preliminary, 28-16. Campbell and Degnan were high for Catholic High with five points each, while Savage paced the winners with 14

CATHOLIC HIGH.

	F.G.	F.B.	T.P.
Kelly, f.	4	4	12
Ryan, f.	1	5	7
Murray, c.	1	0	2
Trombley, g.	5	2	12
Quinn, g.	0	0	0
Conway, g.	1	0	2
Totals	12	11	35

ST. MARY'S.

	F.G.	F.B.	T.P.
Howlan, f.	1	0	2
Johnson, f.	2	0	4
Oldrych, c.	5	4	14
Isabel, g.	3	0	6
Langley, g.	3	0	6
Kelley, g.	0	1	1
Totals	14	5	33

Referee, Cassidy; scorer, Blakely; timer, Farley; score at half time, 18-13, C. C. H. S.; team fouls called, 11-8, St. Mary's.

ROWE PLAYERS TO MEET BERLIN

The Rowe Five, conquerors of the high-flying St. Adalbert's quintet of Schenectady last Tuesday, will tackle the tough Berlin Bearcat team tomorrow night at Berlin, in a contest that brings together two of the fastest teams of this area.

The Rowe players will meet at the rooms, 2212 Fifth Avenue, at 7:30 p.m. to make the trip. The tentative starting lineup for the Troy team is Phillips, LeMay, Krambuhl, Finkle and Harrington, formerly of Siena, while Passinelli and a new member, Jim Graham, will be in reserve. "Rip" Rielly, a veteran of three seasons with the Rowe's, will assume his new duties as coach for this game.

Bill Bolton, former Syracuse star who started the season with the Troy Pros, is still on the sick list and will not be on the Bearcats lineup. Bolton is slated to appear for the Rowe's here next Wednesday when they take on the Troy Boys' Club.

Fishing for $$$

Joe DiMaggio, still casting for a salary hoist from New York Yankees, fondles fishing pole reflectively at St. Petersburg.

SEVERAL LEADING PLAYERS UNSIGNED IN BIG LEAGUES

By JUDSON BAILEY.

New York (AP)—Little has been heard of contract controversies in the major leagues this winter for various reasons, but a check yesterday showed that many outstanding players still are unsigned on the eve of the training season.

Joe DiMaggio, who will be the highest salaried star in baseball this year, has returned his contract at least once without a signature. More amazing, perhaps, is the fact that only pitcher Lefty Gomez and shortstop Phil Rizzuto of all the regulars among the world champions have agreed to terms.

The New York Giants opened their training camp at Miami Monday with no more than a dozen performers signed and several other clubs similarly have big groups of players outside the fold.

Not all the players unsigned are discontented. The war has posed so many before more important problems for the magnates that some contracts were not mailed out until last week and a majority were not offered the players until the first week in February.

As the result some players will bring their signed contracts into camp with them and others will come to terms as soon as they get on the scene and have a chance to talk over their desires.

Set Sensational Record.

DiMaggio, who set a sensational record by hitting in 56 consecutive games last summer, leading the Yankees to the World championship and earning the most valuable player award for himself, reportedly was offered a contract for $37,500, the same amount he received last year. Most observers believe that he and President Edward G. Barrow of the Yanks will compromise on $40,00 with a minimum of argument.

There has been no indication of what is delaying the signing of the other Yankees, whose camp opens next week-end.

Bonus arrangements, which some clubs have written into this year's contracts because of the uncertainty of attendance in war time, have caused some balks. A case in point is first baseman Dick Siebert of the Philadelphia Athletics, who, it is understood, wants a definite commitment in five figures.

Connie Mack said he has given Siebert his final offer, adding, "he can take it or leave it. He has given me trouble every year... always felt he was entitled to more money. That may be all right as far as he is concerned, but I am not going to raise my offer this time."

Kreevich Unsigned.

Mike Kreevich and Bob Johnson also are unsigned among the A's.

Luke Appling, who alone of all the Chicago White Sox has not come to terms, presumably also is opposed to a bonus plan.

First Baseman Elbie Fletcher is the only Pirate not signed and is reportedly at odds with the club over $2,000.

Bobo Newsom, among the Tigers, has been grumbling about a reported pay cut and pitchers John Gorsica and Paul (Dizzy) Trout have made open holdout declarations.

Relief Pitcher Mike Ryba has notified the Red Sox that he is "dissatisfied with the contract terms but is still considering them."

The Indians have not yet signed Jeff Heath, Gee Walker, Hal Trosky and some others, but Trosky is the leading question mark. He has remained silent since his contract was mailed in January.

Eight of the Brooklyn Dodgers, National League Champions, were unsigned when President Larry MacPhail left here by plane for Miami this morning, but he expected to have most of them lined up before the squad flies to Havana today.

FAVORITES TOP FLORIDA TOURNEY

St. Augustine, Fla. (AP)—The "Big Three" favorites in the Club Champions Golf Tournament, defending champion Bill Stark of Jacksonville, Fla.; medalist Carl Dann of Orlando, Fla., and Frankie Stranahan, golfing sensation from Toledo, Ohio, survived yesterday's opening of match play with convincing triumphs.

Stranahan scored an 8 to 6 verdict over Ed Rodgers of Jacksonville, while Stark eliminate F. W. Edwards of Biltmore, N. C., 6 and 5.

Dann, seeking to become the first golfer to win the event three times, was forced to come from behind on the back stretch to defeat L. G. Klipple, Phillipsburg, N. J., 4 and 2.

James Paul, Gulph Mills, Pa., defeated veteran James Nammack, Hempstead, Long Island, 5 and 4.

Other first round results included:

Ward Rodgers, Clearwater, Fla., defeated Joseph Switzer, St. Louis, Mo., 1 up; Fred W. Hooper, Jacksonville, defeated Walter Sefina, New Bedford, Mass., 2 and 1; Dick Van Kleeck, Ponte Vedra Beach, Fla., defeated Joseph Feldman, Inwood, Long Island, 1 up, 22 holes; William McIntyre, St. Petersburg, defeated J. E. Scheffmeyer, New York City, 2 and 1; Dick Doeschler, Jacksonville, defeated Homer Lichtenwalter, jr., Summit, N. J., 1 up, 19 holes; Robert B. Archibald, Jacksonville, defeated Dr. William Connelly, Stamford, Conn., 1 up, 19 holes.

Powell Crichton, Bronxville, defeated Fred Wright, Tuckahoe, 1 up; Jack Ryerson, Cooperstown, defeated Alfred Ulmer, Jacksonville, 2 and 1; Mel Demariais, Portsmouth, N. H., defeated Jules Leitser, Elmsford, 4 and 3.

CANISIUS QUINT TO MEET SIENA CAGERS FRIDAY

The highlight of Siena College's basketball schedule will take place Friday night at Gibbons Hall, Loudonville, when the Canisius College Griffins come to meet the Loudonville Indians in their annual meeting.

Rated sixth in the nation, the Buffalo aggregation boasts of its most powerful team in the history of the school. Canisius has taken the measure of some of the leading teams in the United States, including Oregon, Wyoming, Colgate, Scranton and Niagara. The Griffins have lost to Southern California, 43-39; St. Bonaventure, 44-33 and Long Island University, 46-43, in an overtime period.

The Griffin quintet, coached by Allie Seelbach, line-up with four seniors and one sophomore, and has averaged better than fifty points per game thus far this season.

The team is captained by Joe Niland, also captain last year. A high scoring playmaker, Niland is probably the most feared and respected player on the Griffins roster.

Next comes Bob Gauchat, who has broken Canisius scoring records for the last two year. last winter he established the present total of 299 points. Bob chalked up 22 points against Siena last year.

CENTER QUINT LISTS 3 GAMES

The Troy Jewish Community Center varsity will tackle the strong Mercury Club quintet of Albany at 8:30 p.m. today on the Center court in the first of a home and home series. In their last start, the J. C. C. cagers topped the St. Lawrence five.

The Center squad includes Abe Kaplan, Sonny Kaplan, Don Caswell, Bernard Zyniewski, Milt Klein, Stanley Weiss and Coach Manny Elfenbein.

In an intermediate girls' tussle, the Trojan All-Stars tackle the Delta Psi Stars. The former team includes Ruth Bobbin, Esther Dembrosky, Joyce Lagunoff, Shirley Kaplan, Sue Friedman and Estelle Siegal. The latter team has Toby Gaies, Gloria Vigadi, Dorothy Vigadi, Rosselyn Pufeles, Lee Jaffee, Miriam Rosenberg, Muriel Lurie, and Rose Rosen. This game starts at 7 p.m.

Friday, the Center varsity will go to Newark to meet two of that city's outstanding quints, the Newark Y. M. H. A. and the St. Lucy's C. Y. O. team. The first game will be played Saturday and the second on Sunday. Abe and Sonny Kaplan, Caswell, Klein, Weiss, Zyniewski and Coach Elfenbein will make the trip.

The Y. M. H. A. outfit is undefeated in the New Jersey Jewish Federation League, while the St. Lucy's team boast such performers as Fred Kunz, former St. Peter's all-state player, and Sal Constentio, city scoring leader.

Matches Men

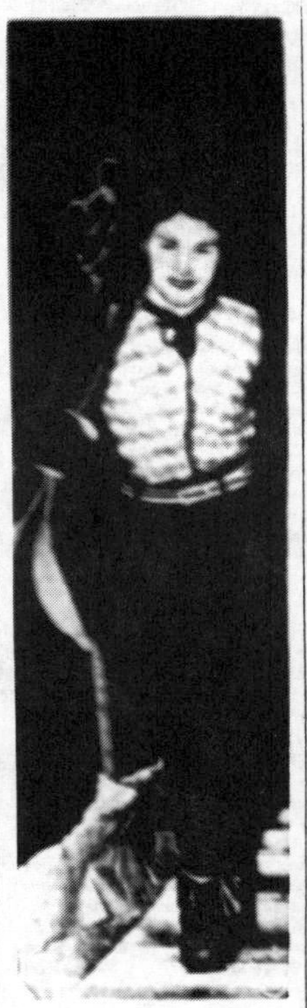

Dorothy Graves of Greenfield, Mass., stirred the crowd at the Bear Mountain, N. Y., Sports Association ski tournament by tying Walter Brostek for first place. Miss Graves jumped 122 and 118 feet for 205.5 points. She finished ahead of 16 masculine experts.

BOSTON TILTS FREE TO ALL SERVICE MEN

Boston (AP)—A plan to admit the uniformed personnel of New England army camps and naval bases to Boston's major league ball parks seven days a week, including holidays, during the 1942 season was outlined yesterday by President Bob Quinn of the Braves, and General Manager Eddie Collins of the Red Sox.

WINTER UPSETS MAKE CHANGES IN WIDENER 'CAP

Miami, Fla. (AP)—A winter of upsets has made the $50,000 Widener Handicap March 7 a wide open horse race—and even the experts may throw away their form charts and jab a pin in a program in trying to pick the winner.

Most of the hubbub has been raised over Alsab's two defeats and Challedon's disappointing performance, but not one of the other 54 eligible thoroughbreds has a season's record conspicuous enough to make him a favorite.

Almost every topnotch campaigner in the country is entered for the only big stake to be offered for older horses until the Massachusetts Handicap is run in July.

Yet in 137 starts at Miami, Widener eligibles have won only 18 times. Up until yesterday, they had 17 seconds and 19 thirds.

A roll call of the early favorites is like a story of failure.

In two starts, W. L. Brann's Challedon could do no better than second, and Pictor failed to win in one opportunity. Al Sabath's Alsab was out of the money the only two times he ran.

Circle M. Ranch's Get Off, second in the Widener last year, won the Palm Beach Handicap but could do no better than show in three other outings. Samuel D. Riddle's War Relic was third in his one attempt.

Louis Tufano's Market Wise was third once, fourth once, and Woodvale Farm's Our Boots ran one race and came in fourth.

Two horses given some early consideration—Arnold Hanger's Dit and John Hay Whitney's Gramps—contributed bright entries for the ledger. Dit won his only start, and Gramps set a Hialeah track record for the mile in winning one of two races

Question marks are Charles S. Howard's ace California performers, Mioland and Porter's Cap, both of which have had fast workouts, but have been given no competition.

Horses which will bear watching on the basis of victories either at Tropical Park or Hialeah include Olympus; Trois Pistoles; He Rolls; Allessandro; Alohort, twice triumphant in sprints; Century Note, in one dead heat; Snow Ridge, winner of his only start; The Chief; City Talk; Cis Marion; Ponty, conqueror of Challedon; Red Dock, and Signator.

CLUB VARSITY FACES DORP TEAM TONIGHT

The Troy Boys' Club varsity will meet the St. Adalbert's A. C. of Schenectady at 8:30 p.m. today at the State Street gym. The Club Rams will seek their fifth straight win against the King All-Stars at 7:30 p.m. in the preliminary.

The Schenectady aggregation, including several former Nott Terrace and Mont Pleasant players, had a ten-game victory string until they lost to Rowe's Five, 26-25, last week. The T. B. C. quint is coleader of the Greater Troy League.

Troy, Lansingburg High Fives Ready For Tonight

A BIT OF THIS AND A BIT OF THAT

By JACK (Peerless) McGRATH

After much dickering and many setbacks, the C. Y. O. boxing program is now definitely in the cards. This corner has long advocated the enterprise and expects it to live up to the fine precedents set by the C. Y. O. in other cities. The boxers are good and the cause is right. What more could anyone ask?

The first show is slated for Monday, March 9, at La Salle Institute's gymnasium. Pete Mooney of the South End will act as matchmaker, pairing the boys according to weight and previous experience to assure fast and equal battles in all the scheduled bouts.

Mooney recently took his Troy C. Y. O. leather-pushers to Gloversville to meet that community's best ring generals. The result was four victories in five bouts for the Trojans. The Hillside coach promises a good scrap for every one of the boys and, on past performances as well as natural competitive spirit, it's safe to say that's just what the fans of this area can expect.

* * *

For the first time in the history of organized baseball the bleacher brigade has been given a voice in the management of its favorite diamond outfit. The Cincinnati Reds are responsible for this revolutionary policy. They asked the fans what they thought about night baseball and allied subjects and they found out.

The answers to the Redlegs' questionnaire were turned in by customers who attended hundreds of games, so that their opinions were based on experience. Outstanding fact revealed in the poll was that the people who pay the freight agree with President Roosevelt on night baseball.

More than four-fifths said they would attend more night games if more are played and about 98 per cent assured the Cincinnati bosses that they didn't care whether any fireworks were provided as extra attraction. In other words, they want their fireworks during the regulation nine innings and not as an entre-act affair.

About 49 out of every fifty persons answering the questions claimed they attended night games and better than 80 per cent of them would like to see the games start at 9 p.m. Nocturnal frays at Crowsley Field will henceforth start at that hour. Public opinion must not be flouted.

The fans prefer Wednesdays and Fridays for their arc light games, with Tuesdays, Thursdays and Mondays following in order of popularity. Reading the handwriting on the wall, the management announces that four contests will be played on Wednesdays and the same on Fridays. Two will be played on Tuesdays, Wednesdays and Mondadys.

* * *

The traditional starting for single weekday tilts, 3 p.m., meets with the approval of better than 80 per cent of the fans and the 2:30 p.m. time for Sunday contests drew about the same response. General Manager Giles also learned that twilight ball is not popular. Starting hours grow progressively less popular as they grow later, until only 6 per cent liked 4:30 p.m. Q. E. D.—No twilight ball in Crosley Field.

This true-or-false has proven a great aid to the Cincinnati brain trust in arranging their home schedule, but it has created some headaches besides. For instance, the women polled favored Saturday for Women's Day, so that office help could take advantage of the occasion. But retail merchants are against it, because it puts a crimp in the traditional Saturday shopping trip.

* * *

Cleveland Indian ballplayers can get ready to have their mistakes and errors pointed out to them this season by the club's staff of coaches, and this information from their own manager, Lou Boudreau. Although only 24 years old, Boudreau has plenty of sage ideas on how to run a ball club.

Boudreau speaks from personal experience. When he played in the Three-I League he was a third sacker and when he switched to Buffalo he switched to short-stopping at the advice of Greg Mulleavy, former White Sox coach.

"If my coaches will help our young players that way," says Boudreau, "I'll be satisfied."

FAIR OR FOUL

BY LAWTON CARVER

New York, (INS)—If I had the endurance to run a whole mile in record time or close to it, with my life wrapped up in whether I made it, I wouldn't want any of my fellow men clocking the performance. I wouldn't question their integrity or doubt their ability for a second. But no matter how good they may be or how long at the business of timing sports events I'd still feel some misgivings over their ability to catch me at the exact instant of starting then again at hitting the tape.

What they would have to provide would be a mechanical timer, if I could run a mile, which heaven's knows I never will. A stroll to the nearest tavern is a workout. And I am not attempting to say that being a fraction off in the time of a mile race is the most important thing in the world in times like these.

Still, one of these nights—perhaps this Saturday night—a record will fall and the setter thereof won't get credit for it because manmade clocking can't possibly be infallible. I know how near to perfect it is, but there still can be mistakes.

What they ought to have is an electrical timer, with the usual clockers as backstops in case anything goes wrong with the mechanical gadget, then if Les MacMitchell steps off that new record as he is almost certain to do sooner or later it will be in the books.

For instance, he is going to run in the mile on Saturday night, in the New York A. C. games, and deliberately try to shatter the indoor standard for distance. Naturally if he does it with considerable to spare there will be no doubt, but suppose he comes close and the clocking is a little cockeyed as it seldom is, but could be?

In that case he would be deprived of his goal, regardless of how unimportant this may be to you and to me.

The thing about this indoor mile record of 4:07.4 (not to be confused with Glen Cunningham's 4:04.4 paced race) is that it has been run four times at Madison Square Garden, beginning in 1938, when that same Cunningham established the mark, Chuck Fenske duplicated it twice in 1940 and MacMitchell reeled off one in the same time last year in the same event as he will be appearing in Saturday night—the Baxter mile of the New York A. C. games.

I just wonder if the electric timer mightn't have knocked that down to a slower time in one of those races. Of course, it might have lifted one of those times, too, but that isn't particularly important for the purposes of this piece.

Dan Ferris, the A. A. U. head man would favor an electric timer if they could be had at a reasonable figure, but they cost too much except for big international meets, the Olympic games and such.

"I think our usual timing is as accurate as man can make it," Ferris said today, "but naturally that human equation enters into it and mechanical timing would be better with clockers to back it up in case of mechanical difficulties.

"The way it works now we have three timers and an alternate. We accept two identical times or in case three differ we take the middle watch. However, there scarcely ever is a time when the difference is more than 1-10. Yet, of course, this is not infallible, as a timer might miss the flash of a gun, or anticipate a start or finish and get a fast time. This is especially true in the sprints. Electric timing would be wonderful if it could be had," he concluded.

I'll butt in further to the extent of saying it should be had.

TWO CONTESTS IN "Y" HOUSE LEAGUE

The Indians defeated the Mike and Johns, 28-20, and the Clan Lads overwhelmed the Panthers, 51-18, last night in Senior House League cage contests at the Troy Y. M. C. A. court. Kirker and Sorenson with eight each were high for the Indians and Turton paced the Johns with 12.

INDIANS.

	F.G.	F.B.	T.P.
Ryan, f.	0	1	1
Kirker, f.	4	0	8
Sorenson, c.	3	2	8
Bowdy, g.	1	0	2
Bessette, g.	4	1	9
Totals	12	4	28

MIKE AND JOHNS.

	F.G.	F.B.	T.P.
Pokrey, f.	0	1	1
Maderosian, f.	1	2	4
Ruff, c.	1	1	3
Turton, g.	5	2	12
O'Connell, g.	0	0	0
Totals	7	6	20

CLAN LADS

	F.G.	F.B.	T.P.
Reid, f.	2	0	4
Ray, f.	5	0	10
Finkle, c.	2	2	6
Zdunycuy, g.	0	0	0
Wachter, g.	5	2	12
Reynolds, g.	1	2	4
Stanille, g.	7	1	15
Totals	22	7	51

PANTHERS.

	F.G.	F.B.	T.P.
Snyder, f.	2	1	5
Dansereau, f.	1	0	2
Meich, c.	0	0	0
Connolly, g.	1	1	3
Grabu, g.	0	0	0
Kelly, g.	1	1	3
Doughney, g.	2	1	5
Totals	7	4	18

WILD LIFE TEAM WINS GUN SHOOT

The Wild Life team last night downed the Hendrick Hudson Stars, 1466-1430, in a Troy Pistol League match. W. Maxwell of the winners was high score shooter with 299, while his team mate J. Spain got 298. Today, the Arsenal Owls will take on the Rensselaer Valve team at 8 p.m. and the Fort Orange outfit tackles the Watervliet Pirates at 9 p.m.

WILD LIFE.

A. Jones	289
A. Card	290
J. Spain	298
W. Maxwell	290
F. Lotz	299
Total	1466

HENDRICK HUDSON STARS.

D. Callahan	277
J. Parslow	293
G. Lindgren	281
R. Patrie	295
E. Buckley	284
Total	1430
Total	1430

Hockey Results.

Brooklyn Americans 6, Boston Bruins 4.

Detroit Red Wings 6, Chicago Blackhawks 1.

AMERKS TOP BRUINS.

New York (AP) — The wobbling Boston Bruins, still fitting new cogs into their damaged machine, last night failed three times to hold a lead and finally were beaten 6-4 in a National Hockey League game by the Brooklyn Americans on three third-period goals.

EDDIE PICKEN'S UNBEATEN CREW INVADES 'BURG

Trojans Are Favorites for Both Tonight's Game and Tomorrow's Against La Salle Institute.

All the Troy and vicinity quintets see action this week-end, with the undefeated Troy High five shouldering the heaviest burden as they engage in their two biggest games of the season on successive nights.

Troy takes on the Lansingburg courtmen on the Knickerbacker Junior High court tonight and tackles La Salle tomorrow night on the Cadets court. Catholic High plays host to Cathedral tonight in the other week-end highlighter. Cohoes and Watervliet clash tonight on the Arsenal City court, while Heatly is at Berlin tonight and at home tomorrow night against Salem.

The Troy-'Burg fracas will mark a new installment in the city's oldest cage rivalry, and has important bearing on Lansingburg's chances in the Public High School League. Troy High has a comfortable lead in the loop and has nine victories to no defeats for the season. The 'Burg five has won its last six starts and has a total of nine wins to two losses.

Sharpshooting forwards Hiram "Tee" Grimes and Lou Cioffi will lead the Trojans through the week-end's heavy firing. The Trojans clipped the 'Burg, 35-19, in a previous tangle this season and stopped La Salle, 30-16, so that they rule as favorites to take both tilts. The Cadets, winner of six out of ten, will be out to redeem themselves after the staggering, 58-17, loss to Cathedral last week.

Troy probably will start Grimes, Cioffi, Walt Willetts, Bob Coonradt and George Collins in both games, while Lansingburg plans to use Chuck Boland, Nick Lennek and Jack Fisher, with the other starting berths undecided. La Salle's first five will include George Rafferty, Jim Pemrick, Jim Mahoney and either Ed Yamin and Jim Duffy or Joe Cahill and Ed Sullivan.

Catholic Central, Catholic Diocesan League pace-setters, can assure themselves of the loop title by taking Cathedral into camp tonight, but Cathedral, fresh from the walloping it gave La Salle, will not be a push over. Cathedral can earn full possession of second place by winning.

Catholic High cagers tamed the Albanians, 37-32, earlier this season, but the invaders are a much improved team since that first engagement. C. C. H. S. likely will start Jim Ryan and John Kelly at forwards, Bill Murray at the pivot post and Bob Trombley and Bob Quinn at guards.

TORGER TOKLE IN PLACID TOURNEY

Lake Placid (AP).—Four Royal Canadian Air Force flyers vie with United States skiers in three days of competition opening today in this Adirondack Mountain resort.

Downhill events on the Whiteface Trail (1 p.m., E.W.T.) launch both the 21st annual Washington's Birthday ski tournament for men and the sixth annual February invitation women's ski tournament. Slalom racing on Rimrock Trail begins tomorrow noon.

Feminine contesting for the Kate Smith trophy held by 16-year-old Marilyn Shaw, Stowe, Vt., is on an official two-country team basis, with a Canadian girls' team from Eastern Canada opposing a United States combination.

Adding to the international flavor is the presence of several other male skiers from across the border, and the leaping Norwegian, Torger Tokle. Tokle will compete with the nationally-known Arthur Devlin, Lake Placid, Monday in the 21st annual ski-jumping tourney for the Beck and Dunn trophies on the intervales 60-meter Olympic ski hill. Devlin recently bested Tokle at Duluth, Minn.

LARRIES' JAYVEES TRIUMPH, 37 TO 21

Mike Gully's St. Lawrence Junior Varsity scored a 37 to 21 win over the Comets at St. Lawrence's gym.

Agars paced the winners with nine fields for 18 points with Comerford adding nine points to the victor's score. Chioddec scored 13 points for the losers scoring more than half their field goals.

After playing a full game in the prelim, Comerford donned a varsity suit and was second high scorer as the Larries defeated the Sacred Heart tossers 50 to 48.

COMETS.

	F.G.	F.B.	T.P.
Donovan, f.	1	0	2
Cronin, f.	1	0	2
Tesber, f.	0	0	0
Chioddec, c.	6	1	13
Valley, g.	0	0	0
Weingartner, g.	2	0	4
Totals	10	1	21

ST. LAWRENCE JAYVEES.

	F.G.	F.B.	T.P.
Comerford, f.	4	1	9
Tapler, f.	3	0	6
Agars, c.	9	0	18
Casey, g.	0	1	1
Walsh, g.	0	1	1
Burke, g.	1	0	2
Totals	17	3	37

Referee, Ruff; scorer, Agars; timer, Weingartner; score at half time, 18-12, St. Lawrence.

PASSES FOR 600,000.

New York (UP).—The New York City Defense Recreation Committee will distribute free passes to more than 600,000 service men during the 1942 season for use at New York's three major league parks.

"Four Horsemen"--Then and Today

The famous "Four Horsemen" of Notre Dame's football teams—left to right, Don Miller, Harry Stuhldreher, Jim Crowley and Elmer Layden—look at a picture of themselves made back in 1924. The first reunion of the quartet since 1931 was held in Cleveland, in honor of Miller's appointment as U. S. Attorney.

Bits Of Sports Reported Briefly

New York (AP)—The Middle Atlantic Skating Association has changed the flag symbol for ice skating to a green ball on a white field.

The new emblem, suggested by Everett M. Vassar, Brooklyn, and George Eckhardt, Jersey City, N. J., was selected in a contest which ended yesterday. The old symbol—a white flag with a red ball in the center—was discarded after the attack on Pearl Harbor.

Boston (AP)—Mrs. Weston W. Adams, wife of the youthful president of the Boston Bruins of the National Hockey League, made her second venture into sports today by taking over a vice presidency of the hockey club. For the past year she has raced a string of thoroughbreds with some success.

Cambridge, Mass. (AP) — Roy Cochran, the Indiana University flash, was ready today for one more competitive effort before hanging up his spikes to enter service at the Great Lakes Naval Training Station. Cochran, who has been working out at Harvard, competes in the special New York A. C. 500 tomorrow night.

Worcester, Mass. (AP)—Prof. Percy Carpenter, athletic director at Worcester Tech, announced today that the freshman rule, installed only last fall at the college, would be dropped at once for the duration of the war. Baseball Coach Bob Pritchard reaps the first benefit.

San Fernando, Cal. (AP)—Baseball at the cocktail hours will be introduced to West Coast fans March 4 in an exhibition game between the Philadelphia Athletics and the Seattle Rainiers.

Lest the customers misunderstand, Business Manager Bill Mulligan of Seattle said cocktail hour was just a catchy expression. None will be served to players or fans.

Boulder, Col. (AP)—Maybe this is why sophomore Heath Nuckolls so coolly sank the two free throws that gave Colorado its 49-48 cage win over Utah.

Capt. Bob Doll told the youngster there were two minutes left to play. In reality there were just three seconds.

Jacksonville, Fla. (AP)—Promoter Mike Jacobs says he plans to pit Billy Conn against Joe Louis this year if conditions allow it.

"Billy Conn's showing against Tony Zale the other night warrants a return match," Jacobs said. "Just because Conn didn't knock Zale out is nothing against him. Billy is a good boy. He'll give Joe a run."

Birmingham, Ala (AP)—Bobby Riggs defeated Frank Kovacs, 6-3, 8-6 and Don Budge downed Fred Perry, 6-4, 6-4, here last night in matches staged by the touring professional tennis troupe.

Durham, N. C. (AP)—Chances are the new queen of American badminta will be a brunette.

Thelma Kingsbury, the blonde Englisthwoman who dominated play in the national tournaments, is ineligible to play in the U. S. championships here April 2-4. All leading candidates for her crown are dark heads.

A new six-year residence rule governing foreign-born players will bar Miss Kingsbury from competition.

Chicago (AP)—Dates of the international Y. M. C. A. invitational basketball championships have been changed to March 30, 31 and April 1, H. G. Imbenhausen, meet chairman, announced today. They were scheduled previously for March 26-28. More than twenty teams from all parts of the United States already have entered.

Chicago (AP)—Ace Gutowsky, former star fullback with the Detroit Lions professional football team, still is bowling over the opposition—only this time in bridge. Gutowsky teamed with Mrs. Phil Spink of Chicago to win the mixed pairs championship of the Chicago Contract Bridge Association's central states competition. Gutowsky took up bridge in 1934, his first year with the Lions. He has more than a dozen cups won in bridge tournaments.

Robinson, Berger In Garden Bout Tonight

New York (AP)—The infantile paralysis fund and Ray Robinson figure to have a winning evening in Madison Square Garden tonight at the expense of Maxie Berger.

The skinny Harlem hammer and Canada's top thumper collide in a 12-rounder at 10 p.m. (E.W.T.), for which Promoter Mike Jacobs expects some 10,000 customers to contribute close to $30,000. The National Foundation for Infantile Paralysis will benefit by a percentage slice 'off the top."

Riding along on a 27-fight winning streak since he turned professional a couple of years ago, Robinson is 1 to 5 in the betting. Berger has been one of the more consistent performers among the welterweights for the last year and a half, but at this writing Roundhouse Ray is rated the No. 1 contender for champion Red Cochrane's crown.

In fact, most of the betting going on centers around Berger's chances of going the route. Robinson has flattened twenty of the 27 pros he has faced. The last fellow for whom he made the birdies sing was Fritzie Zivic, which is quite a trick. The problem now is whether he can do the same for the fast, veteran from Montreal who has had nearly 100 fights.

Back of the main go is an eight-rounder which has Sammy Sekreet, well-regarded Pittsburg welterweight, taking on Norman Rubio of Albany, in his Garden debut.

GLENS FALLS CAGE TOURNEY SETS DATES

Glens Falls (AP)—The 23rd annual Eastern States Scholastic Basketball Tournament, in which Memorial High, West New York, N. J., will defend its title, was set yesterday for March 26-28.

Keep 'Em Swinging--By Art Krenz

3B FINALLY BOWS IN LASALLE GAME

Class 4A performed a feat considered impossible yesterday when they defeated 3B, 34-31, in a La Salle Inter-class League game.

It was the first loss that 3B has suffered in two years of interclass competition. They had triumphed in seven straight contests this season. However, they remained far in the lead in the junior division race. By this victory, their second in five starts, 4A climbed out of the senior division cellar and took second place, a half game ahead of 4C. 4B has already clinched the senior championship.

Holding 3B's high scorers, Jack Stewart and Dick Ryan, to a total of six points, 4A took an early lead and held it throughout the contest, having a 16-12 advantage at half-time. 4A's foul-shooting decided the fracas as the winners counted six charity goals to 3B's three. Both quintets registered 14 field baskets.

Joe Francis with ten and Tony DiMicco with eight led the victors, while Tony Pasinelli had ten for 3B.

4A.

	F.G.	F.B.	T.P.
Englat, f.	2	1	5
Sheehan, f.	1	2	4
Cotch, c.	3	0	6
Ashley, c.	0	1	1
DiMicco, g.	3	2	8
Francis, g.	5	0	10
Totals	14	6	34

3B.

	F.G.	F.B.	T.P.
Stewart, f.	1	0	2
Curran, f.	3	0	6
Ryan, c.	2	0	4
Pasinelli, g.	4	2	10
Kelly, g.	3	0	6
Halpin, g.	1	1	3
Totals	14	3	31

Score at half time—16-12, 4A. Referees — Brother Edward and Law. Fouls committed—9-8, 4A.

TWO HOWARD ACES IN HIALEAH RACE

Miami, Fla., (AP) — Charles S. Howard's ace California horses, Mioland and Porter's Cap, will run at Hialeah Park today in a conditioning race leading up to the $50,000 Widener Handicap.

The thoroughbreds will make their first start of the season in a $1,500 mile and one-eighth race against three other fast horses.

Also entered are Pictor, one of W. L. Brann's chief hopes; Sir Marlboro, the turf course champion, and Cit Talk.

SIENA BASKETBALL CAGERS HOSTS TO CANISIUS TONIGHT

Canisius College's cagers, rated sixth in the nation's rankings, will bring a team record of eight wins and three losses to Gibbons Hall, Loudonville, tonight when the Griffins oppose Siena College's Indians.

Siena, boasting of upset victories over Villanova and Scranton, will take the floor with a six win-four loss mark.

Whatever hopes of victory Siena entertains seems to rest squarely on the fact that they must stop Captain Joe Niland and Bob Gauch from scoring. This pair is the backbone of the Canisius outfits, and pack most of the offensive punch.

Siena College's jayvees will play host to Sacred Heart, Troy CYO leaders, in the preliminary at 7:30 o'clock.

Bowling News

The Brownie Bowling League started its fourth and final round this week at the Alpha Alleys, with the Kesslers making a clean sweep against the Seven Crowns. Captain Bill Carley paced the winners with games of 180, 202 and 180 for 562 and "Cookie" Bloomingdale helped out with a 487. Wally Rogers was high for the losers with [illegible].

The Vos snatched a pair from the Morrises as Pepper Cooney showed the way with 451, followed by Lou Merkle with 450. Jim Canavally with 481 and Ed Hogan with 470 topped the losers.

The Fitzgeralds took a couple from the Zibros on the strength of "Chesty" Kirkner's 491 and Joe Bloomingdale's 473. "Monk" Bloomingdale batted out a 491 and Griffen got 450 for the losers.

The Bolands finished the program with a [illegible] game win over the Five Crowns. "Porky" Kasarjian rolled 469 and Eddie Bauer had 450 for the winners and Joe Claessens got 519 and Bill Sharpe 453 for the losers.

Railroad Afternoon.

Following the latest outing of the Troy Union Railroad Afternoon League, the teams line up in this order: Clums, Ryans, Doyles, Kanes, Pillsworths and Zarlengos. The Clums enjoy [illegible] .905 percentage with [illegible] wins in 21 starts.

The Doyles took all from the Zarlengos this week as Captain Mickey spilled a 573 and Floyd Nelson got 542. For the Zarlengos, it was Chris Bladen with 473 and Lee Billingham with 437. The Ryans got three more from the Kanes as Willie Ryan hit 541 and Harley Bump spilled 516, while "Flash" Flanigan paced the losers with 458 and Eddie Kane got 436.

The Clums made their usual clean sweep with the Pillsworths as their victims this time. Bill Burdick was the heavy hitter for the winners with 534, while "Howie" Warren got 511. For the Pillsworths Jack Burke hit 561 and Joe Tucker came through with 429.

Watervliet Churches.

The Third Avenue Methodists, with Clarence Ray's 200—560, Chris Drescher's 201—550, Earl VanAntwerp's 208—541 and Olsey's 536, took everything in sight in their Watervliet Church League match with the First Avenue Methodist No. 2 team, for whom Art Rosekrans rolled 201—549 and Ben Franklin got 205—511.

The First Presbyterians, with Floyd Tucker's 536 and Herman Neeb's 503, took all from the Baptists. Len Yetto's 261—567, Al Mangene's 515 and Len Mitchell's 510 blanked the Levings for the Trinity Episcopalians, while the First Avenue Methodist No. 1 team shut out the Lutherans, without either team turning up a 500 tally.

Alpha Beta.

Wager walked off with the honors this week in the Alpha Beta loop, with high single of 181 and high triple of 483. Other good scores were Peak's 465, Cote's 437, Woodworth's 437, Davis' 418, Perrine's 412, Heath's 411, Hebert's 410, Wooster's 406, Ray's 403 and Sweeney's 403. In the team results, the Hopes took three from the Olesens, the Charleys took a pair from the Seven Ups, the Commodores nicked the Boswells in two and the Dions got a couple from the Pommers.

Church of Christ.

The Sparrows and Lions took two points each in matches this week, the Sparrows outpointing the Eagles and the Lions downing the Robbins. Only three bowlers hit over 500 headed by Kinnicutt who had games of 167, 216 and 178 for 563. Others were Al Ives of the Lions with 505 and C. Penn[illegible] of the Robins with 506.

Troy Club.

The Rousseau's scored a clean sweep over the Weavers in the Troy Club bowling this week with the losers failing to come within 85 pins of the winners in any of the three games. H. McGrath opened a 203 single but "cooled off" and failed to get 500. He paced both teams with his 498 with Roberts hitting 470 and Phelps getting 468 for the winners.

Troy Merchants'.

A 637 triple gave the bowlers in this loop plenty to shoot at this week with Jake Pettinelli putting together games of 23[illegible], 206 and 195 for this tally. "Ace" Acierno hit 594 and Jack Martin hit 583. Acierno's single game of 239 went for high, but he couldn't keep up the pace.

Team scores gave Higgins and

Dead-eye Dear

Helene Stiles, best U. S. woman pistol shot, takes aim at movable targets of Miami Palmetto Pistol Club range, which is to be duplicated by Marine Corps. It is a two-and-a-half-ton traveling crane, 160 feet long, which advances from rear of range to firing line.

HIGBE PLANS TO STAY IN FLORIDA

Miami, Fla. (AP)—Kirby Higbe, star Brooklyn pitcher who declined to accompany the team to Havana when he learned his wife would not be allowed to go, disclosed yesterday he plans to work himself into shape here.

"I'll do some running and play golf, and get myself into pretty good shape by the time they get back," he said, adding there was a possibility he would work out with a local high school team.

The Brooklyn club did not invite players' wives, Secretary John McDonald said, "because we're the first ball club ever to train outside the United States during a war, and we didn't want to add any complications. Besides, we are using planes and there isn't room for them."

Burleigh three points from the Open Door, Cahill's took two from Wagar's Dairy and Saratoga Dryes won two from Butler Stores.

Five hundred hitters were Fred George Murphy, 558; Waldo Wagar, George Murph, 558; Waldo Wagar, 556; Jimmy Crossen, 544; Doc Reeves, 542; Tom Duke, 516; Cy Wagar, 514; Les Schumann, 511; Felix Padula, 506; Patsy Simmons, 504; Jack Naumowitz, 502; and George Allen, 502.

Weekly prize winners were Martin, Kramer, Acierno, Claydon, Pettignelli and Bill Wagar.

St. Mary's, Waterford.

Mary Gast stepped out with a 488 triple to pace the women's league this week with Fran Acierno pressing her closely with 469. Miss Gast's triple came from games of 172, 155 and 161. Other top scores were rolled by Bea Vertefeuille, 448; Mary Doud, 444; Margaret Hartnett, 436; Kay Gemmelli 409; and Leona Doud who hit a 186 high single with Kay Gemmelli tying her in this division. Adell Inglis, whom the girls have dubbed "Miss America" hit a 149 single and a 402 triple.

Second Wartime Contingent Of 47 Cohoes Men Leaves For Army Service

HUGE CROWD JAMS CITY HALL TO BID GROUP FAREWELL

Departing Draftees Presented Gifts by Mayor Rudolph Roulier; Michael Ensel Named Leader.

An estimated 300 relatives, friends and officials jammed City Hall this morning to bid farewell to the largest and the second wartime contingent of 47 Cohoes men.

It was the largest group of residents that gathered in the City Hall in recent years. The departing men were presented with shaving kits from Mayor Rudolph Roulier as a gift from the city.

Rev. Adrien J. Bechard, pastor of St. Marie's Church, represented the clergy. Final instructions of the board were given by Angus D. MacAffer, secretary.

The Joseph Gadoua Garrison, Army and Navy Union, band played patriotic marches while women of the Cohoes Chapter, American Red Cross, passed out candy, post cards and magazines to the draftees.

Michael Ensel, 4 Broadway, was named leader and Carter J. Higgins, former employee of the city treasurer's office, was named assistant leader.

Meantime, the Cohoes Selective Service Board has placed a large number of men in Class 1-A after they had been given their physical examinations recently.

Forty Hours' Devotion.

Forty Hours' Devotion is scheduled to open at the 8 a.m. mass Sunday at St. Agnes Church, according to an announcement by Rev. Joseph A. Franklin, pastor. Children of the parish will take part in a procession.

The devotional period will be concluded Tuesday night, March 17. Featuring the closing service will be a procession in which men of the parish, members of Cohoes Assembly, Fourth Degree Knights of Columbus, and representatives of the cadet battalions of LaSalle Institute and Christian Brothers Academy, with the national and regimental colors, will act as guard of honor to the Blessed Sacrament.

YOU GIRLS!
13 to 25 Who Suffer
DYSMENORRHEA
Which Makes You
Tired, Nervous—

If at such times pain and distress of functional monthly disturbances make you feel weak, dragged out, cranky, nervous—try Lydia E. Pinkham's Vegetable Compound—made *especially for women!*

Pinkham's Compound not only helps relieve monthly pain (cramps, headache, backache), but also helps soothe nervousness of such days when due to this cause. Taken regularly through the month—it helps build up resistance against such symptoms. Thousands upon thousands of women helped! Follow label directions.

WURLITZER PIANOS
Follett Piano Co.
at
"Growing Through Service"
(Miller's Music Store, Est. 1855)
73 Fourth St., Troy Phone 5239

YOUR FRIENDS AND NEIGHBORS
Are Doing It, Why Not Join Them

Your Government requests that you do not spend your Surplus earnings unwisely but invest them in United States

DEFENSE BONDS

During February your Friends and Neighbors invested their Surplus earnings in Defense Bonds; they bought $47,800 worth of bonds and $857.00 worth of Defense Stamps. Don't be left behind—join them.

"YOU'LL BE GLAD YOU SAVED YOUR MONEY"

Cohoes Savings Bank
COHOES' OLDEST BANK

Largest Group Leaves for Training From Cohoes

Assembled on the steps of the Cohoes City Hall, the largest group of draftees from that city since introduction of the Selective Service System, prepares to leave following simple ceremonies of farewell this morning conducted by city officials in the presence of friends and relatives.

METER RECEIPTS DROP TO LOWEST MONTHLY INTAKE

Average Daily Income in February Was $37.78 as Compared to $41.06 in January.

Parking meter receipts in Cohoes dropped to their lowest monthly intake since the installation month when $868.94 was taken in during February, the report of the city treasurer's office to Mayor Rudolph Roulier showed.

The average daily income for the last month was $37.78 while the January daily average was $41.06. Last March the daily average was only $30.84 but it was not for a complete month because the meters were installed during the second week.

The addition of last month's receipts brought the total figure to $12,104.95 for 11 months. Of this $9,078.73 has been sent to the meter company while $3,026.25 was retained by the city.

KNIGHTS TO MEET ST. PATRICK'S DAY FOR YEARLY EVENT

Past Grands To Be Honored at Council Quarters; March 22 Set for Communion Breakfast.

Plans for several events to take place in the near future are being outlined by Cohoes Council, Knights of Columbus.

The group has completed arrangements for the St. Patrick's Night gathering Tuesday night, March 17. "Past Grand Knights' Night" will be observed at that time. A ham and cabbage supper will feature the gathering, which will be held at the council quarters on Remsen Street. Thomas Burns, sr., is general chairman of the affair.

Sunday, March 22, has been set as the date for the council's annual communion breakfast. Members will receive Holy Communion in a body at Sacred Heart Church, following which the breakfast will be served in the cafeteria of Keveny Memorial Academy. Announcement of the speaker for the occasion and other details of the program will be made within the next few days. Preliminary plans are being made for the group's annual Easter Ball, to be conducted at Moonlight Garden, Green Island.

NAME MISS CARTER TO SCHOOL FACULTY

Announcement of the appointment of Miss M. Janet Carter, daughter of Dr. J. H. Carter and Mrs. Carter of 22 Mann Avenue, to the faculty of Cohoes High School, was made today by James V. Marra, president of the board of education.

Miss Carter will serve in the commercial department and the appointment is effective immediately. She was graduated from Cohoes High School and the College of St. Rose.

VAN SCHAICK SCHOOL SELLS $775.50 IN BONDS AND STAMPS

Defense bonds and stamps totaling $775.50 have been sold to date in the campaign being conducted at the Van Schaick Island School. It was announced today. This week's stamp sales aggregated $87.05.

John Monast of the seventh grade is listed as having purchased $12 worth of stamps this week. Purchase of $5 worth each were made by Joan Bernard of the second grade, Joanne Manoni of the kindergarten and Carol Soltys of the first grade.

RICHARD BOLTON GETS FIRST SERIAL NUMBER IN DRAFT

Order Numbers Will Be Assigned Registrants After National Lottery at Washington Next Tuesday.

The registration card of Richard E. Bolton, 21, 205 Remsen Street, student, was marked No. T-1 in the serial number lottery conducted by the Selective Service Board 345 yesterday afternoon.

The first card was drawn out of the wire revolving drum by Miss Mary Y. Archibald, assistant city librarian. The board members, Daniel J. Coagro, chairman; Angus D. MacAffer, and Arthur L. Lalonde, member, were in charge of the drawing.

The first ten new registrants to receive their serial numbers besides Bolton were: Edmond J. Carmel, 126 Central Avenue, T-2; James E. Reed, 63 Canvass Street, T-3; Rene J. Vautrin, 21 Olmstead Street, T-4; George S. Martin, 44 Younglove Avenue, T-5; Faida LaBonte, 172 Bridge Avenue, T-6; John J. Sheehan, jr., 59 Younglove Avenue, T-7; Raymond F. Van Slett, 12 Richmond Street, T-8; Clement J. Clifford, 96 Myrtel Street, T-9, and Charles H. Maguire, jr., 71 Reservoir Street, T-10.

At the conclusion of the drawing all 1,387 Cohoes men registered in the third national registration received their serial numbers. In the following step, order numbers will be assigned to prospective draftees after the national lottery next Tuesday. The questionnaires will be sent out in the order the order numbers are drawn.

Wins College Honor.

Tufts College Dental School has announced the award of an honor to a former Cohoes resident.

The school has announced that Frank W. Archibald, son of Dr. H. N. Archibald, formerly of Cohoes, has been appointed Carnegie University. In making the announcement the Tufts bulletin described him as the "outstanding member of the senior class" at the dental school.

Under the grant Archibald will spend one year in clinical work and the next year will be resident in oral surgery at Rochester University.

Veterans' Session.

A meeting of Cohoes Post, Veterans of Foreign Wars, is scheduled to be conducted Thursday at 8 p.m. at the rooms on Remsen Street. Commander David Mayeroff will preside during the business session, which will be followed by a social time.

Hospital Unit Meets.

Members of the Women's Auxiliary of Cohoes Hospital will meet today at 2:30 p.m. in the Nurses' Home. Mrs. Francis M. Noonan, president of the group, presided during the business session, which was followed by a social period.

To Plan Banquet.

Plans for the annual present and past officers' banquet to be conducted by Cohoes Chapter, No. 166, R. A. M., will be outlined at a meeting of the group tomorrow night at the Masonic Temple. Charles E. Dawson is general chairman of the arrangement committee.

Decision Reserved.

The combined negligence action of Alphonse Berger of Latham against Joseph Lasek, 4 Strong Place, was tried this morning before City Judge W. Stanton Ablett. Decision was reserved. Berger, plaintiff in the first action, asks $435 for damages to his car while Lasek in the second case asks for his machine. The accident occurred Nov. 16, 1940, on Route 9.

DEFENSE DISCUSSED BY DR. ARCHIBOLD AT SILLIMAN CLUB

Dr. James MacF. Archibold, chairman of the Medical Division of the Cohoes Defense Council, was the speaker at a meeting of the Silliman Club of Silliman Memorial Presbyterian Church conducted last night in the church house.

Having as his topic "Defense—What Are We Doing About It?" the physician gave an outline of the local medical defense program, including the establishment of casualty stations and the assigning of doctors and nurses to the various sites. He pointed out the various ways in which the public can cooperate in the program. Questions relative to defense were answered by the physician following the address.

The speaker was introduced by Mrs. Douglas Fletcher, president of the group, who presided. Mrs. Gilbert C. Bindewald was in charge of the program.

During the business session arrangements were discussed for a "foodless" food sale the last week of this month. Following the meeting a social period was enjoyed and refreshments were served.

Honor Roll Totals 43.

Forty-three Cohoes High School students made the honor roll last month, Charles E. Wheeler, principal, announced. Of the group, 18 were seniors, 8 juniors, 15 sophomores and 7 freshmen.

Church Unit to Meet.

A meeting of the Mothers' Society of St. John's Episcopal Church is scheduled to be conducted tomorrow at 2:30 p.m. at the residence of Mrs. M. P. Morse, 75 Broadway.

Obituary.

Mrs. Augusta Mossey Webb, widow of George W. Webb, died yesterday at the residence of George A. Webb, 181 Remsen Street, Cohoes, after a short illness. She was born in Northside and had been a resident of Cohoes most of her life. She was a communicant of St. Joseph's Church, Cohoes. The survivors are one daughter, Mrs. Edna Perras; one granddaughter, Miss Caroline Perras; two sisters, Mrs. Mary J. Dufort and Mrs. George LaPorte and two brothers, Arthur N. and William H. Mossey, all of Cohoes.

Funeral services will be held Thursday at 8:30 a.m. from the James S. Calkins and Son Funeral Parlors, 108 Mohawk Street, Cohoes, and at 9 a.m. from St. Joseph's Church where a solemn requiem mass will be sung. Burial will be in St. Joseph's Cemetery, Waterford.

The funeral of Joseph Duclos was held this morning from the A. G. Boivin's Sons, Inc., funeral home, 70 Congress Street, and later from St. Joseph's Church, where a solemn mass of requiem was celebrated by Rev. Leo H. Paradis with Rev. Augustus Supernant as deacon and Rev. Celas A. Robitaille as subdeacon. Rev. L. A. Lavigne, M.R., and Rev. Raoul A. Lavalee were seated in the sanctuary. The Gregorian funeral mass was sung by Mrs. Gertrude Cone, Miss Cecile M. Rivet and Henry P. Pellegrin with Max Pellegrin at the organ. "Pie Jesu" was rendered at the offertory. Bearers were Emilien Isabel, Amedee Girard, John LeClair, Romeo Lefebvre, Rosario Ouimet and Archille Vautrin. Interment will take place tomorrow at Sherrington, P. Q., Canada.

The funeral of Charles E. Borden was held this morning from the funeral home of A. G. Boivin's Sons, Inc., 70 Congress Street. St. Patrick's Church where a requiem high mass was celebrated by Rev. Thomas A. Flanagan. Bearers were Fred J. Bouchard, William Dubrey, George Granger, George Godfrey, Wallace Riberdy and John J. Van Hoamer. Interment will be in St. Joseph's Cemetery, Waterford. A delegation from Cohoes Lodge, 1332 I. O. O. M. conducted services at the funeral home last night and attended the funeral today.

E. T. RUANE POST PLANS TO OBSERVE 23RD ANNIVERSARY

Members of Group To Be Guests of Ladies' Auxiliary at Birthday Party Sunday.

The 23rd anniversary of the founding of E. T. Ruane Post, American Legion, will be marked by a birthday party to be tendered members of the group Sunday afternoon by the Ladies' Auxiliary. The gathering will be held at the Legion quarters on Oneida Street and will open at 4:30 p.m.

Dinner will be served and several speakers are scheduled to address the units, their names to be announced later. A program of entertainment will be presented.

Plans for the function were outlined at a meeting of the auxiliary last night at the rooms, with Mrs. Mary Kilduff, president, presiding. Mrs. Catherine Dennehy and Mrs. Sarah Holleran were chosen as co-chairmen of the arrangement committee, which includes Mrs. Eva Connors, Mrs. Mary Landry, Mrs. Margaret Willett, Mrs. Mary Plouffe, Mrs. Pearl Smith, Mrs. Anna Mae Patnode and Mrs. Elizabeth Parker. Reservations are under the direction of Mrs. Dennenny, Mrs. Holleran and Mrs. Kilduff.

At last night's session plans were also outlined for the county auxiliary gathering to be conducted here Friday night, March 20. Mrs. Andrew Deheus of Elsmere, county chairman, will preside.

A social under the joint auspices of the post and auxiliary will be conducted at the rooms Thursday night. Mrs. Smith and Alvin P. Bullock are co-chairmen of the arrangements committee.

CERTIFICATES FOR TIRES ISSUED TO THREE RESIDENTS

Two Wholesale Food Dealers Included in List; Purchase of Car Approved by Rationing Board.

Three additional tire certificates were issued today by the Cohoes Rationing Board. At the same time, the board issued its first certificate permitting the purchase of a new car.

Those allowed to buy tires were: Raymond Lynch, 90 Willow Street, two light tires and one tube for wholesale delivery of food. John J. Gabriel, 50 Champlain Street, two light tire and tube, wholesale food delivery. Leo Phoenix, Boght Road, one light tire, wholesale milk delivery.

The certificate allowing the purchase of a car was issued to William Wygert, 78 Rensselaer Avenue, on the reason that it was essential to his work in war industry.

MOTORISTS BUY 75 AUTO TAX STAMPS

Cohoes motorists purchased 75 auto use tax stamps which are being sold for $1.67 this month at the Cohoes Postoffice. The price of stamps will decline each month until July 1 when the $5 tax stamps will go on sale.

Nearly 8,000 auto stamps for $2.09 were sold in Cohoes prior to Feb. 1, which was the first deadline for obtaining the federal tags. The Postoffice has been filled daily this week as income tax payers rushed to obtain money orders to be enclosed with the income tax blanks.

Garrison Will Meet.

A meeting of Joseph Gadoua Garrison, Army and Navy Union, will be conducted today at 8 p.m. at the rooms on Mohawk Street. Commander Myer Cramer will preside during a brief business session, following which members of the group will visit the home of the late Patrick Thomas Daly, 28 Garner Street.

Leaves Hospital.

One of the three women taken to Cohoes Hospital Sunday night as a result of injuries sustained in a three-car crash in Ontario Street, Mrs. Anna Macejka of 1214 Fifth Avenue, Schenectady, returned to her home.

Mrs. Anna Spaan of R. D. 1, Cohoes, who sustained injuries to her forehead and left eye and who is also suffering from shock, and Mrs. Josephine Dufresne of 71 Third Street, Northside, remain at the hospital.

TROY PASTOR WILL CONDUCT SERVICE AT FIRST CHURCH

Rev. Frederick Allen, D.D., To Give Communion Meditation at Baptist Program Thursday Night.

WATERFORD

Rev. Frederick Allen, D.D., pastor of the First Baptist Church of Troy, will conduct a communion service at the First Baptist Church here Thursday evening. The program of the service is as follows:
Prelude "Communion"   Nolte
Processional
Invocation and Choral Amen
Hymn "Lord, As We Thy Name Profess"
Anthem "Saviour, Thy Dying Love"   Nolte
Prayer and choral response
Anthem "Remember Calvary"   Meredith
Sung by the choir
Communion Meditation—
Rev. Frederick Allen
Vocal solo—"Jesu, Jesu Miserere"   Nevin
Sung by Miss Hazel Abrams
Hymn of Fellowship "Blest Be the Tie That Binds"
Benediction with choral response
Postlude—

The choir will be under the direction of Miss Hazel Abrams, and Miss Winifred Hicks will preside at the organ.

To Hold Supper.

The Philathea Class of the First Baptist Church will hold a covered dish supper Friday evening in the chapel of the church at 6:30 p.m.

Auxiliary To Meet.

The Ladies' Auxiliary of the Knickerbocker Steamer Co. will hold its regular meeting today at 8 p.m. in the rooms on Pearl Street. Mrs. Mary Kane will preside.

Conduct Contest.

Troop 31, Boy Scouts, will hold its regular meeting today at 7:30 p.m. in their rooms at the Methodist Church, with G. Raymond Anderson, scoutmaster, in charge. A personal contest is being conducted by members of the troop.

Camp Fire Girls Plan Party.

The Tatapochon Camp Fire Girls will hold a meeting today at 7:30 p.m. in the Methodist Church. Plans will be made for the kitchen caper party to be held at the meeting next week. Work on the birthday.

---

day honor will be checked to determine the number to receive the honor.

Schedule Pinochle Game.

The next game in the pinochle tournament being conducted by teams from the Waterford Council Knights of Columbus, and Clinton Lodge, F. and A. M., will be held at the Masonic Temple Thursday at 8 p.m. The K. of C. is leading in the series with a total score of 569,670 to 567,960 for the Masons.

Ionic Chapter Meets.

Ionic Chapter, Order of Eastern Star, met last night in the Masonic Temple, with Mrs. Miriam Hidings worthy matron, and Milford E. Frost, worthy patron, presiding. Mrs. Elizabeth Mill and Mrs. Vera M. Chemberlin were the hostesses for the social time which followed the business session. The chapter will hold a brief meeting March 23 at 8 p.m. and will go from the Temple to attend the visitation of the Grand Matron of the state at the Ten Eyck in Albany.

To Address Group.

The Waterford Parent-Teacher Association will hold its next meeting Monday at 8 p.m. in School 2 in Northside, with Mrs. Raymond Conklin presiding. Dr. Mary Blaghner of Troy will speak on the subject, "Sustaining Mental Health." There will be a motion picture on "Fishing." A committee will be appointed at this meeting to nominate for the election of officers to be held at the April meeting. The hostesses for the meeting will be Mrs. Roland Juenger and Mrs. Frank Jones.

If Your Child Catches Cold Listen—

—listen to millions of experienced mothers and relieve miseries with the IMPROVED Vicks treatment that takes only 3 minutes and makes good old Vicks VapoRub give BETTER THAN EVER RESULTS! IT ACTS 2 WAYS AT ONCE to bring relief.

2 WAYS AT ONCE

PENETRATES to upper breathing passages with soothing medicinal vapors. STIMULATES chest and back surfaces like a warming poultice.

Works for hours to ease coughs, relieve muscular soreness or tightness, and bring real, honest-to-goodness comfort.

To get this improved treatment... just massage VapoRub for 3 minutes ON BACK as well as throat and chest, then spread thick layer of best and cover with warmed cloth.

VICKS
VapoRub
The Improved Way

AT UNION HOME FURNISHERS

FOR EXPERT WINDOW
WASHING, CLEANING
AND POLISHING

CALL

THE TROY WINDOW &
HOUSE CLEANING CO.
Jos. Sullivan, Pres. & Treas.
Phone Troy 2127

REPAIR TYPEWRITERS
AND ADDING MACHINES
FOR DEFENSE
WE REPAIR ALL MAKES
AGENCY
FOR NEW L. C. SMITH and
CORONA TYPEWRITERS
Victor, Corona and Barrett
Adding Machines

COPELAND TYPEWRITER
AGENCY
416 Fulton St.
Telephone Troy 3556
Our Truck Picks Up and Delivers

THE WEATHER

Series 1942 No. 61.

THE TIMES RECORD

TROY, N. Y., FRIDAY EVENING, MARCH 13, 1942

PRICE THREE CENTS

Jap Fleet Near Solomon Islands

Seven Convicted German Spies Given Prison Terms Ranging Up To 20 Years

POLICE SUPPRESS ANTI-AXIS RIOTS IN RIO DE JANEIRO

Brazilian Throngs Stage Angry Demonstrations Against Nazi Attacks on Nation's Shipping.

Rio De Janeiro (U.P.)—Police fired into the air today in an effort to disperse angry crowds of rioters demonstrating for the second day against Nazi sinkings of Brazilian ships.

The shots were fired when a new demonstration broke out in front of a German-owned drugstore in the heart of Rio's downtown business district.

First reports said no one had been injured and it was believed the officers' guns were loaded with blank cartridges.

Crowds roamed through the streets, congregating in front of Axis commercial establishments and shouting demands that they raise the Brazilian flag.

Heavy Police Patrols.

Police, anticipating a renewal of the demonstrations, had taken up strategic positions in the areas where Axis establishments are located.

The demonstrations started yesterday afternoon and continued into the night when crowds smashed several German bars and restaurants in the aristocratic Copacabana district around midnight.

Police squads were reported to have broken up several attempted demonstrations by speedy action and the use of blank cartridges.

Reports from interior Brazil points revealed that similar demonstrations have broken out at many points.

Reports from Bahia said that several German concerns were attacked by mobs.

Rio In Festive Garb.

The downtown area of Rio today had a festive appearance. All foreign firms hoisted their national flags and there was a sunburst of American and British colors. Brazilian firms flew the Brazilian colors. Axis businesses did not fly Axis flags and in most instances hoisted that of Brazil.

Several thousand police were on duty with riot squads stationed at all principal intersections.

Crowds demonstrated in front of Japanese firms, including the offices of the Asaka Shipping Line and the firm of Hachiya Brothers, a toy concern.

The crowds paid little or no attention to Italian firms. The Brazilian press, it was noted, never has treated the Italian war effort seriously.

RUSSIA PERSISTS IN CHARGE NAZIS HAVE FRENCH WARSHIPS

London (U.P.)—Russia, persisting in its charge that the Vichy government is handing over French warships to Germany, said today that the Germans were operating special naval schools at numerous French ports to train German seamen to operate the ships.

It was asserted that several thousand German seamen were now at Toulon, the great Mediterranean naval base in unoccupied France, to form crews for the 26,500 ton battleship Dunkerque.

Further, it said, Grand Admiral Erich Raeder, German naval commander in chief, had issued a secret order for formation of German crews for ships handed over by the French, to be ready by April 10.

Russia broadcast its charge over the Moscow radio, quoting a Cairo dispatch of the official news agency Tass.

Sergeant Honored for Pearl Harbor Alert

Staff Sergt. Joseph L. Lockard (center), who was a private when he gave the un-heeded alarm that planes were approaching Pearl Harbor Dec. 7, received the Distinguished Service Medal from Undersecretary of War Robert P. Patterson (left) in Washington. At the right is Rep. Forest A. Harness (R., Ind.).

WAGE CONTROL IS UNDER STUDY

President Reveals Subject Being Considered as War Measure.

Washington (AP)—The question of wage control as a war measure is under study, President Roosevelt asserted today.

The Chief Executive declined at a press conference to go into the question of putting a ceiling on wages as an anti-inflation step but he did disclose that the whole problem was under consideration.

Asked whether he was considering "positive action on wage control," he replied crisply, it is under study.

To another question, whether any progress was being made on controlling inflation, Mr. Roosevelt said, in some ways, yes, and in some ways, no. He placed the action of the House in voting to ban sales of government-owned surplus farm products at below parity prices in the category of those things on what he termed the no side.

Proponents of a wage ceiling have contended it is necessary to cut down purchasing power of individuals if inflation is to be checked, just as it is necessary to control prices.

Mr. Roosevelt was asked whether he had arrived at any opinion on how the Canadian system of wage control might work in this country. He said he did not know and had no news on the matter. This is only one factor of the situation which is under study, he said.

While Mrs. Roosevelt had written in her newspaper column of a meeting at the White House at which wage control was discussed, the Chief Executive said he had not participated in the meeting.

ARLINGTON, VA., MAY INCORPORATE AS CITY

Richmond, Va. (AP)—Virginia may get a new city.

The general assembly has granted authority to citizens of Arlington County to incorporate as a city if they so desire. The small county, just across the Potomac River from Washington and once a part of the District of Columbia, has a population of over 57,000—and it is growing rapidly as the nation's capital grows.

If the voters decide in a referendum to incorporate as a city, Arlington will be the fourth in size in the old dominion, exceeded only by Richmond, Norfolk and Roanoke.

Man, Thrice Saved At Sea, Killed by Taxicab

Newark, N. J. (AP)—The borrowed time on which Captain Bennett D. Coleman had been living since his schooner was wrecked at sea last week ended abruptly last night in an automobile crash.

The 73-year-old mariner three times escaped a seaman's death, but a taxicab in which he was a passenger and an automobile collided at South Orange Avenue and Twentieth Street last night. Captain Coleman was dead before arrival of an ambulance.

Just a week ago in a storm off Cape Hatteras the Falmouth Heights, Mass., Skipper was rescued for the third time by the Coast Guard when his four-masted schooner the Anna R. Heidritter with a cargo for Philadelphia out of Charleston, S. C., foundered in a storm.

GIRL, 15, HELD FOR SLAYING FATHER

Farm Child Tells Police Story of Frequent Beatings by Parent.

Valley View, Pa. (AP)—A motherless, 15-year-old girl who tearfully complained that her father had abused her once too often shot and killed him last night, state police reported today.

Private H. E. Bell of the state motor police said Peter Peoletti, 44-year-old farmer, had been killed by a shotgun blast in the back of the head.

With Schuylkill County Detectives Louis Buono and Bruce Clayton, Bell related that Peoletti's young daughter told them that her father had beaten her frequently. She was taken into custody by the detectives but no charges have been filed.

Bell reported that father and daughter had lived alone on a little farm in an isolated section near this eastern Pennsylvania community since Mrs. Peoletti died. Last midnight, he said the girl told him, Peoletti tried to abuse her again. She snatched up a shotgun and fired, later fleeing to the home of two brothers who lived nearby.

The officers said the brothers also told of ill-treatment at the hands of their father.

YOUTH DIES IN CRASH.

Watertown (AP)—Walter S. Brezezinski, 19, Lafargeville, was killed early today when the automobile he was operating was struck by another car near here.

PRESIDENT MAY VETO FARM BILL

Clause Banning Disposal of Surplus Products Flouts War Policy.

Washington (AP)—A high administration source said today that President Roosevelt was considering veto of the $695,000,000 farm supply bill because it bans disposal of government-controlled stocks of farm products at less than parity.

The President was beaten both in Senate and House on his plea that the prohibition be eliminated to help prevent a further rise in the cost of living. He was reported to believe that only by a veto could he win his point.

The Senate recently passed and sent to the House a bill containing the ban. The House, which is still considering the appropriation bill, has refused to remove a clause to prohibit the Commodity Credit Corporation using any administrative funds in connection with sales of its surplus stocks below parity, with minor exceptions.

A veto would mean that the measure, carrying money for the administration's farm programs beginning July 1, would be returned to Congress for further consideration. Legislators said that it would have to be approved in some form soon after that date to avoid suspension of farmer benefit payments.

SUB RAMMED INTO LIFEBOATS, SHIP SURVIVORS CLAIM

Philadelphia, (AP)—The tale of an unmerciful submarine crew which first sank a tanker by shellfire and then ran down and smashed through two lifeboats and a life-raft was entered today in the ever-growing sea legends of the second World War.

It was told by four survivors of a crew of 38 aboard a medium-sized U. S. tanker which went down in the Caribbean Sea Feb. 28.

For more than a week they drifted on two small rafts after the submarine, striking without warning, fired about 200 shells into their ship. It was not torpedoed, they said, but sank within five hours after the attack.

The quartet was picked up by another ship on March 5 and landed here Tuesday night.

EXECUTE SLAYER OF WIFE, FIVE CHILDREN

Montgomery, Ala., (AP) — Esker Washington Gibson, 32, convicted of burning his wife to death and accused of destroying his five children in the same fire, died in Kilby Prison's electric chair early today.

Gibson's plea for clemency was denied yesterday by Gov. Frank Dixon. Gibson's wife and five children perished in the family's flame-swept home at Irvington, Ala., the night of April 24, 1941.

POST EDITOR RESIGNS.

Philadelphia (U.P.) — Wesley Winans Stout has resigned as editor of the Saturday Evening Post, effective Monday, because of a "firm but friendly disagreement with the company on policy," and will be succeeded by Ben Hibbs, editor of the Country Gentleman, the Curtis Publishing Co. said today.

Pullman Company Granted Rate Boost

Washington (U.P.)—The Interstate Commerce Commission today authorized the Pullman Co. to increase its rates, fares, and charges by 10 per cent.

The commission found that existing revenues of the company are inadequate, and that the increase would be "just and reasonable."

The increased rates may be made effective upon not less than ten days' notice to the commission.

"It is important, especially in the present national emergency, that those services be maintained at the maxmium of efficiency," the commission said.

But it added that the company could not be expected to continue "to pay in expenses and taxes more than 96 cents out of every dollar earned, as it did in the last four years, and in addition bear increased wages and payroll taxes of about $6,000,000 annually, not to mention increased costs of materials and supplies, without jeopardizing the maximum war effort."

On the basis of 1941 revenues the 10 per cent increase would bring the company about $5,000,000 annually.

SIX MEN, WOMAN, NAZI AGENTS, ARE JEERED BY CROWD

Kurt Ludwig, Leader of Ring, Borchardt and Froelich, Former U. S. Soldier, Get Maximum Terms.

New York (UP)—Six men and a woman convicted of spying in the United States for Nazi Germany were sentenced today to prison terms ranging from 12 to 20 years by Federal Judge Henry W. Goddard.

A crowd which jammed the halls of the Federal Building booed and hissed the prisoners when they were led from the court room at the conclusion of the first espionage trial since the United States entered the war.

Kurt Frederick Ludwig, brains of the ring, Paul T. Borchardt, a former major in the German army in the first World War and Rene Froehlich, who was drafted into the United States Army last year, were given the maximum sentence of 20 years.

Lesser Sentences.

Hans Helmut Page, who admitted his guilt after the trial began, Mrs. Helen Pauline Mayer, a housewife whose husband fled to Japan last year, and Karl Victor Mueller, 36-year-old machinist, were given terms of [illegible] years.

Frederick Edward Schlosser, 20, drew the lightest sentence, 12 years.

Lucy Boehmler, 18-year-old secretary to the spy ring, and Carl Hermann Schroetter, a Miami boat captain, pleaded guilty before the trial began. They will be sentenced later. Miss Boehmler was the government's star witness in the lengthy trial.

Former Soldier Denounced.

Judge Goddard, castigating each defendant as he imposed the individual sentences, was particularly concerned over the role played by Froehlich, the United States soldier. Froehlich, he said, was the "most treacherous because he gave information to the ring both as a citizen and as a soldier."

In the cases of the others, the court commented:

Mrs. Mayer: "This woman thought she could get away with being a spy because she was a woman. Anyone on a boat sunk by a German torpedo is not given special consideration because that information is passed on by a woman."

Borchardt and Ludwig: "This man (Borchardt) is of equal prominence with Ludwig in this case, but he was more skillful in keeping his activities in the background."

Sent Information Abroad.

Trial testimony developed that the ring gathered information about United States shipping, Army camps, morale, defense production and Army movements, and sent this information, many times in secret writing, to agents in Spain and Germany.

In pleading for his client, Froelich, Defense Atty. Charles Oberwager, characterized him as a mental case, but Judge Goddard commented that "you would be more successful in describing him as a shrewd actor."

The defense asked that Froehlich be permitted to rejoin the Army and Judge Goddard asked: "Would it be fair to loyal soldiers in our Army to sen back into their midst a spy?"

"A great lesson in the American system of justice has been learned at this trial," Oberwager said, adding that "emotion of the war

(Continued on Page 6).

YOUNG MOTHER AND MALE FRIEND FOUND DEAD IN AUTOMOBILE

New Bedford, Mass. (AP)—A young mother of two children and a Manchester, Conn., construction worker were found dead in a parked automobile today in what medical examiner William Rosen described as a case of murder and suicide.

Police Chief Samuel McLeod said the victims were Mrs. Irene Bollea, 28, and Jarvis Webster Presley, 33.

He added that a .32 calibre revolver was found in Presley's hand, and that a note in the car asked that Presley's brother, Leon, of Lacona, Oswego County, N. Y., be notified.

Police Inspector Stephen J. Downey said Mrs. Bollea had been separated from her husband and that she had been friendly with Presley since a year ago last Christmas.

PARIS HAS AIR ALARM.

Vichy (AP)—The Royal Air Force was over the Paris area again today, but no bombs were dropped. Sirens in the French capital sounded the alarm at 3:15 p.m. (9:15 a.m., E.W.T.).

FBI Agent Slain In Gun Battle With Army Deserters

Blackout Area

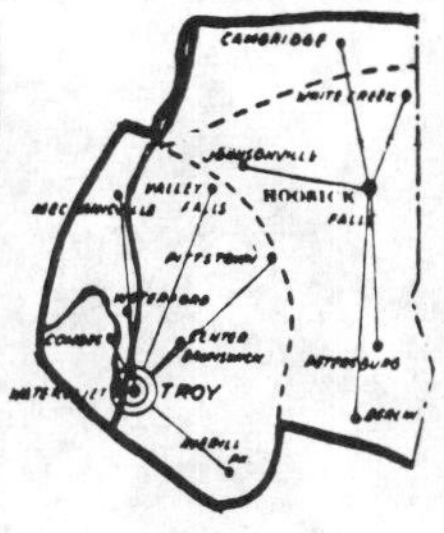

Pictured above is the Troy warning area which will participate in a special blackout some night next week between Sunday and the following Wednesday.

SPECIAL BLACKOUT PLANNED FOR TROY DURING NEXT WEEK

Comes Between Sunday and Wednesday; No Further Announcement on Failure of Test Recently Held

The Troy area warning center will have a special blackout test of its own sometime between Sunday and the following Wednesday night, John J. Farrell, state deputy director of civilian defense, announced today.

"Due to the unfortunate occurrence last Wednesday night when the blackout was conducted, another test will be held between March 15 and March 18 just for the Troy warning area," Mr. Farrell stated.

Meanwhile no further announcement was made following the investigation to determine why Troy failed to receive the red or "lights-out" warning signal Wednesday night.

Conference Held.

Mayor Frank J. Hogan, chairman of the Troy Defense Council, revealed that he had held a long conference yesterday with Col. Thomas Sherman, attached to the State Civilian Defense Office at Albany.

It was implied that as a result of this and other conferences the special test for the Troy warning center was ordered.

Chief communities in the Troy warning center are Troy, Watervliet, Cohoes, Mechanicville, Waterford, Green Island, Northside, the county area south to the City of Renaselaer and not including the City of Rensselaer, Averill Park, Berlin, Petersburg, Pittstown, Valley Falls, Johnsonville, Hoosick Falls and Cambridge.

The Troy warning center map reproduced with this story shows the exact area which will participate, including some communities located within the area and not listed above.

Purpose of Test.

The chief purpose of the special Troy warning center blackout is to determine what happened last Wednesday when Troy failed to receive the red warning or at least to give the communications system a further test.

Meanwhile Boston authorities announced today that the third regional blackout for Massachusetts will be held next Monday night between 9 and 9:20 p.m. Thirty-seven cities and towns in Western Massachusetts, including nearby Williamstown, North Adams, and area cities will participate. The area covered will total 1,053 square miles and will blanket 79,100 persons.

SLIGHT FIRE ON NORMANDIE.

New York (U.P.)—A small fire broke out today in the hulk of the burned liner Normandie, but was extinguished quickly by firemen without damage.

Second Federal Man Wounded in Attempt to Arrest Two Fugitives in Virginia Restaurants.

Abingdon, Va. (AP).—Two Army deserters who shot and killed one F. B. I. agent and wounded another seriously were captured in an abandoned house on the outskirts of Abingdon this afternoon.

More than a hundred Federal, state and local officers surrounded the house and a number of shots were exchanged before tear gas forced the soldiers out.

Abingdon, Va. (AP) An F B I agent was slain and another seriously wounded today in a gun battle in a restaurant where they had gone to arrest a pair of Army deserters.

Agent Hubert J. Treacy, jr. 28, was shot to death and Charles L. Tignor, 29, was wounded five times. They were attempting to arrest two soldiers from Fort Oglethorpe, Ga., Charles J. Lovett, 21 and James Evans Testerman, 22.

The soldier pair, who blazed away as soon as the agents identified themselves in the all-night cafe, had been sought since Thursday when, according to H. I. Bobbitt, special agent in charge of the Richmond F. B. I. office, they stole a supply of pistols and ammunition from the Fort, kidnaped a taxi driver and escaped into Tennessee.

The driver of the taxi was released at Cleveland, Tenn., and the men drove on to Abingdon, where Treacy and Tignor, tipped by the Nashville F. B. I office, were on the lookout.

F. B. I. Agent Slain.

Wallace Ford, another agent, said Treacy was killed instantly and Tignor was wounded in the arm in the cafe as the men, still in Army uniforms, ran out. Tignor, giving chase, fell on the street with four bullet wounds in his chest.

Ford said the pair, each holding two pistols, attempted to commander a car owned by Andy Hilton, of Abingdon, but Policeman Troy Combs jammed his machine into Hilton's. Combs exchanged gunfire with the men as they fled.

The men attempted to take over another car driven by Mrs. Elizabeth Kreger, but she pulled the keys out and tossed them across the street.

The soldiers then ran off in the direction of Lebanon and this morning were the objects of an intensive search throughout Southwest Virginia.

All state troopers in the area were mobilized immediately and they were joined by 65 local officers attending an F. B. I. School at nearby Bristol.

Sentry Badly Beaten.

W. H. Murphy, chief of the F. B. I. office in Knoxville, said there that the pair beat a Fort Oglethorpe sentry severely before commandeering the taxicab. The sentry was identified at Fort Oglethorpe as Sergeant Clifton Hall of Rossville, Ga., and his condition was described as critical today.

Murphy said that both the men were privates in the Third Cavalry assigned to Fort Oglethorpe and gave Lovett's home address as 667 52nd Street, Philadelphia, Testerman's as P. O. Box 76, Lynchburg, Va.

The F. B. I. agent said that after beating up Hall, the soldiers armed themselves with four .45 caliber revolvers and 100 rounds of ammunition. They then held up the Chattanooga cab driver, Charles F. Landreth at Rossville, Ga., and forced him to drive them to Cleveland, Tenn., where they put him out of the cab and drove on. The cab was found abandoned at Sweetwater, Tenn.

WAR BRINGS ABOUT INCREASE OF 5,000 IN WELFARE CASES

Albany (AP)—Feeling the sudden impact of war New York's $152,000,000 social welfare program incurred the burden of more than 5,000 additional public assistance cases from the month preceding Pearl Harbor through January of this year.

Result Of Aluminum Drive Still Mystery

Washington (AP)—The Office for Emergency Management is still trying to find out what happened to all the pots and pans donated by housewives in the aluminum salvage drive nearly seven months ago.

The information division of the office has telepgraphed the 29 aluminum smelters which handled the scrap asking for the exact status of utensils still at the smelters or already in ingot form.

Some of the questions which O.E.M. has been unable to answer, in the face of repeated inquiries, are: How much aluminum, if any, has not yet gone to the smelters? How much aluminum collected during the campaign actually has gotten into war production? How much of it was bought by the R.F.C. Metals Reserve Co. and how much of it was sold by the smelters direct to industrial users?

One War Production Board spokesman said comparatively little of the aluminum reclaimed from the pots and pans went into plane production because of its inferior quality, but that the campaign produced a highly valuable stock of secondary aluminum capable of being used in a wide variety of military items.

Last Sept. 24 the O.P.M. and the Office of Civilian Defense reported jointly that an estimated 11,835,139 pounds of pots and pans were collected. These would yield approximately 7,000,000 pounds of aluminum, they figured.

NIPPONESE MOVE MAY HINT THRUST AT NEW ZEALAND

British Join Forces With Chinese North of Rangoon; Lone U. S. Sub Sinks Four Enemy Ships.

BY THE ASSOCIATED PRESS.

Japan's offensive against Australia, still taking form in the welter of islands curving along the vast northern shore of the continent, has speared off in a tangent of naval penetration of the Solomon Islands.

In the second chief theater of the war with Japan, the British imperials withdrawing north of Rangoon, have for the first time joined Chinese troops, attempting to consolidate a front between two main routes out of Rangoon, sixty to eighty miles from the abandoned port city of the Irrawaddy Delta.

In the Philippines, the United States reported no change in the Bataan Peninsula situation — a watchful waiting for the next all-out Japanese attack on General MacArthur's forces.

Warship Force Sighted.

Japan's Solomon Islands move was evidently either a feint to distract attention from establishment of New Guinea bases for the prospective lunge at Australia or actually a thrust toward the New Hebrides and New Zealand along the island chain pointed at the United Nations sea route to Australia, ahead of any direct attempt to invade the continent.

The move was disclosed by Australian air reconnaissance over the Australian-mandated part of the Solomon group. The warship force was sighted three days ago off Kessa, on tiny Buka Island, a stepping stone from New Britain to the Solomons. There was no further indication that the Japanese had landed there.

Buka is 150 miles southeast of Japanese-occupied Rabaul, New Britain, and 900 miles northeast of Australia's northeastern extremity, the Cape York Peninsula.

Bomb Enemy Airfields.

Australian bombers smashing at the potential island route toward New Zealand attacked the enemy-held airfield at Gasmata, on the south coast of New Britain, yesterday.

"All our bombs fell in the target area and columns of smoke rose from the ground," a communique said. Counter-attacking Japanese fighting planes were beaten off.

The Japanese offensive was crippled to some extent in the sinking or damaging of seven ships by air attack last Tuesday off Salamaua, a Japanese foothold in New Guinea. Closer at home for the enemy, a single United States submarine has picked off four vessels, boosting to 149 the total of Japanese ships destroyed or damaged by U. S. forces.

U. S. Airmen Triumph.

The war department announced that five Japanese planes were destroyed two days ago by five United States Army heavy bombers in a raid on Japanese-held airdromes at Salamaua and Lae, both in New Guinea.

All the airdrome buildings were destroyed and a harbor pier at Lae was hit directly.

Again Japanese fighters challenged the raiders, but five were shot down and the big bombers escaped unscathed.

The war department's announcement, paralleling an Australian communique yesterday which credited the Lae-Salamaua attacks to

(Continued on Page 24.)

FAMILIES OF CIVILIAN WAR CASUALTIES TO GET FEDERAL HELP

Washington (AP)—Families of civilians who are killed, disabled or captured by the enemy in American outposts will receive temporary benefit payments ranging from $30 to $85 a month, the Security Administrater announced today.

A widow or wife without children will receive between $30 and $45 monthly; with one child between $40 and $60; with two children between $50 and $75; and with three or more children between $60 and $85. The scale is based on monthly earnings of the persons affected by enemy action.

The benefits are restricted to families of civilians affected by enemy action outside the continental United States.

Under another program, announced last night, civilians in America who are injured by enemy action, including sabotage, will be given free hospital treatment.

The Index

CLAYTON SHAW, JR., AGAIN PRESIDENT OF COUNTRY CLUB

Woman's Society of Christian Service To Meet at 3 P.M. Tomorrow at Methodist Church.

HOOSICK FALLS

Clayton E. Shaw, jr., president and Harry McGrath, vice president, were reelected last night at the organization meeting of the directors of the Hoosick Falls Country Club. John MacMurtrie, secretary last year, was elected secretary and treasurer, the latter office having been held by Oliver N. Rathbun who declined reelection. The various standing committees were appointed.

Fifty Attend Dinner.

Although the attendance was affected by the blackout there were about fifty persons, including members of both organizations at the dinner given last night by Hoosick Post, No. 40, American Legion, in honor of Cristoforo Colombo Lodge, American Sons of Italy. Past Commander James McLucas was in charge of the menu which featured corned beef and cabbage. Following the dinner an informal social was enjoyed which was interrupted by the blackout during which the hosts and guests sat in the darkness.

Society To Meet.

The Women's Society of Christian Service of the Methodist Church will meet tomorrow at 3 p.m. in the church parlors. The program will include a short play, "The Health of India," by a cast composed of Mrs. Grant Smith, Mrs. J. Earle Percy, and Misses Elva Brenenstuhl, Doris Yetter, Marjorie Beaumont, Marjorie Hutt and Janet Stewart. The Men's class will have its monthly fellowship meeting and supper at 6 p.m. in the church kitchen. Immediately following the nominating committee of the quarterly conference will meet. The monthly meeting of the Official Board will be omitted because of the fourth quarterly conference to be held this month. Choir rehearsal will be held at 7 p.m.

Brevities.

Thursday's meeting of the Potter Hill unit, at the Episcopal Hall in Boyntonville, starting at 8 p.m., will feature a program in the interest of the Red Cross by the "Health Hunters."

A clam chowder sale will be conducted tomorrow afternoon in St. Mark's parish house by St. Hilda's Guild. Mrs. Lucina Roys and Mrs. Stella Shaw are the chairmen. Patrons will be expected to bring their own containers.

The final lesson in the refinishing of furniture will be given at tomorrow's meeting of the Hoosick Falls unit of Rensselaer County Home Bureau in the [illegible]can Legion rooms by Miss Dorothy Bradley, [illegible]

Pride of Asiatic Squadron Sunk in Battle of Java Watervliet Man's "Home"

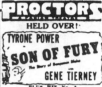

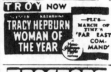

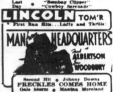

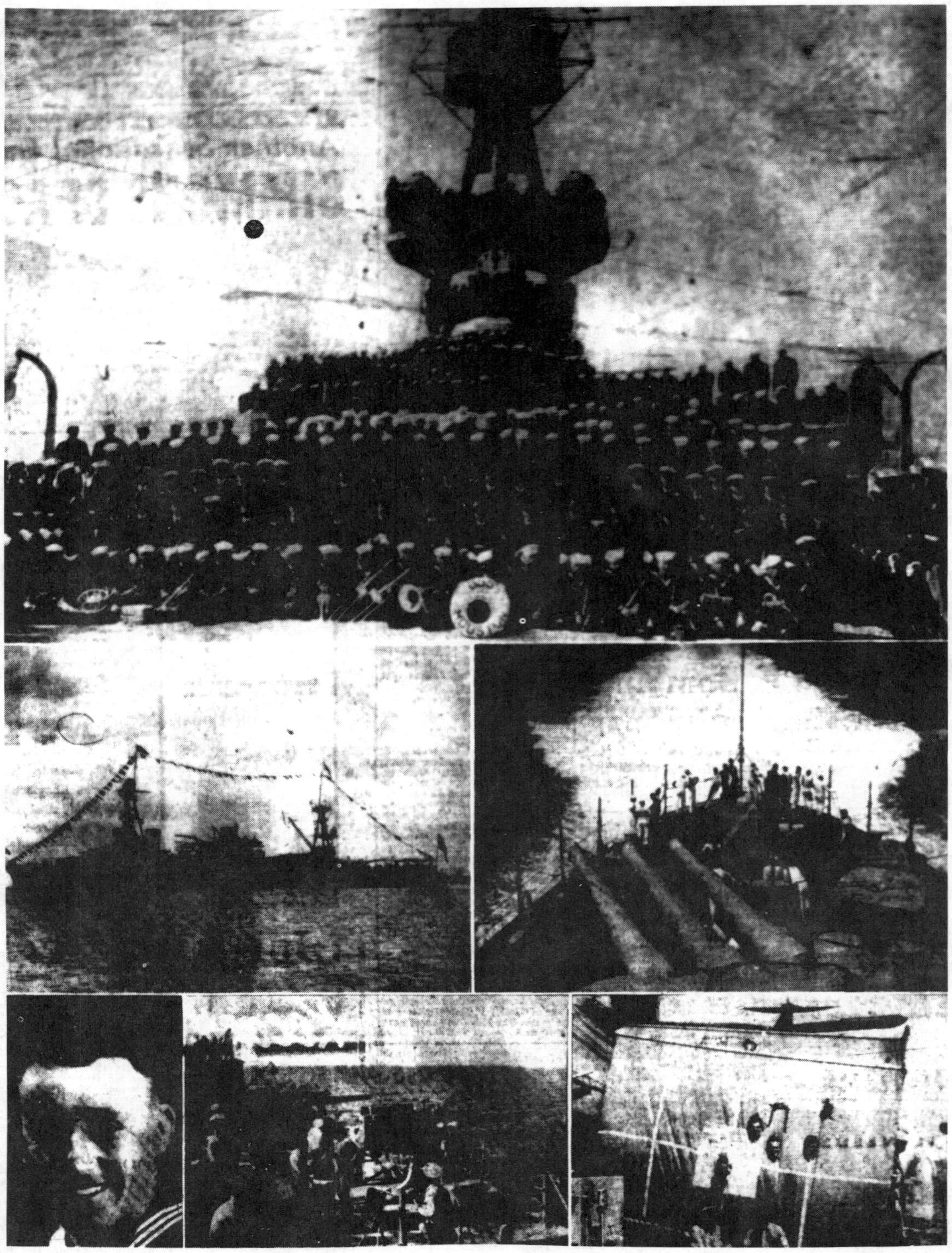

The U. S. S. Houston, one time flagship of the Asiatic squadron, on which Earl C. Patenaude of Watervliet served a few years ago, now lying on the ocean's bottom, victim of the Japanese in the Battle of Java. On top is the ship's entire complement in 1933, with Admiral Montgomery M. Taylor in front center with his Filipino band before him; middle left, the Houston in full dress at China station in observance of Navy Day; middle right, a speed run in China waters with the aft turret showing the "heavy" 9-inch guns; lower left, Patenaude as he was while serving on the Houston; lower center, the Houston coming on range with the 5-inch guns being trained on the target; lower right, the target shot by the Houston to break the 5-inch record for the Navy.

WATERVLIET MAN RECALLS DUTY ON CRUISER HOUSTON

Earl C. Patenaude Served Aboard U. S. Vessel Sent to Bottom During Battle in February.

"That was a real home and it certainly makes my heart ache to think of her lying at the bottom of the ocean," Earl C. Patenaude of 2120 Fourth Avenue, Watervliet, said today as he commented on the sinking of the U. S. S. Houston, 10,000-ton cruiser destroyed in the battle of Java on Feb. 27.

Patenaude served almost his entire enlistment period in the U. S. Navy aboard the Houston, mostly in Eastern waters, while it was the flagship of the Asiatic squadron.

The young man was enlisted at Albany in 1931 and, after his preliminary training at the Training Station at Newport, R. I., was sent immediately to serve on the Houston, then only two years past its launching. He was discharged four years later with a rating of seaman, first class.

Assistant Coxswain.

While on the Houston, which was flagship for Admiral Montgomery Meggs Taylor, then commander of the Asiatic fleet, he served as assistant coxswain on the admiral's barge and was privileged to see many things not grantd to most seamen.

Twice they visited Japan, once to bear condolences for the death of Admiral Toga, hero of the Russo-Japanese war, and paid visits of goodwill to most of the ports of China and the East Indies. While its home port was at Manila, the cruiser spent most of its time in traveling, he said.

Then, in the spring of 1932, reveille was sounded at midnight, the ship took on a detachment of marines and a full supply of fuel and steamed away toward China, arriving off Shanghai just as a Japanese cruiser was shelling the international settlement.

Signal flags were run up for the Jap ship to cease firing so the American vessel could go through and the order was obeyed, but as they passed the belligerents' ship one of its turrets was swung so that the guns commanded the American vessel.

Held Their Fire.

"For a time," Patenaude says, "we thought we were in for some fireworks, but the Japanese continued to hold their fire until we were beyond range. Americans were at their battle stations, ready for war if need be.

They landed the Marines to protect the municipal power works of Shanghai and prevent contamination of the water supply or cutting of the electric lines.

The ship was held in the river ready, if necessary, to evacuate refugees and from its decks Patenaude and the others watched the Japs bomb the city and toss shells into the international settlement.

"She was a sweet ship," Patenaude, now a guard at the Watervliet Arsenal, mourns, "and, for her sake if for nothing else, I will be ready to go back into service when they call me."

MISS HANSON DIES OF HEART ATTACK

One Time Owner of Delicatessen Here Passes Away in Albany.

A few hours after she had completed the sale of Hanson's delicatessen store at 86 Ferry Street, Miss Martha Hanson, 26, died of a heart attack at 2 a.m. yesterday at the home of her aunt, Mrs. Etta Rosenthal, 325 Larch Street, Albany.

Miss Hanson recently disposed of the store to Timothy Sweeney and went to Brooklyn to live with her sister, Mrs. [illegible] Weinstein. She returned to [illegible] Sunday to complete details of [illegible] transaction whereby the store which had been owned by the Hanson family for forty years was sold to Timothy Sweeney.

At the home of her aunt in Albany, she complained of chest pains upon retiring at 11 p.m. At 2 a.m. yesterday she died. A post-mortem examination conducted by Dr. O. A. Brenenstuhl revealed that death had been caused by a heart attack. Miss Hanson had come into possession of the family store upon the death last fall of her brother, Paul Hanson. She was a daughter of the late Mr. and Mrs. Jacob Hanson of Troy.

Survivors include her sister, two aunts, Mrs. Rosenthal and Mrs. Rudnick of Brooklyn and an uncle, Morris Azie of Albany. Rabbi Isaac K. Teicher and Cantor Isaac Werlin of the River Street Synagogue conducted the funeral services at noon today from the Silberg Memorial Chapel, 8[illegible] Madison Avenue, Albany. Burial was in the Congregational Cemetery in Troy.

POWNAL.

Nanette Trimarche returned Saturday to her home in North Adams after a week with her grandparents, Mr. and Mrs. H. Green Brimmer.

Seven tables were in play at the P.-T. A. card party Friday evening at the home of Mrs. Martha Ames. Prizes were awarded to Mrs. Byron F. Towslee, Mrs. Gordon Niles and Frank Buck.

Parent-Teachers will meet at 7:30 p.m. tomorrow with an interesting and instructive program. Norman W. Fuller of the Bennington Y. M. C. A. is expected to speak on "Safety." Superintendent of Schools Francis S. Irons will meet with teachers and school board the same evening in the same building, and it is hoped they can adjourn in time to attend the other meeting. The teachers are to be instructed in their task of issuing sugar rationing cards and, circumstances permitting, Mr. Irons will explain the plan to the larger group.

● ANSWERS TO WAR QUIZ

Questions on Page 3

1. Four stars, full general; three, lieutenant general; two, major general; one, brigadier general.

2. A tin fish is a submarine; a tin can a destroyer and an ash can a depth bomb.

3. Jackson, William H. Harrison, Taylor, Grant, Hayes, Garfield, Benjamin Harrison and Theodore Roosevelt.

DAIRY FARMERS ARE BEING POLLED

New York (AP)—N. J. Cladakis, administrator of the New York metropolitan milk marketing area, said yesterday that ballots were being mailed to 57,145 dairy farmers in the six-state New York milk shed for the referendum on an amended marketing order.

Cladakis, named referendum agent, said the ballots were to be returned to him and must bear a postmark not later than 11:59 p.m. (E.W.T.) Saturday.

Vegetables Take Spotlight At Show

New York (AP)—If you were stranded on an island in the Pacific which would you rather have, a bunch of carrots or a bunch of orchids?

Even if you don't like carrots the answer is obvious—and the same sentiment is in evidence at the 29th International Flower Show, opening in New York yesterday.

In most of the displays, lowly vegetables and flowers occupy first place, while luxury hot-house flowers take a back seat.

Estate gardeners who used to import tulip bulbs from Holland and orchid plants from Java make the most of petunias (now called "glamour blossoms"), bachelor buttons, carrots, marigolds, radishes, candy tuft, peas, portulaca, beans, phlox tomatoes and nasturium.

Veteran gardeners — Commercial growers and garden club ladies— wandering among the sweet-smelling displays at Grand Central Palace, remarked, "it's like pre-war days."

The meant pre-World War I. For it seems the old-fashioned vegetable-and-flower gardens went out of style in the 1920's, giving place to imported plants and delicately-bred hybrids. Even the famous "American Beauty" rose was an artifically-bred product of the jazz age.

Now the American Beauty is no more, its strain having run out, and the sweet and simple five-cents-a-package flowers are in again. Zinnias and anemones aren't fussy about where and how you plant them. They'll share a flower bed with Rosemary and potato plants without a complaint.

The amateur planter, eager to grow a "victory garden," can't fail to produce something either pretty or edible if he makes use of one of the dozens of vitamin-packed plant foods developed within the last few years.

Gardens representing various sections of the United States were "make the most of what you have" productions, demonstrating the wisdom of planting according to local climatic conditions instead of bucking nature.

"Utility gardens" intended for small plots of grounds such as those found in a typical defense housing project, were remarkably compact assemblages of table vegetables and easy-to-grow flowers. They were to be judged for "plan, economy and the greatest utility for a small family."

Most discussed new flower was the "Mrs. Douglas MacArthur sweetpea," originated by David Burpee. It is more vigorous, longer-stemmed, and richer in color than ordinary sweetpeas. Mrs. George C. Marshall, wife of the U. S. Army chief of staff, visited the flower show and accepted a bouquet of these in the name of Mrs. MacArthur.

SENATOR REDUCES FOR ARM.

Albany (UP)—After walking off 67 pounds, State Senator Phelps Phelps is in the Army. Overweight, the senator was rejected last summer. He began walking six to eight miles daily to reduce. He "came in" at 189.

Interpreting The War News

By KIRKE L. SIMPSON.
Wide World War Analyst.

On any other Nazi lips but Hitler's own a vow to defeat Russia during "the coming summer" would be but meaningless rhetoric. It could do little to reveal actual Nazi plans.

In Hitler's mouth, however, that commitment has meaning. His personal prestige, not only with his suppressed people but with his army, is at stake. That army has tasted defeat for the first time in Russia, and under his personal captaincy.

Only complete and final victory in Russia could restore him to his pedestal in the eyes of his troops, and Hitler knows it. That was the price he paid for ousting his top generals and risking the dangers of "Napoleon's fate in 1812," he now admits.

Danger May Not Be Passed.

Whether that danger is yet passed, as Hitler intimated, remains to be seen. There is considerable winter and a long spring thaw yet to be reckoned with in Russia.

Accept the view that his promise of complete victory this summer is a definite Hitler commitment to atone for terrible German losses, and it follows that every future German move, except against Russia, must be regarded as a diversion. Russian armies can be annihilated only in Russia, not on any other front.

Just when and where the summer drive will come depends probably on the weather. The unprecedented winter, the worst in a century or so, must be followed by an unprecedented spring. It will be late June probably before the ground is hard enough in the central and northern Ukraine, and northward to the Leningrad front, for mechanized warfare.

The weather moderates earlier in the southern Ukraine. However, during the thaw season, that area receives the run-off drainage of all western Russia south of the Valdai Hills. The Black Sea and the Sea of Azov receive those spring floods, making every waterway a torrent, every marshland a morass. It probably will be late May or even mid-June before the Nazi "summer offensive' can get going even in the south, and that is the road to oil, the resource above all others Hitler soon must reach.

Japanese, Too.

Oddly enough, June seems also the most probable month for a possible assault on Russia's Vladivostok fortress and Siberian armies. Ice conditions in the northern end of the Sea of Japan tend to forbid any earlier Japanese move to match a Hitler attack on Russia from the west.

That lends color to Chinese and other speculation as to a possible combined Nazi-Japanese squeeze against Russia. It gives added significance to Hitler's fulsome references to "heroic" Japanese victories in the Pacific theater. It is what he hopes for, if not what Japan is yet willing to undertake.

Vladivostok, despite Russian-Japanese non-aggression pacts, is a menacing threat at Japan's back. But if Tokyo has some understanding with Berlin calling for a joint offensive against Russia, it must follow that further Japanese advances in the south against Australia or in Burma are to be restricted to what can be quicly attained. She dare not risk simultaneous major action on three far separated fronts in addition to her China campaign.

The probabilities are that Tokyo would await developments of the Nazi offensive in Russia and strike northward only if it appeared certain to be crowned with success.

JOB ABOLISHED.

Santa Cruz, Cal. (UP)—The city council abolished the position of wharfinger because the amount of work did not justify continuation of such expenditure. Allen S. Lozier, who has held the position, says he hasn't docked a boat in three years.

Monk Simons, New Head Football Coach For Tulane, Started As Mascot

ALSO WAS GREAT STAR FOR SCHOOL SOME YEARS AGO

His Father is Trainer There; Charley Rucker, 1928 Captain, Named Chief Assistant.

New Orleans (AP)—"The Trainer's Little Boy," the gangling kid who used to carry the water bucket, is going to head coach of the Tulane green wave.

Claude "Little Monk" Simons, jr., last night was named boss man of Tulane football—culminating a career that started as mascot of that team and included a period as one of the greatest athletes ever to wear the Olive and Blue.

He will succeed Lowell "Red" Dawson, who resigned Saturday to become an assistant coach at Minnesota, where he was an aide to Bernie Bierman before taking over here in 1936. Simons has been on the staff since 1938, for two years as assistant freshman coach and two as varsity backfield coach.

When "Little Monk" takes charge it probably will be the first time that a major college football team has ever had a father-and-son combination with the son as head coach and the father as trainer.

"Big Monk"—who is about two-thirds the size of his 28-year-old, six-foot-plus, 220-pound son — has been a coach and trainer at Tulane since 1919. He brought "Little Monk" in rompers to watch the team practice and play, and the youngster has been around ever since except for three years as athletic director and football coach at Transylvania College just after he graduated from Tulane in 1936.

Both father and son have coached Tulane baseball and basketball teams, and "Little Monk" is now head tutor in the latter sport. His father also has handled track and boxing, but now sticks to his duties as trainer and instructor in physical education.

Line Coach Charley Rucker, who captained the 1928 team, was named chief assistant of the all-alumni staff.

Racing Notes

By The Associated Press.

New York racing authorities and other patrons of the sport have resumed their drive to provide Uncle Sam with all the binoculars his Navy needs. The sailors desire the loan of thousands of the type used by owners, trainers and handicappers at the track.

To facilitate the immediate delivery of the glasses to the Navy, the sportsmen have established an office and will even provide messengers for collecting purposes in the metropolitan area.

Because the Navy cannot accept gifts, $1 will be paid each person turning in glasses which fill the requirements. After the war, efforts will be made to return each glass to its owner.

More than 50,000 sets were turned over to the Navy during World War No. 1 and all but one glass was returned.

Don Meade will ride either Sir Marlboro or Bull Reigh in the Coral Gables Handicap Saturday if Johnston goes to the post in the Rowe Memorial at Bowie, a stake he won last April, the little man who led the nation's riders during 1942 will fly to Maryland for that race.

Market Wise, Lou Tufano's Cinderella horse, will not race in the Gables Handicap. Trainer George Washington Carroll says the horse suffered several leg cuts in its disappointing appearance in the Widener and will be rested until mid-April.

Col. Ed Bradley's Best Seller, surprise second-place horse in the Widener, carried the stable's Green and White silks to the front in the St. Patrick's Day purse at Tropical Park yesterday.

Sterling Young gave the Blue Larkspur 4-year-old a smart ride and came home a length and a half in front of Mrs. C. S. Bromley's In Question.

Best Seller was the 11 to 20 choice and was clocked in 1:41 2-5, just a fifth of a second off the track record. Third went to Ruth Sidell's Displayer.

Intra-Mural Tourney Opens at R. P. I.

Action in two of the five bouts yesterday in the first round of the R. P. I. Intra-mural Boxing Tourney is shown in these pictures. In the upper photo, Bob Thurston takes aim for a wallop as Ken Borden tries to skip out of harms way. Thurston won. The referee is Walter McNary, boxing instructor at R. P. I. and former well-known fighter. In the lower photo, George Frank misses with a haymaker thrown at Ray Silver. Frank didn't miss them all, however, and emerged the winner.

Three Candidates Loom For Yale Post

BY HUGH FULLERTON, JR.
Wide World Sports Columnist.

New York—Dartmouth's basketballers, who'll tackle Princeton tonight in the Eastern Intercollegiate League playoff at Philadelphia, and then jump to New Orleans for the N. C. A. A. tournament Friday and Saturday, probably will be pleased to know that they won't be unduly fatigued by the chore...Doc. H. C. Carlson, the Pitt coach, has been making a study of the subject and his conclusion is that the athletes ease up late in the game before reaching their limit of stamina... Only if the Indians let up, they'll likely get licked...Latest on the Yale coaching situation via George Trevor of the New York Sun is that the field has been whittled to three candidates—Henry Frnka of Tulsa, Bob Kubale of Southwestern (Memphis) and Jess Neeley of Rice.

Winter Sports Association, which runs the Sugar Bowl show, never saw a football game until the first Sugar Bowl scrap between Tulane and Temple in 1935...Lou Tufano has insured his $1,500 hoss, Market Wise, for $75,000. But that doesn't insure any bets on him.

Today's Guest Star.

Walter Stewart, Memphis Commercial Appeal: "George Washington Case, the Senator base burglar, has a separate source of income. His father left him a secret formula for horse liniment. It's in great demand on trotting tracks, but must be pretty useless in the Washington dressing room. For few of Griff's hands are fast enough to raise a trot."

Shear Nonsense.

Jack North of the Des Moines Tribune claims Hal Trosky will be back with the Indians "providing he finds a good headache remedy and Cleveland raises the salary offer."...Philadelphia Bulletin reports that Ethel Kaumeyer, secretary of the Penn athletic publicity office for 18 years, has been elected secretary of an organization dedicated to the perpetuation of old Philadelphia landmarks. Sounds like a case of self-preservaton...An unidentified Denver Post writer says: "Bing Crosby's La Zonga is a candidate for the Arkansas derby. All the crooner needs to do now is put a little la zinga in La Zonga."

One-Minute Sports Page.

Red Rolfe, who has been undergoing treatment for colitis by a Toledo specialist, plans to report at the Yankees Florida camp this week...The national clay courts tennis tournament, tossed overboard by Chicago on the excuse of "war conditions," probably will be played in St. Louis...Joe David, new head of the New Orleans Mid-

HIRAM GRIMES GIVES GOLDEN BALL TO HIGH SCHOOL

At the underclass assembly at Troy High School yesterday morning Capt. Hiram Grimes, of the basketball quintet, presented to W. Kenneth Doyle, principal, the gold basketball he was awarded last Saturday at R. P. I. for being the outstanding basketball player from high schools in this area.

Mr. Doyle thanked Grimes in behalf of the school for the award and he further stated that it will be placed, along with other trophies, in the school trophy case. Motion pictures about the Marine Corps were shown and the school band, under the direction of Frank Catricale, played several well known selections.

Kolloway, White Sox Infielder, Gets 6 Base Hits In Two Days

By the Associated Press.

St. Petersburg, Fla. Funniest incident of the spring training season happened yesterday when the New York Yankees' shortstop, 5-foot 5-inch Phil Rizzuto, stood right up and argued with 6-foot 4-inch Umpire Cal Hubbard about a third strike.

Hollywood, Cal.—Young Don Kolloway, the Chicago White Sox second sacker, got six hits against the Chicago Cubs and the Philadelphia A's in the last two days.

Orlando, Fla.—Catcher Jake Early of the Washington Senators has found out that the Brooklyn Dodgers can be rough even in an exhibition game. He was thoroughly shaken up in yesterday's encounter with Johnny Rizzo.

St. Petersburg, Fla.—The St. Louis Cardinals, seeking their ninth straight Grapefruit League triumph, designated Bill Lohrman, Lon Warneke and Harry Breechen to pitch today against the Boston Red Sox. So effective were Max Lanier and John Beazeley in yesterday's 1 to 0 triumph over Cleveland the Card outfield had only two chances.

Daytona Beach, Fla.—Kirby Higbe, one of Brooklyn's better pitchers, will see today what a

period of rest has done to the "catch" in his shoulder. He is slated to take the mound against the Detroit Tigers.

Clearwater, Fla.—The New York Giants came here today for the first of 15 games with the Cleveland Indians, who are gloating over the pitching ability of Ray Poat, up from Cedar Rapids of the Three-Eye League. Poat yesterday limited the St. Louis Cardinals to one hit in five innings.

Ontario, Cal.—Rumors that Phil Cavarretta might be sold to the Philadelphia Athletics were sidetracked today by Manager Jimmy Wilson's remark that the three left hand hitting outfielders intended to keep for the Chicago Cubs' National League campaign were Cavarretta, Bill Nicholson and Charley Gilbert.

Sanford, Fla.—After watching Nanny Fernandez, Boston Brave rookie third baseman, develop a sore right arm, Casey Stengel chided him. "Oh, it is nothing," the youngster said, "just keep me in the line-up and I'll work it out."

Deland, Fla.—The St. Louis Browns moved over to Orlando today for a tussle with the Washington Senators. Don Gutteridge, pride of the Brownie rookie infielders, got half of team's six hits yesterday and scored the run that beat Kansas City, 7 to 6, in ten innings.

Miami, Fla.—Hank Leiber, husky New York Giant outfielder, played only one inning of yesterday's 16 to 2 defeat by the Cincinnati Reds because of blistered feet. His ailment gave Barna a chance to shine in the outer garden.

Sarasota, Fla.—Joe Dobson, who turned in one of the Boston Red Sox's best pitching performances of 1942 by going five hitless innings against the Washington Senators last week, shares the mound duties against the St. Louis Cardinals today with Mike Ryba.

Tampa, Fla.—Rookie Ray Lamanno, apple of Manager Bill McKechnie's eye, will be on the shelf for a few days. The Cincinnati Reds' rookie catcher injured two fingers yesterday on a foul tip off the bat of Johnny Mize.

San Bernardino, Cal.—President Bill Benswanger of the Pittsburg Pirates, terms "preposterous" the report that the club would let Jim Wasdell go to the Philadelphia Athletics. Wasdell, last year a utility player with the Brooklyn Dodgers, now looms as the Pirates' regular right fielder.

Miami Beach, Fla.—Frank Melton took over in the seventh yesterday when the Syracuse Internationals threatened to go ahead of the Phils and fanned six men in the ensuing three and a third innings.

BORDEMAN, SABIA, VANVELSOR, ZIMET WIN THEIR BOUTS

The R. P. I. elimination boxing tournament got under way yesterday afternoon with five fast matches in the '87 gymnasium.

In the first match Ken Bordeman of the class of '45 defeated Bob Thurston, a classmate, by a decision. These boys were originally in the 135-145 pound class, but were shifted shortly before the bout to the 145-155 pound class. Bordeman showed promise as he used all the tactics of a real fighter. Thurston made a good stand after a poor start. Bordeman will fight Martin Roberts, class of '44, today.

The second bout of the 125-135 pound class saw Bill Sabia defeat St. John, both of the class of '45, by a decision. Sabia was fast and landed often. St. John was on the defensive most of the time and was unable to land very many punches. Sabia will fight Dick Duda today.

In the 135-145 pound class another frosh, Harry Van Velsor, jr., son of the head of the physical education department, won from Dick Kyte, a sophomore. During the first round Van Velsor received a left to the nose drawing blood, but failed to hinder him. The second round was fast with both boys landing punches. However, Van Velsor had the edge during this period. Toward the end of the third round Kyte had a sudden spurt but Van Velsor covered up well to take the match by a decision.

In the 165-175 pound class Art Zimet defeated a brother freshman also by a decision. Irvine looked good during the first round but he tired half way through the second round. From then on Zimet led the fighting, landing several good punches in a row to the face during the third round. Zimet will meet Ed Sewall today.

In the fifth and final bout George Frank beat Ray Silver, both juniors, in the unlimited weight class by a technical knockout. Frank knocked Silver down during the first round for the count of three. The blow stunned him so that Referee McNary stopped the fight. Frank will meet Bob Schoenlank, class of '44, today.

All bouts were three-minute rounds.

145-155 lb. class—Bordeman (146) defeated Thurston (149) by a decision.

125-135 lb. class—Sabia (133) defeated St. John (134) by a decision.

135-145 lb. class—Van Velsor (145) defeated Kyte (145) by a decision.

165-175 lb. class—Zimet (174) defeated Irvine (170) by a decision.

Unlimited weight class — Frank (190) defeated Silver (192) by a technical knockout.

Referee, Walter McNary; judges, Graham and Donald; timer, Donald.

GOLDEN GLOVES ENTRANTS INCLUDE WATERVLIET BOY

To date the Troy Area has just one entrant in the Golden Gloves show scheduled for Vincentian Institute in Albany March 25 and 26, but several Troy mittalingers are expected to send in their names for the annual Adirondack A.A.U. title show this week.

The lone Troy Area entry is Tom Cavanaugh of Watervliet who will seek honors in the 147-pound class along with Doug Scaccia of Rome; John Mezzenolte of Schenectady; Wally Trafton of Sharon Springs, and Tony Marco of Schenectady.

The entry list for the two-day show will be completed within a couple of days and will be sent in by Ben Becker, director of the bouts.

Trip to New York Prize Awaiting CYO Winners

A trip to New York to meet the Archdiocesan Basketball League champions of that city i- this month will be the prize awaiting the winners of the Senior and Intermediate C. Y. O. League champions of Troy in the playoff finals tomorrow night at La Salle gym. It was announced last night by Rev. Harold B. Hinds, diocesan director.

No exact date for the intersectional championships has been set, but it will come sometime after March 26, when the New York champs will be crowned after their final round. The trip this year is an added incentive to the Troy quintets.

The winners of the C. Y. O. division in Albany will be the next opponents of the Troy winners Sunday afternoon at La Salle gym, according to plans now nearly completed. The finals for the Trojans tomorrow, starting at 7 p.m., climaxes a full schedule of league competition and two playoff rounds in three leagues.

SECOND ANNUAL COURT TOURNEY TO OPEN FRIDAY

The second annual La Salle Institute Grammar School Basketball Tournament, slated for Friday and Saturday, has drawn entries from last year's first, second and third place teams as well as almost a score of others.

Defending champs are St. Luke's of Schenectady, with Hillside of Troy last year's runner-up and St. Augustine's of Troy the third place outfit. Entries will be received until noon today.

Other Troy teams entered are St. Paul's, St. Patrick's, St. Peter's, St. Mary's, St. Michael's, St. Lawrence's, St. Anthony's, Sacred Heart and Our Lady of Victory. From Mechanicville comes St. Paul's, from Watervliet St. Bridget's and Sacred Heart and from Cohoes St. Joseph's.

Other teams have been entered from Stillwater and Schaghticoke, but missing this year will be two from Saratoga, St. Peter's and St. Clement's.

TORONTO WINNER OF INITIAL CONTEST IN HOCKEY PLAYOFFS

Toronto (AP)—The first game in the National Hockey League's Stanley Cup playoff series will be played here Saturday, the management of the Maple Leafs said last night.

Officials of the Toronto and the title-winning New York clubs reached an agreement last night on the switch from the previous

LOU ELKAN WINNER OVER BEN CLARKE

New York (AP)—Lou Elkan of Hartford, Conn., defeated Ben Clarke of Newark, 40 to 35, in a 35-inning Eastern States three-cushion billiard tournament match yesterday. Clarke's high run was a six compared with Elkan's four.

AMATEUR PLAYER CARRIES LOAD IN MANY TOURNEYS

St. Augustine, Fla. (AP) — The pros pocket the $3,000 in cash prizes and get the headlines in the National Amateur-Professional Golf Championships, opening its eighth session here today, but often it is their lesser-known amateur partners who carry the load and get in the deciding putts.

Take the championship combination of Sam Snead and Wilford Wehrle of Racine, Wis., for example. They teamed their shots to win the National Amateur-Pro title last year with slammin' Samuel drawing the gallery and in the end putting $1,000 in first money in his pocket.

But it was Wehrle who turned the trick. He knocked in the winning putt on the 36th hole against Jack Grout and Fran Allan, another fine amateur from Pittston, Pa. The match was hanging all even coming to the last green and Wehrle planted a great second shot five feet from the pin. With the rest of the foursome carding par fours, he took careful aim and dropped his putt for a birdie three. It was a $500 putt for partner Snead.

Likewise, it was Allan who kept his pro partner in the running. When the going was tough he canned a 40-footer to keep his side in the match.

It was nearly the same story in 1940 when Horton Smith teamed with Marvin (Bud) Ward, National Amateur Champion from Spokane, Wash., to beat Henry Poe, Reading, Pa., and Harold Manley, Westerfield, Conn. Then it was Smith's hot putter that brought about a 4 to 2 win, but it was up to Ward to close out the match on the 34th hole by sinking a great 20-foot putt.

Go back over the years when Jimmy Hines, Gene Sarazen, Henry Picard, Frank Moore and Denny Shute bagged top money. Their amateur partners did more than their share by scoring a birdie at the right time or knocking in a putt that counted from the edge of the carpet.

This year's field is made up of some of golf's best amateurs, many of whom know the St. Augustine links like a book.

---

arrangements which had the two teams opening the series at New York Sunday.

Under present plans the second game will be played in Madison Square Garden on that date with the third billed for the same site on March 24 with the fourth here March 28.

If fifth, sixth and seventh contests are necessary they will be played in New York March 29, Toronto March 31, and New York April 2, respectively.

THE WEATHER

THE TIMES RECORD

Series 1942 - No. 68. TROY, N. Y., SATURDAY EVENING, MARCH 21, 1942. PRICE THREE CENTS

Troy And Cohoes Men Held By FBI

Melbourne Throngs Roar Wild Welcome To Gen. MacArthur

President Orders Railroad Seized

U. S. WILL OPERATE TOLEDO, PEORIA AND WESTERN LINE

Roosevelt Acts Under War Powers as Railway Executive Ignores Arbitration Request.

Washington (AP) — President Roosevelt today ordered seizure of the Toledo, Peoria and Western Railroad and its operation by the government, in the interests of the "successful prosecution of the war."

The President acted after a long series of unsuccessful government efforts to get George P. McNear, jr., president of the 239-mile road, to arbitrate a strike of 104 workers.

Mr. Roosevelt issued an executive order authorizing Joseph B. Eastman, director of the Office of Defense Transportation, to take immediate possession of the property and to "operate or arrange for the operation of such railroad in such a manner as he deems necessary for the successful prosecution of the war."

Prior to the issuance of his order, the Chief Executive conferred with Chairman William H. Davis of the War Labor Board, the fourth government agency which had attempted to persuade McNear to arbitrate the nearly three-months-old dispute.

Acts Under War Powers.

At one point in the exchanges McNear asked that the government either protect the line and its employees from violence or operate the road itself.

The President's action was taken under his constitutional authority and his powers as commander-in-chief of the Army and Navy.

The latest reply from McNear to the President's demand for arbitration came in the form of a 17-page telegram which the White House said was sent collect.

It was added, however, that Davis, pressing McNear at the President's behest for a quick answer, had asked the railroad president to telegraph a copy of his airmail letter addressed to the White House Thursday.

The President's order declared that representatives of labor and industry had agreed that there shall be no strikes or lockouts during the war and that all labor disputes shall be settled by peaceful means. It added that the company had "refused and continues to refuse" to submit a dispute with its employees to arbitration.

Eastman to Manage Road.

The order directed Eastman to manage the road "under such terms and conditions of employment as he deems advisable and proper, pending such termination of the existing labor dispute as may be approved by the National War Labor Board."

The Toledo, Peoria and Western Railroad is only 239 miles long and only 104 workers are involved in the dispute over a new contract, but its uninterrupted operation is especially vital in wartime because it affords a bypass around Chicago for transcontinental freight shipments.

Since the strike began Dec. 28 settlement was sought unsuccessfully by the National Railway Mediation Board, the Office of Defense Transportation, the United States Conciliation Service and the War Labor Board.

All proposed arbitration and the W.L.B. ordered it. But McNear, 51-year-old mechanical engineer who bought the faltering shortline for $1,300,000 in 1926 and put it in the black in 45 days, stood his ground.

Last 5 Callers Were Too Late

RANGE, electric Westinghouse, in good condition, grey enamel. Will sell reasonably to quick buyer. Troy 546-W.

Six persons inquired about the electric range described in this recent Classified Ad in The Record Newspapers but the last five were too late — the first party decided to buy it! For quick sales, use Classified Ads!

Just Phone TROY 6100

Guess What Day It Is?

—why, obviously, it's the first day of spring.
(Copyright, 1942, NEA Service, Inc. Printed in U. S. A.)

DATES FOR SUGAR REGISTRATION SET

Consumers to Sign Up at Nation's Schools, May 4, 5, 6 and 7.

Chicago (UP)—Frank Bane, national field director of the Office of Price Administration, announced today that the nationwide registration for sugar rationing will be held April 28 and 29 for commercial concerns and May 4, 5, 6 and 7 for consumers.

Bane revealed the registration dates at a conference of 48 state and ten regional rationing administrators, called to work out the details of the sugar rationing program.

Registration for regular consumers will be at the nearest grade school and for industrial and retail concerns at the nearest high school.

Bane said the commercial registration would embrace such industrial users as bakers, candy and confection manufacturers, tobacco processors and wholesale and retail establishments.

Industrial rationing will be on the basis of a percentage of normal use.

Individual consumers will get one pound every two weeks or three-quarters of a pound every week—the rationing administration hasn't decided which.

Individuals must use their own rationing books, but that does not mean that a mother cannot take all the books to the store and collect for her whole family. It does mean that Jones cannot transfer his book to Smith.

Bane said the coupon books would be distributed at the time of the registration.

FORMER MINISTRY STUDENT NOW ON M'ARTHUR'S STAFF

Des Moines, Ia. (AP)—Master Sergt. Paul P. Rogers of Des Moines—a divinity student who quit his studies to enlist in the Army because he felt the war was "a challenge"—was one of the 15 Army men who accompanied Gen. Douglas MacArthur from the Philippines to Australia.

A secretary on General MacArthur's staff, he was the only non-commissioned man chosen to make the trip.

The 22-year-old sergeant gave up his studies for the ministry at William Jewell College, Liberty, Mo., last September and told his parents, Mr. and Mrs. L. P. Rogers, that he was going to enlist in the Army.

His father explained that "Paul felt the war was a challenge to him—that he would be a better man for going."

Spring Arrives; Ban on Rolled Stockings Off

Newark, N. J. (AP)—Spring arrived today—and approximately 8,000 girl office workers at the Prudential Insurance Co. were permitted to roll stockings below their knees or even go stockingless for the first time in many years. The company, taking note of the war-time clothing emergency, lifted its requirement that full-length stockings be worn.

Girl workers say the object of the requirement has been to prevent distraction of male employees.

Generally, however, as spring arrived officially at 2:11 a.m. (E.W.T.) the nation as a whole looked back upon one of the mildest winters in many years.

BENNY GOODMAN WEDS IN NEVADA

"King of Swing" and Vanderbilt Heiress on Honeymoon.

New York (AP)—Benny Goodman, whose magic clarinet lifted him from poverty in Chicago to the throne of New York's swing king, was honeymooning today with his bride, the former Mrs. Alice Hammond Duckworth, great-great granddaughter of Commodore Cornelius Vanderbilt.

The marriage, announced in New York by the bride's parents, Mr. and Mrs. John Henry Hammond, took place yesterday at Las Vegas, Nev.

The idol of the nation's jitterbugs and the pretty blonde Vanderbilt descendant remained at Las Vegas for their honeymoon and won't return to New York until the end of the month. It was the first marriage for 32-year-old Benny, the second for 36-year-old Alice Duckworth.

She obtained a divorce at Las Vegas last Jan. 26 from George Arthur Victor Duckworth of London, to whom she was married in March, 1927.

Her marriage was performed by Judge George E. Marshall, with a sister of the bride, Mrs. Rachel McClenahan, and a friend, Miss Ann Emmons, as the only witnesses.

Through his marriage, the king of swing moves into the most elect of New York's social circles and his bride's socially-prominent family speedily indicated their pleasure over the event.

YOUNG MOTORIST KILLED.

Buffalo (UP)—Alfred K. Swartz, 19, of Akron, died in a Buffalo Hospital today several hours after his automobile overturned in suburban Amherst.

JAP SUB SUNK AT CHRISTMAS ISLAND

Shore Batteries Destroy Raider That Attacked Norwegian Ship.

New York (UP)—Shore batteries at the Port of Spain on Christmas Island in the Indian Ocean sank a Japanese submarine after it had torpedoed a Norwegian steamer, the Australian radio reported today.

Two submarines attacked and sank the Norwegian ship before the shore bateries scored a direct hit on one of the enemy raiders, the broadcast, recorded by CBS, said. The action was said to have occurred "recently.'

"All torpedoes were fired by two submarines before the ship went down," it said. "As the submarine surfaced, shore batteries opened up and quickly forced it down again. Later the submarine came close to the shore. Gunners from one of the shore batteries sighted her and opened fire. They scored a direct hit. The submarine came to the surface, rolled over, showed her keel, and then disappeared."

The broadcast said the Norwegian ship's crew was rescued and later removed from the island by an unidentified allied warship now in Australia.

SAYS BRITISH LABOR IN BETTER POSITION THAN THAT OF NAZIS

London (AP) — Labor Minister Ernest Bevin told a London audience today that "on the labor side, we are in better position than Germany."

"The demands on our manpower have been and still are tremendous," he said. "Our reserves have had to be heavily drawn upon but by careful manipulation of our resources I think I can see daylight from the manpower point of view, even if the war has to be carried on for a long time yet."

METAL HOUSEHOLD FURNITURE BANNED

Washington (INS) — Production of metal household furniture—everything from tables and chairs to mirror frames and shoe racks—will be stopped after May 31, the WPB announced today.

The order is designed to conserve critical materials. Conversion of the industry to war production also is planned.

The ban includes porch and garden furniture, ornamental wall brackets, beach and lawn umbrellas, kitchen cabinets, medicine cabinets, smoking stands and ash trays, porcelain table tops and coat and hat racks.

ALLIED CHIEFTAIN CONFIDENT JAPS WILL BE CRUSHED

Cautions Against Hopes for Early Offensive; Nipponese Cruiser Bombed and Sunk.

BY THE ASSOCIATED PRESS

Gen. Douglas MacArthur, greeted by wildly cheering thousands, declared in Melbourne today he had every confidence of "ultimate success" in the battle to crush Japan's far-flung invasion armies, but cautioned against too eager hopes for an immediate allied grand offensive

As the hero of Bataan began to plan strategy to wrest the initiative from Japan, a war department bulletin reported that defenders of the Philippines still were carrying on the MacArthur tradition of aggressiveness.

A Washington communique said American and Filipino troops made a surprise attack on Japanese forces near Zamboanga on Mindanao Island, 600 miles south of Bataan, and inflicted heavy casualties on the enemy.

Harbor Defenses Shelled.

The communique said Japanese artillery, including eight-inch guns, subjected American harbor defenses of Manila Bay to "extremely heavy" shelling but caused little damage of military consequence. By harbor defenses, the communique apparently referred to Corregidor and other island fortresses guarding the entrance to Manila Bay.

"Our guns effectively returned the fire," the War Department said, adding that the lull in fighting on Bataan Peninsula itself continued.

Officials said the reference to American troops on Mindanao might have been to Philippine Scouts, or forces sent to the islands from the continental United States before the Pacific war, or both. The scouts, although Filipinos, are an integral part of the United States Army but limited to service in the islands.

Jap Cruiser Sunk.

Who is in command in Mindanao was unannounced. In early stages of the fighting for the large southern island, Lieutenant Colonel Roger Hilsman was in command of forces which were forced out of the Port of Davao.

While great crowds accorded General MacArthur a hero's welcome, United Nations airmen were officially credited with sinking another Japanese heavy cruiser in a daring raid on Rabaul, New Britain.

Australia's Prime Minister John Curtin said the cruiser—the 64th enemy warship sunk or damaged in the Far Pacific theater—was sent to the bottom, smoking and aflame, by bombers which attacker through violent anti-aircraft fire in daylight, beat off enemy pursuit planes and returned to their base intact.

Japs Reported at Papua.

It was the 27th on the list of Japanese warships and merchant vessels sunk or damaged in less than two weeks in the battle for the approaches to Australia.

Meanwhile, the German radio quoted Tokyo dispatches as asserting that Japanese shock troops had reached the Gulf of Papua, on the southern side of New Guinea island, and that "the last decisive attack for complete occupation of New Guinea" had begun.

The broadcast said other Japanese forces striking down from the north were executing a pincer movement against Port Moresby, New Guinea capital of the Gulf of Papua, only 300 miles from the Australian mainland.

Conquest of New Guinea, when

(Continued on Page 2.)

CONGRESS TO PROBE DRIVES SUPPORTING ANTI-STRIKE LAWS

Washington (UP) — Plans were underway in Congress today for an investigation of mail and telegraphic campaigns directed at pressuring Congress into enacting anti-strike legislation and suspending the 40-hour week.

Chairman Harry S. Truman, D. Mo., of the special Senate Defense Investigating Committee, announced he would conduct an inquiry if formally requested to do so by Chairman Elmer Thomas, D., Okla., of a Senate sub-committee on military appropriations.

Thomas, whose group has been holding hearings on the labor-production situation, said he intends to ask for an investigation.

He is convinced by four days of testimony on strikes, production and allied problems, he said, that "the way things are now, Congress isn't justified even in pressing hearings" on measures proposing restrictive labor legislation.

Alleged Lottery Operators

RAYMOND D. BARGER

EDWARD BORDEN

HOWARD BRENNAN

RUSSIANS STORM FOUR NAZI BASES

Vichy Says Red Army Has Smashed Its Way Into Staraya Russa.

BY THE ASSOCIATED PRESS.

Russia's armies, crowding the Germans off balance before Hitler can launch his spring offensive, were reported storming against four key Nazi bases on the 1,200-mile front today, and a Vichy radio broadcast declared Soviet troops had already fought their way into Staraya Russa.

Other Russian assaults were aimed at Bryansk, Kharkov and Taganrog.

Staraya Russa, 150 miles below Leningrad, is the base headquarters of the trapped German 16th army which has been cut off for weeks in the frozen marshlands around Lake Ilmen.

A bulletin from Hitler's field headquarters acknowledged the increasing violence of Russian assaults, declaring that Nazi troops had beaten off six fierce attacks yesterday southeast of Lake Ilmen, in the Staraya Russa sector, but gave no details on the fate of Staraya Russa itself.

Admit Red Pressure.

"Many dead were left on the field and numerous prisoners were taken," a German communique said.

The high command also conceded that the Russians were pressing the offensive in the Crimea, in the Donets River basin of the Ukraine, and on the central (Moscow) and northern (Leningrad) fronts.

From Vichy, Leningrad and Moscow came details—reports that Red Army troops had penetrated Kharkov fortifications but were forced back; that there was hard fighting north of Taganrog, Azov Sea anchor of the German lines; that 455 Germans were killed and ten blockhouses were demolished on the Leningrad front.

Severe Cold Continues.

Russian guerrillas were officially declared to have killed 1,000 Germans near Bryansk, a railway city 220 miles southwest of Moscow, and audaciously entered its heart to burn German supplies and post Russian pamphlets on German bulletin boards.

Despite the calendar, bitterly cold weather swept the fronts and wintry clouds forced aircraft to fly low.

Soviet dispatches declared soldiers were shooting down German aircraft with rifles and machine-guns. A ski unit was credited with knocking out two transports. A detachment on the northwestern front was said to have shot down a transport carrying two tons of flour and oats to German troops.

ARNOLD PICTURES ORGANIZED LABOR BUSINESS MENACE

Assistant Attorney General Sees Farmers, Public and Trade "At Mercy" of Unions.

Washington (AP) Thurman Arnold, assistant attorney general, accused organized labor today of "injuring and destroying" independent business and said that farmers, consumers and business men were "at its mercy."

He flatly told the House Judiciary Committee that a measure to require government registration of unions and trade associations "doesn't go far enough" in protecting the public from practices of organized labor.

"When you look at the entire picture," Arnold asserted, "the situation is putting a very substantial handicap on the distribution of all civilian necessities.

"It is impeding the distribution of housing and food and is injuring or destroying the independent business man at a time when we are trying to save the consumer and independent business man."

He told the committee that "no other group in our society" could do anything like the things he said have been done by labor unions.

Specific Charges.

Unions alone, he said, have been able to do these things without being subject to prosecution.

Arnold charged the unions with:

1. Exploitation of farmers.
2. Undemocratic procedure, "including packing its membership to insure elections."
3. Impeding transportation.
4. Making it "impossible to get cheap, mass production of housing."
5. Forcing business men to employ "useless" labor.
6. Restricting "efficient use of men and machines."

"Independent business men all over the country are completely at the mercy of any organized labor group," he declared.

"Farmers Exploited."

"Labor," Arnold told the committee, "can tell any independent business man to stop business, either by refusing to deal with him, or by putting too great a burden on him in the form of useless and unnecessary employees."

And he maintained also that unions, "particularly large unions" want to deal with large organizations, adding:

"Small organizations get in the way, so they simply eliminate them."

This, he contended, was done usually by jurisdictional strikes. He said that a jurisdictional strike and a boycott by labor in Chicago had "forced on consumers a luxury system of milk delivery."

He charged that unions had exploited the farmers by stopping delivery of their produce.

Cites California Case.

To back up his contention that unions were restricting efficient use

(Continued on Page 2.)

FOUR ARMY FLYERS KILLED IN CRASH

Greenfield, Ind. (AP)—Four Army flyers were killed near here last night in the crash and explosion of a two-motor bomber apparently crippled by engine trouble.

The victims, the only occupants of the airplane, were Lieut. Paul F. Hawkins, Ponca City, Okla., pilot; Lieut. James P. Van Story, Lincolnton, N. C., co-pilot; Lieut. Lawrence J. Rux, Henderson, N. C., navigator, and Sergt. Robert W. Morgan, Uniontown, Pa., mechanic.

AGENTS ARREST 73 IN DRIVE AGAINST GAMBLING RINGS

Series of Raids Made Over Extensive Territory; Seize Printing Plant in Spindle City.

sons were arrested in raids in cities from Maine to Florida, the ring having operated along the entire Atlantic seaboard with one of its main cogs being situated in Cohoes, according to Arthur J. Cornelius, chief of the Albany F. B. I. office.

The Troy and Cohoes men arrested were Raymond D. Barger, 20 Collins Avenue, Troy; Edward Borden, 68 Edward Street, Cohoes and Howard Brennan, 10 Congress Street, Cohoes.

This morning at Myrtle Beach, S. C., the F. B. I. arrested Gerard Damiano of Syracuse another alleged member of the $10,000,000 a year racket. The F. B. I. said that Damiano was closely associated with Frank Cohen of South Manning Boulevard, Albany, one of the reputed leaders of the ring.

U. S. Attorney Ralph L. Emmons announced today at Albany that he expected to arraign the Troy and Cohoes men as well as all others seized in this section of the state before U. S. Commissioner Lester T. Hubbard in Albany, probably on Monday morning.

This will be the second time that Barger will face federal authorities on a lottery charge he having been fined $2,000 in Federal Court at Albany on May 2, 1938 after a big lottery cleanup in Cohoes and throughout the eastern states in that year.

Working simultaneously in 36 cities from Maine to Florida and as far west as St. Louis, F. B. I. agents seized thousands of dollars worth of equipment including printing presses, staplers, paper cutters, stitchers and other printing accessories, and literally tons of steel and paper.

Charged with Mail Violation.

The Troy Area men are charged with conspiracy to violate the federal statute governing use of U. S. mails for transportation of lottery tickets, and their actual duty in the ring, it is believed, was the operation of a printing plant in an "Old red barn" located at the rear of 1 Lincoln Avenue, Cohoes.

In this barn F. B. I. agents seized 70,000 tickets, 200 pounds of paper to be used for tickets, two printing presses, paper cutters, staplers, and stitching machines and rolls of steel to be used for staples for the tickets.

Another similar printing establishment was discovered operating in Schenectady and still another at Fort Plain, according to Mr. Cornelius. Arrests were made in these and other places in this state by agents from the Albany office working simultaneously with agents throughout Eastern Seaboard states.

All Detained.

The warrants were issued on information given by U. S. Attorney Ralph L. Emmons, and all those arrested are being detained in fed-

(Continued on Page 9.)

SCHENCK CONVICTION UPHELD BY COURT

New York (INS)—The conviction of movie executive Joseph Schenck and his confidential associate, Joseph H. Moskowitz, on charges of evading the payment of federal income taxes was affirmed today by the U. S. Circuit Court of Appeals.

Schenck, former chairman of the board of 20th Century-Fox Films, and Mosowitz were convicted last April and since have been free on bail pending a decision on their appeal. Schenck was sentenced to a three-year prison term and Moskowitz to a year and a day. Schenck was fined $20,000 while his associate was assessed $10,000.

The Index

THE WEATHER
U. S. Weather Bureau.
Tonight—Rain, warmer.

THE TIMES RECORD

FINAL EDITION

Series 1942—No. 84.

(Entered as Second Class Matter at the Postoffice at Troy, N. Y., under the Act of March 3, 1879.)

TROY, N. Y., THURSDAY EVENING, APRIL 9, 1942.

(Published Daily Except Sunday)

PRICE THREE CENTS

BATAAN DEFENDERS OVERCOME; 36,853 FACE DEATH, CAPTURE

BRITAIN LOSES TWO CRUISERS TO JAPS IN INDIAN OCEAN

Admiralty Also Announces Sinking by Submarine of Italian Warship in Mediterranean.

London (INS)—Loss of two British cruisers to Japanese action in the Indian Ocean and the sinking of a 10.000-ton Italian cruiser in the Mediterranean were announced by the Admiralty today.

One of the British cruisers lost was the 9,975-ton Dorsetshire, previously perhaps the most envied vessel in the Royal Navy. It was the Dorsetshire that on May 27, 1941, gave the giant German battleship Bismarck the coup de grace.

Her captain, Commander A. E. S. Agar, was privileged to give the order which sent a final torpedo into the huge Nazi dreadnaught, sending her to the bottom after a dramatic battle with ships and planes of the British Navy.

The other vessel lost was the 10.000-ton cruiser Cornwall. A total of 1,100 men were saved from both ships.

Axis Make Heavy Claims.

The Dorsetshire and the Cornwall, like the Prince of Wales and the Repulse, were both sunk by Japanese bombing and torpedo-carrying planes in the course of extended action in the Indian Ocean during which enemy planes bombed the great naval base of Trincomalee on the Island of Ceylon.

(Editor's Note: In announcing loss of the cruisers, the British government confirmed merely one of a host of Axis claims. The Berlin radio asserted that Japanese forces had landed at an undisclosed spot on the Bay of Bengal, which could be in India proper or Burma, and said that Nippon troops "which are now north of Akyab" were advancing along the road to Calcutta. A recent Chinese announcement that the Japanese had seized Akyab was found to be erroneous. Meanwhile, the Japanese claimed to have sunk 21 and heavily damaged 23 merchant vessels in the Indian Ocean. as well as shooting down sixty planes in recent activities. All of these assertions went without confirmation in any reliable quarter).

The Italian cruiser was torpedoed and sunk. It brought to five the number of Italian vessels of this class sent to the bottom since the war began. Italy entered the war with only seven 10,000-ton cruisers.

An Admiralty communique confirming earlier Japanese claims

(Continued on Page 2.)

R. A. F. SMASHES AT HAMBURG AND PORTS IN OCCUPIED FRANCE

London (UP)—A strong force of R. A. F. bombers, daring bad weather to continue their nightly assaults on Germany, attacked the key port of Hamburg and other objectives in northwest Germany last night, the Air Ministry reported today.

Docks at the German-occupied French port of Le Havre also were bombed, the communique reported.

Six bombers were lost in the forays, it was said.

Torpedo bombers of the coastal command yesterday afternoon attacked a convoy of enemy supply ships off the coast of Jutland but the air ministry said results of the attack could not be observed. The British said they lost two coastal command planes.

BABY SUFFOCATED

Buffalo (UP)—A five weeks' old baby boy, Neal J. Kotok, was suffocated yesterday when he rolled on his face while asleep in a buggy on the porch of his home. Firemen worked over the child for half an hour before a physician pronounced him dead.

RENTED

The First Day!

WATERVLIET, lower, near Arsenal and D. & H Furnished home and garage to small adult family; privilege of room and board by owner. Inquire 598 5th Ave., North.

The Watervliet accommodations described in this Classified Ad were snapped right up by a man the first day the ad was published in The Record Newspapers. With the demand for living quarters in the Troy Area a vacancy is an unnecessary expense.

To Get A Tenant
Phone Troy 6100

Prosecutor's Movie Photos Show Brooklyn Graft Payoff

This series of pictures shows money actually being paid a Brooklyn cop by a New York bookie according to John Harlen Amen, special assistant attorney general, who charges police received approximately $1,000,000 in graft from racketeers. Above: Cop stands at corner, looks around, and . . .

. . . an alleged bookmaker walks out of a nearby store. In his right hand, according to charges in a presentment handed up by a special grand jury, is a sum of money. The bookie walks to the corner and . . .

. . . shakes hands with the uniformed policeman. During the handshake, according to Amen, the bookie transferred the money to the cop, as allegedly shown . . .

. . . by the emptiness of the bookie's right hand while he stands at the corner with the officer after the handshake. Then, without wasting any time . . .

. . . the bookie and the cop part company and go about their regular business. The dramatic series of photographs was obtained with a small movie camera and used as evidence against the policeman, one of the 49 high ranking officers and patrolmen accused of misconduct.

ORDER SUSPENSION OF 32 POLICEMEN ACCUSED IN GRAFT

Departmental Trials To Be Given Officers Named in $100,000,000 Brooklyn Gambling Syndicate.

New York (INS)—Police Commissioner Lewis J. Valentine today ordered departmental trials for 32 policemen accused of being paid protectors of an alleged $100,000,000-a-year Brooklyn gambling syndicate.

Named with 17 others in six presentments returned by an extraordinary grand jury investigating alleged official corruption in Kings County. The policemen were suspended immediately from active duty.

Fourteen of the original 49 listed as sharing in more than $1,000,000 in protection payments annually escaped penalty because they are no longer on the police force.

Included in the presentments which climaxed nearly a year of inquiry under the direction of Special Prosecutor John Harlan Amen were motion pictures purporting to show policemen in alleged Brooklyn bookmaking establishments.

Warning that police protection of gambling extends to all boroughs of the city, Amen asserted that mere changes in personnel would not alter the system. He added, however, that no criminal prosecution is contemplated against the policemen since many witnesses have moved away or are dead.

THIRTY MILES OF UPPER BRONX WILL UNDERGO BLACKOUT

New York (INS)—Thirty miles of the upper Bronx will undergo a blackout test from 9 to 9:20 tonight, affecting 895,000 persons from Riverdale to Pelham Bay and from Baychester to Tremont Avenue.

With 15,000 air wardens on duty, Mayor F. H. LaGuardia and Commissioner Lewis J. Valentine will tour the area to see that preparations are complete, while an Army plane will observe overhead.

For the first time in the city's tests, part of a transit system will be blacked out, at the request of the Army, lights being extinguished on the I. R. T. Pelham Bay line terminus, elevated structure at Middleton Road and Westchester Avenue.

Cars from Westchester and Connecticut will be barred from entering the borough during the test, and all street traffic inside the area must halt.

Order Further Curtailment Of Gasoline Deliveries

Washington (UP)—The War Production Board today cut gasoline deliveries to filling stations and other bulk consumers in the east and west coast curtailment areas from the present 80 per cent to 66 per cent of the average amounts they received in December, January and February.

The order is effective April 16.

The curtailment areas include the 17 eastern seaboard states, the District of Columbia and the Pacific northwest states of Washington and Oregon.

The City of Bristol, Tenn., was added to the restricted area because it is in both Tennessee and Virginia.

The order provides that seasonal variations may be adjusted in computing the delivery figure on which the 66 per cent volume is computed.

MALTA ATTACKED BY 300 BOMBERS

Intensity of Raids Exceeds Anything Experienced by Island.

London (UP)—Germany sent more than 300 bombers and fifty fighter planes against Malta in the Tuesday raids whose intensity exceeded anything experienced by the island informed sources said today.

It was estimated that many of the bombers made up to three trips to the island, and that Germany was using about 500 planes in all in trying to knock Malta out of the war.

"The bombers were mostly Junkers-88 (dive bombers) and Italian bombers were not often seen, it was said here. Several days earlier, he said, the Germans used 180 bombers in one attack and on another raid used more than 200.

"They evidently are trying to break Malta before Malta breaks them," an observer said.

Because of Malta's size — 17 by eight miles—it is easy for the enemy pilots to concentrate their fire and the island has become known as the most frequently bombed place in the world.

CHURCHILL SEES DANES FREED FROM GERMAN TYRANNY

London (INS)—The day will come when Denmark will be freed from Nazi tyranny, Prime Minister Winston Churchill said today in receiving a check for 38,000 pounds sterling ($153,200) collected by 'Free Danes" in England.

"We shall never give in, never weary and never pause in our struggle, nor will our great American and Russian allies," he said.

"I have very little doubt that the day will come, perhaps sooner than it would be prudent or sensible to hope, when Denmark is free and able to resume her independent honored place among the free peoples and states of Europe."

TEXTILE DEMANDS CERTIFIED TO WLB

General Pay Raise, Bonus Sought by 54,000 Workers in 47 Mills.

Washington (AP)—Secretary of Labor Perkins today certified to the War Labor Board wage demands involving 54,000 workers in 47 textile mills in 19 cities in New England and Utica.

The major demand is a general 10-cents-and-hour pay raise on undisclosed scales. Other demands involve a 7 per cent bonus for third shift workers, automatic increases based on living cost indices, paid vacations and overtime pay.

One dispute involves 11 mills in the New Bedford, Mass., area and the United Textile Workers of America (A. F. L.) and its affiliate, the New Bedford Textile Council.

The other dispute is between textile manufacturers and the Textile Workers Union of America (C. I. O.) and involves 40,000 workers..

The cities in which there are mills involved in the C. I. O. demands include Lewiston, Biddeford and Saco, Me.; Fall River, Taunton, South Attleboro, New Bedford, Fitchburg, East Boston, Salem, Holyoke and Westfield, Mass.; Willimantic, Jewett City and Putnam, Conn.; Pawtucket and West Warwick, R. I.; Nashua and Suncook, N. H., and Utica.

RECORD EARTHQUAKE OF GREAT INTENSITY IN YELLOW SEA AREA

Bombay, India (AP)—An earthquake of great intensity, apparently centering in the Yellow Sea, between Japan and the China coast, was recorded here last night at 9:19 o'clock (1:49 p.m., E.W.T. Wednesday).

Two more shocks of lesser intensity were recorded today at 1:08 a.m. and 5.35 a.m.

The epicenter was calculated to be about 3,160 miles from Bombay, near latitude 35 north, longitude 122 east.

INSURANCE AGENTS TO VOTE ON UNION

A state-wide vote will be taken late this month by insurance agents of the Prudential Life on tthe question of organizing as locals of the United Office and Professional Workers of America, C.I.O. Union representatives have set up offices at 38 King Street.

Recentlty the State Labor Relations Board certified to an election of Prudential agents in New York, but declined to authorize one on a state-wide scale. In order that the state-wide vote could be taken the union has decided to surrender its rights under the SLRB order and abide by the result of the April vote.

TWO MEN HELD FOR SLURRING REMARKS

Los Angeles (INS) — Allegedly slurring remarks about Gen. Douglas MacArthur today had led to federal indictment of Robert Noble and Ellis O. Jones, leaders of the reputedly pro-Axis "Friends of Progress" organization.

Both were ordered held under $20,000 bond each for uttering seditious statements. They were scheduled for Federal Court hearings next week.

REPORT ALL-INDIA LEADERS AGREE TO NEW BRITISH PLAN

Proposal Said to Provide Immediate Establishment of Indian National Government.

New Delhi, India (UP)—A new proposal for settlement of the Indian problem today was reported to provide immediate establishment of an Indian national government controlling all portfolios, including defense.

Usually well-informed quarters said the Nationalist All-India Congress has decided to accept the formula, but this was not immediately confirmed.

(The All-India radio, heard in London, said there would be "no difficulty or delay" in establishing a national government. The broadcast said the working committee of the All-India Congress would publish its reply to the British proposals "tomorrow, or not later than Saturday.")

It was understood the formula provided that the new national government must agree to leave actual military direction under Gen Sir Archibald P. Wavell, British commander-in-chief in India, because of the "present critical situation."

Such functions as civil defense and mobilization of troops, it was said, would be in charge of the national government.

Differences still were said to exist between the Congress and Sir Stafford Cripps, British Lord Privy Seal, over the delegation of defense and military powers. Some Congress leaders, reports said, insisted that such functions as acquisition of equipment and the training of national guards and home militia remain with the native defense minister.

Advocate New Proposal.

Those opposed to the new formula were said to advocate a new proposal not including voluntary abdication of major military power to Wavell.

Several other points were reported under discussion, including provisions for establishing a constitutional body and the rights of Indian provinces.

Informed sources predicted additional time would be necessary to bring the various Indian factions into agreement.

The new proposal, a revision of one previously advanced by the Indian Nationalists, was submitted by Louis A. Johnson, President Roosevelt's special envoy, to Jawaharlal Nehru, Nationalist leader. The Nationalist formula had been proposed as the "last hope" for agreement between British and Indian political

(Continued on Page 2.)

NAME SEVEN BABIES AFTER MACARTHUR

New York (INS)—Health Department records showed today that seven baby boys have been named Douglas MacArthur in honor of the United Nations' commander in the Pacific. In addition six others were named Douglas Arthur while a 13th baby with the surname MacArthur was given the first name of Douglas. Three of the little Douglas MacArthur's are Negroes, one apparently Scandinavian and another Slavic.

PROBE $200,000 FIRE IN DEFENSE FACTORY

New York (INS)—Fire of undetermined origin today razed the suburban College Point factory of the Superior Steel Door & Trim Corp. which holds war contracts Damage was estimated at $200,000.

Police asserted that the blaze, which swept the block-square three-story wooden structure, didn't appear to be of suspicious origin but an investigation was launched After the rear walls and roof collapsed firemen brought the blaze under control about three hours after it was discovered.

Outbreak of Typhus In Berlin Reported

Moscow (UP)—More than 1,250 cases of typhus have been registered in Berlin in the last two weeks, creating an epidemic that is "daily assuming more threatening proportions," Tass reported today.

At Kuestrin, Germany, Nazi military authorities were compelled to delay the dispatch of reinforcements to the front because of an outbreak of typhus among the troops, the Soviet news agency declared.

WHITEHALL YOUTH FALLS TO DEATH

George Foy, 17, Plunges in Sleep from 18th Floor of New York Hotel.

The Easter vacation of 52 students of the Whitehall High School spent in New York had a sad ending last night when George Foy, 17, a member of the senior class, fell from the 18th floor of the Hotel Taft to instant death on the pavement below, according to Ambrose H. Gilligan and Miss Helen Layden, members of the school staff who were chaperoning the group. Foy walked in his sleep through a window in his room.

The rest of the class, which had been in New York since Monday, started on the return trip this morning.

Foy is survived by his parents, who reside in First Avenue, Whitehall; two sisters, Loretta and Jane Foy, and a brother, Joseph Foy. His father is an engineer on the Delaware & Hudson Railroad.

Ernest Murphy, principal of the school, was informed of the tragedy early this morning. Arrangements are being made to return the body to Whitehall.

SCHENECTADY MAN FROM SUNKEN BOAT REACHES U. S. SAFE

Robert Morris Sherman, 20, grandson of Mr. and Mrs. Edward M. Dreher, 806 Grant Avenue, Schenectady, a sailor who had been serving on the Aircraft Tender Langley, which the Navy Department reported sunk in battle off Java late in February, has arrived safe in the United States.

In a telegram to his grandmother, filed from San Francisco April 6, young Sherman informed her that he had just arrived and "am O. K."

Mrs. Dreher said the youth had been slightly wounded in January during a previous engagement between the Langley and an enemy force.

Important Dates In Philippines Battle

Washington (UP)—Here are the important dates in the four-month battle of the Philippines:

Dec. 10—First landings of Japanese troops confirmed by the War Department.

Dec. 22—Eighty enemy ships carrying from 80,000 to 100,000 troops reported in Lingayen Bay. Other landings are made south of Manila.

Dec. 29—Manila is declared an open city, but is bombed nevertheless.

Jan. 2—Japanese enter Manila after American and Filipino forces concentrated for a defense of Bataan Peninsula.

Jan. 21—American and Filipino troops counterattack, retaking some lost territory and inflicting heavy casualties.

By the end of January Japanese reinforcements had arrived on Luzon, and the Manila Bay guns had smashed a concentration of enemy launches in the bay.

Jan. 26—Another American offensive reestablished the Bataan lines, driving the Japs back as far as five miles. Shortly afterwards Gen. Masahuru Homma was reported to have committed suicide to atone for his failure to take Bataan and Gen. Tomoyuki Yamashita, the conqueror of Singapore took command.

March 17—Gen. Douglas MacArthur was appointed commander of United Nations forces in the Far Pacific and arrived in Australia.

March 22—Surrender demanded by Yamashita. He received no answer.

March 28—Japs break Bataan line after many assaults, but it was restored.

April 5—Jap shock troops make gains they were able to extend the next day.

April 7—Defenders forced to withdraw to new positions during the night. Japs immediately start the heaviest assaults of the campaign.

April 9—American and Filipino east flank is beaten back, and the physically-exhausted troops cannot hold the enemy onslaugh. Bataan is "probably overcome."

Exhaustion Ends Heroic Battle Of American Forces

Washington (AP)—Capture or death at the hands of invading Japanese hordes faced the bulk of 36,853 gallant American-Filipino defenders of Bataan Peninsula today, closing an heroic three-months battle against numerically overwhelming forces.

Exhausted by short rations and disease, and virtually cut off from supplies despite costly efforts which provided some ammunition but did not relieve the food shortage, the doughty defenders fell back before the Japanese who already had overrun the rich Dutch Indies and Britain's Singapore and Malaya.

Secretary of War Stimson related the first details concerning the defenders today, after a special communique had announced that the defense of Bataan had probably been overcome, and said President Roosevelt had authorized the Philippine commander to make any decision he deemed necessary in the light of events.

There was a round-about radio report from Berlin, quoting a Shanghai newspaper report that Lieut. Gen. Jonathan M. Wainwright, commander on Bataan, had sought an armistice, but this was not confirmed in any other quarter.

Only Temporary Loss, Stimson Says.

Latest reports, Stimson said, indicated that Corregidor and other fortresses guarding Manila Bay were still in United States hands, as was about half of the area of the Philippines, but he declined to make predictions how long the forts could be held. He said he saw no reason why resistance by small, isolated forces would not continue.

"This is only a temporary loss," Stimson said. "We shall not stop until we drive out the invaders from the islands."

Stimson said the figure of 36,853 effectives was in the report received yesterday from General Wainwright. He stressed that this figure included only the men fighting on Bataan at that time.

Excluded were American and Filipino troops guarding the defenses of Corregidor and the other islands, the wounded, nearly 20,000 civilian refugees, and some 6,000 Filipino laborers who were non-combatant.

Stimson disclosed that under the direction of Brig. Gen. Patrick J. Hurley, former secretary of war who is now minister to New Zealand, urgent efforts were made beginning last January 11 to reinforce the besieged Philippine forces.

From a base in Australia several ship loads of supplies were sent to the Philippines, and part of these supplies reached Corregidor and Bataan.

"But for every ship that arrived, we lost nearly two ships," Stimson said.

Never Short of Ammunition.

Because of these supplies, the defenders were never short of ammunition, the secretary said, but had been on short rations.

Stimson said he saw no reason why resistance by isolated, relatively small forces should not continue in northern Luzon, on the island of Mindanao and elsewhere where blows have been struck, aside from further defense of Corregidor.

The War Department's sober early morning communique stating "the probability that the defenses on Bataan have been overcome" was the latest news the War Department had received up to 10:30 a.m., Eastern War Time, today, Stimson said.

"Our troops, outnumbered and worn down by successive attacks by fresh troops, exhausted by insufficient rations and the disease prevalent in that peninsula, finally had their lines broken and enveloped by the enemy," the secretary said.

"We do not know the details of what has happened since that communique, but it is evident as stated therein that the defenses on Bataan have been overcome.

"A long and gallant defense has been worn down and overthrown.

"We have nothing but praise and admiration for the commanders and the men who have conducted this epic chapter in American history."

Stimson emphasized also that both General Wainwright and Gen. Douglas MacArthur, his predecessor, had nothing but praise for the Filipino soldiers, who had been

(Continued on Page 2.)

GOVERNOR SIGNS HEALTH MEASURE

Bill Provides $100,000 to Continue Study of Long-range State Program.

Albany (AP)—Governor Lehman approved today formulation of a long-range health program for New York State, signing into law a bill appropriating $100,000 to continue study of the plan another year.

For the past year, a legislative committee has been surveying the state's health facilities in an effort to mobilize "all services and skills pertaining to health" for state and national defense purposes.

The executive also signed a bill continuing the flood control commission until next April and appropriating $17,500 for the joint Federal-State program. He signed last week a bill allowing the state to acquire property for flood control projects.

Lehman vetoed as a "non-essential construction project" a measure which would have appropriated $40,000 for acquisition of land and construction of a fish hatchery on Chautauqua Lake.

"This type of capital project," the Governor asserted, "should be referred to the post war planning commission when it is established."

BUFFALO YOUTH KILLED.

Buffalo (UP)—Merle Matthews, 16, was killed and a girl companion, Sarah De Lillis, 16, was critically injured last night when an automobile struck their bicycles while they rode across a bridge. Matthews was pronounced dead on arrival at a hospital. He was the city's 19th traffic fatality of the year.

NEW YORK CITY HAS LIGHT SNOWFALL

New York (INS)—A touch of winter returned to New York City in a post-Easter display today and by noon the entire metropolitan area was lightly covered by a continuing snowfall.

Weather Bureau officials said the fall extended along New York State's southern border, with little or no precipitation north of Westchester County. The fall put a damper on the opening of the metropolitan racing season at Jamaica.

U. S. Has Four More Philippine Footholds

Washington (UP) — The collapse of Lieut. Gen. Jonathan M. Wainwright's defenses on Bataan Peninsula means that the last major American footholds in the Philippines are four small rock-bound islands in Manila Bay.

The largest of these is Corregidor, an almost solid piece of rock about five miles long and three miles wide. The Spaniards first fortified it, and American forces have turned it into a bristling arsenal with 12-inch guns which command the entrance to Manila Bay.

Fort Mills is the main fortification on Corregidor, and its anti-aircraft gun crews have established a reputation for accuracy by shooting down more than thirty of the hordes of Jap bombers which have attacked it. Big galleries and tunnels have been hewed out of the rock for storerooms and shelters for the Corregidor garrison. How many supplies there are on Corregidor is not known.

The other Manila Bay forts, all smaller than Fort Mills, are Drum, Hughes and Frank. Fort Drum was built about 25 years ago in the form of a battleship, whose revolving turrets of 12-inch guns can fire in any direction. It is of steel and concrete construction, and like the other bay fortresses has withstood the hammering of Jap shore batteries and dive bombers with only minor damage.

The guns from all four fortresses have protected the rear lines of Bataan, breaking up a half dozen enemy attempts to concentrate barges and ships for a sea-borne attack. In addition, they control a system of electric mines in the harbor entrance.

The problem of holding the islands will probably be one of supply and defense against sea assaults, because the rock shelter tunnels and the heavy concentration of anti-aircraft batteries have already demonstrated their ability to withstand air attacks. The British island of Malta in the Mediterranean, also rockbound, has taken the heaviest bomb pounding of the war without being subdued.

The Index

THE WEATHER
U. S. Weather Bureau.
Tonight—Snow and rain.

THE TIMES RECORD

FINAL EDITION

Series 1942—No. 85. (Entered as Second Class Matter at the Postoffice at Troy, N. Y., under the Act of March 3, 1879) TROY, N. Y., FRIDAY EVENING, APRIL 10, 1942. (Published Daily Except Sunday) PRICE THREE CENTS

Japanese Cruiser Sunk By American Torpedo Boats In Philippines Battle

Troy Record Voted "Best" In Class In Newspaper Contest

The Troy Record has been awarded first honorable mention in the less than 10,000 circulation classification in the 12th Annual Exhibition of Newspaper Typography, conducted by N. W. Ayer & Son, Inc.

Second honorable mention in that classification went to the Alexandria (Va.) Gazette, and third honorable mention to Public Opinion, Chambersburg, Pa. The New York Times received the F. Wayland Ayer Cup, highest recognition in the competition.

The winners were selected from among a total of 1,326 entries in the exhibition, which was open to all English language dailies in the United States. The award was made on the basis of excellence in typography, makeup, and presswork.

Honorable mentions were awarded to papers in the following other circulation and format groups:

Standard size papers of more than 50,000 circulation: First honorable mention, New York Herald Tribune; second honorable mention, the Christian Science Monitor; third honorable mention, the Evening Sun, Baltimore, Md.

Standard size papers of from 10,000 to 50,000 circulation: First honorable mention, the News, Lynchburg, Va.; second honorable mention, the Billings (Mont.) Gazette; third honorable mention, Rutland (Vt.) Daily Herald.

Tabloids, regardless of circulation: PM, New York.

Judges for the exhibition were Dr. M. F. Agha, art director of Conde Nast Publications; Ernest K. Lindley, chief of the Washington bureau of Newsweek, and Lewis W. Trayser, vice president of the Curtis Publishing Co.

In studying the entries, they commented on the fact that the average newspaper has improved its typography and general appearance during the last year. The excellence of makeup, they pointed out, is especially notable

(Continued on Page 20.)

Tops Field of 750 National Newspapers

The blue ribbon for papers of less than 10,000 circulation in the 12th Annual Ayer Exhibition of Newspaper Typography was won by The Troy Record, morning edition of The Record Newspapers, left above. Second and third honorable mention went to The Alexandria (Va.) Gazette, center, and Public Opinion, Chambersburg, Pa. The Troy Record last year received third honorable mention and the Alexandria Gazette, second.

"Old Glory" Waves On Corregidor But Enemy Wins Bataan

Nipponese Warship Guarding New Invasion Forces Sent to Bottom Off Island of Cebu; Fate of Bataan Defenders Not Revealed; Tokyo Says Fighting Continues on Peninsula; Japs Claim More British Warships Sunk in Indian Ocean.

Washington (AP)—Most of an estimated 3,500 Marines and Bluejackets in the original American forces in the Bataan sector of the Philippines are presumed to have been evacuated to the fortress island of Corregidor, the Navy announced today, reporting they were removed under cover of darkness when collapse of peninsula defenses appeared imminent.

Corregidor, a tiny island fortress, proudly flaunted the Stars and Stripes before besieging Japanese armies today while southward, in the Philippine Archipelago, American torpedo boats sank a Japanese cruiser guarding new invading forces.

But on bloody Bataan Peninsula, just five miles across Manila Bay from Corregidor, it was apparent that Japanese hordes had crushed the last American-Filipino resistance.

To President Roosevelt, as commander-in-chief, came this message from Lieut. Gen. Jonathan M. Wainwright, commander in the Philippines:

"Our Flag still flies on the beleaguered island fortress of Corregidor."

Then the General tersely noted that the enemy was apparently landing troops in Cebu, some 350 air miles south of Manila, and "our torpedo boats attacked the enemy vessels, sinking a Japanese cruiser."

The President revealed his message from General Wainwright at a press conference shortly after the War Department had released a communique—the first in 17 hours after a special bulletin early yesterday announced the probability that the Bataan defenses had been overcome.

The communique left unanswered whether large numbers of the Bataan defenders had surrendered, or how many had reached Corregidor.

Mr. Roosevelt said that of course we all feel badly about Bataan and that there was no further news concerning the 36,853 effectives known to have been facing the Japanese there Wednesday except that he had received what he called a grand message from General Wainwright in reply to a message he had sent.

Neither message was released in full, and Mr. Roosevelt read only the single sentence from Wainwright's communication, that the Flag still flies over Corregidor.

This communication came in this morning.

Cebu Invasion Begins.

The Japanese cruiser sunk was one of an armada of five warships and ten transports landing troops in Cebu.

(In San Francisco, the Radio Corp. of America reported that wireless communication with Cebu was suspended at 8:50 a.m. today.)

This indicated that the Japanese were extending their conquest of the 7,000 islands in the Philippine archipelago, where native Filipino guerrillas and possibly a few United States troops are rasisting.

Cebu lies 350 air-line miles south of Manila.

Aside from Luzon, the Japanese have occupied Masbate and several points in Mindoro, both immediately south of Luzon. They also have occupied Jolo, in the extreme southwest, Davao and Zamboanga, important ports on the southernmost major island of Mindanao.

The War Department said General Wainwright sent a message to President Roosevelt reporting that "everything possible had been done to hold Bataan" but that "the overwhelming air and artillery superiority of the Japanese finnaly overcame the dogged resistance of the hungry and exhausted defenders."

Japs Admit Fighting.

President Roosevelt had given General Wainwright authorization to take whatever action he saw fit, in view of the extreme peril of the battle-exhausted, hopelessly outnumbered defenders.

As an added fillip of nightmare shock to the American and Filipino soldiers, Japanese dispatches said a violent earthquake rocked the whole peninsula during the final stages of the battle, collapsing Filipino huts and starting landslides.

But after asserting that the men of Bataan had "begged for a halt in hostilities after six days of fierce Japanese assault," the Japanese acknowledged that General Wainwright's troops continued to fight today.

Earlier, a Domei dispatch said: "Details of the conditions of surrender are not yet disclosed. Nor

(Continued on Page 18.)

PRESIDENT SAYS WOMEN 18 TO 65 MAY BE ENROLLED

Chief Executive Reports "Voluntary Registration" Plan Being Considered for War Work.

Washington (AP) — President Roosevelt disclosed today that, in connection with studies for mobilization of man-power for war industries, the government was considering voluntary registration for all women 18 to 65 years old.

Probably within a week, Mr. Roosevelt asserted, some decision will be reached on how to go about channeling man power into war jobs.

One difficulty in registering women, he asserted at a press conference, is inherent in the number of persons who would come forward to enroll. This would create mechanical difficulties, he said, remarking that the preparation of cards alone would be a tremendous task.

He said there had been talk of a voluntary registration for women on the next registration day for men up to 65, on April 27. If, and he emphasized the if, it is decided to register women, a date will be set later on.

A cabinet committee which has been tussling with the problem of channeling men into war production activities thus far has made only an oral report, the Chief Executive said. But the question is discussed, he added, at nearly every cabinet meeting.

One of the real problems in setting up the machinery, after it is determined what is to be done with available man power, Mr. Roosevelt explained, lies in a determination whether a completely new governmental agency should be created or whether there should merely be some central supervision of a great many governmental agencies already engaged in allocating and using man and woman power.

"No Army Has Ever Done So Much With So Little" . . . MacArthur

Melbourne (AP)—Gen. Douglas MacArthur said today of the defenders of Bataan: "No army has ever done so much with so little."

The supreme commander, hero of Bataan's first successful defense, said:

"The Bataan force went out as it would have wished—fighting to the end of its flickering, forlorn hope.

"No army has ever done so much with so little.

"Nothing became it more than its last hour of trial and agony.

"To the weeping mothers of its dead I only say that the sacrifice halo of Jesus has descended upon their sons and that God has taken them unto Himself."

The supreme commander wrote this tribute to the Bataan defenders in his hotel suite.

It was read to newspapermen from a ruled sheet of paper on which the words were written in pencil in the general's own hand.

RED ARMY SWEEPS ACROSS FRONTIER INTO WHITE RUSSIA

British and Axis Armies Reported Engaged in Violent Battle on Desert in North Africa.

BY THE ASSOCIATED PRESS.

British and Axis troops fought with increasing violence on the North African desert today, while on the Soviet front, Vichy radio reports via Stockholm said Red army troops had crossed the frontier into White Russia and were continuing their advance.

The drive into White Russia, a Soviet republic, was said to have taken place in a sector 75 miles northwest of Smolensk, between Vitebsk and Novel.

If continued, the thrust would be a serious threat to the important Vitebsk defenses guarding the flank of the German "escape corridor" from Moscow on the old Napoleonic road to Smolensk.

The Vichy radio, quoting German news agency dispatches, also reported mounting Soviet pressure in the Orel and Kharkov sectors, south of Moscow, and around Sevastopol, the long-besieged Russian naval base in the Crimea.

In North Africa.

A bulletin from Adolf Hitler's field headquarters acknowledged heavy Red Army attacks on the Kerch Peninsula in the Crimea, but declared they had been repulsed and that Nazi gunners had knocked 82 Russian tanks out of action.

In North Africa, British headquarters reported that British troops in the renewed Libyan desert fighting had attacked two Axis columns and set tanks on fire.

Italy's high command said new clashes between British and Axis vanguards "resulted again to our complete advantage," and the German communique reported several British armored cars and guns destroyed or captured in the desert warfare.

The German account told of continued day and night assaults on bomb-battered Malta, British

(Continued on Page 18.)

WORKERS WANT LINDBERGH FIRED

Ford Employees Call Flyer "Pro-Nazi" and Demoralizing Influence.

Detroit (INS)—The removal of Charles A. Lindbergh from the payroll of the Ford Motor Co. was asked today in a resolution of workers in the firm's foundry unit which asserted that the famous flyer "is a demoralizing influence on the laboring man" and charged him with a "pro-Nazi attitude in the past."

The resolution, reportedly having the full approval of the 10,000 U. A. W.-C. I. O. workers in the foundry, was sent to President Roosevelt, Gov. Murray D. Van Wagoner and Ford Co. officials. There was no immediate comment from company officials.

Lindbergh was hired by the Ford Motor Co. a few weeks ago and it was said he would work at the company's Willow Run bomber plant.

The resolution said that the hiring of Lindbergh by the Ford Co. "is a slap in the face" to labor in the United States.

"...Lindbergh's pro-Nazi attitude in the past does not speak for national unity...is a demoralizing influence on the laboring man of the nation..." the resolution said.

The resolution was signed by Hosea Young, recording secretary of the union at the production foundry, and four members of the resolution committee.

QUISLING JAILS BISHOP OF OSLO

Three Other Pastors Interned for "Rebellion" Against Nazi Puppets.

Stockholm, Sweden (UP)—Nazi-Quisling authorities of Norway, facing open revolt by the united Protestant clergymen of the country, arrested Bishop E. J. Berggrav of Oslo and three other pastors today on charges of instigation to rebellion, an Oslo dispatch to the newspaper Tidningens reported.

It asserted that Bishop Berggrav and Pastors Indreboe, Carlsen and Wisloeff had been sent to the Bretvedt concentration camp.

At the same time Vidkun Quisling, head of the puppet regime, issued an ultimatum to 1,100 pastors of the Norwegian church who had resigned that if they did not notify him by 2 p.m. Saturday that they were resuming their duties they would be dismissed.

Confronted by the determination of 1,100 resigned clergymen to preach next Sunday as free men, and undoubtedly to denounce the persecution of the Christian church against which their resignations were directed, the Nazis and their puppets decided to act first.

Bishop Berggrav, whose stout defense of his country and his church had enraged Nazis and Quislings alike, and his three associates, were arrested on the charge that they had "instigated" the collective resignation of the patriot clergy, and that this was considered an "act of rebellion."

Quisling's ultimatum had been timed so that if, as was believed certain, the clergymen defied him, he would have time to seek fellow Quislings to invade Norwegian churches Sunday and profess to take the place of the pastors, it was indicated.

NAZIS THREATEN SLAV GUERRILLAS

Germans Say 16,000 Will Be Executed If Warfare Continues.

London (UP)—German authorities have posted proclamations in Yugoslavia demanding an end to guerrilla warfare by Monday and threatening execution of 16,000 hostages, a Yugoslav refugee government spokesman said today.

The statement followed disclosure that the Germans had "invited" Gen. Draja Mihailovich, leader of the guerrillas, to surrender and threatened that his family and the families of other Serb leaders would be arrested as hostages and held responsible for acts of the guerrilla leaders against the Axis.

The spokesman said that the new proclamation threatened the slaughter of hostages unless the guerrilla warfare ends within 24 hours from Saturday morning—or some time on Sunday.

The Germans, preparing for their spring offensive, have withdrawn all their troops from Yugoslavia and left the country in the hands of Bulgarian divisions under the command of Gen. Milutin Neditch, the spokesman said, with instructions to massacre women and children as well as men if the guerrilla resistance did not stop.

Mihailovich earlier wired the Yugoslav government here that he had ignored the order.

WOMAN JAILED FOR BEATING BOY

Charged With Attacking 4-Year-Old Nephew With Broomstick.

New York (AP)—Helen Krushinski, 29, was held in $5,000 bail today for grand jury action on a charge of felonious assault in the beating of her 4-year-old nephew with a broomstick while he was bound hand and foot with apron strings.

Mrs. Elsie Weeks, 23, mother of the child, William, said she found her sister raining blows upon the lad last Saturday with a 2½-foot long broom handle and quoted her as saying:

"I'm going to teach him not to call me bad names."

Mrs. Weeks said the boy—one of whose feet was in a plaster cast as the result of a fall which injured his ankle several days before the alleged beating—"seemed ill" on Sunday.

William is gravely ill.

He is in Cumberland Hospital, Brooklyn, in serious condition with a possible brain concussion, a possible spinal injury, a black eye and bruises about the body.

NAZIS HINT SIEGE COMING IN BREST

German Warning Indicates Invaders Fear Subversive Activities.

Vichy (AP)—German authorities notified the population of the coastal city of Brest on the English Channel today to be ready for a proclamation of a state of siege without advance notice.

The state of siege would be proclaimed because of "the existence of elements x x x which might, when the moment appeared favorable, permit themselves to engage in manifestations which could have unpredictable repercussions," the German notice said.

(The tenor of the German announcement indicated it was concerned with subversive activities among the French population of the German-occupied city rather than in preparation for meeting a possible invasion attempt by allied forces.)

The declaration, published in the newspaper Depeche De Brest, said the state of siege, if proclaimed, would last indefinitely.

ENGAGED 50 YEARS, GET LICENSE TO WED

Pasadena, Cal. (AP)—William C. Smith, 75, and Jennie E. Renslow, 72, celebrated the golden anniversary of their engagement by applying for a marriage license.

"Now that we've got the license, I suppose we'll be married right soon," Smith said. He didn't explain the fifty-year wait.

FREIGHTER SINKS AFTER COLLISION

Baltimore, Md. (INS)—Shipping circles disclosed today that a large Argentine freighter has gone down in lower Chesapeake Bay after colliding with an American freighter during a heavy fog.

FIVE KILLED IN CRASH OF BOMBER

Bakersfield, Cal. (INS)—A twin-motored advance training plane, one of seven which started out last night from Sacramento, Cal., to Tucson, Ariz., crashed in the Mojave Desert, near Bagdad, killing its crew of five, Army authorities revealed today at Bakersfield.

The entire flight ran into unexpected conditions, but six of the planes were landed safely, four of them at Tucson. Two others landed at Palmdale, Cal.

STATE'S FEBRUARY TRAFFIC DEATHS WORST IN YEARS

Albany (UP) — Traffic fatalities among New York State's walking and driving populace during February was the worst in four years, Motor Vehicle Commissioner Carroll E. Mealey announced today.

The commissioner reported that there were 5,220 accidents resulting in 147 deaths compared with 4,580 accidents resulting in 140 deaths in February, 1941.

Pedestrian fatalities rose from 69 in February, 1941, to 103 this year. Acts of pedestrians contributing most to the high death toll were crossing between intersections and crossing intersections against traffic lights, the commissioner's analysis reported.

HOME GIRLS FORM "HEART CLUB" FOR BOYS IN SERVICE

St. Paul (AP)—The sweetheart of the first Yank to land in Ireland with the A. E. F. of World War II, 20-year-old Iola Christensen, Hutchinson, Minn., blonde, laid campaign plans today for the girls who have sworn to remain true to their Army boy friends.

Plump Miss Christensen was drafted as national commander of the "Always in My Heart Club," an organization with members now in 23 cities, each member pledged to keep faith with her fighting sweetheart.

Iola wasted no time in telling the girls what their objective should be. "Everything will be kept status quo until the boys come home," she remarked. Any girl who promises to be true to her soldier is eligible for enrollment. While they may go out on dates, the serious side is out for the duration, Iola said.

Doggone!

ENGLISH BULLDOG lost in North Troy; chain collar; male; brindle with black face; reward. M. J. Day, 966 Third Ave. North 7.

Vexed indeed was a North Troy resident when his dog was gone. Doggone pleased was he when this Classified Ad in The Record Newspapers brought about return of the pet within 24 hours.

If Something's Lost

PHONE TROY 6100

Japs Claim Quake Rocked Philippines

San Francisco (INS)—Declaring that a temblor struck in the Philippines several hours before the American and Filipino defenders "asked for a halt of hostilities," the imperial Japanese government today made its first mention of the fall of Bataan Peninsula.

The Domei (Japanese) news agency gave the report, which was intercepted by the CBS short-wave listening station in San Francisco. In code, and dated "with the Japanese on Bataan, April 9," it read:

"Sixty thousand Filipino-American troops resisting the Japanese on Bataan Peninsula asked for a halt in the hostilities this morning after six days of fierce Japanese assault, which was launched on April 3."

"Details of the conditions of surrender are not yet disclosed, nor is it known yet whether Japanese forces have decided to accept the terms."

Domei said that several hours before the American forces offered to surrender, "the whole of Bataan Peninsula was rocked by an intensive quake."

"The main force of the temblor," said the dispatch, "lasted five minutes, causing Filipino huts to crumble and starting several landslides."

(Editor's Note: Washington dispatches made no mention of the temblor, and there was no confirmation of Axis reports that Gen. Jonathan W. Wainwright had asked an armistice.)

Brewed From Golden Grain and Hops Utica Club Pilsner Lager or XXX Cream Ale is nature's kindliest gift to man. Ask for it; sold everywhere.—Adv.

FOOD PRICES SHOW ANOTHER INCREASE

Washington (AP) — Retail food prices rose 1.5 per cent from mid-February to mid-March, the Labor Department announced today, to the point where it cost $1.20 to buy the food which sold for $1 a year ago.

The increase in the average for all goods was due particularly, the department said, to large gains in prices for pork, fruit and canned vegetables. Substantially higher prices were reported also for shortening, coffee, tea, rice and rolled oats.

TWO OFFICERS DIE IN BARRACKS FIRE

Rockford, Ill. (INS)—Maj. Ira Brown of Chicago and Capt. Harry S. Gorelick of Detroit were fatally burned early today when fire razed an officers' barracks at Camp Grant, southeast of Rockford. Two other officers were severely burned. The fire was extinguished after raging for an hour. Authorities would not comment on the possible cause of the blaze.

The injured were Capt. Francis Williams of Detroit and Capt. Herbert L. Corke of Waukegan, Ill., both of whom were in serious condition.

Jones And Capital Publisher In "Bout"

Washington (INS)—The officials fight, into the night, deep in the heart of Washington. They swing and shake but don't cause an ache, deep in the heart of Washington.

Noted for its notoriously bad boxing bouts, the National Capital today was recovering from a fast one rounder between two newcomers to the fight game—Secretary of Commerce Jesse Jones and Eugene Meyer, Washington publisher.

Before a ringside group that included such notables as two Supreme Court justices and members of Congress, Jones and Meyer stretched the rubber situation into a private fist fight. It happened in the little ballroom of the Willard Hotel last night.

Both were guests at a dinner held by the Alfalfa Club and during the course of the evening Meyer, who published an editorial blaming Jones for the rubber shortage, was the subject of heated glaring by the cabinet official. When Meyer attempted to leave after the dinner, Jones stepped up and seized the publisher rather violently.

Jones, who doubles as Federal loan administrator, practically picked Meyer up by the shoulders and shook him severely. Meyer lost his glasses, but recovered quickly, swinging a right. It missed. The publisher let fly another right but Jones neatly side-stepped.

When Meyer failed to connect with a third blow, a combination left jab, hook and what-have-you, Jones again took the offensive with his shaking tactics.

At this point, bystanders stepped in and abruptly ended the fracas, rushing the two battlers off into the night.

The editorial that apparently caused the battle was entitled "Mr Jones' Excuses," and declared that the cabinet member had repeatedly tried to blame the rubber crisis on others and had attempted to shield himself behind President Roosevelt

Jones, a 6 foot, 3 inch Texan, is 68, and himself a newspaper publisher. Meyer is two years younger, but weighs 30 pounds less than his erstwhile opponent.

Among the ringside guests were Supreme Court Justices James F. Byrnes and Stanley F. Reed, Sens Tom Connally (D-Tex), and William Bulow (D-N D) and Maj. Gen Edwin Watson, President Roosevelt's military aid.

Attention Joe Louis: Your title is still safe.

The Index

VIOLA AND MARRA WILL BE RETRIED AT TERM IN JUNE

Prosecution To Act Promptly in Cases Where Appellate Division Reversed Judgments.

Anthony Viola and Nicholas Marra of this city—whose convictions for burglary, third degree, and petit larceny in connection with the theft of $21.05 worth of dates and nuts from the store of Henry J. Powell at the public market Dec. 8, 1940, were reversed by the Appellate Division Wednesday— will be retried at the June term of Rensselaer County Court, Dist. Atty. Earle J. Wiley said last night.

The county prosecutor declared that the cases will be moved for trial June 1, the opening day of County Court. Both men will be tried jointly as was the case when they were previously convicted.

In directing a new trial, the Appellate Division, through an opinion written by Associate Justice Sidney F. Foster, held the convictions should be reversed because of several incidents during the trial, including reference to previous alleged crimes.

Court's Opinion.

After reviewing the circumstances surrounding the theft, as brought out in testimony during the trial before County Judge Harry E. Clinton, Justice Foster set forth in the opinion that:

"It may be readily seen from this resume that the People had a strong case and unless substantial error can be pointed out, there would be no justification for a reversal of the convictions. Some of the errors assigned by appellants have no substance as a matter of law. Such, for instance, is the claim raised by demurrer that the indictment was insufficient because, among other things, it failed to allege a felonious intent. The indictment charged a breaking and entering the premises with the intent to commit a crime therein, which is the language of the statute, and is sufficient (Penal Law, Section 404). Nor does the argument that the evidence was not sufficient to establish burglary, because there was no breaking, have any support as a matter of law.

"The term 'breaking' has a greatly extended significance as defined by statute, and includes opening by any means whatever, any outer door of a building or by obtaining entrance by any artifice (Penal Law, Section 400). There is no requirement that violence must be shown, nor is there any requirement that the door must be tightly closed. If it is closed to such an extent, or in such a manner, so that some effort must be made to open it far enough to admit the body of a person, and it is opened for that purpose, the element of breaking is present. If the jury accepted the People's testimony, they were justified in finding a breaking under the statute.

Improper References.

"Appellants assert that evidence of previous crimes was improperly admitted. We do not find that any such evidence was left in the record, but there are some instances where some references, more or less damning, were made to previous crimes.

"With the one exception, the trial judge did all that was possible under the circumstances to protect the rights of appellants, and to limit the consideration of the jury to the issue at hand. Nevertheless, an insidious impression of other crimes must have been implanted in the minds of the jurors. Considered in conjunction with the remarks of the district attorney, when he referred to the failure of appellants to produce character witnesses, these detrimental references to other crimes may well have exercised a powerful influence in creating an atmosphere decidedly prejudicial to appellants."

Justice Foster also set forth that "another error assigned was the ruling of the trial judge in refusing appellants' request to produce evidence that their confessions were not voluntarily made." It was pointed out that after examination of police officers concerning both oral admissions and written statements and the circumstances under which they were made by the appellants, these statements were offered in evidence over the objections of defense counsel, the trial judge stating that he would leave it to the jury to say whether the statements had been freely and voluntarily made.

Requests Denied.

Counsel for appellants then asked for permission to produce witnesses to show on an examination preliminary to the admission of the statements in evidence that one had been obtained under promise of immunity and the other under duress. These requests were denied by the court and the written statements were then admitted in evidence.

"This refusal to permit appellants to produce evidence that their written confessions were not voluntarily made before the same were admitted in evidence, we are compelled to regard as error. Whether the appellants could have produced such evidence, we are not called upon to determine, nor was the trial judge authorized to determine that question without giving appellants an opportunity to be heard."

"Freeze" Will Stop This

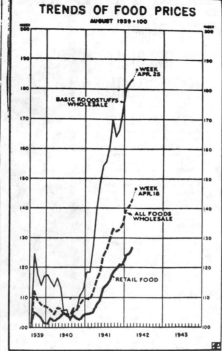

TRENDS OF FOOD PRICES
AUGUST 1939 = 100

This chart, prepared by the U. S. Department of Labor, shows how prices of food have risen since August, 1939, the month before outbreak of the war in Europe. The government's new price control program is designed to prevent further rises.

BEMAN PARK.

Bethany Chapel Sunday School will be held at the chapel at 2:30 p.m. Sunday. Leo Messner, superintendent, will conduct opening devotions.

Personal.

Mrs. Alfred B. Carr and daughters, Doris and Shirley, have returned to Yonkers after a four weeks' stay as guests of Mrs. Carr's parents, Mr. and Mrs. Wallace Bryce, 2353 Seventeenth Street.

Schedule of Masses.

Masses Sunday at the Church of St. Paul the Apostle will be at 7:30, 8:45, 10 and 11 a.m., the last mass to be followed by benediction of the Most Blessed Sacrament. The members of the Rosary Society will receive Holy Communion at the first mass and meet with the pastor at 4 p.m. for their May conference. Mass will be said by Rev. Walter J. Torpey, pastor, and Rev. Michael E. Breen, assistant pastor

---

WELFARE BUREAU TO PROVIDE SEEDS FOR CLIENTS' USE

Commissioner John J. Givney Announces Free Distribution; Continues Last Year's Plan.

Troy Welfare Department clients and WPA workers will have an opportunity to provide food for their households this summer by raising vegetables in their backyard gardens, John J. Givney, commissioner of welfare, announced today.

Seeds have arrived at the Welfare Department for a large variety of vegetables, Mr. Givney stated. The seeds may be obtained at the surplus food outlet at 200 River Street.

The department's garden program will be carried on in cooperation with the Rensselaer County Victory Garden organization.

Later on the department will receive onion and tomato plants for issuance to garden growers.

Last summer about 300 clients had gardens in their backyard or at plots near to their homes, Mr. Givney stated.

TROJAN CONTRIBUTES TO WAR CHILD FUND

Miss Ellen A. Freeman of 54 Second Street is one of fifty residents of New York State who contributed toward the support of children of the United Nations in Great Britain through the Foster Parents' Plan for War Children, Mrs. Edna Blue of New York, plan executive chairman, announced yesterday.

On receipt of an application one becomes a foster parent, the Plan makes arrangements to take a war child from a subway shelter or a bombed-out settlement into one of the Foster Parents' colonies. As soon as possible the foster parent receives a photograph and life history of the child and pays $15 a month for its support.

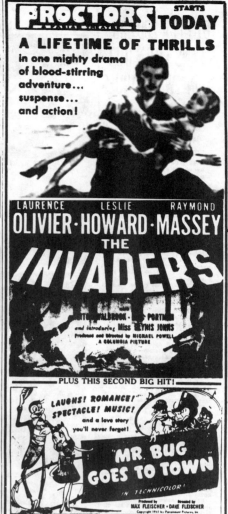

Cards And Pirates Threaten League Lead As Dodgers Drop Two Games

BETTER 200,000 FANS TURN OUT IN TWO LEAGUES

Yankee Stadium Has Season's Largest Throng of 65,800; Brooklyn's Margin One Game.

BY AUSTIN BEALMEAR
Associated Press Sports Writer

Brooklyn's champion Dodgers still rule the roost in the National League, but the St. Louis Cardinals and Pittsburg Pirates have them hanging on the ropes in what is rapidly shaping up as the hottest three-way argument since junior learned to drive the family automobile.

Still reeling from the effects of a one-two punch that absorbed at Pittsburg, Durocher's dandies staggered into St. Louis and were flattened twice by a Cardinal team that finally discovered what bats were for.

A total of 135,654 customers paid their way into American League parks yesterday and 87,090 turned out in the National League. Yankee Stadium in New York boasted the season's greatest throng, 65,804.

Reduces Margin.

At St. Louis, 24,871 watched the Cardinals clip the Dodgers, 16-0, in a long-winded opening game and 4-2 in the afternoon, which was held to five and a half innings because the daylight ran out.

The double defeat reduced Brooklyn's margin to a single game over the second-place Pittsburg Pirates, who missed their chance to share the lead by dividing a doubleheader with the Boston Braves.

The Dodgers and Cards went at it hammer and tongs, but Cardinal catcher Ken O'Dea decided the issue in the opening game with a grand-slam homer that routed Whitlow Wyatt in the first inning and a three-run double that broke a 10-10 tie in the seventh.

Kirby Higbe issued a trio of untimely walks in losing the second game. With the bases filled on passes in the fourth inning, Jimmy Brown, tripled to bring in all the runs St. Louis needed, and came home himself on an outfield fly.

Both managers and three players were chased from the field for differing with the umpires on various decisions. Leo Durocher and Billy Southworth were waved to the showers in the opener, along with Freddie Fitzsimmons of the Brooks, while Dodgers Wyatt and Dolph Camilli were banished during the nightcap.

Pressure finally caught up with the Cleveland Indians, two lengths to the good in the American League, and the Boston Red Sox cashed in on a trio of errors for an 8-4 triumph that snapped the Tribe's winning streak at 12 games. The Boston crowd of 32,123 was the second biggest of the day.

Snap Deadlock.

Rudy York's sixth and seventh home runs of the season carried the Detroit Tigers to an 8-7 victory over the Philadelphia Athletics, but Phil Marchildon pitched a sparkling two-hitter in the nightcap to give the A's an even break, 1-0.

The New York Yankees snapped a deadlock with the Red Sox and moved to within a half game of the second-place Tigers by sweeping a bargain bill from the Chicago White Sox, 6-4 and 3-1. A two-run homer by Charlie Keller paced the White Sox attack in the opening game and Atley Donald kept the Sox under control in the second by scattering seven hits.

The St. Louis Browns and Washington Senators divided their doubleheader bill, Washington 'taking the opener 9-5 on Stan Spence's two-run triple in the ninth and St. Louis coming back for a 5-1 decision in the second with the help of effective pitching by Al Hollingsworth. Spence collected six hits in ten appearances for the day, two of them three-baggers.

Pittsburg ran its winning streak to three by downing Boston 6-3 in the first game behind the seven-hit pitching of Max Butcher, but the Braves came back with a 14-hit attack to square accounts, 12-3. Eddie Miller hit a home run with the bases loaded for Boston in the nightcap, while Babe Phelps drove in all of the Pirates runs with a pair of four-masters.

The New York Giants knocked Bucky Walters out of the box in the second inning and went on to trip the Cincinnati Reds, 5-4, as Bob Carpenter went all the way.

At Chicago, the Cubs downed the Philadelphia Phils, 3-1, but the Phils took the second game, 8-1.

DWYERS TRIM 4-H CLUBBERS IN 11TH

The Dwyer All-Stars yesterday battled to an 11-inning victory 7-6, over the Rensselaer County 4-H Club in their sole-league opener at Geer Field. Pitcher Bill Everton won his own ball game in single that brought in the final run.

| 4-H | 201 000 030 00—6 |
| Dwyers | 000 222 100 01—7 |

SCHOOL GOLFERS TO COMPETE IN JUNE

The Ninth Annual Scholastic Golf Tournament sponsored jointly by Section 2, of the New York State Public High School Athletic Association and the Troy Country Club will be staged either June 6 or 12 over the Troy course, it was announced over the week-end.

P. H. Russell will supervise the Troy Country Club's participation in the tournament which is expected to draw teams from at least a dozen schools in the area, and W. Kenneth Doyle, Troy High School principal, will represent the scholastic faction.

Shut Out Leads Them Home

Shut Out (No. 3 foreground) above comes home the winner in the 68th running of the Kentucky Derby. Alsab (right behind Shut Out) was second in a photo finish. Valdina Orphan (No. 16) was third and With Regards (No. 17, on rail) fourth. Below, Shut Out, with Jockey W. D. Wright up, receives the wreath of roses.

American League

(box scores — partially illegible)

R. P. I. TRACKMEN WIN, TWO OTHER TEAMS DEFEATED

Rensselaer Tech athletic teams fared poorly in their week-end engagements; the track team turned in the only victory, downing City College by 74½ to 51½, while the baseball team lost to Stevens Institute, 2-1, the frosh nine bowed to Albany Business College, 15-2, and the lacrosse team went down, 17-0, before Cornell's stickmen.

The most successful team on the Hill this spring, the cinder striders took the C.C.N.Y. into camp in their Lewisohn Stadium meet, with the help of Frank Barclay's 18 points on firsts in the 120 high hurdles, 220 low hurdles and high jump and second in the broad jump.

The Engineer diamond delegation seemed well on the way to its first victory of the season as Ken Hecht pitched runnless ball through seven innings and R. P. I. collected a counter in the fifth on consecutive doubles by Dick Gans and Charley Horsfall. Stevens tied the game in the eighth with two-baggers by Paster and Mitterman.

12-Inning Battle.

The game went into extra innings with Hecht continuing to hurl masterful ball, but the Trehmen missed their chance for victory in the 11th when, with one out and men on first and second, Hal Wright fanned and Horsfall forced Gans at second. Walt Taverna, Stevens backstop, put on the clincher as the first man up in the 12th with a lusty wallop that went for a circuit trip.

The yearling nine, weakened by the loss of its stars to the varsity team, was never in the ball game with Albany Business College, scoring all their runs in the second inning after the opposition had taken a three-run lead. The winners scored in every inning and pitcher Mel Flowers allowed the Engineers only three hits. Porten and Dickson, pitching for the losers, gave up only nine bingles, but their team mates committed seven errors.

Although the R. P. I. and Cornell lacrosse teams both had had their first three encounters of the season, the Big Red had things all their own way as Campbell got five goals and Foster three to compile the impressive total of 17 goals to none for the Engineers.

Track.

120 yard hurdles—Won by Frank Barclay, RPI; Bob Mangum, CCNY; Dick Alleyne, CCNY, third. Time—15.6 seconds.

100 yard dash—Won by Tom Hanley, RPI; John Rehmer, RPI, second; Evan Heyman, CCNY, third. Time—10.4 seconds.

One mile run—Won by Jim Harding, RPI; Lou Cantor, CCNY, second; Fred Davis, RPI, third. Time—4:31.4.

440 yard dash—Won by Rubin Gause, CCNY; Wm. De Carteret, RPI, second; Harry Van Velsor, RPI, third. Time—53.8 seconds.

2 mile run—Won by Verne Hartley, RPI; Fred Navis, RPI, second; George Burke, CCNY, third. Time—10:08.4.

220 yard low hurdles—Won by Frank Barclay, RPI; Sy Levin, CCNY, second; Bob Miner, CCNY, third. Time—26.4 seconds.

220 yard dash—Won by Ben Marshall, RPI; Jerry Livingston, CCNY, second; Evan Heyman, CCNY, third. Time—24.0.

880 yard run—Won by Lou Cantor, CCNY; Rubin Gause, CCNY, second; Al Voorhees, RPI, third. Time—2:02.6.

High jump—Won by Bob Mangum, CCNY; Dick Alleyne, CCNY, and Ken Bordeman, RPI, tied for third. Height, 5 feet, 10 inches.

Shot put—Won by Allan Zweidling, CCNY; George Frank, RPI, second; Stan Sadowsky, CCNY, third. Distance 40 feet 1½ inches.

Discus throw—Won by Stan Sadowsky, CCNY; George Frank, RPI, second; Al Voorhees, RPI, third. Distance 128 feet, 7 inches.

Pole vault—Won by Jim Dukes, RPI; Al Jenkins, RPI, second; Ray Baumrind, CCNY, third. Height 11 feet.

Javelin throw—Won by Meyer Kaston, CCNY; Walter Haswell, RPI, second; Vladimar Giglivitch, CCNY, third. Distance 168 feet, 1 inches.

Broad jump—Won by Tom Hanley, RPI; Frank Barclay, RPI, second; Bob Fabrey, RPI third.

SLOW VICTORY BY SHUT OUT SEEN AS DISAPPOINTMENT

Louisville (AP)—Out of the rosy nostalgic clouds which enveloped Shut Out's Derby win for his daddy, speculation spread yesterday over the war-time future of America's number one horse race and the possibility that the best horse in the 68th classic may have been in his barn when the heat was run.

Naturally, you can't take a thing away from Equipoise's son for the way he went all out to win the big end of the poor—$64,225—by 2½ lengths, thereby topping off the comeback of both himself and "Tough Luck Goldey"—Wayne Wright to you. Nor can you overlook the way Alsab came a-winging from 'way back to grab second place and boom out of the "bust" class to which he's been consigned this year.

At the same time, however, you couldn't help wondering what Sun Again, backed by Ben Jones' Missouri miracles of training, might have done in this race, if he hadn't been scratched at the last minute Saturday. He was only a neck away from ringing the bell in the Derby Trial mile run in a snappy 1:36 last Tuesday. Saturday, the mile was clocked three seconds slower on the way to a slow 2:04 2-5 mile and a quarter.

Churchill Downs showed it was in there pitching when Col. Matt Winn turned over a $50,000 check to the Red Cross. However, driving back from the picturesque ragging plant after the shindig was over, one veteran newspaperman in Derbytown pointed out that although a near-record of $1,983,011 was bet by the cash contributors, and concessionaires did a land office business, the Defense Bond booths in the clubhouse and grandstand sold the grand total of $200 worth of stamps and bonds all day.

The Derby babies were packing up yesterday and getting ready to shove off for the Preakness and 'way points. Shut Out and Devil Diver, the stablemate who was supposed to be the "big boss" until Saturday, shipped yesterday along with William Woodward's Apache, Al Sabath's Alsab and Mrs. Payne Whitney's Douglas' Fair Call. The rest go today, Saturday they'll all tangle with one or more threats, notably R. Sterling Clark's Colchis, in the Preakness.

Meantime, Eddie Arcaro came out flatly and said he wasn't going to change his "wrong guess" of the Derby when, as Mrs. Payne Whitney's contract jockey, he chose Devil Diver for his mount and gave the ride on Shut Out to Wright. This was giving away the victory and he got only sixth place for himself.

As usual, the estimate of the crowd varied widely. Most observers thought it was about 80,000. Col. Matt Winn estimated 100,000.

It's Over That Way Fellows

Al Watson, president of the Troy Pistol League, points to the target for the benefit of the competitors in the first national pistol tournament sponsored by the league at the range on River Street. Center is Ed Collins, vice president, tallying one of the scores, while Jack Sheridan of the National Rifle Association looks on.

Sharkey To Referee Navy Relief Bout

BY HUGH FULLERTON, JR.
Wide World Sports Columnist

New York—Walter Hagen starts his "comeback" today when he hooks up with actor Bob Hope, Jimmy Demaret and Mayor Jeffries of Detroit in a war relief match at Detroit . . . You can look for Sir Walter to finish second in that field . . . Report from Louisville says Ben Jones' reason for scratching Sun Again from the Derby was not because he didn't figure the colt was ready but because he didn't like the post position he drew . . . Sun Again likely will be a Preakness starter although Ben claimed he wasn't sure when he shipped him to Pimlico . . . Jack Sharkey is listed to referee the Red Cochrane-Garvey Young Navy Relief fight at Boston Friday. Wonder how the old gob will feel if he has to give Marine Young the decision over Sailor Cochrane?

Monday Matinee

Lew (the honest brakeman) Diamond is listening to an offer of $25,000 from Pittsburg's Dapper Dan Club to have Gus Lesnevich defend the light heavyweight title against Mose Brown and Cleveland wants Gus to put it on the line against Jimmy Bivins . . . So if Lesnevich can get loose from the Coast Guard for a while, says Lew, he did quite a bit of half-backing for Brown a decade ago . . . Ken Silvestri, who was third string catcher for the Yankees before he went into the Army, is spending his furlough from Camp Custer (Mich.) at the Yankee stadium doing bull pen duty . . . Louisville sportsmen are arranging to invite service men on leave to accompany them on week-end fishing trips after the season opens and even figure on providing the tackle . . . Ben Foord, former British Empire heavyweight champion, has been serving on the North African front for the last two years. Writing to Franny Murray, the ex-Penn footballer, Ben admitted it wasn't so much fun, especially when he was hit on the hand by a bit of shrapnel, but he escaped a lot of sleepless nights when the baby was teething.

Today's Guest Star

Art Edson, Oklahoma City Times: "It isn't whether you win or lose, but if you insist on doing the lasy, you'll never be bothered by those stuffy big crowds."

Service Dept.

When George (Bud) Svendsen was playing football for Minnesota and the Green Bay Packers, Bob Swisher was performing for Northwestern and the Chicago Bears. They've buried their rivalry for the duration and are doing temporary recruiting for Naval Aviation in . . .

ST. PAUL'S NINE DEFEATS JUNIORS

St. Paul's C. Y. O. nine yesterday nosed out the Troy Boys' Club Juniors, 13-12, at Catholic High Field, with both teams collecting 19 safeties. Lemke and Collins hit for the circuit for the Clubbers and P. Conway homered for the Saints.

Pafundi and Rowe led the hit department with four each and Lemke and Collins each got three for the Club Horgan bingled four times, Ryan and P. Conway three each for the opposition. Merola started on the mound for the Club but gave way to Sargent in the sixth, when Flynn relieved McCarthy for the Saints.

| Club Juniors | 130 114 200—12 19 8 |
| St. Paul's | 310 105 201—13 19 5 |

BITS ABOUT GOLFERS

Golfers at the municipal course at Frear Park yesterday staged their first blind bogey of the current season with Joe Bovasso and Seymour Myers splitting top honors. The "bogey" was set at 85 with Bovasso carding an 89 with a seven handicap for 82, with Myers hitting 102 with a 14 handicap for 88.

Other scores with handicaps were: Dave Weisberg, 95-15, 80; Pete Zomrich, 80-25, 55; Dick 100-11, 89; H. F. Polk, 87-22, 65; Charles Brendfoer, 80-20, 60; Jerry Carpenter, 82-3, 79; John McGrath, 79-10, 69; K. Hyde, 140-24, 114; P. Hyde, 142-8, 134, and Frank Ball, 128-3, 125.

The "play for pay" golfers of the Northeastern New York Professional Golf Association tee off at 9 a.m. today over the Troy Country Club course in the sectional qualifying round for the National P. G. A. tournament. The event will be 36-hole medal play.

Three places for the National meet to be held May 25-31 at Atlantic City will be awarded winners of the sectional qualifying test. Troy Creavy, Albany Country Club, automatically qualifies for the Nationals by virtue of being runner-up in the 1941 meet.

Eddie Schultz, home club professional; Jack Patroni, Alex Gerlak, Joe Creavy and Johnny Gaucas are among the area professionals expected to compete in the sectionals.

SPORTS MIRROR

By The Associated Press.

Today A Year Ago—Cleveland Indians moved three and a half games in front in American League race by defeating Washington, 12 to 4, for tenth straight victory.

Three Years Ago—Larry MacPhail advanced to presidency of the Brooklyn Dodgers.

Five Years Ago—Although knocked out of box in seventh inning, Carl Hubbell of New York Giants received credit for his third win of the season and his 19th in a row over a two-year stretch.

It's "Horse Sense"—
There's Big Demand For Places To Rent

Lots of folks like to wait until after the May First rush before they move. Others want to see what desirable places become available then, while families with youngsters often want to wait until school's nearly over before moving. And of course there are always new residents coming here to work in Troy area war plants. There's just one sure way to get in touch with these prospective tenants—a Classified Ad in The Record Newspapers.

TELEPHONE TROY 6100

Ask for the low 6-time Order Rate

THE WEATHER
U. S. Weather Bureau.
Tonight—Warmer.

THE TIMES RECORD

FINAL EDITION

Series 1942—No. 107. (Entered as Second Class Matter at the Postoffice at Troy, N. Y., under the Act of March 3, 1879.) TROY, N. Y., WEDNESDAY EVENING, MAY 6, 1942. (Published Daily Except Sunday) PRICE FOUR CENTS

CORREGIDOR SURRENDERS TO JAPS AFTER TERRIFIC ATTACK

British Storm Madagascar Naval Base

Two French Cruisers Are Reported Missing

Vichy (U.P.) — Two French cruisers—the Marseillaise and the Lamotte Picquet—today were reported as missing since the British attack on Madagascar. It was not known whether they had rallied to the British cause or were attempting to rejoin French warships in Indo-China.

The Marseillaise is a new cruiser, finished about the time the war started. She is of 7,600 tons.

The Lamotte Picquet, of 7,250 tons, was built in 1926.

AXIS SUBMARINE SENT TO BOTTOM BY U. S. DESTROYER

Shell Blasted Hole in Undersea Raider, Navy Reveals; Nazi Seamen Rescued.

New York (AP)—"The debris in the water left no doubt that the sub had gone straight to the bottom—and for good."

And so, the Third Naval District disclosed today, another Axis undersea raider was eliminated by the Atlantic patrol. The job was done by an old four-stack destroyer.

The story, told by an officer aboard the destroyer, was formally released by the naval district.

It was in the middle of the first watch, between 2 a.m. and 3 a.m. The destroyer was sliding quietly along through calm blackness. On deck no lights were showing. Below, the blue battle lights were sombre pin-points. No signs of life were visible, but silent officers and men were at every station.

Suddenly, a low, dark shape loomed up ahead. At the same moment the destroyer's spotlight stabbed out and revealed a submarine lying on the surface, charging her batteries, while startled members of the submarine crew attempted to get to cover.

On the destroyer, a chief boatswain's mate manning a machine gun sent fiery tracer bullets zinging out at the submarine, forcing some of the crew to leap into the sea.

The submarine fired two torpedoes, both of which were wide. Then from the destroyer came the sharp crack of a four-inch gun fired at almost point blank range. There was a dull boom and a gaping hole showed in the side of the submarine, which slowly rolled over and disappeared.

The destroyed charged on and dropped a pattern of depth bombs over the spot where the submarine was last seen, then crossed back and dropped more. The destroyer's officers and men reported that there was no doubt about that one.

With the action over, the destroyer picked up survivors and resumed patrol.

LIMIT SPENDING OF ITALIAN OFFICIALS

Berlin (German Broadcast Recorded by United Press in New York)—Premier Benito Mussolini has decreed that Italian officials must abstain from spending money "unless it is absolutely necessary," a German Trans-Ocean News Agency dispatch from Rome said today. It said Mussolini had declared that spending must be devoted to the war effort.

MASONIC VETERAN DEAD.

Hornell (INS)—The oldest Master Mason in Steuben County was dead today. Philip M. Nast, jr., 94, a Mason for 72 years, died at Bethesday Hospital after a long illness.

BOY'S BODY FOUND IN HUDSON RIVER AT ADAMS STREET

Five-year old John Drewecki of 30 River Street Missing from Home Since Monday Evening.

The body of 5-year-old John Drewecki, son of Mr. and Mrs. Nicholas Drewecki of 30 River Street, was recovered from the Hudson River about 1 p.m. today by state troopers and Troy police who had been dragging the river at the foot of Adams Street where the boy had last been reported seen Monday night.

When all indications appeared that the missing boy had fallen in the river the State and Troy police began dragging the stream about 10:30 a.m. today and in a little more than two hours the body was located.

Coroner Charles J. Cote ordered the removal of the body to the John J. Burke Funeral Home and gave a verdict of accidental drowning.

The dragging operations were under the direction of Capt. Michael B. Shea of the First Precinct, and those taking part included Plainclothesman James Cassin and Patrolmen Raymond C. O'Bryan and Edward Maloney.

The state police included W. J. Sullivan and D. F. Lang.

The boy was the youngest of a family of seven children. Monday night he had been playing near the river and had been warned by one of his older brothers to stay away from the water. He then left but apparently returned to the river bank.

AMBASSADOR LEAHY REACHES LISBON ON WAY TO WASHINGTON

Lisbon (U.P.)—Admiral William D. Leahy, United States ambassador to Vichy, today awaited transportation aboard the next clipper plane to Washington where he will "report" to President Roosevelt.

Leahy, a secretary and the body of Mrs. Leahy arrived by train last night. The ambassador was met by his son, Lieut. Commdr. William H. Leahy, assistant Naval attache at the American embassy in London; Bert Fish, United States minister to Portugal; representatives of the Portuguese government, and members of the English embassy.

Mrs. Leahy's body received by the Portuguese administration and English Chaplain Fullford Williams, will remain at an English cemetery awaiting transportation to the United States. She died following an operation in Vichy.

NEGRO HUNTED FOR SLAYING WIFE AND FOUR OTHER PERSONS

Hamlet, N. C. (U.P.) — Two airplanes, bloodhounds and a posse of more than 300 men hunted through the swamps today for Will Dawkins, 50, a Negro carpenter who killed his 18-year-old wife, two of her sisters, a nephew and Police Chief John Fallaw, 48.

Dawkins and his wife, Orenna, were estranged.

Late yesterday, he went to plead with her to return to him. A quarrel started, and Dawkins killed his wife first, then her sisters, then Jack Quick, 2, son of one of the sisters.

Fallaw found him near the edge of town. Fallaw ordered him to surrender. Dawkins snapped a shotgun to his shoulder and shot Fallaw in the head and fled into the swamps.

CHILD FOUND DEAD IN NEARBY SPRING

Three-year-old Ronald Beswick, last seen by his mother, Mrs. Howard C. Beswick, Lake George at 3 p.m. yesterday was found dead about an hour later in a 4-foot spring about 100 yards at the rear of his home.

The spring is surrounded by a circular wall which was covered with loose boards and it is thought that the boy was walking on these when one gave way.

Dr. H. H. Dier was summoned and Robert Smith, who assisted with the pulmotor and artificial respiration. Dr. P. H. Huntington of Warrensburg, Warren County coroner, gave a verdict of accidental drowning.

"MOTHER'S DAY" PROCLAIMED.

Albany (AP)—Proclaiming Sunday Mother's Day, Governor Lehman today urged communities to "join with mothers and fathers of men in service in an expression of the pride and love we feel for these young men."

Madagascar--Invaded by British Troops

The harbor of Diego Suarez, Vichy France's naval base on Madagascar, fourth largest island in the world, invaded by British Empire Commandos. Island, which lies athwart United Nations' supply routes to China, India and the Middle East, was being eyed by Japanese.

BULOW DEFEATED IN SOUTH DAKOTA

Senator Loses Democratic Primary Battle to Former Governor Berry.

BY THE ASSOCIATED PRESS.

Sen. W. J. Bulow, South Dakota Democrat, lost renomination for a third trem to an out-and-out Roosevelt supporter who charged him with pre-war isolationism, incomplete returns from the headline contest in primary voting of four states indicated today.

Former South Dakota Gov. Tom Berry held better than a 2 to 1 lead over the 72-year-old senator, who since Pearl Harbor has pledged support to the war effort but reserved the right to criticize administration domestic policies.

Gov. Harlan J. Bushfield appeared certain to be Berry's Republican opponent, holding a decisive lead over Olive A. Ringsrud, secretary of state. Rep. Karl Mundt (R) was renominated. He will be opposed by Fred Hildebrandt, a former representative who retired in 1940 to run for the senate.

The state's four-way Republican gubernatorial race was so close it probably must be decided at the June party convention.

Unofficial results of voting yesterday in the other states:

Indiana—Rep. Schulte (D), a labor leader, trailed Ray J. Madden; six other representatives were unopposed; the other five incumbents held safe leads.

Alabama—Senator Bankhead and six representatives, all Democrats were unopposed; Rep. Grant (D) was renominated, and two incumbent Democratic representatives, Patrick and Jarman, faced the prospect of a run-off primary June 2 because of close contests. Chauncey Sparks led four other Democratic candidates for governor.

Florida—Four Democratic Congressmen were renominated; Rep. Green led Democratic balloting for a new sixth seat gained through reapportionment, but both this race and that for the fifth seat, which Green vacates, appeared headed for May runoff primaries.

U. S. CITIZENS WILL SAIL FROM SWEDEN

Stockholm (U.P.)—Seventy-five American citizens sail May 23 for the United States aboard the Swedish liner Gripsholm, chartered for the repatriation of American and Japanese diplomats and nationals. It was reported the ship also would carry an unspecified number of passengers from Finland and possibly some from Norway and Denmark.

Reds Warn Tokyo of More Bombs to Come

Moscow (U.P.) — The Soviet Army's official organ Red Star asserted today that Japan's industrial centers and strategic bases are threatened with further attacks by American bombers in an Allied shift "from defensive to offensive tactics."

The recent bombing of Tokyo and two other Japanese industrial centers by American bombers showed tremendous distances mean nothing to modern aircraft, Red Star said. The Soviet paper also pointed out that where Allied planes have engaged the Japanese airmen, "results proved favorable to the allies."

STATE HOSPITAL OPEN TO DRAFTEES

Attorney General Rules Kings Park Institution May Care for Service Men

(Staff Correspondence)

Albany—Residents of New York State inducted into the country's armed forces under the Selective Service Act and discharged since the declaration of war may be admitted to the veterans' unit at Kings Park State Hospital under a ruling today by Atty. Gen. John J. Bennett, jr.

His opinion was asked by Dr. William J. Tiffany, state commissioner of mental hygiene, after hospital officials questioned whether selectees were admissible.

Bennett held that, while a 1923 law authorized the unit for treatment of World War veterans only, a subdivision enacted in 1932 extends its facilities to "discharged soldiers, sailors and Marines of all wars who volunteered or were commissioned, warranted or inducted into service from the state of New York."

REPORT AIR ALARM SOUNDED IN PARIS

Vichy (AP)—Advices from Paris said today that an air alarm sounded in the German-occupied French capital during the night.

At the same time there was mounting attention to recurring air activity over unoccupied France by what Frenchmen generally assumed to be British planes, although an information office statement mentioned no nationality.

CURTIN ACCLAIMS CORREGIDOR ARMY

Australian Prime Minister Says American Heroes Gained Objective.

Canberra, Australia (AP) — Prime Minister John Curtin declared today that "there will be no dismay at the news of the fall of Corregidor; rather will there be a feeling of pride and admiration."

"The fact is," he continued in a statement, "that a very small force of brave men has held the world's attention by an amazing stand against the armed might of a foe greatly superior in manpower and machines.

"The government and people of Australia send to the government and people of the United States at this moment a message of congratulation and thanks for what their men did at Corregidor. The stand there upset Japan's war strategy and gained precious time.

"Corregidor takes its place in world history. We had our Tobruk. America has its Corregidor.

"Standing to that spirit of dauntless gallentry we cannot lose. Our heads are high; our hearts are not heavy. We shall go on.

"General MacArthur said when he came to our country that he would go back to the Philippines. That is a solemn pledge we shall most certainly help him keep."

VANDERBILT LEAVES ESTATE TO WIFE, SON AND DAUGHTER

New York (AP)—Brig. Gen. Cornelius Vanderbilt left his entire estate—unofficially estimated at several millions—to his wife, Mrs. Grace Vanderbilt; his son, Cornelius Vanderbilt, jr., and his daughter, Mrs. Robert Livingston Stevens.

The will, filed for probate yesterday, formally appraised the estate at "more than $10,000." The financier and soldier died March 1 at Biscayne Bay, Fla. He was 68.

Except for several $500 bequests to servants, the entire estate was halved, one part ordered into trust for his wife, and the other divided equally between his son and daughter.

Disclosure of the disposition of General Vanderbilt's will followed by 24 hours the filing of the will of Gertrude Vanderbilt Whitney, the general's sister. Between them, the two wills cover the disposal of a majority of the famous Vanderbilt fortune, founded more than a century ago by the late Commodore Cornelius Vanderbilt, great-grandfather of General Vanderbilt and operator of a fleet of ferry boats.

COMMANDOS PUSH INTO OUTSKIRTS OF DIEGO SUAREZ

Vichy Indicates Fall of City Imminent; U. S. May Seize French Possessions in Caribbean.

BY THE ASSOCIATED PRESS.

Tank-led British commandos were reported battling French colonial troops on the outskirts of Diego Suarez today as Vichy reports indicated that the fall of that key naval base on Madagascar island was imminent.

R. A. F. warplanes dominated the skies over Diego Suarez, on the northern end of the big island, and British warships were reported in firm command of the surrounding seas.

The commandos, leading the assault, had plunged twenty miles through the jungles against "stiffening French resistance" to reach the gates of the naval base.

Meanwhile, Washington considered a possible United States move against Vichy-controlled bases flanking the Panama Canal since Vichy France has defied a United States warning against resistance to the British on Madagascar.

Chief of the Vichy government Pierre Laval reported on Madagascar to the cabinet, which a communique said fully approved the French resistance and "paid homage to the troops and their leaders, which despite great numerical inferiority opposed with heroic resistance the Anglo-Saxon forces."

Washington diplomatic sources said the Vichy government's fight against British occupation at Madagascar Island could be construed as hostile to the United Nations and that it raised the question of whether French bases in the Caribbean—Martinique, Guadeloupe and French Guiana should be allowed to remain in Vichy hands.

A bulletin from French headquarters on Madagascar said the island's entire air force had been thrown into action against renewed British bombing attacks and declared:

"We are resisting along the first line of redoubts."

British Admist Resistance.

London military quarters said the British commandos, infantry and marines who landed on the 1,000-mile-long island at dawn Tuesday were now closing in on the key Diego Suarez naval base.

These quarters acknowledged that the island's defenders, under orders from Vichy to fight to the end, were putting up sharp resistance but said the British advance was progressing "satisfactorily."

Vichy reports last night said the British, estimated by the French at 20,000 troops, had reached the town of Andrakaka, only four miles from Diego Suarez.

The German-controlled Paris radio said: "Fighting has been going on in Madagascar for 24 hours, and a handful of French colonials, without hope of help or reinforcements from the home country, has been fighting step by step against the British aggressors."

Laval Ignores U. S. Warning.

Acting with the full consent of the United States, the British moved into Madagascar to prevent a threatened Axis seizure of the strategic island, which commands Allied sea communications to the Middle East, India and China.

France's pro-German Premier Pierre Laval bluntly ignored the warning contained in an American note to Vichy that "any warlike act permitted by the French government against the government of Great Britain or of the United States would, of necessity, have to be regarded as an attack upon the United Nations as a whole."

While French planes fiercely attacked the British occupation forces, a Madagascar communique disclosed that the French had lost two out of three light naval units which dashed out of the Diego Suarez base yesterday in a desperate foray against British warships.

Two French Ships Sunk.

The communique said British gunners sank the 1,379-ton submarine Beveziers and the Bougainville, variously described as an auxiliary cruiser and a light cruiser, and damaged a small French auxiliary cruiser. Most of the crews were saved.

Madagascar's land forces were estimated in London at 1,500 Frenchmen and 3,700 colonials.

Vichy dispatches said several British planes were shot down by anti-aircraft guns and some of the light British tanks put ashore had been destroyed.

Newspapers in unoccupied France

(Continued On Page 14)

NOTED ARCHITECT DEAD.

Buffalo (U.P.)—Charles F. Reif, 78, nationally-known architectural designer, died at his home here last night. He was the father of Col. Allan F. Reif and Maj. Charles A. Reif of the 74th Regiment, New York Guard.

WPB Orders 50 Per Cent Cut In "Gas" And Fuel Oil For East

Washington (AP)—A gasoline limit of five to six gallons a week for many Eastern motorists was indicated today in a War Production Board order cutting consumption in the seaboard area to one-half that of last year starting May 16, when rationing becomes effective.

Gasoline consumption in the East and Oregon and Washington already is cut to two-thirds normal. The new order made no mention of the Northwestern states and there was speculation that restrictions might be lifted there because of immproved supply conditions.

The WPB order also limited consumption of light fuel oil, the kind used in house heating, to 50 per cent of normal beginning May 16 in the 17 Eastern states and the District of Columbia. The order applied to deliveries to suppliers and was the first cut on heating oil.

Although the overall curtailment of gasoline consumption in the East will be one-half, it was explained that since necessary vehicles will continue to receive their full requirements, the non-essential users will be cut by about 60 per cent.

The supply available under a 50 per cent cut would mean that many motorists would have to get along on five or six gallons weekly but there was on officiahint as to the ration allowance for each motorist under the card system. A temporary emergency plan will go into effect in the East on May 16 and continue until July 1, when a more elaborate program will be put in operation.

Motorists of the whole country were warned by Joseph B. Eastman, Defense Transportation Director, that automobiles and tires now on the road are a "national and not a private resource."

"Every owner of a motor vehicle in public or private service should realize that he holds this vehicle in trust for the national war effort and that it should be used only for purposes of necessity," Eastman said.

American-Filipino Garrison Suffers Heavy Casualties

General Wainwright's Troops, Weary and Hungry Afte[r] 27 Days of Continuous Attack, Forced to Yield When Big Japanese Guns Sweep Away Beach Defenses; Nipponese Land From Bataan in Stee[l] Barges; President Acclaims Heroic Garrison.

BY THE UNITED PRESS.

The exhausted, bomb-battered little American garriso[n] surrendered Corregidor Fortress and Manila Bay to Japanes[e] assault troops today as fighting raged to new peaks in the South west Pacific and Indian Oceans.

Gen. Jonathan M. Wainwright and his 7,000 men an[d] Army nurses went down after a 27- battle against impossibl[e] odds at an hour when Japanese armies in Burma were increas[-] ing the threat to China and India and when British occupatio[n] forces were fighting fiercely at the big French naval base o[n] Northern Madagascar Island.

The fall of Corregidor and three other fortresses guardin[g] the entrance to Manila Bay was announced in a special com[-] munique at headquarters of Gen. Douglas MacArthur, in Aus[-] tralia, where announcement also was made of damaging ne[w] allied air attacks on the Japanese invasion bases of Lae an[d] Rabaul.

MacArthur, who pledged that his forces one day will re[-] turn to the Philippines in triumph, said that Wainwright wa[s] forced to surrender the islands after a powerful Japanese a[t-] tack had been made across three miles of water from Bataa[n] Peninsula.

Corregidor went down to defeat only after new concen[-] trations of heavy caliber Japanese guns had swept away beac[h] defenses and inflicted heavy casualties on the weary, hungr[y] and disease-ridden American and Filipino defenders.

New .4-inch batteries concentrated in the mountains o[f] Bataan high above the fortress rock at the entrance to Manil[a] Bay accomplished what nearly five months of incessant bombin[g] and shelling had failed to do.

Barbed wire entanglements, machine gun nests and othe[r] American installations were destroyed. Then in the darknes[s] of last night the Japanese swarmed across the three miles o[f] water separating the fortress from Bataan. They came in stee[l] barges. And they established a beach head which the weak[-] ened defenders could not dislodge.

The communique indicated that the Japanese, now that the Manila bay forts have been captured, were proceeding without pause in efforts to end resistance elsewhere in the Philippines.

The surrender came 44 years after Dewey's victory at Manila Bay and at the end of five months of American participation in the war. It gave Japan control, for the first time, of one of the most valuable naval bases in the Pacific but it found American and Filipino forces still fighting guerrilla actions on the major islands.

There are 7,000 Philippine Islands and American military circles said that resistance would be continued over a long period in guerrilla warfare, such as is now in progress on Mindanao Island.

One of his last messages before he had to surrender Corregidor, General Walwright reported that the Japanese had landed reinforcements in western Minanao, the Philippines' second largest island, in the vicinity of Malabang near Cotabato.

Japs Sweep Up River.

Enemy troops in steel invasion barges, the communique said, are moving up the Pulangi River in Mindanao and heavy Japanese pressure is being exerted on American-Filipino forces near Digos on the same island.

Military observers estimated that about 7,000 American and Filipino soldiers, sailors and marines and 3,000 civilians were on the Manila Bay fortresses when they fell. Included in the total were 68 Army nurses who had been removed from Bataan when that peninsula fell April 9.

The communique detailing the last fighting on Corregidor—whose defenders a few hours before had been called by President Roosevelt the "living symbol of our war aims and the guarantee of victory"—told how the fortress' 12-inch naval guns had fired back at the enemy almost to the end.

Under Continuous Fire.

But the big guns were handicapped by total lack of aerial observation. They did succeed in smashing enemy truck columns on Bataan. But they were unable to spot and destroy the heavy guns that blasted down on Corregidor from the slopes of Mount Mariveles.

Ever since the fall of Bataan, the communique said, the Japanese had subjected the island forts to unremitting aerial and artillery bombardment.

On April 29 the enemy assaults became "much heavier," the War Department said, "and from then until May 5 there was little respite."

On the last day of fighting, and for the fourth consecutive day, the Japanese made 13 separate air attacks on the 1,300-acre rock, but the communique said it was enemy artillery fire which in the end proved disastrous.

Heavy Casualties Indicated.

The communique gave no details of American losses in killed and wounded in the last few days of the battle but said:

"There were many casualties among our troops and the damage to military installations was severe."

The Japanese in capturing the island forts after nearly five months of never-ending attack won a ma[-] jor strategical victory. Militar[y] men pointed out, however, that th[e] forts' value to the enemy canno[t] now be nearly as great as it woul[d] have been three months ago.

In that respect, officials said to[-] day, the garrisons on Corregido[r] Island and on her sister forts ca[r-] ried out their assignment—la[st] ditch resistance while inflicting th[e] greatest possible loss on the enem[y].

"The defenders did their job an[d] did it well," one official said. "Th[e] Japanese have paid a high price [to] control Manila Bay."

President's Tribute.

Lieut. Gen. Jonathan M. Wai[n-] wright and his heroic men receive[d] only yesterday, before the Japane[se] invasion of Corregidor Island, [a] stirring tribute from their com[-] mander-in-chief, President Roos[e-] velt.

"You and your devoted followe[rs] have become the living symbols [of] our war aims and the guarantee [of] victory," the President said in h[is] message to Wainwright.

And as what had been inevitab[le] for many weeks became fact, of[fi-] cers, enlisted men, high officia[ls] and the man in the street spoke [of] Corregidor and her heroic defen[d-] ers with awesome reverence.

There was no doubt in Washin[g-] ton that every man had given [his] all to resist the overwhelming Ja[p-] anese hordes.

President Roosevelt revealed y[es-] terday that hunger, disease, [ex-] haustion and lack of supplie[s—] those allies that aided the ene[my] in the jungles of Bataan—h[ad] played their ugly roles on Corre[gi-] dor, too.

Message to Wainwright.

He had just dispatched his me[s-] sage to Wainwright, telling of [his] admiration of the heroic sta[nd] against the mounting intensity [of] bombardment by enemy planes a[nd] heavy siege guns.

(Continued On Page 5)

SCHENECTADY NURSE SAFE IN AUSTRALI[A]

Lieut. Pauline Serafino, Schen[ec-] tady's first nurse to volunteer [for] service in the U. S. Army, is [safe] in Australia, according to word [re-] cently received by her parents, [Mr.] and Mrs. Angelo Serafino, of [...] Foster Avenue, Schenectady.

The Schenectady girl notified [her] parents she had arrived safel[y in] Australia sometime in March [and] assured them that "all is well."

The Index

SIX AREA YOUTHS GIVEN WAR WINGS AT PILOT SCHOOLS

Young Men From Troy, Rensselaer, Ballston Lake, Palmer and Salem Are Now Lieutenants.

Six Troy Area youths were among the fighter-flyers of Class 42-E, receiving war wings at seven different pilot schools of the Gulf Coast Air Force Training Center today. It was the largest class in history, and represented every state in the union.

The area young men, who with others of the class, are now preparing to stream forth to every continent under the sun to fight Uncle Sam's sky battles, are:

Lieut. George K. Shako, jr., of 2256 Burdett Avenue, Troy, graduated from the Lubbock pilot school.

Lieut. John A. Mancini, Ballston Lake, graduate of Moore Field.

Others Graduated.

Lieut. Edwin J. Moses of Palmer, Saratoga County, graduated from Foster Field.

Lieut. Lester D. McCluskey, 1333 Second Street, Rensselaer, graduated from Ellington Field.

Lieut. Kenneth James Murphy, 1401 Second Street, Rensselaer, graduate of Moore Field.

Staff Sergt. William A. Gillis, Salem, graduate of Kelly Field.

"Unusual" was the name for this class.

For example:

Class 42-E—the sixth post-Pearl Harbor brood—was the largest in history (phraseology that has become standard every five weeks).

Class 42-E was the last to wear the traditional cadet blue garb.

Class 42-E grinds out from more schools than ever before (four in March, six in April, seven this time.)

Besides the "home-town" boys who made good, were other significant names, including Lieut. U. S. Bond, of Wentworth, S. D., who skyrocketed to fame through the remarkable coincidence of his name-letter combination; Lieut. Arthur L. Foster, jr., who graduated at the field named after his pilot-pioneer father, Foster Field, Victoria, Tex.

Trained in Texas.

Lieutenant Bond's finishing school was Lubbock, Tex., advanced multiengined base, as is Ellington Field, near Houston. Single engined advanced schools included were: Kelly Field and Brooks Field, near San Antonio; Foster Field, Moore Field, Mission, Tex., and Lake Charles, La., which produced its first class of pursuit pilots. Closely following upon the "cloudheels" of the pilots was a record-smashing class of bombardiers the "cell from Heaven Men," and navigators—also flying officers who round out the three-man air crew.

According to custom, wings were pinned on finished fledglings and simultaneously mailed to "honorary" members of Class 42-E," the mothers and girl friends of the ex-cadets back home.

AUXILIARY GROUP WILL WORK DEGREE

Mrs. Florence H. Brown will be pianist for the degree team of the Auxiliary to the Sons of Union Veterans of the Civil War which will exemplify ritual at the Utica convention next month. The team is composed of past department presidents, including Mrs. Mary E. Stapleton, national vice president.

Mrs. Brown and Miss Mary I. Weaver attended a meeting of the Mizpah Club at the home of Mrs. Susie Smith, Schenectady, Saturday. Mrs. Gertrude Clothier presided at the business meeting at which Miss Weaver gave the secretary's report.

Troy District Flyers Get Air Corps "Wings"

LIEUT. G. K. SHAKO, JR.

LIEUT. J. A. MANCINI

LIEUT. E. J. MOSES

LIEUT. L. D. McCLUSKEY

LIEUT. K. J. MURPHY

STAFF SGT. W. A. GILLIS

MEMORIAL RITES HELD BY CHAPTER OF EASTERN STAR

Flaring Up of Oil Stove at Trimble Home Results in Call for Fire Apparatus; Little Damage Caused.

HOOSICK FALLS

The semi-annual memorial service was the outstanding feature of Friday night's meeting of Van Rensselaer Chapter, O. E. S. The ceremony, conducted by the officers of the chapter, memorialized Mrs. Sarah Tuck and Mrs. Sadie Dorr, members of the chapter who died since the preceding memorial, also Laverne Twining, grand patron of the order in 1939-1940 and a past grand trustee.

During the meeting Mrs. Mary Rudd, junior past matron of the chapter, acting on behalf of the chapter, presented a gift of silver to Miss Helen Wright, worthy matron of the chapter, whose marriage to Lieut. F. Albert Chamberlain, takes place Wednesday.

Mrs. Ethel Gooding "drew out" of the merchandise club. Following the meeting a social session with refreshments was enjoyed.

Personal.

Among the week-end visitors in town were Thomas K. Beaumont and Edward Albergine of Fort Monmouth, N. J.

Oil Stove Flares Up.

The flaring up of an oil stove on the enclosed porch on the rear of the residence of Mrs. Emma Trimble, 17 Willow Street, Saturday morning shortly before noon brought the fire truck to the scene but the blazing stove had been brought under control. Mrs. Trimble was upstairs in the house at the time and had the smoke emanating from the porch not been noticed by residents of Nixon Street it is probable that the firemen would have had work to do. Damage was slight, being confined to the porch.

Brevities.

St. Mary's Alumni Association will meet tomorrow at 8 p. m. in the Immaculate Conception parish hall for the purpose of starting on plans for the association's annual reunion.

Rev. Walter D. Kring, pastor of First Presbyterian Church, will be the principal speaker at the annual meeting and spring rally of the Troy Local Union of Christian Endeavor tomorrow evening at Third Presbyterian Church in Troy.

Lieut. Gov. John B. Wood of Albany, head of the Division of New York State Kiwanis in which the Kiwanis Club is located, will make an official visit to the club tomorrow noon in Masonic Hall. In view of his visit a full attendance of the membership is expected.

MELROSE.

Monarch Lodge will sponsor a card party at I. O. O. F. Hall tomorrow evening.

Melrose Grange will hold a card and domino party at the home of Mr. and Mrs. Charles Wetsel on May 29.

The Women's Society of Christian Service met Thursday afternoon at the home of Mrs. Joseph C. Booth, Mrs. Clyde Sumner had charge of the devotional service. Plans for the next meeting on June 11 were made.

The Willing Workers' Society of St. John's Lutheran Church met Thursday afternoon at the home of Mrs. Charles Divinell. Ten members were present. Plans were made for the annual picnic. Because of the gas rationing the affair will not be held at Babcock Lake as usual, but instead at a nearby unannounced destination known only to one member. Members are asked to meet at the church.

ALPS.

Mrs. Charles Boughton has returned from Florida.

Mr. and Mrs. George Eichler have returned from New York City.

The 4-H Alpine Hustlers will meet Thursday at the home of Mary Jackson's at 7:30 p. m.

The flowers on the altar at the Baptist Church Mother's Day were in memory of Mrs. Edith Alderman and given by her daughter, Mrs. Edward Palmer.

Mr. and Mrs. Harold Gundrum and son Edward have moved into their new home in Averill Park.

Mr. and Mrs. Robert Nelson and sons, James and Robert spent the week-end with her parents, Mr. and Mrs. George Boughton.

The funeral of the late Charles D. Boughton was held Saturday at Larkin's Funeral Parlor. Interment was in the Sand Lake Cemetery.

Charter New Troop Of Boy Scouts

Howard Gorham, second right, commissioner of Troy Area Council, Boy Scouts of America presenting to Donald Warenfield, chairman of the troop committee of newly organized Troop 27 in Eagle Mills, the troop charter. Scouts looking on are left to right, Jack Robb, Allen Decker, Donald Gutbrodt and John O'Neil. At extreme right is the scoutmaster, Paul Diehl.

CHURCH CALENDAR

Oakwood Presbyterian.
Today—6:15 p. m., Annual fellowship supper by the Woman's Missionary Society with Miss Gertrude Hodgman as speaker.
Tomorrow—10 a. m., Sewing session at Red Cross rooms. 7:45 p. m., Boy Scout meeting. 6:30 p. m., Troy Local Union of Christian Endeavor dinner at Third Presbyterian Church.
Thursday—7 p. m., Meeting of the Girl Scouts.

Levings Methodist.
Thursday—2 p. m., Meeting of Afternoon Workers at the home of Mrs. James Ralston, 26 Thomas Street.
Friday—7 p. m., Choir rehearsal.

Ninth Presbyterian.
Today—8 p. m., The Session will meet at the church. 8 p. m., Woman's Missionary Society meeting at the home of Mrs. E. I. Hodkins, 15 Eaton Road.
Tomorrow—6:30 p. m., Christian Endeavor dinner at Third Presbyterian Church. 7 p. m., Meeting of the Camp Fire Girls.
Wednesday—7:30 p. m., Boy Scout troop meeting. 8 p. m., Aunt Lizzie Clum's Class meeting in the chapel rooms.
Thursday—6:30 p. m., Chapel choir rehearsal. 8 p. m., Meeting of Group 2 at the home of Mrs. Adam Ross, 2nd.

Woodside Presbyterian.
Tomorrow—2 p. m., Home nursing class. 8 p. m., Rehearsal for variety show. 8 p. m., Completion of arrangements for 75th anniversary of church.
Wednesday — 7:15 p. m., Boy Scouts.
Thursday — 7:30 p. m., Home nursing class. 8 p. m., Dress rehearsal for variety show.
Friday—8 p. m., Variety show in the First Baptist Church hall, Cohoes.

St. John's Episcopal.
Today—8 p. m., Girls Friendly society garden service.
Tomorrow—8 p. m., Meeting of the Daughters of St. John at the rectory, 23 Myrtle Avenue.
Wednesday—8 p. m., Senior auxiliary choir rehearsal.
Thursday—10:30 a. m., Meeting of women of the church to sew for the Church Mission of Help, Red Cross and the Samaritan Hospital. A box luncheon will be served at 12:30 p. m.
Friday—4:30 p. m., Church school choir rehearsal. 8 p. m., Address by Rev. Michael Coleman, vicar of All Hallows Cathedral, London.

Second Presbyterian.
Today—6:15 p. m., Supper meeting of the Women's Guild. 8 p. m., Meetings of the deacons and board of trustees.
Tomorrow—10 a. m., All day sewing session for hospitals and the Red Cross.

First Church of Christ, Scientist.
Wednesday—8 p. m., Testimonial meeting. Reading room open daily except Sunday, from 10 a. m. until 5 p. m.

Salvation Army.
Tomorrow—4 p. m., Band of Love; Corps Cadet class. 6:30 p. m., Boys' Red Shield Club. 7:30 p. m., Ladies' Home League.
Wednesday—4 p. m., Sunbeams; young people's songster practice. 6:30 p. m., Girl Guards. 8 p. m., Torchbearers.
Friday—7 p. m., Young people's band practice. 8 p. m., Holiness meeting.
Saturday—7 p. m., Senior songster practice. 8 p. m., Senior band practice.

St. Paul's Episcopal.
Today — 8 p. m., Girls' Friendly Society.
Tomorrow—10 a. m. (beginning), Knitting for soldiers. 7:30 p. m., St. Elizabeth's Guild.

Liberty Presbyterian.
Monday—Boy Scouts.
Tuesday—Music and art club, Louis Pignanelli instructor.
Wednesday—8 p. m., Fellowship of prayer service.
Thursday—7:30 p. m., Young People's choir rehearsal.
Friday—7:30 p. m., Friday night social.

First Presbyterian, Lansingburg.
Today—10 a.m.—4 p. m., Red Cross at Trinity parish house. 7:30 p. m., Boy Scouts, Troop 11, in chapel.
Tomorrow—7:30 p. m., Red Cross home nursing course in chapel.
Wednesday—10 a.m.—4 p.m., Red Cross in Trinity parish house. 7:30 p. m., Concluding union prayer meeting in chapel, Rev. Ernest F. Tripp, St. Mark's Methodist Church, preacher.
Thursday—6:30 p. m., Ladies Guild in chapel; covered dish supper. 7:30 p. m., Mortgage committee in primary room. 7:30 p. m., Monthly meeting of Troop 11 committee with Burton M. Follett, 34 Glen Avenue.
Friday—7:30 p. m., Choir rehearsal. 7:30 p. m., Cub pack in chapel.

Church of Christ, Disciples.
Today—8 p.m., Official board, Howard W. Coonley, presiding. 8 p.m., Dorcas Circle with Mrs. Helen Temple, 1203 Hutton Street.
Tomorrow—Triangle Club with Miss Marjorie Coonley, 22 Woodrow Court Miss Virginia Simpson leader.

Trinity Evangelical Lutheran.
Today—8 p.m., Men's Club.
Wednesday—6:30 p. m., Committee on records and publications.

Trinity Episcopal.
Today—10 a.m., Sewing for Red Cross. 7 p.m., Camp Fire Girls. 8 p.m., Woman's Council.
Wednesday—Sewing for

St. Barnabas' Episcopal.
Tomorrow—7:30 p. m., Holy Communion.
Wednesday — 3 p. m. Church school.
Wednesday afternoon and evening—Red Cross sewing units.
Thursday—7:30 a. m., Holy Communion. 8 p.m., Committee of the Whole.
Saturday—7:30 a. m., Holy Communion.

First Baptist.
Tomorrow—2:30 p. m., Women's Missionary Society meeting and installation.
Wednesday—7:45 p. m., Midweek prayer service.
Thursday—4 p. m., Junior choir rehearsal.

Grace Methodist.
Today—6:30 p. m., Mother and daughter banquet by W. S. C. S.; Mrs. H. C. Bennett, Latham, speaker.
Tomorrow—7:30 p. m., District youth rally at Latham church; business, games, installation.
Wednesday—12, noon, Fidelity Class luncheon, church parlors.
Thursday—7:30 p. m., Choir rehearsal.

Fifth Ave.-State St. Methodist.
Today—8 p. m., Young Women's Division of Christian Service meeting in the home of Mrs. John C. Manchester, 143 Sixth Avenue. 8 p.m., Woman's Society for Christian Service meeting in the church house, program, "Decorating the Home." Devotions in charge of Mrs. Lowell H. Bryce, program in charge of Miss Elsie M. Diefendorf. Hostesses, Mrs. William Herbert, Mrs. Sally Lobdell, Mrs. Harry Bills, Mrs. Elizabeth Jacobie, Mrs. Embury P. Moston, Mrs. Harold S. Wiltsey, Miss H. Staley and Mrs. J. F. Fellows.
Tomorrow—7:30 p. m., Troy subdistrict youth rally at the Methodist Church at Latham.
Wednesday—7:45 p. m., Midweek church service.
Thursday — 6:30 p. m., Covered dish supper and birthday party of Mrs. Fellows Bible Class in the church house. Annual election of officers and business meeting. Hostesses, Mrs. Dennie Riggs, Mrs. Elizabeth Meredith, Mrs. J. F. Fellows, Mrs. Warren L. Potter and Miss Eva Podmore.

Millis Memorial Baptist.
Tomorrow — 2:30 p. m., Cottage prayer meeting in church parlors.
6:30 p. m., Philathea Class meeting at Y. W. C. A.
Friday—7:30 p. m., Bible study and prayer. 8:30 p. m., Choir practice.

Church of Christ, Disciples (continued)

Red Cross. School of religious education suspended until fall.

Central Lutheran.
Today—4 p.m., Confirmation class.
Tomorrow — Meeting of Roses and Flax Society at the home of Mrs. Burdett Niles, 52 Fifth Avenue.
Wednesday—11 a. m., Luncheon.

Christian and Missionary Alliance.
Wednesday — 7:30 p. m., Prayer service.

Christ Episcopal.
Today—6:30 p. m., Girls Friendly Society.
Wednesday—7:30 p. m., Choir rehearsal.

Sixth Avenue Baptist.
Wednesday—8 p. m., Church school officers and teachers.
Thursday—7:45 p. m., Prayer service.
Friday—10:30 p.m., Annual meeting of the Women's Missionary Society of the Hudson River Baptist Association North at Tabernacle Baptist Church, Schenectady.

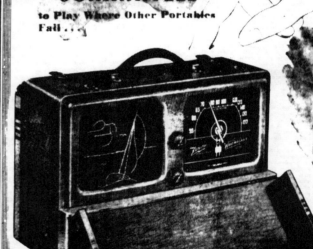

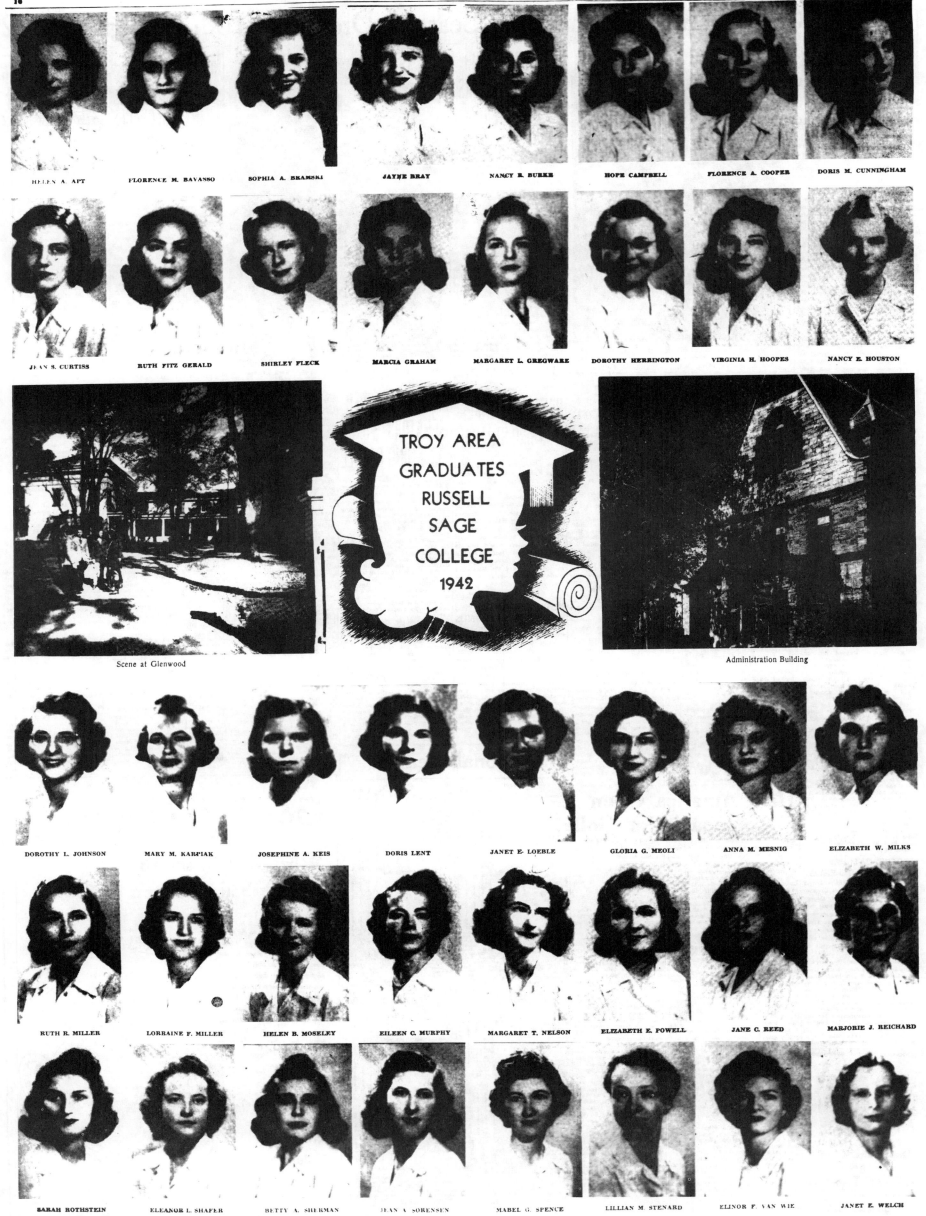

HELEN A. APT   FLORENCE M. BAVASSO   SOPHIA A. BRAMSKI   JAYNE BRAY   NANCY B. BURKE   HOPE CAMPBELL   FLORENCE A. COOPER   DORIS M. CUNNINGHAM

JEAN S. CURTISS   RUTH FITZ GERALD   SHIRLEY FLECK   MARCIA GRAHAM   MARGARET L. GREGWARE   DOROTHY HERRINGTON   VIRGINIA H. HOOPES   NANCY E. HOUSTON

TROY AREA
GRADUATES
RUSSELL
SAGE
COLLEGE
1942

Scene at Glenwood

Administration Building

DOROTHY L. JOHNSON   MARY M. KARPIAK   JOSEPHINE A. KEIS   DORIS LENT   JANET E. LOEBLE   GLORIA G. MEOLI   ANNA M. MESNIG   ELIZABETH W. MILKS

RUTH R. MILLER   LORRAINE F. MILLER   HELEN B. MOSELEY   EILEEN C. MURPHY   MARGARET T. NELSON   ELIZABETH E. POWELL   JANE C. REED   MARJORIE J. REICHARD

SARAH ROTHSTEIN   ELEANOR L. SHAFER   BETTY A. SHERMAN   JEAN A SORENSEN   MABEL G. SPENCE   LILLIAN M. STENARD   ELINOR F. VAN WIE   JANET E. WELCH

Pirates Get Worst Thrashing of Season, Dropping 10th Straight, 17-2

BROOKLYN EASILY WINS GAME FROM SLIPPING PIRATES

Pathetic Pittsburgers Now Have Lost 16 of Last 18 Contests; Giants Crush Cubs.

BY JUDSON BAILEY.
Associated Press Sports Writer.

If there ever are times that Frank (Onkel Franz) Frisch yearns to return to radio announcing today must be one of them.

The Pittsburg Pirates, who started the season in splendor, have become more futile and pathetic than even the Philadelphia Phils, who haven't been out of the National League cellar since the first day of the campaign.

Pittsburg has lost ten straight games and 16 of its last 18 and humiliated yesterday by the worst thrashing of the season in the senior circuit—17 to 2 by the Brooklyn Dodgers.

Just before the Dodgers barged into the Smoky City Manager Frisch optimistically asserted that the Pirates would get going soon. "We aren't this bad a ball club," he claimed. "We can't be."

Get Twenty Hits.

But the Dodgers yesterday made twenty hits—including five in succession by Pete Reiser — while rookie Les Webber was checking Pittsburg on five.

There were two other five-hit pitching performances in the National League yesterday — thrown against each other by old Si Johnson and young Elmer Riddle in a ten-inning dual which the Phils took from the Cincinnati Reds 1-0.

Over the regulation route Riddle, who has won only one game this season and been defeated six times, allowed three hits with Johnson was giving five. Then in the tenth the Phils pushed across the lone run on two singles, an error and a long fly by Tommy Livingston.

Hal Schumacher, who hadn't won a game since April 22, kept nine hits scattered at Chicago and the New York Giants hailed the Cubs 5-1 with a 13-hit attack in which Willard Marshall, Mel Ott and Johnny Mize each got three blows and Schumacher two.

John Beazley, young relief hurler for the St. Louis Cardinals, did a spectacular job to save a 4 to 3 decision over the Boston Braves for Mort Cooper. Cooper weakened in the ninth and permitted Sibby Sisti to triple a pair of runs home with only one out. Beazley trudged in from the bull pen to retire the side.

Saves the Day.

Mel Harder stepped into the breach for the Cleveland Indians at Boston by holding the Red Sockers to six hits and winning 7-2. The Tribe has been in a sticky slump, losing nine of their last 11 games and it was Harder who accounted for one of the two victories. Yesterday he had the help of a 14-hit offensive by his teammates, including homers by Jeff Heath and Les Fleming.

Two great pitching performances were turned in under the lights with Early Wynn, the Washington youngster, stopping the St. Louis Browns 4 to 1, and Virgil (Fire) Trucks of the Tigers applying the first coat of whitewash to the Athletics this season, 3 to 0.

Wynn was touched for only five hits, one of which was George McQuinn's homer, and cracked out a double to aid his own cause. The payoff blow, however, was Bobby Estalella's fifth-inning single with the bases loaded that drove in a pair of runs.

Trucks allowed the Athletics only one blow in the first five innings and kept five others well enough scattered to gain the shutout.

TIGERS' CATCHER ATTEMPTS TO ENLIST

Detroit (AP)—Maj. Frank Denny of the Army Procurement Division disclosed yesterday that George (Birdie) Tebbetts, 27-year-old catcher of the Detroit Tigers, had applied for enlistment in the Army Air Corps. Tebbetts has completed the physical examination, he said, and the application has gone to Washington.

Tebbetts underwent the physical tests at Selfridge Field, Mich., Monday before the Tigers headed east for a 14-game American League road trip, the officer said. He gave no hint when the ball player would be called if accepted.

Tebbetts is unmarried but has had 3-A draft classification because of the dependency of his mother, who lives at Nashua, N. H.

The Tigers have one other catcher, Edward (Dixie) Parsons.

Corp. Jim Turnesa returns to Fort Dix a hero despite his defeat by Sam Snead in P. G. A. final at Seaview, 2 and 1. Note captain, right, doing shoulder duty.

English Colt Equals Record at Belmont

New York (AP)—Fairaris, English-bred colt that was third to Alsab in the Withers Mile, bounced back into the spotlight by equalling Belmont Park's record of 1:48 2-5 for a mile and a furlong in winning the third running of the Peter Pan Handicap.

Fairaris, a $4.50 for $2 choice, did the six furlongs in 1:09 3-5 and was caught in 1:35 at the mile.

His dazzling speed was too much for Warren Wright's Col. Teddy who was a length and a half to the rear in second place. Another English-bred colt, Louis B. Mayer's King's Abbey, took third.

It was the third victory in four U. S. starts for Fairaris, owned by R. S. McLaughlin, the Canadian automobile builder.

Take Wing made it two straight victories at Lincoln Fields yesterday by romping home in front in the featured mile. The four-year-old gelding, owned by W. B. Simpson, caught the front running Sis Baker in the stretch and won by two and a half lengths. Sis Baker was second and Shortening third. The time was 1:39½ with Take Wing returning $12.00.

Charm Bracelet, from the Barns of the Pine Tree Farms, annexed Suffolk Downs' Aspinwall Purse, finishing a length in front of Louis B. Mayer's Two Ton Tony. Walter G. McCarty's Lassator came from far back to win third place.

The winner was clocked in 1:11-2-5 for the six furlongs and was worth $10.60.

Seamanlike, Mill Creek's creditable entry in the Withers Mile, made his appearance at Delaware Park yesterday and galloped off with the featured six furlong race. Eddie Wielander broke the axe of Halcyon and Shipshape on top and he was first at every pole the entire race. Free Double was the nearest pursuit all the way and finished second with third going to Wind Whither.

Seamanlike, paying $3.30 for $2, needed 1:15 2-5 for the distance over a tough track.

MONTREAL, CHIEFS SPLIT DOUBLE BILL

Syracuse (AP) — Syracuse and Montreal swapped identical 4 to 2 victories in a twilight-night doubleheader here as Tom DeLacrux limited the Royals to five hits in the opener and Chet Kehn came back to yield only five hits to the Chiefs in the nightcap.

Bobby Adams, young Syracuse second-sacker, hit home runs in each game with nobody on. The wildness of Albosta, who relieved Max Macon in the fifth inning of the first game, let the Chiefs collect their two-run margin of victory, while Nate Andrews put himself behind in the first inning of the second game by issuing four bases on balls, which let in the first two Montreal runs.

Hale America Open Comeback for Golf

BY HUGH FULLERTON, JR.
Wide World Sport Columnist.

New York—The United States Golf Association, which drew a lot of criticism for its hasty cancellation of the Open and Amateur Championships, seems to be making a great comeback with the Hale America open tournament....The sectional qualifying rounds this week-end will take in virtually all the top-ranking pros and amateurs available and the ones who don't have to qualify will play exhibitions anyway....About the only important names we can think of that will be missing are Sam Snead, Porky Oliver, Bud Ward, Willie Turnesa, Charlie Yates and Johnny Fisher, who will be too busy with their Army and Navy duties....Jim Turnesa, the Army's No. 1 golfer right now, reports his putting was so hot during the P. O. A. tournament because he didn't have much chance to practice anything else.

Last Straw.

When Jack Dunn, 3rd, who is a pretty good college ball player besides being traveling secretary of the Baltimore Orioles, was playing for Princeton against the soldier team at Ft. Monmouth, N. J., the other day, he rolled one into the stands....The spectator who got the ball hesitated about throwing it back, and a soldier shouted from the field: "Please return all balls, and we will give them to the Phillies."...The fan tossed it back.

Sports Mention.

Les Steers, who was breaking high-jump records for the University of Oregon last year, now is performing for O. S. C.—it isn't Oregon's old enemy, Oregon State College, but the Oregon Shipbuilding Corp. and Les is helping to break records building liberty ships....Denny Galehouse, the Brown's pitcher, is taking a mail order law course....Leland (Bunky) Morris of Syracuse University, pitched three ball games this spring without a victory or defeat on his record; one

was a 15-inning tie, another was all square when he was taken out and the third was a relief job....Barney Berlinger, the old Pennsylvania weight-tossing star, still is throwing things around. He recently cast a five-ounce plug 230 feet to win a tournament.

Today's Guest Star.

Sam Atcheson, Memphis Commercial Appeal: "Nothing will ruin a golf club quicker than letting nature take its course."

Service Dept.

June 14 has been set for the opening game of the Army Hockey League season at San Francisco; two Coast Artillery units and one shipyard squad will summer are in the service; Stroke Bill Campbell recently joined a hospital unit training in Louisiana; Joe Ludwig is a parachutist at Fort Benning, Ga.; his brother Franz is at Fort Jackson, S. C.; George Hutchinson is the Marines at Parris Island, S. C., and Herb Koening in the Army Air Corps in Texas.

Some Phone, Eh?

Eddie Collins tells one about the time Tom Yawkey telephoned from Alaska to see how the Red Sox were doing. They were a run behind in the ninth, and Yawkey listened to a ball-by-ball description until Jimmy Foxx fanned with a man on base. Then he hung up the phone in disgust, and it wasn't until two weeks later that he learned Joe Cronin had socked the next pitch for a game-winning homer.

TROY BOYS' CLUB BEATS PANTHERS BY SCORE OF 4-1

The Troy Boys' Club last evening snapped its eight game losing streak with a 4-1 triumph over the Panthers at Prospect Park behind the five-hit pitching of Rev. John Stuart, pastor of the Third Presbyterian Church of Albia.

Joe DeLucia extended his streak of consecutive games in which he has hit to ten, when he lined out a sharp single in the sixth, the Clubbers' big inning.

Bradley started it by reaching first on an error and gaining third on DeBonis' single. DeLucia singled the first run home and, after an error, Winney's single brought in two more tallies. Winney was out stealing, but Liney walked and Grimes tripled him in with the final run.

Lou Maslan's Cats got their only counter in the seventh, when Whitney worked his way to second as his grounder was bobbled and Al Bosco, pinch-hitting for Joe Carney, rapped out a single to bring him in. The Panthers had five hits to the T. B. C. six and four errors to two.

The Boys' Club takes on the 4-H Club at 6:15 p. m. today at the 116th Street Field in another Greater Troy League contest.

RIVERSIDES TAKE THIRD STRAIGHT

The Riverside A. A. defeated the Ridge Runners in a closely fought contest last night at Laureate Park, 5 to 0.

Kaville, Grannon, Snyder and Painton starred for the winners. It was the third straight win for the Riversides, who previously defeated the Pal O'Mine and Presidents while losing to St. Lawrence's.

The Riversides would like to book games with leading softball teams in the Troy Area. This is an open date and the Riversides would like to arrange a road game with some fast club.

For games call 6075 any time.

NOTRE DAME FIVE TO PLAY CANISIUS

Buffalo (AP)—Notre Dame University's basketball team will meet Canisius College in Buffalo Memorial Auditorium next Feb. 15, Dr. James H. Crowdle, Canisius graduate manager of athletics, said yesterday.

The Irish will play in one of ten intercollegiate double-header programs to be booked for the 1942-43 season under joint promotion of Ned Irish of Madison Square Garden and the Canisius Athletic Association, Crowdle added. Eight double-headers were played here last season.

Switch Swing Sammy

The swing's the thing: Sammy Byrd as New York Yankee outfielder and top-notch professional golfer.

BARONS WIN OVER SENATORS, 3-0, IN 13-INNING BATTLE

After their first extra-base blow of the game had set up a scoring chance, the Wilkes-Barre Barons shifted to finesse in the 13th inning last night and bunted and stole their way to a 3-0 victory over the Albany Senators at Hawkins Stadium.

Sammy Liberto started the fateful 13th with a double near the rightfield corner—the third hit of the game off Albany's Reggie Grabowski. Liberto pulled up at second with a leg injury and Joe Pennington was sent into run for him. Gusak laid down a bunt and Pennington slid under Rice's throw to third. Kordenbrock grounded to Cullinane who forced Gusak at second, but Pennington couldn't advance.

Then Manager Earl Wolgamot of the Barons flashed the squeeze sign to Tony Renna, slowest man on the club and with Pennington running on the pitch, he scored easily. Rensa's bunt was so good he beat it out and went to second on Cullinane's wild throw. Then Pitcher Ollie Reynolds duplicated the trick, bunting down the first base line for another single and another run. Eddie Turchin tried another bunt, but the Barons played the squeeze safe and Rensa was nailed off third. Reynold's however, reached third on the play.

Wolgamot switched his strategy once more and called a double steal. As soon as Rice threw all

the way in an effort to get Turchin, Reynolds scored standing up, and the other runner slid safely into second. Lotshaw drew his third walk of the game and Woodling, only other pass-wangler, collected his second to fill the bases before Frierson, ninth man to bat, grounded sharply to Cullinane, who made the force at third. All runs were earned as the only error—Cullinane's overthrow was not of the out-making variety.

Ben Drake fouled out and Ray Rice flied to right in the Senators' half of the frame, but Hank Camelli, batting for Grabowski, walked to keep hopes alive. The game ended a moment later when Bernie Snyder, after working the count to 3-and-1, hit a unintentional foul strike and then fanned.

Reynolds, hanging up his second win against two defeats, held the Senators to three safeties, all singles. He fanned 15 men, and was never in trouble although his mates made three errors.

Grabowski allowed five hits, three of them in the final inning, and was the victim of two errors.

SENATORS	AB	R	H	O	A
Snyder, cf	5	0	0	3	0
Johnson, 2b	5	0	0	2	5
Cullinane, 3b	5	0	0	1	1
Brubaker, ss	5	0	0	1	0
Riner, rf	4	0	0	1	0
DeWeese, lf	5	0	0	3	0
Drake, rf	5	0	0	2	0
Rice, c	4	0	0	9	2
Grabowski, p	4	0	0	0	3
zCamelli	0	0	0	0	0
Totals	40	0	3	42	12

z—Batted for Grabowski in 13th.

WILKES-BARRE	AB	R	H	O	A
Turchin, ss	5	0	1	5	0
Lotshaw, 1b	2	0	0	14	0
Woodling, rf	4	0	1	1	0
Frierson, rf	5	0	1	3	0
Liberto, lf	5	1	1	3	0
Gusak, 2b	4	0	0	3	3
Kordenbrock, 3b	4	0	0	0	1
Rensa, c	4	1	1	6	1
Reynolds, p	5	1	2	1	0
zPennington	0	1	0	0	0
Totals	43	3	5	39	11

z—Ran for Liberto in 13th.
Wilkes-Barre .... 000 000 000 000 3—3
Albany .... 000 000 000 000 0—0
Errors—Turchin, Rensa, Reynolds, Gusak, Grabowski. Runs batted in—Rensa, Reynolds. Two base hit—Liberto. Sacrifices—Gusak. Double plays—Johnson to Brubaker; Wilkes-Barre 2. Left on bases—Albany 7, Wilkes-Barre 7. Bases on balls—Off Grabowski 3, Reynolds 6. Struck out—By Reynolds 15, Grabowski 6.

MEDWICK BACK WITH BROOKLYN IN GOOD GRACES

New York (AP) — Joe (Muscles) Medwick has won his way back into the good graces of the Brooklyn Dodgers by that .322 batting average he was sporting up till yesterday.

The official family of the National League champions was decidedly cool toward the veteran slugger in the spring and it was freely forecast that Medwick not only wouldn't be a regular for Brooklyn this season, he probably would not even be with the ball club.

The fellow who was a star outfielder for the St. Louis Cardinals for eight years before being traded to the Dodgers in 1940 apparently had not recovered from his beaning by Bob Bowman soon after coming to Brooklyn.

The fact that he had batted .318 last season was obscured in the south by his helplessness against righthanded pitchers generally and sidearmers specifically. He was overweight and there was a noticeable restraint in his relations with Manager Leo Durocher, who had been his most intimate friend in or out of baseball, even when they were on different clubs.

They didn't pal together and when Medwick showed signs of his old form the manager said he should look better. Once Durocher made a not-too-vague declaration that "I have a good friend on this ball club who is not going to be in the lineup unless he starts showing something."

Medwick refused to be ruffled. "Leo is just doing his duty and acting for what he considers the best interests of the team," he said. Medwick was in his familiar leftfield position when the season opened, but for a few days he had to share the work with Augie Galan. Then Dolph Camilli got hurt and Galan had to fill in at first base and before Camilli returned Galan became seriously ill with influenza.

Thus by force of circumstances Medwick remained a regular and circumstances have helped swell his batting average, too.

Because most of the Dodgers' leading hitters are lefthanded batters—Dolph Camilli, Pete Reiser, Arky Vaughan and Dixie Walker opponents have been using southpaws against them at every opportunity. This persistent policy has made the batting average of Camilli, last year's league leader in home runs and runs batted in, fade to almost .200.

But it has helped the righthanded Medwick attain a ten-game batting streak and given him new confidence at the plate. He has had to face few, if any sidearmers, this season but he no longer flinches at every head-high pitch by a righthander and as long as the other National League clubs keep feeding the Dodgers on southpaws, he is sure to be a vital force at the plate. In addition he has slimmed down to playing weight and made many spectacular fielding plays.

SYRACUSE CREW CAPTAINS.

Syracuse (AP)—The bow portion of the Syracuse University crew was honored here yesterday as Arthur Hughes, bow, and Richard Willenborg, No. 2, were elected co-captains of the 1943 varsity. Hughes halls from Newton, Mass., while Willenborg's home is in Weehawken, N. J.

The Baseball Standings

Games Today.

NATIONAL LEAGUE.
New York at Chicago.
Brooklyn at Pittsburg, night game.
Philadelphia at Cincinnati, night game.
Boston at St. Louis, night game.

AMERICAN LEAGUE.
Chicago at New York.
Cleveland at Boston.
Detroit at Philadelphia, night game.
St. Louis at Washington, night game.

EASTERN LEAGUE.
Wilkes-Barre at ALBANY.
Scranton at Binghamton.
Williamsport at Springfield.
Elmira at Hartford.

Yesterday's Results.

NATIONAL LEAGUE.
Brooklyn 17, Pittsburg 2.
New York 5, Chicago 1.
Philadelphia 1, Cincinnati 0, 10 innings.
St. Louis 4, Boston 3.

AMERICAN LEAGUE.
Cleveland 7, Boston 2.
Chicago at New York, postponed, weather.
Washington 4, St. Louis 1.
Detroit 3, Philadelphia 0.

INTERNATIONAL LEAGUE.
Buffalo at Jersey City, postponed, weather.
Rochester at Newark, postponed, weather.
Toronto at Baltimore, postponed, weather.
1—Syracuse 4, Montreal 2.
2—Montreal 4, Syracuse 2.

EASTERN LEAGUE.
Wilkes-Barre 3, Albany 0.
Scranton 5, Binghamton 0.
Springfield 6, Hartford 0.
Only games scheduled.

The Standings.

NATIONAL LEAGUE.

	Won	Lost	Pct.
Brooklyn	33	13	.717
St. Louis	26	18	.591
Boston	23	23	.561
New York	24	23	.511
Cincinnati	22	23	.489
Chicago	21	25	.457
Pittsburg	18	26	.404
Philadelphia	15	32	.319

AMERICAN LEAGUE.

	Won	Lost	Pct.
New York	31	11	.738
Cleveland	25	21	.543
Detroit	27	23	.561
Boston	23	21	.523
St. Louis	23	25	.479
Chicago	18	26	.409
Washington	18	27	.400
Philadelphia	19	31	.380

EASTERN LEAGUE.

	Won	Lost	Pct.
Scranton	20	10	.667
ALBANY	18	11	.621
Binghamton	15	12	.600
Wilkes-Barre	15	15	.545
Hartford	15	15	.500
Elmira	13	20	.394
Williamsport	12	19	.387
Springfield	9	19	.321

National League

BOSTON

	AB	R	H	O	A
Holmes, rf	5	1	3	0	0
Waner, rf	5	1	3	0	0
Miller, ss	4	0	0	0	2
Fernandez, ss	4	0	1	1	0
Lombardi, c	4	0	2	4	0
zMast	1	0	0	0	0
West, 1b	5	0	1	2	0
Demaree, lf	4	0	1	2	0
Sisti, 2b	4	0	1	2	3
Totals					

x—Ran for Lombardi in 9th.

ST. LOUIS

	AB	R	H	O	A
Brown, lf	5	0	1	2	0
W. Cooper, c	4	0	1	8	0
Slaughter, rf	4	0	0	1	0
W. Cooper, c	4	0	1	5	0
Walker, lf	4	1	2	3	0
Hopp, 1b	4	1	1	9	0
Kurowski, 3b	4	1	1	1	3
Marion, ss	4	0	1	4	4
M. Cooper, p	3	0	0	0	2
Beazley, p	0	0	0	0	0
Totals					

Boston .... 000 100 002—3
St. Louis .... 100 000 00x—4
Errors—None. Runs batted in—Waner, Slaughter, Marion 2, Sisti. Three base hit—Sisti. Stolen base—T. Moore. Sacrifices—W. Cooper, M. Cooper. Double plays—M. Cooper to Marion to Hopp; Brown, Marion and Hopp. Left on bases—Boston 9, St. Louis 7. Bases on balls—Off Tobin 1, off M. Cooper 3, off Beazley 1. Struck out—By Tobin 2, by M. Cooper 3. Hits—Off M. Cooper, 5 in 8 1-3; off Beazley, 0 in 2-3. Hit by pitcher—By M. Cooper (Miller). Passed ball—W. Cooper. Winning pitcher—M. Cooper. Umpires—Barr and Conlon. Time—2:05. Attendance—11,148.

NEW YORK

	AB	R	H	O	A
Werber, 3b	4	0	0	1	2
Marshall, rf	5	1	3	2	0
Ott, rf	4	1	2	2	0
Miss, 1b	4	1	3	9	0
Barna, lf	4	0	0	2	0
Danning, c	3	1	1	5	1
Jurges, ss	4	0	0	2	3
Schumacher, p	4	0	2	0	1
Totals					

CHICAGO

	AB	R	H	O	A
Hack, 3b	4	0	1	1	2
Sturgeon, ss	4	0	2	2	3
Cavarretta, rf	4	0	0	2	0
Nicholson, rf	4	0	0	4	0
Russell, lf	3	0	0	2	0
Novikoff, lf	3	0	1	2	0
Dallessandro, lf	3	0	0	2	0
McCullough, c	3	1	1	2	0
Merullo, ss	3	0	1	1	4
Totals					

New York .... 000 110 300—5
Chicago .... 001 000 000—1
Errors—Werber, Runs batted in—Marshall 2, Ott 2, Miss 2, Danning, Russell. Two base hits—Schumacher, Marshall, McCullough, Miss, Merullo. Home run—McCullough. Stolen base—Hack. Double plays—Jurges and Miss 2; Hack, Sturgeon and Cavarretta. Left on bases—New York 7, Chicago 4. Bases on balls—Off Wilkie 3, Webber 1. Struck out—By Schumacher 4, by Wilkie 7 in 7 innings. Losing pitcher—Wilkie. Umpires—Magerkurth, Jorda and Barr. Time—2:13. Attendance—3,287.

PITTSBURG

	AB	R	H	O	A
Gustine, 2b	4	0	0	2	3
Barrett, rf	4	0	0	2	0
Wasdell, 1b	4	0	1	8	0
Elliott, 3b	4	1	1	0	1
Van Robays, lf	4	0	1	2	0
DiMaggio, cf	4	0	1	2	0
Anderson, ss	4	1	0	3	2
Lopez, c	4	0	1	6	0
Baker, c	3	0	0	0	0
Wilkie, p	2	0	0	0	3
Jungels, p	0	0	0	0	0
zRikard	1	0	0	0	0
Totals					

z—Batted for Jungels in 9th.
Brooklyn .... 304 142 210—17
Pittsburg .... 011 000 000— 2
Errors—Elliott. Runs batted in—Vaughan 2, Reiser 4, Owen 2, Herman 2, Van Robays, Lopez, Medwick, Kampouris. Two base hits—Reiser, Rizzo, Reese. Two base hits—Reese, Herman. Left on bases—Brooklyn 7; Pittsburg 7. Bases on balls—Off Wilkie 3, Webber 1. Struck out—By Webber 3, by Jungels 4. Hits—Off Wilkie, 8 in 3 innings; Jungels, 12 in 6. Home runs—None. Losing pitcher—Wilkie. Umpires—Reardon, Goetz and Pinelli. Time—1:58. Attendance—(Actual)—4,260.

BROOKLYN

	AB	R	H	O	A
Reese, ss	5	3	2	2	4
Vaughan, 3b	5	2	1	1	1
Riggs, 3b	0	0	0	0	1
Galan, cf	5	2	2	1	0
Medwick, lf	4	1	2	2	0
Rizzo, lf	1	0	1	1	0
Walker, rf	4	1	1	2	0
Bordagaray, rf	1	0	0	0	0
Camilli, 1b	5	2	2	9	1
Dahlgren, 1b	0	0	0	3	0
Owen, c	5	1	2	2	0
Sullivan, c	1	0	0	1	0
Herman, 2b	5	2	3	2	5
Kampouris, 2b	1	0	0	0	1
Webber, p	5	1	1	0	3
Totals	46	17	20	27	10

PHILADELPHIA

	AB	R	H	O	A
Waner, cf	4	0	1	2	0
Benjamin, cf	0	0	0	0	0
Murtaugh, 2b	4	0	1	2	3
Etten, 1b	4	0	0	11	0
Litwhiler, lf	4	0	0	2	0
Glossop, 2b	4	0	1	2	3
Northey, rf	4	0	1	2	0
Bragan, ss	4	0	1	2	3
Livingston, c	4	0	2	6	0
Totals	36	1	8	30	9

CINCINNATI

	AB	R	H	O	A
Joost, ss	4	0	0	2	3
Frey, 2b	4	0	1	2	3
Marshall, rf	4	0	1	2	0
Tipton, lf	4	0	1	3	0
Walker, cf	4	0	0	2	0
Abreu, 3b	4	0	0	1	2
Vollmer, 1b	4	0	0	11	0
Lamanno, c	4	0	1	6	0
Riddle, p	3	0	0	0	3
xGoodman	1	0	0	0	0
Totals					

x—Batted for Riddle in 10th
Philadelphia .... 000 000 000 1—1
Cincinnati .... 000 000 000 0—0
Two base hit—Bragan. Sacrifices—Murtaugh, Hack. Double play—Murtaugh to Etten. Left on bases—Philadelphia 5, Cincinnati 5. Bases on balls—Off Johnson 3, Riddle 1. Struck out—By Johnson 2, Riddle 5. Umpires—Sears, Stewart and Ballanfant. Time—1:53. Attendance—1,864.

LIST NAVY RULES ON GRID ELIGIBILITY

Athens, Ga. (AP)—Cadets, officers and enlisted men all will be eligible for the varsity football team at the Navy's Pre-Flight Training School opening here this month.

Capt. C. E. Smith, the commanding officer, outlined this broad policy yesterday and his announcement was believed to be the first regarding this question at any of the four Naval pre-flight schools. Others are at Chapel Hill, N. C., Iowa City, Iowa, and St. Mary's Cal.

The Athens school has a tentative schedule of ten games, including several big time college teams. Officers and enlisted men include several former college and professional standouts.

THE WEATHER
U. S. Weather Bureau.
Tonight Warmer

THE TIMES RECORD

FINAL EDITION

Series 1942—No. 135. (Entered as Second Class Matter at the Postoffice at Troy, N. Y., under the Act of March 3, 1879.) TROY, N. Y., TUESDAY EVENING, JUNE 9, 1942. PRICE FOUR CENTS

AMERICAN AIR FORCES IN CHINA

Twelve Feared Dead After Navy Blimps Collide In Mid-Air

BODIES OF THREE VICTIMS FOUND IN ATLANTIC OCEAN

Only One Known Survivor of Crash Off New Jersey Coast; Civilians Among Missing.

Lakehurst, N. J. (AP)—Coast Guards recovered today three bodies and wreckage from one of two Navy training blimps lost in what apparently was a mid-air collision over the Atlantic Ocean while on an unexplained "experimental mission."

Only one survivor was known.

Still missing were nine of the 13 naval and civilian occupants of the G-1 and the smaller L-2 when they set out last night from the naval air station at Lakehurst. The airships plunged into the ocean about four miles off Manasquan, which is 16 miles northeast of Lakehurst.

Three Bodies Recovered.

Among those missing was Ensign Frank A. Tortter of Toms River, N. J., internationally famous free balloon racer. Former pilot for an Ohio Rubber and Airship Co., he was missing for nine days in with Ward Van Orman when their balloon landed during one race in the Canadian wilds.

Three bodies were recovered:

Lieut. Comdr. Clinton S. Rounds, 39, Toms River, senior officer aboard the two craft.

Aviation Chief Machinist's Mate R. C. Poteet, 28, Langdon, Kan.

Dr. A. B. Wise, civilian scientist, 9 Shirley Lane, New London, Conn.

Ensign Rescued.

Rounds is survived by his widow and 6-year-old daughter, Carmella.

All occupants of the blimps were equipped with lifejackets for use should the craft be forced down on the water. They were about 400 feet above the sea when they apparently collided.

The Navy declined to discuss the purpose of the flight except to say it was "an experimental mission involving some hazard.

Ensign Howard Fahey of Scarsdale, N. Y., was rescued and brought ashore by Coast Guards early today. He suffered an apparent fracture of an arm in the crash, but swam about until picked up.

Coast Guard boats patrolled the area for possible other survivors and grappled for the G-1.

A clock in the gondola of the L-2 had stopped at 10:20 p.m.

Missing and Feared Dead.

Ensign Tortter, lighter than-air pilot since 1929 and observer on several of the dirigible Hindenburg's transatlantic flights. Survived by wife, Marjorie. Pilot of the G-2.

Ensign Clarence C. Ross, 27, son of Mr. and Mrs. John Ross, R. D. 1, Jacksonville, Fla. Commissioned here less than a month ago. Copilot of G-1.

Ensign K. G. Lee, New London, Conn., attached to Bureau of Ordnance and doing research work.

Ole V. Roos, 39, aviation chief machinist's mate, 201 East Seventh Street, Lakewood; born Dunbar, Neb.; wife, Mary.

W. H. Herndon, jr., boatswain's mate first class, Lakehurst. Born Jacksonville, Fla.; wife, Bessie.

Dr. Charles R. Hoover, 19 Wesleyan Place, Middletown, Conn.; Wesleyan University chemistry professor; wife and two sons.

L. S. Moyer, 622 Southeast Fifth Street, Minneapolis, Minn.

I. H. Tilles, 3344 Talbot Street, San Diego, Cal.

Dr. F. C. Gilbert, 9 Shirley Lane, New London, Conn.

WAR ORPHANS WILL GET SCHOLARSHIPS

Albany (UP)—Forty war orphan scholarships covering $200 a year toward college expenses will be awarded this year, the State Education Department announced today.

Eligible for the scholarships are children of men who died in the armed service of their country. Regular Regents' examinations will be the basis for the awards.

10 Asked About This Troy Flat

HIGHLAND AVE., 1726 — Lower flat; recently decorated. Stall for one car. Rent $40 per month. Call Troy 290 or 2435.

Once you have prospects to look at attractive property renting it is easy. This Classified Ad in The Record Newspapers brought 10 inquiries and the owner reports that he now has a new tenant.

Ask for the Low 6-Time Order Rate — Phone TROY 6100

Hitler Planned To Wed Bavarian Girl, Oechsner Declares

Outbreak Of War Sidetracked Romance With Eva Braun, Twenty Years His Junior; Fuehrer's Sweetheart Twice Tried Suicide; She Buys His Ties And Pajamas And Resents His Attentions To Other Women; Presides As Mistress Of Reichs-chancellory In Berlin And At Berchtesgaden Mountain Retreat.

Editor's Note: In the second of his series of dispatches on the personal life of Adolf Hitler, Frederick C. Oeschner, who studied the man at close range for 12 years as head of the Berlin bureau of the United Press, discusses the Nazi dictator's relationship with women.

BY FREDERICK C. OECHSNER,
(Copyright, 1942, by United Press).

New York (UP).—Adolf Hitler almost certainly would have married a stocky young Bavarian girl if the outbreak of war had not directed his attention and energies to battles.

He wanted to turn over the actual running of the Reich to Marshal Hermann Goering and become the husband of Eva Braun, twenty years his junior and his mistress for seven years. This, Hitler felt, would give him the opportunity to devote himself to lofty plans and theories for the whole of Europe.

Close observation of Hitler over 12 years has enabled me to state these facts about his emotional life:

He became attracted, in middle age, to Eva Braun and the romance progressed far enough for him to buy her an engagement ring and a wedding present.

This romance led to two attempted suicides by Fraulein Braun, probably in an attempt to create sympathy for herself and distract Hitler from other women. It also caused three attempted or successful suicides by her younger admirers, but it is doubtful whether Hitler ever knew the real reason for their acts.

A competent medical authority in Germany told me categorically that Hitler had homosexual traits and there seems to be no doubt that he was completely cold to women until he meet Eva Braun.

Since meeting Eva Braun, Hitler has become attracted at times to other women, including the British girl, Unity Mitford. But their relationship remained on an idealistic plane. He was attracted to her because he considered her a perfect example of noridic beauty. She was attracted to him by an idealization so intense that when her country and Germany went to war she inflicted a pistol wound upon herself.

Indulged In Revels.

Hitler indulged occasionally in revels at which nude dancers performed, but maintained that his interest in them was purely artistic.

Eva Braun was a young assistant to Heinrich Hoffman, Hitler's official photographer. Hoffman sent her to Obersalzberg to take some photographs of Hitler in his home there. Hitler became attracted to this olive-skinned, brown-eyed, healthy young woman. He began showing her little favors and courtesies and asked Hoffman to let her continue to take pictures of him. She appeared at many of the Nazi functions, never actually escorted by Hitler but chaperoned by the wives of men like Hess and Frick, and sitting at Hitler's table.

By midsummer of 1938, she had her own apartment in the reichschancellory in Berlin and at Berchtesgaden, and the staffs at both places were calling her "Die Chefin," the femine form for chief, as Hitler was called by his staff among themselves. At that time I was all set to file a dispatch on Hitler's impending marriage to Eva Braun. I know that she had the ring, that Hitler had a wedding gift—a beautiful Mercedes custom-built touring car—prepared for her and that all that remained to be settled was the actual date of the ceremony.

War Halted Wedding Plans.

As it developed, I could not send the dispatch because the steady rolling up of war peril made it evident that Hitler had decided that marriage was not possible.

Maybe he was relieved. Eva Braun had attempted twice to kill

(Continued on Page 12)

MIDWAY VIEWED AIR FORCE VICTORY

Experts Say Battle Shows Ability of Planes to Defeat Warships.

Washington (UP)—The battle of Midway was another demonstration of the ability of land-based aircraft to repulse superior naval force.

On the basis of incomplete reports available, it seemed that, when the final accounting is made, a large share of the toll of Japanese would be credited to Army and Navy flyers.

Even before Midway, according to Lieut. Gen Henry H. Arnold, the Army air force alone, had destroyed 33 Japanese warships. Those figures apparently included the battle of the Coral Sea which Admiral Ernest J. King, commander-in-chief of the fleet, had described as a decisive set-back for the enemy. Big Army bombers played a major role in that battle which drove off an invasion fleet aimed at Australia.

During the early months of the war, experts said, Japanese successes were mainly a result of air superiority and possession of land bases. Recent events have demonstrated the growing strength of American air power in the Pacific.

The battle of the Coral Sea, these experts said, provided the United States with its first chance to use heavy land-based bombers in large numbers against a Japanese naval force. The battle of Midway, a sequel to the Coral Sea, provided an even greater opportunity for land-based aircraft because of the proximity of the Hawaiian Islands and Midway.

Since it is known that great distances were involved in the Midway battle, it could be deduced that heavy land-based bombers of the Boeing flying fortress or Consolidated B-24 types were the Army's major contribution. Those planes are capable of flying long distances—they were used in the recent American raid on the Philippines from Australia—with tremendous bomb loads. They can operate in altitudes beyond the effective range of Japan's best plane, the Zero fighter.

BUFFALO BOY DROWNS.

Buffalo (UP) — Coast guardsmen grappled today for the body of 12-year-old Salvatore Guzzo who drowned when he dove from a raft in Buffalo River yesterday.

ASKS CHEERFUL LETTERS.

Indianapolis (INS) — Letters to soldiers of the American Army should be messages of cheer and of "hope and courage." Capt. J. Hobart Miller of the Army counseled parents today. He added: "The idea that soldiers want sympathy is false. Above all, keep your sympathy and your own troubles out of the letters you write them."

Nazis Threaten To Avenge Heydrich

London (UP)—A threat to "avenge without mercy" the assassination of Reinhard Heydrich was broadcast to the occupied countries today in the midst of a state funeral in Berlin for the slain deputy chief and purge master of the gestapo, attended by Adolf Hitler.

Hitler, returning from his headquarters on the eastern front, spoke briefly at the funeral services held in the ornate mosaic hall of his new chancellory but the chief role was played by Heinrich Himmler, gestapo chief.

Into a microphone that carried the services to all Germany and all the occupied countries, Himmler shouted:

"We promise to avenge his death and pursue without mercy his work of fighting the enemies of the reich."

Himmler revealed that his 38-year-old subordinate, victim of a rifle and bomb atack on May 27, almost was killed last year when Russian anti-aircraft guns shot down his plane as he flew over the Russian front.

Heydrich managed to return to the German lines, Himmler said.

FINE BEER

When taken in moderate quantity Utica Club Pilsner Lager or XXX Cream Ale has a friendly influence upon health and life.—Adv.

DEFENSE OFFICE TAKES CONTROL OF BUS OPERATIONS

Routes Ordered Frozen, Competitive Services Pooled; Edict Hits All Amusement Resorts.

Washington (AP) — The Office of Defense Transportation took wartime control today over all of the nation's inter-city bus operations, ordering present routes frozen, competitive service pooled, and all express service discontinued. The order is effective July 1.

After that date, ODT directed, no inter-city busses may be operated "for the primary purpose" of serving golf courses, athletic fields, race tracks, theaters, dancing pavilions, or "other places conducted primarily for the purpose of amusement or entertainment."

Order Hits Resorts.

An ODT spokesman said this would affect bus service to beaches and other resorts provided the busses were used pirmarily to take passengers to such places.

In addition, except for one daily round trip, bus companies must discontinue schedules which fail to show an average load in both directions of more than 40 per cent of the seating capacity of the busses used. Operators are required to keep records of passenger miles and seat miles and report to ODT any round trip schedule which fails to meet the seating capacity requirement.

"Inter-city bus service," as defined by the order, excludes runs within 15 miles of city limits and schedules on which the average fare is 35 cents or less.

Extension Prohibited.

The order prohibits any extension of bus routes July 1 without special permission of ODT. Operators of competing lines must plan jointly for maximum use of equipment through pooling of services, staggered schedules, exchange of operating rights, or other means, ODT declared.

Such plans, or a statement as to why no plans were agreed upon, must be submitted to ODT by July 30.

Express service was ordered stopped, ODT said, to release vehicles needed in local service.

The nationwide control followed two special orders based on operators' plans affecting four bus lines operating New York and Washington and two lines operating in the West. Other special orders covering particular routes and lines are forthcoming, ODT noted.

May Delay Gas Rationing.

Postponement of any nationwide gasoline rationing until a comprehensive survey is made of the country's available scrap rubber was predicted in congressional quarters today.

Senate Democratic Leader Barkley (D., Ky.) said he understood such a survey was being contemplated and other informed legislators added that it was likely President Roosevelt would await the results before deciding whether it was necessary to put all private automobiles on short fuel rations.

Barkley told reporters there were all kinds of estimates on the amount of rubber that could be reclaimed from the scrap pile, ranging from the 10,000,000 ton estimate of one big business executive down to a War Production Board expert's guess that only 700,000 tons could be obtained.

A Senate committee considering a bill to permit the allocation of 3,500 tons of crude rubber and 85,000 tons of reclaimed rubber each year for recapping and retreading of tires was told today that this would permit operation of "at least 20,000,000 passenger cars."

"I believe it has been definitely established," Senator Ellender, (D.-La.), informed the Senate banking committee, "that in order for this country to carry on its war production program and maintain a sound civilian economy, we must have at least that number of passenger cars in operation."

Normally, there are about 30,000,000 passenger cars in operation.

STATE WAR BALLOT COMMISSION NAMED BY ALBANY LEADERS

Albany (AP)—A temporary state war ballot commission of two Republicans and two Democrats was named today to administer the new absentee voting law for New Yorkers in the armed forces at home and abroad.

All are veterans of World War 1 and will receive $5,000 annually.

Republican appointees, announced by Assembly Speaker Oswald D. Heck and Senate Majority Leader Joe R. Hanley, are George M. Clancy, Rochester, and William T. Simpson, Brooklyn.

Democratic selections made by Senate Minority Leader John J Dunnigan and Assembly Minority Leader Irwin Steingut are William T. Larkin, Mt Morris, and Neil M Lieblich, Brooklyn.

The commission was appropriated $100,000 by the 1942 Legislature.

The Caption Is Superfluous

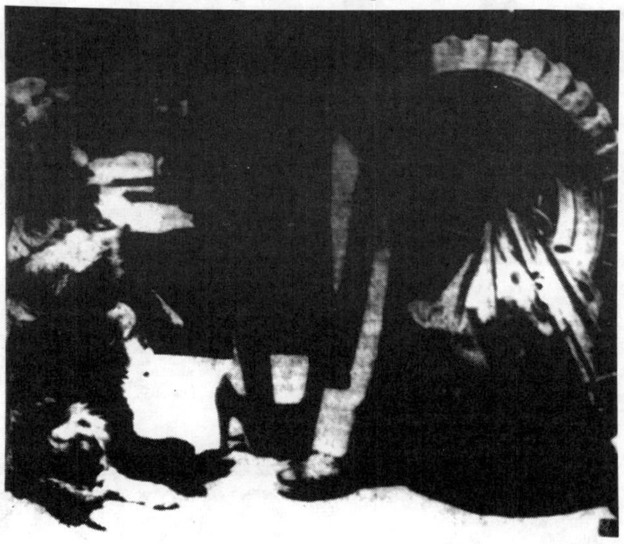

An old Chinese proverb says: "A picture is worth 10,000 words." An Army photographer took the above picture and proved it. It is a soldier saying farewell at an embarkation point. That's all the Army could say as embarkation points and troop movements are military secrets. But who needs words.

URGE CITIZENS TO BOARD WORKERS

Mayors Told of Program Designed to Alleviate Housing Shortages.

Syracuse (UP)—Private home owners who have never rented out rooms were confronted with an appeal today to open their residences to "war guests" to relieve a serious housing shortage among war workers that threatens to become increasingly worse.

Edward Weinfeld, state housing commissioner, told delegates to the annual meeting of the State Conference of Mayors that shelter must be provided for an additional 30,000 to 40,000 war workers during the next six or seven months.

Three-Point Program.

He recommended a three-point program, as follows:

1 One hundred per cent utilization of all suitable existing housing. This means opening to "war guests" homes that never have rented a room but consider it their patriotic duty to do so now.

2 The construction of temporary housing to be built through federal agencies.

3 Construction of sound, well planned homes by private enterprise with the aid of the state housing program in communities anticipating permanent increases in population.

City Manager Ralph Klebes of Elmira illustrated how municipalities can prepare for the post war period by adopting a reserve plan for capital improvements to be undertaken when community workers no longer have a place in the defense set-up.

Elmira Adopts Plan.

Klebes told the conference that Elmira had already started such a plan. "In this year's budget $50,000 has been set up and we propose, over the next few years, to place approximately $100,000 each year in the budget so that an accumulation of funds will be available when needed," he said.

Government must cooperate closely with business, labor and agriculture to avoid a serious post-war unemployment problem, Oswald D. Heck, speaker of the State Assembly, told the conference.

He declared the State Legislature has laid the foundation for a reservoir of post-war projects which will benefit both labor and industry while plants are being retooled after the war.

"TOWN CRIER" LOSES PROVINCETOWN JOB BECAUSE OF WAR

Provincetown, Mass. (AP)—The "town crier," an institution in this resort, has lost his job because of the war.

Members of the Town Criers Association announced today that business conditions did not warrant an appropriation for his salary.

Bell in hand, and wearing buckled shoes, breeches and hose, and long cloak, the "town crier" has strolled the streets every summer for half a century.

In earlier years, he served as a newsgathering and dispensing agency and was employed by the town to call out various notices of meetings and other civic affairs. However, in recent years merchants paid him and he spent most of his time meeting vacationists at the pier and calling out the times of tides.

"Lily of Mohawks" Nears Beatification

Vatican City, (From Italian Broadcasts) (UP)—The Congregation of Rites, meeting today in the presence of Pope Pius, advanced one step nearer the beatification of the Indian maiden, Catherine Tekakwitha.

In today's session the congregation formally discussed the heroism and virtues of the Indian girl.

Catherine Tekakwitha, who may become the first American Indian saint, was known as the "Lily of the Mohawks."

She was one of the converts at the Mohawk village of Gandaouaque where she was baptized into the Catholic faith in 1675. She died in 1680 while serving at the Iroquois mission of St. Francis Xavier Du Sault.

STEAMER ARRIVES WITH U. S. CITIZENS

Liner Gripsholm Sailed from Sweden Under Safe-Conduct Pledge.

Jersey City, N. J. (AP) The 18,134-ton passenger liner Gripsholm arrived today from Gotheburg, Sweden, a day late on her mission to exchange Japanese and American diplomats and nationals.

The white-painted Swedish American liner, which has not been seen in this country in several years, carried 193 Swedish and other Scandinavian-Americans.

On the pier was the baggae of Japanese, who will board the ship for its first exchange voyage to Lourenco Marques, Portuguese East Africa. Americans from Japan will board the ship there for the return voyage to the United States

The baggage included crated bicycles and sewing machines. Many of the trunks bore emblems of the rising sun.

They were permitted to make the trip by all belligerents who inspected the passenger list before the ship sailed under safe conduct from all warring na ions.

Like her sister exchange ship, the Drottningholm, the Gripsholm had huge Swedish flags painted on her white sides and the word "diplomat" prominently displayed.

Nelson Sees 60,000 Planes U. S. Output

Columbia, Mo. (INS)—War Production Czar Donald M. Nelson said today that the nation is now "making munitions in undreamed-of volume" and will produce 60,000 airplanes this year.

Speaking to the graduating class of the University of Missouri, where 31 years ago he received a degree in chemical engineering, Nelson said

"The ingenuity and resourcefulness which formerly made peacetime commodities cheaper are now making munitions in undreamed-of volume.

"This year we shall make 60,000 airplanes, and by the end of the year we shall still be picking up speed for an even vaster production in 1943."

The WPB chief said that many of the new war factories built in the past year are now producing at a greater rate than originally anticipated.

"In other words, we have found that our total production of war goods is higher than we had any reason to suppose it could be when we looked at the blueprints," he said.

"We have somehow brought about an enormous release of energy in this country, and we are today in the position of men who realize that they are actually doing the impossible."

Nelson served a grim warning to the graduates, however, that they are going forth "into a very confused, disorganized and tortured world."

Nelson said there is no need for a "terrible slump" that would bring the nation's economy "down about our ears after the war."

"We shall have no one to blame but ourselves if it does happen," he said.

WPA BILL GIVEN COMMITTEE O. K.

President's Request for Drastically Curtailed Fund Approved.

Washington (UP)—The House Appropriations Committee approved today President Roosevelt's request for $280,000,000 to operate a drastically curtailed Works Projects Administration program during the fiscal year beginning July 1.

The fund will provide WPA employment for an average of 400,000 workers during the year, and is expected to force dismissal this summer of about 350,000 relief workers.

Mr. Rosevelt asked $465,000,000 for WPA in the budget message he submitted to Congress in January, but in a recent message he lowered the figure to $280,000,000 because war industries are taking up much of the slack in unemployment.

In recommending the WPA appropriation bill for House passage, the committee reported that despite the war production drive there still would be some unemployment because of such factors as industrial dislocation and a growing labor force.

Acting WPA Administrator Francis Dryden told the deficiency appropriations subcommittee that WPA rolls will have to be pared immediately to less than 400,000 so that the agency will have sufficient funds to meet unforeseen emergencies next summer.

The committee estimated that unemployment in the current fiscal year averaged 4,000,000 and that next year it will drop to between 2,500,000 and 3,000,000. It cited bureau of labor statistics estimates that employment will drop about 8,000,000 in civilian industries but rise about 10,000,000 in war industries.

DAY TO RETIRE.

New Haven, Conn (INS)—George Parmly Day, treasurer of Yale University, founder and director of the Yale University Press and senior officer of the university in point of service will retire at the end of the present academic year, President Charles Seymour announced today. He will remain a director of the Press, chairman of the president's committee on university development and as university director of the Yale Alumni Fund.

CHUNGKING ALSO REPORTS ARRIVAL OF BRITISH FLYERS

Japanese People Being Prepared for "Bad News" as Defeated Fleet Limps Home from Midway.

BY THE ASSOCIATED PRESS.

Dispatches reaching London from Chungking today reported that British and American air force units have arrived in China. The United States units presumably are in addition to the "Flying Tigers" of the American volunteer group, commanded by Brig. Gen. Claire Chennault, which already is operating in China.

(Chennault, together with Maj. Gen. Lewis H. Brereton, commander of United States air forces in India, and Lieut. Gen. Joseph W. Stilwell, American commander of Chinese forces in the battle of Burma, flew to Chungking last week for conferences with Generalissimo Chiang Kai-shek).

Generalissimo Chiang Kai-shek's armies, meanwhile were reported to have thrown a strategic Japanese victory into reverse.

Chinese Recapture City.

A Chungking spokesman said that a Japanese force which penetrated the walled city of Chuhsien in Chekiang Province had been wiped out after three days of violent fighting and that the Chinese were again in full possession of the city.

Chekiang, on China's east coast, is important as a potential base for Allied air attacks on Japan.

The Chinese had previously acknowledged loss of the Chuhsien airport and a Japanese thrust into the town itself, following a Tokyo claim to a full victory there Saturday.

A Chinese government spokesman expressed China's gratitude for what he called a prompt and generous response to appeals for help from both the United States and Great Britain, but declared that "the situation remains grave."

"The next few months will be very critical," he said.

Jap Fleet Limps Home.

While Japan's battered sea armada retreated from Midway Island—battle contact was lost Saturday night—Pearl Harbor observers predicted that the enemy fleet, with reinforcements, would probably return for another "face saving" attack on American defenses in the Pacific.

Official reports said that before contact was lost, the enemy suffered at least three warships sunk, 11 more heavily damaged and the accompanying air arm practically wiped out.

United States losses were listed as one destroyer sunk, an airplane carrier damaged and an unspecified number of planes destroyed.

Thus, whatever dream Japan may have had for occupation of the Hawaiian Islands—such apparently was the ultimate aim of the invaders—was turned into a nightmare of destruction.

Tokyo Prepares "Bad News."

Without specifically mentioning the Japanese naval disaster at Midway, Tokyo dispatches quoted by the Berlin radio today suggested that Japan may be preparing her people for bad news.

"One cannot always expect victories but must also be able to stand losses," the broadcast quoted an unnamed Japanese admiral as saying.

He added that "if the war should be protracted both sides would be greatly exhausted. The situation could never be such that one side could continuously gain brilliant victories while the other side endured only losses. Hence in the long run that side would lose which first tired of the struggle."

So far, the Tokyo radio has maintained silence on the Midway sea fight.

CHINESE ENVOY HONORED BY YALE

New Haven, Conn. (UP) — Yale University awarded honorary degrees to nine distinguished personages today, including T. V. Soong, China's foreign and finance minister, and Charles Merz, editor of the New York Times.

Soong, president of the Bank of China, was awarded a doctor of laws degree, and Merz the degree of doctor of letters.

The Index

HISTORY OF CHAPTER AT WESLEYAN CITES FELLOWS FAMILY

The Fellows family of Troy appears frequently in the pages of a current book, Seventy-five Years of Gamma Phi, by James E. Stiles, publisher of the Nassau Daily Review-Star. It is a history of the Wesleyan chapter of Delta Kappa Epsilon.

J. Franklin Fellows of this city, a member of the class of '85, started the family tradition at Wesleyan, according to the history, in 1881, having been graduated from Centenary Collegiate Institute that spring. He had two brothers, Hervey William Fellows and Frank Fellows, both in the class of '88. J. Franklin Fellows, a Trojan, sent his son, Haynes H. Fellows, to Wesleyan and into the fraternity in 1909. The son's younger brother, F. Edward Fellows, was graduated in 1921, and Haynes Fellows' son, of the same name, was in the class of 1940.

The original Wesleyan Fellows, J. Franklin, resides in this city. His son, born here, is now a physician and resides in Maplewood, N. J. The grandson is in the Army. There are a number of others from Troy and several now residing in Rensselaer County who appear in the pages of the book. It is a handsome quarto, richly illustrated and, competently written. It may be doubted whether any chapter history in any fraternity has ever been written and published which will compare with this for beauty of page and completeness of story.

BALLET MASTER IN SHIPYARD

Portland, Ore. (UP)—The war has wrcught many changes. It even made a shipyard worker of a ballet dancer. For 30 years, Alexander Oumansky danced and directed ballets in every part of the world. Now, because "I wanted to do my part," he's building ships.

NEW ADDITIONS TO TROY PUBLIC LIBRARY

The following new books, which have been added at the Troy Public Library, will be on exhibition there for one week.

Concert Life in New York, Richard Aldrich, a volume of carefully chosen articles from the scrap-books of Richard Aldrich, the noted music critic; Sherwood Anderson's Memoirs, Sherwood Anderson, an unconventional autobiography; It's About Time, P. M. Chamberlain, a comprehensive treatment of the history and development of clocks and watches; Victory Through Air Power, A. P. De Seversky, tells how America can win the war by air power; My Yankee Mother, H. E. French, an entertining book about a genuinely delightful person; Good Housekeeping Cookbook, Good Housekeeping Institute, New York, a complete guide to home food problems; Heroes of the Atlantic, Ivor Halstead, the epic story of the seamen who struggle to keep our life lines open; Defense Will Not Win the War, W. F. Kernan, the author shows his conception of the only way to win the present war; Napoleon's Invasion of Russia, E. V. Tarle, presents the complete story of the most dramatic event in Russian history; Simon Bolivar, Mrs. E. D. (Jenkinson) Waugh, the exciting story of the great liberator of South America.

Fiction—Floods of Spring, Henry Bellamann; Old Soldiers Never Die, James Ronald; Fear Stalks the Village, E. L. White.

LOCAL RED CROSS RECEIVES SHIPMENT OF NEW MATERIAL

A new shipment of material has arrived at the Red Cross production house, 106 Second Street, Mrs. Norman F. Coons, production chairman has announced to complete the present War Relief quota.

The sewing room at the house will be open daily under the chairmanship of Mrs. Maude Betham and Mrs. Charles A. Brown.

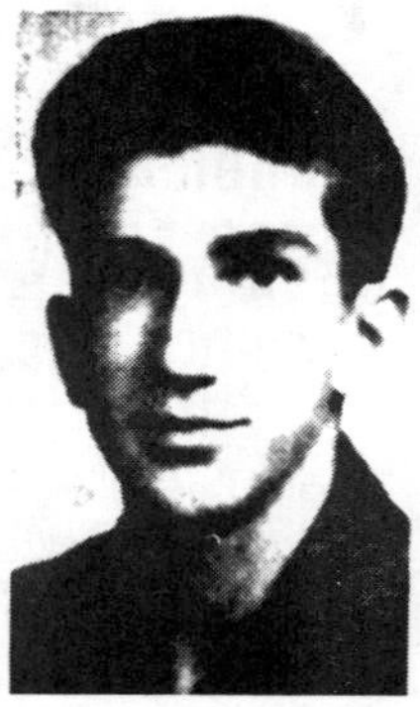

WILLIAM F. AUSTIN

Bill is graduating from Cambridge Union School, where he played baseball, basketball and football and was on the track team. He was president of the Aviation Club and builds model planes, hopes to continue his interest in things aeronautical in the Army Air Corps. A carrier six years.

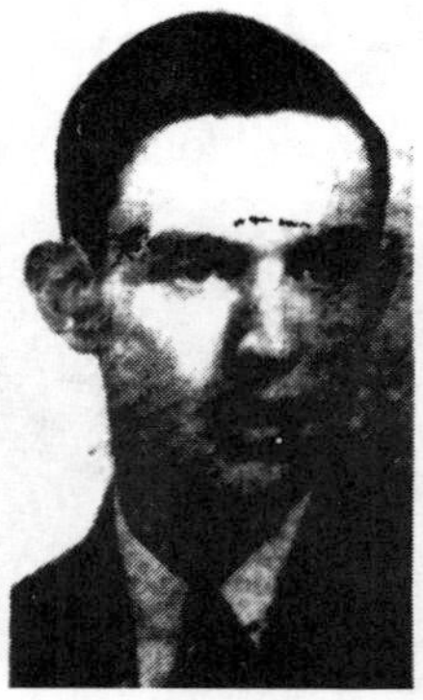

DONALD T. BIRKMAYER

A Sycaway carrier two years, Don is graduating from Troy High School. He's interested in mechanics, so it's not surprising he hopes to go to R. P. I. Don is a coin collector.

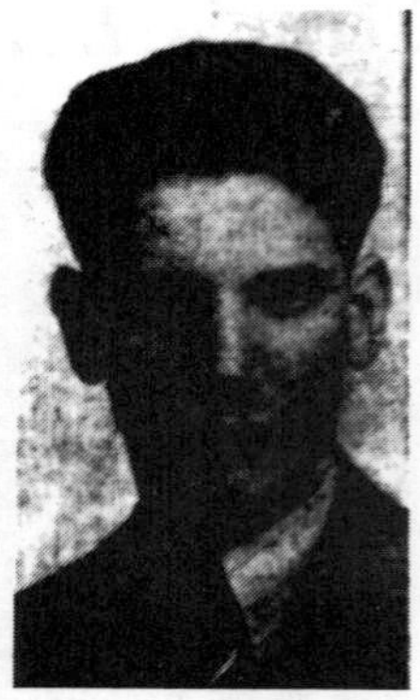

ROWLAND E. BLATCHLEY

Rowland played football and baseball at Cambridge Union School, where he was president of the Radio Club, vice president of the Aviation Club and secretary of his class. An amateur machinist and plane-builder, he's aiming for the Army Air Corps or the General Electric plant. A carrier for one year.

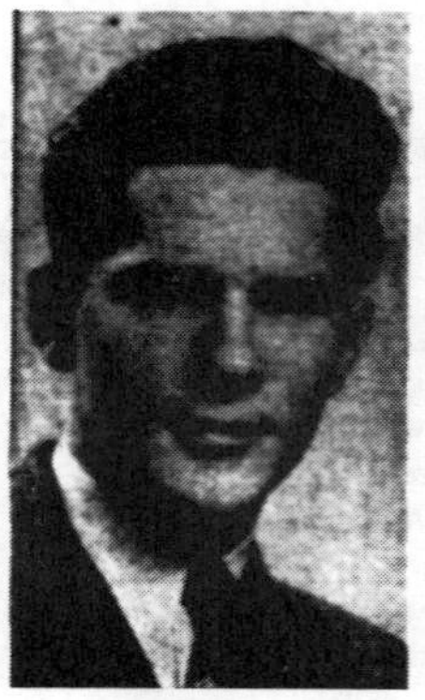

EARL L. BOISEN

Earl is graduating from Lansingburg High School, where he was captain of the track team and treasurer of the Hi-Y Club. He has been a Lansingburg carrier for six years. He plans to go to work, but week-ends and holidays you'll find him hunting and fishing.

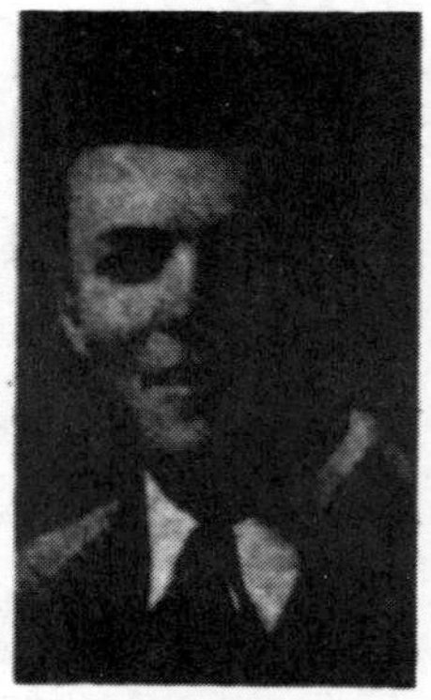

E. DONALD BRENNAN

In addition to being a carrier for four years, Don has served as Watervliet High School correspondent. He's played baseball, basketball and tennis, was a cheer leader and a member of the Hi-Y Club. His plans are still indefinite.

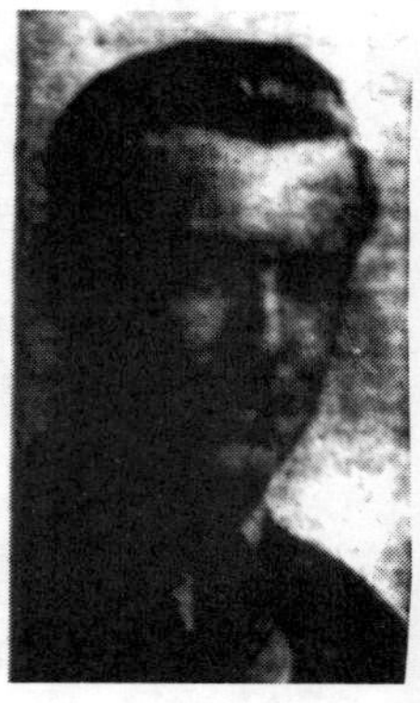

DONALD E. BRINKMANN

An industrial arts graduate of Troy High School, Don has served as a messenger for The Record Newspapers. He was president of the school Radio Club last year and is the operator of Station W2NMF. He's going with the General Electric Co., hopes to attend R. P. I.

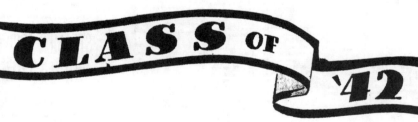

CONGRATULATIONS

To the Carriers, Correspondents and Other Young Men of Our Organization Graduating in the

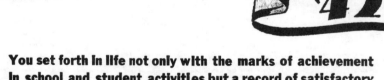

CLASS OF '42

You set forth in life not only with the marks of achievement in school and student activities but a record of satisfactory service in business.

We are proud to have had you associated with our organization and feel confident that the added experience you have thereby gained will prove of constant value to you.

Congratulations and good luck!

THE RECORD NEWSPAPERS

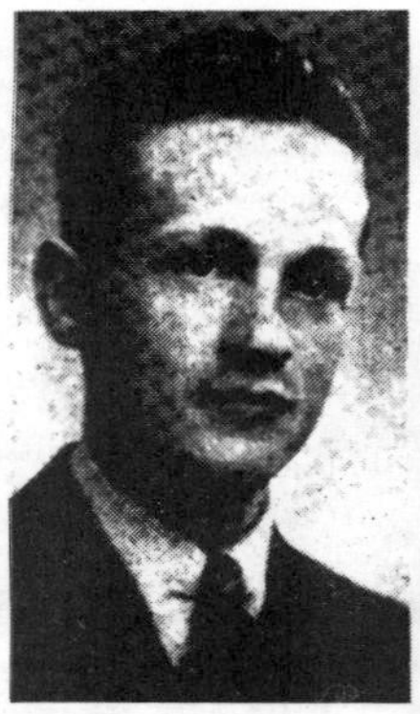

WARREN S. BRUNDIGE

Warren is salutatorian and vice president of the Waterford High School Seniors. He played varsity soccer and baseball, was on the year book staff and was a member of the Newspaper Club. A carrier for three years, he is going to college and wants to be an auditor.

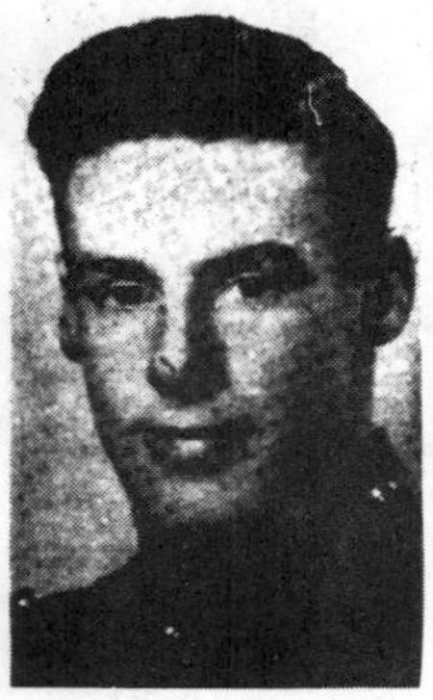

CHARLES G. BRYANT

"Chuck" is among the La Salle Institute graduates. He's a ski enthusiast and a fisherman. He has work d in the mail room for one year, is now a galley boy in The Troy Record composing room and plans to become a printer.

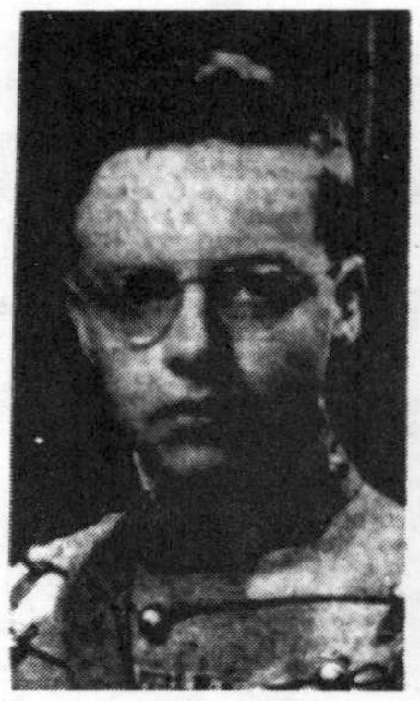

JOHN D. CARROLL, JR.

John was correspondent at La Salle Institute, where he was lieutenant colonel. He was on the fencing team two years, was manager of varsity football and basketball, earned first honors in English and languages and won a scholarship to Manhattan College.

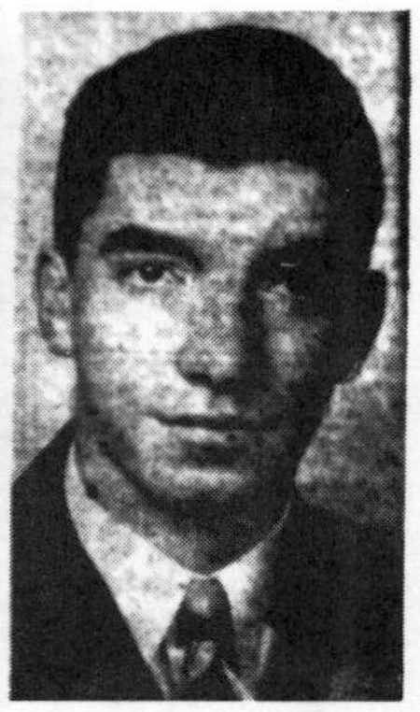

MARTIN W. CONNELL

Martin is graduating from Catholic Central High School. He was a member of the Dramatic Club and sports are his big interest. He has served as an East Side carrier for six years. He plans to go to college.

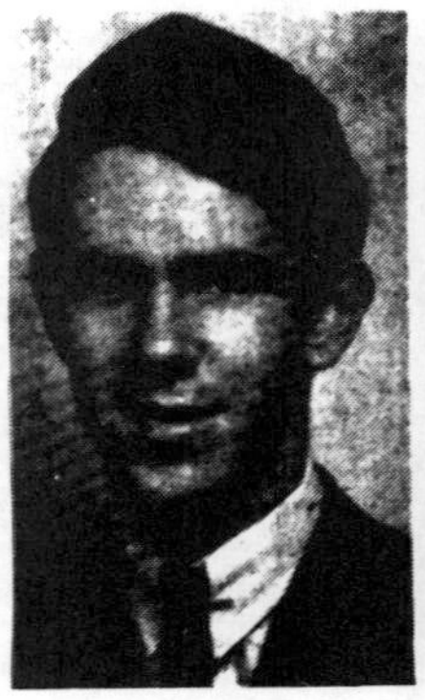

JAMES D. COUGHTRY

Jim is a Catholic Central High School graduate. He was a member of the school dance band. Skiing, model plane-making and music are his hobbies. A Watervliet carrier one year, he expects to go to college to become a pharmacist.

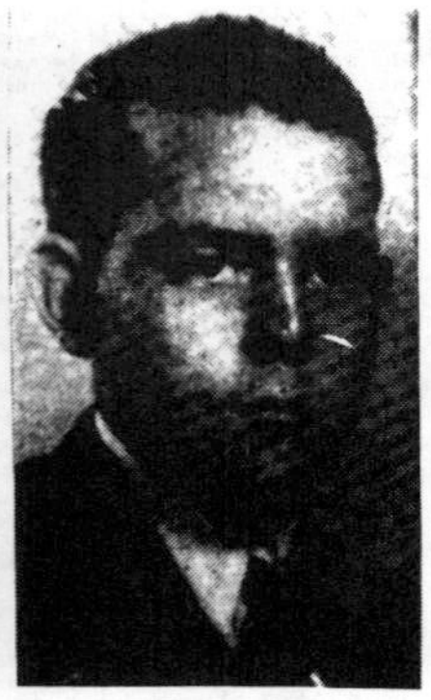

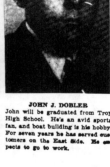

JOHN J. DOBLER

John will be graduated from Troy High School. He's an avid sports fan, and boat building is his hobby. For seven years he has served customers on the East Side. He expects to go to work.

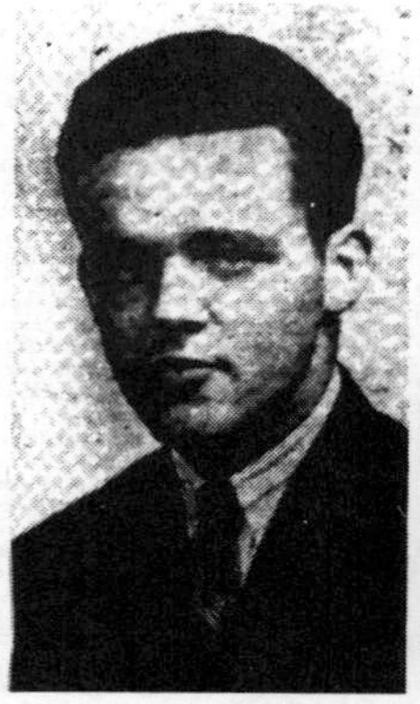

EUGENE A. GILCHRIST

Gene is among the graduates of Catholic Central High School, where he was co-captain of cheerleaders. He has had a route in Watervliet for five years. He expects to go to Siena College.

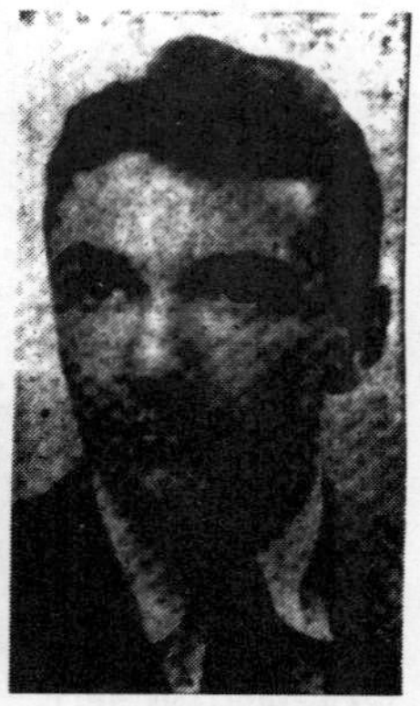

LEONARD A. HUMPHREYS

Leonard is salutatorian of the Lansingburg High School graduating class, of which he was president last year. He was on the track team, is interested in Scouting and mechanics and hopes to enter West Point. A Sycaway carrier six years.

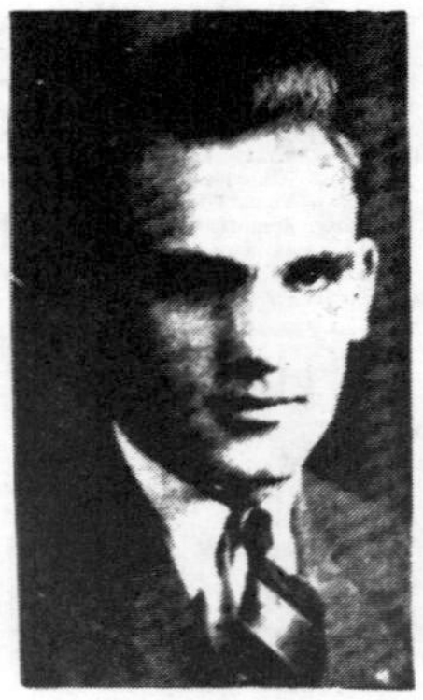

WILLIAM KOSTUN

Bill, for two years a street salesman, is graduating from Watervliet High School, where he was on the honor roll three years. He played junior varsity basketball. Drafting is his hobby, one that fits in well with his aim to become a machinist.

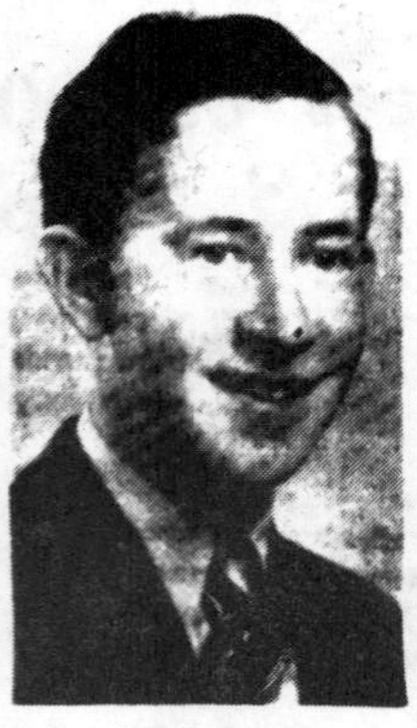

JOHN P. LARGE

John is graduating from Lansingburg High School and has been a Lansingburg carrier for one year. Building model planes and playing baseball are his hobbies. He plans to go to work.

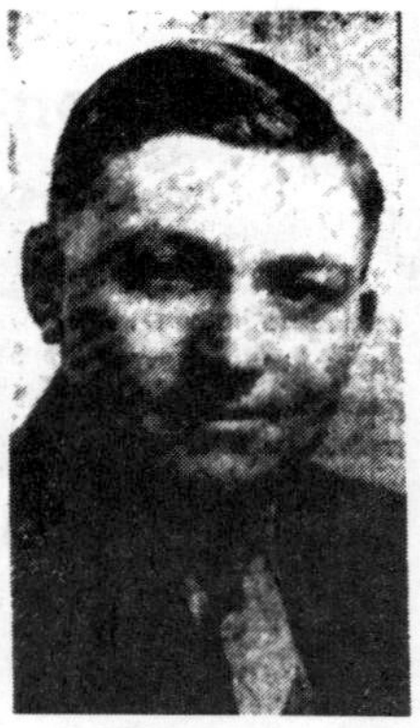

EUGENE LEWIS

A Troy High School graduate, Eugene has been a carrier in Sycaway for two years. He's done an outstanding job as a Treasury Department Defense Agent, having sold more than 34,000 ten cent War Stamps. A stamp collector and fisherman, he's going to college.

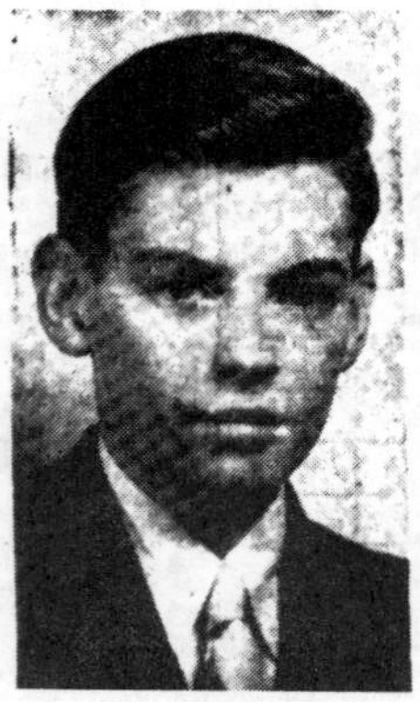

DANIEL M. MAHONEY

Dan completed the course at Catholic Central High School in 3½ years. He was "mayor" of Troy's Boys' Day, is president of his class and belonged to the CYO and French Club. He'll attend Siena College, has been an East Side carrier for a year.

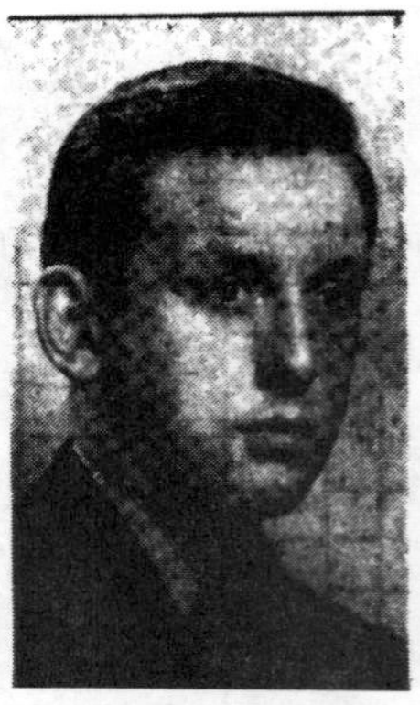

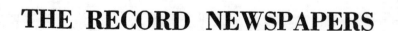

RICHARD A. MULLINS

Dick has been correspondent at Lansingburg High School, where he was a member of the Beacon staff, the Hi-Y and the Dramatic Clubs. He was in the Senior play. Writing is his hobby, and he hopes to work on a newspaper.

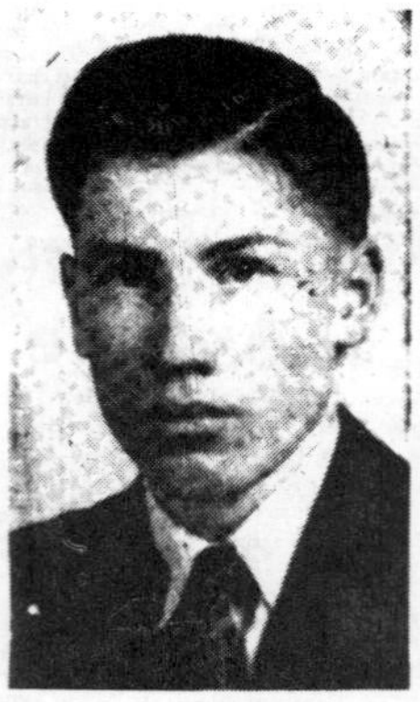

FRANK T. O'DONNELL

A Central Section carrier five years, Frank has been on the honor roll at Catholic Central High School for four years, is fifth highest in the class. He's been active in debating, likes baseball and hopes to go to college to study law.

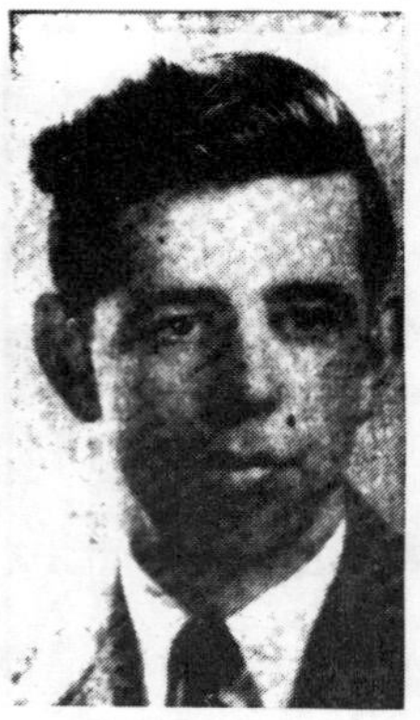

THOMAS F. TURLEY

Tom will graduate from Lansingburg High School. He has been a Lansingburg carrier for two years. Soap carving and photography are his hobbies. He expects to go to work in the Watervliet Arsenal.

THE WEATHER
U. S. Weather Bureau.
Tonight—Warmer.

THE TIMES RECORD

FINAL EDITION

Series 1942—No. 156. (Entered as Second Class Matter at the Postoffice at Troy, N. Y., under the Act of March 3, 1879) TROY, N. Y., FRIDAY EVENING, JULY 3, 1942. (Published Daily Except Sunday) PRICE FOUR CENTS

AXIS FORCES RETREAT AFTER GREAT TANK BATTLE IN EGYPT

COHOES RESIDENT FATALLY HURT IN TRUCK ACCIDENT

Employee of Fitzgerald Brothers Brewing Co. Died Today in Chestertown Road.

Wallace Riberdy, 40, of 67 Mohawk Street, Cohoes, a truck driver for the Fitzgerald Bros. Brewing Co., of this city, was killed early this morning when his truck, proceeding north in the new Warrensburg-Chestertown Road, left the highway and plunged down a forty-foot bank just north of Tripp Lake.

Mr. Riberdy was the Republican leader of the Second Ward, Cohoes, and had been the party's candidate for supervisor of that ward in the last election.

No Eye-Witnesses.

So far as could be learned today, there were no eye-witnesses to the accident, which apparently had happened several hours before it was discovered by Grant Hill, state highway patrolman from Chestertown, who was on his way to work with a crew of men when he noticed the broken guard rail. Investigating, the men found the wreckage of the truck at the foot of the bank and Riberdy's body several feet away. The victim's watch was stopped at 2:50 indicating this might have been the time of the fatal accident.

The truck, fully loaded, was demolished and its cargo almost a complete loss.

Dr. J. E. Goodman of Warrensburg, Warren County coroner, investigated and gave a verdict of accidental death due to a broken neck.

At his home in Cohoes, it was stated that Mr. Riberdy had not felt well yesterday and Mrs. Riberdy had urged him not to go to work.

He had been employed by the brewey for several years and was described at the company office this morning as "a reliable man and a conscientious worker."

Active in G. O. P. Circles.

He had been active in the affairs of the Republican Party in Cohoes for a number of years and had served as a committeeman for several years.

Survivors include his wife, the former Aurore Thouin; one daughter, Claire; two sisters, Mrs. Alice Lavigne and Mrs. Blanche Morin; his stepmother, Mrs. Victoria Riberdy, and three brothers, Donald, Raymond and Lawrence Riberdy, all of Cohoes.

The body will be removed to the funeral home of A. G. Boivin's Sons, Inc., 70 Congress Street, Cohoes. Funeral arrangements have not yet been completed.

Killed

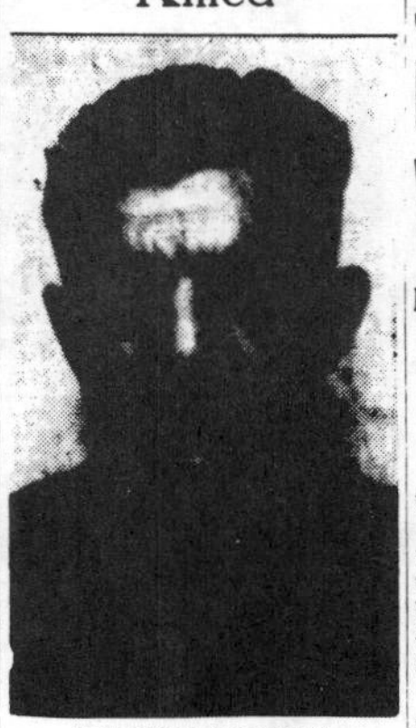

WALLACE RIBERDY

WOMAN INFORMER WOUNDED BY TWO PARIS BICYCLISTS

Vichy, Unoccupied France (AP)—Two bicyclists shot and seriously wounded the woman manager of a Paris apartment house in an attack which police termed in reprisal for informing German authorities of subversive activities of a tenant, reports reaching here today said.

It was the first recorded shooting of a woman in the long series of assaults against pro-Nazi collaborationists.

French civil and German military law requires apartment house employees to report suspicious activities of tenants. Large rewards including money and extra food ration coupons have been offered by German officials for spying on individuals.

Additonal reports from occupied France told of the arrest of 12 youths at Deziers in a raid on a clandestine print shop where anti-German leaflets and stickers were being turned out.

ARMY WILL BEGIN INDUCTING MEN IN SERVICE CLASS 1-B

Draftees With Minor Physical Defects To Be Assigned to Corps Area Commands.

Washington (AP)—The Army announced intention today of starting the induction of regular quotas of men placed in the deferred 1-B Selective Service class because of minor physical defects.

Beginning Aug. 1, men with only one eye or complete deafness in one ear, among others, will be inducted for limited military service, provided they otherwise meet requirements.

They will be assigned to duty with corps area service commands and the War Deparment overhead organization, and thereby release an almost equal number of fully qualified soldiers for service with task forces.

Induction, under the new standards, "will be limited to those with minor physical defects who are able to bring to the Army a useful vocation which was followed in civil life," the War Department said.

Men found upon reexamination to be qualified for full military service will be inducted as 1-A registrants.

Among those now classified as 1-B who would be eligible under the new ruling for limited service status are men: Whose weight and chest circumference do not meet 1-A standards but do not fall in Class 4; who have minimum 20-40 sight in one or both eyes if correctible with glasses to 20-40 in either eye; whose hearing in one or both ears is not less than 5-20, with complete deafness in one ear permitted if hearing in the other is 10-20 or better; who have insufficient teeth if the defect is correctible by dentures.

GIRL, 9, SACRIFICES HAIR FOR UNCLE SAM

Fitchburg, Mass. (U.P.)—Nine-year-old Carleen Gabriel was happy today in the knowledge that she had done her part in the war effort by contributing her 20-inch, brown curls.

Carleen, a third-grade pupil, decided several weeks ago that she would like to help and she had her long locks cut. The hair will be sent to the Bendix Corp., of Baltimore, which previously tested a sample and found it perfect for use in precision instruments.

$180,490 RAISED BY TROY PLAN IN VICTORY DAY DRIVE

Retail Merchants Report Figure at Ceremony at Homesite of Uncle Sam Wilson.

This city reported to the nation today that the Troy Plan works.

The U. S. Treasury department was informed by telegram that Retailers for Victory Day, Wednesday, had brought an investment of $180,490 in War Bonds during one day in Troy, and total is still rising.

It went up another $400 two seconds after the telegram was sent. One "small" merchant who had reported his day's sales as $100, handed in a check for $500 to be invested in War Bonds.

Before the last Victory merchant has turned in his report, it is believed that the total will reach $200,000.

This total represents the amount invested in War Bonds by retail merchants who had pledged their entire day's proceeds for that purpose and also the amount of War Bonds and Stamps sold over the counters of stores here Wednesday.

Uncle Sam Gets Huge Sum.

The ceremony of presenting the huge sum for tanks, guns and bullets to Uncle Sam took place at 11 a.m. at Second and Ferry Streets in front of the plaque marking the homesite of Uncle Sam Wilson, the Troy merchant who stamped "U. S." on barrels of meat bound for the Army during the War of 1812. The initials stood for United States and also for Uncle Sam. Thus came the name Uncle Sam as a designation for the United States.

Uncle Sam was impersonated by lanky Leo Trumbull. The Armed Forces of the nation were represented by Sergt. T. S. Ogden of the U. S. Army and Thomas Rhodes, yeoman second class, of the Navy.

Robert A. Block, chairman of the Retail Merchants' Bureau, handed Uncle Sam a scroll embossed with the figure $180,490 and tied with red, white and blue ribbions. Present at the ceremony were James F. O'Crowley, chairman of the Retailers for Victory Committee; Mayor Frank J. Hogan, and assistant Corporation Counsel John P. Judge, Mrs. James H. Donnelly, chairman of the County War Savings Committee, Women's Division; Mrs. Thomas Trowbridge, chairman of the city division, and members of Mr. O'Crowley's committee.

Merchants Thanked.

Mr. O'Crowley thanked all retail merchants of the city who took part in the drive. Practically all stores sold War Stamps and Bonds exclusively over their counters from noon to 12:15 p.m. Wednesday and more than 300 pledged their total day's sales for the purchase of War Bonds.

He also expressed the gratitude of the merchants for the aid given by the county and city War Savings Committee, both men's and women's divisions, and to the Chamber of Commerce and its president, Samuel W. McCochrane.

"It has been a most successful effort," Mr. O'Crowley said, "and the retail merchants and business men of the city have brought honor to the name of Troy as a progressive and patriotic city and one of the first to answer the call of our country in a particularly unique way to stimulate War Bond and Stamp buying. The public was generous in its support. The people certainly turned out and bought plenty of Bonds and Stamps."

MINES KILL 14 PERSONS.

Tunis (AP)—Fourteen persons, including five children in swimming, have been killed by floating mines in Tunisian waters, authorities announced today.

Uncle Sam Gets $180,490 for War Bonds from Troy

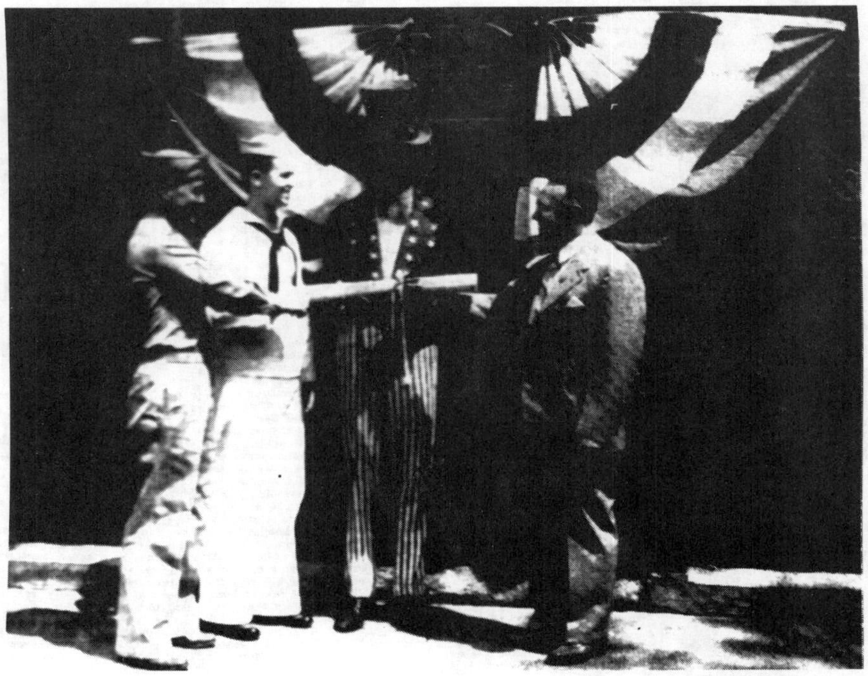

Robert A. Block, right, chairman of the Retail Merchants' Bureau, hands Uncle Sam, impersonated by Leo Trumbull, a scroll embossed with the figure $180,490. The amount represents the results of Retailers' Victory Day in Troy Wednesday. It includes the total reported by more than 300 merchants pledged to invest their entire day's proceeds in War Bonds, plus the total amount of War Bonds and Stamps sold over store counters Wednesday. At the left are Sergt. T. S. Ogden of the Army and Thomas Rhodes, yeoman second class, of the Navy. The group stands in front of the plaque marking the homesite of Uncle Sam Wilson, Troy merchant in the War of 1812, from whose name and initials "Uncle Sam" came to designate the United States.

33 LIVES LOST AS CARGO SHIP SINKS

British Vessel Torpedoed in Gulf of Mexico on June 29.

A Gulf Coast Port (U.P.) An Axis submarine, aided by a bright moon set a medium-sized British cargo ship afire with two torpedoes in the Gulf of Mexico on June 29 and a few minutes later 33 men died when their two lifeboats caught fire and were destroyed, the Eighth Naval District announced today.

Fourteen men escaped in a third lifeboat, the only one to clear the burning ship, and were picked up by a coast guard auxiliary at 5 a.m., EWT, three hours and 15 minutes after the attack. The ship burned and sank at 10 a.m.

The survivors, nine in serious condition, were taken to a gulf port for treatment of burns and bruises.

Third Engineer J. Steel, a victim, was "pointed out for particular heroism" by Capt. Hugh Bradford Bentley (of Ronceval Higher Brith Road, Tarquay, England.)

Bentley said the vessal was making 11 knots when the torpedoes struck, too fast to permit the lauching of the lifeboats. Steel stopped the engines so the lifeboats could be lowered.

A periscope was sighted about a half mile off the port beam, but there was no time for the alarm to be given since the first torpedo hit amidship two or three seconds later. It was followed by a torpedo a few moments afterward. The second torpedo struck further aft. As a result, the ship's guns never were used.

HARRY HOPKINS TO WED LOUISE MACY, FASHION AUTHORITY

New York (AP)—Mrs. Louise Macy, attractive fashion authority and former Paris editor of Harper's Bazaar, said today that she and Harry Hopkins, presidential aide, would be married in about a month.

Mrs. Macy said that she met Hopkins about six months ago through their mutual friends, Mr. and Mrs. Averill Harriman.

Asked when they would be married, Mrs. Macy said:

"You know Mr. Hopkins is a very busy man, and we haven't had an opportunity to discuss wedding plans fully. We definitely will be married in about a month, however.

"I expect to see Mr. Hopkins over the week-end, and perhaps we can then decide."

Hopkins, 52, is a close personal friend of President Roosevelt and lives at the White House, as does his daughter Diana.

It will be Hopkins' third marriage. He was separated by divorce from his first wife, by whom he had three children, and his second wife, Mrs. Barbara Duncan Hopkins, mother of Diana, died Oct. 7, 1937.

Mrs. Macy is 36.

U. S. Troops in Egypt, Berlin Paper Reports

Stockholm (U.P.) — American troops are fighting with the British Imperial Army at El Alamein in Egypt, the Berlin correspondent of the newspaper Allehanda reported today, quoting German advices from Egypt.

The dispatch said the troops were members of the "first American Expeditionary Corps" and were several thousand strong and excellently equipped.

(There were rumors several days ago that U. S. armored forces had landed in the Middle East and would shortly go into battle against the Axis in Egypt, but they never were confirmed. Today's reports originated in Berlin and conceivably were disseminated by the German military in hopes of drawing enlightening comment from a United Nations source.)

NEW YORK BOARD BACKS DISMISSAL OF 40 TEACHERS

New York (AP) A resolution dismissing 40 high school teachers and first assistants, which surperseded a previous order calling for the dismissal of 125 regularly appointed high school instructors, was passed by the Board of Estimate yesterday by a 4 to 3 vote.

The dismissed teachers were assigned to their positions nine years ago without formal appointment and are eligible for retirement when their dismissals become effective Aug. 31.

The superintendent of schools was directed last month to prepare a list of 125 teachers whose dismissal would save $140,000. He found that the dismissal of 40 teachers, because of their higher salaries, would save $180,000.

ROOSEVELT SIGNS GIANT ARMY BILL

Will Provide Most Powerful Air and Ground Forces in World.

Washington (U.P.) President Roosevelt has signed the $42,820,003,067 Army appropriation bill for 1943, the largest single appropriations measure in history and designed to provide the most powerful air and ground forces in the world, the White House announced today.

The bill contains $11,316,892,910 for 23,550 planes and equipment for the Army Air Forces, and $9,948,319,237 for "almost 100,000 tanks" and other mechanized equipment.

To pay and maintain the Army as it approaches the 4,500,000 mark the strength scheduled to be reached during the 1943 fiscal year the bill provides $10,739,559,34[illegible]. Figured in that is the recently enacted legislation increasing the base pay of privates from $30 to $50 a month.

The President is authorized by the bill to allocate a maximum of $12,700,000,000 for lend-lease purposes.

The House Appropriations Committee reported that the 23,550 planes in the bill would "complete the War Department's part of the program enunciated by the President on Jan. 6, 1942, calling for the production of 60,000 airplanes in the calendar year 1942, and 125,000 airplanes in the calendar year 1943."

The bill brings total war expenditures and contractual authorization to approximately $228,000,000,000.

BRITISH BOMBERS ATTACK BREMEN

Many Fires Blazing in German U-Boat Base Following Raid.

London (U.P.) — A strong fleet of long range bombing planes, estimated to number upwards of 300, made the fourth large Royal Air Force raid in eight nights on Bremen, key German submarine and war factory area, during the night, it was announced today.

Many fires were left burning in the city, already devastated by three previous raids in the first of which, on the night of June 25, a force of upwards of 1,000 big planes, each with tons of bombs, hurled destruction on factories, docks and building yards.

An air ministry communique, reporting that 13 bombers were missing, indicated the size of the raid.

It was estimated that in eight nights a total of 2,400 planes had bombed Bremen.

The bombing planes shot down one enemy night fighter which challenged them in the raid last night, the communique said.

Short range planes heavily attacked German airdromes in Holland and Belgium in diversionary attacks designed to keep some enemy fighters occupied and permit the Bremen raiders more freedom.

Coastal command forces of Lockheed Hudson planes attacked enemy shipping off the Netherlands coast.

Germany in its first reports of the British raid on Bremen claimed only 11 planes downed and said that the raid had "little effect."

DESERT CONFLICT STILL RAGING IN EL ALAMEIN ZONE

Rommel's Armies Meet First Setback in Sweep Toward Nile; Heavy Fighting on Russian Front.

London (AP)—The British light cruiser Hermione, four British destroyers and one Polish destroyer were lost in the recent effort to reinforce Malta and British forces in Libya before they were pushed back into Egypt, it was announced officially today.

Besides the 5,456-ton Hermione, the destroyers were the British Bedouin, Hasty, Grove, Airedale and the Polish Kujawiak.

BY THE ASSOCIATED PRESS.

Britain's Egyptian armies clashed with the Axis in violent battle west of El Alamein again today after driving Field Marshal Edwin Rommel's African corps into at least temporary retreat in the three-day-old "battle of the bottleneck."

Dispatches from the front said the British, rallying at the eleventh hour, were striking furiously at the Axis invaders.

Details were lacking as to whether Rommel had returned after withdrawing last night or whether the British, seizing the initiative, were pursuing the Axis forces.

A bulletin from British imperial headquarters said Rommel's army "withdrew to the west, leaving our positions intact," after a fierce tank battle last evening at El Alamein, less than seventy miles west of Alexandria.

Italian headquarters yesterday claimed the capture of El Alamein, which was described as the last British stronghold guarding the great Alexandria naval base.

Front-line dispatches said the twilight tank battle in the desert, the first major setback for General Rommel's armies in their sweep toward the Nile, climaxed bitter all-day fighting in which the invaders launched a general attack against El Alamein.

Rommel Calls Retreat.

"Our mobile and armored forces counter-attacked the enemy flanks," a British communique said, inflicting such heavy losses that Rommel called a retreat.

"Throughout the battle our light bombers, fighter-bombers and fighters were employed in increasing numbers and heavily attacked enemy concentrations southwest of El Alamein," the British said.

Italy's high command, locating the scene of battle as "southeast of El Alamein," asserted that 2,000 more British troops had been captured and declared Axis operations were developing favorably.

"Strong enemy forces were wiped out," the Italian communique said.

The British communique reporting the German-Italian invaders had withdrawn west of El Alamein disputed the Axis claim yesterday that Rommel's forces had broken through the main British position.

El Alamein is the northern anchor of the 35-mile British line protecting the "bottleneck" gateway to Alexandria. The line extends from the Mediterranean coastal escarpment to the desolate Qattara salt sink.

Nazis May Be Trapped.

Bolstered by "very considerable reinforcements," which Prime Minister Churchill announced yesterday were arriving at the front, Gen Sir Claude Auchinleck's imperial armies were said to be throwing everything they had in-

(Continued on Page 2.)

U. S. COMPTROLLER ISSUES BANK CALL

Washington (AP)—The comptroller of the currency today issued a call for a statement of the condition of all national banks at the close of business Tuesday, June 30.

The request for condition reports was the usual mid-year checkup by all federal banking agencies. Similar calls were issued by the Federal Reserve Board and the Federal Deposit Insurance Corp.

Altogether, approximately 13,460 banks, both national and state, were requested to file statements of their assets and liabilities.

Classified Ads

Taken Tonight

Till 10 O'Clock

To sell, rent, buy, find, hire, fill other wants use Classified Ads in The Record Newspapers.

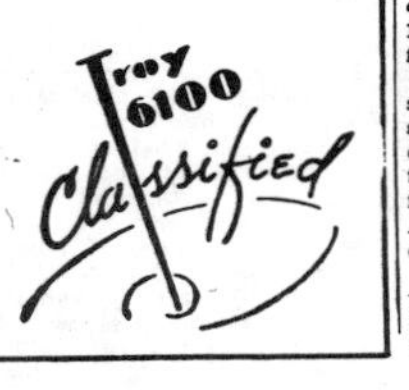

Auto Stamp Sales Exceptionally Poor

Washington (AP)—Indications that large numbers of automobile owners were staying away from the $5 Federal use tax stamp window sent top Treasury officials into a huddle today over various proposed methods of enforcing the levy.

The first auto stickers, which have been required since Feb. 1, expired Tuesday night, but scattered reports indicate "exceptionally poor" sales of the stamps covering the fiscal year starting July 1. On a proportionate basis, the first stickers cost $2.09.

Technically, persons who do not show the stamps on their windshields are liable to a fine of $25 or a jail term of 30 days. Actually, the Treasury has no adequate funds to police the millions of cars. A few arrests were made because of failure to exhibit the first sticker, but the Treasury has no reports of anyone going to jail for the offense.

A stab at rigid enforcement in the East was made recently when the Treasury got the Office of Price Administration to require motorists to report the serial numbers of their tax stamps before obtaining gasoline ration books.

But this plan is deemed by some officials to be inadequate because many car owners are apt to invent a number. The stamp must be glued to the windshields and can't readily be brought before the rationing boards. Besides, there is no gasoline rationing in most of the country.

Another complication is the fact that thousands of cars have been laid up for lack of tires, and the Treasury doesn't have any idea of how many stamps ought to be sold. The tax applies only to the "use of a motor vehicle," and laid-up cars are exempt.

About 29,800,000 stamps were sold in the last fiscal year.

WITH YOUR MEALS
In your favorite restaurant it's smart to say "UTICA CLUB XXX Pale Ale or Pilsner Lager for mine."—Adv.

"Glorious Fourth" Not To Halt Wheels In U. S. War Factories

BY THE ASSOCIATED PRESS

A nation fighting to protect the freedom it won in other wars celebrates tomorrow its first wartime Fourth of July in a quarter of a century under conditions that may make it really "safe and sane."

Most war factories will hum on, many fireworks have been abandoned and, on the populous eastern seaboard, gasoline rationing will keep the greater part of the area's 10,000,000 motorists off the highways.

True, many of the 54,000,000 residents of the 17 gas-starved Atlantic coast states plan to make their usual holiday trips by train or bus, and some municipalities—mostly in the Midwest—are to stage huge fireworks displays, but travel generally will be in the form of parades and fireworks in the form of speeches.

Army warnings that fireworks displays and large gatherings might present opportunities for token air raids and for saboteurs and actual bans on such celebrations on the east and west coasts as well as the gulf states indicated that those areas would observe the holiday quietly.

In the nation's capital, Washington's annual municipal fireworks display was cancelled and it was announced that work would go on in all government offices connected with the war effort.

Inland, however, in some central and southwestern states, where the danger of possible air raids is less than that on the coasts, many big events were planned to attract great throngs of celebrants, unhampered by gas rationing.

Typical of these will be Minneapolis' annual American Legion show at Powderhorn Park, where 200,000—largest crowd in the event's 13-year history—are expected to attend an all-day program featuring the mass induction of 1,500 Navy recruits.

All war plants in the beehive Detroit area will operate as usual, as will the North American bomber plant at Kansas City, where Nat Milgram, president of the American War Dads, has issued an appeal to celebrants to buy war stamps and bonds instead of firecrackers.

New Yorkers, prohibited from using fireworks and many unable to get fuel for cars, are expected either to stay home or do their whooping up by train and bus travel and indications are that there'll be plenty of the latter.

The New York Central and Pennsylvania Railroads reported that they were prepared to use every piece of available equipment for the annual rush by millions both into and out of the city.

The Index

Freak Homer By Rudy York Wins For A. L. All-Stars By 3-1 Tally

FANCY EXPLOITS BY LOU BOUDREAU FURNISHES SPARK

Leads Off With Homer in First; Owen Clouts One for Only N. L. Run.

By JUDSON BAILEY.

Polo Grounds, New York (AP)—The American League made a travesty of the tenth major league all-star spectacle in one inning last night, knocking the National Leaguers groggy with three runs on two homers in the first frame and coasting to a 3 to 1 triumph.

With the major leagues' bat and ball fund as the recipient, 33,694 fans paid $95,000 to pass through the turnstiles.

It was the American League's seventh success in the annual classic and entitled the stars of the junior circuit to head for Cleveland where tonight they will engage Lieut. Gordon (Mickey) Cochrane's service stars in the big municipal stadium. A crowd of 60,000 will view the game.

This knitted into the picture of last night's tussle perfectly for it was Lou Boudreau, the 24-year-old shortstop manager of the Cleveland Indians, whose sensational exploits furnished the impetus for the American League victory.

He led off with a tremendous homer into the upper left field stands in the first inning after looking at only one pitch from Morton Cooper, the rugged right hander of the St. Louis Cardinals who has dominated the pitching scene in the senior loop all season.

It was the first time an all-star game ever had been opened with a homer and it picked right up where the American League left off last year when Ted Williams clouted a mighty drive in the ninth inning at Detroit to beat the National Leaguers 7 to 5.

Boudreau's homer came after the fans had waited nearly an hour for the game to get under way because of weather conditions, a factor that put the finish on the start of a citywide blackout that started at 9:30 p.m.

The shouting of the fans had barely subsided over the Cleveland manager's blow before Tommy Henrich of the New York Yankees drove a double into right and after Cooper had succeeded in stopping Williams and Joe DiMaggio, powerful Rudy York of the Detroit Tigers tried to dodge out of the way of an inside pitch and the ball bounced off his bat and into the nearby right field stands for another homer.

It was all so easy that most of the spectators settled down resignedly to see a rout and no amount of fine hurling by four National League aces later could change the complexion of the game.

After that opening outbreak the American League made only four fruitless hits, but even this restoration of National League pitching prowess failed to outshine the hurling of Spurgeon (Spud) Chandler of the Yanks and big Al Benton of the Detroit Tigers, who shared the entire pitching chore for Manager Joe McCarthy and allow only six hits—one of which was a pinch home run by little Mickey Owen of Brooklyn in the eighth inning to save the Nationals the embarrassment of a shutout.

Chandler, winner of nine games against two defeats for the world champions this season, served the first four innings and allowed only two hits in a flawless performance and received credit for the victory in the first all-star game he ever worked.

Both Chandler and Benton, who was somewhat wild and in trouble frequently in his five-inning stretch, received marvelous support.

Boudreau handled nine fielding chances, some of them almost miraculous, and took part in two double plays.

The crowd, although smaller than expected because of weather conditions which forced the covering of the infield and delayed the start, was as vocally powerful as many larger turnouts and the customers alternately cheered and jeered with great enthusiasm.

Joe DiMaggio, the Yankee clipper, came into disfavor by grounding out in the first inning and popping to the catcher on his next turn at bat. As a result he was booed and hooted until echoes rang when he came to bat later in the game. He jabbed back at his tormentors, however, by getting two singles in his last two turns.

Ted Williams got one of the American League's other singles and Bob Johnson of the Philadelphia Athletics, completed his team's hitting with a pinch single while batting for Chandler in the fifth.

Joe Gordon, who paced the American League in hitting for many weeks, fanned his first three times up and grounded out weakly in the ninth and altogether the National hurlers piled up seven strikeouts.

Two were by Cooper, who fanned Gordon to end the rollicking first inning, four others were by lefty John Vander Meer of Cincinnati, who pitched impressive two-hit ball for three frames, and the last was by Claude Passeau of the Chicago Cubs, who allowed one hit in the two stanzas he served. Bucky Walters of Cincinnati came in to work for the final inning and set the American Leaguers down in order.

After the first inning the Americans got only one runner past first and that was in the sixth inning when DiMaggio singled and reached second as Jimmy Brown of St. Louis dropped a throw from Arky Vaughan of Brooklyn in what would have been an easy forced play.

The National Leaguers got nowhere against Chandler until the fourth when Pete Reiser, Brooklyn's league batting champion, beat out a scratch single and advanced to second on a passed ball only to be left stranded.

Benton got away to an equally solid start, and in the sixth when Danny Litwhiler of the Phils, pinch hitting for Vander Meer, singled, he was promptly erased in a sparkling double play engineered by Boudreau. Benton walked Vaughan, but he was left on base.

With two out in the seventh Enos Slaughter of St. Louis singled and big Ernie Lombardi of Boston waited out a walk, but Boudreau snatched down a liner by Pee Wee Reese of the Dodgers to snuff out the threat.

Finally Owen, batting for Passeau at the start of the eighth, bunted foul once and then lifted a homer into the lower right field stands. Subsequently Bob Elliott of Pittsburg singled, but the rally died when Frank McCormick of the Reds grounded to Boudreau for a force out.

The game barely beat the 9:30 p.m. deadline for a blackout ordered in New York City and the crowd had to remain seated in the stands for some thirty minutes.

The American League players, however, hastily changed into civilian clothes and rushed for the Cleveland train with Manager McCarthy announcing that Jim Bagby of the Indians and Buddy Rosar of the Yankees would form his battery against the service stars tonight.

AMERICAN.

	AB.	R.	H.	O.	A.
Boudreau, ss.	4	1	1	4	5
Henrich, rf.	4	1	1	2	0
Williams, lf.	4	0	1	0	0
J. DiMaggio, cf.	4	0	2	2	0
York, 1b.	4	1	1	11	3
Gordon, 2b.	4	0	0	1	4
Keltner, 3b.	4	0	0	0	1
Tebbetts, c.	4	0	0	4	1
Chandler, p.	1	0	0	3	1
xJohnson	1	0	1	0	0
Benton, p.	1	0	0	0	1
Totals	35	3	7	27	16

x—Batted for Chandler in 5th.

NATIONAL.

	AB.	R.	H.	O.	A.
Brown, 2b.	2	0	0	1	0
Herman, 2b.	1	0	0	0	0
Vaughan, 3b.	2	0	0	1	2
Elliott, 3b.	1	0	1	1	2
Reiser, cf.	3	0	1	3	0
Moore, cf.	1	0	0	1	0
Mize, 1b.	2	0	0	3	0
F. McCormick, 1b.	2	0	0	3	0
Ott, rf.	4	0	0	1	0
Medwick, lf.	2	0	0	1	0
Slaughter, lf.	2	0	1	1	0
W. Cooper, c.	2	0	1	7	0
Lombardi, c.	1	0	0	2	0
Miller, ss.	2	0	0	2	1
Reese, ss.	1	0	0	0	1
M. Cooper, p.	0	0	0	0	0
zMarshall	1	0	0	0	0
Vander Meer, p.	0	0	0	0	1
zzLitwhiler	1	0	1	0	0
Passeau, p.	0	0	0	0	0
zzzOwen	1	1	1	0	0
Walters, p.	0	0	0	0	0
Totals	31	1	6	27	7

z—Batted for M. Cooper in 3rd.
zz—Batted for Vander Meer in 6th.
zzz—Batted for Passeau in 8th

Americans	300 000 000—3
Nationals	000 000 010—1

Error—Brown. Runs batted in—Boudreau, York 2, Owen. Two base hit—Henrich. Home runs—Boudreau, York, Owen. Double plays—Gordon, Boudreau and York; Boudreau and York. Left on bases—American 5, National 6. Earned runs—American 3, National 1. Bases on balls—Off Benton 2 (Vaughan and Lombardi). Struck out—By Cooper 2, (Gordon and Tebbetts); by Chandler 2 (Ott, Miller); by Vander Meer 4 (York, Gordon 2, Henrich); by Benton 1 (Ott); by Passeau 1 (Tebbetts); by Walters 1 (Keltner). Pitching summary off Cooper, 4 hits 1, 3 runs in 3 innings; off Vander Meer, 2 hits, 0 runs in 3 innings; off Chandler, 2 hits, 0 runs in 4 innings; off Benton, 4 hits, 1 run in 5 innings; off Passeau, 1 hit, 0 runs in 2 innings; off Walters, 0 hits, 0 runs in 1 inning. Hit by pitcher—By Chandler (Brown). Passed ball—Tebbets. Winning pitcher—Chandler. Losing pitcher—Cooper. Umpires—Ballanfant, National League at plate and ... Stewart, American League. Barlick, National League, second base; McGowan, American League, third base for ... 4½ innings. McGowan, American League at plate. Barlick, National League, first base; Stewart, American League, 2nd base; Ballanfant, National League, 3rd base (second 4½ innings). Time—2:07. Attendance—33,694.

Heavy Hitters

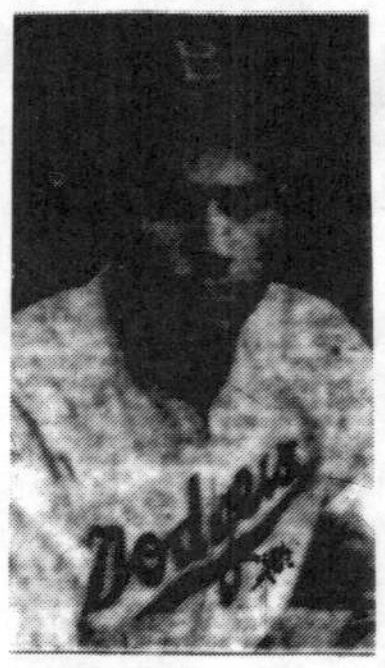

MICKEY OWEN.

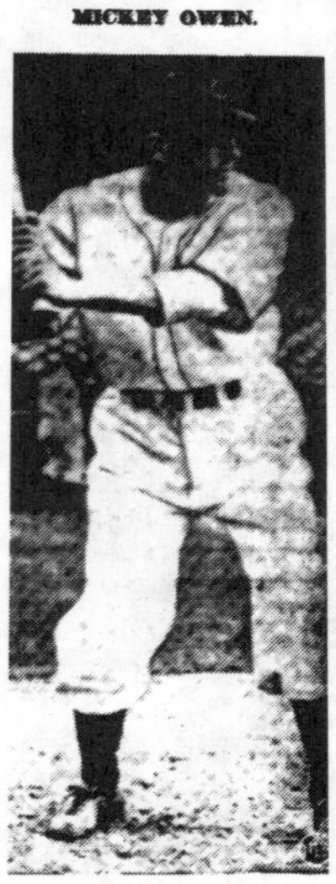

LOU BOUDREAU.

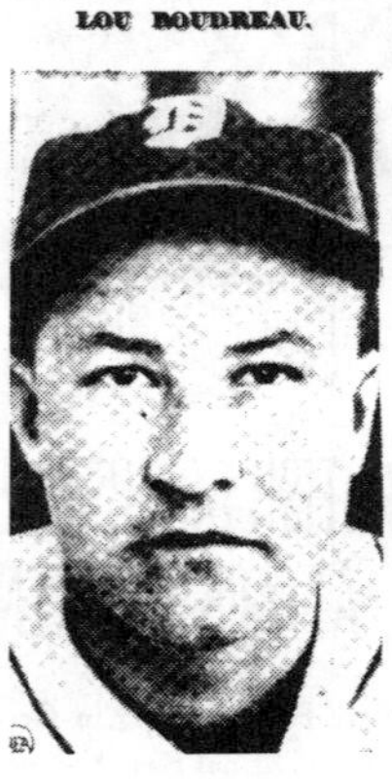

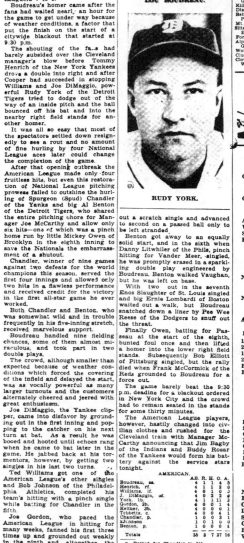

RUDY YORK.

BEAUNIT MILLERS, FORD TEAMS LEAD INDUSTRIAL LOOPS

The Beaunit Millers continued undefeated this week at the top of the Division A standings in the Industrial A. A. Softball League, while the Ford Motors duplicated the performance in Division B. The Millers have won four straight and the Fords three, since the second round began.

Beaunit notched its triumph by a narrow 3-2 margin over the determined Arsenal outfit. The Fords were more impressive in their victory, turning back the Alphas, 11-6. In Division A, other results were Allegheny-Ludlum over Coverts, 9-2, and Behr-Manning over Diamond Rock, 21-12. In Division B, Mt. Ida downed Sliters, 10-6 and Cloverleaf walloped Cluetts, 31-19.

Today's schedule fololws: Division A, Diamond Rock vs. Beaunit, Behr-Manning vs. Allegheny-Ludlum and Coverts vs. Arsenal; Division B, Alphas vs. Mt. Ida, Coca Cola vs. Sliters and Cloverleaf vs. Fords. Below are the team standings:

Division A.

Team	Won	Lost	Pct.
Beaunit	4	0	1.000
Allegheny	3	1	.750
Behr-Manning	3	1	.750
Coverts	1	3	.250
Arsenal	1	3	.250
Diamond	0	4	.000

Division B.

Team	Won	Lost	Pct.
Fords	3	0	1.000
Cloverleafs	3	1	.750
Mt. Ida	2	1	.667
Alphas	2	2	.500
Cluetts	2	2	.500
Coca Cola	0	3	.000
Sliters	0	0	.000

This week's scores:

Coverts	200 000 000—2
Allegheny	520 010 010—9

Goering and Mirpin; Blichko and Frawley.

Arsenal	010 000 001—2
Beaunit	001 000 02x—3

Grimm and Peperian; Charbonneau and Killian.

Diamonds	000 324 3—12
Behr-Manning	936 003 0—21

Prout and Ott; Bonjukian and Graber.

Mt. Ida	003 030 031—10
Sliters	001 032 00x— 6

Evers and Peckham; Daniels and Miers.

Fords	104 004 110—11
Alphas	002 210 100— 6

Grady and VanArnum; Keleher and Wolfe

Cluetts	223 210 324—19
Cloverleaf	602 506 66x—31

Wood and Schultz; Hansen and Griffen.

The Baseball Standings

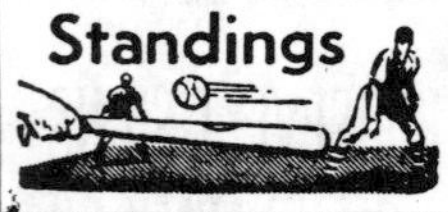

Games Today.

NATIONAL LEAGUE.
Open date.

AMERICAN LEAGUE.
Open date.

EASTERN LEAGUE.
ALBANY at Hartford.
Wilkes-Barre at Williamsport.
Scranton at Elmira.
Binghamton at Springfield.

Yesterday's Results.

NATIONAL LEAGUE.
No games scheduled.

AMERICAN LEAGUE.
No games scheduled.

EASTERN LEAGUE.
All games postponed.

INTERNATIONAL LEAGUE.
1—Baltimore 5, Toronto 0.
2—Toronto 16, Baltimore 1.
1—Montreal 4, Newark 1.
2—Montreal 7, Newark 3.
Buffalo 4, Jersey City 3.
Rochester at Syracuse, postponed.

The Standings.

NATIONAL LEAGUE.

	Won	Lost	Pct.
Brooklyn	52	21	.712
St. Louis	43	29	.597
Cincinnati	41	34	.547
New York	40	37	.519
Chicago	38	41	.481
Pittsburg	34	40	.459
Boston	34	47	.420
Philadelphia	21	54	.280

AMERICAN LEAGUE.

	Won	Lost	Pct.
New York	49	26	.653
Boston	46	29	.613
Cleveland	45	34	.570
Detroit	43	38	.531
St. Louis	37	40	.481
Chicago	31	44	.413
Philadelphia	33	50	.398
Washington	28	51	.354

EASTERN LEAGUE.

	Won	Lost	Pct.
Wilkes-Barre	43	27	.614
Scranton	38	25	.603
ALBANY	37	27	.578
Binghamton	35	30	.538
Hartford	35	33	.515
Williamsport	31	35	.470
Elmira	27	42	.391
Springfield	18	45	.286

LEAGUE MOGULS AVOID DISCUSSION OF SERIES TOUR

New York (AP)—Officials and club owners of the major leagues, meeting in three lengthy sessions yesterday, discussed the possibility of altering the plans for the 1942 World Series, but left the final decision to the advisory council.

A long joint session, which followed separate league meetings and lasted almost till time for the all-star game, wound up with both leagues leaving the series entirely in the hands of the council, composed of Commissioner Kenesaw M. Landis, President Will Harridge of the American League, and President Ford Frick of the National League.

Leslie O'Conner, secretary to the commissioner, said after the final meeting that the only definite plan for the World Series called for the contribution of a part of the receipts to War Relief. All other details will be worked out by the advisory council, which did not set a date for a meeting. The council usually holds a regular session about a month before series time.

Considerable talk in baseball circles had involved the possibility of playing a World Series longer than the usual seven games and taking the later games on a "tour" of several cities and it was assumed that such an arrangement was among the matters discussed

A request of Clark Griffith owner of the Washington Senators to play all of Washington's remaining homes games this season at night with the exception of Sundays and holidays was turned down in the joint meeting with Commissioner Landis casting the deciding vote.

The American League approved Griffith's request at its meeting but then the National League voted against it and in the joint session Landis sided with the senior circuit.

Washington already is operating under a special ruling allowing the Senators 21 night games at home this season seven more than any other major league club

The American League also discussed condensing the 1943 season by two weeks although adhering to a 154-game program. President Harridge said the junior circuit considered starting the season a week later than usual and ending it a week earlier Such a schedule would make for many more double headers It was not brought up at the joint session

A suggestion made several days ago by Jack Zeller general manager of the Detroit Tigers that the clubs give up spring training trips to Florida and California next season never was discussed

AMATEURS TEE OFF IN WESTERN GOLF TOURNAMENT TODAY

Spokane, Wash. (AP)—Amateur golf's last big fling of the year, and probably for the duration of the war, gets under way today in the forty-third playing of the Western Amateur Championship.

Although a number of the links sharpshooters are in military service, the field of nearly a hundred shaped up impressively, headed by Corp. Marvin (Bud) Ward, National and Western Champion.

Ward, stationed at nearby Fort Wright, returned from a California honeymoon in time for a last minute fairway tune-up. He's the man to beat for the title and the long, fairly flat par 72 Manito course is made to order for his game.

Lucky Fish

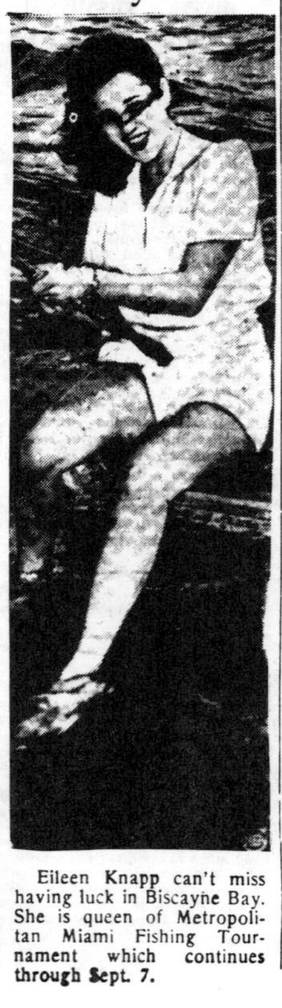

Eileen Knapp can't miss having luck in Biscayne Bay. She is queen of Metropolitan Miami Fishing Tournament which continues through Sept. 7.

Climbing Coast Guardsmen--Outdoor and In

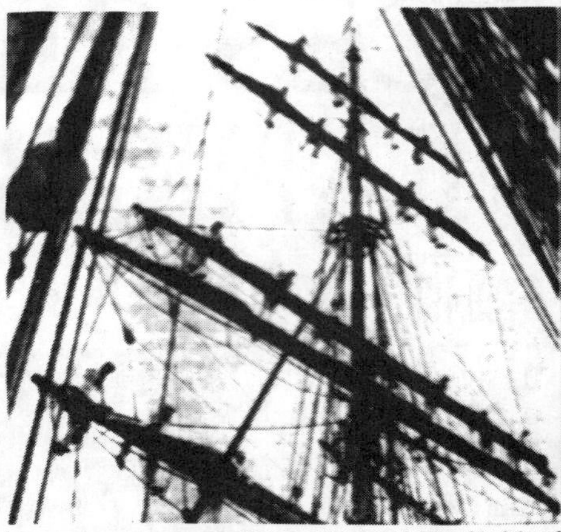

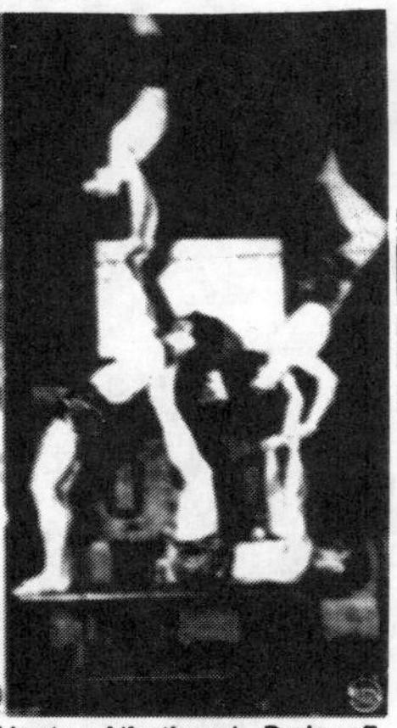

During the day Coast Guardsmen swarm over rigging of training ship at an Atlantic port. During off hours, they take mailman's holiday with gymnastics in USO club house.

PROSPECT PARK TENNIS TEST TO OPEN SATURDAY

Members of the Adirondack Lawn Tennis Association will take to the courts at Prospect Park this week-end in an attempt to gain or regain ranking for the season, when the annual Troy Open Tourney opens at 11 a.m. Saturday.

The results of two other tourneys will be used, together with the Troy Open affair, to determine the seedings. Approximately forty net artists are expected to compete, according to Seth Smith, tourney director. The event is sponsored by the city recreation department.

All entries must be filed by Thursday with Seth Smith, Box 136, Troy. Among those expected are last year's champ Phil Englebardt of Schenectady and runner-up Smith. Englebardt teamed with Marv Dwore to take the doubles title last year but, since the latter has retired from competition, will pair with Smith this season.

Among the Trojans to compete are Lou Travers, Bill Cavanaugh, Warren O'Neill, Red Harley and Howard Buchanan. Others are Calvin McCracken, Schenectady County champ and former Princeton University netman; Randall Whitbeck of Albany, Walt D'Arcy of Rensselaer, Monty Paige of Albany and Bill Emmerich of Gloversville. McCracken-Leo Glenn and Sutherland-Perle of Albany are likely doubles combinations.

WILLIAMS AT TOP OF HITTING HEAP

Chicago (AP) — By less than one percentage point Ted Williams, the 1941 American League batting champion, yesterday took over the lead in this year's swat race.

The Boston Red Sox outfielder hit at an even .500 pace last week to rise 21 points. This coincided with an 18-point drop by Joe Gordon of the Yankees and enabled Williams to move in front with a mark of .3473 to Gordon's .3467.

Thus, last year's .406 slugger led the league's top ten for the first time this year.

Besides Williams' phenomenal gain, young Vernon Stephens of the St. Louis Browns climbed from the sub-.300 ranks to .314, good enough for seventh place. But the rest of the top hitters either recorded slight gains or lost ground. The Cleveland Indians' Les Fleming was among the latter, dropping 16 points to .332. Last week Fleming was in second place. Now he's fifth.

After Williams and Gordon came Boston's Bobby Doerr at .346; John Pesky of the Red Sox .336; Fleming, .332; Bill Dickey, New York, .316; Stephens, .314; Stan Spence, Washington, .313; and Lou Boudreau, Cleveland Indians manager, .304.

Taft Wright, the Chicago White Sox' long-ailing outfielder who only recently got back to work, saw his mark drop last week from .375 to .331, lodging him between Fleming and Dickey in the ratings. But Wright is not officially entitled to a place in the top ten, being 11 "at bats" short of the current qualifying mark of 150.

Besides holding down the batting lead, Williams continued to set the pace in runs batted in with 80, in home runs with 18, and in runs scored with 72. Spence led in total hits with 101, Doerr showed the way in two-baggers with 29 and Jeff Heath of Cleveland had the most triples, eight. George Case of Washington led in stolen bases with 14.

Hank Borowy of the Yankees suffered his first hurling setback last week but continued to lead the pitchers with six wins and one loss. Next were Spud Chandler of the Yankees with 9 and 2 and Ernie Bonham of the Yanks with 9 and 3.

Raceway Program Halted by Weather

Weather canceled last night's program at the Saratoga Raceway, but followers of the trotting game will have an opportunity tonight to see the card that was slated for last night and tonight's original card will be seen tomorrow evening.

Scranton On Top Most In E. L. Race

By The Associated Press.

Scranton, trying to win its third pennant in four years, has occupied first place more than any other club during the first ten weeks of the Eastern League championship.

A table showing the leaders at the end of each of the ten weeks discloses Scranton has been on top on five occasions. Albany has led twice and Binghamton and Elmira each once. Wilkes-Barre, striving for its second consecutive pennant, now tops the circuit with 43 wins against 27 setbacks, jumping into first place last week-end.

The table compiled by the Associated Press after all of last night's games were postponed, follows:

End of	Leader	W.	L.	Pct.
1st week	Elmira	5	1	.833
2nd week	Scranton	9	4	.692
3rd week	Bingh'ton	12	5	.706
4th week	Albany	15	6	.714
5th week	Scranton	19	10	.655
6th week	Scranton	22	12	.647
7th week	Scranton	23	15	.605
8th week	Albany	27	18	.600
9th week	Scranton	32	21	.604
10th week	W.-Barre	43	27	.614

Tonight's Games.

Albany at Hartford, night doubleheader, 6.30 p.m.

Scranton at Elmira, night doubleheader, 6:30 p.m.

Binghamton at Springfield, night doubleheader, 7 p.m.

Wilkes-Barre at Williamsport.

ARMY-PROS' GRID SCHEDULE OKAYED

New York (AP)—The War Football fund, handling the military gridiron setup for Army Emergency Relief, yesterday approved an eight-game coast-to-coast schedule between the Army's squad of 80 players and teams of the National Professional League. A game may be approved later.

The Army squad may be split into two groups, Eastern and Western, but "it is likely players will be interchanged," officials of the fund announced.

The team's coaching staff will be announced later this week. It will be drawn from a list of some ten of the country's leading pilots, both in and out of the Army.

All the players are now in the Army. They include both college and pro performers in civilian life. Details for pre-season training will be ironed out later, with the possibility that half the players will work out on the West Coast to prepare for the opening game August 30 against the Washington Redskins in Los Angeles Coliseum, and the others getting ready here to begin action against the New York Giants September 12 in the New York Herald-Tribune's annual charity game.

Fund officials arranged tentatively for a Sept. 20 game, with the Chicago Bears at Syraucse, but said nothing definite would be done about this yet.

GOPHER ACE IN NAVY.

Great Lakes, Ill. (AP)—Bruce Smith, Minnesota's All-America fullback, entered the Great Lakes Naval Training Station yesterday. The Gopher football star reported with a group of newly enlisted men from Minneapolis and immediately began training as an apprentice seaman.

SHEARY CAPTURES EKWANOK CROWN

Jack Sheary, 17-year-old recent graduate of La Salle Institute and a member of the Troy Country Club, captured the historic Robert Todd Lincoln Cup Golf Tourney at Ekwanok Country Club in an upset victory over Powell Crichton, 1 up.

Sheary had scored another upset earlier by eliminating Ray Billows of Poughkeepsie, state champion, by 2 and 1 to gain the semi-finals. He earned the crack at the championship by downing Eddie Driggs of Siwanoy.

Pierce H. "Bud" Russell, a club mate of Sheary's and a former state champion himself, bowed out to Crichton in the semi-finals after having won medalist honors.

Sheary was the main stay of the recent highly successful La Salle links team and has performed capably in local tourneys, but his success in the Manchester, Vt., event was unlooked for even by those who had seen him play here. It was considered the major upset in the tourney's long history.

Fights Last Night

By The Associated Press.

Chicago — Willie Joyce, 137½, Gary, Ind., outpointed Harvey Dubs, 146½, Windsor, Ont., (10).

Baltimore — Luther (Slugger) White, 132¼, Baltimore, outpointed Jimmy Hatcher, 132, Lake City, S. C., (10).

Newark—Al Hart, 223, Washington, D. C., outpointed Eddie Blunt, 217, New York, (10).

Pittsburg — Mose Brown, 175½, Pittsburg, won by technical knockout over Frank Zamaris, Detroit, (7).

Makes Races Close

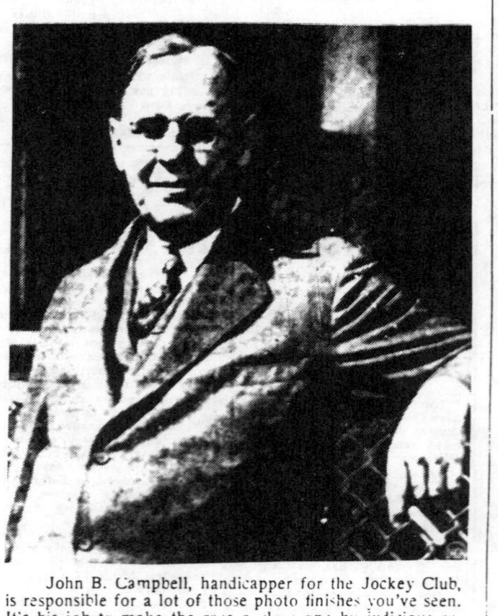

John B. Campbell, handicapper for the Jockey Club, is responsible for a lot of those photo finishes you've seen. It's his job to make the race a close one by judicious assignments of weight to the bangtails entered. If you had your deuce on Whirly in the Butler 'Cap when he spotted Tola Rose 29 pounds, you can thank Campbell for a neat bit of handicapping.

LISTS SIDELIGHTS OF POLO GROUNDS BASEBALL CLASSIC

By AUSTIN BEALMEAR

New York (AP)—They shoved the major league All-Star game in between a military secret and a blackout.

Mayor LaGuardia scheduled the blackout for 9:30 p.m., but Lou Boudreau and Rudy York of the American League beat him to the punch by a couple of hours, making things look pretty dark for the National Leaguers about 7:30.

The start of the game was held up nearly an hour by the weather, and by the time the first inning was over, Mort Cooper, the National League's starting pitcher was hoping for more of the same. Boudreau pickled the second ball Cooper pitched and York, another right-hander, sliced his home run into the right field stands after Tommy Henrich doubled.

Spud Chandler, the starting American League pitcher, reversed Cooper's procedure. The first man up hit Cooper, but Chandler hit the first National Leaguer to bat, Jimmy Brown. Manager Joe McCarthy of the American Leaguers, tipped his hand when he let Chandler pitch four innings, saving plenty of hurlers for the game with the Service All-Stars in Cleveland tonight.

It looked for a time as if the game wouldn't start before today, but 33,694 baseball fans can't be wrong. Having come into the Polo Grounds while the sun was shining, they kept up a continual clamor for the game, and got it—eventually. In the meantime, they helped the band play "Deep in the Heart of Texas," and 33,694 pairs of hands can do a lot of clapping. After watching the American League win, 3-1, the entire crowd sat in the pitch-dark stands for 30 minutes during a test city-wide blackout.

It looked a little like a replay of the last World Series, or perhaps a preview of the next one. There were four Yankees and three Dodgers in the starting lineups. Although his American Leaguers were in a foreign park, Manager McCarthy should have felt right at home. In addition to eight players and their manager the Yankees contributed a coach, a trainer, a batting practice pitcher, and a bull pen catcher.

The National League was supposed to have the pitchers and the American League the hitters. As it turned out, the American League not only displayed both the best pitching and hitting, but also the best fielding. All members of the American League's inner defense came up with fielding gems and Joe Gordon worked double plays just as easily with Lou Boudreau as he does with his own keystone partner, Phil Rizzuto.

If you wonder why the National League picked only seven pitchers, while the American League selected nine, look at the record of their total victories—71 this season for the seven National Leaguers and 59 for the nine American hurlers. Mort Cooper and Walker Cooper formed the first brother battery ever to play in the All-Star game. In 1937, the Washington Senators put Wes and Rick Ferrell on the American League squad, but Wes didn't pitch and Rick didn't catch.

Pinch Hitter Mickey Owen tried a bunt, which was foul by inches, just before smashing his homer. Like York, Owen hit into the right field stands, although he bats right-handed. The game was over only three minutes before the blackout deadline. It produced something like $95,000 for the baseball equipment fund for the armed forces. The All-Star players got wallets and $25 war bonds.

When Lieut. Mickey Cochrane manages the All-Star Service team against the American Leaguers in Cleveland's Municipal Stadium tonight, he'll find a familiar background. Cochrane, then Detroit pilot, managed the American League All-Stars against the Nationals there in 1935, when Jimmy Foxx's home run won the game for the Americans, 4-1.

Troy Area Golfers In Women's State Tourney

Miss Marjorie Harrison of Troy Country Club and Miss Peggy Delahant of Schuyler Meadows Country Club yesterday led the local contingent in the medal play of the New York State Women's Golf Tourney at Lake Placid, but trailed 19-year-old Ann Winslow of Frankfort, who captured the medal with a 79, one over par.

Miss Harrison, who won the state title in 1940 at the Troy Country Club, ran into trouble on the back nine and carded an 38. She lives now in Ausable Forks, but maintains her T. C. C. membership. Miss Delahant was the titlist in 1939 at Rochester but could do no better than 86 yesterday.

According to the Associated Press scores, Mrs. Dan Chandler of Newburg took runner-up honors with a card of 80 on a pair of 40's. Third was the defending titleholder Mrs. Virginia Guilfoil Allen of Syracuse with 40-41—81. She was the only one of the former champs to threaten the school girl's top spot.

Mrs. Charles Leichner of Flushing, well known here like most of the other leaders, tied Miss Delahant at 86. Those qualifying yesterday will start match play today and continue through Saturday.

TROOP G MEMBERS SPEAK AT SESSION OF DEFENSE CLASSES

More than 300 civilian protection volunteers attended the opening session yesterday of the defense instruction class held in the auditorium of the Glens Falls Senior High School. Sergt. E. C. Updike, of the Latham outpost, Troop G, New York State Police, was the principal speaker. The school will continue today with Trooper D. F. Lang, of Troop G, speaking on "Chemical Agents and First Aid."

Sergeant Updike, addressing the group, comprising air raid wardens and auxiliary policemen of Warren County, outlined the duties of civilian protection volunteers, charging them with the duty of instilling confidence in the civilian population in their territory.

He warned against "spy-hunts" by civilian protection workers and asked that such action be left to persons specially trained in the task.

GAME PROTECTORS GET JOBS HELPING IN CIVIL DEFENSE

State's 163 Wardens Augment Other Police Agencies in Patrol, Investigation, Observation Work.

New York's game protective force, 163 strong, is leading a changed way of life, and it's all of their own choosing. The war and the necessity for increased vigil at all times has added additional responsibilities to their already full time jobs.

Without relaxing their efforts to bring about a proper understanding of the law protecting wildlife, game protectors have volunteered their services in practically every line of war and defense activity.

Information reaching Conservation Department offices in Albany discloses the fact that because of their regular duties as law enforcement officers, they are well qualified to augment federal and state agencies in general police work. Of major importance has been their assistance in the investigation of enemy aliens and the patrolling, observation and inspection of vital defense areas within their own districts and searches for escaped enemy war prisoners near the Canadian border. In their patrols, game protectors have been assigned to guard high tension power lines, reservoirs, dams, river fronts, railroad bridges and trestles.

Other activities have included local defense work where they have been called upon to assume major roles in community effort. Many game protectors have already completed approved first aid courses in connection with air raid warden requirements, while others have become identified with auxiliary police and firemen organizations. Several protectors have donated blood to the blood banks.

Lansingburg Day Campers Turn to Craft Work

Between hiking and swimming and other athletics, including the ever-popular softball, lads attending the day camp of the Lansingburg Boys' Club find time for craft work. Camp meets three days a week and one of these days, Wednesday, is devoted almost entirely to craftwork. Top picture shows craft class in session with David Seymour, one of the older boys, teaching clay modeling and mask making. Woodworking is pictured below with Paul S. Young, director of the club, supervising boys sandpapering a kayak made by Harry Murphy, 16, junior at the Lansingburg High School, who plans to use the boat on Indian Lake in the Adirondacks later this summer. Camp boys who passed strength tests in Victory Volunteer program at the club yesterday afternoon were Raymond Zeto, Raymond Haskins, James Kane, James Bagley, David Seymour, George Maloney, Paul Beyer, Jimmy Janak, Hugh Muckle, Thomas Muckle, Edward Keene, Carl DeMartin.

RAILWAY PROTESTS BUS CHARTERING BY STATE EMPLOYEES

A protest by the Schenectady Railway Co. against the action of a group of state employees living in Schenectady who chartered a bus to transport them to their work in Albany is today in the hands of the State War Transportation Committee.

The company alleges that the George Welcome Lines, owner of the chartered bus, solicited business on a route for which the company had a franchise. Members of the "commuter-charter" group, including John L. Halpin, secretary of the state Conservation Department, and John Kelly, assistant executive officer of the State Liquor Authority, assert that the idea was their own and that they were not solicited by the Welcome Lines.

Halpin stated that "by hiring the bus we take 17 cars off the road," and pointed out further that in addition to saving tires and gasoline, members of the party save from thirty minutes to an hour each morning.

While the company is pressing the complaint, members of the commuters group are attempting to "line up" additional bus riders. Under the present plan each member pays $3 per week, with the bus being chartered at $14.50 per day. There are in all 26 members of the group, all state employees.

The man-made Lake of the Ozarks in southwest Missouri has more shoreline than Lake Michigan.

BURNS CLUB WILL CONDUCT OUTING

Auxiliary To Join in Picnic Event at Glenwood on July 18.

The Troy Burns Club and Auxiliary will hold the summer basket picnic Saturday afternoon, July 18, at the home of Treasurer William Miller at Glenwood. Sports will be enjoyed by old and young, prizes being awarded in war stamps. William Miller and Gavin Lawson will have charge. At 5:30 p.m. supper will be served. Robert E. Urquhart heads the committee. Community singing and dancing will conclude the program.

In a recent issue of the Evening News, Glasgow, Scotland, an interesting news item appears in the "Talk of the Town" column, under the caption "Troy, N. Y., and the Duke of Atholl." The article refers to the interest taken by the late Duke of Atholl in the Troy Burns Club and of his having entertained eighty members of the organization visiting Scotland during his twenty years of honorary membership. Each of the guests were presented a "cromak" or cane made by the Duke from wood on his 2,000-acre estate. The interest of the Duke of Atholl in the Troy organization originated in the space given by the Scottish and overseas press in its activities.

THE WEATHER
U. S. Weather Bureau
Tonight—Warmer.

THE TIMES RECORD

FINAL EDITION

Series 1942—No. 161.
(Entered as Second Class Matter at the Postoffice at Troy, N. Y., under the Act of March 3, 1879)
TROY, N. Y., FRIDAY EVENING, JULY 10, 1942.
(Published Daily Except Sunday)
PRICE FOUR CENTS

R.P.I. Graduate May Be Summoned To Trial In Military Court As Nazi Spy

ADMIRAL NIMITZ, CORAL SEA HERO, GETS NAVY D.S.M.

President Honors American Commander for Great Fleet Victories Over Japanese.

Washington (UP)—Admiral Chester W. Nimitz, 57, commander-in-chief of the Pacific fleet, recently escaped serious injury when an airplane in which he was traveling crashed at a west coast airfield, the Navy announced today.

Nimitz received minor injuries which did not interrupt his journey, the Navy said. Lieut. Thomas Morton Roscoe, 29, of Oakland, Calif., co-pilot of the plane, was killed in the crash and several other passengers were slightly injured.

A West Coast Port (UP)—Admiral Chester W. Nimitz, who directed America's victories against the Japanese navy at Coral Sea and Midway, has been awarded the Distinguished Service Medal for "exceptionally meritorious service as commander in chief of the United States Pacific fleet," it was disclosed today.

Admiral Ernest J. King, commander-in-chief of the U. S. fleet, made the citation and presentation to Admiral Nimitz aboard a warship in a brief, simple ceremony witnessed only by a small group of naval officers and newsmen.

Sank 15 Jap Warships.

American airmen and warships, attacking jointly under Admiral Nimitz' Pacific command, sank more than 15 Japanese ships and damaged more than twenty others in the battle of the Coral Sea; and sank at least ten Japanese ships, including four aircraft carriers, and damaged at least eight others in the Midway battle.

Admiral King came to the Pacific coast from Washington, D. C., to present the award to Admiral Nimitz in behalf of President Roosevelt and Secretary of Navy Frank Knox. Due to wartime exigencies, it was not possible for Admiral Nimitz to go to Washington to receive the medal from the President, as the Chief Executive would have liked, Admiral King announced.

President's Citation.

Admiral Nimitz received the following citation from the President:

"For exceptionally meritorious service as commander-in-chief, United States Pacific fleet. In that position of great responsibility he exercised sound judgment and decision in his employment and disposition of units of the Pacific fleet during the period immediately following our entry into war with Japan.

"His conduct of the operations of the Pacific fleet, resulting in successful actions against the enemy in the Coral Sea in May, 1942, and off Midway Island in June, 1942, was characterized by unfailing judgment and sound decision, coupled with skill and vigor. His exercise of command on all occasions left nothing to be desired."

Admiral Responds.

Admiral Nimitz responded:

"In accepting this honor I do so with the distinct knowledge it was made possible by the devoted service of the officers and men under my command and the loyal service of the staffs and the rank and file of the Army and Marine Corps who made up the task forces participating in the action."

The Distinguished Service Medal is the highest among the decorations Admiral Nimitz has received for service to his country. The 56-year-old, 6-foot admiral who replaced Admiral Husband E. Kimmel as Pacific fleet commander Dec. 17, 1941, has several other service awards, including one for risking his life while saving a seaman who had fallen overboard and could not swim.

British Subs Sink Two Ships Bound for Libya

London (UP)—The admiralty today said that British submarines had sunk two enemy ships bound for Libya, and that two motor torpedo boats last night challenged six enemy minesweepers in European coastal waters and sank two and damaged three.

One submarine accounted for both enemy ships in the Mediterranean.

"The submarine torpedoed and sank a medium sized merchant-ship in a strongly escorted convoy carrying supplies to Libya," the communique said. "Later a medium-sized naval auxiliary vessel was intercepted and attacked by the same submarine. The enemy vessel, which was southbound, was hit by torpedoes and sunk."

The attack on the minesweepers was carried out without loss or casualties.

MAN SWEPT OVER FALLS.

Niagara Falls, (UP)—A man identified as Anthony C. Wolda, 25, Niagara Falls, waded into the Niagara River and was swept to his death over the American Falls yesterday in full view of a large number of sightseers.

Nazi Army Crosses Upper Don River At Several Points

AXIS FORCED INTO NEW RETREAT ON EGYPTIAN FRONT

U. S. Army Air Corps Bombers Aid in Devastating Attack; Battle Line Shortened.

Cairo (UP)—British imperial mobile columns attacked Axis forces at the southern end of the Alamein line and forced them to move northward toward the coast, a middle eastern command communique announced today.

United States Army Air Corps heavy bombers, operating in conjunction with British and South African air forces in a devastating offensive, shot down two enemy fighter planes which challenged them, the communique said.

In the clash at the southern end of the line running southwestward from El Alamein, the imperial lightning columns, made up tank, armored car, artillery and motorized infantry units, struck so savagely the Axis forces, which included tanks, were compelled to give their defensive positions and draw up toward the coast.

Battle Line Shortened.

As a result, the imperial battle line was shortened and strengthened. For days, the British columns had kept up their pressure at the southern end of the line, threatening constantly to get in behind the enemy.

The Axis line originally had started just west of El Alamein and extended eastward toward, eastward, First British pressure forced German Field Marshal Erwin Rommel to flatten out his line, so that it went southward from El Alamein for about 20 miles and then veered westward.

Now, it was understood, the line starting west of El Alamein goes directly southeastward.

Air Forces Blast Axis.

Aside from the southern end of the line, artillery and patrol action continued.

Today's communique, issued jointly by the Middle Air Force command and the Royal Air Force, made it plain that the allied air forces, including United States Army bombers, were continuing the biggest aerial offensive ever seen in the Middle East.

British fighter-bombers destroyed more than 50 enemy transport vehicles in one of many raids, the communique said.

Moscow Reports Violent Battles Raging on East Bank; Red Army Launches Counter Attack

BY THE ASSOCIATED PRESS.

Adolf Hitler's invasion armies have swept across the upper Don River at several points, Soviet dispatches acknowledged today, while the Red Cross are battling a dangerous new thrust into the Rossosh sector 100 miles south of Voronezh on the Moscow-Rostov railway.

The Nazi advance across the upper Don, ten miles west of Voronezh, came after the Russians reported they had beaten off a series of violent assaults and inflicted bloody losses on the enemy.

Front line dispatches said furious battles were developing on the east bank of the river as the Germans attempted to widen their wedges into Red Army defense lines.

The bulk of the fourth German tank army was said to be massed on the west bank to reinforce the offensive against Voronezh.

A bulletin from Hitler's field headquarters declared broadly that Russian forces in retreat were being pursued "on a broad front" in the south—evidently referring to the Voronezh and Rossosh sectors.

Russians Withdraw.

"Local resistance was broken," the Nazi command asserted.

"Enemy attacks supported by tanks to relieve pressure northwest of Voronezh broke down with heavy casualties."

The Nazi high command still failed to reiterate its claim, however, that Voronezh had fallen.

Dispatches to Red Star, the Soviet army newspaper, said the fighting had swelled to a gigantic scale, with the Germans pouring in masses of fresh reserves and tanks. Russian estimates had previously declared the Nazi grand offensive was powered by 1,000,000 troops.

"Conditions west of Voronezh are becoming more complicated," Red Star said.

Front line dispatches said the Russians withdrew in good order toward Rossosh to avoid being flanked, but conceded that the invaders had penetrated into Russian defenses in depth.

Reds Counter Attack.

While vast battles raged over the Don stepper for control of the vital rail line to the Caucasus, Red Star said an important Red Army counter-attack to relieve pressure on Voronezh was threatening the German left flank.

"Stubborn battles there may have a serious influence over the position near Voronezh," the newspaper said.

It did not disclose the scene of the Soviet counter-blow, but Hitler's headquarters said the Russians were attacking with strong infantry and tank forces north and northwest of Orel, a major German base, 165 miles northwest of Voronezh.

The Nazi command said the Rus-

(Continued on Page 2.)

SENATORS APPROVE BOOST IN FUNDS FOR HENDERSON OFFICE

Washington (UP)—A Senate appropriations subcommittee approved today an appropriation of $120,000,000 to operate the Office of Price Administration for the current fiscal year—$90,000,000 less than Administrator Leon Henderson originally requested but $45,000,000 above the sum voted by the House.

The committee stipulated that none of the $120,000,000 was to be used for the payment of subsidies and amendment insisted upon by Senator Russell (D-Ga.) who has been outspoken in his criticism of OPA for allowing an increase of 2½ cents a gallon in the price of gasoline in rationed eastern states.

OPA contended the increase was necessary to pay increased transportation costs resulting from hauling the fuel overland instead of by ocean tankers.

Sailors Gave Lives To Save Comrades

San Francisco (UP)—Fifteen men, survivors from a bombed U. S. Navy tanker in the Coral Sea, willingly went overboard from their lifeboat to make room for wounded comrades, it was disclosed today.

Only four survived the pounding seas, but the wounded were rescued.

The story of sacrifice was told by Ed A. Flaherty, 22, electrician's mate third class from St. Louis, Mo., and Douglas J. Nelson, 22, signalman third class from Laurel, Mont.

Both men previously were aboard a cruiser when they were transferred to the tanker—the Neosho—as "passengers." Flaherty received severe burns in the bombing of the Neosho. Nelson was uninjured, and was placed in charge of a group of wounded.

"The wounded," Flaherty said, "were taken into two whale-boats. The boats were overcrowded. Lieut. Henry Bradford ordered every uninjured man overboard to shift for himself. The lieutenant went first and 14 enlisted men followed.

"The lieutenant and three others later were saved. The rest drowned. The sea was very rough and it must have been tough swimming."

Flaherty said the fight started for them on May 6. Two waves of Japanese planes made level bombing runs and two more waves dove. Between thirty and forty planes participated in each attack.

MOTHER OF HERO WILL BE WITNESS AGAINST NAZI SPY

American Soldier, Missing on Bataan, Gave Haupt Beating; Trial Continues in Secrecy.

Washington (UP)—The mother of an American battle hero was expected to testify against one of the eight Nazi saboteurs whose secret trial before a special military commission entered its third session today.

The prospective witness was Mrs. Agnes Jordan of Chicago, mother of Larry Jordan, wounded and reported missing while serving as a tank battalion sergeant on Bataan. She volunteered to testify against 22-year-old Herbert Hans Haupt, former Chicagoan who went to Germany to master the art of sabotage under gestapo tutelage and then returned to this country, aboard a submarine, to practice his treacherous craft.

Gave Haupt Beating.

Mrs. Jordan's son, it was disclosed, once gave Haupt a beating because "Hans was a Nazi."

The third session of the trial, with the defendant's lives at stake, brought no rift in secrecy which has shrouded the proceedings from the start.

Despite efforts of Elmer Davis, director of the Office of War Information, to obtain censored reports of the trial's progress, the military commission of seven generals headed by Maj. Gen. Frank R. McCoy issued no morning "communique."

Witnesses were taken into the justice building through corridors and elevators closed to the public, apparently in an effort by officials in charge to prevent speculation as to their identity and testimony.

Used Hero's Name As Alias.

Taken to the building in Army automobiles, they went by private elevator to the fifth floor trial room which is barricaded by newly installed double doors blocking off the corridors.

Coincident with Mrs. Jordan's offer of testimony against Haupt, her husband, Anthony Jordan, disclosed in Chicago that the young Nazi had used his son's name as an alias during the brief period of freedom he enjoyed after disembarking with the other saboteurs from German submarines.

Haupt once invited young Jordan to a party in the Haus Vaterland in Chicago, the father said. When the real Larry Jordan arrived at the dance he found Haupt in a storm trooper's uniform. The upshot was that young Jordan knocked Haupt down and "stalked home still angry and told me that Hans was a Nazi," the father said. McCoy was not expected to issue any statement today until the end of the session. In one of two issued yesterday he explained that the trial was secret because the testimony involved "the security of the United States and the lives of its soldiers, sailors and citizens."

Seven Witnesses Testify.

He revealed that seven witnesses had testified in the first two days of the trial, and added:

"Each of these witnesses, as well as all other persons present in the courtroom, except the prisoners, have been placed under oath not to reveal any part of the proceedings unless and until authorized by competent authority. Violation of this oath is punishable by contempt."

Considering the care with which the saboteurs were guarded, there was little chance of their revealing anything.

"Counsel for the defense," General McCoy disclosed, "were given the opportunity to cross-examine each" of the seven witnesses.

The witnesses, it was believed, were the most damning the government could produce. Among them were Coast Guardsmen whose vigilance helped to frustrate the saboteurs' diabolically laid plot, Federal Bureau of Investigation counter-espionage agents who tracked them down and Mrs. Gerda Melind of Chicago.

Widow Jilted Spy.

Pretty Mrs. Melind, 24, a widow, was the fiancee of Haupt, one of the defendants. Shortly after a submarine landed him in this country he rushed to Chicago and asked her to marry him. She accepted him, then jilted him when she heard what he was up to. Although the testimony against the saboteurs was secret, the case against them was not. The F.B.I. revealed their plot shortly after it caught them.

Four were landed by a German submarine on Long Island. Four more were similarly landed near Ponte Vedra, Fla. In rubber boats they carried to shore enough tools of their trade—explosives, wire and fuses to last them two years. These they buried in the sand.

They had more than $150,000 with them to buy helpers and ease their task. But the F. B. I. caught them before they had spent much of their money and were able to dig up their tools.

Recall Residence Here of Alleged Spy

Upper picture, in this home at 1328 Fourth avenue, Watervliet, the wife of Herbert K. F. Bahr, graduate of R. P. I. who is accused of being a Nazi spy, lived until recently, when she went to Buffalo to work. She is the former Miss Ruth Neeb, her mother, Mrs. Thoralf M. Madsen, still resides here. In the right foreground is the young stepsister of Mrs. Bahr, the only member of the family at home this morning. Lower picture, this rooming house at 728 Federal Street. Inset is a picture of Bahr taken after his arrest by federal agents in Newark, N. J.

DELAY GRANTED IN KUNZE TRIAL

Former Bund Leader and Two Others To Face Court on July 28.

Hartford, Conn. (UP)—The government consented today to delaying until July 28 the trial of Gerhard Wilhelm Kunze and two others accused of espionage to permit the German-American Bund leader to prepare a defense against charges he was an Axis agent.

Kunze, held under $50,000 bond, Tuesday entered a plea of innocent to an indictment that he was entrusted by a spy group with transmitting military information to Germany and Japan.

The first fruits of that happenshu early this week in the start of a new phase of their apparent campaign to establish a rail route from Shanghai to Singapore. Their conquest of Chekiang Province and its Kiangsi gave them lines from Shanghai to Nanchang.

The high command said fighting also had flared anew in Chekiang Province, where the Japanese, more than 10,000 reinforcements, struck south toward Kwangtung Province and Changshu, where the invaders had reached the Kiangsi-Hunan Railway.

The Japanese had taken Changshu early this week in the start of a new phase of their apparent campaign to establish a rail route from Shanghai to Singapore. Their conquest of Chekiang Province and its Kiangsi gave them lines from Shanghai to Nanchang.

The trial originally was scheduled for July 15.

Standing trial with Kunze will be Dr. Wolfgang Ebell, El Paso, Tex., a former German imperial army officer, and Rev. Kurt E. B. Molzahn, Philadelphia Lutheran minister, who served in the German imperial army as a cavalry officer and was decorated with the Iron Cross. Both were charged with aiding in the escape of Kunze to Mexico and with helping him keep contacts in this country since his flight.

HERBERT K. B. BAHR, CLASS '38, SEIZED ON SWEDISH LINER

Admitted Espionage Work for Gestapo; Deserted Wife and Son to Return to Germany.

Charges of Nazi espionage, passport fraud, unlawful possession of United States money and smuggling of secret writing chemicals were made today in Newark, N. J., against Herbert Karl Friederich Bahr, 29, German born graduate of Rensselaer Polytechnic Institute and husband of the former Miss Ruth Neeb of Watervliet.

Bahr was arraigned in federal court at Newark this afternoon and Judge William F. Smith ordered the former R. P. I. man held without bail for the grand jury. He had no counsel and a plea was not entered. Judge Smith said he would assign the defendant a lawyer immediately.

Bahr who once wrote officials of R. P. I. "You will find I shall do my best to be worthy of the confidence placed in me," was seized aboard the Swedish liner Drottningholm, charged with being the key figure in a Nazi plot to slip a spy into the United States aboard the diplomatic exchange ship.

In Washington, it was said in some Justice Department circles that Bahr might be tried before the special military commission now hearing charges against eight Nazi saboteurs. He would appear to fall within the definition of enemies of the country as outlined by President Roosevelt in his proclamation setting up the commission.

Mother-in-law Angry.

In Watervliet today his mother-in-law, Mrs. Thoralf M. Madsen of 1328 Fourth avenue, said she wished she had known Bahr better "so I could give more information against him for the harm he tried to do our country."

Mrs. Madsen, the front door of whose cottage displays several patriotic emblems pasted on the glass, said frankly that she had never liked Bahr because of the way he had treated her daughter.

The couple were married June 9, 1938, according to the marriage certificate on file in the Watervliet city clerk's office by Rev. Ingolf Torkelsen, pastor of Our Saviour's Lutheran Church in Lansingburg. The wedding took place four days before Bahr was graduated from the institute. Three months later Bahr returned to Germany. Mrs. Bahr's family said that the young woman had not heard from him since 1939.

Today Son's Birthday.

Their 3-year-old son, Herbert, now in a home for children at Albany, celebrated his birthday today. Officials of the home said that the father never had visited his son there. The little boy lived with his grandmother, Mrs. Madsen, in Watervliet until a few months ago, when his mother went to Buffalo to work as a domestic in the home of a doctor.

"Bahr never did anything for the baby except buy one pair of shoes," Mrs. Madsen said angrily, "and give him some clothing that he himself had when he was a baby. I never liked the man and only met him a few times when he was a student at R. P. I."

In a complaint drawn up in Newark in preparation for Bahr's arraignment, it is alleged that the young man conspired "with Karl Bauer and other persons unknown."

Enter the United States.

"(as a German agent and obtain information respecting national defense."

"Obtain documents to be transmitted back to Germany.

"Use a 'mutilated' passport.

"Use unlawfully possessed U. S. currency.

"Concealing on his person 'certain chemicals to be used in the manufacture of ink capable of invisible writing."

Federal agents identified "Karl Bauer," named in the complaint, as one of those who gave Bahr

(Continued on Page 11.)

TWENTY MEN DIE IN MINE EXPLOSION

Bodies of Victims Located in Coal Shaft Near Morgantown, W. Va.

Morgantown, W. Va. (UP)—Crews, digging in relays of ten because of narrow tunnels, were shoveling through 100 tons of debris today for the bodies of twenty miners, killed in an explosion four miles underground.

The explosion, in the Pursglove Coal Corp. No. 2 mine, occurred after 70 members of the night shift had reported for work.

"It was about three miles inside the mine when the explosion let go," Ferrell Grove, section foreman of Fairmont, W. Va., said. "I turned back to get my men, but it was useless I didn't get out of the mine myself until almost three hours later."

"We have found all of the victims in the 20-foot right section about four miles underground," Joseph H. Stewart, chief company clerk, announced last night.

Digging crews made slow progress, and 9,000 miners and relatives of the victims stood silently around the drift opening throughout the night. State police had to restrain some, who tried to break through to question rescue workers.

Timekeepers identified some of the victims as Glenn Taylor, 27, Sabreton, W. Va.; Byron Dusenberry, Pursglove; John Lewis, Pursglove; Albert McDonald, Dellslow, W. Va., father of seven children; Leslie Stanton, 30, Pursglove, father of five; Joe Oliberio, near City, W. Va.; John Wilson, 37, Osage, W. Va.; Russel Saffron and the following five whom addresses were not available; Mike Barbus and Andy Judik, Ernest Lambert, Charles Andy, James Poro-heruff, Vernon Hickey, Richard Carr, Eddie Wilson and Joseph Boken.

The mine is three miles from the Christopher Coal Co. No. 3 mine where an explosion less than two months ago killed 56 miners.

CHINESE REPORT CHUNGSHU TAKEN

Japs Meet New Setback in Push Along Kiangsi Railway Line.

Chungking (UP)—The Chinese high command announced today the recapture of Chungshu, 45 miles southwest of Nanchang, in a new set-back of the Japanese and a sharp set-back of the invaders' latest push along the Kiangsi rail line to Hunan Province.

Also recaptured, the Chinese said, was the town of Tsungjen, seventy miles south of the Japanese base at Nanchang.

The high command confirmed Chinese dispatches which reported yesterday that a Japanese force of 30,000 had been ambushed and beaten back to the north and east in heavy fighting in Kiangsi.

The first fruits of that happshu early this week in the start of a new phase of their apparent campaign to establish a rail route from Shanghai to Singapore. Their conquest of Chekiang Province and its Kiangsi gave them lines from Shanghai to Nanchang.

The high command said fighting also had flared anew in Chekiang Province, where the Japanese, more than 10,000 reinforcements, struck south toward Kwangtung Province and Changshu, where the invaders had reached the Kiangsi-Hunan Railway.

The Japanese had taken Changshu early this week in the start of a new phase of their apparent campaign to establish a rail route from Shanghai to Singapore. Their conquest of Chekiang Province and its Kiangsi gave them lines from Shanghai to Nanchang.

NOTED COMPOSER OF CHURCH MUSIC DEAD

Dayton, O. (AP)—Edward Simon Lorenz, 88, well known composer of church music and editor, died today. Dr. Lorenz was known throughout the world for his inspiring hymns "Tell It To Jesus Alone," "Joy Cometh in the Morning," "The Name of Jesus So Sweet" and "Thou Thinkest, Lord of Me."

Tom Pierce, Rutland Star, Captures Troy Country Club Golf Crown

DEFEATS RUSZAS, OF SHAKER RIDGE, IN FINALS, ONE UP

Winner Had To Come From Behind To Conquer Albanian; Large Crowd Views Match.

Tommy Pierce of Rutland Club, former Vermont state champion, annexed Troy Country Club's ninth annual invitation tourney honors yesterday when he nosed out Joey Ruszas of Shaker Ridge, 1 up, in a ding-dong 18 hole final on the Brunswick Road links.

Pierce, who was runnerup to Ray Billows in the State Amateur on this same course last year as representative of the T. C. C., had to come from behind to turn back the Albany star, who still holds the amateur record on the Troy layout by virtue of a sparkling 66 he fired in the state meet last year.

Ruszas, winner of the Albany city championship the last time it was conducted, jumped into a 2 up lead on the first two holes but Pierce had evened the match before the turn. Then on the back stretch the Vermont representative won three holes as compared with two for his opponent.

In capturing the finals, Pierce monopolized all the tourney honors, having annexed the medal in the qualifying round with a card of 72, one over par, Friday.

Both fired 38's, two over par, on the outgoing stretch and Pierce carded a two-over par 37 coming home as compared with a 38 for Ruszas. Considering the high wind, which made many shots difficult, some good golf was displayed in the final.

Ruszas went out front on the first hole as he rammed down a 30 foot putt for a birdie three as Pierce was getting a regulation four and the Albany shotmaker added to this lead as he won the second hole with a par three. On this hole Pierce had a trapped shot and took a bogie four.

The third hole was halved in regulation four's, both getting on in two and two-putting but Pierce won the fourth hole with a par five as compared with a six for Ruszas. Pierce was off to the right of the green in the rough with his second shot and short with his third but he put his fourth shot two feet from the pin and holed out. Ruszas, off the far edge of the green with his third, got on in four and two-putted.

Pierce squared the match on the next hole, where he was on in two and down in two for his four as Ruszas was taking a five after being trapped with his second shot.

The next four holes were halved, sending the finalists around the turn all even.

Pierce jumped into the lead for the first time on the 10th hole, where he chipped his third shot inches from the pin and holded out for a regulation four as Ruszas was taking a five after leaving himself a long putt because of a weak chip.

Ruszas Squares on 11th.

Ruszas bagged a birdie four at the 11th to square the match once more as Tommy was taking a five. The Albany player put his third shot three feet from the pin and rammed down the putt as his opponent was taking four to get on the green after putting his tee shot into the trees to the left of the fairway.

Pierce went ahead again at the 12th, where he was on in two and sank a three-foot putt for his par three as Ruszas was getting on in two and two-putting from 18 feet.

The next two hales were halved in par four's. At the 13th, Ruszas got home with a drive and a brassie and two-putted, while Pierce, who was over with a driver and an iron, chipped four feet past the pin and holded out. At the 14th, Ruszas was on in two and two-putted while Pierce was forced to sink an 18-foot putt after taking three to get on. The Vermonter hooked his drive into the rough to the left of the fairway but made a fine recovery shot.

Pierce won the short 15th with a par three to increase his lead after getting on with his tee shot. On this same hole Ruszas' tee shot was off to the left of the green and he left himself a 25-foot putt which he missed.

Samson Finish.

Ruszas cut down his opponent's lead at the 16th, however, where he was on in two and sank a six-footer for his birdie three. Pierce was on in two and two-putted from 35 feet for a par four.

The 17th was halved in bogie five's, both getting on in three and two-putting.

Then came the 18th and Ruszas' last chance to overtake the Vermonter.

Both finalists were straight out in the fairway with their drives but Ruszas' second shot, an iron shot, was on the edge of a trap while Pierce's No. 5 iron was on the far edge of the green. Ruszas' third was on the green, 30 feet from the pin but he two-putted for a five and his last chance faded as Tommy rolled his putt up close enough to get down in five for a half.

Par for the course follows:

Out	434 544 534—36
In	453 443 444—35—71

Cards of the finalists:

Pierce—	
Out	444 544 544—38
Ruszas—	
Out	334 654 544—38
Pierce—	
In	453 443 455—37—75
Ruszas—	
In	544 444 355—38—76

Pierce wins 1 up.

Tourney prizes were presented by Furber Marshall at ceremonies on the lawn late yesterday afternoon.

Semi-Final Results.

Pierce gained the final with a 3 and 2 victory over Lonnie Parks, Eastern Golf Association champion from Edison Club, while Ruszas advanced with a 4 and 3 triumph over Dave Daniels of Wolferts Roost, one of the tourney darkhorses.

Pierce and Parks staged a seesaw battle on the outgoing stretch with the Vermonter winning the first and fourth holes and Parks taking the sixth. Parks overapproached the green at the first hole and took a bogie five to his opponent's four while Pierce won No. 4 hole with a birdie four, chipping up close with his third and sinking the short putt.

Both made mistakes at the sixth with Parks taking a bogie five after a trapped shot and Pierce taking a two-over-par six after going over the green with his second shot.

Rounding the turn 1 up, Pierce halved the first two holes with Parks but added to his lead at the short 12th, which he won with a birdie two after putting his tee shot a foot and a half from the pin. The Vermonter jumped 3 up by taking the 13th with a bogie five and the next three holes were halved ending the match.

Ruszas and Daniels were all even after nine holes, each carding 40 on the outgoing stretch.

Daniels took the early lead with a birdie three at the first hole, where he sank a 14 footer but Ruszas got back on even terms at the second, winning with a perfect three. Ruszas went ahead at the third which he captured with a par four as his opponent over-chipped but Daniels squared the match at the fifth which he won with apar four as Ruszas was three-putting for a five.

The next two holes were halved and then Daniels went ahead as he captured the eighth with a par three. Ruszas squared the contest again at the ninth, winning with a par four as Daniels was taking a five after being short to the left of the green with his approach.

Ruszas went 1 up at the 10th, which he captured with a par four and he added to his lead at the next hole, winning with a birdie four after a pretty second shot left him just short of the green.

The 12th was halved in par threes but Ruszas went 3 up at the 13th, which he captured with a perfect four as Daniels was taking a five after getting into the rough. Ruszas went 4 up at the 14th, which he took with a par four and the match ended on the next hole which was halved in par threes.

Semi-final cards:

Pierce out	434456534—38
Parks out	534555534—39
Pierce in	5425434
Parks in	5436434
Ruszas out	434654644—40
Daniels out	345644635—40
Ruszas in	443443
Daniels in	553553

Home Club Threats Out.

The two big home club threats—Bud Russell and Jack Sheary—fell by the wayside Saturday.

Russell, frequent winner of the Troy classic, couldn't get started in the tourney and went out in the opening round, Saturday morning. Dave Daniels of Wolferts Roost defeated him, 2 and 1.

Russell was off form in the qualifying round, Friday, when he needed a 77 to qualify and he played the same type of golf Saturday although he gave Daniels a battle a times.

Sheary one of the pre-tourney favorites as a result of his victory in the Lincoln Cup classic at Manchester, Vermont, recently, got by the first round but fell out of the picture in the second round, Saturday afternoon.

Sheary defeated Charles Martin of Van Schaick Island, 1 up, in the opening round but fell before Ruszas in the second round. Ruszas won, 3 and 2.

Officials Pleased.

Despite the fact the tourney entry list was not quite as large as in other years, tourney officials declared the tourney was highly successful.

What the field lacked in numbers it made for in quality. The first division was one of the strongest in the history of the event.

The summaries follow:

First Division.

Semi-finals—Tommy Pierce, Rutland. defeated Lonnie Parks, Edison Club, 3 and 2; Joey Ruszas, Shaker Ridge, defeated Dave Daniels, Wolferts Roost, 4 and 3.

Final—Pierce defeated Ruszas, 1 up.

Beaten Eight.

Semi-finals—C. W. Snow, Schuyler Meadows, defeated Don Hesnor. Stanford, 1 up; Bill Ramsay, Van Schaick Island, defeated John Doolittle. Schuyler Meadows, 1 up.

Final—Snow defeated Ramsay, 4 and 3.

Second Division.

Semi-finals—C. W. Benedict, Whipporwill, defeated Elmer Facteau, Van Schaick Island, 1 up; Walt Ewing, Troy C. C., defeated K. V. Bennett, Mohawk, 4 and 2.

Final—Benedict defeated Ewing, 2 up.

Beaten Eight.

Semi-finals—Ed Mazur, Van Schaick, defeated C. L. Cook, Frear Park, 1 up (22 holes); A. B. Lesneski, McGregor Links, defeated Paul Fisher, Van Schaick, 2 and 1.

Final—Mazur defeated Lesneski, 3 and 2.

Third Division.

Semi-finals—Ray Maloy, Normanside, defeated R. S. O. Polk, Frear Park, 4 and 2; Ralph Bullock, Schuyler Meadow, defeated Clarence Scott, Troy C. C., 2 and 1.

Final—Bullock defeated Maloy, 4 and 3.

Beaten Eight.

Semi-finals—G. E. Hatfield, Albany, defeated George Kirk, Normanside, 3 and 1; R. F. Delahant, Wolferts Roost, defeated A. Smith, Albany, by default.

Final—Delahant defeated Hatfield, 2 and 1.

Fourth Division.

Semi-finals—George Radz, Troy, defeated S. A. Romolo, Garden City, 5 and 4; H. P. Prout, Van Rensselaer, defeated Ralph Bigelow, Drumlins, 2 and 1.

Final—Prout defeated Radz, 3 and 2.

Beaten Eight.

Semi-finals — Harrison Bullock, Whipporwill, defeated A. A. Schulz, Normanside, 2 and 1; Jim Hare, Shaker Ridge, defeated Irving Walsh, Troy, 2 and 1.

Final—Hare defeated Bullock, 4 and 2.

Fifth Division.

Semi-finals—E. E. Heath, Van Rensselaer defeated Bill Manning, Troy C. C., 6 and 5; Chet Graham, Van Rensselaer, defeated W. M. Porter Drumlins, 3 and 2.

Final—Heath defeated Graham 1 up.

Beaten Eight.

Semi-finals—A. B. Counsel, Troy C. C., defeated L. C. Anderson, Mohawk, 1 up; William Sloan, Troy, defeated J .R. Stevenson, Troy, 1 up.

Final—Counsel defeated Sloan, 6 and 5.

Sixth Division.

Semi-finals—R. C. Royer, Van Rensselaer, defeated Hugh Kling, Shaker Ridge, 8 and 6; Dr. N. J. Patterson, Normanside, defeated Kennedy Boone, Mt. Anthony 1 up.

Final — Dr. Patterson defeated Royer, 1 up.

Beaten Eight.

Semi-finals—H. Lewis, Troy, defeated William Czaja, Frear Park, 2 up; William Shannon, Troy, defeated Tom Dougherty, Troy, by default.

Final—Lewis defeated Shannon, 2 and 1.

Champ in Action at Country Club Golf Tournament

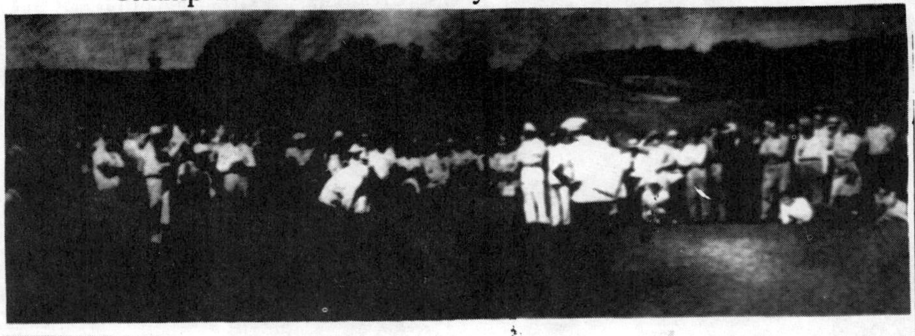

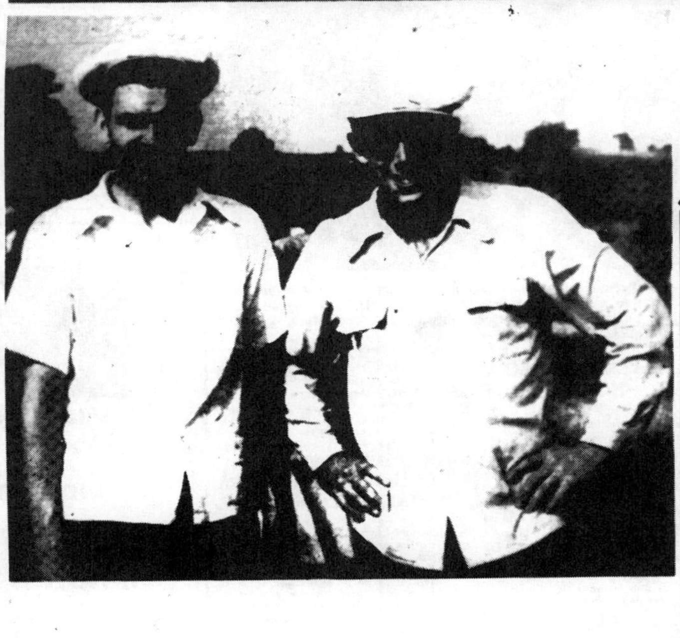

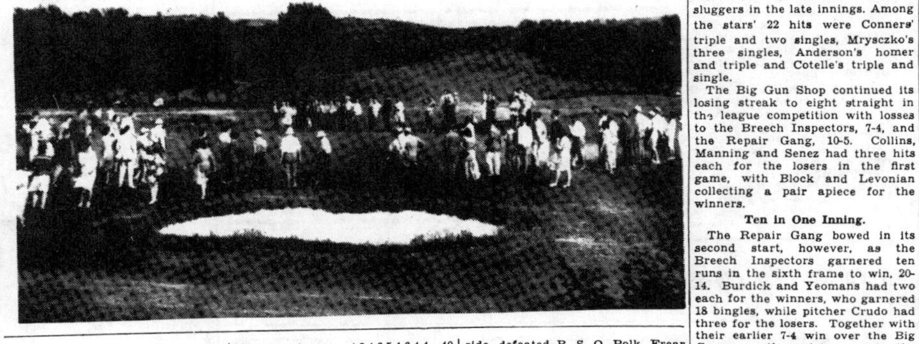

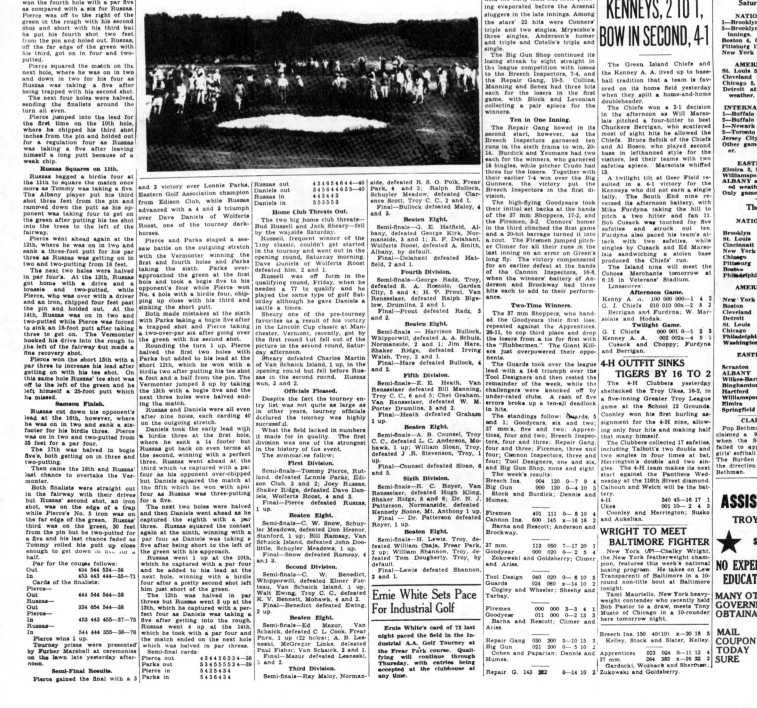

The gallery at the Troy Country Club's ninth annual invitation golf tournament, above, watches Tommy Pierce of Rutland, Vt., the 1942 champion, putt. Center, Pierce, right, with Joe Ruszas of Shaker Ridge whom Pierce defeated in the finals, 1 up. Below, finalists on 18th green.

Ernie White Sets Pace For Industrial Golf

Ernie White's card of 73 last night paced the field in the Industrial A.A. Golf Tourney at the Frear Park course. Qualifying will continue through Thursday, with entries being accepted at the clubhouse at any time.

LEADERS FAIL IN SOFTBALL LEAGUE, ALL-STARS WIN

The Guards became the vanguard of the Arsenal 4:30 p.m. Softball League last week with a victory over the Tool Designers, while the Goodyears dropped their first two decisions to wind up in the second spot, one-half game ahead of the fast-rising 37 mm Shop, which won two.

While the league standings were undergoing these alterations, the loop's all-stars trounced the Faith Millers of the Industrial A. A. Softball League, 21-8. The Millers played a cagey bunting game to hold the early lead, but their pitching evaporated before the Arsenal sluggers in the late innings. Among the stars' 22 hits were Conners' triple and two singles, Mrysczko's three singles, Anderson's homer and triple and Cotelle's triple and single.

The Big Gun Shop continued its losing streak to eight straight in the league competition with losses to the Breech Inspectors, 7-4, and the Repair Gang, 10-5. Collins, Manning and Senez had three hits each for the losers in the first game, with Block and Levonian collecting a pair apiece for the winners.

Ten in One Inning.

The Repair Gang bowed in its second start, however, as the Breech Inspectors garnered ten runs in the sixth frame to win, 20-14. Burdick and Yeomans had two each for the winners, who garnered 18 bingles, while pitcher Crudo had three for the losers. Together with their earlier 7-4 win over the Big Gunners, the victory put the Breech Inspectors in the first division.

The high-flying Goodyears took their initial set backs at the hands of the 37 mm Shoppers, 17-2, and the Firemen, 3-2. Connors' homer in the third clinched the first game and a 20-hit barrage turned it into a rout. The Firemen jumped pitcher Climer for all their runs in the last inning on an error on Green's long fly. The victory compensated for an earlier defeat at the hands of the Cannon Inspectors, 16-8, when the winners' battery of Anderson and Brockway had three hits each to add to their performance.

Two-Time Winners.

The 37 mm Shoppers, who handed the Goodyears their first loss, repeated against the Apprentices, 26-11, to cop third place and drop the losers from a tie for first with the "Rubbermen." The Giant Killers just overpowered their opponents.

The Guards took over the league lead with a 14-6 triumph over the Tool Designers and then rested the remainder of the week, while the challengers were knocked off by under-rated clubs. A rash of five errors broke up a ten-all deadlock in hits.

The standings follow: Guards, 5 and 1; Goodyears, six and two; 37 mm's, five and two; Apprentices, four and two; Breech Inspectors, four and three; Repair Gang, four and three; Firemen, three and four; Cannon Inspectors, three and four; Tool Designers, one and six, and Big Gun Shop, none and eight.

The week's results:

Breech Ins. 004 120 0—7 9 4
Big Gun 000 130 0—4 10 5
Stock and Burdick; Dennis and Humes.

Firemen 401 111 0— 8 10 4
Cannon Ins. 600 145 x—16 18 2
Barna and Rescott; Anderson and Brockway.

37 mm. 113 050 7—17 20 1
Goodyear 000 020 0— 2 5 4
Zokowski and Goldsberry; Climer and Ariss.

Tool Design 040 020 0— 6 10 5
Guards 024 080 x—14 10 2
Cogley and Wheeler; Sheehy and Tarbay.

Firemen 000 000 3—3 4 1
Goodyear 011 000 0—2 13 3
Barna and Rescott; Climer and Ariss.

Repair Gang 030 200 5—10 15 3
Big Gun 021 200 0— 5 10 2
Cohen and Paparian; Dennis and Humes.

Repair G. 143 222 0—14 10 2
Breech Ins. 150 40(10) x—20 18 5
Kelley, Stock and Slater, Kelley.

Apprentices 023 024 0—11 12 4
37 mm. 264 383 x—26 22 2
Gardocki, Woznack and Sherman; Zukowski and Goldsberry.

SWEETSER SAYS NELSON NO. 1 MAN IN GOLF WORLD

St. Petersburg, Fla. (AP)—Byron Nelson, the master of the long irons, got another vote yesterday for the mythical title of the World's Greatest Golfer.

Jess Sweetser, who's seen them come and go since the days he ruled the amteur roost in the early twenties, said the Toledo, O., star is "simply unbeatable when his putts are dropping."

Sweetser, first American-born golfer to win the British Amateur title, was quick to explain why he placed Nelson ahead of Ben Hogan, the Hershey, Pa., pro who won the coveted Vardon Trophy last year.

"Nelson and Sam Snead (who's now in the Navy) take to the game more naturally than Ben does," he declared. "Did you ever notice how calloused Hogan's hands are because of a tight grip and constant practice?"

Hogan's tremendous power is no mystery, Sweetser declared.

"It's because he has unusually large hands and large forearms for a small man," he asserted.

Sweetser looked at golf today and contrasted it to the game in 1922, when he won the U. S. Amatuer title.

"They're shooting lower scores today because of several factors—closer competition, improved equipment, a livelier ball and better conditioned courses.

"The intense competition has put 20 good golfers in every field where there used to be five or six. The longer ball is making the game too easy, since golfers can reach every green in two except on long holes where the terrain is a factor."

He added that golfers today have a more open swing, which gives much greater distance off the tee than was obtained by the early stars "who had a habit of bending their left arm and keeping the club closer to their bodies."

CHIEFS DEFEAT KENNEYS, 2 TO 1, BOW IN SECOND, 4-1

The Green Island Chiefs and the Kenney A. A. lived up to baseball tradition that a team is favored on its home field yesterday when they split a home-and-home doubleheader.

The Chiefs won a 2-1 decision in the afternoon as Will Marsolais pitched a four-hitter to best Chuckers Berrigan, who scattered most of eight hits he allowed the Chiefs. Bruce Sefcik of the Chiefs and Al Bosco. who played second base in lefthanded style for the visitors, led their teams with two safeties apiece. Marsolais whiffed 13.

A twilight tilt at Geer Field resulted in a 4-1 victory for the Kenneys who did not earn a single tally. The South End nine reversed its afternoon battery, with Mike Furdyna taking the hill to pitch a two hitter and fan 11. Bob Cusack was touched for five safeties and struck out ten. Furdyna also paced his team's attack with two safeties, while singles by Cusack and Ed Marsolais sandwiching a stolen base produced the Chiefs' run.

The Island nine will meet the Cohoes Merchants tomorrow at 6:15 in Veterans' Stadium.

Linescores:

Afternoon Game.

Kenny A. A. 100 000 000—1 4 2
G. I. Chiefs 010 010 00x—2 8 2
Berrigan and Furdyna; W. Marsolais and Hodak.

Twilight Game.

G. I. Chiefs 000 001 0—1 2 3
Kenney A. A. 002 002x—4 5 1
Cusack and Choppy; Furdyna and Berrigan.

4-H OUTFIT SINKS TIGERS BY 16 TO 2

The 4-H Clubbers yesterday shellacked the Troy Ukes, 16-2, in a five-inning Greater Troy League game at the School 12 Grounds. Coonley won his first hurling assignment for the 4-H nine, allowing only four hits and making half that many himself.

The Clubbers collected 17 safeties, including Talbott's two double and two singles in four times at bat, Herrington's double and two singles. The 4-H team makes its next start against the Panthers Wednesday at the 116th Street diamond. Calhoun and Welch will be the battery.

4-H 340 45—16 17 1
Ukes 001 10— 2 4 3
Coonley and Herrington; Susko and Aukelian.

WRIGHT TO MEET BALTIMORE FIGHTER

New York (AP)—Chalky Wright, the New York featherweight champion, features this week's national boxing program. He takes on Lew Transparenti of Baltimore in a 10-round non-title bout at Baltimore tonight.

Tami Mauriello, New York heavyweight contender who recently held Bob Pastor to a draw, meets Tony Musto of Chicago in a 10-rounder here tomorrow night.

The Baseball Standings

Games Today.

NATIONAL LEAGUE.
Philadelphia at Cincinnati.
Only game scheduled.

AMERICAN LEAGUE.
Detroit at New York.
Cleveland at Washington, night game.
Chicago at Philadelphia, night game.
Only games scheduled.

EASTERN LEAGUE.
Hartford at ALBANY.
Only game scheduled.

Yesterday's Results.

NATIONAL LEAGUE.
1—Brooklyn 2, Pittsburg 1.
2—Pittsburg 6, Brooklyn 4.
1—New York 6, Chicago 2.
2—Chicago 8, New York. 3.
1—St. Louis 5, Boston 1.
2—St. Louis 9, Boston 3.
1—Cincinnati 2, Philadelphia 0.
2—Cincinnati 2, Philadelphia 1.

AMERICAN LEAGUE.
1—Detroit 6, New York 4.
2—New York 3, Detroit 1, 13 innings.
1—St. Louis 1, Boston 0.
2—St. Louis 10, Boston 6.
1—Cleveland 9, Washington 7, 10 innings.
2—Cleveland 5, Washington 0.
1—Philadelphia 3, Chicago 2, 10 innings.
2—Chicago 11, Philadelphia 1.

INTERNATIONAL LEAGUE.
1—Newark 5, Baltimore 1.
2—Newark 5, Baltimore 1.
1—Jersey City 2, Syracuse 0.
2—Syracuse 2, Jersey City 0.
1—Rochester 8, Toronto 4.
2—Rochester 7, Toronto 4.
1—Buffalo 8, Montreal 2.
2—Buffalo 8, Montreal 3.

EASTERN LEAGUE.
1—ALBANY 2, Hartford 1, 10 innings.
2—ALBANY 3, Hartford 0.
1—Wilkes-Barre 2, Williamsport 0.
2—Wilkes-Barre 3, Williamsport 0.
1—Binghamton 7, Springfield 1.
2—Binghamton 5, Springfield 2.
1—Scranton 4, Elmira 1.
2—Elmira 5, Scranton 4.

Saturday's Results

NATIONAL LEAGUE.
1—Brooklyn 5, Cincinnati 0.
2—Brooklyn 3, Cincinnati 2, 15 innings.
Boston 4, Chicago 2.
Pittsburg 12, Philadelphia 5.
New York 8, St. Louis 3.

AMERICAN LEAGUE.
St. Louis 5, New York 2.
Cleveland 3, Philadelphia 1.
Chicago 5, Washington 3.
Detroit at Boston, postponed weather.

INTERNATIONAL LEAGUE.
1—Buffalo 11, Syracuse 1.
2—Buffalo 5, Syracuse 4.
1—Newark 6, Toronto 3.
2—Toronto 5, Newark 2.
Jersey City 12, Rochester 3.
Other game postponed, weather.

EASTERN LEAGUE.
Elmira 3, Scranton 2.
Williamsport 4, Wilkes-Barre 1.
ALBANY at Hartford, postponed weather.
Only games scheduled.

The Standings.

NATIONAL LEAGUE.

	Won	Lost	Pct.
Brooklyn	56	23	.709
St. Louis	47	30	.610
Cincinnati	44	37	.543
New York	42	40	.512
Chicago	37	41	.474
Pittsburg	37	41	.474
Boston	36	50	.419
Philadelphia	21	58	.266

AMERICAN LEAGUE.

	Won	Lost	Pct.
New York	53	28	.654
Boston	48	32	.600
Cleveland	49	36	.576
Detroit	45	41	.523
St. Louis	40	43	.482
Chicago	34	45	.430
Philadelphia	35	54	.393
Washington	29	54	.349

EASTERN LEAGUE.

	Won	Lost	Pct.
Scranton	43	27	.614
ALBANY	43	29	.597
Wilkes-Barre	45	31	.592
Binghamton	39	33	.542
Hartford	31	38	.449
Williamsport	32	41	.438
Elmira	32	43	.427
Springfield	20	49	.290

CLAIM FORFEIT.

Pop Bethman's Maplewood Tigers claimed a 9-0 forfeit yesterday when the Schaghticoke Wildcats failed to appear for a scheduled girls' softball team at Burden Lake. The Burden Lake team is under the direction of Joe Hepp and Ed Bethman.

FORDS DOWNED BY CLUETTS BUT MAINTAIN LEAD

While the Beaunit Millers continued their blitz conquest of the A Division in the Industrial A. A. Softball League, the Ford Motors, heretofore undefeated, bowed to the Cluetts but maintained their B Division lead by a comfortable margin.

The Beaunit outfit ran its string of consecutive victories to six by walloping the Allegheny-Ludlum nine, 17-1. Other results in the upper bracket were the Behr-Manning's 12-9 triumph over the Coverts and the Arsenal's 15-0 shellacking of the Diamond Rock nine.

The Fords suffered their first defeat in five starts at the hands of the Cluetts, 9 to 7, the latter taking a tie for second place. Other lower bracket scores were: Sliters over Alphas, 8-5, and Mt. Ida over Coca Colas, 17-13.

Tuesday's schedule is: Diamond 1, Allegheny-Ludlum vs Watervliet Arsenal; Diamond 2, Cloverleaf vs. Sliters; Diamond 3, Behr-Manning vs. Beaunit; Diamond 4, Coca Cola vs. Ford Motors; Diamond 5, Diamond Rock vs. Coverts, and Diamond 6, Cluetts vs. Mt. Ida.

The current standings follow for the A Division: Beaunit, six and none; Behr-Manning, five and one; Allegheny-Ludum, three and three; Watervliet Arsenal, three and three; Coverts, one and five; Diamond Rock, none and six. For the B Division: Fords, four and one; Cloverleafs, three andtwo; Cluetts, three and two; Mt. Ida, three and two; Alpha, three and three; Sliters, two and three, and Coca Cola, none and five.

The linescores:

Behr-Manning 040 013 112—12
Coverts 241 000 002— 9
Bonjukian and Graber; Slichko and Frawley.

Arsenal 780 000 000—15
Diamond Rock 000 000 000— 0
Evertsen and Peperian; Haldeman and Ott.

Beaunit Mills 400 103 072—17
Allegheny-Lud. 000 100 000— 1
Charbonneau and Killian; Goering and Miroin.

Cluetts 041 010 102—9
Ford Motors 004 020 001—7
Woods and Schultz; Jupin and VanArnum.

Alphas 013 001 000—5
Sliters 000 005 12x—8
Keleher and Wolfe; Daniels and Hayner.

Coca Cola 220 401 004—13
Mt. Ida 020 031 425—17
Buher and Keegan; Evers and Ward.

CUBS SEND ROOKIE EDDIE HANYZEWSKI TO MILWAUKEE CLUB

Chicago (AP)—Jim Gallagher, general manager of the Chicago Cubs, announced last night that Eddie Hanyzewski, right-handed rookie pitcher, had been optioned to Milwaukee of the American Association subject to 24 hour recall.

The Cubs picked up Hanyzewski direct from the South Bend. Ind., sandlots last winter. His record with the Cubs is one victory and no defeats.

CANAL ZONE HAS HOUR AIR ALERT

U. S. Army Headquarters, Panama Canal Zone (AP)—The vital Panama Canal Zone underwent a one-hour general air raid alarm yesterday afternoon after a friendly plane not immediately identifiable had touched off the strategic waterway's elaborate defense system.

The plane was first spotted while heading toward Panama across the Gulf of Chiriqui at an estimated speed of 250 m. p. h. It was soon identified, but Lieut.-Gen. Frank M. Andrews, commander of the Caribbean defense zone, decided to prolong the alarm for a full test of the Canal's defenses.

The alarm, the first since shortly after the United States entered the war, lasted from 2:20 p.m. to 3:23 p.m. E.S.T. (3:20 p.m. to 4:23 p.m., E.W.T.)

Physical requirements for an airline stewardess are, in some respects, even stiffer than those for U. S. Army cadets. Age group is especially stringent—girls must be between 23 and 26. Top weight is 120 pounds; maximum height, 5 feet, 5.

Playground Street Dance Attracts Large Crowd

With Mann Avenue for their floor, the sky for their ceiling and the neighborhood for their audience, children danced all last evening to the music of a phonograph on the porch of Mr. and Mrs. Alexander C. King, 276 Mann Avenue. It was the second street dance there in as many weeks and it attracted about 150 people, including adults. Edward A. Wachter, commissioner of recreation, was a guest.

Japanese Railroads Seen As Targets For Raids By U.S. Bombers

Washington (INS)—Following the successful bombing of Japanese cities by American planes, Nippon's 17,000-mile transportation system, interlacing the Empire's many islands, today takes on added importance as the target of future attacks.

Japan's chief railroad trunk line, on which its major political and industrial centers are situated, runs along the east coast of Honshu Island. In its interior, this island is mountainous, with volcanic peaks, and generally unsuitable for the construction of an extensive rail system. Hence, the nation's railway lines are limited for the most part to the coastal areas.

In terms of an American aerial offensive against Japan, a National Geographic Society bulletin points out, this means that an effective bombing raid could disrupt a major portion of the entire system almost immediately.

Dependent on Rail Lines.

The initial U. S. raid was directed at Tokyo, Yokohama, Kobe, and Nagoya—all located within a radius of 300 miles, as the airplane flies, in the southern section of Honshu Island.

A scattered, multi-island unit, the Japanese Empire is completely dependent upon an efficient transportation system. Conveyance of passengers and freight between its widely segregated areas must be effected by ferry service or, as in the case of its newest project, by underwater tunnel.

This tunnel, which is reported to have been opened April 13, 1942, links Honshu and Kyushu Island, just to the south. Described as two and a half miles long, with double track, it is considered especially important to the Japanese war effort because of its location in the center of the vitally important industrial region.

The bulletin points out that with three of her ferry points and all of her main rail terminals thus situated, bombing attacks on Japan could be concentrated on an area with a radius of approximately 200 miles.

Introduced by Perry.

Admiral Perry introduced rail transportation into Japan in 1852 at Yokohama, where he set up a model line on the ocean beach. By 1872, an 18-mile line was completed along the coastal section, thereby connecting Yokohama and Tokyo. A few years later, following the merger of separate lines, a single trunk system was established and extended to Kobe.

Although British capital built the first Japanese railways, United States equipment and mechanical ideas have kept them in operation. In 1938-39 more than 125,000,000,000 passengers were carried on government lines alone. As an industrial enterprise, the state railways employed more than 227,000 persons in 1937, while private companies hired over 40,000 workers.

STUDENTS LEARN CAMOUFLAGE FOR USE IN CONFLICT

Columbus, O. (INS)—Sand tables, on which model houses, factories, airports and other structures appear, occupy a classroom at Ohio State University.

It is not a kindergarten, either, as you might suppose from a quick glance. It is, instead, the subtle art of camouflaging.

Students at the university are being taught this summer types of camouflaging needed for industry and military objectives and personnel. Morris E. Trotter, jr., who recently completed the camouflage course given at Ft. Belvoir, Va., is the instructor.

One group of students is given a military objective and instructed to work out a plan of concealing it from bombers. Paint and other materials are employed in covering the model buildings to make them appear as part of the terrain from the air.

Photographs of the problems are taken before and after camouflaging to prove pictorially effectiveness of the students' work.

BLAMES CAPITAL FOR COMPLACENCY

Washington (AP)—Rep. Mason (R-Ill.) told the House yesterday that the administration had taken the attitude that "the American people did not have the courage or the stamina to receive bad news and stand up under the blows of adversity."

As a result, Mason said, "many people have remained more or less complacent because the information given them by the propaganda agencies and the press agencies of the bureaucracy at Washington has been such as to justify their complacency."

"This complacency," Mason contended, "is the direct result of the administration's policy of applying the soft pedal to our war reverses and the loud pedal to our war successes, thereby creating a false impression of the war situation."

FLYER SENDS BONDS HOME TO MOTHER

Dallas, Tex. (INS)—E. W. Hix, Navy radioman, third class, believed in purchasing war bonds. But he couldn't see why his mother kept asking him to send the bonds home for safe-keeping.

He carried four of them in his pocket during the Jap raid on Pearl Harbor and Wake Island. They were still with him when his plane went aloft in the battle of Midway Island.

The bomber to which Hix was assigned was shot down. For four and a half days the crew, unharmed, awaited their eventual rescue.

Back at Pearl Harbor once more, Hix wrote his mother immediately—enclosing the bonds.

"I understand now why it's better for me to send them home for safe-keeping," he wrote, "after keeping them in my pocket for four days while I doubted whether I'd ever get home again."

COHOES BOY RANGERS TAKE SECOND PLACE

The Boy Rangers of Cohoes won second award Sunday afternoon during a drum corps competition of the International Drum Corps Alliance at Whitehall. The Liberty Drum Corps of Whitehall, host to the competitors, gave a special exhibition but did not enter the contest. A street parade preceded the competition.

The Frank I. Stiles Drum Corps of North Adams took top honors.

"E" Awarded Men Behind the Men Behind the Guns

Brig. Gen. Burton O. Lewis, left above, chief of the Boston Ordnance District, awarded the Army and Navy "E" to the Watervliet Arsenal yesterday in recognition of the extraordinary production record of the cannon plant. With General Lewis, left to right, Gov. Herbert H. Lehman, a speaker at the exercises; Brig. Alexander G. Gillespie, Arsenal commandant; Capt. John S. Phillips, commanding the R. P. I. Naval R. O. T. C. and who awarded the "E" pins to the Arsenal workers, and Dwight Marvin, editor of The Record Newspapers and master of ceremonies. General Gillespie receives the pennant, below, from General Lewis.

ARMY-NAVY "E" FLIES AT ARSENAL CITING WORKERS

Nation's Highest Production Award Goes to Watervliet Gun Plant; 8,000 See Ceremony.

(Continued From Page 5.)

of naval science and tactics at Rensselaer Polytechnic Institute, told the audience that he wished to give them "the reactions of a Naval officer at sea in the Pacific at the very beginning of the war."

"I was operating in the Pacific at that time and for some months thereafter," he said.

"In the mornings, at noon and in the evenings broadcasts came over a loud speaker right below the bridge. We heard broadcasts from Japan in which Mr. Tojo said that we were yellow, that we could not fight, that it would be an easy matter for the Japanese to clear the Pacific of the U. S. Navy.

"We heard outbursts from Mr. Hitler that labor and management in the United States could neither coordinate their efforts nor cooperate in building up the desired war production industry. Each time these broadcasts were heard I read in the faces of my men a grim determination to prove that they were not yellow, that they could fight and that they would fight. Believe me, they demonstrated that in true American fashion. You have demonstrated that management and labor can cooperate and that they have cooperated. No one doubts what the ultimate outcome will be."

Mr. Mead in accepting the award said:

"We know that this is not an idle gesture but recognition of our service to our government. I have been here in two wars and I can say that never before have I seen such activity or better cooperation between management and workers. We accept this award with pride, and trust that we deserve it."

Workers Give Up Sleep.

A few minutes before the time set for the ceremony, workmen in overalls and carrying lunch pails, and women workers in slacks poured out of the Arsenal buildings. Thousands more came in the gates, either reporting for duty or members of the midnight shift who had sacrificed some of their sleep to see the "E" pennant awarded.

Mounted guards patroled the grounds. Other guards acted as ushers to seat the families of Arsenal officials and members of the Twenty Year Club who occupied seats of honor directly in front of the grandstand.

Among the guests on the grandstand were Rep. E. Harold Cluett; Lieut. Col. D. L. Martin of the office of the Chief of Ordnance, Col. M. H. Shute, commander of the Northern New York Military District; Col. Lester C. Higbee, commanding the Second Regiment. State Guard; Lieut. Comdr. H. M. Denty of the N. R. O. T. C., Lieut. Thomas B. Kiely, chief of the Navy public relations bureau in this area. The ceremonies closed with the singing of "America" by the assemblage led by the Arsenal Choral Society.

IRON CHIEF — Hiland G. Batcheller, appointed head of War Production Board, Iron and Steel branch, by Chief Donald Nelson. He is president of the Alleghany-Ludlum Steel Company, 56, and a New Yorker.

REV. T. S. SLATTERY, NATIVE OF COHOES, DIES IN HOSPITAL

Pastor of St. Thomas' Church, Schenectady, Succumbs at St. Peter's Hospital in Albany.

Rev. Thomas S. Slattery, 59, native of Cohoes, and pastor of St. Thomas' Church, Schenectady, for the last seven years, died yesterday afternoon at St. Peter's Hospital, Albany, to which he was taken Tuesday for treatment.

Father Slattery was born in Cohoes, Sept. 24, 1883, the son of the late Mr. and Mrs. John Slattery. After receiving his early education at St. Bernard's Academy in Cohoes, he studied at Niagara University from which he received both the A. B. and M. A. degrees. He prepared for the priesthood at Dunwoodie Seminary, Yonkers, and was ordained May 21, 1910, at the Cathedral of the Immaculate Conception in Albany.

His first charge was as assistant pastor at St. John's Church, Albany, a post to which he was named shortly after ordination. He was made pastor of St. Paul's Church at Hancock in 1919 and became pastor of St. Joseph's Church at Dolgeville in 1923. He became pastor of St. Thomas' Church in Schenectady seven years ago.

The body will be taken to St. Thomas' Church tomorrow at 4 p.m. to lie in state until Saturday at 11 a.m. when a solemn high mass of requiem, coram episcopo, will be chanted. Vespers will be chanted on arrival of the body at the church tomorrow. Burial will be in St. Mary's Cemetery, Waterford.

Father Slattery's only survivor is his aunt, Miss Catherine Slattery, who lived with him.

NORTH HOOSICK.

The Home Bureau will meet at the school Wednesday at 1:30 p.m.

The Women's Society of Christian Service will meet at the Methodist Church at 2 p.m. tomorrow.

Pvt. Raymond Searles of Fort Devens, Mass. spent the week-end with Mr. and Mrs. Robert Mooney.

Mrs. George Lippert returned Saturday from spending several weeks with relatives in Verona, N. J.

The South Cambridge church which is on this circuit will sponsor a Harvest Supper starting 5:30 p.m. today.

The Youth Fellowship will meet with the pastor, Rev. A. J. Cambridge, at the church Monday night.

Pvt. Donald A. Hillman and Corp. Karl Gibbs of Fort Ethan Allen spent the week-end at the former's home here.

Miss Grace Wright will leave this week to spend a considerable time as employee in the home of Mrs. H. B. Elger at Jackson Heights.

World Communion Service will be held in the Methodist Church Sunday. The sacrament of the Lord's Supper will be given and a special collection will be taken.

Extensive plans are being made for the turkey supper to be served at the Methodist Church parlors Thursday night, Oct. 29, by the Women's Society of Christian Service.

Several from here and Wollomsac attended the miscellaneous shower Sunday evening at the home of Mrs. Vincent LeBlanc of East Hoosick in honor of Miss Mary Wolfrum whose marriage to James Hoag will take place Saturday. There were sixty relatives and friends present. A good attendance was present at the "Family Night" supper served at the Methodist Church Tuesday night. About $35.00 was realized. An auction sale of fruits and vegetables helped to raise the proceeds. Mrs. John Cathcart acted as auctioneer and sold all the fall products.

Announcement have been received in town that Miss Frieda Wolfrum of New York, daughter of John Wolfrum of this town, will be married to Dr. Alfred B. Clements, son of Mr. and Mrs. J. Clements of New York, Oct. 11 by Rabbi Schorr of Temple Adath Israel of New York. The bride-to-be is a graduate of Hoosick Falls High School and Mount Sinai Nurses Training School in New York. Dr. Clements is a graduate of City College in New York and received his medical degree at Long Island Medical College.

STREET CARS CUT STOPS.

Denver (UP) — Street cars and busses in Denver are now making "victory stops" to speed up their service. Under the new arrangement, the tramway cars stop only at every other corner.

Miss Dix Advises Women To Face Grim Realities Of War And Prepare For Future

Mother's Milk Best Food For Infant, Says Expert

The article below is another in a series of exclusive stories on infant care written by Mrs. Theodore Hall. Mrs. Hall is not only an authority on children, but a young mother herself.

BY MRS. THEODORE HALL.

This morning as I was feeding Timothy Hall, I carried on an imaginary conversation with young Mrs. Mother-to-Be.

"Young Mrs. Mother-to-Be," I said, "Do you know the name of a baby food worth $10 a quart?" She didn't.

"A food so precious that mothers of premature babies would give any price for it? Can you guess?" She couldn't.

"Mother's milk!" said I impressively. "No food on earth is as good for young babies as mother's milk. Formulas often do a very good job of imitation but listen to this." And down the list I went.

I told her how mother's milk is the easiest of all foods for a baby to digest. That breast-fed babies have fewer colicky pains and are rarely constipated. That mother's milk has the food elements in the proper proportions for babies to thrive on. And it is always clean, warm, and ready to drink.

Baby Feels Secure.

Breast-fed babies are less likely to develop allergies. In fact, they receive elements in mother's milk that keep them from catching certain diseases. The exercise of

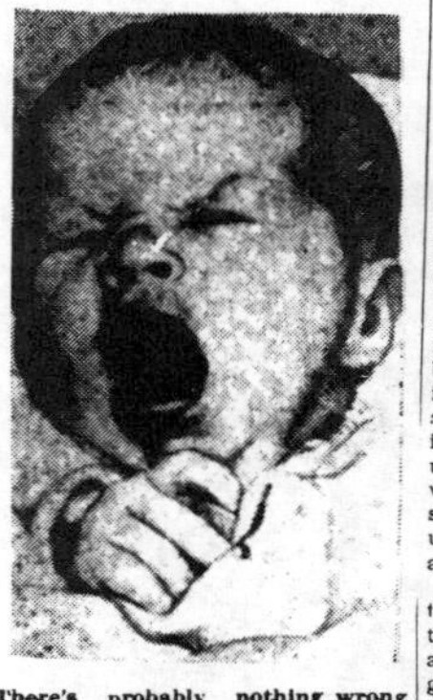

There's probably nothing wrong with this lusty youngster. Maybe he's just askin in his own way for some o the most precious of all baby s: mother's milk

nursing dev ps the baby's face and jaw mu les far more than the easier act of sucking a rubber nipple.

But most important, the close warmth of nursing from the mother gives the baby the feeling of being loved and secure.

Not only is nursing best for the baby, but a young mother owes herself its advantages. She will have very little energy to spare after the baby arrives and nursing will be easier than making up a formula. If she is careful not to eat fattening foods, it need not cause her to put on extra weight.

"Young Mother-to-Be," I urged, "Make up your mind right now to nurse your baby!"

Many a young mother has gone to the hospital, hoping to—but has come home with directions for a formula—a disappointed lady. This often happens because she was not prepared to meet the real difficulties that nursing can present.

First of all, she needs to have her husband on her side. And she must choose a doctor who makes her feel confident that she can nurse. A doubtful doctor or a doubtful husband makes a doubtful mother, and successful nursing often depends on a mother's confidence.

Nursing Not Easy.

Now a new mother can hardly be expected to look forward to nursing—it is new and strange to her. But she usually expects it to be natural and easy. With some this will be the case. On the other hand, she should be prepared to find it one of the hardest adjustments she ever made.

Nursing is often painful, particularly at the beginning. And young babies do not always want to nurse. They find the rubber nipple on their supplementary bottle so easy that they refuse to work for their food when put to the breast.

So a new mother must be prepared to teach her baby to nurse, and keep him awake and feeding. For only in this way will she get a good supply of milk for him. Once she has some milk, she stands a very good chance of giving more, and eventually, enough for the baby's entire needs, providing she persists.

Housewife Should Conserve Clothesline, Pins

War is such a huge and costly thing that homemakers sometimes find it hard to realize that small household economics make contributions toward victory. In homemaking, seemingly insignificant savings can be effected to release funds for war stamps on the one hand, and release materials for the war effort on the other.

Take the washline, for instance. It consists of scores or perhaps hundreds of feet of rope or wire, which are inexpensive and easy to replace in peace time. Now, however, they are among the war scarities. By taking care of the washline, keeping it usable by keeping it clean, the homemaker helps the war by releasing vital war products and saving the money required for replacement. The rope line can be kept in condition by churning it in the washer once a month, and by taking it down and winding it carefully between washdays, unless it is attached to pulleys. The wire line should be wiped with a soap-dampened cloth before every use, and it too, can be taken down and wound neatly.

Clothespins are other small items that have been treated casually in the past, because they were cheap and easy to replace. Now it is good policy to pick up every one that drops, and to keep all of them clean. Nothing is so irritating to a housewife, nor so easy to prevent, as clothespin marks on otherwise clean clothing. Just treat the pins to a monthly sudsing. They rarely need more than to float in a tub of warm soapy water. Even rinsing isn't necessary. They should be dried in the air or sun. It will help to keep them clean if the pins are always kept in a thoroughly clean clothespin bag. Sturdy bags can be made of bed ticking or denim, both of which are easily washed.

How To Drive Your Family Really Mad

Some people become so immersed in their own plans that they forget everything else.

They talk of the things they expect to do until everyone within earshot grows weary. Or else they become so wrapped up in their schemes that their conversation is confined to monosyllables.

Anything which hinders their progress in carrying out their plans provokes a discourtesy—a sharp word to the telephone operator who gives a wrong number, a frown to the waitress who is slow with the menu, impatience that rises to anger over any delay.

Sometimes they stew over details connected with a plan to the neglect of responsibilities beyond it. If they are cleaning house, they keep it upset for days, until the family complains there isn't a comfortable place to sit down. If they are sewing they work until almost dinner time, then scramble together a hasty meal which is neither appetizing nor nourishing. If they are immersed in a sport, they take time out from the office routine.

Feminine Factory Workers Balk at Cast-off Overalls

Hand-me-down Problem Solved With Smart New Work Clothes

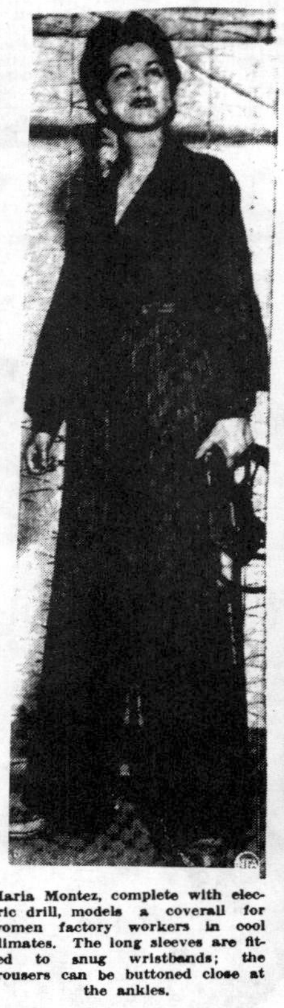

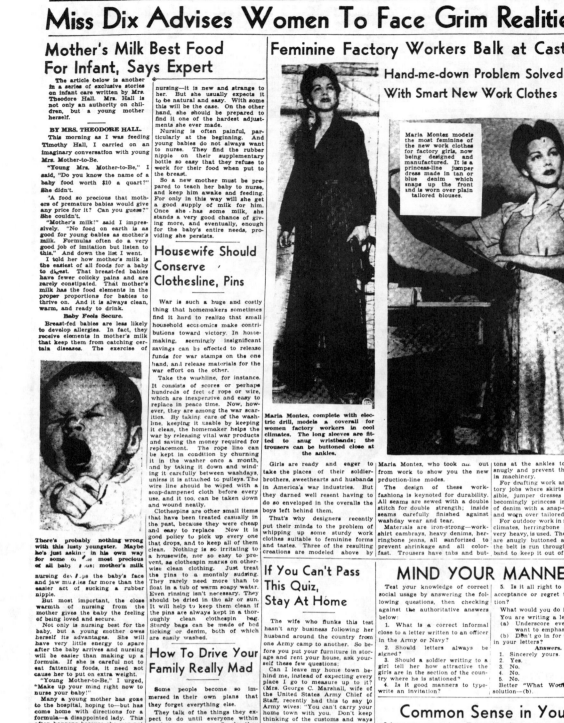

Maria Montez, complete with electric drill, models a coverall for women factory workers in cool climates. The long sleeves are fitted to snug wristbands; the trousers can be buttoned close at the ankles.

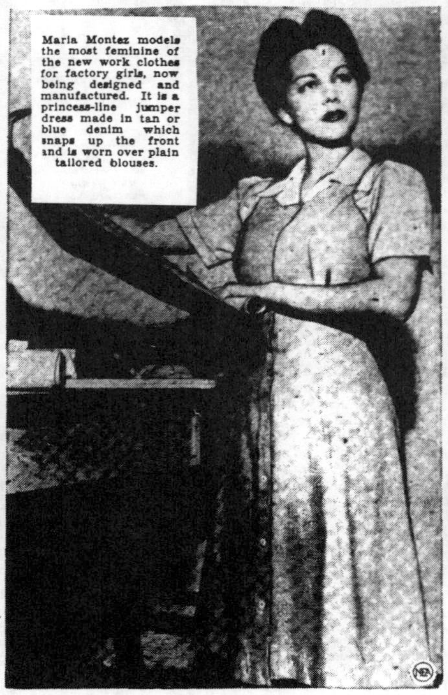

Maria Montez models the most feminine of the new work clothes for factory girls, now being designed and manufactured. It is a princess-line jumper dress made in tan or blue denim which snaps up the front and is worn over plain tailored blouses.

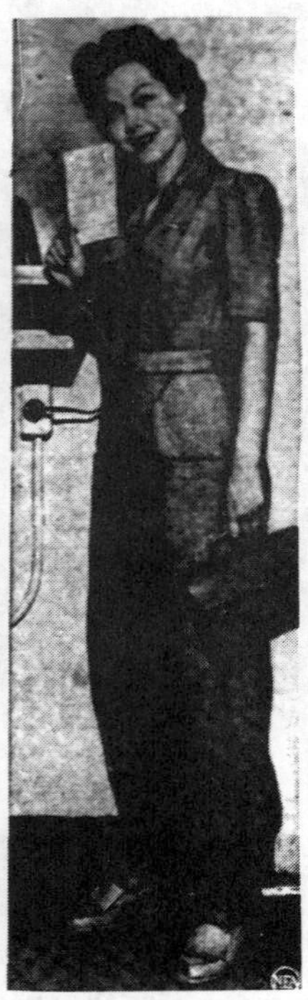

Aircraft factory girls prefer this model, illustrated by Marie Montez. Short-sleeved, and open-throated its front-closing is a warp-around for perfect fit which eliminates all but the one button at the waistband.

Girls are ready and eager to take the places of their soldier-brothers, sweethearts and husbands in America's war industries. But they darned well resent having to do so enveloped in the overalls the boys left behind them.

That's why designers recently put their minds to the problem of whipping up some sturdy work clothes suitable to feminine forms and tastes. Three of the resulting creations are modeled above by Maria Montez, who took out from work to show you the new prduction-line modes.

The design of these work-fashions is keynoted for durability. All seams are sewed with a double stitch for double strength; inside seams carefully finished against washday wear and tear.

Materials are iron-strong—work-shirt cambrays, heavy denims, herringbone jeans, all sanforized to prevent shrinkage and all color-fast. Trousers have tabs and buttons at the ankles to bind them snugly and prevent their catching in machinery.

For drafting work and other factory jobs where skirts are permissible, jumper dresses are offered, becomingly princess in line, made of denim with a snap-closing front and worn over tailored blouses.

For outdoor work in not too warm climates, herringbone jean cloth, very heavy, is used. The long sleeves are snugly buttoned at the wrist; the belt is run through a covering band to keep it out of harm's way and there is a huge pocket on the hip for tools.

A lighter weight design, excellent for airplane factories, is made in work-shirt cambray, with an open throat and short sleeves. The front closing is artfully fitted to wrap around and eliminate buttons except for one at the belt, while tabs hold the trousers in at the ankles.

These are only a few of the designs already being accepted all over the country by America's new army of feminine factory workers.

If You Can't Pass This Quiz, Stay At Home

The wife who flunks this test hasn't any business following her husband around the country from one Army camp to another. So before you put your furniture in storage and rent your house, ask yourself these few questions:

Can I leave my home town behind me, instead of expecting every place I go to measure up to it? (Mrs. George C. Marshall, wife of the United States Army Chief of Staff, recently had this to say to Army wives: "You can't carry your home town with you. Don't keep thinking of the customs and ways back home.")

Could I be happy living in a house or a room that is far less comfortable and convenient than what I have been used to?

Could I withstand the temptation to share all my small worries and problems with my husband, and be willing to assume all responsibility for running the house and taking care of the children?

Could I get along with the wives of my husband's associates?

Could I find enough to do to keep busy, so that my husband wouldn't have a dissatisfied, lonesome woman on his hands?

Could I keep my nose out of my husband's business, instead of encouraging him in being dissatisfied or becoming jealous of the man above him?

Would I try to make life easier and more pleasant for my husband, or would I expect him to worry about keeping me happy and contented?

If she can't say "Yes" to every one of these questions, a service man's wife had better not follow him around the country. She would just be in the way.

White Floors Found To Improve Lighting

White floors for kitchens may become the rule of the future. According to a well-known industrial color consultant, whose services have been used in many of the new war production plants, white, or at least light tinted floor coverings provide a better background for work than the dark floors which were formerly favored because they did not show dirt. White floors, he points out, improve visibility by reflecting lights upward and toning down shadows.

As good lighting is important to the housewife, especialy in the kitchen, the suggestion of the color expert may solve a problem for rooms which are poorly provided with sunlight. Light paint or light linoleum may give just the extra visibility which will make artificial lighting unnecessary.

Both painted floors and linoleum-covered ones can be wiped up readily with a sudsy cloth. Too much water should be avoided. While a light floor undoubtedly shows more quickly the presence of dirt, in a kitchen this should be an advantage, for if there is one room above another that should be immaculate it is the one in which meals are prepared. Healthfulness calls for cleanliness, and white or light colored floors should help make cleanliness sure.

MIND YOUR MANNERS

Test your knowledge of correct social usage by answering the following questions, then checking against the authoritative answers below:

1. What is a correct informal close to a letter written to an officer in the Army or Navy?
2. Should letters always be signed?
3. Should a soldier writing to a girl tell her how attractive the girls are in the section of the country where he is stationed?
4. Is it good manners to typewrite an invitation?
5. Is it all right to typewrite an acceptance or regret to an invitation?

What would you do if—

You are writing a letter—

(a) Underscore everything you want to emphasize?

(b) Don't go in for underscoring in your letters?

Answers.

1. Sincerely yours.
2. Yes.
3. No.
4. No.
5. No.

Better "What Would You Do" solution—(b).

Common Sense in Youth

I have seen young Anne Baxter in two pictures recently—and find her refreshingly natural and sweet in comparison with some of the artificial youngsters who are featured in a film or two and then dropped. Not only is she a good actress, but her sincerity is carried into her roles—she is earnest, ambitious, and hard-working—qualities that are sure to bring her to success. It disturbs me to find some young people today who think that good positions, big incomes, and recognition should be theirs simply because they have put in four years at college—or have had a little experience. Occasionally some of these boys and girls find their way to our house with a group of others—and I just ache to take them down a peg or two when they begin to "hold forth." But, of course, I mind my own business, knowing full well that their eyes will be opened for them one day—the sooner the better.

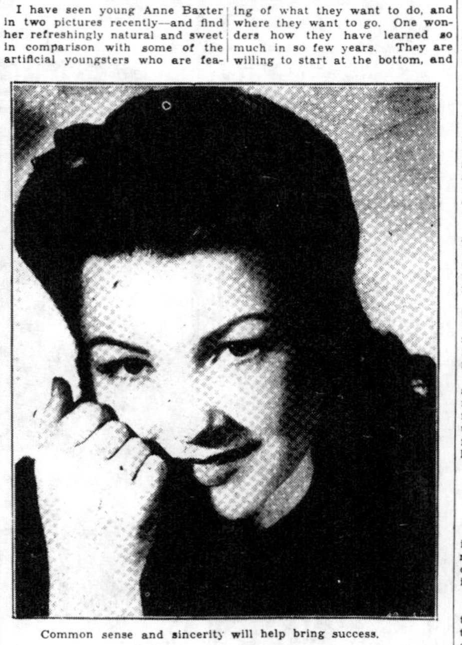

Common sense and sincerity will help bring success.

Then, on the other hand, one often finds young people who have an amazing amount of good, common sense, and a keen understanding of what they want to do, and where they want to go. One wonders how they have learned so much in so few years. They are willing to start at the bottom, and humbly learn the practical application of all the theories they have studied in school—because that is what school should do; teach the theories, make the student more capable to think and plan out a problem—then when the opportunities come of making constructive changes and improvements in their chosen work, they will avoid costly and embarrassing mistakes. That type of person finds success and satisfaction in his work, early in life.

When sending for material, offered you in my column, please remember always to enclose a self-addressed, three-cent stamped envelope. Address me in care of The Times Record, Troy, N. Y. Remember, too, that I cannot make personal replies for personal diagnosis, consultations, or treatment, you must consult some recognized beautician or your personal physician.—V. D.

Wife Who Urges Hubby to Join Army Good Sport

There are two ways a childless wife can answer her husband's "Honey, what do you thing about my volunteering?"

She can say, "What about me? If you really loved me, you wouldn't think about going off and leaving me. And what about the home we're buying, and all our nice furniture? We would have to let the house go and store the furniture. After all, you have a wife to think about. You just wait until they call you. Personally I don't think married men ought to be called at all."

Or, she can say, "That is a decision I think you ought to make yourself. If you really feel that you should be in, it is all right with me. I'll miss you dreadfully, of course. But I can get along all right. I'll bet I could even get my old job back. If not, I know I could get another one.

"And, we would get along all right. If we couldn't manage the payments on the house, we could sell it, and I could move into an apartment. It won't be any fun for either of us. But I think you ought to be free to do what you think is right."

The women who give the second answer may not have their husbands with them as long as the other women. But their men and their marriages will be stronger for their attitude.

And, if you hear any husbands bragging about their wives, it will be the husbands of the girls who say, "You do whatever you think is right—and don't worry about me. I'll get along fine."

The only men who will go around quoting their "What about me?" wives will be the men who fell called on to explain, "I'd volunteer in a minute if it weren't for my wife. But she juts won't hear of it."

Handy Hints

For extra nutrition and flavor interest mix three tablespoons peanut butter into one cup mayonnaise or boiled salad dressing and serve it on top of fruit salad.

When cooking a meal outdoors take along a pair of asbestos gloves to protect the hands when cooking over the camp fire.

Curried apricots are something new with broiled chops, fried chicken or browned liver. Arrange the apricots on a shallow pan. Brush lightly with melted butter (about 3 tablespoons) with 1/8 teaspoon each of curry powder, salt, paprika and celery seed. Broil or bake until well browned. Serve warm.

The attachments of vacuum sweepers make easy work of cleaning hard-to-reach places such as behind radiators, down registers and around the back of a fireplace.

Never let old rugs or woolen rags lay around the house. They might attract insects and moths. Wash and pack the cloths away when they are dry and clean.

Always close zippers on washable clothes before putting them in the laundry.

They Should Forget Romance And Come Down to Earth

BY DOROTHY DIX

Wake up, girls. Rub the sleep from your eyes. Face reality. Fit yourselves to look the world in the face and tell it where to go. From time immemorial the pipe dream of every woman has been love and marriage, a husband and children, a home and security. Heretofore there has been enough probability of the dream coming true for every girl to believe that she was being vouchsafed a prophetic vision of her future and that it wasn't much use for her to bother about learning any way to support herself when heaven would supply her with a meal ticket.

But the war has changed all of that. The pleasant romantic era of sturdy oaks and clinging vines is gone, never to return. The social upheaval of the world has, in particular, changed the whole status of women. It has made a new heaven and a new earth and also a new hell for them, unless they fit themselves to meet the changed conditions.

So, girls, rouse yourselves from your sentimental trances. Forget your wishful thinking. Waste no more time looking for a fairy prince to come riding down your street and trying to decide whether you will have a swell church wedding or marry at home under a floral bell.

Instead, concentrate all your thoughts upon the present and use every bit of intelligence you have in trying to get a preview of the future and preparing yourself to meet it. If you are single accept the bitter truth that you cannot count upon marriage. For you and millions of other girls like you, there will be no love life. You will never know the sweet dependence of wifehood, the thrill of having your baby's head upon your breast, for the men who should have been your husbands are lying in graves over half the world they died to save.

Be on Own.

This means, in the first place, that you will have no strong man to lean upon. You will be on your own. You will have to earn your own bread and butter or starve. In the second place, it means that you will have to take this new life and like it. You will have to acquire a new philosophy and to substitute acquired tastes and habits for the old instinctive ones of your sex. In other words, you will have to espouse a career instead of a man, absorb yourself in your ambitions instead of your home, and let the knowledge that you are being of use in the world compensate you for having missed your heart's desire.

If you should chance to be a war widow, or one of the wives whose husbands come back to them wrecked in body or mind, you will have even greater need than the single girl to have some trade or profession by which you can support not only yourself but those dependent upon you. For upon your salary may depend whether you can keep your children with you or have them sent to some orphanage, whether you can give your sick husband the medical attention and rest and freedom from worry that will restore him to strength and health again, or leave him a permanent invalid.

In any case, even when your husband comes home from the war unscathed, as please God he may, he will have to begin his business life over again; and a wife who is a good little money-maker will be a mighty handy thing to have about the house.

Do Men's Work.

Therefore, girls, in this time of dreary waiting for you know not what, quit mooning over vine-wreathed cottages and all that went with them, and gird yourselves to meet this new hard life that will need hard, strong women to do men's work instead of embroidering doilies and knitting pink baby socks. Find out what Nature intended you to do and learn how to do it.

Don't kid yourself into thinking that it isn't worth while trying to learn how to do anything well because your job is going to be only a temporary bridge between the school-room and the altar. The chances are that it is going to be your lifework and how much you get paid for doing it will depend altogether on your skill. You will have to work just as hard for a thin pay envelope as for a fat one.

This war has flung every door of opportunity wide open to women. It has been proved that they can do any kind of work that men can do except the heavier labor. The government, colleges, the industries themselves have established training schools for women in which they can fit themselves to do good work and earn large pay. Take advantage of these opportunities and you will have taken out the best insurance you can against whatever vicissitudes Fate has in store for you.

• • •

Dear Miss Dix: I am a girl of 15. For sometime now I have been taking care of a neighbor's children when they step out nights. I have always admired and respected the handsome young couple who seemed very happy together. However a few weeks ago while I was minding the children, the husband came home from work early. He sat down next to me and, to my amazement, put his arms around me and began kissing me. Twice since then he has tried the same thing. His kissing was not given in a joking manner. What shall I do about it? I am afraid of a scandal if I tell my parents or his wife.

BEWILDERED GIRL.

Tell your mother about it and do not let anybody persuade you into going back to that house where you will be alone with the man, and unable to protect yourself against him.

Don't let anyone put you off your guard by telling you that he just looks upon you as a child, that his kisses meant nothing, and that they were given to you as one would caress a child. You sensed his amorous kisses, and that they put you in danger.

Any married man who deliberately would try to seduce a 15-year-old girl, the daughter of a neighbor, is a cad so low that he deserves to be ostracized from decent society. Be afraid of him, my dear, and keep away from him.

(Released by The Bell Syndicate, Inc.)

Record Pattern

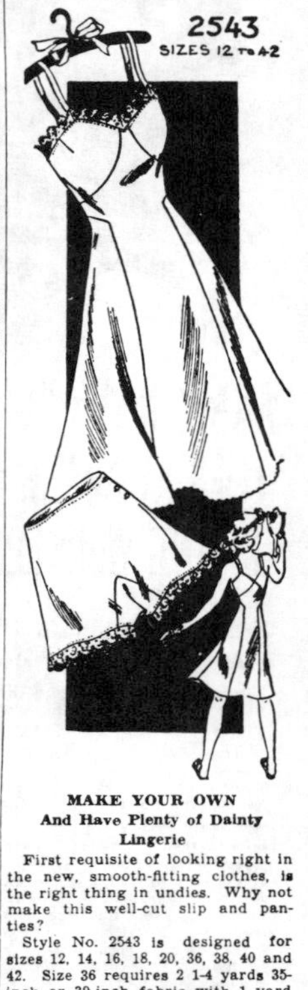

MAKE YOUR OWN
And Have Plenty of Dainty Lingerie

First requisite of looking right in the new, smooth-fitting clothes, is the right thing in undies. Why not make this well-cut slip and panties?

Style No. 2543 is designed for sizes 12, 14, 16, 18, 20, 36, 38, 40 and 42. Size 36 requires 2 1-4 yards 35-inch or 39-inch fabric with 1 yard lace, for slip; 1 1/8 yards with 1 1/2 yards lace, for panties.

Send 10c for Pattern. Write your name, address and style number. Be sure to state size you wish.

The Fall-Winter Fashion Book brings you a new peak in style—and the most practical suggestions for style at a saving. Send for the Fashion Book. Price 10c.

Address Pattern Department, The Times Record, Troy, N. Y.

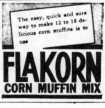

"Old Man" A. A. Stagg Overruled His Prexy On Football Crisis

By HUGH FULLERTON, JR.
Wide World Sports Columnist

New York—New York doesn't show much outward excitement over a little thing like a World Series, but just try to get a hotel room here for the week-end. . . . And the telephone company reports a jump of 100,000 calls during the time the ball games were on in St. Louis from folks who wanted to know the score. . . . Looks as if it ought to be a great series for guys who never get anywhere on time. Most of the excitement in the opener was in that ninth inning and yesterday the big noise was in the eighth. . . . and whatever became of that idea that Cullenbine and Hassett were a couple of weak spots in the Yanks' lineup? . . . Babe Pinelli, the National League umpire, says the test of a great ball club is its behavior on the field. . . . If that's so, the Yanks and Cards must be a couple of great clubs.

Today's Guest Star

Bill Tobitt, Oakland (Calif.) Tribune: "Those colleges who took the last vestige of tradition out of football by substituting steel goal posts for wooden ones can now revert to lumber. In that way two interests are served—the nation gets the steel and the customers on the winning side get splinters."

Shorts And Shells

Carrying out Mayor Fiorello (Butch) LaGuardia's orders to bear down on horse-race gambling, a few cops took over the office of a local racing wire service yesterday. When the customers began asking why the entries hadn't been sent on the wires, the only answer they got was "Ask Butch" . . . The Detroit Tigers haven't signed any players to 1943 contracts yet, preferring to wait and see what will happen before spring. And the athletes were told to take their uniforms and equipment home with them . . . Dick Durrance, the old Dartmouth ski star, is working for a west coast airplane company, turning out educational films . . . Denver is ready to bid for its ninth consecutive A. A. U. basketball tournament—if they hold one next spring.

Stagg At Bay

Dr. Tully C. Knoles, president of the College of the Pacific, gives this explanation of how he and "old man" A. A. Stagg decided to continue varsity football this season . . . "I explained to Mr. Stagg that many of his players would not return; that his squad would be very small. Besides, that he was old enough to take a rest. Therefore that the college of the Pacific would give up football." . . . Stagg listened politely and replied: "Mr. Knoles, College of the Pacific will continue varsity football this fall." . . . And that was that.

Service Dept.

Sergt. Alex Gizzi, former Long Branch, N. J., athlete, reports that Australian boys are pretty hot stuff at basketball, although his Army outfit won 22 straight games from them . . . Lieut. Col. Bernie Bierman's latest moan is because his Iowa Seahawks footballers have lost two men on the evening of the Minnesota game. Tackle Al Greenwood and Quarterback Fred Folino moved on to flight training this week . . . Boston's kraut kids, who went into the R. C. A. F. last winter, should get some real competition during the coming hockey season if they're not too busy fighting a war. When the rangers checked up on their regulars they found Neil and Mac Colville and Alex Shibicky had joined the Canadian army together and four other "varsity" men also were in uniform.

Recovered Fumbles

Continuing the football guessing game for Saturday, we like Boston College over West Virginia, Penn over Harvard, Navy over Virginia, Notre Dame over Georgia Tech, Texas over Northwestern, Tulane over Auburn, Iowa Seahawks over Minnesota and Fordham over Tennessee.

LOMBARDO TO START FOR ARMY ELEVEN

West Point (AP)—The Army team which faces Lafayette in its opening football game probably will be composed of four seniors, two juniors, four sophomores and one plebe.

Coach Earl Blaik indicated yesterday that Tom Lombardo, plebe from St. Louis, would be in the starting backfield along with the veterans—Herschel Jarrel, Capt. Han Mazur and Ralph Hill.

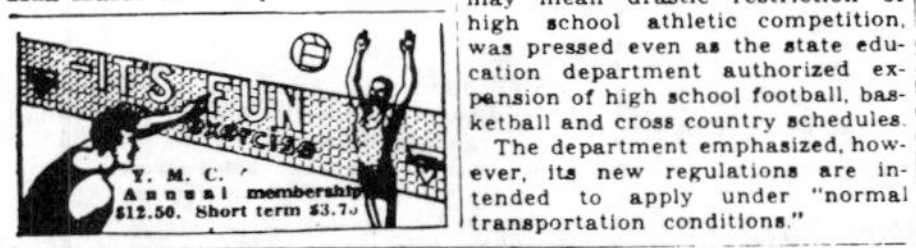

LANSINGBURG AND TROY TEAMS MEET TONIGHT AT R. P. I.

A pep rally is scheduled this morning at Troy High in preparation for tonight's football game with Lansingburg High at R. P. I. North Field. The contest, one of the high spots of the local season, is scheduled for 8 p.m.

Coach Eddie Picken of Troy High is not certain if his ace running back George Koshgarian will be in condition for the game. Koshgarian injured his right knee in last week's encounter with Nott Terrace after he had scored Troy High's only touchdown.

While the Pickenmen made all their yardage last week by end runs by George Koshgarian and Jimmie Van Wert and by Joe Muscatello's center plunges, they might use a passing attack tonight. Picken tried the passing battery of Muscatello and Bob Stacy in the Nott Terrace game and although Bob Stacy is a little green yet, he has shown to advantage as a receiver.

Starting lineup for Troy High will be Jim (Zip) Gordon, right end; Bob Coonradt, right tackle; Charlie Foster, right guard; Mick Rubino, center; Charlie Testo, left guard; Walter Winney, captain, left tackle; Irwin Berger, left end; Bill Houser, quarterback; Jimmie Van Wert, left halfback; George Koshgarian or John Menillo, right halfback, and Joe Muscatello, fullback.

PLAN REVISION IN SCHOOL LEAGUES

Albany (AP)—Revision of high school sports "league" setups was predicted today as an "almost certain" result of state efforts for a maximum saving of bus tires and gasoline in transporting athletic teams.

The State Education Department and State War Transportation Committee currently are studying interscholastic sport schedules, primarily to eliminate wherever possible the use of school-owned or private busses.

"It appears almost certain," a participant in the study said, "that the sanctity of local league setups will be out for the duration of the war. Bus transportation to distant 'league' cities when a school might schedule games in a neighboring, non-league town seems like a waste of gasoline and rubber."

Other possibilities he foresaw as a result of the study were:

1. Required team travel by common carrier—train or commercial busses—wherever possible, despite inconvenience and higher costs.

2. Repeated playing of games with the same teams.

"High school athletics are being considered in their relation to their value in the war physical fitness program," he explained. "As far as physical benefits are concerned, the student derives as much from repeated contests with the same teams as in games with a variety of opponents."

The study of schedules, which may mean drastic restriction of high school athletic competition, was pressed even as the state education department authorized expansion of high school football, basketball and cross country schedules.

The department emphasized, however, its new regulations are intended to apply under "normal transportation conditions."

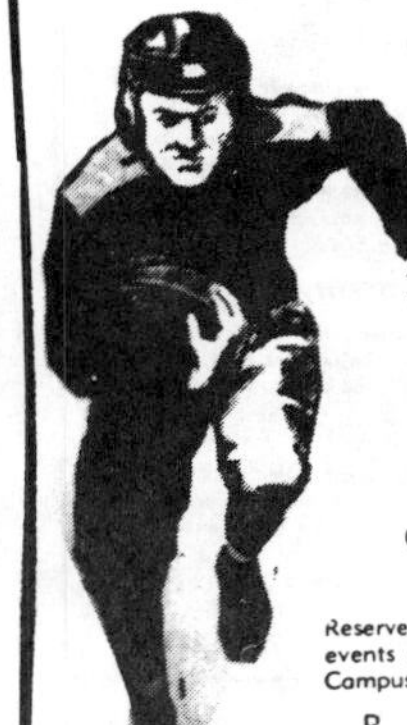

R. P. I. Opens Season Against Hamilton Tomorrow

HOPE TO AVENGE 1941 DEFEAT IN '86 FIELD BATTLE

Locals Lost Last Year, 21 to 0; Visitors To Have Experienced Team for Battle; Many in Service.

Rensselaer Polytechnic Institute's Fight Engineers will be out to avenge last year's 21-0 defeat by Hamilton College when they open the 1942 season tomorrow on the '86 Field against the Continental eleven.

While the Hamilton College gridders will throw a fully experienced line into the game, there will be only two lettermen in the backfield. On the other hand, Rensselaer's Coach Graham wil lhave an experienced backfield, including Warren Lemke, last year's sophomore sensation and the team's high scorer, behind a line which includes four lettermen.

But Two Lettermen.

The No. 1 Cherry and White backfield is strictly a veteran group, with Lemke, of Troy, at fullback; Don McFarland, Tenafly, N. J., at tailback; Eddie Haller, Buffalo, on the wing, and Bill Baker, of Old Hickory, Tenn., as blocker. Alternating with McFarland, who is the team's only triple-threater, will be Ben Browne, New York, a light but shifty running back and the team's second high scorer from last season. Among the sophomore backs who should help out are George Cook, East Orange, N. J.; Niel Marshall, Hempstead, and Dick McLaughlin, Newton Center, Mass.

Desspite the absence of Foster Bentley, 215 pound tackle from Niagara Falls, who is out with a recurrence of old shoulder injury, the starting line looks relatively strong. Bob Peck, a Troy sophomore, who did well throughout practice despite his lack of experience, will probably fill in for Bentley.

Fortunately for Hamitlon, one of teh two backfield lettermen is the thoroughly dependable Milt Jannone, eastern touchdown ace, who ran wild last year against the Engineers. The other is "Cowboy Bob" Enery, a 160 pound back from Oklahoma. Phil Dodd, one of the Continental backfield aces, will be missing for the firts three or four weeks of the season while he undergoes an operation to qualify for the Navy's V-7 enlisting program.

Something Added.

Rounding out the Hamilton backfield will be two sophomores, one of whom Chuck Redmond, quarterback, never played football before he showed up at spring practice. The other is Bob Cowan, halfback.

R. P. I. may find that something new has been added to Jannone's bag of tricks, if last week's scrimmage at Clinton is any indication of what Coach Campbell Dickson has in mind. The Continental squad has taken to the air with aJnnone on the passing end.

Last year Forest Evashevski, Hamilton's grid coach who is now in the Navy together with "Duke" Nelson, R. P. I. mentor, said the Hamilton team didn't have any system; or if it did it was one in which everyone blocked for Jannone. But whatever it was that enabled Hamitlon to run up five victories in seven starts for the best season in years is not likely to be interfered with by Coach Dickson who, like Evashevski, is a Crisler-school produce. Dickson served Crisler as end coach and scout for seven years at Princeton and Michigan and in the war emergency has added coaching football in his previous job of dean.

With 15 gridmen enrolled in the Army, Navy, or Marine Reserves, Hamilton has preserved last year's squad pretty well intact barring the loss of seniors. Six lettermen were graduated in June. But, however the squad shapes up, much will depend on Jannone who ran up 16 touchdowns against seven opponents last year. Used sparingly, aJnnone was given the ball only 103 times during the season and on those occasions he advanced for an average of seven yards per try.

R. P. I. Gridders Pry Off Lid with Hamilton

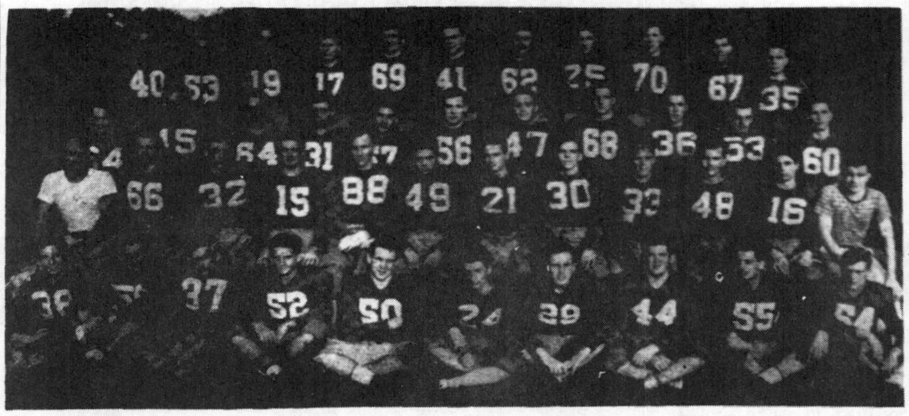

Grouped above are members of Rensselaer Polytechnic Institute's 1942 football squad. They get under way tomorrow against Hamilton on the home field. With several returning veterans, the Engineers hope for another successful season, now under the guidance of Coach Paul Graham.

In the photo are, first row, left to right: Richard Wulf, Troy; Newell Whitcomb, Lyons; Robert Watchmaker, Brookline, Mass.,; Grant H. Lennox, Springfield, N. J.; Martin T. Davis, West Hartford, Conn.; Seymour Margulies, Montville, Mass.; William A. Miller, Pittsburg, Pa.; Stanton Parrish, Salem; Paul Jacobson, Brooklyn; John P. Reimherr, Troy.

Second row, left to right: Coach Paul Graham; Warren Lemke, Troy; Robert Landon, Winnetka, Ill.; Dale H. Brown, South Orange, N. J.; George Frank, Staten Island; Alfred E. Krug, Yonkers; Donald McFarland, Tenafly, N. J.; Louis Nieliwocki, Albany; Edward Haller, Buffalo; Robert M. Curran, Cohoes; Benjamin Browne, New York City; Manager John E. Flavin, jr.

Third row, left to right: John L. Cummings, Schenectady; Richard Nickerson, Cranston, R. I.; Foster Bentley, Niagara Falls; David Lurie, Mt. Vernon; Jack Richards, Montclair, N. J.; Augustus Brinnier, Kingston; Joseph Klopotowski, Paterson, N. J.; Robert Peck, Troy; George A. Harper, Middlebury, Conn.; George Powell, Baldwin; Arthur Zimet, Great Neck.

Top row, left to right: Arnold Beckhardt, Coatesville, Pa.; Hubert Mattice, Middleburg; Neil Marshall, Hempstead; William J. Baker, Old Hickory, Tenn.; Richard Bacon, Hermosa Beach, Cal.; Charles Horsfall, Ossining; Barrett Sand, Schenectady; George D. Cook, East Orange, N. J.; Elwin Stevens, Hoosick Falls; Stephen Yerazunis, Pittsfield, Mass.,; Lyance Littlejohn, Westhampton.

NICK ALEXANDER FACES BEARCATS IN SUNDAY GAME

Like Ol' Man River, Nick Alexander of the Amsterdam pro gridders, who will come to Troy Sunday night to face the Troy Bearcats, just goes on and on.

Year after year, the big back, who played first for Amsterdam High and then for Providence College, appears for the Carpet City club and though he did seem to be slowing down last season, still packs plenty of punch when ramming the opposition's line.

Sunday marks the first appearance of the "new Bearcats," as fans have chosen to call them since the war has caused better than a 50 per cent turnover in personnel. Many are anxious to see LeRoy Collier, Albany Negro, who dazzled fans in this area as a scholastic ball carrier.

Over the long period of years that the Bearcats and Amsterdam club have been meeting, the Trojans hold a 7 to 3 advantage in games won and lost.

Last year the Bearcats wound up their very successful season by defeating the Amsterdam club, 25 to 7, on Thanksgiving Day. Three of the players who figured strongly in the scoring of the Bearcat touchdowns in that game will be present and in the Bearcat lineup Sunday night.

One is Pete Stanish, the Albany back, who caught one of the two touchdowns passes heaved by Mike Gully. Second is Tom Zippitelli, who caught another Gully-heaved score. And third is Pete DeMarco, who made his only tally as a Bearcat when he gathered in a fumble and ran 45 yards to score. Missing, along with Mike Gully, will be Art Laurence who ran 71 yards for the fourth Troy score. Both are in the Army.

Sunday's game will be at 8:15 with Walt Eckerson and Sven Rosengren doing the refereeing and umpiring.

JOINS FOOTBALL GIANTS.

New York (AP)—Harold Hall, former Springfield College center, has joined the New York football Giants and will be used as relief for Mel Hein. The Giants also announced that Ward Cuff, veteran back, has been engaged to coach the Cardinal Hayes High School of New York squad but will continue to play with the New York club.

Robinson Favorite For Tonight's Bout

BY JACK CUDDY

New York (U.P.)—They're trying to get young Ray Robinson licked tonight. They believe that a beating will be the best thing that ever happened to Robinson, the streamlined young Negro who has registered 35 straight professional victories.

So they've tossed him into the ring with a middleweight, Jack La Motta of the Bronx, who will outweight Robinson about 158 pounds to 144—or 14 pounds.

Robinson accepted this match because he figures there's no more worth-while competition in the 147-pound division because (1) Champion Freddie Cochrane, now in the Army, has been ordered to Pearl Harbor, (2) Fritzie Zivic is campaigning in the west, and (3) Jackie Wilson of Los Angeles is in the Army and may not be permitted to fight

Hence it is that young Robinson, Harlem's dancing dynamiter, moves out of his class for an oponent. He is willing to pack the saddle-load of about 14 pounds to square off against the "Human Tank," La Motta, who has suffered but four defeats in his 39 bouts. And La Motta at 21, is the same age as Robinson, and a guy who's been fighting middleweights.

They're fighting only ten rounds at Madison Square Garden, but that distance is quite enough to determine whether slender Robinson shall continue in his role as one of the greatest fighters that ever lived or whether he must bow to a grand "club fighter" in the division above him.

Personally we believe that Robinson will overcome the weight handicap and knock out the bigger man. We expect Ray to belt out his bigger adversary within six rounds.

Robinson, the greatest all-around fighter we ever have seen, enters the ring a 2-1 favorite, despite the difference in poundage. And we say the odds are right because we believe that no human being within fifty pounds of Robinson's weight has any chance against him. He's that fast—that clever—and that explosive with either hand. Moreover, Robinson has the footwork. He can knock you dead with either hand while he's sliding away.

But it may be that La Motta will give him plenty of trouble. La Motta is a body-punching specialist who will go to work on Robinson's wasp waist. La Motta is a guy who keeps pressing forward—always in close, where Robinson doesn't like to fight. And La Motta is a tough kid who never has been knocked out — and who has beaten such promising middleweights as Jimmy Reeves and Jimmy Edgar.

If La Motta licks Robinson, that will be a story, indeed, and he might do it if he doesn't get hit on the chin by either of Ray's explosive fists."

Racing Notes

By The Associated Press.

A return duel between Alsab and Whirlaway was assured today after Trainer Sarge Swenke announced that Al Sabath's Chicago charger would be a definite starter in tomorrow's Jockey Club Gold Cup at Belmont.

The Sab came out of his easy triumph in Tuesday's Lawrence Realization in fine condition and the stable intends to send him after the winner's share of the $25,000 added money in the two-mile classic run under weight-for-age conditions.

Alsab will re ridden by Carroll Bierman and Whirlaway by George Woolf. That makes the setup for tomorrow's race the same in every respect, except for distance, as when the two met ten days ago in the Narragansett Championship, which Alsab won by a scant nose.

The Gold Cup is exactly thirteen-sixteenths of a mile longer than the Narragansett affair.

Others expected to go to the post tomorrow include T. B. Martin's Bolingbroke, conqueror of Whirlaway in the Manhattan Handicap last Saturday at a mile and a half; Maxwell Howard's Party Buster, and L. B. Mayer's King's Abbey.

Most jockeys have a favorite saddle or a lucky whip, but George Woolf has both. He has used them in winning stakes races that add up to more than $1,500,000, and he has used them in overnight events.

He will use them both at least twice at Belmont tomorrow, on Whirlaway in the Jockey Club Gold Cup and on Occupation in the Futurity.

The saddle was worn by Phar Lap in the last $100,000 Agua Caliente Handicap. The Australian jockey who rode Phar Lap gave it to Woolf when he sailed for home after the great horse died.

It is a large saddle of the English type but is surprisingly light for its size. It weighs only three pounds and Woolf says it fits horses better than any saddle he ever saw.

Mrs. Tilyou Christopher's Doublerab, the season's outstanding sprinter, suffered a stunning defeat at Belmont yesterday, finishing last in the seven-horse field in the Vosburgh Handicap, won by C. V. Whitney's Parasang.

It was the third straight failure for the 4-year-old sprint champ since he suffered a filled ankle at Saratoga in August. He was forced to carry 132 pounds in his 54th outing of the year.

Parasang, under 112 pounds, scored by a length and a half with Don Mead in the saddle, covering the seven furlongs in 1:23 flat and paying $13.10 for $2. The Greentree Stable's Devil Diver was second, five lengths in front of G. D. Widener's Rosetown.

With the Maryland Futurity only eight days away, owners of home-bred 2-year-olds are pointing their charges for the $5,000 six-furlong affair which always is one of the highlights of the Laurel meeting.

Among those regarded as certain to start in the Futurity, Oct. 10, are A. J. Abel's Dot's Key, W. L. Brann's Persita, either Rough Oney or Rough Doc from the Yancey Christmas Barn, Alan T Clarke's Nellie Mowlee, Mrs. R. H. Heighe's Adroit, O. L. Bonifay's Little Hoops, Jerome H. Loucheim's Ecomint, Mrs. Chester A. Lyon's Gallant Mowlee, A. G. Vanderbilt's Zanzibar and S. B. Casilear's Lost and Found.

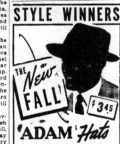

Cullenbine Safe After Fancy Slide

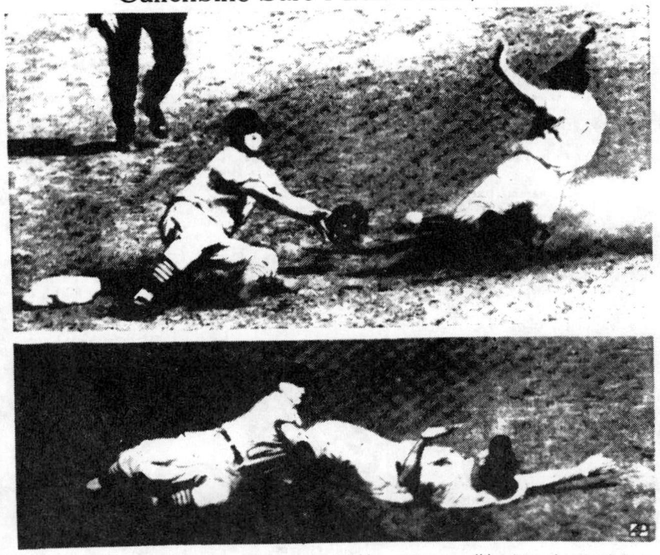

Hands up, Roy Cullenbine, Yankee rightfielder, starts a slide toward second base (above) as he steals in the eighth inning of the second World Series game at St. Louis. He comes in safely (below) on his back, as Jimmy Brown, Cardinal second baseman, drops the ball. Cullenbine later scored the first Yankee run, but the Cards won, 4-3.

CORNELL PRIMED FOR BATTLE WITH ANDY KERR'S MEN

Albany (AP)—Cornell's sophomores, who have done it before, will try it again tomorrow at Ithaca against Andy Kerr's Colgate football team, primed this time to win its first decision in six starts against the Big Red.

Kerr's veteran-sprinkled Red Raiders are a slight choice but acutely aware that "Green" Cornell clubs sprawled Colgate, 40-7, in 1937 and 21-2 last autumn.

The clash between the "Big Three" members heads an upstate card in which the largest bloc of minor interest centers on Bud Degroot's powerful little Rochester University outfit.

The Yellow Jackets, who had their best season in years last fall and are rated even better by Degroot, collide with Washington and Jefferson at Rochester. Rochester opened with a 26-0 verdict last week over Depauw.

Syracuse, the other big team, plays Boston University under Archbold Stadium lights tomorrow night.

Six sophomores probably will start for Cornell which has had only one close shave with Colgate—a 14-12 in 1939—since they resumed their arguments in 1937.

Carl Snavely's team barely survived a closing Lafayette rush last week for a 20-16 decision, but as a young outfit is bound to profit by the experience. The Leopards are rated higher than little St. Lawrence which Colgate stiff-armed, 49-0.

The sophs concern Colgate. One, Wally Kretz ripped off 65 and 75-yard touchdown trips fired a payoff aerial against Lafayette. Another, win Wright, will operate at fullback and a third, Jack Saylor, a bruising blocker, will make an interloper of "Old" Charlie Robinson, a junior halfback who does the punting. Junior speedster Sam Pierce, who scored twice last year against Colgate, is on the injury list this time.

Syracuse, 58-6 winner over Clarkson last week, will have to go a little faster against Boston University's Terriers in the night game that will permit Coach Ossie Solem to scrutinize both Cornell and Colgate in the afternoon.

The rest of the Saturday card:

St. Lawrence vs. University of Buffalo; Union vs. Hobart at Geneva; Cortland Teachers vs. Clarkson at Potsdam; Hamilton vs. Rensselaer Poly at Troy, and Hartwick vs. Penn Military College at Chester, Pa.

Ithaca College opens its season tonight at Reading, Pa., against Albright. Canisius and St. Bonaventure duel in a western New York little three classic Sunday at Buffalo.

TECH SOCCERMEN OPEN TOMORROW AGAINST HAMILTON

With the return of Freeman Hartnell, captain-elect and high scorer of the soccer team two years ago, the R. P. I. booters are looking forward to another successful season and are working out regularly under the eye of Coach Dick Schmelzer in preparation for their opening game against Hamilton at Clinton tomorrow.

Hartnell, who was not in school last year, was the spearhead of attack for the 1940 aggregation and scored ten out of the 11 goals made by the Cherry and White that season. His presence again at center forward should give Schmelzer's booters a real scoring punch.

Hamilton is not expected to give the Fighting Engineers stiff opposition. Last year the R. P. I. booters staged an impressive 5 to 1 victory over the Continentals on the home field.

Returning from last year's team, many outstanding players will again represent the Institute. In the goal will be Fred Schultz, Stillwater, a junior who played a great game in the cage last season. Capt. Fred Schubert, a senior from Rochester, will hold down the left fullback position where he has been outstanding for two years. Schubert is considered by Schmelzer and coaches of opposing teams to be one of the outstanding fullbacks in collegiate circles. William Sloan, a junior from La Grange, Ill., will fill the other fullback spot vacated by his classmate Dick Knoeckel, who is now in the Air Corps.

At center halfback the likely candidate is again Henri Montero, of Lima, Peru, a junior, while the left halfback position will be played by George Mohn, Robesonia, Pa., another junior. Sophomores William Peace of Akron, O., and Robert Fischer, of Guatemala, will alternate at right half back.

Outside and inside left will be well taken care of by the Teran brothers, Manuel and Felix, juniors from Yucatan, Mexico. Manuel was leading high scorer last year while Felix finished as runner-up. On the other end of the forward line, James Dukes, of Fort Leavenworth, Kan., a senior, will play the outside position while Alvaro Calero, Cali, Colombia, junior, will fill the inside spot.

Among the sophomores are several regulars from last year's frosh team, including Robert Campbell, Watertown, Mass., and Lindsay Collin, Westfield, N. J. The Cherry and White is further strengthened by several freshmen reserves who are now eligible for varsity competition.

SPORTS MIRROR

By the Associated Press.

Today a Year Ago—New York Yankees' string of ten successive World Series victories was snapped by Whitlow Wyatt of Brooklyn Dodgers as he beat Yanks, 3-2, in second game of series.

Three Years Ago—Ceferino Garcia won world's middleweight championship (New York-California version) by knocking out Fred Apostoli in seven rounds at New York.

Five Years Ago—Minnesota suffered its second defeat in five years at Golden Gophers were upset by Nebraska, 14-9.

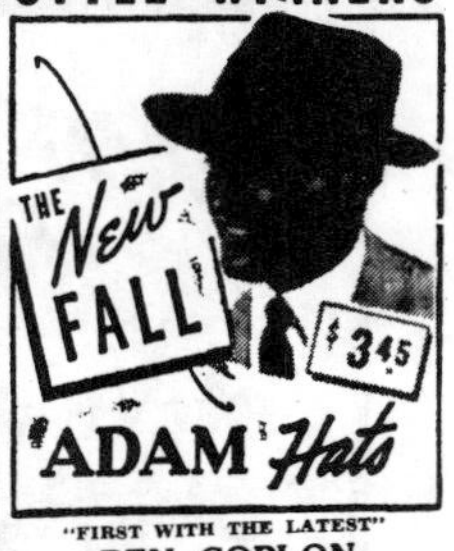

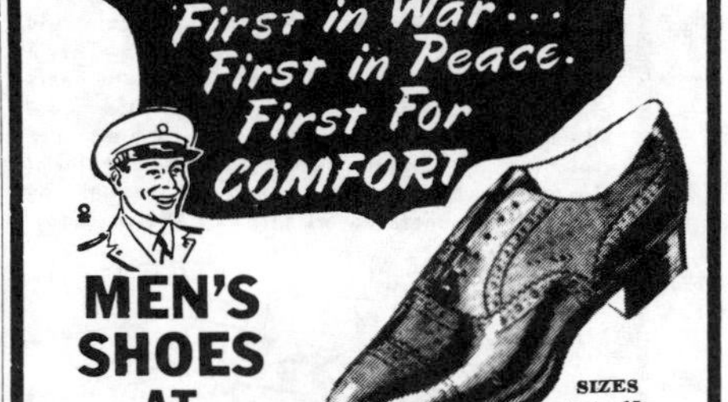

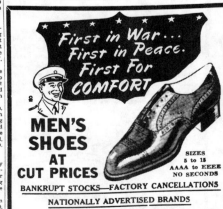

Only 25¢ PENETRO COLD MISERIES
for colds' coughing, sniffles and muscle aches get the salve with the base of old-fashioned mutton suet Grandma liked.

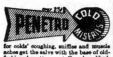

CADET VISITS HOME.

Flight Cadet C. Fred Schwarz, jr., who has completed his primary training at Massachusetts State College, is visiting his parents, Mr. and Mrs. C. Fred Schwarz of 451 Broadway. He will return to Amherst within a week for his secondary training.

NOT EVERY WOMAN IS UNDER TWENTY

We believe a woman looks lovely when her hair is styled as suits the age she appears to be. So if you look past twenty—let us suggest an appropriately stunning hair style for you—whom added years make beautiful in a very special way!

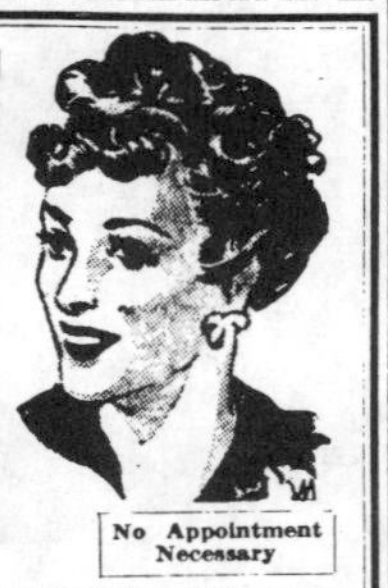

"VAPER-CURL"
A NEW STYLE CROQUIGNOLE PERMANENT WAVE $2
No Appointment Necessary

STEAM and OIL PERMANENT WAVE Complete $3.00	"VONETTE" Includes Feather Bob Hair Style $4.00	Water Processed MACHINELESS Permanent Wave $4.50
"EMPIRE" Including $1.50 Haircut & Shaping $5.00	'PARK AVENUE' Machineless A deluxe Permanent $6.50	"Little Princess" A Permanent Wave for the 6 to 12s $3.50

CHARM BEAUTY SALON
CLAFFEY OPERATED
5 THIRD ST. TROY 6943
Open 8 A. M. to 9 P. M.—With or Without Appointment

CLERGYMEN ATTEND FUNERAL SERVICES FOR COUNTY PASTOR

Clergy of the Troy Conference of the Methodist Church attended and took part in funeral services yesterday for Rev. William B. Goodman, pastor of the Center Brunswick Methodist Church, who died Thursday. A prayer service with Rev. Edward Bowers, former pastor, in charge, was held at the parsonage at 2 p.m. Rev. Cassius J. Miller, D. D., former district superintendent, officiated at the funeral held at 2:30 p.m. from the church. Rev. Samuel Spear of Broadalbin and Rev. Robert B. Leslie, retired Methodist pastor, also took part in the services.

Members of the official board of the church acted as bearers: Howard E. Wagar, John Howe, William Keyes, Harold Keyes, Robert Manderville and Francis Both. Two of the official board members, Harold E. Wilson and Frank Banker, also aided in the arrangements. Burial was in Elmwood Cemetery, Schaghticoke.

THREE HURT WHEN AUTO STRIKES POLE

Forced off the Saratoga Springs-Albany highway two miles north of Round Lake yesterday afternoon, Ambrose Gambrell of Port Henry drove his car into two poles, causing injuries to three companions. Marcel Freeman, a boy, was cut about the face; Mildred Torrante, 17, suffered fractured ribs and a bruised right leg; Rosemary Gambrell, 6, sprained her right ankle. State Trooper John B. Miliman of Spa Barracks investigated.

THREE TROY AREA PILOTS COMPLETE TRAINING SCHOOL

Trio Will Be Commissioned Lieutenants in Army Air Forces at Exercises Tomorrow.

Three Troy Area youths, members of the eighth class of aviation second lieutenants in the army air Flying School near Columbus, Miss., will be commissioned as second lieutenants in the army forces upon their graduation from the school tomorrow.

The three lieutenants are: John W. Willcox, 22, son of Mrs. G. E. Moore of Route 1, Watervliet; Homer J. Phoenix, 24, son of Mr. and Mrs. W. E. Phoenix, 335 Fourth Street, Troy, and George W. Gregware, 22, son of Mr. and Mrs. Eugene Gregware 156 Hudson Avenue, Green Island. They entered pilot training in January and attended flying school at Avon Park, Fla, and Greenville, Miss., before enrolling in the advanced flying school from which they have just graduated.

Two other Troy soldiers, Pvt. Francis J. Hope, son of Mr. and Mrs. F. S. Hope of East Park Place and Pvt. Nicholas F. Walsh, jr., son of Mr. and Mrs. Nicholas F. Walsh, sr., of Bouton Road, have been recently graduated from the Army Air Force Technical School at Scott Field, Ill., where they studied radio operation.

At the Navy Training Station at Newport, R. I., three Troy Area men have completed their basic training and have been selected to attend Navy trade schools: Guy C. Nickerson, 20, of 31 George Street, Green Island, son of Mr. and Mrs. G. Nickerson; William F. Banker, 20, of 834 Fifth Avenue, Troy, son of Mr. and Mrs. William F. Banker, and Nicholas J. Ferramosca, 24, of 33 Hoosick Street, son of Mrs. Julia Ferramosca. Ferramosca, who will attend a school for hospital corpsmen, was employed by Cluett, Peabody & Co., after his graduation from the Troy High school in 1937.

Nickerson was active in sports at Heatly High School from which he was graduated in 1941. He was employed by Montgomery Ward and will now attend a school for radio men.

Banker attended Lansingburg High School and worked as a pipefitter at the American Locomotive Co. in Schenectady before he entered the Navy. His wife is the former Helen E. Nolin.

At Camp Upton, Mayor Charles G. Maloy of Rensselaer, who volunteered to enter the Army, has passed through the processing line and is bound for the fighting front as a private. Aged 38, he is a member of the law firm of Kahn and Maloy.

Local Youths Earn Wings

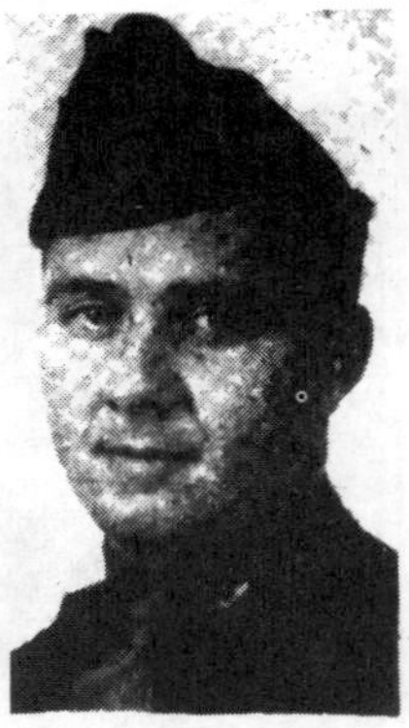

HOMER J. PHOENIX.

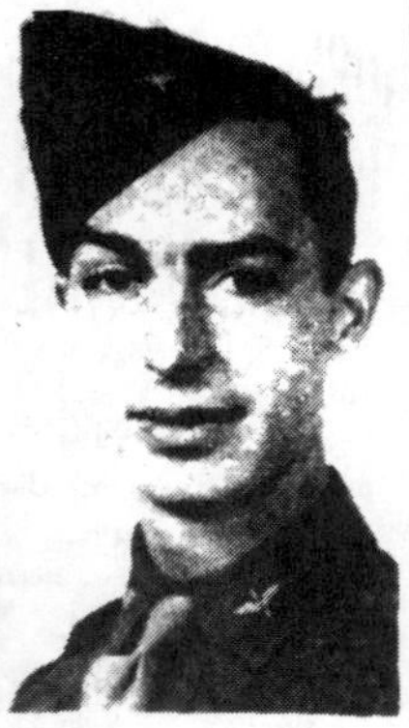

JOHN W. WILLCOX.

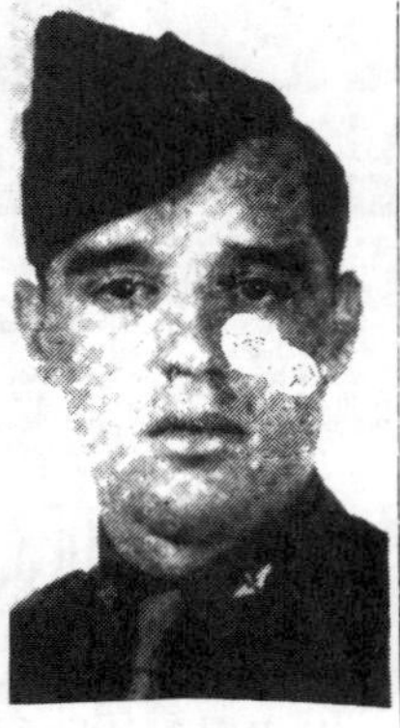

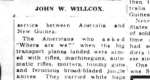

GEORGE W. GREGWARE.

WALLACE URGES NEW TYPE STATE AFTER WAR ENDS

Vice President Would Blend American and Soviet Systems Into Common Democracy.

New York, (AP)—Vice President Wallace said yesterday that Americans and Russians alike are deeply interested in fashioning a new "democracy of the common man" for the post-war world.

"This new democracy will be neither communism of the old-fashioned internationalist type nor democracy of the old-fashioned isolationist sort," he predicted in an adress prepared for the Congress of American-Soviet Friendship at Madison Square Garden.

Instead, he said, it should be a blend of "political bill of rights democracy," economic democracy, ethnic democracy educational democracy and democracy in the treatment of the sexes.

An "international T. V. A." and an international bank must be organized, he added.

"The first article in the international law of the future is undoubtedly the United Nations' Charter," Wallace said, explaining that document included the Atlantic Charter originally agreed upon by President Roosevelt and Prime Minister Churchill and now signed on behalf of thirty nations.

As "a starter" for a post-war public works program, the Vice President suggested "a combined highway and airway from southern South America across the United States, Canada, and Alaska, into Siberia and on to Europe with Feeder highways and airways from China, India and the Middle East.

He said he broached that project to Vyacheslav Molotov, the Soviet foreign commissar, when the Russian visited the United States last spring. Wallace recalled that Molotov's first reaction was "no one nation can do that by itself," but later he said, "you and I will live to see the day."

Declaring that the various kinds of democracy "must be woven together into a harmonious whole," Wallace declared:

"Some in the United States believe that we have overemphasized what might be called political or bill-of-rights democracy. Carried to its extreme form, it leads to rugged individualism, exploitation, impractical emphasis on states' rights, and even to anarchy.

GIRLS MARK STOCK BOARD.

San Francisco, (U.P.)—For the first time in the history of the San Francisco Stock Exchange girls now are being used for marking up quotations.

AIR-BORNE YANKS THREATEN JAPS ON NEW GUINEA

Probable Sinking of Two Nipponese Warships in Solomons Zone Reported by U. S. Navy.

By THE ASSOCIATED PRESS

Jungle-trained U. S troops menaced the Buna-Gona Japanese beachhead on the northeast New Guinea shore from all sides today after a bold mass movement of the troops by air from Australia, the greatest military transfer of infantrymen by plane in the nation's history.

These hardened fighting men, clad in motley green fatigue uniforms, had filtered through central and northern Papua and appeared to have flanked a tough nest of Japanese resistance at Oivi, 45 miles south of Buna, where Australian troops were fighting after driving over the rugged Owen Stanley Range.

Gen. Douglas MacArthur said his men now controlled all of Papua—the long eastern stretch of New Guinea except the Buna-Gona area.

The probable sinkings of a Japanese light cruiser and a destroyer in the vicinity of the Solomons Saturday was announced yesterday by the Navy in Washington in a communique which reported that the advance of American troops eastward on Guadalcanal Island was continuing.

Motor torpedo boats attacked two enemy destroyers north of the American positions on Guadalcanal Saturday morning, and one of the ships was believed to have been sunk. That afternoon American planes attacked enemy surface ships about 150 miles north of Guadalcanal, badly damaging a light cruiser and one of ten destroyers.

The Navy said the cruiser possibly was sunk, and that the enemy also lost twelve planes which attempted to intercept the attacking American aircraft. However, four of the American planes failed to return.

All Japanese remnants in the Milne Bay sector of New Guinea at the extreme eastern tip had been cleared and Allied forces had occupied Goodenough Island, the westernmost of the Dentrecastreaux group thirty miles northeast of Milne Bay.

The great plane - transported odyssey was flown 600 miles across the exotic Coral Sea from Australia in October, unhindered by Japanese opposition. Troop carriers swiftly reinforced the sky troopers by sea in a swift ferry shuttle service between Australia and New Guinea.

The Americans who asked "Where are we?" when the big transport planes landed were armed with rifles, machineguns, automatic rifles, mortars, tommy guns and ferocious broad-bladed jungle knives. They carried white bags filled with rice, a trick learned from the Japanese. The number of air-borne troops was not disclosed but they were in considerable force, well trained, well equipped and eager "to give those little men plenty of condensed hell," as Pvt. Kyle Granger of Los Angeles put it.

Swiftly, after the American transport planes landed, the Americans plunged into the task of working their way by devious means across New Guinea's mountains and northwestward along the coast through one of the world's most difficult battlefields.

For days the bivouacked Americans had been awaiting orders to close in on the Japanese from their positions in Central and Northern New Guinea. Among troops under the American command were Mexicans, Arabians and Chinese.

The invasion of Goodenough Island was a short, sharp action on Oct. 23 in a raging tropical storm. The strongly entrenched Japanese garrison soon was routed and the remnants escaped to a nearby island where they were removed by an enemy warship Oct 27. The Japanese landed on Goodenough Sept. 26 with 400 men and probably were reinforced.

Whether the Americans in the Buna-Gona vicinity had yet opened siege on the Japanese base, first taken July 22, was not indicated.

Australian reports said the Japanese at Oivi obviously had been given orders to resist to the death, which was coming to them swiftly by gun, bayonet and by Douglas bombers. Japanese air support was almost wholly lacking.

The flowering of Gen. MacArthur's carefully laid plan for the reconquest of northeastern New Guina gave life to the commander's words upon assuming command in the Southwest Pacific. He said then that the campaign for Australia would be fought in New Guinea.

Never before had the United States moved such large numbers of soldiers by air. It was the first time also that Gen. MacArthur had sent his American foot soldiers into combat with the Japanese since the Philippines campaign.

One of those arriving by plane was Sgt. Frank Peterson of New Haven, Conn., who said that during the trip he crouched in an aisle reading a magazine. He said he was too excited to sleep.

Women Defense Workers
KNITCRAFT SHOPPE
9 Third St., Troy
offers
Slack Sets
Sizes 12-52
*Gabardine
Flannels
*Corduroy
Also Slacks $1 up
Complete line of Sweaters and Skirts (Debs to Stouts)

Saturdays 9 to 6
Office Hours 9 to 8 Daily
DR. F. V. SUTLAND
DENTIST
30 FOURTH ST
TROY N. Y.
Phone 6406

MACHINE OPERATORS!
DO YOUR PART IN THIS CRITICAL WAR EFFORT AND MAKE GOOD MONEY
NEED OPERATORS ON SINGLE AND DOUBLE NEEDLE MACHINES, MACHINE BUTTONHOLERS, MACHINE BUTTON SEWERS, MACHINE BARTACKERS AND ALSO CAN USE SOME LEARNERS.
(People already engaged in war production work need not apply).
WULTEX FACTORY
CONGRESS AT FIFTEENTH ST.

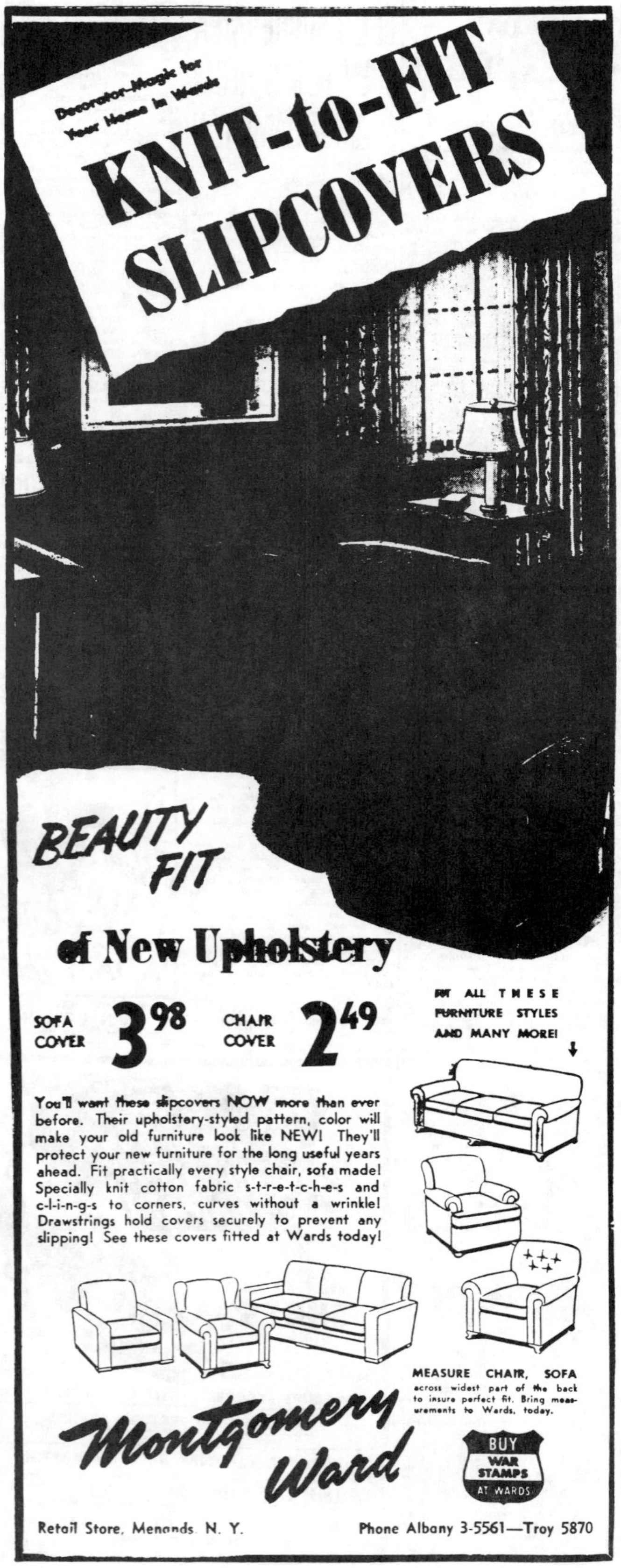
Decorator-Magic for Your Home at Wards
KNIT-to-FIT SLIPCOVERS
BEAUTY FIT of New Upholstery
SOFA COVER 3.98
CHAIR COVER 2.49
FIT ALL THESE FURNITURE STYLES AND MANY MORE!
You'll want these slipcovers NOW more than ever before. Their upholstery-styled pattern, color will make your old furniture look like NEW! They'll protect your new furniture for the long useful years ahead. Fit practically every style chair, sofa made! Specially knit cotton fabric s-t-r-e-t-c-h-e-s and c-l-i-n-g-s to corners, curves without a wrinkle! Drawstrings hold covers securely to prevent any slipping! See these covers fitted at Wards today!
MEASURE CHAIR, SOFA across widest part of the back to insure perfect fit. Bring measurements to Wards, today.
BUY WAR STAMPS AT WARDS
Montgomery Ward
Retail Store, Menands, N. Y.
Phone Albany 3-5561—Troy 5870

16 3rd ST., TROY
BERNER'S
Gift Center

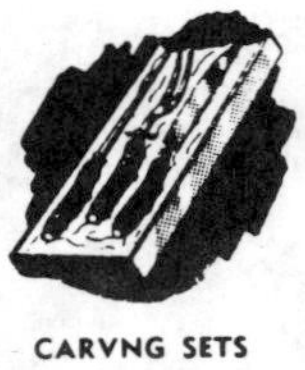

CARVNG SETS
FOR YOUR THANKSGIVING TURKEY
From 4.95 up
16 3rd ST., TROY

Just by Keeping Well YOU can help Win this War!

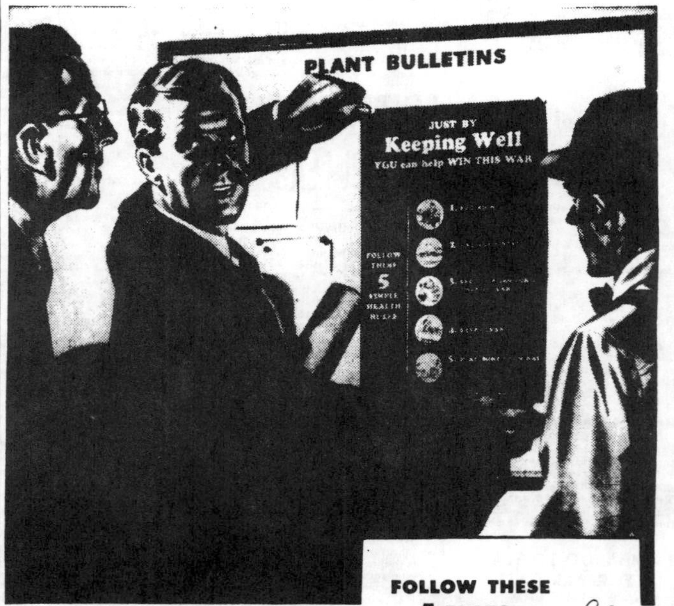
PLANT BULLETINS
JUST BY Keeping Well YOU can help WIN THIS WAR
FOLLOW THESE 5 SIMPLE HEALTH RULES

Salute to the men behind the scenes

You have heard of the country's growing doctor shortage. You know what it means—that while our doctors are away at war those of us at home must face the risks of epidemics and illnesses with fewer men of medicine and their professional aides.

• • •

But what is being done about this? What are we doing to protect ourselves to be sure that sickness doesn't reduce our all-important war production?

For one thing, your government is at work on the problem through the U. S. Public Health Service and many other agencies. You have probably seen other messages like this in your newspaper, which are the contribution of the Institute of Life Insurance to this important job.

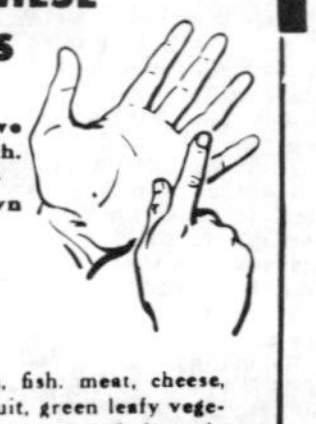

But the work hasn't stopped in the pages of your newspaper. Behind the scenes, thousands of life insurance agents throughout the country are doing a valuable part in helping you, your officials and health authorities to get by this wartime risk, without disaster.

• • •

Doubtless right here in your community, your city officials, your remaining doctors, your civic and business leaders and your own life insurance agent are co-operating in this vital health crusade.

Posters are being placed in school rooms, factories, and public buildings. Millions of copies of the five health rules are being distributed.

You can best show your co-operation with this crusade by following the five simple rules of health which are the backbone of the whole drive—the ways in which *you* can help to keep yourself and your own family well.

FOLLOW THESE 5 RULES

Memorize these five keys to good health. Follow them carefully—for your own welfare and for victory.

1. Eat right
Milk, butter, eggs, fish, meat, cheese, beans and peas, fruit, green leafy vegetables and the yellow ones, whole-grain or enriched cereals and bread—these are the *key* foods. Eat plenty of them. *And* eat 3 meals a day!

2. Get your rest
Regularity counts most. You can't catch up on *lost* sleep or *missed* relaxation! Try to keep on a regular schedule every day. Take it easy for a little while after lunch and dinner. Go to bed on time, get up on time.

3. See your doctor once a year
You have your *car* checked and serviced every thousand miles. Do as much for your body. Physicians can *prevent* many diseases and illnesses for both children and grownups nowadays. Give your doctor a chance *now*, BEFORE you get sick. Go to see *him!*

4. Keep clean
Plenty of baths, lots of soap. Clean hands, clothes, houses, beds! Get fresh air, sunshine. Drink lots of water.

5. "Play" some each day
Romp with the family, visit with friends, take walks, play games—or do whatever you like to give your mind and body a change from the daily grind on the job. "All work and no play makes Jack a dull boy."

Life insurance has provided the means to keep millions of Americans in health and security. This message is one way life insurance companies believe they can help you to win this war.
INSTITUTE OF LIFE INSURANCE, 60 EAST 42nd STREET, NEW YORK CITY

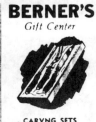

BELLS OF CHURCHES RING AGAIN IN BRITAIN

London (AP)—For the first time since June, 1940, Britain's church bells will ring Sunday in thanksgiving for the Eighth Army's victory in Egypt.

Church bells were silenced by the government when Hitler's invasion threat hung — over these islands and were ordered rung only in case of attack.

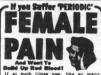

DOOLITTLE BARELY ESCAPES DEATH AS AIRPLANES BATTLE

Flying Fortress Proves More Than Match for Four German Pilots in Northern Africa

By WES GALLAGHER.
U. S. Correspondent with the A.E.F. in Africa.

Allied Headquarters in North Africa (AP)—Because a Flying Fortress proved more than a match for four German pilots who did not know what big game they were stalking, Brig. Gen James H. Doolittle, chief of the 12th Air Force, is continuing to direct the U. S. air attack against the Axis instead of lying dead.

Doolittle and 12 staff officers were attacked by four enemy planes. The co-pilot was wounded in a running gun battle and Doolittle took his place in the fighting ship.

This is the story of how the short-handed young Fortress crew led by Pilot Lieut. John C. Summers, of Lexington, Tenn., saved Doolittle and his staff officers, some of whom did not know they had been in a fight until the co-pilot fell to the floor covered with blood from a machine gun bullet in his shoulder. Among the officers on the Fortress was Lieut. Col. Joe Phillips, of New York.

The Fortress flew a few feet above water most of the time and it was short handed because of the large number of officers aboard.

When the four enemy planes were sighted the crew jumped to their posts. Most of the staff officers in the bomb bay were unaware of the approach of the planes.

The pilot turned and the enemy gave chase.

Just skimming the waves, the Fortress was not at its best operational height and in a few minutes the enemy took position above, ready to peel off on the speeding plane whose guns now were spitting fire.

The lead German plane dove down and met a burst from the Fortress' top guns. It wobbled and staggered off, badly hit.

The staff officers inside had heard the guns but, except for Doolittle and Phillips, who had seen the planes, they said nothing. They said later they thought the crew was "practicing."

The second and third Nazi planes attacked almost simultaneously. Machine-gun bullets smashed into the Fortress and the lieutenant co-pilot was hit in the shoulder. He fell to the floor.

One of the German planes was believed damaged badly enough. It appeared to be having difficulty gaining height.

Officers heard the bump of the co-pilot's fall. Opening the door to the pilot's cabin, they saw him on the floor, pulled him out, while General Doolittle, his floppy flyers' cap cocked tighter around his head, climbed in and took the co-pilot's place.

The last German plane turned in, made a half-hearted attack, and turned away.

"If those Germans had known we had the Commanding General of the 12th Air Force aboard they damn well would have stuck around or maybe the Fortress was just too much for them," one officer said.

Doolittle, with Summers, whose flying skill played a large part in the battle, flew the plane to its destination and the co-pilot was taken to a hospital.

In a few minutes after his arrival, the leader of the Tokyo raid was at his desk directing operations of his planes in North Africa. Nor was that the only aerial feat on this front. American parachutists staged the longest airborne invasion in history when they flew in transport planes 1,500 miles nonstop from England to participate in the assault on Oran.

The troops, led by Col. Ed. Raff of New York, 34-year-old West Point graduate, and wearing camouflaged battle suits, boarded planes early Saturday night and flew continuously for eight hours across Europe and the Mediterranean to land at dawn, Sunday near Oran.

None of the parachutists except Raff knew when they started where they were going.

Maj. Gen. Mark Clark, in discussing the feat, said "I called in Raff and told him what we planned and asked him if he thought it possible. He said 'Give me some time to think it over.'

"I had to leave the office, but in a few moments he came back and left me a note," the deputy supreme commander said. "It read: 'We can do it. But first I want my own battalion to do the job and I want personally to lead them.'"

Both requests were granted.

Despite the long night trip the troops arrived fighting fit.

The longest known previous airborne troop movement was in the Norwegian invasion when the Germans flew parachutists from fields near Namsos to Narvik, which is less than 400 miles. Nazi parachute troops attacking Crete had only a short jump.

HUNTING GUN STOLEN.

J. E. Damto of 18 North Church Street, Cortland, reported to the Detective Bureau yesterday that a hunting gun, valued at $25 was stolen from the trunk of his automobile while parked at Fulton and Front Streets.

Lose Something?

U. S. Men Shoot French Only On Resistance

By NOLAND NORGAARD
U. S. War Correspondent with the A.E.F. in North Africa

Headquarters of the Twelfth Air Force in Algeria, Nov. 10 (Delayed) (AP)—Broken remnants of a strong French tank and artillery column which was beaten away from this American-held airdrome straggled back to its base today unmolested by American planes.

The column which moved against this field from the French Foreign Legion base at Sidi Bel Abbes had been battered while moving to the attack but the Spitfires of Brig. Gen. James H. Doolittle's airmen didn't harass it in retreat and airforce officers explained:

We don't want to shoot Frenchmen and their troops won't be attacked except when they are moving to attack us.

The U. S. forces found that where the French decided to fight they fought well but there was equally strong evidence that many Frenchmen were just as anxious to avoid killing Americans as the Americans were eager to avoid killing Frenchmen.

A number of French prisoners already have asked permission to serve with the American troops and the ranks of these converts are expected to mount swiftly now that Oran has fallen.

The French and Arabs alike displayed strong resentment against the German-Italian Armistice Commission which systematically has stripped French North Africa of food, cotton cloth and other essentials.

News travels slowly in this land of few radios and poor communications and many Arabs in this vicinity learned only today of the Americans' arrival.

Outside Oran, scattered resistance continued throughout the day and sniping was reported from some towns and along roads.

Fighter planes sought out isolated gun positions, several of which were silenced by planes, cannon and machine-gun fire. Pilots reported destruction of six French tanks.

Along with the bullets went thousands of leaflets bearing Gen. Henri Giraud's call to the French to welcome the Americans as friends and avoid sabotage.

INDUSTRY NEEDS 5,000,000 MORE WOMEN WORKERS

Pittsburgh (AP)—Paul V. McNutt, chairman of the War Manpower Commission, declared yesterday that women are capable of doing 80 per cent of all war jobs and said that 5,000,000 more of them would be needed in industry and on the farms by the end of 1943.

"Women constitute our biggest single labor pool," he said in an Armistice Day speech prepared for delivery at a luncheon meeting of the Pittsburgh Chamber of Commerce and American Legion, adding "and they can perform many operations better than men."

McNutt said the nation's labor force would grow from 54,000,000 to "somewhere around 62,000,000 people," and declared manpower would have to be borrowed from civilian industries to get those extra 8,500,000.

FRENCH TRICOLOR RAISED AT BUFFALO

Buffalo (AP)—The French tricolor was restored to the walls of the Buffalo Navy Recruiting Station yesterday, a few hours after the Nazis marched into "unoccupied" France.

Capt. William A. Maguire, chaplain, who was in the thick of the Pearl Harbor attack, watched as the French colors were placed between flags of Norway and Great Britain. Flags of other United Nations also are hung from the walls of the station.

FRENCH REPORTED READY TO REVOLT

Member of DeGaulle Committee Addresses Hunter College Group.

New York (AP)—Andre Philip, commissioner of interior and labor in Gen. Charles de Gaulle's French national committee in London, declared last night that "there is complete unity among the French people who have been waiting to revolt."

"We have been slowly building a movement of resistance that today is expressing itself in the return of France into the war," said Philip, former leader of the underground movement in France. He asserted that the resistance of the French people "will continue despite the Nazi invasion of Unoccupied France."

He addressed an Armistice Day rally at Hunter College sponsored by France Forever, official organization of de Gaulle sympathizers in the United States.

"American troops in North Africa have again given France the hope of the return of liberty, truth and justice to her nation and have made possible the organization of a French government on French soil," Philip said.

DE BECK, FAMOUS CARTOONIST, DIES

New York (AP)—William Morgan "Billy" de Beck, 52, cartoonist who created "Barney Google" and many other comic strip characters, died yesterday after a long illness. His wife was at the bedside.

De Beck began his famous comic strip, in which many contemporary slang phrases were born, in 1919 when he joined King Features in New York.

The strip introduced the immortal "Spark-plug," a squint-eyed race horse which in cash earnings outran Cavalcade, Gallant Fox, War Admiral, Sea Biscuit and many other turf stars.

The inner part of a bread loaf is called the "crumb."

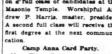

WATERVLIET NEWS

BRANCH OFFICE: 1715 BROADWAY — PHONE WATERVLIET 1593

YOUTHS WILL BE DEFERRED UNTIL CLOSE OF SCHOOL

Seven 'Teen Agers, Who Became 18 This Month, Have Enrolled With Selective Service Board.

Under the interpretation by Selective Service Board No. 346 of the regulations governing induction of students, 18 or twenty boys of this district who registered as 18 years old in December and January will be given deferrment from induction until the end of the present school year and the same will apply to more than half those expected to register between now and June.

The board calls attention of high school students now entering the second half of the school year to the fact that they are deferrable from induction until the end of the school year, according to the board's interpretation. This the board points out, applies to those who have not yet received notice of induction and who may, on completion of their questionnaires, apply formally to the board for postponement of induction until the end of the school year.

In addition they must file with the board a statement from their principal attesting to their standing in the institution. The ruling does not apply to college students.

Up to the present time, only seven have registered as having become 18 years old this month and it is not expected that many more will be registered. Warning, however, is given that the young men, on attaining their 18th birthday anniversaries, must register with the board that day or on the following day should the birthday anniversary fall on Sunday or a holiday.

Tonight the board will conduct examinations for those 'teen-agers who registered in December who will go to make up the March call. Quite a number have beaten the call by volunteering and about twenty of these will go in February.

The following volunteered yesterday to serve in the Navy: Francis Edward Wood of 104 Third Avenue, James Edward Byrnes of 1524 Avenue A and Leo John Boyland of 1908 Eighth Avenue.

Card Party Hostess.

Mrs. George Crall og 1519 Fifth Avenue will be the hostess at a card party Tuesday night at her home for the benefit of the Mothers' Club of the Sacred Heart of Mary School.

A. O. H. Will Meet.

Division No 1 A O H. will meet tomorrow night at 416 Fifteenth Street where a report will be received on the social last Saturday night from Owen Gilmutray, chairman.

To Conduct Socials.

Lieut. John A Patten Post, American Legion, will open its second series of socials tomorrow night in American Legion headquarters on Broadway. Albert Shorkey will be in charge.

Confer First Degree.

Rising Star Lodge, F and A M last night conferred the first degree on a full class of candidates at the Masonic Temple. Worshipful Andrew P. Harris, master, presided. A second full class will receive the first degree at the next communication.

Camp Anna Card Party.

Mrs. Ellen Buchanan and Mrs. Mrs. John J. Fitzgerald won the awards for high score at a card party last night sponsored by Camp Anna, R. N. of A., in the rooms, 416 Fifteenth Street.

The next party will be held Tuesday night in the association room.

WHY THOUSANDS OF DOCTORS ORDERED

Pertussin FOR Bad Coughs (DUE TO COLDS)

Pertussin must be good when thousands upon thousands of Doctors have prescribed it for so many years. Pertussin acts at once to relieve your coughing. It loosens and makes phlegm easier to raise. Safe and effective for both old and young. Inexpensive!

WEEKLY SOCIAL
8:30 P. M.
THURSDAY
Lt. John A. Patten Post
AMERICAN LEGION
1553 Broadway — Watervliet

GIRL SCOUT TROOP COLLECTS OLD SILK IN SALVAGE DRIVE

Yvonne Taylor, Lorraine Marchand, Jane Donnelly Win Prizes for Largest Amounts Taken Up.

Yvonne Taylor was awarded first prize among members of Troop 45, Girl Scouts, meeting at Jermain Memorial Presbyterian Church, Watervliet, last night for the collection of women's old silk and nylon stockings in connection with the present salvage drive being conducted for them. She collected 300 pairs.

Second prize went to Lorraine Marchand and third prize was won by Jane Donnelly. One of the prizes was donated by Harry Willis, chairman of the Watervliet salvage committee.

Special study groups were conducted at the meeting of the troop. Mrs. Norman Jacobsen, dramatics teacher at Watervliet High School, instructed the group working for their dramatic badges, and Mrs Reuben Graves was in charge of the group seeking design badges. Other study groups that were conducted were food, cooking, flag etiquette, and second class work (first aid).

Letters of appreciation from the Red Cross for money donated for ditty bags for soldiers, and toys donated at Christmas, were received.

MARCH OF DIMES WORKERS NAMED BY MISS FOGARTY

Rosary Society, Royal Neighbors of America, Thalian Group To Furnish Volunteers.

Miss Margaret Fogarty, chairman of the women's division of the March of Dimes campaign, today announced the workers who will serve in the collection booths at the National Bank of Watervliet and the Postoffice.

The Rosary Society of St. Bridget's Church has named the following women to be in charge at the bank from 9 a.m. to 2 p.m.: Mrs. C. B. Leonard, Mrs. George Lawlor, Mrs Margaret Farmer, Mrs Mary Schanz, Mrs John McMahon, Mrs Charles MacComber, Mrs Joseph Rainey, Mrs. James Dorgan, Mrs. Albert Dommer and Mrs. Frank Carr.

At the Postoffice tomorrow morning the Royal Neighbors of America will be in charge. The workers include Mrs Delia Hughes, Mrs Anna Leonard, Mrs. Betty Gilmurry and Mrs Margaret Shaughnessy.

The Thalian Society has named the following group to work tomorrow afternoon including the Misses Jean Fox, Agnes Fennessy, Gloria Dumont, Julie Behuniak, Marcia Voris, Betty Williams, Gloria Baker and Margaret Alston.

RED CROSS GROUP TO MAP CAMPAIGN FOR FUND RAISING

Executive Committee Will Meet Friday to Plan Details of Collecting Double Last Year's Total.

A newly appointed executive committee for the Watervliet division of the American Red Cross, which will arrange all details for the forthcoming fund campaign in March, will have its initial meeting Friday at 8:45 p.m. in Watervliet City Hall.

James D. McNary is general chairman of the executive group, with Mayor James F. Donlon as the honorary chairman. The members include J. Gregory Nealon, Joseph A. O'Hare, Joseph L. Lamb, Frank A. Mooney, C. A. Warren Davenport, Harry A. Rettie, Richard A. Hennessy, James A McLean, John J. Lapinski, John Dzbinski, Joseph D. Foley, William S Richmond, Earl W. Sargent, Mrs Valentine R. Gray, Mrs. Thomas Dowling, Mrs. Thomas Cavanaugh, Mrs. Harry Doust, Mrs. Thomas Berry, Mrs. John H. McMahon, Miss Ruth Gardner and Mrs. William Doring.

At Friday's meeting this group will complete organization plans and study details for the campaign in Watervliet.

It marks the first time that Red Cross activity in Watervliet has been guided by an executive committee and is in preparation for what will be the city's largest campaign. Last year's record collection of $16,000 is expected to be only half the sum to be collected this year.

The city will observe the Red Cross campaign dates on the same basis as other communities in the nation, starting March 1, and continuing for the month.

However, because of the number of industrial plants where much time and effort must be directed, the executive committee plans to have its activity well underway by the March 1 starting date.

AXIS BROADCASTERS WERE WRONG AGAIN ON ALLIED PARLEY

Washington (AP). The Axis radio was wrong again.

Only three hours before last night's announcement of the Roosevelt-Churchill conference, the radio station at Calais said:

"Churchill, who as is well known at present is staying in Washington, has been confronted by the Americans with new territorial demands in Trinidad and Jamaica as a result of which Halifax has tendered his resignation as British ambassador. After the conclusion of his visit to Washington Churchill will proceed to Moscow."

At 10:15 p.m. (E.W.T.) 15 minutes after the news of the conference had been made public in Allied countries, the Berlin radio in an English-language broadcast to North America reported "rumors that Churchill is again visiting Roosevelt and Eleanor in Washington" and added that "we would not be surprised if London came out one of these days with a lot of big noise about it."

Finally, at 11:30 p.m. (E.W.T.) the Berlin radio broadcast a brief, correct news summary of the conference without comment.

In December Axis broadcasters said Prime Minister Churchill had come to North America for another conference. Reporters on December 28 asked Stephen Early, White White secretary, whether Churchill was here and received the response:

"I don't know that he is and I don't know that he isn't, and if I did know I wouldn't tell you."

EAST SIDE.

A successful white elephant sale was conducted last evening at Mrs. David Wilkins' home, 32 Ford Avenue. Proceeds will go towards the treasury of the Women's Guild of the Third Presbyterian Church. The affair was arranged by the January group of that society. Assisting Mrs. Wilkins was Mrs Mae Mealey as cochairman; Mrs. Willard Ramsdall, donations; Mrs Harry E. Duran and Miss Betty Post, waitresses; Mrs. Charles Brunelle, auctioneer; Mrs. Berton Smith and Mrs. Karl Pendt, assistant auctioneers, and Mrs. Marie Dunham and Mrs Frank Whalen, wrappers.

Personal.

Mrs Elmo E. Oakhout of 29 Maple Avenue is visiting her brother and sister-in-law, Mr. and Mrs. Raymond M. Snyder and family at Indianapolis, Ind.

Talks on "Prayer."

Rev. John M. Stuart, pastor of the Third Presbyterian Church will continue his talks on "Prayer" today in the church at 7:45 p.m. Choir rehearsal will follow. Sewing for the Red Cross will be held tomorrow from 10 a.m. until 4 p.m. in the Sunday School rooms. Mrs. James Beale will have charge of the distribution of work.

REPORTED MISSING.

Edward A. Murtaugh, son of Edward A. Murtaugh of Hampton Manor, has been reported missing in action in the Navy's newest casualty list.

WATERVLIET ELKS' SOCIAL
EVERY WEDNESDAY NIGHT AT 8:30

Historic Conference Site

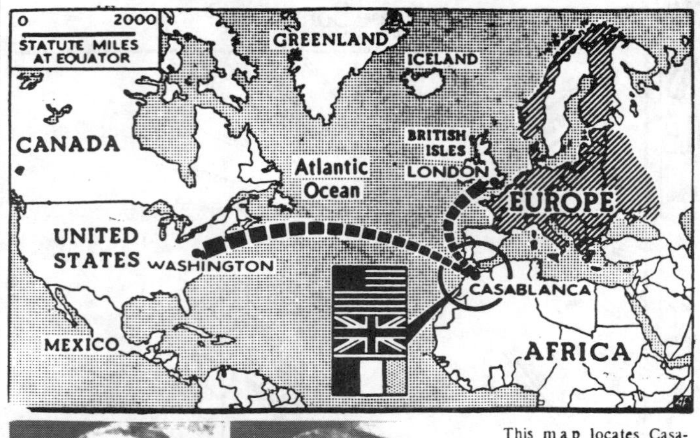

This map locates Casablanca, on the coast of Morocco where President Roosevelt, Prime Minister Churchill and other Allied leaders conferred secretly on the strategy and progress of the war. President Roosevelt flew to Africa for the meeting, and visited United States troops. The four men at the left were important conferees. Above, Prime Minister Winston Churchill and President Roosevelt; below (left) Gen. Charles DeGaulle, leader of the Fighting French, and Gen. Henri Honore Giraud, North African commissioner.

Invasion Courses Believed Mapped At African Parley

(Continued From Page 1.)

portance, recovering large sections lost a week ago by the French.

French troops had been driven back several miles by German armored forces 25 miles southwest of Pont Du Fahs.

Rains still hampered large-scale operations.

Lorient, Naples Bombed.

Other American forces in the region of Maknassy, 35 miles inland from the Gulf of Gabes, poised a threat to the rear of the French-built Mareth Line which lies near the Libyan - Tunisian frontier. Front line dispatches said the Americans were also in a position to cut off Rommel's "escape corridor" with a thrust to the gulf coast between Sfax and Gabes.

A broadcast by the German controlled Paris radio said Rommel's legions had already made contact with Col. Gen. Jurgen Von Arnim's Tunisian army behind the Mareth fortifications.

In the western air war, Britain's big home-based bombers renewed the assault on the German U-boat nest at Lorient, France, ending a two-night lull, and this morning the English Channel skies were alive with planes crossing and recrossing the coast.

Other R. A. F. planes pounded the French port of Bordeaux.

Simultaneously, an Italian communique reported that Allied bombers last night raided Naples, a chief port of reinforcement and supply for Axis forces in North Africa.

Smashing Blows Expected.

While Germany and her satelites sought to discount the importance of the Roosevelt-Churchill meeting, conveniently forgetting that the three earlier meetings of the Allied leaders resulted in momentous developments, United Nations capitals generally acclaimed it as the prelude to smashing new blows.

Authoritative quarters in Washington expressed belief that Mr Roosevelt and Mr. Churchill had agreed on a general European offensive as soon as possible after the conclusion of the African campaign.

Similarly, London quarters declared it was believed that the Roosevelt - Churchill communique covered many untold decisions and British military observers said that the long-waited invasion of Hitler's so-called "European fortress" might be expected sooner than was thought possible a few months ago.

London sources also declared it would be no great surprise if Lieut.-Gen. Dwight D. Eisenhower, American commander-in-chief of Allied forces in North Africa, returned to Britain to help plan the European offensive.

High Spots Of Parley.

These are the high spots of the conference, which Roosevelt and Churchill agreed was unprecedented in history and may decide the fate of the world for generations to come:

One—The leaders of America and Britain, both military and civil, have agreed on a war plan for 1943 designed to maintain the initiative in every theater of the war.

Two—Churchill and Roosevelt agreed that peace can come only through "unconditional surrender" of Germany, Italy and Japan.

French Generals Meet.

Three—Generals Giraud and DeGaulle, meeting for the first time under the sponsorship of the President and Prime Minister, are negotiating for a United French movement designed to put French armies, a navy and an air force again into the field against the Axis.

Four—Premier Joseph Stalin of Russia was kept informed of the results of the conferences. In fact, Churchill and Roosevelt offered to meet Stalin "very much farther to the east" but the Russian chief was unable to leave the U.S.S.R., due to the need of his directing the present Red Army offensives.

The President and Prime Minister also have been in communication with Generalissimo Chiang Kai-Shek and "have appraised him of the measures which they are taking to assist him in China's magnificent and unrelaxing struggle for the common cause."

Five—Maximum material to Russia and China will be one of the prime aims of the U. S. and Britain.

President Visits Troops.

Six—Roosevelt visited American troops in the field in North Africa —the first American President to visit an active war theater since Abraham Lincoln.

The meetings were held in a closely-guarded, barbed-wire-surrounded inclosure at a hotel in Casablanca under the greatest secrecy.

Prime Minister Churchill arrived for the meeting first. When President Roosevelt arrived by plane a few hours later, he dispatched Harry Hopkins to the Churchill villa, and the Prime Minister immediately came to start the meetings.

The first began at 7 o'clock in the evening of January 14 and lasted until three o'clock the next morning.

President Roosevelt met correspondents in the garden of his villa Sunday afternoon.

Planes Guard Conference.

Protecting American fighters and Spitfires roared overhead as the conference was held. The only woman present was WAAC captain Louise Anderson of Denver, Colo., a stenographer from Lieut. Gen. Dwight D. Eisenhower's headquarters.

Hopkins was among the first to arrive, along with the President's flying son, Lieut. Col. Elliott Roosevelt, who was wearing the Distinguished Flying Cross recently awarded him.

While the President's envoy, Robert Murphy, flitted in the background, Generals Giraud and DeGaulle, clad in French army uniforms, appeared from the President's quarters. They were closely followed by Roosevelt himself, wearing a light grey suit with the usual cigarette holder held at a jaunty angle.

Churchill, in a dark grey suit and with the inevitable cigar, followed them to the four chairs in the garden.

As DeGaulle and Giraud shook hands for the benefit of photographers, the President opined that it was a momentous moment.

Giraud and DeGaulle immediately went back into the house and the press conference began.

The President on behalf of the Prime Minister and himself, expressed regret at the death of the Canadian Broadcasting Corp. war correspondent, Edouard Baudry, who was killed by a machinegun bullet when the plane in which he was riding with other correspondents enroute to the meeting was lost over Spanish Morocco and was fired upon by Spanish ground defenses.

The President then went into the background of the meeting, saying that it became clear when the North African campaign was launched that a meeting between himself and the Prime Minister would be necessary.

He said Stalin had been kept advised on all details worked out at the meeting, and in the words of the communique added that Stalin had been "cordially invited to meet the President and Prime Minister, in which case the meeting would have been held very much farther to the east." Stalin, however, was "unable to leave Russia at this time on account of the great offensive which he himself as commander-in-chief is directing."

While the Prime Minister nodded assent, the President said the conference had reached "complete agreement" on war plans for 1943 to bring about the "unconditional surrender" of the Axis nations.

The President and Prime Minister both said the Allies were determined to maintain the battle initiative in every part of the world, and said that theater by theater every campaign had been discussed.

This was taken to mean that Gen George C Marshall, chief-of-staff of the U. S. Army, Gen. Sir Alan Brooke, chief of the imperial general staff, Admiral Ernest J. King, commander-in-chief of the U. S. Navy, and Admiral of the Fleet Sir Dudley Pound along with other generals had mapped invasion plans and probably also picked the generals for such field commands.

The President said the meetings in the past ten days had been unprecedented in history, while the Prime Minister chimed in to add that they surpassed anything in his World War one experience.

One of the main decisions of the conference was to lend all material aid to the Russians, who are draining German manpower and war materials, the President said, and he added that China was to get a full measure to help to end forever the Japanese attempt to dominate the Far East.

The President said "unconditional surrender" of Germany, Italy, and Japan did not mean destruction of the populations but destruction of the philosophy of these countries based on conquest and reigns of terror.

All resources of the United Nations have been pooled and will be administered according to one central plan decided upon at the conference, the President said, but he gave no hint of when or where the military strength of the United Nations would smash against the Axis.

The President and Prime Minister stressed the sterength of their friendship and Churchill said nothing had ever come between him and the President.

In speaking of the Allied landings in North Africa, the Prime Minister, after the President had finished the first part of the conference, said this great enterprise had altered the whole strategy of the war and given the Allies an initiative which they would never lose.

In discussing the fighting in the Middle East, Churchill described Marshal Erwin Rommel as a fugitive from Egypt who now would like to pose as the deliverer of Tunisia, but said the Eighth Army would never let go of him.

That the ten-day conference had developed the long-discussed Allied master battle plan for the war was clear in both the President's and Prime Minister's statements.

Churchill, waving his cigar, declared that despite the fact that there may be some delay at times, there is a design and purpose and unconquerable will to enforce "unconditional surrender" upon the criminals who plunged the world into war.

Churchill, wearing an American Distinguished Service Order given him by Gen. John J. Pershing in the World War, declared the present conference had surpassed anything in his long experience.

The President and Prime Minister repeated the words of the communique describing the Giraud-DeGaulle meeting, saying they felt the moment "made it opportune to invite General Giraud to confer with the combined chiefs of staff and to arrange a meeting between him and General DeGaulle."

President Roosevelt praised the valor of French fighting men, pointing out they lay side by side with Americans in graves in Africa, but now stand united in common cause.

A brief announcement near the end of the day describing the meeting between DeGaulle and Giraud said:

"At the conclusion of their first conversations in North Africa General DeGaulle and General Giraud make the following joint statement:

" 'We have met. We have talked. We have registered entire agreement on the end to be achieved, which is the liberation of France and the triumph of human liberties by the total defeat of the enemy.

" 'This end will be attained by the union in war of all free Frenchmen fighting side by side with all the Allies.' "

The President toward the end of the press conference said of his visit to the field troops that he was the first President to go to the Eastern Hemisphere since the visit of President Woodrow Wilson in 1919.

"I have seen the bulk of several divisions," the President said, permitting himself to be directly quoted. "I have eaten lunch in the field and it was a darn good lunch too."

The President said American troops were equipped with the best weapons in the world, weapons superior to anything the enemy had developed.

"They had a band at one place I visited which played for lunch" he said. "It was a good band but I had to move upwind so I could hear it."

He said he had visited Port Lyautey, where some of the heaviest fighting took place, and placed wreaths on the graves of American soldiers.

The President praised the French for bravery in battle and said with the coming peace they are now helping us to carry out our common objective.

Waving his finger at correspondents seated in a semicircle in front of him, he said: "Our soldiers are eager to carry on the fight and I want you to tell the folks back home that I am proud of them."

The President in conclusion said America was determined to help the French civilians in North Africa with food and clothing until such time as they could recover from the stripping done by the Axis.

He said he had given a dinner for the Sultan of Morocco and his son and had gotten on extremely well with both of them.

At the moment he was fingering what is probably the most rare autograph book in the world. It is bound in leather and contains the signature of all those dignitaries attending the conference.

The book would go to the government museum at Hyde Park, the President said.

In flying to the meeting President Roosevelt was in a plane for the first time since 1932, when he flew to the national democratic convention in Chicago upon receiving the presidential nomination.

Fiery Smarting of minor **Burns**
Quick use of this soothing ointment gives wonderful relief in little burns
RESINOL

AUXILIARY INDUCTS NEW OFFICERS AT EVENING PROGRAM

Mrs. Lida Van Hoesen Installed as President of Webster-Bailey Group of Union Veterans.

GREEN ISLAND

The new officers of the Webster-Bailey Auxiliary of the Sons of the Union Veterans of the Civil War were installed with patriotic ceremonies Monday night in the Cohoes G. A. R. Hall by Charles Van Hoesen of N. G. Lyons Camp, Sons of Union Veterans.

The following were inducted: Mrs. Lida Van Hoesen, president; Mrs. Mary Patrick, vice president; Miss Jennie DeLong, past president; Mrs. Charlotte M. Bailey, Mrs. Mary Waddington and Miss DeLong, trustees; Miss Hilda A. Bailey, treasurer; Mrs. Minnie Terry, patriotic instructor; Mrs. Waddington, chaplain; Mrs. Eva May Mylott, guide; Mrs. Helen B. Connolly, assistant guide; Mrs. Margaret Brock and Alice Waddington, color guards; Mrs. Lillian Eoose, inside guard; Mrs. Lucinda Rouse, outside guard; Mrs. Bailey, press correspondent; Mrs. Beatrice Fitzgerald, secretary; Miss Iva May Terry, pianist; Walter K. Bailey, councilor.

Visiting auxiliaries and corps included Tibbits and McConihe Auxiliaries from Troy, Sheridan Auxiliary, Albany, Ten Eyck Camp, Albany; N. G. Lyons Camp, Cohoes; Gademic Auxiliary, Army and Navy Union, Cohoes; Mollie E. Titcomb and 1942 Auxiliaries, Army and Navy Union, Troy and Camp Collins Ross, U. S. W. V., Cohoes. Refreshments were served and social hour followed.

Classes to Meet.

The men's physical fitness class will meet at the auditorium of Heatly High School today at 7 30 p.m.

Appratus Received.

The village has received three roof-ladders to be added to the auxiliary fire-fighting equipment loaned by the Federal Government.

Meeting Tonight.

The Cottage Prayer Meeting and Advocate Reading Club of the Green Island Methodist Church will meet tonight at the home of Miss Isabelle Miller, 53 Hudson Avenue, Green Island, at 7 45 p.m.

Attended Dinner.

The following members of Legnard-Curtain Post, American Legion, last night attended the legislative dinner in the Ten Eyck Hotel, Albany: Frank J. Tilley, Francis J. Legnard, Andrew Doyle, Flanagan, Oliver A. LaFlame.

Intra-Mural Games.

The boys' intra-mural teams at Heatly High School met on the basketball court in the gym yesterday. In the senior league, Dartmouth won over Yale, 18 to 2, with Paul Volk, Robert Dupont and Lawrence Geiser rolling up the most points for the winning side, and George Demarest and Robert McAuliffe scoring high for Yale.

Princeton took Harvard, 14 to 12, with William Ivimey and Robert Anderson netting the most points for Princeton and Julius Iannone scoring for Harvard.

William Harris of the student body acted as referee.

Yesterday's games bring senior league point standings to the following totals: Yale 11, Dartmouth 11, Harvard 7, Princeton 7.

In the junior league Navy won over Siena yesterday by 12 to 7. Navy players scoring high were Bernard Cusack and Richard Stoliker. Siena scorers were Roy Bryce, Anthony Bologna and Lou Colley. John Cietek, a student, was referee.

Junior league point standings are: Navy 10, Notre Dame 5, Siena 2, Army 1.

ALEXANDERSON SAYS RADIO ECHOES WILL GUIDE AIRPLANES

Radio echoes will guide airplanes of the future through mountain ranges, in clouds and darkness, a General Electric engineer, Dr. Ernst F. W. Alexanderson said late night at Schenectady in a prepared G. E. Science Forum address. The development, he said, will allow aircraft to land safely without the pilot seeing the ground.

The radio echo was tested in 1928, he added, and "the aviation industry has shown repeated interest, but the finished device, which may be carried by every airplane, is still to be developed. But it is safe to predict that, in the future, airplanes will be piloted by radio echo."

Make Your Job Easier with Ice-Mint Feet

It's a trick well worth knowing — as many a defense plant worker might tell you —just use Ice-Mint on your feet to help keep them cool and comfortable—on the job. See, too, how Ice-Mint helps soften up stinging corns and tough old callouses. For people who stand all day on tired, burning feet—Ice-Mint can't be beat. Get a jar from your druggist today!

READY MONEY FOR TAXES

The safest, surest way to get out of debt is by small, systematic weekly payments.

Troy Prudential Association makes many hundreds of easier weekly payment loans $25 to $2,500 for 50 or less weeks.

Anyone can apply for a Prudential Loan. Simply call at 251 Broadway (between Second and Third Sts.) or phone Troy 308. Talk with the manager confidentially regarding any financial problem.

COST OF PRUDENTIAL LOANS

Amount of Loan	Interest 6 Per Cent	Service Charge	Cash You Receive	You Pay Wkly
$25.00	$1.00	$1.00	$23.00	$2.00
50.00	1.50	1.00	47.50	2.00
100.00	6.00	2.00	92.00	2.00
250.00	15.00	5.00	230.00	5.0
500.00	30.00	7.50	462.50	10.00
1000.00	60.00	12.50	927.50	20.00
2000.00	120.00	20.00	1860.00	40.00
2500.00	150.00	20.00	2330.00	50.00

Prudential Loans are paid back in small convenient weekly deposits and are the easiest loans to pay.

TROY PRUDENTIAL ASSOCIATION, Inc.
251 BROADWAY — TROY, N. Y.
(A Locally Owned Industrial Bank)

DO YOUR PART—BUY WAR BONDS and STAMPS

WORLD NEWS FEATURE PICTURES

JAPS LEFT IT—U. S. soldiers drive into camp with jeep-load of Jap equipment left when Japs surrendered on Guadalcanal. Food, medical supplies were picked up

SAUSAGE MEN — These men, from left: Karl Acherman of Swiss descent, Rudolph Brauch of German descent and Felix Zocchi of Italian descent, are all wrapped up in their work. They formerly were sausage makers in San Francisco, but now they've turned wartime pipe coverers.

FAMILY PORTRAIT—Charming picture of Britain's Queen Elizabeth and her daughters, Princess Elizabeth, standing, and Princess Margaret Rose. Picture taken in Buckingham Palace by Cecil Beaton.

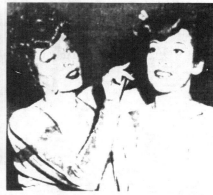

LADY MARINE—Mrs. Ruth Cheney Streeter, 47, of Morristown, N. J., director of new Women's Reserve Corps of U. S. Marine Corps, with rank of major. She holds commercial pilot's license.

ONE IS LUPE — Screen star Lupe Velez and close friend, stand-in and double, Sandra Lynn, look so much alike that even Hollywood folk have difficulty in distinguishing them. That's Lupe at left.

HO-HUM! LIFE'S A BORE—That's what Cote Neige Beau Rene and Great Pyrenee pal, Cote de Neige Vivante, seem to say at Westminster Kennel Club show, New York. See if they make you yawn, too.

KILLED TO AID MOTHER—Daniel Glecier, 15, tells sister Sally how he fatally shot soldier breaking into cabin home near Camp Roberts, Cal., to attack mother. Boy's father is officer in camp.

HURRY - UPPER — Hugh Short, of Georgetown U slated to resume cup hunting at 75th meet of New York Athletic Club, at Madison Square Garden, New York. He was favored in 500-yard dash.

JAPS GAVE UP—These Japs preferred to be taken prisoner rather than fight it out and die, as Japs capitulated on Guadalcanal to Yanks.

NEIGHBORS—Tito Guizar, singer, left, known as Latin-American Ambassador of Good Will, at the Waldorf-Astoria, New York, with three Ambassadors. They are: Rodolfo Michels, Chile; Francisco Castillo Najera, Mexico, and Herman Figueroa, from Chile to Spain

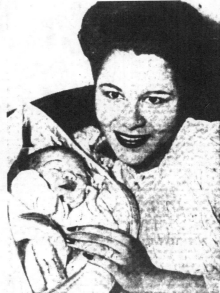

COP'S HELPERS—U. S. Army and Navy sightseers in Fiji Islands glad to aid native barefoot traffic cop. This way, that way—any way to oblige pedestrians.

CHAMP'S BABY—Here's boxing champion Joe Louis Barrow's new daughter Jacqueline, with her mother, former Marva Trotter, in Chicago. Sergeant Joe hurried from Fort Riley for brief visit with new arrival.

ABROAD—Most Rev. Francis J. Spellman, Catholic Archbishop of New York, visiting Pope Pius in Vatican in Rome. En route, he celebrated mass at Cathedral of San Isidro, Madrid.

HAS DEBT TO PAY—Jack Rogers signs consent papers, in Birmingham, Ala., permitting son Hugh, 17, left, to enlist in Navy. Hugh has debt to Japs, who killed his three brothers.

Distr. by United Feature Syndicate, Inc.

LaSalle Captures Principals' Flag

CATHOLIC CENTRAL CAGERS DEFEATED BY 42 TO 27 TALLY

Cadets Take Early Lead in Winning; Second Win of Year Over the Purples And Second Title.

La Salle Institute fastened another pennant to its flagstaff last night by handing Catholic Central High a 42-27 defeat at the Cadets' gym.

The victory, second of the year over the Purples, enabled the Cadets to clinch the Principals' League flag in addition to the Catholic Diocesan title they gained last week.

After Catholic Central opened the scoring with a field goal by Bob Degnan, the home forces surged into a 9-2 lead as the first stanza ended. They lengthened it to 29-8 at halftime and then coasted home.

Jim Pemrick, who is a wizard under the loop, used his talent to befuddle the Purples and pass off to teammates from that post last night. But he assumed a new shooting role by flipping in popshots from the sides to account for 15 points. Jim Mahoney and Joe Cahill scored ten each to keep up the trio's average of 35 per game.

Degnan, who got the visitors off to a neat start, was high with nine and John Kelly and Dan Quinn accounted for the bulk of the scoring with six each.

After Degnan tallied at the outset for C. C. H. S., Cahill tallied on a foul toss to start the Cadets. Then in order came two-pointers by Sullivan, Mahoney and Pemrick (twice) to complete the first period scoring.

At the start of the second stanza the Cadets picked up where they left off. Pemrick started it with a toss from the floor and then Mahoney, who used his left hand advantageously, flipped in three goals to widen the margin to 17-2. At that point, Kelly scored from the foul line for the Purple, but La Salle started anew. Pemrick and Cahill tallied two-pointers. Kelly and Ed Sullivan of La Salle matched field goals. Then Jim Ryan tossed in a goal from the floor before Pemrick scored twice in succession. Jim Ryan then added a foul, but Mahoney scored once more from the floor before the half ended at 29-8, La Salle.

Opening the third period, Cahill scored five points himself, with two free throws, a floor toss and another penalty counter to make it 34-8, the widest margin the Cadets enjoyed. The Purples immediately cut into it with 12 points in a row. These came on a field goal by Jim Ryan, foul points by Kelly and Degnan, Dowd's field goal, a pair of floor hoops by Quinn and another two-pointer by Degnan. That ended the visitors' spurt, but a foul by Pemrick closed out the scoring for the stanza. The tally was 35-20, LaSalle.

Each side scored seven points in the final period. Catholic Central got the jump, with six in a row as Quinn tossed in a field shot and Degnan added a pair. LaSalle came back to get its seven points for the period at this juncture, with Pemrick getting a two-pointer, Furdyna a penalty point, and Pemrick and Sullivan duplicate baskets. The final tally was a foul point by Joe Dowd of C. C. H. S.

In the junior varsity preliminary, LaSalle won, 28-17, with Bill Doody's seven topping the Cadets and Jack Gully and Dan Yamin sharing C. C. H. S. honors. In a frosh encounter it was 22-19, Catholic Central. Crawley and Holmes had eight each for the Eighth Streeters, while Ryan and Dwyer paced the losers with three apiece.

LA SALLE.

	F.G.	F.B.	T.P.
Mahoney, f.	5	0	10
Russo, f.	0	0	0
Cahill, f.	3	4	10
Pemrick, c.	7	1	15
Yamin, c.	0	0	0
Sullivan, g.	3	0	6
Wheeler, g.	0	0	0
Furdyna, g.	0	1	1
Totals	18	6	42

CATHOLIC HIGH.

	F.G.	F.B.	T.P.
T. Ryan, f.	0	0	0
Egan, f.	0	0	0
Kelly, f.	2	2	6
Conway, f.	0	0	0
McCarthy, c.	0	0	0
Dowd, c.	1	1	3
Degnan, g.	4	1	9
J. Ryan, g.	1	1	3
Quinn, g.	3	0	6
Totals	11	5	27

LaSalle	9	20	6	7—42
C. C. H. S.	2	6	12	7—35

Referees—Wittner and Dowling.
Fouls called—10-7, LaSalle.

GOING UP—Jim Pemrick, La Salle center, (in white jersey) outjumps Jim Ryan of Catholic Central for a tap-in shot as the Cadets routed the Purple, 42-27, last night at La Salle gym. Watching anxiously (left to right) are: John Kelly (7), C. C. H. S. forward; Joe Cahill (11), La Salle forward; Ed Sullivan (16), La Salle guard; Bob McCarthy (3), C. C. H. S. center, and Bob Degnan (6), C. C. H. S. guard. Referee Flip Dowling (back to camera), watches play.

A BIT OF THIS AND A BIT OF THAT

By JACK (Peerless) McGRATH

Devil's Thumb, winner of the rich Hopeful at Saratoga last year, will develop into a really great horse this year, according to Cecil "Dutch" Wilhelm, his trainer.

Wilhelm is aiming him at the Kentucky Derby, May 1, and according to reports he's shaping up fine.

Devil's Thumb was the most unpredictable of the 2-year-olds of 1942. In some races he would step to the front with the opening of the gates, sizzle into a long lead, only to check down in the stretch. In others he wouldn't turn a lick for two or three furlongs, then charge on a like a wild horse.

W. E. Boeing, the Seattle, Wash., airplane builder, bought him at the Saratoga Sales Stakes for $3,000 and named him after a mountain peak near Boeing's back yard. He proved to be the outstanding bargain of the year, because by his starting performances at the Spa last August, he pushed his earnings to $62,875.

Boeing was able to get the colt for such a small sum because no one else figured that this son of Grand Slam, an unproven sire, which was only a fair success during his racing career, and out of a dam, Daintiness, which never had raced, was not worth so high a gamble as $3,000. And for a long, long time even Boeing wasn't sure that he hadn't made a financial mistake.

Devil's Thumb could pick up only one second and one third portion of the money in his first eight starts, finally scoring in his ninth trip to the post, which was at Arlington Park, but there was nothing impressive about that winning performance.

Wilhelm shipped him to Saratoga, and decided to equip the colt with blinkers for the first time. Devil's Thumb became a horse transformed. He made six starts at the historic course, won five stakes races and was second in the other.

In his inaugural at the Spa he was second to Breezing Home. Wilhelm switched jockeys for the next start, substituting Con McCreary, and magic resulted.

Devil's Thumb won the U. S. Hotel Stakes, the Saratoga Sales, the Sanford, the Grand Union, and the Hopeful in succession. Nothing could match strides with this colt, which on Chicago form, had class only for the "leaky roof" circuits.

In the Hopeful, his fnal start of the year, Devil's Thumb broke slowly, swerved on the backstretch, and seemed to be favoring an ankle as he turned for home. But when called upon for the best he had—and all of it—Devil's Thumb charged straight and fast, wore down the leaders, and won by a length in 1:18 for six and a half.

Boeing immediately retired him and Wilhelm began treating the ankle at Belmont. Some months later, when the colt was shipped to winter quarters, in Columbia, S. C., the ankle appeared to be completely cured.

Devil's Thumb did not hook up with either Count Fleet or Occupation in 1942.

"He'll get his chance at Count Fleet in the Kentucky Derby," said Wilhelm. "And nobody will need to make apologies for him. He ought to do quite all right on any track, under any conditions, over any distance, and no matter who is in there with him."

• • •

Chicago Cubs are getting a shortstop who can hit and think in Eddie Stanky, who is the son-in-law of Milton Stock, the old National League third baseman and minor league manager. The most valuable player in the American Association, young Stanky led the loop in batting with .342, a remarkable figure for a shortstop.

"Stanky hasn't the best arm in the world and he isn't fast, but he thinks twice as rapidly as any man he wants to outguess and plays ahead of the opposition," says Charley Grimm, who managed him in Milwaukee. Stanky, a native of Philadelphia, was once the property of the Athletics and did a stretch with the Macon club.

• • •

R. P. I. and Union clash tonight at the '87 gym here. One of the biggest crowds of the year is expected to turn out for this traditional battle. R. P. I. dropped the decision to Union in Schenectady a few weeks ago and the Trojans will be out for revenge tonight. Anything can happen when R. P. I. tangles with Union.

• • •

Answering the mail: Jimmy Foxx hit 58 home runs for the Philadelphia Athletics back in 1932. He was born in Sudlersville, Md., on Oct. 22, 1907. He bats and throws right-handed.

AVERILL PARK FIVE BEATS CASTLETON

Averill Park defeated Castleton yesterday afternoon at Castleton, 38 to 22.

Karpiak topped Averill Park with 18 points. Spring was high man for the losers with eight.

CASTLETON.

	F.G.	F.B.	T.P.
Rickert, f.	1	0	2
Spring, f.	4	0	8
Relyea, c.	0	0	0
Van Buren, g.	3	1	7
E. Rickert, g.	1	0	2
Nichols, g.	1	0	2
Gietz, g.	0	1	1
Totals	10	2	22

AVERILL PARK.

	F.G.	F.B.	T.P.
Connick, f.	5	0	10
Bekner, f.	3	2	8
Willibrant, c.	1	0	2
Wilkins, g.	0	0	0
Karpiak, g.	8	2	18
Totals	17	4	38

Plenty of Action In Greco-Shans Bout

BY HUGH FULLERTON, JR.

New York (AP)—Thoughts while listening: Branch (two words for the price of one) Rickey is a well-named guy . . . You ought to hear how he can branch off on another subject after starting to answer a question . . . And if it takes as long to rebuild the Dodgers as to renovate their downtown offices, them Bums won't be in the pennant race this year . . . What with Dolf Camilli's and Arky Vaughan's ranches, the farm that Rufus Melton bought (but can't tell where its located) the Dodgers are having more farm troubles now than when they were operating a dozen minor league clubs . . . No wonder a scrib suggested they might settle their problems by putting Victory Gardens outside Ebbets Field.

Encore.

During the border conference basketball tournament, the West Texas Buffaloes were having some tough going against Arizona State of Flagstaff . . . Then Capt. Norman Trimble brought the ball down the floor, yelled "23" and passed to Chat Johnson, who pitched the ball through the basket without even touching the rim . . . One fan, watching intently, turned to his neighbor and remarked: "There's nothing difficult about that play; they ought to run it again."

Quote, Unquote.

Coast Guardsman Bill Shirley (ex-sportswriter and ball player): "The only good thing I can detect in the elimination of baseball is that it would keep the Phillies from winding up in the National League cellar. But, even then, the new proprietors of the club would no doubt be very glad to spend the summer in the cellar if it would aid the cause."

One-minute Sports Page.

For sheer action, last night's Johnny Greco-Cleo Shans fight was the best we've seen this season, but we can't say they're the best fighters . . . As for Sal Bartolo-Pedro Hernandez, there was no pep, Willie or other, in that one . . . Holly Beach Farm, famous hoss-breeding establishment at Annapolis, Md., has been taken over for the construction of a Naval Air Field . . Jack Welsh, Penn's crack football and basketball player, also can pole vault 13-3 but will be too busy on the court to complete in the I. C. 4-A meet next week . . . After serving as his club's press agent for three weeks, owner Fred Mandel of the eDtroit Lions had to leave for six weeks' rest at Palm Springs, Cal. . . . Tough racket, this tub-thumping.

Today's Guest Star.

Frank B. Ward, Youngstown (O.) Vindicator: "Since shoe leather is precious, those umpires who order players to take a walk may get in bad with the OPA."

Service Dept.

A couple of guys who tried to get by Chief Boatswain's Mate Fred Hitchman's post carrying cameras should have known better. Any hockey player could have told them there never was a more reliable guy on a defense post than the Hitcher . . . The Fort Monmouth, N. J., public relations office reports plenty of "big names" in the recent post "Golden Gloves" tourney entries included a Baer, a Simon, a Johnson and a Johnston—not to mention a Shakespeare and a Whitehouse from Washington, D. C. . . . To make sure that future naval aviators won't have to be bailed out if they have to bail out, the swimming program at the North Carolina Pre-flight School has been placed under the direction of Lieut. John Miller, formerly a noted tank coach at Mercersburg (Pa.) Academy, and Ensign Peter Fick, Olympic free-style record breaker.

TOO LATE TO CLASSIFY by Loring

"Say, Mom, there'll be other women answering that Classified Ad in The Record Newspapers offering that bargain oriental rug; don't you think I'd better go, too?"

RENSSELAER TECH SWIMMERS TOP ROCHESTER TEAM

Superiority in the relay tests last night gave Rensselaer Tech's swimming team a 42-33 victory over University of Rochester at '87 pool to even their activities for the R. P. I. earlier had dropped a telegraphic meet to Virginia Tech.

Rensselaer won both the medley and 400 yard relays to cop the decision as Rochester took three first and several seconds and third to pile up a point advantage in the individual events.

Hennrich led the visitors by scoring victories in the 200 and 400 yard freestyle events. He was the only double winner of the meet.

In keeping at the .500 mark for the season, Tech showed some strong freshman swimmers. Ed Flack of Troy, who copped the 50-yard freestyle; Ted Anning, the backstroke winner, and Siff, who anchored the 400-yard relay are all freshmen.

Rensselaer will conclude its swimming season at 2 p.m., today by opposing an unofficial Union swimming club at '87 pool. Tech is highly favored.

COURT STANDINGS IN THREE LOOPS

Principals' League.

	W.	L.	Pct.
LaSalle	8	1	.889
Watervliet	5	3	.625
Catholic Central	5	5	.500
Troy	3	4	.429
Lansingburg	3	5	.375
Cohoes	0	8	.000

Class AB P. H. S. League.

	W.	L.	Pct.
Troy	5	2	.714
Watervliet	5	2	.714
Lansingburg	5	3	.625
Albany	5	3	.625
Hudson	2	6	.250
Cohoes	1	7	.125

Catholic Central.

	W.	L.	Pct.
LaSalle	8	1	.889
St. Mary's, Amst.	5	3	.625
C. B. A.	5	4	.556
Catholic Central	4	5	.445
Cathedral	4	5	.445
Vincentian	0	8	.000

FUNNY BUSINESS.

"It's the fuel administration's office giving the Treasury Department the dickens for making people burn midnight oil figuring their income taxes!"

TIPPIE AND "CAP" STUBBS — Not A Thing — By EDWINA

ELLA CINDERS — Man of Mystery — By CHARLES PLUMB

BOOTS AND HER BUDDIES — ! ! ! ? ? — By EDGAR MARTIN

FRECKLES AND HIS FRIENDS — Looking Ahead — By MERRILL BLOSSER

RED RYDER — Ready for the Dance — By FRED HARMAN

OUR BOARDING HOUSE ... with ... MAJOR HOOPLE

OUT OUR WAY — By J. R. WILLIAMS

DRIVE SUCCESSFUL AT SAVINGS BANK

The Troy Savings Bank is the first business establishment in Troy to complete its Red Cross War Fund drive and receive a 100 per cent award. The bank employees gave two and one half times as much as last year.

The drive was in charge of Harold M. J. Lewis of the banking section of the public service division. George Matthews heads the division.

Not even strong acids compare with water as a dissolver of chemical substances.

MEETING PLANNED ON CONSERVATION OF PROTEIN FEEDS

Manufacturers, Dealers and Farmers' Participation To Be Discussed at Farm Bureau Session Thursday.

A protein conservation program in which feed manufacturers, dealers and farmers are being asked to cooperate will be discussed at a meeting of retail feed handlers of Rensselaer County at the offices of the County Farm Bureau in the Troy Postoffice building at 1:30 p.m. Thursday.

County Agricultural Agent Elton K. Hanks will preside at the meeting which will be attended by a representative of the State Feed Dealers' Association who will tell what plans have been drawn up in the voluntary program. Dealer cooperation with these plans will be asked.

Feed manufacturers and dealers are taking the initiative to work out a voluntary protein conservation program so that the government will not be forced to take steps for rationing the available protein supply.

Minimum To Be Set.

Feeding of only the necessary amounts of animal protein in all poultry and livestock feeds, it is pointed out, will enable New York farmers to continue dairy and poultry production in the face of dwindling protein supplies.

Under the voluntary plan, the basic ration of protein in poultry, hog and cattle feeds will be set at the minimum amount that will permit good growth and continued food production. Present huge numbers of livestock and their heavy feeding to produce more food have absorbed the greatly increased output of soybean and other crop protein feeds at the same time that the supply of animal proteins for feedstuffs has been reduced.

In the program, first worked out by the feed industry council and the U. S. Department of Agriculture, nutrition specialists have adjusted the protein levels for wartime feeding. Voluntary cooperation in the plan will prevent the red tape of official regulation and will enable farmers to get balanced feed rations for their stock through this year and through next winter, when the greatest pinch is expected to come.

Protein Contents.

The feed program, expected to go into effect in New York and other states in the near future, limits protein content of dairy feed to 16 per cent, except where hay is poor. It limits the weight of animal protein in poultry feeds to 1.125 per cent of total protein in all-mash growing ration, 2 per cent in chick and duck starter and broiler mash, 2.25 per cent in growing and laying mashes fed with grain, 2.5 per cent in turkey starter mash, and 4.5 per cent for breeding mashes fed with grain. Poultry supplements used for home mixing of rations are also limited to 3.375 per cent animal protein for 26 per cent total protein mixtures, 4.5 per cent for the 32 per cent protein mixture and 5 per cent for the 36 per cent protein mixture.

Calf starters are limited to 3 per cent of animal protein, calf starters fed with grain, to 6 per cent.

For swine, animal protein will be limited to 1.5 per cent for hog fatteners; 2 per cent for sow and pig feeds; 3 per cent for hog supplements fed with grain and 4 per cent for sow and pig feeds fed with grain.

HIGH SPOT OF PLAY—Wedding guests register astonishment as the bride in "She Married a Minister" stands revealed as the scullery maid. The two-act comedy will be presented at 8 p.m. today in St. Mark's Methodist Church house by members of the congregation. Left to right are Miss Myrtle Grandjean, Mrs. Raymond Foster, one of the bride's attendants; Constance Foster, flower girl; Mrs. Paul Derrick, the bride; Mrs. George Harris, one of the guests; Frances Young, the second flower girl, and the Misses Olive Nichols, Julia Ann Aird, Anita Kenyon, Mildred Johnson, Marjorie McNeary and Carolyn Gowie, attendants and guests. Mrs. Mahlon P. Wemple is the director.

FEDERAL AGENT IN TROY TO ARRANGE FOR FARM LOANS

Will Be Here Each Thursday and Friday to Provide Funds for Agriculture Needs.

Erwin R. Herrington of the Regional Agricultural Credit Corporation was in Troy yesterday and today to assist Rensselaer County farmers in obtaining emergency loans to assure a maximum production of needed farm products for wartime use. He will be here each Thursday and Friday until further notice, making his headquarters in the offices of the United States Department of Agriculture War Board, Room 409, Cannon Building.

The farmers can obtain the loans to purchase feed, seed, fertilizer, machinery repair parts, gasoline and oil, cattle, poultry and to pay for minor construction jobs, current interest and taxes. No loans can be obtained for purchase of real estate, major improvements or for refinancing debts.

Rate of interest on the RACC loans is 5 per cent; the usual term one year, though loans for heavy machinery may be extended to three years.

The loans are strictly for emergency use by farmers, according to Ralph Y. DeWolfe, chairman of the New York State U. S. D. A. War Board, under whom the new credit agency is set up. They are intended only to supplement the borrowings by farmers from established agencies such as local banks, Production Credit Associations, the Farm Security Administration and the Crop and Feed Loan Service.

Farmers are liable for the entire amount of the loan, even though the crop financed does not repay the debt, except when the farmers grow certain war crops: soybeans for grain, three or more acres of potatoes, dry beans, smooth-seed, dry peas, tomatoes, snap and lima beans, peas, carrots and cabbage, sweet corn and beets for processing.

WELLINGTON SENTENCED.
John J. Wellington, 20, Schenectady, has been sentenced to three years and ten months in prison for failing to report for Army induction. Sentenced yesterday in Federal District Court, he claimed membership in a religious sect opposed to war participation.

SCHENECTADY TEAM WILL LEAD SERVICE AT LOCAL CHURCH

Sunday evening at 7:45 another in the series of special Sunday evening services will be held at the Sixth Avenue Baptist Church. The service will be in charge of a gospel team from the Christian Men's Fellowship in Schenectady.

Thomas Schuyler, for a number of years organist of the Mt. Pleasant Reformed Church in Schenectady, will be the organist for the service. Orla Wood, executive secretary of fellowship, will be in charge of the group. Both Mr. Wood and Mr. Schuyler are employees of the General Electric Co. in Schenectady.

The Christian Men's Fellowship is an outgrowth of the meetings which were conducted by Gypsy Smith, the international evangelist when he was in Schenectady in 1940. The group has grown from eighty men at its inception to 230 men at the present time. It is composed of laymen and preachers. At a meeting held recently it was said that about ten or 15 of the members will be present at the meeting in the Troy church.

The program will be composed of inspiring testimonies in song and word. The public is invited.

TWO MEN NAMED TO WAR COUNCIL

Appointment of Dr. F. Herrick Conners, superintendent of Cohoes schools, and Charles H. Conrad, secretary-treasurer of the Cohoes Savings Bank, as members of the Cohoes War Council was announced today by Frank S. Ablett, chairman. The appointments were made by Mayor Rudolph I. Roulier.

FILES TRADE NAME.

Walter Warren, 36 First Street, Hoosick Falls, has filed a certificate in the county clerk's office to the effect that he is conducting business at First and Center Streets, that village, under the name of Walt's Market.

NAVY WORKING OUT NEW SYSTEMS FOR PACKING SUPPLIES

Goods Must Be Prepared for Handling Under Varying Circumstances With Loss Eliminated.

Washington (AP) — Total war has drastically changed the way in which supplies are shipped, handled and prepared for our armed forces.

A special organization of about 100 persons has been created by the Navy to develop new containers and packaging methods for speeding the greatest volume of goods in the shortest possible time. It early became apparent that Iceland, the Solomons and North Africa as destinations for millions of tons of supplies where places whose climate and dock facilities were different, demanding new methods of transporting and packaging fighting supplies.

In Guadalcanal, for example, a shipment of canned goods was dunked in the surf washing the labels from the cans. As a result, unhappy Marines ate canned corn for five successive days. But this monotonous diet will not be repeated. Contents of the cans are now revealed by an embossed legend printed directly on the can.

Are Floated Ashore.

When docking facilities are lacking, unloading of supplies is usually a hasty affair, carried, on at the same volume before the war night and involving the throwing of supplies overboard so that they can float to shore. Ordinary wooden boxes and cardboard cartons were unsatisfactory because they disintegrated.

The Navy found the answer to this problem. It developed what is known as V-board which resists rough handling much better than standard container material.

Again, when the places of male dock workers in many foreign ports were taken by women, supplies had to be packaged so that women could handle them.

The containers themselves, once they have been emptied, are made to serve other purposes. Thus gasoline cans become water containers, and are even used in the building of sheds, dugouts and other structures. Filled with sand they become convenient building blocks. Walls of these cans are said to be excellent protection against bomb splinters.

Platforms Make Shelters.

The wooden platforms from which supplies are now unloaded to serve as floors and walls in temporary shelters.

When 23,000,000 pounds of soap was shipped recently, the space utilized was 19 per cent less than that occupied by shipments of the same volume before the war.

Store Workers to See Red Cross Pictures

Members of the Retail Merchants Bureau will keep their stores closed until 9:30 a. m. Monday. At 9 a. m. clerks and other personnel will meet at The Hendrick Hudson to see the Red Cross moving picture showing activity of the organization since Pearl Harbor was attacked by the Japanese.

The meeting will last about twenty minutes.

Plain Unflavored Gelatin Turns Leftovers Into Delicious Dishes

Invent Your Own Recipes To Use Up Food On Hand

No longer will left-overs be the Cinderellas of the refrigerator. With the food situation what it is today, they have come into their own. As members of the Home-Front Army, it is our job not to waste a single thing. Instead, we must apply a great deal of thought and ingenuity to the planning of our menus and turn every bit of food into a delicious dish of some kind.

Plain unflavored gelatin is a magic wand that turns leftovers into good-to-eat salads, main dishes and desserts. tI also extends small amounts of foods into generous servings. Keep a covered dish in the refrigerator and tuck away small amounts of fruits, vegetables and meats that would ordinarily be thrown away. When you have collected a cup or so of vegetables for instance, combine them with an envelope of plain gelatine and presto, you have a delectable salad.

Basic Recipes.

Basic recipes that will fit any left-overs are musts in a 1943 recipe file. Here are three that will prove to be the handiest ones you've ever had. Any dsired combinations of fruits, vegetables or meats may be folded into them. We are giving you a few suggested combinations as starters and you can invent your own according to what you have on hand.

We know you are busy trying to do three times as much in each day as you used to do. That is another reason why you'll like these plain gelatine recipes. They may be made up early in the morning (or the evening before), tucked away in the refrigerator and they "cook" while you go ahead with the rest of your day's activities. When you get home, they are all ready to serve.

Basic Vegetable Salad
(Serves 6)

1 envelope plain unflavored gelatine
1-4 cup cold water
1 cup hot water
1-4 cup mild vinegar
1 tablespoon lemon juice
1/2 teaspoon salt
1 or 2 tablespoons sugar (or more to taste)
Dash of pepper
1 tablespoon finely minced onion
1 1/2 cups diced or shredded vegetables, cooked or raw

Soften gelatine in cold water and dissolve in hot water. Add vinegar, lemon juice, salt, sugar and pepper. Cool. When mixture begins to thicken, fold in vegetables. Turn into one large or individual molds that have been rinsed in cold water first, and chill. When firm, unmold onto salad greens and serve with desired dressing.

Suggested Combinations.

1. 1/2 cup each cooked peas, diced or shredded raw carrots, celery.
2. 1/2 cup each cooked string beans, peas and carrots.
3. 1/2 cup each diced cooked beets, shredded raw cabbage and chopped celery.
4. 1 cup diced left-over meat (veal, pork, beef, chicken, etc.) 1/2 cup chopped celery or some other left-over vegetables such as peas or carrots.
5. Or any other desired combination of fresh or canned vegetables.

Basic Fruit Salad.
(Serves 6)

1 envelope plain unflavored gelatine
1-4 cup cold water
1 cup hot water or fruit juice
1-4 cup lemon juice
1-4 cup sugar (or more to taste if very tart fresh fruits are used)
1-4 teaspoon salt
1 1/2 cups diced mixed fruits

Soften gelatine in cold water and dissolve in hot liquid. Add lemon juice, sugar and salt. Cool and when mixture begins to thicken, fold in diced fruits. Pour into one large or individual molds that have been rinsed out in cold water first, and chill. When firm, unmold onto salad greens and serve with real mayonnaise. Note: If home canned fruits are used, use a little less sugar, as they are usually sweeter than commercially canned ones.

Suggested Combinations.

1. 1/2 cup diced strawberries, apple and pears.
2. 3/4 cup each diced strawberries and melon.
3. 1/2 cup each halved grapes, peaches and melon.
4. Or any other desired combination of canned or fresh fruits.

Basic Blanc Mange.
(Serves 6)

1 envelope plain unflavored gelatine
2 cups milk
1-4 teaspoon salt
1-8 cup sugar (or 1/4 cup light syrup)
1/2 teaspoon vanilla

Scald one and one-half cups milk with sugar. Soften gelatine in remaining one-half cup cold milk. Add to hot milk and stir until dissolved. Cool slightly, add flavoring and salt. Turn into one large or individual molds that have been rinsed out in cold water first and chill. When firm, unmold and serve with cream, chocolate sauce or crushed fruit juice. Dessert may be molded directly in serving dishes, in which case, it is not necessary to unmold.

Variations

1. Increase sugar to 1/2 cup or corn syrup to 3/4 cup. Cool mixture until it begins to thicken. Fold in 1 cup sliced canned or fresh fruit. Turn into molds and chill.
2. Allow Blanc Mange to cool until it begins to thicken. Arrange alternate layers of Blanc Mange and crushed sweetened fruit in dessert glasses or dishes. Chill until firm.
3. Add 1 square melted chocolate or 3 tablespoons cocoa and 2 tablespoons more sugar or 3 tablespoons light or dark corn syrup, to scalded milk. Stir until blended. Proceed as above.
4. Line serving dishes with cut up pieces of left-over cake or cookies. Pour in pudding and chill until firm. Pieces of cake or cookies may be folded into pudding before pouring into dishes or molds.

Plan to Use Meat Alternates For Family Dinner

Let's do some planning in the face of the meat situation we have several alternatives. We can go all-out and serve the old-time roast, as often as our meat ration will permit, and omit meat from other dinner menus. If that is the verdict in your family, you'll want to plan a meatless main dish for the meatless dinners. Here is a suggestion which should soothe the ruffled feelings of members of the family who, having eaten their roast, are counting the days until the next one makes its appearance.

Gnocchi With Spanish Sauce.

One cup milk, 1/2 teaspoon salt, 1/2 cup wheat-meal, 3/4 cup grated American cheese, 1 egg, well beaten; paprika.

Heat meal in saucepan. Add salt and wheat-meal gradually, boil and cook and stir 3 minutes. Remove from heat. Add 1-4 cup cheese and egg and blend. Pour into shallow pan. Chill. Place spoonsfuls, or 2-inch squares in shallow baking dish and cover with Spanish sauce. Sprinkle with remaining cheese and paprika. Bake in hot oven (400 degrees Fahrenheit) 15 minutes, or until cheese is melted.

Spanish Sauce.

One and one-half tablespoons butter, 3 tablespoons chopped onion, 3 tablespoons chopped green pepper, 4 tablespoons diced celery, 1 1/2 cups canned tomatoes, 1-4 teaspoon salt, dash of pepper.

Melt butter in skillet; add onion, green pepper, and celery and cook slowly until onion is golden brown. Add tomatoes and seasonings. Cook slowly until sauce is thickened. Makes about 1 cup sauce.

Use Oats As Meat Extender

If you know your oats about extending your voluntary meat supply you'll move the quick cooking kind you had for breakfast right on to the dinner table in the Upside Down Meat Loaf posing prettily for its picture. It's a thrifty and nutritious way to make meat go further with vitaminized margarine playing both roles. Here's how to do it without further ado:

Upside Down Meat Loaf.

1/2 cup quick oats
1 teaspoon salt
1/2 cup water
1 pound ground beef
1-3 cup vitaminized margarine
3 cups sifted self-rising flour
1 tablespoon minced onion
2 tablespoons chopped parsley
2 tablespoons chopped green pepper
1/2 raw carrot, grated
1 egg
Milk or water

Combine quick oats, salt, water and ground beef, mix well. Form into balls; brown in vitaminized margarine. Arrange in greased casserole. (Make gravy with drippings in pan to serve with finished casserole.) Combine flour, onion, parsley, green pepper and carrot. Break egg into measuring cup; fill to 1 cup mark with milk or water. Add to dry ingredients; mix lightly. Drop by tablespoons on meat balls. Cover tightly with waxed paper or cheese cloth. Place casserole in large pan partly filled with boiling water. Cover tightly; place over heat. Steam 30 minutes or until dumplings are cooked. Do not remove cover during cooking. Turn dumplings and meat mixture out upside down on platter. Serve hot with gravy. Serves six.

TUMBLE JUMBLE SALAD.

1 cup cubed tangerines
2-3 cup diced grapefruit
1 cup diced apples
1 tablespoon lemon juice
1/2 cup salted peanuts
1 cup shredded cabbage
1-3 cup broken nuts
4 tablespoons salad dressing
Chill ingredients, blend.

Study Meat-Saver Recipes For Meal Planning

The first recipe in a new book, "100 Meat-saving Recipes," shows why it's an important contribution to our wartime menu planning.

Potatoes Stuffed With Codfish.

Allow a medium size potato for each person to be served. Bake the potatoes, making sure to grease the skins first. For the stuffing, a standard size box of shredded codfish is enough for every 3 potatoes. Cover the codfish with cold water, bring to a boil and drain. Do this 3 times and the last time do not drain but let the codfish keep on cooking until it is tender. All this takes about half an hour.

When the potatoes are soft halve them crosswise. Scoop the insides into a bowl, add a tablespoon of butter or fortified margarine and one of top milk for each half together with the cooked codfish and some freshly ground black pepper. Don't salt without tasting, because codfish is often salty enough.

Beat all the ingredients together vigorously until the mixture is very smooth, light and fluffy. Then refill the potato shells, sprinkle the tops with grated American cheese and paprika, put half a teaspoon of butter on each one and bake in a hot oven at 400 degrees Fahrenheit, until the tops are brown, which takes about 15 minutes. (A pan of sliced tomatoes, sprinkled with bread crumbs and dotted with butter, will cook in about the same time and go well with the stuffed potatoes.)

Potato Stuffing.

Three potatoes, 1 box shredded codfish, 7 tablespoons butter or fortified margarine, 6 tablespoons top milk, American cheese, paprika, pepper.

HONEY COOKIES.

1/2 cup honey
1/2 cup shortening
2 eggs, beaten
1-4 teaspoon salt
1 teaspoon cinnamon
1 teaspoon vanilla
1/2 teaspoon cloves
1 teaspoon soda
1-4 teaspoon baking powder
2 1-4 cups flour
1/2 cup chopped nuts

Heat honey and shortening until blended. Cool and add eggs. Beat well. Lightly stir in remaining ingredients and chill dough if convenient. Break off small bits of dough and flatten down 3 inches apart on greased baking sheet. Bake 12 minutes in moderate oven. Cookies with honey in them will scorch easily so watch them carefully while baking.

Under a new process steel propeller blades are being manufactured from chrome-nickel-molybdenum steel tubing.

Lima Loaf Spares Meat

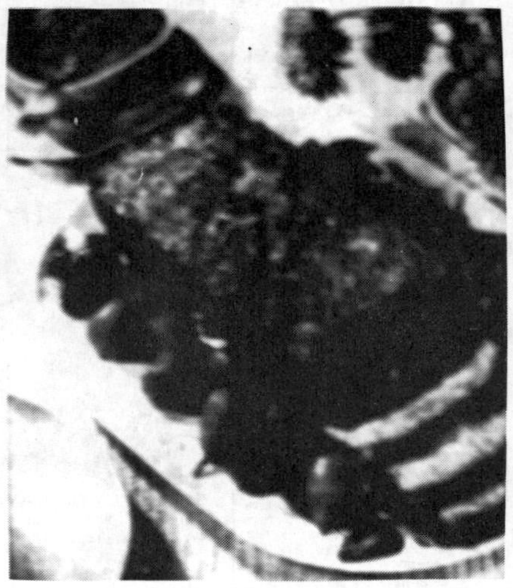

Lima beans are a nutritionally sound meat extender for they are good sources of vegetable protein, "B" vitamins and iron. Today's meat sparing entree stars limas in a savory loaf made as follows. Brown 1/4 cup minced onion and 2 tablespoons chopped green pepper in 2 tablespoons butter. Add 2 cups cooked, pureed dried lima beans, [illegible] cup cracker crumbs, 1/2 cup ground ham, 2 tablespoons chopped parsley, 1/2 cup shredded cheese, 1/2 cup milk, 2 tablespoons chili sauce and 2 well-beaten eggs. Mix well, pack in greased loaf pan and bake at 350 degrees for fifty minutes. Baste frequently with 1/2 cup meat stock. Serve with tomato sauce.

WYNANTSKILL.

Mrs. Sanford Osterhout, chairman of the Red Cross Drive, announced this week that the total received was $428.51. A card party is planned to be held at a later date, proceeds for the Red Cross War Fund. Mrs. Osterhout thanks all those who contributed to make this drive a success.

DON'T FEAR LOSS OF HEARING!

WARTIME OPPORTUNITIES!

Good War Jobs! Defense Work!

Hard-of-hearing people are needed! Needed in wartime jobs with big pay! Needed in volunteer war service and defense groups!

10 to 1 you are not deaf—and can hear well with a little help . . . Trial is proof. Your own use of the Western Electric Hearing Aid is your best proof of successful results.

Write Today for Free Home Demonstration or for Booklet.

Western Electric HEARING AIDS

CAPITOL DISTRICT AUDIPHONE CO.
W. G. G. RENWAY, Mgr.
90 STATE ST., ALBANY
Room 1215 Tel. 4-1812

HAVE YOUR STORM WINDOWS CLEANED BY THE

THE TROY WINDOW & HOUSE CLEANING CO.
1905 Seventh Ave., Troy, N. Y.
Prices subject to change without notice.
Phone Troy 2127
Joseph Sullivan, Pres. and Treas.

CHROMATICS OPEN LOCAL CAMPAIGN FOR NEXT SEASON

Laurence McKinney Gives Address at Dinner Meeting; Community Concerts Plan Aid Attends.

Music is the most universal of the arts. In the midst of a war with Germany, we play themes written by a German and hear them conducted probably by an Italian, Laurence McKinney, president of the Albany Symphony Orchestra, declared last night in The Hendrick Hudson at the dinner meeting of the Troy Chromatics Concerts, Inc., which has begun its annual public campaign for subscriptions.

"In our orchestra in Albany, I see the Catricalas of Watervliet and Troy, the Rosenbergs of Schenectady and Albany and others from Pittsfield and Hudson, all working together to enjoy music and to give music to others," Mr. McKinney said.

And what is so inexpensive as music. You can get two seats for four concerts for little more than two bottles of whisky, he said. When you hear music, even the same music, you are laying away an investment which pays continuous dividends, the speaker said.

Mrs. Jean Fish, Bridgeport, Conn., field representative of the Community Concerts Plan and the campaign manager, declared that as the war is brought closer to every home, "you will want to hear more and more music."

Mrs. Fish urged the members to present the best concert series ever presented here and explained that the efforts of every member will be required in order to promote a good season.

Plans for the campaign were outlined by Herman J. Rosenthal who is chairman of the subscription campaign. Dwight Marvin, member of the executive board, introduced Mr. Rosenthal. Mrs. Elmer C. Schacht and Miss Lillian M. Russ were in charge of the dinner arrangements.

Persons who wish to attend the concerts sponsored by Chromatics at the Music Hall must subscribe to the entire season's series during the present drive which will be concluded Saturday.

Holders of subscriptions had until last night to renew their membership or to change their seats.

CHROMATICS OPEN DRIVE—Laurence McKinney, second left, president of the Albany Symphony Orchestra, spoke at last night's dinner meeting launching the subscription campaign of Troy Chromatic Concerts, Inc. With the speaker are Herman Rosenthal, campaign chairman, Mrs. Elmer C. Schacht, dinner chairman, and Mrs. Jean Fish, right, campaign manager.

What whiskey is so supremely fine that it has come to be associated with Nature's loveliest flower... the Gardenia?

ANSWER: PM DE LUXE
86.8 Proof
Rye or Bourbon

National Distillers Products Corp., N.Y. Blended Rye Whiskey. 49% grain neutral spirits.

UNTHINKINGLY many people are permitting urgently needed things to lie unused and going to waste in their storerooms, cellars and attics.

Among Articles Recently Advertised For:

Baby Stroller, Baby Carriage, Bedstead, Bicycle, Canoe, Electric Drill, Ice Cream Cabinet, Invalid's Chair, Oscilloscope, Refrigerator, Sewing Machine, Taylor Tot

Look at the "Wanted to Buy" ads in today's Classified Section of The Record Newspapers and see if someone is seeking some article you have. If there are things you have stored away that you know are in demand, you can quickly get a buyer for them by phoning a "For Sale" ad to Troy 6100. For best results at lowest cost ask for the 6-time rate.

MOTION DENIED TO SET ASIDE VERDICT

Saunders-Roner Decision Against Bus Company To Stand, Court Rules.

Verdicts for the plaintiffs granted at the January term of the Saratoga County Supreme Court in Ballston Spa in the actions of Hazel and William Saunders, Ballston Spa, and Raymond Roner against the Champlain Bus Corporation were upheld by Justice O. Byron Brewster in Saratoga County Supreme Court, as he denied a request to set aside the previous verdict.

Defendant's counsel moved that verdicts of $5,000, $3,000 and $2,000 for the respective plaintiffs be set aside as excessive.

It was the second trial of the case, the first having resulted in verdicts of $3,000, $1,000 and $200 for the plaintiffs as named. They were reversed by the Appellate Division because of an exception taken by the defendant.

The action grew out of an automobile accident, March 2, 1941 in Schenectady, when a car driven by Roner, in which Mr. and Mrs. Saunders were riding, collided with a bus. Roner, who is in the Army, was not present at the second trial.

WOOD VS. COAL.

Used with good furnace equipment, a cord and a quarter of heavy hardwood will yield as much heat as a ton of anthracite, experts say.

Need $30 UNTIL PAY DAY?

$30 for 2 weeks costs you only 35c

This is the total cost to you. No extras, no special charges. Other amounts up to $250 or more are in proportion. Loans are made on your own signature and outsiders are not involved.

SPECIAL SERVICE FOR WOMEN
Women, as well as men, can readily get a Between-Pay-Day loan to tide them over. Prompt, friendly, time-saving service. No long rigmarole. No embarrassment.

1-VISIT LOANS
Phone us now and tell us how much you need. Then come in on your lunch hour by appointment to sign and get the cash.

Personal FINANCE CO. of New York
342 BROADWAY (Corner 3rd St.) Troy
Phone: Troy 1500
Ask for Mr. Oshel

ON THE AIR

Radio Programs From Local Stations

TONIGHT.

1,000—WTRY—TROY—980.
P. M.

- 5:00—Hop Harrigan.
- 5:15—Dick Tracy.
- 5:30—Jack Armstrong.
- 5:45—Captain Midnight.
- 6:00—Terry and the Pirates.
- 6:15—Roy Shudt News and Sports Review.
- 6:30—Dinner Music.
- 7:00—Victor Borge.
- 7:05—Ella Fitzgerald.
- 7:15—Men, Machines, and Victory.
- 7:30—Pop Stuff.
- 8:00—Earl Godwin.
- 8:15—Lum and Abner.
- 8:30—Duffy's.
- 9:00—Famous Jury Trials.
- 9:30—Spotlight Bands.
- 9:55—Little Known Facts.
- 10:00—Raymond Gram Swing.
- 10:15—Gracie Fields Victory Show.
- 10:30—Uncle Sam.
- 10:45—Wohl's Saphisticates.
- 10:50—Jim Healey.
- 11:00—Music for Listening.
- 11:30—Music You Want.
- 12:00—News.

370—WGY—SCHENECTADY—810.
P. M.

- 5:00—When a Girl Marries.
- 5:15—Portia Faces Life.
- 5:30—Just Plain Bill.
- 5:45—Front Page Farrell.
- 6:00—News.
- 6:05—News by Douglas Campbell.
- 6:15—Varieties.
- 6:30—Dinner Dance.
- 6:45—Lowell Thomas.
- 7:00—Fred Waring in Pleasure Time.
- 7:15—John W. Vandercook.
- 7:30—Science Forum.
- 8:00—Johnny Presents.
- 8:30—Treasure Chest.
- 9:00—Battle of the Sexes.
- 9:30—Fibber McGee and Molly.
- 10:00—Bob Hope Variety Show.
- 10:30—Red Skelton.
- 11:00—News.
- 11:05—On With the Dance.
- 11:15—Harkness of Washington.
- 11:30—Club Conga.
- 12:00—News.

305—WOKO—ALBANY—1460.
P. M.

- 5:00—Madeleine Carroll.
- 5:15—Mother and Dad.
- 5:30—Dancetime.
- 5:45—Keep the Home Fires Burning.
- 6:00—Transradio News.
- 6:15—The Human Side of the News.
- 6:30—Frazier Hunt.
- 6:45—John B. Kennedy.
- 7:00—I Love a Mystery.
- 7:15—Harry James and his Music Makers.
- 7:30—American Melody Hour.
- 8:00—Lights Out.
- 8:30—Al Jolson.
- 8:55—Cecil Brown and the News.
- 9:00—Burns and Allen.
- 9:30—"Su-pense."
- 10:00—Jazz Laboratory.
- 10:30—"Congress Speaks."
- 10:45—Mary Small, Songs.
- 11:00—Transradio News.
- 11:15—State Police News.
- 11:25—Interlude.
- 11:30—Charles Molina's Orchestra.
- 12:00—Voices of Freedom.

TOMORROW.

1,000—WTRY—TROY—980.
A. M.

- 6:45—Farmer's Almanac.
- 6:55—News.
- 7:00—Good Morning Newspaper.
- 7:05—Timekeeper.
- 7:30—News.
- 7:45—Timekeeper.
- 7:55—News.
- 8:00—Martin Agronsky.
- 8:15—Timekeeper.
- 8:30—Rise 'n' Shine.
- 8:45—Timekeeper.
- 8:55—News.
- 9:00—Breakfast Club.
- 9:30—Breakfast Club.
- 9:45—Breakfast Club.
- 10:00—Morning Market Basket.
- 10:15—Roy Porter.
- 10:30—Troy Chapel Service.
- 10:45—Texas Rangers.
- 11:00—Breakfast at Sardi's.
- 11:30—Little Show.
- 11:45—Little Jack Little.
- 12:00—Noon Edition.
- 12:15—Texas Rangers.
- 12:30—Sweet and Swing.
- 12:45—Interlude.
- 12:55—Melody Time.
- 1:00—Baukhage Talking.
- 1:15—Little Show.
- 1:30—Kay Moser's Matinee.
- 2:00—U. S. Marine Band.
- 2:15—Mystery Chef.
- 2:30—James McDonald, News.
- 2:45—Piano Ramblings.
- 3:00—Morton Downey.
- 3:15—Music to Remember.
- 4:00—Catholic Hour.
- 4:15—Treasury Star Parade.
- 4:30—Maurice Concert Trio.
- 4:45—Ted Powell.
- 4:50—Melody Time.
- 4:55—News.
- 5:00—Hop Harrigan.
- 5:15—Dick Tracy.
- 5:30—Jack Armstrong.
- 5:45—Captain Midnight.
- 6:00—Terry and the Pirates.
- 6:15—Roy Shudt News and Sports Review.
- 6:30—Dinner Music.
- 7:00—Victor Borge.
- 7:05—Army Emergency Relief.
- 7:15—News.
- 7:30—The Lone Ranger.
- 8:00—Earl Godwin.
- 8:15—Lum and Abner.
- 8:30—Manhattan at Midnight.
- 9:00—John Freedom.
- 9:30—Spotlight Bands.
- 9:55—Little Known Facts.
- 10:00—Raymond Gram Swing.
- 10:15—Gracie Fields Victory Show.
- 10:30—Alec Templeton Time.
- 10:35—Uncle Sam.
- 10:50—Jim Healey.
- 11:00—Music for Listening.
- 11:30—Music You Want.
- 12:00—News.

370—WGY—SCHENECTADY—810.
A. M.

- 6:00—Farm News.
- 6:05—Morning Melodies.
- 6:10—News.
- 6:15—Church in the Wildwood.
- 6:30—Otis and Eleanor.
- 6:45—Morning Watch.
- 7:15—Uncle Sam.
- 7:30—News.
- 7:35—Time to Shine.
- 7:45—Musical Clock.
- 8:00—News.
- 8:15—Musical Clock.
- 8:30—Neighborhood Call.
- 8:45—Market Basket.
- 9:00—Morning Moods.
- 9:15—Everything Goes.
- 9:30—News by Gene O'Haire.
- 9:45—Aunt Jenny's Stories.
- 10:00—Big Sister.
- 10:15—The O'Neills.
- 10:30—Help Mate.
- 10:45—A Woman of America.
- 11:00—Road of Life.
- 11:15—Vic and Sade.
- 11:30—Snow Village.
- 11:45—David Harum.
- 12:00—News.

P. M.

- 12:05—Otis and Eleanor.
- 12:10—Noontime Melodies.
- 12:15—News.
- 12:30—Farm Paper of the Air.
- 1:00—Musical Matinee.
- 1:15—Scissors and Paste.
- 1:30—Household Chats.
- 1:45—Educational Series.
- 2:00—Light of the World.
- 2:15—Lonely Women.
- 2:30—The Guiding Light.
- 2:45—Hymns of all Churches.
- 3:00—Story of Mary Marlin.
- 3:15—Ma Perkins.
- 3:30—Pepper Young's Family.
- 3:45—Right to Happiness.
- 4:00—Backstage Wife.
- 4:15—Stella Dalla.
- 4:30—Lorenzo Jones.
- 4:45—Young Widder Brown.
- 5:00—When a Girl Marries.
- 5:15—Portia Faces Life.
- 5:30—Just Plain Bill.
- 5:45—Front Page Farrell.
- 6:00—News.
- 6:05—News by Gene O'Haire.
- 6:15—Varieties.
- 6:30—N. Y. S. Income Tax Talk.
- 6:45—Lowell Thomas.
- 7:00—Fred Waring in Pleasure Time.
- 7:15—John W. Vandercook.
- 7:30—Writers War Board Dramatic Program.
- 8:00—Mr. and Mrs. North.
- 8:30—Tommy Dorsey and Orchestra.
- 9:00—Time to Smile.
- 9:30—Mr. District Attorney.
- 10:00—Kay Kyser's College of Musical Knowledge.
- 11:00—News.
- 11:05—On with the Dance.
- 11:15—Harkness of Washington.
- 11:30—Rice Ensemble.
- 12:00—News.

305—WOKO—ALBANY—1460.
A. M.

- 6:45—Sacred Heart Program.
- 7:00—Transradio News.
- 7:05—Minute Man.
- 7:45—Transradio News.
- 8:00—Musical Clock.
- 9:00—Newsflash.
- 9:05—Interlude.
- 9:15—School of the Air.
- 9:45—This Life is Mine.
- 10:00—Valiant Lady.
- 10:15—Kitty Foyle.
- 10:30—Amanda of Honeymoon Hill.
- 10:45—Morning Melodies.
- 11:00—Food News Roundup.
- 11:15—Second Husband.
- 11:30—Bright Horizon.
- 11:45—Louise Benay.

P. M.

- 12:00—Transradio News.
- 12:06—Timely Tunes.
- 12:11—Luncheon Music.
- 12:30—Romance of Helen Trent.
- 12:45—Our Gal Sunday.
- 1:00—Life Can Be Beautiful.
- 1:15—Ma Perkins.
- 1:30—Vic and Sade.
- 1:45—The Goldbergs.
- 2:00—Young Dr. Malone.
- 2:15—Joyce Jordan, M.D.
- 2:30—We Love and Learn.
- 2:45—Pepper Young's Family.
- 3:00—Forrest Willis.
- 3:15—Landt Trio.
- 3:30—Master Works.
- 4:00—Public Service Uncle Sam.
- 4:15—Green Valley, U. S. A.
- 4:30—Joe and Ethel Turp.
- 4:45—Four Smart Boys.
- 5:00—Madeleine Carroll Reads.
- 5:15—Mrs. Harold Milligan.
- 5:30—Dancetime.
- 5:45—Keep the Home Fires Burning.
- 6:00—Transradio News.
- 6:15—State Income Tax Talk.
- 6:30—Keep Working—Keep Singing America.
- 6:45—Interlude.
- 6:55—Meaning of the News.
- 7:00—I Love a Mystery.
- 7:15—Harry James and His Music Makers.
- 7:30—Easy Aces.
- 7:45—Mr. Keen, Tracer of Lost Persons.
- 8:00—Sammy Kaye's Orchestra, Guests, Chorus.
- 8:30—Dr. Christian.
- 8:55—Cecil Brown and the News.
- 9:00—Mayor of the Town.
- 9:30—Milton Berle.
- 10:00—Great Moments in Music.
- 10:30—Corliss Archer.
- 11:00—Transradio News.
- 11:15—State Police News.
- 11:25—Interlude.
- 11:30—Guy Lombardo's Orchestra.
- 12:00—Voices of Freedom.

RAYMERTOWN.

Mrs. Marvin Bonesteel will entertain the Dorcas Circle Friday, April 16.

Mrs. Ella Robinson of Hoosick Falls is visiting at the home of Mrs. M. C. Snyder.

Mrs. Charles Bulson recently entertained the Ever Ready Class for the April meeting.

Mrs. Anna Robbins and Miss Ada Stickney have returned after spending the winter in Troy.

The Women's Missionary Society will meet at the home of Mrs. Everett Wright Tuesday afternoon April 13.

Mr. and Mrs. Lester Herbert and son Richard of Schenectady spent the week-end with Mrs. Herbert's parents, Mr. and Mrs. Lester Campbell.

Mrs. Earl Cushman had for week-end guests Mrs. Grace Frier of North Hoosick and the Misses Helen and Esther Herrington of Center Brunswick.

DANGER FIN.

The angel fish is equipped with long appendages which warn it when too near the sea floor and in danger of damaging its delicate lower fins.

Modernella Beauty Salon
.. for a CHARMING HAIR-DO for EASTER BEAUTIES

Our flattering permanent will keep your hair lovely for Easter and months to come.

EASTER SPECIAL! ARLETTE $10
Your Individual Oil Permanent ......

Shampoo and Set 70c

Feather Cut — Feather Bob Favorite For You. $7 Wave Specially Priced — $4
Duart Wave — A nationally advertised permanent that you will like. — $5
$10 Empress Special — A grand permanent for gray, dry, dyed or difficult hair. — $6
Remote Control — One of our finest oil waves especially priced for this sale. — $8

HOURS 8:30 A.M. TO 7 P.M. OPEN ALL DAY SATURDAY

Always Comfortable HERE

MODERNELLA BEAUTY SALON
13 THIRD ST. PHONE 6300

ONE OF FIVE

HORIZONTAL

1 Depicted body of water, —— ——
10 Bachelor of Art (abbr.)
11 Resident physician in a hospital
12 Music note
14 Obtained
15 Negative word
16 Siamese coin
17 Tavern
19 Bamboolike grass
21 Provide
23 System of signals
24 Mistake
26 Fish eggs
27 Inflexible
28 Like
29 Vegetables
31 French article
33 Symbol for silver
34 Lower case (abbr.)
36 Paradise
38 Exist
39 Fineness
41 Harem room
43 Sharp
44 Severe
46 At sea
50 Auricle
51 Hawaiian wreath
52 Portuguese territory in India
54 Sea eagle
55 Northwestern (abbr.)
56 Those who expiate
58 Symbol for nickel
59 Adaptation

VERTICAL

1 More recent
2 Relative
3 Son of Seth (Bib.)
4 Musteline mammals
5 Compass point
6 Journey
7 Poker stake
8 Soak
9 Constellation
10 South African Huguenots
13 Terminates
14 It is the smallest of the five —— ——
18 Born
20 Diamond-cutter's cup
22 Artificial language
23 Symbol for cerium
25 Prepared
30 Era
32 First woman
35 Spotless
36 Division of geological time
37 Knickknack (colloq.)
38 Bargeman
40 Genus of snow partridges
42 From
44 Caterpillar hair
45 Model
47 Dispatched
48 Silkworm
49 Any
51 Gibbon
53 Enzyme
57 Norwegian (abbr.)

Answer to Previous Puzzle

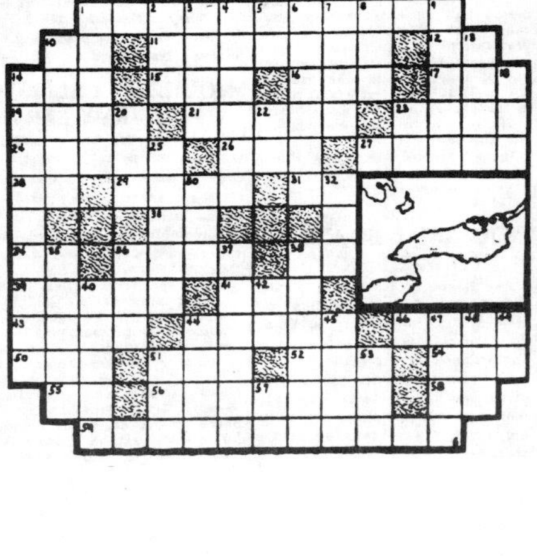

SPENCER CASSEDY, HALFMOON, NAMED FOREMAN OF JURY

Justice Daniel F. Imrie of Glens Falls Presides as Supreme Court for Saratoga County Convenes.

Supreme Court for Saratoga County convened yesterday at Ballston Spa with Justice Daniel F Imrie of Glens Falls presiding there for the first time. Clarence Kilmer of Saratoga Springs, president of the Saratoga County Bar Association, was on hand to welcome him to the court.

Judge Imrie appointed Spencer D Cassedy of the Town of Halfmoon, chairman of the Saratoga County Board of Supervisors, as foreman of the grand jury and Benjamin H. Denton of the Town of Day, a former supervisor, as assistant foreman.

Six of the grand jurors were excused from service. The trial jurors were called this morning.

Eighteen of 22 applicants for naturalization were granted citizenship in the only business of the court for the day. Three of the other applicants were not present when their names were called and the application o. the other remaining person was dismissed.

Those granted citizenship were:

John Lumnianik, Joseph Kafka and Antonina Gaweys of Ballston Spa; Leo Friedman, Sophie Quchlicki, William Vardy, Albert Sandy, John J. Pabalja and John A. Soltis of Mechanicville; Edwin Smith and Elena Aranjo of Saratoga Springs; Carl Tobler and Elizabeth J. Morgan of Waterford; Bartholomew Riordan of South Glens Falls; Laurence Jolly of Northside, Cohoes; Isaac Brewer of Hadley; Marguerite Duguay of Corinth, and Anne Muller of Greenfield Center.

WILLIAM GROVES OF SARATOGA SPA KILLED BY TRAIN

Identified by Brother; Man Believed to Have Been Walking Along Tracks in Search of Work.

William Groves, 50, of Jackson Street, Saratoga Springs, was instantly killed yesterday afternoon when he was struck by the Montreal-bound "Laurentian," D. and H. passenger train, near the West Avenue crossing in Saratoga Springs.

Dr. Frederick G. Eaton, Saratoga County coroner, directed the removal of the body to a funeral home and permitted the train to continue to Montreal.

Identification of the body was made by a brother, Malcom Groves, last night at 8 p.m. Dr. Eaton is continuing his investigation. It is believed that Groves was looking for work in that vicinity and was walking along the tracks.

Charles Manell of Whitehall was engineer of the train that struck Groves. Other members of the crew were John J. Bower, Troy, baggageman; Lawrence Hogan, Troy, trainman; Roscoe Crannell, Watervliet, flagman, and Truman Kilburn Whitehall, conductor.

BENJAMIN C. ACKER, LOCAL CONTRACTOR, EXPIRES IN GEORGIA

Benjamin C. Acker, well known contractor and resident of the Sycaway section, died Sunday at the University Hospital, Augusta, Ga., after an illness of three weeks. Mr. Acker was spending a vacation in Florida and was taken ill on his way home.

He was a lifelong resident of this city and was the son of Mrs. Rose Acker and the late Joseph Acker. He had been in the contracting business for thirty years and erected many of the homes in the Sycaway section.

He is survived by his wife, the former Jessie Film; his mother, Mrs. Rose Acker; two sisters, Mrs. Rose Perry and Mrs. Lillian Gilbert, and a brother, William Acker.

The funeral will be conducted from the residence, 562 Hoosick Street, Thursday at 2:30 p.m., with Rev David J Livingstone, pastor of the Memorial Methodist Church, officiating. Interment will be in Mount Ida Cemetery.

BY OTHER NAMES . . .

Our name "automobile" was adopted over such suggestions as gasmobile, autovic, carleck, autogo, kineter, autokinet and ipsomotor.

+ RED CROSS WEEK +
AT THE NATION'S MOTION PICTURE THEATRES
APRIL 1 — 7

TROY NOW See it!
AIR FORCE
Plus "OZZIE NELSON & ORCH."
"Blitzwolf" News
"Arsenal of Might"

PROCTORS
HELD OVER!
Spencer TRACY
Katharine HEPBURN
KEEPER of the FLAME
HIT NO. 2 EDDIE ALBERT ANNE SHIRLEY in "Lady Bodyguard"
EXTRA ADDED ATTRACTION TOMORROW NITE!
Direct from 7 Months in New York
BERT KING
Star of Stage and Radio
ON THE STAGE—IN PERSON
WITH HIS FAMOUS
"BLIND DATE QUIZ PARTY"
A RIOT OF LAUGHS!

COHOES
TODAY ONLY!
RICHARD TRAVIS
VIRGINIA CHRISTINE
"TRUCK BUSTERS"
HIT NO. 2
ROY ROGERS
"SUNSET SERENADE"
PLUS
BIG PARTY TONITE
STARTS TOMORROW
Ginger Rogers, Cary Grant
"ONCE UPON A HONEYMOON"
LINDA DARNELL
"CITY WITHOUT MEN"

NEW GRISWOLD
2 BIG HITS Today Thru Wed.
THE TWIN HIT SHOW IN TOWN!
IDA LUPINO
DENNIS MORGAN
JOAN LESLIE
JACK CARSON
GLADYS GEORGE
The Hard Way
ALSO
MY HEART BELONGS TO DADDY

AMERICAN
Tomorrow Night
AT 9:30
IN PERSON
FRANK
Bring 'Em Back Alive
BUCK

LINCOLN Now 2 BIG HITS
Bonita Granville and Tim Holt in
HITLER'S CHILDREN
THE SCREEN'S SUPER-SENSATION
ALSO
"IT COMES UP LOVE"

BIJOU
Tonight—Tomorrow—Thursday
ROBERT YOUNG
JEANETTE MAC DONALD
REGINALD OWEN
"CAIRO"
—ALSO—
KATHRYN GRAYSON
VAN HEFLIN
MARSHA HUNT
"SEVEN SWEETHEARTS"

AMERICAN NOW 2 BIG HITS
REVEILLE WITH BEVERLY
MILLER 4 GREAT BANDS
Bob Crosby • Freddie Slack • Duke Ellington
Count Basie -- Frank Sinatra
2nd HIT! DEAD END KIDS
"MUG TOWN"

NEW EMPIRE
COHOES
TONITE 2 • • • • FIRST RUNS
RICHARD DIX in
"THE ROUNDUP"
Hit 2
'THERE'S MAGIC IN MUSIC'
With ALAN JONES

Palace NOW
TO THE LADIES TONIGHT
"BOLERO BLOSSOM"
DINNERWARE ITEM!
SOUP PLATE
You Can Still Start the Set
CLAUDETTE COLBERT ★ JOEL McCREA
RUDY VALLEE
"PALM BEACH STORY"
PLUS James Craig • Bonita Granville
"7 Miles from Alcatraz"

FAMILY WATERVLIET TODAY
"THAT OTHER WOMAN"
Virginia Gilmore and James Ellison
"EYES OF THE UNDERWORLD"
Lon Chaney and Richard Dix
Beautiful Bolero Dish Night

CASINO WATERFORD TODAY
"WINGS AND THE WOMAN"
With Anna Neagle, Robert Newton
—Also—
"SHERLOCK HOLMES AND THE VOICE OF TERROR"
With Basil Rathbone, Evelyn Ankers, Nigel Bruce
BEAUTIFUL BOLERO DISHES FOR THE LADIES!

RIVOLI TONIGHT
"EAGLE SQUADRON"
Starring Robert Stack and Diana Barrymore—Also
"FANGS OF THE WILD"
Starring Dennis Moore and Luana Walters—Also
Fun and Excitement Around 8 P.M.

STATE DOUBLE HIT SHOW TONIGHT
Ellen Drew—Richard Denning
"ICECAPADE REVUE"
2nd Hit
Basil Rathbone—Evelyn Ankers
"SHERLOCK HOLMES AND VOICE OF TERROR"
GIVE TO RED CROSS

But Seven Players Report For Initial Practice Of Albany Club

SENATORS HAVE DISMAL TRAINING SESSION AT PARK

Team Adds Two Players in Reinforcement Move; Other Additions Expected Shortly.

The Albany Senators started their 1943 spring training dismally yesterday. There were only seven players on hand, the weather was too bad for a practice session and Manager Jimmy (Ripper) Collins was hors de combat with a bad cold.

But there was one bright note: Any change will be for the better.

The changing started, in fact, shortly after Collins called it a day at Ridgefield Park around noon time. There were three rapid-fire developments, which boosted the Albany roster:

1—Pitcher Leonard Gilmore and Outfielder Ernie Sites, who had had workouts with the Pirates, reported to Collins right after yesterday's drill.

2—President Tom McCaffery announced he had bought 39-year-old George (Tony) Rensa, former major league catcher, from Trenton of the Interstate League.

3—Toronto of the International League announced it was sending Tommy Davis, infielder, and Eddie Black, outfielder, to Albany via release. But McCaffrey turned down the offer of Davis temporarily.

The arrival of Gilmore and Sites was just a forerunner of several other additions to the squad expected soon. Both Bill Nagel and Virgil (Hook) Brown of last year's team, who have signed contracts, have reported they're en route and expect to reach Albany today or tomorrow

Altogether, Collins expects to have about 20 players on hand out of a total roster of 32.

Signing of Rensa, who was with Wilkes-Barre in the Eastern League part of last season, solves what looked like a first class problem for the Senators. They were uncertain as to wheth.r Ray Rice and Hank Camelli of last year's receiving staff would return.

Rensa gives them plenty of protection. Despite his 39 years, he'll probably do O. K. in the league this year. He is 5:10, weighs 180 and is right-handed all the way. He caught 90 games last year, should do as much this season. He spent several seasons in the big show with the Yanks, Tigers, Red Sox and Phillies.

Camelli, first string catcher last season, is a railroad fireman, and Rice, his understudy, is busy in his father's electrical business. Of the two, Camelli is more likely to report.

Addition of Black—and possibly Davis a little later—came as a surprise. The announcement was made by Peter Campbell, head of the Toronto Club, which lis Albany works with the Pirates.

In approving the assignment of Black, McCaffrey commented that he was not interested in Davis until his status had been cleared up. Hitch in the Davis case is the fact that Toronto bought him conditionally from a now-defunct club and it's up to W. G. Bramham, minor leagues' czar, to determine who owns him now.

The Leafs also said they were going to release Pete Gray the farfamed one-armed outfielder, "for light hitting," but McCaffrey said he wasn't nterested.

"He is terrifically fast on his feet and has a good arm but I don't think Gray would help us," McCaffrey commented "Swinging with only one arm he has no power. Last season, he got only I think two extra base hits"

Collins, still uncertain of what schedule he'll follow in conditioning the team, has called the squad to report at 11 a.m. today in the Albany Y. M. C. A. But judging from the weather forecasts, they won't do any baseball work.

Those to took part in yesterday's workout were: Fred Pfeifer and Mike Brutchak, infielders; Vic Noon and Henry Sweeney, first basemen Murray Rothma., outfielder, and Al Treichel and James Walsh pitchers. All except Pfeifer and Rothman are signed to contracts, but even these two have some previous pro experience

ELMIRA MANAGER WON'T END SEASON

Elmira produces the story of a manager signing with the knowledge he won't finish the season at the helm of the club. But it's his own doing. He has to leave the club in August to begin coaching at a high school near his home town in Portland, Ind.

Brubaker, who was signed last week, is visiting the Indiana training camps of three American Association training camps to look for talent.

RIPPER AND ROOKIES—Kept idle by a heavy cold, Manager Jimmy (Ripper) Collins of the Albany Senators yesterday directed seven of his players through their first drill at Ridgefield Park, Albany. At top he's shown giving Outfielder Murray Rothman (left) and Infielder Fred Pfeifer instructions of getting in shape. The lower photo was taken as the Senators jogged and puffed around the slightly muddy field.

COIN FLIP SENT HOCKETT HOME

Ft. Banjamin Harrison, Ind. (AP)—The Indians' payroll was caught off base by the spring training season's neatest squeeze play because a flip of a coin sent Outfielder Oris Hockett heading for home.

The stocky gardener disclosed yesterday this part of the story of his week-end absence which left the Indians only two fly chasers, forcing them to meet at least part of holdout Jeff Heath's terms to avoid starting the regular campaign with a pitcher patrolling left field.

Then Hockett, who stirred up the hectic week-end by deciding to quit baseball, changed his mind after thinking things over at his Dayton, O., home.

Returning to the club Sunday night, he walked into the hotel lobby, drew a 50-cent piece from his pocket and asked if anyone could change it.

"I want to get rid of this so-and-so," he declared, "the other morning, when I got down to the depot, I pulled a half-dollar out of my pocket and said to myself: 'Heads I go, tails I stay.' I flipped—and it came up heads."

Hockett conceded he had told Manager Lou Boudreau he was quitting baseball, but declined to say why. **"When the season's over I'll tell you all about it," was the** hustling 31-year-old fly chaser's only comment.

His leave-taking was all the more pointed since it came only two weeks after Fabian Gaffke, originally Cleveland's fifth outfielder and never replaced, likewise departed without formality. Gaffke left a note behind, saying he despaired of making the major league grade.

Nobody said whether as happened last summer a salary raise might have changed Hockett's mind about retiring. Several Indians did remark that he deserved at least a slice of the extra money promised Heath, then holding out at Seattle. Hockett set up a neat unscheduled double play and the Tribe front office is out.

BISSONETTE HOPES FOR IMPROVEMENT

Del Bissonette, former Albany first baseman, started his Hartford Laurels on their training grind yesterday under almost the same conditions as did Collins. Few players reported and the weather at Hartford was (censored). **It also was censured** by the Laurels.

Bissonette looks forward to great improvement over his poor debut year. But he still hasn't seen most of his players.

Charley George, veteran left-handed pitcher, has completely recovered from a broken leg, which kept him idle most of last year. He has signed his contract, thus giving Hartford a nucleus of three tried pitchers. The others are Ernie Johnson, who joined the club last season, and Johnny Dagenhard who was with the team in 1941.

The team is to practice at an airplane plant's field from which the public will be barred by Army orders.

New Draft Revision Will Help Baseball

BY JACK CUDDY.

New York (U.P.)—President Ford Frick of the National League believes that the new draft revision, putting "pre-Pearl Harbor" fathers in Class 3-A, **will permit the major leagues to play ou. the 1943 season.**

Discussing the revision at league headquarters, Frick admitted that there had been considerable uncertainty in baseball circles about prospects of continuing play after Labor Day or even July 4.

"But now," he said, "it seems virtually assured that we can play out the season at least in the National League. Naturally I do not know about the manpower situation in the American League, but I presume it's quite similar to ours."

Until the major league brass hats learned definitely of the government's policy regarding pre-Pearl Harbor fathers (with children born prior to last Sept. 15), they were uncertain how long the game could carry on and were operating in the hope that such fathers would not be drafted before October.

Frick said, "Now that selective service has announced its policy regarding these fathers, I am convinced that they will no. be called up until late autumn, at the earliest—although nothing is absolutely certain in wartime.

"I believe the draft boards will be busy until after the baseball season handling the 2,880,000 men whose dependency deferments have been eliminated by the new revision—men who support only wives or collateral dependents. They'll be busy also with the new crop of 18-year-olds coming up.

The senior-circuit prexy said there were about 200 players currently available among the eight clubs in the National League Of these, he estimated that about 137 were pre-Pearl Harbor fathers. About 15 others are in 4-F because of various disabilities. Five are Latin Americans. The others are unclassified, including some who will be benefitted by the new regulations.

Frick emphasized, "under the draft rule, our league will lose a few men, but we will be assured of enough to carry on in satisfactory fashion. I can tell you, it's a great relief to learn the government's policy about fathers."

Frick said he was looking forward to an excellent season and a hard-fought pennant race. All the clubs seem to be in good physical condition despite northern training, he said, and were eager for the campaign to get under way.

ANGEL, POPE WIN SHOW FEATURES

Inspired perhaps by the biggest crowd of the season—more than 800 attended—The Angel (Maurice Tillet) used his superior weight to defeat George Macricostas in the three-fall main event at the Capitol Arena in Albany last night.

The Angel, a glandular freak, used a pickup and body press with all his 270 pounds behind it to take the first fall in 14:23. After Macricostas evened the match by using a leg twist at 6:27, Tillet came back to win by using a bear hug in 7:09.

The other best of three falls match had an anti-climactic ending. Irish Eddie Pope lost the first fall to Chief Chewocki when he missed a flying tackle, plunged out of the ring and was counted out in 28:34. He hurt his shoulder in the plunge, and Chewocki body-slammed him on that shoulder to win the second f ll at 2:48.

In the preliminary, Steve Budynas of Schenectady flattened Ace Freeman with a reverse jackknife in 26:37.

INDUSTRIAL BOARD TO MEET TONIGHT

The Board of Governors of the Industrial Athletic Association will meet at 7:30 tonight at the Y. M. C. A. to consider plans for spring and summer sports activities.

T. Frank McClester will preside at the session. Operation of a softball league and plans for golf probably will be taken up at the meeting.

BRIDGE CHAMPS START DEFENSE

New York (AP)—Last year's champions, representing the New York Bridge Whist Club, last night began defense of their title as the 16th annual Blue-Ribbon Vanderbilt Cup National team-of-four contract bridge tournament got under way.

Many of the players who competed in the Masters Individual championship which ended Sunday were entered in the Vanderbilt. Defending champions are Richard L. Frey, Lee Hazen and Sam Staymen, all of New York; Sigmund Dornbusch, Newark, N. J., and Sylvester Gintell in place of Lester Bachner, New York.

McQUILLEN CALLED FOR ARMY SERVICE

St. Louis (AP)—Glenn McQuillen will not be in left field for the Browns when they play the third of their seven spring exhibition games with the World Champion Cardinals today. **He is scheduled for induction into the Army at Jefferson Barracks.**

McQuillen went hitless Sunday in what may be his last major league game for the duration.

Manager Billy Southworth of the Cards plans to use these pitchers in an effort to take the series lead —rookie George Munger, southpaw Howard Pollet and right hander Howard Krist. Since Denny Galehouse has a chest cold Manager Luke Sewell of the Browns is undecided on his hurling staff.

BOWLERS CONDUCT ANNUAL BANQUET AT WYNANTSKILL

The Wynantskill Bowling League has written another season into its history. The group held its annual banquet at Madsen's Restaurant, Averill Park Road.

Two members, Nelson Brott and Earl Shortsleeves were given a farewell in honor of their departure this week for the armed forces. Frank Milanese sang, accompanied by Pete Bertasso. Other entertainers included: Angela and Irene DeThomas, Bob Christie and Nelson Brott.

The committee in charge of the affair included the officers: Sanford Osterhout, president; Henry Hanney, vice president; Joe Vogel, secretary, and Tom Whalen, treasurer.

WELTERS LEADING A. A. U. RING MEET

Boston (AP)—A quartet of iron-fisted amateur battlers, two of them service men, thrilled the National A. A. U. boxing tournament's opening night crowd with their punching prowess as they smashed their way into the 147-pound semifinals last night at the Boston Garden.

Outstanding in that group of sluggers was **Pvt. Billy Tiger, an Indian from Fort Sill, Okla., who turned in a pair of one-round knockouts against rugged Melvin** Hawkins of New York, and Pvt. Art Saulsgiver, stationed at Smyrna, Tenn., to qualify for tonight's competition.

Tony Vero, a fighting U. S. Marine from Albany, appeared in danger of being torpedoed until his fighting spirit jumped to the whiteheat point in the second round, when he flattened Edward Timbers of Pittsburg, a really clever boxer. It was their first tournament start, for both drew byes in the opening round.

Charlies Cooper, the Washington welterweight entry, was another to advance on a pair of knockouts, he stopped both Calvin Courtney of Columbus, Ohio, and Connie Frizzi of Boston, in the second round. The other survivor in that class, the experienced Eddie Gettys of New Orleans, demonstrated his punching ability by knocking out George Espina of Washington, before outpointing Tony Brush of Cleveland.

Leroy Jackson of Cleveland, last year's 112-pound national champion, qualified for the semi-final round in the bantamweight division by knocking out Pvt. Barry Darby of Fort Sill, Okla., in the second session after drawing a bye.

Another of last year's competitors who returned with added weight was Charlie Hunter of Cleveland, a former 118-pounder, who qualified for the 135-pounds semi-finals by outpointing Melvin Johnson of Chicago.

WEATHER RUINS GIANTS' GOOD DAY

Fort Dix, N. J. (AP)—The Giants jumped on Bob Chipman for four runs in the first inning to take a 4-0 lead over the Dodgers before the weather forced abandonment of play at the start of the second half of the second inning.

Bill Jurges drove in the last run with a double but made the third out when he tried to stretch the hit into a triple. Buster Maynard, Giant centerfielder, suffered a cut on his right leg sliding into the plate. The Dodgers got one hit off Tom Sunkel in their only appearance at the plate.

where they have their annual city series with the Cubs starting Friday.

Meanwhile, the Sox cripple list was growing. Jim Grant, prospective regular third baseman, is nursing a lame arm for the second week; Julius Solters' legs still are keeping him from much action, and Rookie Outfielders Thurman Tucker and Frank Kalin are slowed down with injured ankles.

Cardinals, Yankees Choice Of Fullerton

BY HUGH FULLERTON, JR.

New York (AP)—The season is at hand for selecting this year's major league pennant winners, though we can't see what good it will do this year when the team you pick in April may be just a bunch of individuals in Uncle Sam's uniforms by October . . . Why not just wait until the end of the season and then say: "See, I told you so?" . . . At any rate, here's what this dept. has to offer in the day of selections:

National League.

To pick a winner, just pick a Card:
They're full of pep and try so hard
But never overlook the Dodgers,
A bunch of ancient, draft-free codgers.
The Reds rely on muscle magic
If they're not third, it will be tragic.
The Giants, Pirates and Cubs come next,
As pennant contenders they're all hexed.
The Braves and Phillies are in the rear
With very little hope or cheer.

American League.

The first-place vote goes to the Yanks,
As hard to stop at Sherman tanks.
Boston comes second, on a guess,
Because we like the Indians less.
Despite the ballyhood for St. Looey
The Browns are fourth, and that's no hooey.
Then Tigers, White Sox, Senators, A's,
Who are lucky if in the league they stays.

Today's Guest Star.

C. M. Gibbs, Baltimore Sun: "With the parking lot at Pimlico open during the forthcoming spring meet this means drivers may enter and park—at their own risk . . . Having done this, they may then go in and bet—also at their own risk."

One-Minute Sports Page.

Manufacturers are working on two different kinds of plastic golf balls and expect to come up with an acceptable substitute for rubber soon . . . The Women's International Bowling Congress not only bought a bomber for Uncle Sam with $1.50 contributions, but the members have "adopted" its two-man crew, Capt. William J. Crum and M. Sgt. William B. Morehead . . . Clair Berry, the Tigers' traveling secretary, never goes to ball games because he's afraid he might become a baseball fan and "let my prejudices as a fan interfere with my work with the boys." . . . Louis Messina, promoter of Friday's Charley Burley-Kid Cocoa fight at New Orleans, has invited 5,000 service men to see it on the cuff and claims to be the first promoter to play Santa Claus to so many men.

One Hit, One Error.

Bill Brandt, who takes considerable pride in the accuracy of his National League "Green Book," is the first to spot a mistake in the records of games won and lost at home and abroad. The headings were reversed, thus giving every culb in the league a better record on the road than at home.

Service Dept.

First Class Specialist Max Marek, who once outpointed Joe Louis in Joe's amateur boxing days, is at Floyd Bennett Field, instructing sailors in boxing, wrestling and judo . . . When Lieut. Dan Pollock, director of physical training at Moore Field, Tex., started from his Southern Illinois home to become a star athlete at St. Edwards University in Texas some years ago, he had just $6 in his pocket. His first hitch-hike ride was with some city slickers who relieved him of a fin in a shell game . . . The Army can't teach Dan anything about the old Army game.

Bowling Notes

Team 6 won three games from Team 4 in the Arsenal Girls League. Alida Dougherty with 432 topped the winners. Nan Schillinger had 335. Pauline Marcott with 387 and Janet Anderson with 372 were high for the winners.

Florence Knipple posted 423 as Team 3 took two from Team 1. Stella Vaicunas with 384 and Sophia Semon with 363 were best for the losers.

Dorathea Campbell with 444 and Peggy Rice with 427 showed the way as Team 2 dropped two games to Team 5. Vivian Jones with 431 and Evelyn Miller with 407 topped the winners

• • •

Hudson Women.

Emma McConbrey turned in a triple of 466, the highest for the week in the Hudson Women's League. She had scores of 145, 169 and 152. She was closely followed by Kay Tybush who posted games of 148, 170 and 147 for a triple of 465.

Other 400 scores were Lynn Davis, 184-464; Clara McPhail, 167-462; Kay Reuter, 182-455; Elinor Wells, 170-448; **Josie Lampariello, 161-441; Margaret Van Duesen, 161-431; Dolly Rich, 145-414 and Gladys Mason, 169-402.**

In team competition the Reuters took three from the Davis team while Toussaint girls captured two from the Baileys.

• • •

Marvin Neitzel.

The Cuffs won from the Gowns, the Aprons trimmed the Caps and Collars whipped the Uniforms in the Marvin-Neitzel League.

The scores:

Anna Kirik, 179-473; Eunice VanPatten, 154-441; Marion VanZandt, 164-430; Rosemary Reineke, 171-428; Mary Sweeney, 157-424; Hasel Champine, 150-419; Helen Owens, 158-418; Ruth Page, 154-414; Berniee Brown, 146-412; Anna Felock, 144-406; Claire Banister, 147-404; Virginia Messick, 143-402.

Mary Howansky had a single of 164, Nicoline Strunk, 155 and Mary Farley 151.

• • •

Pal O'Mine.

The Pal O'Mine bowling league completed their 1943 season and are now looking forward to the high-low and annual banquet that will be held at the Pawling Inn. The winning team for the third round was the Cains; Captain Fisher, Nesta, Swan, VanZandt and Burleigh. Second place was taken by the Coons; Captain Kelly, Walter, Sestito, Montanye and Meyers. Third place went to the Claessens; Captain Wagar, Claessens, C. Joslin, J. Acierno and Pillsworth.

The following prizes were taken by the following: High Average—Class A, Wagar 186, high triple—Mochan 619 and high single—Reeves 255. Class B, high average, Burleigh 165, high triple, Swan 601 and high single, Ros 217. The following were awarded prizes for perfect attendance: Wagar, Langlots, Montanye, Kelly and Claessens.

• • •

St. Mary's, Waterford.

F. Acierno with 151, 178, 165—494 topped St. Mary's Women bowlers of Waterford. Other scores were M. Vrooman, 170-486; M. Doud, 166-471; K. Gemmelli, 168-469; M. Gast, 163-465; A. Inglis, 161-424; B. McLeod, 155-415 and B. Vertefeuille, 145-409.

ERNIE LOMBARDI STRONG-SILENT TYPE OF HOLDOUT

New York (AP)—Of all the baseball holdout cases we ever heard of, that of Ernie Lombardi is the most confusing, as from all we have been able to gather there hasn't been a clear-cut statement from either side as to just what is behind it all.

From Lombardi's angle, this is understandable, as the big, likeable catcher is something of a word miser and keeps his troubles strictly to himself, and unless you can interpret short grunts you are somewhat in the dark as to just what he means.

He is as reticent about disclosing his physical ailments or injuries as he is about his dealings with the front office, and he stoically took all kinds of derisive comment after that fantastic play at home plate in the 1939 World Series rather than offer the obvious explanation that he was injured.

There have been numerous unsubstantiated reports as to the reasons for his failure to get together with the Braves on a 1943 contract. His father was very ill, and he had decided to remain in California, one report said. Another idea was that he was dissatisfied with the salary terms, and still another wa. to the effect that the club was ignorant of any salary difficulties as it had not received any notice from him that he was dissatisfied.

The Giants, for one, would take the big guy as quick as you could say "it's a deal," if the terms were right. They lost Harry Danning, a top-flight receiver, and with Johnny Mize also gone they could use Lombardi's catching and his heavy bat very nicely.

According to New York reports, Bob Quinn is willing to dispose of the silent one, wanting only a controlling interest in the Empire State Building and the Giant ball club in return. Quinn just wants about $50,000 in cash and two of the best Giant players, it was said.

We'd like to see Old Schnoz line up somewhere, whether in Boston, or New York, or Pittsburg, or anywhere. He's too good a man to be idle, and in that peculiar, negative way of his that some players, such as Joe Di Maggio, have, he has color. **When he walks up to that plate you look for something to happen, and it's worth the price of** admission just to see him lumbering down to first base on one of his two-base singles.

We missed what must have been one of the milestones of baseball. That was when LOMBARDI BEAT OUT A RUN IN BROOKLYN. It would have to be Brooklyn, of course.

ATHLETICS STOP NATIONALS' STREAK

Fort George C. Meade, Md. (AP)—The Nationals tossed in three errors where they counted most yesterday and gave the game to the Athletics, 5 to 2. The result ended a seven-game win streak for Washington.

The game was called at the end of the fifth inning.

The Athletics built up a 3 to 0 lead in the first inning with only one hit, a homer by Dick Siebert. But they were helped by Rookie Dewey Adkins, Washington pitcher, who walked the first man, they then threw wild to second on a sacrifice bunt.

WILLIAM LYONS, 5, STRUCK BY AUTO IN HOOSICK STREET

Machine Driven by Schenectady Man; Cohoes Resident's Car Blew Shoe, Hit Power Pole.

William Lyons, 5, of 522 River Street, suffered an abrasion to the right leg below the knee about 4:40 p.m. yesterday when he was struck by an automobile owned and driven by Eugene E. Abba, 1137 Third Avenue, Schenectady, in Hoosick Street, east of Fifth Avenue. He was taken to the Troy Hospital.

The driver told Central Station police he was proceeding east in Hoosick Street and that the boy was playing ball in the street and ran into the left front of the automobile. He fell to the roadway the report claims.

Daniel P. Whinnery, 113 Maple Avenue, Cohoes, reported to First Precinct police yesterday morning that he was driving his coach north in Fourth Street, between Tyler and Harrison Streets, and that the left front tire blew out. The machine struck and damaged a power company pole and the two-story frame house at 563 Fourth Street, owned by Michael Mazur, same address, and a pole about four feet high in front of 565 Fourth Street, owned by John F. Shea, same address. The accident happened about 3 a.m.

HERE are silhouettes of the U. S. warplanes—Army, Navy and Marine—that will help you to recognize them at a distance. Shown are three views of the planes—when flying head on, when directly above in the sky, and as they look from the side. Given are the company names for the planes and the popular names for them which are now used in Army and Navy communiques.

Student Rescues Dog From Narrow Ledge

A curly-haired white and tan dog of the uncertain ancestry sometimes unkindly referred to as a "mutt" was the object of daring rescue early yesterday afternoon from the Mt. Ida falls of the Poestenkill.

Marooned on a six-inch shelf of ground just back of the Second Baptist Church, with the falls on one side, water on the second, and a 25-foot perpendicular drop on the third, the dog finally attracted attention of passersbys by his shrill barks and whines.

Among those attracted were husky Austin "Red" Moore, Buffalo, a Naval flight student at R. P. I. and his companion Robert Mirabello, Brooklyn, another student.

With the aid of firemen from the Farnam Steamer House who supplied a long rope, and police, Moore slid down the rope to the narrow shelf at the water's edge, grasped the dog in one arm, and then hung on with the other while the men above hauled him to safety.

Once on familiar ground, the dog disappeared without a backward glance. He was believed to have fallen into the creek above the Pawling Avenue bridge and somehow managed to climb to the narrow shelf just before being swept over the falls.

BERLIN.

Tuesday the Kayingehaga group of Camp Fire Girls held its meeting at the home of Mrs. Nels Nelson, who is a member of their sponsoring committee. The girls tied a quilt. The Odakanya group and the Blue Birds together held a council fire in their clubroom. The Wohelo candles were lighted by Eleanor Whitney, Shirley Ann King and Nancy Vail. Candles for the seven parts of the Camp Fire Law were lighted by Ruth Schiff and Merle Fifield, Blue Birds, and Olive King, Jean Rose, Dorothy Stevens, Helen Crandall and Nancy Vail, Camp Fire Girls. The pledge of allegiance to the American Flag was given. Honor beads were awarded to Nancy Vail and Eleanor Whitney. Roll call of the Blue Birds was taken by Fay Jorgensen, and of the Camp Fire Girls by Eleanor Whitney. Three Blue Birds, Constance Jorgensen, Fay Jorgensen, and Jessie Ford, were made Camp Fire Girls with an appropriate ceremony, the changing of their Blue Bird ties for the red ones of the Camp Fire Girls. Certificates stating that they are eligible to become Camp Fire Girls were presented to them by their Blue Bird leader, Mrs. Hubert Wing. Blue Bird symbols were presented to Helen Crandall, Olive King Constance Jorgensen, Fay Jorgensen, Nancy Vail, Eleanor Whitney, Jessie Ford and Norma Shaw by Mrs. Wing. Songs were sung. Nature stories were read by Nancy Vail and Eleanor Whitney. The ceremony was conducted by the guardian of the Odakanya group, Miss Norma Shaw.

ROUND LAKE.

William H. Belton is convalescing here following an operation at the Albany Hospital.

Mrs. Bessie Morrison has returned from Detroit where she had been a guest of her son, Cecil Morrison.

Mrs. Robert Van Horn and sons, Henry and Robert of Mechanicville, are spending some time at the home of her father, Dan L. Van Horn.

Dr. and Mrs. Clarence A. MacMinn have returned from Haddonfield, N. J., where they had been visiting their daughter, Mrs. Mulford M. Brandt, and family.

Mrs. H. O. Stills of Montreal has been visiting her cousin, Mrs. Richard Read, and Miss Edith Read. Mrs. Stills is returning from spending the winter in Florida.

The Woman's Round Lake Improvement Society will meet in Library Hall at 3 p.m. tomorrow. Mrs. Edwin H. Van Deusen, president, desires to meet her executive committee at 2:46 p.m.

The Canteen Group, in charge of Mrs. Carl W. Robbins, served an emergency lunch at the Red Cross Rest Center in the basement of the Methodist Church after the blackout Thursday night. Those served included firemen, police, air raid wardens and messengers. Mrs. Harrison Goddard was in charge of the menu planning. " a preparation committee served the lunch. Mrs. Steben E. Merritt was chairman of the housekeeping committee.

ALPS.

Ervin Pratt has returned from the Samaritan Hospital.

Mr. and Mrs. O. Gile of West Stephentown have moved into the house owned by Walter Teal.

Mr. and Mrs. John Barry and family of Stephentown have purchased the home of A. Face.

CENTER BRUNSWICK.

A clinic for children will be conducted tomorrow from 9:30 a.m. at the school when children will be inoculated against diphtheria and smallpox. Dr. F. W. F. Caird, health officer, will be in charge assisted by Miss Ada M. Fass, county health nurse.

SANCTORUMS MEET, PLAN JOINT PICNIC FOR SUMMER DATE

Members of Adaran Sanctorum, Ancient Mystic Order of Samaritans, joined with Fayuom Sanctorum at Schenectady Saturday night in a meeting to plan a joint picnic at Schenectady Sunday, July 25.

During the business session, a degree was conferred on a class of candidates Abe Wolin, district deputy elect of Rensselaer district, headed the Troy delegation.

Meetings of Odd Fellows groups planned this week include: Hudson Valley Lodge, tomorrow at the 112th Street Temple; Troy Encampment, Wednesday night at Diamond Rock Hall; Athenian Lodge at Diamond Rock Hall Friday night.

ELECTED AT COLLEGE.

Miss Marie DeChene, daughter of Mr. and Mrs. Joseph DeChene of South Third Avenue, Mechanicville, a sophomore at New York State College for Teachers, has been elected secretary of the college Newman Club.

SARATOGA COURT ISSUES LETTERS ON AREA ESTATES

Susan L. Keane of Waterford Takes Whole Estate Left by Mother; Other Proceedings.

Susan L. Keane of Waterford will receive all property, including the home and its contents, by terms of the will of her mother, Ellen M. Keane, of Waterford, which has been admitted to probate. Miss Keane is named executrix.

Agnes A. Post and Kathleen H. Knickerbacker of Ballaton Spa are named executrixes in the will of their mother, Harriet A. Hayes, Town of Milton. The will has been admitted to probate by Surrogate George O. Tuck in Saratoga County. Two sons-in-law, W. Elmer Finley of Teaneck, N. J., and Dr. Ralph B. Post of Ballaton Spa, each receive $1,000. The remainder of the estate is divided equally among three daughters, Mrs. Post, Mrs. Knickerbacker and Mrs. Alma E. Finley, of West Hartford, Vt. Personal property exceeds $5,000; real estate exceeds $2,500.

Real estate is valued at $10,000 in the estate of Margaret Redmond Cunningham of Saratoga Springs, on which letters of administration have been granted to her husband, David Cunningham.

Harvey E. Karr of Stillwater is executor and sole legatee in the will of his wife, Masie Elizabeth Karr. Personal property does "not exceed" $6,200.

Letters of administration in the estate of their father, Fred B. Downing of Corinth, have been granted Arthur C. Downing of Staten Island and Ruth C. Hopkins of Mechanicville.

Letters of administration in the estate of Hattie M. Dibble of Clifton Park have been issued to her husband, Coe H. Dibble.

Celeste Van Deusen of Charlton receives all property of her husband, Charles K. Van Deusen, according to the terms of the will. She is named executrix.

Alice B. Nolan of Stillwater has been appointed administratrix of the estate of her husband, William H. Nolan, Stillwater. Surviving children are Anna N. Custer of Stillwater, Helen Nolan Neil of Washington and James W. Nolan of Syracuse.

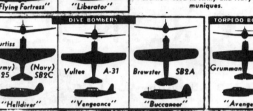

WATERVLIET NEWS

BRANCH OFFICE: 1715 BROADWAY   **PHONE WATERVLIET 1593**

RESIDENTS OF CITY REQUESTED AGAIN TO SALVAGE PAPER

Lack of Wood and Metal for Containers Creating Great Demand for Substitute Materials.

Alf C. Meneely, secretary of the salvage committee of the Watervliet War Council, today called on citizens of this city to save waste paper again.

He pointed out that, owing to the lack of wood and metal for manufacturing shipping containers, the demand of the Army and Navy for containers made of paper has been tremendously increased.

He said that, owing to the lack of manpower in the woods, a shortage of wood pulp from which to make this paper has developed.

Mr. Meneely advised that the primary grades which fit this requirement are used brown paper bags, corrugated boxes, used brown wrapping paper and brown paper containers. All materials of this type, he said, that can be accumulated in economic quantities for shipment can be readily used.

The committee secretary stated that householders saving this paper should do it from a patriotic standpoint rather than for commercial gain because collectors will pay little if anything for the paper. Because of their shortage of help, he pointed out, it doesn't pay them to handle it in small quantities if they have to pay for it.

One of the reasons why local waste material dealers have not been accepting mixed or folded newspapers, he stated, is because they haven't the help to properly sort it and prepare it for shipment to the mills.

"It takes only a little effort to save the paper needed," Mr. Meneely said, "and you'll know you may be helping to save a life by so doing you may be helping in providing a carrier of ammunition or other material so badly needed by the men fighting for you in foreign lands."

MRS. SCHANZ AGAIN RENAMED AS HEAD OF COURT REGINA

Annual Election of Officers Held by Court Group at K. of C. Hall Last Evening.

Mrs. Bertha Schanz was reelected grand regent of Court Regina, C. D. of A., at a meeting and election of officers last night at the K. of C. Hall.

Others elected to office include Miss Elizabeth Moore, vice regent; Miss Kate McMahon, prophetess; Mrs. John H. McMahon, lecturer; Mrs. Elizabeth Dahlen, financial secretary; Miss Anna K. McCarthy, treasurer; Miss Mabel A. Law, historian; Mrs. Marian Munson, monitor; Miss Emma Walsh, organist; Mrs. Ann Brennan, inside sentinel; Mrs. Joseph Decker, Miss Nellie Walsh and Mrs. Anna Bassett, trustees. Rev. Paul F. Flynn, assistant pastor of St. Patrick's Church, was named chaplain.

A social hour followed and a period of games was enjoyed. Refreshments were served under the direction of Mrs. Schanz.

AUXILIARY FIREMEN TESTING NEW PUMPS

Auxiliary firemen of Watervliet last night held a drill and put in use the recently acquired pumps issued by the Office of Civilian Defense. Four lengths of hose were connected for practice purposes. Pumps were manned by William Riley and Charles Cramer and George Roe and E. Haffman were hosemen.

Fourteen members of the organization were present for the drill which was under the direction of Fire Chief James J. Corbett and the supervision of Lawrence Kehoe.

Girl at Five Headed For Newspaper Work

Watervliet has an embryonic Dorothy Thompson in the person of 5-year-old Dianne Charlotte Powell, daughter of Mr. and Mrs. Frank L. Powell, 902 Nineteenth Street.

Dianne aspires to be a reporter. She got her inclination toward newspaper work by visiting the Watervliet branch office of The Record Newspapers with her brother, Ronald, a carrier.

The little scribe contributes personals frequently, in most of which Dianne Charlotte Powell features, but she also contributes bona fide news concerning her playmates and even of adults.

She scorns the business world. When asked if she wouldn't like to help the circulation manager count money, she tossed her head and replied, "I want to write news," and putting action to her words, made for the typewriter.

FOR SERVICEMEN—Beaupre and Spencer, above, well known local magicians, will present a program tomorrow night at Pulaski Hall in Watervliet for the Amalgamated Clothing Workers' fund for servicemen's gifts.

LOCALS WILL GIVE BENEFIT PROGRAM FOR SERVICEMEN

Magicians, One-act Play, Other Entertainment To Feature Party to Raise Money for Gifts.

Beaupre and Spencer, well known local magicians, will feature the entertainment program at a party for the benefit of area men and women of the Amalgamated Clothing Workers now in the armed services. The party sponsored by Locals 71, 163, 196 and 314, will be held tomorrow evening at the Pulaski Club in Watervliet.

The Amalgamated Clothing Workers union in this area has 225 men and women in the various branches of the armed forces, according to Edward S. Harley, chairman of the committee planning the party. The locals have kept in touch with members in the service by sending gifts to them on holidays. The purpose of tomorrow's party is to provide funds for Memorial Day gifts.

Also listed on the entertainment program, besides the magicians, is a one-act play, "Toots Joins the WAACS" with members of Local 71 appearing in the principal roles. The play was written by Mrs. Gladys Trembley. Others contributing to the program are Bernadette Piche, Laura White and a barber shop quartette. Dancing will be enjoyed and refreshments served.

Assisting Mr. Harley is a committee of sixty members of the union headed by Mrs. Mabel Bracken, reception; Mrs. Rose Avakian, entertainment; George Mallinson, tickets; Mrs. Eleanore Tandy, refreshments Miss Mary Valenti, waitresses, and Harold Aurelius, waiters.

SHORKEY ASSIGNED TO SOUTH PACIFIC

Harold J. Shorkey, son of Mr. and Mrs. Albert C. Shorkey, who entered the Naval Training Station at Jacksonville, Fla., as a seaman second class, has been graduated with a rating of aviation ordnance machinist third class, and assigned to duty in the South Pacific.

He is a graduate of LaSalle Institute, '39, and entered service in the Navy July 9, 1942.

MISSIONARY WILL TELL ABOUT AFRICA IN TALK TONIGHT

Africa will be the subject of Rev. Price Stark's sermon today at 7:30 p.m. at Wesleyan Methodist Church. Mr. Clark is the president of the Champlain Annual Conference and for six years was missionary to Sierra Leone, West Africa.

Mr. Stark recently returned from Africa, has a number of curios which will be on display. He will tell of the customs of the inhabitants of that country which is now in the battle area of the present conflict. He returned from Africa in 1940 and expects to return soon and continue in missionary work.

COLLISION OF CARS RESULTS IN BLAZE, DRIVER TELLS POLICE

Theodore Krill of 1 Craig Street, reported to police today that the fire in the automobile of Frank Rogers of Troy early yesterday apparently had been caused by a collision with the Krill machine.

He said that he was driving south in Second Avenue about 3:40 a.m. when the car of Rogers came from the west and struck his machine damaging a headlight in his machine.

Firemen were called ten minutes later by an alarm from Box 43 to extinguish a fire in Rogers' car.

HONOR PUPIL—Miss Virginia Mary Hannon, honor senior at Watervliet High School, whose name was inadvertently omitted from the list yesterday. Miss Hannon, who resides at 1427 Fifth Avenue, Watervliet, received an average of 89.567.

DAY HOME BUREAU ELECTS OFFICERS FOR COMING YEAR

All Executives Renamed With Mrs. William B. Gilbert as Chairman; Mrs. Hunt Treasurer.

GREEN ISLAND

The Green Island Day Unit of the Albany County Home Bureau held its annual meeting yesterday afternoon, reelecting all officers.

They are Mrs. William B. Gilbert, chairman; Mrs. John B. Berghamer, vice chairman; Mrs. Martin J. Doyle, secretary; Mrs. Willard I. Hunt, treasurer.

Plans were made for entertaining the new county agent, Mrs. Vera A. Caulum, at the meeting Thursday, June 10. Mrs. Willard F. Simmons was named chairman for the reception.

Members of the unit are in charge of the War Stamp and Bond booth at the Central Market this week.

Spring Play.

The seniors of Heatly High School yesterday afternoon gave a preliminary showing of their spring play "Sixteen in August" to the school children of the village in the school auditorium. It will be presented to the general public at 8:15 p.m. today. The cast is composed of Thomas Lawrence, Arthur Khutz, Armand Charron, Ann Chevalier, Lois Crandall, Ann Warren, Helen Chesky, Marian VanBuskirk, Gloria Wiese, Gloria Swisher, Ruth Davenport and Grace McLoughlin. The class officers are Claud Spaswick, president; Armand Charron, vice president; Gloria Swisher, secretary, and James Falasco, treasurer. The committee in charge is composed of Robert Grathwod and Thomas Lawrence, stage; Harriet Sickler, properties; Agnes Bailey and Grace McDermott, program; Michael Valente, Francis Mitchell and James Falasco, scenery; Adele Koughan, Amelia Muller, Patricia Harrington and Doris Shepard, ushers; Claud Spaswick, Alfred Bills, Francis Bolles and Richard Wade, advertising; Miss Mary G. Fitzgerald is a director, Miss Rosemary Boll of activities, Howard Roda of scenery, Miss Edna M. Ryan of costumes and Mrs. Frances R. Smith of programs as faculty committee members.

Speaking Contest.

Preliminaries in the oratory contest in Heatly School were held yesterday and out of the 18 contestants, the following were selected to take part in the finals Friday, June 4: Girls, Jean Cary, Shirley Rivett, Evelyn Spanswick and Gloria Swisher with Mary Mae Sabol as alternate; boys, James Hills, John Ivenay, Eugene Rogers and Stafford Willis with Robert McAuliffe as alternate. Judges were Mrs. Frances Smith, Miss Margaret M. Kenney and Francis Cnaln. Miss Marcella Keating, principal, was in charge.

To Start Gardening.

Walter A. VanBergen has called on those who have victory gardens in Plot A at the northern section of the village near the dyke, to start planting tonight. He will be there with his committee from 5 to 8 p.m. to advise and obtain assistance for those that need it. The land is all ready for planting, he says. Those who have not received allotments of land for victory gardens and who want them are advised to see him there tonight.

Methodist News.

Rev. Fred C. Bennett, pastor of the Methodist Church, will preach on the subject, "A Lesson in Praying," at the 10:30 a.m. service Sunday. Sunday School will convene at 11:45 a.m. The Sunday School Board will hold a supper meeting in the church parlors Monday at 6:30 p.m. Hostesses will be Mrs. Burton L. Deuel and Mrs. Harry Giles.

Presbyterian Notes.

At the Presbyterian Church at the 10:30 a.m. service Sunday the pastor, Rev. Henry D. Smith, will speak of "The Four Freedoms."

The Sunday School will convene at 11:45 a.m. The Men's club will meet at the church Monday at 8 p.m.

Court to Meet.

Court St. Joseph, C. D. of A., will meet Monday at 8 p.m. in the American Legion rooms. Mrs. Clara Gaynor will be in charge of the business session. A social hour will be held under direction of Miss Mary Stebbins.

Society to Meet.

A special meeting of the Italian Mutual Aid Society of Green Island has been called for Sunday at 2 p.m. in the rooms on George Street. The scheduled meeting of last Tuesday was postponed. Ralph Choppy, president, will preside.

St. Mark's Church.

The celebration of the Holy Eucharist will be held Sunday at 8 a.m. in St. Mark's Church. Morning prayer and the sermon by the rector will be at 10:30 a.m., and Sunday school will be conducted at noon.

Observe Arbor Day.

Children of the eighth grade in Heatly School this morning, during the activities period, presented a play in double observance of Arbor Day and I Am An American Day.

Letters Sent Parents.

Honor letters for the six-week course period ending last week today were sent parents of students in the senior and junior sections of Heatly High School.

EAST SIDE.

Mrs. John De Lee was elected president of the Parent-Teacher Association of School 16 at the last meeting of the season yesterday in the school auditorium. Others elected for the ensuing year include Mrs. Lloyd Austin, vice president; Mrs. Arleigh Fish, second vice president; Mrs. L. E. Hoogstoel, recording secretary; Miss Marjorie Dougherty, secretary and Miss Pauline Raymond, treasurer. Mrs. Sanford Cluett addressed the meeting in regard to the need for home nurses and nurses' aids. Tea was served at the conclusion of the meeting. An announcement was made of the desert bridge and food sale to be held in the school next Thursday beginning at 1:30 p.m.

Tendered Luncheon.

Mrs. Ralph D. Williams, vice president of the Parent-Teacher Association of School 16 for the past year and who has held other executive offices with the association, was tendered a luncheon yesterday in the school. The affair was arranged for members of the board and faculty and was held prior to the general meeting yesterday. Mr. Williams, who is with the Hudson Valley Coke Co., has been transferred to Maplewood, N. J.

Brevities.

The usual Friday evening social will take place today in Odd Fellows' Hall on Pawling Avenue at 8:30 p.m.

A meeting of the Board of Trustees of the Third Presbyterian Church will be held today at 8 p.m. in the church.

The Community Couples Club will collect old newspapers and scrap metal tomorrow in this section. Anyone wishing to donate may have someone call for the material by calling either T-6304 or T-1856-W.

REUNITED ABROAD—Gazing upward at planes are former New York Governor Herbert H. Lehman, right, director of Foreign Relief and Rehabilitation, and his son, Flight Officer Peter Lehman. Father and son were reunited when dad visited airport somewhere in England.

THALIAN SOCIETY ELECTS—The Thalian Society of the Watervliet High School this week chose officers to serve for next year. This society is composed of members of the three upper classes. Left to right are Dorothy Cox, critic; Joan O'Brien, vice president; Rita Gavreau, president; Marjorie Pryor, treasurer; Mary Lou Ellrott, secretary, and Frances Holmes, reporter.

THE WEATHER
Tonight—Unchanged.

THE TIMES RECORD

FINAL EDITION

Series 1943—No. 136. (Entered as Second Class Matter at the Postoffice at Troy N. Y., Under the Act of March 3, 1879.) TROY, N. Y., THURSDAY EVENING, JUNE 10, 1943. (Published Daily Except Sunday) PRICE FOUR CENTS

Ickes Fines Miners $1 Day For Strike

Shattering New Air Raids Announced On Italians' Gibraltar At Pantelleria

D. A. V. SEEKS LAW ASSURING JOB OF DISABLED SOLDIER

Veterans Would Protect Men Wounded in Present War; Several Recommendations Accepted.

Laws "with teeth" to force employers to rehire disabled veterans of World War II were the first recommendation made by Disabled American Veterans who opened their annual state convention at The Hendrick Hudson this morning.

The opening session accepted recommendations made by Abraham Janko, national rehabilitation officer for the state departments of the D. A. V. in New York and New Jersey, stationed at Base Hopital 81, the Bronx.

Janko recommended that the state department work for laws "without loopholes" to require reemployment of the disabled in this war who are "facing the same problems that we were at the end of the last war."

The recommendations accepted by the state department with Dr Carl K. San Jule of Tonawanda, state commander, presiding included

Six months' "adjustment pay" to each honorably discharged soldier sailor or marine so that he may have funds to clothe himself properly and adjust himself to civilian life.

Rights and Privileges.

The issuing to each service man with his discharge of a leaflet containing all rights and privileges to which he is entitled.

That the proceeds of private and government insurance paid ... beneficiaries, particularly widows, not be considered "income" when claims are filed for pension benefits for the reason that during his lifetime the veteran paid premiums for the protection of his family and payment of such obligation as accrued incident to his death and thereby deducted from income which would otherwise accrue to the benefit of his family during his lifetime.

That disabled veterans and their dependents be given absolute preference in civil service.

Adequate provision for a disabled veteran unable to work and provide for himself or his family pending outcome of his claim so that he will not be forced to seek public welfare or become a public charge.

Mayor Frank J Hogan addressed the opening session, saying

"We all have prayer in our

(Continued on Page 13.)

PAST COMMANDERS—Three past state department commanders of the Disabled American Veterans talked over old times this morning as the annual state convention opened at The Hendrick Hudson. Left to right, Henry C. Johnson of Liberty, Milton D. Cohn of Buffalo and Andrew W. Knebel of Addison served in World War I.

SICILY HIT AGAIN, RAF ATTACKS AXIS SHIPS OFF GREECE

Few Casualties Suffered in Commando Thrust at Island of Lampedusa, Eisenhower Office Announces.

BY THE ASSOCIATED PRESS

Shattering new assaults on Italy's "Gibraltar" at Pantelleria and a British commando attack on Lampedusa Island were announced by Gen. Dwight D Eisenhower's headquarters today, while in London the belief persisted that momentous operations were imminent.

"Official news of landing expected this morning," said Lord Beaverbrook's London Daily Express, headlining the siege of Pantelleria.

The volcanic little island, athwart the trans-Mediterranean invasion route to Sicily and the Italian mainland, underwent its 18th successive day of aerial attack yesterday after rejecting an Allied ultimatum for unconditional surrender.

At the same time, American heavy bombers from the Middle East kept up the pounding of Italy's Sicilian stronghold, blasting the airdrome at Gerbine and the town of Catania, and R. A. F. planes swept over the Aegean Sea to strafe Axis ships off Nazi-occupied Greece.

Italian headquarters listed 41 killed and 91 injured in an attack by multi-engined bombers at Catania.

Raid on Lampedusa.

Confirming previous Axis reports Allied headquarters announced that British commandos raided Lampedusa Island, 80 miles south of Pantelleria, on Monday night, apparently as part of the "war of nerves" against invasion-worried Italy.

A communique said the commandos encountered fire from two field guns and machine-guns on the beach in Monday's attack, but suffered few casualties and withdrew after accomplishing their mission.

Other developments at a glance.

RUSSIA Moscow stresses violent air battle as prelude to 1943 summer campaign; Red armies beat off German attacks in two sectors, destroying two German infantry companies on Leningrad front.

UNREST—Yugoslav patriots battle tank-led Axis troops in Montenegrin mountains.

AIR WAR R.A.F. lists 874 planes lost in first five months of great Allied aerial offensive against Europe, 252 lost in May.

SOUTHWEST PACIFIC—Australia Prime Minister says hour near for Allied drive against Japanese.

BURMA R. A. F. planes bomb

(Continued On Page 2.)

Developments on Strike Front Across United States

BY INTERNATIONAL NEWS SERVICE

COAL—Hopes to avert a new coal strike June 20 grew today following agreement of Central Pennsylvania operators and United Mine Workers' Union officials over a new wage contract.

BEARINGS—War Labor Board appeals direct to striking machinists of the Redwood, Cal., plant of the National Motor Bearing Co. in an effort to get them to return to work.

RUBBER—All work stopped at the United States Rubber Company's Providence, R. I., plant with a walkout of 1,000 workers in an unauthorized strike.

STEEL—Representatives of striking C. I. O. United Steel Workers at the Bonney-Floyd Co., Columbus, O., charge company refused to meet with union to discuss grievances. Five hundred walked out Tuesday.

HIGHER SOFT COAL PRICES DEMANDED BY MINE OWNERS

War Labor Board Hears Appalachian Conference Report Deadlock Over Wage Negotiations.

Washington (INS)—Coal Czar Harold L. Ickes today announced he had fined the nation's coal miners $1-a-day for their recent 5-day strike as it was disclosed United Mine Workers President John L. Lewis may win a $1.47-a-day wage increase for members of his union.

Further, it was estimated, that if the pay increase is granted, the nation's coal bill will be boosted $180,000,000-a-year.

Ickes, at a news conference, said that the 540,000 members of Lewis' union who engaged in the general strike in the nation's coal mines from June 1 to June 5 would be assessed the fine. Through this, he would not tolerate strikes while it is running the coal pits. Ickes also made it clear that the miners would be fined again if they engage in any further walkouts.

Reaction Uncertain.

It was not known how Lewis or the miners would react to Ickes' action.

While Ickes clamped down his virtual "no strike" edict, the War Labor Board in Washington conducted a public hearing into the wage dispute between the miners and the coal operators. Charles O'Neill, leader of the Central Pennsylvania Coal Producers Association, revealed that he had made a separate agreement with Lewis providing for a "wage settlement" of $1.30 a day for portal-to-portal pay for the miners. With working charges and increased vacation benefits already granted the miners by the WLB, this would mean a pay raise of $1.47 a day for the miners, O'Neill said.

He estimated that it would increase coal costs thirty cents a ton, and boost the annual cost of coal by the $180,000,000 figure. However, the agreement made by O'Neil, which is expected to serve as the "model" for the entire industry, has yet to be approved by the WLB.

Sees Return of Mines.

O'Neill said that the agreement would lead to quick return of the mines to the operators. Since May 1, when a first general strike occurred, Ickes had been operating the mines in the name of the government.

Ickes maintained that the fines were in accordance with the contract between the miners and operators. After government "seizure of the mines, he continued operation of the old contract," Ickes maintained, and the contract contains a clause calling for a $1 fine every day a miner engages in a wildcat strike. Thus, every miner in the nation who participated in the second walkout starting June 1, will be fined $5, according to Ickes.

"The fines," Ickes continued, "will be withheld from the miners' pay envelopes and the money will be donated to a charity. That is according to the contract, too."

"Customary Thing"—Ickes.

Ickes stated that the fines will be deducted next pay day. If another strike occurs, he added, the miners will be fined a $1 a day for every day they stay out.

"This fine is not new," Ickes insisted again and again. "It has been done before in the history of the coal fields. It is the customary thing."

Ickes' announcement came after Northern and Southern soft coal

(Continued On Page 2.)

RATIONING OF MILK BEING CONSIDERED

Federal Agencies Studying Problem, According to Official of WFA.

Sacramento Cal (UP) Milk may be the next commodity to be rationed, a federal authority disclosed today.

The War Food Administration, the Office of Price Administration and the dairy industry are studying ways of limiting civilian consumption of milk, expecting a decline in supplies later this year, said T. G. Stitts, chief of dairy and poultry in the WFA.

Stitts, in a speech prepared for delivery before the California Dairy Council, said food officials had concluded that the government must curtail consumption of fluid milk or cut down on the manufacture of such products as butter, cheese, evaporated and dried milk. The latter alternative was said to be out of the question because manufactured products now meet only essential military and civilian needs.

These four methods of limiting consumption of fluid milk are under study, the dairy official said:

Rationing of fluid milk on a coupon basis, somewhat like gasoline.

Restricting transportation of milk, thereby limiting, and possibly reducing, the size of urban milk sheds. This would cut out the importation of so-called "emergency" milk brought in from long distance.

Eliminating sales of cream and cream by-products.

Allocating supplies to dealers or to markets.

Stitts said it was possible that a combination of these methods might be used.

Whatever restrictions might be imposed would be nation-wide, he said.

FORMER SULTAN DEAD.

Tetuan, Spanish Morocco (AP) Muley Abd-Aziz, 65, who was Sultan of Morocco from 1894 to 1908, when he abdicated, died here yesterday.

SWIMMER DROWNED.

Lockport (AP)—Shirley Cutler, 17, drowned last night while swimming in Bond's Lake near here.

Announce Route of Veterans' Parade

Charles H. Burkhardt, grand marshal of the D. A. V. convention parade at 7 p.m. today, has announced the following line of march:

Formation at Broadway and Second Street, then east in Broadway to Fourth Street, to Grand Street, to River Street, to Third Street, to Washington Park and dismiss for memorial services at the monument to the late Rev. Francis A. Kelley.

Among the marchers will be convention delegates and visitors, the First Battalion, Second Regiment, New York State Guard; veterans' organizations and American Red Cross.

MUNDA AIR BASE BOMBED BY YANKS

Japanese Casualties on Attu Placed at 1,845 Known Dead.

Washington (UP) Flying Fortress heavy bombers, escorted by fighter planes, again have bombed the Japanese air base at Munda in the Central Solomons, the Navy announced today.

The attack, second on Munda in three days, was carried out without loss to the Americans.

The renewal of American air attacks on Munda suggested the possibility that the Japanese had succeeded in putting the base into operational use again following the destructive series of raids on that position in the early months of this year.

The Navy also announced that 19 more Japanese soldiers were killed yesterday in continuing mopping up operations on Attu Island in the Aleutians. In addition, five more prisoners were taken. This raised Japanese casualties in the Attu fighting to 1,845 known dead and 20 prisoners.

American forces still are searching Attu for enemy survivors and preparing permanent housing and defenses for themselves on that Aleutian Island, Secretary of War Henry L. Stimson declared.

U. S. DOUBLES AIR FORCE IN EUROPE

Will Be Doubled Again by September, Declares General Eaker.

U. S. Bomber Base, England (UP) Maj. Gen. Ira C. Eaker, head of the American Air Forces in the European theater, said today that the United States Air Force in Britain had been doubled since March and would be doubled again by September to "carry its full share" of the aerial onslaught against the Axis.

The American Air Force is increasing by 15 to 30 per cent monthly, Eaker said.

"By the end of the summer the U. S. A. A. F. will be carrying its full share of the bombing offensive with the R. A. F.," he said.

The increase in American planes is in both bombers and fighters, he added with a preponderance of bombers, both heavy and medium.

"The great factor, of course—and it will be the determining factor in a way—lies in the fact that we can replace our losses and the enemy cannot replace his," Eaker told a press conference.

"Our air force is on the build-up and his is on the wane. He has reached the peak if, indeed, he has not passed it. We are still growing and at a very satisfactory rate."

PRESIDENT SIGNS PAY-GO TAX LAW, EFFECTIVE JULY 1

Washington (AP)—America's 44,000,000 individual income taxpayers were put on a pay-as-you-go basis today, as President Roosevelt signed into law legislation abating 75-to-100 per cent of one year's taxes and imposing a 20 per cent withholding levy against wages and salaries, effective July 1.

GIRAUD AGREEABLE.

London (AP)—A Reuters dispatch from Algiers said today that Gen. Henri Giraud had "accepted in principle" an invitation to visit Washington. It said he was not likely to leave Algiers under present circumstances, however.

ICKES ONCE MORE DEMANDS INCREASE IN CRUDE OIL PRICE

Washington (INS)—Secretary of the Interior Ickes, revealing that stricter gasoline rationing for the Middle West was not in immediate prospect, today disclosed that he is renewing his request for a 35 cents-a-barrel increase in the price of crude oil.

He indicated that if it is turned down by the OPA he will appeal to the President.

Ickes described the oil production situation in this country as "so serious that we are right now on the edge of becoming an importing nation instead of an exporting nation."

"We have gone along like a bunch of cheerfully ignorant little children in our belief that our oil supply is inexhaustible," Ickes told a committee of 12 eastern states congressmen. "The situation is really serious."

ROMMEL SPEEDS FRENCH DEFENSES ON SOUTH COAST

Berlin Radio in Particularly Boastful Broadcast Dares Allies to Invade Continent of Europe.

London (UP) German Marshal Erwin Rommel is frantically speeding the construction of defenses along the French Mediterranean Coast, a Madrid dispatch said today while the Berlin radio dared the Allies to invade Europe, "the sooner the better."

Reports reaching Madrid from Vichy said that Rommel has been named commander of the so-called Mittelmeer Wall, the name loosely applied to the Axis defenses in the Mediterranean from the Spanish to the Turkish borders.

For unexplained reasons, however, Rommel apparently has not been given authority over the defenses of Sardinia, Sicily or any part of Italy and deeply resents it, Madrid said.

Broadcast Boastful.

Little work had been done toward defending the South Coast of France before he arrived, the dispatch reported, and Rommel has been spurring construction units into building more and better forts, more artillery emplacements and more anti-aircraft batteries.

Rommel also was said to have visited Corsica several times to advise on the construction of defenses. Before going to France, he was reported to have strengthened the Anti-invasion defenses in the Balkans.

The German radio, in an especially boastful broadcast last night, said that every man landing on European soil with arms in his hands would "either end up in a coffin or in a prison camp."

"Let there be no mistake on this point, please," the broadcaster said. "We are ready and waiting for your would-be second fronters—and the sooner the better."

"Bigger and Bloodier."

Another German broadcast said that any attempt to land on the French Atlantic Coast would result in a "bigger and bloodier catastrophe than the first attempt to invade Dieppe."

"The wall of steel and concrete which defends the coasts of the European continent is constantly reinforced and new fortifications in depth are added everywhere," the broadcast said. "The British and Americans who still doubt whether the wall is really so strong are cordially invited to make a trial."

The Daily Mail reported that Hitler already has started to recall his submarines from the Atlantic to help defend Europe from invasion. The submarines are being concentrated at La Pallice and Lorient on the Bay of Biscay, in the Scheldt estuary in Southern Holland and at Trondheim, Norway.

Vice Admiral Luetzow, German naval commentator, said in a German broadcast that naval activities were increasing in the English Channel.

TROOPS ARRIVE.

London (UP) Another contingent of United States, Dominion and Royal Air Force troops recently arrived in the United Kingdom the Ministry of Information announced today.

NEW TAX BATTLE NEARS IN DEMAND FOR 16 BILLIONS

Treasury Favors Spending Levy While House Members Back 10 Per Cent National Sales Impost.

Washington (UP) — A tax fight which some House members say may dwarf even the pay-as-you-go dispute was shaping up today over the various proposals for meeting President Roosevelt's unprecendented demand for at least $16,000,000,000 in additional revenue this year.

The big fight was expected to be between the Treasury, which favors a spending tax, and House members, who favor a 10 per cent national sales tax. The Treasury's proposal would be a tax on money spent after allowing deduction for such items as debt repayment, insurance premium payments, increases in bank balances and purchases of bonds or other capital assets.

Conference Called Today.

Congressional sources said that some aspects of this and other phases of the general tax question might be ironed out today at a conference called by War Mobilization Director James F. Byrnes. Economic Stabilization Director Fred M. Vinson, Budget Director Harold Smith and Treasury General Counsel Randolph Paul, representing Secretary Henry Morgenthau, jr., were to attend the conference. Morgenthau presented his pay-as-you-go tax views to President Roosevelt a week ago, it was said. He and Undersecretary of Treasury Daniel Bell are conferring in New York on future war financing programs.

Byrnes made it clear that the conference was to deal with future administration tax policy and indicated that details would be sent to Congress in a presidential message approving the pay-as-you-go income tax bill.

So far as Congress was concerned, two questions stood out. How much new revenue does the

(Continued On Page 2.)

MUSSOLINI NEARS END HE DESERVES, HULL TELLS PRESS

Washington (UP)—Secretary of State Cordell Hull said today that Italian Dictator Benito Mussolini rapidly is approaching the timely end which he deserves.

Hull was referring to prospects that Italy soon may be driven out of the war and into collapse, rather than to Mussolini's personal health which has been reported as bad.

His remarks were made at a press conference in response to requests for comment on the third anniversary of Italy's entrance into the war.

Hull said that Mussolini had been false to all his people and false to every law and rule of organized society, while on the other hand being as loyal as his nature permits to Hitler and Hitlerism, and to all the infamies which that comprises.

Hull started to refer to an untimely end for Mussolini but quickly changed to timely, saying that Mussolini is approaching a doom in harmony with his actions.

CZECH TO MARRY GIRL WHO TAUGHT HIM TO PROPOSE

Wellesley, Mass. (INS) The romance of a wounded Czech soldier and a British censor who taught him to propose in English culminated today in their marriage.

The bride is Eleanor Mary Brackenbury of Hull, England; the bridegroom, Charles Victor, a veteran of the battle of France and of an heroic escape from Africa to Bermuda by canoe.

Wounded in France, Victor posed as a French officer to make his escape. Of the 190 men in his company five survived. Two of the five disappeared but with his captain and a corporal Victor made his way to Africa.

They persuaded natives to build them a 15-foot dugout and in this craft the three men set out on a three-month journey to Bermuda.

His two companions were released after a short stay in the Bermuda Hospital but Victor stayed long enough for his romance with Miss Brackenbury, employed as a censor, to bloom.

TARS LEAP INTO PIT AS BEARS CLAW GIRL

San Diego, Cal (AP)—Two sailors leaped into a bear pit at the San Diego Zoo, fought off three Malayan sun bears, and rescued 12-year-old Joyce Howlett.

She had been clawed and bitten severely.

The zoo director, Mrs. Belle Benchley, said the girl must have climbed over a fence and leaped a moat to get in the pit yesterday.

Her rescuers, W. H. Fields, aviation machinist's mate and Leon Chriskurtz, Naval Training Station sailor, first fought off the bears with clubs, then subdued them by turning a stream of water on them from a hose.

CUNNINGHAM NAMED.

London (INS)—Vice Admiral Sir John Cunningham has been appointed commander-in-chief of British naval forces in the Levant in succession to Vice Admiral Sir Ralph Leatham, the Admiralty announced today.

German Morale Sagging, Himmler's Police Tighten Grip

Stockholm (AP)—Heinrich Himmler's police are tightening their grip on Germany because of sagging morale, reliable reports coming out of Germany indicated today, and for this reason keen observers here believe a crackup in Germany is unlikely until absolute military collapse also is at hand.

Supplementing the stories that leak out of Germany is the plain fact that Nazi leaders and party orators are stumping the country, setting up a strange screen of appeals for fatith in victor yand threats that "weak" Germans will be purged. Behind this screen the Gestapo head was at work with efficiency, pointing up the oratory of Paul Joseph Goebbels and Labor Front Leader Robert Ley; Josef Wagner, the Gauleiter for Alsace, and Erich Koch, the Nazi commissioner for the Ukraine.

Sources here said "Himmler's Gestapo is not applying any new methods in combatting discontent, unrest and activities endangering the war effort but is acting on a much wider scale.

"Where it used to crack down on tens or hundreds, now it is striking at thousands," they said.

These same sources said, too, that "the Gestapo has its worries: For the first time signs of organized opposition to the Nazis, in Austria, for example, are appearing; for the first time, also, the arming of such opposition is no problem. Three kelograms of coffee (about 6½ pounds) is worth a machine-gun in a country pinched for food, such as is Germany.

"It is even easier in occupied lands," the sources added. "Moreover, the Nazis' enemies are shooting down Gestapo agents with increasing frequency. Garbed as SS men, they are even known to have invaded Gestapo offices."

In Austria, where the morale is said to be especially low, more than 140 Austrians were reported executed by the SS since November for underground anti-Nazi activity. All those were announced in the press—but actually they were said to represent only a fraction of the executions in that period.

General dissatisfaction and restiveness also were seen in the character of court convictions recorded in the press during May. There were 78 sentences for war crimes such as talking disparagingly about soldiers or the Nazi party, for spreading rumors of black marketing, and for plundering in blackouts.

The charges mainly brought prison terms of from five to 15 years, but there were 23 death sentences. The Nazi policy has been to publish only a few of such cases to serve as a frightening example.

Other small incidents also show the changing temper of the people.

Travelers reaching here report, for example, the Germans now commonly greet one another with a "Heil," dropping the "Hitler," or have reverted to the old salutation "Gruess Gott"—a simple, colloquial "good day" translated out of the linking of the words for greeting and for God.

A Swedish business man returned from a visit to Stuttgart expressed his surprise at a schoolboy who used the "Gruess Gott" salutation instead of a "Heil Hitler."

"We're beginning to teach our children differently," his host told the visitor.

In Munich, an equestrian statute of Field Marshal von Hindenburg was placarded with a sign one day which read, translated: "Come down, proud rider, your corporal doesn't know how to continue." The corporal, of course, is Hitler.

Goebbels is said to have received as many as 40 highly critical "crank" letters a day, but Hitler seldom has been publicly attacked.

Now, however people were reported beginning to talk a bit more openly about the fuehrer and even the SS organ, Das Schwarze Korps, recently attemtped to apologize for him by declaring its readers should not expect him to be infallible.

The streets are full of war invalids, adding to the general sense of depression. Vienna especially is referred to as a city of war hospitals, and with the wounded said to dominate the streets, the once lighthearted capital's cafe life is subdued, with wine a scarcity.

The only young men in evidence are party functionaries, particularly the SS men, and the reaction against them is most severe in Austria and Southern Germany, it was said.

In Northern Germany, on the other hand, the attitude was said to be an indifferent "we don't care" feeling, although the Germans were reported complaining "it seems as though every PG (party member) has something the matter with him which exempts him from service at the front."

It was reported here that the Nazis in increasing numbers prefer not to wear lapel party badges. Listening to forbidden foreign broadcasts was said to have increased sharply, although the penalties still are great for that practice.

There is a standing unwritten rule not to speak within earshot of children or servants who might betray the conversations, and it is said that where three Germans gather nothing is said in confidence because of susspicion that the Nazi spy system may be at work.

The Index

SNATCHES BABY'S PURSE.

San Jose, Cal. (UP)—Carl Milton Taylor began his first experience with purse snatchers when he was only 2½ years old. He was standing with his mother at a bank teller's window where she was about to make deposit, holding a purse in his own hands. The purse snatcher, evidently supposing it contained the money his mother was about to deposit, snatched it and ran. It contained the magnificent sum of 18 cents.

MANY STYLES OF VACATION TRAVEL USED IN CANADA

Iron Horse, Saddle Horse and Shanks' Mare Placed in Service by Holiday-seekers.

New York (INS)—Summer vacationists on "civilian furlough" will have reason to bless the iron horse, the saddle horse and shanks' mare in 1943. These three will be the chief means of Canadian holiday travel this summer, whether the objective be the Canadian Rockies or Ontario's wooded lakes or French-Canada's countryside. In quieter times we went in for noisier vacations, but in a busy time we hanker for quiet holidays. Even the word "streamlined" has, in its popular sense, assumed a new and truer meaning. It used to mean de luxe, patrician, full of fancy trimmings; today it suggests something slim, practical, trimmed of all excess. Our sterner times have brought a new realism into "streamline" and every traveler secretly feels that his civilian sacrifices have turned a good word into a better.

Reserve Tickets Early.

In the Canadian Rockies, summer hotel luxury will be curtailed for the war's duration, but Banff and Lake Louise remain the region's twin capitals. The Canadian Pacific Railway brings the vacationist to these as to other points in the Dominion, but urges the traveler to reserve space in good time, for passenger facilities are not as ample as in former years. From Eastern seaboard cities the tourist can go to Montreal or Toronto whence the C.P.R's main line proceeds direct to Banff or else by Soo Line via Chicago, St. Paul and Moose Jaw to Banff.

In the foothills of the Rockies is where the cowboy's Canadian west begins. There the saddle horse remains monarch of the range, and will again prove his title at the annual Stampede at Calgary from July 5 to 10. Those ranchers and cowhands who are still tending the range will again show their skill as bronco busters, calf ropers, steer decorators, wild cow milkers and chuckwagon drivers. Indians of the Stoney tribe come down from their nearby reserve at Morley to compete in the Stampede events or to admire the reckless riding of the paleface cowboys.

Trail Ride in July.

Eighty miles west of Calgary the village of Banff continues to dominate the summer scene. The Banff Springs Hotel is closed this year but two of its long-sponsored events go on as before. The annual Trail Ride and the Trail Hike, each of them starting and ending in Banff. The Trail Riders of the Canadian Rockies have set their five-day trek for July 30 to Aug. 3, their objective being the 8,000-foot levels of Simpson Pass. Led by President Marshall H. Sheely of Woodbury, N. J., the riders and their train of pack ponies canter forth from Banff on this fifty-mile trip along Brewster Creek, past Fatigue Mountain, Simpson Summit and over Simpson Pass, spending each night under canvas. They complete their snaky circle trail at Banff where the year's Pow Wow is held.

Contemptuous of horse and motor alike the Sky Line Trail Hikers of the Canadian Rockies, headed by Sidney Hollander of Baltimore, Md. now plan to stretch their four-day trek to five days, just to show they can "take it." Pitching their main camp near Banff on the Spray River where it joins Goat Creek, the hikers can look directly up at several alpine objectives, Mount Rundle (9,389 feet) and Goat Range (8,340 feet). All about are rarely traveled trails through forest and slope, routes that summon the pioneer in every hiker.

Small Camps Open.

In the Banff-Lake Louise area there will be ample accommodations in the smaller year-round and summer hotels and camps. Jim Brewster's Sunshine Camp near Banff and Deer Lodge at Lake Louise, will be open during July and August, and so will Erling Strom's Mount Assiniboine Camp, some forty miles from Banff.

Two Ontario camps will be open this summer—Jack Strathdee's French River Chalet Bungalow Camp in the Georgian Bay district, and the Devil's Gap Lodge at Kenora, Ont. Both camps are noted for fine fishing, good golfing and canoeing. French River lies 215 miles north of Toronto and can be reached from there or else from Sudbury, Ont. on the main line. Kenora station is 800 miles due west of Sudbury.

All of the Canadian Pacific's year-round hotels, of course, remain open: the Chateau Frontenac in Quebec City expecting a good summer. In French-Canada generally, and notably in the Laurentian district, most of the summer hotels will be in full operation.

UNDER THE TREES—In Mrs. Miles Hewett's garden at Latham, members of the Woman's Society for Christian Service of Calvary Church were guests at the annual picnic yesterday. Standing left to right are Mrs. Walter Willder, president, Mrs. William Williams, chairman of picnic arrangements; Mrs. Hewett, the hostess, and Mrs. Caroline Hammond of Gloversville, the guest of honor who is a sister of Rev. Howard C. Bennett, pastor of the church, here for a visit.

rudely stopped momentarily by gas, or soldiers relaxing on the sidelines, cleaning their weapons, may have to stop for quick grabs at their protectors before proceeding.

Speed Stressed in Gas Warfare Training

Camp Stewart, Ga. (INS)—Trainees at Camp Stewart have to be "fast on the draw" with their masks in gas warfare training under the present realistic program.

For, according to Colonel Kenyon P. Flagg, director of training, realism has been increased by the use of "visible tear gas."

As a result troops may be moving along very peacefully at one moment, but an instant later find themselves in the middle of a gas barrage. These attacks are likely to come anywhere, anytime, as the post without advance warning.

For instance, a battalion may be engaged in a brisk session of anti-aircraft firing at towed targets, when suddenly the smoke gas surrounds them from nowhere. On a given alarm it is sounded, troops don masks and firing continues as though nothing had broken into their game. A night march may be

THE WEATHER
Tonight—Continued warm.

THE TIMES RECORD

FINAL EDITION

Series 1943—No. 161. (Entered as Second Class Matter at the Postoffice at Troy, N. Y., Under the Act of March 3, 1879.) TROY, N. Y., SATURDAY EVENING, JULY 10, 1943. (Published Daily Except Sunday) PRICE FOUR CENTS

SICILY INVADED BY ALLIES

PRESIDENT SEES SICILY INVASION 'BEGINNING OF END'

Chief Executive Tells General Giraud France Will Be Liberated by Allied Troops.

Washington (AP)—President Roosevelt views the invasion of Sicily as "the beginning of the end" for Hitler and Mussolini.

He used that phrase, it was disclosed today, in dramatically announcing the invasion to a White House dinner party last night in honor of Gen. Henri Honore Giraud, French commander-in-chief.

Mr. Roosevelt, toasting a unified France, promised that while this invasion was not directed at the shores of France itself, eventually all of France would be liberated.

White House Secretary Stephen T. Early said reports of the Allied invasion of Sicily began reaching the President at about 9 o'clock during the dinner.

All but two of the guests were military or naval persons. Giraud sat on the President's right and Gen. George C. Marshall, chief of staff, was at the President's left. Secretary of State Cordell Hull sat across the table from Mr. Roosevelt.

Shortly before 10 o'clock, as the dinner was drawing to a close, Mr. Roosevelt made the dramatic announcement of the landings.

"I've just had word of the first attack against the soft underbelly of Europe," the President told his guests.

Mr. Roosevelt asked those present not to say anything about invasion until midnight because of the arrangement for simultaneous announcements at that time in North Africa, Washington and London.

"Operations Have Begun."

Mr. Roosevelt, after telling of the attack and landing, continued:

"The operations have begun. We won't get definite news until later. But the news will be coming in from now on."

Then he said:

"This is a good illustration of the fact of planning not the desire for planning, but the fact of planning.

"With the commencing of the expedition in North Africa with complete cooperation with the British and ourselves—that was followed by complete cooperation with the French in North Africa. The result after landing was the battle of Tunis. That was not all planning. That was cooperation. And from that time on we have been working in complete harmony.

"There are a great many of objectives, of course, and the major objective is the elimination of Germany. That goes without saying, as a result of the step which is in progress at this moment. We hope it is the beginning of the end.

"Last autumn the Prime Minister of England called it 'the end of the beginning.' I think we can almost

(Continued on Page 2.)

REPORT ROLLBACK OF COFFEE PRICES ABANDONED BY OPA

Washington (UP)—The administration has abandoned the projected rollback of retail coffee prices and will limit the subsidy-rollback program to butter and meat, it was learned today.

Price Administrator Prentiss M. Brown reportedly gave such assurances to Congress this week, a fact that generally is credited with enabling the administration finally to defeat congressional attempts to outlaw all subsidy-rollbacks.

Abandonment of the subsidized roll-back theory, except for the programs already under way, was disclosed by Sen. Robert F. Wagner, D., N. Y., strong administration supporter and chairman of the Senate banking committee, when he was asked whether the issue would dominate the fall session of Congress.

"They (roll-back subsidies) won't be an issue any more," Wagner replied. "There won't be any more such programs."

THOMAS W. WALLACE.

LIEUT. GOVERNOR CRITICALLY ILL

Thomas W. Wallace Fighting for Life in Schenectady Hospital.

Albany (AP)—Lieut. Gov. Thomas W. Wallace is critically ill with pneumonia and under oxygen tent treatment in a Schenectady hospital, the office of Governor Dewey announced today.

The 43-year-old Republican Lieutenant Governor, a resident of Schenectady, was placed in the tent at Ellis Hospital last night. His illness began with an attack of chicken pox which developed last Saturday.

Dr. James Smith, one of the attending physicians, said at Schenectady that Wallace "is very seriously ill." Pneumonia developed Thursday and he was taken to the hospital yesterday.

Wallace, former Schenectady County district attorney, was elected Lieutenant Governor by a close margin over Democratic Charles Poletti, the incumbent, last November in a political upheaval that gave New York its first Republican administration in twenty years. He assumed office simultaneously with Governor Dewey, Jan. 1.

Wallace became the Republican candidate for Lieutenant Governor after going to the party's state convention at Saratoga a candidate for nomination for attorney general. He accepted second place on the ticket at the request of county chairman, who wanted a New York City resident for attorney general.

Born in Schenectady, Jan. 24, 1900, Wallace was educated in its public schools, at Union College and Albany Law School.

HINES IS DENIED JUDICIAL REVIEW OF PAROLE RULING

White Plains (AP)—James J. Hines, former Democratic district leader now serving a four to eight-year sentence in Sing Sing Prison, has been refused a judicial review of a state parole board decision denying him a parole.

Supreme Court Justice Gerald Nolan yesterday turned down Hines' application, contending that the "petition does not contain a plain or concise statement of material fact. The objectionable portions are so interwoven with allegations of fact that it is impossible for the court to separate."

Hines contended the board failed to comply with the law in its refusal to parole him and in arguing the motion on June 28 before Justice Nolan his attorney said that when Hines was interviewed by the board the sole matter discussed was whether he was guilty of the crime.

Hines was convicted three years ago on four counts of contriving a lottery.

CHAMPLIN ELECTED V. F. W. COMMANDER

Utica (UP)—Frank O. Champlin, New York City, an R. H. Macy and Co. executive, today began his term as commander of the State Veterans of Foreign Wars after election at the 24th convention. He succeeds Adrian J. Goldsmith, of Solvay.

Other officers elected as the encampment was brought to a close yesterday were: Junior vice-commander, Francis C. Dale, of Coldspring, Putnam County, and senior vice-commander, Jacob A. Latona of Buffalo, a captain in the New York State Guard. The convention voted unanimously to hold the 1944 encampment in Buffalo.

PLANE SCARE CAUSES DROWNING OF SISTERS

Santa Rosa, Cal. (AP)—Three sisters screamed, then stumbled into a deep waterhole as two planes roared low over the Russian River resort where they were wading.

Two of the sisters, Rose and Louise Guidotti, aged 24 and 19, of Salinas, Cal., were drowned yesterday. The third, Marie, returned safely to shallow water. None of the girls could swim.

Coroner Vernon Silvershield is trying to learn if the planes were on maneuvers or were stunting over the resort to give bathers a thrill.

LONDON OBSERVER HINTS NEW ALLIED INVASION MOVES

Coordinated Drives in Mediterranean Possible; Prolonged Fighting Expected in Sicily.

London (AP)—The invasion of Europe now under way through Sicily should not be regarded as "the only landing, nor even as the landing" planned by the Allies, a British observer told correspondents today.

He also warned that "hard and prolonged fighting must be expected" against the island's total defense forces, estimated at 400,000.

Deployment of the Allied striking power along the upper coast of North Africa suggested a strong possibility that the assault on Sicily might be accompanied at any moment by coordinated moves elsewhere along the Mediterranean front, it was said.

This possibility also was strengthened by Gen. Dwight D. Eisenhower's statement in his personal message broadcast to Europe that the "battle of Europe" had now begun.

The total strength of the Allied forces in the Mediterranean area has never even been suggested by Allied sources, but Axis feeler broadcasts reported 44 infantry divisions, from 15 to 20 tank divisions, two air-borne divisions, and a parachute battalion ready in northwest Africa and the Middle East.

Warn of Heavy Losses.

London sources declined to comment on the chain of command under General Eisenhower, although there had been no indication of any change in the team which swept Tunisia clean. This had Gen. Sir Harold Alexander in charge of ground forces and Air Chief Marshal Sir Arthur Tedder commanding in the air.

British newspapers warned readers to prepare for heavy losses and possible setbacks before Sicily is taken.

Workers in war factories cheered announcement of the invasion news over loudspeaker systems.

"This news gives up heart. We know we really are working for something now," was a typical remark.

Selection of Sicily for the first assault was no surprise, for a cleanup of the Mediterranean islands has been plainly hinted as the Allies' next step.

"Sicily is the only target in the Mediterranean against which the full weight of Allied material superiority could be brought to bear upon the enemy," said the Evening Standard's military correspondent.

Other Divisions Ready.

With dozens of other Allied divisions standing by between Morocco and Syria, it was emphasized in London that this landing is not likely to be the only one of the summer.

Unofficial hints from Washington, reported by Reuters, tended to confirm London correspondents' estimates that neither the veteran British Eighth Army nor the eager American Fifth Army had been thrown into the Sicily assault. There was nothing to suggest that the French army—75,000 of whom are reported fully-equipped—had joined the attack, and the British Ninth and Tenth Armies also are standing by in the East for new jobs.

The threat of action from these forces is likely to deter the Axis from heavily reinforcing the Sicilian garrison from either Italy or the Balkans.

"Even larger forces" than those of the Mediterranean were disclosed by Prime Minister Churchill to be gathering in Britain, and on June 30 he promised that "very probably there will be heavy fighting in the Mediterranean and elsewhere before the leaves of autumn fall."

YOUNG SEMINARIAN DROWNS IN LAKE

Point Chautauqua (UP)—Frank T. Borrasca, 18-year-old Buffalo seminarian, drowned in Lake Chautauqua yesterday despite a rescue attempt by another Buffalo youth, Eugene Radm, 21.

Borrasca was swimming to a raft when he suffered cramps and sunk beneath the water. Radm, boating some distance from his friend, saw Borrasca go down for the first time, and hurried to the spot in a canoe.

Making several dives in rapid succession, Radm, surfaced finally with Borrasca in his left arm, struck out for shore. Resuscitation was applied for three hours but failed.

STOCK EXCHANGE TO EMPLOY WOMEN

New York (AP)—The New York Stock Exchange for the first time in its 151-year history will employ women on the exchange floor starting Monday morning, it was announced.

After a course of training 36 young women have been selected as pages and "quote girls," to take over duties formerly looked after by men now serving in the armed forces.

Eighteen of the women had worked for the exchange in administrative departments and the remainder are new employees.

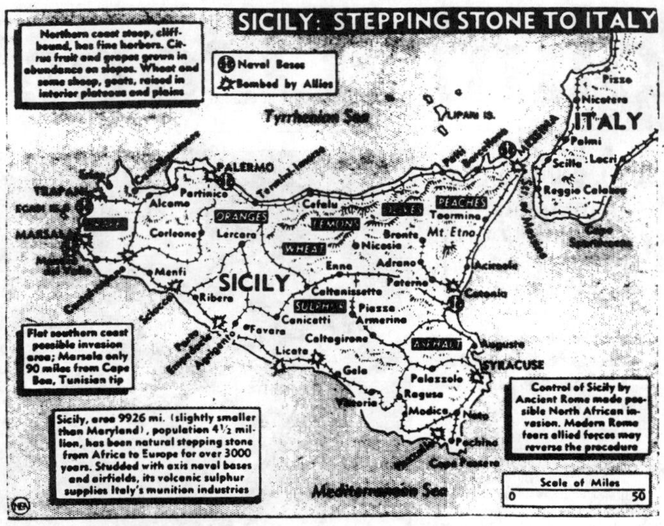
SICILY: STEPPING STONE TO ITALY
Northern coast steep, cliff-bound, has fine harbors. Citrus fruit and grapes grown in abundance on slopes. Wheat and some sheep, goats, raised in interior plateaus and plains
Naval Bases
Bombed by Allies
Tyrrhenian Sea
ITALY
SICILY
Palermo
Trapani
Marsala
Alcamo
Partinico
Corleone
Menfi
Ribera
Lercara
Cefalu
Nicosia
Bronte
Mt. Etna
Enna
Adrano
Paterno
Caltanissetta
Canicatti
Licata
Piazza Armerina
Caltagirone
Gela
Vittoria
Ragusa
Modica
Noto
Pachino
Cape Passero
Palazzolo
Augusta
Syracuse
Catania
Palmi
Locri
Reggio Calabria
Pizzo
ORANGES
LEMONS
WHEAT
SULPHUR
ASPHALT
PEACHES
Flat southern coast possible invasion area; Marsala only 90 miles from Cape Bon, Tunisian tip
Sicily, area 9926 mi. (slightly smaller than Maryland), population 4½ million, has been natural stepping stone from Africa to Europe for over 3000 years. Studded with axis naval bases and airfields, its volcanic sulphur supplies Italy's munition industries
Control of Sicily by Ancient Rome made possible North African invasion. Modern Rome fears allied forces may reverse the procedure
Mediterranean Sea
Scale of Miles
0
50

PRESS SWARMS ASHORE IN SICILY

Allied Forces Accompanied by Large Number of War Correspondents.

An Allied force command post in North Africa (AP) With Allied soldiers landing in Sicily today carrying the latest death-dealing weapons went war correspondents and photographers carrying typewriters, notebooks and cameras.

They will give the people of the United Nations first-hand accounts in words and pictures of the first direct thrust into Hitler's European stronghold.

A total of 54 American, British, Canadian and Australian correspondents went with the combat forces invading the island gateway to Italy. At least twenty of them were scheduled to land with the troops fighting their way first on the beaches and then inland.

Twenty-nine others were assigned directly to naval forces participating in the operations, and the remainder to the field headquarters of commanders.

It is the largest force of correspondents and photographers ever taken on such a venture and every one of them carried only the weapons of his trade and no instruments for killing.

As long ago as June 12 Gen. Dwight D. Eisenhower took the correspondents in North Africa numbering nearly 100 into his confidence on some aspects of the Allied plans for the first direct smash threatening Italy and the Axis great European fortress.

Then the correspondents began to disappear singly to join units with which they were to go in the landings.

STRIKERS BLOCK MINE ENTRANCES IN PENNSYLVANIA

Pittsburg (AP) While a federal investigation of coal mine work stoppages was under way, insurgent strikers blocked entrances today at the big gates mines of the H. C. Frike Coke Co. near Brownsville and prevented some 500 diggers from going back to work.

It was at this mine that workers burst through picket lines yesterday but today a larger force, estimated between 140 and 170 pickets, was on the scene.

State Police broke up a traffic jam when pickets stopped a bus carrying miners, by ordering the pickets to move on, but neither the bus nor automobiles following it attempted to drive to the mine entrance.

Sicily Is Natural Road Into Italy

Reports Hint Three Landings in Sicily

BY THE ASSOCIATED PRESS.

Axis and Allied reports indicated today that Gen. Dwight D. Eisenhower's sea-borne invasion forces landed in at least three areas of Sicily.

Italian headquarters said Allied troops, spearheaded by parachutists, landed on the southern and eastern coasts.

A German broadcast said the Allies landed "in the southeastern part of Sicily," and declared it could not be stated whether landing attempts had been made at other points on the island.

An Algiers radio report said Allied forces also swept ashore on the rock-studded western tip of the island, near the bomb-ruined port of Trapani.

MEAT SHORTAGE BLAMED ON OPA

Republican Committee Charges Utter Failure of Control Program.

Washington (AP) A Republican committee studying the food situation blamed the Office of Price Administration (OPA) today for domestic meat shortages.

"We have the paradox of the largest inventory of live animals in the history of the United States, and yet the flow of meat products through the regular trade channels has been slowed up and almost stopped entirely," said the report of a committee of Republican congressmen headed by Representative Chenoweth (R., Col.).

Asking: "What has caused scarcity in this land of plenty?" The report declared "it is the utter failure of the OPA, through its meat control section, to properly appraise the situation and then take the necessary steps to insure adequate supplies of meat at all times."

The group asserted that wholesale price ceilings have been too low, and that "every animal slaughtered has resulted in a loss."

"Packers cannot obtain live animals in competition with the black market bidder," the committee said.

Price ceilings have discouraged the feeder—have left no margin for him to finish cattle and "as a result, millions of pounds of beef have been lost to the American consumer," the report declared.

The fixing of slaughter quotas at 70 per cent of the 1941 kill was described as "another tragic mistake."

Mountainous Island Has Been Battle Scene for Ages; Only Two Miles From Mainland.

BY THE UNITED PRESS

Mountainous Sicily, scene of battle for ages, is the natural road into Italy.

Jutting out from the toe of the Italian boot, the triangular-shaped island is actually more like a continuation of Italy itself.

Knowing this, the Axis reportedly has made the island its strongest bastion of the many fringing the continent.

Italy lies only two miles away from the island shore across the Straits of Messina at the closest point.

How far the Axis defenses have progressed is not known for sure but it is certain that strong fortifications and defense positions vulnerable only to the strongest assault have been set up and that the fighting will bear no resemblance to the collapse of Pantelleria and Lampedusa, small Italian islands in the Mediterranean which succumbed to air bombardment.

Sicily contains about 4,000,000 people. Its area is 9,936 square miles, including some minor nearby islands. Most of the island tops 500 feet above sea level, rising to the highest point, volcanic Mount Etna, 10,868 feet. The mountain has a base of 400 square miles.

Fighting on the island would range through vineyards, big flowered slopes and orchards, including orange and lemon groves. There are many good roads.

The southern part of Sicily is famous for its olive, orange and lemon groves. With a climate similar to that of California, Sicily has had snow only seven times in the last forty years. Rain rarely falls during the summer months.

The largest city in Sicily, Palermo, has a normal population of 417,000. It is on the north side of the island and has better communications with the interior than any Sicilian port except Catania. It is

(Continued on Page 2.)

MME. CHIANG'S PLANE ALMOST LANDED IN JAPANESE TERRITORY

Chungking (AP)—Mrs. Chiang Kai-shek, wife of the Chinese generalissimo, who returned here last Sunday after an extended tour of the United States and Canada, disclosed today that the plane carrying her home became lost on the flight from India and almost landed in Japanese territory.

She told newsmen that the plane piloted by an American crew, accidentally followed the beam of a Japanese air field in Burma but that the pilot had a sudden hunch and pulled away just as he was on the verge of landing and turned back to Chungking.

"If it hadn't been for his hunch we would today have been the state guests of the imperial Japanese government," said China's first lady.

After flying continuously at 24,000 feet for seven hours, Mrs. Chiang said, she didn't care where she landed.

The Index

Eisenhower Urges French To Be Calm

Allied Headquarters, North Africa (UP)—Gen. Dwight D. Eisenhower, supreme commander of Allied forces in North Africa, told the French people by radio today that the Allied landings in Sicily marked the "first stage in the liberation of the European continent."

He called on the French people to remain calm and not expose themselves to reprisals through premature action.

"When the hour of action strikes, we will let you know," he said. "Until then, help us by following our instructions."

The text of Eisenhower's broadcast, made over the Algiers radio:

"The Anglo-American - Canadian armed forces have today launched an offensive against Sicily. It is the first stage in the liberation of the European continent. There will be others.

"I call on the French people to remain calm, not to allow themselves to be deceived by the false rumors which the enemy might circulate.

"The Allied radio will keep you informed on military developments. I count on your sang-froid and on your sense of discipline. Do not be rash, for the enemy is watching. Keep on listening to the Allied radio and never heed rumors. Verify carefully the news you receive.

"By remaining calm and by not exposing yourselves to reprisals through premature action, you will be helping us effectively.

"When the hour of action strikes, we will let you know. Till then, help us by following our instructions. That is to say: Keep calm, conserve your strength. We repeat: When the hour of action strikes, we will let you know."

American, British, Canadian Armies Storming Island

Meager Reports From Mediterranean Battle Zone Indicate Early Success of Allied Smash; President Tells Pope Vatican Domains Will Be Respected; Axis Rushes Reinforcements Across Messina Strait; Heavy Fighting Reported.

London (UP)—The Rome radio broadcast tonight that Italian naval forces had gone into action off Sicily.

The broadcast also said that Italian torpedo bombers, attacking Allied invasion ships, had hit and damaged three transports—of 7,000, 10,000 and 12,000 tons.

Violent air battles involving "masses of planes" were described.

BY THE ASSOCIATED PRESS.

A huge Allied invasion army of American, British and Canadian troops stormed ashore on the gun-studded beaches of Sicily today, landing in perhaps three or more key zones, and as the hours passed there was every indication of at least preliminary success.

By noon, more than 15 hours after the invasion began, the enemy made no claim of having turned back any part of the multi-pronged assault which President Roosevelt described in Washington as "the beginning of the end" of Hitler's Europe.

Zero hour for the invasion was 3 a.m., European time this morning (9 p.m. Eastern War Time last night.)

An Algiers broadcast at noon today said "everything is going according to plan" in the momentous assault which rang up the curtain on the battle of Europe.

(United Press reports from Madrid and large numbers of Allied troops were already ashore in Sicily and were establishing bridge-heads and pushing inland.)

President Roosevelt advised Pope Pius XII today that as American and British soldiers fight to rid Italy of fascism "the neutral status of Vatican City as well as of the papal domains throughout Italy will be respected."

The President's message to the Pope, given out at the White House, clearly held forth the prospect that the invasion of the Italian island of Sicily would be followed by similar operations against the Italian mainland.

Mighty Allied Invasion Host.

Axis estimates indicated that a mighty host of at least thirty Allied divisions—perhaps 450,000 troops—had been thrown into the invasion, together with 2,000 planes.

London sources pictured the attack as being evenly divided between battle-hardened American and British troops, supported by Canadian forces moved into the Mediterranean since the battle of Africa ended June 10.

Sicily's importance, both to Italy and as the gateway to Europe, was emphasized long ago when Garibaldi issued his famous proclamation: "Here we make Italy or we die."

A bulletin from Italian headquarters said Allied parachutists spearheaded the assault and reported that fighting was in progress along the southern and eastern coasts, nearest to Italy.

First unofficial reports, according to the British news agency Reuters, said operations were going "according to plan."

Heavy Axis reinforcements were reported streaming across the narrow Messina Strait from Southern Italy to combat the invasion.

London quarters hinted that the assault on Sicily might be accompanied at any moment by coordinated moves elsewhere along the Mediterranean front.

Message to Pope Pius.

The President's message to Pope Pius follows:

By the time this message reaches Your Holiness, a landing in force by American and British troops will have taken place on Italian soil. Our soldiers have come to rid Italy of fascism and all its unhappy symbols, and to drive out the Nazi oppressors who are infesting her soil.

"There is no need for me to reaffirm that respect for religious beliefs and for the free exercise of religious worship is fundamental to our ideals. Churches and religious institutions will, to the extent that it is within our power, be spared the devastations of war during the struggle ahead.

"Throughout the period of operations the neutral status of Vatican City as well as of the papal domains throughout Italy will be respected.

"I look forward, as does Your Holiness, to that bright day when the peace of God returns to the world. We are convinced that this will occur only when the forces of evil which now hold vast areas of Europe and Asia enslaved have been utterly destroyed. On that day we will joyfully turn our energies from the grim duties of war to the fruitful tasks of reconstruction. In common with all other nations and forces imbued with the spirit of good will toward men and with help of Almighty God, we will turn our hearts and our minds to the exacting task of building a just and enduring peace on earth.

Dispatches from Ankara said there was a strong possibility of action in the Balkans this week-end, with the Germans feverishly reinforcing their defenses in the traditional "powder-keg" countries as well as key islands in the Aegean Sea.

British newspapers warned readers to expect heavy losses and possible setbacks before the conquest of Sicily, Italy's strongest island bastion, is completed.

Landed By Moonlight.

"The enemy started last night, with support of strong air and sea formations and with dropping of parachutist units, the attacks against Italy," a Fascist communique said.

"Axis armed forces are decisively counter-attacking the enemy's action."

Dispatches from Allied headquarters said Gen. Dwight D. Eisenhower's combined forces swarmed ashore in bright moonlight, under cover of a terrific barrage by Allied warships.

Sicily lies 260 airline miles from Rome and its eastern tip is only two miles across Messina Strait from the "toe" of Italy.

"The battle of Africa is over; the battle of Europe has begun!" an Algiers broadcast said, in a message to the conquered nations of Europe.

Hours after the great test began, the enemy made no claim of having beat off or defeated any part of the Allied sea-borne forces—nor was there any claim of the shore-bound Italian fleet having swung into action.

Tersely the German high command said the Allies "immediately encountered strong defenses on the ground and in the air. Fighting is still progressing."

Heavy Fighting Reported.

A Nazi propaganda broadcast asserted that Allied parachutists were "encircled and rendered harmless" and declared that Axis coastal batteries and bombers sank a number of landing craft filled with troops and supplies.

"The invasion forces were immediately engaged in heavy fighting which proved extraordinarily costly for them," the Berlin radio said.

Dispatches from Gen. Eisenhower's headquarters said Allied troops, slipping ashore in snub-nosed, shallow-craft boats from convoys a mile or more off the coast, cut through wire barriers and hot machine-gun defenses and then, with hardly a moment's pause, began battering their way inland.

Swarms of Allied planes filled the skies, forming a vast aerial umbrella over the invasion forces and smashing at Axis fortifications.

The Algers radio said Allied forces swept ashore from landing barges on the rock-studded western tip of Sicily, near the bomb-ruined port of Trapani.

London quarters said the grand-

(Continued on Page 2.)

THE WEATHER
Tonight—Showers.

THE TIMES RECORD

FINAL EDITION

Series 1943—No. 174. (Entered as Second Class Matter at the Postoffice at Troy, N. Y., Under the Act of March 3, 1879.) TROY, N. Y., MONDAY EVENING, JULY 26, 1943. (Published Daily Except Sunday) PRICE FOUR CENTS

Martial Law Imposed On Italy; Mussolini Drops From Sight

ESSEN BOMBED IN GIANT RAID TO CAP RECORD WEEK-END

Deep New Inroads Made on Hitler's Production in Assaults on Hamburg, Cologne and Other Points.

London (U.P.)—Allied planes, including heavy bombers, attacked targets on the European continent throughout today, following up the heaviest week-end air offensive of the war in which Essen, Germany's greatest arms center, was bombed during the night.

Allied planes crossed and recrossed the English coast all day. Anti-aircraft guns could be heard frequently on the French coast and heavier explosions indicated that bombs had been dropped near the coast.

Every type American and British plane in the European arsenal participated in day and night raids, ranging as far north as Trondheim, as far south as Leghorn and deep into Germany.

Maintaining the round-the-clock schedule, other formations of bombers and fighters roared across Dover Strait in daylight today.

Twenty-five bombers were lost in last night's "very heavy" attack on Essen and a smaller-scale raid by swift wooden Mosquito bombers on Hamburg and Cologne, Germany's second and third cities respectively. The raid on Hamburg was the third in a little more than 24 hours.

Essen Factories Hard Hit.

The British bombers, flying through good weather, hit Essen for the 57th time in an attack probably not much smaller in scale than the record assault on Hamburg Saturday night in which 2,300 tons of explosives were dropped.

First reports indicated the Essen raid made deep new inroads on industrial production for Hitler's war machine. Five enemy fighters were destroyed by the bombers and by planes operating over Western Europe.

The American part in the week-end assaults found the Eighth U. S. Air Force putting in its greatest day of bombing yesterday and making its deepest penetration of Germany in the war. Fighters and bombers attacked over Germany, France, Holland and Belgium in the record-breaking raids.

May Beat June Record.

Despite a lull of five days previous to the Hamburg attack Saturday, it appeared possible the Allied planes would equal and possibly exceed June's mark of 15,000 tons of explosives dropped on Germany.

German planes made weak re-

(Continued on Page 18.)

NATIONAL PARLEY ON FOODS CALLED BY FRANK GANNETT

Rochester (U.P.)—Frank Gannett of the Gannett Newspapers announced today that as a result of appeals from the heads of Departments of Agriculture in 16 states and from several U. S. Senators, he has called a national food conference to be held in the Hotel Sherman in Chicago on Sept. 9 and 10

"The state agrcicultural leaders, in urging me to take leadership in arranging this conference, pointed out that food is an essential weapon in waging war," Gannett said. "They believe it is imperative that we immediately find ways and means for increasing our food production next year and that we must have better handling of our present food supply, so that we may be able to feed our armed forces and have sufficient food to sustain the health and morale of our civilian population providing the implements of war."

LOST—

PIN — Shape of crescent moon, solid gold, set with stones. Lost in Proctor's or on River St., Troy. Finder please phone Cohoes 791.

FOUND—

The owner of the pin was "mighty glad" to have it back.

It's inexpensive to recover an article of financial or sentimental value, by placing your "Lost" sign at the crossroads, where thousands pass daily.

The Classified Section of The Record Newspapers

Rumors Spring Up In Wake Of Mussolini

BY UNITED PRESS.

Benito Mussolini appeared to have vanished from public view amid the ruins of his Fascist regime today but there were countless rumors that he was fleeing to exile, was under arrest or was critically ill.

Reports seeping through neutral sources speculated that the ousted Italian dictator had:

1—Fled to Switzerland.
2—Fled to Germany.
3—Been arrested, with other Fascist leaders, by the Italian army leaders to be turned over to the Allies for trial on "war guilt" charges after a peace deal is made.
4—Made a deal under which he would seek to save his own skin by arranging an escape through the Vatican, where his son-in-law is ambassador.

ALLIES IN SICILY CAPTURE TERMINI, SEIZE 7,000 MORE

Six Italian Generals and Admiral Added to List of High Officers Taken Prisoner.

Allied Headquarters in North Africa (AP) Allied troops are squeezing tighter upon Axis last-stand defenses in Northeastern Sicily against bitter resistance, it was announced today, and American troops mopping up Western Sicily have captured Termini, twenty miles east of Palermo, and taken 7,000 more prisoners, including six Italian generals and an admiral.

"Further pressure on the enemy was maintained in all sectors" by American, Canadian and British forces closing in on the Catania-Etna-Messina area, the Allied communique declared.

Canadians striking east from Central Sicily "continued to advance, but their progress was slowed in the face of bitter resistance," it added.

Some units of the U. S. Seventh Army driving toward Messina are far to the east of Termini, and its capture consolidates the grasp upon the northern coastal area of the island.

More than 70,000 prisoners now are in Allied hands of whom 56,000 were taken by Americans. The six Italian generals and the admiral were not immediately identified.

To date, ten generals and two admirals have surrendered.

It was officially estimated that three and a half German divisions and three Italian divisions were bottled up in the northeastern corner of Sicily. One of the Nazi units in the Messina bridgehead was identified as the 29th Division, named for the German unit destroyed by the Russians at Stalingrad.

This division was rushed across

(Continued on Page 2.)

MOSLEM LEADER KNIFED IN BOMBAY

Bombay (AP)—Mahomed Ali Jinnah, president of the All Indian Moslem League, was slightly wounded today by a Moslem who knifed him during an interview.

Jinnah suffered minor injuries on the chin and one hand. His assailant was arrested. (This dispatch did not bring out the reason for the attack. Jinnah, a wealthy lawyer, advocates creation of a separate state for India's 90,000,000 Moslems).

LATE FOR WORK.

Cheektowaga (AP)—Fire Chief Valentine Mandel had a good answer to why he was late for his war plant work. He was boarding a street car when it was hit by lightning. Debarking, he ran to his fire house, summoned his men, went back and helped extinguish the trolley fire, then headed for work again.

U. S. INDICTS EIGHT FOR BROADCASTING IN BEHALF OF AXIS

Americans Accused of Treason in European Talks Face Death Penalty When Caught.

Washington (AP)—Eight Americans, including two women, who have broadcast regularly from Germany and Italy in behalf of the Axis war effort, were indicted today for treason, and Attorney General Biddle said they would be brought to trial when caught.

The indictments, involving a charge which carries the death penalty, were returned before Federal District Judge James W. Morris in the District of Columbia as the culmination of many month's of preparation by the Justice Department.

The indictments are similar, each alleging that the defendant named aided this country's enemies by repeated broadcasts designed "to persuade citizens of the United States to decline to support the United States in the conduct of the war."

Six Native Americans.

Seven of those charged have been broadcasting from Germany, one from Italy. Six are native Americans, the other two are naturalized Americans of German birth.

The defendants, with a summary of their backgrounds as outlined by the Justice Department, are

Ezra Pound, 57, a native of Hailey, Ida., educated in the East and a former resident of New York City; a poet and writer who has lived in England, France and Italy since 1911; only one of the group who broadcasts from Italy.

Robert H. Best, 47, a native of Sumter, S. C., former United States Army officer and long a correspondent for American interests in Europe.

Frederick Wilhelm Kaltenbach, 48, a native of Dubuque, Ia., where he was fired from a high school teaching position after organizing a Brown Shirt group among students; a former Army officer; worked as a translator and free lance writer in Germany beginning in 1933; described as the Nazi's American counterpart of "Lord Haw-Haw."

Douglas Chandler, 54, a native of Chicago who was reared in Boston; served in the United States Navy; worked as a reporter in Baltimore; entered the advertising and later the brokerage business in New York; has been in Europe since 1930; broadcast from Germany as "Paul Revere."

Others Accused.

Edward Leo Delaney, 57, born in Olney, Ill.; for many years a bit player in stock companies, motion pictures and musical comedies; went to Europe in 1939; known on the Nazi radio as "E. D. Ward" before his broadcasts were stopped in June, 1942.

Constance Drexel, 48, a native of Darmstadt, Germany, who acquired citizenship through her father's naturalization when she was four years old; grew up in Roslindale, Mass., worked as a reporter in Boston, went to Europe as a correspondent in 1915, later working for newspapers in this country; worked on a WPA writer's project in Philadelphia, which she claims as her home.

Jane Anderson, 50, born at Atlanta, went to New York City at the age of 16 and then to London, where she worked as a reporter; was saved from death by the intercession of the United States' State Department after being arrested as a spy by the Spanish Loyalists; her Nazi broadcasts ceased in April, 1942.

Max Otto Koischwitz, 41, a native of Germany who was educated there and in France; went to New York in 1925, taught German at Columbia University, transferred to the Hunter College faculty in 1931 and became a citizen through naturalization in 1935; he is known as "O. K." on Nazi broadcasts.

PRINCIPALS IN ITALIAN SHAKEUP—Here are the principals in the Italian government shakeup, King Vittorio Emanuele (left), Premier Mussolini (center), and Marshal Pietro Badoglio (right), as they attended a flag ceremony April 3, 1937, in Rome.

GERMANS WRECK OREL IN DESPAIR

Reds Expected to Find Only Ruined City on Their Entrance.

Moscow (U.P.)—Soviet military advices said today that the Germans were wrecking Orel in apparent preparation for withdrawal and the Red Army was expected to drive into it at any time.

Front reports said a Russian column driving behind Orel from the north had cut the railroad to Bryansk and advanced to bring under fire the highway roughly paralleling the line about 20 miles to the south.

The plight of the German garrison was described as critical. Its sole route of retreat from Orel, against which Soviet troops were advancing from three directions, was said to be a dirt road angling down to the southwest.

That the Germans realized their peril was indicated by reports that they were engaged in the methodical demolition of Orel which evidently made clear their intentions of giving it up rather than face the growing threat of another Stalingrad disaster.

CHURCHILL PLANS TALK ON MUSSOLINI

London (U.P.) — Prime Minister Winston Churchill will address the next sitting of the House of Commons about the resignation of Italian Premier Benito Mussolini, it was stated reliably today.

Four Articles Tell Mussolini's Story

From harsh-spoken epithets: Tough . . . Turncoat . . . Pacifist . . .

To high-sounding names: The Modern Caesar . . . The Man of Destiny . . . The Leader . . .

To more-recent nicknames: The Clown . . . The Stooge of Hitler . . . The Betrayer of Italy.

Between these extremes lies the story of the Great Chin—Benito Amilcare Andrea Mussolini.

Richard G. Massock, chief of The Associated Press Bureau in Rome when Italy declared war on the United States, traces the career of the Fascist leader in four daily articles, starting today on Page 6.

Drinks On House, Says Italian Boniface

Washington (U.P.)—Ciro Gallotti, proprietor of a popular Italian restaurant, celebrated last night.

"I haven't had a drink for 13 years, but tonight's different," he shouted to startled guests when he learned of Mussolini's resignation.

He pushed aside guests trying to pay their dinner checks, ordered drinks on the house, and brought out his French horn for renditions of "Anchors Aweigh" and "The Caissons Go Rolling Along."

30 INDICTED AFTER SOFT COAL STRIKE

True Bills First Since Enactment of Connally-Smith Anti-strike Law.

Pittsburg (AP)—A Federal Grand Jury investigating recent unauthorized strikes in the soft coal fields of Southwestern Pennsylvania today indicted thirty persons, charging conspiracy to prevent production of coal in violation of the law.

The indictments were the first since enactment of the Connally-Smith Anti-strike Law on June 26.

The indictments charged defendants specifically with "combining, conspiring and confederating together to interfere by strike and other interruptions with the opera-

(Continued on Page 16.)

ITALY MUST STILL SURRENDER—HULL

Casablanca Terms Apply to Whoever Rules There, Says Secretary of State.

Washington (U.P.)—Secretary of State Cordell Hull said today that the Casablanca terms of unconditional surrender still apply to Italy.

Questioned at his press conference about this government's attitude toward the resignation of Benito Mussolini, Hull said he did not anticipate any change in the announced policy that the Axis countries would be dealt with only on the basis of unconditional surrender.

There has been no information of any impending change in policy either from President Roosevelt—or from the War Department, Hull said.

Hull said that in his opinion, the timely and appropriate end of Mussolini is the first major step toward the early and complete destruction and eradication of every vestige of Fascism, both nationally and internationally.

The Secretary said he had been convinced for a long time that Fascism carried within it the seeds of its own destruction and that events were bearing out this belief

Hull, who appeared in particularly good humor, said there was no truth whatever in reports that the United Nations had been in contact with Marshal Badoglio.

The question of whether the United Nations would deal with the House of Savoy had not come up in his conversations with President

(Continued on Page 2.)

Start Of Italy's End, Observers Indicate

BY THE UNITED PRESS.

Persons in all walks of life today hailed the ouster of Benito Mussolini as the beginning of the end for Italy and a definite sign that the Axis structure is crumbling.

Comment included:

Former President Herbert Hoover: . . . The downfall of one of the world's greatest persecutors . . . will give heart to every persecuted man and woman in the Axis-occupied world and it is the hand-writing on the wall for his colleagues.

Vice President Henry A. Wallace: Surely it won't be long now as far as Italy is concerned.

Mayor F. H. LaGuardia of New York: I anticipate the complete capitulation of Italy within the next few days. He (Mussolini) will go down in history as the betrayer of Italy.

Prime Minister John Curtin of Australia: The repercussions on occupied countries cannot be overstated. Hitler sees in the fate of his ally the handwriting on the wall for himself.

Foreign Minister Ezequiel Padilla of Mexico: The machinery of the Axis is breaking up.

Count Carlo Sforza, foreign minister of Italy before the rise of Fascism: Mussolini's end is a happy

(Continued on Page 2.)

Badoglio Lukewarm To Fascists' Ideals

BY THE ASSOCIATED PRESS.

Field Marshal Pietro Badoglio, 72-year-old veteran of six Italian wars, has stepped from retirement into the premiership vacated by Benito Mussolini to face a conflict upon two fronts alongside of which all of his other campaigns pale into insignificance.

The hard-bitten soldier comes to the leadership of his country at an hour which finds it threatened by victorious Allied armies from without and with the home front crumbling under the sledge-hammer blows of Allied aircraft and the ebbing morale born of defeatism.

Long a close friend of King Vittorio Emanuele and never a member of the Fascist clique which surrounded Mussolini he has, nevertheless, been a dominant figure in Italian affairs from World War I until he resigned as chief of staff of the Italian army on Dec. 6, 1940, after the crushing defeats in the Greek campaign.

His opposition to various aspects of Mussolini's leadership since Italy's entrance into the present war have given rise to frequent rumors that he was the leader of a move for a separate peace for Italy.

It is no secret that he has been out of step with the Fascist Party,

(Continued on Page 22.)

Badoglio Forms New Government With No Fascists

Regime Sponsored By King Watched Closely In World Capitals To See Whether Il Duce's Successor Will Continue War Aggressively Or Seek Peace After Token Resistance.

London (UP)—The Rome radio tonight announced Marshal Pietro Badoglio, new premier of Italy, had formed a new Italian cabinet. The announcement followed the new premier's proclamation of nationwide martial law and unconfirmed reports that ousted Premier Benito Mussolini had fled into exile or arrested as a war criminal to be turned over to the Allies. The cabinet follows:

Chief of Government: Marshal Pietro Badoglio.
Foreign Minister: Raffaele Guariglia.
Minister of Interior: Bruno Forancari.
Minister of War: Antonio Sorice.
Minister of Navy: Rear Admiral Rafaello DeCurten.
Minister for Italian Africa: Gen. Melchiable Gatta.
Minister of Justice: Gaetano Ozzariti.
Minister of Finance: Domenico Bartolini.
Air: Renato Tandagli.
Education: Leonardo Severi.
Public Works: Alessandro Brizzi.
Communications: Gen. Frederico Amoroso.
Corporations: Leonardo Piccardi.
Popular Culture: Guido Rocco.
Currency: Giovanni Campora.
War Production: Gen. Carlo Savagasta.
Undersecretary to President of Council: Dr. Pietro Daratono.

Announcement of the new cabinet, from which all of the former Fascist leaders were cleaned out, was preceded by a statement that "His Mapesty, the King Emperor, at the suggestion of the head of the government, the Prime Minister" had nominated the new cabinet members.

An authoritative source said that Britain was ready to talk peace terms with the new Italian regime, but there still was deep mystery around Badoglio's intentions regarding a separate peace as well as around the fate of the fallen Duce.

The German propaganda line was intended to convince Europe that the Italians would fight on with the Nazis. Rumors circulated in Stockholm, however, suggested that the new premier at Rome might desire to make a deal with the United Nations and turn Mussolini over to them for trial—if he could get out from under German domination. The rumors lacked any official support.

Germans in Italy Chief Problem.

It appeared likely that the true position of the new Italian government would emerge only after considerable delay, although an expected speech by Prime Minister Winston Churchill at the next sitting of the House of Commons may clarify the outlook.

The outstanding question regarding Italy concerned the position of German armed forces in that country and of Italian troops in the Nazi-conquered Balkans. It was estimated that the Germans have from seven to nine divisions (possibly 130,000 men) in Italy and Sicily and there has been much speculation that the Nazis eventually would seek to set up a defense line protecting the northern industrial area of Italy above the Po River.

Although Badoglio was known to have opposed the Nazis as well as the Fascists in the past, there was no concrete evidence that he would try to oust the Germans and seek peace with the Allies.

Badoglio emphasized that the Fascist organization was being liquidated as such by removing Blackshirt guards at the Swiss border and replacing them with regular military police but he gave no hint as to the whereabouts of Mussolini, who frequently has been reported thin and gaunt recently as a result of illness.

Mussolini Arrested?

Stockholm newspapers, usually a center for Axis propaganda feelers, also appeared to be without information of a definite nature but did produce the usual rumors and speculation. One such rumor was that Mussolini had fled to Switzerland or Germany. No source was indicated. Another and conflicting rumor in Stockholm was that Badoglio had arrested Mussolini and other high Fascists and that he would later seek to use them in negotiations with the Allies, possibly offering to turn the Fascists over to the United Nations for trial on "war guilt" charges.

Madrid reports said that Spanish newspapers pointed out that Mussolini's resignation "presumably" was due to illness. Madrid also reported that the ouster was received with wild joy in occupied Europe, especially in France.

May Call On Vatican.

There was also speculation that Mussolini might have sought to save himself by some negotiations through the Vatican, where his son-in-law, Count Galeazzo Ciano, has been ambassador and where the Ciano family was expected to take refuge.

The German propaganda line was the obvious one. The Nazi broadcasts took the position that Mussolini was ill and that the government change at Rome would have no effect on Axis relations and that Italy would fight on with Germany. This position was taken by Nazi Propaganda Minister Joseph Goebbels after considerable delay. The Japanese broadcasts even delayed 16 hours in announcing Mussolini's resignation.

Badoglio quickly established a drastic military regime in all of Italy.

Dusk-to-Dawn Curfew.

He also ordered a dusk-to-dawn curfew and banned all public meetings in what may have been a move to prevent a civil war between ousted Fascists and supporters of the new royalist regime.

Signs multiplied that the new government, while seeking to maintain a semblance of Italian resistance in order to strengthen its bargaining position, soon will begin feeling out the Allies regarding peace terms, presumably through Pope Pius XII, Turkey, or Sweden.

If the Badoglio government does ask for terms, an authoritative British diplomatic commentator said, Britain wil be prepared to deal with him "provided that it is evident he exercises full authority in Italy."

The only "terms" acceptable to the Allies, as specified by President Roosevelt and Prime Minister Churchill, will be unconditional surrender. However, both the United States and Britain had refused even to discuss a separate peace for Italy so long as Mussolini remained at the helm.

Badoglio's Actions Watched.

The British Cabinet will meet soon to examine the implications of Mussolini's deposal and decide its attitude toward the new government, the commentator said. The government was said to be watching closely to see whether the Badoglio regime will overthrow the whole Fascist system or merely

(Continued on Page 18.)

The Index

THE TIMES RECORD

COHOES BRANCH OFFICE, 296 ONTARIO STREET — TROY, N. Y., WEDNESDAY EVENING, AUGUST 4, 1943. — PHONE COHOES 511

State War Council Cites Cohoes As Outstanding City In Paper Salvage

ISSUES BULLETIN IN WHICH WORK RECEIVES PRAISE

System of Firemen's Association in Carrying Out Program is Held Up as Example to Others.

The work being accomplished in the collection of waste paper and magazines here by the Cohoes Paid Firemen's Association in cooperation with the local Salvage Committee has been made the subject of a release which the New York State Committee, cooperating with the State War Council, has sent to all salvage committee units throughout the state.

It is stated in the release that "The City of Cohoes has always salvaged in a quiet, orderly and businesslike way, which has resulted in great productivity."

Included in the bulletin is the report of William Vandercar, chairman of the local Salvage Committee, as follows:

"The Salvage Committee of the Cohoes War Council has enlisted the aid of the Cohoes Paid Firemen's Association in the launching of a waste paper salvage collection service. This organization will function for the duration.

"These men are systematically covering every street in the city. We have also canvassed every industrial plant in our drive for corrugated box board.

"The John Legget Box Co. of Cohoes donated the use of a 1½-ton truck to be used in this salvage program. Other equipment such as a baler, scales, etc., have been donated by the Kennedy Knitting Co. and the Lowenthall Manufacturing Co.

"The collections are made daily and an average of two tons of waste paper, newspaper, magazines and corrugated cartons are being secured each day. Arrangements have been made with the paper manufacturers in this vicinity for the disposal of all material collected and ceiling prices are received.

"The Firemen's Association receives 50 per cent of the net proceeds, the balance going into the Salvage Committee Fund.

"Posters, window cards for housewives and other literature secured from the Albany office are being used with good results.

"The firemen are solving two problems in this drive. Fire hazards are being eliminated by these men through clearing up waste paper accumulations in cellars and under stairways.

"All in all, this campaign is proving very successful. A total tonnage of approximately thirty tons have been secured in three weeks."

WILLIAM VANDERCAR,
Chairman,
Cohoes City Salvage Committee.

In sending you the above, we hope that it will give you some idea as to how to proceed in your waste paper collection plans.

OFFICIALS, STOVE DEALERS ATTEND OPA CONFERENCE

A group of local officials and stove dealers last night attended the conference conducted at the New York Power and Light Corp. auditorium in Albany under the auspices of the Albany district and regional offices of the Office of Price Administration, at which discussion was held reative to the rationing of stoves, which is scheduled to become effective late this month.

Attending from Cohoes, in addition to several local dealers, were Mrs. Jane Maney, chief clerk of the Cohoes War Price and Rationing Board; Mrs. Marjorie Bolton and Mrs. Mildred Weiler of the board's staff and members of the fuel oil panel, including Raymond S. Van Santvoord, chairman; John C. Callaghan and Robert G. Hanlon.

MRS. ETHEL BROWN BACK FROM PARLEY

Mrs. Ethel brown, executive secrtary of the Cohoes War Council, has returned from Lake Placid, where she attended the conference on juvenile delinquency conducted under the auspices [illegible] the New York State War Council.

Appointment of a [illegible] committee to deal with the problem of delinquency to function under the direction of [illegible] [illegible]cil is planned for the near future.

To Conduct Social.

The Ladies' Auxiliary of E. T. Ruane Post, American Legion, will conduct a social today at 8:15 p.m. Mrs. Pearl Smith is chairman. At a meeting Monday night final plans will be made for participating in the annual state convention in New York City Thursday, Friday and Saturday, Aug. 12, 13 and 14. Mrs. Smith and Mrs. Elizabeth Dundon are the delegates, the alternates being Mrs. Sarah Halloran and Mrs. Josephine Hildreth.

JAMES F. BRACKLEY

JAMES BRACKLEY, VETERAN, DIES AT BRONX HOSPITAL

Well-known Business Man, Who Fought in World War 1, Native of North Adams, Mass.

James F. Brackley, well known Cohoes resident and business man, died yesterday at Veteran's Hospital in The Bronx. Mr. Brackley was a veteran of World War I and saw service overseas. He was a member of E. T. Ruane Post, American Legion, and the Last Man Club of the post.

He was born in North Adams, Mass., the son of the late James P. and Margaret McGuillan Brackley and for the last 15 years was assistant manager of Welsh & Grey Lumber Co. of Cohoes. He was also a member of C. B. A. Men's Association and active in the affairs of the Christian Brother's Academy in Albany. He was a member of St. Bernard's Church and the Holy Name Society of the church.

Survivors include his wife, the former Mary A. Ryan; a son, Pvt James F. Brackley, jr., U. S. M. C. R., stationed at Cornell University; and four brothers, George F. Napanoch; Joseph E., Andrew J. and A. Leo Brackley, all of Cohoes.

Funeral services will be held from the residence, 84 Amity Street, Cohoes, Saturday at 9 a.m. and at 9:30 a.m. from St. Bernard's Church where a requiem mass will be celebrated. Interment will be in St. Agnes' Cemetery.

MILITARY HONORS PAID VETERAN OF LAST WORLD WAR

Services Conducted This Morning for Daniel J. Hogan; Military Police Fire Volley Over Grave.

Military honors were accorded at the funeral of Daniel J. Hogan, veteran of World War 1, today at 9 a.m. from the residence, 264 Remsen Street, and at 9.30 a.m. from St. Bernard's Church, where a requiem mass was celebrated by Rev. Joseph A. Kelly, assistant pastor. Rev. Joseph A. Franklin, pastor of St. Agnes' Church, was seated in the sanctuary.

Miss Mary Coyle presided at the organ and Miss M. Loretta Hayden and James McManus sang during the mass. At the offertory Mr. McManus rendered "Ave Maria" and at the conclusion "Softly and Tenderly Jesus Is Calling" was sung by Miss Hayden.

Bearers included James and Raymond Tierney, Frank Bechard and Alphonse Nolin.

Rev. William P. Brennan, pastor of the church, officiated at the grave in St. Agnes' Cemetery. A salute was fired by a squad of members of Company C, 767th Military Police Battalion, Albany, commanded by Corp. Arthur P. Auger and composed of Pvts First Class Michael Longo, Frank Boutelier, Stanley Orgel, George Kugis, John Howard and Thomas Gormley. "Taps" was sounded by Pfc. George Farrington. Members of the squad acted as a guard of honor from the residence to the church.

Garden Party Held.

A garden party under the auspices of the Ladies' Auxiliary of Cohoes Post, Veterans of Foreign Wars, was conducted last night at the home of Mrs. Frances Offenbacker, 187 Park Avenue. Refreshmants were served and a social time enjoyed.

Completes Course.

Aviation Cadet Michael J. Slater of this city has been graduated from the 61st Flying Training Detachment at Avon Park, Fla., and will be transferred to a basic school. The local youth previously trained at the Pre-Flight Pilot School at Maxwell Field, Ala.

MAYOR APPOINTS GROUP TO ACT ON REQUESTS FOR GAS

Committee Will Pass Applications of City Employees for Supplementary Supplies.

Announced as being for the purpose of ending existing confusion, a Municipal Transportation Committee has been appointed by Mayor Rudolph I. Roulier for the purpose of acting on applications made by city employees for supplementary gasoline supplies for use on official business.

The city executive heads the group, other members of which are S. Earl McDermott, commissioner of public safety; Willaim Marra, superintendent of the Water Bureau of the Department of Public Works and Dr. F. Herrick Conners, superintendent of schools.

Under the new system, each member of the committee will have charge of the consideration of all applications for additional gas made by members of their respective departments.

Approval by the committee of such applications must be given before they are submitted to the Cohoes War Price and Rationing Board. It is pointed out, however, that such approval, has no bearing on whatever action the ration group may take in each instance.

In connection with the new system it has been pointed out that there are numerous occasions on which it is necessary for city workers to use their private cars on official business. Such use obviously cuts their own supply of gasoline for regular driving and makes necessary the submission of applications for supplementary amounts.

Heretofore there has been no set plan for consideration of these applications and the newly-created committee has been named in order to terminate existing confusion.

COMMON COUNCIL TAKES ACTION ON ARREARS IN TAXES

City Treasurer Authorized to Accept Sum in Settlement of Levy on Rolling Mill Buildings.

Two ordinances pertaining to settlement and tax arrears were adopted in a meeting of the Common Council last night.

One measure authorized the city treasurer to satisfy arrears in taxes for 1942 and 1943 assessments on property owned by the Cohoes Rolling Mill Co.

Parcel One includes the former puddling mill, rolling mill, pipe shop, mill yard and miscellaneous buildings, the assessment on which is listed as $177,000.

Parcel Two is listed as a brick and steel building on Saratoga Street the assessment of which is given as $35,000.

In regard to the second parcel the ordinance declares that whereas the Cohoes Rolling Mill has conveyed the building to the Star Woolen Co., and the assessment has been severed, the city treasurer has been authorized to accept the sum of $1,055.82 in full settlement of state, city and county taxes, water rents and special assessments provided that such payment is made on or before Aug. 9.

The second ordinance approves an agreement entered into between Corporation Counsel John J. Doherty, Walter H. Wertime, sr., and Katherine E. Anderson as trustees of the Charles H. Adams estate terminating certiorari proceedings relative to assessments for 1942 and 1943.

New valuations approved on three parcels of property owned by this estate are as follows: Parcel One, $23,000; Parcel Two, $32,500 and Parcel Three, $500.

The city treasurer is directed to collect 1942 and 1943 taxes on these properties based on the new valuations.

SURPRISE SHOWER GIVEN BRIDE-TO-BE BY EASTERN STARS

Miss Elaine Adriance, daughter of Mr. and Mrs. Charles Adriance of 193 Congress Street, whose marriage to Joseph Hutchinson, son of Mr. and Mrs. E. E. Hutchinson of LeRoy will take place Saturday, Aug. 21, at 2 p.m. in the First Baptist Church, was tendered a surprise shower last night by her fellow officers of Imperial Chapter, O. E. S.

The function was held at the residence of Mrs. Mildred Bowen, 52 Saratoga Avenue, Northside. Mrs. Martha Cole was general chairman.

Cards were played and a buffet luncheon was served from a table attractively decorated in pink and white and having as a centerpiece a large cake surmounted by the figures of a miniature bride and bridegroom.

The bride-to-be was the recipient of a table lamp, the presentation being made by Charles J. Ellett, worthy patron of the chapter.

Welfare Clinic Held.

Seventeen patients attended the child welfare clinic held yesterday at the City Hall under the auspices

FILE INSPECTORS OF ELECTION LIST AT BALLSTON SPA

Jones Manufacturing Co. Employees Have Annual Roast; Textile Local Will Meet Tomorrow.

WATERFORD

The following list of inspectors of election for the town of Waterford has been filed with the board of elections at Ballston Spa:

Dist. No. 1, Harold Vrooman and Josie Conroy, Republican; Margaret Bernardo and Ursula Fitzgerald, Democrat; Dist. No. 2., Olive Lawrence and Isabelle Smith, Republican; Florence Murray and Roger Herney, Democrat; Dist. No. 3, Prudence Van Steenberg and Louise Reimherr, Republican, and James French and Sephora Keating, Democrat; Dist. No. 4. Levi Gilbert and William Beddow, Republican; Mary Kennedy and Jane Craven, Democrat.

Choir Rehearsal.

The choir of the First Baptist Church will meet for rehearsal tomorrow at 8 p.m. in the chapel of the church under the direction of Norbury Smith.

Local To Meet.

The United Textile Local 898 of the Ford Manufacturing Co. will hold its regular business meeting tomorrow at 8 p.m. at the union rooms on Broad Street.

Corps To Rehearse.

St. Mary's Sponsored Corps of the Charles J. Brady Post, American Legion, will meet for rehearsal today at 7 p.m. at St. Mary's Hall under the direction of William E. Houlihan.

Annual Employees' Roast.

The Jones Manufacturing Co. held its annual hot dog and corn roast for its employees and friends recently at the home of Miss Marion Fero on the Waterford-Mechanicville Road. Mrs. Clara Whalen and Wellington Jones entertained with several vocal solo selections during the afternoon. Games were enjoyed following the luncheon.

Surgical Dressing Unit.

The surgical dressing unit of the Red Cross will fold bandages tomorrow at its meeting at the John House Memorial of the First Presbyterian Church under the direction of Mrs. B. Emerson Devitt, chairman. All women of the village who have available time are urged to aid in this necessary service. The group will meet from 9.30 a.m. to 4 p.m.

Brevities.

The naming committee of the Waterford Methodist Church will meet today at 8 p.m. at the church

of the Health Department. Three vaccinations and two toxoid inoculations were administered, the remaining patients being examined and advised. Dr. M. J. Keough, health commissioner, was in charge, assisted by Mrs. Mary Lynch, city nurse.

FUNERAL OF RIVER DROWNING VICTIM CONDUCTED TODAY

The funeral of Clarence H. Jerome of R. D. 1, Waterford, who was drowned Sunday in the Mohawk River at Halfmoon Beach, was held today at 9 a.m. from the funeral home of A. G. Boivin's Sons, 70 Congress Street, and at 9.30 a.m. from St. Mary's Church, Crescent, where a requiem mass was celebrated by Rev. William Skelton. Miss Mary Devery presided at the organ and sang during the mass.

Bearers included Raymond Prescott, George and Albert Jesmain, Donald Riberdy, Harry Brandt and Edward Martin.

Rev. Edward Hinkle officiated at the grave in St. Joseph's Cemetery, Waterford.

On Furlough Here.

Corp. Edwin S. Vickers of the Army, who is stationed at Camp Crowder, Mo., is spending a ten-day furlough with his parents, Mr. and Mrs. Robert Vickers of 3 Simmons Avenue.

Social Slated.

A social under the auspices of N. G. Lyon Camp, Sons of Union Veterans of the Civil War, is scheduled to be conducted Saturday night in the G. A. R. rooms. Walter Bailey is chairman.

Personal.

Frank Broomhead of 98 Remsen Street, Joseph Raymond of 11 Main Street, Euclid Snay of 19 Sargent Street and Peter Laporte of Central Terrace are spending a week at Putnam, on Lake Champlain.

Obituary.

Funeral services for George H. Conboy were conducted today at 9 a.m. at the residence on North Mohawk Street and at 9:30 a.m. at St. Patrick's Church, where a requiem mass was celebrated by the pastor, Rev. Thomas A. Flanagan. Bearers included Frank Wright, John McCarthy, Charles Bailey, John Walsh, James Hickey and Paul Surprenant. Father Flanagan officiated at the grave in St. Mary's Cemetery, Waterford. Members of Cohoes Lodge of Elks visited the home last night and conducted a ritualistic service.

HASTY EXIT: Roomers in the three upper floors of a four-story brick building at 250 River Street, occupied by the Lenox Hotel, were forced to make a hasty exit about 1:30 a.m. today when smoke, originating from a fire in the rear of the first floor restaurant swept through the building. Thomas J. Keary, a roomer, was aided to safety by firemen. One fireman, Thomas Evers, injured his hip in a fall.

HUNGARY VEERING TOWARD ALLIES

London Believes Axis Satellite May Surrender with Italy.

London (INS)—Astute observers in London today believe that when Italy surrenders Hungary will either give up simultaneously or shortly afterward.

Hence, they are keeping one eye cocked in the direction of Budapest for any indication that anti-Nazi Charles Peyer, Socialist, is about to take over the premiership.

Peyer is believed to have maintained underground communication with high-ranking British labor leaders to assure the best of relations between the two countries when Premier Miklos De Kallay is ousted.

Nevertheless, it should not be overlooked that these friendly approaches place British officialdom in a dilemma, in view of the fact that Czecho-Slovakian President Eduard Benes and his foreign minister, Jan Masaryk, haven't forgotten Hungary's carcass-nibbling at the time Germany gobbled up Czecho-Slovakia and Yugoslavia. Some circles believe Prime Minister Winston Churchill would have made direct offer to Hungary if the attitude of Benes and Masaryk did not stay his hand.

Regent Nicholas Horthy of Hungary is reported fence-sitting, but lately apparently veering toward the Alilied side. He reecntly baited Adolf Hitler by refusing to permit garrisoning of Hungarian troops in Czecho-Slovakia and Yugoslavia.

The Hungarian Socialist organ Pestihirlad is now read openly in Budapest and other Hungarian cities. Heretofore it was covertly circulated. Now the paper openly criticizes German and Hungarian Nazis.

SENATOR WHEELER DENOUNCES PLAN TO DRAFT FATHERS

Washington (AP)—Senator Wheeler (D-Mont.), today assailed the Selective Service plan for drafting pre-Pearl Harbor fathers after Oct. 1. asserting "it would seem that the only purpose is the psychological effect on Russia at the peace table, if and when she attends a peace conference."

"We should not play politics with American lives," Wheeler said in a statement issued from Belton, Mont.

The Montanan, who has six children, said "the latest edict to call up the pre-Pearl Harbor fathers adds to the confusion caused by the War Manpower Board." He described the action as contrary to expressed congressional sentiment as reflected in House passage of the Kilday Bill to defer fathers until all single men within a state have been exhausted, and approval by the Senate Military Affairs Committee of his own bill to exempt fathers from the draft until Jan. 1, 1944.

GEORGIANS APPROVE LOWER VOTING AGE

Atlanta (AP)—Steadily climbing majorities indicated today that Georgians had approved an amendment to their state constitution which would lower the legal voting age from 21 to 18.

Youthful Governor Elllis Arnall said he was confident the proposal would be adopted and announced that "I and my friends in the Georgia delegation will be on the floor insisting that the [illegible] of the voting age from 21 to 18 be written into the 1944 Democratic platform." The unofficial vote from 206 of the state's 1,735 precincts showed 16,810 for the proposal and 5,265 against in yesterday's election.

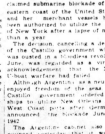

THREE SONS IN SERVICE—Mr. and Mrs. Timothy J. Shaughnessy, 305 Fourteenth Street, Watervliet, are the proud parents of three sons in service. They are, left to right, Corp. Timothy J. Shaughnessy, stationed "somewhere in the Pacific," Pvt Michael Shaughnessy, at Fort Benning, Ga., and Corp. William J. Shaughnessy, also "somewhere in the Pacific." Timothy and William enlisted in October, 1940, and Michael in January, 1941. All three were formerly with the Civilian Conservation Corps, and Timothy and William were members of the 105th Infantry.

FIREMAN INJURED, DAMAGE OF $2,000 CAUSED BY BLAZE

Three Upper Floors of Lenox Hotel and Restaurant Filled with Clouds of Smoke.

One fireman was injured and about $2,000 damage was caused to the four-story brick building at 250 River Street, occupied by the Lenox Hotel and Restaurant, when fire broke out at 1 30 a.m. today

Hoseman Thomas Evers of the Central Fire Station suffered a slight injury to a hip when he fell in a cellarway.

A smoldering blaze which started in the basement of the restaurant at River Street and Broadway poured smoke into the three upper floors causing roomers to make hasty exits. Thomas J. Keary, one of the residents of the hotel, was carried down a fire ladder to safety by Driver John Slattery of Central Fire Station.

Patrolman Harry Anslow of the Central Police Station said smoke was so thick on the third floor where Keary was sleeping that he fell to the floor while trying to make his escape. Several other roomers were awakened before smoke penetrated the upper floors.

The building, according to the fire report, is owned by Theodosio Vanvakias. The first floor is occupied by Joseph Vaccarelli.

The fire provided the initial test for Troy's new $12,000 pumper. Manned by Chauffeur John Maldney, the pumper drew praise from firemen.

GERMANS BEGIN GENERAL RETREAT FROM OREL BULGE

Nazi Army of 250,000 Seeks to Escape Trap as Russians Near City from Three Directions.

(Continued From Page 1.)

retained supremacy, checking enemy dive-bombing attacks and supporting their own ground forces. Seventy-six German planes were shot down in aerial combat south and southwest of Orel yesterday, including 70 out of a formation that attacked a force of Russian tanks emerging from a forest.

The capture of Orel, held by the Germans since 1941, would cave in the whole central front and pose a potent threat to Bryansk, 80 miles to the west, main Axis bastion opposite Moscow.

The Germans sacrificed 2,000 men, 13 tanks and 15 guns yesterday alone in their futile attempts to stem the Soviet advance from the northwest.

Another 1,600 Germans were killed in fighting Russian advances south and southwest of Orel.

Converging Russian armies already were within sight of Orel from the north, east and south. Advances of 3½ to 6 miles yesterday yielded more than fifty additional towns and villages, including Stish on the Kharkov railroad five miles to the south, and Domnino, on the Yelets railorad less than seven miles to the east.

WORKERS POISONED.

Rochester (UP)—Health officers today investigated food served in the cafeteria of the Eastman Kodak Co.'s Kodak Park plant after 33 plant employees were stricken with food poisoning last night.

Clothing in Britain is strictly rationed on a coupon system. If a woman bought 2 pairs of stockings a month, and one apron a year, she would have no coupons left to buy other clothes.

MANAGEMENT TO BE INCLUDED IN COURSES AT R. P. I.

Preparatory Training for Foremen, Supervisors and Department Heads To Be in Free Classes.

Note: This is the last of a series of articles describing the new war production training program to open in August at R. P. I. for men and women civilians of the Tri-City Aera.

A series of courses in the field of production management are among the 22 part-time, tuition-free evening courses starting the latter part of August at Rensselaer Polytechnic Institute for civilians, both men and women of the Tri-City Area.

The basic course, production supervision, provides broad training and is intended for training first-line foremen, supervisors and department managers in the processing and operating departments of war industries. Subject matter includes organization of the internal administration of a plant or company, principles governing the location of plants and their general design and lay-out, and management of materials, the planning and control of production, motion and time study and work simplification, cost accounting, the management of personnel.

Stemming from this broad basic cours are several courses which deal more extensively with specialized phases of production management.

A course in motion and time study provides training in the principles of work simplification through methods study.

A course in production planning and control has as its purpose development of the ability to analyze the factors in production schedules and to prepare such schedules. It includes a study of the lay-out and sequence of work and its control in connection with both small and large scale business.

In the field of accounting two courses are offered, one in corporation and manufacturing accounting, the other in cost accounting.

A related course in advanced traffic management deals with the routing and shipping of materals.

Another subject, important to those concerned with production supervision, is industrial safety. A nation-wide campaign has been in progress to make both labor and management more "safety-conscious" and thus to reduce the loss of man hours through industrial accidents. In cooperation with this campaign, R. P. I. offers a course in industrial safety engineering especially intended for group leaders, foremen and supervisors who are responsible for safety methods and procedures in their organizations.

Previous courses have culminated in the formation of two permanent organizations in this area—one of graduates of the course in industrial safety engineering and the other of graduates of the course in production supervision.

A pamphlet has been prepared which describes the courses in detail. A copy may be obtained by addressing the E. S. M. W. T. office at the Institute. Registration for the courses will close Aug. 11.

ARGENTINA IGNORES NAZI BLOCKADE OF EASTERN U. S. COAST

Buenos Aires (AP)—Argentina has decided to ignore the German-proclaimed submarine blockade of the eastern coast of the United States and her merchant vessels have been authorized to utilize the port of New York after a lapse of more than a year.

The decision, cancelling a decree of the Castillo government which was ousted in a bloodless revolt in June, was regarded as a virtual acknowledgement that the Nazi U-boat warfare had failed.

Although Argentina, as a neutral, enjoyed freedom of the seas, the Castillo government ordered its ships to utilize New Orleans and West Coast ports after Germany announced the blockade June 6, 1942.

The Argentine cabinet also announced yesterday that it would press a campaign against Communism in Argentina "until this scourge which threatens to destroy society in its very fundamental bases is finished."

TURKISH GIRL SLAIN.

London (UP)—The German transocean news service reported today that the daughter of the Wali (governor) of Istanbul, Turkey, had been killed by a stray bullet while driving through the streets of Rome during a fight between Fascists and anti-Fascists.

INVASION OF KISKA SEEMS IMMINENT; AIR RAIDS CEASE

Last Bombing Carried Out Week Ago, When Single Flying Fortress Attacked Heavily Defended Base.

Washington (UP)—The invasion of Kiska, isolated but heavily defended Japanese base in the Aleutians, appeared imminent today in the opinion of military observers.

Although the end of comparatively moderate weather in the Aleutians is but a matter of weeks away, military analysts noted a number of signs which they believe indicate that American forces will shortly attempt invasion.

One of these is the cessation of the almost daily air attacks on Kiska. The last air raid was carried out on last Thursday when a single Flying Fortress dropped bombs through the overcast.

The experts pointed out that a somewhat similar period of aerial inactivity preceded the invasion of Attu last May. Attack planes remained grounded from May 6 until May 11, when the landings were first made.

The cessation of air attacks, the experts suggested, may be necessary to service the planes and lay in and conserve supplies that will be needed when the amphibious landing operations get under way.

The severe aerial mauling and intermittent bombardment by surface ships during July undoubtedly was part of the pre-invasion "softening up" process. There were 61 separate air attacks on Kiska in July. There were eight different surface bombardments, the last on July 30. Japanese shore guns failed to reply on all but two occasions.

PROMOTED—Word has been received by Mr. and Mrs. William P. Dauchy of Ford Avenue of the promotion of their son, Charles H. Dauchy, from ensign to lieutenant, j.g., in the Navy Reserve. Lieutenant Dauchy is now an executive officer at Great Lakes Naval Training Station, Chicago, Ill. He entered the service as an ensign in July. He is a graduate of Rensselaer Polytechnic Institute. His brother, William P. Dauchy, has recently been commissioned a second lieutenant in the Army Air Forces and is now stationed in Texas.

WHEELER MAY ASK CONGRESS' RETURN

Bleton, Mont. (UP)—Senator Wheeler (D-Mont.) said yesterday he would ask Congress to return immediately to Washington to deal with national Selective Service unless War Manpower Commissioner Paul V. McNutt modified a proposal to induct pre-Pearl Harbor fathers after October 1.

Wheeler said he would telegraph McNutt in Washington today demanding that the order be rescinded.

MULES REFUSE TO EAT SUGAR COUPONS

Shelby, N. C. (UP)—A farmer here sought a new sugar certificate on the ground that his mules had eaten the original, lost in some shucks. The next day he was back to report to the rationing board that he had made a mistake. His sugar-loving mules had spurned the certificate, which he found undamaged in the feed trough.

EAST SIDE.

The picnic planned by Triumph Rebekah Lodge to be held Saturday at the home of Mrs. Emma Wait and her sister, Mrs. Theodore Miller, 56 Brookview Avenue has been postponed. The new date is Saturday, Aug. 21.

To Occupy Pulpit.

Rev. Clayton VanDuesen of Chatham will occupy the pulpit of Third Presbyterian Church Sunday at 11 a.m. during the pastor's absence.

Personal.

Mrs. James Gavin, a former Trojan, who is now residing at Cairo was a recent guest of Mr. and Mrs. Edward Ramroth, 15 Munro Court.

Leland Palitech of the Seabees, stationed at Camp Endicott, R. I., was a recent visitor of his parents, Mr. and Mrs. Otto Palitsch, 28 Winter Street.

Mr. and Mrs. John J. Strohecker of 1704 Highland Avenue are entertaining Miss Anita Sorensen of Bridgeport, Conn., and Mrs. Strohecker's brother, Julius Frandsen of Newport, R. I.

Mrs. Charles H. Shortsleeve, Jr., of 494 Pawling Avenue left today to spend some time with her husband, Sergeant Shortsleeve who is stationed at Greensboro, N. C. She is the former, Miss Virginia Boyle.

FBI CAMPAIGNS TO STOP FORGERY OF FEDERAL CHECKS

Ask Cooperation of Merchants Who Cash Them; Directions Given by Secret Service Agents.

The Record Newspapers Bureau, Washington, D. C.

In a campaign to stamp out forgery of government allotment and allowance checks, the United States Secret Service is conducting a campaign among New York merchants who cash government checks and persons who receive them.

For example, all dependents of men in the armed forces receiving government checks should have locks placed in their mail boxes and should try to be present or have some member of the family present on the days when checks are expected. If payees change their addresses they should promptly report the change to the postoffice and to the disbursing office which sends the checks.

They also should make a practice to try to cash their checks at the same place and should never endorse the checks except in the presence of the persons accepting same. Payees should never allow relatives or members of their families to endorse the checks for them. In cases where payees are unable to write their names, they should endorse the checks by mark and have two persons who know them to sign the checks as witnesses, giving their addresses in full.

CHILD KILLED IN FALL FROM HOTEL SIXTH FLOOR ROOM

New York (INS)—Stephen Rowe Bradley, 3rd, 9, of 56 Fairmont Street, Lowell, Mass. was instantly killed early today when he fell from his sixth floor room at the Hotel Weylin, here.

The child's body was discovered by his father after the elder Bradley entered the room and saw the bed empty.

The Bradleys registered at the hotel several days ago upon their arrival from Lowell.

LONE CLUE SPURS OREGON QUEST FOR KIDNAPED INFANT

Mother Makes Appeal for Return of Her Three-day-old Daughter; Abducted Tuesday.

Albany, Ore. (UP)—Mrs. W. B. Gurney appealed yesterday for the return of her kidnaped three-day-old daughter, Judith, while clue-short officers investigated a drugstore purchase of infant's supplies by a young woman who did not know what formula to buy.

L. W. McCartney, assistant manager of a drugstore at Portland, Ore., said a young woman, carrying a baby in her arms, bought a nursing bottle, nipple and chemical formula Tuesday night. Although a formula ordinarily is prescribed by a doctor, he said, the woman selected one at random from many displayed after asking which was best.

McCartney said he was informed by a clerk that a man came into the store with the woman but waited at the door while she made the purchase.

Appealing for her baby's return, Mrs. Gurney said:

"I bear no malice toward anyone. All I want is my baby back."

Mrs. Gurney is the wife of an Albany plywood plant foreman and local labor union official. Grief-stricken, she still was too unhappy in the hospital from which the baby was abducted early Tuesday morning.

During 1942, American forces stationed in Australia and New Zealand received through reverse Lend-Lease eighty million pounds of fruits and vegetables and thirty million pounds of beef, veal, lamb and mutton.

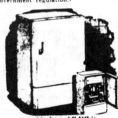

THE WEATHER
Tonight—Cool.

THE TIMES RECORD

FINAL EDITION

Series 1943—No. 211. (Entered as Second Class Matter at the Postoffice at Troy, N. Y., Under the Act of March 3, 1879.) TROY, N. Y., WEDNESDAY EVENING, SEPTEMBER 8, 1943. (Published Daily Except Sunday) PRICE FOUR CENTS

ITALY SURRENDERS

ITALIANS OF TROY OVERJOYED WITH SURRENDER NEWS

Those Who Have Relatives in Homeland Glad They Will Be Spared Further War.

News of Italy's unconditional surrender to the United Nations swept through Troy like wildfire. It was hailed merely as a confirmation of the long-expected inevitable. Reaction was sober-minded. No one crowed that the Axis major powers — Germany and Japan — might now crack up. Italy's abandonment of the Axis was merely considered as having demobilized a small wing of the Axis armies thereby permitting the use of Alliedl power in other offensives and hurrying forward the day when the United Nations will clinch with Germany and Japan for the final kill.

Trojans of Italian descent, many of whom have close relatives in Italy, not only shared the feelings of others but had additional cause for hailing the surrender inasmuch as it would probably mean that relatives in Italy would be spared many of the horrors of war which otherwise would have been suffered by them. Many of those Trojans were confident that thousands of Italians would now seek to join the Allied forces to turn on Germany whom they never liked but with whom they were forced to fight because of the decision of the Fascist leader who drove an unwilling people into war.

At War Plants.

War workers took the important information in stride. Checks on several important war industry plants in the Troy Area showed there was not a moment's stoppage as word of the surrender seeped through the plants. On the contrary there was a noticeable pickup. The announcement served as a stimulant. Administrative officials in most of the establishments said there appeared an even stronger determination to maintain maximum production so that the Axis can be hurried down "the last long mile."

Cessation of hostilities was looked upon by Italian American citizens of Troy today as "the best thing that could happen as far as Italians are concerned."

Inquiry among numerous Italian-Americans revealed almost the same identical opinion a few moments after the surrender of Italy to Gen. Dwight D. Eisenhower had been announced.

"Just think of the lives that will

(Continued on Page 9.)

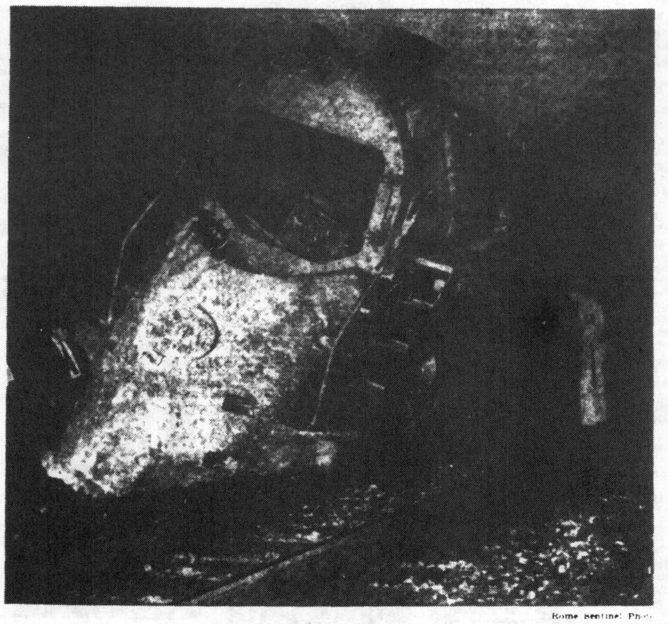

Rome Sentinel Photo

BLAST-WRECKED LOCOMOTIVE—All that remained intact of the Locomotive of the ill tated New York Central Twentieth Century Limited, wrecked when the engine blew up near Canastota, killing three crew members and injuring several persons. Twelve of the 18 cars on the train were derailed.

ALLIED VICTORY IN WAR CERTAIN, MARSHALL SAYS

Plans to Smash Hitler's European Fortress Virtually Complete, Army Staff Chief Asserts.

Washington (AP)—Allied preparations for smashing Germany's European fortress including an invasion of northwestern Europe are virtually complete, Gen. George C. Marshall disclosed today, and plans for decisive triumphs over Japan are well advanced.

"The end is not yet in sight," the Army chief of staff said of history's greatest war, "but victory is certain."

That the long heralded "second front" was plotted as long ago as the Casablanca conference in January was made clear by his disclosure that "the plans for air and other operations in Northwestern Europe were reviewed and confirmed" at that meeting.

Marshall's conclusion as to the invincibility of Allied arms was set forth in an extraordinary report to Secretary of War Stimson in which he reviewed the early months of heartbreaking defeat suffered because of inadequate forces, revealed the swift measures taken to stem Axis aggression, told of historic decisions made in Casablanca and Washington, and showed how the enemy had at last been forced on the defensive road to defeat.

Progress In Pacific.

"Strategically the enemy in Europe has been reduced to the defensive and the blockage is complete," Marshall declared. "In the Pacific the Japanese are being steadily ejected or rather eliminated from their conquered territory.

"In the South and Southwest Pacific two facts are plainly evident to the Japanese command as well as to the world at large: our progress may seem slow but it is steady and determined, and it has been accompanied by a terrific destruction of enemy planes and surface vessels. This attrition must present an appalling problem for the enemy high command."

"In brief," he said, "the strength of the enemy is steadily declining while the combined power of the United Nations is rapidly increasing, more rapidly with each succeeding months.

"There can be but one result and every resource we possess is being employed to hasten the hour of victory without undue sacrifice of the lives of our men."

Five Phases of War.

Marshall divided the war into five phases, dating the fifth and last phase from the start of the offensive against Gaudalcanal last Au-

(Continued on Page 7.)

Russian Forces Capture Stalino In Donets Basin

Red Army Wins Back Two-thirds of Rich Ukraine Zone; Berlin Admits Evacuation.

London (AP)—Capture of fiercely defended Stalino by the Russians was acknowledged by the German today, restoring the last of the great industrial cities of the Donets Basin to the Red Army which already has won back two-thirds of the Ukraine's rich grain lands.

The Red Army advance also crossed the rail line to Mariupol, 65 miles southwest of Stalino on the Sea of Azov, making it almost certain that Nazi forces which have been fighting east of that town must withdraw to escape entrapment by the southward turning move.

The Red Army newspaper Red Star reported that other units had severed the main railroad from the Donets Basin Dnieperopetrovsk, 115 miles west of Stalino.

The German communique, recorded by the Associated Press, said Stalino, Russia's 12th largest city, had been evacuated "to shorten the front" after all military installations had been destroyed.

Russian dispatches indicated Stalino fell in flanking moves rather than by direct assault.

This new victory followed upon Moscow's announcement that the Red Armies had killed more than 420,000 Germans, wounded 1,080,000 and captured 38,600 in taking back at least 30,000 square miles of occupied territory since July 5.

Stalino, a city of about 500,000 pre-war population, was taken by the Germans in October, 1941, and the Russians never had been able to wrest it back until now.

At the hub of a railways system serving the Donets Basin, Stalino is an excellent base for a possible thrust southwest to pinch the invaders completely out of their foothold in the Kuban and in the Crimea.

The German war bulletin said the Donets battle was raging with "undiminished violence."

The Russians said their armies were advancing all along the 600-mile front, and the Germans, as in the case of Taganrog and other cities, were the first to announce that Stalino had fallen.

The tremendous German casualties were announced in a special

(Continued on Page 2.)

NAZIS EXECUTE DANISH ENGINEER

Berlin Reports Victim Was Put to Death for Sabotage.

London (AP)—A Danish engineer has been executed for sabotage and another Dane was slain while trying to escape when caught caching a large quantity of explosives dropped by British planes, according to a Copenhagen dispatch broadcast by the Berlin radio today.

The name of the executed man, who is believed in London to have been the first Dane to be put to death for sabotage, was given by the Berlin radio as Paul Edwin Soerensen of Aalborg. The broadcast was recorded here by the Associated Press.

The Berlin broadcast quoted Nazi occupation authorities in Denmark as saying that Soerensen was one of a group of Danes engaged in blowing up trains carrying German troops and war material.

Despite severe reprisals and the offer of bribes to Danish citizens to betray the saboteurs, the Berlin radio disclosed in another broadcast that attacks on railroads were continuing.

Life in northern Jutland, Danish coastal region heavily fortified by German military authorities, has been disrupted during the past few days, the Berlin radio said, as the result of forays by "irresponsible elements, mainly of foreign nationality."

WAYLAND WRECK VICTIM EXPIRES

Rochester (AP)—The death toll in the wreck of the Delaware, Lackawanna and Western's Evening Flyer Aug. 30 stands at 29 today.

Latest victim was Miss Jean Rankine, 27, daughter of Mr. and Mrs. Adam Rankine of Rahway, N. J., who died last night. She was brought here for treatment.

Husband and Father of Wreck Victims Suicide

New York (AP)—Morris Borden, 48, who last night in a Philadelphia morgue identified three of the victims of the wreck of the Pennsylvania Congressional Limited as his wife and two children, was found dead today at his Brooklyn home.

After identifying bodies of his wife, Grace, 42, his daughter, Irma, 14, and his son, Stephen, 7, Borden returned to Brooklyn to arrange for funeral services.

He was found in his kitchen with five jets on the gas stove turned on. Police listed the case as a suicide.

Borden was a clerk in the Brooklyn main postoffice.

HOUSE COMMITTEE MEETS TO STUDY NEW TAX PROGRAM

Washington (UP)—The House Ways and Means Committee will meet today to complete a fall program designed to place a new tax bill on President Roosevelt's desk sometime in December.

Peace has been restored between the committe's agents and the Treasury, and Chairman Robert L. Doughton, D. N. C., said Secretary of Treasury Henry Morgenthau, jr., had "expressed a desire to cooperate" in the formulation of the new tax program.

Rep. Harold Knutson, R., Minn., ranking Republican member of the committee, suggested that Economic Stabilization Director Fred M. Vinson be invited to sit in when tax conferences open.

Knutson said in a statement that "Congress must go slow in imposing new and additional taxes," but added "war may drive us to it."

He said new sources of revenue would be necessary, and predicted that "compulsory savings is out and the corporation tax can't be increased much more, but excises may be boosted a little."

GUERRILLAS READY TO ASSIST ALLIES

London (AP)—Albanian guerrilla forces anticipate an Allied invasion of the Balkans within a month and the Germans are moving men and equipment from Yugoslavia into Albania to meet a possible thrust across the Strait of Otranto from the Italian heel, Istanbul press dispatches reported today.

Leaders of the Albanian guerrilla bands met recently near Tirana to decide how best they could aid an invading Allied force, these reports said.

The Index

WOMAN KIDNAPER PLEADS INNOCENT

Albany, Ore. (UP)—Mrs. Catherine Wright, 26, confessed kidnaper of two-day-old Judith Gurney, pleaded innocent to a baby-stealing charge today on grounds she "was insane at the time the act was committed."

Edward E. Cox, Mrs. Wright's attorney, said he would produce evidence that she was out of her mind when she convinced her husband and neighbors she was pregnant and then stole the new-born Gurney baby from an Albany hospital.

PEOPLE OF ITALY PAY PENALTY FOR "STAB" AT FRANCE

Mussolini's Dream of Safe, Easy War, Boomerangs Into Frightful Catastrophe at Home.

BY ALTON BLAKESLEE
(Associated Press Foreign Staff)

A safe easy war that boomeranged into frightful calamities gnawed like acid into Italian morale, finally toppled that nation as the first Axis victim of World War II.

Preceding it in inglorious finale went Benito Mussolini, the prophet and artisan of modern-day Fascism who sought a Twentieth Century Roman empire.

Italy fell after Allied armies battered in her front door of Sicily and put her cities including Rome under devastation from the air.

The Italian rallying cry changed to "peace" from the drum-thumping days of Nice, Corsica and Tunis and proclamations of the Mediterranean as Mare Nostrum "our sea."

It was a confident Mussolini who launched his "stab in the back" march on France on June 10, 1940, when France was collapsing, when Britain stood alone, when speedy and absolute victory seemed so close to the dictators' grasp. For Mussolini, conqueror of Ethiopia and Albania, it seemed almost like a bloodless coup.

Duce Guessed Wrong.

It was a criminal miscalculation. In three years and several months the war has boomeranged to strip him of his African empire, to tear Sicily from Italy, to bring invaders to the mainland, to bottle up the Mediterranean, to bring the air siege to all Italians and drain the country of manpower and shatter much of her navy.

For Mussolini, leader of the black shirts and would-be dictator of the Roman conquerors, it was the last hand in the game of intrigue and power he started with his "march" on Rome in 1922 to become a dictator. Mussolinin was ousted July 25, and his Fascist regime began to shred to ruins.

The first few months of war were benign and glorious for Italy. They brought a share in the spoils o fbeaten France more of a "place in the sun."

Missed Chance in Egypt.

In September, 1940, Italian legions were sent driving into Egypt, 300,000 strong, but they stopped after a seventy-mile penetration. The British War Office later disclosed that Mussolini was facing only a handful of imperial froops, that he had missed a golden chance to seize all of Egypt and Africa. So began the African campaign so ill-fated for Italy.

In October, 1940, after subjecting Albania, Mussolini lashed at Greece, with every expectation of a quick victory. But the astonishing Greeks threw him back nearly into the Adriatic Sea, and inflicted enormous losses in men, arms and prestige upon the modern-day Romans. Mussolini was saved only by Hitler, whose formidable armored columns smashed the Greeks and their British allies, to achieve victory in April, 1941. Since

(Continued on Page 2.)

SEE "GREEN HANDS" PARTLY TO BLAME FOR TRAIN WRECKS

Washington (UP)—Government and labor officials today blamed the use of "green hands" and the strain on existing equipment on railways for recent major train wrecks.

Emmett C. Davison, general secretary of the International Association of Machinists, condemned draft boards for "indiscriminate drafting" of experienced trainmen, and denounced the present practice of using women for inspectors as being "just out of their line."

Transportation Director Joseph B. Eastman said the railroads were having a tremendous turnover in employment, were getting many "green hands," and pointed out that he warned only last Saturday that the nation is heading for a railway manpower crisis.

Eastman cited the tremendous strain on the railroad's physical equipment and their manpower troubles. He said they were being forced to "drive their equipment as it never has been driven before."

Philadelphia Wreck Death Toll Now 78

Philadelphia (AP)—The death toll in the Labor Day wreck of the Pennsylvania Railroad's Congressional Limited stood at 78 today as a procession of men and women with dread-haunted faces filed past the rows of gnarled bodies in the city morgue seeking friends or relatives among the 23 still unidentified victims.

Railroad workers searched too, in the rubble along the northeast Philadelphia curve where nine of the flyer's 16 cars wrenched loose for still other bodies, and physicians said at least six of the 90 injured who remained in hospitals might not live through the day.

One of the 541 passengers who boarded the Washington-to-New York train, Mrs. Marian Berry McCauley, 35, of New York, was missing, and the list of dead and injured gave no answer to her 6-year-old son Ian's plea.

"Where is my mama?"

A friend of Mrs. McCauley's, Mrs. William Barbour of New York, visited Ian in a hospital, where he was treated for slight back and

(Continued on Page 14.)

Allies Grant Military Truce To Government Of Marshal Badoglio

Gen. Dwight D. Eisenhower Announces Capitulation of Rome Regime as Berlin Reports New Allied Landings on Italian Peninsula; Some Nazi Troops May Be Trapped by Surrender of Axis Partner and Collapse Is Viewed Grave Blow to Hitler; Terms Were Approved by United States, Great Britain and Russia Last Friday.

BY THE ASSOCIATED PRESS

Gen. Dwight D. Eisenhower today announced unconditional surrender of Italy in the greatest knockout victory for Allied arms in the four years of war, even as Axis broadcasts asserted sea-borne American forces were moving toward new goals in Hitler's beleaguered Europe.

Battered and bleeding, with no heart for the war, Italy capitulated to the Allies last Friday, it was disclosed, and Premier Marshal Pietro Badoglio indicated that Italian troops themselves would combat any further German attempt to make Italy a battleground.

"The Italian forces will cease all acts of hostility against the Anglo-American forces wherever they may be met," Badoglio said, in a proclamation.

"They will, however, oppose attacks from any other quarter."

The five-day delay in revealing Italy's surrender—which actually came on the day British Eighth Army troops first invaded Southern Italy from Sicily—was arranged so that "the armistice should come into force at the moment most favorable to the Allies" and to forestall possible German interference.

Russia as well as the United States and Britain approved the granting of the armistice. The terms will be imposed later, it was announced, and in the interim a military armistice has been granted the kingdom.

Hitler's "European fortress was cracked, the way was opened for new offensives, the course of World War II immeasurably shortened.

Eisenhower called on the Italians to join the Allies in helping to eject the Germans from their country, and promised that all who do so will have the "assistance and support of the United Nations."

Marshal Pietro Badoglio's proclamation for the Italian armed forces to cease fighting but oppose attacks "from any other quarter" was closely related to this.

General Eisenhower's disclosure of the electric news—perhaps the best single piece of news for the Allies in the four years of war—did not make clear whether the Germans would agree to the surrender. Nazi radios were silent on the collapse of their Axis partner and it was entirely possible the Germans would make a fight for the northern section of the kingdom, without Italian help.

The still-powerful but long shore-bound Italian fleet had already left its hase at Taranto, on the heel of the Italian boot, and presumably will fall to the Allies.

Sir Andrew Browne Cunningham, Allied naval commander in the Mediterranean, broadcast a message to the Italian fleet and merchant marine, telling them:

"The German armed forces have become the open enemy of the Italian people and intend to seize your ships."

Commanders of Italian ships were told to make Allied ports, or at worst, neutral ports.

As soon as the announcement was made, Allied planes roared over Italy—not to bomb but to bring the Italians the news that the Allies no longer are fighting them.

The planes droppd pamphlets telling the Italians that the opportunity has come to take "vengeance on the German oppressors."

The pamphlets declared:

"Italians! Backed by the might of the Allies, Italy now has the opportunity of taking vengeance on the German oppressors and aiding in the expulsion of the eternal enemy from Italian soil."

Only a few hours earlier, the German high command had acknowledged a new Allied landing on the Gulf of Eufemia, forty miles north of the British Eighth Army's original beachhead, and a Berlin broadcast said that two large Anglo-American convoys had sailed from Palermo, Sicily.

The broadcast said the new Allied expeditions totaling "roughly 200 merchant and transport vessels" indicated that American forces "are about to carry out further landing attempts somewhere."

Extensive Allied ship movements in North African harbors, especially in Tunisia, were also reported.

Berlin said four or five British infantry battalions landed at Pizzo on the lower part of Eufemia Gulf in a drive to cut off "German rearguards to the south and southwest."

This indicated that at least some Nazi troops were cut off by the surrender.

The collapse of Italy, within a few short weeks after the downfall of Premier Benito Mussolini, meant a body blow to the Germans, who had made every effort to keep Italy in the war and thus postpone the inevitable day of an Allied invasion of the German homeland itself.

With Italy, the junior partner of the Berlin-Tokyo-Rome Axis, driven out of the war, the Allies presumably will soon be in a position to bomb Germany from the south—as it is now being mercilessly blasted from the British Isles in the North—and may well shorten the European conflict by many months.

Germany had hoped to make Italy a battleground and it had been reported that tens of thousands of German reinforcements had poured into Italy in recent weeks with a view to defending at least the rich industrial areas of Northern Italy, particularly in the Po River Valley.

Prime Minister Churchill had characterized Italy's strength as one-tenth that of Germany.

The announcement came as dispirited Italian troops by the hundreds surrendered to British and Canadian troops advancing up the Calabrian Peninsula, where the Allies landed last Friday on the heels of a 38-day Sicilian victory which sent the Germans fleeing to the mainland.

American armies which took part in the Tunisian and Sicilian victories have not participated in the Calabrian invasion, and the Italian surrender leaves them free to strike elsewhere in Europe.

Axis radio stations broadcast nothing immediately on the capitulation.

Today's communique said the terms of the armistice had been approved by the governments of Great Britain, the United States and Russia, and "both parties have bound themselves" to abide by the terms of the agreement.

General Eisenhower said the agreement was signed by his representatives and those of Marshal Badoglio.

All hostilities will terminate at once, Eisenhower added.

The commander-in-chief promised "all Italians who assist in the fight against the Germans will have the support of the United Nations."

President Roosevelt was seated at his momento-crowded desk in the White House offices and Prime Minister Churchill of Great Britain was busy elsewhere in the executive mansion when the world heard today that Italy had capitulated.

Both obviously had known the news for some time, since the terms were agreed upon last Friday. But from neither of the leaders was there immediate formal comment.

It was "big stuff" elsewhere. Suppressed excitement was evident among the White House staff when news dispatches gave the story to a jubilant American capital.

Allied headquarters said the capitulation terms were signed last Friday—the day that British and Canadian troops moved on to the Italian mainland.

The headquarters announcement:

"Some weeks ago the Italian government made an approach to the British and American governments with a view

(Continued on Page 2.)

Questions Rise On Surrender

BY THE ASSOCIATED PRESS

These questions arose from the Italian surrender today:

1. What becomes of the Italian fleet, which is built around seven battleships and is split between Pola on the Adriatic and Spezia on the Italian West Coast?

2. Will the Germans retire from the Po valley in the north where they have been reported to have as many as 15 or 20 divisions?

3. What happens to the 25 to 30 Italian garrison divisions in the Balkans and France? And to the 250,000 Italian workmen estimated in Germany?

4. What effect will the Italian surrender have on the wavering morale of Hitler's Balkan satellites of Hungary, Rumania, Bulgaria and Croatia? Hungarian policy has been linked more closely with increasing signs of war weariness.

5. Does the surrender include the French island of Corsica, barely 30 miles from Southern France which the Italians occupied when the Allies landed in North Africa?

6. Will the scattered German units still in Southern and Central Italy be allowed to return to Germany?

FIRST LADY VISITS AMERICAN WOUNDED

Sydney, Australia (AP)—Making friends with Australian service groups and meeting "as many Americans as I can," Mrs. Eleanor Roosevelt spent two hours at 118th General Hospital and then made brief visits today to Australian hospitals.

She visited many battle casualties from the Pacific (which now is gaining full momentum in the Lae and Salamaua area.

WELSH SAILOR, ON VISIT HERE, EATS FIRST SWEET CORN

Air Fitter on British Carrier Happy Over Experiences in Troy; Has Seen Heavy Action.

By MICHAEL DANYLA.

Wilfred Roberts, of hedge-cropped Beddgelert, Caernorvan Shire County, North Wales, is a very happy man. For the first time he has (1) eaten sweet corn (2) had a hot dog, "kindly cover it with mustard, sir" (3) been taken out by two girls.

For Joe Bloke living up the block, this is old stuff. For shy, good-looking Roberts, whose home in Wales snuggles at the foot of 4,000 foot high Mt. Snowden and who ran the Nazi Mediterranean gantlet aboard a British aircraft carrier in the famed Malta convoy, it was an education. He likes to talk about these homely pleasures and tells of his home and travels—but not of the battles he has seen.

While his ship has the barnacles scraped off its tough hide at an Atlantic base, Roberts is in Troy, guest of Mr. and Mrs. John P. Nugent, 2245 Fifteenth Street.

This Is How It Came About.

Reason for his being in Troy is a story in itself, that can best be told in the over-the-backyard-fence fashion: Roberts has a sister in Wales who married a distant relative of Mrs. Nugent who has never seen her relative but with whom she corresponds. Mrs. Nugent wrote her relative who told Roberts's sister who wrote Roberts that if he ever gets to the States to look up Mrs. Nugent.

All of which led staff of the American Red Cross station, Fulton and River Streets, where Roberts spent yesterday morning, to exclaim the inevitable: "Isn't it a small world!"

Arriving here Thursday from Pearl Harbor where he saw no evidence of the December 7 debacle, Roberts spent Saturday at Union Station hobnobbing with British tars and Tommies en route to and from Canada.

Yesterday he told the local Angels of Mercy he had twenty pounds of sugar aboard his ship which he would have to bring into Wales "by underhand methods," five pounds being the limit. The Welsh rate sugar the number one delicacy.

Not Home in 18 Months.

Over the week-end he had a "banana sundae," the well known "split." Saturday night two girls took him to the movies. Did he have a girl? "I had one," he said, "but I haven't been home in 18 months."

Spencer Tracy and Larraine Day are Welsh movie favorites, he says, and a weekend in Liverpool is considered the ultimate in vacations. He thinks New York is "terrific" and rates bomb-scarred London a close second.

He was in a taxicab in London once when an air raid alarm sounded. The cabbie kept right on going. "They are the most mercenary people I have ever met," he said.

After plowing through the gales of the North Atlantic, once last winter, his ship arrived in Murmansk looking like a "big, fat icicle." In Iceland, he found the natives unusually aloof, and the buildings in Reykjavik, capital and chief port, built mostly of wood.

On a recent voyage from the South Pacific, his ship carried three Jap prisoners, one of whom spoke excellent English. They were put ashore in Hawaii.

Showing a Welsh newspaper, he said he spoke Welsh until he entered high school at the age of 12. The paper was a paradox; stories were printed in Welsh, advertisements in English. The largest ad read: "Are your sheep afflicted with fleas?", while a lower corner ad trumpeted the arrival of a truss expert.

Welsh printing looks like backstage double talk, sounds like Sanskrit. Roberts read from the paper. It was impossible to understand him.

He can't accustom himself to the universal use of refrigerators in America. Giving no leeway to a mechanical age, he still calls them "ice boxes." In Wales, they are very exclusive, he said, and are practically unobtainable.

Willing to Learn.

He can't jutterbug, but asks only for a couple of months in this country—then watch!

He claims to be still a little wobbly on his sea legs. "Every time I sit down," he says, "I feel like going to sleep. Aboard ship he sleeps in a hammock. In the South Pacific where the heat was unbearable, he threw himself on deck and slept on the boards. He thinks the mattress he sleeps on at the Nugent home is like something out of a king's guest room.

Three years ago, Roberts spent a lot of time fishing in the stream that ripples through mountain-hemmed Beddgelert. He was an apprentice mechanical engineer. When he was 20, he enlisted in the Navy and holds the rank of air fitter, first class, aboard a carrier.

There are five girls in the family, he says with expanded chest, and a brother in Saskatchewan, Canada, who he has never seen.

Today Roberts leaves for his ship, then back to the British Isles. Asked if he had a particular wish, he said, "Yes, I wish I could swim."

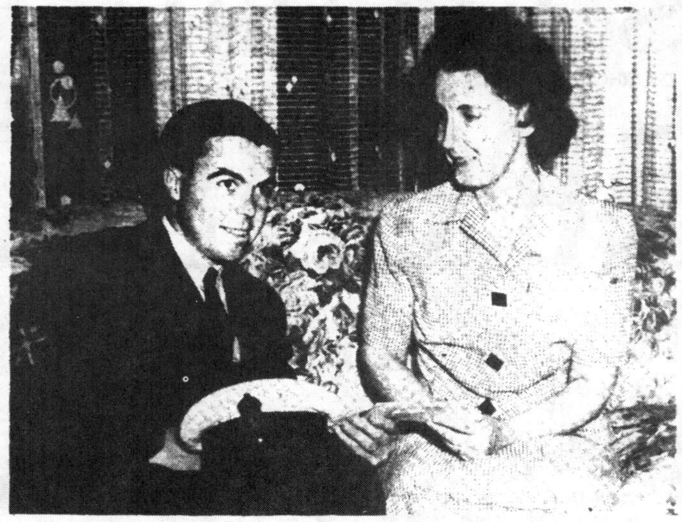

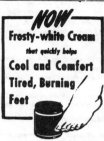

UNITED BY WAR—Most unusual visitor in Troy over the week-end was Welshman Wilfred Roberts, an air fitter aboard a British aircraft carrier now in drydock at an American port. He was the guest of Mr. and Mrs. John P. Nugent, of 2245 Fifteenth Street, to whom he is related by marriage. A veteran of the famed Malta convoy and sea battles in the North Atlantic, he shows Mrs. Nugent pictures taken aboard the carrier.

HOOSICK.

Mrs. John D. Blake was operated upon Saturday in the hospital at Cambridge.

Samuel Cipperly and daughter, Miss Audna Cipperly, of Speigletown called on relatives Sunday.

Miss Geneva Armstrong of Glens Falls is visiting at the home of her nephew and family, Harry E. Cipperly.

John Fitzgerald of Schenectady is passing a few days with his daughter and family, Mrs. Joseph Strever.

Mrs. Clyde Tomlinson and daughter Marcia of North Hoosick called Sunday on Mrs. James D. Paddock.

Mr. and Mrs. Albert Sabin and son Herman of Halfmoon were Sunday guests of Mr. and Mrs. Everett F. James.

Mrs. Nellie J. Marshall passed the week-end in North Petersburg with her sister and brother-in-law, Mr. and Mrs. George Tatro.

At the Hoosick Baptist Church Suunday Rev. J. J. Gould will preach at 9:30 a.m. on "Never Again." Sunday School at 10:30 a.m.

Mrs. Helen Crandell of Troy was the week-end guest and Mr. and Mrs. Ralph Hammond and son Timothy of Center Brunswick passed Sunday with Mrs. George Rifenburg.

At All Saints' Episcopal Church Sunday Rev. William Garner will preach and celebrate communion at 11 a.m. He will have charge of the Mission of the Holy Name, Boyntonville, at 9 a.m.

Pvt. Donald Hillman, who has just returned from maneuvers in Tennessee; Douglas Rudd from Camp Alamogordo, N. M., and Carl Stevens are on furloughs with their parents and families here.

The Loyal Workers of the Baptist Church will meet Wednesday, Sept. 15, at the home of Mrs. Jannette Green, North Petersburg. Mrs. Edward Goodermote and Mrs. Earl Philpott will be the assisting hostesses.

Mr. and Mrs. William Spath and daughter and Mrs. William Frank and children of Rensselaer called on Mr. and Mrs. Harry N. Hawks Monday. Mr. and Mrs. Hawks, with their son, George A. Hawks, and family of Hoosick Falls spent the week-end at Hedges Lake.

GREENWICH.

Miss Helen Roberson of Albany spent the holiday week-end at the home of her parents, Mr. and Mrs. Charles B. Roberson, at Beech Hill.

Mr. and Mrs. Ernest Ringer and two daughters, Kingston, spent the week-end and Labor Day with Mrs. Ringer's mother, Mrs. Harry Toomey, at her home at Center Falls.

Richard Crozier and Ralph Barber, who enlisted in the Navy a few weeks ago, returned to Sampson today after being home on leave following their "boot" training at Sampson naval base.

Edward G. Stiles, son of Mr. and Mrs. George Stiles of this village, who Aug. 30 received his wings and commission as second lieutenant in the Army Air Corps at Yuma, Ariz., arrived home Friday for a brief leave. He left Monday to return to Albuquerque, N. M., for assignment to duty. Lieutenant Stiles volunteered under the Selective Service Act for duty in April, 1941, and before being transferred to the Air Corps was stationed for some time at Fort Jackson, S. C., in the Medical Corps.

CAMBRIDGE.

Rev. Pascal Parente of Washington, D.C., is visiting his brother, Thomas Parente.

Miss Margaret J. Agan died Aug. 22 in North Adams where she had made her home for many years with her brother, the late John Agan. Miss Agan was a native of Cambridge, daughter of Michael and Margaret Tobin Agan. She had been ill for three months. The funeral was held at St. Francis' Church with a solemn high mass of requiem Aug. 25 and the body brought to Cambridge for interment in St. Patrick's Cemetery, Rev. Francis D. Ronan, O.S.A., in charge of the committal service. One sister, Mrs. Mary McClellan of Cambridge, and two nieces, the Misses Rita and Loretta Agan of North Adams, survive.

POWNAL.

Pfc. Edward Brookman of Camp Pickett, Va., is home on furlough.

Lieut. William C. Haag, who is stationed in Arkansas, is at Cherry Court.

Seaman Francis E. Haley surprised his parents by arriving from Philadelphia for the week-end.

Mr. and Mrs. Wilfred Proud have returned from visiting his brother, Archie Barbeau in Woodford, Vt.

A farewell party for Earl Leonard was held at Righthome Monday evening prior to his leaving for service in the Navy.

Miss Maybelle Abbot of Worcester, Mass., was a week-end and holiday guest of Mr. and Mrs. John L. Mason at Melody Farm.

STATE COUNCIL TO CONVENE HERE FOR TWO-DAY SESSIONS

Public, Church Leaders Invited to Attend Meetings to Build "Top Efficiency," Cleric Says.

A two-day convention under the auspices of the New York State Council of Churches is scheduled to take place at the First Baptist Church in Troy Wednesday evening, Sept. 22, and the next day. The meeting will be one of ten scheduled throughout New York State from Sept. 19 to Oct. 1.

The public is invited to attend the sessions, and "all church leaders, interested in building top efficiency in their churches are eligible to share in the features of the convention." Rev. William A. Perry, pastor of the Waterford Methodist Church, is in charge of convention arrangements.

First on the convention program will be a mass meeting Wednesday night, beginning at 7:30 p.m. Rev. Stewart Herman, jr., D.D., former pastor of the American Church in Berlin and author of the book, "It's Your Souls We Want," will be the speaker. Rev. Norman R. Adams, Ph.D., pastor of Westminster Presbyterian Church, will conduct the worship service. Mr. Perry will be the presiding officer.

Several seminars and a general meeting are among the features of the second day of the convention. Delegates from area churches will register at 8:30 a.m.

Rev. E. Stanley Jones, D.D., author, lecturer and widely known minister, will be the speaker at the mass meeting the second day. Both of the general meetings will take place beginning at 7:30 p.m.

Other convention speakers will include Rev. Roy Williamson, D.D., executive secretary of the New York State Baptist Missionary Convention and president of the Council of Churches; Rev. Wilbur T. Clemens, D. D., Albany, head executive officer of the Council of Churches and described as an authority on rural churches; Rev. Anthony Luidens, D.D., pastor of Brighton Reformed Church, Rochester, and Rev. L. R. Loomis, D.D., professor at Keuka College, Keuka Park. The latter two men will conduct a seminar in "Leadership Education," in which the chairman will be Rev. Dr. E. Fritts, pastor of Redeemer Lutheran Church.

SALEM.

Miss Adele Moore has returned to Ithaca after visiting her father, Carl Moore.

Miss Stella McIntyre and Mrs. Leroy Munson of Watervliet recently spent several days in town with friends.

Mrs. Edward J. Blanchfield, who has been receiving treatment at the Troy Hospital, returned here Saturday.

Mr. and Mrs. Evariste Lavigne and family have returned to Albany after visiting her parents, Mr. and Mrs. Thomas Stanton.

Mr. and Mrs. Harold E. Blanchfield and family of Albany recently visited their parents, Mr. and Mrs. Peter Dunnigan, and Mr. and Mrs Edward J. Blanchfield.

Dr. Edward B. Mates and family left yesterday for Evansville, Ind., where he has accepted appointment as assistant to a leading surgeon in the hospital in that city.

Mr. and Mrs. Charles Mitchell of this village announce the marriage of their daughter, Thelma, to Vincent Pekins of Troy. The marriage took place Aug 21 at Troy. Mr. and Mrs. Pekins are both former residents of Salem.

INCREASE PRICES FOR WOOD, LUMBER

Ceiling Raised on Essential Materials for Building, War Work and Fuel.

Increases in the price of softwood lumber and ceilings on cord wood have been announced by the Office of Price Administration. Price ceiling injunction proceedings are now impending against nearly half the lumbering concerns in the 16 counties in the district as a result of a reported violations of ceiling prices.

The increase amounts to as much as $4 per 1,000 board feet. Other increases allowed $1.50 for round-edge white pine lumber; $3 for spruce, jackpine and Norway pine lumber; $4 for hemlock lumber; $1 per 1,000 pieces of spruce lath and $1 per square for white cedar shingles. The increases are applicable to the base mill price. Otherwise, all lumber ceilings remain.

The softwood lumber is used for crating and boxing heavy war materials and for essential home and building construction.

The cord wood will range from $6.75 a quarter cord for 12-inch wood to $25 for the same size a full cord delivered to the consumer. Due to the shortage in coal and oil the firewood situation is expected to show an increased demand this fall and winter.

Beginnings of Chinese books are on what would be the last page of American books.

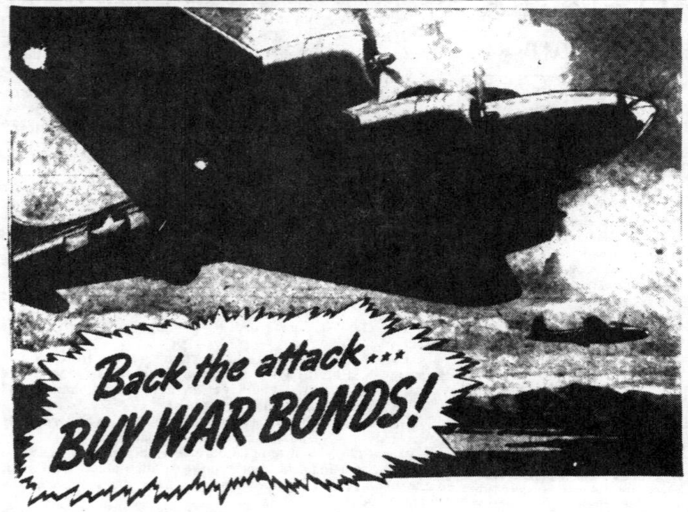

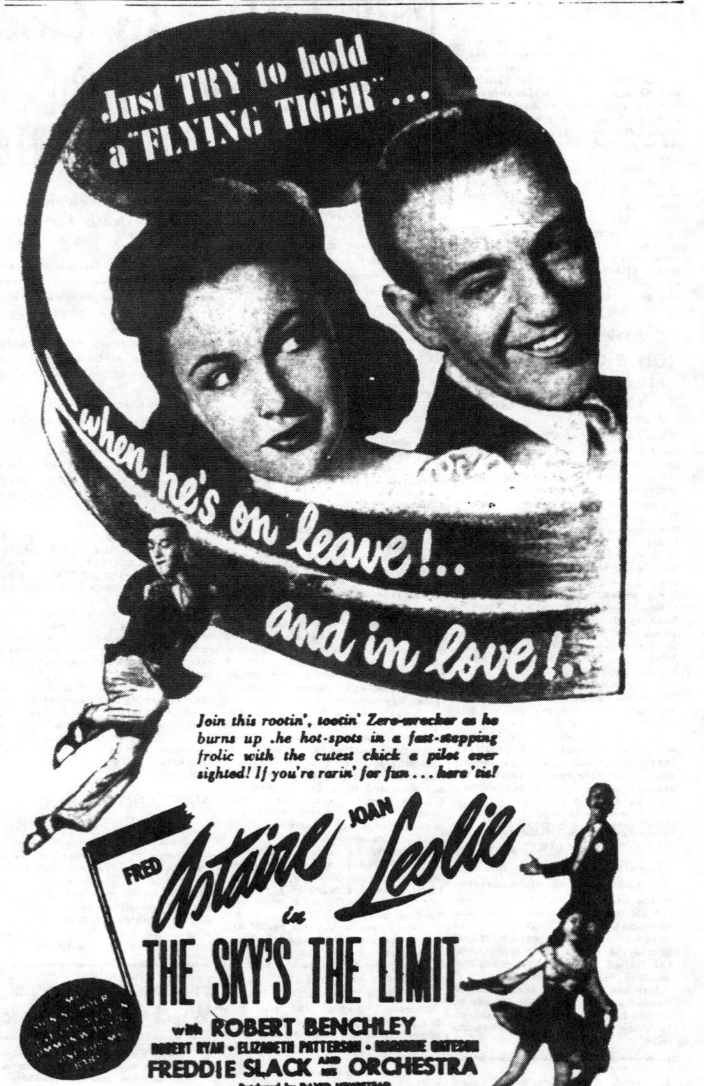

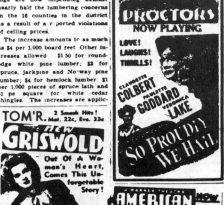

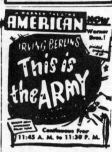

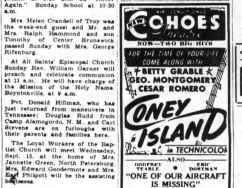

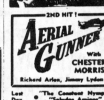

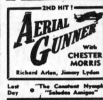

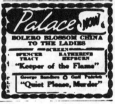

CHAPTER HONORS FORMER OFFICERS OF EASTERN STAR

Charter Members Also Guests of Honor at Session Last Night

STILLWATER

The charter members and past matrons and patrons were honored last evening at a meeting of Upton Chapter O. E. S.

Ten charter members and matrons and patrons were present and a degree in their honor was presented by the matron, Mrs. Isabel Wilbur, Miss Irene Brownell, Mrs. Myra Truland, Miss Janet Bradley, Mrs. Ellen Dean and Mrs. Helen Doughty. A gift was presented to each guest by Miss Irene Brownell.

The worthy matron announced that Mrs. Margaret Talmadge, a past matron of Upton Chapter, has been appointed district deputy grand matron of the Saratoga District. Mrs. Talmadge will be installed at Grand Lodge sessions next week at the Hotel Astor, New York City. A reception in her honor will be held Nov. 3 by Upton Chapter.

The social committee appointed for the next meeting includes Mrs. Lillian Mitchell, Miss Helen Case and Mrs. Helen Doughty. The entertainment committee is Mrs. Bernice Booth and Mrs. Pauline Osgood.

The worthy matron asked that members have a table of cards to raise money for this month. Games were played following the meeting and awards given to Miss Irene Brownell, Mrs. Etta Haight, Mrs. Gertrude Coons, Mrs. Lillian Mitchell, Alfred Brownell, Mrs. Helen Doughty, Miss Cordelia Pitney and Mrs. Bernice Booth.

Card Club Entertained

Mrs. John Hammond was hostess last evening to the Wednesday Evening Bridge Club. Prizes were awarded to Mrs. Lyman W. Smith, Mrs. Lawrence McDonald and Mrs. David Dyer. The club will be entertained next by Mrs. W. E. Deyoe.

Men's Club

The Men's Club of the Schoonmaker Memorial Presbyterian Church met last evening at the home of Earl G. Hayner in Bemis Heights. A covered dish supper was served at 6.30 p.m. Following supper a program of games was enjoyed.

Attend Presbytery

Several members of the Missionary Society of the Presbyterian Church attended the semi-annual session of the Troy Presbytery today in the Westminster Church, Troy. Those attending were Mrs. E. G. Hayner, Mrs. Fred Lamb, Mrs. E. C. Lawrence and Mrs. Lyman A. Talman.

To Hold Family Night

"Family" night will be observed tomorrow evening in the Methodist Church. All families of the church are invited to a covered dish supper and program. Rally Day will be observed on Sunday and the family get-together is in preparation for Sunday. Supper will be served tomorrow at 6.30 p.m. followed by a program under the direction of Miss Vera Ashley, school music director.

Obituary

James Baldwin, 28, a lifelong resident of Stillwater, died this morning in Hurn Memorial Hospital at Albany where he had been confined for three years and critically ill for the past three weeks. He attended Stillwater schools and St. Peter's Church and was employed at the former J. B. Lyon Printing Co. in Menands before his illness. Survivors are his parents, Mr. and Mrs. Patrick Baldwin, six sisters, Mrs. Frank Welch of Schenectady, the Misses Lela, Corrine, Verna and Patricia Ann of Stillwater, and Miss Mary Quinn of Albany, and five brothers, Pvt. Earl Baldwin in Oregon, Pfc. Stanley Baldwin in Africa and Norman, Kenneth and David Baldwin of Stillwater.

THREE SERVING—Mrs. Margaret Cassino is mother of three men serving in the armed forces, two in the Navy and one in the Army. Left to right above they are shown: Adolph J. Cassino, seaman, first class, who is on submarine duty in the South Pacific, having enlisted two years ago; Corp. Joseph Cassino, who has been in a year and now is at Camp Weingarten, Mo., and Frank Cassino, who has been in the Navy ten years and now is stationed at Memphis, Tenn. Joseph and Frank are married and the corporal has one child.

WALLACE CERTAIN THIS IS CENTURY FOR COMMON MAN

Vice President Appears in Tip-top Health on His 55th Birthday.

BY FRANCIS J. KELLY.

Washington (AP)—Vice President Henry A. Wallace, 55 years old today, is more certain than ever that this is the century of the common man because he has "faith in the peace to come."

The common man of the world will have the food and the jobs and the decent standards of living and the freedom from fear of future war which he has so long desired, Wallace declared in an interview.

The only barrier to this end "lies in the realm of politics and the common man can take care of that if he really wants to do so," the vice president said.

He figures the common man's century, a forecast and an expression he first made two years ago, will really get under way as soon as the war is won, and that Americans will have a big hand in it. In that connection he remarked, no one "should assume that the United States is going to feed other people, or give its resources to other people, except on an emergency basis.

"It may be good business for the United States to save tens of millions of people from starvation now," he observed, "but it also would be good business to get those tens of millions producing for themselves at the earliest possible moment. When they become productive, they'll become potentially good customers of the United States."

Wallace suggests self-liquidating public works in various parts of the globe as a valuable outlet for some of this country's surplus production capacity and engineering ability. He estimated that surplus, however, at only about 5 or 10 per cent of the nation's potential, "because 90 or 95 per cent of our resources and skills will be needed to give our own folks proper food, housing, good educational facilities and modern transportation."

He added enthusiastically:

"We've just started making these United States a fine place to live." "Full employment in the United States can do an awful lot to promote world-wide prosperity," he said. "For instance, if we're fully employed, we would buy more coffee from Brazil, more minerals from Bolivia, Peru and Chile, and so on."

Wallace, busy presiding over daily sessions of the Senate and receiving distinguished foreign visitors, appears in tip-top health.

EAST SIDE.

Triumph Rebekah Lodge held a short business meeting Tuesday in the Odd Fellows' Hall to allow the members who are on the staff and escorts of the D. D. P. Mrs. Verna Hammersley to attend installation at Minehaha Lodge, Mechanicville. Those who made the trip included: Mrs. Barbara Moreland, Mrs. Betty Mohl, Mrs. Catharine Lloyd, Mrs. Catharine Munson, Mrs. H. Barbara Osterhout, Mrs. Mae Degen, Miss Louise B. Barber and Mrs. Hammersley. Triumph Lodge will hold its own installation ceremonies Tuesday. Nov. 2, Mrs. Marion Quandt will be installed Noble Grand.

Personal.

Mrs. George Murray of Jesse Court is confined to the Troy Hospital with pneumonia.

Mr. and Mrs. Andrew F. Krieger of Pawling Avenue are expected home this evening after spending a few days in New York.

Church Notes.

Tomorrow in Trinity Methodist Church hall there will be an informal gathering including games and committee meetings of the Youth Fellowship group. Miss Edna Ward is superintendent of the group The time is 7.30 p.m.

The executive board and group leaders of the Women's Guild of the Third Presbyterian Church will meet tomorrow with Mrs. W. E. Baylis, McChesney Court at 8 p.m. Today the Women's Missionary Society will meet with Mrs. Albert T. Baylis, 14 Blakeley Court.

NO ROOM ON BUS; BITES HER WAY IN

London (AP)—Wartime London busses are very crowded and it's mighty exasperating for everyone, but Magistrate J B Sandbach decided that Vilma Gall went too far in showing her annoyance when conductor Mrs Jessie Rontree refused her admission to an already full bus.

Vilma bit Jessie's wrist and now she must serve seven days in jail.

COMICAL COMMAS.

Springfield, Mo. (AP)—Something happened to all the periods and commas in the typesetting machine of the Seymour comma Mo period comma Citizen and the weekly newspaper came out without any periods

It was comma the editor indicated comma a period of a comma comma period

ONE DAY'S FIRING.

A single infantry division may use up 540 tons of Army Ordnance ammunition in one day's firing A single armored division uses more than 600 tons every day it is in action.

CHAPLAIN—Lieut. Hiro Higuchi, native of Hawaii, of Japanese descent, is second such chaplain to receive commission in U. S. Army. He trains at Harvard. He represents Congregational Christian communion.

ACHIEVEMENTS OF BOY GARDENERS TOLD AT ROTARY

John E. Sambrook Reveals Work Accomplished by 27 Club Members

An account of the achievements of 27 youngsters of the Troy Boys' Club in turning twenty acres of farmland into successful victory gardens during the last summer was given to the Rotary Club today, at its luncheon meeting in The Hendrick Hudson by John E. Sambrook, Troy business man and owner of the farm.

Present at the meeting, as guests for the occasion were five of the boys who won prizes for their accomplishments in connection with the work. The prize-winning boys who were introduced to the Rotarians by Mr. Sambrook, were: Albert Meleti, most productive garden; Harold Temple, best kept garden; Michael Pascarelli, canning; Louis Anthony, attendance; Anthony Kasparian, largest display at fair held at close of the season.

Mr. Sambrook narrated briefly how he had conceived the idea of turning part of his idle farm acreage into victory gardens and cast about to find people willing to go to work on the project; and how he finally found the desired volunteers in the Troy Boys' Club. He then told how these boys went to work on their victory gardens, under the supervision of Edward A. Kane, director of the club. The average age of the boys, he said, was about 10 years.

The speaker emphasized the lively interest which he said the boys showed in the work, and praised their conduct, which he said, was excellent. He also praised Mr Kane for his part in the endeavor.

Mr. Sambrook was introduced by Julian W. Williams. At the conclusion of his talk, a rising vote of appreciation was moved by W. Frank Leversee.

ONE ARRESTED, OTHER TAKEN TO HOSPITAL AFTER FIGHT IN YARDS

A fight in the Boston & Maine Railroad yards this morning sent one man to the Troy Hospital and a second to Troy Police Court.

Luther Wilson, 54, Negro of Boston, was taken to the Troy Hospital in a police radio car for treatment for a head laceration. Wilson was treated but refused to remain at the hospital. He was conveyed there by Patrolmen William J. Cunningham and Dominick Campana.

Later Joseph R. Chambers, 66, also a Negro from Boston, was arraigned before Judge James F. Byron in Troy Police Court on a charge of assault, third degree. Police charge Chambers with hitting Wilson with a club.

The case was adjourned to Thursd-- morning.

SUR--ATE ACTIVITIES IN WASHINGTON COUNTY

The following are among the proceedings in the Washington County Surrogate's Court for the week ending yesterday:

Orders entered in the following estates exempting said estates from tax under the estate tax law: Estate of Sarah A. Hamilton, Jackson, and estate of John Von Pomer, Fort Edward.

Estate of Cornelius J. Cronin, Fort Ann; order entered determining the tax under the estate tax law.

Estate of Mary E. Buckley, White Creek; amended order entered determining the tax under the estate tax law.

Orders entered in the following estates directing the county treasurer to make the appraisal: Estate of Ambrose Arnott, Jackson; estate of Joseph Lyttle, sr., Greenwich; estate of Newcomb S. Pratt, Greenwich; estate of Frank W Stockton, Kingsbury; and estate of Catherine Tierney, Salem.

Estate of Grace E. Gooding, White Creek; probate of last will adjourned to Nov. 16, at Salem.

Estate of Mabel Fish Clark, Whitehall; probate of heirship adjourned to Nov. 10, at Hudson Falls.

Estate of Edgar DeWitt Flower, Salem; last will admitted to probate; letters testamentary issued to Eva T. Flower.

Estate of William J. McCon-t, Argyle; citation issued in probate of last will, returnable Dec. 6 at Hudson Falls.

Estate of William C. Bernard, Kingsbury; citation issued in judicial settlement of the account of executor, returnable Nov. 16 at Salem.

Estate of Frank A. Garrett, Greenwich; last will admitted to probate; letters testamenatry issued to Grace F. Garrett.

Estate of Napoleon Paquette, Fort Edward; receipts, releases and waivers in judicial accounting of administration filed.

Estate of Anthony Scott, Whitehall, limited letters of administration issued to Catherine Scott.

Estate of Royal E. LaGrange, Fort Ann; inventory filed.

GETS SUSPENDED TERM; ORDERED TO LEAVE CITY

For throwing a kitten into the street during a neighborhood quarrel recently, Arthur Mundell of 141 Madison Avenue, Pittsfield, Mass. yesterday received a two months' suspended sentence in the House of Correction and an order from the judge to leave the city. He was also found guilty of an assault and battery charge brought by Mrs. Beatrice Beaupre who said he had hit both her and her husband after the latter had asked Mundell to stop insulting his wife.

JOHN PAUL JONES IS IN NAVY ONCE AGAIN

John Paul Jones joined the Navy today.

The namesake of the father of the U. S. Navy, John Paul lives in Glens Falls and was 17 years old on Navy Day.

"It took some coaxing to get my mother to sign my papers," the youth said; "but she finally agreed x x x." He said he did not know whether he was a descendant of the famed commodore.

SAFE FROM PENTAGON'S FANS—Clasping his hands across his stomach, Capt. Clark Gable, erstwhile movie star, faced the press in the Pentagon building in Washington, safe for the moment from the surging crowds of girls and women in the corridors outside. The War Department would not allow pictures of him as he passed through the admiring women workers of the Pentagon going to and returning from the press conference.

Financial News

N. Y. Produce Market.

New York, Nov. 2 (AP)

FLOUR Steady

Spring patents (100 lbs)	3 73	a	3 78
Soft winter straights (98 lbs.)		a	4 01
Hard winter (100 lbs)	3.70	a	3.75

RYE FLOUR Steady.

Fancy patents (100 lbs)	3 35	a	3 50

CORNMEAL -Steady.

(per 100 lbs) white granulated		a	3 43½
Yellow		a	2 99½

BUCKWHEAT—Nominal. No quotations.

FEED -Steady.

Western bran, per ton, basis Buffalo		a	41 55

POTATOES—Higher. Long Island, 100 lb. sack.

Cobblers, including dark color No. 1	2.50	a	2 75
Chippewa, No. 1	2.65	a	3 00
Green Mountain, No. 1	2 75	a	3 10
Size "B"		a	1 60
50 lb. sack Green Mountain No. 1	1 40	a	1 50
Maine, 100 lb. sack Green Mountain and Katahdin	2 65	a	2 85

BUTTER—(2 days' receipts) 739,760; firm.

Maximum prices set by OPA for bulk butter in cartons, delivered New York:

Creamery, higher than 92 score and premiums marks (AA)	a	42¼
92 score (A)	a	41¾
90 score (B)	a	41¼
89 score (C)	a	41

(Tubs ½ cent a pound more on all grades).

CHEESE—(2 days' receipts) 344,678; nominal.

No quotations.

EGGS—(2 days' receipts) 18,449; firm.

The following are first receivers' selling prices:

(Paying prices to shippers or producers are 1 3-10 cents below these prices and joubers selling prices are 1½ cents above these quotations.)

U. S. specials (average net weight per 30 dozen.)

48 lbs 56.3; 46 lbs 55.3; 44 lbs 53.8; 43 lbs 53.1; 40 lbs 50.8; 38 lbs 49.3; 36 lbs 47.8; 34 lbs 46.3.

Current receipts 43 lbs 46.3; dirties 45.3. Checks 45.3.

Poultry quotations are wholesale sellers' prices which include 1½ cent allowance above ceiling levels for first hand distribution costs and commissions.)

Dressed firm. Fresh: Boxes, fowls, all weights 33½; chickens, all weights 37½. Old roosters 29 Turkeys, boxes or bbls, dry packed and iced, hens and toms 6-16 lbs 45½; 16-20 lbs 43½; over 20 lbs 42 Frozen, boxes, fowls, all weights 33½. Chickens, all weights, 37½. Old roosters 29. Turkeys, boxes or bbls, dry packed and iced, hens and toms, 6-16 lbs 45½; 16-20 lbs 43½; over 20 lbs 42.

Live firm. By freight and express. Broilers, fryers and roasters 30-32. Fowls 26½-28½. Old roosters 22½-24½. Turkeys, young, under 18 lbs 37½-39½; 18-22 lbs. 36-38; 22 lbs and over 35-37; old turkeys, under 18 lbs 35½-37½; 18-22 lbs. 34-36; 22 lbs and over 33-35. Ducks 26½-28½.

FARMERS' MARKET.

Nov. 2, 1943 About the only "vicinity" item showing noticeable strength this morning was cauliflower. With produce dealers box pears are slightly easier while sweet potatoes touch $4.50 per bushel, an advance of approximately $1.00. Pomegranates are to be had in boxes of forty specimens at $3.50.

TOMATOES, basket	1 50@2.00
Green, basket	@1 00
POTATOES, bushel	@1 75
CELERY, doz bu	@1.00
CABBAGE, bushel	@1 25
Savoy	@1.00
KALE, bas.	@ 50
CAULIFLOWER, cr.	@3.25
BROCCOLI, doz. bu.	@1.75
SQUASH, basket - Acorn	1.00@1.25
Hubbard	1 00@1.25
PUMPKINS, pie, bas.	@1.00
PARSLEY, doz bu	@ 40
RADISHES 100 bchs.	@3 00
BEETS, bu	1.75@2.00
TURNIPS, bu.	1.50@1.75
CARROTS, doz. bchs.	@ .60
Bushel	1.75@2.00
SPINACH, bu	.65@ .75
ENDIVE, basket	@ .75
PARSNIPS, basket	@2 00
BEETS, doz. bchs.	@ .60
APPLES, bushel	2 00@3 25
CHICKENS Live weight, lb.	@ 40
ORANGES, Fla.	5.25@5.50
GRAPEFRUIT, Fla.	4.75@5.00
PEARS, box	@6.50
PEPPERS, bu	@2.50
BEANS, hpr	@4.25
TOMATOES, lugs	@3 00
RUTABAGAS, 50 lbs.	1.50@1.65
LEMONS, crate	@7 50
GRAPES, box	@3 50
NUTS, mixed, lb.	@ 45
FIGS, lb pkg doz	@6.75
CRANBERRIES, box	@5 25
LETTUCE, Iceberg, cr	@6 25
POTATOES, 100 lbs.	3 00@3 50
Idaho, 50 lbs.	@2 50
ONIONS, 50 lbs.	@3.25
SWEET POTATOES, bu.	@4.50

CORNELL TEAM POINTS FOR PENN STATE TILT

Ithaca (AP) Cornell football practice was back on normal basis and Carl Snavely began pointing his Redmen for Saturday's final home game with Penn State. There was a long dummy scrimmage and the climax was a tough game in which passing was specialized. Al Dikdebrun was at the controls for the first team at tail back, while others in the backfield were Howie Blose at right half, Capt. Meredith Cushing at quarterback and Schneider at full. Nathan Sheer operated at left end in place of the departed Tommy Lascalla. He was converted to that spot from fullback.

TO INSTALL OFFICERS.

Mrs Versa A. Hammersley, district deputy president, will visit Triumph Rebekah Lodge, her home lodge, to install officers this evening in the Albia Odd Fellows' Hall.

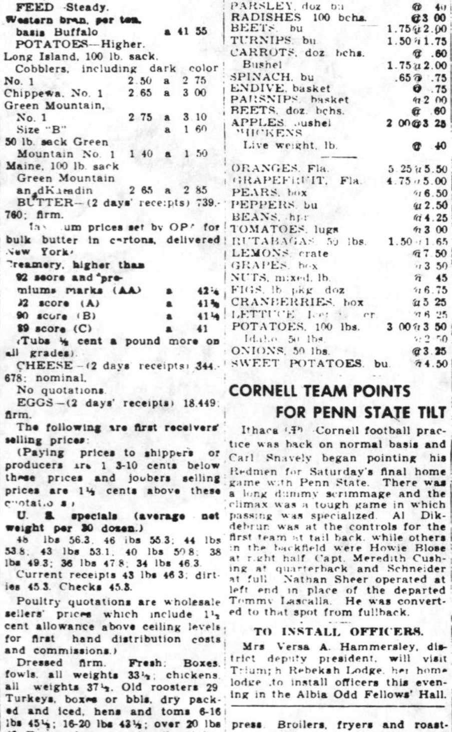

DAVIS CAUGHT—West Point's Galloping Glenn Davis, center, swivel-hipped his way past clutching hands of the four Penn tacklers seen at right, but couldn't elude Quaker Quillen (No. 42) who downed him after a three-yard gain in the first quarter. Army and Penn both remained unbeaten when their rain-swept battle at Franklin Field ended in a 13-13 tie.

EXPERT PREDICTS HOUSING RUSH IN POST-WAR DEMAND

Most Popular Home To Be Ready-constructed Five-Room Model

Chicago (INS)—The most popular postwar house, a five room structure complete with all electrical appliances, will cost between $2,500 and $3,000 and will be ready for occupancy within a month after it is selected. This prediction was made by Bror Dahlberg, a nationally recognized housing authority.

"That $2,500 house," he continued, "will be far better built and equipped than anything costing $10,000 today. It will have air change apparatus fuel-cutting insulatoin and electrical cleaning gadgets"—but it will still look like a house.

Dahlberg doesn't believe people want to live in something that resembles a tear drop or hat box. "People will want to live in the country," he said, "in a house as beautiful and functional as a city skyscraper but cozy and homelike, and they'll want to pay around $3,000."

Ready Immediately.

That house will be available immediately after the war, he emphasized, because the building industry, through war time necessity, has learned more about construction in the past two years than in the preceding two decades.

"The most important thing learned," Dahlberg stated, "is the fact that houses can be completely built in a factory and set up on a lot in a few weeks without losing individuality and at a fraction of the former expense.

"After the war a couple will go to the builder, tell him the size and type of house they want, and select their variation from hundreds of 'basic' samples. The kitchen, for instance, can come in any color, in any of a dozen shapes and sizes, but it will come as a complete unit, from windows to toaster."

The largest saving in the postwar house will be a result of the wall construction, Dahlberg explained. They won't be put up laboriously on the lot by a few workmen paid by the hour for months. Instead they will consist of a single material, turned out by an assembly line, cut to fit the individual house. At the same time they will be insulated, exterior and interior and can be painted, papered or stuccoed to fit the type of house.

Insulated Walls.

The new walls will be such good insulators that the interior will remain cool in summer and cut furnace tending to a one-in-a-few-days chore in winter.

The furnace, within a few years, Dahlberg contends, will be the size of a small filing cabinet and as easy to care for.

Hundreds of thousands of war marriages, returning servicemen who will want to live in a house as soon as possible and the present dissatisfaction with old fashioned, crowded city dwellings will force the building industry to institute mass production of low-priced houses, Dahlberg believes.

He predicts that there will be a migration to the country due to improved transportation, helicopter service and the post-war shorter work week.

"About 1,500,000 new homes are needed immediately after the war. The building industry wouldn't be able to supply them the old-fashioned, expensive, time-consuming way. People will buy houses as they buy ready-made clothes, and the houses they live in will be just as individual as the way they look," Dahlberg declared.

SEEK MISSING HUNTER IN HERKIMER COUNTY

Rome (AP).—State Police continued today their search for Adam Cegielski, Rome Air Depot employee lost since Sunday in the woods near McKeever, Herkimer County.

Trooper Gardner Vaughn said Cegielski's hunting companions reported him missing after his automobile was found parked in a gas station. Cegielski's home address is 71 James Street, Wilkes-Barre, Pa.

WEST SAND LAKE.

The Woman's Society for Christian Service will meet at the parsonage this evening with the president, Mrs. James Hargrave in charge.

The Executive Committee and those who are selling tickets for the father and son banquet will meet at the Methodist Church today at 8 p.m.

The Loyal Berean Class will serve a swiss steak supper Thursday evening at the church. In connection with the supper, the class will have a fair and sale of fancy articles. All members of the class are requested to bring something to sell.

The prayer meeting will be omitted this week, but Robert Bicknell will show the pictures, "Chaos and the Way Out," at the midweek service at the Pawling Avenue Methodist Church Wednesday. Those wishing to attend should consult Mr. Lavender or Mr. Bicknell.

AVERILL PARK.

William Warger is home from the Samaritan Hospital.

Eugene Warren of the Naval Training Station at Sampson is home on a week's leave.

Mrs. Herbert Hemple of Essex is spending the winter with Rev. and Mrs. Orrin Iveson, jr.

Dr. and Mrs. J. D. Livingston of Rochester were recent guests of Mr. and Mrs. Alfred Bauer.

The Red Cross members will hold an all day meeting and sewing at the Engine House Thursday at 10:30 a.m.

The Ladies' Aid Society of the Hoags Corners Methodist Church will hold its monthly meeting with Mrs. Wonderling Thursday at 2 p.m.

NAVY TEAM PREPARING FOR CONTEST WITH PENN

Annapolis, Md. (AP) — Showing little signs of wear and tear from the Notre Dame tilt, Navy's football squad began preparations yesterday for the Pennsylvania game Saturday at Philadelphia pepped up by the return of Bobby Jenkins, speedy left halfback.

Jenkins, former Alabama University player, was injured in the Duke game almost a month ago, and has seen little action since, but Capt. John E. Whelchel, Navy head coach, said the 190-pound speedster was about ready to go again.

The Middies came out of the Cleveland game with a very few scratches, Navy coaches said.

LAST MINUTE PLAY DISCUSSED BY FANS

New York (AP)—Gather round, you Monday quarterbacks, and debate this question? Did Penn do the right thing in running with the ball on fourth down in midfield in the last minute of its game with Army at Philadelphia?

Picture the situation: two unbeaten, untied teams are tied 13-13 with 71,615 spectators feeling thrills running up and down their spine. Penn has the ball in midfield, 4th down, 10 yards to go, and only 60 seconds to play.

Would you gamble by passing or running or play safe by kicking?

Quarterback Bob Odell, of the Red and Blue, elected to call a running play. Joe Kane gained three yards on the play, but it wasn't enough so Army took over on its own 47 with 20 seconds left, plenty of time to get off a possible long forward pass for a winning touchdown.

As it turned out Army had time to try two aerials. One fell incomplete, the other was completed for a first down on the Penn 30 as the final gun sounded.

And what about Steve Filipowicz's backward run in the Tulane-George Pre-Flight game at New Orleans?

The Pre-Flight boys were ahead by a 14-13 and had the pigskin on the Tulane 30 with fourth down coming up. There was 11 seconds left to play. Filipowicz took the pass from center, executed an about face and ran all the way back to his own 34 as the game ended.

Just supposing he had been chased back over his own goal line for a safety, giving Tulane a 15-14 victory?

That is what Odell did in his sophomore year at Penn when the Red and Blue played Columbia at Franklin Field in 1941. Penn was ahead, 19-14, when Odell deliberately ran fifty yards in reverse for a safety. The play gave Penn an opportunity to get off an onside kick without the possibility of it being blocked. It worked out, too, Penn winning, 19-16.

HAVANA QUINTET BOOKS THREE CONTESTS IN U. S.

New York (AP)—The University of Havana basketball team, winner of the Pan-American Olympic title last winter, will play a trio of games in the United States this season, opening its campaign in Madison Square Garden against Long Island University on December 25.

The Cubans also will oppose Canisius College at Buffalo on December 28 and Temple University at Philadelphia on January 1.

FUNNY BUSINESS.

"In case some driver gets fresh, I let him have it!"

TIPPIE AND "CAP" STUBBS — Well, She Tried to Help — By EDWINA

ELLA CINDERS — Vindication — By CHARLES PLUMB

BOOTS AND HER BUDDIES — A Life Saver — By EDGAR MARTIN

FRECKLES AND HIS FRIENDS — Between the Boys — By MERRILL BLOSSER

RED RYDER — Vengeance Bound — By FRED HARMAN

OUR BOARDING HOUSE . . . with . . MAJOR HOOPLE

OUT OUR WAY — By J. R. WILLIAMS

POESTENKILL

Services beginning at 11 a.m. Sunday in the Church of Christ, Poestenkill, will be conducted by Fay E. Derby of Auburn.

Final plans for the rummage sale to be held in Troy Nov. 19 and 20 in conjunction with the Loyal Friends Class will be made Monday at 2 p.m. when the Ladies' Aid Society will meet at Church of Christ.

The Ladies' Aid Society will sponsor the apron party which will be held at the church at 8 p.m. Nov. 19. Mrs. Ralph Andrews, Troy, will present readings as a feature of the evening's entertainment. Other articles will be sold in addition to the aprons. Refreshments will be served.

A Glamor Touch To Graying Hair

Give new beauty, color, luster, to those graying locks. Look years younger, more attractive! Hide your gray hair with the easy-to-use Barbo recipe below. Get a professional looking hair tinting job right at home at small cost.

Get from your druggist one box Barbo Compound. Mix in half pint of pure water as directed on package. This makes a big bottle of one of the best gray hair preparations you can use. Simply comb the hair as directed. Gray, faded, streaked hair is given a soft, glossy, lustrous color that will not wash out, rub off, stain the scalp, or affect permanents. This color is uniform, natural looking, most beautiful and easy and economical to maintain. Try the popular Barbo recipe today. See how much younger you will look, and forget you ever had gray hair.—Adv.

NOTED BIOGRAPHER PREDICTS END OF WAR THIS WINTER

Emil Ludwig Addresses Civic Forum at Jewish Community Center

"The Germans will break down this winter in the same way as they did in 1918," Emil Ludwig predicted in his address last night to a capacity audience at the Jewish Community Center.

Dr. Ludwig, noted biographer and authority on international affairs, was the first speaker in this year's civic forum series of the Center. The chairman of the Center's cultural activities, Herman J. Rosenthal, presided, and Rev. Robert Campbell, D.D., introduced the lecturer.

"What Kind of Peace Shall We Make with Germany" was Dr. Ludwig's topic.

Preferred Hitler.

Twenty-five years ago the German republic was founded. With it came the hope of a new era for Germany, but the character of the Germans themselves made it impossible for them to accept a Democracy, and they were easily led into Hitler's regime—not only because they preferred it, Dr. Ludwig said. We, in America, think that we are not fighting the German people, only the Nazis. What we do not seem to realize is that we are fighting the German temperament, the German training, in other words, the German people themselves, the speaker said. They are trained to command and to obey, and unless the Allies show strength and constant supervision after the war is won, the Germans will soon find a way to revert to their natural way of life, which is obedience to power as exemplified by a uniform.

Dr. Ludwig's proposals for a peace plan are these:

First there must be a complete disarmament of all the Germans, the leaders, the people, even the policemen.

Hundreds of their terrifying leaders must pay for their crimes by death.

An army of occupation, comprised of soldiers of all the Allies must supervise the German government, industries and education.

To reeducate the "Hitler Youth" will be one of the biggest problems facing the Allies warned Dr. Ludwig. German professors who believe in the democratic way of life must teach once again the old German literature, music and philosophy. They must educate the young people of Germany toward democracy, and away from dictatorship. This will take time, of course, as will all the program of rehabilitation. Ten years of supervising at least will be necessary before the Germans can be trusted to take over the control of their own government, he felt.

Must Repair Ruins.

Production in factories must be supervised by the occupation army, the speaker said, and Germans must work to rebuild and repair the ruins they have created in Europe.

Most important of all, plans should be formulated now, before the end comes, so that there will be no dissention among the Allies as to what shall be done.

Dr. Ludwig after his address answered a few questions asked by the audience.

The program was opened by the singing of "The Star Spangled Banner" led by Miss Olive Bonelli. City Judge John J. Sweeney spoke on the Allied Communities War Chest campaign now under way.

WHITEHALL

Sergt. Robert Royal who is stationed in Florida, is visiting his sister, Miss Edna Royal.

Capt. Fred Nelson, Air Forces is spending a furlough with his father, Warner B. Nelson.

Archille De Celia has returned from Pittsfield, Mass. where he was called by the death of his sister, Miss Arcellia De Celia.

Avon Swinton Gregory, a former resident of Whitehall is spending a twenty-day furlough at the home of his aunt, Mrs. Archie Camp of Bennington.

Irwin Charpentier is visiting his wife and parents, Mr. and Mrs. Albert Charpentier, Robert Charpen

tier, is also visiting at Camp McKall, N. C., is also visiting his parents.

John Baker of the Naval Reserves has returned to Hobart College to continue his studies after spending an eight-day leave with his parents, Mr. and Mrs. Roy Baker.

Corp. Marilyn Trumbull of the Canadian Woman's Corps visited her mother, Mrs. Joseph Cavaller this week-end. Joseph Cavaller is also the guest of Mrs. Zayachek, his mother-in-law.

After serving more than three years in the armed forces and taking part in several campaigns, Angelo Rovelli has been honorably discharged. He was discharged with the rank of sergeant. Rovelli left here with the Anti Tank Company October 1940, and served in the Hawaiian Islands and the Guadalcanal. While in the latter place he was stricken four times with malaria fever and for that reason and an injured knee he received his honorable discharge.

At a recent meeting of Whitehall Grange the following officers were elected: Master, Edson Ayera, overseer; Rufus Norton, lecturer; Sarah Ormandy, steward; Clifford Chadwick, assistant steward; Claude Kingsley, chaplain; Amy Moore, treasurer; James J. Sullivan, secretary; Mrs. Mary Norton, gatekeeper; Alice Kilburn, Ceres; Florence Ayers, Pomona; Marjorie Chadwick, Flora; Ethel Kelly, lady assistant steward. Bernadette Kingsley, executive committee for three years, George Brown.

POWNAL

Mrs. Carolyn Prezi is confined to her home by illness.

Mrs. Alice Willetts spent the week-end in Boston.

Miss Fay Willette has returned from visiting friends in Valley Falls.

Misses Victoria Davis and Julia Robb of Bennington were recent guests of Mrs. Jay Buck.

Chief Yeoman Harold J. Arbour of Palm Beach, Fla. is spending a short leave at his home in North Pownal.

The Baptist Ladies' Auxiliary will meet at 7:30 Friday evening at the home of Mrs. Floyd B. Lewis of North Church Street.

Mr. and Mrs. Frank C. Paddock are entertaining their daughters, Mrs. Arthur Fielding of Cleveland, O. and Mrs. K. L. Stevens of Philadelphia. The latter is accompanied by her two children, Margaret and Julia.

A complimentary copy of "Men in Motion" by Henry J. Taylor has been received at the library. This is a very recent work by the last American permitted in or out of Germany before Hitler declared war on the United States. Told in story form, it deals with international situations and problems of the present and of the future.

SOUTH CAMBRIDGE.

Victor Royal was reelected master and Harold Hamilton, overseer, at the annual elections of officers at Pleasant Valley Grange Friday night. Other officers elected were Lecturer Charlotte Babcock, steward; Clifford Burch, assistant steward, Philip Babcock, chaplain; Mary Hungerford; treasurer; Fred Buckley, secretary; Pauline Brownell, gate keeper; Malcolm Hamilton; ceres, Frank Bennett, pomona, Alura Pearson, Flora, Helen Hamilton, executive

BUREAU LEADERS SEE PREPARATION OF WARTIME MEAL

Food Drippings Instead of Fats Used in Demonstration

More than thirty leaders of Home Bureau units throughout the county attended a demonstration on cooking wartime meals at St. John's Church recently. Miss Theresa Wood, nutrition expert of Cornell University, was in charge of preparing a meal cooked with food drippings, instead of purchased fats. The dinner stressed use of cereals and soybean products.

A feature of the meal was a green salad prepared by grinding a whole lemon and mixing it with shredded carrots. This was served on apple rings and placed on a bed of entire soybean cookies were served as dessert.

Reports on use of soybeans and soybean products in cooking were delivered by several leaders.

Armed with the latest knowledge in nutrition development the leaders will teach more than 1500 Home Bureau members throughout the county. For those who were unable to attend community demonstrations recipes are available at the Home Bureau office in the Postoffice.

It was announced that Miss Margaret Murphy, education staff member of an Odah ma glass jar company will present two canning demonstrations this week. The first will be at St. John's Church.

Rensselaer at 8 pm tomorrow and the second at 2 pm Friday at St. John's Church, Troy. Interested homemakers are invited.

More than 3,000,000 cans of fruit and vegetables have been canned in the county this year. It was revealed.

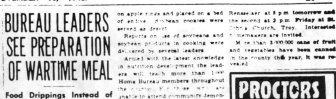

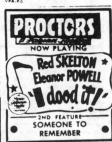

DR. LUDWIG LECTURES—Emil Ludwig, second right, noted biographer, predicted collapse of Nazi Germany this winter in a lecture last night at the Jewish Community Center opening the center's civic forum series. With the speaker are Fred Glass, left, director of the center; Miss Olive Bonelli, Rev. Robert Campbell, D.D., who introduced Dr. Ludwig, and Herman J. Rosenthal, right, chairman of the cultural activities committee of the center.

TROOPS SWEATED WAY TO ASSAULT ON JAP ISLANDS

Men Sweltered in Crowded Transport But Had Fine Spirit

BY WILLIAM HIPPLE

Pearl Harbor (AP)—American assault forces invading Japanese-held tropical islands, literally sweat their way to the point where they clamber off their hot, crowded transports into landing boats, burning with hatred for the enemy.

It was so sweltering and cramped for the Marines who invaded Tarawa in the Gilbert Islands, that the men who had never seen action were filled with this hate. It was hatred not aroused by propaganda or second hand information but it stemmed from the discomfort the Japanese made them go through to reach Tarawa.

the men perspired until they were wringing wet in their packed compartments deep in the ship. They slept naked, and still the sweat poured off them. They awoke groggy from the bad air.

Perspiration dripped from their eyes and their noses as they ate and as they daily watched the running of Hollywood's class B movies.

Sleep on Deck.

Until the night before the invasion the Marines found nooks and corners of the topsides of the transports and lay on the hard decks trying to catch a breath of breeze. But on the last night it was forbidden, for if an enemy bomb hit the deck crowded with men, it would be disastrous.

Prowling the weather decks of a blacked out ship on previous nights it wasn't unusual to step inadvertently on a part of some Marine's anatomy. This usually got a grunt out of the Marine, but no anger. He had probably stepped on somebody else himself previously.

Men learn to live together peaceably on a transport area more crowded and compact than any city tenement. Officers said there had been no fist fights between the Marines on the ships I rode, although the men had been packed aboard her for weeks.

The Marines amused themselves by a sort of endless chatter about their past experiences, like back home, where they had been, what they would like to be doing now, the inevitable grousing about food (which wasn't bad), and friendly ridicule of each other.

Find Old Magazines.

They had little reading matter, partly because the packs must be light and partly because books donated by the homefolks never seem to reach that far. But they managed to drag from the depths of the ship some tattered old books and magazines from two to ten years old.

One Marine showed me an eight-year old magazine warning that some day we might have to fight the Japs. "We should have listened to that guy," the Marine said.

These enlisted men showed complete confidence in themselves, their comrades, their officers and their weapons, and each was confident that he wouldn't be killed. I have never seen such spirit as among these men, sailing in an ocean full of aircraft carriers, battleships, cruisers, destroyers and transports, stretching around the ship as far as the eye could see.

The chaplain said "there's been a heavy increase in the number of confessions as we neared the Jap base." But the Marines appeared light-hearted. I heard them harmonizing sourly but spiritedly on the Marine hymn with "shore of Tarawa" substituted for "shores of Tripoli."

When I asked one of the Marines if he worried about the outcome, he said, "Hell, no! Haven't you heard, mister. We are the Marines."

FIRST AT ARSENAL—The War Department for the first time in its history made service awards to civilians yesterday at the Watervliet Arsenal. The ceremonies staged at noon during the lunch hour are pictured above. The service awards were made by Brig. Gen. A. G. Gillespie, commanding the gun plant, to representatives of the various departments.

ON THE AIR

Radio Programs From Local Stations

TONIGHT.

1,000—WTRY—Troy—980.

P. M.

5:00—Hop Harrigan
5:15—Dick Tracy
5:30—Jack Armstrong
5:45—Captain Midnight
6:00—Terry and the Pirates
6:15—Roy Shudt
6:30—Gift Bar
6:40—Dinner Music
7:00—Organ Interlude
7:05—House on "Q" St.
7:30—Fighting Coast Guard
8:00—Earl Godwin
8:15—Lum and Abner
8:30—Town Meeting
9:30—Tony Pastor
9:55—Melody Time
10:00—Raymond G'm Swing
10:15—Star Parade
10:30—Wings to Victory
11:00—Music for Listening
11:30—Music You Want
12:00—News

370—WGY, Schenectady—810

P. M.

5:00—When A Girl Marries
5:15—Portia Faces Life
5:30—Just Plain Bill
5:45—Front Page Farrell
6:00—News
6:05—News, Bob Banes
6:15—Varieties
6:30—Dinner Dance
6:45—Lowell Thomas
7:00—Fred Waring
7:15—John W. Vandercook
7:30—Bob Burns
8:00—Variety Program
8:30—The Aldrich Family
9:00—Music Hall
9:30—Davis and Haley
10:00—Abbott and Costello
10:30—March of Time
11:00—News
11:05—Melodie Moods
11:15—Harkness
11:30—Music
12:00—News

306—WOKO, Albany—1460.

P. M.

5:00—Four Smart Boys
5:15—Say It With Music
5:45—American Women
6:00—News
6:15—Supper Melodies
6:30—Major Eliot
6:45—World Today
6:55—Meaning of News
7:00—I Love a Mystery
7:15—Harry James
7:30—Mr. Keen
8:00—Suspense
8:30—Death Valley Days
8:55—Bill Henry, News
9:00—Major Bowes
9:30—Dinah Shore
10:00—The First Line
10:30—Dick Haymes
11:00—News
11:15—Joan Brooks, Songs.
11:30—Raymond Scott's Or.

TOMORROW.

1,000—WTRY—Troy—980.

A. M.

6:45—Top of the Morning
6:50—Goood Morning
6:55—News
7:00—Timekeeper
7:10—Morning Melodies
7:25—Timekeeper
7:30—News
7:45—Timekeeper
7:55—News
8:00—Timekeeper
8:15—Rise 'n' Shine
8:30—Timekeeper
8:55—News
9:00—Breakfast Club
9:30—Breakfast Club
9:45—Breakfast Club
10:00—Household Diary
10:15—Roy Porter
10:30—Troy Chapel Service
10:45—Humbard Family
11:00—Breakfast at Sardi's
11:15—Breakfast at Sardi's
11:30—News—Gil Martyn
11:45—Mary Gaynor
11:50—Melody Lane
12:00—Noon Edition

P. M.

12:15—Texas Jim Lewis
12:30—Sweet and Swing
12:55—Melody Time
1:00—Baukhage Talking
1:15—Salon Orchestra
1:30—Kay Moser
2:00—Trombini and Small
2:15—Mystery Chef.
2:30—Ladies Be Seated.
3:00—Morton Downey.
3:15—Muic to Remember.
3:55—News.
4:00—Blue Frolics.
4:30—News.
4:45—Melody Time.
4:50—Phill Ohman.
5:00—Hop Harrigan.
5:15—Dick Tracy.
5:30—Jack Armstrong.
5:45—Captain Midnight.
6:00—Terry and Pirates.

370—WGY, Schenectady, 810

A. M.

6:00—Farm News
6:00—Poultry Journal
6:10—News
6:15—Church in Wildwood
6:30—Otis and Eleanor
6:45—Song Shop
7:00—Song Shop
7:30—News
7:35—Time to Shine
7:45—News
8:00—Time to Save
8:15—Meet the Band
8:30—Otis and Eleanor
8:45—Market Basket
9:00—Morning Moods
9:15—Big Sister
9:30—News
9:45—Aunt Jenny
10:00—Lora Lawton
10:15—The Open Door
10:30—Helpmate
10:45—Recipe Contest
10:50—Song Parade
11:00—Road of Life
11:15—Vic and Sade
11:30—Brave Tomorrow
11:45—David Harum
12:00—News

P. M.

12:05—Noontime Melodies
12:15—News
12:30—Farm Paper
1:00—Musical Matinee
1:15—Scissors and Paste
1:30—Household Chats
1:45—Carey Longmire
2:00—The Guiding Light
2:15—Lonely Women.
2:30—Light of World.
2:45—Betty Crocker.
3:00—Woman of America.
3:15—Ma Perkins.
3:30—Pepper Young.
3:45—Right to Happiness.
4:00—Backstage Wife.
4:15—Stella Dallas.
4:30—Lorenzo Jones.
4:45—Young Widder Brown
5:00—When A Girl Marries.
5:15—Portia Faces Life.
5:30—Just Plain Bill.
5:45—Front Page Farrell.
6:00—News.

306—WOKO—Albany, 1460

A. M.

6:45—Sacred Heart
7:00—News
7:05—Vista Grande
7:15—Minute Man
7:45—News
8:00—Musical Clock
9:00—Newsflash
9:05—Interlude
9:15—American School
9:45—Forrest Willis
10:00—Valiant Lady
10:15—Kitty Foyle
10:30—Burl Ives
10:45—Interlude
10:55—Receipe Contest
11:00—Amanda
11:15—Second Husband
11:30—Bright Horizon
11:45—Louise Benay
12:00—News

P. M.

12:06—Timely Tunes
12:11—Interlude
12:15—Kate Smith
12:30—Helen Trent
12:45—Our Gal Sunday
1:00—Life Beautiful
1:15—Ma Perkins
1:30—Bernadine Flynn
1:45—The Goldbergs
2:00—Young Dr. Malone
2:15—Joyce Jordan.
2:30—We Love and Learn.
2:45—Perry Mason.
3:00—Mary Martin.
3:15—Red Cross Program.
3:30—Yours Truly.
4:00—Home Front Matinee.
4:25—Neighbors.
4:30—Master Works.
5:00—Four Smart Boys.
5:15—Say it With Music.
5:45—American Women.
6:00—News.

CANADIANS WILL GET PERMITS TO PURCHASE TIRES OR TUBES HERE

Washington (AP)—The Office of Price Administration today made eligible to buy reclaimed or used tires and new tubes in this country those Canadians in the United States who drive for occupational or essential reasons.

Although Canada permits Americans to buy tires and tubes in the Dominion, Canadian drivers on this side of the border, in the past, have not been eligible for tire purchases because no basic gasoline ration is issued them. They have received "special" rations, instead.

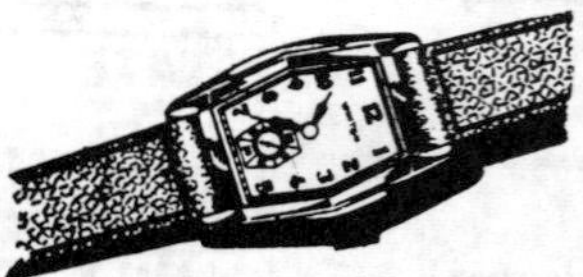

Canadians who receive "special" rations—up to 15 gallons a year—solely for tourist travel will continue to be ineligible for tires. The change is effective Dec. 14.

The Army's 155 mm. guns mounted on pneumatic tires and weighing about 15 tons, hurls a 95-pound projectile more than 15 miles.

ST. LAWRENCE PLAN HIGH ON SENATE'S LIST OF AGENDA

"New Yorker in Washington" Finds Other Bits of Home State News

BY HOWARD DOBSON

Washington (AP)—High on the Senate's "Let's-put-that-off-until-next-year" agenda is the controversial St. Lawrence power development and seaway project, on which hearings will begin soon after the holiday recess.

Senator Overton (D., La.) is chairman of a special subcommittee of the Senate Commerce Committee, which will conduct hearings on a bill introduced in September by Senator Aiken (R., Vt.).

Other Democrats on the subcommittee are New York's Senator Mead, and Senator Radcliff of Maryland. Republicans are Vandenburg of Michigan and Burton of Ohio.

The bill would permit immediate start on electric power and navigation facilities on the St. Lawrence under an agreement with Canada. Mead said the hearings were put over until after the first of the year because subsidy, tax and soldiers-vote bills before the Senate are taking more time than was expected.

The bill would authorize the President to negotiate a transfer to the New York State Power Authority of power facilities constructed in New York, along with the right to use waters at the project sites for producing electric power. However, the state would have to pay $93,375,000—the present estimate by Army engineers of the cost of power developments in the total project.

Payment could be made over a period of fifty years, interest on the debt to be compounded annually at 3 per cent.

Finds Living High.

When you speak of high war-time taxes, shed a tear for the New York Congressman who says his pre-war "take home" of $9,800 (out of his $10,000 salary) is now down to $6,500 . . . Also, he adds with understandable pain, he has to maintain a full time residence here, whereas he formerly lived in Washington only about six months a year . . . Costs back home haven't dropped, either.

P. O. Disapproves.

The Postoffice Department has disapproved, "from a purely administrative standpoint," of Rep. Walter Lynch's bill to bar from the mails false and defamatory printed matter aimed at religious or racial groups? . . . The resulting "hear," says the New York City Democrat, "has been terrific" . . . Postmaster General Walker asked Lynch recently, "What did you do to us—and why?"

"Stop Roosevelt"—Landon.

Most New Yorkers who attended the 78 Club (made up of freshman Republican members of the 78th Congress) party for Alf Landon expected him to make a "Stop Willkie" speech, but report it was more of a "Stop Roosevelt" plea instead . . . The 1936 G. O. P. presidential candidate did not mention Governor Dewey, they add, although it is understood here that Landon prefers Dewey to Willkie for the 1944 race.

Stump for WAC.

The current WAC recruiting drive has had the aid of two New York Representatives, both Republican freshmen . . . "Pat" Kearney of Gloversville, whose daughter is in the WAC, made a speech two weeks ago urging enlistments in the corps . . . Last week Winifred Stanley of Buffalo suggested inclusion of the corps in plans for rehabilitating liberated territories as combat troops advance.

WILSON'S WEEKLY Bulletin

By George Rector
Food and Nutrition Consultant to Wilson & Co.

LOW-POINT MEATS HIGH IN FLAVOR

Back in the days when Rector's was the meeting place of food connoisseurs, we did not have to think about points . . . flavor was the chief test which food had to pass. However, many of the dishes that were most famous in our dining rooms were the ones that used meats which are now of low point value. It's truly remarkable how much flavor can be coaxed out of these meats when they are given their rightful share of attention and care in preparation. Today I am passing on to you two of my favorite recipes, modernised with both points and food value in mind.

Spaghetti Dinner
Italian Spaghetti with B-V Meat Sauce
Pear Salad
Hard Rolls Olives
Baked Custard
Peanut Butter Cookies
Milk Coffee

In making spaghetti today the trick is to stay within your meat points and at the same time serve it forth with Italian sauce that even a Caruso would approve. In the old days gourmets usually used large amounts of meat in the sauce. Let's see what a half pound will do and incidentally, I predict that this sauce will take a permanent place in all spaghetti schemes, henceforth.

Italian Spaghetti

1 clove garlic, sliced
4 cups tomatoes
1 tbsp. sugar
¼ tsp. mace
4 whole cloves
½ bay leaf
2 tsp. Wilson's B-V
½ lb. hamburger
1 onion, chopped
3 tbsp. bacon drippings
1½ tbsp. flour
½ cup sliced mushrooms
2 stalks celery, sliced
1 pkg. spaghetti (8 oz.)
½ cup grated cheese

Simmer garlic, tomatoes, and next four ingredients, covered, for ½ hr. Strain. Dissolve Wilson's B-V in 2 tbsp. hot liquid and add to first mixture. Brown meat and onion in fat, stir in flour, add celery, mushrooms and tomato mixture and simmer 15 min. Meanwhile boil whole spaghetti in salted water 10 to 15 min. until just barely tender. Drain, rinse with hot water, drain again. Serve hot sauce over spaghetti. Sprinkle grated cheese over top. Serves 6.

Tasty Vitamins

Here's a dish that's really delicious. And is it plenty nutritious, what with both pork liver and sausage in it! The meat supplies large amounts of protein, iron, Vitamin A, thiamine, riboflavin and niacin. One serving insures almost a day's needs of iron and Vitamin A.

Liver and Sausage Loaf

1 tsp. Wilson's B-V
½ cup boiling water
1 tsp. grated onion
½ lb. Wilson's Certified Pork Sausage
½ lb. pork liver, ground
1 cup dry bread crumbs
1 tbsp. ketchup
1 tbsp. horseradish
1 egg, beaten

Dissolve B-V in the hot water and mix well with remaining ingredients. Bake in an oiled loaf pan 1¼ hours, 325° F. Serves 6.

Besides being nutritious, Wilson's B-V spreads an indescribably good, richly delicious flavor throughout any main dish. Use it, too, to add delicious meat flavor to gravy, soup, and casserole dishes.

Yours for flavorful nutrition,
GEORGE RECTOR

BRITISH ADMIRAL GIVES PICTURE OF PAST NAVAL CRISIS

Says Allied Cause Might Have Been Lost After Crete

Washington (U.P.)—After the battle for Crete, the British battle fleet in the Mediterranean consisted of only three cruisers and if the vastly heavier-gunned, numerically-superior Italian fleet had been willing to risk action, the Allied cause might have been as good as lost.

This picture was presented today by Admr. Sir William James, naval information chief of the British Admiralty in an article for the forthcoming "United States At War" issue of the Army and Navy Journal.

"It was fortunate that the enemy did not know, or, if he did have an inkling of the truth, that he failed to put it to an acid test of decisive action," he wrote.

Had Mussolini's fleet come out to do battle against this weak British fleet—the only force between Gibraltar and the Red Sea—Italo-German forces might have been free to crush British resistance in North Africa, to open the back door to Soviet Russia and even to reach the Indian Ocean to link arms with Japan, James said.

Fortunately, he added, it became possible to reinforce the Mediterranean fleet with ships such as the aircraft carriers Eagle, Formidable and the Wasp, the latter the U. S. Navy carrier which subsequently was sunk in the Pacific. These ships ferried about 700 R. A. F. planes to Malta, rebuilding that island into the formidable fortress that its strategic position in the Central Mediterranean merited.

The British admiral said Britain faced an earlier crisis in the Mediterranean when Italy entered the war. Then the Axis had available six battleships, 19 cruisers and a large number of destroyers, submarines and other craft.

"To that array Great Britain was able to oppose only four battleships, seven cruisers, one aircraft carrier and an assortment of small craft," James said. "Just one floating airfield against the chain of land airfields hostile or passively unfriendly, and stretched from Gibraltar to the borders of Egypt."

But, he said, the then British Mediterranean commander-in-chief Sir Andrew Cunningham, kept the Italians checked with a policy of aggressiveness.

"Many times in the ensuing months did the British fleet try to force a decisive action but whenever contact was made, the enemy retired as if tacitly accepting the mastery which the Royal Navy possessed only in offensive spirit," he added.

Of the present, James said:

"The Royal Navy under the good providence of God, by the side of the Allies, and now that it has the real means, will soon give the enemy its answer."

WYNANTSKILL.

Rev. A. A. Seso is confined to his home with illness.

Mrs. Joseph Haughney has returned from a visit to New York City.

Mrs. Floyd Pierson and Mrs. Duane Vroman of Watervliet have returned from a visit with friends in Springfield, Mass.

Mrs. Thomas J. Ryan left this week to join her husband, who is stationed in California with the Seabees. Mrs. Ryan was formerly Miss Helena Pitts of 12 Brookside Avenue.

Mrs. LaVerne Smith, sr., of Buffalo has returned home after visiting her grandsons and daughter-in-law, Mrs. LaVerne Smith, jr., the former Miss Nettie Bump, whose husband is in the Army and is now stationed at Camp Stewart, Georgia.

CHRISTMAS MUSIC TO BE FEATURE IN VILLAGE CHURCHES

Carols, Holiday Anthems Scheduled on Calendars For Tomorrow

HOOSICK FALLS

Christmas services will be held tomorrow in the Baptist, Methodist and Presbyterian churches.

At the First Baptist Church the order of service at 10:30 a.m., as announced by Rev. Wallace E. McCoy, pastor, will be as follows: Organ prelude, "O, Holy Night" (Adam), Osmond R. Eldredge; carol, "Praise to God in Heaven" (Curry), junior choir; vocal solo "Night of Nights" (Van De Water), Mrs. Ethel Bentley, choir director; offertory instrumental trio, "Christmas Bells" (Johnson), Mrs. Frederick Strait, Edward Cusson, Mr. Eldredge; anthem, "Song in the Air" (Loreas); organ postlude, "Joyous Postlude" (Mallard), Mr. Eldredge. Mr. McCoy will preach on "A Tower and a Manger."

The Methodist service at 10:30 a.m. has been announced as follows by Rev. Mark Kelley, D.D., pastor: Organ prelude, "Offertory for Christmas Season" (Barret), Miss Elma Rowley; carol, "Holy Night" (Franz Gruber); call to worship, Dr. Kelley; processional hymn, "Adeste Fidelis" (No. 96); prayer of confession; silent prayer; words of assurance, Dr. Kelley; the Lord's Prayer with choral Amen; anthem, "Christmas Hymn" (Jungst); responsive reading, Gloria Patri; affirmation of faith; Scripture lesson, Luke 2:8-20; choral sentence, "We Would See Jesus;" pastoral prayer, choral response; anthem, "Behold, I Bring You Glad Tidings" (Semper); offertory, "O, Holy Night" (Adam); doxology; hymn 98, "There's a Song in the Air;" sermon, "The Theme Song of Christmas," Dr. Kelley; prayer; hymn 92, "It Came Upon the Midnight Clear;" benediction, Danish three-fold Amen; organ postlude, "Christmas March," Miss Rowley.

At the Presbyterian Church, because the choir director, H. Bradford Cole, is in the armed forces and the pastor, Rev. Walter D. Kring, has joined the Navy Chaplain Corps, the service at 11 a.m. will be very simple, the instrumental and congregational singing featuring Christmas music. Rev Harold C. Harmon of Cambridge, a native of Hoosick Falls, will conduct the service and preach. Miss Marion Jones is organist and Lynn McEachron, clarinetist.

Sunday School Party.

The Advent Christian Sunday School, Southwest Hoosick, will have its annual Christmas party Monday at 7 p.m. in the church.

Class To Have Party.

The United Class of West Hoosick Baptist Church will have a Christmas party with grabbag Monday at 8 p.m. at the home of Mrs. Lester Pine.

The annual turkey social of the Derby Community Club will be held Monday evening in the American House. The meeting will include nomination and election of officers for the coming year.

Schools Close.

The schools of the village closed yesterday for the Christmas vacation. Christmas parties and programs were held in every classroom and at St. Mary's Academy the juniors gave the seniors a party. Classes will be resumed on Jan. 3.

Holds Achievement Day.

The Hoosick Falls Home Bureau held an Achievement Day Thursday afternoon in the American Legion rooms. Baskets, pressing pads, home made toys and weaving, all done by the members, were on display. The program of entertainment included carol singing, a reading by Mrs. Carolyn H. Thomas, a short talk by Miss Florence Titcomb, assistant county agent, and games. Refreshments were served.

Tree Exercises.

The annual Christmas tree exercises of the First Baptist Church School will be held Monday at 7 p.m. in the church hall under the charge of Mrs. Ethel Bentley, superintendent of the elementary department. The young men of the church, whose names are on its honor roll, will be remembered in a prayer by Rev. Wallace E. McCoy, pastor. Santa Claus is expected to pay a visit. The choir will lead in the carol singing. Refreshments will be served by the Philathea Class. Parents are asked to attend with their children.

Sunday in the Churches.

Baptist, Rev. Wallace E. McCoy, pastor—10:30 a.m., morning worship; 11:45 a.m., Church School; 6 p.m., Youth Fellowship.

St. Mark's Episcopal, Rev. Jerrald C. Potts, rector—8 and 10:30 a.m., Holy Communion with sermon by the rector at the latter service; 9:45 a.m., Church School.

Immaculate Conception, Rev. George C. Egan, O. S. A., pastor—Low masses at 6, 8 and 10:45 a.m., with benediction following the late service. High mass at 9:15 a.m.

Presbyterian—10 a.m., Sunday School; 11 a.m., morning worship. There will be a special meeting of the Troy Presbytery at 3 p.m. to officially consider the resignation as pastor of Rev. Walter D. Kring and to appoint a moderator of the church.

Court Has Party.

The Christmas party of Court St. Mary, Catholic Daughters of America, Thursday night in the Immaculate Conception parish hall, was well attended. The hall was appropriately decorated and the tables were adorned with candles with a small Christmas tree on the center table. Supper was served at 6:30 by a committee of which Mrs. Mrs. Joseph Kempf was chairman. The blessing was asked by Rev George C. Egan, O. S. A., chaplain of the court. Christmas carols were sung with Miss Phyllis White at the piano, and Rev. James P. Ambrose, O. S. A., and Miss White sang solos. Short talks were given by Father Egan and Father Ambrose, Rev. Paul K. Lynch, O. S. A., and Miss Elizabeth Armstrong, grand regent of the court. There was a grabbag and the evening was concluded with games. Mrs. James M. Brahan was chairman of the dining room committee, and the entertainment was arranged by Miss Margaret Curtis.

THE TRAPP FAMILY SINGERS.

President Reveals Nazi Conspiracy To Kill "Big Three"

Washington (AP)—President Roosevelt said yesterday that the Russians got wind of a Nazi plot to kill him, Prime Minister Churchill and Marshal Stalin while they were in Teheran for their momentous war conferences.

That was why, he explained to a news conference, he took up lodgings in the Russian embassy compound where Stalin also was staying. He noted that the British embassy was next door and the move meant none of the three principals would have to go through the streets to get together for their talks.

The President said the conference area in the Middle East was within range of German planes and that air transports were like sitting ducks on the water. It was in an air transport that he journeyed to Teheran, he said.

Tanned and looking fit, the President leaned back at his desk and related with evident relish the bare outline of the story during nearly an hour's exchange of questions and answers with reporters which developed these other chief points:

1 The talks at Teheran and the Anglo-American-Chinese discussions at Cairo were a success in every way and he hopes they laid the foundation for a postwar era of peace which will last at least through the lives of the present generation. That hope, he added, is shared by Churchill, Stalin, and President Chiang Kai-shek of China.

2 Important military decisions were reached but he would not, he said in response to a question, make any predictions that they will bring the European war to a close next year. All of us, he said, are working as hard as we can to defeat Hitler as early as possible.

3 He intends to pack into a Christmas Eve address, to be broadcast at 3 p.m., Eastern War Time, all over networks, as full a report as possible on the conferences. He will speak from his home at Hyde Park, and intends to spend Christmas Day there. Whatever may be left over in the way of news on the conferences will go into a report to be made later to Congress.

4 There may or may not be later meetings with Stalin, Churchill, or Chiang Kai-shek. The way to phrase it, he said, is that all four of them are on call.

The President said Stalin had lived up to his highest expectations and that he had been glad to meet also with Generalissimo Chiang Kai-shek. Meeting those two men, he said, makes for excellent relations in the future.

In response to inquiries, Mr. Roosevelt said he had called Stalin marshal and that while conversations took place through interpreters, the discussions were not stodgy and sometimes the answers came out before the translations were completed.

The President arrived in Washington at 9:30 yesterday morning, held an impromptu reception for congressional leaders at the White House, and plunged into a busy day.

He had successive conferences with diplomats representing Britain, China, Russia, Turkey, Iran and Egypt—all nations which figured in one way or another in his conferences abroad. Secretary of State Hull was a luncheon visitor and a Cabinet meeting followed.

Shortly after 4 p.m., the President received reporters. Having had little chance to talk with him, Mrs. Roosevelt also attended the conference as did their daughter, Mrs. John Boettiger, and Lieut. and Mrs. Franklin D. Roosevelt, jr., their son and daughter-in-law.

Apparently not at all tired by his 36-day trip, the President gaily asked the reporters whether anything happened around here while he was gone and indulged in other quips.

He would like to tell about his method of travel, he said, but didn't want any trouble with the Army and Navy and all he could say was that he went to Teheran by plane.

When he got to Teheran, he related, he went to the American embassy. That night he got word from Stalin of a German plot. The Soviet marshal pleaded with him to go down to the Russian embassy, so the next morning he went there to stay.

He supposed it would have made a pretty good haul for the Germans, the President chuckled, if they could have got all three of them going through the streets of Teheran.

He gave no other details of the reported plot, but observed that there must be a hundred or more German agents in Teheran.

Mr. Roosevelt explained the mid-afternoon hour for his Christmas Eve speech by saying it was intended primarily for service men overseas. He noted the hour would be 9 p.m. in Cairo, 10:30 p.m. in Iran and Christmas morning in the Southwest Pacific.

Hundreds of office-bound government workers knew of the President's return to the Capitol some minutes before the official announcement, when they saw the executive's entourage sweep down historic Constitution Avenue an whirl into the White House drive.

TRAPP FAMILY TO PRESENT CONCERT WITH RARE MUSIC

Folk Songs Will Be Given In Peasant Costume on Jan. 10

The Trapp Family Singers will present a program of rare old church and folk music at Music Hall, Monday, Jan. 10, under the auspices of the Troy Catholic Associates. In native Tyrolean costume, the Baroness Maria Augusta von Trapp and her nine gifted daughters and sons will entertain with a capella singing, and performances on such long-neglected musical instruments as the block-flute, spinet and viol de gamba.

Full length dirndls of handsome woven fabrics of black and white, the formal evening version of their native dress, will be worn for the first part of the program, which is a presentation of the early pre-classical music. A change to gay colors, bright shawls and aprons, for the second part of the program will be appropriate for the lusty yodels and gay folk songs which will follow the religious airs.

Trojans will be able to observe at first hand authentic originals of the colorful peasant costumes of native Austrian mountains.

The program will be conducted by the Family's priest and musical director, Father Franz Wasner.

U. S. SENATE APPROVES MUSTERING OUT PAY FOR ARMED SERVICES

Washington (AP)—With breakneck speed, the Senate approved overwhelmingly and sent to the House yesterday a "Christmas Gift" measure to provide mustering out pay ranging from $200 to $500 for men and women in the armed forces.

The Senate acted after only a little more than an hour's debate roll call vote after Democratic leader Barkley (Ky.) had urged a "Christmas present" to the fighting forces.

Under the measure, $500 would be paid to each man and woman up to and including the rank of colonel who had served 18 months or more overseas or in Alaska. One third of the sum would be paid on termination of service and the remainder in two monthly installments.

The mustering out pay would be $400 for 12 to 18 months overseas service and $300 for less. Persons who served more than 12 months in this country would get $300 and those serving less than that $200. All payments except that of $200 would be in three equal installments, the latter being paid in two monthly checks.

Estimates of the over-all cost of this reward for service, recommended in a message to Congress by President Roosevelt, ranged from $3,000,000,000 fixed by Barkley to $4,000,000,000 estimated by Senator Johnson (D.-Colo.), who headed a subcommittee which whipped the bill into shape.

INFANT EXPIRES AFTER SLAPPING, WOMAN HELD

Rockford, Ill. (AP)—Nine-month-old Sammy Aiello died yesterday of a brain hemorrhage and state's attorney Max Weston said Mrs. Leona Lemery, 23, admitted she slapped the baby twice "because the child got on my nerves with its whining and crying."

The prosecutor said Mrs. Lemery was held in jail pending completion of the investigation.

FIRE DAMAGES FORD'S WAYSIDE TRADE SCHOOL

Sudbury, Mass. (AP)—Fire caused damage which Fire Chief W. E. Davison estimated at $15,000 yesterday at Henry Ford's Wayside trade school yesterday.

MISS BETTY OOTHOUT.

TROY GIRL MAKES RADIO CITY DEBUT IN SONG ENSEMBLE

Soloist for Seven Years at Silliman Church, Cohoes

Miss Betty Oothout, daughter of Marshall P. Oothout of Hackensack, N. J., and Mrs. Marshall Oothout of Troy, made her debut with the Christmas stage show at Radio City Music Hall which opened Thursday. She is a member of the singing ensemble.

Miss Oothout long has been recognized in music circles of Troy for her exceptionally fine messo-soprano voice. For seven years she was soloist for the Silliman Memorial Church of Cohoes. She has sung over WTRY, and was a feature of "Dreamin' Time," a WGY presentation during 1941.

In that year she sang on the Albany concert stage, accompanied by George H. Pickering, her vocal teacher. The Niagara - Hudson Choral Club presented its tenth annual concert with Miss Oothout as one of its guest soloists.

For the last summer she has been singing at St. Bartholomew's Church in New York.

Miss Oothout uses the professional name Bette Holland.

WARTIME PROFITS OF GREAT CORPORATIONS HIT ALL-TIME PEAK

Washington (AP) — Corporation profits for 1943, after taxes, will reach an estimated $8,000,000,000, an all-time high, the Department of Commerce said yesterday.

Profits before taxes are expected to range between $22,000,000,000 and $23,000,000,000, likewise a new peak, the department added.

"Taken together," it said in a statement, "these figures indicate that while performing miracles of war production the corporations are pouring back into the United States Treasury in the form of taxes roughly two-thirds of their unprecedented earnings."

Profits after the taxes for the first nine months of this year aggregated $5,900,000,000, a rise of 11 per cent over the same period of 1942, while aggregate corporate profits before taxes for the nine months period were $16,000,000,000, 20 per cent above the corresponding 1942 total.

CROP PRODUCTION TOPS AVERAGE FOR 5 YEARS

Washington (AP)—The Agriculture Department, in final figures for the year, reported yesterday that total crop production this year fell about 6 per cent below the record harvest of 1942 but topped the average of the five preceding seasons by 9 per cent.

Total production of all foods, however—including such live stock products as meats, milk, poultry and eggs produced largely from feed grown in previous years—set a new record of about 4 per cent above last year to meet unprecedented wartime requirements.

The Department said this year's output was remarkable in the light of shortages of manpower, supplies, equipment, and delays with [illegible] weather and floods. It said [illegible] per week and more Sundays than in [illegible]eration.

YULE PAGEANT TO BE PRESENTED AT BAPTIST CHURCH

Mrs. George Martin To Be Director of Christmas Program Tomorrow

STILLWATER

A pageant, "Christmas Is a Miracle," will be presented at the Second Baptist Church tomorrow at 7:30 p.m. under the direction of Mrs. George Martin.

The public is invited and the offering taken will be for the World Emergency Forward Fund.

Personal.

George De Zuba left yesterday to join the Navy.

Guild To Be Entertained.

The World Wide Guild of the Second Baptist Church will hold its postponed meeting Monday evening at the home of Miss Mildred Hayner.

Entertains Club.

Mrs. Charles Dyer entertained the members of her bridge club last evening at her home. Two tables of contract were in play, with the awards going to Mrs. Aurelia Palmatier. The club will meet next with Mrs. Aurelia Palmatier.

Church Notes.

Rev. John C. Elliot will preach at 10:30 a.m. tomorrow in the Methodist Church. Church School at 11:45 a.m.

Masses will be held at 9:15 a.m. and 11:15 a.m. tomorrow in St. Peter's Church. Rev. Lawrence P Kelly is pastor.

Church service tomorrow will be at 10:30 a.m. in the Second Baptist Church with Rev. Wendell P. Stanford preaching a Christmas sermon on "A King Is Born." There will be special music. Church School will be at 11:45 a.m. The Stillwater Baptist Youth Fellowship will not meet tomorrow evening because of the pageant.

Rev. Lyman A. Talman will preach tomorrow at 10:30 a.m. in the Schoonmaker Memorial Presbyterian Church. The sermon topic will be "A King Afraid of a Baby." Church School will be at 11:45 a.m. Westminster Youth Fellowship will be at 6:30 p.m. Special music will be rendered at the 10:30 a.m. service which will include: Prelude, "Gloria in Excelsis;" processional, "Adeste Fidelis;" postlude, "Adoration." Choir numbers will include "The Song of the Magi," by Holton and "Good Tidings of Great Joy." Shaw.

TARAWA ATTACK WAS SKILLFULLY EXECUTED, VANDEGRIFT DECLARES

Washington (AP) — The Senate Naval Committee received assurance from Lieut. Gen. A. A. Vandegrift, commandant of the Marine Corps, yesterday that the Tarawa attack was "well planned and skillfully executed" together with a blunt warning that losses in such attacks in the future also will be heavy.

Tarawa, bloodiest fight in Marine Corps history, cost the American victors 1,026 dead and 2,557 wounded in 72 hours of battle.

Vandegrift wrote to Chairman Walsh (D.-Mass.) of the Naval Committee in response to an inquiry as to why losses were so heavy. After discussing the difficulties of the operation, and grimly commenting that "there are no fox-holes off shore" for the men who storm beaches, Vandegrift added:

"No one regrets the losses in such an attack more than does the Marine Corps itself. No one realizes more than does the Marine Corps that there is no royal road to Tokyo. We must steel our people to the same realization."

TWO POLICEMEN HURT IN AUTO COLLISION IN SCHENECTADY STREET

Two Schenectady policemen were injured in a two-car collision in upper State Street last night.

The injured officers, Patrolman John Mullen, 26, and Patrolman William Miller, 28, were removed to their homes after being treated by the police surgeon, Dr. William Nealon, for shock and contusions.

The two officers, off duty at the time, were traveling west in Mullen's car when it collided with a car driven by John Graves, 37, who was attempting to make a left turn into a driveway. Graves, whose car was struck in the rear, was also shaken up, police said. A passenger in his car escaped injury.

PREDICT EISENHOWER TO DIRECT INVASION

Washington (AP)—In a story credited to "well informed sources," the Army and Navy Register declared today that Gen. Dwight D. Eisenhower will direct an invasion from Britain and that Gen. George C. Marshall will be retained in Washington as chief of staff.

The Register, unofficial but usually authoritative service weekly, observes that "this is a reversal of the previous intention to send him (Marshall) to London, sometime this winter, to take command of Allied forces to invade the continent of Europe from the British Isles.

FOOD SUBSIDIES GIVEN TEMPORARY EXTENSION

Washington (AP)—Both Houses of Congress voted for a temporary continuance of food subsidies and the Commodity Credit Corporation yesterday but the Senate's sixty-day extension plan was rejected by the House in favor of only a 35-day reprive, until February 5.

This prompted the Senate to schedule an unusual Saturday session today to decide what to do about the House's action. Majority Leader Barkley (Ky.) said he thought a compromise on the extension date could be reached.

Allies Find Road To Rome No Speedway

By WES GALLAGHER.

Allied Headquarters, Algiers (AP)—After 105 days of bloody fighting since the first Allied troops set foot on Italy, Rome is still far away in a military sense with little prospect that it will be liberated soon.

There is no disguising the fact that Allied attack has gone much more slowly than had been expected, and there is little chance that it can be speeded up. This slow progress has been largely attributed to terrain and weather, which played a part, but the following factors have played as large a role, if not larger:

1. The Italian surrender has produced far less in a military sense than had first been hoped for Italian guerrilla activity and sabotage has been negligible, and the Italian armed forces have not yet proved of any great value, especially on land.

2. This Mediterranean theater does not enjoy the favored position that it did last winter in the matter of supplies and troops and is competing in priorities with other theaters which figure higher in Allied plans.

3. Militarily there is little value outside of prestige in capturing Rome and it would not be worth the tremendous infantry casualties necessary to bring the campaign to a quick end.

These three factors, along with terrain and weather, are so closely linked that it is difficult to tell which is most important.

There is no doubt the Allies hoped to capitalize more than they did on the chaotic conditions which followed Italian capitulation. It was hoped that thousands of Italian troops and millions of civilians might turn wholeheartedly against the Germans, making it impossible for them to wage a successful campaign in southern Italy.

The Germans feared this too, for they started destroying ports and other military facilities as far north as Florence.

But the Italians merely put down their arms and sat, watching the Allies and Germans fight.

Criticism has also been offered that the Allies tried to conduct the Italian invasion on a shoestring in that the initial Eighth Army Force landing in Southern Italy and the Fifth Army initial landing in Salerno were conducted by only a part of the strength available.

It was apparent during the battle of the Volturno that the time for lightning advances had passed. With typical thoroughness the Germans had sown every inch of the way with mines and flooded the Pontine Marshes, closing the lowland approach to Rome, and had fortified every mountain strong point along the way.

The terrain ruled out the use of armor and heavy rains left no choice except to depend on infantry, artillery and air bombardment.

Two courses were open to Allied commanders. One was to call for unlimited numbers of infantry divisions, throw tens of thousands of men wholesale into battle all along the line engaging the Germans until they collapsed from sheer exhaustion.

Such a course would have resulted in heavy casualties.

It was a question of weighing these casualties against the military advantage of this type of operation.

The second choice was to bring up a preponderance of artillery and with the airforces pound German strong points with high explosives one by one until the infantry could take them with comparatively small losses.

This much slower, but less costly process, is being followed, as the Allies pound and jab the Germans back from one defense line to another.

It does not mean Rome will not fall this winter but it means capture of the capital will not come in a matter of weeks.

Much has been written about the number of divisions the Germans have been forced to keep in the Balkans and Italy because of the Allied campaign but it is doubtful if the Italian campaign made much difference in the fighting on the Russian front.

Eleven or so Nazi divisions are facing the Fifth and Eighth Army in the fighting area.

On the debit side of the ledger, as far as the Allies are concerned the conquest of southern Italy has brought an economic headache. An apathetic population must be fed, clothed and kept warm to a large extent at the cost of Allied shipping which might be devoted to military purposes.

PLAN TO TAX WHISKY REVIVED IN U. S. SENATE

Washington (AP)—The chairman of the Senate's liquor shortage inquiry revived last night the plan to force stored liquor on the market through taxes, despite its one-sided rejection by the Finance Committee.

There will be a campaign on the Senate floor, said Senator Van Nuys (D.-Ind.), to add the proposal to the pending revenue bill when this measure comes up for debate early next month.

The proposed amendment, reducing from eight to five years the length of time during which aging liquor may be held in government-bonded warehouses free of taxes was rejected by the Finance Committee Thursday on a 17-2 vote.

Chairman George (D.-Ga.) has estimated that the amendment would force 117,000,000 gallons of whisky out of storage. It would make these gallons immediately subject to tax—$9 a gallon in the new revenue bill.

HOUSE APPROPRIATES FARM LABOR FUNDS

Washington (AP)—Without dissent on a voice vote, the House yesterday passed and sent the Senate legislation appropriating $33,750,000 for continuance of the farm labor recruitment program for the next twelve months.

The House followed a recommendation of its appropriation committee that the program be handled by the federal extension and the state extension services.

2 DROPS
Just 2 drops Penetro Nose Drops in each nostril help you breathe freer almost instantly, so your head cold gets air. Only 25c—2½ times as much for 50c. Caution: Use only as directed. Penetro Nose Drops

CHRISTMAS TREES
1,000 FRESH CUT
BALSAMS
75c up 171 Fourth St.

WANTED!
GIRLS
We need you to do light assembly work on gas masks for the Navy. All you need is quick nimble fingers and we will show you how to use them. Working conditions are excellent. You will receive full pay while learning, with time and one-half for over 40 hours!
Apply Employment Department, Entrance No. 1
Busses Stop at Door
Cluett, Peabody & Co. Inc.
TROY, N. Y.
Must have statement of availability if essentially employed.

SCHOOL 2 PAGEANT—Pictured above are pupils of the fourth, fifth and sixth grades of School 2 as they appeared in the pageant entitled "The Christmas Story" which they presented to the Parent-Teacher Association of the school at the December meeting of the organization held Thursday in the school auditorium. Other features of the Christmas entertainment given by the students included a playlet, "Toys Around the Christmas Tree," recitations, vocal selections and Christmas carols.

Troy, 'Vliet, Cohoes, La Salle Heatly, C. C. H. S. Teams Busy Tonight

PICKEN'S CHARGES WILL BE GUESTS AT ARSENAL CITY

Cadets Meet 'Burg Tomorrow While Cohoes Is Host to Nott Terrace

Topped by the Principal's League game between Troy High and Watervliet tonight, the week-end's scholastic cage schedule for the city of Troy area is filled to overflowing with choice basketball morsels.

Ed Picken's charges will invade Watervliet for a contest with the 'Vliet quint tonight at 9 p.m. in the feature of the six-game slate.

La Salle Institute's quintet will be host to Cohoes High in the second Principal's League game of the evening.

Catholic High travels to Albany for a Catholic League contest with Cathedral and Heatly, High opens its season against St. Ann's of Albany at the Green Island school.

That rounds out tonight's program and tomorrow evening's forum contains two games, which will send La Salle and Cohoes into action for the second time over the week-end.

The Cadets meet Lansingburgh High in a Principal's League game at the Knickerbocker Junior High gym and Cohoes is host to Nott Terrace High of Schenectady.

Troy High, originally picked to play two games this week, will only take on Watervliet tonight. A contest scheduled with Albany High to be played tomorrow at Albany was postponed to a later date.

Shifting his lineup in order to have two teams available for service, Picken has moved Sherman Wilson and Bob Stacy up to fill starting roles. The pair will team up with Teddy Bayer and "Cap" Seibert, at forwards, and Bill Deegan at center, three starters in the 'Burg game which saw Troy lose in the overtime period. The second team will be Richard "Zip" Gordon, jumping center; Bruce Campbell and Bernie Samioff at forward and Jack Newman and Bernie Cohen at guards.

Watervliet High, with a record of two and one, will bid for a higher spot in the Principal League standings with its starting lineup unchanged. The Garnet and Gray cagers, under the direction of Ed Bennett, will start Ed Ogden and Tony DiBacco at forwards; Andy Swota and Dave Torncello at guards and Stan Bajor at guards.

An injury to Don Lynn, high scoring Cohoes center, will force Pete Mooney to shift his starting lineup to fill the gap. "Bub" Ferris will take the place of Lynn, who will be kept on the sidelines for about three weeks with a busted ankle. Victors in two of three games, the Spindle City quint will be favored to chalk up a win over La Salle tonight and Nott Terrace tomorrow. The game with the Dorpians was added this week to Cohoes' schedule.

La Salle's Cadets will bid for their seventh win after drilling all week on offensive tactics. Tomorrow night's engagement with Lansingburg at Knickerbocker gym, will provide the Fourth Streeters with an opportunity to gain in the Principal's League standings.

Heatly High opens its season tonight with St. Ann's of Albany. The game with Berlin, originally scheduled for tomorrow night, has been postponed to a later date.

Catholic High's undefeated basketball forces will attempt to keep their top ranking spot in the Catholic League when they meet Cathedral tonight at Albany in their fourth road contest of the season. Returning after being out of action since the opener against V. I, Ed Whitney will be available for service with Bill Carley's charges.

The C. C. H. S. starting lineup will have John Kelly, the area's leading scorer, and Tom Ryan at forwards; Tom Egan at center; and Bob Degnan and Phil Barrett at guards.

Lansingburgh High's varsity, winners of one of three games played will be after its second Principal's League win when they tangle with La Salle tomorrow. Walt Eckerson will use Harry Cote and Jack Wittman at forwards; George Winkler at center, and Gene Lennek and Irv Goldsberry at guards.

PROS FAVORED IN GOLF TOURNAMENT

Los Angeles (AP)—The winner of the $12,500 Los Angeles Open golf championship, resuming today at the Wilshire Country Club, probably will come from the touring topnotch professionals, but there are a couple of real threats among those who have been wintering here.

Ellsworth Vines, for instance. The former tennis champion seldom has been out of the sixties. He lacks tournament experience but he may be ready for a great competitive game.

Then there is Olin Dutra, the Santa Monica, Cal., veteran. He recently played the Wilshire course in 69 and came back with a 67. He's the best pro, too.

Byron Nelson of Toledo seems to be favored among the competitors themselves. He covered Wilshire Wednesday in 66, two under par, and recently, in a pro-amateur match, fired a 66.

There was no action yesterday after Wednesday's 36-hole qualifying round. Medalist honors of 72-70—142 were won by Harry Bassler, local professional.

After 18-hole rounds today and tomorrow the field will be cut to sixty for Sunday and Monday. Twosomes of the better known players did not have to qualify.

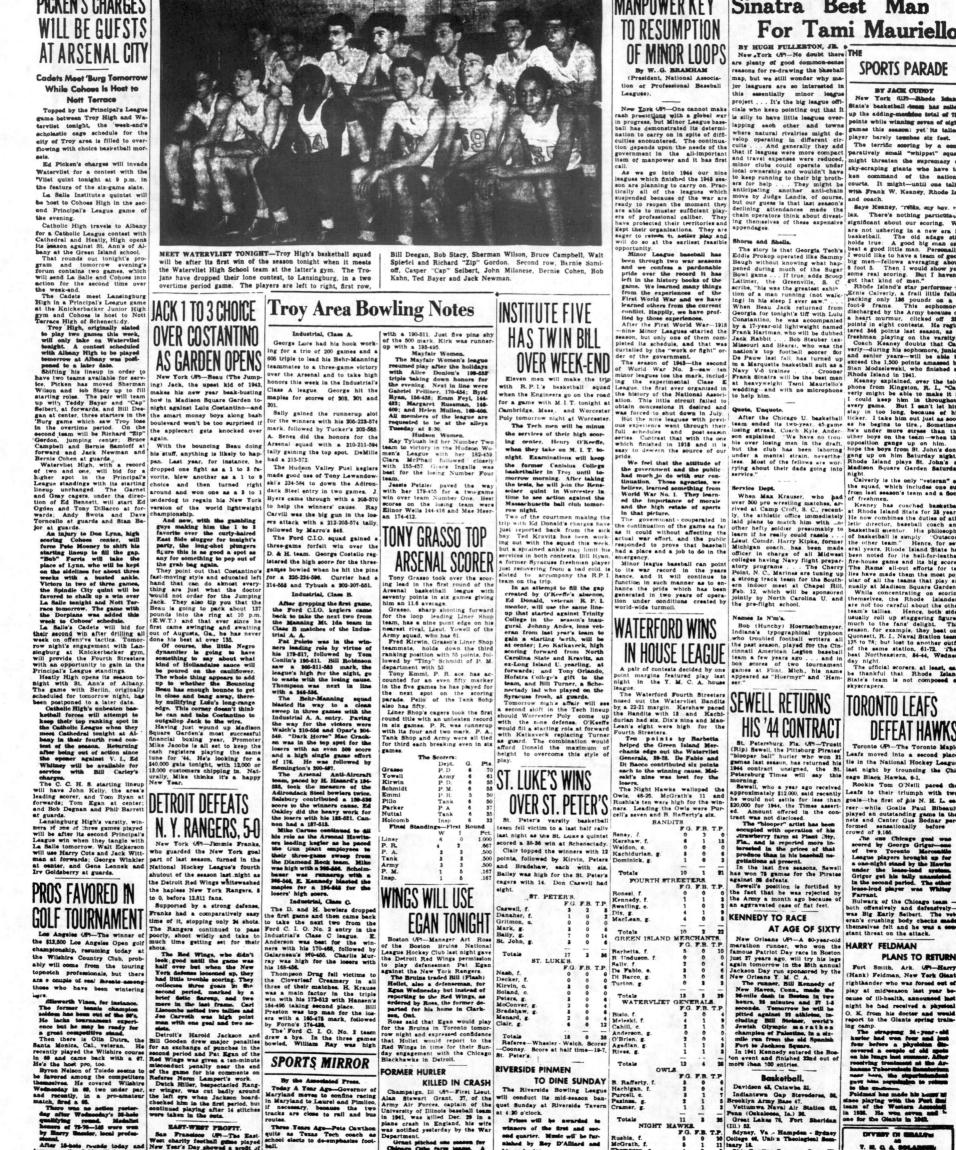

MEET WATERVLIET TONIGHT—Troy High's basketball squad will be after its first win of the season tonight when it meets the Watervliet High School team at the latter's gym. The Trojans have dropped their lone contest, to Lansingburgh, in a two overtime period game. The players are left to right, first row, Bill Deegan, Bob Stacy, Sherman Wilson, Bruce Campbell, Walt Spielel and Richard "Zip" Gordon. Second row, Bernie Samioff, Casper "Cap" Seibert, John Milanese, Bernie Cohen, Bob Kahn, Ted Bayer and Jack Newman.

JACK 1 TO 3 CHOICE OVER COSTANTINO AS GARDEN OPENS

New York (AP)—Beau (The Jumping) Jack, the upset kid of 1943, makes his new year beak-bursting bow in Madison Square Garden tonight against Lulu Costantino and the smart money boys along bash boulevard won't be too surprised if the applecart gets knocked over again.

With the bouncing Beau doing his stuff, anything is likely to happen. Last year, for instance, he dropped one fight as a 1 to 3 favorite, blew another as a 1 to 9 choice and then turned right around and won one as a 1 to 1 underdog to regain his New York version of the world lightweight championship.

And now, with the gambling guys making him the 1 to 1 favorite over the curly-haired East Side slugger for tonight's party, the long-shot plungers figure this is as good a spot as any for something to pop out of the grab bag again.

They point out that Costantino's fast-moving style and educated left hand that can do almost everything are just what the doctor would not order for the Jumping Jack. They also tip you that the Beau is going to pack about 137 pounds into the ring at 10 p.m. (E.W.T.) and that ever since he first came swinging and swatting out of Augusta, Ga., he has never done his best at over 135.

Of course, the little Negro dynamiter is going to have something to say about what kind of Hollandaise sauce will be poured on the cauliflower. The whole thing appears to add up to whether the Bouncing Beau has enough bounce to get in close and bang away, thereby nullifying Lulu's long-range edge. This corner doesn't think he can and take Costantino to outgallop Jack to the wire.

Having just wound up Madison Square Garden's most successful financial boxing year, Promoter Mike Jacobs is all set to keep the cash registers playing the same tune for '44. He's looking for a $40,000 gate tonight, with 12,000 or 13,000 customers chipping in. Naturally, Mike thinks it's a happy New Year.

DETROIT DEFEATS N. Y. RANGERS, 5-0

New York (AP)—Jimmie Franks, who guarded the New York goal part of last season, turned in the National Hockey League's fourth shutout of the season last night as the Detroit Red Wings whitewashed the hapless New York Rangers, 5 to 0, before 12,811 fans.

Supported by a strong defense, Franks had a comparatively easy time of it, stopping only 24 shots. The Rangers continued to pass poorly, shoot wildly and take to much time getting set for their shots.

The Red Wings, who didn't look good until the game was half over but when the New York defense loosened up, they had little trouble scoring. They collected three goals in the second period, marked by a brief Battle hassup, and two more in the last frame. Carl Liscombe netted two tallies and Joe Carveth one high point man with one goal and two assists.

Detroit's Harold Jackson and Bill Gooden drew major penalties for an exchange of punches in the second period and Pat Egan of the Red Wings was given a ten-minute misconduct penalty near the end of the game for his comments on Referee Norm Lampert's work.

Troy Area Bowling Notes

Industrial, Class A

George Luce had his book working for a trio of 200 games and a 606 triple to lead his Behr-Manning teammates to a three-game victory over the Arsenal and to take high honors this week in the Industrial's Class A league. George hit the maples for scores of 203, 201 and 201.

Sally gained the runnerup slot for the winners with his 206-223-574 mark, followed by Tucker's 202-585. A. Senes did the honors for the Arsenal squad with a 210-211-594 tally gaining the top spot. DeMille had a 215-572.

The Hudson Valley Fuel keglers made good use of Tony Lewandowski's 234-584 to down the Adirondack Steel entry in two games. J. Byers came through with a 203-570 to help the winners' cause. Ray Carvill was the big gun in the losers attack with a 212-203-574 tally, followed by Marro's 546.

The Ford C.I.O. squad gained a three-game forfeit win over the D. & H. team. George Costello registered the high score for the three-games bowled when he hit the pins for a 225-224-596. Currier had a 214-553 and Tybush a 203-207-551.

Industrial, Class B

After dropping the first game, the Ford C.I.O. keglers came back to take the next two from the Manning Mt. Ida team in Class B matches of the Industrial's loop.

Pat Poleto was in the winners leading role by virtue of his 179-517, followed by Tom Conlin's 195-511. Bill Robinson saw a 206-511-563 mark, the league's high for the night, go to waste with the losing cause. Thompson was next in line with a 546-534.

The Behr-Manning squad blasted its way to a clean sweep in three games with the Industrial A. A. entry. Paving the way for the victors were Walsh's 210-556 and Opar's 204-549. "Dark Horse" Mac Cracken was in the top spot for the losers with an even 500 score and a high single game effort of 176. He was followed by Remington's 200-487.

The Arsenal Anti-Aircraft team, paced by H. Hazard's 194-538, took the measure of the Adirondack Steel bowlers twice. Salsbury contributed a 189-530 score to the winners cause. Ed Oakley did the heavy work for the losers with his 185-521. Cannon had a 187-513.

Mike Carvan continued to All his role as the Arsenal bowlers leading kegler as he paced the Gun plant employees to their three-game sweep from the Diamond Rock team. Mike was high with a 208-564. Scheimhauser was runnerup with a 206-546. E. Kennedy blasted the maples for a 194-545 for the losers' high score.

Industrial, Class C

The D. and H. bowlers dropped the first game and then came back to take the next two from the Ford C. I. O. No. 2 entry in the Industrial's Class C league. E. Anderson was best for the winners with his 170-468, followed by Galarneau's 160-455. Charlie Murray was high for the losers with his 168-456.

Thompson Drug fell victims to the Cloverleaf Creamery in all three of their matches. H. Kvasae was a main factor in the triple win with his 173-513 with Hansen's 184-495 taking second place. Bill Preston was top man for the losers with a 165-475 mark, followed by Forno's 174-459.

The Ford C. I. O. No. 2 team drew a bye. In the three games bowled, William Ray was high

with a 190-511. Just five pins shy of the 500 mark, Kirk was runnerup with a 193-495.

Mayfair Women

The Mayfair Women's loop resumed play after the holidays with Alice Donlon's 190-553 triple taking down honors for the evening. Next in line were Gabriel Pelliner, 170-584, Byrd Ryan, 156-453; Emm Feyl, 144-453; Margaret Russman, 148-400; and Helen Mullen, 160-400. All members of the league are requested to be at the alleys Tuesday at 8:30.

Hudson Women

Kay Tybush led her Number Two team to victory in the Hudson Women's League with her 182-459. Clara McPhail followed closely with 155-457. Grace Ingalls was best for the losing Number Four team.

Jessie Petzler paved the way with her 179-455 for a two-game win over team Number One. Best scores on the losing team were Elinor Wells 144-416 and Mae Heeran 174-412.

INSTITUTE FIVE HAS TWIN BILL OVER WEEK-END

Eleven men will make the trip with R.P.I.'s basketball squad when the Engineers go on the road for a game with M.I.T. tonight at Cambridge, Mass., and Worcester Poly tomorrow night at Worcester.

The Tech men will be minus the services of their high scoring center, Henry O'Keeffe, when they take on M. I. T. tonight. Examinations will keep the former Canisius College basketballer in Troy until tomorrow morning. After taking the tests, he will join the Rensselaer quint in Worcester in time to see action against the Massachusetts ball club tomorrow night.

Two of the courtmen making the trip with Ed Donald's charges have just reported back from the sick bay. Ted Kravitz has been working out with the squad this week but a sprained ankle may limit his services in both contests. Bill Flynn, a former Syracuse freshman player just recovering from a bad cold, is slated to accompany the R.P.I. team on the trip.

In an attempt to fill the gap created by O'Keeffe's absence, Ed Donald, veteran R. P. I. mentor, will use the same lineup that started against Trinity College in the season's inaugural. Johnny Andre, lone veteran from last year's team to gain a starting berth, will be at center; Leo Katkaveck, high scoring forward from North Carolina State and Kravitz, an ex-Long Island U. yearling, at forwards; and Tony Orlando, Hofstra College's gift to the Tech men and Bill Turner, a Schenectady lad who played on the Syracuse frosh, at guards.

Tomorrow night's affair will see a second slant in the Tech lineup should Worcester Poly come with the zone defense. O'Keeffe would fill a starting role at forward with Katkaveck replacing Turner as guard. The combination would afford Donald the maximum of height to combat this style of play.

WATERFORD WINS IN HOUSE LEAGUE

A pair of contests decided by one point margins featured play last night in the Y. M. C. A. house league.

The Waterford Fourth Streeters nosed out the Watervliet Bandits by a 22-21 margin. Kershaw paced the Bandits with 13 and Kachidurian had six. Dix's nine and MacLean's eight were high for the Fourth Streeters.

Ten points by Barbetta helped the Green Island Merchants edge out the Watervliet Generals, 29-22. De Fabio and Di Bacco contributed six points each to the winning cause. Meleski's nine was best for the losers.

The Night Hawks walloped the Owls, 46-25. McGrath's 11 and Rushla's ten were high for the winners. Leading the Owls were Purcell's seven and R. Rafferty's six.

ST. LUKE'S WINS OVER ST. PETER'S

St. Peter's varsity basketball team fell victim to a last half rally last night as the St. Luke's quintet scored a 38-36 win at Schenectady. Clair topped the winners with 12 points, followed by Kirvin, Peters and Bradshaw, each with six. Bailey was high for the St. Peter's cagers with 14. Don Caswell had eight.

ST. PETER'S			
	F.G.	F.B.	T.P.
Caswell, f.	6	2	14
Danaher, f.	1	0	2
Gritmon, c.	0	0	0
Mark, g.	0	0	0
Baily, g.	7	0	14
St. John, g.	3	0	6
Totals	17	2	36

ST. LUKE'S			
	F.G.	F.B.	T.P.
Nash, f.	0	1	1
Decker, f.	3	0	6
Kirvin, c.	3	0	6
Boland, c.	0	0	0
Peters, g.	3	0	6
McConver, g.	2	0	4
Bradshaw, g.	3	0	6
Menard, g.	2	0	4
Clair, g.	5	2	12
Totals	19	0	38

Referee—Wheeler. Welch, Scorer—Cooney. Score at half time—19-7.

RIVERSIDE PINMEN TO DINE SUNDAY

The Riverside Bowling League will conduct its mid-season banquet Sunday at Riverside Tavern at 4:30 o'clock.

Prizes will be awarded to winners of the first and second quarter. Music will be furnished by Roy D'Alliard and his orchestra.

The second half of the league will swing into action next Wednesday.

TONY GRASSO TOP ARSENAL SCORER

Tony Grasso took over the scoring lead in the final round of the Arsenal basketball league with seventy points in six games giving him an 11.6 average.

Grasso, sharp shooting forward for the loop leading Liner Shop team, has a nine point edge on his nearest rival, Lieut. Yowell of the Army squad, who has 61.

Pat Poleto was in the winners leading role by virtue of his 179-517, followed by Tom Conlin's 195-511...

Fred Kirwin, Grasso's Liner Shop teammate, holds down the third ranking position with 55 points, followed by "Tiny" Schmidt of P. M. department with 53.

Tony Emmi, P. R. ace, has accounted for an even fifty marker in the five games he has played for the next spot on the scoring parade. Pillo of the Tank Shop also has fifty.

Liner Shop's cagers took the first round title with an unbeaten record in five games. P. R. was runnerup with its four and two mark. P. A. Tank Shop and Army were all tied for third each breaking even in six games.

The Scorers:

	Dept.	G.	Pts.
Grasso	P.D.	6	70
Yowell	Army	6	61
Kirwin	P.D.	6	55
Schmidt	P.M.	6	53
Emmi	P.R.	5	50
Pillo	Tank	6	50
Parker	P.A.	6	37
Nuttal	Tank	6	35
Holcomb	Insp.	6	33

Final Standings—First Round

	W.	l.	Pct.
Liner	6	0	1.000
P. R.	4	2	.667
P. A.	3	3	.500
Tank	3	3	.500
Army	3	3	.500
P. M.	1	5	.167
Insp.	1	5	.167

WINGS WILL USE EGAN TONIGHT

Boston (AP)—Manager Art Ross of the Boston Bruins National League hockey club last night gained the Detroit Red Wings permission to play defenseman Pat Egan against the New York Rangers.

The Bruins traded Bill (Flash) Hollet, also a defenseman, for Egan Wednesday but instead of reporting to the Red Wings, as ordered by Ross, the former departed for his home in Clarkson, Ont.

Ross said that Egan would play for the Bruins in Toronto tomorrow night and expressed confidence that Hollet would report to the Red Wings in time for their Sunday engagement with the Chicago Blackhawks in Detroit.

SPORTS MIRROR

By the Associated Press.

Today A Year Ago—Governor of Maryland moves to confine racing in Maryland to Laurel and Pimlico, if necessary, because the two tracks are close to rail and bus routes.

Three Years Ago—Pete Cawthon quits as Texas Tech coach as school elects to de-emphasize football.

Five Years Ago—Wesley Wallace of Fordham sets new world record at 1:04.4 for 500 meters at indoor track meet.

FORMER HURLER KILLED IN CRASH

Champaign, Ill. (AP)—First Lieut. Alan Stewart Grant, 27, of the Army Air Forces, captain of the University of Illinois baseball team in 1941, was killed Dec. 29 in a plane crash in England, his wife was notified yesterday by the War Department.

Grant pitched one season for Chicago Cubs farm teams. A baseballer, he had been overseas for three months. His parents are Mr. and Mrs. Alfred Grant, of Los Angeles, Cal.

MANPOWER KEY TO RESUMPTION OF MINOR LOOPS

By W. G. BRAMHAM
(President, National Association of Professional Baseball Leagues).

NEW YORK (AP)—One cannot make rash predictions with a global war in progress, but Minor League baseball has demonstrated its determination to carry on in spite of difficulties encountered. The continuation depends upon the needs of the government in the all-important item of manpower and it has first call.

As we go into 1944 some nine leagues which finished the 1943 season are planning to carry on. Practically all of the leagues which suspended because of the war are ready to reopen the moment they are able to muster sufficient players of professional caliber. They have protected their territories and kept their organizations intact. They are eager to return to active play and will do so at the earliest feasible opportunity.

Minor League baseball has been through two war seasons and we confess a pardonable pride over the record it has left in the history books of the war. We learned many things from the experience of the First World War and we have learned others from the current conflict. Happily, we have profited by these experiences.

After the First World War—1918 —nine Minor Leagues started the season, but only one of them completed its schedule, and that was curtailed by the "work or fight" order of the government.

The season of 1943—the second of World War No. 2—saw ten minor leagues toe the mark, including the experimental Class E League, the first ever organized in the history of the National Association. This little circuit failed to obtain concessions it desired and was forced to shut down in July.

But the nine leagues with previous experience went through their full schedules and post season series. Contrast that with the one which finished in 1918 and it is easy to discern the source of our pride.

We feel that the attitude of the players and the public has and done much to do with our continuation. These agencies, we believe, learned something from World War No. 1. They learned the importance of morale and the high retain of sports in that picture.

The government—cooperated in the continuation of the game as far as it could without affecting the actual war effort, and the public responded to prove that baseball has a place and a job to do in the emergency.

Minor league baseball can point to its war record in the years hence, and it will continue its function in such manner as to enhance the pride which has been generated in two years of operation under conditions created by world-wide turmoil.

Sinatra Best Man For Tami Mauriello

BY HUGH FULLERTON, JR.

New York (AP)—No doubt there are plenty of good common-sense reasons for re-drawing the baseball map, but we still wonder why major leaguers are so interested in this essentially minor league project . . . It's the big league officials who keep pointing out that it is silly to have little leagues overlapping each other and towns where natural rivalries might develop operating in different circuits . . . And generally they add that if leagues were more compact and travel expenses were reduced, minor clubs could operate under local ownership and wouldn't be so keep running to their big brothers for help . . . They might be anticipating another anti-trust move by Judge Landis, of course, but our guess is that last season's declining attendance made the chain operators think about divesting themselves of these expensive appendages.

Shorts and Shells.

The story is that Georgia Tech's Eddie Prokop operated like Sammy Baugh without knowing what happened during much of the Sugar Bowl game . . . If true, adds Scoop Latimer, the Greenville, S. C. scribe, "his was the greatest exhibition of a man running (not walking) in his sleep I ever saw." When Beau Jack returned from Georgia for tonight's tiff with Lulu Constantino, he was accompanied by a 17-year-old lightweight named Frank Hartman, who will be dubbed Jack Rabbit . . . Bob Steuber (ex-Missouri and Bears), who was the nation's top football scorer for DeSuwe last fall, has turned up in a Marquette basketball suit as a Navy V-5 trainee . . . Crooner Frank Sinatra will be the best man at heavyweight Tami Mauriello's wedding—and with no microphones to help him.

Quote, Unquote.

After the Chicago U. basketball team ended its two-year, 45-game losing streak, Coach Kyle Anderson explained "We have no trouble keeping men in the draft, but the club has been laboring under a mental strain, nevertheless. Most of the fellows are worrying about their dads going into service."

Service Stuff.

When Max Krauser, who had one day of pro wrestling matches, arrived at Camp Croft, S. C. recently, the athletic office immediately laid plans to match him with another hefty soldier presumably to learn if he really could rassle . . . Lieut. Comdr. Harry Kipke, former Michigan coach, has been made officer in charge of all Midwest colleges having Navy flight preparatory programs . . . The Cherry Point, N. C. Marines are tuning up a strong track team for the Southern indoor meet at Chapel Hill, Feb. 12, which will be sponsored jointly by North Carolina U. and the freshir, ship school.

Names is N'm's.

Bob (Hunchy) Hoernschemeyer, Indiana's typographical typhoon who troubled football writers all the past season, played for the Cincinnati American Legion baseball team a few years ago . . . and in box scores of two tournament games at Flint, Mich., his name appeared as "Hoermyr" and "Hemser."

SPORTS PARADE

BY JACK CUDDY

New York (UP)—Rhode Island State's basketball team has rolled up the adding-machine total of 720 points while winning seven of eight games this season; yet its tallest player barely touches six feet.

The terrific scoring by a comparatively small "whippet" squad might threaten the supremacy of sky-scraping giants who have taken command of the nation's courts. It might—until one talks with Frank W. Keaney, Rhode Island coach.

Says Keaney, "relax, my boy, relax. There's nothing particularly significant about our scoring. We are not ushering in a new era in basketball. The old adage still holds true: A good big man can beat a good little man. Personally, I would like to have a team of good big men—fellows averaging about 6 foot 5. Then I would show you some real scoring. But I haven't got that kind of men."

Rhode Island's star performer is Ernie Calverly, a frail little feller packing only 136 pounds on a a foot-9 frame. This sophomore, discharged by the Army because of a heart murmur, clicked off 346 points in eight contests. He registered 346 points last season, as a freshman playing on the varsity.

Coach Keaney doubts that Calverly—during the sophomore, junior and senior years—will be able to exceed the 1,500 points amassed by Stan Modzelewski, who starred at Rhode Island in 1941.

Keaney explained, over the telephone from Kingston, R. I, "Calverly might be able to make it if I could keep him in throughout every game. But I can't let him stay in too long, because of his heart condition. Sometimes he's under more stress than the other boys on the team—when the opposition gangs up on him. I hope the boys from St. John's don't gang up on him Saturday night." Rhode Island plays St. John's at Madison Square Garden Saturday night.

Calverly is the only "veteran" on the squad, which includes one sub from last season's team and a flock of freshmen.

Keaney has coached basketball at Rhode Island State for 23 years. He now combines the duties of athletic director, baseball coach and basketball mentor. His philosophy of basketball is simply "Outscore the other team." Hence, for several years, Rhode Island State has been noted for its hell-for-leather, fire-house game and its big scores. The Rams' all-out efforts for tallies have made them the most popular of all the teams that play annually at Madison Square Garden.

While concentrating on scoring themselves, the Rhode Islanders are not too careful about the other team's tallies. Hence, both sides usually roll up staggering figures, much to the fans' delight. This season, for example, they beat one Quonsett, R. I. Naval Station team, 125 to 76; but lost to another outfit of the same station, 61-72. They beat Northeastern, 54-44, Wednesday night.

The official scorers, at least, can be thankful that Rhode Island State's team is not composed of skyscrapers.

SEWELL RETURNS HIS '44 CONTRACT

St. Petersburg, Fla. (AP)—Truett (Rip) Sewell, the Pittsburg Pirates' "blooper ball" hurler who won 21 games last season, has returned his 1944 contract unsigned, the St. Petersburg Times will say this morning.

Sewell, who a year ago received approximately $12,000, and recently he would not settle for less than $20,000 for 1944, the Times asserted. Amount offered in the contract was not disclosed.

The "blooper" artist has been occupied with operation of his strawberry farm at Plant City, Fla., and is reported more interested in the prices of that produce than in his baseball negotiations at present.

In the last five seasons, Sewell has won 70 games for the Pirates against 56 defeats.

Sewell's position is fortified by the fact that he was rejected by the Army a month ago because of an aggravated case of flat feet.

KENNEDY TO RACE AT AGE OF SIXTY

New Orleans (AP)—A 60-year-old marathon runner, who won the famous Patriot Day race in Boston just 27 years ago, will try his luck again tomorrow in the 26th annual Jackson Day run sponsored by the New Orleans Y. M. C. A.

The runner, Bill Kennedy of New Haven, Conn., made the 26-mile dash in Boston in two hours, 26 minutes and 71 1-5 seconds. Tomorrow he will be pitted against 37 athletes, including Bill Steiner, world's champion of Palestine, in a six-mile run from the old Spanish Fort to Jackson Square.

In 1941 Kennedy entered the Boston event and finished 22nd out of more than 100 entries.

TORONTO LEAFS DEFEAT HAWKS

Toronto (AP)—The Toronto Maple Leafs moved into a second place tie in the National Hockey League last night by trouncing the Chicago Black Hawks, 6-1.

Rookie Tom O'Neill paced the Leafs to their triumph with two goals—the first of his N. H. L. career—while Goalie Paul Bibeault played an outstanding game in the nets and Center Gus Bodnar performed sensationally before crowd of 8,160.

The one Chicago goal was scored by George Grigor—one of two Toronto Mercantile League players brought up for a one-night stand by the Hawks under the lease-lend system. Grigor got his tally unassisted in the second period. The other lease-lend player was Whitey Farrant.

Bulwark of the Chicago team—both offensively and defensively—was Big Early Seibert. The veteran's crushing body checks made themselves felt and he was a constant threat on the attack.

HARRY FELDMAN PLANS TO RETURN

Fort Smith, Ark. (AP)—Harry (Hank) Feldman, New York Giant righthander who was benched late last season, plans to play ball again next season but not because of ill-health, announced last night he had received a physical O. K. from his doctor and would report to the Giants during spring training camp.

The strapping 24-year-old hurler had won four and lost four before a physician began a course a couple of old spots covered a course of treatment at the Arkansas Tuberculosis Sanitarium near here, the superintendent announced.

Feldman has made his home by since playing with the Fort Sal team all this winter in 1932. He was served well one for the Giants in 1943.

Basketball.

Davidson 46, Catawba 31.
Indiantown Gap Stevedores 56, Brooklyn Army Base 47.
Vottumwa Naval Air Station 41, Penn (Oskaloosa, Ia.) 26.
Lincoln (Mo.) 64, Port Sheridan (Ill.) 52.
Sidney, Va.—Hampden - Sydney 40, Union Theological Seminary 18.
Ohio Bowling Green 52, Oklahoma Aggies 43, Phillips U.

EAST-WEST PROFIT.

San Francisco (AP)—The East-West charity football games played New Year's Day showed a profit of $77,104, an audit showed yesterday. The money will be turned over to the local Shriners' Crippled Children's Hospital.

NIGHT HAWKS			
	F.G.	F.B.	T.P.
B. Rafferty, f.	0	0	0
Hachigan, f.	2	0	4
Purcell, c.	3	1	7
Pasinas, g.	2	1	5
Cramer, g.	2	0	4

BANDITS			
	F.G.	F.B.	T.P.
Seney, f.	0	3	9
Kershaw, f.	6	1	13
Weldon, c.	0	0	0
Kachidurian, g.	2	2	6
Dominick, g.	1	0	2
Totals	9	3	21

FOURTH STREETERS			
	F.G.	F.B.	T.P.
Ronesi, f.	4	0	8
Kennedy, f.	1	0	2
Swatling, c.	1	0	2
Dix, g.	1	0	2
MacLean, g.	4	0	8
Totals	10	2	22

GREEN ISLAND MERCHANTS			
	F.G.	F.B.	T.P.
Barbetta, f.	5	0	10
B. Finduson, f.	0	0	0
Kelly, c.	2	0	4
De Fabio, g.	3	0	6
Di Bacco, g.	3	0	6
Turton, g.	0	0	0
Totals	13	3	29

WATERVLIET GENERALS			
	F.G.	F.B.	T.P.
Bislo, f.	3	0	6
Meleski, f.	4	1	9
Cahill, c.	0	0	0
Anderson, g.	0	0	0
O'Brien, g.	1	0	2
Agadian, g.	2	0	4
Rives, g.	0	0	0
Totals	13	4	22

OWLS			

NIGHT HAWKS			
	F.G.	F.B.	T.P.
Rushla, f.	4	1	10
McGrath, f.	5	0	11
Snyder, g.	2	0	4
Ballantyne, g.	2	1	5

THE WEATHER
Tonight—Fair

THE TIMES RECORD

FINAL EDITION

SERIES 1944—NO. 18 | (Entered as Second Class Matter at the Postoffice at Troy, N. Y. Under the Act of March 3, 1879) | TROY, N. Y., SATURDAY EVENING, JANUARY 22, 1944. | (Published Daily Except Sunday) | PRICE FOUR CENTS

ALLIES LAND FAR BEHIND GERMAN LINES IN ITALY

DEMOCRATS NAME ROBERT HANNEGAN PARTY CHAIRMAN

Roosevelt "Fourth Term" Talk Applauded at Capital

Washington (AP)—The Democratic National Committee unanimously adopted today a resolution "earnestly soliciting" President Roosevelt "to continue as our great world humanitarian leader."

The committee approved a resolution, submitted by a committee headed by Senator Green (D.-R.I.), asserting the belief that "our allies are praying with us" that the President be reelected.

Washington (AP) — The Democratic National Committee today elected by acclamation Robert E. Hannegan as chairman to succeed Postmaster General Frank C. Walker, who resigned.

Putting an accent on youth, the committee chose the 40-year-old St. Louisian to head a campaign drive in which most of the Democratic faithful at the meeting believe will find President Roosevelt running for a fourth term.

Hannegan, was nominated by James P. Aylward, Missouri national committeeman, who said Hannegan was eminently qualified to lead the party to "a grand and glorious victory in the election of Franklin Delano Roosevelt to a fourth term."

Aylwards reference to a fourth term provoked spirited applause by the national committee members present at today's session, called to fix the date and place of this year's national convention.

Resigns Revenue Post.

The Missouri commiteeman said that Hannegan, who replaces 57-year-old Walker, as chairman, would "equal in energy and activity James A. Farley of New York," former national chairman who broke with President Roosevelt and opposed a third term. There was a smattering of applause when Farley's name was mentioned.

Immediately after his election, Hannegan tendered his resignation from the Internal Revenue Commission and President Roosevelt accepted it, effective today.

Secretary of the Treasury Morgenthau designated Harold N. Graves, assistant commissioner, to be acting internal revenue commissioner.

Walker "Proud" of Record.

Without reference to a possible fourth term for President Roosevelt, Walker told the committee it was with genuine regret that he offered his resignation as chairman. He said the war had brought fresh problems and a constantly growing volume of business to the Postoffice Department, which he said required the full attention and energy of the postmaster general.

"Let there be no misunderstanding as to my attitude," Walker said. "I am proud of the accomplishments of the Democratic Party. x x x Looking back over the years since March, 1933, during which the responsibility for government has been entrusted to the Democratic administration, we find a record of magnificent service.

"More than once, I have called that period the glorious decade. I think that historians of the future, noting the advances made by the cause of humanity in those years, will not challenge my estimate."

"Oh," President Says.

Walker asserted that the most important issue in this year's election is the selection of a president and Congress who will lead in winning the war and bringing about a peace "which would be approved by God and which would answer the aspirations of the human heart."

He voiced confidence that the Democratic Party "is closer than any other political group to the aspirations of the American people," adding:

"The needs of the country call for the devoted service, and the proven leadership which our party alone is preeminently qualified to give."

A pre-meeting conference of Midwest Democrats yesterday adopted a resolution calling for Mr. Roosevelt to run again. When the President was told about it he said:

"Oh!"

That was all.

Appeals for Unity.

Hannegan, appearing before the national committee to accept the chairmanship, appealed for "teamwork" and party harmony.

"I am a plain, ordinary, everyday, straight 100 per cent organization Democrat and I am not angry at any Democrat," the black-haired athletic-looking new chairman told the committee.

Hannegan avoided any reference to a fourth term for Mr. Roosevelt.

Predicting that the November election would bring victory if the Democrats work together as a team, Hannegan paid tribute to the work of former chairmen, including Farley. He said he was proud to have worked under Farley and hoped that he might some day approach the New Yorker in organization ability.

ROBERT E. HANNEGAN

ALLIED AIR, SEA UNITS BLAST JAPS IN RAMU VALLEY

Two-pronged Drive Hints Possible Smash at New Guinea Bases

BY THE UNITED PRESS.

A two-pronged drive on the Japanese base of Madang, New Guinea, appeared developing today as official reports told of Allied air and sea units blasting Japanese positions in the Ramu Valley and enemy attempts to reinforce his New Guinea garrisons.

Allied medium bombers and fighters rained 74 tons of bombs on Japanese-held areas in the upper Ramu Valley and American P-T boats sank four enemy troop-laden barges off Madang while medium bombers and fighters sank twenty barges and damaged others at Hansa Bay, 100 miles north of Madang.

A spokesman at Gen. Douglas MacArthur's headquarters said that concentrated attacks in the Ramu Valley indicated a possible offensive with limited objectives for veteran Australian jungle troops who continued to improve their positions only thirty miles south of Madang.

Other Allied ground forces pushing up the coast extended their control of the coast to a point 45 miles below Madang.

Crews of the American P-T boats reported that equipment of 160 Japanese troops killed in the sinking of the barges indicated they were replacements and were not being evacuated.

Other Allied planes damaged a 1,000-ton freighter off Wewak 200 miles above Madang while heavy bombers ranging over the Dutch East Indies dropped 45 tons of bombs on the naval base at Ambon on Amboina Island, shooting down five enemy fighters and losing two Allied planes.

The Japanese Domei news agency, in a dispatch reported to the OWI, said that 180 planes raided Rabaul Thursday, but said that no damage was done and that 38 of the raiding planes, including four "probable" were shot down.

On Bougainville, American bombers blasted an airfield on the southern coast and naval units bombarded enemy shore installations at the northern tip of the island while 45 more Japanese dead were counted as U. S. troops suffered light casualties in patrol activity.

U. S. Army and Navy bombers raided three Marshall Islands atolls, damaging two cargo vessels and losing two planes.

Two night bombing raids on the Japanese naval base on Paramushiru in the Kurile Islands Friday night were reported today, by the Navy Department, foreshadowing a possible renewal of activity in the North Pacific.

All of the American planes, Aleutian-based Navy bombers, returned safely. The Navy did not announce the results of the attacks.

BRITISH BOMBERS HIT MAGDEBURG IN HEAVY ATTACK

Nazis Retaliate With Raids on London and Southeast England

London (AP)—The R. A. F.'s campaign to flatten German industrial targets crushed the city of Magdeburg in Saxony last night under more than 2,000 long tons of bombs as the major phase of a great aerial operation which included a smaller attack on Berlin.

The new blows against Germany, following up a heavy 2,200 long ton assault on the capital the previous night, cost the R. A. F. 55 bombers, one of the heaviest losses suffered in a year.

They came while the Germans themselves were stabbing at London and Southeast England with two sharp raids by a force of approximately ninety bombers.

Probably 1,000 planes took part in the widespread operatons of the R. A. F. during the night, striking also into Northern France and laying mines. This made it the second 1,000-planes Allied offensive within 14 hours. Approximately that number of American and British aircraft attacked the Pas De Calais area in daylight yesterday.

Magdeburg Rail Center.

The night's losses were the heaviest since 58 bombers went down during a great assault on Berlin last Aug. 23. Fourteen of the missing bombers were Canadian.

Magdeburg, a city of 300,000 on the left bank of the Elbe River, about 83 miles southwest of Berlin, is a junction point for the main railways to Leipzig, Kassel and Hamburg all previously hit heavily.

Magdeburg itself was bombed exactly a week before by Mosquitos while a big fleet of British bombers concentrated on the aircraft manufacturing center of Brunswick, 26 miles away, which some neutral sources now say "ceases to exist."

The air ministry described last night's blast at Magdeburg as "a very heavy attack" and said great fires were left burning.

The R. A. F. force which returned to Berlin, where fires still blazed from the 2,300 long ton bombing of the night before, included both four-engined Lancasters and the swift little Mosquitos.

At the same time other bombers struck unidentified targets in France, following up yesterday's 1,000-plane daylight assault on the so-called "rocket gun coast" in the neighborhood of Pas De Calais.

Germans Bomb London.

The Germans, goaded into making a counter blow, sent one group of bombers across the channel before midnight and another in the early hours of this morning.

They operated mainly over Southeast England, but about thirty of the invaders struck into the London area.

A communique said, "Bombs were dropped at a number of places. Damage was caused and there were a number of casualties, some of which were fatal." Eight enemy aircraft were destroyed.

The Nazi retaliation, although puny by present-day Allied bombing standards, was the heaviest in months and spectacular enough to remind many Londoners of the "old days." Guns thundered, the skies were alight, and incendiaries as wel las high explosives were dropped in the London area and other parts of Southeast England.

Damage and casualties were heavier than usual, and throughout the early morning hours rescuers dug for victims by the light of lamps along the Thames Estuary. The first raid, before midnight, cost the Germans eight planes, the largest number of night raiders downed over Britain in ten months.

53 DIE IN GERMAN WRECK.

London (AP) — The Berlin radio announced today that 53 persons had been killed in "a railway disaster" near Hanover, in North-central Germany. The broadcast gave no details.

Predicts Red Army Will Occupy Berlin

London (INS)—A Russian general predicted today that the Red Army will occupy Berlin. The Moscow radio reported the prediction in an account of a meeting of the Soviet war leaders headed by Premier Marshal Stalin, called to commemorate the anniversary of Lenin's death.

Addressing the meeting, Deputy Commissar for defense Lieut. Gen. Scherbakov said: The Germans are eager to shorten their front line. Let them shorten it, by all means. The day will come when it will run along the Spree." The Spree is a river in Central Prussia which leads directly into Berlin.

HITLER SHUFFLES DEFENSE SETUP IN OCCUPIED EUROPE

Marshal Rommel Named Inspector General; Von Runstedt Transferred

London (AP)—Adolf Hitler has completed his anti-invasion command with the appointment of Marshal Erwin Rommel as inspector general for the defense of Europe, a London newspaper reported today as Allied transport chiefs in Britain announced completion of a "shadow" supply service for the armies that will attack Western Europe.

Hitler has completely reshuffled his high command in preparation for the Allied attack from Britain, according to neutral reports quoted by the Daily Express.

In his new role, Rommel holds a post corresponding to that of Col. Gen. Heinz Guderian, inspector general of tank forces and Maj. Gen. Adolf Galland, inspector general of the German air force. None will be a field commander but each will be in supreme control of their respective services, it was said.

Von Runstedt Shifted.

Field Marshal Karl von Runstedt has been transferred from command of the western defenses of Europe to Southeastern Europe, where he will be in charge of the areas behind Field Marshal Fritz von Mannstein's armies retreating from Russia, the Express said. Field Marshal Maximilian von Weichs, who last was reported in charge of German forces in the Balkans, apparently has been dropped from the German defense setup.

Col. Gen. Eduard Dietl, according to the Express' informants, has been recalled from Finland and place in command of reserve forces inside Germany proper, while the commands of Gen. Nikolaus von Falkenhorst in Norway and Hermann von Hannecken in Denmark have been confirmed by Hitler.

Field Marshal Georg von Kuechler, now in command of German forces in Northern Russia and General Fromm, commanding German home forces, will divide command of the armies on the shortened Russian front.

General Christensen of the Ger-

(Continued on Page 2.)

ANTHONY J. D. BIDDLE, JR., QUITS DIPLOMATIC POST

Washington (UP) The White House announced today that President Roosevelt has accepted the resignation of Anthony J. Drexel Biddle, jr., as ambassador-minister to the Allied exile governments in London to accept a military position on the staff of Gen. Dwight D. Eisenhower.

Biddle will be assigned to the staff of the supreme Allied commander to act as liaison officer with the same governments-in-exile. No plans were made for the appointment of a new ambassador to the post. The White House announced that Biddle's duties will be carried on by a charge d'affaires while he is in the military service.

GERMAN FORCES RACING TO ESCAPE RED ARMY TRAP

Russians Clear Nazis From Railway Between Leningrad and Moscow

Moscow (UP)—Red Armies cleared the Germans from a second direct railway between Leningrad and Moscow today and pressed on in pursuit of enemy units fleeing in disorder from their shattered northwestern front defenses.

The Soviet high command said the remnants of German divisions which besieged Leningrad for more than two years were abandoning one stronghold after another and casting aside their arms in a panicky attempt to escape a Soviet trap that threatened to annihilate 300,000 of them.

Enemy forces immediately south of Leningrad were squeezed into a 35-mile wide corridor that was disintegrating rapidly under Soviet pressure from three sides. Considerable prisoners were being rounded up, the Soviet high command said.

Capture Rail Junction.

Gen. Leonid A. Govorov, commander of the Leningrad armies, and Gen. Kyril A. Meretskov, liberator of Novgorod, reopened the second direct railway line between Moscow and Leningrad yesterday with the capture of Mga, five-way railroad junction 29 miles east southeast of Leningrad.

Occupation of Mga and several surrounding localities cleared the Germans from the Leningrad-Mga-Kirishi-Moscow railroad. Previously, the Soviets had to rely on an emergency line skirting Lake Ladoga from Volkhovstroi on the Volkhov River to Schusselburg and thence over a short line to Leningrad for communication between the country's two largest cities.

It was over the emergency line, built following the smashing of the Leningrad blockade in December, 1942, that the Russians relieved the hard-pressed population of the former Czarist capital with food and fuel and rushed arms, equipment and ammunition to Govorov to mount his present offensive.

Govorov's armies, advancing on a 21-mile front south and east of Leningrad, and Meretskov's northern wing, advancing on a 16-mile front, joined forces at Mga after capturing a score or more localities in their respective sectors.

2,000 Germans Slain.

Govorov seized Tortolovo, 33 miles southeast of Leningrad to wipe out a Nazi salient that had narrowed the Soviet lifeline corridor below Lake Ladoga to Leningrad to nine miles.

Meretskov was credited with capture of Vinyagolovo, 18 miles southeast of Mga and 46 miles southeast of Leningrad, and Karbusel, nine miles southeast of Mga.

Soutwest of Leningrad, Govorov's western wing, killed 2,000 Germans, captured 29 guns and routed an enemy infantry regiment in pushing to within 43 miles of Estonia with the capture of Vitino, 27 miles from Leningrad.

Some 100 miles south of Leningrad, Meretskov's main forces continued to sweep westward from Novgorod. The Germans put up bitter resistance only in isolated sectors, the Soviet high command said, and even in these were "unable to withstand the onslaught of Soviet infantry."

Nearly 2,000 Germans were killed in one sector, while in another 800 fell in a futile counter-attack.

NEW HAVEN PROBATE COURT CLERK SHOT; GUNMAN CAPTURED

New Haven, Conn. (UP)—A man walked into the office of the New Haven Probate Court today, shot Clerk Clifford Sturgess three times and was overpowered by other members of the court staff, according to police. The assailant was identified tentatively as Pasquale La Vorgna.

Sturgess, who is judge of the East Haven Town Court, was removed to New Haven Hospital, where his condition was said to be serious.

He was wounded in the chin and wrist, and another bullet was believed to have penetrated his back.

Hospital attendants said he was weakened by loss of blood and that his name had been placed on the danger list. Police took the assailant into custody and Police Chief Henry P. Clark, aside from announcing his identity, kept him incommunicado for questioning.

SEAMAN MISSING AFTER ATLANTIC COLLISION

Lewes, Del (AP) A small coastwise tanker caught fire in a collision with a liberty ship in the Atlantic Ocean five miles off the Delaware Capes last night and a Navy officer reported today that one tanker seaman was missing.

Fifteen of the craft's crew of 16 were landed at the Fort Miles Del Army dock after abandoning ship. The tanker was last reported under tow into the Delaware breakwater its flames under control. The cargo ship was not badly damaged.

Japs Score Victory Over Old Oil Drums

Guadalcanal (UP) — Japanese artillery on Bougainville today was credited with what the Tokyo radio probably will describe as a "great naval victory over an enemy fleet."

A number of oil drums washed off the U. S.-held beach recently and drifted today in Empress Augusta Bay, offering a menace to Allied shipping. Dive bombers were assigned to strafe and sink them, but the Japanese were on their toes. Apparently thinking they had spotted a group of boats or a submarine, they cut loose with a heavy barrage, sinking all the drums. Allied dive-bomber pilots confirmed the "victory."

WAGE CONTROL PLAN SET UP FOR FARM WORKERS

Food Administrator Puts Maximum Ceiling at $2,400 Per Year

Washington (AP) In a move unprecedented in all American farm history, a wage control program for agricultural workers, with maximum ceilings of $2,400 a year, has been ordered by War Food Administrator Marvin Jones.

Aides of the administrator, who disclosed the plan, said War Food Administration labor offices have been directed to set up state farm wage boards to hold hearings and establish maximum wages.

These groups would function much in the manner of the War Labor Board in determining the ceilings for industrial workers. Director Fred M. Vinson put farm wages under the supervision of the WFA but officials did not consider it necessary to take any immediate general action toward control.

Wages Now at Peak.

Now however, farm wages have reached the highest point in twenty years. Many workers have gone into war plants. Those who have remained on the farms have repeatedly received what amounts to a blanket deferment from Selective Service. There are few restrictions on their transfer from one farm to another. Thus they are in a position to bargain.

This, it was disclosed, has played a big part in leading the WFA into the unprecedented wage control program.

A recent report of the Bureau of Agricultural Economics stated that in every section of the country farm wages had shown a sharp increase in the previous 12 months.

For the year 1943, wages stood at 264 per cent of the 1910-14 average, and 64 points above the 1942 level. Present rates are said to average $63 a month, with board, compared with $50.91 a year ago and with $26 for the 1935-39 average. In some areas wages are considerably higher than the average.

Will Set Ceilings.

The farm wage boards will be instructed to set ceilings only for specific types of work or farm operations for certain designated areas. Wages considered substandard will not be affected. However, ceilings below the $2,400 level may be set if boards consider it necessary.

Increases in pay above the $2,400 level would be permitted only with the approval of the food administrator, expect in cases of increases above $5,000, where control rests with the Commissioner of Internal Revenue.

WFA officials said the farm wage regulations would subject violators to serve penalties. Under provisions of the stabilization act, maximum penalty is a fine of $1,000, and imprisonment for a year. Both employers and employees would be liable.

The regulations also prohibit reductions in wage rates below the highest wage or salary paid for the particular work between Jan. 1, 1942, and Sept. 15, 1942.

Invaders Swarm Ashore Only 28 Miles From Rome

American Rangers and British Commandos Spearhead Fifth Army Landing Near Tiber Estuary; Situation Progressing Satisfactorily, Allied Headquarters Reports; Germans Taken by Surprise and Resistance Is Feeble; Maneuver Must Quickly Decide Fate of Rome.

Allied Headquarters, Algiers (UP)—Thousands of American and Allied troops striking their greatest blow to throw the Germans out of Italy landed far behind the enemy lines today and swarmed inland from a miles-long beachhead in a surprise invasion which may decide the fate of Rome.

The German radio said the Allied amphibious force splashed ashore 28 miles from Rome in the area of the Tiber Estuary and occupied the port of Nettuno, 32 miles from the capital, but early reports here did not specify the landing place.

Gen. Harold R. L. G. Alexander, supreme commander of the new Allied Central Mediterranean force, in his first report to headquarters flashed tersely:

"Initial landing successful—situation progressing satisfactorily."

The invasion by picked units of the Fifth Army, spearheaded by United States Rangers and British Commandos, posed a direct threat to Rome and to the German divisions between the beachhead and along the old battlefront to the south.

Rome Virtually Blockaded.

Rome already was reported virtually blockaded by a paralyzing aerial bombardment which had cut most of the radiating transport lines and knocked out all but one of its fighter plane bases.

The clandestine Radio Atlantic said today that the Germans had begun the evacuation of Rome, moving administrative and other facilities northward.

The broadcast said Pope Pius intended to remain in the Vatican, even in case of fighting near Rome, although the Germans had advised him to leave.

The Cairo radio reported today that there were indications the Germans were preparing a general withdrawal before the Allied Fifth Army in Italy.

Rear Adm. Frank J. Lowry of the United States Navy commanded the Allied sea forces—American, British, French, Greek and Dutch—which carried the invaders to the beaches and covered the landing with a bombardment synchronized with a terrific Allied aerial assault.

Unofficial front line reports said the landings were not seriously contested by the Germans.

Preparatory blows against German air bases helped keep German fighter plane opposition to a negligible minimum in the early phases of the dawn invasion. United Press correspondent Robert Vermillion reported that in a later flight over the new battlefront the aerial resistance had increased.

(German broadcasts said the Allies had occupied the port of Nettuno, 32 miles south of Rome, and had won footholds "between Nettuno and the Tiber Estuary"—the latter 16 miles southwest of Rome.)

Invaders Sweep Inland.

Paced by United States rangers and British commandos, the Allied invasion force of the Fifth Army swarmed ashore in an unidentified sector of Italy's west coast and fanned out inland. The first major blow in the battle for Rome was struck after other Fifth Army forces to the southeast had ripped into the German defense line, breaking through at three key points.

The concerted assaults by Lt. Gen. Mark W. Clark's army threatened to cut off and chop up the formidable German forces manning the crumbling fortifications in the Liri Valley 65 miles below Rome.

A special communique announced the new invasion, the greatest since the Fifth Army landing on the Salerno beaches last Sept. 9, which was carried out under a shattering bombardment by Allied planes and warships.

"Initial landing successful—situation progressing satisfactorily," Gen. Sir Harold R. L. G. Alexander, commander of the central Mediterranean force, messaged headquarters hours later.

A steady stream of Allied troops and trucks were pouring ashore with virtually no opposition from the German air force, the first American pilots to return from flights over the new beachhead reported.

The assault forces closed in against the beaches through fairly calm seas and landed on the shore white with a heavy frost, the airmen said.

"I was over the area for an hour and 15 minutes, and I saw only two enemy planes which were attacking our naval vessels," Capt. Lewis R. Raffanelli of Richfield, O., said on his returned to an advanced American air field in Italy at which he is executive officer.

By the time he left, Raffanelli

(Continued on Page 2)

SAYS LUFTWAFFE WILL BE SMASHED

Spaatz Says Knockout May Come This Summer

U. S. Army Air Force Headquarters, England (UP) Lieut. Gen. Carl A. Spaatz said today that with a reasonable break in weather the Allied air forces hope to knock out the Luftwaffe this summer.

In his first press conference as commanding general of the United States strategic air forces over Europe, the tanned veteran of the Tunisian, Sicilian and Italian campaigns told almost 100 British and American correspondents that the Schweinfurt ball-bearing plant raids, plus subsequent attacks on fighter assembly plants, had reduced by 40 per cent the "planned German fighter production."

Spaatz side-stepped the question whether four more raids of the magnitude of the Jan. 11 Oschersleben and Brunswick attacks would knock out German fighter production, but he countered:

"Given the same sort of weather we had in the Mediterranean for a while, I do not think the German air forces would last very long."

Asked if he anticipated that the Luftwaffe would be knocked out during the summer, given reasonable weather, Spaatz replied:

"That is what we expect to do. The German air force can be pretty well knocked out, given reasonable weather."

STRIKE CALLED OFF.

Seattle (UP) A four-day strike of 6,000 molders and foundrymen, which tied up war production in 79 plants in Washington and Oregon, ended today when the strikers voted to return to work pending a National War Labor review of their wage demands.

Bombs Destroy German Post Concealed Near Pope's Home

An Advanced Airbase in Italy (AP)

A German front line Air Corps headquarters, carefully hidden in what was previously considered "neutral" territory because of its proximity to the summer residence of Pope Pius XII, was reported destroyed today by dive bombing A36 Invaders from the Twelfth Air Support Command.

Returning pilots, who had been painstakingly briefed for the special mission said the Pope's summer home and surrounding areas of Castel Gandolfo, south of Rome never felt a thing."

The German "Flieger Corps" headquarters was housed in a villa near Frascati, south of Rome and only about five miles from Castel Gandolfo. The entire area had been voluntarily restricted by the Allies and our planes forbidden to fly over it. Apparently the Nazis learned of the restrictions and slipped in a headquarters to take advantage of it.

Two flights of eight Invaders each peeled out of a formation 10 minutes apart shortly after noon and scored 26 direct hits on the headquarters villa. Two bombs landed on the west wing of the building, causing a tremendous explosion which the pilots said enveloped the entire villa, sending up clouds of black smoke.

"Most of our bombs hit the target and I'm sure we knocked out the whole building," said Lieut Marin J Snider of Elkton Mich, leader of one of the flights "There was no activity around the villa and no flak. It looked like we surprised them."

"The Germans thought they'd pull a fast one when they put their headquarters so near the Pope's home," said Lieut William M Fox of Washington, D. C. the other flight leader "but our bombs were right on the target and Castel Gandolfo never felt a thing."

Lieut Col Harold E Kofahl of Fellows, Cal the Invader group commander, said the pilots were carefully briefed for the mission and that they carried photographs of the German headquarters villa to make doubly sure their bombs hit the right target.

The special mission was timed and planned in advance by Maj Gen Edwin J House and his staff officers of the Twelfth Air Support Command.

Fired From Union, Fast Workers Say

Edgewater N. J. (INS) The threat of a strike still hung over the assembly plant of the Ford Motor Co. at Edgewater today as two test drivers allegedly ousted from their C. I. O. union because they worked "too fast" continued at their jobs despite a closed shop contract.

In an effort to avert a walkout of the 4,400 employees at the war plant, heads of U. A. W. Local 906, went to Detroit for a conference with officials of the Ford Co. and Harry Schulmann, $25,000-a-year arbiter who handles the disputes arising between the company and the union.

The ousted test drivers were John Elvin 45 a veteran of World War I and father of seven children, and Neil Smith, 28, both of whom have been employed at the plant for seven years. Elvin appealed to President Roosevelt to intervene and help them.

Elvin charged that he and Smith were booted out of the local because they tested cars twice as fast as other employees. The union, however contended that they were ejected because they "complained" without justification to the management that the other drivers were not doing their utmost.

Elvin, in a telegram to the President and to Secretary of War Henry Stimson explained that the cause of his union expulsion was the fact that he and Smith delivered twice as many trucks to the Army and Navy per day as did other union members.

The union has asked for the men's discharge but so far the company has refused to fire them.

The Index

CARD PARTY HELD BY AMARANTH COURT AT 81 FOURTH ST.

A public card party was conducted by Apollo Court, O. of A., after a brief meeting last night in the rooms, 81 Fourth Street. Mrs. Minnie Newbold was chairman of the arrangements committee. Awards were presented and refreshments were served.

The short business meeting was in charge of Mrs. Sara G. Hughes, acting royal matron, and John C. Neal, acting royal patron. The activities committee appointed for March includes Mrs Hughes, Mrs Dalla Miner, Mrs Gertrude Woods and Mrs Edith Smith.

At the next meeting, Thursday, March 2, a rehearsal of ritual work will be conducted.

FALSE TEETH
That Loosen Need Not Embarrass

Many wearers of false teeth have suffered real embarrassment because their plate dropped, slipped or wobbled at just the wrong time. Do not live in fear of this happening to you just sprinkle a little FASTEETH on your plates. This pleasant powder gives a remarkable sense of added comfort and security by holding plates more firmly. No gummy, gooey, pasty taste or feeling. It's alkaline (non-acid). Get FASTEETH at any drug store.

"GAS HOUSE GANG" ANTICS UNFOLDED BY "RIP" COLLINS

Elks' Father-and-Son Diners Hear Albany Baseball Manager

The antics of the St. Louis Cardinals, the "Gas House Gang," were described last night by Jimmy "Ripper" Collins, former member of the Cardinals and present manager of the Albany Eastern League baseball team at the father and son dinner of the Troy Lodge of Elks in the lodge rooms.

Collins said life with the Cardinals was a mixture of hard work and plenty of horse play. His anecdotes kept the audience of more than 150 men and boys in laughter for the half hour he spoke.

Collins was introduced by Charles E. Young, Albany Elk and sports editor of the Knickerbocker News.

Earlier, Exalted Ruler John L. Fleming, jr. welcomed the group and expressed gratitude for the large turnout. He said he hoped the dinner would become an annual affair.

Recently returned from Boston where he attended a national conclave of Elks, the exalted ruler said the Department of Justice has asked lodges throughout the country to aid in curbing juvenile delinquency. The Troy Lodge was far ahead of the others, he explained and pointed out last night's dinner as being just what the department ordered.

He traced the history of Elkdom for the benefit of the boys and closed with the hope they would follow in their fathers' footsteps and become Elks when they reached maturity.

Arthur W. Mace, loyal knight, chairman, made the opening remarks and introduced Dr. J. Edward Gallico, past state president, toastmaster.

Joseph N. Blase, exalted ruler of the Albany Lodge, was introduced by Dr. Gallico. He spoke briefly as did Past District Deputy John J. Sweeney and Roy Shudt.

Following the speeches a program of entertainment was offered in charge of Edward J. Flanagan. And then the boys went to the bowling alleys where they were initiated, many of them at least, to the game of duckpins and big pins. This part of the program was in charge of Paul J. Lynch.

ROUND LAKE.

Mrs. Lillian C. Lavery has been visiting Mr and Mrs. Ralph Fargo at Pattersonville.

Service at All Saints Episcopal Church, Sunday, will be Holy Communion and prayers, Rev. W. L. Fielding Haylor, rector.

Mrs. M. G. Cole, Troy Conference promotion secretary of the Woman's Society of Christian Service, spoke at the meeting of the society in the Methodist Church, Ballston Spa last evening. Her topic was "For The Facing of This Hour."

Methodist Church services, 10.30, devotions, Rev. Chester A. Finch, pastor; 11.45, Church Bible school; William M. Lighthall, superintendent, children's hour, 3 p.m., at the parsonage. Mrs. Finch, leader, 7.30 p.m., Young Peoples' Hour, Rev. C. A. Finch leading.

The Malta Home Bureau will hold a card party at the home of Mrs. Frank Brownell at 221 Third Street, Mechanicville, Saturday evening, Feb. 26 at 8 o'clock. Refreshments will be served. The affair will be under the auspices of the social committee of the bureau, with Mrs. Reginald MacKinley, chairman; Mrs. William McDermott and Mrs. Emmett Smith.

The monthly meeting of the Woman's Society of Christian Service of the Methodist Church was held in the church Wednesday with a covered dish luncheon. Mrs. M. G. Cole and Mrs. Grace S. Carlton were hostesses. Mrs. Rodney O. Winans presided at the business meeting. It was planned to hold a tea-time social in March. At that time all as they turn in the dollar which they have earned, will tell the method of earning it. The resignation of Mrs. G. Fred Bond as secretary of local activities was accepted and Mrs. Robert Kopp and Mrs. Harry P. Ruhle were elected in her place. The president appointed Mrs. Ada M. Harwood, Mrs. G. Fred Bond and Mrs. Barbara MacLauchlin to draw names for the various groups for another year. Mrs. Chester A. Finch led the devotional period. Mrs. C. E. Hemet had prepared a program, which Mrs. Rodney O. Winans conducted. The topic was "Students in our Schools." Those representing schools of different nations were Mrs. Ada M Harwood, Mrs. Edna Flannagan, Mrs. John W. Morris, Mrs. William M. Lighthall and Mrs. Leslie G. Brown. The next meeting will be held the third Wednesday in March when the luncheon hostesses will be Mrs. Chester A. Finch and Mrs. Rodney O. Winans.

FATHER-AND-SON DINNER—Joseph N. Blase, exalted ruler of Albany Lodge of Elks, speaks at last night's father-and-son dinner of Troy Lodge. Seated at the right is the principal speaker, James "Ripper" Collins, Albany baseball team manager.

ON THE AIR
Radio Programs From Local Stations

[Radio program listings]

ACADEMY SENIOR BALL SCHEDULED MONDAY EVENING

Looms as Outstanding Pre-Lenten Affair in Village; Robert Smith Chairman

HOOSICK FALLS

The fourth annual senior ball of St. Mary's Academy, to be held Monday evening in the Immaculate Conception parish hall, gives every indication of being the outstanding pre-Lenten social event of the community. It will be opened at 9 p.m. and continue to 1 a.m., with music by Harry Hart's Virginians. A grand march will be one of the features.

Robert Smith is general chairman and Patricia Hyland, cochairman in charge of arrangements, assisted by the following sub-committees: Decorations Adelia Davendonis, James Coleton, Marie Sukuskas, Anne Yankus; floor—William Burns, James Coleton, Joseph Haynes, Benny Nowik; orchestra and publicity—James Coleton, Benny Nowik, William Archer; tickets and programs—Anne Brahan, James Monahan, Katherine Nolan, John Driscoll; refreshments—Anne Yankus, Arthur White, Adela Davendonis, Marie Sukuskas, Ann Maleady.

To Conduct Ritual.

Members of the Knights of Columbus will assemble today at 7.30 p.m. at the K. of C. clubhouse to go to the home of their late fellow member, James F. Mooney, 181 Church Street, to recite prayers for the repose of his soul.

No Jurisdiction Over Coal.

Announcement has been made by Peter Seward, chairman of the Hoosick Falls Rationing Board, that the board has no jurisdiction over coal and that requests for assistance in obtaining coal cannot be handled by the board.

Leap Year Dance.

A leap year dance will be sponsored tonight at the High School gymnasium by the junior class of Hoosick Falls High School. The committee in charge is composed of Claire Allen, Margaret Tilton, Marie Gehrean, A. Liporace, James Kinney and Forrest Haswell.

For Story Hour.

Dorothy Hughes, one of the juvenile patrons of Cheney Public Library, will read her favorite story at this week's story hour at Cheney Library tomorrow at 1.30 p.m. This feature, recently introduced into the story hour's program, has aroused great interest among the children, all of whom are looking forward to being heard with their favorite stories.

Personal.

Lucille Oliver suffered a deep cut on her right leg Monday evening when she fell on ice. She was attended by Dr. Robert E. Maderer.

James M. Brahan, editor of The Standard Press, was elected a director of the New York Press Association at that organization's annual meeting last week in Syracuse.

Carleton Viets, F 1/c, U. S. Navy, son of Mrs. Frances Viets, Wilder Avenue, was graduated Saturday from the Machinist Mate's School, Wahpeton, Minn. He is home on a seven-day leave and goes Feb. 23 to Newport, R. I., to be assigned to a ship. Prior to being sent to Wahpeton, he received his "boot" training at the Naval Training Station at Sampson.

Brevities.

Tonight's meeting of Van Rensselaer Chapter, O. E. S., will be followed by a Valentine party.

Hoosac-Walloomsac Chapter, Daughters of the American Revolution, will meet tomorrow at 3 p.m. at the home of Mrs. Edwin Surdam, Hoosick. The assisting hostesses are the Misses Finney and Ruth Howe of Troy and Mrs. Phebe Armsby.

MOSCOW PEOPLE HAVING TROUBLE WITH MOSQUITOS

Unseasonably Warm Weather Bringing Plague of Insects to Muscovites

BY EDDY GILMORE

Moscow (Delayed)—(AP)—Lots of Muscovites are scratching mosquito bites when they should be nursing frosen noses.

"I have been in Moscow since I was 8 years old, said bearded, 82-year-old Vaselei Feydovitch Baranov, "and I remember nothing like this. I'm an old man now and I haven't even had a cold chill." He said, yes, mosquitos have been bothering him too in the last few days. The mosquitos are not hearsay with me. They are in my room and twice last night I had to get up to hunt them.

Afanassi Danliovitch Chuprenko, who came to the Soviet capital when a boy and now near seventy, said he remembered a winter before the revolution when there was strangely warm weather, but it was not like the winter of 1943-44.

"I almost thought I was getting young again," he said, "until the doctor said the reason my joints are not troubling me is because it hasn't been cold." He's has mosquito trouble, too.

There's another old fellow I know who calls the weather downright insulting.

"I arranged my life," said Dyedooshka, "where it was adjusted to the summer in summertime and to the winter in wintertime. I've learned to live that way. Now this has me all upset. I think the war has something to do with it."

Dyedooshka has a theory there's been so much firing on the front—so many shells and so many bombs exploded—that it's warmed up the air to the point where we've got a war-conditioned winter.

Scientists have publicly advanced no explanation for a winter which in February sees signs of spring in the Ukraine, heavy thaws as far north as the Baltic and unfrozen streams in Siberia.

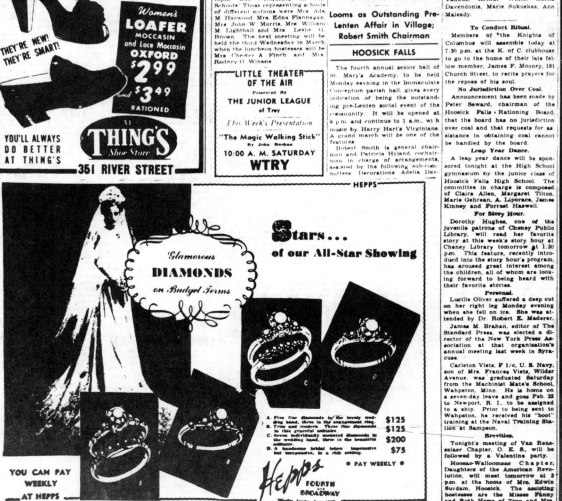

WATERVLIET NEWS

BRANCH OFFICE: 1715 BROADWAY   PHONE WATERVLIET 1593

SCHOOL 7 PUPILS PRESENT PLAY AT BIRTHDAY PARTY

Total of $1,025 in Bonds and Stamps Purchased as Admissions

A Washington Birthday entertainment was presented by the members of the sixth grade of School 7 assisted by the pupils of the seventh and eighth grades yesterday at the school as a part of the Fourth War Loan project. The affair was under the direction of Miss H. Dorothy Hayford, teacher, and Miss Maybelle P. Reynolds, principal.

A total of $1,025 in War Bonds and $367.05 in stamps were purchased as the price of admission. The cast consisted of Miss Eleanor Paley as Martha Washington and Louise Choiffi as George Washington; Henry McGrath as "Mammy;" Joseph Czjakowski as "Peter, the slave;" Cynthia Hills, a "Southern belle;" Robert Curtin and Albert Pardis, drummers, Robert Gaffigan, Washington as a small boy; David Shenton, Gerald Firth, Melvin Stewart, Louis Paley, Patrick Morelli, Nelson Vandenburgh, and Burham Lamkins, Boy Scouts; Audrey Cooney as Miss America, and Lois Prue and Bertha Natee, dancers. Eleanor Catricala was the soloist.

ALTAR SOCIETY WILL HOLD PARTY, DANCE

The Altar Society of Our Lady of Mt. Carmel Church has completed plans for the Washington birthday party and social to be held today at 8 p.m. in the new recreation center. Mrs. Sophie Carafano and Mrs. Minnie Razzano are in charge of the arrangements.

Other committee members are Mrs. Cora Zaccarino, Mrs. Frances Julian, Mrs. Lena Dinino, Mrs. Anthette Tedesco, Mrs. Theresa Chouffi, Mrs Mary Consuelo and Mrs. Mary Grillo. Refreshments will be served and special prizes will be awarded.

To Distribute Ashes.

Tomorrow, Ash Wednesday, ashes will be distributed after mass, after school and at 7.30 p.m. in all of the Catholic Churches of the city. The Stations of the Cross will be offered Friday at 7:30 p.m

SCHOOL 7 ENTERTAINS—Above pose members of the sixth grade at School 7, Watervliet, in the costumes they wore in the school play presented at the school yesterday to promote the sale of War Stamps and Bonds. The above group was under the direction of Mrs. Dorothy Hayford.

ROYAL ARCANUM COUNCIL HOST TO GRAND OFFICERS

Fifty-year Pin Presented Robert Laurie; Candidates Installed

Wyoma Council, Royal Arcanum, was host to the grand officers at a meeting last night in the Knights of Columbus Hall. Guests of honor were Daniel J. Gilvey, grand regent; Robert W. Quigley, vice grand regent and Edmond, A. Knopple, supreme orator.

A fifty-year pin was presented Robert Laurie of Watervliet. Members receiving 25-year pins last night were Frank B. Knight, Frank Knight, Jr., Chester Gardener and Edward H. Nutting.

A class of candidates was installed by the Fort Orange Council of Albany.

REVENUE BUREAU MEN GIVING ASSISTANCE IN FILING TAX RETURNS

Local residents yesterday and today thronged the City Hall to receive aid in making out income tax forms.

Thomas F. Brierton and William J. Lundy of the Internal Revenue Bureau, Albany, held office hours from 9 a.m. through 4 p.m. yesterday and today, to assist citizens with the income tax forms. The bureau representatives will remain at the City Hall for consultation tomorrow and will be at the Cohoes City Hall Thursday, Friday and Saturday to assist Cohoes residents

MRS. DENNIS HOSTESS FOR JERMAIN GROUP

The Jermain Guild of the Jermain Memorial Presbyterian Church held a meeting last night at the home of Mrs. Frank Dennis of 722 Eighth Avenue Mrs. Ernest Gloeckner presided. The devotions were led by Mrs. Robert Welch

The next meeting will be held Monday, March 6, at the home of Mrs. Albert Whittaker of 514 Sixth Avenue.

BOARD 346 CALLS 52 FOR SERVICE UNDER NEW PLAN

Army Inductees Expected to be Sent to Fort Dix, N. J.

Selective Service Board 346 has received the first group of induction calls under the new arrangements.

The group of selectees, examined two weeks ago at the Albany Induction station, will receive notice of their induction through the mail. They will leave for active service two weeks from tomorrow.

The 52 inductees will receive the calls through the mail. The calls are separate for the Army and Navy but both units will go to Albany together, the Army group to the Albany Union Station for expected transfer to Fort Dix, N. J., and the Navy selectees proceeding to the Navy Recruiting and Induction station at the Albany Post-office building. Rev. Ivan H. Ball, rector of Trinity Episcopal Church, will officiate at the farewell ceremonies.

Leo Francis Norton, among the selectees, is a volunteer for the Army Air Forces. Volunteers for the Navy Ship Repair unit include Charles Francis Pinning of Green Island and Frank Romano, Patrick Donald McGrath, Anthony Joseph Stellons, Watervliet, and Austin McGrath of Cohoes.

The remaining selectees to leave for service two weeks from tomorrow include the following Watervliet residents: Edwin Frank Tracy, Nicholas William Patalino, Richard H. Spratt, John Charles Carlo, William Alexander Millette, Walter Aloysius Tracey, Harry Albert Moore, Jr., Francis Wesley Totten and John William Rosenberger, Army selectees, and John Henry Farrell, William Burnham Knapp, Charles Francis May, Joseph Marwood Turton, Thomas Edward Fahey, Metro Warika, Stephen Krill, Angelo Charles Morisio, Anthony Daniel Montepare, Eugene Everett Deyette, George Franklin Belonga, John Thomas Sherlock and Charles Joseph Austin, jr., Navy selectees.

Green Island selectees to leave March 7 are Paul Robert Guynup, Melvin James Wagner, Richard Joseph Sheehan, John Thomas Green, Dominick Peter Altobello and James Laird, Army selectees; Arthur Aloysius Heffern, James Aloysius McCallen, Ellis Wilbur Crandall and Francis Joseph McGovern, Navy selectees.

Troy residents to leave for Army service include Rocco Mario Favata, and those to leave for Navy service are Benjamin Franklin Wheatley, Anthony Sgritta and George James Costello.

Andrew Dooley Petregal of Latham and Raymond Gerry Bodell of Averill Park will both leave for Navy service.

BIRTHDAY PARTY HELD FOR GLORIA HEINER

Mrs Fred Heiner of 1621 Second Avenue entertained Saturday night with a birthday party in honor of their daughter, Gloria.

Games were played and refreshments were served at a table decorated in pink, blue and yellow with a large birthday cake as the centerpiece. The guests were the Misses Gloria, Cynthia and Linda Leahy of Loudonville, Betty Jane Hauser and Shirley Flubacker of Troy, Joan Marie Bell, Gail Stewart, Gail Martinucci, Margaret Fox, Claire Houben and Mrs A. J. Schlomberg.

Sale For Blind.

The women of the Third Avenue Methodist Church will be in charge of the sale of articles for the benefit of the blind Friday from 11 a.m to 3 p.m in the Legion rooms in Broadway. The members of the church will attend the World Day of Prayer observance Friday at 2 30 p m in the Jermain Memorial Chapel

COUPLE ENTERTAIN FOR THIRD SON WHO LEFT FOR SERVICE

Mr and Mrs. George Wido of this city entertained at a farewell party Saturday night in honor of their son, Joseph Wido, who left yesterday for service with the armed forces. A program of songs and music was presented followed by a series of games. A buffet luncheon was served.

The guests included Mr. and Mrs. Augustine Halupka, Mr. and Mrs. Walter Evertsen, Mr. and Mrs. Frank Chioffi, Mr. and Mrs. Samuel Debonis, the Misses Mary Skelly, Harriet Smith, Jean Mae Hoftin, Jean Normandin, Lucille Provost, Dorothy Morrissey and Julia Mazzda, Bernard Wido, John Nucci, Rudy Razzano, Edward Marelli, Christy Maio, Jerry Butler, John Musca, Russell Bodo and Michael Dugar. Mr. Wido received many gifts.

Mr. and Mrs. Wido have two other sons in service. Staff Sergt. George Wido is flying with bomber crew somewhere in the South Pacific, and Corp. Bernard Wido is serving in the Air Transport Command in California.

ELKS' LODGE INITIATES SEVENTEEN CANDIDATES

Seventeen candidates of the Watervliet Lodge of Elks were initiated at the annual past exalted ruler's night in the lodge rooms yesterday. Judge Daniel H. Prior of Albany, guest speaker, talked on "Americanism and Elkdom."

The evening's program was in charge of the past exalted rulers of the lodge led by Joseph W. Keis, chairman; George J. Halpin, Charles L. Roberts, Edward J. Bulger, James Gilmore, Charles S. Christianson and John H. Looby.

Card Party Hostess.

Mrs. Edward Edwards will be the hostess for a card party today at 8 p.m. in the eighth grade classroom of the Sacred Heart of Mary School. The party is for the benefit of the Mothers' Club.

Communion Service.

Rev. Ivan H. Ball, rector, will officiate at the communion service tomorrow at 8:30 a.m. at St. Gabriel's Chapel. The sermon and Litany will be held at 7:30 p.m. Holy Communion service will be held at the Trinity Episcopal Church tomorrow at 7:30 a.m.

Holy Communion will be distributed Friday at 7:30 a.m. at the Trinity Episcopal Church. The Litany and sermon will be held at 7:30 p.m.

WIFE HID IN CAR TRUNK TO SPY ON HUSBAND

Baltimore (AP)—A Baltimore divorcee, seeking $10,000 for alienation of affections, testified yesterday that she spent five hours in the trunk of her husband's car—with the temperature at 23 degrees while he made love to another woman.

"It was cold," Mrs. Verna W. Mace told a common pleas court jury in her suit against Mrs. Jean A. Landsman, also of Baltimore.

Asserting that "I loved my husband very much but watched him very hard," the auburn-haired Mrs. Mace named three dates when she had hidden in the trunk to spy on him.

Mrs. Mace and James H. Mace were divorced last autumn.

DENIAL OF JAMES HINES PAROLE HEARING UPHELD

New York (AP) The appellate division of the Supreme Court of Brooklyn yesterday upheld the decision of a judge who refused to review the action of the State Board of Parole in withholding a parole from James J. Hines, former Tammany leader.

The 66-year-old Hines is serving a four to eight year sentence in Sing Sing as a result of conviction of contriving a lottery.

NO DOGS IN RUSSIA.

Algiers (INS)—A U S Army surgeon, back from Russia, said he did not see a single dog in the Soviet Union. They had been killed and used for food.

MONTREAL TRAMWAY WORKERS ARRESTED

Montreal (AP)—Five employees of the Montreal Tramway Co., were arrested last night on charges based on recently enacted provincial legislation prohibiting strikes in public services.

The arrests were an outcome of a thirty-hour strike of tramway employees which was ended early Sunday.

The walkout involved refusal of Canadian Congress of Labor to work with American Federation of Labor men on the same trams.

ARMY TO DETERMINE STATUS OF STUDENTS

Washington (AP)—The Army is going to keep "advanced" medical, dental and engineering students at their studies in its college program but the Army itself is not quite sure what it means by "advanced" students.

THE WEATHER
Tonight—Fair, colder.

THE TIMES RECORD

FINAL EDITION

SERIES 1944—NO. 68 (Entered as Second Class Matter at the Postoffice at Troy, N. Y., Under the Act of March 3, 1879.) TROY, N. Y., TUESDAY EVENING, MARCH 21, 1944. (Published Daily Except Sunday) PRICE FOUR CENTS

Hungarians Fight Nazi Invaders

Allied Submarines And Planes Sink 27 Jap Ships In Pacific

Draft Dodger, Jailed, Demands Nazi Lawyer

New York (INS)—Ivar Haug, 25-year-old native Norwegian Nazi, was in the federal house of detention today, awaiting trial on a draft-evasion charge after demanding that a Nazi lawyer be assigned to defend him.

Since Haug has $1,400 in the bank, Federal Judge Simon H. Rifkind directed the Norwegian to get his own legal counsel, but remarked: "You'll have trouble finding a member of the New York bar who is also a member of the Nazi Party." Haug previously served a disorderly conduct sentence after praising Hitler and denouncing the United States in a New York tavern.

STASSEN SAYS HE WOULD ACCEPT G.O.P. NOMINATION

Former Minnesota Governor Not to Seek Honor, He Informs Knox

Washington (U.P.)—Lieut. Comdr. Harold E. Stassen, former governor of Minnesota, has notified Secretary of Navy Frank Knox that while he will not seek the Republican presidential nomination he will accept if nominated.

Knox said that Stassen made his position clear in a letter which came through official channels from the South Pacific where the former governor is serving on the staff of Admr. William F. Halsey, jr., commander of the South Pacific area.

Stassen's Letter.

Stassen's letter to Knox follows:

"In recent weeks there have been numerous questions by representatives of the press in the South Pacific as to my attitude toward the current inclusion of my name in the presidential nomination discussions.

"The same questions have been raised in the public press on the mainland, accompanied by an increasing amount of conjecture and speculation and attempts at interpretation and misinterpretation.

"I have therefore concluded that it is desirable and in the best interests of my naval service that my position be clearly, concisely, promptly and publicly stated.

Public Statement.

(The following, Knox said, is the statement Stassen wished to make publicly.)

"In reply to the questions that are being asked as to my attitude toward the current inclusion of my name in the presidential nomination discussions, I will frankly and directly state my position.

"I do not seek and will do nothing personally to secure the nomination. If, notwithstanding this position, I were to be nominated, I would consider it to be my plain duty to accept and would do so, requesting inactive duty for a sufficient time to discuss with the people the issues and problems of the future.

"I wish to make it equally clear that I will make no statement on political issues while on active duty, that I do not wish any publicity of my activities in the Navy to be used in a political manner, and that no one is authorized to make personal comitments on my behalf.

"I will continue to carry out to the best of my ability those naval duties assigned to me."

Knox made no comment on the letter.

PRESIDENT REMAINS IN WHITE HOUSE QUARTERS TO NURSE HEAD COLD

Washington (AP) — President Roosevelt was treated for a head cold today and, upon the advice of his physician, remained in the residential quarters of the White House for a second successive day. He cancelled all appointments.

Mr. Roosevelt stayed in his quarters yesterday and had no engagements, but the White House did not announce until this morning that he had a cold.

Presidential Secretary Stephen Early said, however, that Mr. Roosevelt was "all right" and was not running a temperature. He did sneeze through the night, so his physician, Vice Admr. Ross T. McIntire, suggested that he stay away from his office, particularly the regular Tuesday afternoon press-radio conference which would have brought him in contact with several score persons.

Report Sextuplets Born in Nicaragua

Managua, Nicaragua, (AP)—Sextuplets, four boys and two girls, were reported today to have been born to Paula Esquivel in Potosi, near Rivas. No confirmation was available immediately.

AMERICAN BOATS SENT 15 ENEMY SHIPS TO BOTTOM

British Destroy Seven Nipponese Vessels Off Dutch East Indies

BY THE ASSOCIATED PRESS.

The sinking of at least 27 Japanese ships was announced today by Allied headquarters—22 of them by submarines—as indications mounted that one of Japan's by-passed fortresses in the Marshall Islands was about ready for the final assalut.

American submarines accounted for 15 ships in Pacific and Far East waters, the Navy announced, bringing to 642 the number of Japanese vessels sunk, probably sunk or damaged by undersea craft.

Included in the American submarines' toll were two transports, two tankers and 11 freighters.

In London, the British Admiralty earlier had announced that British submarines had sunk seven Japanese ships and damaged three in Far Eastern waters. In addition, Gen. Douglas MacArthur reported that American flyers wiped out all five ships of a Nipponese convoy Sunday near Wewak, New Guinea.

Allied Subs Cooperate.

Secretary of the Navy Frank Knox, in announcing the bag of 15 Japanese ships, referred to sinkings of American submarines by the Japanese and said it is "inevitable that practice makes them more perfect in combating submarines." American submarine losses since the war started now total 22, all but three of which have been lost in Pacific waters.

Asked about a British Admiralty announcement of sinkings of ships in Japanese waters, he said that British and American submarines are working together but that the seven ships reported sunk in the Admiralty announcement were entirely separate from the American bag of 15.

The skill of American submarine men is increasing at such a rate that they are outdistancing the improved techniques of the Japanese in anti-submarine activities, he continued.

Convoy Destroyed.

Seven Japanese ships were sunk and three damaged by submarines off islands in the Dutch East Indies, the British admiralty said. A large river steamer, a smaller vessel of undesignated type and a supply ship were the only victims specified.

A five-ship convoy, including two transports and three Corvettes, got within sight of Japan's bomb-battered base at Wewak, New Guinea, before it was obliterated by more than 100 Fifth Airforce planes in a furious four-day battle.

In the central Pacific, Adm. Chester W. Nimitz brought in his mighty battleship guns to assist carrier-based planes soften up Mili Atoll, once one of Japan's strongest bases in the Marshalls.

1,500 Japs Drowned.

Continuance of the Mili assault was indicated by the fact that Nimitz, in announcing the combined battleship-carrier plane attack last Sunday, lifted for the first time in more than a month his policy of not designating raid targets in the eastern Marshalls because Allied positions in the western and central Marshalls have cut the Japanese communication lines and Tokyo might not know all the details of the eastern Marshalls condition.

Pilots returning from the Wewak convoy battle estimated about 1,500 Japanese were killed or drowned. The convoy apparently was attempting to sneak into Wewak with reinforcements.

While planes poured 113 tons of bombs into Wewak's defenses during the ninth consecutive daily attack, destroyers steamed boldly into Wewak's harbor to shell shore installations.

Other planes hit Rabaul, New Britain, with sixty tons of fire bombs and raided Ponape, in the eastern Caroline Islands, and five targets in the Marshalls.

SCENE OF FATAL BUS PLUNGE: Skidding on the icy pavement, a crowded bus crashed through the rail of this Market Street Bridge in Passaic, N. J., and plunged into the deep channel of the river below. Actual break-through occurred in the section next to the watchman's shelter.

THIRTEEN BODIES RECOVERED AFTER PASSAIC TRAGEDY

River Being Dragged for Ten to 16 Others Reported Missing

Passaic, N. J. (U.P.) – Thirteen bodies had been recovered today and between ten and 16 persons still were missing from the 20-year-old bus which crashed through a bridge railing and plunged into the icy waters of the Passaic River yesterday.

Eight bodies were in the bus when it was raised from the river bottom by a crane late last night. Bodies of the others had been recovered earlier, including that of Walter Leroy Thomas, a pedestrian who was struck by the bus as it went out of control. Seven persons were rescued and were being treated for submersion. Rescue workers resumed the search for other bodies at dawn today.

Divers who examined the bus on the river bottom yesterday afternoon estimated there were about 25 bodies inside.

Dr. George Surgent, Passaic County physician, said his estimate of the number of missing was based on inquiries received by police from relatives of missing war workers.

The bus, operated by the Comfort Bus Co., was carrying workers to war plants in Wallington, East Rutherford, and Woodbridge, N. J., when the driver, Irwin Urbach, Clifton, N. J., lost control as the vehicle skidded on the ice-covered bridge. Shortly before Urbach had remarked to a passenger, "This is my last trip. I'll soon be home, thank God!"

Until rescue work was halted last night, workers groped for bodies with long poles, equipped with hooks. As the bodies were recovered from the river, they were placed on cots in a temporary morgue set up at the Passaic Elks Club.

As relatives identified the bodies they were removed to private funeral homes.

CHAPLIN TRIAL STARTED.

Hollywood (U.P.) A subdued Charlie Chaplin shoved his way through a crowd of noisy fans today to begin his fight to convince a federal court jury that red-haired Joan Barry lied when she called him a white slaver.

ARABIAN PIPELINE PLAN BACKED BY SECRETARY KNOX

Will Solve Problem of Dwindling U. S. Supply, He Declares

Washington (AP) – Secretary of the Navy Knox declared today that "a lot of selfish oil companies" should not be permitted to interfere with planned construction of a trans-Arabian pipeline to move oil. From Saudi Arabian fields for use by the United Nations.

Knox disclosed that the decision to build the pipeline, reached by the joint chiefs of staffs, was primarily a military move and secondarily an attempt to meet the problem of a rapidly dwindling supply of petroleum reserves in the American hemisphere.

The proposal, he said, calls for tapping a billion barrel reserve of oil which would play a major part in assuring a continued supply of fuel oil for naval craft and petroleum products for planes.

"Any new source in the European area during the war is found to reduce the amount of American oil used and also shorten the haul, which means a saving in tankers," he said after pointing out that 90 per cent of the oil used thus far has come from American reserves.

Knox declared that if adequate refining facilities were made available, the pipeline would "take care of all the needs in the Mediterranean."

Advantage to America.

He added that it would be "to our long range advantage" to utilize the Arabian oil for European and Far Eastern needs during the war.

"Both militarily and economically," he said, "a new source of oil in the Mediterranean is exceedingly important and for future safety and security to create there or in any area a reserve of a billion barrels of oil adds to our security."

Knox contended that pipeline transportation of the oil would cost only about half as much as hauling it by surface craft through the Red Sea.

"In money as well as in saving of tankers," he stated, "the pipeline is an economical operation."

The Navy secretary said that "because of optimism about the end of

(Continued on Page 2.)

FIFTH ARMY MEN SCORE NEW GAINS ON CASSINO FRONT

New Zealand Infantrymen Take Hotel Stronghold at Bayonet Point

Allied Headquarters, Naples (U.P.)—Allied Fifth Army troops were reported advancing slowly through the last German defenses in the southwestern end of Cassino today as a communique acknowledged that the Nazis again had succeeded in reinforcing their garrison and were counter-attacking heavily in the surrounding hills.

Driving forward yard by yard over mounds of rubble that provided perfect bunkers for the German gunners, New Zealand infantrymen fought their way through Cassino at bayonet point. Allied tanks and artillery supported the soldiers, laying down a heavy barrage on the Nazi strongpoints and on concentrations of fresh enemy troops trying to slip into the town.

Headquarters said 220 enemy prisoners had been captured by the New Zealanders since they began mopping up the ruined town after the record Allied aerial and artillery bombardment last Wednesday.

Nazis Surrenders.

They disclosed, however, that Nazi Panzer Grenadiers had filtered into the southwestern end of the town to reinforce the tough paratroop units already entrenched there, and it was indicated that the Allies still faced a slow, costly battle to clear out the remaining enemy positions.

Almost 200 of the paratroopers, who had boasted they would hang on to Cassino "indefinitely," threw down their guns and quit yesterday when the veteran Maoris slugged their way into the ruined lobby of the Continental Hotel, the major enemy stronghold in the town.

The Nazis held out inside the hotel under two days of incessant attack, but their stubborn defense collapsed after the Maoris knocked out two tanks emplaced in the lobby.

On the slopes of Mount Cassino overlooking the town, German troops still held on to one of the heights they won back in their counter-attack Sunday, and it was disclosed that the Nazis were using a dry watercourse northeast and north of the wrecked Benedictine Monastery as a passage for reinforcements.

Lull in Beachhead Battle.

Three miles southwest of Cassino, Allied and German combat patrols fought a savage night action near San Angelo while both sides exchanged a thunderous artillery fire across the lower Garigliano Valley on the western flank of the main Fifth Army line.

The battle of the Anzio beachhead to the north continued stalemated, although long-range German and Allied cannon duelled continually.

British combat patrols, supported by heavy shellfire, made two successful raids on the German lines along the western end of the beachhead early Sunday and withdrew after inflicting heavy casualties.

German fighter-bombers attempted a heavy attack on the Anzio port area early Monday, but they were fought off by patrolling Allied Spitfire pilots who sent four of the Nazi planes crashing in flames.

On the long-dormant British Eighth Army front, violent patrol clashes were reported throughout the day and night. Repeated skirmishes were fought in the Ortona sector and around Tollo, where Allied artillery and machine gun fire blasted a number of enemy positions.

Railway Targets Bombed.

American Marauder and Mitchell Medium bombers again paced the Allied aerial assault. The Marauders centered their attacks on the west coast ports into which German blockade runners have been attempting to run supplies from Southern France, hitting dock installations at Piombino and Porto Ercole and a railway bridge at Poggibonsi.

The Mitchells struck heavily at railway bottleneck points on the Florence-Rome line, hitting the Orvieto and Terni railway yards. Harbor installations at San Stefano also came under the Mitchells' bombsights.

Swarms of lighter Allied bombers also were on the attack over the Cassino Area and the Anzio beachhead, with Invaders, Warhawks and Bostons bombing and machinegunning enemy troops and gun emplacements along the battle lines.

In all, the Allied air forces flew some 1,100 sorties at a cost of three planes. Six Nazi planes were shot down in yesterday's operations, including the abortive raid on Anzio.

THREE JURORS PICKED AT LONERGAN'S TRIAL

New York (U.P.) The task of selecting a jury continued today in the state's second effort to try Wayne Lonergan, R. C. A. F. aircraftman for the candlestick murder of his heiress wife, Patricia Burton Lonergan.

Three jurors were selected yesterday. They were William J. Byrne, a claim examiner and jury foreman; Peter F. Reilly, a banker, and Lowell Wilson, milk company executive.

Russians Report Germans Fleeing Across Rumania

Red Army Now Pouring Into Bessarabia on Front Fifty Miles Wide

Moscow (U.P.)—Marshal Ivan S. Konev drove Soviet spearheads through Bessarabia to within 35 miles of the Rumanian frontier today and the government organ Izvestia said that "smashed German regiments are retreating across Rumania."

(Since the Soviets regard Bessarabia as a part of Russia, the Izvestia report of a Nazi retreat "across Rumania" apparently meant that the Germans are pulling back beyond the Prut River, the boundary between Rumania and Bessarabia.)

As the second army of the Ukraine poured into Bessarabia on a front more than fifty miles wide, the official Soviet army journal Red Star proclaimed jubilantly.

"Germany has lost the battle of the south. The Red Army offensive is spreading like a spring flood.

"The Red Army has crossed the last river barrier in the Soviet south. The Dniester is behind us. There is increasing anxiety among Hitler's vassals, especially the Rumanians."

Push Toward Carpathians.

To the northwest, Marshal Gregory Zhukov's First Army of the Ukraine pushed toward the Carpathians and stepped up the pressure of Marshal Fritz Von Mannstein's salient stretched taut between the Lwow approaches and Proskurov.

With the nipping off of the Vinnitsa end of the salient the German position now was narrowed to a precarious foothold, at many points only sixty miles wide, between the Soviet northern pincers and the forbidding Carpathian walls.

Increasing Soviet pressure from the north raised the possibility of a break-through which would encircle the German garrisons of Proskurov and Tarnopol.

Brody, about fifty miles northeast of Lwow, Already was three-quarters encircled, front dispatches said. Its fall would open the way for a straight shoot down the railroad to Lwow.

Rumanians Cover Retreat.

Field reports said the Germans were relying on Rumanian divisions to cover their retreat at many points. Two Rumanian divisions with German stiffening elements were charged with the defense of Migilev-Podolski. There on the elbow of the Dniester the Russians feinted attacks in several directions, threw the defenders off balance, seized the river bridge and

(Continued on Page 2.)

CHINESE FORCES DRIVE AHEAD IN NORTHERN BURMA

British Battle to Curb Jap Offensive Aimed at Imphal, India

New Delhi (U.P.) Chinese forces which swept the Japanese out of the Hukawng Valley pushed into narrow Jambu Bum Pass today for a drive to clear the Mogaung Valley in Northern Burma while on the central front British Imperial troops fought to stem a three-pronged enemy offensive aimed at the Indian city of Imphal.

Lieut. Gen. Joseph W. Stilwell's Chinese, aided by American infantrymen, were reported fighting their most difficult battle since the Northern Burma campaign began, facing a long forty-mile march through strongly fortified Japanese hill positions before they will reach level ground in the Mogaung Valley.

They captured Jambu Bum, a small rugged mountain between the Mogaung and Hukawng Valleys, Sunday, Stilwell's 61st birthday anniversary, to make good the American general's prediction nine days earlier that the entire Hukawng "will soon be ours."

Advance 175 Miles.

Frank Hewlett, United Press war correspondent with the Chinese-American troops, reported that Stilwell's men had advanced 175 miles into Burma with the capture of Jambu Bum and were only 65 miles from the town of Mogaung, northern terminus to the Burma railway.

The battle for the mountain between the two valleys lasted two days as the Chinese fought uphill, handicapped by recent rains which turned roads and trails into a mass of knee-deep mud, Hewlett reported.

To the southwest just inside Burma from the Indian border, three Japanese columns were attempting to drive into India, but reports on action there were more optimistic yesterday than at any time during the last week.

Three Separate Drives.

The Japanese offensive on this central front appeared to be coordinated even though it comprised three separate actions.

In the first, at least three strong enemy columns crossed the Chindwin River at several points south of Tamanthi, driving westward over jungle and mountain trails toward Imphal, capital of India's Manipur State in the Manipur Valley.

A second Japanese force was attempting to move up the narrow Kaban Valley through which a road leads from the port of Chindwin to Imphal through the Indo-Japanese border town of Tamu.

The third enemy drive was moving through difficult mountain country in an attempt to outflank Tiddim and reach the Manipur Valley along the Tiddim track.

38 ESCORT CARRIERS DELIVERED TO BRITAIN

Washington (U.P.) Secretary of the Navy Frank Knox announced today that 38 escort aircraft carriers built in the United States have been delivered to Great Britain under lend lease.

Knox said at a press conference that the United States has approximately fifty of these vessels of about 10,000 tons each operating with the fleet. Escort carriers, he said, are part of the anti submarine fleet of the Allies.

AIRMEN RESUME HUNT FOR FLYERS ADRIFT ON ICE IN ST. LAWRENCE

Montreal (U.P.) Twelve civilian and military aircraft searched the ice clogged lower Gulf of St. Lawrence today for three men marooned beside a stranded air liner on a big ice floe for a week.

Improved flying conditions sent every available plane into the air. While an icebreaker bucked a heavy sea of ice up the coast of Newfoundland toward the narrow strait of Belle Isle to head off the floe before it drifts to sea.

The three men were two unidentified employees of Canadian Pacific Airlines and a passenger. They were aboard a company plane forced down by fog on to the floe in the gulf near Harrington Harbor, 800 miles east of Quebec City at 9 p.m. last Tuesday. The pilot radioed he had made a safe landing and the plane was located from the air next day when supplies were dropped to the men. It has not been seen since Saturday when supplies were dropped to the men.

GERMANS OCCUPY BALKAN COUNTRY IN "SNEAK" COUP

Nation's Leaders Reported Kidnaped; Imredi Named Puppet Premier

London (U.P.) Upwards of 100,000 German and Rumanian troops were reported occupying Hungary today against the growing threat of Russian armies a bare 100 miles from the borders of the expanded Balkan kingdom.

Some scattered fighting sprung from the occupation but there was nothing to suggest any serious difficulties for Hitler. Top-flight Hungarian leaders including the regent, Admr. Nicholas Horthy, and foreign ministers and possibly Premier Nicholas Kallay were believed virtually kidnaped in Germany, whence they had been summoned to receive peremptory demands for all-out military assistance.

Bela Imredi, former premier and foreign minister and a Hungarian Nazi, was reported establishing a government. He was said to have convoked parliament for tomorrow at which time he was expected to assume Horthy's powers.

Russians Near Frontier.

The Russian columns in Old Poland were nearest war-weary Hungary.

Red troops at Tarnopol were 100 miles from Transylvania, the province amputated from Rumania with German connivance. Red troops in the old Rumanian province of Bessarabia were 150 miles from the Carpatho-Ukraine territory which Hungary wrested from Czechoslovakia. Others advancing on Lwow were within 125 miles.

A German foreign office spokesman was quoted by the Berlin radio as saying "no detailed discussion of the Hungarian problem was possible as long as certain phases in the development were not yet concluded." The German press was silent.

Stockholm dispatches said there was some indications that the satellite gateway kingdom to Nazi communications in the Balkans might become a new area of partisan activity directed against German transport and military operations. One report was that Marshal Tito's Yugoslav partisans had recently been in Hungary organizing units.

The newspaper Tidningen of Stockholm said German troops had hidden in boats on the Danube near Budapest and burst forth to occupy strategic points in the capital at a given signal.

Advices filtering from Hungary later today said that Imredi had grown reluctant to head a new government and that the Naziphile editor of Pester Lloyd, George Ottlik had gone to Berlin to discuss the possibility of becoming the chief of state. Those conversant with the Hungarian tangle expressed belief that Imredi might assume pro tem powers of the regent Horthy, but that Ottlik would emerge as premier.

Hungarian Army garrisons in the southern part of the country were reported in the Stockholm newspaper Aftonbladet to have clashed with the Germans at several places. The Budapest radio left the air during the morning hours and one report was that it had been damaged in fights between Regulars and Imredi's troopers. Sporadic clashes were said to have taken place along the frontier from Arad to Oradea in the north.

Hungarians Fight Invaders.

Some Hungarians were reported fighting this new invader at the call of their leaders, but the Nazis

(Continued on Page 2.)

U. S. BOMBERS SMASH AT FRENCH INVASION COAST

London (U.P.) American heavy bombers switched the weight of their daylight offensive back to the French invasion coast today in the wake of a small-scale R. A. F. night assault on a Nazi explosive works in Southern France.

Headquarters of the U. S. Eighth Air Force announced that a force of Liberators struck across the channel under a Thunderbolt fighter cover at the bomb-battered Pas De Calais area – where the Germans reportedly have installed rocket guns and other anti-invasion defenses. There were no immediate details of the assault, beyond the terse announcement that enemy "military objectives" were bombed.

Lava Flow From Mt. Vesuvius Destroys Two Italian Towns

Naples (AP)—A great stream of hot lava poured out of the crater of Mount Vesuvius at a speed of forty miles an hour at noon today without signs of subsiding, and the molten river licked at a third village on the northwest slopes after destroying two.

After burying most of San Sebastiano and Massa Di Somma, tht lava stream, thirty feet high and 200 yards wide, swept on toward Cercola, below San Sebastiano. Its pace slowed as it wound down the mountain.

The 5,000 inhabitants of Cercola were hurriedly evacuated as the white-hot rock flowed to within 150 feet of its town hall. U. S. Army trucks completed evacuation of the 7,000 inhabitants of the other two villages during the night. No casualties were reported.

Worst Eruption Since 1872.

The eruption, the worst since 1872, caused great property loss, not only from the burial of the towns but also from destruction of orchards and vineyards on the slopes.

A food dump for refugees was set up in the village of Pollena by Lieut. Col. James L. Kincaid of New York City, Allied administrative chief for the city of Naples. From this center bread and soup were distributed to various villages where the refugees found shelter. Medical supplies were made ready for delivery to any spot on short notice.

Kincaid remained on the volcano's slopes directing rescue work after Lieut. Col. Charles Poletti of New York, regional commissioner for the Allied military government in Naples, returned from all-night duty at the scene.

Villages Evacuated.

Evacuation of the villages was carried out expeditiously, although many of the Italian villagers were reluctant to leave their homes until the scorching lava was at the door. Allied authorities allowed each to take what possessions they wished.

Capt. Arthur Carter, former mayor of Amsterdam, N. Y., administrative officer in charge of the Vesuvius region, assisted in the work. Capt. John N. Lummus of Miami, Fla., from Kincaid's office in Naples, rushed out supplies as requests came from the scene.

The evacuation was begun at 4 p.m. yesterday as the molten river, flowing at a rate of five to ten feet a minute, reached a point less than a half-mile from San Sebastiano.

The famed volcano which wiped out Pompei in the days of ancient Rome, killing possibly 2,000 persons, began erupting Saturday afternoon. About 100 feet of a scenic railway winding around the mountain was quickly engulfed as three distinct rivers of lava moved downward. Only the flow on the northwestern slope threatened any damage.

Allied Air Tactics Baffling Germans

Editor's Note: The following dispatch was written by a correspondent fresh from internment in Germany tells some of the Allied air tactics which have baffled the Germans and made a "rusty sieve" of Goering's boasted "curtain of steel" to protect the reich from aerial attack. It is written by the former United Press director for France, who spent 13 months interned at Baden Baden.

BY RALPH E. HEINZEN.

New York (U.P.) Germany's Atlantic wall and its supporting defensive barriers remain to be tested but 13 months in German internment at Baden Baden gave ample evidence that the German fortress has no roof.

In more than 200 raids on the reich the war has been carried to 30,000,000 Germans in more than seventy big cities. Night after night I heard the warning sirens wail. I saw the Fortresses flying over on the first great American daylight raids of the war. I watched the bombing of Mannheim, Offenbach, Frankfort and Stuttgart. I could feel the shock of the explosions miles away.

Never once did I see the American and British bombers driven off their objectives. I saw some of them drop out of the skies in flames. I also saw German fighters crash.

The Germans know now that Germany was caught short on her air defenses. Fuehrer Adolf Hitler believed the boast of his pompous Air Reichs-marshal Herman Goering that the Allies never would overtake the lead his luftwaffe had established at the beginning of the war.

They know that Goering's boast that he had erected a curtain of steel an impenetrable barrier of

(Continued on Page 13.)

The Index

SNAP BEANS EASY TO GROW, PROVIDE MUCH GOOD FOOD

Mature Quickly in Any Home Garden; Make Three Sowings

By HENRY L. FREE
Written for NEA

Beans are easy to grow, quick to mature, and provide the home gardener with large returns for the space occupied and the time spent. There are many satisfactory varieties. Beans prefer a light, rich, alkaline soil, and lime should be added to soils which are acid in reaction.

Green snap beans are Bountiful, maturing in fifty days, Tendergreen, 52 days, and Streamliner, 55 days, are excellent in quality and among the most productive of all bush beans. An excellent gardener could make three sowings of Bountiful during the average garden season and secure a splendid yield from each planting.

Wax and bush beans (we call them butter beans) and Golden Bountiful Wax, mature flat, thick six-inch pods with purplish seeds in 55 days; Pencil Pod Wax, 52 days, bears abundantly over a long period. The pods are nearly round and very fleshy. Round Pod Kidney Wax, 88 days, is highly recommended for canning.

Lima beans should be planted a little later than other bush beans and in a more favorable location, as they mature late. Always plant with the eye down. The bush lima bean is more easily grown, earlier and more economical of space than the tall, but the pole varieties will provide a greater yield.

Seed may be sown a week after frost proof date. Cover two inches and thin plants to five inches apart in the row. Seed best picked clean will bear till frost; Fordhook Bush, 78 days, is the best; while Baby Potato, 72 days, runs a close second. The earliest of the pole limas is Surcliniese, 75 days to maturity, and King of the Garden, 85 days, the most productive tall variety.

Green pole beans yield heavily and because they are less hardy, should not be planted until the weather is settled. Set the poles two to three feet apart and in each hill plant six to eight beans, thinning out all but the best three or four. The old favorite Kentucky Wonder, ready in 65 days from planting, and Decatur, 65 days, the 1942 All-America silver medal winner, are my recommendations.

Stakes for high-yielding pole lima beans are set out, and seeds planted at base of each pole.

LOYAL JAPS FORBIDDEN TO SERVE IN PACIFIC

San Francisco (AP) The War Department will not use any of the 10,000 Japanese-Americans in U. S. uniform as combat soldiers against the Japanese Imperial Army because of possible enemy retaliation and "considerable confusion and increasing hazards of enemy infiltration," the Army notified the War Relocation Authority yesterday.

ON THE AIR
Radio Programs From Local Stations

(radio program listings)

CORINTH MAN DIES ON ITALIAN FRONT

Second Lieut. Robert L. Holland has been reported killed in action in Italy on April 5, according to a War Department telegram to his parents, Mr. and Mrs. Walter A. Holland of Corinth. After enlisting in 1942, the 21-year-old youth was sent overseas as a pilot in January, 1943. He was a graduate of Corinth High School and prior to his enlistment was employed at the Russell pharmacy in the village.

4-H CLUB TO OPEN CAMP ON JULY 30

Committee Decides Site Will Be Used This Year

"War or no war priorities or not," the 4-H Club youngsters missed their summer camping last summer and they aren't being hesitant in letting the seniors of the organization know about it.

The camp committee meeting yesterday in the office of Samuel R. Dorrance, Rensselaer County agent, decided that the camp would open on July 30 for two weeks at Camp Rotary if there is capacity registration. That means that seventy will have to sign for each week.

"It'll be a case of first come first served," Mr. Dorrance stated, and added, "With five counties it won't take long. Our biggest problems will be personnel and food. The youngster will need the best supervision and camping sharpens their appetites."

The program will include all sorts of summer sports with swimming being especially featured. In conjunction with this, first aid will be taught. This will require two waterfront directors. Instruction will be given in several types of crafts. Interesting field trips will be planned for the nature study which intrigues all children.

Applications will be received by Mr. Dorrance, secretary and treasurer of the camping committee, at the 4-H Club office in the Troy Postoffice.

EAGLE MILLS.

There will be no Red Cross sewing meeting this week

(local news items)

PROTEST MADE AT ACCOUNTING FILED IN DE FABIO CASE

Creditors of Late Green Island Resident Make Complaints

Objections to an accounting filed in the estate of the late Erminio DiFabio, Green Island contractor, by the executor, former Sheriff John J. McNulty, were made yesterday by creditors before Surrogate Edward G. Rogan.

A "proper" inventory of the estate was not made by McNulty, the creditors claimed. They said a value of $12,000 he placed on 33 shares of stock in Green Island Construction Co. Inc, was too low. They objected to his alleged failure to defend foreclosure on this stock and certain real estate by the First Trust Co.

Objection was also made to a $2,500 fee paid the law firm of Cooper, Erving and Savage for services as the executor's attorney and it was contended any acts of the firm were "not beneficial" to the estate because the same firm represented the First Trust Company, the largest single creditor.

Among the creditors who participated in yesterday's hearing were Pietro Santacrore, represented by Kenneth S. MacAffer, Republican chairman of Albany County; John Averan, Watervliet; the Cloverleaf Dairy, Inc., Troy, and Lee R. Chait, doing business as the Mill End Shop, Albany.

The objections said DiFabio, who died in August, 1940, had posted the 33 shares of the Green Island Construction Co. stock with First Trust Company as security for a loan. Mr. DiFabio was owner of the Moonlight Gardens at Green Island which was also taken over in foreclosure action by the bank. Eugene Steiner appeared as attorney for Mr. McNulty.

LIBERTY COUNCIL TO HOLD BANQUET

Daughters of America Plan to Mark 43rd Anniversary

Liberty Council, Daughters of America, will celebrate the 43rd anniversary of the founding of the organization at a banquet Monday, May 8, at the Tavern. Plans were completed at a meeting last night in the Chasan Building.

Mrs. Bernice E. Kehn of Albany, a national representative and past councilor, will speak. More than 100 members from councils in Ravena and Schenectady have been invited.

A rehearsal for the district meeting at Ravena, May 18, will be held at Albany Council rooms Wednesday night, Mrs. Bertha Simpkin, president, announced. Members of

PLAN D-DAY SERVICE

Rev. H. Boardman Jones, rector of Christ Church, has announced that on the evening of the day of invasion, a special service of intercession will be conducted at the church at 8 p.m. The chapel will be open all day for those who wish to offer prayers for the success of the invasion.

A brush council is scheduled by Liberty Council for Wednesday, May 10, at the rooms in the Chasan Building. A social will follow.

The committee in charge of the anniversary banquet includes Mrs. Simpkin, Mrs. Thelma Hiller, Mrs. Mary Storm and Miss Ruth Craver.

The degree team from Liberty Council will attend.

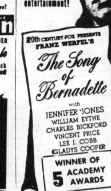

"The world's chief supply of helium, the gas used in our dirigibles, lies in certain sections of Texas, Colorado, Kansas and Utah.

MARINES SIT OUT U.S. OCCUPATION OF MARSHALLS ATOLL

Assault Force Fidgeted as Unarmed Native Rounded Up Japs

Majuro Atoll (AP)—True story of the American occupation of the neighboring atoll of Arno:

A strong assault force sat and fidgeted and fingered its weapons—while an unarmed native boy rounded up the few Japanese, conferred with them at length, and finally persuaded them to surrender.

"Even the natives had hidden when we went ashore," recalls Lieut. Eugene F. Bogan, former Washington, D. C., and New York tax lawyer trained as a civil administrator for occupied territory.

"A couple from Majuro finally filed back, reassured that we would not hurt them. They said the Japanese were hiding in a bomb shelter a couple of miles away.

"We finally decided to let one native boy see if he could persuade them to surrender. It seemed like a long time and everyone was getting pretty tense—it was nearly dark—when along came a motley little procession.

"It was our native boy and the three Japanese. One of them was shouting:

"'My English, she is so scarce—my English, she is so scarce! But please do not hurt my wife!'"

The native reported he had found the three men and the wife of one of them talking of suicide. The woman, he said, was trying to get her husband to kill her first.

"I don't know what our native boy told them, but he must have been quite an orator to get them to surrender.

"We persuaded the married man he should take his wife into captivity with him, and the next morning she came tremblingly out of the native village and joined him. Then two small native kids came out, too, and fell all over the old guy. Come to find out, he'd had a native mistress and family, too—two complete homes."

Majuro, also occupied without resistance two months ago is less than twenty miles west of Arno—and its circle of narrow coral islands encloses one of the finest fleet anchorages in the whole Pacific.

The 700 Majuro natives are segregated from the occupation forces. They live peaceably and quietly on one large island while the Army, Navy and Marines use the remainder of the atoll and huge warships ride at anchor in the wide lagoon.

One Marine tent, amid a thick forest of similar canvas homes, bears a boldly-painted sign: "American Embassy."

Snuffy Snedeker, Maitre D'Majuro, has a new sign painted for his lodging house, too: "The New Rita Hotel."

Snuffy (William) Snedeker is a former Los Angeles newspaper pressman who served a hitch in the last war and has a son in this one. His 80-cot hostelry serves transient officers. There is running water, after a fashion—you run out to a nearby shed to get some.

Snuffy glowers at all his guests—all the while coddling them with every necessity and luxury that he can buy, beg or borrow for them.

Let a guest leave a call for 7 a.m. and Snuffy will arouse him gently and usually manages to dig up a truck or a jeep and personally deliver the visitor to the nearest mess hall for breakfast. Brings him back, too; and all for free!

Meanwhile he growls: "The hotel business? Ahhh, I don't pay no attention to it. I'm just stuck with it; nothing I can do."

Whereupon this morose petty officer rushes out to his wash shed—he's wangled two electric washers, somewhere—and starts his daily laundry chores.

"Snuffy," remarks a Marine lieutenant, "takes damn fine care of you!"

Japan's highest possible aircraft production is believed to be 1,000 a month, whereas the U. S. is currently turning out upwards of 8,000 a month of all types.

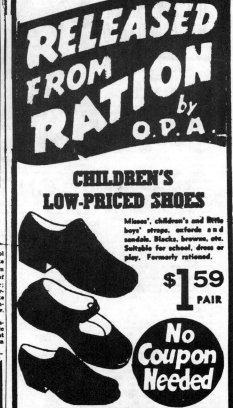

AIR WAC SHOW OPENS—Lieut. Beatrice M. Mutton of the Air WAC recruiting team, currently booking WAC enlistments in Troy for assignment to the Army Air Forces, is pictured above as she familiarizes Mrs. John Molloy with some of the Air Force emergency equipment at the opening of the three-day Air WAC show at Frear's store yesterday. The five-man rubber life raft and the small emergency radio set shown in the picture are part of the equipment display which includes a score or more of equally interesting articles.

DEFER PAGE TRIAL UNTIL NEXT WEEK

Adjourn Case of Broome County Surrogate

The trial of Broome County Surrogate Roy M. Page, scheduled for May 16, was postponed yesterday by Supreme Court Justice Ely W. Personius until May 22. Page is charged with illegal collection of state employees' salaries while he was a state senator. Page will be defended by E. Stewart Jones, Troy corporation counsel, and Daniel H. Prior, Albany attorney.

Page was indicted April 19 by the grand jury, ordered by Governor Dewey to investigate legislative spending, on 52 counts of first degree grand larceny and three counts of corrupt bargaining for appointments.

The grand jury heard five witnesses yesterday, including Norman R. McMasters of Canton, clerk to Senator Rhoda Fox Graves; Sol Lothenberg, New York real estate man; Benjamin Uchitell, Brooklyn real estate man; Orton Gillett of Chateaugay, Senate doorkeeper; and Charles Assin, New York, formerly employed as a real estate adviser to the joint legislative committee on assessments and review.

The Navy's new M-class non-rigid airships built for Atlantic patrol work carry 50 per cent greater volume of helium than their predecessors.

THE WEATHER
Tonight—Fair.

THE TIMES RECORD

FINAL EDITION

SERIES 1944—NO. 127 | (Entered as Second Class Matter at the Postoffice at Troy, N. Y., Under the Act of March 3, 1879.) | TROY, N. Y., MONDAY EVENING, MAY 29, 1944 | (Published Daily Except Sunday) | PRICE FOUR CENTS

Allies Advancing Toward Rome

Bombers Blast Nazi Targets In Germany, Poland And Austria

HITLER'S EUROPE TREMBLES UNDER TERRIFIC ATTACK

American Bombers Pound Poznan, Kreising, Leipzig and Vienna Areas

London (UP)—Two great American air forces totaling perhaps 3,700 heavy bombers and fighters struck synchronized blows from Britain and Italy today at eight Nazi aircraft factories and two airdromes in Eastern Germany, Poland and Austria.

A near record fleet of more than 2,200 bombers and fighters flew up to 1,300 miles to hammer six factories on a half moon arc swinging wide around Berlin and into Poland.

Up to 750 Flying Fortresses and Liberators shepherded by a comparable number of fighters swarmed up from Italy and smashed at two airdromes and two aircraft plants in the Wiener Neustadt area below Viena.

While the U. S. Eighth and 15th Air Forces were clamping the bombing pincers on the plants supplying the German air force on invasion eve, other hundreds of Allied bombers chuttled against the defenses of Western Europe throughout the morning and into the afternoon.

Raids on Huge Scale.

Preliminary reports of big scale activity supplementing the two heavy bomber broadsides suggested that the day's sorties might approach if not exceed a total of 6,000.

The eighth air force's 1,000 bombers with an escort of more than 1,200 fighters bracketed Berlin with bombs at a distance ranging up to 150 miles in the six-way attack on Poznan and nearby Kreising in Poland, and Leipzig, Sorau, Cottbus, and Tutrow, Germany, on three sides of the capital.

While the Americans were on the way home, the German radio claimed 45 U. S. bombers and five fighters were shot down over Northern Germany in violent air battles.

Austrian Plants Hit.

The first fighter pilots back from the long range mission with the bombers said the Germans did not try seriously to interfere with the formation they were protecting. A Mustang group led by Col. Don Blakeslee of Fairport Harbor, O., accompanied the heavies over Poland.

The targets of the Italy-based Forts and Liberators were the Wiener Neustadt Nord and Wollersdorf airdromes along with the Noll aircraft factory near Wiener Neustadt and the Atzgersdorff plant six miles southwest of Vienna.

Intense anti-aircraft fire was encountered over all the Austrian targets, headquarters at Naples announced and considerable numbers of German planes challenged the raiders.

Bridges Destroyed.

About 400 American Marauders and Havocs, the biggest force of its kind ever mobilized, this afternoon attacked bridges in Northern France and Belgium and the Achiet air field in France.

Reconnaissance planes which flew over three of the bridges ten minutes after the bombers left said one was completely broken, a span of another was toppled into the river, and the third had a row of bomb craters across it. Bomber crews reported at least 12 hits on

(Continued on Page 2.)

Revolt Reported At Quito, Ecuador

Quito, Ecuador (UP)—A revolution broke out today among military forces and civilians. The movement was led by supporters of Velasco Ibarra, former president, who is in exile and has been living near the Ecuadorean border in Colombia.

Ecuador is amid a heated presidential campaign, with elections scheduled June 2-3. Some groups opposing the present regime desired Velasco Ibarra to return to the country as a candidate, but the government refused him a visa from Chile. Velasco Ibarra then went to Colombia, where he previously lived several years in exile.

The Liberal candidate in the elections is Miguel Angel Albornoz, who is opposed by the Velasco Ibarra forces.

NAZIS PRESS POPE TO ABANDON ROME FOR SAFER REFUGE

Pontiff Reported Determined to Remain in Vatican City

Washington (INS) With the Allied armies advancing on Rome, a message dispatched from the Vatican to Washington revealed today that the Pope is being pressed to abandon the ancient and holy seat of the church for a safer refuge within Hitler's Europe.

The move is being urged by the Nazi command, for the avowed purpose of "protecting" the Pope from the Allied armies, now almost within artillery fire of the Holy City.

But Washington officials saw another motive - the desire of the Germans to enjoy the prestige of the Pope's presence, and to prevent the Allies from claiming they had "rescued" him from the German invasion.

High church circles in Washington declared emphatically that the Pope will accept no such invitation and will respond to no Nazi pressure, but will make a stand at the Vatican.

In fact, there was every indication that the Pope and other Vatican dignitaries would welcome the Allies as liberation forces, not only for themselves but for thousands of persons who have sought refuge in the various buildings and properties of the Vatican which are scattered, like neutral islands, throughout the area of Rome.

It is estimated that thousands of refugees are sequestered on one property alone, the papal palace at Castel Gandolfo. Other refugees have been received at the Lateran Palace and Basilica, the Palace of Propaganda Fide, the School of the Noble Eccliastics, at the Palace of Cardinals, and at various Vatican congregations and seminaries.

Though the majority of the refugees are Italian civilians whose anti-Nazi attitude made life dangerous, great numbers are escaped Allied prisoners of war. The release of these prisoners, officials said, will be one of the great and surprising stories at the moment of the liberation of Rome.

It is believed the normal population of Rome has doubled with the influx of refugees from Southern Italy. Therefore, when Rome falls there will be the problem of feeding not one million, but two million persons.

All of them have been suffering food shortages under the Germans. Present bread rations in Rome are only one-fourth of normal. A black market flourishes and prices are extremely high. Medicines are scarce, fuel stocks are low and there is a general disruption of transportation and facilities.

AMERICANS DRIVE FOR JAP AIRFIELD ON BIAK ISLAND

Australian Prime Minister Hints Philippine Invasion in Few Months

Allied Headquarters, Southwest Pacific (UP)—Acting Prime Minister Francis M. Forde of Australia suggested today that Gen. Douglas MacArthur's forces may invade the Philippines before "many more months" go by.

His indirect prediction of an early assault came as American jungle troops closed in on Mokmer airfield, 900 miles southeast of the Philippines, after landing on Biak Island Saturday in a 200-mile invasion jump from the north coast of New Guinea.

"I hope that it will not be many months before we will go back to the Philippines with a bang, then on to "Formosa and Japan," Forde said at a luncheon of the Australian Natives' Association.

MacArthur himself, in announcing the landing on Biak Island, said that it secured bases "for the advance to (the Japanese Empire's) vital areas in the Philippines and the Netherlands East Indies."

Drive On Airfields.

Tanks, planes and naval guns were supporting infantrymen in their drive toward Mokmer airfield, one of three on the island. The fall of Bosnek, main village on the island, within the first few hours of the invasion secured the new beachhead and probably doomed the airfields.

From Bosnek, the invasion units smashed 4¼ miles toward Mokmer airdrome, seven miles to the southwest, while other troops ran into desperate Japanese resistance at Soriari, 1½ miles northeast of Bosnek.

There are three airdromes on the island. The other two, Sorido and Boroki, are west of the Mokmer field.

The Boroki airfield is 5¼ miles west of Mokmer while Sorido is a mile and a half beyond that. At Sorido, Allied forces would be only 595 miles south of Palau, one of the Japanese eastern defense outposts of the Philippines.

Coast Defenses Bombed.

Japanese aircraft attacked the beachhead and four enemy fighters and five bombers were shot down. One unidentified American fighter pilot shot down the four fighters and one bomber, while naval antiaircraft fire downed four Japanese bombers. One enemy plane fell in flames on a small naval escort vessel, causing damage and casualties.

Liberators dropped 288 tons of explosives on Japanese coastal positions on Biak and infantrymen captured several enemy heavy guns, including two 6-inch, four 5-inch and three 2-inch pieces. While no Americans were killed in original landings because "the enemy didn't shoot straight," MacArthur reported, the U. S. units were suffering some casualties at Soriari.

REPORTS DROP IN APRIL MUNITIONS PRODUCTION

Washington (AP) Chairman Donald M. Nelson of the War Production Board has disclosed that munitions production in April was 3 per cent behind schedule, and 2 per cent under the March quota.

Nelson said in a week-end report that the 1944 production has been cut from an original objective of $82,000,000,000 to "somewhat less" than $69,000,000,000.

The WPB chief said, however, that most of the "must" items on the military schedule were well up on the production schedule. These include aircraft, landing craft, heavy artillery, ammunition, tractors and trucks.

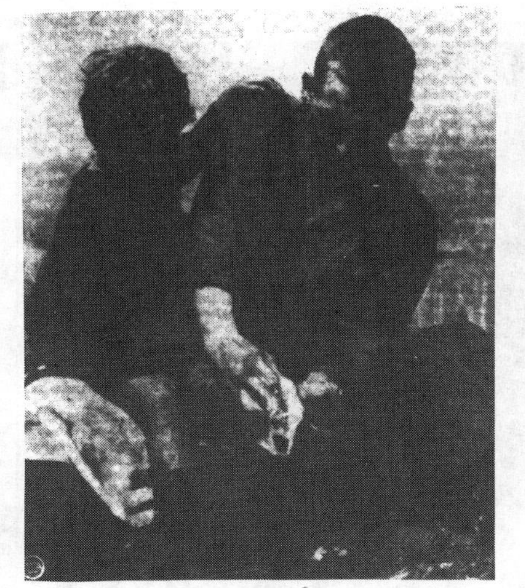

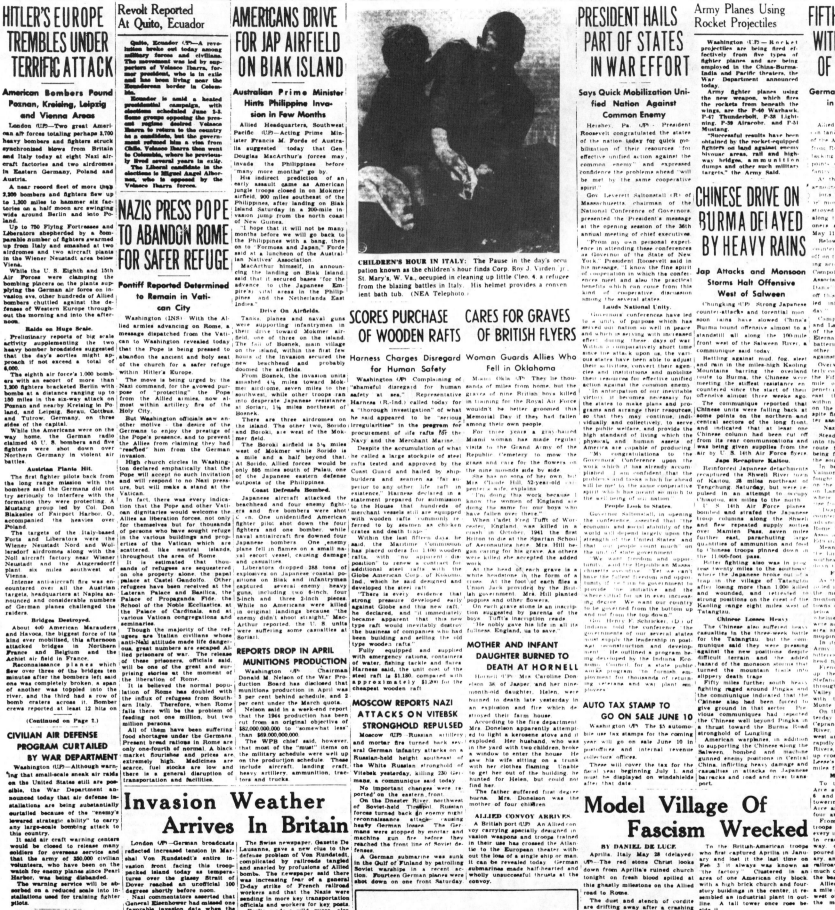

CHILDREN'S HOUR IN ITALY: The Pause in the day's occupation known as the children's hour finds Corp. Roy J. Virden, jr., St. Mary's, W. Va., occupied in cleaning up little Cleo, 4, a refugee from the blazing battles in Italy. His helmet provides a convenient bath tub. (NEA Telephoto.)

SCORES PURCHASE OF WOODEN RAFTS

Harness Charges Disregard for Human Safety

Washington (AP) Complaining of "shameful disregard for human safety at sea," Representative Harness (R.-Ind.) called today for a "thorough investigation" of what he said appeared to be "serious irregularities" in the program for procurement of life rafts for the Navy and the Merchant Marine.

Despite the accumulation of what he called a large stockpile of steel rafts tested and approved by the Coast Guard and hailed by shipbuilders and seamen as "far superior to any other life raft in existence," Harness declared in a statement prepared for submission to the House that hundreds of merchant vessels still are equipped with wooden rafts "commonly referred to by seamen as chicken crates and death traps."

Within the last fifteen days, he said, the Maritime Commission has placed orders for 1,400 wooden rafts, with "no apparent disposition" to renew a contract for additional steel rafts with the Globe American Corp. of Kokomo, Ind., which he said designed and developed the steel raft.

"There is every evidence that strong pressure developed early against Globe and this new raft," he declared, and "it immediately became apparent that this new type raft would inevitably destroy the business of companies who had been building and selling the old type wooden rafts."

Fully equipped and supplied with emergency rations, containers of water, fishing tackle and flares Harness said, the unit cost of the steel raft is $1,180, compared with approximately $1,200 for the cheapest wooden raft.

MOSCOW REPORTS NAZI ATTACKS ON VITEBSK STRONGHOLD REPULSED

Moscow (UP)—Russian artillery and mortar fire turned back several German infantry attacks on a Russian-held height southeast of the White Russian stronghold of Vitebsk yesterday, killing 230 Germans, a communique said today.

No important changes were reported on the eastern front.

On the Dnester River, northwest of Soviet-held Tiraspol, Russian forces turned back an enemy night reconnaissance attack causing heavy German losses. The Germans were stopped by mortar and machine gun fire before they reached the front line of Soviet defenses.

A German submarine was sunk in the Gulf of Finland by patrolling Soviet warships in a recent action. Fourteen German planes were shot down on one front Saturday.

CARES FOR GRAVES OF BRITISH FLYERS

Woman Guards Allies Who Fell in Oklahoma

Miami, Okla (UP) They lie thousands of miles from home, but the graves of nine British boys killed in training for the Royal Air Force wouldn't be better groomed this Memorial Day if they had fallen among their own people.

For three years a gray-haired Miami woman has made regular visits to the Grand Army of the Republic Cemetery to mow the grass and care for the flowers on the nine mounds side by side.

She has no sons of her own, but Mrs. Claude Hill, 52-year-old carpenter's wife, explains:

"I'm doing this work because I know the women of England are doing the same for our boys who have fallen over there."

When Cadet Fred Tufft of Worcester, England, was killed in a crash in October, 1941 the first Briton to die at the Spartan School of Aeronautics here, Mrs. Hill began caring for his grave. As others were killed she accepted the added work.

At the head of each grave is a white headstone in the form of a cross. At the foot of each flies a Union Jack provided by the British government. Mrs. Hill planted poppies and other flowers.

On each grave stone is an inscription suggested by parents of the boys. Tufft's inscription reads:

"He nobly gave his life in all its fullness, England, us to save."

MOTHER AND INFANT DAUGHTER BURNED TO DEATH AT HORNELL

Hornell (UP) Mrs. Caroline Donelson 38, of Jasper, and her nine-month-old daughter, Helen, were burned to death late yesterday in an explosion and fire which destroyed their farm house.

According to the fire department Mrs. Donelson apparently attempted to light a kerosene stove and it exploded. Her husband, who was in the yard with two children, broke a window to enter the house. He saw his wife sitting on a trunk with her clothes flaming. Unable to get her out of the building, he hunted for Helen, but could not find her.

The father suffered first degree burns. Mrs. Donelson was the mother of four children.

ALLIED CONVOY ARRIVES.

A British port (UP) An Allied convoy carrying specially designed invasion weapons and troops trained in their use has crossed the Atlantic to the European theater without the loss of a single ship or man, it can be revealed today. German submarines made half-hearted and wholly unsuccessful thrusts at the convoy.

PRESIDENT HAILS PART OF STATES IN WAR EFFORT

Says Quick Mobilization Unified Nation Against Common Enemy

Hershey, Pa. (AP) President Roosevelt congratulated the states of the nation today for quick mobilization of their resources "for effective unified action against the common enemy" and expressed confidence the problems ahead "will be met by the same cooperative spirit."

Gov. Leverett Saltonstall (R) of Massachusetts, chairman of the National Conference of Governors, presented the President's message at the opening session of the 36th annual meeting of chief executives.

"From my own personal experience in attending these conferences as Governor of the State of New York," President Roosevelt said in his message, "I know the fine spirit of cooperation in which the conferences meet and also the practical benefits which can come from this kind of cooperative discussion among the several states.

Lauds National Unity.

"Governors' conferences have led to a unity of purpose which has served our nation so well in peace and which is serving with increased effect during these days of war. Within a comparatively short time since the attack upon us, the various states have been able to adjust their activities, convert their agencies and institutions and mobilize their resources for effective unified action against the common enemy.

"In anticipation of our inevitable victory it becomes necessary for the states to make plans and programs and arrange their resources, so that they may continue, individually and collectively, to serve the public welfare, and provide the high standard of living which the physical and human assets of America are capable of producing.

"My congratulations to the Governors' Conference upon the work which it has already accomplished. I am confident that the problems and tasks which lie ahead will be met by the same cooperative spirit which has meant so much to the well being of our nation."

People Look to States.

Governor Saltonstall, in opening the conference, asserted that "the economic and social stability of the world will depend largely upon the strength of the United States" and that "our people count much" on the unit of state government.

"We want freedom and opportunity," said the Republican Massachusetts executive. "Yet we can't have the fullest freedom and opportunity if we turn to government to provide the initiative and the wherewithal for us in ever increasing degree. We want our country to be governed from the bottom up and not from the top down."

Gov. Henry F. Schricker, (D.) of Indiana told the conference "the governments of our several states must supply the leadership in postwar reconstruction and development." He outlined a program being developed by the Indiana Economic Council, for a state public works program "to furnish employment for thousands of returning veterans and war plant employees."

AUTO TAX STAMP TO GO ON SALE JUNE 10

Washington (AP) The $5 automobile use tax stamps for the coming year will go on sale June 10 in postoffices and internal revenue collectors' offices.

These will cover the tax for the fiscal year beginning July 1, and must be displayed on windshields after that date.

Army Planes Using Rocket Projectiles

Washington (UP)—Rocket projectiles are being fired effectively from five types of fighter planes and are being employed in the China-Burma-India and Pacific theaters, the War Department announced today.

Army fighter planes using the new weapon, which fires the rockets from beneath the wings, are the P-40 Warhawk, P-47 Thunderbolt, P-38 Lightning, P-39 Airacobr, and P-51 Mustang.

"Successful results have been obtained by the rocket-equipped fighters on land against enemy bivouac areas, rail and highway bridges, ammunition dumps and other such military targets," the Army Said.

CHINESE DRIVE ON BURMA DELAYED BY HEAVY RAINS

Jap Attacks and Monsoon Storms Halt Offensive West of Salween

Chungking (UP) Strong Japanese counter-attacks and torential monsoon rains have slowed China's Burma bound offensive almost to a standstill all along the 100-mile front west of the Salween River, a communique said today.

Battling against mud, fog, sleet and rain in the miles-high Kaoling Mountains barring the overland route to Burma, the Chinese were meeting the stiffest resistance encountered since the start of their offensive almost three weeks ago.

The communique reported that Chinese units were falling back at some points on the northern and central sectors of the long front, and indicated that at least one Chinese column had been cut off from its rear communications and was being given supplies from the air by U. S. 14th Air Force flyers.

Japs Recapture Kaitou.

Reinforced Japanese detachments recaptured the Shweli River town of Kaitou, 28 miles northeast of Tengchung, Saturday, but were repulsed in an attempt to occupy Chiaotou, six miles to the north.

U. S. 14th Air Force planes bombed and strafed the Japanese troop columns along the Shweli and flew repeated supply sorties over Mamien Pass, seven miles further east, parachuting large quantities of ammunition and food to Chinese troops pinned down in the 11,000-foot pass.

Bitter fighting also was in progress twenty miles to the southeast where the Japanese broke out of a trap in the village of Tatangtzu after losing more than 1,000 killed and wounded, and retreated to strong positions on the crest of the Kaoling range eight miles west of Tatangtzu.

Chinese Losses Heavy.

The Chinese also suffered heavy casualties in the three-week battle for the Tatangtzu, but the communique said they were pressing against the new positions despite difficult terrain and the added hazard of the monsoon storms that turned the mountain trails into slippery death traps.

Fifty miles further south heavy fighting raged around Pingka and the communique indicated that the Chinese also had been forced to give ground in that sector. Previous communiques had reported the Chinese well beyond Pingka in a thrust toward the Burma Road stronghold of Lungling.

American warplanes, in addition to supporting the Chinese along the Salween, bombed and machine gunned enemy positions in Central China, inflicting heavy damage and casualties in attacks on Japanese barracks and road and river transport.

FIFTH ARMY MEN WITHIN 16 MILES OF ETERNAL CITY

Germans Battle Desperately in Futile Attempt to Halt Allies

Allied Headquarters (AP)—American tanks have struck to the slopes of the Alban hills less than 16 miles from Rome's outskirts, and are attacking German mobile strongpoints of armor, artillery and infantry, a front dispatch said today.

At the same time headquarters announced that three German divisions totaling possibly 24,000 men or more had been virtually destroyed out of the 18 engaged all along the front. The bag of prisoners since the offensive opened May 11 rose above 15,000.

Below Rome sharp German counter attacks have been beaten off on the Fifth Army flank extending across a road from Lanuvio to Campoleone, a dispatch from Associated Press Correspondent Daniel De Luce said, and "fighting off this danger to the flank, tank-led infantry made progress all day."

Campoleone, 16 miles from Rome, and Lanuvio are two strongpoints of the enemy line protecting the Eternal City. The Fifth Army was battering toward them and two other fortress cities farther east against fierce resistance.

Overwhelming Aprilia, once bitterly contested beachhead fortress, the Fifth punched north within a mile of Compoleone the closest penetration toward Rome. To the east the Fifth Army advanced within 2,000 yards of Valmontone, on the shell-torn Via Casilina, despite flame-throwing German counter assaults.

Nazi Escape Route Shelled.

Steady artillery fire was pumped into the Via Casilina, main escape route for eight German divisions being forced back on the front to the southeast.

In between on the Campoleone-Valmontone line other forces fought in the outskirts of Velletri on the Appian Way, and closed up on Lanuvio four miles southwest, where the Alban Hills begin to rise from the Pontine plain.

Despite several sharp German counter attacks, the Americans are advancing in the direction of Rome, a battlefront dispatch from Associated Press Correspondent Edward Kennedy declared.

Meanwhile the Eighth Army in the Liri and Sacco Valleys to the southeast pushed ahead breaking down German rear guard stands.

French Drive Forward

As the sound of the great battle rolled into Rome, the enemy in the the mountains southeast of Valmontone was driven out of the towns of Sermoneta and Bassiano below Norma, which was overwhelmed yesterday. Snipers still were active in the hills beyond this area and Fifth Army patrols were mopping them up.

In its northward drive the Fifth Army slashed across two of the bitterest battlegrounds of the beachhead fights of last February.

French forces meantime followed up their seizure of Ville Santo Stefano by taking off northward through the hills toward the Liri Valley making only casual contact with the enemy and capturing Monte Siserno, 2,400 feet high.

On the heels of the capture yesterday of the important town of Ceprano on Highway 6 and the Liri River, the Eighth Army pushed west and north. Throwing bridges rapidly across the Liri and Sacco Rivers, where the enemy had blown up crossings, Lieut. Gen. Sir Oliver Leese's troops swept westward six miles from Ceprano to Pofi.

Monte Oreo Surrounded.

To the north, in the area of Arce at the junction of Highways 6 and 82, they surrounded the towering Monte Oreo, dominating Arce and surrounded Santo Padre, four and a half miles northeast.

From the beachhead Fifth Army troops met stubborn resistance every inch of the way in their drive to crack the Anzio-Albano Highway, down which the Germans poured vicious attacks last February, and past the Aprilia highway, railroad and factory area, scene of much of the bloodiest fighting since the beachhead was established.

Allied forces pounding to within a mile and a half of Lanuvio, southwest of Velletri, ran into some of the most determined counter-at-

(Continued on Page 2.)

CIVILIAN AIR DEFENSE PROGRAM CURTAILED BY WAR DEPARTMENT

Washington (UP)—Although warning that small-scale sneak air raids on the United States still are possible, the War Department announced today that air defense installations are being substantially curtailed because of the "enemy's lowered strategic ability" to carry any large-scale bombing attack to this country.

It said air craft warning centers would be closed to release many soldiers for overseas service and that the army of 350,000 civilian volunteers, who have been on the watch for enemy planes since Pearl Harbor, was being disbanded.

The warning service will be absorbed on a reduced scale into installations used for training fighter pilots.

CATHEDRAL EGG-TOSSER DETAINED AT BELLEVUE

New York (UP)—Frank Hahnl, 52, a tailor, was under observation at Bellevue Hospital today after tossing two eggs at Archbishop Francis J. Spellman as he sat on his throne at St. Patrick's Cathedral during a solemn Pentecostal mass.

Hahnl, who explained only that the prelate "said something I didn't like," aimed poorly and neither of the eggs struck the Archbishop. He was rushed from the church, as the ritual continued without interruption, and was found to have two other eggs in his pocket. Hahnl was to be held at the hospital pending trial on June 7 on a disorderly conduct charge.

Invasion Weather Arrives In Britain

London (AP)—German broadcasts reflected increased tension in Marshal Von Rundstedt's entire invasion front facing this troop-packed island today as temperatures over the glassy Strait of Dover reached an unofficial 100 degrees shortly before noon.

Nazi commentators asserted that General Eisenhower had missed one favorable invasion date when the tides and weather were perfect and cried out: "Germany would prefer for the invasion to come today rather than tomorrow."

That suggested that enemy defenses at least once already had been brought to a nerve-wracking peak of alertness, only to find that Hitler's command had guessed wrong.

"It is no longer a secret that the British have already missed one invasion date," the German transocean agency said, quoting a foreign office spokesman. DNB, the official enemy news agency, said "there can be no doubt that the original date fixed for invasion has passed but there are so many symptoms and speculations in connection with the next date that Germany cannot possibly be taken by surprise."

The Swiss newspaper, Gazette De Lausanne, gave a new clue to the defense problem of Von Rundstedt, complicated by railroads tangled and snarled by profusions of Allied bombs. The newspaper said there was increasing fear of a general D-day strike of French railroad workers and that the Nazis were sending in more key transportation officials and workers for key posts.

Berlin made a wild guess, also, that "General Eisenhower is waiting for fresh troops from America" before giving the go-ahead for the western assault.

"The Allied high command has allowed the past week—most favorable both from the point of view of tides and weather—go by because it has discovered flaws in armament and preparations of the invasion forces," proclaimed the German-controlled Brussels radio.

There was invasion tenseness in this armed island over the sunny Whitsun week-end. The people remembered with gratification during these Dunkerque evacuation anniversary days how the war in Europe has swung in a full cycle from the dark days four years ago. Newspapers again told of invasion tenseness in the United States also.

ATTENTION

Memorial Day—Tuesday, May 30th, 1944

The Troy Record will be published and distributed on Memorial Day as it has been the custom in past years. However, because of the shortage of newsprint, no advertising (Classified and Legal excepted) will be published in the Memorial Day issue.

Model Village Of Fascism Wrecked

BY DANIEL DE LUCE

Aprilia, Italy May 28 (delayed) (AP)—The red stone Christ looks down from Aprilia's ruined church tonight on fresh blood spilled at this ghastly milestone on the Allied road to Rome.

The dust and stench of cordite are drifting away after a crashing German bombardment, and Corp. William Sweeney of Liverpool, England, who fought at El Alamein in North Africa, has just carried a wounded Tommy out of the rubble.

Aprilia was in German hands last night. It was a no man's land this morning. At 3 p.m. it fell to the British when Maj. Henry W. King of Burton-on-Trent, Derbyshire, sent his riflemen from the Robin Hood country into its mutilated streets.

Ironically this model village of fascism, which has changed hands five times since the Anzio beachhead was established and has cost the lives of thousands of Allied and German soldiers, was occupied without a hand to hand struggle.

Eighteen miles away lies Rome, and our offensive is rolling onward.

To the British-American troops who first captured Aprilia in January and lost it the last time on Feb. 3 it always was known as "the factory." Clustered in an area of one American city block, with a high brick church and four-story buildings in the center, it resembled an industrial plant in outline. A tall tower once rose beside it.

Battered by hundreds of American heavy bombers and shelled daily for more than four months, Aprilia no longer has a tower or a roof to any of its buildings. Every wall is shell torn. Each street is pitted with craters.

The big red brick church is completely gutted and the rubble is four feet deep inside. But on one wall a plaque of Christ on Calvary somehow remained untouched.

In the corner sandwich shop, Where Mussolini is reported to have eaten a snack after reaping wheat from the land he had given his fascist devotees, a percolator and an ice cream machine lie half buried under broken bricks.

Aprilia was dedicated to fascism less than a decade ago. Now the town at last is dead.

The Index

THE WEATHER
Tonight—Cloudy, cooler.

THE TIMES RECORD

FINAL EDITION

SERIES 1944—NO. 133 (Entered as Second Class Matter at the Postoffice at Troy, N. Y., Under the Act of March 3, 1879.) TROY, N. Y., TUESDAY EVENING, JUNE 6, 1944. (Published Daily Except Sunday) PRICE FOUR CENTS

ALLIED INVASION ARMIES PUSH DEEP INTO FRANCE

PRESIDENT'S PRAYER FOR INVASION FORCES

Washington, (UP)—Following is President Roosevelt's prayer for success of our arms in their task—a prayer in which he asks all to join when he utters it by radio at 10 o'clock EWT tonight:

My fellow Americans:

In this poignant hour, I ask you to join me in prayer:

Almighty God: Our sons, pride of our nation, this day have set upon a mighty endeavor, a struggle to preserve our republic, our religion, and our civilization, and to set free a suffering humanity.

Lead them straight and true: Give strength to their arms, stoutness to their hearts, steadfastness to their faith.

They will need Thy blessings. Their roads will be long and hard. The enemy is strong. He may hurl back our forces. Success may not come with rushing speed, but we shall return again and again; and we know that by Thy grace, and by the righteousness of our cause, our sons will triumph.

They will be sore tired, by night and by day, without rest—till the victory is won. The darkness will be rent by noise and flame. Men's souls will be shaken with the violences of war.

These are men lately drawn from the ways of peace. They fight not for the lust of conquest. They fight to end conquest. They fight to liberate. They fight to let justice arise, and tolerance and good will among all thy people. They yearn but for the end of battle, for their return to the haven of home.

Some will never return. Embrace these, Father, and receive them, Thy heroic servants, into Thy kingdom.

And for us at home—fathers, mothers, children, wives, sisters and brothers of brave men overseas—whose thoughts and prayers are ever with them—help us, Almighty God, to rededicate ourselves in renewed faith in Thee in this hour of great sacrifice.

Many people have urged that I call the nation into a single day of special prayer. But because the road is long and the desire is great, I ask that our people devote themselves in continuance of prayer. As we rise to each new day, and again when each day is spent, let words of prayer be on our lips, invoking Thy help to our efforts.

Give us strength, too—strength in our daily tasks, to redouble the contributions we make in the physical and material support of our armed forces.

And let our hearts be stout, to wait out the long trail, to bear sorrows that may come, to impart our courage unto our sons wheresoever they may be.

And, O Lord, give us faith in Thee; faith in our sons; faith in each other; faith in our united crusade. Let not the keenness of our spirit ever be dulled. Let not the impacts of temporary events, of temporal matters of but fleeting moment—Let not these deter us in our unconquerable purpose.

With Thy blessing, we shall prevail over the unholy forces of our enemy. Help us to conquer the apostles of greed and racial arrogancies. Lead us to the saving of our country, with our sister nations into a world unity that will spell a sure peace—a peace invulnerable to the schemings of unworthy men. And a peace that will let all men live in freedom, reaping the just rewards of their honest toil.

Thy will be done, Almighty God.

AMERICAN FLEET TAKING PART IN FRENCH INVASION

U. S. Battleships, Cruisers and Destroyers Back Landing Forces

Washington (UP)—Admr. Royal E. Ingersoll revealed today that U. S. battleships, cruisers and destroyers are participating in the invasion of Western Europe.

Ingersoll, commander-in-chief of the U. S. Atlantic fleet, said that the ships, requisitioned from his command, had arrived in British waters in ample time to participate in covering our operations and in shore bombardments.

He did not know exactly where the ships were assigned.

Asked at a news conference arranged by Secretary of Navy James Forrestal, how the American ships were being used, Ingersoll replied:

"I presume they are being used in the same way as at Kwajalein and other places—for shore bombardment.

He said that everything that was needed for the invasion in the way of supplies and material already was "over there" and that from now on the Atlantic fleet's task would be easier because it would be charged largely with seeing that enough supplies get overseas to take care of combat expenditures.

Telling of the success of the Atlantic fleet in combating the submarine menace, Ingersoll said that since Jan. 1, 1942, ships of his fleet had taken across under escort over 7,000 vessels. Of these only ten were lost in the Atlantic and not a single troop transport was lost.

FLIES 20 MILES, FAILS TO SEE GERMAN GUN

New York (AP)—An NBC reporter who flew over twenty miles of the invasion coast this morning said "not a single German coastal gun was firing in the entire invasion zone," and NBC said this indicated "we have completely knocked out the initial line of defenses of the much-vaunted Atlantic wall."

PRESIDENT CALLS NATION TO PRAYER FOR ALLIED ARMS

Asks Divine Aid for Peace That Will Permit Men to Live in Freedom

Washington (AP). — President Roosevelt called upon a hopeful nation today to join him in a prayer for divine aid in speeding the invasion to victory and "a peace that will let all men live in freedom, reaping the just rewards of their honest toil."

The Chief Executive wrote the prayer last night as he sat up late at the blacked out White House to hear up-to-the-minute reports on progress of the great battle of liberation.

He will read it over a nationwide broadcast at 10 p.m., Eastern War Time, tonight, but its text was issued at mid-day to permit Americans to familiarize themselves with its wording so that they might join him in the recital.

Mr. Roosevelt dispatched the prayer to the House by motorcycle messenger, and it was read on the floor shortly after Dr. James Shera Montgomery, House chaplain, departed from custom to ask members to join him in the opening invocation.

Again the members stood, this time in silent prayer. At its conclusion Minority Leader Martin of Massachusetts reminded his colleagues that "many heart-breaking days lie ahead."

During the morning Mr. Roosevelt summoned the Army and Navy high command to the White House for his first personal conference with the commanders since troops began hitting the beaches during the night.

Gen. George C. Marshall, Army chief of staff; Gen. H. H. Arnold, head of the Army Air Forces, and Adm. Ernest J. King, chief of naval operations, arrived at 11:20 a. m. General Marshall appeared worn, as if after a sleepless night.

Presidential Secretary Stephen Early, who described Mr. Roosevelt's activities to reporters, said the President went to his bedroom early last evening and began working on the prayer shortly after he delivered a nation-wide radio broadcast on the fall of Rome.

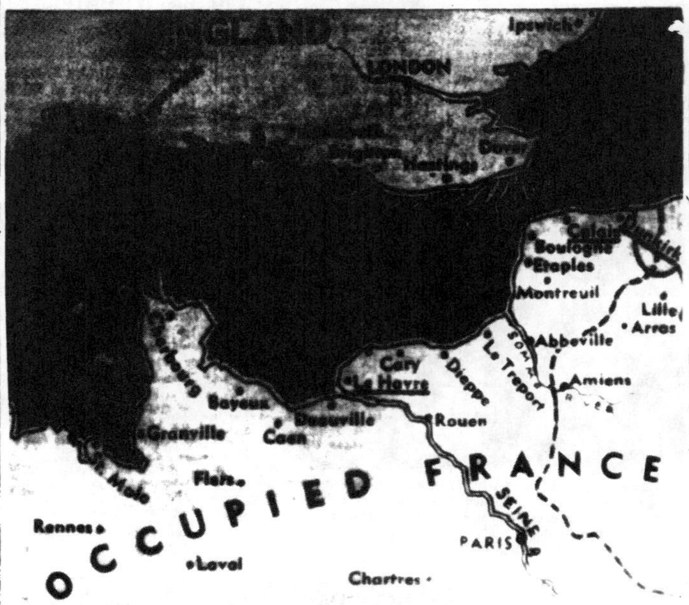

WHERE ALLIED INVASION TROOPS LANDED—The long-awaited invasion of Fortress Europe began early this morning with combined Anglo-American operations covering the entire coastline between Le Havre and Cherbourg. One blow was struck from the sea and another from the air. Large scale amphibious operations were launched between the Seine Estuary and the mouth of the Vire River. Early D. N. B. reports indicated invasion was launched from the 120-mile coastal area of England, between Portsmouth and Dover.

TROY FOLKS GREET NEWS OF INVASION GOING TO CHURCH

All Edifices in City Will Remain Open During Day; Some Plan Services

Those who said with surprise this morning, "Isn't the city quiet for invasion day?" had not been into the churches to see the kneeling women or to watch their faces. They would have known the reason why.

The city greeted D-Day, not with flag-flying or jubilation, but with prayers for the safety of its sons.

All the churches will remain open throughout the day. Many will hold special services of prayer this evening.

There have been people in the churches almost since the first messages of the invasion came. At the Wayside Chapel in St. Paul's Episcopal Church, the book in which those who pray write the names of the men for whom the prayers are offered had two pages covered with June 6 visitors by 9 a.m. today. After the names of many of the men was written, "In England."

The Army and Navy observed the day as "routine in the business of war."

At R. P. I. the Navy students went about their studies as usual. No special services were planned according to naval procedure at a time such as this.

Broadcast at Arsenal.

At Watervliet Arsenal, the night shift workers were among the first in the area to hear the news. It was broadcast throughout the shops over the public address system. At their machines, many of the workers stopped involuntarily as the voice of the army officer announced the invasion. Some of the women wept and knelt to say brief prayers. Then the work went on. As the night shift left the gun plant, where many of the guns for the invasion have been made, the workers streamed into the churches before returning to their homes.

When the first flash came, the New York Telephone Co. sent extra workers to the Troy office. The company had been prepared for this for many days. The wires, however, were surprisingly quiet until 7 a.m.

At that hour, the city woke up to the fact that the invasion had begun. The wires were busy for a few hours, Frank Phelps, manager of the Troy office, said. Mr. Phelps

(Continued on Page 11.)

Beware of Axis Lies On Allied Invasion!

Washington (UP)—Director Elmer Davis of the Office of War Information, advised Americans today to be wary of Axis reports on the progress of invasion fighting.

"Anything the Axis radio puts out, is in their own interest," Davis told a handful of correspondents gathered in his office in early morning hours.

As soon as General Eisenhower's first communique was received, 17 of OWI's 28 transmitters at New York began beaming it to Europe. Other transmitters, including those in London, started bombarding the airwaves in 22 languages.

INVASION APPEARS TO BE HEADED FOR PARIS, AFTONBLADET STATES

Stockholm (AP) The Berlin correspondent of the Aftonbladet asserted in a dispatch today that the Allied invasion attack "seems directed against the most heavily defended section of the French coast and aimed directly at Paris."

The dispatch declared that "warships of all kinds, including battleships, threw tons of shells at the coast, covering the landings."

Berlin said newspapers were jammed with calls as word of the invasion spread through the Reich.

Other Stockholm dispatches from Berlin said the Allies landed at 12 points between the mouths of the Orne and Vire Rivers on the Normandy coast, with the central assault directed at Caen.

EVERY DOUGHBOY IN INVASION ARMY WALKING ARSENAL

Troops Relieved of Overcoats and Money Before Leaving Britain

Washington (UP)—A War Department report from "a front line town" on the coast of England said today that the jumpoff of Allied troops for the invasion of Europe "began in a small way" from that point.

"First, several advance parties of the assault troops marched into the landing stages of this port, clambored aboard the blunt-nosed assault craft and a little later climbed on the larger craft swinging at anchor farther out in the harbor," the report said.

"Second, gangs of service troops began loading the rations that will sustain the task force while seaborne between England and the European continent.

"An officer said that there were enough rations put aboard LCI's to last eight days, plus one day of emergency combat rations."

Carried Light Rations.

None of the food loaded by the service troops was intended for use on the beaches after the assault troops land. For the first day of land operations, each soldier has been issued one day's emergency rations. After that time, field kitchens will be in operation, and hot food served, the War Department promised.

These final preparations were carried out "very quietly and without tension" by the Army and Navy, "almost under the noses of the civilian populace of this town without attracting the slightest bit of attention," the Army dispatch said.

The report said that the assembly areas along the British coastline were changed into marshalling areas beginning on Sunday and troops were briefed as to their exact missions and reshuffled from

(Continued on Page 4.)

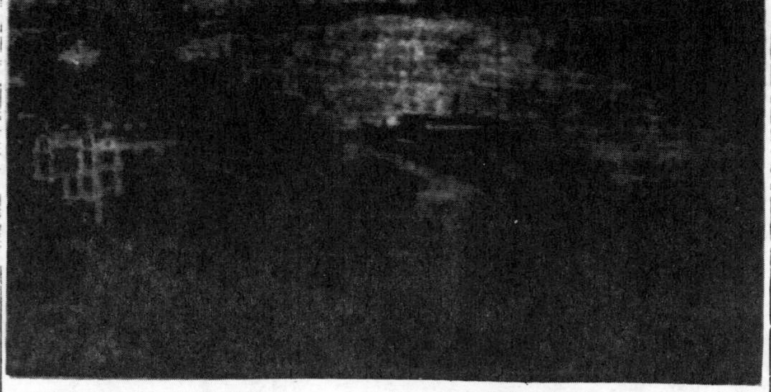

ALLIES INVADE LE HAVRE—Air view of Le Havre shows the Seine Estuary, where Allies landed troops by sea and air. One of the mightiest fleets in history laid down an earth-shaking bombardment of the coast to cover landings of Anglo-American troops by ship and parachute.

Highly-Vaunted German Defenses Pierced From LeHavre To Cherbourg

Americans, British and Canadians Land Under Protection of Gigantic Aerial Umbrella of 11,000 Warplanes and Combined Surface Fleets; German Opposition Weaker Than Anticipated; Allied Losses During Early Phase of Battle Reported Light; Nazi Coastal Guns Silenced.

London (UP)—The German Transocean News Agency said tonight that the Allied "offensive area" had been extended to the entire Norman peninsula.

Supreme Headquarters, Allied Expeditionary Force (AP)—Allied forces landed in the Normandy area of Northwest France today and have thrust several miles inland against unexpectedly slight German opposition and with losses much smaller than had been anticipated.

The grand assault—scheduled for yesterday but postponed until today because of bad weather—found the highly-vaunted German defenses much less formidable in every department than had been feared.

Air-borne troops who led the assault before daylight on a history-making scale suffered "extremely small" losses in the air, headquarters disclosed tonight, even though the great plane fleets extended across 200 miles of sky and used navigation lights to keep formation.

Naval losses for the sea-borne forces were described at headquarters as "very, very small," although 4,000 ships and several thousand smaller craft participated in taking the American, Canadian and British troops to France.

German Batteries Silenced.

Coastal batteries were virtually silenced by the guns of the British, American and Allied fleets, including battleships, and the beachheads were speedily consolidated.

The German radio said the scene of the landings was a 100-mile stretch of coast from Cherbourg to Le Havre, around the bay of the Seine and the northeast shore of the Normandy peninsula.

Britain's Prime Minister Churchill, in announcing the successful invasion to the House of Commons at noon—six hours after the first sea-borne troops landed—said the landings were "the first of a series."

In a statement early tonight (Tuesday) Churchill said the Allied troops had penetrated several miles inland in France.

Churchill disclosed that 11,000 Allied planes were available as needed for the battle. The Allied bombers, climaxing 96 hours of steady pounding, as the German air force up till noon had flown only fifty sorties against the invading forces.

The Germans were known to have probably 1,750 fighters and 500 bombers to meet the attack. Why they did not use them at the start was not apparent, but Allied airmen warned that a violent reaction might be expected soon, noting that Herman Goering in an order of the day had told his air forces, "the invasion must be beaten off even if the luftwaffe perishes."

German opposition apparently was less effective than expected, although fierce in many respects, and the Germans said they were bringing reinforcements continuously up to the coast, where "a battle for life or death is in progress."

The seaborne troops, led by Gen. Sir Bernard L. Montgomery, surged across the channel from England by 4,000 regular ships and additional thousands of smaller craft.

They were preceded by massed flights of parachute and glider forces who landed inland during the dark.

Channel Isles Also Invaded.

The initial landings were made from 6 to 8:25 a.m. British time (midnight to 2:25 a.m., EWT.). The Germans said subsequent landings were made on the English Channel isles of Jersey and Guernsey and that invasion at new points on the continent was expected hourly.

Aside from confirming that Normandy was the general area of the assault, supreme headquarters of the Allied Expeditionary Force was silent concerning the location for tactical reasons.

From Moscow came word that the Russian army was massing in preparation for another great attack from the east as its part in defeating Germany.

Prime Minister Churchill said tonight that a record-shattering number of Allied parachute and glider troops were battling the Germans in Caen, nine miles inland, and had seized a number of important bridges in the invasion area.

All reports from the beachhead, meager though they were in specific detail, agreed that the Allies had made good the gamble of amphibious landing against possibly the strongest fortified section of coast in the world.

Reconnaissance pilots said the Allied troops had secured the beaches and were slashing inland, some of them actually running in a swift advance. The unofficial word at headquarters confirmed this, while the Vichy radio admitted the Allied drive inland was going right ahead.

Navy Pounds Nazi Fortifications.

More than 640 naval guns, ranging from 4 to 16-inch, hurled many tons of shells accurately into the coastal fortifications which the Germans had spent four years preparing against this day.

Prime Minister Churchill was able to tell Parliament that the shore batteries had been "largely quelled," the underwater obstructions had proven less dangerous than feared, and the whole operation was "proceeding according to plan."

Allied planes preceded the landings with a steady 96-hour bombardment which reached its pinnacle in the hour before the troops hit the beaches.

The air attack was thrust home through cloud banks 5,000 feet high.

German naval opposition was confined to destroyers and motor torpedo boats which headquarters said succinctly were being "dealt with." The Germans, as expected, blared on their radios all sorts of claims of vast destruction done to Allied fleets and forces, but with no confirmation.

Germans Admit Landings.

In one defiant gesture, some of the German cross-channel guns opened a sporadic fire on Dover during the afternoon.

Unconfirmed reports said Adolf Hitler was rushing to France to try his intuition against the Allied operation. Presumably Field Marshals Karl Gerd Von Rundstedt and Erwin Rommel were directing the defenses from their headquarters in France.

German accounts through Sweden admitted that steady streams of Allied troops were continuing to land, particularly in the vicinity of Arromanches, about midway between Le Havre and Harfleur, and that tanks were ashore at several places. They said there was especially bitter fighting at the mouths of the Orne and Vire Rivers.

The airborne troops' principal scenes of operations were placed by the Germans at Caen and Harfleur. The Germans said the American 82nd and 101st parachute divisions had landed on the Normandy Peninsula, along with the American 28th and 100th airborne divisions. They said the British First and Sixth airborne divisions were operating in the Seine Bay area. The Germans complained that at some points dummy parachutists were dropped, exploding on touch.

The tenor of their accounts lent support to Prime Minister Churchill's assertion that "there already are hopes that actual tactical surprise has been attained" and that "we hope to furnish the enemy with a succession of surprises during the course of the fighting."

Normandy Initial Beachhead.

If the Germans were correct about the locations, the Allied plan apparently was to seize the Cherbourg Peninsula and

(Continued on Page 8)

U. S. BLOCK ISLAND LOST IN ATLANTIC

Aircraft Carrier Destroyed by Enemy Action

Washington (AP) The Navy, in new accountings of the war at sea, reported yesterday the loss of a U. S. escort carrier and the sinking of 16 more Japanese merchant ships by American submarines.

The small aircraft carrier Block Island was sunk by enemy action in the Atlantic last month with "light" casualties, the Navy said in a communique. She was the 158th Navy ship lost during the war.

In another communique, the Navy gave a fortnightly report on its submarine warfare against the Japanese. The 16 enemy merchant ships reported in yesterday's announcement lifted the total of Japanese ships sunk by American submersibles to 589.

The announcement about the Block Island did not say how she went down—whether by submarine action, gunfire, aerial bombs or mines.

Troy Man In Crew Of Escort Carrier

William J. O'Neil, jr., 19, son of William J. O'Neil, 4 McKinley Avenue, was a radar operator aboard the escort carrier Block Island which the Navy yesterday announced as having been sunk in the Pacific as a result of enemy action.

O'Neil enlisted in the Navy a year ago and, after boot training at Sampson, was sent to Norfolk, Va., where he was assigned to the carrier. No word has yet been received from him.

June 6 Momentous Date In World War II

San Francisco (UP)—June 6 will go down at least twice as a momentous date in World War II—in 1942 and 1944.

Exactly two years ago, it marked the finale of the battle of Midway, now recognized as Japan's greatest thrust at the Western Hemisphere. Planes of the U. S. Navy, Army and Marines hurled back a huge Nippon fleet in flaming battles which marked the turning point in the Pacific war.

Jean Buckland Engaged To Captain Evans

Rev. and Mrs. Harold W. Buckland of Schenectady, formerly of this city, have announced the engagement of their daughter, Miss Jean Millar Buckland, to Capt. Hiram J. Evans, son of Mrs. David J. Evans of Schenectady and the late Mr. Evans of Granville.

Miss Buckland is a graduate of Russell Sage College in the class of 1940 and has been on the faculty of Draper High School in Schenectady for the last four years.

Captain Evans, an alumnus of Hamilton College, received his master's degree from Williams College and his doctor of philosophy degree from Harvard University. He has been in the Army Air Force for the last two years and is now stationed at Elgin Field, Fla. No date has been set for the wedding.

Hospital Party Benefits Ambulance Fund

Approximately 75 tables of bridge were in play at the annual card party conducted Wednesday afternoon and evening by the Library Committee of the Leonard Hospital at McKean Staff House.

Individual table prizes were attractively boxed handkerchiefs and special awards were home baked cakes. Refreshments were served by junior members of the Library Committee. They included the Misses Sally Comeskey, Bernice Bornt, Sally Baker, Shirley Myers, Joyce Eagle, Geraldine Toohey, Jane Campbell and Dorothy Marsh.

The committee consisting of Mrs. John T. Comeskey and Mrs. Raymon L. Mason, cochairmen, Mrs. William A. Toohey, Mrs. Thomas F. Van Allen, Miss Toni Marchese and Mrs. Irene H. Campbell presented the proceeds of the affair to Miss Frances Dalton, superintendent. The proceeds will augment the ambulance fund for which they have been working for several years.

Gladys Moon Bride Of J. H. A. Choquette

Miss Gladys Margaret Moon, daughter of Mr. and Mrs. Edgar Moon, 6 Ball Street, Hoosick Falls, and Joseph H. A. Choquette, son of Mrs. Yvonne Choquette of North Aadms, Mass., and the late Mr. Choquette, were married at a nuptial mass today at 10 a.m. in the Church of the Immaculate Conception, Hoosick Falls, by Rev. Paul K. Lynch, O. S. A. Miss Phyllis White, organist of the church, played the wedding marches.

Miss Kathleen Moon, sister of the bride, was bridesmaid, and Theodore Dargis, North Adams, cousin of the bridegroom, was best man.

The bride, who was given in marriage by her father, wore an afternoon dress of magnolia white crepe with large navy blue hat and a shoulder bouquet of blue violets. Her sister wore an afternoon dress of rose crepe, with small white hat and a shoulder bouquet of white roses and blue sweetpeas.

The reception, at the home of the bride's parents, was attended by about fifty guests, including relatives and friends of the bridal couple from Watervliet, North Adams and Adams, Mass. Assisting in receiving were the mothers of the bridal couple, Mrs. Moon wearing a blue crepe suit and Mrs. Choquette a navy blue dress. Each had a shoulder bouquet, Mrs. Moon of roses and Mrs. Choquette of gardenias.

Mr. and Mrs. Choquette left on a wedding trip to an unannounced destination, the bride wearing a plain white dress with navy accessories and a shoulder bouquet. They will reside in Pittsfield, Mass.

The bride attended St. Mary's Academy, Hoosick Falls, and the bridegroom Plunkett Junior High School, North Adams. He served nine months in the U. S. Marine Corps, after which he was given a medical discharge, and is now engaged on war work in the General Electric plant at Pittsfield.

Private Bradley Feted While Home

Pfc. George Bradley, U. S. A., has returned to duty after a furlough spent with his parents, Mr. and Mrs. George Bradley, at their home in Berlin. He was tendered a furlough party recently attended by thirty guests. Dinner was served and square dancing enjoyed by the guests. Several Cherry Plain and Stephentown persons attended.

Marian Lodge
LAKE LUZERNE, N. Y.
CAMP FOR GIRLS
1944 Season, July 9th to Aug. 13th.
Chartered Bus From Schenectady, Albany and Troy.
RATES: ONE WEEK, $15.00
For any longer period, $14.00 per week
Albany Catholic Ass'n, Inc.
For Information Address:
MISS HELEN A. WARREN
Menallen Ave., Albany, N. Y.
TEL. ALBANY 3-2307.

WEDDING GOWNS
Our complete stock of Bridal Apparel assures you of a large selection of the newest in style. We can outfit your entire wedding party *immediately.*
LOU ANN *"The Bride's Shop"*
ALBANY-TROY ROAD, MENANDS
Bus Stops at the Door
Open Tuesday and Friday Evenings, Daily Until 5:30

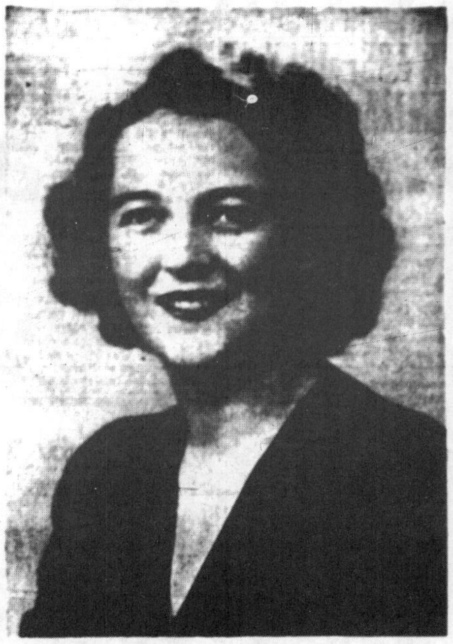

MISS JEAN MILLAR BUCKLAND

Dorothy Bussey Wed in Double Ring Rites to Richard P. Doody, Jr.

Miss Dorothy Ann Bussey, daughter of Mr. and Mrs. Charles M. Bussey of 2327 Fifteenth Street, became the bride this morning of Richard P. Doody, jr., son of Dr. Richard P. Doody and the late Mrs. Doody of 1 Eaton Road.

The double ring ceremony was performed at 9 a.m. in St. Paul the Apostle's Church by Rev. Walter J. Torpey. Miss Theresa Hennessy, organist, played a program of wedding music and accompanied the soloist, Miss Frances Wallace, who rendered, "Ave Maria," "On This Day, O Beautiful Mother" and "Bless Us Sweet Saviour Ere We Go." Palms formed the church decorations.

Miss Eva K. Bussey was maid of honor for her sister and James McManus served as best man. The ushers were Robert Bussey, brother of the bride, and Gordon C. Neitzel.

The bride wore a white mousseline de soie wedding gown made with a sweetheart neckline and flounced skirt. Her fingertip length veil of tulle was held in place with a tiara of flowers and she carried a Colonial bouquet of white roses.

Her attendant was attired in blue mousseline de soie with a square neckline and bracelet sleeves. She wore a matching picture hat and carried a Colonial bouquet of pink roses.

A reception followed the ceremony at The Hendrick Hudson. Mrs. Bussey received the guests wearing a pink crepe dress with a hat to correspond. Mrs. Elizabeth Dunn, grandmother of the bridegroom, also in the receiving line, was dressed in a grey crepe afternoon gown with white accessories. Both wore shoulder bouquets of gardenias.

The bride is a graduate of Catholic Central High School and is employed by Cluett, Peabody & Co., Inc., in the Sales Record office. Mr. Doody, a graduate of LaSalle Institute, attended Rensselaer Polytechnic Institute. He served in the Navy and was recently honorably discharged. He is employed by Behr Manning Corp., in the technical department.

The couple left on a wedding trip to New York and Atlantic City, Mrs. Doody traveling in a blue silk faille suit with white accessories and a corsage of white orchids. Upon their return, they will reside at 853 Second Avenue. Among the out-of-town guests present was Mrs. Sarah Miller of Hudson.

Gloves Will Arm You for Every Occasion

New York.—Playing the most versatile roles in their fashion lives, summer gloves give you the sole whoop-de-do that you need for an outfit; make covers for arms that shouldn't be exposed; supply motifs that are easy to repeat for clever ensembling, and provides changes as fresh as Monday's wash to revive a wilted costume.

Supply Excitement.

They supply excitement with no help, thank you, from other accessories, when they're made of any giddy print as, for instance, a dizzy gauntlet made of scarf silk with black spotted zebras romping over a background of aquamarine. There's another example in a rayon fringed jersey arm climbing gloves.

Capable of playing a solo role—and heavily dramatic—are femme fatal black mesh arm-length "mitts," in a popular peek-a-boo crochet stitch.

Glove Trimmings.

Among the glove trimmings that beg you to repeat their decorative motifs elsewhere in a costume are whopping buttons in gay colors, such as is seen on a white capeskin shortie. Buttons to match only bigger can be bought over the counter for use on a blouse, a jacket or a dress.

Other motifs are hand-painted on a glove such as a butterfly decorated cotton shortie and repeated on sweaters and stockings of resort ensembles.

Because chic hand-crocheted shorties are made clean with a dip or two in the basin, dry quickly and can go anywhere, they're a foremost glove favorite for both a city and suburban summer this year.

Troy Council To Meet Thursday

The Troy Council of Parents and Teachers will hold its June dinner-meeting at 6:30 p.m. Thursday at the Memorial Methodist Church. Mrs. Nelson H. Schmay, president, has appointed Mrs. Lloyd Austin, general chairman; Mrs. Justin Driscoll, in charge of reservations and Mrs. Carl Martin program chairman.

Mr. and Mrs. Hans Lund will entertain. He is well known as an impersonator and his wife will give piano selections.

All reservations must be made by Monday.

SCATTER RUG SAVER.

To prolong the life of your hooked scatter rugs and keep them from folding up like an accordion every time you walk over them, line with sail cloth, burlap or other sturdy material.

To cut a lining, place material flat on floor and your rug over it, then cut, allowing for a turn-in seam.

Sew lining to rug all along the edge underneath with a whipstitch. If lining buckles in the center, use a few quilting stitches to make it lie flat.

Bible Class Holds Luncheon Meeting

The Women's Bible Class of the Woodside Presbyterian Church staged a luncheon meeting yesterday with Mrs. LeRoy Bryce, Mrs. James Geddis, Mrs. Milton Dobert and Mrs. John Gundrum acting as hostesses. Mrs. Milton Dobert, class president, conducted the business session and reports were read by Mrs. Thomas Wells, treasurer, and Mrs. William Young, secretary. A song service dedicated to the men in service followed the meeting.

Nurse Graduates

Miss Madeliene Mary Summermatter, daughter of Alex Summermatter of this city, was graduated in May from the Philadelphia General Hospital. She will join the Navy in the near future.

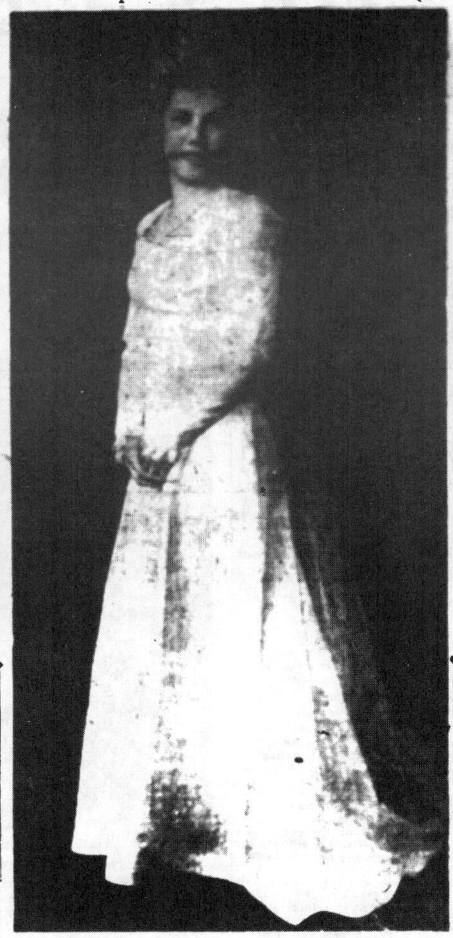

Photo by Booth Studio.

DR. PARK'S BRIDE—Mrs. John Morris Parks, who was married to Dr. Parks, a member of the department of metallurgy at Rensselaer Polytechnic Institute, on Thursday evening, is the former Miss Martha MacElhose, daughter of Mr. and Mrs. Irving H. MacElhose of Schenectady. The couple will reside at 207 Pawling Avenue.

ABOUT TOWN

HERE FOR GRADUATION

Mr. and Mrs. Raymond B. Bowen of New Rochelle and Miss Theodora Olcott of New York City arrived last night and are staying at The Hendrick Hudson. They will attend the graduation tomorrow at Emma Willard School of Miss Barbara Bowen. Mrs. Bowen is the former Miss Virginia van Santvoord of this city.

SUPPER PARTY

Edgar H. Betts will entertain this evening at a supper party at his home, "Orchard House" in honor of a group of seniors at Emma Willard School and their parents. Assisting him will be his daughters-in-law, Mrs. Robert G. Betts and Mrs. Edgar H. Betts, jr.

VISITOR RETURNS

Miss Katherine Rossiter of Longmeadow, Mass., returned to her home yesterday after being the houseguest of the Misses Marilyn and Grace Eiseman, daughters of Mr. and Mrs. Norman W. Eiseman of Maple Avenue. Miss Rossiter attended the wedding on Thursday of Miss Margaret Fitzgerald and Lieut. Paul H. Andrae.

HOME FROM NEW YORK

Miss Trent Cluett returned today from New York City where she was the guest of Mrs. Fritz Pruyn.

WEEK-END GUESTS

Miss Mary Louise Carlock of Brooklyn and Miss Merrill MacArthur of Hanover, N. H., are the week-end guests of Mrs. Charles A. MacArthur and Miss Judy MacArthur.

ON FURLOUGH

Aviation Cadet Robert P. Kahn is spending a ten-day furlough with his parents, Dr. and Mrs. Philip E. Kahn. His fiancee, Miss Jean Orth, who has been visiting him at Maxwell Field, Ala., where he is stationed, returned to town with him.

Social Situations

THE SITUATION: Your telephone is on a party line, and during a chatty telephone conversation which you are having the other party lifts the receiver from the hook in an attempt to use the line.

WRONG WAY: Keep right on talking and let the other party wait, since you were on the line first, and since you don't feel that you use the telephone any more than your share.

RIGHT WAY: Bring your conversation to a close, and give the other person a chance. (The efficiency of a party line depends on how considerate the persons are who use it.)

Future Bride Tendered Shower

A miscellaneous surprise shower was given by the Zeta Chapter of Delta Gamma Delta Sorority for Miss Olive Elder on Thursday night. The affair was held at the home of the sorority advisor, Mrs. Robert Prins. Table decorations were in silver and white and a shower cake formed the centerpiece.

The guest of honor, who will be married June 24 to James Law of Montreal, Can., was presented with a corsage of red roses and received many gifts. There were 22 guests present.

Business Women To Stage Picnic

The Business and Professional Women's Club will hold a picnic Monday night at the Pawling Sanitarium. Cars will be at the end of the Albia bus line at 6 p.m. to transport those attending.

The committee in charge includes Miss Katharine Gray, Miss Cora Tobin, Miss Edna Engle and Miss Catherine Bross.

Soldier Returns

Pvt. William E. Cutler returned last night to Fort Leonard Wood, Missouri, after spending a ten-day furlough with his wife and daughter at 10¼ Munro Court, Troy. Private Cutler has been in the service since July 12, 1943.

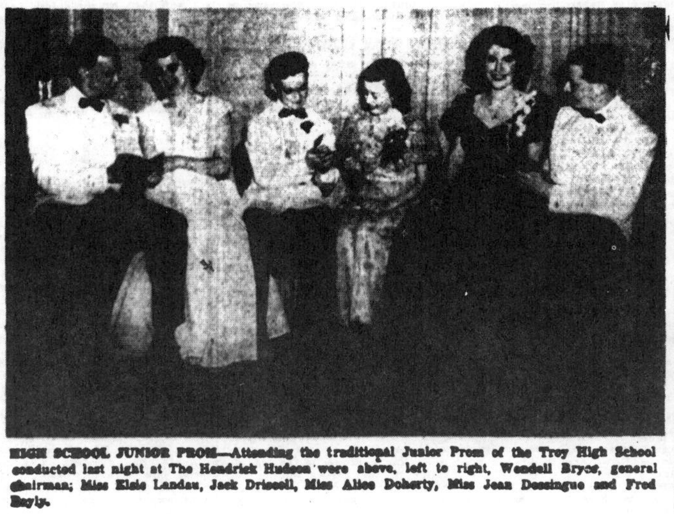

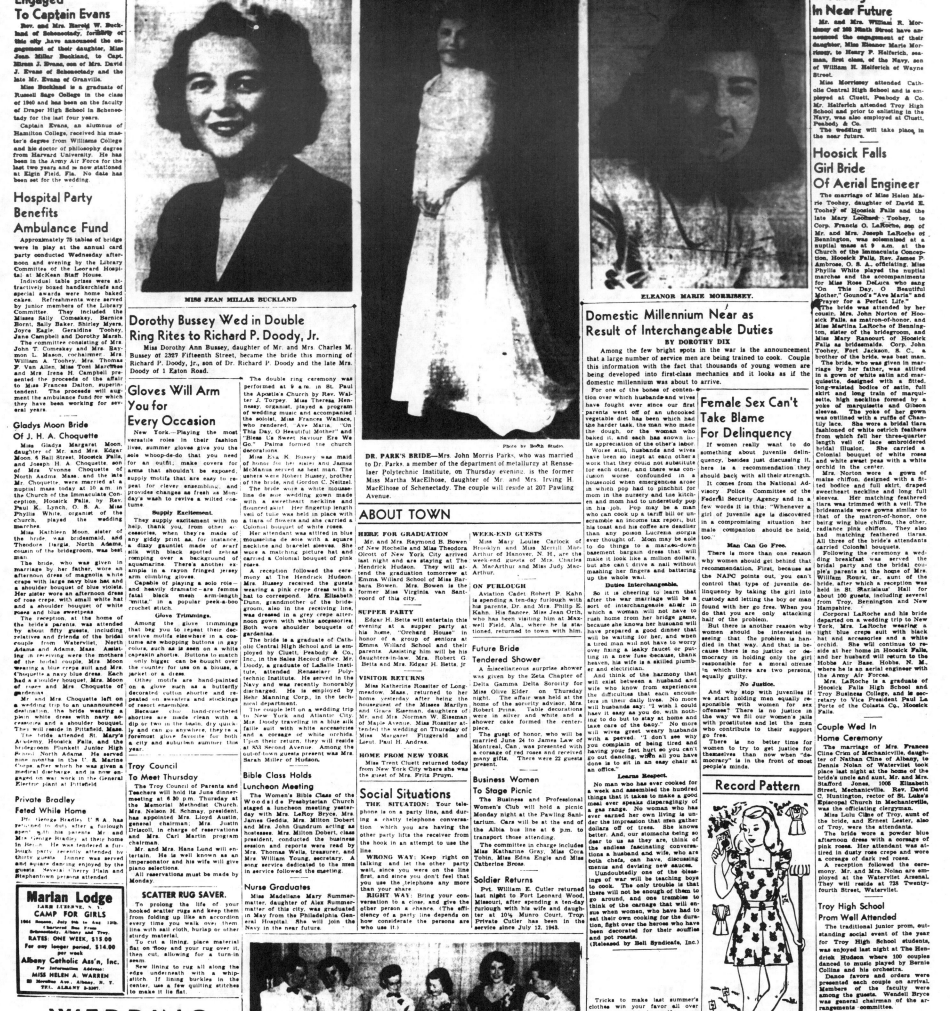

HIGH SCHOOL JUNIOR PROM—Attending the traditional Junior Prom of the Troy High School conducted last night at The Hendrick Hudson were above, left to right, Wendell Bryce, general chairman; Miss Elsie Landau, Jack Driscoll, Miss Alice Doherty, Miss Jean Dessingue and Fred Bayly.

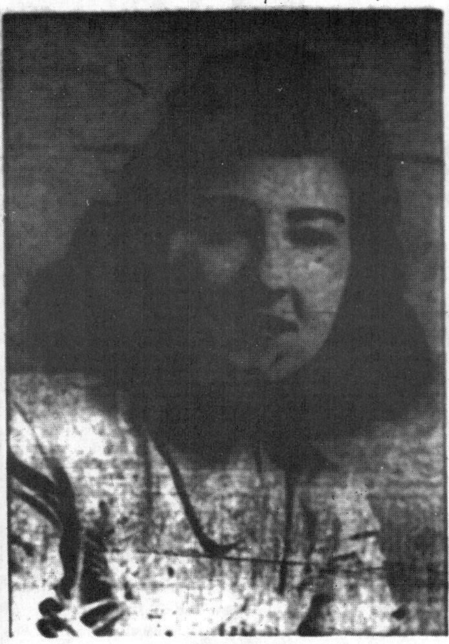

ELEANOR MARIE MORRISSEY.

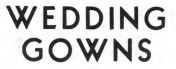

Domestic Millennium Near as Result of Interchangeable Duties

BY DOROTHY DIX

Among the few bright spots in the war is the announcement that a large number of service men are being trained to cook. Couple this information with the fact that thousands of young women are being developed into first-class mechanics and it looks as if the domestic millennium was about to arrive.

For one of the bones of contention over which husbands and wives have fought ever since our first parents went off of an uncooked vegetable diet has been which had the harder task, the man who made the dough, or the woman who baked it, and each has shown little appreciation of the other's labor.

Worse still, husbands and wives have been so inept at each other's work that they could not substitute for each other, and there was confusion worse confounded in a household when emergencies arose in which pop had to pinchhit for mom in the nursery and the kitchen and mom had to understudy pop in his job. Pop may be a man who can cook up a tariff bill or unscramble an income tax report, but his toast and his coffee are deadlier than any poison Lucrezia Borgia ever thought of. Mom may be able to do things to a marked-down basement bargain dress that will make it look like a million dollars, but she can't drive a nail without mashing her fingers and battering up the whole wall.

Duties Interchangeable.

So it is cheering to learn that after the war marriage will be a sort of interchangeable affair in which a woman will not have to rush home from her bridge game, because she knows her husband will have prepared a good dinner that will be waiting for her, and when a tired man will not have to worry over fixing a leaky faucet or putting in a new fuse because, thank heaven, his wife is a skilled plumber and electrician.

And think of the harmony that will exist between a husband and wife who know from experiences the difficulties that each encounters in their daily lives. No more will husbands say: "I wish I could haev it easy as you do, with nothing to do but to stay at home and take care of the baby." No more will wives greet weary husbands with a peeved. "I don't see why you complain of being tired and having your feet hurt so you can't go out dancing, when all you have done is to sit in an easy chair at an office."

Learns Respect.

No man who has ever cooked for a week and assembled the hundred things that it takes to make a good meal ever speaks disparagingly of a gas range. No woman who has ever earned her own living is under the impression that men gather dollars off of trees. She knows better. And, our stomachs being so dear to us as they are, think of the endless fascinating conversations a husband and wife, who are both chefs, can have, discussing menus and devising new sauces.

Uundoubtedly one of the blessings of war will be teaching boys to cook. The only trouble is that there will not be enough of them to go around, and one trembles to think of the carnage that will ensue when women, who have had to eat their own cooking for the duration, fight over the heroes who have been decorated for their souffles and pot roasts.

(Released by Bell Syndicate, Inc.)

Female Sex Can't Take Blame For Delinquency

If women really want to do something about juvenile delinquency, besides just discussing it, here is a recommendation they should back with all their strength.

It comes from the National Advisory Police Committee of the Federal Security Agency and in a few words it is this: "Whenever a girl of juvenile age is discovered in a compromising situation her male companion should be held, too."

Man Can Go Free.

There is more than one reason why women should get behind that recommendation. First, because as the NAPC points out, you can't control that type of juvenile delinquency by taking the girl into custody and letting the boy or man found with her go free. When you do that you are only attacking half of the problem.

But there is another reason why women should be interested in seeing that the problem is handled in that way. And that is because there is no justice or democracy in holding only the girl responsible for a moral offense in which there are two persons, equally guilty.

No Justice.

And why stop with juveniles if we start holding men equally responsible with women for sex offenses? There is no justice in the way we fill our women's jails with prostitutes and let the men who contribute to their support go free.

There is no better time for women to try to get justice for themselves than now when "democracy" is in the front of most people's minds.

Tricks to make last summer's clothes win your favor all over again are good to know, if you are a bit fickle but would like to keep these faithfuls in service. Suggestions come from the alteration experts of one of New York's swankiest shops, who says it is neglect of the little details that keep good clothes out of the running.

Best trick, she says, to give an old dress a new lease on life is to re-hem it. Even it up, re-measure the length, and tack with care.

Fit your dress to your this-year's figure, if your weight has changed. A good fitting job will give your dress new attractions that will charm you all over again.

Change the buttons. Sometimes it's a good idea, even if last year's crop is intact and in good condition, because new buttons—particularly if you'll look around for exciting ones—will receive your interest.

Freshen the neckline of the dress. That may mean only a new binding. But if that's not enough, splurge on some fancy neckwear.

Record Pattern

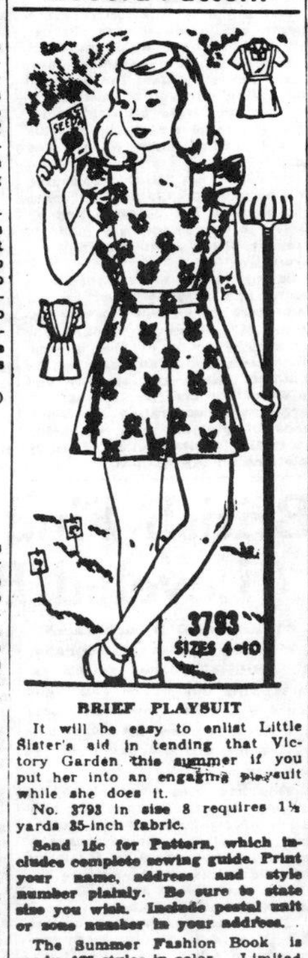

BRIEF PLAYSUIT

It will be easy to enlist Little Sister's aid in tending that Victory Garden this summer if you put her into an engaging playsuit while she does it.

No. 3793 in size 8 requires 1⅛ yards 35-inch fabric.

Send 15c for Pattern, which includes complete sewing guide. Print your name, address and style number plainly. Be sure to state size you wish. Include postal unit or zone number in your address.

The Summer Fashion Book is ready, 175 styles in color. Limited supply. 15c a copy, or only 10c with a pattern.

Address Pattern Department, The Times Record, 121 West 19th St., New York 11, N. Y.

Local Couple Plans Wedding In Near Future

Mr. and Mrs. William R. Morrissey of 103 Ninth Street have announced the engagement of their daughter, Miss Eleanor Marie Morrissey, to Henry P. Helferich, seaman, first class, of the Navy, son of William H. Helferich of Wayne Street.

Miss Morrissey attended Catholic Central High School and is employed at Cluett, Peabody & Co. Mr. Helferich attended Troy High School and prior to enlisting in the Navy, was also employed at Cluett, Peabody & Co.

The wedding will take place in the near future.

Hoosick Falls Girl Bride Of Aerial Engineer

The marriage of Miss Helen Marie Toohey, daughter of David E. Toohey of Hoosick Falls and the late Mary Leonard Toohey, to Corp. Francis O. LaRoche, son of Mr. and Mrs. Joseph LaRoche of Bennington, was solemnized at a nuptial mass at 9 a.m. at the Church of the Immaculate Conception, Hoosick Falls, Rev. James P. Ambrose, O. S. A., officiating. Miss Phyllis White played the nuptial marches and the accompaniments for Miss Rose DeLuca who sang "On This Day, O Beautiful Mother," Gounod's "Ave Maria" and "Prayer for a Perfect Life."

The bride was attended by her cousin, Mrs. John Norton of Hoosick Falls, as matron-of-honor, and Miss Martina LaRoche of Bennington, sister of the bridegroom, and Miss Mary Rancourt of Hoosick Falls as bridesmaids. Corp. John Toohey, Fort Jackson, S. C., a brother of the bride, was best man.

The bride, who was given in marriage by her father, was attired in a gown of white satin and marquisette, designed with a fitted, long-waisted bodice of satin, full skirt and long train of marquisette, high neckline formed by a yoke of marquisette and Gibson sleeves. The yoke of her gown was outlined with a ruffle of Chantily lace. She wore a bridal tiara fashioned of white ostrich feathers from which fell her three-quarter length veil of lace embroidered bridal illusion. She carried a Colonial bouquet of white roses and white sweet peas with a white orchid in the center.

Mrs. Norton wore a gown of maize chiffon, designed with a fitted bodice and full skirt, draped sweetheart neckline and long full sleeves. Her matching feathered tiara was trimmed with a veil. The bridesmaids wore gowns similar to that of the matron-of-honor, one being wing blue chiffon, the other, radiance pink chiffon. They also had matching feathered tiaras. All three of the bride's attendants carried Colonial bouquets.

Following the ceremony a wedding breakfast was served the bridal party and the bridal couple's parents at the home of Mrs. William Rourk, sr., aunt of the bride, after which a reception was held in St. Stanislaus' Hall for about 100 guests, including several from Troy, Bennington and New Hampshire.

Corporal LaRoche and his bride departed on a wedding trip to New York, Mrs. LaRoche wearing a light blue crepe suit with black hat and accessories and a white orchid. She will continue to reside at her home in Hoosick Falls, and her husband will return to the Hobbs Air Base, Hobbs, N. M., where he is an aerial engineer with the Army Air Forces.

Mrs. LaRoche is a graduate of Hoosick Falls High School and Troy Business College, and is secretary to Vice President Paul La Porte of the Colasta Co., Hoosick Falls.

Couple Wed In Home Ceremony

The marriage of Mrs. Frances Cline Crim of Mechanicville, daughter of Nathan Cline of Albany, to Dennis Nolan of Watervliet took place last night at the home of the bride's uncle and aunt, Mr. and Mrs. Stafford Jones, 1005 Elizabeth Street, Mechanicville. Rev. David C. Huntington, rector of St. Luke's Episcopal Church in Mechanicville, was the officiating clergyman.

Miss Lulu Cline of Troy, aunt of the bride, and Ernest Lester, also of Troy, were the attendants.

The bride wore a powder blue afternoon dress with a corsage of pink roses. Her attendant was attired in dusty rose crepe and wore a corsage of dark red roses.

A reception followed the ceremony. Mr. and Mrs. Nolan are employed at the Watervliet Arsenal. They will reside at 728 Twenty-fourth Street, Watervliet.

Troy High School Prom Well Attended

The traditional junior prom, outstanding social event of the year for Troy High School students, was enjoyed last night at The Hendrick Hudson where 100 couples danced to music played by Bernie Collins and his orchestra.

Dance favors and orders were presented each couple on arrival. Members of the faculty were among the guests. Wendell Bryce was general chairman of the arrangements committee.

Lawn Party Monday

The annual lawn party and bake sale of the Beth El Sisterhood will be held Monday afternoon at 2 p.m. at the home of Mrs. A. C. Goldstein at the head of Joseph Street. In case of rain the affair will be staged in the vestry rooms of the Beth El Temple.

BEAUTICIANS WANTED
Exceptionally good salary to start plus COMMISSIONS, IDEAL WORKING CONDITIONS.
ALLURE
BEAUTY SALON
91 Third St. Troy 2626

THE WEATHER
Tonight—Cloudy, warmer.

THE TIMES RECORD

FINAL EDITION

SERIES 1944—NO. 141 | (Entered as Second Class Matter at the Postoffice at Troy, N. Y., Under the Act of March 3, 1879.) | TROY, N. Y., THURSDAY EVENING, JUNE 15, 1944. | (Published Daily Except Sunday) | PRICE FOUR CENTS

Super-Fortresses Bomb Japan

Americans Advancing In Normandy

JAPANESE HINT AT U. S. LANDINGS IN MARIANAS ISLES

Tokyo Communique Reports "Heavy Fighting" on Saipan, Tinian

BY THE UNITED PRESS.

A Japanese Imperial Headquarters communique said today that U. S. troops attempted to land this morning on Saipan and Tinian Islands in the Marianas, 1,500 miles southeast of Tokyo, and indicated the Americans had gained a foothold on the islands.

The communique, broadcast by the Japanese Domei News Agency and recorded by FCC, said "heavy fighting is in progress between Japanese units and enemy forces."

The dispatch followed an earlier report by Domei that American troops twice had attempted to land on Saipan, just north of Tinian in the southern part of the Marianas group.

The Navy Department, in line with its usual policy of keeping silent on enemy claims, said it had no comment today on the report of the Japanese news agency that American forces had attempted to land on Saipan.

Domei's first broadcast, an English-language transmission beamed to the United States, said the first American attempt to land was repulsed and in reference to the second attempt said "heavy fighting" is now going on.

Heavily Shelled By Fleet.

The communique, beamed in Japanese to occupied East Asia areas, said landings were attempted at both Saipan and Tinian, but did not claim that the Americans were thrown back, indicating that the invasion forces had at least reached the beaches. Domei's original report said the American "invaders" employed seventy landing barges and twenty to thirty special barges in the invasion efforts following a series of "raids."

The "raids" apparently referred to the three-day assault delivered by a powerful Pacific fleet task force which shelled and bombed Saipan in a series of attacks on the Marianas during the week-end.

Possesion of the Marianas, which include the former American island of Guam, would give the Allies control over Japan's Central Pacific supply routes and open the way for a possible direct drive to the China coast—the goal of Admr. Chester W. Nimitz, commander of the Pacific fleet.

Northwest of Truk.

Saipan, which was attacked by two big naval task forces in five months, is only 650 miles northwest of the big enemy base at Truk in the Carolines, 1,100 miles almost due west from the American-held Eniwetok in the Marshalls, and 1,300 miles northeast of the Philippines.

There has been no Allied information of American activity in the Marianas since Nimitz' communique yesterday which said that battleships, cruisers and destroyers had shelled Saipan and Tinian Monday in a follow-up of three days of carrier-based attacks on the two islands, and also on Guam, Rota and Pagan.

In that assault, big guns of the warships were concentrated on Tanatag Harbor, Charan-Kanoa and the Saipan's largest town, Garapan, which has a population of 10,000.

Aerial fleets from the same task force battered the five principal islands in the group from Saturday through Monday, ranging from, 150 miles south of Saipan, to Pagan at the northern end.

The Domei enemy agency reported that twenty transports appeared off Saipan about 6:30 a.m. Tokyo

(Continued on Page 2.)

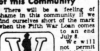

Air Dreadnaughts Hit Nippon From Far East Bases

Targets Not Identified But War Department Says Planes Came From China-Burma-India Theater; General Marshall Hails New Type of Offensive Against Enemy; First Smash at Jap Homeland Since Doolittle Raid in 1942.

Washington (UP) — American "Super-Fortress" B-29 bombers attacked Japan proper today in what Gen. George C. Marshall hailed as the opening step in a new-type of offensive against the Japanese.

The raid on the enemy's homeland—the first carried out by American airmen since the epic Doolittle raid of 1942—was announced by the War Department in a brief statement which gave no details but said only:

"B-29 Super-Fortresses of the United States Army Air Forces Twentieth Bomber Command bombed Japan today."

The Super-Fortresses hit Japan from distant bases somewhere in the China-Burma-India theater, the War Department disclosed.

The China-Burma-India theater is a vast territory covering millions of square miles. But General Marshall pointed out that the B-29s are capable of striking from "remote bases" and indicated that they might have flown from almost any part of that theater.

The department's announcement disclosed for the first time the existence of the Twentieth Air Force, a new organization which will have jurisdiction over all Super-Fortress activities.

It was the first time the big new "super Fortresses" were revealed to have been in action, although their existence has been known for some time.

Information made public coincidental with announcement of their attack revealed that they could have dropped their bombs from a height of more than 30,000 feet, that they could have cruised toward their objective at more than 300 miles an hour, and that they are half again as large as Flying Fortresses and Liberators.

Major Task Force.

General Marshall said since the power of the new bombers is so great, the Twentieth Air Force would not be confirmed to a single theater. The new organization will remain under central control of the joint chiefs of staff, with Gen. Henry H. Arnold, chief of the Army Air Forces, directing B-29 operations throughout the world.

"The planes will be treated as a major task force in the same manner as the naval task forces are directed against specific objectives," Marshall said.

Arnold said the use of the ships in combat "brings actuality to an Air Forces' plan made years in advance for truly global aerial warfare."

He hailed the B-29 as "a highly complicated and most deadly airplane, capable of delivering the heaviest blows yet known through air power."

"I assume the heavy responsibility for its employment under the joint chiefs of staff with full confidence in its potential use," he said.

"This employment of the B-29 makes possible the softening up attack on Japan very much earlier than would be possible with aircraft

(Continued on Page 24.)

PRESIDENT MAPS U. S. PROGRAM FOR POST-WAR WORLD

Elective Security Body and International Court Features of Plan

Washington (UP)—President Roosevelt today for the first time outlined the government's plans for an international postwar security organization to be built around "a council, annually elected by the fully representative body of all nations."

In a statement issued shortly after he met with Secretary of State Cordell Hull and postwar planning experts of the State Department, the President said this government proposed that the council concern itself "with peaceful settlement of international disputes and with the prevention of threats of the peace or breaches of the peace."

"There would also be an international court of justice to deal primarily with justiciable disputes," the President said.

"We are not thinking of a superstate with its own police forces and other paraphenalia of coercive power," the President said in the first authoritative, public outline to come from this government.

"We are seeking effective agreements and arrangements through which the nations would maintain, according to their capacities, adequate forces to meet the needs of preventing war and of making impossible deliberate preparation for war, and to have such forces available for joint action when necessary."

He added that "all this, of course, will become possible once our present enemies are defeated and effective arrangements are made to prevent them from making war again."

Saying that the maintenance of peace and security must be the joint task of all peace loving nations, Mr. Roosevelt defined the primary purpose of the international security organization as "to maintain peace and security and to assist the creation, through international cooperation of conditions of stability and well-being necessary for peaceful and friendly relations among nations."

MERCHANTS ASK OPA TO PROBE "48-HOUR" SHOE

Buffalo (UP)—Acting on evidence that an unrationed "ersatz" shoe which lasts only about 48 hours is being distributed in the Buffalo area, the Greater Buffalo Shoe Retailers' Association today petitioned the Office of Price Administration for investigation of the source of the product.

George W. Cooke, president of the association, last night exhibited to a meeting of the group a child's shoe with canvas top and felt bottom which, he said, sold for approximately $2 a pair.

"It was purchased on Saturday and worn out completely on Monday," he said.

British Find Tilly Leveled By Barrage

BY RICHARD D. McMILLAN

With the British in Normandy (UP)—British armored patrols entered Tilly Sur Seules today and found it a ghost town, shattered and smoking under the bright blue sky of the first fine day since the invasion.

Tilly had been smashed by a mighty "Monty Barrage" of hundreds of big guns, stacked hub to hub in a great armored square of tanks—a new offensive formation adapted in this roaring, surging battle for vital ground around the German defense hub of Caen.

The barrages are named for Gen Sir Bernard L. Montgomery, commander of Allied assault forces, and who first employed massed artillery to send Marshall Erwin Rommell fleeing from the gates of Alexandria.

Allied aviation started the destruction of Tilly. Then Montgomery moved up the tanks, which formed big hollow squares to enclose and protect the artillery. When the big guns were through, no German defense of Tilly was possible. It was nothing but a heap of smouldering rubble in which no German—or tarrying Frenchman—could have survived.

Today the tanks confirmed that the Germans had fled.

American mobile guns and British artillery teamed up to fight off new armored stabs by the German panzers early this morning as the British position was consolidated in high ground just to the rear of the farthest advance south of Caen and St. Lo yesterday. The Germans were reported to have thrust new divisions, including panzers, into the area south of Bayeux from their reserves deeper in France.

A German tank corporal questioned by his captors said the odds already were heavily against Rommel on the western front.

ALLIES CAPTURE HUNDREDS OF NAZI TROOPS IN ITALY

Germans Resume Big Retreat as Resistance Cracks Over Wide Front

Allied Headquarters, Naples (UP)—Allied Fifth and Eighth Army troops broke through the makeshift German hill defenses on a broad front fifty to eighty miles above Rome and swept on to the north today, rounding up hundreds of battle-weary Nazi rear guards left behind by the fleeing enemy.

German resistance cracked all the way from the Tyrrhenian Sea coast around the northern end of Lake Bolsena and down to Terni, seventy miles east of the advanced Allied coastal columns.

At the same time, the enemy was in full retreat from the entire Adriatic sector, pulling back so radidly that Eighth Army flying columns were unable to make contact with his covering rear guards.

Fresh German reinforcements rushed down from the north to stem the Allide advance from Rome were in headlong flight on the heels of the broken Nazi Fourteenth Army, after putting up a savage three-day battle in the hills bordering the Etruscan Plain.

Yanks Capture Magliano.

American troops drove northward on the coastal highway to Bengodi, eight and one-half miles north of Orbetello and less than 15 miles short of the important road junction of Grosseto, while other elements fanned out to the east along Highway 74 to join American spearheads pushing westward from Lake Bolsena.

Seven miles inland from the Tyrrhenian coast and five miles north of Highway 74, the Americans captured Magliano, the last important hill town south of Grosseto.

A communique said the entire 37-mile lateral highway had been cleared of enemy troops, including cavalry units and anti-tank gunners who fought to the death in a vain attempt to halt the converging American forces.

More than 300 German prisoners were rounded up on the coastal sector within 24 hours by a single American unit, and headquarters spokesmen said large groups of Nazis were surrendering at other points on the Allied line.

French Push Forward.

French troops also pushed northward along the west side of Lake Bolsena, while British Eighth Army columns on the east side cracked through the enemy defenses at Bagnoregio and raced on six miles to capture Orvieto.

The advance from Orvieto to the sea poised a serious threat to the big railway center of Florence, now only eighty to 85 miles north of the onrushing Allied columns.

Twenty-five miles southeast of Orvieto, British tanks and infantrymen drove the Germans from Narni and pushed on toward the industrial and communications center of Terni, seven miles to the northeast and fifty airline miles above Rome.

Front reports said the retreating Germans studded their line of flight with thousands of land mines and shot off every available artillery shell to prevent their falling into Allied hands.

Bombers Hammer Nazis.

On the Adriatic front, Eighth Army forces expanded their foothold on the north bank of the Saline River and sent armored patrols into the abandoned enemy stronghold of Aquila, 26 miles northwest of captured Popoli and 39 miles inland.

Allied medium bombers hammered at enemy communications lines all across the center of the peninsula from Livorno (Leghorn) to Pesaro, on the east coast, while swarms of fighter-bombers hit the highways in the rear of the retreating Germans, finding few transport targets left to attack.

The Allied air forces flew more than 2,000 sorties yesterday, including heavy bomber attacks on enmy oil refineries in Hungary and Yugoslavia, at a cost of 18 planes. An equal number of enmy planes were destroyed.

British Halifaxes, Wellingtons and Liberators followed through after nightfall with an attack on the locomotive yards and railway repair sheds at Nis, Yugoslavia.

DEMOCRATS NAME KERR AS KEYNOTE SPEAKER

Chicago (AP)—Gov. Robert S. Kerr of Oklahoma, an advocate of a fourth term for President Roosevelt, was selected today as the keynoter for the Democratic National Convention opening here July 19.

The choice was made by the party's convention arrangements committee, but recommendation of a permanent chairman for the conclave was deferred until later.

GESTAPO OFFICIAL EXECUTED

London (AP)—A Reuthers dispatch from Geneva said today reports reached Switzerland that Gen. Werner of the German Gestapo had been captured and executed by French partisans near Pontarlier.

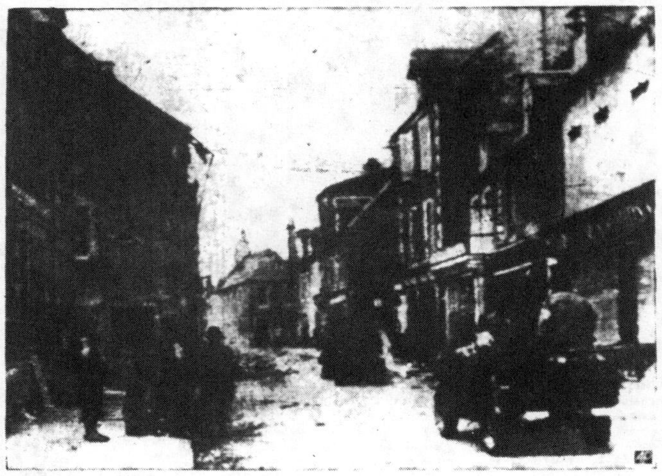

AMERICAN TROOPS IN CARENTAN: American troops, resting beside a walkie-talkie (left), watch jeeps hauling light artillery (center) and hospital corpsmen (right) through the outskirts of Carentan, one of the first cities to fall to the Allies in the Normandy coast area of France. (AP Wirephoto from Signal Corps Radiophoto).

HOUSE TAKES UP HUGE ARMY BILL

Solons Told Measure Seals Doom of Hitler

Washington (AP) Conveying the "hope" for military leaders that Germany will be knocked out of the war by next Jan. 1. Representative Snyder (D-Pa.) urged the House today to approve unanimously a $49,109,002,795 "Hitler Doom Bill."

The big bill, to finance the War Department for the year starting July 1, was described by the chairman of the appropriations military sub-committee as one that also "will soften Tojo for his doom that shortly will follow" the downfall of Germany.

It boosts to approximately $390,000,000,000 war and defense obligations incurred since July 1, 1940.

"This bill x x x provides General Eisenhower with his knockout punch," the Pennsylvanian told a House waiting to give its overwhelming approval to the measure. "The first round started June 6. The day of the last round we just cannot predict, but we can fervently hope that it will come before the snow flies again."

"It is the hope of our military leadership that Germany will be out of the war before another year begins," he added.

The bill carries $15,436,031,795 in new funds and $33,672,971,000 in reappropriations of funds previously allotted.

VICHY COLLABORATORS REPORTED CONSPIRING TO OVERTHROW PETAIN

London (UP) Vichy French collaborationists faced with increasing sabotage and violence from underground armies were reported today to be seeking Hitler's permission to overthrow the Petain government and declare war on the Allies.

A pro-Nazi group, headed by Secretary of State Joseph Darnand is organizing a coup, according to unconfirmed Swiss reports, to remove Marshal Henri Philippe Petain, chief of state, and Pierre Laval, chief of government, to Germany. The Berne reports said the new government could be expected to move swiftly and ruthlessly against the resistance movement.

French partisans, reinforced with guns and ammunition dropped by Allied planes in the last 48 hours, were reported today to be striking new blows at the Germans in Haute Savoie and elsewhere.

FIFTH WAR LOAN DRIVE PASSES 8 PER CENT OF INDIVIDUAL SALES GOAL

Washington (AP) The Fifth War Loan drive passed 8 per cent of the goal of individual sales during its second day.

Reported purchases through Tuesday night were $484,000,000 toward the $6,000,000,000 goal for individuals, the Treasury announced last night.

The Treasury said War Bonds now buy more and better war equipment than they did a year ago. For example:

A heavy bomber, listed at $500,000 a year ago, now costs $250,000.

A fighter plane, which cost $150,000 last year, now is listed at $50,000. A 4,000-pound blockbuster used to cost $872, now is $778. A Garand rifle was $80 a year ago, now $35

But the price of Army mules has gone up. The average a year ago was $190. Now it's $225.

PRESS CHIEF DEAD.

Clarkson, Ont. (AP)—J. F. B. Livesay, 69, for twenty years general manager of the Canadian Press, and a pioneer in the organization of the news-gathering cooperative, which now embraces almost all of Canada's daily newspapers, died today.

U. S. Fishing Boat Shelled By Nazi Sub In Atlantic

Crew Machine-gunned but Boat Arrives Safely in Boston

Boston (AP)—A German submarine invaded the North Atlantic fishing grounds recently, shelled and machine-gunned a Boston trawler and forced all but two of her crew to abandon ship.

The submersible finally left, her skipper apparently thinking the trawler would sink. Then the crew put the vessel in shape and brought her into port early today, her hull and superstructure looking almost like a sieve.

Details of the attack were given at a press conference by Capt. James L. Abbott, 35, skipper of the fishing vessel the Lark, owned by F. J. O'Hara Brothers, Boston operators. The vessel is 145 gross tons.

The sub first was sighted about 2:30 a.m. Captain Abbott said, but was mistaken at first for a friendly patrol boat. Then John Aspell, at the wheel, got a good look in the moonlight night and Abbott immediately roused the crewmen who were sleeping.

Fired On Fishermen.

The enemy fired one shot across the bow and then opened up with machineguns as the fishermen scrambled into their dories. Captain Abbott, his 74-year-old cook Dan Maloney and the ship's dog, Rex, remained aboard.

The sub fired from about 300 feet, the captain said, but there were no casualties. Then the undersea craft vanished and the men pulled about a mile from their ship. One dory started back, however, and the U-boat returned.

This time she circled, slamming shells into the Lark.

"There were 500 holes in the sails," Abbott related. Seven large holes were ripped in the hull. Abbott said a third type of weapon which he could not describe also was used.

Ship Hit Many Times.

When the sub opened up the second time, Abbott was in the pilot house. A shell screamed through it. He dropped to the deck and then sought safety near the bow. But more shells and machine gun bullets sprayed all around him.

"I said a few prayers," the captain asserted. "I knew a lot of boys were losing their lives over there and I thought I would take my medicine."

Eventually, he reached the stern and remained there unharmed.

Tracer bullets hit the Lark many times, he said, but failed to start any fires.

After twenty minutes the sub pulled away, leaving the ship apparently helpless with a damaged engine. The U-boat then went among the dories but did not fire.

Return To Port.

So close did the U-boat come to a dory that one fisherman, Herman Bichard, reached out and struck it with an oar, which broke. Five others were in the same dory.

During the shelling, Dan Maloney remembered he was the cook and set out to prepare food to take off if he had to abandon ship. The men in the dories had had no time to take either food or extra clothes.

The dories eventually returned to the Lark and the men got the Diesel motor started and then manned the pumps. The Lark shipped water en route home but the pumps averted further danger.

The Lark brought its catch in safely—105,000 pounds of ground fish, 70,000 pounds short of ca capacity.

Captain Abbott previously skippered the famed racing Gloucester fisherman, Gertrude Thebaud. He took that ship to the Chicago World Fair in 1933.

ROONEY INDUCTED AS DEFERMENT EXPIRES

Los Angeles (AP) The screen's Mickey Rooney has a new role and a new salary today. The Army gave him both.

A barracks bag slung over his shoulder, the 22-year-old inductee told reporters at nearby Fort MacArthur:

"This is the biggest thing in my life. It makes me happy to know they've accepted me."

Rooney inducted yesterday following a deferment granted to complete film work when he passed his physical last March. In March, 1943, Rooney was rejected for military service because, his mother said, Army doctors found he had a heart flutter and high blood pressure.

Predict Accord On Price Control Bill

Washington (UP)—Prominent Republican and Democratic congressmen predicted today that Senate-House conferees will be able to work out a compromise price control extension bill that will satisfy most OPA critics and still be acceptable to President Roosevelt.

The highly-amended measure was sent into conference late yesterday when the House completed action after a last minute decision to eliminate several provisions opposed by the administration.

Although the bill still contains sections opposed by the administration, Chairman Brent Spence, D., Ky., of the House Banking Committee and two ranking minority members, Reps. Jesse P. Wolcott, R., Mich., and Ralph Gamble, R., N. Y., believed the prospects for avoiding a presidential veto were improved.

They were confident that the conferees, who are scheduled to begin work tomorrow, would be able to compromise the House and Senate versions into a "good bill."

The conferees will go into their work mindful that Mr. Roosevelt can veto any measure which he thinks would destroy the price control program, thereby threatening congressional hopes to recess next week-end for the national political conventions.

Administration opposition to the House version appeared directed at amendments dealing with enforcement of OPA regulations. Richard Field, chief OPA counsel objected to amendments sponsored by Reps. Everett M. Dirksen, R., Ill., and Angier L. Goodwin, R., Mass.

The Dirksen amendment provides for District Court reviews of OPA regulations and the Goodwin amendment permits alleged violators to defend themselves on grounds that violations were not willful and were committed only after due precaution had been taken to prevent them.

ALLIES HOLD FIRM ALONG 100-MILE INVASION SECTOR

Yanks Six Miles from Last Cherbourg Rail Line; Nazi Losses Heavy

Supreme Headquarters Allied Expeditionary Force (AP)—American troops have surged powerfully ahead in their stab into the Cherbourg neck, Allied headquarters announced today, and Berlin reported that less than six miles separated the spearhead from the last west coast communications linking Cherbourg with France. The gains were hammered out in spite of furious counter-attacks all along the 100-mile invasion front in which the Germans had thrown about twenty divisions and 600 tanks.

Allied headquarters, confirming that American infantry and parachute troops, supported by tanks, had scored further gains west of Carentan, said Allied soldiers were holding firm everywhere else despite the massive nature of the German counter-stroke and were inflicting heavy losses on the enemy.

German Attacks Smashed.

This was after it was acknowledged that the British at the eastern end of the line had been forced to give up Troarn, their anchor nine miles east of Caen, and Villers-Bocage, one of their two advance points 15 miles southwest of Caen.

Further heavy counter-attacks in the Villers-Bocage area were turned back yesterday evening, headquarters said, and the British were still secure in their hold on Caumont, their other most advanced point, twenty miles southwest of Caen.

Seventeen German tanks, including eight sixty-ton Tigers, were knocked out in the fierce armored battling yesterday, headquarters said. The other eight tanks were Panthers armed with 77 mm. guns.

At the western end of the line, the Americans first moved forward on a nine-mile front to the Les Sablons-Baupte area, south of Ste. Mere Eglise and only about seven miles from high ground overlooking La Haye Du Puits on the west coast road and rail line leading to Cherbourg.

Yanks Back in Montebourg.

The Berlin radio commentator, Ludwig Sertorius, then reported that they had gained another three and one-half miles to the west, reaching Pretot, which is less than six miles from La Haye Du Puits itself.

The Americans also fought their way back into Montebourg, 14 miles from Cherbourg, and headquarters said street fighting was in progress. But the fighting here was fluid, and the Germans in mid-afternoon claimed they were again in possession of the town.

American troops also were engaged in heavy fighting in the Pont L'Abbe area, four miles north of Pretot, and along the road from Montebourg to Quineville on the coast.

The Americans hammered out gains, both in the Pont L'Abbe area and around Quineville, which represents the Allied right flank headquarters said.

Battle Approaches Climax.

The heavy nature of the fighting was plainly indicated by the German high command, which said the battle is "approaching a climax" and growing more violent every day with the Allies hitting hard in all directions to enlarge their beachhead.

The American advance was on a nine-mile front westward from Carentan toward high ground controlling the last German roads leading to Cherbourg.

Violent German reaction to the threat to the lifeline was expected, and it was likely that further American advances would be only after the costliest fighting.

American artillery was shelling the road from Montebourg to Valognes to the northwest, and the doughboys controlled the road from Quineville, on the coast, to Montebourg, but the town itself changed hands from hour to hour.

American airborne troops spearheaded the fighting around Carentan and besides pushing to the west shoved the Germans back more than a mile south of the town.

Allied troops driving southward along the central sector of the front were engaged in heavy fighting around Caumont and Villers-Bocage, with the Allies in Caumont

(Continued on Page 2.)

The Index

THE WEATHER
Tonight—Fair, cool.

THE TIMES RECORD

FINAL EDITION

SERIES 1944—NO. 172 (Entered as Second Class Matter at the Postoffice at Troy, N. Y., Under the Act of March 3, 1879.) TROY, N. Y., SATURDAY EVENING, JULY 22, 1944. (Published Daily Except Sunday) PRICE FOUR CENTS

German Naval Revolt Reported

Democrats Name U. S. Senator H. S. Truman For Vice President

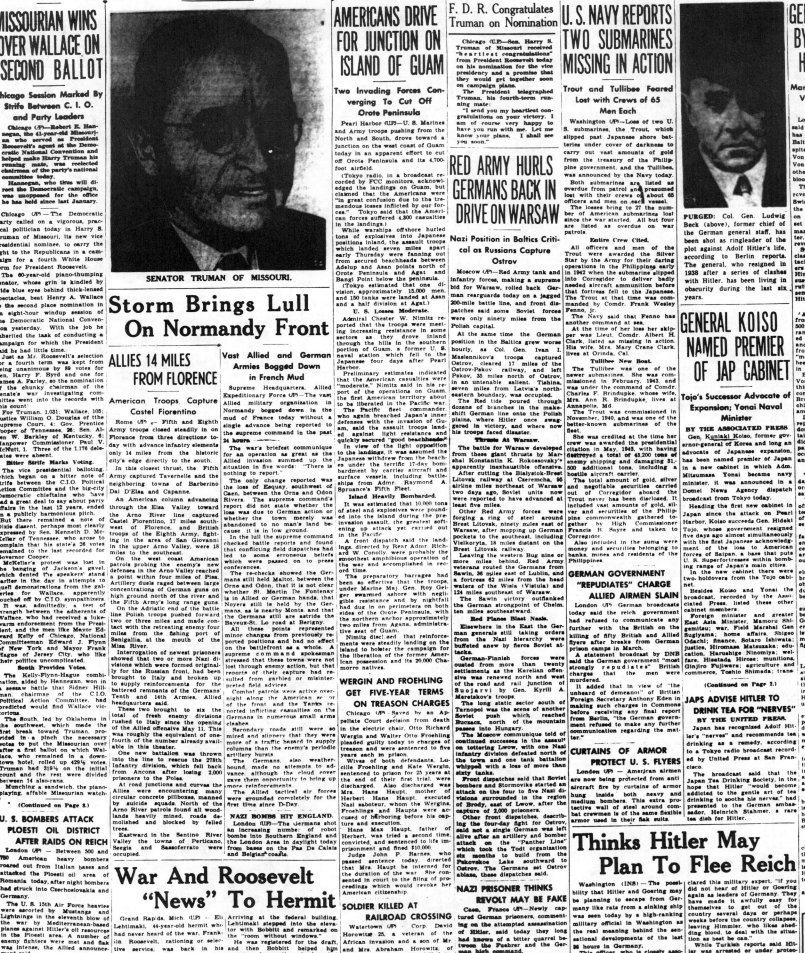

MISSOURIAN WINS OVER WALLACE ON SECOND BALLOT

Chicago Session Marked By Strife Between C. I. O. and Party Leaders

Chicago (AP)—Robert E. Hannegan, the 41-year-old Missourian who served as President Roosevelt's agent at the Democratic National Convention and helped make Harry Truman his running mate, was reelected chairman of the party's national committee today.

Hannegan, who thus will direct the Democratic campaign, was unopposed for the office he has held since last January.

Chicago (AP) — The Democratic Party called on a vigorous, practical politician today in Harry S. Truman of Missouri, its new vice presidential nominee, to carry the fight to the Republicans in a campaign for a fourth White House term for President Roosevelt.

The 60-year-old piano-thumping senator, whose grin is kindled by wide blue eyes behind thick-lensed spectacles, beat Henry A. Wallace to the second place nomination in an eight-hour windup session of the Democratic National Convention yesterday. With the job he inherited the task of conducting a campaign for which the President said he had little time.

Just as Mr. Roosevelt's selection for a fourth term was kept from being unanimous by 89 votes for Sen. Harry F. Byrd and one for James A. Farley, so the nomination of the chunky chairman of the Senate's war investigating committee went into the records with this count:

For Truman, 1.031; Wallace, 105; Justice William O. Douglas of tthe Supreme Court, 4; Gov. Prentice Cooper of Tennessee, 26; Sen. Alben W. Barkley of Kentucky, 6; Manpower Commissioner Paul V. McNutt, 1. Three of the 1.176 delegates were absent.

Bitter Strife Marks Voting.

The vice presidential balloting, which began on a bitter note of strife between the C.I.O. Political Action Committee and the big-city Democratic chieftains who have had a great deal to say about party affairs in the last 12 years, ended on a publicly harmonious pitch.

But there remained a note of Dixie dissent, perhaps most clearly expressed by Sen. Kenneth D. McKellar of Tennessee, who arose to complain that his state's 26 votes remained to the last recorded for Governor Cooper.

McKellar's protest was lost in the banging of Jackson's gavel, which dented the speakers' stand earlier in the day in attempts to quell demonstrations from the galleries for Wallace, apparently touched off by C.I.O. sympathizers.

It was, admittedly, a test of strength between the adherents of Wallace, who had received a lukewarm endorsement from the President, and the men like Mayor Edward Kelly of Chicago, National Committeeman Edward J. Flynn of New York and Mayor Frank Hague of Jersey City, who like their politics uncomplicated.

South Provides Votes.

The Kelly-Flynn-Hague combination, aided by Hannegan, won in a seesaw battle that Sidney Hillman, chairman of the C.I.O. Political Action Committee, had predicted would find Wallace victorious.

The South, led by Oklahoma in the southwest, which made the first break toward Truman, provided in a pinch the necessary votes to put the Missourian over after a first ballot on which Wallace, who remained in a downtown hotel, rolled up 429½ votes. Truman had 319½ on the initial count and the rest were divided between 14 also-rans.

Munching a sandwich, the piano-playing, affable Missourian watch-

(Continued on Page 8.)

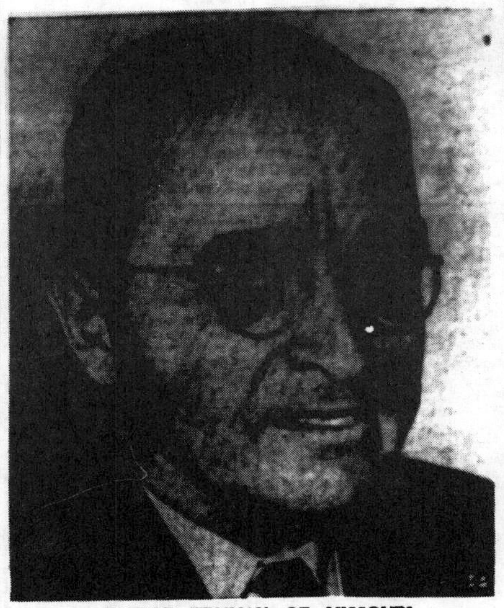

SENATOR TRUMAN OF MISSOURI.

Storm Brings Lull On Normandy Front

ALLIES 14 MILES FROM FLORENCE

American Troops Capture Castel Fiorentino

Rome (AP) — Fifth and Eighth Army troops closed steadily in on Florence from three directions today with advance infantry elements only 14 miles from the historic city's edge directly to the south.

In this closest thrust, the Fifth Army captured Tavernelle and the neighboring towns of Barberino Dal D'Elsa and Capanne.

An American column advancing through the Elsa Valley toward the Arno River line captured Castel Fiorentino, 17 miles southwest of Florence, and British troops of the Eighth Army, fighting in the area of San Giovanni in the upper Arno Valley, were 18 miles to the southeast.

On the west coast American patrols probing the enemy's new defenses in the Arno Valley reached a point within four miles of Pisa. Artillery duels raged between large concentrations of German guns on high ground north of the river and the Fifth Army's long range guns.

On the Adriatic end of the battle line Polish troops pushed forward two or three miles and made contact with the retreating enemy four miles from the fishing port of Senigallia, at the mouth of the Misa River.

Interrogation of newest prisoners showed that two or more Nazi divisions which were formed originally for the Russian front, had been brought to Italy and broken up to supply reinforcements for the battered remnants of the Germans' Tenth and 14th Armies, Allied headquarters said.

These two brought to six the total of fresh enemy divisions rushed to Italy since the opening of the Allied offensive May 11. This was roughly the equivalent of one-fourth of the number already available in this theater.

One new battalion was thrown into the line to rescue the 278th Infantry division, which fell back from Ancona after losing 2,000 prisoners to the Poles.

At road junctions and curves the Allies were encountering many circular concrete pillboxes, manned by suicide squads. North of the Arno River patrols found all woodlands heavily mined, roads demolished and blocked by felled trees.

Eastward in the Sentino River Valley the towns of Perticano, Seegia and Sassoferrato were occupied.

Vast Allied and German Armies Bogged Down in French Mud

Supreme Headquarters, Allied Expeditionary Force (UP)—The vast Allied military organization in Normandy bogged down in the mud of France today without a single advance being reported to the supreme command in the past 24 hours.

The war's briefest communique for an operation as great as the Allied invasion summed up the situation in five words: "There is nothing to report."

The only change reported was the loss of Esquay, southwest of Caen, between the Orne and Odon Rivers. The supreme command's report did not state whether the loss was due to German action or whether the town merely was abandoned to no man's land because it is in low ground.

In the lull the supreme command checked battle reports and found that conflicting field dispatches had led to some erroneous beliefs which were passed on to press conferences.

The re-checks showed the Germans still held Maltot, between the Orne and Odon, that it is not clear whether St. Martin De Fontenay is in Allied or German hands, that Noyers still is held by the Germans, as is nearby Monts, and that the Germans still are astride the Bayeux-St. Lo road at Berigny.

All these points represented minor changes from previously reported positions and had no effect on the battlefront as a whole. A supreme command spokesman stressed that these towns were not lost through enemy action, but that reports of their capture had resulted from garbled or misinterpreted field advices.

Combat patrols were active overnight along the American sector of the front and the Yanks reported inflicting casualties on the Germans in numerous small arms clashes.

Secondary roads still were so mired and slippery that they were more of a traffic hazard to supply columns than the enemy's periodic artillery bursts.

The Germans, also weather-bound, made no attempts to advance, although the cloud cover gave them opportunity to bring up more reinforcements.

The Allied tactical air forces were grounded completely for the first time since D-Day.

NAZI BOMBS HIT ENGLAND.

London (UP)—The Germans shot an increasing number of robot bombs into Southern England and the London Area in daylight today from bases on the Pas De Calais and Belgian coasts.

War And Roosevelt "News" To Hermit

Grand Rapids, Mich. (UP) — Eli Lehtimaki, 44-year-old hermit who had never heard of the war, Franklin Roosevelt, rationing or selective service, was back in his country shack today after the F. B. I. called his attention to the draft laws.

Howard Bobbitt, agent in charge at the Grand Rapids office of the Federal Bureau of Investigation, said Lehtimaki had been brought in because he had not registered for selective service.

The ride into Grand Rapids marked one of the few times the bearded, long-haired recluse had ridden in an automobile, and he said he never had been on a train.

Arriving at the federal building, Lehtimaki stepped into the elevator with Bobbitt and remarked on the "room without windows."

He was registered for the draft, and then Bobbitt helped him register for ration books, but Lehtimaki was dubious of their value to him, since he lives by hunting and fishing with occasional stretches of work at a lumber camp.

However, he avoided other workers at the camp for the same reason he originally took to the woods - he "hated people."

He was uninterested in stories of the war or of politics, and hurried back to the seclusion of his shack near Marquette after complying with all regulations.

U. S. BOMBERS ATTACK PLOESTI OIL DISTRICT AFTER RAIDS ON REICH

London (AP) — Between 500 and 750 American heavy bombers roared out from Italian bases and attacked the Ploesti oil area of Romania today, after night bombers had struck into Czechoslovakia and Germany.

The U. S. 15th Air Force heavies were escorted by Mustangs and Lightnings in the eleventh blow of the war by Mediterranean-based planes against Hitler's oil resources in the Ploesti area. A number of enemy fighters were met and flak was intense, the Allied announcement said.

By night, British Mosquitos bombed Berlin, and Italian-based bombers struck into Czechoslovakia for the second time in less than 24 hours, hammering an oil refinery at Pardubice, sixty miles east of Prag (Prague).

GEOLOGIST TO RETIRE.

Albany (AP) Dr Chris A. Hartnagle, state geologist, will retire in the fall, he disclosed today. He has been with the State Education Department for 44 years.

AMERICANS DRIVE FOR JUNCTION ON ISLAND OF GUAM

Two Invading Forces Converging To Cut Off Orote Peninsula

Pearl Harbor (UP)—U. S. Marines and Army troops pushing from the North and South, drove toward a junction on the west coast of Guam today in an apparent effort to cut off Orote Peninsula and its 4,700-foot airfield.

(Tokyo radio, in a broadcast recorded by FCC monitors, acknowledged the landings on Guam, but claimed that the Americans were "in great confusion due to the tremendous losses inflicted by our forces." Tokyo said that the American forces suffered 4,300 casualties in the landings.)

While warships offshore hurled tons of explosives into Japanese positions inland, the assault troops which landed seven miles apart early Thursday were fanning out from secured beachheads between Adelup and Asan points north of Orote Peninsula and Agat and Bangi Point below the peninsula.

(Tokyo estimated that one division, approximately 15,000 men, and 150 tanks were landed at Asan and a half division at Agat.)

U. S. Losses Moderate.

Admiral Chester W. Nimitz reported that the troops were meeting increasing resistance in some sectors as they drove inland through the hills in the southern portion of Guam, a former U. S. naval station which fell to the Japanese four days after Pearl Harbor.

Preliminary estimates indicated that the American casualties were "moderate." Nimitz said in his report of the operations on Guam, the first American territory about to be liberated in the Pacific war.

The Pacific fleet commander, who again breached Japan's inner defenses with the invasion of Guam, said the assault troops landed against light resistance and quickly secured "good beachheads."

In view of the light opposition to the landings, it was assumed the Japanese withdrew from the beaches under the terrific 17-day bombardment by carrier aircraft and surface vessels, including battleships from Admr. Raymond A. Spruance's Fifth Fleet.

Island Heavily Bombarded.

It was estimated that 10,000 tons of steel and explosives were pounded into the island during the pre-invasion assault, the greatest softening up attack yet carried out in the Pacific.

A front dispatch said the landings, directed by Rear Admr. Richard W. Conolly, were probably the smoothest amphibious operation of the war and accomplished in record time.

The preparatory barrages had been so effective that the troops, under Marine Maj. Gen. Roy Geiger swarmed ashore with negligible resistance and by nightfall had dug in on perimeters on both sides of the Orote Peninsula, with the northern anchor approximately two miles from Agana, administrative seat of Guam.

Nimitz disclosed that reinforcements were steadily landing on the island to bolster the campaign for the liberation of the former American possession and its 20,000 Chamorro natives.

WERGIN AND FROEHLING GET FIVE-YEAR TERMS ON TREASON CHARGES

Chicago (AP) - Saved by an Appellate Court decision from death in the electric chair, Otto Richard Wergin and Walter Otto Froehling pleaded guilty today to charges of treason and were sentenced to five years each in prison.

Wives of both defendants, Lucille Froehling and Kate Wergin, sentenced to prison for 25 years at the end of their first trial, were discharged. Also discharged was Mrs. Hans Haupt, mother of Herbert Hans Haupt, executed Nazi saboteur, whom the Wergins, Froehlings and Haupts were accused of harboring before his capture and execution.

Hans Max Haupt, father of Herbert, was tried a second time, convicted, and sentenced to life imprisonment and fined $10,000.

Judge John P. Barnes, who passed sentence today, directed that Mrs. Haupt be interned for the duration of the war. She consented in court to the filing of proceedings which would revoke her American citizenship.

SOLDIER KILLED AT RAILROAD CROSSING

Watertown (AP) - Corp. David Horowitz, 25, a veteran of the African invasion and a son of Mr. and Mrs. Abraham Horowitz, of New Haven, Conn., was killed today when his automobile struck a New York Central train. Horowitz recently was assigned to Pine Camp.

BRAZILIAN SHIP SUNK.

Rio De Janeiro (INS)—The Brazilian government announced today that the steamship Vital Olivetra has been sunk in the South Atlantic by an Axis submarine. Most of the crew from the Brazilian vessel has been landed safely in Rio De Janeiro, the statement added.

F. D. R. Congratulates Truman on Nomination

Chicago (UP)—Sen. Harry S. Truman of Missouri received "heartiest congratulations" from President Roosevelt today on his nomination for the vice presidency and a promise that they would get together soon on campaign plans.

The President telegraphed Truman, his fourth-term running mate:

"I send you my heartiest congratulations on your victory. I am of course very happy to have you run with me. Let me know your plans. I shall see you soon."

RED ARMY HURLS GERMANS BACK IN DRIVE ON WARSAW

Nazi Position in Baltics Critical as Russians Capture Ostrov

Moscow (AP)—Red Army tank and infantry forces, making a supreme bid for Warsaw, rolled back German rearguards today on a jagged 200-mile battle line, and front dispatches said some Soviet forces were only ninety miles from the Polish capital.

At the same time the German position in the Baltics grew worse hourly, as Col. Gen. Ivan I. Maslennikov's troops captured Ostrov, cleared 17 miles of the Ostrov-Pskov railway, and left Pskov, 35 miles north of Ostrov, in an untenable salient. Tishina, seven miles from Latvia's north-eastern boundary, was occupied.

The Red tide poured through dozens of branches in the make-shift German line onto the Polish plains, where Hitler once swaggered in victory, and where now his troops faced disaster.

Thrusts At Warsaw.

The battle for Warsaw developed from these giant thrusts by Marshal Konstantin K. Rokossovsky's apparently inexhaustible offensive.

After cutting the Bialystok-Brest Litovsk railway at Czeremcha, 95 airline miles northeast of Warsaw two days ago, Soviet units now were reported to have advanced at least five miles.

Other Red Army forces were forging a ring of steel around Brest Litovsk, ninety miles east of Warsaw, after mopping up German pockets to the southeast, including Vielkoryta, 18 miles distant on the Brest Litovsk railway.

Leaving the western Bug nine or more miles behind, Red Army veterans routed the Germans from Sawin, 36 miles east of Lublin, and a fortress 62 miles from the head waters of the Wisla (Vistula) and 124 miles southeast of Warsaw.

The Sawin victory outflanked the German strongpoint of Chelm, ten miles southeastward.

Red Planes Blast Nazis.

Elsewhere in the East the German generals still taking orders from the Nazi hierarchy were buffeted anew by fierce Soviet attacks.

German-Finnish forces were ousted from more than twenty settlements as the Karelian offensive was renewed north and west of the road and rail junction of Suojarvi by Gen. Kyrill A. Meretskov's troops.

The long static sector south of Tarnopol was the scene of another Soviet push which reached Buczacz, north of the mountain passes into Hungary.

The Moscow communique told of continued successes in the assault on tottering Lwow, with one Nazi infantry division defeated north of the town and one tank battalion whipped with a loss of more than sixty tanks.

Front dispatches said that Soviet bombers and Stormoviks started an attack on the four to five Nazi divisions surrounded in the region of Brody, east of Lwow, after the capture of 2,000 prisoners.

Other front dispatches, describing the four-day fight for Ostrov, said not a single German was left alive after an artillery and bomber attack on the "Panther Line" which took the Todt organization six months to build from the Pskovskoe Lake southward to Ostrov. The Germans set Ostrov ablaze, these dispatches said.

NAZI PRISONER THINKS REVOLT MAY BE FAKE

Caen, France (AP)—Newly captured German prisoners, commenting on the attempted assassination of Hitler, said today they long had known of a bitter quarrel between the Fuehrer and the German high command.

"The generals want to get Hitler out and make a quick end of the war," said Corporal Werner, 19, of Munster, a member of an Elite Nazi division. He was captured at 7 p.m. yesterday near Cagny.

"Of course the whole thing may be a fake to whip up sympathy of the German people for Hitler. Many of our people are sick to death of the war but when they hear the leader narrowly escaped death they say, 'what a terrible thing to attack our poor dear Fuehrer.'"

U. S. NAVY REPORTS TWO SUBMARINES MISSING IN ACTION

Trout and Tullibee Feared Lost with Crews of 65 Men Each

Washington (AP)—Loss of two U. S. submarines, the Trout, which slipped past Japanese shore batteries under cover of darkness to carry out vast amounts of gold from the treasury of the Philippine government, and the Tullibee, was announced by the Navy today.

Both submarines are listed as overdue from patrol and presumed lost with their crews of about 65 officers and men on each vessel.

The losses bring to 27 the number of American submarines lost since the war started. All but four are listed as overdue on war patrols.

Entire Crew Cited.

All officers and men of the Trout were awarded the Silver Star by the Army for their daring operations in the Philippines early in 1942 when the submarine slipped into Corregidor to deliver badly needed aircraft ammunition before that fortress fell to the Japanese. The Trout at that time was commanded by Comdr. Frank Wesley Fenno, jr.

The Navy said that Fenno has another command at sea.

At the time of her loss her skipper was Lieut. Comdr. Albert H. Clark, listed as missing in action. His wife, Mrs. Mary Crane Clark, lives at Orinda, Cal.

Tullibee New Boat.

The Tullibee was one of the newer submarines. She was commissioned in February, 1943, and was under the command of Comdr. Charles F. Brindupke, whose wife, Mrs. Ann R. Brindupke, lives at Annapolis, Md.

The Trout was commissioned in November, 1940, and was one of the better-known submarines of the fleet.

She was credited at the time her crew was awarded the presidential citation in May, 1943, with having destroyed a total of 43,200 tons of enemy shipping and damaging 31,500 additional tons, including a hostile aircraft carrier.

The total amount of gold, silver and negotiable securities carried out of Corregidor aboard the Trout never has been disclosed. It included vast amounts of gold, silver and securities of the Philippine commonwealth gathered together by High Commissioner Francis B. Sayre and taken to Corregidor.

Also included in the sums were money and securities belonging to banks, mines and residents of the Philippines.

GERMAN GOVERNMENT "REPUDIATES" CHARGE ALLIED AIRMEN SLAIN

London (AP) German broadcasts today said the reich government had refused to communicate any further with the British on the killing of fifty British and Allied flyers after breaks from German prison camps in March.

A statement broadcast by DNB said the German government "most strongly repudiates" British charges that the men were murdered.

It added that in view of "the unheard of demeanor of Britian Foreign Secretary Anthony Eden in making such charges in Commons before receiving any final report from Berlin, "the German government refused to make any further communication regarding the matter."

CURTAINS OF ARMOR PROTECT U. S. FLYERS

London (AP) — American airmen are now being protected from anti aircraft fire by curtains of armor hung inside both heavy and medium bombers. This extra protective wall of steel around combat crewmen is of the same flexible armor used in their flak suits.

Thinks Hitler May Plan To Flee Reich

Washington (INS) — The possibility that Hitler and Goering may be planning to escape from Germany like rats from a sinking ship was seen today by a high-ranking military official in Washington as the real meaning behind the sensational developments of the last 36 hours in Germany.

This officer, who is closely associated with the combined chiefs of staff, predicted that the German people may not hear from Hitler or Goering again.

He pointed out that Hitler has handed Germany over to Himmler, and Goering, though always jealous of his command of the Luftwaffe, has appointed another supreme commander (Colonel General Stumpf), and he and Hitler have said, "You can expect to get orders from someone else."

"I wouldn't be surprised," declared this military expert, "if you did not hear of Hitler or Goering again as leaders of Germany. They have made it awfully easy for themselves to get out of the country several days or perhaps weeks before the country collapses, leaving Himmler, who likes shedding blood, to deal with the situation as best he can."

While Turkish reports said Hitler was arrested or under protective custody, this view seemed to be strengthened by a broadcast from the clandestine German radio, "Atlantic," which declared that a four-motored transport plane, able to fly 10,000 miles, is standing by at a secret air base in Germany for Hitler's use.

According to this broadcast from within Germany, Hitler may be preparing to leave the country on this long-distance plane, the same plane which last year flew non-stop from Germany to Japan.

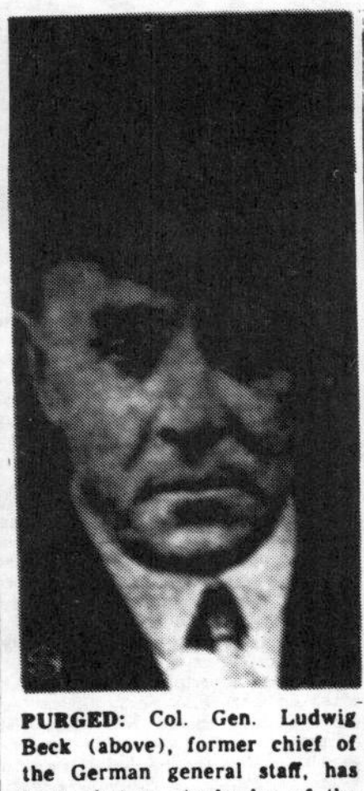

PURGED: Col. Gen. Ludwig Beck (above), former chief of the German general staff, has been shot as ringleader of the plot against Adolf Hitler's life, according to Berlin reports. The general, who resigned in 1938 after a series of clashes with Hitler, has been living in obscurity during the last six years.

GENERAL KOISO NAMED PREMIER OF JAP CABINET

Tojo's Successor Advocate of Expansion; Yonai Naval Minister

BY THE ASSOCIATED PRESS

Gen. Kuniaki Koiso, former governor-general of Korea and long an advocate of Japanese expansion, has been named premier of Japan in a new cabinet in which Adm. Mitsumasa Yonai became navy minister, it was announced in a Domei News Agency dispatch broadcast from Tokyo today.

Heading the first new cabinet in Japan since the attack on Pearl Harbor, Koiso succeeds Gen. Hideki Tojo, whose government resigned five days ago almost simultaneously with the first Japanese acknowledgment of the loss to American forces of Saipan, a base that puts U. S. Superfortresses within bombing range of Japan's main cities.

In the new cabinet there were two holdovers from the Tojo cabinet.

Besides Koiso and Yonai the broadcast, recorded by the Associated Press, listed these other cabinet members:

Foreign minister and greater East Asia Minister, Mamoru Shigemitsu; war, Field Marshal Gen Sugiyama; home affairs, Shigeo Odachi; finance, Sotaro Ishiwata; justice, Hiromasa Matsuzaka; education, Harushige Ninomiya; welfare, Hisatada Hirose; munitions, Ginjiro Fujiwara; agriculture and commerce, Toshio Shimada; trans-

(Continued on Page 2.)

JAPS ADVISE HITLER TO DRINK TEA FOR "NERVES"

BY THE UNITED PRESS.

Japan has recognized Adolf Hitler's "nerves" and recommends tea drinking as a remedy, according to a Tokyo radio broadcast recorded by United Press at San Francisco.

The broadcast said that the Japan Tea Drinking Society, in the hope that Hitler "would become addicted to the gentle art of tea drinking to soothe his nerves," had presented to the German ambassador, Heinrich Stahmer, a rare tea dish for Hitler.

GERMANY SWEPT BY BLOOD PURGE; HUNDREDS SLAIN

Marshals Von Runstedt and Von Brauchitsch Among Gestapo Victims

London (UP)—Swiss dispatches said today that a revolt in Germany has spread to naval units at the Baltic bases at Kiel and Stettin despite the execution of Marshal Gerd Von Runstedt, Marshal Walther Von Brauchitsch and hundreds of other officers in a growing Nazi blood purge.

The report that naval units had revolted came from Basel on the Swiss-German frontier and recalled the World War I mutiny at Kiel on Oct. 29, 1918—the spark that set off a revolution and led to Germany's capitulation a fortnight later. No details of the purported revolt were available, Basel said.

Swiss dispatches also reported clashes between regular army detachments and Nazi storm troopers and Gestapo units as Heinrich Himmler's raiding squads arrested suspects by the thousands in a ruthless effort to wipe out all semblance of opposition to Adolf Hitler.

Hundreds Executed.

A London daily mail dispatch from Stockholm estimated that 5,500 German officers of various ranks, including many from trusted SS divisions, had been arrested, and travelers arriving in Malmo from Berlin said they heard that "many hundreds" of officers had been executed in the greatest purge in German history.

Bern said frontier reports said Von Rundstedt, removed earlier this month as supreme German commander in the west, and Von Brauchitsch, former commander-in-chief of the German army, were among those put to death.

Despite the run of sensational reports of uprisings reaching London, Hitler appeared to be maintaining firm control of German radio stations, news agencies, newspapers and other key points whose occupation would be necessary for any successful revolt.

Hitler Denounces "Traitors."

The DNB news agency said today that Hitler yesterday issued an order of the day to the army which said:

"A small circle of unscrupulous officers committed a murderous attempt on me and the general staff of the armed forces in order to seize power in the state.

"Providence made the crime a failure. By the immediate and energetic intervention of loyal officers and soldiers of the home army, the traitor clique was wiped out or arrested within a few hours.

"I had not expected anything else. I know you are fighting bravely as up to now in exemplary obedience and loyal fulfillment of duty until in the end victory will be ours in spite of everything."

Responsible sources in London suggested that many stories were being spread purposely from non-German sources in order to increase the confusion presently existing in Germany and to undermine morale on German home and fighting fronts.

Army Revolt Rumored.

Unconfirmed reports reaching London from European sources said that army units in East Prussia had rebelled and been shot, that heavy fighting was going on in Bavaria and even that Adolf Hitler had been arrested or put under protective custody.

There appeared no doubt, however, that Heinrich Himmler, empowered by Hitler to restore order at all cost, was pressing ahead with his purge of anti-Nazi elements with a fury unparalleled even in the 1934 massacre.

The Germans themselves admitted that Hitler was determined this time to wipe out not only those involved in the incipient revolt and attempt on his life, but also all elements regarded as potential sources of opposition.

Dr. Robert Ley, Hitler's red-faced, bull-necked labor front leader, lashed out repeatedly as "blue-blooded swine" in a speech over Berlin radio that bordered constantly on hysteria.

Blames "Moscow Jews."

Addressing arms workers, Ley charged that "Moscow Jews gave the order for the heaviest caliber mine to be imported from England" and it was planted beside Hitler by German counts and aristocrats.

"These creatures must be annihilated," he said. "Every single Ger-

(Continued on Page 2.)

The Index

	Page
Classified	12-13
Cohoes	9
Comics	10
David Lawrence	6
Editorial	6
Obituary	2
Pulse of the People	6
Radio	10
Society	4
Sports	11
Theaters	8
Woman's Features	4

ALLIED FRIENDSHIP BEING SOUGHT AFTER BY ITALIAN LEADER

Rome (AP)—Premier Ivanoe Bonomi, taking over the Italian foreign ministry yesterday, said his government was a fervid friend of "all peoples which Fascism assaulted" and pledged future collaboration with the United States, Britain, Russia and France in order that "we may return to our past."

He described the armistice conditions which Italy accepted as "very hard," but said his government would respect them entirely. It would be unjust, however, he declared, if Italy were to be treated as a conquered nation, the same as those nations still allied with Germany.

SAVE THAT TIN!

Thirty-three pounds of tin are required to solder the electrical connections and alloy the bushings and bearings of a medium tank. This is approximately the tin content of 5,000 tin cans.

TROY SECTION HAS FIRST BLACKOUT IN THREE MONTHS

Municipal Officials Tour City; Four Violations Reported

With the element of complete surprise figuring heavily throughout, Troy acquitted itself excellently last night as the city experienced its first summer practice blackout for this year and, incidently, the first test in three months.

The entire warning period lasted nearly an hour, although the city was in complete darkness for only ten and one-half minutes from 9:30½ to 9:41 p.m. Homes were in darkness for a total of 35 minutes while the practice went through two blue warning periods as well as the red "danger" time.

Satisfactory Here.

For Troy, it was an adequate test for the functioning of the rearranged warning and control center which, from the time that blackouts were initiated, was the focal point for blackout controls but which now serves merely as the message and signal transmission center. The new arrangement functioned to perfection.

Trojans were momentarily in a quandary as the sirens sounded but speedily slipped back into routine. Wardens reported that with the first blue warning, many homes failed to darken although the greater percentage remembered past lessons. The delinquents speedily were brought into line.

In the entire city there were only four reports of major violations, with lights showing throughout the blackout and with no facilities for extinguishing them. Warnings will be issued in all cases with the admonition that future violations will bring penalties. All four cases were in the center of the city.

That Trojans were taken by surprise was evidenced by the fact that four presons called The Record Newspapers and, with indignant voices, protested the unfairness of a surprise blackout particularly since they had been led to belive that blackouts would be discontinued.

This belief apparently existed in the face of recent announcements by the State Office of Civilian Protection that practice blackouts may be expected at least at intervals of three months.

Tour City.

During the blackout period, the city was toured by Mayor John J. Ahern, Police Chief Frank B. Kendall and Commissioner of Public Safety Frank M. Ames. They reported few instances of noticeable violations except the four major cases, and it was noted that air raid wardens were prominently in action. During their twenty minute ride about the city they found volunteer protective workers in evidence everywhere.

With the new arrangement at the control center, operations are in charge of a small group including the mayor and police officials, City Clerk James M. McGrath and Thomas J. Larkin, superintendent of the fire alarm system. Last night, Dr. James C. Boland, new city health commissioner, was present at the control center to witness the general functions in the first blackout in which he has participated in official capacity.

Other services which normally were part of the control center functioned in their regular offices. These included Chief Carl A. Smith in charge at central fire headquarters: William F. Luby, commissioner of public works, at his office; Edward L. Ryan, chief air raid warden, at his office; George D. Gray and George Matthews, at the office of the New York Power and Light Corp.

Control Setup.

The control center now receives all calls and complaints and issues all signals and messages. Complaints or calls for assistance are rerouted to their proper destination. Under the previous system, such calls were given to individuals in the control room and then were transmitted to proper destination by direct wire.

Signals, as received at the Troy center and then transmitted to surrounding cities and to rural Rensselaer County and points in Washington and Saratoga Counties, were noted on the following schedule: Yellow warning, 9:03 p.m.: preliminary blue warning, 9:21 p.m.; red signal 9:30¼ p.m.; secondary blue, 9:41 p.m.; all clear, 9:56 p.m.

The blackout, for which permission was given by the Army's Second Service Command, embraced most of the state north of New York. War plants merely tested control switches and then continued in operation.

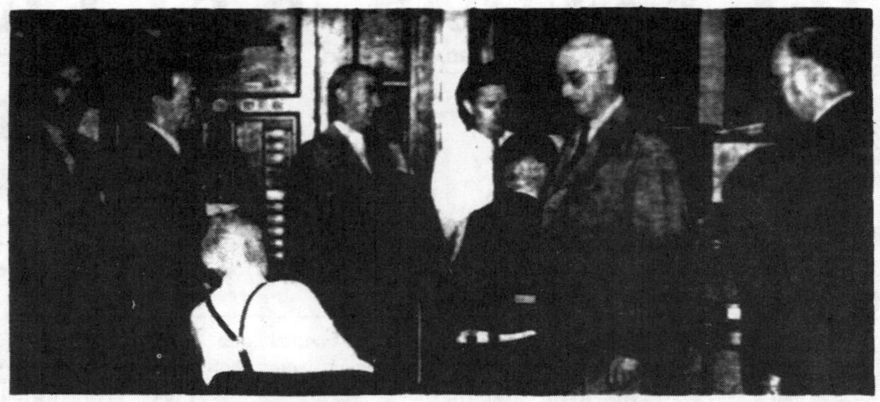

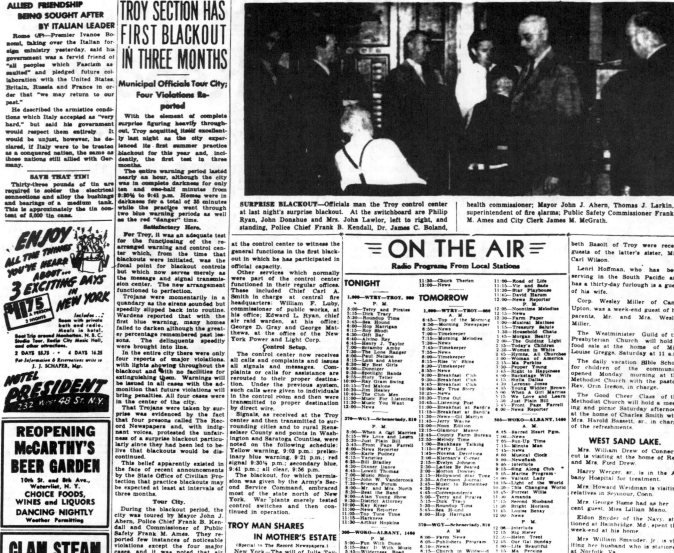

SURPRISE BLACKOUT—Officials man the Troy control center at last night's surprise blackout. At the switchboard are Philip Ryan, John Donahue and Mrs. John Lawlor, left to right, and standing, Police Chief Frank B. Kendall, Dr. James C. Boland, health commissioner; Mayor John J. Ahern, Thomas J. Larkin, superintendent of fire alarms; Public Safety Commissioner Frank M. Ames and City Clerk James M. McGrath.

TROY MAN SHARES IN MOTHER'S ESTATE

(Special to The Record Newspapers.)

New York—The will of Julia Taylor Rhodes, who died on June 17 last and was the mother of Benjamin C. Rhodes of 10 Eaton Road Troy, on file for probate here with Surrogate James A. Delehanty, leaves to the son one-quarter of the residuary estate outright. All personal effects are to be distributed by him, according to a letter left for his guidance.

Among others is divided the remaining three-quarters of the residue, plus $7,000.

As yet no date has been set for the proving of the document, executed on April 2, 1937, and which names Benjamin Rhodes, son, as the executor of the estate which according to the petition, is "more than $20,000" in personal property.

GRAFTON.

Bobby Cone visited his cousin, Jack Gapp, the last week.

Frank Corbin is building John Church's house on the South Road.

Jackie Powers celebrated her third birthday with a party Saturday.

Walter W. Poole of Sampson is spending a few days at his home here.

Rev. and Mrs. Paul Maxon of Berlin were Sunday dinner guests of Mrs. Nettie Klaus.

Miss Joan Mullahey of Watervliet spent the week-end with Miss Marilyn Harlow and family.

Sharon Gapp fell from her bicycle recently, cutting her chin; three stitches were taken.

William Odell was operated on at the Mary McClellan Hospital at Cambridge Thursday for appendicitis.

Jack Gapp and Billy Hogan went on a fishing trip with their grandfather, John Foley, to Lake Champlain.

Miss Marie Clancy, Mrs. Mae Scheafer and David Callahan, all of Troy, are spending the week at Mrs. F. A. Babcock's.

The Pioneer Club was organized July 18 by John Gapp, president; Edward Sheridan, chairman; Robert Foster, treasurer; Ronny Lamphere, secretary, and Donald Raymond, assistant secretary. The other members are Harold Foster and Jerry Simmons.

ROUND LAKE.

Mrs. Burr D. Vail was hostess to the summer group of her contract club recently.

Miss Mabel Blanchard has been entertaining Mrs. Bernadine Boyd of St. Petersburg, Fla.

Mr. and Mrs. Waley Wilson of Lake Placid are guests at the home of their son, Lawrence S. Wilson, and family.

Malta Grange will meet Thursday evening. Mr. and Mrs. George W. Corp and Mrs. Mary Adams are in charge of the refreshments.

Mrs. Jesse W. Pitts has returned from visiting her son-in-law and daughter, Mr. and Mrs. Carl Anderson, at West Hartford, Conn., the last six weeks.

Mr. and Mrs. Rufus G. Sutherland of Albany were week-end guests of Mr. and Mrs. Dalton H. Blanchard. Mr. and Mrs. Sutherland were summer residents here many years.

At the recent meeting of the Board of Education the following officers were named: President, Mrs. W. Merritt Goddard; treasurer, George F. Turpit; collector (district), Mrs. Emma McKean; janitor and attendance officer, H. Beecher Williams. The position of clerk remains to be filled.

ON THE AIR

Radio Programs From Local Stations

TONIGHT

1,000—WTRY—TROY, 980

P. M.

5:00—Terry and Pirates
5:15—Dick Tracy
5:30—Roundup Time
5:45—Sea Hound
6:00—Hop Harrigan
6:15—Roy Shudt
6:30—Gift Bar
6:40—Alvino Rey
6:45—Henry J. Taylor
7:00—Scramby Amby
7:30—The Lone Ranger
8:00—Paul Neilson
8:15—Lum and Abner
8:30—My Best Girls
9:00—Dunniger
9:30—Spotlight Bands
9:55—Story Teller
10:00—Ray Gram Swing
10:15—Ted Malone
10:30—Jim Healey
10:40—The Club Men
11:00—Music For Listening
11:30—Music You Want
12:00—News

370—WGY—Schenectady, 810

P. M.

5:00—When A Girl Marries
5:15—We Love and Learn
5:30—Just Plain Bill
5:45—Front Page Farrell
6:00—News Reporter
6:05—Earle Pudney
6:15—Varieties
6:25—Bill Bradley
6:30—Dinner Dance
6:45—Lowell Thomas
7:00—Music Shop
7:15—John W. Vandercook
7:30—Science Forum
8:00—Mr. and Mrs. North
8:30—Beat the Band
9:00—Alan Young Show
9:30—District Attorney
10:00—Kay Kyser
11:00—News Reporter
11:05—Top Tune Time
11:15—Harkness
11:30—Arthur Hopkins

305—WOKO—ALBANY, 1460

P. M.

5:00—Fun With Dunn
5:15—Say It With Music
5:45—Wilderness Road
6:00—News
6:15—Lynn Murray
6:30—Supper Melodies
6:45—The World Today
6:55—Meaning of the News
7:00—I Love a Mystery
7:15—Passing Parade
7:30—Easy Aces
8:00—Allan Jones
8:30—Dr. Christian
8:55—Bill Henry
9:00—Jack Carson
9:30—Mildred Bailey
10:00—Moments in Music
10:30—The Colonel
11:00—News
11:15—Harold Stern
11:30—Chuck Therien
12:00—News

TOMORROW

1,000—WTRY—TROY—980

A. M.

6:45—Top of the Morning
6:50—Morning Newspaper
6:55—News
7:00—Timekeeper
7:15—Morning Melodies
7:30—News
7:45—Timekeeper
7:55—News
8:00—Timekeeper
8:15—Rise 'n' Shine
8:30—Timekeeper
8:55—News
9:00—Breakfast Club
9:30—Breakfast Club
9:45—Breakfast Club
10:00—My True Story
10:25—News
10:30—Time Out
10:45—Listening Post
11:00—Breakfast at Sardi's
11:15—Breakfast at Sardi's
11:30—News—Gil Martyn
11:45—Jerry Wayne
12:00—Noon Edition
12:15—Glamour Manor
12:45—County Farm Bureau
12:55—Melody Time
1:00—Baukhage Talking
1:15—Party Line
1:45—Novena Devotions
2:00—Kiernan's Corner
2:15—Evelyn Johnson
2:30—Ladies Be Seated
3:00—Morton Downey
3:15—Hollywood Star Time
3:30—Afternoon Journal
3:45—Music to Remember
4:30—News
4:45—Correspondents
5:00—Terry and Pirates
5:15—Dick Tracy
5:30—Roundup Time
5:45—Sea Hound
6:00—Hop Harrigan

370—WGY—Schenectady, 810

A. M.

6:00—Farm News
6:05—Publishers Program
6:10—News
6:15—Church in Wildwood
6:30—Voice of the Army
6:45—Song Shop
7:00—News Reporter
7:35—Time to Shine
7:45—News
8:00—Morning Melodies
8:15—Meet the Band
9:00—Mirth and Madness
9:15—Morning Moods
9:30—News
9:45—Aunt Jenny
10:00—Lora Lawton
10:15—Robert St. John
10:30—Finders Keepers
10:45—Recipe Contest
10:50—Victory Garden
11:00—Road of Life
11:15—Vic and Sade
11:30—Star Playhouse
11:45—David Harum
12:00—News Reporter

P. M.

12:05—Noontime Melodies
12:15—News
12:30—Farm Paper
1:00—Musical Matinee
1:15—Treasury Salute
1:30—Household Chats
1:45—Morgan Beatty
2:00—The Guiding Light
2:15—Today's Children
2:30—Women in White
2:45—Hymns, All Churches
3:00—Woman of America
3:15—Ma Perkins
3:30—Pepper Young
3:45—Right to Happiness
4:00—Backstage Wife
4:15—Stella Dallas
4:30—Lorenzo Jones
4:45—Young Widder Brown
5:00—When A Girl Marries
5:15—We Love and Learn
5:30—Just Plain Bill
5:45—Front Page Farrell
6:00—News Reporter

305—WOKO—ALBANY, 1460

A. M.

6:45—Sacred Heart Pgm.
7:00—News
7:05—Sun-Up Time
7:15—Minute Man
7:45—News
8:00—Musical Clock
9:00—Newsflash
9:05—Interlude
9:15—Sing Along Club
9:45—Marine Program
10:00—Valiant Lady
10:15—Light of the World
10:30—This Changing World
10:45—Forrest Willis
11:00—Amanda
11:15—Second Husband
11:30—Bright Horizon
11:45—Louise Benay
12:00—News

P. M.

12:05—Interlude
12:15—Big Sister
12:30—Helen Trent
12:45—Our Gal Sunday
1:00—Life Beautiful
1:15—Ma Perkins
1:30—Bernadine Flynn
1:45—The Goldbergs
2:00—Portia Faces Life
2:15—Joyce Jordan, M. D.
2:30—Young Dr. Malone
2:45—Perry Mason
3:00—Mary Marlin
3:15—The Jubilaires
3:30—Yours Truly
4:00—Broadway Matinee
4:25—Interlude
4:30—Program
4:45—Hollywood Soundstage
5:00—Fun With Dunn
5:15—Say It With Music
5:45—Wilderness Road
6:00—News

POWNAL.

Mr. and Mrs. Sidney Clayton of Yonkers are at the home of her parents, Mr. and Mrs. George H. Dunn, for this week.

Victory Guard and 4-H members, with their parents and local and county leaders, held a picnic Sunday at Sand Springs.

Mrs. James H. Krom will entertain the Women's Society at Hinge Hutch, her summer home on Northwest Hill, tomorrow afternoon.

Mrs. Charles Moon, accompanied by her two children and her young brother, of Philadelphia, are visiting Mrs. Jennie Moon of Mountain Street. Her husband is on duty with the Pacific war fleet.

AVERILL PARK.

Mr. and Mrs. James Cox of Schenectady are the guests of Mrs. Howard Stouring.

Miss Sarah Hans of Troy was a recent guest of Mr. and Mrs. George Kershner.

Miss Florence A. Helms of East Schodack is a guest of Mr. and Mrs. Lester Helms.

Mrs. Sarah McCullean, who spent the last two years in Florida with relatives has returned home.

Charles R. Roney, A. S., who is in the V-12 at Dartmouth was a week-end guest of his parents, Mr. and Mrs. Garner Roney.

Misses Sylvia Zimmer and Elizabeth Basolt of Troy were recent guests of the latter's sister, Mrs. Carl Wilson.

Lenri Hoffman, who has been serving in the South Pacific and has a thirty-day furlough is a guest of his wife.

Corp. Wesley Miller of Camp Upton, was a week-end guest of his parents, Mr. and Mrs. Wesley Miller.

The Westminister Guild of the Presbyterian Church will hold a food sale at the home of Miss Louise Greggs, Saturday at 11 a.m.

The daily vacation Bible School for children of the community opened Monday morning at the Methodist Church with the pastor, Rev. Orin Ireson, in charge.

The Good Cheer Class of the Methodist Church will hold a meeting and picnic Saturday afternoon at the home of Charles Smith with Mrs. Harold Bassett, sr., in charge of the refreshments.

WEST SAND LAKE.

Mrs. William Drew of Connecticut is visiting at the home of Rev. and Mrs. Fred Drew.

Harry Werger, sr., is in the Albany Hospital for treatment.

Mrs. Howard Weidman is visiting relatives in Seymour, Conn.

Mrs. George Bame had as her recent guest, Miss Lillian Mano.

Eldon Snyder of the Navy, stationed at Bainbridge, Md., spent the week-end at his home.

Mrs. William Smauder, jr., is visiting her husband who is stationed at Norfolk, Va.

Mr. and Mrs. Robert Hastings and sons are spending the week at Lake George.

Mr. and Mrs. Edward Bower of Lyndhurst, L. I., are visiting Mr. and Mrs. George Bame here.

The members of the Trinity Lutheran Sunday School will hold their annual picnic Saturday on the church grounds.

Prayer service will be held at the Salem Evangelical Church Thursday at 7:45 p.m. The Sunday School will hold their picnic Saturday, Aug. 23, on the church lawn.

TROY CHAPLAIN'S HEROISM CITED IN MAGAZINE ARTICLE

"Padre of Piva Trail" Depicts Career of Rev. Robert J. Cronin

The exploits of Navy Chaplain Lieut. (j.g.) Robert James Cronin, which earned for the former assistant pastor of St. Peter's Church, of Troy, the Silver Star, are recounted in a national pictorial magazine article.

In an installment of an "American Heroes Series," entitled "The Padre of Piva Trail," the article describes the action which took place during and after the invasion of Bougainville by the Marines' Third Raider Battalion.

The article describes the action in part by saying:

"He went in with the first waves. He pushed forward, risked his life time and time again helping the wounded, dying and the dead. In a crisis on Piva Trail, he thought quickly and made it possible for the Marines to pass the ammunition up front. Lieutenant Cronin, who had volunteered for his perilous assignment, stuck with the Raiders throughout their two months on Bougainville, and was awarded the Silver Star."

Lieutenant Cronin, 38, is a native of Glens Falls, was educated at Holy Cross and Niagara University, and was stationed at St. Peter's and the Cathedral of the Immaculate Conception in Albany.

LEVINGS METHODIST CHURCH PLANS TO SELL STOW HILL MISSION

The Board of Trustees of the Levings Methodist Church has been authorized to sell a piece of property known as Stow Hill Mission by Judge Harry E. Clinton at a special term of County Court held in chambers. The property, located on the north side of Cottage Street, will be purchased by William J. Hipwell for $500.

The church corporation has no use for the chapel, and its sale was authorized by more than a two-thirds vote of the corporate body at a congregational meeting called especially for the purpose of deciding upon the disposition of the building. The cash received from the sale will be used for repairs and improvements on other church property. Pastor of the church is Rev. William H. Kroeger.

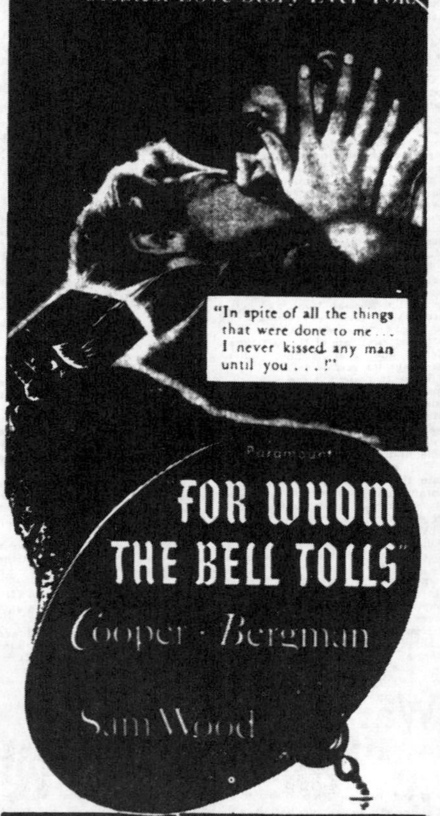

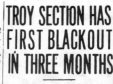

Zarilla's 654 Hitting Spree Keeps Browns At Top Of American League

GETS THREE HITS AS ST. LOUIS CLUB DEFEATS A'S, 8-5

Has Garnered 17 Hits in His Last 26 Times at Bat

BY JACK HAND.
Associated Press Sports Writer.

Al Zarilla's amazing hitting spree for a .654 average in the last seven Brownie games was accepted today in baseball circles as one of the chief factors keeping the St. Louis Americans out front in the junior loop flag chase despite the rush of Boston and Cleveland.

When Zarilla stepped into the lineup last Sunday to replace Left Fielder Chet Laabs, who had set the league on fire with a home run streak two years ago, he was just another guy from Toledo. Last night's three hits as the Browns thumped Philadelphia, 8-5, upped his total to 17 in his last 26 at bats and boosted his all-season mark to .301. Most of his appearances have been reserved for opposition right handed pitching and he has been hitting them like he owned them.

As the Browns finished business with the A's and prepared to welcome the slumping Washington Senators, they had won 7 of 12 starts against eastern clubs on the current home stand and boasted a 3½ game lead on New York and Boston, virtually tied for second although the Yanks held a 1-point edge.

Boston clubbed Detroit's Dizzy Trout for a lopsided 15-5 pasting yesterday as Emmett O'Neil chalked up his third win. In taking 7 of 11 from the western teams, the Sox hit the ball at a .315 clip to make up for spotty hurling. The Yanks split their set with Cleveland by taking a 13-7 verdict for Ernie Bonham's sixth straight victory. Nick Etten and Johnny Lindell chipped in homers to help hand Al Smith his eighth loss.

Chicago got a neat 8-hit job by rookie Ed Lopat to trim Washington, 8-2. Johnny Dickshot's bases-loaded triple off Lefty Lefebvre sparked a 5-run Chicago third inning as the White Sox pulled even with the .500 mark and sent the Sens down for their 11th loss in 12 games. Jimmy Dykes' men, who have played fewer games than any other club in the league, moved to within six lengths of the top to again become serious contenders.

Bill Voiselle of the New York Giants blanked Pittsburg, 4-0, for his 13th victory and first shut out to take over the strike out lead of the majors at 101.

Bob Chipman defeated his old Brooklyn mates for the second time as he hurled Chicago to a 4-1 edge with the help of some heavy clouting by Stan Hack and Ival Goodman. Philadelphia, Boston, St. Louis and Cincinnati were not scheduled in the National.

RACE RESULTS

ROCKINGHAM.

1st.—Cl., 4 yr. up, 6 f., off 2:32½.
Lucky B. (V. Bovine) 10.20 5.00 4.20
Flaming High (H. Claggett) 4.20 3.20
Balmand (C. Bachman) 6.00
Time—1:15 2-5. Mack's Dream, Chant Thru, Back Tooth, Cute Eye, Sun Ivy, Private Earl also ran.

2nd.—Cl., 3 yr., 6 f., off 3:01½.
Good China (W. Turnbull) 29.40 13.00 7.40
Light Sandwich (P. Patterson) 11.00 5.50
Payable (J. Brennan) 3.60
Time—1:15 4-5. Dear Bridget, Renraw, Walloon, Peach Cobbler, Dear Miss, Emerson, Barnacle, Miss Menow also ran.
DAILY DOUBLE: Lucky B. and Good China paid $305.00.

3rd.—Cl., 2 yr., 5½ f., off 3:33.
Fijord (W. Turnbull) 16.20 6.00 4.20
Cat Lady (H. Trent) 3.80 3.00
Queensnon (C. Bachman) 5.00
Time—1:09 1-5. Lovan Day, Exit, Dark Morning, Oakling also ran.

4th.—Cl., 3 yr. up, 6 f., off 4:04.
Lost Gold (H. Claggett) 5.00 3.00 2.80
Fire Kabo (E. Blanco) 6.00 5.00
Hardship (P. Patterson) 4.80
Time—1:14 2-5. Torch Lee, Halycon Boy, Hy-Cop, Cherriko, Over Ice, Friar's Scout also ran.

5th.—All., 3 yr. up, 6 f., off 4:34½.
dhVim (E. Gross) 2.60 2.20 2.00
dhEllen Mist (H. Trent) 4.00 3.60 3.20
Railreader (V. Bovine) 11.00
Time—1:14 2-5. Tracelette, Eaglestone, Calm Port, Pompous Fox, Jes Lov Me, Sweep Call, Madam Mamie, Smoothy, Alport also ran.
dh—Dead heat for first position.

6th.—All., 3 yr. up, 1 1-16 mi., off 5:04½.
Darby Ducat (W. Balzaretti) 5.80 3.00 2.40
Scotch Abbot (E. Gross) 3.80 2.80
Midnight Ride (E. Blanco) 3.80
Time — 1:50. Procia, Ancipital, Total Eclipse, Sir Kid also ran.

7th.—Cl., 3 yr. up, 1 1-16 mi., off 5:35.
Rest Awhile (G. McMullen) 21.80 9.20 5.40
Credentials (H. Trent) 7.00 5.20
Bowling Green (L. Kerr) 10.20
Time—1:52. Thalel, First Girl, Big Raid, Galful, Nediana, Dark Cluod also ran.

8th.—Cl., 4 yr. up, 1 3-16 mi., off 6:04½.
Janca (E. Gross) 5.00 3.80 2.00
Straight Lead (M. Fator) 23.00 6.40
Helen Mewise (H. Trent) 3.60
Time — 2:04 4-5. Ovando, Cumshaw, Stormy Night, War Communique also ran.

GARDEN CITY.

1st.—Cl., 4 yr. up, 1 1-16 mi., off 2:33.
a-Satin Cap (W. Cook) 11.10 4.80 3.80
Alhalon (J. Breen) 3.30 2.60
Grand Stop (W. Vassar) 7.40
Time—1:55 3-5. Miss Kalola, Lauerman, Swell Time, Kaltain, a-Sally of Erin, Mickey Curran, Peacemaker, Milky Moon also ran.
a—Garisto and McCallum entry.

2nd.—Spc. wgts., 3 yr., 6 f., off 3:11½.
Balburnie (W. Mann) 11.80 5.80 3.70
Chanco Bras (W. Cook) 22.60 12.00
Sting Lee (A. Daniels) 10.30
Time—1:15 2-5. Be Favored, Lanlast, War Peak, Susan's Trick, If It also ran.
DAILY DOUBLE—Satin Cap and Balburnie paid $78.00.

3rd.—Cl. 3 yr., 6 f., off 3:40½.
Doctor Jeep (S. Clark) 6.60 4.30 4.10
Postwar Style (J. Breen) 9.10 6.20
New Flame (R. Best) 12.00
Time—1:14 4-5. Parasun, Mabel Daubel, Black Africa, Little Milly, Triple Scotch also ran.

4th.—All., 2 yr., 6 f., off 4:09.
[illegible]eating (J. McCoy) 19.20 7.80 5.00
Lycotna (J. Gilbert) 4.20 3.60
Rax (L. Knapp) 4.40
Time—1:15 1-5. Belpast, Belwyn, Belfonda, Ginokum also ran.

5th.—All., 3 yr., 6 f., off 4:46½.
[illegible] (J. Breen) 10.70 4.70 3.40
Fortify (J. Becker) 3.80 2.70
Mahatone (N. Coule) 6.80
Time—1:13 2-5. Sumoor, Riar Red, Hi.. Fox, Bride's Biscuit, Pin Up Girl a.. ran.

[illegible] yr. up 1 mi., off 5:07.
Bright Argosy (T. Luther) 63.10 18.80 7.80
Barford (S. Mondo) 3.80 3.70
Phantom Player (N. Bernardo) 3.60
Time—1:41 4-5. Pittsburg, Top Transit, Mugwump, Mae Case also ran.

7th.—Cl., 3 yr. up, 1 mi. and 70 yds., off 5:36½.
Red Rosette (R. Root) 11.80 4.30 3.20
Orpheum (J. Breen) 3.00 2.60
Elbanga (S. Clark) 3.40
Time—1:46 3-5. Dandy Fox, Arakan also ran.

8th.—Cl., 3 yr., 1 1-16 mi., off 6:06.
Paola's Star (F. Zehr) 8.60 4.70 3.20
a-Big Punch (W. Gorieck) 7.00 4.50
Consignment (A. Snellings) 3.80
Time—1:51 4-5. Tigmore, Sun Tip, Shell Rock, Nida Barker, a-Rennie also ran.
a—Schoch and Haggerty entry.

JAMAICA.
(Empire City Meet.)

1st.—Cl., 2 yr., 5½ f., off 1:38.
Ellen's Slam (T. Atkinson) 4.10 3.10 2.80
Princess R. L. (F. Maschek) 7.00 4.90
Torch Ginger (M. Lindberg) 4.90
Time—1:06 4-5. Victory News, King Appell, Genial Sam S., Watch Henry, Hada Bar, Zacawon also ran.

2nd.—Cl., 3 yr. up, m., 1 1-6 mi., off 2:08½.
Omaloe (T. Atkinson) 21.80 8.30 6.10
Bay Magic (D. Meade) 8.00 4.70
Edahaste (L. Leveridge) 17.30
Time—1:48. Flame Opal, Agrarist, Briarlass, Pinefa, Jetta T., Didi B., Clan O'Gale, Oakford, Sun Banner also ran.
DAILY DOUBLE: Ellen's Slam and Omaloe paid $62.80.

3rd.—Cl., 3 yr. up, 6 f., off 2:45.
Sirlette (J. Longden) 15.20 3.80 3.00
Hubbub (B. Mills) 6 3.80 3.00
Miss Sugar (T. Atkinson) 3.00
Time—1:11 4-5. Buzalong, My Zaca, Showtown, Capetown, Sea Convoy also ran.

4th.—Mdn., 2 yr., 5½ f., off 3:17.
March Scholar (D. Meade) 29.10 16.00 6.80
Miss Zibby (T. Atkinson) 16.00 8.80
Smart Bit (A. Snider) 5.30
Time—1:06 3-5. Dine 'n' Dance, Meadow Maid, Mai, Sis Brownie also ran.

5th.—H'cap, 3 yr. up, 6 f., off 3:52.
Westwood Belle (F. Zufelt) 7.60 4.00 2.90
Bed Grey (H. Woodhouse) 8.70 5.50
Lou-Bre (D. Meade) 4.00
Time—1:12 2-5. Sir Drake, Change Here, Wild Rice, Return Call, Okapi Lancer, Seal Rock also ran.

6th.—All., 3 yr. up, 1 1-6 mi., off 4:23½.
Moon Maiden (T. Atkinson) 3.10 2.40 2.30
Peppy Miss (R. Merritt) 3.00 2.60
Barlided (R. Guerin) 3.30
Time—1:45 1-5. Esterita, Blue Flight, Dairy Lady, Hopeville, Crystal also ran.

7th.—Cl., 4 yr. up, 1 1-16 mi., off 4:56½.
Sun Flame (D. Meade) 9.30 5.40 3.40
This Air (H. Jones) 16.80 6.00
Art of War (R. Guerin) 4.80
Time—1:46 2-5. Brown Saxon, Sight, Yukon, Chance Grey, Ben Gray, Psychiatrist, Baruna, Dead Level, Betty's Bobby also ran.

Sam Riddle Still Active Around Oval

BY FRITZ HOWELL
(Pinch-hitting for Hugh Fullerton.)

New York (AP)—Bits of this and that from here and there.

Hal Trosky of the Chicago White Sox chews tobacco in bed...Johnny Dickshot of the same club packs in snuff and sleeps like a babe from curew until breakfast...Marty McManus, the old St. Louis Brownie, is still in baseball—managing the Kenosha Comets in the American Girls Professional League... Herman Taylor, Philly boxing promoter who used to smoke four packs a day, quit just like that four years ago and hasn't touched a cigarette since...The St. Louis Cards are winning so easily and often that the baseball bookies are planning to "build a fence around 'em" so far as betting is concerned ...George Magerkurth, the umpire, had 76 professional fights before turning to baseball—and he hasn't lost a decision as an arbiter.

Do You Know, Dept.?

No. 1—Who was the only player to win the home run championship in both major leagues?

No. 2—Who was the only pitcher to lead both major leagues in winning percentages?

(Don't look now—the answers are at the end.)

Introducing—

Ford Andrews, the Huronite, Huron, S. D.: "Two men are outside," an usher said to the manager just before Sunday's game. "They want passes to the game—said they were friends of the umpire."

"Throw 'em out," replied the manager. "They're imposters. No umpire ever had two friends."

Pitter-Patter.

The Holy Cross team of New Orleans, which sent Pitcher Dick Callahan to the Boston Red Sox, and was winner of the Louisiana American Legion title with a 31 to 0 conquest of Baton Rouge, has challenged the Southern Association Pelicans to a contest—and probably will get it...After Thursday night's Phillie-Card twi-night doubleheader at Philadelphia the loud-speaker announced "no game tomorrow"—and 12,000 Phillie fans applauded...Just 16 years ago today, July 29, 1928, the Cleveland Indians scored 17 runs in the first two innings against the World Champion Yankees...Samuel D. Riddle, owner of Man o' War and "Laird of Glen Riddle, Pa.," is still active around the Garden State Park race paddock despite his 83 years.

Bowlers Back 'Em.

The Bowlers Victory Legion has pledged to raise $1,000,000 during 1944-45 for recreation equipment for battle area service men. Last season the ten-pin topplers raised $187,000 which went for 200,000 decks of cards, 325,000 pocket-size fiction books, 17,254 fishing kits, 100,000 pocket-size games of various kinds, and 100,000 sewing kits. The bowling leagues also invested $248,000,000 in war bonds. Nice going, fellahs!

Answers to Questions.

No. 1—Sam Crawford, 16 homers for Cincinnati in 1901, and seven for Detroit in 1908.

No. 2—Jack Chesbro, 28-6 for Pittsburg in 1902, and 41-12 for New York in 1904.

Fights Last Night

By the Associated Press.

New York—Lee Q. Murray, 206¾, New York, outpointed Turkey Thompson, 207¼, Los Angeles (10). Dorsey Lay, 137½, Philadelphia, stopped Vince Dell Orto, 134¼, New York (5).

Jacksonville, Fla.—Buddy Scott, 188, Tampa, outpointed Gunnar Barlund, 201, New York (10). Chuck Taylor, 146, Pittsburg, outpointed Merald Tidwell, 145, San Francisco (8).

San Francisco—Jackie Ryan, 149, San Francisco, and Auriel Coutoure, 145, Bangor, Me., drew (10).

VLIET AND COHOES TEAM PLAN TILT TOMORROW NIGHT

The Sacred Heart team of Watervliet will meet the Cohoes All-Stars tomorrow on the Watervliet High School diamond.

The game is scheduled for 6:15 p.m.

The Watervliet team has chalked up an impressive record on the diamond this season and will be making every effort to keep it intact tomorrow night.

Manager Tom Halpin probably will use his ace hurler, Lefty Karafanda.

NINE RACES ON SARATOGA CARD

Saratoga Springs — Two stakes and a total of nine races are scheduled for Saratoga Raceway tonight. The stakes are the $2,000 Amsterdam and the $1,200 Mechanicville.

The Amsterdam has drawn the same field of top pacers which raced in the $5,000 Saratoga Pacing Derby. The entries are headed by Prince Yakima, winner of the Derby. Also included is Mose Dale which Vic Fleming kept well in front of the Prince in one heat of the Derby until a collision which broke his sulky and forced him to drop back.

Watson E. Direct and Hopeworthy Lee which raced second and third to Prince Yakima are also slated to go as is Mr. Voici, left at the post in the feature last week, but capable of staying well up in the field.

The Mechanicville has drawn seven trotters including Gypsy Hanover and Mountain Maid, both winners in overnight heats this year. The ninth race has been added to a usual eight race program to give the Saturday night racegoers a chance to see all the harness racing which can be offered them.

First Race—Purst $250, trotting. One mile. For three-year-olds and upwards:
1. Verna Hanover (R. Dracksley).
2. Blitsco (C. Femling).
3. Princess Harriet (F. Phillips).
4. Margaret Scott (E. Dunwoody).
5. Josephine Knight (F. Church, jr.)
6. Miss Rutherford (H. Stout).
7. Oletta Aubrey (W. Dyke).
8. Kernel Siliko (F. Sargent).

Also eligible: Roya Abbey (A. Rodney), What's New (J. Devlin).

Second Race—Purse $300, pacing. One Mile. For three-year-olds and upward:
1. Abbe Cheer (J. Broderick).
2. Tony Grattan (C. Masten).
3. Wolf Tone (no driver).
4. Eria Reynolds (no driver).
5. Sarasota (H. Myott).
6. Peter Watts (G. Tingley).
7. Indian Chief (J. Porter).
8. Bell's Nairn (G. Bulger).

Third Race—Purse $300, pacing. One mile. For three-year-olds and upwards:
1. True Tone (C. Hatchell).
2. Yosmite (S. Spie).
3. My Grattan (L. James).
4. Ima Star (R. Dracksley).
5. Red Breast (M. Van Auken).
6. Oxford Lad (S. Craig).
7. Tarton (J. Devlin).

Fourth Race—Purse $250, pacing. One mile. For three-year-olds and upward.
1. Tillie Athlone (F. Church, jr.)
2. Hava Hanover (W. Smart).
3. Lucy Grattan II (S. Craig).
4. Anthony (H. Myott).
5. Judge Patchen (H. Fry).
6. Jessie Rector (W. Greth).
7. Fast Tempo (E. Dunwoody).
8. Rose Abbe (H. Dailey).

Fifth Race — The Amsterdam, purse $1,000, pacing. One mile. For four-year-olds and upwards.
1. Hopeworthy Lee (S. Sipe).
2. Mr. Voici (E. Dunwoody).
3. Volo H. (W. Wathen).
4. Prince Yakima (W. Dennis).
5. Watson E. Direct (W. Smart).
6. Phillipus (C. Hatchell).
7. Mose Dale (V. Fleming).
8. Dan Grattan (R. Reeves).

Sixth Race — The Mechanicville, purse $600, trotting. One mile. For four-year-olds and upward:
1. Gypsy Hanover (A. Rodney).
2. Mountain Maid (H. Myott).
3. Mr. Van (L. James).
4. All Spencer (H. Livingston).
5. Chuck Signal (J. Brown).
6. Dixie Spencer (C. Hodgins).
7. Seven Up (C. Fleming).

Seventh Race—Purse $250, pacing. One mile. For three-year-olds and upward:
1. Lucy Grattan II (S. Craig).
2. Fast Tempo (E. Dunwoody).
3. Jessie Rector (W. Greth).
4. Rose Abbe (H. Dailey).
5. Hava Hanover (W. Smart).
6. Tillie Athlone (F. Church, jr.)
7. Anthony (H. Myott).
8. Judge Patchen (H. Fry).

Eight Race — The Amsterdam, purse $1,000. One mile. For four-year-olds and upward.
1. Mose Dale (V. Fleming).
2. Prince Yakima (W. Dennis).
3. Mr. Voici (E. Dunwoody).
4. Volo J. (W. Wathen).
5. Watson E. Direct (W. Smart).
6. Phillipus (C. Hatchell).
7. Dan Grattan (R. Reeves).
8. Hopeworthy Lee (S. Sipe).

Ninth Race—The Mechanicville, purse $600, trotting. One mile. For four-year-olds and upward:
1. Seven Up (C. Fleming).
2. Dixie Spencer (C. Hodgins).
3. Mountain Maid (H. Myott).
4. Mr. Van (L. James).
5. Chuck Signal (J. Brown).
6. Gypsy Hanover (A. Rodney).
7. All Spencer (H. Livingston).

Horses listed according to post positions. First post 8:15 p.m.

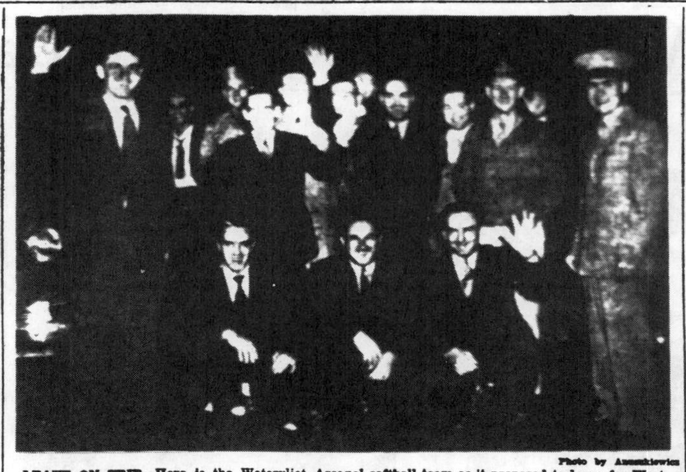

Photo by Anuszkiewicz

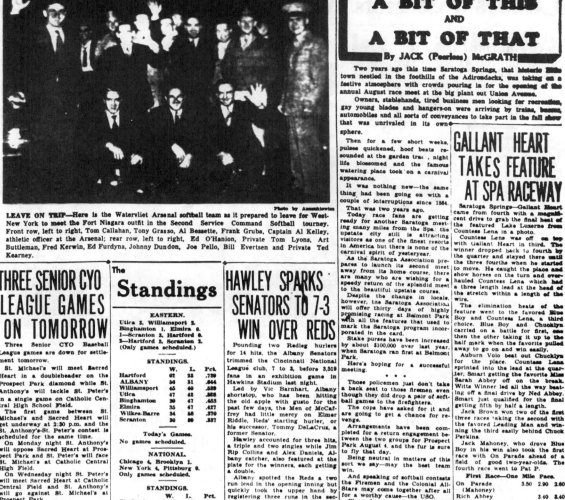

LEAVE ON TRIP—Here is the Watervliet Arsenal softball team as it prepared to leave for West-New York to meet the Fort Niagara outfit in the Second Service Command Softball tourney. Front row, left to right, Tom Callahan, Tony Grasso, Al Bessette, Frank Gruba, Captain Al Kelley, athletic officer at the Arsenal; rear row, left to right, Ed O'Hanion, Private Tom Lyons, Art Buttleman, Fred Kerwin, Ed Furdyna, Johnny Dundon, Joe Pello, Bill Evertsen and Private Ted Kearney.

THREE SENIOR CYO LEAGUE GAMES ON TOMORROW

Three Senior CYO Baseball League games are down for settlement tomorrow.

St. Michael's will meet Sacred Heart in a doubleheader on the Prospect Park diamond while St. Anthony's will tackle St. Peter's in a single game on Catholic Central High School Field.

The first game between St. Michael's and Sacred Heart will get underway at 2:30 p.m. and the St. Anthony's-St. Peter's contest is scheduled for the same time.

On Monday night St. Anthony's will oppose Sacred Heart at Prospect Park and St. Peter's will face St. Michael's at Catholic Central High Field.

On Wednesday night St. Peter's will meet Sacred Heart at Catholic Central Field and St. Anthony's will go against St. Michael's at Prospect Park.

In tomorrow's doubleheader with St. Michael's Sacred Heart will use Jack O'Brien, Tink Breen or Tom Quest on the mound with B. Walthers receiving.

SPEAKER, RUTH TO BE AT MACK FETE

Philadelphia (AP)—The committee arranging Connie Mack's managerial golden jubilee celebration at Shibe Park Aug. 4 announced yesterday that Babe Ruth and Tris Speaker have accepted invitations to attend as members of an all-star living baseball team selected by Mr. Mack.

Acceptances previously were received from George Sisler, Eddie Collins, Honus Wagner, Frank (Home Run) Baker, Bill Dickey, Walter Johnson and Lefty Grove, with final decisions still awaited from Ty Cobb and Mickey Cochrane.

JUNIOR GOLFERS IN SEMI-FINALS

Play in the junior championship golf tourney at Frear Park was brought down to the semi-finals yesterday with Billy Burke, Al Bibb, jr., Jack Moynihan and Jack Joslin still in the running.

Burke defeated Buster Trombley, 2 and 1 while Bibb disposed of Tim Anderson, 4 and 3.

Moynihan, son of Johnny Moynihan, Frear Park pro, defeated Marvin Anderson, 4 and 3, and Jack Joslin turned back Ed Flanigan, 6 and 5.

The semi-finals will take place Monday with Burke meeting Bibb and Moynihan opposing Joslin. The winners will clash in the 18-hole final, Tuesday.

The junior tourney, first of its kind attempted in this section in some time, is being run off under the supervision of the Troy Recreation Department.

The Standings

EASTERN.

Utica 3, Williamsport 2.
Binghamton 1, Elmira 0.
1—Scranton 3, Hartford 0.
2—Hartford 3, Scranton 2.
(Only games scheduled.)

STANDINGS.

	W.	L.	Pct.
Hartford	62	23	.729
ALBANY	56	31	.644
Williamsport	45	40	.529
Utica	47	42	.528
Binghamton	39	47	.453
Elmira	35	47	.427
Wilkes-Barre	34	58	.370
Scranton	30	59	.337

Today's Games.
No games scheduled.

NATIONAL.

Chicago 4, Brooklyn 1.
New York 4, Pittsburg 0.
Only games scheduled.

STANDINGS.

	W.	L.	Pct.
St. Louis	65	24	.730
Cincinnati	51	39	.567
Pittsburg	48	38	.558
New York	43	48	.473
Chicago	38	47	.447
Philadelphia	37	51	.420
Boston	37	54	.407
Brooklyn	36	54	.400

Games Today—
Probable Hurlers:
Chicago at Philadelphia (night) —Passeau (5-7) vs. Gerheauser (6-10).
Pittsburg at Boston — Sewell (10-8) or Starr (4-2) vs. Tobin (11-11).
St. Louis at Brooklyn (2)—Lanier (10-5) and Wilks (8-1) vs. Gregg (6-12) and Webber (4-4).
Cincinnati at New York (2)—Heusser (8-5) and Shoun (7-5) vs. Allen (1-2) and Brewer (1-1).

AMERICAN.

New York 13, Cleveland 7.
Boston 15, Detroit 5.
Chicago 8, Washington 2.
St. Louis 8, Philadelphia 5.

STANDINGS.

	W.	L.	Pct.
St. Louis	55	42	.657
New York	49	43	.533
Boston	50	44	.532
Cleveland	49	47	.510
Chicago	45	45	.500
Detroit	46	49	.484
Washington	42	52	.447
Philadelphia	40	54	.426

Games Today—
Probable Hurlers:
Washington at St. Louis (night) — Haefner (7-7 vs. Hollingsworth (5-6).
New York at Detroit—Roser 4-2) or Borowy (12-6) vs. Gentry (5-11).
Philadelphia at Chicago—Newsom (7-10) or Harris (8-7) vs Wade (1-3).
Only games scheduled.

International

1—Rochester 2, Jersey City 0.
2—Rochester 7, Jersey City 0.
1—Newark 3, Buffalo 2.
2—Newark 3, Buffalo 0.
1—Baltimore 14, Montreal 3.
2—Baltimore 2, Montreal 0.
Syracuse 4, Toronto 3.

HAWLEY SPARKS SENATORS TO 7-3 WIN OVER REDS

Pounding two Redleg hurlers for 14 hits, the Albany Senators trimmed the Cincinnati National League club, 7 to 3, before 3,519 fans in an exhibition game in Hawkins Stadium last night.

Led by Vic Barnhart, Albany shortstop, who has been hitting the old apple with gusto for the past few days, the Men of McCaffrey had little mercy on Elmer Riddle, Reds' starting hurler, or his successor, Tommy DeLaCruz, a former Senator.

Hawley accounted for three hits, a triple and two singles while Jim Rip Collins and Alex Daniels, Albany catcher, also featured at the plate for the winners, each getting a double.

Albany spotted the Reds a two run lead in the opening inning but quickly took the upper hand by registering three runs in the second frame. The Senators went further ahead with three runs in the third and it was in this inning that they drove Riddle, winner of 21 games last year, but a victim of a sore arm this season, from the mound.

Two men were away in the third when Riddle left the mound after yielding six hits.

DeLaCruz was nicked for eight hits and single runs in the fourth and the eighth as he finished up.

Chuck Hawley, Albany's starting pitcher, went the route and hurled splendid ball, letting the National League representatives down with eight hits which he kept well scattered.

Hawley was at his best last night and would have given any opponent a tough time.

After that first inning when the Reds chalked up the two runs to jump into the lead, Hawley had things well in control. He blanked the Redlegs from there in save in the seventh when they were able to squeeze across a single run.

Two singles and a walk produced the seventh inning tally.

The first two Cincinnati runs resulted from Frank McCormick's home run over the left field wall with Tony Criscola on base.

Before the game Joe McCaffrey, vice president of the Albany Club, introduced Manager Bill McKechnie of the Reds; Bucky Walters, ace pitcher, the Redleg coaches and Bill McCorry former Albany manager, who is road secretary of the National League Club.

McCorry urged upper Hudson District fans to support the home club to keep the old game of baseball going. He also thanked the fans for the support they gave him in this section.

Despite the fact they were idle from Eastern League play, the Senators picked up half a game in the championship race as Hartford's league-leading Laurels broke even in a doubleheader with the lowly Scranton Miners.

CINCINNATI

	AB.	R	H	O.	A
Williams, 2b.	3	0	0	1	3
Criscola, rf.	5	1	2	2	1
Walker, cf.	2	0	1	1	0
Clay, cf.	2	0	0	1	0
McCormick, 1b.	4	1	1	6	4
Just, c.	3	0	0	6	2
Tipton, lf.	4	0	2	4	0
Mesner, 3b.	3	0	0	1	0
[illegible]er, ss.	1	0	0	0	1
Aleno, ss.	2	0	0	0	1
Riddle, p	1	0	0	0	0
De La Cruz, p	2	1	1	2	1
aCrabtree	1	0	1	0	0
Totals	34	3	8	24	1[illegible]

a—Batted for De La Cruz in 9th.

ALBANY

	AB	R	H	O	A
Rodgers, rf.	5	0	1	1	0
Brooks, 2b.	3	1	2	1	1
Cayton, 2b.	1	0	1	0	0
Giontriddo, cf.	4	0	0	3	0
Barnhart, 3b.	4	2	3	3	3
Collins, 1b	3	1	2	4	0
Morrow, 1b.	1	0	0	4	0
Mayhew, lf	3	1	2	4	0
Luzansky, lf.	1	0	0	1	0
Daniels, c.	3	1	2	0	3
Lewis, ss	3	1	2	0	3
Hawley, p.	4	0	0	0	1
Totals	36	7	14	27	8

CINCINNATI 200 000 100 – 3
ALBANY 032 100 01x – 7

Errors Lewis, Miller, Just. Runs batted in McCormick 2, Collins 2, Mayhew 2, Daniels, Brooks, Criscola, Rodgers. Two base hits Collins, De La Cruz, Daniels, Crabtree. Three base hits—Barnhart, Mayhew. Stolen base—Barnhart. Double plays Criscola to Just; De La Cruz, McCormick, Just and Mesner. Left on bases —Cincinnati 8, Albany 6. Hits—Off Riddle 6 in 2 2-3 innings, De La Cruz 8 in 5 1-3. Bases on balls—De La Cruz 1, Hawley 4. Strikeouts—Riddle 1, De La Cruz 3, Hawley 5. Losing pitcher—Riddle. Umpires—Rafferty and Connolly. Time—1:48.

NEW ORLEANS MEET.

New Orleans (AP) — Chairman John S. Letellier of the newly elected board of directors of the Fair Grounds Breeders and Racing Association said last night that tentative opening date for the 75-day winter racing season here has been set for Thanksgiving Day.

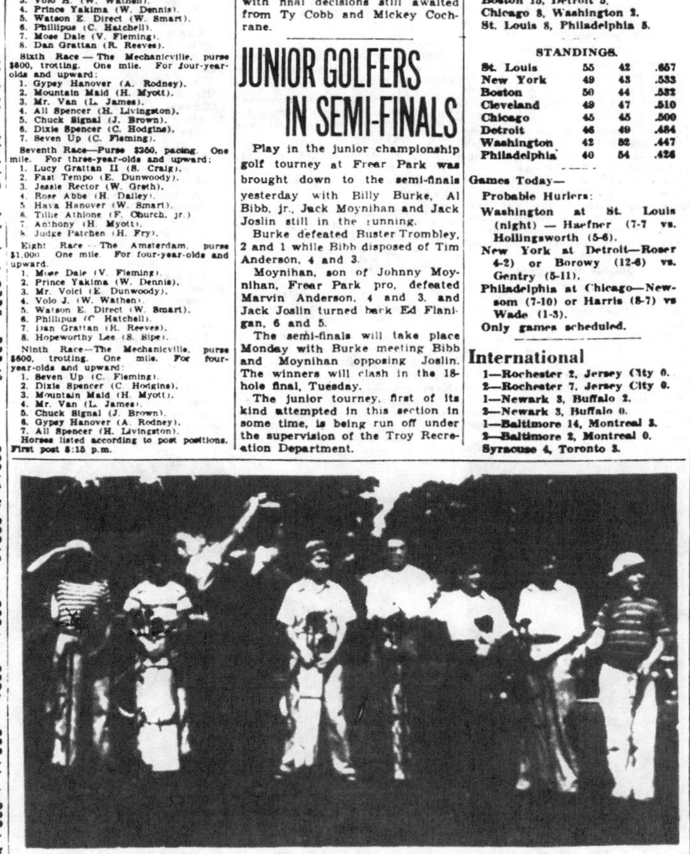

JUNIOR GOLFERS HAVE DAY—Jack Moynihan, son of Johnny Moynihan, Frear Park pro, tees off as match play gets underway in the junior championship tourney at Frear Park. Other competitors, looking on, are, left to right, Marvin Anderson, jr., Jackie Joslin, Albert Bibb, jr., Edward Flanigan, Alfred Trombley, Billy Burke and Tim Anderson.

A BIT OF THIS AND A BIT OF THAT

By JACK (Peerless) McGRATH

Two years ago this time Saratoga Springs, that historic little town nestled in the foothills of the Adirondacks, was taking on a festive atmosphere with crowds pouring in for the opening of the annual August race meet at the big plant out Union Avenue.

Owners, stablehands, tired business men looking for recreation, gay young blades and hangers-on were arriving by trains, busses, automobiles and all sorts of conveyances to take part in the fall show that was unrivaled in its own sphere.

Then for a few short weeks, pulses quickened, hoof beats resounded at the garden trac , night life blossomed and the famous watering place took on a carnival appearance.

It was nothing new—the same thing had been going on with a couple of interruptions since 1864.

That was two years ago.

Today race fans are getting ready for another Saratoga meeting many miles from the Spa: the upstate city still is attracting visitors as one of the finest resorts in America but there is none of the carnival spirit of yesteryear.

As the Saratoga Association prepares to launch its second meet away from its home course, there are many who are wishing for a speedy return of the splendid meet to the beautiful upstate course.

Despite the change in locale, however, the Saratoga Association will offer thirty days of highly promising racing at Belmont Park with all the features that used to mark the Saratoga program incorporated in the card.

Stake purses have been increased by about $100,000 over last year, when Saratoga ran first at Belmont Park.

Here's hoping for a successful meeting.

• • •

Those policemen just don't take a back seat to those firemen even though they did drop a pair of softball games to the firefighters.

The cops have asked for it and are going to get a chance for revenge.

Arrangements have been completed for a return engagement between the two groups for Prospect Park August 4, and the fur is sure to fly that day.

Being neutral in matters of this sort we say—may the best team win.

And speaking of softball contests the Firemen and the Colonial All-Stars may come together after all for a worthy cause—the USO.

Plans for a game between the two outfits are in the making and despite controversies over lineups, players and what not, all signs point toward an early engagement.

Incidentally the All-Stars have announced that Frankie Laureate is their coach and a guy named "Ed," well known Trojan, is acting as manager. The latter tells us he will have sufficient talent to turn back the Firemen when and if a game can be arranged.

• • •

Tony Lupien's father, like Tony himself, was a Harvard man, and a good ball player, but never played on the Harvard team. The father's zeal played a big part in the career of the Phillies' first baseman.

He used his ball-playing talent to earn his living while studying, playing semi-pro ball weekends and all summer. By the time Ulysses, jr., arrived at college age Ulysses, sr., was State civil service director of Massachusetts and Tony didn't have to semilpro his own way through the classic halls at Cambridge.

• • •

And now, so long for awhile. We'll be seeing you at the Saratoga meeting in Belmont.

GOLFERS IN AREA FACE BUSY CARD

Troy Area golfers are in for another busy week-end with play in the quarter final round of the annual industrial championship tourney at Frear Park topping the card.

A battle between Joe Ruszas of Shaker Ridge, state amateur champion, and Ernie White of Mannings, runnerup in the qualifying round, is expected to be one of the hardest fought tilts in the Indus meet.

Judging from his fine performance in winning the Eastern New York Golf Association event at Van Schaick Island Golf Club, Cohoes, last Sunday, Ruszas is playing in top form.

The state amateur king is favored to win his match but may receive plenty of opposition from White, who has carded several low scores on the Frear Park layout.

Another feature quarter final struggle will bring together two brothers, Dan Gormley and Tom Gormley, both representing General Electric Company at Schenectady. Dan Gormley, Eastern New York Golf Association champion, won the tourney medal with a sub-par 69 and will be favored to survive play.

A third quarter final match will find Capt. Roy Fry of Watervliet Arsenal meeting Ed Tofte of Cohoes Textile.

The fourth quarter final event was run off two days ago with Lou Forget of D. and H. defeating Jerry Carpenter of Frear Park, 6 and 5.

Quarter final play also will be in order in three lower divisions over the week-end.

There also will be considerable activity on the Troy Country Club course and the Van Schaick Island Golf Club course.

Play in the annual president's cup meet will begin at the former course. This is a 72-hole medal play affair and entrants have the privilege of playing the 18 holes rounds at any time. The winner, the low net scorer, will have his name inscribed on the president's trophy.

GALLANT HEART TAKES FEATURE AT SPA RACEWAY

Saratoga Springs—Gallant Heart came from fourth with a magnificent drive to grab the final heat of the featured Lake Luzerne from Countess Lena in a photo.

Countess Lena was off on top with Gallant Heart in third. The winner dropped back to fourth by the quarter and stayed there until the three fourths when he started to move. He caught the place and show horses on the turn and overhauled Countess Lena which had a three length lead at the head of the stretch within a length of the wire.

The elimination heats of the feature went to the favored Blue Boy and Countess Lena, a third choice. Blue Boy and Chucklyn carried on a battle for first, one then the other taking it up to the half mark when the favorite pulled away to go on and win easily.

Auburn Volo beat out Chucklyn for the place. Countess Lena sprinted into the lead at the quarter, Smart getting the favorite Miss Sarah Abbey off on the break. Witts Winner led all the way beating off a final drive by Ned Abbey. Smart just qualified for the final getting fifth by half a length.

Jack Brown won two of the first three races taking the second with the favored Leading Man and winning the third easily behind Chuck Perkins.

Jack Mahoney, who drove Blue Boy in his win also took the first race with On Parade ahead of a field of good two-year-olds. The fourth race went to Pat P.

First Race—One Mile Pace.

On Parade (Mahoney) 3.50 2.90 2.60
Rich Abbey (Brown) 3.40 3.40
Kohnny Casey (Stout) 3.30
Also started — Cooperage, Guy, Yardley, Calumet Miss, Ferdinand, Copper Queen. Time—2:13¼.

Second Race—One Mile Trot.

Leading Man (Brown) 3.60 2.20 2.50
Johnnie M. (W. Berry) 2.50 2.60
Peter Aileen (Dean) 3.30
Also started—Best Hanover, Bobby Perkins. Time—2:13¼.
Daily Double—$7.50.

Third Race—One Mile Trot.

Chuck Perkins (Brown) 5.20 3.30 2.60
Black Annie (Casey) 3.40 2.40
Allie Watts Aubrey (Stout) 2.80
Also started — Well Off, J. T. Barnes, Scrantonian. Time—2:12.

Fourth Race—One Mile Pace.

Pat W. (W Berry) 11.20 6.80 3.80
Hartley (Fry) 7.10 3.50
R. A. Grattan (S. Craig) 3.60
Also started — Marie C. Brook, The Pike, Calumet Ethan, Joe C. Abbe, Allworthy Favour. Time—2:07.

Fifth Race—The Lake Luzerne One Mile Trot.

Blue Boy (Mahoney) 4.40 3.20 2.70
Auburn Volo (Brown) 4.80 3.10
Chucklyn (V. Fleming) 3.60
Also started—Dutchess Hanover, Gallant Heart, Fletcher Daq, Josedale Lynn. Time—2:10¼.

Sixth Race—The Lake Luzerne One Mile Trot.

Countess Lena (Witt) 3.40 4.60 3.80
Ned Abbey (Church) 9.30 3.60
Kate Volo (C. Fleming) 10.80
Also started — Cherokee, Miss Sarah Abbey, Friscowyn, Charming Sister. Time—2.08½.

Seventh Race—One Mile Pace.

Pat W. (Berry) 7.30 5.80 3.70
Marie C. Brooke (Casey) 34.60 7.00
Hartley (Fry) 4.20
Also started—R. A. Grattan, Allworthy Favour, The Pike, Joe C. Abbe, Calumet Ethan did not finish. Time—2:09.

Eighth Race—The Lake Luzerne Final—One Mile Trot.

Gallant Heart (Harvie) 20.00 9.50 7.00
Countess Lena (Witt) 3.40 2.40
Dutchess Hanover (Hatchell) 15.80
Also started — [illegible]te Volo, Auburn Volo, Miss Sarah Abbey, Nel Abbey, Chucklyn, Blue Boy, Cherokee. Time—2:08.

SPORTS MIRROR

By the Associated Press.

Today a Year Ago—Rip Sewell chalked up 16th victory for Pittsburg as Pirates beat Giants, 3-2.

Three Years Ago—Freddie "Red" Cochrane won welterweight boxing title by outpointing Fritzie Zivic in 15-rounder at Newark, N. J.

Five Years Ago—Andy K., 38 to 1 outsider, won $47,820 Arlington Futurity after E. R. Bradley scratched his two entries in protest against decision by Illinois racing authorities barring Jockey Don Meade.

Cohoes Assessors Will Conduct Grievance Days August 29-September 2

TAX BOOKS MAY BE INSPECTED AT CITY HALL OFFICE

Records Will Be Sent Later to Albany County Board of Supervisors

Grievance days during which property owners will be given an opportunity to file objections to their valuations in the 1945 assessment roll will be held by the board of assessors Tuesday, Aug. 29, through Saturday, Sept. 2, at its quarters in the City Hall, it was announced today.

The work of preparing the roll has been completed and it is now open for public inspection and will remain so until the grievance period.

Following the last grievance day the roll will again be open for inspection for a period of 15 days, after which a copy will be sent to the Albany County board of supervisors to be used in preparing the state and county tax rates.

JEANETTE PHOENIX OF BOGHT ROAD WED TO EDMUND G. COUTU

Miss Jeanette Phoenix, daughter of Mr. and Mrs. Edward Phoenix of Boght Road and Edmund G. Coutu, son of Mr. and Mrs. Emile Coutu of Manor Heights, Cohoes, were married Sunday at St. Agnes Church in a double ring ceremony performed by Rev. J. A. Franklin, pastor.

The bride was attired in a gown of mousseline de soie and Irish point lace, cap effect, fingertip veil and carried a colonial bouquet of white roses and American Beauty white gladioli.

Miss Fawn Coutu, sister of the bridegroom, was the maid of honor and wore a gown of light orchid organza with a shoulder length veil and tiara of orchid and carried a colonial bouquet of yellow roses, American Beauty, gladioli and orchid asters.

Stanley Novak served as best man.

The church was decorated with gladioli and nuptial music was provided by the church organist, Mrs. James Cox. The music included "O Promise Me," "Ave Maria" and the "Wedding March."

A reception was held at the bride's parents, Mrs. Phoenix receiving the guests in a gown of pale green silk and a shoulder bouquet of peach colored gladioli. Mrs. Emile Coutu, mother of the bridegroom, wore a flowered silk jersey dress and a shoulder bouquet of orchid gladioli.

Following the reception, Mr. and Mrs. Coutu left for an undisclosed destination. The bride wore a travel costume of flowered jersey silk with matching accessories. They will reside at 22 Younglove Avenue after September 1.

SACRED HEART SCHOOL TO HAVE NEW TEACHERS

Two changes in the staff of Sacred Heart School, Cohoes, have been announced by the Sisters of the Holy Names in Montreal. Sister Mary Georgette will go from Cohoes to Silver Springs and be replaced by Sister Therese Anysia of Florida. Sister Ovide Albert will go to Montreal and be replaced by Sister Mary Petronille of Rome.

Soldier Returns

Corp. Robert Walther has returned to Camp Hood, Texas, where he is stationed with the Army. He has been spending a furlough with his parents and their summer home in Dunsbach Ferry. During his visit he was guest of honor at a birthday party.

SINUS, CATARRH SUFFERERS FIND CURB

SERGEANT BORDEN RECEIVES D.F.C. AT ENGLISH AIR BASE

Gunner Flew in Support of Invasion Forces During Normandy Landing

Technical Sergt. Kenneth L. Borden, son of Mr. and Mrs. Arthur D. Borden of 174 Manor Avenue, Cohoes, recently received the Distinguished Flying Cross for extraordinary achievement over enemy territory in Europe.

Sergeant Borden is a radio operator and gunner with an Eighth Air Force Liberator group stationed in England. His outfit has recently completed 100 bombing missions, many of them made in support of the initial landings made by ground troops during the invasion of France. The award was made to Sergeant Borden after completing his thirtieth mission. The citation reads:

"For extraordinary achievement while serving in thirty bombardment missions over enemy occupied continental Europe. Displaying great courage and skill, Sergeant Borden has materially aided in the success of these missions and his actions are an inspiring example for his fellow flyers. His courage, coolness and skill on these occasions reflect the highest credit upon himself and the armed forces of the United States."

Sergeant Borden, whose wife lives at 101 Vliet Boulevard, attended La Salle Institute, Troy, and Siena College in Loudonville.

TAX, WATER RENT BILLS FOR CITY WILL BE PUT IN MAILS ON AUG. 31

Second half tax bills and water rent bills for the period from Jan. 1 to July 1, are being prepared in the city treasurer's office and will be placed in the mails Thursday, Aug. 31.

Taxes for the second half-year period are due Friday, Sept. 1 and can be paid through Oct. 1. In cases where the first half charges were not paid in March a 1 per cent penalty charge is added which is retroactive to March 1.

Heads Committee

Mrs. Mae Maxwell will have charge of the committee which will conduct the weekly sale of bonds and stamps at the special booth in Woolworth's store on Saturday.

VACATION BIBLE SCHOOL HOLDS FINAL SESSION AT SALVATION ARMY HOME

The concluding session of the Dailiy Vacation Bible School which has been conducted during this week at Salvation Army headquarters, 76 Oneida Street, was held today.

Closing exercises for the school, which was originally scheduled for earlier this summer but which was deferred, are scheduled to be held Sunday at 6.30 p.m. In connection with the program exhibit of articles made by those in the handicraft class will be shown.

The school was conducted under the direction of Adjutant Mrs. Victor Stay and Lieut. Margaret Broadribb, local officers-in-charge.

DRAFT BOARD 345 WILL SEND SMALL INDUCTION GROUP

Notices Will Be Placed in Mail Early Next Week

Local Selective Service Board No. 345 has received its quota for September and notices will be placed in the mail early next week, it was announced today.

The size of the contingent which will leave for induction next month was not announced but it is understood that the group will be a small one.

Next month also a group of registrants will undergo preinduction physical examinations at the area induction center.

To Receive Communion.

Members of the Children of Mary Sodality of St. Agnes' Church will receive Holy Communion in a body at the 8.15 a.m. mass Sunday.

To Sell Bonds, Stamps.

Members of the Ladies' Auxiliary of Cohoes Post, Veterans of Foreign Wars, will sell War Savings Bonds and Stamps tomorrow at the special booth in the Woolworth store on Remsen Street.

Society Meeting Scheduled.

The Ladies of St. A. of St. Marie's Church will hold a meeting Monday evening in the church basement. A card party will follow the meeting with Mrs. Alphonse Forget as chairman of the committee on arrangements.

Birthday Party.

A birthday party for Gerald

GIDEON PRESIDENT TO BE SPEAKER AT VILLAGE CHURCH

Robert MacAuley Will Preach at Methodist Service Sunday

WATERFORD

Robert MacAuley, president of the Troy Camp of the Gideons, will preach at the worship service Sunday at 10 a.m. at the Waterford Methodist Church. Mr. MacAuley is a member of the Ninth Presbyterian Church. He will tell the story of the Gideons. G. Raymond Anderson will conduct the service. Mrs. Frances Moore will be at the organ. The Church School will meet at 11 a.m. and the Youth Fellowship at 6.30 p.m. Caryl Chapman and Evelyn Smith will be in charge and review the book, "The Apostle," by Asch.

First Baptist.

There will be no service of worship at the First Baptist Church this Sunday.

At Grace Church.

The service at the Grace Episcopal Church Sunday will be conducted by Rev. James T. Kerr, rector, at 9 a.m. with the celebration of the Holy Communion.

Presbyterian Church.

The service of worship at the First Presbyterian Church Sunday will be at 11 a.m. and will be conducted by Rev. Henry D. Smith of Naylor, two-year-old son of Mr. and Mrs. Harry E. Nailor, was given yesterday at their home, 81 Younglove Avenue. Decorations were in blue and white and a birthday cake was the table centerpiece. Among the young guests present were William Ridgeway, Rudolph Cucchi, Kenneth Richelieu, John Benac, Anna May Wager, Roberta Betloff and Carolyn Martin.

Marine Reassigned

Pvt. David Couch, Marine Corps, son of Mr. and Mrs. William Couch of 11 VanVechten Street, who served at Quadalcanal and Bougainville, has been assigned to the Navy V-12 unit which is stationed at Muhlenberg College, Allentown, Pa. Upon completing the course of training, Private Couch will be sent to Midshipman's School Officer Candidate Class for further training leading to a commission as Ensign.

Green Island. Mrs. Chester B. Parkis will sing the offertory anthem. Miss Grace M. Bartholomew will be at the organ.

Corps To Rehearse.

Members of St. Mary's Sponsored Corps of the Charles J. Brady Post No. 230, American Legion, will report for rehearsal at 7 p.m. today at St. Mary's Hall. The rehearsal will be under the direction of George Slater and John Early. On Sunday the corps will attend a competitive drill at Amsterdam under the auspices of the Junior Drum Corps Council and sponsored by the United Textile Workers of America. St. Mary's Sponsored Corps finished in first place in the competition which was held last Saturday at the Nassau Fair Grounds with a rating of 96.8. In second place was the Blanchard Squadron of Delmar with 94.8 and third place the Ukrainian Girls of Cohoes with 94.7. Other ratings were Noble-Callahan Post of Troy, 94.5; Capital Lancers of Albany, 94.3, and All-Girl Fife and Drum Corps from Fort Johnson, 89.8.

Report Sept. 5.

Rose Titus, Stephentown.
Emily Cramer, West Sand Lake.
Enna M. Belaska, 87 College Avenue.
Ruth Schuttenheim, R. D. 3. Troy.
Mrs. Alfred Geerholt, Stephentown Center.
Edward J. VanKuren, 3046 Sixth Avenue.
Patrick Welch, Rensselaer.
Marie Banker, Wynantskill.
Letta McChesney, R. D. 1. Troy.
Joseph Young, Hoosick Falls.
Anna B. Cone, 3251 Sixth Avenue.
Irene S. Blassberg, 1511 Bouton Road.
Mary Reilly, Miller Avenue.
Edward Auple, Rensselaer.
Cecil C. Hicks, 817 Sixth Avenue.
Owen A. Seymour, 574 First Street.
John Vaughn, Rensselaer.
Ellen O'Donnell, R. D. 2 Valley Falls.
Lure Rivers, 517 Fifth Avenue.
Ida Butler, Averill Park.
Solomon Altman, 37 Eighth Street.
Gustave Giller, Castleton.
Olive Butler, R. D. 3, Troy.
Clarence King, North Greenbush.
Charles Hale, jr. 31 Aiken Avenue.
Albert Stewart, Melrose.
Ernest Harner, R. D. 1, Troy.
Edward F. Fallon, 39' First Street.
Giles Beach, Brunswick.
Henry Lurch, West Sand Lake.
John J. Dobler, 61 Ford Avenue.
Helen Kenyon, West Stephentown.
Dennis J. Black, Nassau.
Chester A. Nash, Sand Lake.
Joseph Willi, 4 Sheridan Avenue.
Peter Olinyk, 378 Second Street.

Report Sept. 11.

Lucielle Roney, Sand Lake.
Charles D. Boland, 228 Eighth Street.
Jessie Van Deusen, Valley Falls.
Helen Bailey, 1 Van Every Avenue.
Frank M. Hedrick, Rensselaer.
Clarence Burch, Rensselaer.
James J. Miller, 30 Glen Avenue.
Louis Scrivens, Petersburg.
Watson House, Castleton.
Mary Hale, R. D. 2, Valley Falls.
Margaret M. Mahar, 417 First Street.
John L. Lintner, East Greenbush.

CALL JURY PANELS FOR SERVICE WITH SEPTEMBER COURT

Term Will Be Convened Here by Judge Harry Clinton Sept. 5

The names of grand and trial jurors to serve with the September term of Rensselaer County Court were drawn today by County Clerk Lawrence J. Collins in the presence of Judge Harry E. Clinton and Undersheriff Harry B. Nugent. The court term will be convened on Tuesday, Sept. 5. Those whose names appear on the list of grand jurors and on the first panel of trial jurors will report to Judge Clinton on the opening day of court.

Those whose names appear on the second panel of trial jurors will report in court Sept. 11 and the third panel reports Sept. 18.

Names appearing on the lists are:

Grand Jurors.

Louis Levinson, 161 Third Street.
Thomas Bromley, 30 Mill Street.
Kenneth L. Darrow, R.D. 3, Troy.
Frank J. Connolly, 499 Second Street.
Reuben B. Young, 26 First Street.
Frank J. McManus, 4 State Street.
Thomas E. Guiden, Walloomsac.
Ralph T. Curtis, 10 Balsam Avenue.
John Rall, Brunswick Road.
John T. Caulfield, Berlin.
Arthur C. Ferguson, West Sand Lake.
William F. VanDerzee, Averill Park.
Florence M. Kelly, Ferry Street.
Herbert A. Smith, Buskirk.
George H. Cipperly, West Sand Lake.
George Cundiff, 3 Fonda Avenue.
Joseph G. Mintzer, 10 Georgian Court.
Joseph Patterson, Stephentown.
Ernest H Rowland, R.D. 2, Troy.
Irving R. Herrington, Johnsonville.
Henry R. Felter, 330 Seventh Avenue.
Laudia R. Faden, R.D. 3, Troy.
Thomas H. Monahan, Albia Terrace.
Florence R. Shaver, R.D. 1, West Sand Lake.

Report Sept. 5.

Miss Lois Haines of Glens Falls is visiting her parents, Mr. and Mrs. William Haines.

Mr. and Mrs. Fayette Barber have returned from Newburg where they visited relatives.

Mrs. James Dunnigan and daughter Mary of Cambridge recently visited her sister, Mrs. Melina Arnold.

Miss Eileen McCann has returned to Albany after visiting her parents, Mr. and Mrs. Arthur McCann.

Mrs. Theodore Barkley has returned from South Carolina where she visited her husband who is stationed there.

Dr. Edward Roche has returned to Cincinnati, O. after visiting his brother and sister-in-law, Mr. and Mrs. George Roche.

Fred A. Staedeli, CSK, who has recently returned from service in Africa, Italy and England, is visiting friends in town.

Mr. and Mrs. Charles Dietrich and family of Summit, N. J. are visiting her brother and sister-in-law, Mr. and Mrs. John Cowan.

William Getty of Shushan, who has been ill at his home for several days, was taken to the Mary McClellan Hospital in Cambridge Tuesday for treatment.

Robert Alexander, son of Undersheriff A. M. Alexander, is spending a furlough with his father, having just been graduated from a Navy course at Columbia University, with the rank of ensign. After the expiration of his furlough he will go to Cornell University for further advanced training.

GERMANS FACING GREATEST DEFEAT IN CURRENT FIGHT

Prisoners Pouring into Allied Lines from Two Great Traps

With the British in Pursuit of the German Seventh Army (UP)—The fighting in western France has become a vast battle of annihilation that promises a victory over the Germans greater than any previously inflicted upon the Wehrmacht in western Europe, British staff officers said today.

Allied forces have created two great pockets: the Germans escape from one only to find themselves in another.

Prisoners are pouring in from both the inner and outer pockets admitting complete defeat.

"Those still fighting are madmen," is a typical prisoner statement. Another says: "They have not the slightest hope and they know it is futile to fight any longer."

British officers said that although a considerable number of Panzers had escaped from the inner trap, they faced annihilation on their way to the Seine.

"It has become open warfare almost along our entire front," I was told at a forward headquarters. "We are making swifter progress in cutting up his slowly withdrawing columns."

"Greatest Victory."

"It begins to look as if the entire German Seventh Army would be wiped out before or at the Seine," an officer said. "Some of our men have been fighting without a break for five days. They manage to carry on because they realize they're in on the greatest victory of Allied arms in the west—the greatest defeat the Germans have ever suffered in Europe."

The German race through France in 1940, which drove me out at Dunkirk, was nothing like this. Our forces are bringing in prisoners in droves.

The German communications have been slashed to ribbons and they have no cohesion as an Army any longer.

The SS men who were sent in to hold the gap on the main road south of Falaise fought a desperate battle. They held the gap until they were killed and I saw their bodies, riddled by grenades and machinegun fire, and heard their story from a Canadian who had been their prisoner in a hair-raising adventure.

Pvt. Joseph Archambeaut of Montreal, a stretcher bearer, told his story as we sat in a ruined chateau with German dead all around us. As we talked, litter bearers brought in the bodies of Canadians who had died in the assault on this Nazi strong point.

Fired Building

"I was taken prisoner yesterday by the Nazi lieutenant here," said Archambeaut, indicating the body of the German half buried in rubble near the door.

"He interrogated me inside the priory where there were fifty Germans with a bazooka for every man. He told me, I think we'd hang you."

"After a minute or two he changed his mind and said, 'no, we'll take you back with us to Germany.' After a while, as the Canadians approached, he said, on second thought we've a badly wounded man take him over to the Canadians for medical attention. Come back, because we'll have you covered."

"I did as I was directed but once back I tried Fifth Column tactics. I told a German stretcher bearer the heat way to end the siege would be to set fire to the priory. At first the German was reluctant, then he went upstairs and started the fire. As the smoke poured out of the rooftop, the SS men, the Red Cross men were left. The Nazi stretcher bearer and I walked out under a Red Cross flag."

ALL JAPANESE TROOPS DRIVEN OUT OF INDIA

Southeast Asia Command Headquarters, Kandy, Ceylon (UP)—The last straggling groups of the Japanese 33rd Division were chased across the India-Burma border toward Tiddim Wednesday, completing the repulse of the invasion of India launched by the enemy's 15th Army last March 8.

CROPSEYVILLE.

James Daniels is home on furlough.

Hubert Roscoe of the Navy is visiting Eleanor Hayner.

Clara Newbury is visiting her sister, Mrs. John Morton of Schodack.

Mrs. Walter Hughs of Poestenkill recently spent the day with friends here.

Members of White Lily Lodge, I. O. O. F., will hold the annual clam steam. Saturday at 3.30 p.m.

Mr. and Mrs. A. B. File and Mr. and Mrs. Kenneth Simmons visited Mr. and Mrs. P. J. Colyer at Lawyersville recently.

AMERICANS AN ALLY?

Fort Riley, Kan. (UP)—The school teachers lament that there is one in every class applies even to orientation lectures at the Cavalry Replacement Training Center here. After a discussion of America's Allies and their status in the war recently, a small voice from a far corner of the annex dayroom asked: "What about Arkansas?"

TO HAVE FOOD SALE.

The Westminster Guild of the First Presbyterian Church of Lake will hold a food sale at the residence of Mrs. Louis tomorrow from 11 a.m.

COHOES KNIGHTS INSTALLED—Above are the new officers of the Cohoes Knights of Columbus installed last evening. They are, seated left to right, James Doran, district deputy; William Trombly, grand knight; Thaddeus Bartnick, deputy grand knight; Edward Heffern, district deputy. Standing, left to right, are Harry Dickey, inside guard; Desmond Havern, past grand knight; Frederick MacGregor, council trustee; John Hughes, advocate; Raymond Coutu, organist; Emmett Ryan, treasurer; Thomas Heslin, outside guard; Armand Bourret, chancellor, and Martin Lindsay, warden.

FOUR SONS IN SERVICE—Four sons of Mrs. Jessica Rexford of 47 Lincoln Avenue are serving in the Army. They are, left to right, Pvt. Kenneth D. Rexford, 19, who enlisted in July, 1943, and who is serving with a Medical Corps unit in France; Pfc. Gordon J. Rexford, who entered the service in February, 1943, and who is stationed in England; Pfc. Donald P. Rexford, 23, who was inducted in June, 1943, and who is now in England with an Air Corps unit, and Sergt. William J Rexford, 25, who entered the service in July, 1942, who is a turret gunner in the Air Corps, his base being in England.

THE WEATHER
Tonight—Fair, cooler.

THE TIMES RECORD

FINAL EDITION

SERIES 1944—NO. 199   (Entered as Second Class Matter at the Postoffice at Troy, N. Y., Under the Act of March 3, 1879.)   TROY, N. Y., WEDNESDAY EVENING, AUGUST 23, 1944.   (Published Daily Except Sunday)   PRICE FOUR CENTS

FRENCH LIBERATE PARIS

Yanks Push Toward German Border

Third Invasion Of France Reported In Bordeaux Zone

PRESIDENT SEES LEND-LEASE VITAL UNTIL JAPAN QUITS

Tells Congress Total Aid to Allies Up to July 1 Was 28 Billions

Washington (AP)—President Roosevelt informed Congress today that lend-lease shipments to the Allies reached a total of $28,270,000,000 on July 1 and urged the program be continued after the defeat of Germany to insure a speedier victory over Japan.

In apparent reference to recent discussions on whether lend-lease could not be halted after the war in Europe ends, Mr. Roosevelt warned in his 16th report to Congress:

"We should not permit any weakening of this system of combined war supply to delay final victory a single day or to cost unnecessarily the life of one American boy."

Lend-lease has helped bring the prospect of complete victory "sooner than we had hoped," the Chief Executive said, pointing out that the $28,270,000,000 cost of the program thus far represented but 15 per cent of all U. S. war spending.

Would Continue Program.

"Until the unconditional surrender of both Japan and Germany," he said, "we should continue the lend-lease program on whatever scale is necessary to make the combined striking power of all the United Nations against our enemies as overwhelming and as effective as we can make it."

The present lend-lease law expires June 30, 1945 unless terminated sooner by a joint resolution of Congress. The National Association of Manufacturers said recently that the British had suggested extension of lend-lease after the German defeat to help Britain rehabilitate her domestic economy and make possible a greater contribution to the war against Japan. The State Department, however, said no direct negotiations have been made on the subject.

Mr. Roosevelt's report listed these principal recipients of lend-lease aid: Great Britain, $9,321,549,000; Russia, $5,931,944,000; Mediterranean theater (Italy and Southern France) $3,070,829,000; India and China, $1,402,426,000; Australia and New Zealand, $1,011,885,000; and Latin American countries, $171,970,000.

Outlines Reverse Aid.

Actual lend-lease shipments, including some others to other countries, totaled $21,534,570,000 on July 1, the President reported, but this did not include other goods or services in transit or awaiting shipment under lend-lease.

Mr. Roosevelt again stressed that lend-lease is not a one way proposition. Not only have the Allies supplied about $3,000,000,000 in reverse aid, he said, but they "have been called upon to give more in lives, in destruction to their homelands and in the suffering of their people."

His report showed that U. S. lend-lease aid through the first three months ending June 30 totaled $4,045,000,000, thus falling slightly below the record of $4,233,000,000 in the first three months of this year.

Since the inception of lend-lease March 11, 1941, about 54 per cent of total aid has consisted of fighting equipment, 21 per cent of industrial materials, 13 per cent of food and about 12 per cent of services.

CIVIL LIBERTY ONLY PROMISE IN RUSSIA, JOHNSON DECLARES

Seattle (AP)—Eric Johnston, U. S. Chamber of Commerce president, after praising Russia as a nation of indomitable courage, described it as a land where "civil liberties are only a vague promise" and where, "if there is any religion, it is the worship of Stalin."

The Spokane, Wash., business man, who recently returned from a trip to the Soviet Union, told 500 construction men last night:

"In my travels I have rediscovered America. Never before did I realize the importance of our freedom, our standard of living, our right of habeas corpus, our bill of rights.

"Don't sell America short."

EINSTEIN RESCUED IN LOWER SARANAC LAKE

Saranac Lake (AP)—Prof. Albert Einstein was reported to have suffered no ill effects yesterday when his sailboat upset and he was thrown into the choppy waters of lower Saranac Lake. Einstein, a summer visitor, and several companions were quickly rescued.

U.S. TANK FORCES HEAD FOR TROYES IN FRENCH SWEEP

Capture of Vital Railway Hub Would Cut Nazi Escape Route

Supreme Headquarters, A. E. F. (UP)—Powerful American tank columns pounded eastward within a day's ride of the German frontier today, striking for the key railway hub of Troyes in a bid to close the last direct escape route for all the Nazi armies of Southern France.

Lieut. Gen. George S. Patton's tanks and motorized infantrymen had broken contact with headquarters in their dramatic strike toward the frontiers of the reich, and headquarters maintained strict secrecy on the whereabouts of the advanced American spearheads.

Front dispatches revealed, however, that the Yanks were driving at breakneck speed beyond the ancient fortified city of Sens, which they captured yesterday after a 60-mile thrust around the southern suburbs of Paris, and heading directly for Troyes, 130 miles east of Germany.

With the American breakthrough into Eastern France, headquarters permitted correspondents to state flatly that the battle of France is nearing its end and that the liberation of the entire country is not far off.

Tighten Trap On Germans.

Far behind Patton's flying columns, a powerful American tank army massed around liberated Paris, while other American and Allied armies converged on the Seine River line, tightening a great noose around the broken remnants of the German Seventh Army in Normandy.

One American column slashed deep into the southern flank of the corridor across which the Germans were fleeing, driving 25 miles northwest of Dreux to the Evreux area against light resistance. A second American force drove into the corridor along a parallel path more than ten miles to the northeast between the Eure and Seine Rivers.

Both forces were reported making rapid progress toward the channel coast and the prize port of Le Havre, little more than fifty miles beyond their advanced units.

Only about 93,000 of the more than 400,000 Germans who defended Normandy on D-Day were alive and uncaptured in the narrowing corridor extending from the channel to the northern suburbs of Paris and from the Seine to the Touques and Vie River lines.

And those fleeing remnants were being hounded mercilessly from land and air, bombed and shelled as they raced for the Seine, where Allied planes swept through low-hanging clouds to strafe the river crossings.

A headquarters spokesman yesterday said that between 40,000 and 50,000 German prisoners had been taken from the Argentan trap and that the enemy dead have not yet been counted.

Canadians Take Trouville.

Canadian, British and American troops pushing eastward toward the Seine advanced an average of ten miles all along the line yesterday, with Canadian units along the channel coast sweeping into

(Continued on Page 13.)

SWITZERLAND SEVERS RELATIONS WITH VICHY

London (AP)—Switzerland broke off diplomatic relations with the Vichy government today, asserting Marshal Henri Philippe Petain no longer considered himself chief of state.

An announcement via the Swiss radio said: "The Swiss Federal Council, having taken note of Petain's statement that he has been taken forcibly—from Vichy and no longer considered himself chief of state, have broken off diplomatic representation with the Petain-Laval government."

Nazis Driven Back On Gothic Line In Italy

Rome (AP)—Eighth Army Polish and Italian troops, overwhelming German rearguard resistance in the Adriatic sector south of the Metauro River between Cesena and Mount Maggiore, pushed the enemy northward to within less than 27 miles of the fortified Gothic line, an Allied communique disclosed today.

While the remainder of the front was relatively quiet, the Poles and Italians sent out patrols which gained control of most of the south bank of the Metauro to a point 12 miles inland. Despite a heavy artillery barrage laid down by the Germans from the north bank of the river, Allied forces made gains up to three miles in the more mountainous country southwest of San Giorgio Di Pesaro.

Allied patrols probed both sides of the upper Arno Valley and found the enemy established in new positions further north, the communique revealed. East of Florence, north of the Arno River, British Eighth Army Indian troops took a number of prisoners in an ambush.

Front dispatches reported that approximately forty persons, including women and children, were killed when German shells landed in the midst of a religious procession near the Church of San Lorenzo, which dates back to the fourth century and is the oldest place of Christian worship in Florence.

Shell fragments damaged the church cupola and walls and caused minor damage in the Uffizi galleries.

GENERAL PATTON PLEASED: Lieut. Gen. George S. (Pistol Packin') Patton has good reason for smiling. His troops are sweeping through France like a prairie fire. Here he is adjusting a new six-shooter in its holster.

RAILWAYS CITED IN ANTI-TRUST ACTION

Western Carriers and Two Banking Houses Named

Lincoln, Neb. (UP)—The Department of Justice filed an anti-trust action in Federal Court today charging the Association of American Railroads, 47 western carriers and their chief executives, and two banking houses with collusive rate-fixing.

The civil complaint, charging violation of the Sherman anti-trust act, also accused the railroads of discouraging improvements in service and equipment.

Banking houses named in the complaint were J. P. Morgan and Co., and Kuhn, Loeb, and Co.

Named also as defendants were the officers and directors of the American Railroad Association, the Western Association of Railway Executives and 31 other individuals.

The 40-page complaint charged that the defendants, beginning about 1932 and continuing to the present time, have been engaged in an unlawful combination and conspiracy in restraint of trade and commerce in the transportation of freight and passengers among the several states and with foreign nations" and "are parties to contracts, agreements, arrangements, and understandings in restraint of said trade and commerce".

The restraints were accomplished and continued to be accomplished, the complaint said, by

Imposing upon shippers in the western district freight rates which are higher than those for comparable service in the eastern district.

Preventing western district railroads from initiating freight or passenger rates without approval of defendants and their conspirators in the eastern district.

Fixing rates for the transportation of petroleum and petroleum products both by rail and pipeline at non-competitive levels.

The department seeks the dissolution of the Association of American Railroads and the Western Association of Railway Executives, and an injunction against all the defendants to prevent the revival or continuance of any of the offenses charged, continuance or reinstatement of the western agreement, the "western commissioners" and the "committee of directors" under which the western agreement was operated.

AUSTIN EXPECTS NO CAMPAIGN DISCORD ON SECURITY AND PEACE

Washington (AP)—Sen. Warren R. Austin, (R.-Vt.) said today after an eighty-minute conference with John Foster Dulles, Gov. Thomas E. Dewey's foreign policy adviser, that the presidential campaign will be devoid of "partisan discord" on the issue of postwar security and peace.

Austin said that after discussing security and peace with Dulles he was "more strongly persuaded than ever" that the issue of foreign policy would be treated by Republican and Democratic campaigners "without ripping open this subject on which all Americans agree."

Dulles meets Secretary of State Cordell Hull later today in a conference that may bring Republican proposals for changes in the American plan of world organization.

"MISS LIBERTY" POPULAR

New York (AP)—The Statue of Liberty is the leading attraction here for sightseers of the Allied forces, a compilation by the USO shows. Last month more than 10,000 visitors were listed.

AMERICAN TROOPS ENTER GRENOBLE IN SOUTH FRANCE

Industrial City Taken in Surprise Thrust with Aid of Maquis

Rome (AP)—American troops of the Seventh Army, in a spectacular surprise thrust deep into southern France through German defenses, have entered the large industrial city of Grenoble, 140 airline miles north of the Mediterranean coast, it was announced today.

A swift American armored and motorized infantry column plunged into the city, long a hotbed of the French patriot movement, with "French forces of the interior playing an effective support role," Allied headquarters said.

This quick advance put Maj. Gen. Alexander M. Patch's spearhead within less than 240 miles airline from the most southerly points officially announced as reached by American troops below Paris, and it appeared that the two Allied French fronts would be joined much sooner than originally thought possible.

Grenoble, 58 miles southeast of Lyon and situated on a river leading directly to the Rhone valley thirty miles to the west, is eighty miles or more beyond the last reported Allied positions in southern France.

Other Towns Captured.

Lying in the French Alps, the city has a population of approximately 100,000 and is a rail center on the Paris-Lyon-Marseille route. It also commands access to important mountain passes in eastern France.

Towns taken by the Americans en route to Grenoble included Digne, Sisteron, Aspres, Gap, St. Bonnet and L'Argentiere, the latter 35 miles from the Italian border.

At Grenoble the Americans were roughly only seventy airline miles from the Swiss frontier and for all practical purposes already had sealed off the Nazi forces in southern France from communication with the enemy in northwestern Italy.

The Americans also were in position, by striking westward, to cut off German units reported fleeing from the Mediterranean beachhead along the Rhone valley toward northern France.

(An Associated Press dispatch from Geneva said French forces of the interior were reported attacking Lyon.)

French Patriot Center.

Grenoble, the old capital of the province of Dauphine and the chief

(Continued on Page 2.)

TROPICAL HURRICANE REPORTED HEADING FOR EAST COAST OF MEXICO

New Orleans (AP)—A tropical hurricane emerging from the Yucatan jungles moved into the Gulf of Campeche early today and continued its westward course toward the east coast of Mexico.

The weather bureau here said it was expected to move inland north of Tampico late tonight with winds up to 85 miles an hour near the center and gales over a 100-mile area north of the center.

The weather bureau in a 4 a. m. (E.W.T.) advisory located the storm about 160 miles west southwest of Merida, Mexico, moving about 15 miles an hour.

High winds and tides will begin on the coast of Tamaulipas, Mexico, late this afternoon, the advisory said.

Shipping in the Gulf of Mexico south of latitude 25 degrees and west of longitude 90 degrees was alerted against high winds.

A lesser disturbance brought squally weather to the lower Texas coast after moving inland south of Brownsville, Tex., last night.

NAZI BOMBS CAUSE MORE CASUALTIES IN ENGLAND

London (AP)—South England today suffered its heaviest dawn barrage of flying bombs yet, as Allied armies beat toward the launching platforms in Pas-de-Calais beyond the Seine.

The robots came so fast that gunners had no respite in throwing up a terrific curtain of orange fire. Clouds of smoke over the area indicated the number of bombs brought down in the channel. Others were heard exploding aloft.

A number of casualties, including some deaths, were reported, mostly from bombs striking residential sections. Bomb shelters survived the bombardment. An American Army officer awaiting a bus was killed.

TEA SUPPLY INCREASES.

New York (AP)—The supply of tea in the United States at mid-year totaled approximately 25,252,000 pounds, more than twice the supply on hand a year ago, Benjamin Wood, managing director of the Tea Bureau announced today.

Pershing Happy at Liberation of Paris

Washington (AP)—Gen. John J. Pershing, who commanded the American Expeditionary Force in the First World War, today described the liberation of Paris as "a great step forward along the road to Berlin."

In a statement issued through the Office of War Information, General Pershing said:

"Over four years ago, when the Germans took Paris, my sorrow was beyond words. Paris is the heart of France.

"Today, Paris is free; and the sons of the Americans who fought to preserve the freedom of Paris in 1917 and 1918 had a prominent part in the liberation of 1944. By their cooperation with their British, Canadian and French allies these American soldiers of 1944 have upheld the high military traditions of the United States Army.

"The liberation of Paris is a great step forward along the road to Berlin."

RED ARMY ROLLS ON FROM IASI IN ROMANIAN DRIVE

New Offensive Threatens to Smash Hitler's Grip on Balkans

Moscow (AP)—A new Red Army offensive, probably designed to knock Romania out of the war and break Hitler's grip on the Balkans, smashed forward today on a 150-mile front beyond Iasi to within 180 miles of jittery Bucharest and 155 of the great Ploesti oil center.

Towns taken by the Americans en route to Grenoble included the entry of the German broadcast said the Russians had reached the beaches at Riga, Latvian capital and largest Baltic states city, indicating a new trap for the German 16th and 18th armies.

The Russians outflank Warsaw.

Lieut. Gen. Joseph Pierre Koenig, commander of the French forces of the interior and military governor of Paris, gave this official version of the deliverance of the capital:

"On the morning of Saturday, Aug. 19, the National Council of Resistance and the Paris Committee of Liberation in agreement with the national delegate representing the provisional government of the French republic, ordered a general insurrection in Paris and in the Parisian district.

"French forces of the interior to the number of 50,000 armed men, supported by several hundred thousand unarmed patriots, went into action immediately.

"The Paris police, who had previously gone on strike, seized the police prefecture and the Ile de la Cite. They turned the Ile de la Cite into a bastion, against which German attacks broke down.

"Toward 8 p.m. yesterday, Aug. 22, after a four-day struggle, the enemy had been beaten everywhere and the patriots occupied all public buildings.

"Representatives of the enemy arrested or are in flight.

"Thus the people of Paris have taken a prominent part in the liberation of the capital.

"Long live France!"

PAPER SAYS ROOSEVELT AND CHURCHILL WILL WITNESS PARIS PARADE

London (AP)—The London Daily Herald said today plans were being made for President Roosevelt and Prime Minister Churchill to be present in Paris, "if that is practical," when Allied troops parade under the Arc de Triomphe.

French troops will head the Allied parade, with Gen. Charles De Gaulle probably having the place of honor, the newspaper added.

Declaring the march into the French capital will climb the "campaign of destruction of the German armies zone a stage further," the Daily Herald said special news reel operators already have been detailed to record the event and military bands which will participate now are practicing in France.

"The Daily Mail said a conference between Roosevelt and Churchill would "take place within a matter of weeks on French soil."

Lily Pons Plans To Sing In Paris Again

New York (UP)—"Now," exclaimed Lily Pons, clasping her hands, "now I will sing in Paris again—the Marseillaise and all of France will sing with me."

The way the little coloratura said it was "sweeng" and "weeth" for in her happiness her accent was even more evident than usual.

"Everything in my home is French and everything in my heart is French," she cried. "And now we do not have the feeling of captivity any longer. The weight is lifted from our hearts."

She jumped down the stairs into her living room two steps at a time and tuned in a radio newscast of Brig. Gen. Joseph-Pierre Koenig's announcement of the liberation of Paris.

"Listen . . . listen . . . France is free," she exclaimed.

And suddenly she was crying, her tears running as quickly as her laughter.

"I shall go to Paris," she said after a while. "André has promised me. We shall give a big concert for relief. We will go all over the country for the relief and all the

PATRIOTS CRUSH LAST OF GERMANS IN "CITY OF LIGHT"

Nazi Garrison Slaughtered in Four-day Battle with Maquis, Civilians

London (AP)—Paris loosed the shackles of four years of enemy bondage today and stood free once more, liberated by armed and unarmed tens of thousands of Frenchmen who swept the Nazis from the city's streets, while American armed might drew up around the capital.

A special communique from Gen. Charles DeGaulle's headquarters in London announced the liberation after four days of street fighting that recalled scenes of Bastille Day 155 years ago when the mobs of Paris once before struck an historic blow for liberty.

This time, the communique said, the fight was led by 50,000 organized French forces of the interior, bolstered by hundreds of thousands more who joined in with whatever weapons they could find.

French Announce Victory.

The dramatic announcement touched off broadcasts to Frenchmen everywhere as the triumphant strains of "La Marseillaise" sounded again to the news of a French victory.

There was no word immediately that American troops had entered the city.

But the French said they had seized all public buildings, won complete control of the situation, and captured all the Vichy representatives who had not fled.

The battle for Paris reached its bloody climax yesterday when patriots equipped wearily back to artillery that apparently had been run into the city from the American rear guards, began shelling the last Nazi positions. The Germans were said to have spent their last strength in an unsuccessful attempt to retake the Ile de la Cite from the patriots.

(There was no immediate indication whether the famous Notre Dame Cathedral, on the Ile de la Cite, had been damaged in the fight.)

Koenig Describes Liberation.

Lieut. Gen. Joseph Pierre Koenig, commander of the French forces of the interior and military governor of Paris, gave this official version of the deliverance of the capital:

German shock troops tried to stiffen war-weary Romanian divisions as Russian tanks rolled at least ten miles south of Iasi—Tukhin's drive through Bessarabia headed cross-country for a junction with Malinovsky in the Galati area, the capture of which would make much of the Balkan area untenable for the enemy. Advances ranged to 44 miles. The Bessarabian capital of Chisinau was left trapped in a deep pocket on the Dnestr.

Russians Outflank Warsaw.

In northern Poland, the Russians gradually were outflanking Warsaw and splitting German forces between that besieged Polish capital and East Prussia. The Russians moved 16 miles southeast of Lomza, communications hub. Desperate German attempts to salvage her Baltic positions brought new tank attacks in the direction of Jelgava, which controls road and rail routes to Latvia.

As the Red Army drive into Romania went through its fourth day, Bucharest was reported in panic with many of Premier Antonescu's formerly fanatical supporters openly discussing the chances of suing for peace. Each mile the Red Army advanced strengthened peace tremors in Bulgaria, too, and gave new hope to Yugoslavia and Greece. Romania, besides being Ger-

(Continued on Page 2.)

"City of Light" Free Again.

Paris, the city of light, was back in French hands just four years and 74 days from the time Adolf Hitler's troops marched in. German troops, then at the flood tide of conquest, entered June 14, 1940.

The city became the first continental capital of a full-fledged ally to be freed from German domination. Rome has been taken, but

(Continued on Page 25.)

money that comes in will go to those who have nothing left now."

She wondered, she said, if her two sisters in Paris would be there still. She has no way of knowing what has happened to them.

"But they are all right. My mother and my niece with me here—we know they will be all right," she said. "They will come to my concert and help me dress."

Miss Pons has dreamed, she said, of staying again at the Hotel Crillon on the Place de la Concorde, of singing at the Salle Playeux. She will give a concert for her own French charity, for those who live at Pont-Aux-Dames.

"They are the artists, the ones who now are tired and so old they cannot sing or paint or write, and we who are still young, we give the benefits for them," she said. "That way, you see, they can live in a castle."

She cannot go to Paris for at least three months. She must sing the opera in New York and San Francisco, "because I am the American too." But then she will come back.

WAR CHEST DRIVE HEADS APPOINTED BY WESLEY WOOD

Bert Baker and Benjamin Levine Cochairmen for County Division

The appointment of Bert Baker and Benjamin Levine as cochairmen of the Rensselaer County Division of the Allied Communities War Chest drive was made yesterday by J. Wesley Wood, jr., general chairman of the War Chest campaign.

Together with organizing the drive in rural areas, Mr. Baker and Mr. Levine will supervise District 1 which includes Hoosick, Pittstown and Schaghticoke. Three other units comprise the Rensselaer County division and the co-chairmen named Granville Hicks, chairman of District 2, John S. Finch, chairman of District 3, and Lewis Griffin, chairman of District 4.

District 2 covers Grafton, Petersburg and Brunswick; District 3 includes Schodack, Nassau, East Greenbush and North Greenbush, while District 4 takes in Stephentown, Berlin, Poestenkill and Sand Lake.

The district chairmen will be charged with the task of lining up volunteer workers in their territories for the drive which opens on Oct. 11 and runs to Oct. 20.

Clinton E. Rose, Troy Area Council Boy Scout executive, will be secretary of the county division.

The 22 agencies of the National War Fund including the USO, the

WAR CHEST LEADERS—Bert Baker, left, and Benjamin Levine, second left, were appointed rural district co-chairmen for the War Chest campaign yesterday by J. Wesley Wood, jr., seated, general chairman. With the chairmen at the Allied Communities War Chest conference are Clinton E. Rose, right, Boy Scout Council executive, who will be secretary of the county division and James C. Turner, executive secretary of the Troy Council of Social Agencies.

United Seamen's and the Prisoner's Aid plus twenty agencies of the Troy Community Chest are included in the drive.

SCHAGHTICOKE.

Miss Lois Pecor is spending a week's vacation with her parents Mr. and Mrs. James Pecor.

Mr. and Mrs. Harry O'Connor have moved from Mechanicville to the Pinkham flat on Main Street.

Corp. Thomas F. Mitchell, U. S. M. C. of San Diego, Cal., is spending a furlough with his parents, Mr. and Mrs. John Mitchell, sr.

Pfc. Charles Leason of Atlantic City, N. J., is spending a furlough with his parents, Mr. and Mrs. Fred Leason. He has recently returned from the South Pacific.

Mrs. Joseph Macri and daughters, Mr. and Mrs. Wolfgang and children of Albany and Mr. and Mrs. William Viall and daughter of Lebanon, Pa., were recent guests of Mrs. Marion Williamson and family.

Mrs. Leon Bevia will entertain the Nimble Needle Club at her home this evening. Miss Mildred Hanks will have the white elephant. Mrs. E. R. Curtis will present her money-making idea. Mrs. Frank Conley will have charge of the games.

The September missionary meeting of the United Society of the Presbyterian Church will be held tomorrow at the home of Mrs. Louis Martin. Mrs. Chauncey Verbeck will be the leader. Mrs. Charles Connolly will have charge of the devotions.

MELROSE.

The Women's Society of Christian Service of the Methodist Church will hold a food sale and clam chowder sale on the lawn of Mrs. Albert Stuart on Saturday at 2 pm. In case of rain it will be held at Diefendorf's store. Mrs. Orin Reed and Mrs. Agnes Olmstead are cochairmen.

MEDICAL WORLD STUDIES NEW DRUG TO FIGHT LEPROSY

Promin, Sulfonamide Derivative, Now Being Given Test

BY MARY FRANCES PUTMAN

Carville, La. (AP)—The medical world may have an opening wedge into its fight against leprosy in promin, a new sulfonamide derivative and a relative of the now famous sulfa drugs, or some promin successor.

Promin resulted from weary months of research by Dr. Louis Brambas, chemical engineer, bacteriologist and chemist. He put together atoms of nitrogen, carbon, oxygen, sulphur and sodium—and the resulting yellow powder was given the name "promin."

The new drug is one of the sulfones, second cousins of the sulfonamides and a family long overshadowed by the sulfas' spectacular rise to medical prominence.

Formerly physicians could recommend only rest, good diet and protection from injury in treating leprosy. Chaulmoogra oil, derived from nuts of an Indian tree, is the only drug weapon which leprologists had to fight the disease and many are still highly doubtful about its value as a treatment.

People contracted leprosy, became resigned to the fact, and still had leprosy when they died. Sufferers of the dreaded malady have always been isolated and shunned by society, although leprosy is actually one of the least communicable of diseases.

Only One Leprosarium.

At lonely little Carville, La., sixty miles north of New Orleans, the U. S. Public Health Service operates the only leprosarium in the continental United States. It usually houses about 350 patients. Medical personnel here became interested in reports of experiments with promin in treatment of tuberculosis, which is like leprosy in many respects, and began experimenting on leprosy patients.

Dr. G. H. Faget, staff physician, selected a group of patients and began what he calls "the most encouraging experimental treatment ever undertaken at the national leprosarium."

In a group of 22 patients, each was given one to five grams of promin intravenously daily, except Sundays, for a period of one year. Two-week rest periods, during which they got no injections, were observed three times during the 12 months. They were plied with liver and iron to ward off anemia, the most troublesome toxic manifestation resulting from promin injections.

Results showed that 15 cases definitely improved; the condition of six remained stationary, and only one out of the 22 showed any signs of growing worse. Bacterioscopies (skin smears) of five of the group reverted from positive to negative.

In another experiment, 46 sufferers took a shorter course of promin intravenously. Duration of treatment in this group varies from two to 11 months, and averages eight months. In 17 the conditions were stationary, and only three patients were worse after the treatment period.

Conditions Improved.

Normal skin began to replace coppery leprous patches on patients treated with promin. Open sores healed. Throat and nasal lesions, which clog these passages and cause suffocation, began to subside, and leprous lesions of the eyes, threatening blindness, cleared up. One 34-year-old man, leprotic for 17 years, took 1,522 grams of promin over a period of 17 months. Leprous ulcers of the lips, mouth and nose and eight ulcers of the legs healed completely. Leprous infiltration of the face diminished.

About 100 Carville patients are now taking promin. "So many others are requesting the treatment that we are considering enlarging the group," Dr. Faget said.

Promin doesn't work overnight miracles, and it is not claimed that promin is a specific cure for leprosy. But staff members at Carville think "it is an advance in the right direction in the therapy of this disease" which today afflicts three to five million persons over the world.

Sulfones are not on the market yet, and the promin used in the national leprosarium experiments was donated by Parke Davis & Co. But research men are still digging into sulfone possibilities, in hopes that further synthesis of the sulfones and other sulfa compounds may produce a substance which will save countless lives in this still dark field of medicine.

LATHAM.

Miss Ann Whitney, daughter of Mr. and Mrs. George Whitney, is ill at her home.

The choir of Calvary Methodist Church will meet today at 7:30 p.m. at the church.

Miss Olive MacDowell of the Shaker Road was the guest last week of Miss Olive Peters of Utica.

Mr. and Mrs. Roy Cormie and son Lee, of Stop 38, Troy-Schenectady Road, spent the week-end with their parents in Utica.

The Boy Scouts' Auxiliary will hold a meeting today at 6:30 p.m. at Calvary Hall. A covered dish luncheon will be served.

Pvt. William H. Dearborn, jr. of Creig Field, Ala. is spending 15 days with his parents, Mr. and Mrs. W. H. Dearborn of the Old Loudon Road.

Billie Hopson, son of Mr. and Mrs. Warren Hopson of the Old Loudon Road, has returned from the Samaritan Hospital where he underwent an operation.

Corp. Earl B. Feiden, jr., who is stationed at Wright Field, Dayton, O., is spending an eight-day furlough with his parents, Mr. and Mrs. Earl B. Feiden, sr., of the Shaker Road.

CITY DIVIDED INTO HEALTH ZONES TO FURTHER PROGRAM

Dr. James C. Boland Acts to Promote Public Health Nursing

The Troy Health Department, headed by Dr. James C. Boland, commissioner, has redistricted the city into four zones for a more efficient public health nursing program. A nurse for generalized nursing, exclusive of venereal and tuberculosis cases, has been appointed for each district.

"We expect with this arrangement the nurse will become more acquainted with her patients," the commissioner disclosed, "the public will have more confidence in a nurse whom they know. It will cut down extensively on traveling expenses by this office, together with costs of equipment.

"Some of the duties of these nurses will be to investigate communicable diseases, help control the health of growing children through prenatal, well-baby and child hygiene attention in addition to checking children not yet immunized against diptheria and smallpox. For the latter we refer them to the family physician or the free treatment at our Friday clinics."

Ways and means of carrying out this program were discussed with Mrs. Anna Hudson of the State Health Department at 2 pm today at the Health Center.

Nurses and their newly assigned districts are Mrs. Kathryn B. Matthews, Congress Street, south to city line; Mrs. Eileen Coffey, Congress Street to 101st Street, east as far as Eighth Street; Miss Veronica C. Voltz, district from Eighth Street east, including East Side and Sycaway and Miss Ellen Sheehy, 101st Street, north to city line.

Newfoundland is the oldest colony in the British Commonwealth.

COMPENSATION AWARDS GIVEN APPROVAL BY REFEREE L. A. KILBURN

Referee Lyman A. Kilburn, presiding in Compensation Court, yesterday approved a $1,000 settlement in the case of Ralph Gruen, injured while in the employ of the Circle Inn. Two Behr-Manning Corp. employees, Raymond Hickey and Abraham Rosen, were granted $392 and $207, respectively, for injuries sustained.

For 10 per cent loss of the use of the left hand, John W. Alber, employed by Alber Bros. Garage, Inc., was awarded $549. Wilbur D. Long, injured while at work for the White Flowmatic Corp., received $225 and Albert J. Wiesenforth, employed by the Mack International Truck Corp., received $222.50.

STAFF ASSISTANTS OF RED CROSS TO MEET

The staff assistant corps of the local Red Cross chapter is holding its first fall meeting at 8 p.m. today with Mrs. R. L. Meade, chairman, presiding. It will review the assignments of members to assist in the need for further volunteers to carry out its program. This group of women is trained in the workings of various departments of the organization to serve in making assignments to each.

Mrs. A. L. Darby, chairman of the Volunteer Special Service Committee, and Mrs. Virginia E. Bray, executive secretary, will be present.

White House Quiz Answers

QUIZ XXII. WHAT IT TAKES

(Questions on Page 12)

1. True.
2. False.
3. True.
4. False.
5. False.
6. False.
7. False.
8. True.
9. False.
10. True.

SCHOOL GIRLS OF TROY GUESTS AT TRI-Y SOCIAL TIME

Many Attend "Get-acquainted Night" Conducted at Y. W. C. A.

The Tri-Y held its annual "get acquainted" party last night at the Troy Y. W. C. A. for all girls of high school age of the city.

About 170 girls were in attendance at the affair, which opened the fall schedule of activities. Girls served refreshments at the Cactus Bar and planned for the various fall events in the near future. A get acquainted bingo was held to enable all present to meet their neighbors.

The young women registered for the various clubs which will get under way next week at the Y. W. C. A. Advisors at last night's meeting were Mrs. Andrew C. Bradt, chairman of Younger Girls committee; Mrs. William E. Fitzgerald, jr., Miss Onnie Lee, Miss Mary Bonelli and Miss Margaret Kenny.

A program under the direction of Miss Elvira Jaborg, secretary for work with girls of high school work, and Miss Ann Swensson, secretary in charge of activities of girls of junior high school age, will get under way next week.

Some of the events scheduled are first aid, child care courses; hikes, picnics, sports, dramatics and service project.

This year's service project will be collecting spools of thread and needles to be sent to The Netherlands Aid Society, a group made up of girls of the same age who need the items mentioned to repair pieces of clothing.

"GET ACQUAINTED"—Troy high school age girls were guests last night at the annual "get acquainted" party of the Tri-Y in the Young Women's Christian Association. Pictured at the event are, left to right, Frances Miller, Juliet Casey, Lucy Casparian, Jean Trembley, Patricia Peetz, Vivian Rowland and Miss Elvira Jaborg, Y. W. C. A. secretary and Tri-Y councilor.

ROOSEVELT FAVORS RURAL SCHOOL AID

Washington (UP) — President Roosevelt said yesterday the federal government should provide financial aid where needed to bring country schools up to the educational level of city school systems, but that such aid should "never involve government interference with local administration."

Speaking to a rural education conference at the White House, Mr. Roosevelt said, "frankly, the chief problem of rural education is the problem of dollars and cents" and he added, the basic reason for the variance between rural schools and city schools hinges on the pay for instructors.

The President said the gap between educational standards in the richer communities and those in poorer areas is greater now than it was a century ago. He said the gap must be closed "by raising the standards in the poorer communities."

NAZIS PLANNING GUERRILLA WAR

Berlin Leaders Hope to Nullify Allied Victory

London (UP) — A Nazi blueprint for highly organized and fanatical guerrilla warfare to nullify any Allied victory and make the civil administration of conquered German territory almost impossible was outlined yesterday by Nazi officialdom.

Propaganda Minister Paul Joseph Goebbels, in a speech to German workers on the western front quoted on the Berlin radio by D.N.B., said the Allies had launched an all-out offensive to win the war before winter, but that conditions now favor the German army, and in any event the Nazis were prepared to wage guerrilla war fare to the death.

An article in Das Schwarze Korps said guerrilla fighting plans, to meet conditions already becoming evident around Aachen, were far advanced, and based on everything the Germans had learned in Russia, the Balkans, France and Belgium—where they, as the occupying forces, were harassed by insurgents behind their lines.

Goebbels, declaring the Americans wanted a cheap pre-winter victory to help reelect President Roosevelt and the British because they were war-weary, said:

"It will make no difference whether the Americans are destroying our machinery and factories, or the bolsheviks are dragging our material and population to Siberia," he said. "Neither from one nor the other foe can we expect mercy."

Goebbels denounced Secretary of the Treasury Morgenthau for proposing to "turn industrial Germany into a vast potato field," and called General Eisenhower's orders to the German populace to obey instructions of the Allied Military Government "the impertinent arrogance of a renegade."

=ON THE AIR=
Radio Programs From Local Stations

TONIGHT

President Roosevelt will speak tonight at 10 o'clock, Station WOKO, Albany.

[radio listings]

THOUSANDS KILLED IN ARMY "HOME" CRASHES

Washington (UP) — Eleven thousand lives have been lost in 5,600 fatal Army Air Force accidents in the United States since Pearl Harbor.

The War Department made public these figures yesterday in a statement supplementing its earlier announcement that 17,500 planes had been "lost" in the United States during the same period. Of this total, the department said, only 11,000 were cracked up in wrecks while 4,000 were worn out in flight training and 2,500 were worn out to the extent that they became fit only for ground training.

The total of "lost" planes was slightly more than half the overall losses of 42,000 AAF aircraft in all operations at home and abroad.

FOOTBALL INJURY FATAL.

Detroit (UP) — Injuries suffered in a football game on a neighborhood playground proved fatal to Edward Chwaszczewski, 16. The youth died in receiving hospital last night.

Nervous, Restless On "CERTAIN DAYS" Of The Month?

If functional periodic disturbances make you feel nervous, tired, restless, "dragged out"—at such times—try famous Lydia E. Pinkham's Vegetable Compound to relieve such symptoms. It helps nature! Pinkham's Compound is also a grand stomachic tonic. Follow label directions. Worth trying!

LYDIA E. PINKHAM'S VEGETABLE COMPOUND

ROUND LAKE.

Mrs. Merritt Goddard is still confined to the Albany Hospital. Their daughter, Anne, is also ill there.

Mr. and Mrs. Lewis Lavery and sons, Adelbert and Robert, have returned from a few days in New York.

Rev. Chester A. Finch and Rev. Eliza Duffield have returned from Lake Placid, where they attended the fall conference meeting of ministers and laymen of the Troy Methodist Conference.

Mr. and Mrs. John W. Morris have been entertaining their daughter, Miss Carolyn Morris, cadet nurse, and Miss Marilyn Moore, of Westogue, Conn., a WAVE. Miss Moore, a former resident here, is entering Hunter College.

Mrs. Royal W. Northup, chairman, will meet the members of the library committee of the Women's Round Lake Improvement Society at the library tomorrow at 3 p.m. to formulate plans for the game party to be conducted by the committee.

Mrs. Edgar A. Seabury was hostess recently to the Round Lake Home Bureau at her home in the circle. Plans for the year were discussed. The next meeting will be Friday evening, Oct. 13, at Mrs. Jacob Schaad. Miss Jones, the home demonstration agent of the county, will outline the year's work and start instruction on the making of lamp shades. Anyone wishing to join the group may do so at that time.

The visual education conference opened this morning with meetings to be held in the Methodist Church today and tomorrow. Sessions tomorrow will include at 10 a.m., "Care and Use of Equipment," with demonstrations the building of an advance picture program for the local church, to be followed by demonstration of a silent picture. Luncheon will be served at noon followed at 1:30 p.m. by the showing of the picture "From Across the Border," and discussion of its educational value for the local church and the development of the schedule for several months ahead. An audio visual program will be conducted at 7:30 p.m. Ministers of all denominations are invited. The leader will be Jay S. Stowall, secretary of visual education of the Methodist Church.

MORE SHIPS NEEDED.

Washington (UP)—An increase of "about eight per cent" in the production of ships, planes and ordnance is necessary in the final quarter of this year, Navy Secretary Forrestal reported yesterday. Assault ships, he said, "continue to be the Navy's primary production problem."

STEPHENTOWN.

It was announced at a recent meeting of Taconic Valley Grange that "Neighbors' Night" will be conducted Monday, Oct. 15 with the tenth anniversary being observed the same evening. It is expected there will be a state speaker present to address the Grange. The Grange will furnish a supper for the Farm Bureau town committeemen and their wives Monday evening, Oct. 9, at Grange Hall. The youth committee of the Grange announced there will be a dance in the hall for the young people of the Grange tomorrow evening. The Grange voted to give $5 to the scholarship fund. A rising vote of thanks to Mark Stillman was given by the Grange for the fair exhibit at Schaghticoke. It now hangs in the hall. Sandwiches, coffee and doughnuts were served by the men.

Athlete's Foot Thrives On Damp Perspiring Feet

Athlete's Foot loves nothing better than to take up housekeeping in damp, perspiring feet—especially in the soggy flesh between the toes. So don't let your perspiring feet invite Athlete's Foot. Get Allen's Foot-Ease from your druggist and sprinkle this soothing medicated powder over your feet, between your toes and in your shoes. Allen's Foot-Ease is not a cure or treatment for Athlete's Foot but it does help to absorb excessive perspiration, keep feet dry and odorless and maintain a wholesome foot condition that helps prevent infection by Athlete's Foot. Get Allen's Foot-Ease today—it's a grand, easy, effective way to foot-comfort. —Adv.

TROY CHURCH GETS $2,000 IN MEMORY OF JAMES TAYLOR

Widow's Will Admitted to Probate by Albany Surrogate

The Second Presbyterian Church of Troy was bequeathed $2,000 by Mrs. Harriet E. Taylor, her will revealed yesterday when it was admitted to probate in Albany.

Mrs. Taylor died in Albany on August 31, leaving an estate of more than $5,000, according to the will. The $2,000 was left to the Troy church in memory of her husband, the late James W. Taylor.

The remainder of the estate was willed to Elizabeth M. Reed, Albany, in memory of "her care and devotion to Mr. and Mrs. Taylor, after disposition of the following bequests:

R. William Sterling, a nephew of Meadville, Pa., $2,000; Annie M Sterling, a sister-in-law also of Meadville, and Estelle Webb, Reading, Pa., $1,000 each; Donald McQueen, a cousin from Napa County, Cal., $500; Charles W. and Grace L. Benson, cousins from Warsaw, Harriet Clark of Meadville, Pa., Richard and Tiffany Lawyer, jr., Albany, and Mrs. Charles E. Miller of Pittsburg, $200 each.

The first attempt to breed salmon in America was made in New York City in 1864.

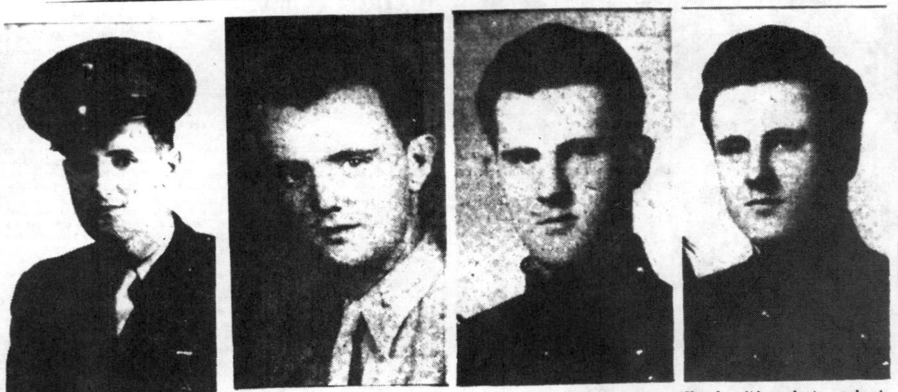

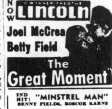

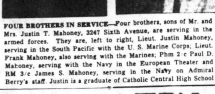

FOUR BROTHERS IN SERVICE—Four brothers, sons of Mr. and Mrs. Justin T. Mahoney, 3247 Sixth Avenue, are serving in the armed forces. They are, left to right, Lieut. Justin Mahoney, serving in the South Pacific with the U. S. Marine Corps; Lieut. Frank Mahoney, also serving with the Marines; Phm 2/c Paul D. Mahoney, serving with the Navy in the European Theater and RM 3/c James S. Mahoney, serving in the Navy on Admiral Berry's staff. Justin is a graduate of Catholic Central High School and the University of Toronto. He also did graduate work at R. P. I. Frank, a graduate of LaSalle and Yale, has been in service since November, 1942. Paul, who has served since September, 1942, is a graduate of LaSalle and attended Siena College and Albany School of Pharmacy. James, a graduate of LaSalle also, entered the Navy in September, 1943, and was a member of the Sampson football team last fall.

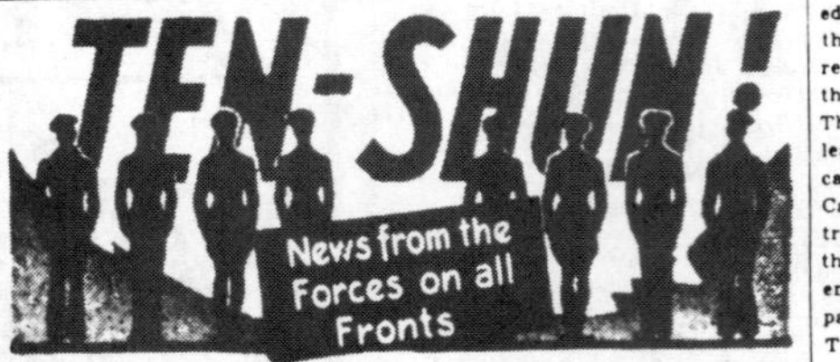

Two local members of a 15th A. A. F. Flying Fortress which has been cited for "heroic performance of duty against the enemy," now wear the blue citation ribbon. They are Staff Sergt. CARL W. MILLER, JR., of 24 Woodlawn Court and Staff Sergt. MICHAEL C. TOMA of 2 East Canal Street, Watervliet. The action for which the organization, the oldest heavy bombardment group in the European Theater, was cited occurred December 24 when they led the beavy bombers of their outfit against the aircraft factory and installations at Steyr, Austria. Despite fierce attacks by more than one hundred enemy fighters against their unescorted formation, the Fortresses fought their way through to bomb the target successfully. The gunners destroyed four enemy fighters, probably destroyed three and damaged two others while their own losses were one man killed and one wounded. Miller is C. C. H. S. and enlisted in the Air Forces March 6, 1943. Toma is Watervliet Hi and was with Behr-Manning, enlisting March 16, 1943. He has the air medal and oak leaf cluster and two battle stars on his ribbons.

Staff Sergt. JOHN H MEALY of 198 Pawling Avenue is an armorer in the B-24 Liberator group which recently completed one hundred bombing missions against enemy targets in 140 days. They showered more than ten million pounds of high explosives on enemy targets in Germany and enemy-held territory . . . Pfc. RALPH J. BONOMO, 381 Congress Street, has been assigned to the supply section of the Air Service Command somewhere in Britain . . . MILLARD L. OSGOOD, Troy, R. D. 4, has been made a sergeant somewhere in Italy. He is tail gunner on a B-24 Liberator and his groups has flown more than 110 combat missions. He is Troy Hi and worked for the United Traction Co.

S1/c DONALD C. WALLACE has returned from Italy to spend a leave with his parents, Mr. and Mrs. Arthur B. Wallace, 349 Second Street. . . . Sergt JOHN T. FITZGERALD, of 154 Liberty Street, serving with a railroad battalion in Italy, writes of the tough going in the mountains there because the rainy season is on but that the boys are giving the Germans no rest. "You never saw such courage, their motto is 'Go and Get 'Em'," he says. The German prisoners taken also have a lot of respect for the courage of the Yanks, he writes.

Corp. FRANCIS ARCHAMBEAULT, son of Mr. and Mrs. Francis Archambeault, sr., 168 Hudson Avenue, Green Island, is a member of a unit which has received a commendation from Brig. Gen. Jesse C. Anton, Wing Commander, for its contribution in aiding an Eighth Air Force fighter group to operate in 11 days after arrival at its English base. Before entering service, in September, 1942, he was employed as a route supervisor by the M. A. Gies Sales Co. At present, he is a propeller specialist at a base in England . . . Also with the unit receiving General Anton's commendation was Pvt. JOHN A. FERRO, son of Mr. and Mrs. Sebastian Ferro, 2315 Third Avenue, Watervliet. An alumnus of Watervliet High, he was employed at the Arsenal before joining up in April 1943. He is a member of the Defense Detachment guarding the airfield . . . Corp. THOMAS L. POLLOCK, son of Mrs. Jennie Pollock, 137 Hoosick Street, has won high commendation for helping to shatter world's production records repairing aircraft propellers, at his Command Depot in England. A mechanic with the Ford Green Island plant before entering service in October, 1942, he received his training at Chanute Field, Ill. . . . Second Lieut. WILLIAM S. PURCELL, son of Mr and Mrs. Edward J. Purcell, 438 Marshland Court, has arrived at Rosecrans Field, a base of the Ferry Division, Air Transport Command, near St. Joseph, Mo. He is at the Missouri base for an advanced pilot training course. A La Salle graduate and former employee of the U. S. Department of Agriculture at Washington, D. C., he was commissioned in February, 1943. His wife lives at South Great Falls, Mont., a brother, EDWARD C. PURCELL, is also in the armed forces. . . . Tech. Fifth Grade JOHN J. TURNER of 179 Fourth Street, was among one officer and 43 enlisted men of the Headquarters Company, 114th Service Command Unit at Camp Edwards, Mass., who were commended by Ma. Gen Sherman Miles, of the First Service Command for rendering valuable service during the hurricane of September 14-15. The men, according to the press release, battled throughout the hurricane to clear a road between the Camp and Falmouth of fallen trees, branches and other debris so that fire department and other emergency vehicles could have passage . . . Radioman PAUL THOMAS AHEARN, aviation radioman third class, of Watervliet, was presented wings of silver and gold, the insignia of a naval aircrewman this week, when he completed the final phase of training at the Jacksonville, Fla., Naval Air Station, and became a member of an air-combat team. Son of Mr. and Mrs Joseph M. Ahearn of 14 Ball Place, Watervliet, he will now be assigned to an operations squadron and proceed to one of the battle fronts either aboard an aircraft carrier or at a naval air station.

DONALD S. BLAIR, seaman second class, of 22 Euclid Avenue, has completed his Navy boot training at Sampson and has been granted a leave to visit home. . . Pvt. EDWARD J. MARKS, son of Mr and Mrs. Michael Suchecki of 654 First Avenue, North Troy, has been graduated from an aviation mechanic school at Amarillo, Tex., Army Air Field, and will be sent to advanced Gunnery School. Upon completion of his training he will be classified as an aerial engineer. Before entering service he was employed at the Eddy Valve Company . . . Carol Lasko, 6-year-old daughter of Dr. and Mrs Joseph P. Lasko, is the proud possessor of invasion money sent to her by Sergt. GERALD B. O'DAY of Troy, a family friend. . . Pfc. DARWIN O. MILLER, son of Edward J. Miller of Averill Park, R. F. D. 2, is a clerk in the engineering section of a 12th Air Force B-25 Mitchell medium bombardment group operating in the Mediterranean theater. . . . JOSEPH A. MILANESE, son of Mrs. Luigia Milanese, 270 Fourth Street, has arrived at Camp Croft, S. C., for basic training. He attended Troy High. . . . ROBERT C. MOORE, son of Mrs. Charles Moore, 23 Van Wert Court, has been promoted to the grade of staff sergeant at Hamilton Field, Cal., Army Air Base. He entered the Army Jan. 3, 1942.

Pfc. WILLARD D. GATES, son of Mr. and Mrs. Harry S. Gates of Eagle Bridge is one of the 88th Infantry Division combat engineers who bridged the Arno river in Italy under enemy fire. . . . Corp. WILLARD J. KILLE, son of Mr. and Mrs. Willard L. Kille, 1035 Twenty-third Street, Watervliet is serving with a 15th AAF group in Italy recently commended for outstanding performances in the European theater of Operations. His wife, Mrs. Ann Kille, lives at 65 109th Street . . . . CHARLES YALE has been promoted to corporal in France, his wife, Mrs. Clara Yale of North Troy, has been informed . . . . Lieut. EDWARD BAUER, with medical administration, has arrived in France, his wife, Sally Bauer of 430 Fifth Avenue, has been informed.

"Your son is a credit to the name of Decatur," a commanding officer has written Mr. and Mrs. Floyd Decatur, sr., of 689 Fourth Avenue about their son, FLOYD DECATUR who is a signalman first class in the Navy. He has been overseas for a year and a half having enlisted in the Navy two years ago. His commanding officer wrote Decatur's parents, "Your son has served me for the last nine months and I consider him one of the most outstanding of all enlisted men in my command. He is a gentleman at all times and in both performance of his duty and in social contacts, his behavior has been examplary. He is a credit to the name of the Naval officer and hero, Stephen Decatur." Signalman Decatur is a graduate of Lansingburg High School where he participated in all sports.

EAGLE BRIDGE.

Tech. Sergt. Douglas Fairbanks of the Army Air Force, who was at one time reported missing in action and later heard from by his parents, Mr. and Mrs. Fred Fairbanks, from Italy, spent several days at his home here recently. He expects to be granted a furlough soon.

The honor roll at Eagle Bridge was unveiled Sunday afternoon. Mrs. Leon Downing, jr., had charge of collections and program. Charles McNally, jr., Rev. Ernest Maguire of North Hoosick, pastor of Eagle Bridge Methodist Church; James Michie, Hoosick Falls; Rev. William Cuddy, pastor of St. Monica's Church of Johnsonville; Pfc. Lawrence Hall home on furlough from Fort Bliss, Tex.; Rev. Howard Hills of Petersburg, former pastor of Eagle Bridge Methodist Church and Mrs. George Gould, gold star mothers, took part.

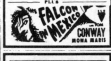

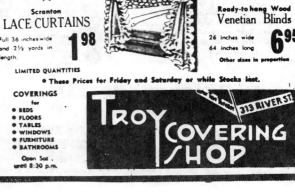

HURRICANE SEASON NEARING END BUT DANGER NOT OVER

Meteorologist Reviews Records; September, October Bad Months

BY JOHN W. WILDS.

Miami, Fla. (AP)—You can take heart from hurricane statistics, if you live on the Atlantic or Gulf Coasts of the United States—but keep your weather eye open.

Figures gathered over a fifty-year span show an average of seven tropical storms blow out of the doldrums—the equatorial area where calms prevail—each year, and already this year the weather bureau has charted eight, including the severe September hurricane that raked 1,000 miles of the East Coast. But—

"Don't read into those figures the assumption that we have had all the 1944 storms we'll have," warned Grady Norton, meterologist and ranking hurricane authority.

"They may indicate only that we're in the middle of a busy season.

Average Takes In Years.

"The average takes in years when only one disturbance was mapped. And it also takes in 1933, when 21 storms were tracked.

"Remember that September and October are the worst months, so far as hurricanes are concerned.

Coastal residents should keep prepared to take precautions against these cyclonic storms until mid-November and we've had them right on up until December."

There is good reason to hope, however, that no other storms this year will compare in ferocity with the one of Sept. 8-14, which already is ranked by the weather bureau among the comparatively few "great" hurricanes.

"It is extremely fortunate," observed Norton, "that the storm did not follow a path fifty miles farther west.

"As it was, the center stayed out to sea almost all of the way during the progress along the eastern shore, and the coast was affected only by the 'weak' side of the hurricane. Winds on the coast exceeded 75 miles an hour anyway. They must have been at least forty miles higher on the 'strong' side, which was out over water."

Move Counter Clockwise.

Hurricane winds whirl counterclockwise. When a disturbance is traveling northward, winds on the east side are stronger because the forward motion is added to the speed of rotation. On the west side, the forward motion serves to lessen the rotary force.

Although no other natural phenomenon packs the energy and the potential destructive power of a cyclonic storm with the size of a hurricane or typhoon, long-range protective forecasting now is impossible.

Atlantic hurricanes are spawned in three areas recognized by weather experts as breeding spots. One is in the vicinity of the Cape Verde Islands, off the African Coast. From here come the big Atlantic storms, such as the one which smacked the Middle Atlantic and New England areas. Another is in the western Caribbean Sea. Here are born most of the early and late summer disturbances. Occasional disturbances come out of the section of the Atlantic Ocean northeast of South America.

These are watery areas of summer doldrums. To the north and the south are the trade winds. Sometimes, meteorologists believe, conflicting trade winds extend unpredictably into the doldrums and collide, setting up a circulation.

Once the warm, moist air starts spinning out over open water—look out!

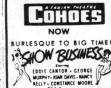

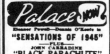

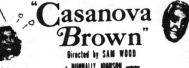

THE WEATHER
Tonight—Fair, colder.

THE TIMES RECORD

FINAL EDITION

SERIES 1944—NO. 264   (Entered as Second Class Matter at the Postoffice at Troy, N. Y., Under the Act of March 3, 1879.)   TROY, N. Y., WEDNESDAY EVENING, NOVEMBER 8, 1944.   (Published Daily Except Sunday)   PRICE FOUR CENTS

President Elected For Fourth Term; Democrats Hold Congress

EXPECT ELSWORTH TO DEFEAT BLISS FOR JUDICIAL POST

Roosevelt Carries Troy by 1,519; Loses County to Dewey by 7,640

With no other results in doubt in the Upper Hudson District sector of New York State, interest today centered on the contest for office of Supreme Court Justice in the Third Judicial District with unofficial returns indicating that Rosco J. V. Elsworth, Kingston Republican, will have a margin of from 1,500 to 2,000 over Judge F. Walter Bliss, Schoharie Democrat.

Actual results may not be known until there is an official canvass in all counties in the district — Rensselaer, Albany, Columbia, Schoharie, Greene, Ulster, Sullivan—but a pretty definite figure is expected to be obtained by tonight as a result of special canvasses being made today by supporters of both men. Such a checkup is being made in the Rensselaer County Board of Elections.

Meanwhile, unofficial returns show that despite this year's "Roosevelt trend," President Franklin D. Roosevelt's strength in Rensselaer County, particularly in the City of Troy, has dwindled in each succeeding campaign since 1932 when he carried the city by 7,354, then went on to win the county by 7,354.

Carried County in 1936

This year President Roosevelt carried Troy by 1,519, but lost Rensselaer County to Gov. Thomas E. Dewey by 7,640 as a climax to a bitter wartime campaign for control of the Federal government.

In 1936 Roosevelt's county majority, four years previously, was not only wiped out but Alf M. Landon carried the county by 3,036 with Roosevelt's previous majority in Troy cut to 5,183.

There are another 3,000 in the Roosevelt vote four years ago when Wendell L. Willkie cut the county by 7,261 with Roosevelt's margin in Troy cut down to 2,404.

Albany this year cut down the normal Roosevelt majorities but Cohoes came through with an unofficial majority for the President of 2,038.

Slumps in Watervliet

Watervliet also cut the Democratic majority for President by approximately 200 as did Green Island.

Waterford showed a Roosevelt upswing with Dewey obtaining a majority of only 180 as against the 405 turned in for Willkie four years ago.

In Mechanicville it was a neck and neck race.

Representatives of both parties today were centering all attention on the Third Judicial contest.

All figures indicate a close race with Elsworth's majority fixed from 1,500 to 2,000 over Judge Bliss.

Ulster County is credited with giving Elsworth a majority of 10,300; Rensselaer, upwards of 5,000. Schoharie, 1,214, Columbia, 2,927, Greene, 2,616, Sullivan, 1,867.

Albany County rolled up a majority of approximately 18,000 for Bliss.

Republicans swept all offices in Rensselaer County.

Van Voorhis Vote.

John Van Voorhis, Republican, carried the county by 7,750 for the office of associate judge of the Court of Appeals after losing by 1,429 to Marvin R. Dye, Democrat.

U. S. Sen. Robert F. Wagner, Democrat, carried Troy by 1,734 but

(Continued on Page 11.)

FRENCH SEEM PLEASED OVER REELECTION OF PRESIDENT ROOSEVELT

Paris (INS) — France generally and American troops in Paris hailed the reelection of President Roosevelt today and expressed extreme gratification.

The French people appeared particularly pleased. Some government circles were especially pleased since among them were those who feared that Gov. Thomas E. Dewey might not, according to their view, have had a sufficient understanding of Europe's problems.

Nine out of ten G. I.'s buttonholed in Paris streets this morning voiced approval of the results which most of them considered a foregone conclusion.

ROOSEVELT APPARENTLY GETS 55 PER CENT OF VOTE

New York (INS)—Best estimates of President Roosevelt's total popular vote indicated today that final returns may show that he received as high as 55 per cent of the ballots cast.

This compares with estimates made by nationwide polls as follows: The Gallup poll gave Roosevelt 51.5 per cent, the Fortune poll 52 per cent, and the Crossley poll 52 per cent. Only Emil Hurja put the majority on the wrong side of the ledger, giving Dewey 52 per cent of the total vote and Roosevelt 48 per cent.

Ten Reported Killed In California Wreck

Colfax, Cal. (UP)—At least ten persons were killed and a score injured early today when a 14-car section of the Southern Pacific Challenger, bound for San Francisco, was derailed three miles west of here, plunging the engine, the baggage car and one coach into a ditch.

Placer County Governor Francis G. West reported from the scene that "at least ten were dead and a score seriously injured."

G.O.P. MAJORITIES IN LEGISLATURE REMAIN INTACT

Defeat of State Senator Dunnigan Most Startling Upset

Albany (AP)—Republican working majorities in the New York Legislature remained intact today as New York City's John J. Dunnigan, minority Senate leader, bowed out of that House after thirty consecutive years' service.

In a surprising upset, Atty. Paul A. Fino ousted Dunnigan, minority leader for the last six years and majority leader for the six years previous, as senator from the 27th District.

Fino polled 68,661 votes to Dunnigan's 55,072, but the balance of power was wielded by the American Labor Party candidate, David Schiosberg, who garnered 14,074 votes.

In the Senate, boosted from 51 to 56 members by reapportionment, the Republican majority stood at 35-21. Republicans previously outnumbered Democrats 31 to 20.

G. O. P. Gains Members.

In the Assembly, where the line-up last session was ninety Republicans, 59 Democrats and one American-Laborite, the G. O. P. raised its total to 92 seats, the Democrats dropping to 56 and the American-Laborite in the larger house when E. Eugene Zimmer of Troy did not seek reelection.

Dunnigan's defeat overshadowed the upsetting of Syracuse's former Mayor Rolland B. Marvin in his bid for the state Senate seat formerly held by G. Frank Wallace.

Marvin, who backed the late Wendell L. Willkie for the presidential nomination, but came out for Governor Dewey after Willkie withdrew from the race, had been expected to lead a Republican grand slam in Onondaga County.

Instead he took an 18,000-vote trouncing from Richard P. Byrne, Democratic and American Labor candidate, and trailed far behind Dewey who captured the county by some 6,000 votes though he lost Syracuse to President Roosevelt.

Another former mayor was the victim in the only upstate race in which an incumbent senator was knocked out. Vincent R. Corrou, Utica, dealt that blow to William H. Hampton, who had been a member of the Senate since 1925.

Assembly Losers.

In Brooklyn, Republican Francis McMullen ended the eight-year tenure of Edgar F. Moran, and Lewis W. Olliffe won reelection over Walter E. Cooke who had been a member since 1943.

Other Democrats defeated were William J. A. Glancy, New York City by Samuel Roman, who had C O P and A L P backing; Frank Rossetti, New York City; by Hamlet O Catennacio incumbent Republican A L P and S Robert Molinari; Staten Island Democrat A L P by Edmund P Radigan who previously defeated Molinari in the G O P primary.

Republicans ousted were Roches-ter's Frank J Sellmayer, beaten by Ray Scheible Democrat A L P; Harry G Convese Deansboro farmer, who lost to incumbent Democrat A L P Frank A Emma of Utica, and John J Lakuile New York City; defeated by Louis De Salvio, Democratic incumbent

DEMOCRATS GAIN IN SENATE AND HOUSE ELECTIONS

Republicans Lose 16 Seats in Lower Branch of Congress

BY THE ASSOCIATED PRESS.

The Democratic Party bored ahead today toward an electoral triumph at the Capitol as well as at the White House.

Smashing yesterday's Republican prediction that the administration would lose control of both houses of Congress, the Democrats made certain of a Senate majority with votes to spare, and snatched 16 seats from the Republicans in the House while losing only two of their own.

With 12 Senate races still to be decided, Democrats counted 51 certain Senate seats compared with 58 they held in the present session. The Republicans tallied up 32, counting holdovers, contrasted with the 37 they now have. The Senate's lone minor party member was not up for election this time.

In the House, forenoon totals showed 187 Democrats elected, 104 Republicans.

Speaker Sam Rayburn of Texas scooted in without opposition, and Representative Rampeck of Georgia, the Democratic whip, won handily. On the other hand, Congresswoman-playwright Clare Boothe Luce traded pointed glares with Mr. Roosevelt and bobbed up a winner in the Fourth Connecticut District.

Senators Reelected.

Eleven incumbent Democratic senators already had been returned: George of Georgia, Overton of Louisiana, Hill of Alabama, Pepper of Florida, Majority Leader Barkley of Kentucky, Thomas of Oklahoma, Tydings of Maryland, Hayden of Arizona, Thomas of Utah, Wagner of New York and Lucas of Illinois.

Democratic senators-elect were Myers of Pennsylvania, Hoey of North Carolina, Clyde T May, North Carolina, and Brien McMahon of Connecticut, who upset Republican Sen. John Danaher.

The Republicans unseated a Democrat, too—Sen Guy M. Gillette of Iowa, who fell to that state's governor, Bourke B. Hickenlooper. Other Republicans winning Senate places were Aiken of Vermont, Reed of Kansas, Morse and Cordon of Oregon, Gurney of South Dakota, Millikin of Colorado and Wiley of Wisconsin.

"Date With Destiny."

Sen Gerald P Nye (R, N.D.) who has served since 1925, was running a weak second in a three way race in North Dakota, with Democrat John Moses holding the lead.

Rep. Hamilton Fish, New York Republican who fought President Roosevelt's pre-war foreign policy, was knocked out by Augustus W. Bennet. Clare Boothe Luce of Connecticut, attractive blonde thorn in the administration's side, slipped through to victory despite a frantic Democratic attempt to unseat her.

The 79th Congress thus will keep its date with destiny next January as predominantly Democratic. The President's intimacy in the Senate can route important international commitments, perhaps even the final peace treaty, through the legislative machinery.

Fish Loses House Seat To Bennet

BY JOSEPH KILGALLEN

United Press Staff Correspondent

Albany (UP)—Rep. Hamilton Fish jr., veteran member of Congress and pre-Pearl Harbor isolationist, was defeated for reelection in the 29th Congressional District by Augustus W. Bennet, Democratic and American Labor Party candidate, almost complete returns showed today.

In returns from all but a few of the reapportioned 29th District's precincts, Democrat Bennet led Fish by approximately 5,000 votes.

Although Bennet, who opposed Fish in the August primary for the Republican nomination, claiming victory early, Fish had refused to admit defeat until it was a certainty.

"I admit, publicly," Fish said as he finally conceded, "that my defeat should be largely credited to Communistic and red forces from New York City backed by a large slush fund probably exceeding $250,000. This slush fund and communistic propaganda had no effect.

where I was known in Orange County but did succeed in decreasing the people in the three new counties (of the reapportioned district).

"I have no regrets whatever as I waged the strongest fight that I knew how and am deeply grateful for the loyal support I was given by my friends in Orange County where I was best known."

The one-time isolationist leader and long-time adversary of President Roosevelt, said that he was "fearful that the overwhelming election of President Roosevelt is a step toward setting up one-man and one-party government in our country."

Fish added that he had "no great desire" to serve as a minority member of Congress and that he hoped to be reelected in order to become chairman of the House rules committee.

Bennet, in a victory statement, said he was "gratified" with the results which he termed well worth the effort and energy put into the campaign.

FRANKLIN D. ROOSEVELT.

YANKS OPEN NEW ATTACK BETWEEN METZ AND NANCY

Americans Capture Four Villages After Crossing Seille River

Paris (UP) — Lieut. Gen. George S. Patton's American Third Army made a new attack between Metz and Nancy in Eastern France today and advanced up to one mile in the first few hours, capturing at least four villages and crossing the Seille River.

The doughboys forced the Seille at several places approximately 13 miles south of Metz and already had outflanked that enemy bastion from the south, United Press War Correspondent Collie Small reported from the south.

On the southwestern approaches to Cologne, a German counterattack drove American First Army troops out of the hamlet of Kommerscheidt, some 13 miles southeast of Aachen, but the doughboys held firmly to high ground 500 yards to the northwest and edged closer to Schmidt, a mile to the southeast.

Doughboys Drive Ahead.

Kommerscheidt was the third town to be won and lost in the period of a few days of the bitter struggle in Germany.

The swaying street battle for Vossenack, a mile and a half northwest of Kommerscheidt, raged on into its third day on a rising scale of fury.

Both the Americans and the Germans threw reinforcements of tanks and infantry into the struggle for Vossenack, field reports said.

Patton sent elements of the 12th Corps under Maj. Gen. Manton Eddy over the top between Metz and Nancy at 6 a.m. after an hour-long artillery barrage in which the Americans used captured German guns and ammunition.

The doughboys slogged ahead over a virtual quagmire churned up by day-long rains yesterday. Leaden skies threatened to rob the troops of air support, but the attack in such inclement conditions apparently caught the enemy by surprise.

Lull on Holland Front.

First reports gave no clue to the scale or scope of the attack, which broke a week-long lull on the Third Army front.

An almost complete lull settled over the 21st Army group front in southwest Holland with the mop-ping up of the last German pocket south of the Maas and the Holland Deep in Moerdijk and other isolated troops in the northwest corner of Walcheren Island the only activity reported.

A dispatch from Antwerp disclosed that Allied minesweepers already had begun the task of sweeping the 80-mile approaches to that port, third largest in the world, to open the way for ships waiting to supply a winter offensive.

The port was captured practically intact, the dispatch said.

NAZI OIL PLANT BOMBED

London (UP)—About 350 Flying Fortresses and Liberators attacked the Leuna synthetic oil plant at Merseburg and rail yards at Thelae today in a renewal of the winter bombing campaign against Germany.

JIM FARLEY CALLS UPON NATION TO SUPPORT F.D.R.

New York (UP) — Former Postmaster General James A. Farley issued a statement early today calling upon the nation to support the Roosevelt administration "to bring about a speedy victory in the war."

"President Roosevelt," he said, "is entitled to congratulations for the confidence bestowed upon him by the American electorate."

Governor Dewey Extends His Congratulations To President

BY THE ASSOCIATED PRESS.

Governor Dewey—"I extend to President Roosevelt my hearty congratulations on his reelection and that his best term will see a restoration of tranquility abroad and lasting peace and the preservation of traditional American rights for all the people.

The Governor added that "every good citizen will accept the will of the people."

President Roosevelt—"I thank you, Governor Dewey, for your statement."

Vice President-Elect Truman—"It was a 'grand' statement by Governor Dewey and it shows American sportsmanship in this political campaign."

Governor Bricker—"I join in the sentiment expressed by Governor Dewey."

Vice President Wallace—"Roosevelt until 1948 means a country confident, moving with full steam ahead."

Democratic National Chairman Robert E. Hannegan—"The overwhelming victory of President Roosevelt means national unity on a program of international collaboration for permanent peace."

Sidney Hillman, C.I.O.-P. A. C. chairman—"The American people have reaffirmed the faith and confidence they repose in a great American and an outstanding leader."

JAPS RESHUFFLE MILITARY CHIEFS

Yanks Destroy 469 More Nipponese Planes

BY THE ASSOCIATED PRESS.

Tokyo's war lords replaced all top-ranking land and air commanders in the Philippines today in an effort to halt the American onslaught which in two successive days wiped out 469 more planes and sank or damaged 29 ships.

Strong units of the 24th Division punched their way slowly through well-entrenched Japanese on Northern Leyte Island yesterday in bitter fighting marked by vicious night counter-attacks and the first heavy artillery duels of the Philippines invasion.

Savagely fighting Japanese slowed down the American advance and, for the first time, shelled Yank positions along Carigara Bay with heavy artillery.

New evacuations of non-essential civilians from 11 major Japanese cities in preparation for "inevitable enemy air raids" were ordered by Japanese militarists.

Reinforcements and supplies were rushed to garrisons in the Kirile and Bonin Islands guarding the northern and southern approaches to Tokyo where American bombers extended their attacks to new targets.

The Nipponese Philippine command was completely reshuffled on the heels of the heaviest recent carrier strike on Manila Bay and surrounding airports on Luzon island. In two days Japanese Manila time Adm. Chester W Nimitz announced 469 Japanese planes were destroyed and 29 ships and a trawler hit.

Strong entrenchment of Japanese was shown in elements of four Divisions fierce counter-attacks and persistent infiltration slowed the advance of the U S 24th Division. Ruthless bullet-headed Gen Tomoyuko Yamashita, Nip who took command of the Nipponese Densharko Okochi, who led holding parties in the 1937 Shanghai incident was transferred to command what's left of Japan's navy in the Philippines.

SOVIETS LAND ON ISLAND IN DANUBE

Suburbs of Budapest Under Artillery Fire

London (UP) Radio Budapest said today that Soviet troops, outflanking the Hungarian capital from the south, had landed on a small island in the middle of the Danube River four miles away from Budapest, the broadcast said adding that Soviet artillery and anti-aircraft guns already were firing from Dunaharaszti, suburban town on the east bank of the Danube also within four miles of the capital.

The Hungarian broadcast gave no details of the landing on the mid-Danube island, but said the attack apparently was designed to build up a base for an assault on 30-mile-long Csepel Island, an industrial center between the eastern and western arms of the Danube below Budapest.

It said "mopping up" operations were in progress against the satellite capital.

Berlin reported the Red Army had launched a strong assault against the 140-mile German defense line along the Tisza River northeast of Budapest and had seized two bridgeheads on the west bank, posing a new threat against the satellite capital.

Roosevelt Lead Points For 407 Electoral Votes

Chief Executive Wins Or Leads in 34 States While Dewey Holds Margin In 14 With Electoral Vote of 124; Big Cities and Big States Favored Roosevelt; Tabulation Continues With Record Vote Probable.

BY THE UNITED PRESS.

The election of President Roosevelt to a fourth term was conceded today by Gov. Thomas E. Dewey as steadily mounting returns from a potential record vote also guaranteed the Democrats numerical control of the House and bolstered the party's strength in the Senate.

The count of the ballot in this first wartime election in eighty years continues, and at 3 p.m., E.W.T. a United Press tabulation showed the following popular vote in the 48 states:
Roosevelt—20,733,119.
Dewey—18,082,672.

That represented about 75 per cent of the expected vote and if the average continues the total ballot may exceed 51,000,000—a figure beyond the expectations of almost all election experts. The vote in 1940 was 49,548,221.

The President had won or was ahead in 34 states with a total electoral vote of 407. Dewey had won or was leading in states with a total electoral vote of 124.

Mr. Roosevelt had won or was ahead in: Alabama, Arizona, Arkansas, California, Connecticut, Delaware, Florida, Georgia, Idaho, Illinois, Kentucky, Louisiana, Maryland, Massachusetts, Minnesota, Mississippi, Missouri, Montana, Nevada, New Hampshire, New Jersey, New Mexico, New York, North Carolina, Oklahoma, Pennsylvania, Rhode Island, South Carolina, Tennessee, Texas, Utah, Virginia, Washington, and West Virginia.

Dewey had won or was ahead in: Colorado, Indiana, Iowa, Kansas, Maine, Michigan, Nebraska, North Dakota, Ohio, Oregon, South Dakota, Vermont, Wisconsin and Wyoming.

The New Deal-Democratic machine, aided this time by a watch works organization of left wing labor, was purring like a post-war motorcar. The popular vote was approximately close and Mr. Roosevelt knew he had been in a contest. Dewey's chief consolation may be that he came, closer than Herbert C. Hoover, Alf M. Landon or the late Wendell L. Willkie did to licking "the champ."

The electoral vote score in those contests was, respectively, 472 to 59; 523 to 8, and 449 to 82.

In most states the vote of the men and women in the armed services was being counted along with the civilian ballots. The trend varied. In some states it was for the President, in others for Dewey.

Dewey lost this 1944 election because he failed to break through Roosevelt defenses in the East. The big cities and most of the big states went for a fourth term. Big New York put 47 electoral votes solidly behind the President. He exceeded his 1940 vote margin of 224,440, piling up a plurality of 391,000 on the basis of tabulations so far.

Labor Party Vote Factor.

The full 1944 election because he failed to break through Roosevelt defenses in the East. The big cities and most of the big states went for a fourth term. Big New York put 47 electoral votes solidly behind the President. He exceeded his 1940 vote margin of 224,440, piling up a plurality of 391,000 on the basis of tabulations so far.

But he would have lost the state to Dewey but for the aid of the American Labor Party, which allegedly is controlled or influenced by the Communists, and the new Liberal Party, an anti-Communist labor organization, making its political debut this election.

"Fighting is going on for big New York City's five counties or boroughs illuminated some of the mysteries of the absentee armed service vote. Of the 242,082 armed service ballots counted in this city Mr Roosevelt got 73 per cent of them. For 15 years were dashing over for Mr Roosevelt even in the two New York boroughs which normally are Republican, Queens and Richmond, although the margins were not great in either.

Dewey Concedes Election.

Dewey conceded Mr. Roosevelt's reelection at 14 a.m. E.W.T. today. The President heard it on the air and replied with a thank

Clare Boothe Luce Wins In Connecticut

Bridgeport, Conn. (UP)—Connecticut's fourth congressional district sent blonde playwright and U S Representative Clare Boothe Luce (R) back to the House for her second term in yesterday's election despite direct intervention by both President Roosevelt and Vice President Wallace on behalf of her opponent.

Even as Mr Roosevelt last night thanked that it would prove a mighty good thing for the country if Mrs Luce were defeated "he vote were pil ng up that would keep her in her seat."

In the end it meant main party ringing a represent tive district Mrs Luce defeated Mayor Jasper McLevy Social ist candidate and Dr John D McWilliams R from his second district seat.

(Continued on Page 2)

you" telegram which pointedly was addressed to his adversary as the "Governor of New York."

Dewey read his concession statement to reporters at Roosevelt hotel campaign headquarters in New York, a smiling, game figure. And then he and Mrs. Dewey smiled out after this reply to questions about his future:

"I have no illusions for 1948."

Dewey and his wife retired immediately afterward to their suite in the Roosevelt Hotel.

President Up Late.

Dewey stayed up until shortly after 3:30 a.m. E.W.T. listening to the news, working his people down to nubs on his own calculations and conferring by telephone with his scattered lieutenants. Between times he joshed with his White House aides gathered with him at Hyde Park and talked to the neighbors who assembled a couple of thousand in the grounds of the "big house" around midnight.

There was no foreboding where Mr. Roosevelt was the host and central figure. Just before midnight his neighbors invaded his estate grounds and he told them that things were going fine.

When Dewey's broadcast came over the radio, the White House office in Poughkeepsie exploded with shouts of "we're in again." People slapped people on the backs. The bellhops at the Nelson House—where the White House staff has been quartered on week-end and day visits for 12 years—were dashing about in a family. They followed the election results by various radios around the gracefully sprawling old house overlooking the Hudson River.

The President interrupted his election night vigils shortly before midnight to greet a traditional torchlight parade of Democrats who whooped down the lane from the Albany Post Road to his house with red flares and a brass band.

The torch bearers represented a Dutchess County minority the

Worked Throughout Night.

The President worked throughout the evening keeping an up-to-the-minute check on how he was doing. His house was full of old-time friends, members of his immediate family.

JAPANESE SOLDIERS BYPASSED BY ALLIES' SUBSIST ON LIZARDS

By THE ASSOCIATED PRESS.

Japanese soldiers isolated on Rabaul, the New Britain Island enemy base by-passed in the Allied offensive toward the Philippines, are subsisting on a diet which includes snakes and lizards and preparing for a long war.

Domei, the Japanese news agency, in a Tokyo broadcast recorded by the Federal Communications Commission, said the Rabaul troops have become farmers, started a newspaper and are "absolutely from ordinary mortal desires."

Besides planting tapioca and taro for food, Domei said, "bananas, papaya and coconuts also help in establishing self-sufficiency. Snakes can also be eaten and lizards are delicious."

Domei said the soldiers there have vowed that "we shall not leave this place until we win. We shall stand firm until the enemy is exhausted and defeated."

HOW TO CONTROL CANCER—Dr. James C. Boland, Troy health commissioner, explained the causes and methods of controlling cancer in an address to the Mother's Club at St. Anthony's Church last night. Pictured, left to right, are: Mrs. Anthony Cesta, club secretary; Mrs. Nicholas Brignola, Dr. Boland, Mrs. J. E. Ray, president of the Mothers' Club; Mrs. Manny DiNova and Mrs. Manuel DiSiena. This was the second of the educational meetings sponsored by the local unit of the Field Army of the American Cancer Society.

SAILOR'S BRAVERY WINS CITATIONS IN TWO INVASIONS

Godfrey E. Anderson, jr., 2112 Fifth Avenue, Now Home on Leave

Seaman 1/c Godfrey E. Anderson, jr., son of Mr. and Mrs. Godfrey Anderson of 2112 Fifth Avenue, is spending a fifteen day furlough with his parents after spending ten months in the European Theater of the war landing invasion troops at Southern France, and Normandy during the D-Day invasion.

For his bravery in landing the troops safely, despite heavy enemy machine gun fire, artillery fire, mines and bombing planes, Seaman Anderson has received two personal citations.

The first citation is for his work in landing troops at the Bay of the Seine on D-Day and the second for successful landings at the beaches of Frejus in France on

August 15. On one occasion, a bomb from an enemy plane fell near the landing barge killing two members of the crew, but Seaman Anderson landed the barge on the beach in spite of the loss. The young sailor entered the Navy in August 1943 and has been overseas since January of this year. His brother, Petty Officer 2/c is serving with the Navy in the South Pacific after a short furlough at home this summer.

Mary Margaret McBride says:

"Building A Happier Home is the basic ideal of every woman. And in working for the mutual understanding which creates real happiness, we all profit most from the actual experiences of others," says famous author and radio columnist Mary Margaret McBride, in a forthcoming issue of TRUE STORY Magazine.

No wonder that TRUE STORY, dealing entirely with the experiences of real people, has long been known as a force for good—as well as a source of absorbing reading for millions each month.

True Story

TEN-SHUN!
News from the Forces on all Fronts

First Lieut. EUGENE FILM, JR., Troy R. D. 3, has been assigned as an engineering officer with the top scoring P-51 Mustang fighter group of the Mediterranean theater attached to the Fifteenth A. A. F. in Italy.

A graduate of Troy High School, Lieutenant Film received his degree in mechanical engineering from the Rensselaer Polytechnic Institute in 1941. From then until January, 1942, he was employed as a junior engineer by the Bridgeport Thermostat Co., leaving to enter the experimental testing department of the Wright Aeronautical Corp.

On April 9, 1942, Film entered the A. A. F. as an engineering cadet and was assigned to Chanute Field, Ill., for training. Receiving his commission as a second lieutenant in August, 1942, he was assigned for duty with a Flying Fortress bomber wing and with it, went overseas, to North Africa. In March of 1943, he transferred to the Twelfth Air Force Fighter Command, serving there through the invasions of Sicily and Italy until December of that year when he transferred, this time to an Air Depot Repair group. In his capacity Lieutenant Film will be responsible for the repair and maintenance of the Mustangs of a group that has one of the most colorful histories among A. A. F. fighter groups in the entire European theater.

Two local young women were sworn in as SPARS at the sub-recruiting station of the Coast Guards in Albany. They are MARY RITA KARLIN, 333 Second Street, this city, and MONICA EVELYN AMYOT. Mary is Troy High and Albany Stenotype Secretarial Studio and was with the G. E. in Schenectady. She has a brother, S 2/c JOHN KAELIN at Fort Lauderdale, Fla. Monica attended CCHS and was with the Boston Meat & Grocery. She has four brothers in service: Corp. JOSEPH AMYOT in Texas, Pvt. ANDRE AMYOT, Scott Field, Ill., Lieut. (j. g.) GERALD AMYOT in the Navy in the Pacific Area, Midshipman PAUL AMYOT at New London, Conn. ... EARL W. COONS, 2654 Sixth Avenue has been made a sergeant with the 15th A. A. F. in Italy. He is an engineer-gunner in a B-24 Liberator group. Earl was a bus driver for the United Traction Co., and entered service in 1942. Pvt. ANNE M. PREDENTIAL of 500 First Street, who has been training at Fort Oglethorpe, Ga., has been assigned to the WAC detachment at Home in the A. A. F. WILLIAM T. FENNELLY, 380 Third Street, has been made Aviation Storekeeper, 3/c at the Naval Air Station, Jacksonville, Fla. He entered the Navy April 6, 1942. LEO DUFTY, son of Mr. and Mrs. Harold Dufty, of Melrose, has entered the service and is stationed at Sampson. He is a brother of S 2/c WARREN DUFTY, who is serving with the Navy in the South Pacific and Corp. HAROLD DUFTY who was killed in action in Italy in July, 1943.

BERNARD W. DAVENPORT, metal-smith 1/c, is spending a thirty-day furlough with his wife at their home, 124 George Street, Green Island, after spending twenty months in the European theater with the amphibious forces. He took part in the invasion of Sicily and Italy and was in England preparing landing craft for the Normandy invasion. He has three stars on his campaign ribbon and was cited by the admiral of the fleet for a special mission. He goes back to Lido Beach, Nov. 26 for further assignment. A brother, Corp. JOHN E. DAVENPORT is overseas 14 months and was in on the invasions of Africa, Italy and Southern France. They are sons of Mrs. F. C. Davenport, 4 Hudson Avenue, Green Island ... Pfc. JOHN J. MAGUIRE of the Marine Corps, son of Mr. and Mrs. Michael Maguire of 4902 Ninth Avenue, Watervliet, is home on thirty days' leave after 23 months in the Pacific with the amphibious forces.

Two local soldiers are members of an ordnance battalion of the Peninsular Base Section in Italy which just celebrated its second anniversary of overseas duty. They are Corp. JOHN J. MALONE of 3282 Sixth Avenue and Pvt. PETER J. BUNK of Melrose. When organized, this battalion was formed of highly-trained experts drawn from advanced Army schools all over the country. These men rebuild, overhaul, repair and maintain thousands of vehicles each month for the section. They served in Africa before going to Italy. Corp. Malone, son of Mr. and Mrs. Patrick Malone, is Troy High and was a machine operator for the G. E. in Schenectady before entering service in 1942. A brother, Corp. THOMAS MALONE, is in the Air Corps. Private Bunk, son of Mr. and Mrs. Thomas Bunk, was with the G. E. as a foundry worker before he entered service some 26 months ago ... GENE LENNEY, 586 Second Avenue, is attending a communication's school at an amphibous training base, Oceanside, Cal. He had five months of training in the radio school at Sampson ... JAMES F. ARNOLD, 49 Christie Street, has been made a sergeant at Camp Beale, Cal.

TEN LIGHT VESSELS LOST TO JAPANESE

Washington (UP)—Loss of one destroyer, two destroyer escorts and seven lesser craft in the Pacific was announced by the Navy last night.

Of the total of ten vessels, the communique said seven were lost through enemy action of the perils of the sea in the Philippines area. But it was specified that they were not casualties of the big battles of October 24-25. The others went down in the New Guinea area.

Losses in Philippine waters were the destroyer Abner Read, the destroyer escort Evermole, the mine sweeper YMS 70, PT's 320 and 321, the fleet tug Sonoma, and the Landing Craft (Infantry) 1065.

The other vessels were the destroyer escort Shelton and the PT's 368 and 371.

SYCAWAY.

The November meeting of the Business Girls of Memorial Methodist Church was held last evening at the home of Mrs. Walter Cantwell, Mellon Avenue. Miss Dorothy McCabe, president, was in charge of the business session. Miss Sally Patterson, Mrs. Ruth Cantwell and Mrs. Mildred Johnston were appointed to decorate the gift booth for the bazaar Thursday, Nov. 30, in the church house. Mrs. Marion Teetsel, Mrs. Mildred Gulli and Mrs. Mary Jensen make up the pricing committee. Mrs. Margaret Banker, Mrs. Edith Humphrey and Mrs. Marie Cooper will have charge of the afternoon sales. Misses Eva Miller and Florence Hull will have the supper hour sales. Misses Maud Miller, Emily Rinaldi and Stella Adams will be in charge of evening sales.

Personal.

Mr. and Mrs. Walter G. Calhoun of 15 South Lake Avenue have moved to Waterford.

Mrs. Joseph Lynch and sons, Joseph and Stephen of Detroit, Mich., are in Troy as guests of Mrs. Lynch's father, Walter Colehamer, and grandmother, Mrs. Carrie Colehamer, of Cooper Avenue.

Plan Home Bureau Luncheon.

Mrs. Marie Cooper, Mrs. Gordon Banker and Miss Esther Pratt will have charge of the dessert to be served by the W. S. C. S. Dec. 4 at the annual Home Bureau luncheon in the Church House. Plans for the Christmas party were made with Misses May Patterson, Esther Pratt, Irene Calhoun, Mrs. Mildred DePuy and Mrs. Ellen Cipperly in charge. The party will be held Thursday evening, Dec. 28, in the Fidelity room of Memorial Church House. Refreshments were served from a table arranged in keeping with Thanksgiving, by the hostess assisted by Mrs. Marie Cooper and Miss Bessie Miller.

TITO IN MOSCOW.

London (UP)—The German radio said today that Marshal Tito was in Moscow.

COHOES SOLDIERS BACK HOME FROM ACTIVE SERVICE

Pfc. Adam Lipin Was in Pacific; Pfc. Michael Glusko, Italy

Two Cohoes soldiers have returned from active duty for a period of rest, processing and reassignment.

Pfc. Adam Lipin, son of Mr. and Mrs. C. E. Lipin of 29 Harmony Street will visit his parents after he has reported at Fort Dix, N. J. He recently completed 30 months of service in the Southwest Pacific.

Pfc. Michael Glusko, son of Mr. and Mrs. John Glusko of 106 Jackson Avenue, in service since Nobember, 1942, and overseas, serving as rifleman and switchboard operator in the U. S. Infantry in Italy, has reported to the Army Ground and Service Forces Redistribution Station at Lake Placid.

CHRISTMAS PARTY TO BE HELD FOR CHILDREN AT SCHOOL 9 TOMORROW

Plans for a Christmas party for children of School 9 will be outlined at a meeting of the Parent-Teacher Association of the school tomorrow at 8p.m. Various specialties are being arranged in connection with the affair.

During the business session reports will be submitted concerning the card party which the group conducted Friday night at the high school. Mrs. Elizabeth Berthiaume was general chairman of the arrangements committee, the cochairman being Mrs. Mae Hines.

Awards for high scores went to Mrs. Catherine Pawlowski, Mrs. Frank Kenny, Mrs. Edward Smith, Mrs. Anna Lavine, Mrs. Joseph McGrath, Mrs. Richard Colaneri, Mrs. Louis Goodness, Mrs. Lottie LaGrand, Mrs. Louis Surprenant, Mrs. Maurice Belanger, Miss Marie McCaffrey, Miss Carol Perry, Miss Katherine Holblock, Miss D. J. Warnock, Mrs. August Neeb, Mrs. Wilfred Perreault, Mrs. Edward Mason, Mrs. Samuel Ringer, Mrs Robert Brehm, Mrs. Hines, David Katz, A. J. Waltzer, Mrs. C. J. Sullivan and Mrs. Ruth Kellogg.

Soldier Returns.

Corp. John Wasenko, son of Mr. and Mrs. Metro Wasenko of 34 Garner Street, has returned to Camp Campbell, Ky., after spending a 14 day furlough with his parents.

Club Meeting Scheduled.

The Mother's Club at Sacred Heart Church will meet today at 8 p.m. in the school hall. Plans for the Christmas party December 12 will be completed. Mrs. Herman Lajeunesse will preside.

Social Slated.

A social under the auspices of Cohoes Lodge of Elks, is scheduled to be conducted Thursday night at the clubhouse on Oneida Street. William Mossey is general chairman of the arrangements committee.

BETTER VISION GREATER SUCCESS

Work quickly and efficiently performed is the springboard for promotion and better pay. Good work requires good vision. Poor vision retards mental and physical reactions, causes fatigue. Good seeing is the result of clear eyesight and ample, well-directed light on every eye task. Have your eyesight examined regularly, defects corrected; and always work under good light.

TIME PAYMENTS At No Extra Cost

T. Brandon Timpane, O.D.
OPTOMETRIST
115 REMSEN ST., COHOES, N. Y.

PFC. TIMOTHY J. HAYDEN.

TIMOTHY HAYDEN OF COHOES KILLED ON ARMISTICE DAY

Had Been Serving in Army Since March; Lost Life in France

Pfc. Timothy J. Hayden of the Army was killed in action in France on Armistice Day, according to a message from the War Department received by his wife, Mrs. Olive Hayden of 52 Younglove Avenue. No details except the date of his death were contained in the telegram.

The soldier, who was born in Cohoes and who was a lifelong resident of this city, attended St. Agnes' School and was a graduate of Keveny Memorial Academy and a communicant of St. Agnes' Church. He was employed in the State Department of Correction prior to entering the service on March 16 of this year.

Private Hayden received his basic training at Camp Croft, S. C., and was sent overseas with an infantry unit in the latter part of August.

Besides his wife, who was formerly Miss Olive Senecal, he is survived by a 2-year-old daughter, Kathleen; his parents, Mr. and Mrs. Timothy E. Hayden, and two sisters, the Misses Monica and Mary Hayden, all of this city.

ROTARY GOVERNOR WILL VISIT COHOES

To Address Club Luncheon Tomorrow Noon

Members of Cohoes Rotary Club will greet Dr. Burchard A. Winne of Johnstown, governor of the 174th District, on the occasion of his official visit at the group's weekly luncheon meeting tomorrow noon at Van Schaick Island Country Club. The visiting official will be the speaker at the session, which will be presided over by Dr. F. Herrick Conners, president.

Directors of the club and chairmen of the various committees will meet with the district governor at 10 a.m. at Dr. Conners' office in the Education Building on Seneca Street.

Common Council to Meet.

The regular meeting of the Common Council will be conducted in the council chambers in the City Hall tonight.

Church Unit To Meet.

A meeting of the Church Work Society of St. John's Episcopal Church will be conducted in the parish house tomorrow at 2:30 p.m.

Bond, Stamp Sales Reported.

Representatives of the Auxiliary of Collin-Ross Camp, United Spanish War Veterans, manned the bond booth in the Woolworth Store Saturday. The committee, composed of Mrs. Mary Collin, Mrs. Margaret Moran, Mrs. Vera Smith, Mrs. Rose Caldwell, Mrs. Mae Archembeault and Mrs. Margaret Riley, disposed of $600 in War Bonds and $181.10 in War Stamps.

Auxiliary to Meet.

Members of the Ladies' Auxiliary of Cohoes Post, Veterans of Foreign Wars, will meet today at 8 p.m. at the quarters on Remsen Street. Mrs. Christine Dewar, president of the group, will preside during the business session, which will be followed by a social. The arrangements committee includes Mrs. Louise Corbell, Mrs. Mary Rettinger and Mrs. Jane Fitzgerald.

SPECIAL THIS WEEK

Nestle Permanent Wave

$5.00

(THIS WEEK ONLY)

BONAT LIFE OIL $6.00

CURLY WAVES $4.00

COLD WAVES $10.00

SPECIAL OIL WAVE $5.00

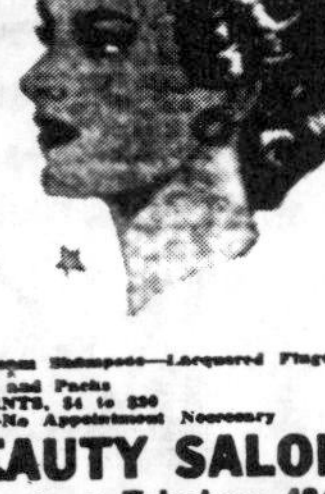

BROADWAY BEAUTY SALON
342 Broadway Telephone 4241

DRAFT CONTINGENT GOES NEXT WEEK FROM BOARD 345

Group Leaving for Induction Expected to be Fairly Small

Registrants who will comprise the December draft contingent have received their official notices and are scheduled to leave for possible induction into the armed forces sometime next week, according to officials of Local Selective Service Board No. 345.

The size of the group has not been revealed but it is believed that it will be a small one as has been the case for the last several months.

A small group of local registrants today underwent preinduction physical examinations at the area induction center.

Members of the draft board are continuing the task of giving new classifications to a large number of registrants, according to recently-adopted directives

Daughters Meet.

Plans for the annual charity card party to be conducted Monday night under the auspices of Court St. Bernard, Catholic Daughters of America, were outlined at a meeting of the group last night in the Knights of Columbus quarters on Remsen Street. Mrs. Florence White, grand regent, presided during the business session. The party committee is headed by Mrs. Charles M. Gildea.

Accidents Reported.

Walter Bouchard of 93 Heartt Avenue, reported to police that his car and a vehicle owned by George Trahan collided at Congress and Newark Streets, Sunday. According to Bouchard, the Trahan car struck the right rear of his machine. Louis LaPlante of 51 Crage Street, Northside, reported that his car was sideswiped by a DelRae taxi in South Saratoga Street, while he was proceeding northward. No damage was reported.

Obituary.

The funeral of Mrs. Sarah Fellows, widow of Judge Isaiah Fellows, was held yesterday at 2 p.m. from her residence, 46 Broadway. Rev. Donald R. Lewis, pastor of the First Methodist Church, officiated. The bearers were Harold Bennett, Donald Scotland, Iver Carlson and Raymond Manning. Burial took place in Waterford Rural Cemetery.

Mrs. Julia Bauman, widow of Henry Bauman, native of Canada and resident of this city for the greater part of her life, died late yesterday following a protracted illness. She was a communicant of St. Joseph's Church. Survivors include a sister, Miss Delia Lajeunesse and several nieces and nephews, all of this city. The funeral will be held Thursday at 8:30 a.m. from the funeral home of Walter J. Duffy, 229 Columbia Street and at 9 a.m. from St. Joseph Church, where a requiem mass will be celebrated. Burial will be in St. Mary's Cemetery, Waterford.

Firemen Summoned.

A telephone call from the Home for Aged Women, 100 Vliet Boulevard yesterday, disclosed that the boiler in the basement of the home was behaving in a peculiar manner. Firemen, acting as an emergency squad, quickly discovered the trouble and corrected it.

ST. ANNE'S CHURCH CLUB NAMES COMMITTEES TO PLAN CHRISTMAS DANCE

Additional committees to complete preparations for the pre-Christmas dance to be staged Sunday at Congoon's Studio on Third Street by the St. Anne's Social Club, were announced last night by officials in charge.

Named to the refreshment committees were Miss Helen Deeb, Miss Alma Deeb, Miss Helen Ziter, Miss Sally Zouky and Miss Della Keyrouze. The decoration committee will include Miss Victoria Rice, Miss Elizabeth Yamin, Miss Ann Deep and Miss Mary Deep.

Music for the dance will be played by Bill Lapp and his orchestra. Frank J. Milanese, local singer, will be the principal vocalist. An exhibition of Spanish dancing will be given by a prominent dance couple of the area.

RECORD EMPLOYEE WOUNDED—Pvt. Eugene P. Broderick, son of Mrs. Martin Broderick of 579 Sixth Avenue and an employee in the mailroom of The Record Newspapers, was slightly wounded in action in France Nov. 15, according to a telegram received from the War Department by his wife, who resides at 14 110th Street. He is in a hospital in France. Gene entered the service in March and has been overseas since August. Two other brothers serve, Sergt. Thomas Broderick in Virginia and Pvt. Charles Broderick who is in the South Pacific.

ANSWER ROLL CALL—Older members of Diamond Rock Lodge, I. O. O. F., respond at the annual roll call meeting of the lodge last night. Left to right are D. Jay Snyder, Irving Schwartz, past grand conductor and guest speaker; Charles Webb, receiving 25-year badge; Arthur W. Morton, oldest member present; Philip H. Pellitier, George Steiner, Charles W. Wend and Warren Strope.

I.O.O.F. LODGE HAS ROLL CALL EVENT AT LANSINGBURG

First Nomination of Officers Slated for Monday, Dec. 11

The annual roll call meeting of Diamond Rock Lodge of Odd Fellows was held last night with Earl Hohn presiding, and Fred W. Whitehouse in charge of the roll call.

Irving Schwartz of New York, past grand conductor of the Grand Lodge, was the principal speaker, stressing Odd Fellowship and its place in the community. He said that 15 per cent of the members were now serving in the armed forces.

A 25-year button was presented by Philip H. Pelletier, past grand, who has served 59 years in Odd Fellowship, to Past Grand Charles Webb. Also honored were Mr. and Mrs. Fred Hunziker on their 25th wedding anniversary.

John W. Whitehouse, oldest member of the lodge, who has served since 1898, was unable to be present. Also absent were William H. Johnson and Nelson Simon, who have been in the lodge since 1896.

Arthur W. Morton, past grand, who joined the lodge in 1897, was named as the oldest continuous member of the lodge attending the roll call. Others present were D. Jay Snyder, 1900; George Steiner, 1906; Charles W. Wend, 1906. Philip H. Pelletier, 1885, by card, 1906; Warren E. Strope, 1894 by card.

Guests included Alexander C. Schafer, grand scribe of the Grand Encampment, who spoke briefly; Maj. Henry E. Page of the Patriarch's Militant, and Cornelius S. Fonda, past district deputy grand master.

The first nomination of lodge officers will be held Monday, Dec. 11.

Willard J. Lamphier and Jesse Darrah also spoke.

The meeting followed a turkey dinner served by Mrs. Josephine Wend, Mrs. Ethel Hunziker and Mrs. Mary Strope. On the social committee were Warren Strope, Fred Hunziker, Charles Hansen and Charles W. Wend.

SOME TIRES TAKEN FROM RATION LIST

Used, Recaps and Damaged Synthetics Now "Free"

Used passenger car tires, including recaps and damaged synthetic tires have been removed from rationing and can now be purchased without any OPA tire certificate, it was announced today by the Albany district OPA office. Used truck tires will continue under rationing, however, the OPA office emphasized.

In removing used passenger tires from rationing, OPA also changed the definition of Grade 1 tires to include factory seconds and tires made of reclaimed rubber. Both of these types, as well as new and undamaged synthetic rubber tires will continue under rationing, and may be purchased only upon presentation of a valid tire rationing certificate, the district OPA office said.

A damaged synthetic rubber tire is a new casing that has been held for sale by a dealer, and which the district OPA has authorized to be reclassified as a Grade III tire after determination by an OPA tire examiner that the tire is so damaged that it cannot reasonably be sold on a certificate, it was explained.

The district OPA office pointed out that all tires, both new and old, are under price control and purchasers should check to see that dealers have the maximum prices of tires posted and note the ceiling prices of any tires they intend to buy.

"Any attempts on the part of sellers to obtain more than the legal ceiling price should be reported to a local War Price and Rationing Board," a district OPA office spokesman said.

The National Audubon Society bird census shows an estimated 5,000,000,000 birds in the United States.

Pfc. JOSEPH F. IOZZO

JOSEPH F. IOZZO IN HOSPITAL WITH BATTLE WOUNDS

Injured in Germany Nov. 11; Had Been Serving Overseas Since May

GREEN ISLAND

Pfc. Joseph F. Iozzo was wounded in action in Germany, Nov. 11, according to word received by his wife, the former Kathryn M. Daniele of Troy, who lives at 49 Paine Street, Green Island. He was wounded in the right hip and is now hospitalized in England. He had been overseas since May and had been in the Army since September, 1942. He is the son of Mr. and Mrs. Anthony Iozzo of the same address.

Stamp Bond Sales.

The students at St. Joseph's School yesterday purchased $420.75 worth of War Bonds and Stamps. The sale is conducted under the supervision of Mrs James Hurley and Mrs. Maurice Van Buskirk.

Knights to Meet.

At a meeting of Green Island Council, K. of C. at 8 p.m. in the council rooms tonight, plans will be completed for a lecture on the mass at the rooms to be given Thursday at 8 p.m. by Rev. John H. Newman of Altamont.

School Sales.

The sale of War Stamps and Bonds in Heatly School yesterday, amounting to $419.75, brings the total for the school year to $3,927.35. Freshmen, seniors and eighth grade students already have reported December sales at more than 90 per cent.

Cheer Leaders Chosen.

The following were chosen cheer leaders for Heatly School during a contest last week Jane MacDowell, Marilyn Chriss, Margaret Lussier, Deloris O'Hara, Anna Mae Sebol, Dorothy Laird, William Cornes and John Kelly. The alternates are Marilyn Denton, Mildred Daudelier and Edward Costigan.

Bond Sale Setup.

Mayor Francis M. Dwyer last night, as chairman of the house-to-house canvass and of the school campaign in the Sixth War Loan Drive, assigned districts to about thirty volunteer workers in the village to conduct a canvass. They will visit each home and ascertain how many bonds have been bought during the period of Nov. 20-Dec. 15, inclusive, so as to discover what credit should be given to the village. H. R. Barnum, cochairman for industry with Joseph V. H. Hayes, addressed the workers last night. He said that the industrial plants in the village will account for all sales made through their medium.

EAST SIDE.

The men of Trinity Methodist Church will get together tomorrow for supper at 6 p.m. The guest speaker will be Rev. George B Cole of Ravena.

Personal.

Reginald Reichard has returned to his home on Brookview Avenue after a recent operation in Samaritan Hospital.

Church Bazaar.

The annual Christmas bazaar in Pawling Avenue Methodist Church will open tomorrow at 2 p.m. and continue until 5 p.m. The pastor, Rev. Arthur H. Landmesser, will formally open the sale which is sponsored by the W. S. C. S. of the church. Thursday the sale will continue in the afternoon and evening with a turkey supper being served at 5:30 p.m. Mrs. Arthur J. Gummer, president, is general chairman, and Mrs Ernest Bonesteel is chairman of the supper.

COUNCIL TO MEET.

The Troy Council of Parents and Teachers will hold its monthly meeting at 1:30 p.m. tomorrow at School 5. According to Mrs. Nelson H. Schmay, president, plans will be completed for the Founder's Day program.

CHEST COLD TIGHTNESS QUICKLY RELIEVED

When chest muscles feel "tight" and sore, due to a cold, rub on Mentholatum. Two vital actions bring quick relief: (1) Mentholatum stimulates surface circulation—helping to "loosen" the tight muscles. (2) Soothing medicinal vapors comfort irritated mucous membranes of nose and throat. Get Mentholatum. Jars, tubes, 30¢.

MENTHOLATUM

What d'ya hear from your highball?

DRINKS mixed with Canada Dry Water even *sound* better. "PIN-POINT CARBONATION" keeps them full of life . . . sparkle lasts to the bottom sip.

Canada Dry Water—the world's most popular club soda—is preferred in the finest bars, hotels and clubs. Its special formula points up the flavor of any tall drink. Serve Canada Dry Water in your home . . . it costs no more than ordinary mixers.

BIG BOTTLE 15¢ Plus deposit

CANADA DRY WATER
WORLD FAMOUS
The Life of the Drink

IONIC TRIANGLE TO HAVE YULE PARTY AT NEXT MEETING

Christmas Program Planned for Dec. 18; Fire Companies Nominate

WATERFORD

Plans for a Christmas party were made by Ionic Triangle, Daughters of the Eastern Star, at its meeting held last evening at the Masonic Temple with Miss June Conklin, beloved queen, presiding. The party will be held in connection with the next meeting, Dec. 18, and will include games, grabbag and refreshments. The committee appointed to be in charge of the affair is headed by Jean Willetts, chairman, and includes the following members: Shirley Le Van, Lois Swatling, Eleanor Waterbury and Mrs. Henry Swatling, supervisor.

Supervisors present were Mrs. Dorothy Gorham, triangle deputy of Waterford Triangle; Mrs. Phyllis Folsom, Mrs. LaVerne Conklin, Mrs. Swatling and Mrs. Dorothy LeVan.

Following the business meeting favors were made to be sent to the Shriners' Hospital at Springfield. A social was enjoyed and refreshments served with Mrs. Conklin, Mary Ruth Spry and Margaret Burgess in charge.

Personal.

Pvt. Frederick Willetts has returned to Fort Mead, Md., after spending a ten-day furlough with his parents, Mr. and Mrs. Alfred Willetts of Upper Third Street.

Auxiliary To Meet.

The auxiliary unit of the Charles J. Brady Post, American Legion, will meet at 8 p.m. today in the Town Hall with Mrs Seena Tracy, president, in charge.

Meeting Slated.

At 8 p.m. today the Altar Guild of Grace Episcopal Church will meet in the parish house and tomorrow and Friday the choir will rehearse at 7:15 p.m. under the direction of Robert Van Steenburg.

Mayor Writes Mead.

Mayor John F. Walsh received recently a communication from Senator Mead concerning the building of a St. Lawrence River seaway. In reply to this Mayor Walsh stated that he felt that the people of Waterford were more interested in enlarging and improving the Barge Canal.

Parish Elects.

The annual parish meeting of Grace Episcopal Church was held last evening at the Clark Memorial parish house. All wardens and vestrymen were reelected as follows: Walter S. Robinson, warden for one year; Harry E. VanKleeck, warden for two years; William H. Law and Donald G. McKay, vestrymen for three years and Edwin J. VanKleeck, vestryman for two years.

Hose Company Elects.

The Ford Hose Company met last evening at its rooms in the Fire House on Division Street with Gerald McNamara, president, presiding. Nominations of members for the annual election of officers for the coming year were made and are as follows: Gerald McNamara, president; Harold Swasey, vice president; Leon Bochard, secretary; Frank Funnucci, captain; James Remmington, first assistant; James Rolston, steward, and Stephen Swasey, trustee for three years. A hamburger steak supper was served following the meeting. The next meeting will be Jan. 8 and will be the annual meeting.

Firemen Buy Bond.

The Knickerbocker Steamer Company voted to purchase its sixth $100 War Bond at its meeting held last evening in the company rooms with Harold Vrooman, president in charge. The annual banquet will be held Jan. 13 at the fire house. Members nominated to be elected at the annual meeting are: Harold Vrooman, president; Edward Shaw, vice president; Frederick Brenz, captain; Gabriel Gentile, first assistant; Richard Tracy, second assistant; J. Ormond Grady, secretary; John Bernardo, steward; James Harris, delegate and George Sorensen, alternate. A roast chicken dinner was served following the meeting under the direction of Mr. Brenze who was assisted by the following committee George Rasmussen, Carl Sorensen, Stephen Faulkner and Harry Tracy.

CLUB TO DINE.

The Twentieth Century Club of the Y. W. C. A., formerly known as the Business and Industrial Girls Club, will have Ventelli, a local magician, as an entertained for its supper-meeting at 6 p.m. Thursday.

★ ★ ★ ★ ★ ★

Help the nation's efforts to keep your living costs DOWN, the buying power of your dollar UP.

★ ★ ★ ★ ★

Today, thrift is a national necessity. Every dollar spent carelessly makes already scarce goods scarcer, forces prices higher, lowers the buying power of the dollar, may lead to widespread economic insecurity later.

It's your duty to save now. Persistent, long-continued, *planned* saving by all of us will lead to greater prosperity after the war. Buy War Bonds regularly—and go to the bank every pay day to deposit as much of your salary as you can. It's your patriotic duty, as well as your duty to yourself and your family.

This advertisement is approved by the Office of Economic Stabilization

BANK OF WATERFORD
WATERFORD, N. Y.
MEMBER FEDERAL DEPOSIT INSURANCE CORPORATION

How Waste Paper Goes to War

PACKED . . . Double-packed in heavy paper, the shell being inserted into the container will travel to the battlefront in perfect condition. Except for the largest sizes, all ammunition is shipped in paper.

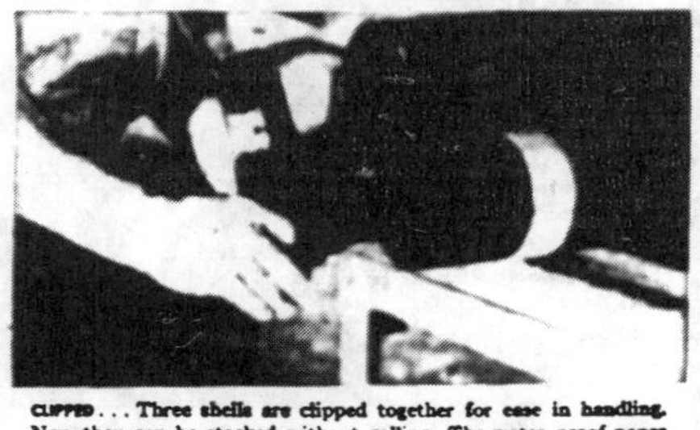

CLIPPED . . . Three shells are clipped together for ease in handling. Now they can be stacked without rolling. The water-proof paper shell containers are strong enough to stand rough treatment.

FIRED . . . by one of our tanks, "dug-in" at the front. These shell containers made from your waste paper have done their job to speed the day of victory!

U.S. VICTORY WASTE PAPER CAMPAIGN

G.O.P. INSURGENTS IN COHOES TO TALK WITH MAC AFFER

Leaders of Revolt Seeking Change in Republican City Leadership

Joseph Kupiec of the Second Ward, said to be leader of the revolt which recently developed within the Republican Party organization in Cohoes, stated today that a majority of organization ward captains met yesterday to discuss the general situation.

It was recently stated by Mr. Kupiec that the movement seeks to have a change in the Cohoes party leadership. Today he declared that at yesterday's gathering, further details of which were not revealed, it was voted to postpone action pending a conference with Kenneth S. MacAffer, chairman of the Albany County Republican Committee.

Although formerly closely associated with Walter H. Wertime, jr., vice chairman for Cohoes of the county G. O. P. committee, Mr. Kupiec has openly declared that the movement which he heads has a change in leadership as its primary purpose.

V. F. W. AUXILIARY HOLDS YULE PARTY

Entertain St. Colman's, Fairview Home Children

Members of the Ladies' Auxiliary Cohoes Post, Veterans of Foreign Wars, entertained children of St. Coleman's Home and Fiarview Home with a Christmas party yesterday afternoon at the group's quarters on Remsen Street.

A buffet luncheon was served from a table attractively decorated in holiday colors and gifts were distributed from beneath a Christmas tree.

Accordion numbers were offered by Robert Ashley and piano selections by Mrs. Mary Lavoie.

Members of the arrangements committee were Miss Marion Murphy, Mrs. hristina Dewar, Mrs. Rita Wood and Miss Ruth Waterhouse.

PARISH MOTHERS' CLUB ENTERTAINS CHILDREN AT ST. AGNES' SCHOOL

The Mothers' Club of St. Agnes' School entertained children of the school with a Christmas party Friday afternoon. Programs were conducted in each of the classrooms and gifts were exchanged.

Mrs. Omer P. Senecal and Mrs. Raymond Lynch were co-chairmen of the arrangements committee, which included Mrs. Robert G. Hanlon, Mrs. Fred Allison, Mrs. William O'Keefe, Mrs. Thomas McGrath, Mrs. William Powers and Mrs. Harry Green.

A meeting of the club will be conducted in Gavin Hall today at 8 p.m. Mrs. Joseph Cox, president of the group, will preside during the business session, which will be followed by a social period.

To Omit Meetings.

Meetings of Group 79, Ladies' Catholic Benevolent Association, will be omitted until after the first of the year, it was announced today by officials of the unit.

YULE LOG REVELS—The 53rd annual Procession of the Boar's Head and Yule Log took place yesterday at Hoosac School. Upper left, the pages escort the Boar's Head Minstrel. The pages are Hadden Wood of Meadowbrook, Pa., and Kendall Simpson of Hoosick. Keith Marvin of Troy, graduate in the class of 1943 and now dormitory master, was the Boar's Head Minstrel for the fourth year. In back of him are David Shaffer of Ringos, N. J., and Donald Smith of Hadley, Mass. Upper right, Kendall Simpson rides the Yule Log, drawn by Joseph Salisbury of Washington, D. C., the Jester. At the left is Charles Stought of Freeport, L. I., and in the rear, Barry McKinley of Scotia, David Hurt of New York and Theodore Simpson of Hoosick. Lower picture, for the first time in the history of the Yule Log revels, girls took part in the pageant. Dancing the gavotte are, left to right, Nina and Olivia Pattison, Jane Sidford and Carol Houston, all of Troy.

COHOES TAX SALE DELAYED PENDING LIST CORRECTION

Owners Appear at Treasurer's Office to Clear Property of Liens

Action by the Cohoes Common Council to authorize City Treasurer John J. Conway to advertise the sale of tax delinquent properties will be delayed pending the correction of the list submitted to the Board of Assessors.

Meanwhile the assessors' office is working on the sheets and when the work is completed, the list will be submitted to the Common Council.

The delay is caused by the number of property owners who have appeared at the treasurer's office to clear their properties of any tax liens levied against them. Taxpayers may have their names removed from the list any time before the sale actually begins by paying all taxes for 1944 and previous years plus the penalties accrued.

HOLIDAY PARTY HELD FRIDAY AFTERNOON AT SACRED HEART SCHOOL

Children of Sacred Heart School were entertained Friday afternoon with a Christmas party under the auspices of the Mothers' Club. Games were played, refreshments were served and Santa Claus distributed gifts from beneath a Christmas tree.

Mrs. Joseph Hervieux and Mrs. Arthur Smith were co-chairmen of the arrangements committee and Mrs. Joseph Zaresky was in charge of the games, awards being given the winners. The refreshment committee included Mrs. Edward Goyette, Mrs. Francis Thibodeau, Mrs John Lavallee, Mrs. Loretta Turcotte and Mrs. Aurore Roberts.

A meeting of captains of the club will be held in the school hall today at 8 p.m.

The group will conduct its annual Christmas party for members Thursday night, Dec. 28. Mrs. Claude McMahon and Mrs. Omer Clermont are co-chairmen of the arrangements committee.

Obituary.

The funeral of Israel Lavigne was held today at 8 a.m. from the Dufresne Funeral Home, 111 Mann Avenue, and at 8:30 a.m. from St. Marie's Church where a requiem mass was celebrated by the pastor, Rev. Adrien J. Bechard. "Domine" was rendered by George Carpo at the offertory and at the conclusion Edward Nadeau and Edward Frament sang "Crucifix." Miss Ellen R. Lapointe presided at the organ. Bearers included Charles Frament, Armand Renaud, Joseph Brun and Francis Choinere. Father Bechard officiated at the grave in St. Joseph's Cemetery, Waterford.

STANLEY WARENDA ELECTED AS HEAD OF POLISH GROUP

Installation Will Be Held at Banquet on Sunday, Jan. 21

Stanley Warenda was elected president of Group 1648, Polish National Alliance, at the group's annual meeting yesterday at P. N. A. Hall on Mohawk Street. He succeeds Edward Adamczyk.

Other officers chosen at the session include Stephen Kowalik, first vice president; Mrs. Anges Sklarz, second vice president; Stephen Mroczka, financial secretary; Vincent Guzek, treasurer; Samuel Bartnick, recording secretary; Wacslaw Kolonczyk, marshal; William H[illegible], sergeant-at-arms and Mr. Adamczyk, Stanley Lis and George Po[illegible].

John Nieckarz, Mr. Guzek and Mr. Adamczyk were elected as members of the Polish-American Congress. Election tellers were Joseph Kupiec, Frank Gorka and Louis Janowski.

Installation ceremonies will take place at a banquet scheduled to be held Sunday, Jan. 21.

Post To Meet.

Members of E. T. Ruane Post, American Legion, will meet today at 8 p.m. at the quarters on Oneida Street. Comdr. Claude C. Foster will preside during the business session.

11 RECLASSIFIED IN DRAFT STATUS BY COHOES BOARD

Four Men Placed in 1-A Category; Several Others in 2-B and 2-B(F)

Eleven registrants were reclassified today by Local Selective Service Board No. 345.

Metro Jubak, Donald L. Trombley, Leslie B. Ashworth and Kenneth J. Hamel have been placed in Class 1-A as being immediately available for possible induction into the armed forces.

Other reclassifications are as follows: John B. Poland, class 2-B; Edward F. Milian and Raymond A. Clement, class 2-B(F); Earl C. Fryer and Donald L. Lewis, class 4-D, and Alfred W. Clark and John J. Walion, class 1-CDisc.

Welfare Clinic Slated.

A welfare clinic under the auspices of the Health Department is scheduled to be conducted at the City Hall tomorrow at 10 a.m. Dr. Hans D. Weiss, health commissioner, will be in charge, assisted by Mrs. Sally Cummings and Mrs. Mary Lynch, city nurses.

Veterans' Session.

Reports on the membership campaign being conducted under the auspices of Cohoes Post, Veterans of Foreign Wars, will be submitted at a meeting of the group Thursday night at the quarters on Remsen Street. The business session will be presided over by Comdr. David Mayeroff and will be followed by a social period.

Elected President.

Harry Hardenburgh yesterday was elected president of the Baraca lass of the First Baptist Church, which is beginning its 49th year of continuous class study in the Sunday School.

Other officers chosen include George Ashby, first vice president; Walter Hartshorn, second vice president; Joseph Waterhouse, secretary; Charles Moquin, treasurer; Egbert Normington, librarian and Rev. George F. McElvein, teacher. Installation ceremonies are scheduled to be conducted Sunday, Dec. 31.

T. H. CLARK, FORMERLY PLUMBING INSPECTOR, DIES AT MENANDS HOME

Thomas H. Clark, who served as municipal plumbing inspector during the administrations of former Mayor John J. Morrissey, died late Saturday at the Home for Aged Men, Menands, following a short illness.

Born in Cohoes, Mr. Clark was a life long resident of this city and a member of St. John's Episcopal Church. His wife, the former Miss Anna Kelly, died about two years ago. Several nieces and nephews survive.

The funeral will be held Wednesday at 11 a.m. from the Tebbutt Funeral Home, 176 State Street, Albany. Rev. Schuyler D. Jenkins, rector of St. John's Church, will officiate. Burial will be in Waterford Rural Cemetery.

GROUP WILL RAISE FUNDS FOR WARD HONOR ROLL

Further plans for the raising of funds for the Fifth Ward Honor Roll to be elected in West End Park will be outlined at a meeting of the committee Wednesday at 7 p.m. in School 5 on Masten Avenue. Howard Van Buskirk is chairman and Edward Pearson cochairman of the committee.

It was announced today that the house-to-house canvass in the interest of the project will be resumed after the first of the year.

Will Hold Party.

A Christmas party for members of the Ladies' Auxiliary of Collin-Ross Camp, United Spanish War Veterans, will be conducted Thursday night in the G. A. R. rooms on Remsen Street. There will be a Christmas tree and a grabbag will be enjoyed. Mrs. Margaret Riely is general chairman of the arrangements committee.

St. John's Episcopal Church.

Children's confirmation instruction class will be held tomorrow at 3 p.m. Wednesday, Ember Day, there will be holy communion at 10 a.m. The Evening Guild will meet at 8 p.m. Wednesday. Thursday, St. Thomas Day, Holy Communion is at 10 a.m. Friday, Ember Day, holy communion service will be conducted at 10 a.m. The children's choir will rehearse at 3 p.m. and adult choir at 8 p.m. Saturday, Ember Day, Holy Communion is at 10 a.m. The Altar Guild will meet at 2:30 p.m. to make plans for decorating the church.

TRADITIONAL YULE EXERCISES HELD AT HOOSAC SCHOOL

Candles Lighted in Memory of Nine Alumni Killed in Service

One of the most successful performances in recent years of the unique Procession of the Boar's Head and Yule Log was given yesterday at Hoosac School for a large audience. More than a score of alumni returned for the 53rd performance of the Christmas revels.

The festivities took place in the candlelit dining hall in Boulton Hall, where they have been held since 1906. The opening ceremony was the lighting of the Yule candle by the youngest boy at the school and the senior prefect, from last year's Christmas Candle. Frank C. Butcher, veteran organist and choirmaster at the school and organist at St. Barnabas' Church here, assisted in the ceremony. Rev. James L. Whitcomb, rector of St. Barnabas', represented the period when he served as headmaster of the school while Rev. Meredith B. Wood, the headmaster, represented the present.

Three candles were lighted in memory of the nine Hoosac School alumni who have made the supreme sacrifice in this war and to whom this year's pageant was dedicated.

Boar's Head Carol Sung.

The procession of the board's head followed. John Pattison of Troy was torchbearer for the herald. Keith Marvin of Troy, dormitory master at the school, and graduate in the class of 1943, sang "The Board's Head Carol" for the fourth year. Carlton J. Anderson of Troy was the yeoman bearing the mince pie. Other important parts in the first half of the revels were Julian G. Hillhouse of the class of 1910, English instructor at the school, as Father Christmas, Joseph Salisbury of Washington as King Wencelas and David Hurt of New York as the page.

After singing of "The Boar's Head Carol," came the procession of the Shepherds of Bethlehem. Eric Messer of Troy was lantern bearer. Rev. R. B. Gutman, rector of St. Mark's in Green Island and former history instructor at Hoosac School, was in the procession.

The procession of the three kings followed. The kings were Robert Howes of Vineyard Haven, Mass., with Edward Pattison of Troy as his page; Rev. George A. Atwater, history instructor, and Brother Herbert, O. H. C.

"The Carol for St. Stephen's Day" was sung as a duet by Lowell Cummings of Bennington, class of 1941, and Mr. Marvin. The recessional to the first half of the revels was "Adeste Fideles."

In the second half of the program, the opening carol "Welcome Yule" was sung by Mr. Marvin and a chorus. The jester was Joseph Salisbury who made his traditional speech and then assisted in bringing in the Yule log. Three carols were sung, "Come Bring With Your Noise," "Now Blazing Yule Logs" and "Christmas in The Olden Time."

Mummers Play Presented.

The Mummers play this year was arranged by Mr. Butcher and Mr. Hillhouse. Carl Anderson of Troy was master of properties. "Jack Finney" was played by Fred Endo of Washington, the "Turkish Knight" by Albert Robinson of Wellesley, Mass., "Father Christmas" by Mr. Hillhouse, the "King Of Egypt" by James Gettings of Boston, "St. George" by John Williams, "Fair Sabra" by Edward Pattison of Troy, the "Dragon" by William McGuckin of Columbus, O., the "Giant" by Albert Morse of Forest Hills, L. I., and the "Doctor" by Hadden Wood of Meadowbrook, Pa.

St. George slew the Dragon, the Turkish Knight and the Giant in rapid succession amid much laughter. The Giant's tombstone was erected and the choristers sang "King George He Was For England."

Then the wassail bowl was carried triumphantly in by two "beefeaters." "The Wassail Song" was sung and the jester performed merrily.

Girls Participate.

An unusual part of the program followed. For the first time in the history of the school, girls took part. The Misses Carol Houston, Olivia, and Nina Pattison and Jane Eidford of Troy danced the sarabande with four Elizabethan gentlemen to incidental music from Mr. Butcher's suite for orchestra, "In Stately Measure." The sarabande music is number one of the suite. They also danced the gavotte to number two of the suite. Both were encored. The dances were arranged by Miss Patricia Gardner of Emma Willard School faculty and Mr. Butcher.

The Elizabethan sword dance was given to "Minuet Caprice," number three of Mr. Butcher's suite.

The pages, leading the rector, then went to the front entrance of the hall and ushered in the waits who sang "God Rest Ye Merry Gentlemen" and "Here We Come A'wassailing." The waits were all alumni. Lowell Cummings sang Mr. Butcher's carol, "Sunny Bank" to the pages as he has for several years. "The Norman Carol" was then sung while the pages tried to drag Father Christmas from the dais. To the tune of "Country Dance" from Mr. Butcher's suite, Father Christmas put reins on the pages and drove them about the hall, distributing candy to the guests.

Three carols were sung around the hearth, "The First Noel," "I Sing of a Maiden" and "The Virgin and Child." Then all faced the embers of the Yule Log in the great fireplace and sang "Silent Night." The school clasped hands and went down the room singing "God Bless Us All," followed by the Hoosac School ode, "Oculos Meos Lavavi."

The orchestra for the revels was from Schenectady.

Meeting Scheduled.

The Women's Society of Christian Service of St. James Methodist Church will meet at the home of Mrs. Thomas Ford, sr., 15 Walnut Street, today at 7:30 p.m.

Veteran Returns

Pvt. James Pettigrew, U. S. A., son of Mrs. Robert Pettigrew of 1 Lewis Street, has returned to this country after 44 months of service in the Southwest Pacific area.

Legion to Meet

E. T. Ruane Post, American Legion will meet today at 8 p. m. at Legion headquarters in Oneida Street. Commander Claude Foster will preside at the business meeting.

Rebekahs to Meet.

Spartana Rebekah Lodge will meet tomorrow at the rooms on Remsen Street with Mrs. Lilia Crier, noble grand, in charge. A social hour will be held after the business meeting.

Club to Hear Miss Reavy.

Miss Grace A. Reavy, former president of the State Civil Service Commission, will address the Cohoes Business and Professional Women's Club at a dinner-meeting today at 6:30 p.m. in the Elks clubhouse. Mrs. Nan Henkes will preside at the busines session.

Firemen Summoned.

An alarm from Box 67 about 6 p.m. Saturday brought firemen to the home of Don Cl[illegible] Park Avenue. An electric iron left on an ironing board ignited the covering. No damage was reported.

First Methodist Church.

A special Christmas service will be conducted at the church next Sunday morning, with special Christmas music. The sacrament of baptism will be administered to infants by the pastor.

A Christmas party, scheduled for tonight and sponsored by the Loyal Daughters Class of the church School has been postponed until further notice.

Assigned to School

Corp. William J. Forant, son of Mr. and Mrs. Wilfred Forant of 88 Lancaster street, has been assigned to the Army Air Forces Training Command Radio School at the Sioux Falls Army Air Field, S. D. The Cohoes soldier will be entered in a twenty-week course and at the completion of his training will become a member of the crew of an army bomber as a radio operator-mechanic. Forant was inducted into the service on January 22 of this year.

Plan Christmas Party

Members of the Ladies of St. Anne Society of St. Marie's Church who have been received into the membership during the year will be feted at a Christmas party today in the basement of the church. The affair will be held following a business meeting at 7:30 p. m. A musical program will be presented under the direction of Mrs. Rose Danis and each member will provide a gift for a grab bag. Mrs. Henry Ouelette is general chairman of the event.

WATCH THE RABBIT—A child patient of Samaritan Hospital watches with glee as a magician pulls a rabbit out of nowhere at the Christmas party Saturday. The party was given by the Twigs, an organization at the hospital, for the children of the out-patient department. There were gifts for all on the tree.

ENLISTED IN NAVY.

Three Mechanicville youths who have enlisted in the Navy left Tuesday for the Naval Training Station at Sampson. They are Edward Hinchey, Louis Cashera and Donald Daley.

STOX
SOUP MIX
CHICKEN-LIKE FLAVOR NOODLES

NEW BILL WOULD PROHIBIT PRACTICE OF ENDORSEMENTS

Proponents Take Cognizance of Heavy Vote Cast in That Manner for F.D.R.

(Staff Correspondence.)

Albany—Revealing an intention on the part of Republican legislative leaders to avoid future criticism of the staffing of both houses of the Legislature, Majority Leader Irving M. Ives of the lower house has submitted a proposal that the responsibility for all clerical appointments in that body be transferred from the clerk to the speaker of the House.

Meanwhile, legislation was drafted to revive the hotly debated proposal of last year to prohibit printing on a primary ballot of the name of a candidate who is an enrolled voter of another party. The measure is directed against the practice of both major parties of seeking endorsement from other parties whose leaders, with the possibility of veto power, have engaged in "political shopping."

A similar bill was defeated 21 to 23 in the upper house last year when eight Republicans joined with 15 Democrats who voted solidly against the proposal. With the possible exception of Rensselaer County, Democrats have benefitted most through other party endorsements.

Write-In Allowed.

The ballot proposal would prevent a candidate from running in primaries of more than one party although he could gain the nomination of a second party through a write-in.

Although the sponsor of the 1944 bill admitted it would have prevented New York City's Mayor La Guardia from seeking either the Republican or Democrate nomination for reelection this year, he denied it was aimed directly at him.

Instead, the sponsor said, it was aimed to prevent what he called an upstate practice "of people running under colors they don't believe in."

The bill appeared certain to arouse opposition in both major parties, inasmuch as both Republican and Democratic legislators have won office with the backing of minority party support.

Renewed interest in the proposal emphasized legislative cognizance of the hefty vote cast for President Roosevelt by the American Labor and Liberal parties last Nov. 7.

The 825,000 A. L. P. and Liberal votes for Mr. Roosevelt were more than double the margin of 316,000 by which he defeated Governor Dewey. The 1944 election marked the third successive year in which Republicans outpolled Democrats.

A. L. P. and Liberal Party nomination of Mr. Roosevelt and Vice President Elect Harry S. Truman resulted in a legal battle which was carried to the Court of Appeals.

The state's highest tribunal ruled that the names of the two Democrats could remain on the A. L. P. and Liberal ballots.

Democrats Take Lead.

On a proposal for the creation of a state juvenile delinquency unit, Democrats beat Republicans to the draw.

Assemblyman Louis Bennett, the Bronx, sponsored the measure, which calls for appropriation of $20,000 for juvenile delinquency division in the executive department.

A Governor Dewey-appointed interdepartmental committee recommended last month creation of a temporary state youth service commission for the same purpose with the committee as a nucleus. It suggested the commission's work be evaluated at the end of five years and "integrated into the permanent structure of the state government." No Republican bill to that end, however, has been presented.

A constitutional amendment proposed by Assemblyman Leo Isacson, (A.L.P., the Bronx) would lower the age requirement for voters from 21 to 18 years. Isacson, only A. L. P. representative in the Legislature, declared war service of men and women under 21 had given them "the right to participate by their vote in the democracy they are defending with their lives."

DEPUTY SCHEDULES VISITS.

William McCall of Hudson Falls, district deputy of the Washington County District of Odd Fellows, has announced the dates for his visitation as follows: Whitehall Lodge, today; Argle, Tuesday, Jane McCrea, Fort Edward, Jan. 18; Salem, Jan. 23; Washington County, North Granville, Jan. 26; Sanatatea Lodge, 849, Hudson Falls, Jan. 29.

EASTERN STAR INSTALLS—Mrs. Gertrude Woods, right, new worthy matron of Bethlehem Star Chapter, O. E. S., was installed last night at the Troy Masonic Temple. With her are the outgoing matron, Mrs. Edna Willetts, and Oliver E. Anderson, worthy patron.

LETHARGY EVIDENT AS G. O. P. ELECTS NEW STATE LEADER

Glen R. Bedenkapp of Lewiston Unanimously Chosen to Succeed Jaeckle

By EDWARD McDONALD.

Albany — Absence, rather than the presence, of protest against party policies provided the ominous note of the session of the Republican State Committee in The Ten Eyck Hotel yesterday, when Glen R. Bedenkapp of Lewiston was unanimously chosen to succeed Edwin F. Jaeckle of Buffalo, resigned, as titular leader of the New York State G. O. P.

Party strategists carefully avoided the presentation of any resolutions which might precipitate controversial arguments on the question of party policies since, for the first time in more than twenty years, Republicans have control of the administrative as well as the legislative branches of the state government.

Behind the Scenes.

Behind the scenes, however there was not only a noticeable lethargy on the part of county chairmen but also predictions that the present top-heavy Republican majorities in both houses of the Legislature would not be "rubber stamps" for recommendations from the administrative branch of government headed by Gov. Thomas E. Dewey. Only Bedenkapp was proposed as a successor to Jaeckle.

On hand were several prominent Republicans who only awaited a signal, or a vehicle, to "have their say." One was former Congressman Hamilton Fish, a scion of the Mann family of Troy, who was anxious to question any resolution which would endorse Governor Dewey's advocacy of state development of the proposed St. Lawrence Seaway project.

The Governor, an avowed foe of Fish, knows or should know that the state cannot make a treaty with a foreign nation, the ex-Congressman told a press conference before attending the meeting of the state committee as a proxy-holder.

Dewey, in his annual message to the Legislature, recommended the state undertake development of the St. Lawrence, potentially for its power resources, if the federal government would not act.

Fish said the federal Constitution plainly prohibited a state from making treaties with foreign powers. Therefore, he added, Dewey knew his proposal was invalid and thus was practicing sheer hypocricy" and "complete defiance" of the fundamental law. Fish said he also was against the St. Lawrence plan "on its merits." He conferred with Assemblyman Wilson C. Van Duzer, Orange Republican, and others opposed to the development. A scheduled public meeting of the anti-St. Lawrence forces failed to materialize.

Fish also indicated that he might be the spearhead of a move next fall, when a new Republican State Committee will be chosen by the enrolled membership of the party, to bring about a rehabilitation of the party's structure.

After the usual speech of acceptance, Bedenkapp said he would stake his leadership of the party on the cooperation of the rank and file of the membership.

Traveling Salesman.

"I want to be a traveling salesman for the Republican Party," he told newsmen after the state committee had chosen him to succeed Jaeckle and the Executive Committee the party's steering group had unanimously named him its chairman. Republican leaders from several sections of the state, in formal resolutions and extemporaneous comment, praised Jaeckle's leadership and expressed regret over his resignation submitted after the General Election last November.

Bedenkapp announced he would resign soon from the State Tax Commission and return to law practice. He formerly practiced in Lockport but he said he would stay in Albany throughout the winter to cooperate with the party's legislative leaders. He may receive a salary as chairman. The question, however, was left open. His tax commission post pays $10,000 a year.

Bedenkapp will visit every county, in so far as possible. "I want to get acquainted with the rank and file," he explained. "I want them to tell me their views."

Bedenkapp, Niagara County chairman since 1930, was nominated by Thomas E. Broderick, Monroe County leader who used the occasion to say Jaeckle had been "a very good chairman" and would continue to work for the party.

J. Russel Sprague of Nassau, a Republican national committeeman, in seconding the nomination voiced regret at Jaeckle's resignation, as did other seconders, including Senate Majority Leader Benjamin F. Feinberg of Plattsburg, Kings Chairman John R. Crews and Jane Todd of Westchester, vice chairman of the state committee.

Jaeckle, who retains his Erie County leadership, received a standing ovation.

Richard W. Lawrence, treasurer, announced the committee had a balance of $212,163, with all bills paid.

The committee adopted resolutions extending sympathy to the families of the late Alfred E. Smith and Wendell L. Willkie.

Governor Dewey was host to committee members at the Executive Mansion after the meeting.

Meanwhile county leaders from throughout the state evinced more interest in future policies of Dewey's administration than they did on who was to head the state committee.

Rensselaer County was represented by Herbert D. Hamm of North Greenbush and Gertrude Cote of Troy.

Congressman Dean P. Taylor Rensselaer County leader, made a hurried trip from Washington to be present. He will return to the national capitol today or tomorrow.

Others on hand from the area were Sen. Gilbert T. Seelye of Burnt Hills, who represents the new Rensselaer-Saratoga County district in the upper house of the Legislature, and Assemblyman John S. Finch of Rensselaer.

With the completion of the business of the committee, county leaders had conferences with legislative representatives as to the appointments to staffs in the current session of the Legislature.

BETHLEHEM STAR CHAPTER INDUCTS OFFICIAL STAFF

Mrs. Gertrude Woods Seated as Worthy Matron at Masonic Temple

Mrs. Gertrude Woods was installed in office as worthy matron of Bethlehem Star Chapter, O. E. S. at a ceremony in the Troy Masonic Temple last night. She succeeds Mrs. Edna Willetts.

Other officers who were inducted were: Oliver E. Anderson worthy patron; Mrs. Sarah Stewart, associate matron; Mrs. Belle McChesney, secretary; Mrs. Florence Pieper, treasurer; Mrs. Helen Jones, conductress; Mrs. Minnie Bowman, associate conductress; Mrs. Edna Willetts, trustee for three years; Mrs. Susan Anderson, chaplain; Mrs. Louise Giles, marshal; Mrs. Lillie Mae Parkes, assistant marshal; Mrs. Alva Armstrong, historian; Mrs. Anna Saunders, warder; Mrs. Gertrude Smith, sentinel; Miss Mary Jane Boyd, color bearer; Miss Irene Melsom, point of Adah; Mrs. Marian Fisher, point of Ruth; Miss Shirley Whittle, point of Esther; Miss Anna Boyd, point of Martha; Mrs. Anna Benard, point of Electa.

Mrs. Anna Gordon, past district deputy president, and Mr. Anderson acted as the installing officers. Their assisting staff included Mrs. Willetts as marshal; Mrs. Hester Xander, assistant marshal; Mrs. Jane Powers, chaplain; Mrs. Della Miner, warder; Mrs. Mae Nelson, sentinel; Mrs. Lottie Bilson, color bearer; Mrs. Belle Lathrop, musician.

A friendship degree was conferred on Mrs. Willetts as she retired from office. During the ceremony she was presented a past matron's jewel, a bouquet and many gifts. Later a rainbow degree was conferred on the new matron, the rainbow ending in a pot of gold filled with gifts from friends.

Guest soloists were Mrs. Jessie Hulstrum and Mrs. Ottie Steinhilber.

A silver tea was served after the meeting, with Mrs. Florence Pieper and Mrs. Anna Gordon presiding at the table. The decorations were based on a centerpiece of flowers.

LOCAL WORKMEN GET COMPENSATION AWARDS

An award of $721.97 was given to William J. Gfroerer in Workmen's Compensation Court yesterday by Referee Lyman A. Kilburn for injuries received while in the employ of the Keller Baking Co., Inc. The case will be continued for one month with compensation.

Two Allegheny Ludlum Steel Corp. employees, John Duval and Alden Alderman, were granted $270.33 and $203.87, respectively, for injuries received while working for the corporation. Alderman's case will continue with compensation for two months. The sum of $209.27 was given to Henry Hughes, injured in the employ of the Troy Hospital Association.

Falling Icicle Hits Boy, Causing Injury To Head

William Connors, six, 320 Third Avenue, was treated at the Leonard Hospital yesterday afternoon by Dr. G. Elmer Martin for a laceration on the top of the head suffered, it was reported, when an icicle fell from the second story roof of his home and struck him while he was playing in the yard. After receiving treatment the boy went home.

More than 70,000 research workers, in 3,400 industrial laboratories, are engaged in chemical research in the U. S.

WAR PLANT
WAR PLANT
?
WASTE PAPER SALVAGE
DROP HERE
JOHN ROSOL

(Reprinted by special permission of The Saturday Evening Post, Copyright, 1944, by the Curtis Publishing Co.)

"THE YOUNG IDEA" By Mossler

"Evidently your gentleman friend doesn't fancy my brand!"

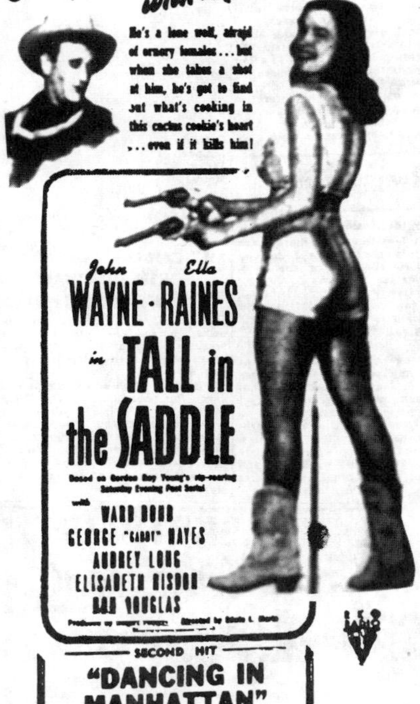

FIVE TROY AREA SCHOLASTIC TILTS ON TOMORROW

Five Troy Area scholastic basketball games are down for settlement tomorrow night.

The spotlight will play on two intra-city contests—one bringing together La Salle and Catholic Central High on the latter's court and the other sending Troy High against Lansingburg High at the 'Burg.

The La Salle-C. C. H. S. clash will count in both the Principals' League and the Diocesan circuit while the Troy-Lansingburg tilt will be a Principals loop affair.

Both games are expected to be hard fought for they bring together natural rivals.

In other Area games tomorrow night Waterford High will entertain Heatly High; Watervliet will tackle Cohoes in a Principals loop affair in the Arsenal City gym and Averill Park will entertain Columbia High of East Greenbush in a Central Hudson Valley League contest.

SKATING STARS TO VIE FOR HONORS IN MEET SUNDAY

Highlighted by Mayor Ahern's three-mile special, an elaborate program of 23 events will be carried out at Belden's Pond, Sunday, as the Troy Recreation Department conducts its eighth annual speed skating championships sanctioned by the Northern New York Skating Association.

The Troy meet originally was scheduled for February 4 but the affair was moved up when Saratoga Springs cancelled its event.

Many of the outstanding skaters of the East will be on hand for the meet in which Hudson Valley outdoor speed skating titles will be at stake.

The program will get underway at 1 o'clock in the afternoon and will include four classes of races—the men's events, midget boys' events, the women's events and events closed to residents of Troy.

There will be five races for boys and girls, 11-17, limited to Troy skaters. Many Troy favorites also will perform in the open events. This group includes Bobby Phillips, Marylin and Jerry McCauley, Anna Mae Murphy, John and William Walthers, Jimmy Riley, Bobby Foz, Bobby Conover and Anna Mae Heitzman.

Another likely entrant is Bobby Phillips, holder of the North American championship as a junior and the New York State title as an intermediate, now stationed at the Sampson Naval Training Station.

Other entries will come from Capitol District, Middle Atlantic, Connecticut and New Jersey skating clubs.

The skating meet is being run off as part of the physical fitness program advocated by the Troy Recreation Department.

Ed Wachter, Troy's superintendent of recreation, says "Skating is an ideal sport for conditioning."

Officials and additional entries for the meet will be announced today or tomorrow.

LINERS BEAT TANKS FOR 7TH IN ROW

The Liners chalked up their seventh straight victory in the Class A Watervliet Arsenal Basketball League last night but they had a real fight on their hands.

The Liners disposed of the Tank Shop, 51 to 48, on the Watervliet High School court by virtue of a second half rally. At the intermission the Tanks led, 24 to 20.

Tony Grasso and John Dundon, with 14 and 15 points, respectively, featured for the winners while Bill Bingham, with 26, was "tops" for the losers.

In another Class A game the Army team snapped out of its losing streak to turn back the Breech quintet, 43 to 30, after trailing 18 to 19 at half time.

Captain Al Kelley and Pvt. Craven, with 13 and eight points, respectively, stood out for the winners while Dave Goldsberry, with seven, was best for the losers.

In the B division the Tank Shop scored its sixth straight triumph by defeating Shop 35, 26 to 13 after holding its opponent scoreless in the first half.

White, with 13, was high for the Tank Shop while Kelleher featured for the losers, playing a fine floor game and tallying three points.

Racing Notes

By the Associated Press.

Seven Mexican-owned horses are entered in the feature 7 furlong Premio Morelia today at the Hipodromo de las Americas.

Irish Bay, Push and Big Bim will carry top weight of 117 pounds. Busy Maid is next with 111, Bienson 108 and Wiseasyou 98.

Pointing out Annapolis Blue as an example, officials of the Hipodromo de las Americas claim that the track's elevation of 7,500 feet makes horses run faster.

The 7-year-old son of Blue Larkspur, a flop in the United States, was sent to Mexico where he made his first start some weeks ago and defeated a field of maidens by five lengths.

Photo by Anuszkiewicz.

INDUS LEAGUE ACTION—Turner, Behr-Manning guard is shown going after the ball during the hectic game with the Arsenal Howitzers in the Troy Indus League this week. Dundon of the Howitzers is second in line while Rudy Czieka of the Behr-Manning outfit is in the background. The Behr-Manning team notched its sixth straight victory as it nosed out the Watervliet aggregation, 19 to 17, in an overtime contest.

WINNERS IN HI-Y COURT CONTESTS

Troy Senior Hi-Y trimmed Troy Junior Hi-Y last night at the Y. M. C. A. court, 85 to 22.

Miles had 37 points for the winners.

In other contests Soph Hi-Y trimmed Cohoes Hi-Y, 21 to 15 and Watervliet Hi-Y turned back Lansingburg Junior Hi-Y.

TROY SR. HI-Y.

	F.G.	F.B.	T.P.
Tutunjian, f.	10	0	20
Miles, f.	18	1	37
McGinnis, c.	8	1	17
Bryce, g.	2	0	4
Sestito, g.	0	0	0
Dickinson, g.	1	1	3
Hughes, g.	2	0	4
Best, g.	0	0	0
Totals	41	3	85

TROY JUNIOR HI-Y.

	F.G.	F.B.	T.P.
Iffland, f.	3	0	6
Bud Walthen, f.	3	0	6
Martin, c.	0	1	1
Gilbert, g.	2	3	7
Gordon, g.	0	0	0
Howe, g.	1	0	2
Totals	9	4	22

Referee — Bachinsky. Scorer — Kelly. Timer McGinnis.

COHOES HI-Y.

	F.G.	F.B.	T.P.
Hebert, f.	0	0	0
Jennings, f.	3	0	6
Mullen, c.		0	0
Brennan, g.	1	0	2
Daley, g.	0	0	0
Monas, g.	1	0	2
Michalski, g.	0	0	0
Forgette, g.	0	0	0
Nystorial, g.	2	1	5
Totals	7	1	15

LANSINGBURG SOPH HI-Y.

	F.G.	F.B.	T.P.
Doyle, f.	0	0	0
Nielson, f.	2	1	5
Cummings, c.	1	0	2
Bogh, g.	2	0	4
Isager, g.	3	0	6
Collopy, g.	2	0	4
Totals	10	1	21

Referee — Bachinsky. Scorer — Kelly. Timer—Paine.

WATERVLIET HI-Y.

	F.G.	F.B.	T.P.
Harris, f.	3	2	8
Michasiw, f.	1	0	2
Squajera, c.	2	2	6
O'Hare, g.	1	0	2
Fabricius, g.	2	0	4
Mosier, g.	0	0	0
Totals	9	4	22

LANSINGBURG JR. HI-Y.

	F.G.	F.B.	T.P.
Conway, f.	2	0	4
Pinkney, f.	1	1	3
Wahelee, c.	0	0	0
Giamel, g.	1	1	3
Malone, g.	3	0	6
Wiley, f.	0	0	0
Maynard, g.	0	1	1
Totals		3	17

Referee — Bachinsky. Scorer — Sestito. Timer—McGinnis.

MEXICAN-OWNED HORSES DOMINATE MEXICO CITY RACE

Mexico City (AP)—Seven Mexico-owned horses are entered in the feature seven-furlong premio Morelia today at the Hipodromo de Las Americas.

Irish Bay, Push and Big Bim will carry top poundage of 117. Busy Maid is next with 111, Menagerie 109, Blenson 108 and Wiseasyou 98.

Except in three of the eight races, today's fields are small. Twelve horses are entered in the second, ten in the fourth and eleven in the eighth.

Boxing Clan Touting Los Angeles Welter

BY LAWTON CARVER.

New York (INS)—Jimmy Doyle, a half-French Irishman whose square name is James J. Delaney, has whipped up as much interest around here as any fighter who has come out of the west in years.

Strangely enough in these times when most prize-fighters are lumbering untutored 4-F's with ailments of one kind or another, this Los Angeles welter is regarded by the habitues of Jacob's Beach as a boxer of the old school. He knows the fundamentals of his trade.

Needless to say, some are already calling him a second Leonard and a second Gans. In fact, they refer to him as the Young Master, not to be confused with the old master, Gans himself. He doesn't hit like an old master or even a young master, but he can box the ears off of a jumping monkey.

He will be making his first start at Madison Square Garden tomorrow night against one Frankie Terry, of Brooklyn, also a Garden debuter. Doyle, or "Deryle" for purposes of Brooklyn identification, will be the favorite and don't tell me he is going to be a flop. These build-ups often go wire-haired in the clutch, but they say Doyle is different.

He has had six fights in the East, and won them all, three by knockouts, to cause observers to go into raves. He is a fine counter-puncher, so they say—I've never seen him fight—and a terrific all-around boxer. His opponent, Terry, is the kind of a hard bun to make him prove it. Terry will hold a weight edge of seven or eight pounds, and is a rough club-fighter, though not a "young master" or young anything except a young man trying to make a living.

Doyle's debut in the Garden will not carry the striking prestige of being the top main event, inasmuch as his fight is one of three tens, and won't even go on last. However it will go no at 10 o'clock in the radio spot and will be the nationally highlighted attraction.

It will be sandwiched in between a closing featherweight brawl between Phil Terranova and Charles (Cabey) Lewis and a heavyweight tussle between Billy Grant and Freddie Schott.

Thus the fight is stamped by Promoter Mike Jacobs as the main event of three main events, regardless of what may precede or follow it.

I nearly forgot to mention that Delaney, Doyle or Deryle, was tutored for a time by Jim Jeffries and later by Jack Johnson. Also, he likes to dance the rhumba and eat apple pie. It just goes to show how much a reporter can dig up on a fellow if he sets out to do it.

Willie Pep, the featherweight champion in some sectors, comes up before Army doctors at Hartford, Conn., next Tuesday for an examination and possible induction, although he was thrown out of the Navy after nearly a year of service because of a perforated ear drum, or some kindred ailment.

He thus is among the first of the 4-F's, or medically discharged, athletes recalled since the work or fight agitation started in Washington.

Meantime, Stan Musial, the Card outfielder and National League batting champion in 1943, has passed his physical and will report for induction on Jan. 19.

UNBEATEN TECH POINTS FOR UNION

Despite the piling up of a team point average per game of 59 and the holding of their opponents thus far to an average of 35, R. P. I.'s basketball team isn't letting down any in intensive practice for Saturday night's contest here against Union College. Anything can happen in this long-standing rivalry and experience has frequently shown that previous performance hasn't meant too much when feelings got running high.

As Coach Ed Donald says: "It isn't how you've been but how you are the night of the game that counts. In addition to psychological aspects generated by traditional rivalries and winning or losing streaks, there are breaks, good or bad."

A desire to win Saturday night's game is even stronger than usual, because if R. P. I. is victorious it will enter the Boston Garden Arena contest against Baldwin-Wallace on Friday evening, Jan. 19, with five straight wins and no defeats.

Tony Orlando, Navy trainee from New York, who did his basketballing for Hofstra College before joining the service, still leads in individual scoring. Adding 20 points in the Rochester game last week, Orlando has now tallied 70. Elliot Kamen, Woodmere, L. I., product, in second place with 37 points, is being threatened by the fast stepping Henry O'Keeffe. O'Keeffe has scored 31 in only two games.

Union College's scoring honors are being monopolized by a 16-year-old civilian student, Al Dingley, former Cohoes High School star, now a freshman at the Schenectady school.

Dingley, who will be appearing for the first time before a home crowd that saw him perform so well as a scholastic cager last season, is at present leading the Union College team. At 5-8 he is one of the shortest players on the starting Dorp drive, but has been the leading factor in Union's wins this season. He makes up with speed and game skill what he lacks in inches.

JOCKEY PERMANE REGRETS HE MADE CERTAIN REMARKS

Miami, Fla. (AP)—Put those brickbats down, fellows. Bobby Permane didn't mean to sound unpatriotic.

The curly-headed little jockey has been ducking ever since he asked, in talking about the racing shutdown: "What good could I do in a war plant?"

Permane went on to explain that he had no mechanical skill, and that by the time a factory could train him, the emergency which led to the turf suspension would be over.

But his remarks drew a verbal barrage. A Chicago plant telegraphed an offer to teach him to work. A postcard brought a threat of a punch in the mouth. Permane's friends didn't fail to tell him that his statement was out of tune with the times.

"I just didn't mean those words like they sounded," he declared yesterday. "You know, I had broken my collarbone in a spill a couple of weeks earlier, and what I wanted to explain was that I couldn't do any work until the shoulder healed. There wasn't anything I could do at the time.

"Believe me, I want to do all I can to help the war effort. I don't think I'm a slacker. I've always played square, and I want people to believe in me.

"I bought $10,000 worth of War Bonds last year, and I only wish I could buy more of them.

"It'll take about three more weeks for my shoulder to heal, then I'm going to do whatever I can. I'd like to get a job here. I like Miami.

"Gosh. The way people understood that story has made me almost ashamed to meet my old friends."

Permane, who will observe his 21st birthday Jan. 21, was turned down three times in Selective Service examinations because of his height, four feet, 11¼ inches, and his weight, 95 pounds.

His step-father, Charles Fairbanks, is with the Army Air Forces in the Pacific.

'VLIET FIVE WINS AS CASWELL STARS

Led by Don Caswell, who chalked up 19 points, the Watervliet Sacred Heart basketball team defeated the Lansingburg Boys' Club quintet, 51 to 37, on the Lansingburg High court last night to notch its second straight victory.

Taking the lead after the first two minutes of play, the Watervliet outfit led the rest of the way, boasting a 31 to 13 margin at half time.

Trombley contributed 12 points to the winners' attack while Blair, with 18 points, stood out for the losers.

The score:

SACRED HEART.

	F.G.	F.B.	T.P.
McGrath, f.	1	0	2
Richardson, f.	0	0	0
Purcell, f.	0	0	0
Caswell, f.	9	1	19
Angstadt, c.	4	1	9
Trombley, g.	4	4	12
Whitney, g.	0	0	0
Kershaw, g.	0	0	0
DiBacco, g.	4	1	9
Rafferty, g.	0	0	0
Totals	22	7	51

LANSINGBURG BOYS' CLUB.

	F.G.	F.B.	T.P.
Meoli, f.	4	1	9
Blair, f.	9	0	18
Collins, c.	0	1	1
Coonrad, g.	2	3	7
Seminick, g.	0	0	0
Singleton, g.	1	0	2
Colligian, g.	0	0	0
Totals	16	5	37

Referee—Karens. Score at half time 31-13, Sacred Heart. Fouls committed—11-9, Lansingburg.

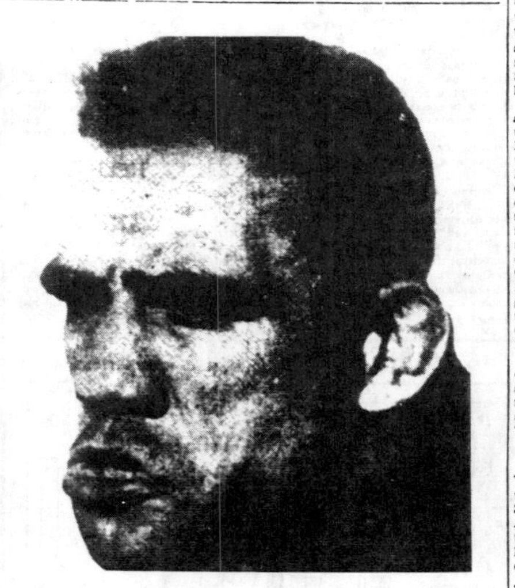

IN ALBANY BOUT—This is a typical expression for Sailor Jack Adams of Florida who will meet Rudy Dusek, Omaha badman, in the feature bout of tonight's wrestling show in the Capitol Arena, Albany.

Rudy Dusek, Omaha grappler, who ran up an impressive string of mat victories at the Capitol Arena in Albany last year, will come back to the Albany scene tonight and attempt to take up where he left off as he faces Sailor Jack Adams of Florida in the main event of the weekly wrestling show.

Dusek is expected to receive plenty of opposition from the experienced Florida grunt and groan artist, who will be seeking his second straight main event victory.

In last week's splotlight contest Adams spotted Jim Austeri of Atlantic City the first fall and then rallied to win two in a row. The bout was well received by the audience which booed Austeri frequently for illegal tactics but applauded Adams no matter what he did.

The feature affair will be a best two-out-of-three fall event.

Tonight's semi-final argument will send Pat Walsh of Atlantic City against Pat Healy of Rochester, who showed up well on last week's card.

Two preliminary events will round out the card.

One of these will send "Bonecrusher" Julius LaRue, employed at the Port of Albany, against Joe Guyon, Schenectady policeman, while the other will pair Young Bull Montana of Utica and Frank Krausse of Schenectady.

The show will begin at 8:30 p.m.

GEORGE LaROVER

STRIKES to SPARE

Alpha Victory League.

Viola Cardish came up with the best triple and single as the Victory League started the second half of it's schedule. Vi's triple was 523 and the single was 202. Two other five hundred scores were handed in also, Rita LaPlante having 519 and Lee Riberdy 501. Other scores of note were: Agnes Herring, 489; Bert Wagar, 475; Mary Jorgensen, 448; Betty Luce, 445; Beryl Blum and daughter, Betty, each with 438 and Ann Johnson, 436.

The league is glad to have Bea Vertefeuille back after a session with a broken arm. If Mary Kane and Grace Hancox must race we wish it would be for high scores and not for low. The league's mid-season party will be held next Monday evening after bowling at the Annex Restaurant.

Troy Merchants.

Philip Celeste and Cy Wagar joined hands to top the Troy Merchants league, each rolling a 629. Celeste also copped the high single a 234. They were followed by Sacala with 609 and Pete Stubel, 608.

The two week layoff evidently sharpened the boys' sights for they crashed the timber with gusto. The 500 circle included: Bill Sokol, 582; Steve Sally, 569; George Clarke, 555; Joe Kelly, 553; Bob Langlotz, 553; Chet Joslin, 550; Jack Martin, 548; Pat Simmons, 541; Jake Pettignelli, 533; Andy Behuniak, 525; Bill Wagar, 519; Al Mochon, 515; Frank Burleigh, 512; George Allain, 508; and Jud Montanye, 500.

Team results were: Simmons Display rolled a season high triple of 2,804 to upset the Saratoga Dry Beverages in three games; Wagars Dairy won two from Cahills, rolling a 958 in the final game for another season's mark; Higgins and Burleigh won two from the Butler Stores.

Weekly prize winners were Cy Wagar, Bill Wagar, Celeste, Langlotz, Pettignelli, Sacala and Sokol.

Inter-City Grill.

The Annex keglers moved into a tie with the Thorns for first place in the Inter-City Grill league by winning all three games from the Webster Turf Inn entry. High scorers for the victors were Morrocco, with a 233 single, and DeStafano a 599 triple. For the losers, Farkas had a 552.

The Thorns kept their hold on at least part of the leadership by taking a 2-1 decision from DeMentos. Bear Beale's 569 was the winners' No. 1 score while Tony DeMento had a 557 to pace his club. Tagues Grill won a pair of contests from the Harveys by a 2-1 margin with Snow's 614 triple showing the way. Bellerose saw a 615 mark go to waste with a losing cause. In the other match, the Camps Grill team defeated the Fifth Avenue entry by a 2-1 margin. Warhurst's single of 239 and triple of 610 helped the victors and Connally's 238-612 was best for the Fifth Avenue Grill.

Next week's schedule which will conclude the first half is: Camps at Thorns; DeMentos at the Annex; Harveys at Webster Turf Inn and Fifth Avenue Tavern at Tagues.

Mayfair Victory.

Mary Clement led the Mayfair Victory league with a 170-480. She was followed by Irene Lewis, 153-397; Ethel Ahearn, 390; and Helen Andrew, 160-383. The Lewises won two from the Clements and the Killions won a pair from the Tague entry.

Troy Business Men.

Falling short of the coveted 600 mark by only one pin, Bowan used a 234-599 score to lead his Coca-Cola teammates to a 3-0 win over the Practical Shoe Repairing team in the Troy Business Men's league. Barrett contributed a 220-573 to the winners' cause. Marinello had a 196-561 for the losers.

With F. Cocca rolling a 208-574 and Rocco a 189-501, the Troy Camera Shop romped to a two-game victory over the Fowlers Heating team. Captain Fowler had a 203-521, and Bloch a 182-507, for the losers' top honors.

Paced by T. Foley's 201-212-212—625, the Mutual Coal keglers rolled to a two-game win over the Dauchy Thorne team. Wild had a 191-539 and Walters a 199-524. Morrison's 203-216-618 and A. Foley's 201-519 were best for the losers. The Berner's Jewelers team defeated the Campus News twice. B. Ross had a 203-533 and B. Beale a 188-529 for the winners and Jack Hallman had a 202-554; Sol Newman a 203-543 and Gilmore a 198-516 for the losers.

New Era Girls.

I. Johnson topped the New Era Girls league with a 213-523 score, high in both departments of play. Other scores were: F. Forcucci, 188-480; K. Zalucki, 186-469; L. Perry, 169-456; G. Berghammer, 188-448; A. Yetto, 166-422; J. Peters, 163-420; F. Headney, 150-416; H. Lake, 148-403.

In team play the Johnsons took two games from the Peters and the Yettos took a pair from the Perrys.

WATERVLIET FIVE TO MEET KELLEYS

Playing its third game in a week, the Watervliet Sacred Heart quintet will meet Captain Al Kelley's Army team from the Watervliet Arsenal on the Watervliet High School court tonight at 9 o'clock.

A secondary feature will bring together the Sacred Heart junior varsity team and the Bandits of the Y. M. C. A. House League at 7:15 o'clock. Both games will be open to the public.

Tom Halpin will start Pete Angstadt at center; Don Caswell and Pierce McGrath at forward and Ray Trombley and Dick DiBacco at the guards. Caswell is a newcomer to the team taking the place of Andy Swota who left for the armed service recently.

Manager Bill Graulty of the Watervliet team still has a few open date for home and home series with fast clubs. For contests, write 1802 Sixth Avenue, Watervliet, or call Watervliet 501 after 6 p.m.

SPORTS MIRROR

By the Associated Press.

Today a year ago: Angelo Bertelli, Notre Dame's great passing quarterback, received the Heisman football award.

Three years ago: New York Baseball Writers association announced Hank Greenberg of the Detroit Tigers will be awarded special plaque for "extraordinary service to baseball" at annual dinner. Greenberg among first of ballplayers to enter Army.

Five years ago: Billy Conn received the Eddie Neil plaque as the outstanding boxer of the year.

Ten years ago: Lou Ambers of Herkimer, N. Y., recognized by New York State Athletic Commission as No. 1 lightweight challenger for champion Barney Ross by outpointing Harry Dublinsky.

GEORGE LA ROVER, IN MAIN MONDAY, HAS GREAT RECORD

George LaRover, hard-hitting New York mittslinger who comes to Troy to meet Art DePietro, Coast star, in the main bout of Monday night's pro boxing show in LaSalle Institute gym, boasts a sensational ring record.

In 41 bouts, many of them with outstanding boxers, LaRover has chalked up 24 knockouts, has won 13 decisions, has gained draws in two bouts and has lost two contests.

His only losses came at the hands of Dorsey Lay and Phil Palmer.

Lay upset LaRover in Philadelphia, scoring a second round knockout, while Palmer decisioned him in New York.

At one time early in his career LaRover scored six straight knockouts.

He kayoed Henry Smothers in the second round in Philadelphia; stopped Carmon Grosso in the fourth at Philadelphia; wound up a battle with Gordon Neil in the second at Wilmington, Del.; kayoed Billy Marcus in the fifth in Hartford, Conn., and stopped Henry Mills in the second at Philadelphia.

Among LaRover's later victims via the knockout route were Carl DePondi, whom he stopped in the first round at Holyoke, Mass.; Marine Brandt of the Royal British Marines whom he kayoed in the third in Philadelphia; Oliver Coin, whom he stopped in the second at Philadelphia; Frankie Carto, whom he stopped in the second in Savannah, Ga.; Charlie Strickland, whom he kayoed in the second in Jacksonville, Florida; Kenny Reed, whom he stopped in the first in Philadelphia; Joe Gills, whom he stopped in second in Boston and Benny Silacto, whom he kayoed in fourth in Philadelphia.

Arrangements for a fast semi-final contest will be completed today by Matchmaker Moe Myers.

Monday's show will be the third to be sponsored by the recently organized Troy Sports Arena Inc.

JACK BROWN PAYS VISIT TO TRACK

Saratoga Raceway—Jack Brown, one of the most popular drivers with the clientele at this track, visited the Raceway a few weeks ago enroute to Canada where he was delivering Cinzano to his new owner in that country.

Cinzano, a pacer with a mark of 2:07 1-2, was a successful campaigner at the summer meeting in Saratoga.

Brown at present is wintering at Harrington, Del., where he has the popular Uncle Scott, Leah Hanover, Chuck Perkins and seven or eight others under his charge.

Horsemen are going to be interested in watching Curley Smart's work with Attorney. Walter J. Michael of Bucyrus, O., bought Attorney at the Fall sales and turned him over to Curley. More horsemen shied away from this crack pacer because of his "stuttering" tactics at the post which made him go a long mile. Smart is an unusually even tempered individual and knowing that Attorney will be a frequent winner if he gets away with the field, Curley is certain to exercise patience galore and should gain the confidence of the colt. It was Attorney who established a world's record at the Village Farm Stakes here last August. He "stuttered" or hesitated at the post and each time was away last. Thus the long miles.

Frank Woodland, racing secretary here, acting for A. W. Pratt of Great Barrington, Mass., has just purchased from Ernest Smith of Washington, D. C., the double-gaited Peter H., a pacer, with a mark of 2:11 3-4. Johnny Broderick down in Chatham is to handle Pratt's newest acquisition.

Marty Burke of Troy, whose stock it at Nassau with Aubrey Rodney, is high on his colt, Olympia Hanover, the Spencer Scott colt who already has shown plenty of trot. His Tompkins Hanover captured a majority of the Nassau Stakes purses last year and Marty hopes Olympia will be a repeat job.

THE WEATHER
Tonight: Fair, colder

THE TIMES RECORD

FINAL EDITION

SERIES 1945—NO. 42. (Entered as Second Class Matter at the Postoffice at Troy, N. Y., Under the Act of March 3, 1879) TROY, N. Y., MONDAY EVENING, FEBRUARY 19, 1945. (Published Daily Except Sunday) PRICE FOUR CENTS

MARINES EXPAND BEACHHEAD AFTER STORMING IWO ISLAND

Churchill Returns From Crimea Parley

London (AP) — Prime Minister Churchill returned to England today from the Crimea conference after stops at Athens and Cairo.

The prime minister is expected to furnish the House of Commons, possibly later this week, a first-hand report on the discussions with President Roosevelt and Premier Stalin.

The house will set aside two days for the review and a debate in which Foreign Secretary Anthony Eden will participate.

RUSSIAN TROOPS NEAR GOERLITZ ON ROAD TO DRESDEN

Other Red Forces Capture Sagan and Naumberg; Germans Trapped

London (AP)—Russian troops pounded out new gains within 16 miles of the industrial city of Goerlitz on the road to Dresden today, and edged nearer Berlin from the southeast after capturing the six-way rail center of Sagan in a bloody two-day fight.

A Soviet communique said the southern wing of Marshal Ivan S. Konev's First Ukraine Army had overrun Naumberg in fighting at the threshold of Saxony. Naumberg is 66 miles east of Dresden.

Konev's northern wing toppled Sagan, site of several German prisoner of war camps. The fate of the internees has not yet been disclosed.

Other Russian troops advancing toward Danzig yesterday broke into the outskirts of the Vistula River stronghold of Grudziadz, city of 50,000 which is 57 miles from the Baltic port.

Moscow said the Third White Russian Army had scored new gains in East Prussia, but these successes were tempered by announcement of the death of that army's brilliant commander, Gen. Ivan D. Cherniakhovsky.

Germans Trapped.

Youngest of the Russian front leaders, this 37-year-old Jewish tank expert died of wounds suffered on the battlefield where his men yesterday killed 2,000 Germans and tightened their stranglehold on the remnants of a force 200,000 Nazis.

Berlin said 100 Soviet divisions were attacking in an attempt to wipe out the trapped Nazis in that sector.

By official Moscow account 7,445 Germans were either captured or killed in fighting along the 800-mile eastern front, bringing to 258,150 the total of Germans and Hungarians reported killed or captured in the last week, including the casualties in the siege of Budapest.

The Paris radio said this morning that the Russians were opening up a huge offensive all along the front and asserted that Marshal Gregory K. Zhukov had assembled enormous masses of materiel for this final assault on Berlin.

Furious fighting was in progress near the confluence of the Bober and Oder Rivers and the Berlin radio said the Russians had crossed the Bober in their drive to turn Berlin's eastern defenses.

Russians Storm Breslau.

Moscow's communiques gave no details of the struggle in this area, but Soviet front dispatches said Russian troops were menacing Cottbus and Guben, 47 and 51 miles southeast of Berlin, and that both places were heavily raided by Soviet bombers.

Moscow announced the liquidation of a large German pocket south of Schwerin, 75 miles east of Berlin, with the capture of 1,.45 prisoners.

Far behind the Oder River a few Germans still held out in the besieged western Polish citadel of Poznan, the Russian communique said.

Pravda said Russian troops had smashed a strong defense ring around beleaguered Breslau, lower Silesian capital of 630,000. Berlin already has asserted that the Russians had penetrated the city.

Attacking on a 15-mile front southwest and south of Breslau, the Russians gained up to three miles by official Moscow account as they deepened the ring around the city. They captured Landau, 14 miles to the southwest and Rudigau, 19 miles south of the city.

COAL PRODUCTION HITS PEAK SINCE NOVEMBER

Washington (AP)—Production of bituminous coal totaled 12,185,000 tons in the week ended Feb. 10, the highest since last November.

Announcing this today, the Solid Fuels Administration attributed the high output to the fact that southern Applacian mines operated Sunday, Feb. 4. Sunday production alone was estimated at 427,000 tons. Anthracite production in the week ended Feb. 10 totaled 1,117,000 tons, compared with 842,000 tons in the previous week.

CHILD DIES OF BURNS.

Jamestown (AP)—Martha Smith, 5, died yesterday of burns received on Christmas Day.

SCOTS BREAK INTO FORTIFIED ROAD CENTER OF GOCH

Heavy Fighting Rages in Streets; Patton Widens Front in Germany

Paris (AP)—Kilted Scots fought into the center of the heavily fortified road center of Goch today as the Canadian First Army advanced within 25 miles of Duisburg, world's largest inland port and western portal of the rich Ruhr arsenal.

British and Canadian troops fought within a mile of Calcar, like Goch an important frontline road center, and pushed the stoutly resisting Germans to the southern edge of the Moylands woods. Casualties were heavy on both sides. The forest extends almost to the edge of Calcar.

Field Marshal Montgomery was said by the Germans to have committed his British Second Army to the intensifying battle between the Meuse and flooded Rhine, a front on which the northern end of the original Siegfried Line has been run through. The marshal himself said the last round of the battle for Germany was on; that the enemy "is going to receive the knockout blow a somewhat unusual one, delivered from more than one direction."

Patton Widens Front.

Lieut. Gen. George S. Patton, jr., widened his U. S. Third Army front in western Germany to 32 miles and captured numerous towns in the Eifel Mountains, some within seven miles of the important road center of Bitburg.

Farther south, Lieut. Gen. Alexander M. Patch's Seventh Army fought back two miles into the German Saar Basin, capturing 1,000 prisoners and Auersmacher, six miles southeast of Saarbrucken.

The American First and Ninth Armies (and perhaps other formations) still were inactive along the Roer River facing Cologne, Bonn and Duesseldorf. It was in this sector east of Aachen that the Germans have been predicting the real battle of decision.

Goch, a city of 13,500 and the center of eight military highways, had been outflanked and virtually surrounded when the Scotch poured into its ruins, created by terrific aerial and ground bombardment. The town is divided by the Niers River and eight miles south of Kleve, and has been fortified since 1291.

Heavy Fighting In Goch.

Enemy opposition, though heavy, was lighter than expected with the Germans concentrating on the flanks of the British Empire troops. Front dispatches called the battle for Goch the heaviest of the 12-day campaign. The Scots drove in from the northeast and northwest through massive outer bulwarks. They battled through a deadly hail of machinegun and mortar fire and fought bitterly, house by house.

On the southern end of the 17-mile attack front the Canadian First Army dealt with strong German resistance along a 3,000 yard anti-tank ditch from the ancient castle of Bijlenbeek, twenty miles north of Venlo, to the swollen Meuse River. The ditch was flooded, and the attacks encountered mines and road blocks.

On the northern and eastern flanks, British and Canadian, Welsh and Scotch troops were within 16 miles of the ruined Ruhr Valley

(Continued on Page 2.)

CONVICTED YANK SEEKS NEW TRIAL IN LONDON

London (AP)—Counsel for Pvt. Karl Gustav Hulten of Cambridge, Mass., appealed for a new trial today in an effort to save the 22-year-old paratrooper from hanging, declaring the presiding judge had failed to sum up the defense adequately for the jury.

Hulten and Mrs. Elizabeth Maud Jones, 18-year-old British strip-tease dancer who also was sentenced to hang for the murder of a London taxicab driver, were in the courtroom when the hearing opened but they did not speak.

Jap Press Clamors For "Home Guard"

London (AP)—The Japanese press is clamoring for a home guard to meet American invasion of the homeland, the Tokyo correspondent of the German news agency Transocean reported today.

"The Japanese people," he said, "have suddenly come to realize that the enemy is at the gates. The press is urgently demanding formation of a Japanese Volkssturm in order to successfully meet the American assault on Japan."

YANKS DIG JAPS FROM TUNNELS ON CORREGIDOR

Americans Hold Both Sides of Fortress; Fighting Continues in Manila

Manila (UP) — American paratroopers and infantrymen joined today in the arduous job of cleaning out hundreds of die-hard Japanese from the tunnels and crevices of Corregidor fortress.

Both sides of the rocky fortress, guarding the entrance to Manila Bay, were secured by the two American contingents which invaded Corregidor from the air and sea. Their sole task was to dig out the Japanese from the recesses where the enemy was expected to make a last-ditch stand.

Gen. Douglas MacArthur hailed the invasion of Corregidor with a tribute to those men of his command who staged the historic defense of Bataan three years ago.

Garrison Saved Australia.

The long struggle on Bataan in 1942 enabled the United Nations to gather strength to resist the Japanese in the Pacific and "prevented the fall of Australia," MacArthur said.

No garrison in history has surpassed that on Bataan in more thoroughly accomplishing its mission, the general asserted, adding:

"Let no man henceforth speak of it as other than as of a magnificent victory."

While units of the 503rd Parachute Regiment and the 34th Infantry Regiment joined in securing the upper and lower parts of Corregidor, observers said the battle for the fortress was just beginning.

The Japanese were lodged strongly in the American-dug tunnels and were harassing the American troops continuously with cannon and machine-gun fire.

A front dispatch disclosed that units of the American fleet entered Manila Harbor for the first time in three years. The mission was carried out by four P-T boats two nights before the invasion of Corregidor. They swept within three miles of the breakwater off Manila's piers to knock out three small enemy craft.

Fighting In Manila.

The mopping up of Manila continued slowly with the 37th Division steadily closing a steel ring on the Japanese garrison in the walled city and Ermita districts.

The drive against the trapped enemy remnants was augmented by big American guns which relentlessly shelled the gates of the thick walls and Japanese strongpoints inside the area.

In pushing to the edge of the walled city, the 37th Division captured the Philippines general hospital and liberated 7,000 persons, including 100 Americans.

Among those safely evacuated from the hospital were 800 patients, among them 42 Americans. The others were residents of the area who had sought safety in the hospital during the battle.

PAT MEANT BUSINESS.

Yonkers (UP)—When Pat Cairnes wants to sleep, he wants to sleep. Margaret, his wife, wanted to talk. Cairnes hopped out of bed, called police and filed a complaint of disorderly conduct against Mrs. Cairnes. She spent the night in jail.

HALSEY WARNS JAPS MAY ISSUE "PEACE FEELERS"

Admiral Urges Prosecution of War Until Nippon is Destroyed

Washington (INS)—Admr. William F. Halsey, commander of the mighty U. S. Third Fleet in the Pacific, called today for prosecution of the war against Japan's "rapidly deteriorating empire" until that nation is destroyed, and warned strongly against acceptance of any peace attempts from Jap industrialists.

Halsey, at a news conference during a surprise visit to Washington, hinted he expected Gen. Douglas MacArthur to head at least a part of United States military forces in the final drive on the Japanese home islands.

He likewise indicated that American forces might by-pass the China mainland on the road to Tokyo.

Asked by reporters if there was any "danger" of MacArthur's seventh fleet getting into Tokyo before his ships, Halsey replied, "we'll go in together. He's a fine man. I've worked under him for two years and we get along swell together."

"Let Them Starve."

In answer to the question of whether Japan can be destroyed without destroying her army on the China mainland, Halsey replied, "let 'em starve." He added, however, "if we have to destroy the army let's go in and destroy it."

Halsey hailed Adm. Marc A. Mitscher's carrier strike against Japan as a "great show against the rapidly deteriorating empire," and predicted that the Iwo operation will be a tough fight, but not as bad as Tarawa because "we've learned a lot since then."

"I have been one of the few to believe that the Japs will break," Halsey said in an hour long news conference marked by the scathing denunciation of the Pacific enemy.

"The industrialists will see that the empire they built up over so long a time is crumbling," he said. "The dollar is just as much to them as any one else.

Warns Against Feelers.

"When they get control over the military they will put out peace feelers. That's the most dangerous time.

"They will appeal to the mothers who will want to save their sons and not think of the grandsons who would have to fight another war. They will try to build up for another war.

"We've got to make them impotent for all time."

Asked about the future of the Mikado, Halsey said: "There shouldn't be any," but added that the Mikado's palace in Tokyo was not a legitimate military objective.

His contemptuous opinion of the Japanese as people he extended also to the Japanese fleet. "I don't think they'll come out and fight during this operation," he said.

"We'll have to go in and dig them out. They haven't much and it's in bad shape."

"How are you going to get them out" he was asked.

"I can't get the rats' frame of mind so I don't know," Halsey answered.

17 BODIES TAKEN FROM WRECKAGE OF MAYFAIR APARTMENT IN TACOMA

Tacoma, Wash. (UP)—Seventeen bodies had been removed from the ruins of the Mayfair apartment house today, and fire department officials estimated that at least eight more were buried in the wreckage.

All but four of the regular tenants of the 40-unit building have been accounted for, but a number of persons were known to have been visiting in the building when fire broke out in a basement candy manufacturing shop early Saturday.

Five men, seven women and five children were included in the dead, all but five of them burned beyond recognition.

Damage was estimated at $500,000.

WITNESS PICTURES STORMING OF IWO BY U. S. MARINES

Island Seems Like Giant Pork Chop Sizzling Under Heavy Fire

BY WILLIAM F. TYREE.
Representing the Combined American Press. Distributed by the Associated Press.

In a Plane Over Iwo Jima (AP) (Via Navy Radio)—American Marines stormed ashore to secure a beachhead on Iwo Jima today, as the tiny gourd-shaped island rocked under one of the heaviest naval bombardments of the Pacific war.

However, the Japanese certainly were fighting back from their underground defenses. Twice as we swung over Mount Suribachi's crater at the south end of the island and around the northern wooded section, the Japanese gave us bursts of anti-aircraft.

While their defenses were being riddled by offshore bombardments some fire twinkled at us from the ground.

As we approached the island hundreds of small craft moved toward the beach, unleashing a fierce barrage of thousands of rockets.

Waves of Marines followed within 45 minutes.

Smoke and dust covered the entire island. Iwo itself looked like a fat pork chop sizzling in the skillet as carrier planes swept in under us, strafing and bombing every installation they could find.

One fighter crashed in flames just inland from where the Marines struggled to consolidate their beachhead. In the calm waters off the island, hundreds of ships maneuvered endlessly while old prewar battleships—New York, Texas, Nevada, Arkansas, Idaho and Tennessee "belched shells from their squat gun platforms.

There wasn't a single Japanese plane in the sky.

Iwo Island appropriately named "Hot Rock" for the occasion of this attack. Our aircraft personnel chattered furiously over the command frequency as they took stations for continuing the fight.

Copilot Ens. John Q. Schell, jr., Asheville, N. C., gave me headphones and we heard the Marines calling for fire support from the fleet. Bursts of orange flames sprang from the muzzles of the battleships and cruisers' big guns and huge columns of smoke and fire rose skyward from the island seconds later.

It was systematic murder and destruction. Suribachi's crater steamed from successive hits along its ridges overlooking the beach. I could see many formidable pillboxes along the beaches as well as a few rusty ship hulls, already put out of action.

The invasion armada had spread out for scores of miles around the island. There was no mistaking the fact that the Americans arrived to stay on Tokyo's doorstep, but the fight looked like it would require a week or more before the finish, and as if an awful lot of blood would be spilled before it was over.

BRITISH WIDEN NEW BURMA BRIDGEHEAD

Hold Vital Point on Irrawaddy Below Mandalay

Calcutta (AP)—British imperial troops who bridged the swift Irrawaddy River in Burma approximately 35 miles below Mandalay were reported today to have the situation "well in hand" after days of fierce fighting with bitterly resisting Japanese.

Indian and Gurkha troops of the 14th Army made the hazardous crossing in the early morning of Feb. 13 under a hail of enemy artillery, mortar and small arms fire. The Japanese reacted violently from their jungle hideouts.

The new bridgehead, first to be established below Mandalay, would keep the enemy from using the river for escape when the city itself finally is assaulted.

British assault troops crossed the stream in hundreds of light river craft. Many were caught in the current and swept downstream out of control.

Troops who gained the left bank of the river in the first wave were forced to dig in at the water's edge after returning Japanese fire from boats for nearly a half-hour. Under constant pressure for five days, the 14th Army troops expanded the bridgehead yard by yard until they gained a ten-mile wide foothold near the village of Myinmu.

Field dispatches described Japanese casualties as heavy and British casualties as having "not been light."

The crossing posed a powerful threat to the Japanese position in Burma and overcame one of the greatest natural obstacles faced by the Allies in the Burmese campaign.

American and British heavy and medium bombers of the Eastern Air Command joined the battle, pounding troop concentrations and supply dumps on the enemy's land routes south of Mandalay.

Frank J. Hogan, Former Mayor Of Troy, Expires

Political Leader and Businessman Dies After Long Illness

FRANK J. HOGAN

Frank J. Hogan, former Troy mayor and a member of the firm John T. Hopkins Coal Co., Inc., died this morning at his residence, 3145 Sixth Avenue.

Mr. Hogan was born in the Town of Halfmoon, Oct. 24, 1880, the son of Patrick and Anna M. (Hopkins) Hogan. He removed with his parents in early childhood to Troy where for many years he had been a business leader.

Educated at St. Patrick's Academy and LaSalle Institute, Mr. Hogan started his career by working as an office boy in the coal office owned by his uncle, the late John T. Hopkins.

Elected in 1937.

He never held political office until he was elected Mayor in November, 1937. He was Mayor for six years. He held the distinction of being the first mayor of Troy elected to serve a four-year term. He was chosen in 1937, winning the mayoralty over Col. James A. McCarthy by a 4,795 plurality. Mr. Hogan ran on the Democratic ticket while Colonel McCarthy was endorsed by the Independent Democratic and Republican tickets.

In March 1939, the Common Coun- passed measure making the office of Mayor a four-year term.

He ran for reelection in 1939, winning over the present Mayor John J. Ahern.

He was active in Troy business and civic affairs. In 1920 he became a member of the firm of John T. Hopkins Coal Co. after serving his apprenticeship.

The former Mayor was a prominent member of Troy Lodge of Elks and was former tiler in the New York State Elks' Association for many years. He also was a member of Troy Council, K. of C. and of the Kiwanis Club.

He was the founder and first member of the Goat Club of the Thirteenth Ward, a social group, and its first president.

He was a former vice president and member of the Board of Directors of the Chamber of Commerce and was chairman of the committee on arrangements for the "Troy On Parade" business and industrial exposition held in the Troy Armory in 1937.

He was active as a communicant at St. Patrick's Church and served 14 years as president of the parish Holy Name Society, and was general chairman of the many benefit parties conducted by the parish.

Named Delegate.

In 1938 he was chosen as a delegate from Rensselaer County to the Democratic state convention at Rochester, and the convention further honored him by selecting him as a member of the powerful resolutions committee. In 1940 he participated in the Democratic National convention at Chicago as a delegate from the 29th Congressional District of New York State.

He was a director of the Security Safety Deposit Company of the Manufacturers National Bank.

He was active in the work of the Salvation Army, taking charge of a campaign in 1937 which netted the organization $4,000.

He also was an energetic worker for the Troy Central Y. M. C. A., Rensselaer County Red Cross, Troy Boys' Club and other organizations. He had served as president of the Kiwanis Club and a member of its Board of Directors.

Previous to becoming Mayor he had been a member of the City Planning Commission, having been appointed in 1927 by former Mayor Cornelius F. Burns.

He was the husband of the late Josephine Kelly of this city.

He is survived by two brothers, Dr. John T. H. Hogan and Joseph A. V. Hogan and several nieces and nephews. He was the brother of the late Mrs. Mary L. Boland.

Mayor John J. Ahern today when informed of the death of former Mayor Hogan issued a statement in which he expressed deep regret.

He also directed that municipal flags be placed at half-staff in honor of Troy's 43rd Mayor.

COURT RULES WACS ARE U. S. SOLDIERS

Buffalo Man Loses Appeal for Harboring A.W.O.L.

Buffalo (AP)—WACS are soldiers, Federal Judge Harold P. Burke ruled today.

The decision denied a defense motion to set aside the guilty verdict which a federal court jury recently returned against Jake Williams, 44, Buffalo, tried on a charge of harboring and concealing WAC Pvt. Irene Alice Way, 30, formerly of Zanesville, O.

The law under which Williams was convicted refers specifically to soldiers. Defense Atty. William B. Mahoney had contended "a soldier is a fighting man while a WAC is a non-combatant who bears arms only under special written authorization for special assignment."

A government brief declared that when the WAC (Women's Army Corps) was organized in place of its predecasor, the WAAC, (Women's Auxiliary Army Corps) the step was taken to make it a "component part of the Army," whose members are subject to laws relating to Army personnel.

Williams will be sentenced Monday in Rochester. Private Way, allegedly absent without leave from Selfridge Field, Mich., has been turned over to military authorities there.

INCREASE IN POSTAL REVENUES FORECAST BY HOUSE COMMITTEE

Washington (UP)—Postal revenues for the fiscal year ending June 30 will exceed expenditures by $117,643,897, the House Appropriations Committee reported today.

The surplus revenue, the committee said in recommending 1946 appropriations for the Postoffice and Treasury Departments, was "brought about by the abnormal amount of mail incident to wartime civilian activity as well as mailings to members of the armed forces."

Postal revenues for 1944 exceeded expenditures by $37,768,028. Estimates for 1946 indicate a possible revenue surplus of as much as $265,214,280, the committee report said.

For operation of the Postoffice Department for the year beginning July 1, the committee recommended $1,342,813,090, which is $59,873,729 less than the current year's appropriation.

HURLEY COMING HOME.

Chungking (AP)—Maj. Gen. Patrick J. Hurley left Chungking today for Washington, presumably to make a personal report to President Roosevelt on the situation in China.

YANKS PENETRATE DEFENSES OF JAP AIRFIELD IN DRIVE

Resistance of Trapped Nipponese Increases; Fleet Shelling Island

Admiral Nimitz's Headquarters, Guam (UP)—Two divisions of U. S. Marines—30,000 men—stormed Iwo Island from an 800-ship armada today and in two hours of bitter fighting, established a two and one-half mile beachhead, extending to the edge of Suribachi Yama Airfield.

Casualties were moderate and the operation was proceeding satisfactorily, Fleet Adm. Chester W. Nimitz said in his latest communique.

Resistance from the trapped enemy forces was increasing as the veteran Marines pushed inland on the tiny eight-square-mile island 750 miles from Tokyo, the communique said.

Two hours after the initial landing was made the Marine veterans had pushed inland on an average of 500 yards and the defenses of Surigachi Yama airstrip were penetrated east of the field, the communique added.

The Marine beachhead extended northward along the southeastern coast from the 546-foot high volcano that forms the southern tip of the island.

Japanese broacasts said American warships completely ringed Iwo and fired shells into the island from virtually every point on the compass.

Radio Tokyo conceded that the Americans had won footholds on the southwest, south and east coasts.

Island Under Heavy Fire.

Swarms of carrier and land-based planes and the 14 and 16-inch guns of battleships were pouring thousands of bombs and shells into the island in support of the invasion troops, but the enemy garrison was putting up a defense reminiscent of Tarawa and Peleliu.

The invasion—an amphibious jump halfway from American bases in the Marianas to Japan—was announced in the second of two jubilant "on to Tokyo" communiques issued only an hour apart by Admiral Nimitz, commander of the Pacific Fleet.

The first communique proclaimed the destruction or damaging of at least 36 ships and 659 enemy planes by aircraft from the world's mightiest carrier fleet in the Tokyo area last Friday and Saturday.

Three Japanese warships were sunk and a fourth overturned in the Tokyo assault, which Nimitz hailed as an "historic and decisive" victory. Forty-nine American planes were lost, but none of the ships in the huge American naval armada was hit.

The invasion of Iwo came on the fourth day of a terrific naval bombardment and the 74th day of an air assault on the tiny patch of land within fighter-plane range of Tokyo.

First Boats Hit Beach.

The first tiny assault boats from hundreds of transports hovering out to sea hit the beaches at Iwo at 9 a.m. (8 a.m. Tokyo time and 7 p.m. Sunday, E.W.T.) shortly after nearly 8,000 rockets had scorched the coastline.

Scrambling ashore against artillery, mortar and machine-gun fire, the green-clad Marine veterans of many another landing in the Pacific campaign quickly struck inland. Wave after wave of reinforcements followed them.

Weblet Edwards, who flew over the island in a Liberator bomber as a representative of the combined radio networks, said he could see the bright flare of flame-throwers as the Marines assaulted inland pillboxes.

Another battle was raging on an island ridge, Edwards said. Troops were landing "far up and down the coast," he said. Carrier planes roared over the Marines at treetop levels, strafing enemy strong points ahead.

Jap Losses Believed Huge.

The entire island was covered by clouds of smoke and dust, broken here and there by bursts of flame as shells and bombs found their mark. Hundreds of Japanese were believed to have been killed in the preliminary bombardment, but the remainder of the garrison of 10,000 to 15,000 was expected to put up a fanatical do-or-die fight.

The immediate prize was three airstrips from which Flying Fortress, Liberators and even fighter planes could attack Tokyo. One

(Continued on Page 2.)

Japs Massacred Sixty Priests, Women And Children In Manila

BY RUSSELL BRINES.

Manila (AP)—The wanton slaying of at least sixty priests and women and children refugees in de LaSalle College in Manila's Malate district by Japanese soldiers was revealed today with recovery of the mutilated remains.

Of seventy caught in the college only eight survived, said one of them, Rev. Francis J. Cosgrove, 47, a Redemptorist father of Sydney, Australia.

Father Cosgrove, recovering from two bayonet wounds in Santo Tomas Hospital, filled in details of the terrible afternoon last Monday.

One Japanese officer and twenty enlisted men shot and bayonetted the American, Filipino, German, Irish and Spanish religious brothers and Filipino refugees.

The bodies, serving as mute and ghastly evidence, were discovered today when the United States 148th Infantry Regiment captured the college area.

Father Cosgrove said the Japanese garrison had remained in one wing of the college, while permitting the priests and refugees to occupy another.

Monday, another tense day on the fringe of the battle area, the Japanese stormed into the priests' room, Father Cosgrove reported. He said the religious group and refugees were just finishing a simple lunch.

The officers screamed something, then fired point-blank with a pistol. Then the Japanese soldiers charged into the sobbing, terrified throng of victims, firing guns and slashing right and left with their bayonets.

Today the bodies lay as they fell in the blood-smeared interior of what once was a modern college near the Rizal Stadium.

They were lying in grotesque helplessness, these slashed and smashed bodies. Some, caught in the first volley, tumbled in the dining room. Others evidently raced out into the first floor hallway. They were cut down after running a few steps.

Still others reached the stairway and started upward toward the chapel. Many failed to reach it and were slaughtered on the stairs or collapsed into a pile at the bottom. One Filipino woman lay on the stairs.

But others reached the chapel before the Japanese killed them.

(Continued on Page 11.)

Superforts Attack Tokyo And Nagoya

Washington (UP)—B-29 Superfortresses took over the air offensive against Tokyo today, dropping hundreds of tons of bombs on the capital while it stil smoldered from a record two-day carrier-based assault.

The Marianas-based raid on Tokyo came simultaneously with an announcement from advance Pacific fleet headquarters that carrier planes had destroyed or damaged at least 36 Japanese ships and 659 aircraft in their raids on the Tokyo area last Friday and Saturday.

A second force of Superfortresses thundered out from bases in India today and bombed military and communications targets on the Malay Peninsula.

A war department bulletin announced the Marianas-based raid merely as against "industrial targets" on the main enemy home island of Honshu. A Japanese communique said 100 B-29s participated, with the main strength attacking Tokyo "and its environs."

At least ten Superfortresses were shot down, the enemy communique said. Damage to Japanese installations was "slight," Tokyo added.

Another Tokyo broadcast said the big Japanese aircraft center of Nagoya, 160 miles west of Tokyo, and targets in Shizuoka prefecture on the [illegible] coast also had been hit.

Japanese broadcasts [illegible] Tokyo must expect more carrier-based raids. Though the [illegible] task force temporarily has moved south to support the [illegible] Iwo, the [illegible] ably will [illegible] home [illegible] troops [illegible] of Iwo."

The Index

FILE TAX REPORT ON MAXWELL AND WEST PROPERTIES

Inheritance Data Presented in County Surrogate's Court

Inheritance tax reports were filed on the estates of Margaret R. Maxwell and Willard E. West in Surrogate's Court yesterday by Edward J. Poland, transfer tax attorney. The papers showed that the Maxwell estate will pay a tax of $32.36, and the West estate will pay $32.

Miss Maxwell, who died April 15, 1944, left a gross estate of $8,993.59. Deductions totaled $758, leaving a net estate of $8,235.59, which goes entirely to Mary E. Maxwell, of Troy, sister of the deceased and executrix of the estate. J. Howard McIsaac is attorney for the estate.

Mr. West, whose death occurred on Nov. 9, 1944, left a gross estate of $4,054.64. Deductions amounted to $855.10, making a net estate of $3,199.54 to be distributed among the five heirs mentioned in the will of the deceased.

Those sharing in the estate include Frank S. West, Hoosick Falls, R. D. 1, a nephew; Rena A. Herrington of Johnsonville, a niece; and Olive M. Case of Hoosick Falls, a niece; each of whom will receive one-fourth of the residue; Irene Marker, Hoosick Falls, R. D. 1, a grandniece; and Morton Hoffman, Hoosick Falls, R. D. 1, a grandnephew; each of whom will receive one-eighth of the residue. Taylor and Taylor are the attorneys handling the estate.

A final judicial settlement of the accounts of Bessie Horowitz, executrix of the estate of the late Adolph Kohn, has been filed in Surrogate's Court. Mr. Kohn left an estate of $19,258.34, which during the course of administration increased by $2,227.36, making total receipts handled by the executrix amount to $21,485.70.

Deductions, including funeral expenses, debts of the decedent, and tax, amounted to $2,016.85, leaving a balance of $19,468.85. The papers show that the executrix is the sole heir to this estate. Henry S. Kahn, of Kahn & Maloy, Albany attorneys, filed the decree.

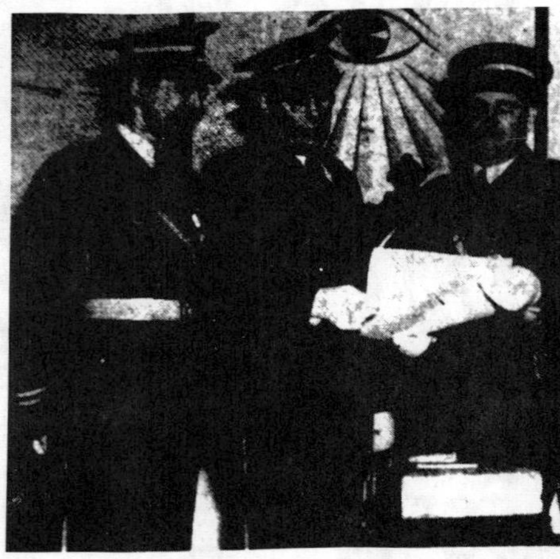

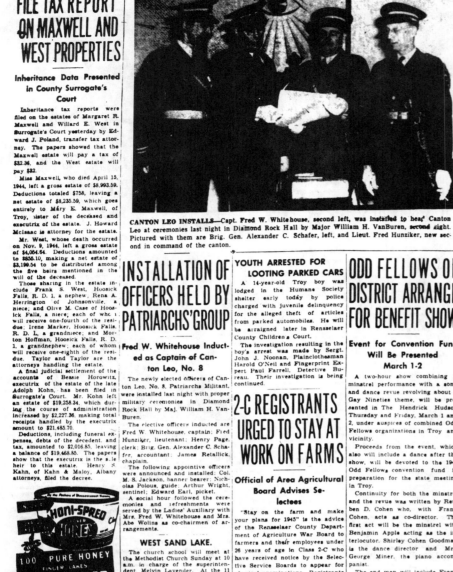

CANTON LEO INSTALLS—Capt. Fred W. Whitehouse, second left, was installed to head Canton Leo at ceremonies last night in Diamond Rock Hall by Major William H. VanBuren, second right. Pictured with them are Brig. Gen. Alexander C. Schafer, left, and Lieut. Fred Hunziker, new second in command of the canton.

INSTALLATION OF OFFICERS HELD BY PATRIARCHS' GROUP

Fred W. Whitehouse Inducted as Captain of Canton Leo, No. 8

The newly elected officers of Canton Leo, No. 8, Patriarchs Militant, were installed last night with proper military ceremonies in Diamond Rock Hall by Maj. William H. VanBuren.

The elective officers inducted are Fred W. Whitehouse, captain; Fred Hunziker, lieutenant; Henry Page, clerk; Brig. Gen. Alexander C. Schafer, accountant; James Retallick, chaplain.

The following appointive officers were announced and installed: Col. M. S. Jackson, banner bearer; Nicholas Polous, guide; Arthur Wright, sentinel; Edward Earl, picket.

A social hour followed the ceremonies and refreshments were served by the Ladies' Auxiliary with Mrs. Fred W. Whitehouse and Mrs. Abe Wolins as co-chairmen of arrangements.

WEST SAND LAKE.

The church school will meet at the Methodist Church Sunday at 10 a.m. in charge of the superintendent, Melvin Lavender. At the 11 o'clock service the pastor, Rev. John A. Lavender, will preach on "Workers Together with God." Special music will be rendered by the choir under the direction of Mrs. Harold Alger. The offering to date for the "Crusade for Christ" is $700, in pledges and gifts. Laymen's Sunday will be observed with a special service Sunday morning, March 4 in in charge of James Hargrave, lay leader.

YOUTH ARRESTED FOR LOOTING PARKED CARS

A 14-year-old Troy boy was lodged in the Humane Society shelter early today by police charged with juvenile delinquency for the alleged theft of articles from parked automobiles. He will be arraigned later in Rensselaer County Children's Court.

The investigation resulting in the boy's arrest was made by Sergt. John J. Noonan, Plainclothesman Harold O'Neil and Fingerprint Expert Paul Farrell, Detective Bureau. Their investigation is being continued.

2-C REGISTRANTS URGED TO STAY AT WORK ON FARMS

Official of Area Agricultural Board Advises Selectees

"Stay on the farm and make your plans for 1945" is the advice of the Rensselaer County Department of Agriculture War Board to farmers and their employees under 26 years of age in Class 2-C who have received notice by the Selective Service Boards to appear for physical examinations. Registrants who qualify as farm workers under the Tydings Amendment to the Selective Service Act are still eligible for deferment, Allen A. Hayner, chairman of the War Board, stated yesterday.

In the opinion of the War Board most of the farm deferred registrants in Rensselaer County meet the qualifications of the Tydings Amendment that provides agricultural deferment for those workers who are found to be "necessary to and regularly engage in" farming and for whom no satisfactory replacement is available.

"There has been no change in the amendment," Mr. Hayner said, "but farm employers and employees have been seriously concerned about the recent Selective Service action. All Selective Service Boards were directed to send all farm workers under 26 in Class 2-C for physical examinations. This led many farm registrants and employers to believe that these men would be taken off farms and inducted into armed services."

ODD FELLOWS OF DISTRICT ARRANGE FOR BENEFIT SHOW

Event for Convention Fund Will Be Presented March 1-2

A two-hour show combining a minstrel performance with a song and dance revue revolving about a Gay Nineties theme, will be presented in The Hendrick Hudson Thursday and Friday, March 1 and 2, under auspices of combined Odd Fellows organizations in Troy and vicinity.

Proceeds from the event, which also will include a dance after the show, will be devoted to the 1945 Odd Fellows convention fund in preparation for the state meeting in Troy.

Continuity for both the minstrel and the revue was written by Reuben D. Cohen who, with Frank Cohen, acts as co-director. The first act will be the minstrel with Benjamin Apple acting as the interlocutor. Shirley Cohen Goodman is the dance director and Mrs. George Miner, the piano accompanist.

The end men will include Frank Cohen, Hans P. Lund, Jack Dembo, Reuben D. Cohen, Harold Turner and John Cohen. Solo performers will be Joan Comiskey, toe tap, "Dance With a Dolly"; Patsy and Shiela McConville, specialty, "Dinah"; Martin Smith, accordion medley; Hans P. Lund, "Strut Miss Lizzie"; Flora Mae Flanders, toe tap, "Give My Regards to Broadway"; Ben Apple, "Together"; Dolores Cupolo, medley, "It Had to Be You"; L. Gale Perryman, "Without a Song"; Janet and Bobby Hoffman, "Don't Fence Me In"; John Cohen, "Aria from Sextette from Lucia"; Eleanor Walsh, "Take It Easy"; Eleanor Bailey, "Smoke Gets in Your Eyes"; Reuben D. Cohen, "Is Yo Is, or Is Yo Ain't My Baby"; Sally Miller, "I'm Making Believe"; Frank Cohen, "You Got to Ac-cen-tu-ate the Positive."

The second act will be titled "Cavalcade of Stars from the Gay Nineties to 1945," or "Saturday Night in Big Mike Slattery's."

Mr. Apple will act the role of Big Mike. Specialties will include: L. Gale Perryman, Charles Dufor, Edwin Dufor, Harry Barnhart, as a quartet singing "Curse of an Aching Heart." Eleanor Bailey as Lillian Russell will sing "A Bird in a Gilded Cage." Sally Miller as Marilyn Miller will sing "Who." Eleanor Walsh, as Elsie Janis, will sing "Over There."

Other individual roles will be: Fred Marr as Diamond Jim Brady, Uriah Williams as Slick Steve," Harrison Bonesteel as Chuck Connors, the "Mayor of Chinatown." John Cohen as the side show barker and Harold Turner as "David" and Eileen Kilgallon, "Little Bit of Heaven."

Song and dance numbers scheduled are: Shirley Cohen Goodman, dance specialty; Patsy Colley, "San Fernando Valley;" Joan Burgess, "Pink Elephants;" Charles Vogt, "You Always Hurt the One You Love," Shirley Walkinshaw "Sweet Dreams, Sweetheart"; Jack Dembo, Russian specialty; military tap finale featuring Dolores Cupolo, Patsy Colley and Joan Comiskey.

Musical accompaniment for the show and for dancing will be played by Toby Middlebrook and his orchestra.

FIVE AREA SOLDIERS ON CASUALTY LISTS

Five area soldiers, killed in action in the European theater of war, are on the latest War Department casualty list. Those names announced today are Pfc. Aloysius C. Gorko, brother of Amelia Gorko of 2629 Fifth Avenue, Watervliet; Pvt. Silvio Pipino, son of Mrs. Josephine Pipino of 113 Lancaster Street, Cohoes; Pvt. Delour A. Hart, son of Delour A. Hart of Stillwater; Second Lieut. Sherwood D. Wishart, son of Mrs. Marie B. Wishart, Rensselaer, and Pfc. Willis H. Lamberson, son of Mrs. Marie J. Lamberson of Castleton.

DR. DAVENPORT HOME.

Capt. Frank S. Davenport, U. S. N. R., Averill Park physician, is home on leave after serving 28 months overseas, in the Peninsula Base Station and in the Mediterranean theater of war. Captain Davenport, who was granted his leave on the rotation plan, will report at Asheville, N. C., March 8.

LOCAL HOSPITAL DIRECTORS HOLD ANNUAL MEETING

Dr. Baker Renamed; Designate New Members at Samaritan

Dr. Ray Palmer Baker was reelected president of the Samaritan Hospital Board of Directors at the annual meeting yesterday afternoon at the Troy Savings Bank. Highlights of the meeting were annual reports which showed the work of the hospital in maintaining efficient service to the community in spite of wartime conditions and the recommendation of the president that the hospital should look ahead now to the role it will play in the postwar world.

Also relected were E. Harold Cluett as first vice president, David B. Plum as second vice president, Ernest L. Warncke as secretary and Edgar C. Stillman as treasurer.

Three New Directors.

Three new members of the corporation and Board of Directors were named. Henry J. Sidford will replace R. O. Kennedy on the board. Stephen H. Sampson succeeds the late Hobart W. Thompson and Arthur H. Wellington replaces Gorham Cluett.

Members reelected to the corporation and to the board for five-year terms are Livingston W. Houston, Harry McGrath, Mr. Plum, William Leroy Shields and Maurice Whitney.

In his annual report, Dr. Baker praised the "loyalty and efficiency" of all members of the professional staffs, employees and volunteers who, under the leadership of the superintendent, Mrs. Helen L. Warren, have "met every crisis with cheerfulness and dispatch."

He said that, because of lack of materials and labor, no important improvements have been undertaken since 1941 and added:

"As the end of the war draws nearer, the Board of Directors may well give thought to the role of the Samaritan Hospital in the community and to the need for development in particular fields. Any survey of this kind should take into consideration not only the facilities now available but also those likely to be provided by the federal government. The possibilities of cooperation among the hospitals of the area should not be overlooked."

Nurses Enter Service.

Mrs. Warren, in giving the superintendent's annual report, pointed out that this year the hospital will feel the pressure of war in the nursing department. Many of the younger nurses, she said, feel that their highest duty is to the armed forces and have applied to enter the Army or Navy Nurse Corps. Eight already are under consideration for duty with the armed forces. She said:

"This is a serious drain on our service but I am proud to have our hospital so honorably represented and I feel confident that with the help of our alumnae and volunteers we shall manage to give adequate and creditable care to our patients."

She spoke of the decrease in number of employees during the year and said that all employees have "assumed cheerfully and without complaint the work which must be done and done well."

Volunteers, both civilian and Red Cross, she said, have given great assistance.

She concluded by reading from an article written by Dr. Joseph C. Doane.

"The open sesame of institutional success is not to be found in town or city, in age or in youth, in poverty or in wealth. Success lies in people, in their sense of fair play, in their vision and intelligence and in their increasing dissatisfaction with present accomplishments. Success lies in the construction by the community of the hospital spiritual."

SALEM.

Miss Jane Lytle of Albany recently visited her parents, Mr. and Mrs. Harry Lytle.

Miss Harriett Fairley of Cambridge recently visited her mother, Mrs. Mina Fairley.

Mrs. William Ston has returned from Lake Placid where she was a guest of Mrs. Edward Kennedy.

Miss Gertrude O'Donnell of Berne recently visited her parents, Mr. and Mrs. William J. O'Donnell, here.

Miss Ruth Ann Fleming has returned to Albany after visiting her parents, Mr. and Mrs. John Fleming.

Mrs. Gretchen Abbott has returned from Oswego where she was a guest of Mr. and Mrs. Morris Selleck.

Mr. and Mrs. Harold Avery and daughter Elsie, of Springfield, Vt., recently visited Mr. Avery's father, David Avery.

M./Sergt. George B. Wagner of Fort Bragg, N. C., is spending a furlough with his parents, Mr. and Mrs. Jacob Wagner.

Mrs. Arthur McCann has returned from Albany where she visited her brother-in-law and sister, Mr. and Mrs. Joseph Whitkop.

Mrs. Helen Lansing, R. N., of Albany, was a dinner guest Monday of Mr. and Mrs. Russell Smith and called on other friends in the vicinity.

Charles A. McNeil, A. M. M. 1/c, who has been stationed at San Diego, Cal., is spending a leave with his sisters, Mrs. James Noon and Mrs. Grace Dunnigan.

Miss Doris Moon has returned to Schuylerville after visiting her parents, Mr. and Mrs. Robert A. Moon.

Mrs. Margaret McKinney has gone to New York where she will visit her son and daughter-in-law, Capt. and Mrs. Alexander McKinney, who are leaving for South America where Captain McKinney will be port captain at Covinas, Colombia.

Sergt. Theodore Barkley of the Army was wounded in action in Luxembourg Jan. 23, according to word received by his family from the War Department. The injury is said to be slight, and it is expected he will be able to return to duty soon.

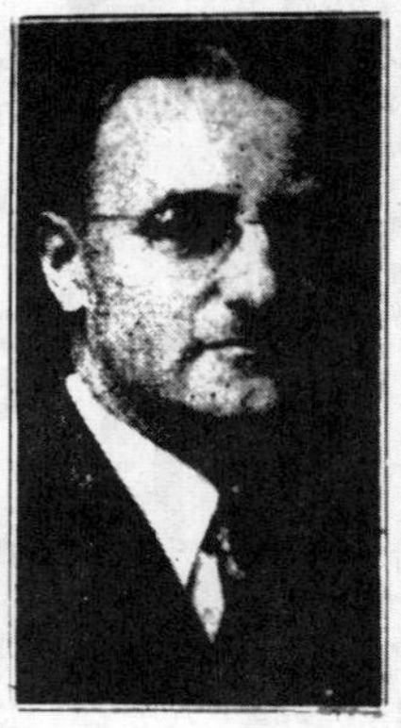

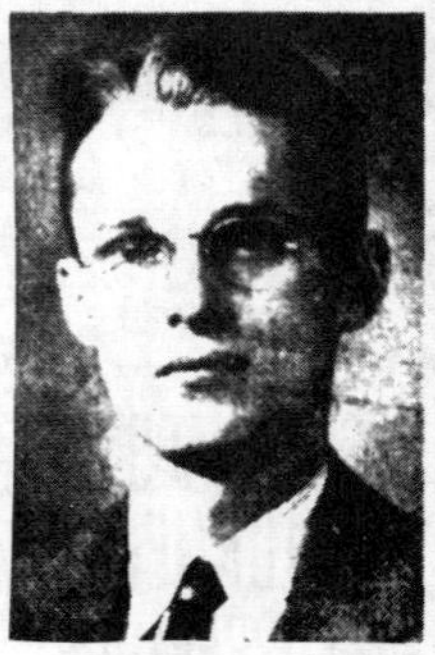

STEPHEN H. SAMPSON

SUIT AGAINST TROJAN ENDS IN COMPROMISE

Supreme Court Justice Harry Schirick, at Albany, yesterday permitted compromise settlement of a negligence action brought by John J. Brown, 540 Morris Street, against Fred A. Pickett, Troy. The amount of settlement was not disclosed.

Brown claimed he suffered an injury to his leg when struck by Pickett's car last June 1. The accident occurred on the grounds of the Watervliet Arsenal where both are employed.

NEITZEL APPOINTS COMMITTEES FOR TROY BOYS' CLUB

Plans Started for Gardening Season at Sambrook Plots on Oakwood Avenue

Raymond P. Neitzel, president of the Troy Boys' Club Board of Directors, recently announced members of the executive committee for 1945 to include E. Harold Cluett, vice president; Charles S. Aldrich, vice president; Ronald B. Hibbard, treasurer; Parker H. Rousseau, secretary; Chester Meneely, W Howard Bumstead and Guy F. Swinnerton.

Committee chairmen named were Thomas W. Rourke, finance; Chester Meneely, entertainment; Parker H. Rousseau, health; Franklin H. Wilson, jr., house; Philip S. Dorlon, Community Chest; Edward A. Wachter, membership; Alfred W. Thompson, senior boys' activities, and Guy F. Swinnerton, garden and camps.

The monthly report submitted to the board by Edward A. Kane, director, revealed that from Jan. 15 through Feb. 15, educational classes that includes carpentry, modeling, cork crafts and other handicrafts attracted 1,157 boys while group games, boxing, indoor baseball and basketball gave physical workouts to 1,866 members.

The Woman's Auxiliary conducted two socials, one community sing and five glee club sessions during the month as entertainment for 403 boys. Other activities including movies and two-way bowling league games were attended by 1,542 members. A total of 4,968 participated in club activities. John E. Sambrook, local florist, for the third year has announced that the Troy Boys' Club will have plots available on his Oakwoood Avenue estate for victory gardening. Mr. Kane is calling the first gardening meeting March 1 when applications for plots by members will be acepted.

Miss Kathryn Sambrook, newly appointed member of the Woman's Auxiliary, and daughter of Mr. Sambrook, is making gardening literature available to boys and their families by the means of a circulating catalogue library.

The first president of the United States who was born in the United States was the eighth President, Martin Van Buren. All of his predecessors were born prior to the signing of the Declaration of Independence.

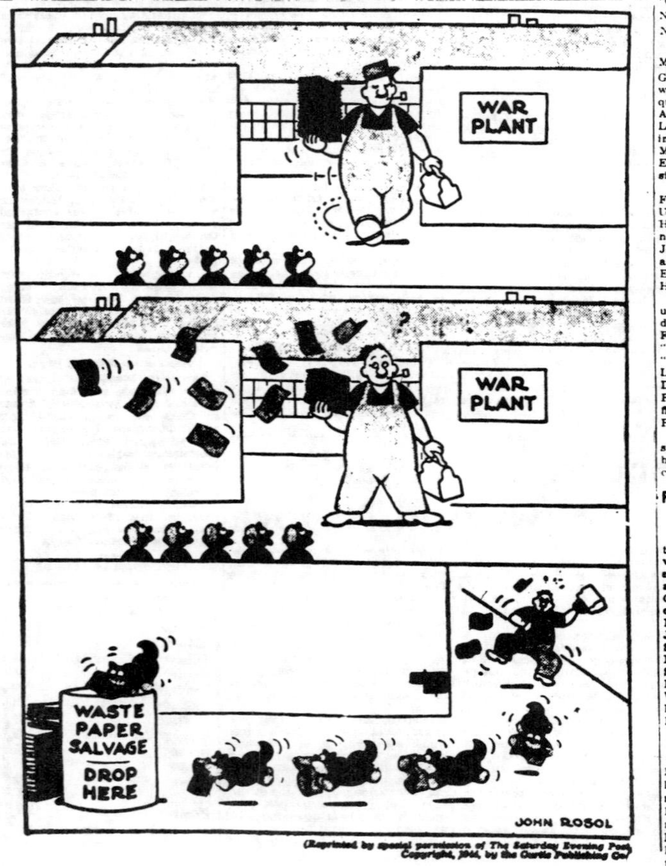

(Reprinted by special permission of The Saturday Evening Post. Copyright, 1944, by the Curtis Publishing Co.)

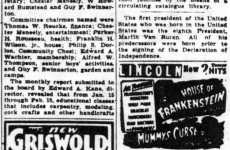

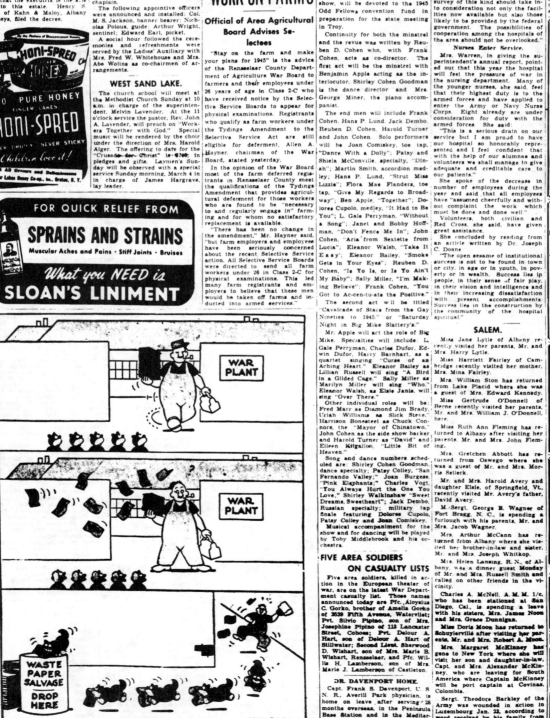

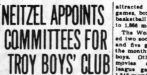

DIOCESAN LOOP TITLE LINEUP STILL IN DOUBT

The Diocesan Basketball League race, apparently won by Catholic Central High School for the second time last Friday, was thrown into doubt last night when Cathedral Academy of Albany forfeited the game it took from St. Mary's of Amsterdam at home, Jan. 26, and thus made possible a deadlock for first place.

Cathedral's action was announced by Rev. J. G. Hart, director of athletics at the Albany school and was based on the ineligibility of John Patterson, a transfer from Vincentian Institute, who helped the Elm Street quintet register its surprise victory over the Carpet City aggregation. This was the first loss suffered by the upstaters in league play this season.

By virtue of Cathedral's action, St. Mary's now boasts a record of seven wins and two setbacks as compared with eight wins and two losses for Coach Bill Carley's charges.

The Amsterdam team will have a chance to knot the count and force a playoff when it meets undermanned Cathedral on the spacious Carpet City court, Friday night, in its final Diocesan loop contest. St. Mary's will be a top heavy favorite in this contest.

In announcing the forfeit Father Hart said:

"We decided to forfeit the game with St. Mary's when we learned John Patterson, whom we used in this contest was ineligible. We used Patterson on Jan. 26 before he had completed a semester at Cathedral after transferring from Vincentian. This was a violation of league rules."

Rev. John Bourke, director of Diocesan athletics sent a letter to all schools on eligibility before the Cathedral-St. Mary's game but due to a series of circumstances this did not come to the attention of Father Hart until after that contest.

Catholic High closed its league season last Friday night with a 42 to 32 victory over Christian Brothers Academy—a victory that to all intents and purposes clinched the flag for the Eighth Streeters for the second successive year.

If Catholic High enters a playoff with St. Mary's for title honors it will be handicapped by the loss of Tom Egan, ace forward, who leaves for service today.

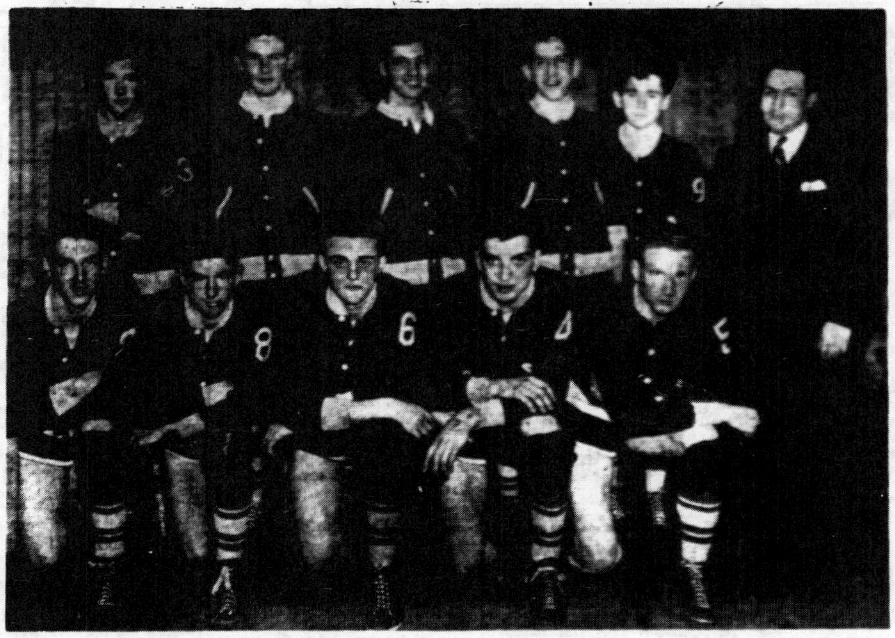

COURT CHAMPIONS—Catholic Central High has definitely clinched the championship in the Principals League for the second successive year and is assured of at least a tie in the Diocesan loop until a playoff despite the fact that Cathedral Academy threw the parochial race into doubt last night by forfeiting a January game to St. Mary's of Amsterdam. Here are the Eighth Streeters after a recent practice session. In the front row, left to right, are Bob Woods, now in the Navy; Jake Gully, Bob Degnan, Bob Gullie and Tom Egan, who enters service today; rear row, left to right, Owen Shanley, Ray Holmes, John Settanny, George Simmons, Dan McCarthy and Coach Bill Carley.

C.Y.O. STARS WILL PLAY 'VLIET FIVE

The Troy CYO All-Stars will meet the Jermain AC of Watervliet in a basketball game on the St. Joseph's Community Center court tonight at 8:15 o'clock.

The CYO team will be selected from the following players: Driscoll, O'Connell, Witbeck, Gray, Lamparello, Bradley, Suciano, Gavin, Bagnaide, Planchat and Testo.

This will be a tuneup game for the return engagement between the Troy All-Stars and the Albany All-Stars in the CYO Center gym, Albany, tomorrow night.

In that contest the Troy team will be seeking its second victory over the Albany outfit, having triumphed at the St. Joseph's Community Center recently.

At 7:15 o'clock tonight the St. Francis quintet will meet the St. Joseph's five for fourth place in the high school division of the CYO League.

The playoffs in the junior and high school divisions will take place Sunday on the St. Joseph's Center court.

'BURG BOYS' CLUB DEFEATS CATSKILL

Tom Rafferty's Lansingburg Boys Club defeated Catskill last night at Catskill, 36 to 31.

The contest was hard fought all the way with the 'Burgers holding the edge throughout.

Blair with 14 points and Collins with eight were high scorers for the North Enders. Tice topped the losers with nine points.

LANSINGBURG.

	F.G.	F.B.	T.P.
Blair, f.	5	4	14
Colligan, f.	1	3	5
Collins, c.	3	2	8
Coonrad, g.	2	1	5
Abrahamson, g.	2	0	4
Totals	13	10	36

CATSKILL.

	F.G.	F.B.	T.P.
N. Meo, f.	3	0	6
L. Seely, f.	0	0	0
Hitchcock, f.	2	0	4
P. Meo, c.	1	2	4
R. Tice, g.	4	1	9
M. Seely, g.	0	1	1
F. Meo, g.	1	0	2
Herringshaw, g.	2	1	5
Link, g.	0	0	0
Totals	13	5	31

Referee—Salamada. Scorer—Rafferty. Timer—Hayward. Score at half time—17-13, L. B. C. Fouls called—13-9, Catskill. Time of periods—8 minutes.

RHODE ISLAND FIVE ACCEPTS TILT BID

New York (AP)—Rhode Island State, one of the highest scoring quintents in the country, yesterday accepted a bid to play in the National Invitation Basketball Tournament opening in Madison Square Gard.n, March 17.

Winner of 18 of its 21 games, with Camp Endicott to be met in the final game tomorrow, the New England team is led by Ernie Calverly and Dick Hale. They have scored 478 and 457 points, respectively. Defeats were by St. Johns, also a tourney entry, Brown and Connecticut.

In addition to St. Johns and Rhode Island State, Tennessee and Muhlenberg also have accepted invitations to play in the tournament. Four other spots remain to be filled. The date for the championship game yesterday was shifted from March 25 to 26.

MAJOR LEAGUE COMMITTEE QUIET ON BASEBALL BOSS

Chicago (AP)—Whoever has the inside track to the baseball commissionership vacated by the death of K. M. Landis is zealously being kept under the hats of a special major league nominating committee which held its first formal huddle yesterday.

The four-member committee met here yesterday morning apparently at the office of Owner P. K. Wrigley of the Chicago Cubs, a member of the all-western screening" board which also includes Sam Breadon of the St. Louis Cardinals, Donald L. Brown of the St. Louis Browns and Alva Bradley of the Cleveland Indians.

General Manager James T. Gallagher of the Cubs released a 48-word statement from the committee shortly before 1 p.m. (CWT). The statement read:

"The four representatives, two from each major league, met yesterday morning to check with each other on progress made to date on gathering data on individuals who appear to be desirable men for the post of commissioner of baseball and is syncronizing their efforts and their methods of working."

Contacted at his office, Wrigley declined to comment on future plans of the committee, what progress had been made or how many candidates were under consideration. "I'm sorry, we can't say any more than is contained in the statement," he asserted.

Gallagher said the statement was "just called to me" and that he had no information whatsoever concerning the meeting.

Wording of the statement further emphasized the unwillingness of the "four representatives" to be termed a committee and indicated the group was in no hurry to suggest candidates to all the club owners who must vote on the new commissioner.

The unannounced session came seven days after a first meeting previously scheduled at St. Louis last Tuesday was cancelled because of publicity.

EVANS BEATS SIKI BEFORE BIG CROWD

While the largest crowd of the season looked on, Don Evans, rough-tough Buffalo grappler, bested Reggie Siki, the Abyssinian panther, in two out of three falls of the feature wrestling bout in La-Salle Institute gym last night.

Judging from the hoots and howls at the ringside, the fans came out to see Evans carry on his villianous warfare on the mat and they weren't disappointed.

In fact, they got a little more than they bargained for because Siki was no slouch himself with the "terror" stuff. He could chew nails just as well as Evans and both grapplers forgot the meaning of the word ethics.

From start to finish the bout was one of those spectacular affairs which kept the fans on the edge of their seats.

After the main-eventers had pummeled each other all over the ring, using all the known holds and many others there weren't in the book, Evans scored the first fall in 24 seconds with a series of body slams.

Siki rallied after the brief intermission and meted out plenty of punishment, much of it by hair-pulling tactics and clouting. He finally turned the tables on his Buffalo foe, however, scoring in ten minutes with a head and hip lock.

The deciding fall came in seven minutes as Evans scored with a face lock and body press.

The semi-final affair was captured by Lou Farina, New York Italian who engaged in a lengthy brawl with Joe Ludlum of Boston. Farina scored in 35 minutes with a pick up and body slam.

Honors in the opening bout went to Tony Morette of Schenectady, who stoopped Frank Krauss, another Schenectady grappler, in 15 minutes with a body press.

Snead Gone Long Way From Virginia Hills

BY LAWTON CARVER.

New York (INS)—Samuel Jackson Snead has gone a long way in a short time since he left the Blue Ridge Mountains of Virginia.

It seems like only yesterday that Fred Corcoran was leading him around by the hand and promising him another big, frothy chocolate ice cream soda if he would go out there and shoot a round of 65 or so just to show all those nice people gathered at the starting tee how the game of golf should be played.

Then more likely than not he would fire a 65—or perhaps even a 61, a card which brough him considerable momentary notice when he was a fledgeling assistant pro at White Sulphur Springs, W. Va.

He and the rest of the touring troupe are headed now for Charlotte, N. C., where on March 16 they will start in a $10,000 open that will be preceded by an old and familiar cry, "Snead is the man to beat." That became the theme song of the Gypsies on the cash-and-carry golf trail in 1938 when he set a money-winning record of $19,354, and the tune hasn't changed much since, except for the period when Snead was in the Navy.

Since he took off the bell-bottom trousers and put back on his seersucker golfing pants he has won six tournaments against four for Byron Nelson the runner-up in point of victories. The latter holds a money edge for the year of $14,468 to $13,849 for Snead, who probably will take care of that little matter in due time.

He's hot now, so hot that you could fry an omelet on the blade of his putter, and he is notorious for staying hot longer than nearly any other man in the game once he begins running a winning temperature.

Byron Nelson may come bouncing back at any moment, but for the time being he has been cooled off, while Jug McSpaden, who was doing a lot of winning awhile back, is beginning to take on the appearance of a permanent frappe.

It's no wonder, the figures show that Snead was 43 strokes under par for 144 holes in capturing the Pensacola and Jacksonville opens successively. In the latter event, over the last week-end, he fired rounds of 69, 65, 66, 66 for a total of 266.

Disregarding the prob.ble difference in playing conditions and competition, that still is just two strokes above the 264 which Craig Wood shot in 1940 for an unofficial world record when he won the Metropolitan Open at Bloomfield, N. J.

The answer to it all seems to be centered in the pains a fellow gets in his back. If you would take 20 strokes off your card arrange to have some floating vertebrae, a spavined sacroiliac, some torn ligaments and general infirminity from shoulder blades to belt line. That does it.

Wood won the National Open playing in a special corset and they recently threw Snead out of the Navy because of some similar difficulty that causes twinges and groans just when a man is concentrating on a 60-foot putt and thinking how easy it would be if he felt well.

What with pills and massage and sleeping on ironing boards and getting a catch in the back every time you stoop over its all a man can do to break par by 8 or 10 strokes. You can almost hear Snead thinking about his troubles.

"It's enough to make a man give plumb up," he says to himself as he bags another birdie, another course record, another tournament and another bale of War Bonds or folding money.

CLIFF BECKETT KO'S LOU SCHWARTZ

Pittsburg (AP)—Three of four eight-round bouts at the Garden here last night wound up in knockouts—two of them in the first frame.

Nearly 2,000 saw wild-swinging Cliff Beckett, 152, Toronto, flatten Lou Schwartz, 150, Columbus, in 1:59 of the first.

Phil Muscato, 174, Buffalo, registered the second first-round kayo in eliminating Tommy Woodward, 174, Columbus, in 2:02.

Other results—Frankie Abrams, 145, Detroit, knocked out Bobby Maloney, 147, Homestead, Pa. (1); Al Gomez, 132, Chicago, decisioned Rene Cantero, 138, Cuba (8).

NATIONAL LEAGUE PLAYOFFS.

At Sheboygan, Wis.—Chicago American Gears 50, Sheboygan Redskins 49.

HOCKEY STAR IN SERIOUS CONDITION

Buffalo, (AP)—Don Webster, Hershey Bears' forward, injured in an American Hockey League game with the Buffalo Bisons Sunday night, is in critical condition, Dr. Louis J. Schmitt, Buffalo team physician, said last night.

Webster's bladder was punctured when the jagged end of a hockey stick was driven into his groin, penetrating the abdominal cavity.

GIANTS SIGN UP FOUR MORE MEN

New York (AP)—The Giants announced yesterday the signing of four outfielders, Joe Medwick, Johnny Rucker, Steve Filipowicz and Danny Gardella. The Giants now have a total of nine men signed for the coming baseball season.

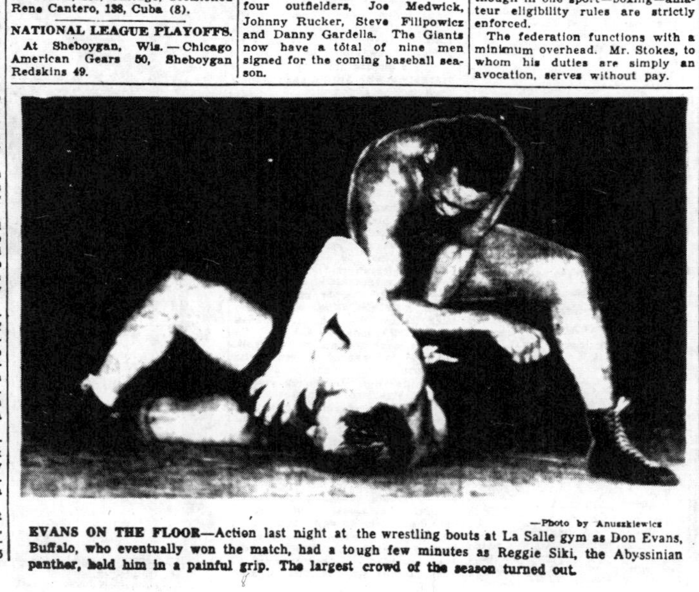

—Photo by Anuszkiewicz

EVANS ON THE FLOOR—Action last night at the wrestling bouts at La Salle gym as Don Evans, Buffalo, who eventually won the match, had a tough few minutes as Reggie Siki, the Abyssinian panther, held him in a painful grip. The largest crowd of the season turned out.

SEE TEXAS PLAN WORKING OKAY IN AMATEUR FIELD

By WHITNEY MARTIN.

New York, (AP)—There will be much emphasis after the war on the physical development of the younger generations, and a million schemes, give or take a couple, will be advanced to organize generally acceptable programs.

There is one plan to encourage voluntary sports participation already functioning in Texas, and it has met with such success that the mechanics of the organization might bear investigation by other states.

The organization is known as the Texas Athletic Federation, a setup something like the Amateur Athletic Union. The chief differences are that members, although pros in another sport, are allowed to compete as amateurs in the sports in which they have no pro affiliation, and the fact that mass participation is encouraged in preference to the development of a few outstanding stars or promotion of big tournaments.

Koger Stokes, a lean, quiet gent from San Antonio who originated the federation idea and is the organization's president, dropped in recently to outline its purpose and accomplishments.

It was organized 20 years ago at Waco, he said, and was the outgrowth of a Sunday school organization he headed at San Antonio. Six cities formed the original group. Now the Federation covers nearly the entire state, with practically all local recreation departments and many sports and athletic associations members.

Mr. Stokes said local and state tournaments are held in various men's competitive sports, such as baseball, basketball, roque, tennis, swimming, track and field, boxing, softball, horseshoe pitching and soccer, as well as in various competitions, but the primary purpose is to provide organized sports for as many participants as possible.

The federation is by no means antagonistic to the A. A. U., Mr. Stokes explained. It "just grew," more or less, filling in a need for organized local competition. With the exception of the eligibility in one sport of an athlete who may be a pro in another, the rules are patterned much after those of the older national organization. He said the two groups work together in many instances.

In recent years the federation has entered in its competition many Army and Navy teams, and the fact the athletes are in the service qualifies them to play, although in one sport—boxing—amateur eligibility rules are strictly enforced.

The federation functions with a minimum overhead. Mr. Stokes, to whom his duties are simply an avocation, serves without pay.

HAGG TO APPEAR SATURDAY NIGHT IN GARDEN RACE

New York (AP)—Gunder Hagg, Swedish ace who finished last in a five-man race last Saturday, said yesterday he would run the mile again this week-end and that he hoped he could cut at least ten sec s off his 4 31 board floor debut.

"I could have lowered my time by about eight seconds last Saturday night but I saw that I was beaten and there was no need to risk possible injury. I'll make no prediction on how I will come out the next time," he said through an interpretor at a luncheon.

Haakan Lidman, English speaking Stockholm sports writer who won the 60-yard high hurdle exhibition Saturday night, said that both he and Hagg were in need of rest and work.

"We honestly don't know how to train for our coming races. If we take the work we need, we won't have enough rest. If we rest, we can't regain our spring. We will have to wait and see what happens," he concluded.

Asked if breathing in the smoke filled arena troubled them, Lidman replied with an emphatic "no."

"Aboard our freighter our two companions always smoked black cigars. The air in Madison Square Garden actually seemed fresh," he continued.

Dan Ferris, secretary-treasurer of the A. A. U., added that he would seek extension of Hagg's visitor's permit in this country and that he hoped to line up a Pacific Coast and southern trip for the two which would terminate with the annual Pennsylvania relays on April 27 and 28.

The gaunt Gunder romped 3,000 yards in an uptown New York park yesterday and said he found the terrain satisfactory but that he planned to spend several afternoons with the New York University squad under Coach Emil Von Elling, who prepared Glenn Cunningham, Leslie MacMitchell and Frank Dixon for their mile efforts.

"That was one of the finest exhibitions I have ever seen," said Von Elling regarding Hagg's mile of last Saturday. "MacMitchell, who now is in the Navy, would need at least six weeks to get in shape for a race like that. Hagg tried it after only fifty hours on shore."

TOMAHAWKS WIN AT CENTER COURT

The All-Stars defeated the Silver Eagles, 12 to 2, in the Girls' League at the J. C. C. court last night.

The Tomahawks won two games. In the first contest they trimmed the J. C. C. All-Stars, 9 to 2, and copped the second game from the Silver Eagles, 18 to 10.

SILVER EAGLES.

	F.G.	F.B.	T.P.
D. Millington, f.	0	0	0
Creech, f.	1	0	2
Pinaha, f.	0	0	0
Testo, c.	0	0	0
Weingartner, g.	0	0	0
M. Millington, g.	0	0	0
Beaydrin, g.	0	0	0
Casey, g.	0	0	0
Totals	1	0	2

ALL-STARS.

	F.G.	F.B.	T.P.
Kendrick, f.	3	0	6
Nadler, f.	0	0	0
Rosenberg, f.	2	0	4
Siegal, c.	1	0	2
Boland, g.	0	0	0
Gallo, g.	0	0	0
Stanger, g.	0	0	0
Totals	6	0	12

Referee—Smith and Adams.

TOMAHAWKS.

	F.G.	F.B.	T.P.
Fran Adams, f.	3	1	7
Betty Spain, f.	1	0	2
Bob Smith, f.	0	0	0
Ellen Randle, g.	0	0	0
Marge Holland, g.	0	0	0
Betsy Ward, g.	0	0	0
Totals	4	1	9

J. C. C. ALL STARS.

	F.G.	F.B.	T.P.
Elaine Nadler, f.	0	0	0
M. Rosenberg, f.	0	0	0
E. Siegal, f.	1	0	2
S. Kendrick, c.	0	0	0
Jo Boland, g.	0	0	0
J. Gallo, g.	0	0	0
R. Stenger, g.	0	0	0
Totals	1	0	2

Referee, Manny Elfenbein.

SILVER EAGLES.

	F.G.	F.B.	T.P.
D. Millington, f.	1	0	2
A. Creech, c.	4	0	8
E. Pinaha, f.	0	0	0
U. Testo, f.	0	0	0
K. Weingartner, g.	0	0	0
M. Millington, g.	0	0	0
M. Beadorn, g.	0	0	0
H. Casey, g.	0	0	0
Totals	5	0	10

TOMAHAWKS.

	F.G.	F.B.	T.P.
Fran Adams, f.	3	1	7
Marge Hulfand, f.	0	1	1
Ellen Randle, c.	4	0	8
Betty Spain, g.	1	0	2
Betsy Ward, g.	0	0	0
Bob Smith, g.	0	0	0
Totals	8	2	18

Referee, Manny Elfenbein.

SINGLETON LOSES IN BOSTON BOUT

Boston (AP)—Gus Mell, 131, employed his powerful right in effective fashion to build up a unanimous decision over Benny Singleton, 137, of Waterbury, Conn., the New England lightweight titlist, in a 10-round feature last night.

While suffering his second setback in his 20 professional starts, the 18-year-old Singleton took a severe head and body beating during the fourth and fifth rounds. But the Canadian, a year older and winner of 30 of his 31 previous starts, was much too eager trying for a knockout and he missed with at least a half dozen terrific right haymakers with Singleton apparently at his mercy.

STRIKES SPARE

Rensselaer Valve Mixed.

Ed Castracani was high scorer in the Rensselaer Valve Mixed League with a 187-517 triple while Bill Taylor's even 200 mark gained him the lead in single scores. Norma Coons topped the women with a 165-465.

Following Ed were Bob Miter, 183-506 and Art Bliss, 174-482. The next highest scorers after Norma were Mabel Bohrer, 168-437, and Frances Cunningham, 152-407.

In team play Art Hintz's team won two games from the Larry Millers and Art Bliss' squad won a pair from Ed Castracani's keglers.

St. Mary's Women, Waterford.

Fran Whinnery gained the top ranking spot in the St. Mary's Women League of Waterford with a 195-187—538, followed by Anita Jordan in second place with a 161-466. Next in line were Fran Acierno, 174-445; Rita Hourigan, 196-442; Helen Brizee, 164-429; Jane Lavin, 161-415; Clara Brundige, 146-402, and Leona Doud a single game of 164 and Julia Bleibtrey, 157.

In team play the Caps won three from the Bank of Waterford and Sophies won two games from the Mohawk Paper Mills.

Railroad "Y."

MacCochran rolled a 212-568 to lead the Brockways to a 2-1 win over the Pratts in the Railroad Y. M. C. A. league. Noonan assisted with a 182-517, for the winners, while Pabst had a 179-509 and S. Pratt a 196-502 for the losers. Coming back strong after a first game setback, the Taylors took the next two from the Greens as Howd rolled a 234-536 and Taylor a 190-521. Peiper's 229-565 and Hallman's 181-534 were high for the losers.

The Hydes swept to a two-game win over the Connors. Hyde's 230-581 and Crawmer's 200-560 were high for the winners and Smyth's 216-497 topped the losers. The Richards scored the only clean sweep of the afternoon, beating the Dunkers in all three games. Schermerhorn had a 213-576 and Smith a 189-532 for the winners and MacLaren a 181-502 for the losers.

DeMento Women.

Marietta DeMento took high honors this week in the DeMento Women's League with a 235 single and a 548 triple. She was followed by Fran Bode, 189-490; Eva DeMento, 178-485; Ida Belogi, 190-487; A. Vergoni, 177-467; R. Choppy, 170-436; Kay Tybush, 167-410; and M. Goerold, 136-402.

Mayfair Victory.

Ellen Clement led the Mayfair Victory League in scoring with a 161-415, nosing out Mabel Millis who had a 143-412. Mary Clement had a 146-394. The Clements took two games from the Killions and the Lewises two from the Tagues.

Troy Church.

In the Troy Church League George Sandholdt grabbed the night's prize after a slow 148 start as he rang up 214 and 205 to end up with a 567 total, the high three of the season in Class B. It was the big noise in the Danish Lutherans shellacking of the Westminster Presbyterians. George's 214 was the night's high single in B class.

Although Milt Lavender came through for the second straight night with the high three, this time with 601 (just two pins lower than his 603 of last week), his Trinity Methodists could snatch but a single game from the St. Mark's Methodists. Helping Milt, also, was Bernie Showalter with a 202 single and a 528 triple. Billy Ray's 503 was tops for the Marksmen, followed by Earl Bronk's 487.

The Grace Methodists' clean sweep over the Green Island Methodists knocked them out of the lead for the first time this season. Jimmy Snow led the winners with an even 600 score that began with 219, the night's high single, while Dom Isabella was next with 533 that closed with a 213 game. For the Greenies Adam Hopson rolled 201—548, while George Dupuis got 509.

The Redeemer Lutherans climbed into first place by one game when they won a 2-1 victory from the First Presbyterians. Their stars were Roy Dexter, 547; Bill Currier, 529; Dave Thorsland, 509, and Ford Trethaway, 200-507.

St. Agnes', Cohoes.

Mrs. Helen Clark rolled high single of 202 and high triple of 495 in games in St. Agnes' League, Cohoes.

Other single and three-game scores were: Mrs. Mary Strauchon, 190-490; Mrs. Kay Lacy, 170-470; Mrs. Gladys Cogley, 169-445; Mrs. Leah Slater, 149-445; Mrs. Mary Jennings, 145-424; Miss Agnes Desmond, 154-411 and Mrs. Estelle Tesh, 143-409. Mrs. Estelle Tesh had high single of 141.

Pal O'Mine.

All games in the Pal O'Mine League resulted in a two-one break. The Cains came off on the long end with the Claessens. The winners were paced by "Ace" Acierno with 542; second place was taken by Dick Goeway with 512 anr Syl Pillsworth finished in the third spot with 501. The losers had only one man in the charmed circle and that was "Old Man" Wagar, who netted a 213-566.

The Ranneys took the odd game from the Camptons but failed to get a man in the 500 class although Al Mochon stopped one pin short at the 499 mark. Mark Fisher set a fast pace when he annexed a 218-554. He was followed by Ed Ryan with 504. The losers out-pinned the winners by 100 pins.

The Coons were best over the Byrons. "Cardinal" Dougherty's 536 was tops for the winners. He was followed by "Roarin" Timmy Britt with 518 and next in order came "Ma" Langlotz with 536. Joe "Smiler" Kelly turned in the best mark for the day, 203-574, for the losers and he had the backing of Chet Joslin with 502.

Mechanicville City.

Arthur Coulson of the Masonic Club team of the Mechanicville City League, heads the average column with a count of 197. The averages of the ten high bowlers are as follows: Anthony Gargano, 195; Arthur Marocco, 190; Gus DeStafane, 190; Armand Izzi, 189; William Cisler, 186; Anthony Iacobelli, 186; Joseph Jackson, 186; Arthur Cavotta, 185; Alfred George, 185, and John Martone, 184.

TOLERANCE ASKED OF BASEBALL FANS BY ED BARROW

First of two articles.

By AL VERMEER

New York (NEA)—Sitting behind a large desk and a pair of shaggy eyebrows, Edward G. Barrow, out-going president of the Yankees, quartered a pair of apples. That is the extent of lunch these days—two apples. If one will keep the doctor away, as is generally supposed, then two certainly should do something about the arthritis which plagues his hands and arms, hopes Mr. Barrow.

Uncle Ed is nearing his 77th birthday and 50 of his years have been devoted to baseball. He believes 1945 will be the most critical of all. The demands of war have taken almost half of the American League's players and threaten to take more. Yet Mr. Barrow feels baseball can survive with reduced rosters. Fans must learn to be more tolerant, he tells you.

"Last summer each club carried 25 men. Maybe we will have to slice that to 20—four outfielders, five infielders, two catchers and nine pitchers. The pitchers will feel the pinch most of all. In the old days we got by with seven or eight, but now most teams carry a dozen.

"Fans demanded this enlargement through their lack of patience. They holler for a new pitcher as soon as the opposing team puts a couple of runs together. In 1945, the fans will find that the starting pitcher often must do the job, no matter how badly things go."

Mr. Barrow does not believe pitchers should be criticized because they fail to match the iron man feats of Joe McGinnity, Big Ed Walsh, Christy Matthewson and others of the old days.

"Those fellows had hair on their chests, but they also had a tremendous advantage. They used old balls, scuffed and blackened, easier to finger. They were permitted the use of the spitter, licorice, emory and pieces of metal with which to nick the ball, which was much deader. Give these privileges to our pitchers and you will get the same results."

Mr. Barrow does not want to see those weapons returned to pitching, however, because the game is better, cleaner and more skillful without them.

* * *

Next: There will be another Babe Ruth.

REPAIR DEFEATS ARMY IN PLAYOFFS

The Repair team defeated Army, 40 to 36, as the Watervliet Arsenal Class A League Foreman's Cup playoffs got underway on the Watervliet High court last night.

The Repair team was out front, 28 to 15, at halftime but Army rallied after the intermission to make a battle of it.

Moxie Attanaseo, with 20 points, paced the winners' attack while Kittrick, with 13 points, and Captain Les Gott, with 12, were best for the losers.

The B division 20 Year Club playoffs also began with the Tank Shop defeating the Liner Shop, 44 to 24.

Don Lamperiello, with 13 points, featured for the Tank Shop which led 23 to 12 at halftime. Jack Mooney, with six, was best for the Liners.

In a special playoff to determine a third team for the 20 Year Club playoffs, the Shop 35 team defeated the Breech outfit, 33 to 20.

Dick Charbonneau, with 10 points, and Steve Scarchill, with seven points, featured for Shop 35 while Val Mackas, with seven points, was high for the losers.

INDUSTRIAL LOOP LISTS THREE TILTS

The Industrial AA Basketball League will continue its campaign tonight with three games on the Central YMCA court.

Top tilt of the night will send the league-leading Behr-Manning quintet against the Cluett Peabody five. This will be the second game on the card and the Behr-Manning club, losers of only one contest to date, will be favored.

In other games the Public Safety team will go against the Allegheny Ludlum outfit which won last year's pennant while the Arsenal Howitzers will clash with the Arsenal Tanks.

The regular league season is scheduled to end March 20 but arrangements must be made for games postponed during the fuel crisis.

Playoffs, involving the top four teams probably won't begin until next month.

ST. PETER'S BEATS ALUMNI, 25 TO 23

The St. Peter's quintet defeated the St. Peter's Alumni outfit, 25 to 23, on the St. Peter Lyceum Court.

Holland, with 10 points, featured for the winners, while Messier duplicated this performance for the losers.

In another game the St. Peter's Juniors trounced Our Lady of Victory, 78 to 10.

Holland tallied 34 points in this game while Carhart, with five, was tops for the losers.

NEW YORK CITY OF ACE FIRST BASEMEN

New York (AP)—No less than five New York boys have attained success as major league first basemen in the last decade.

They are Lou Gehrig and Buddy Hassett of the Yankees, Babe Young of the Giants, Frank McCormick of the Reds and Hank Greenberg of the Tigers.

4

ROMULO TO TELL CONGRESS ABOUT JAP ATROCITIES

Resident Commissioner of Philippines Claims Possession of Evidence

BY EDWARD W. KOEHLER

San Francisco (INS)—A pledge to "indict" the Japanese in the American Congress for atrocities committed during the occupation of the Philippines was made by Brig. Gen. Carlos Romulo, resident commissioner of the Philippines.

Romulo made his statement during an interview upon his return from the islands with his family, a family which fought and hid out from the Japs for more than three years on Luzon.

"I am going to indict the Japanese people on the floor of Congress," Romulo declared, adding:

"I have with me actual Japanese orders, direct from Tokyo, that ordered the wanton destruction of Manila, the Filipino people and anything that would remotely aid in American liberation of my country.

"With me are sworn affidavits of the wanton atrocities that civilians suffered at the hands of the Japanese, together with a newsreel that, I believe with a given distribution in the United States within a few weeks.

"We all recall the rape of Nan-

king by the Japanese. I can say that expedition of Imperial Japanese troops was a picnic compared to the wanton destruction of Manila.

"On orders from Tokyo, for instance, 1,700 Filipino males were herded into Fort Santiago dungeons—the structure was doused with kerosene and set afire. Out of the total, three escaped the flames, two to die from machine gun wounds, and the third to reach American lines safely to tell the story of horror—after breaking his back in an effort to escape."

Escorted by WAC Lt. Anne J. Kupres from Honolulu, the party included the general's wife, Virginia; and their sons, Bobby, 8; Ricardo, 11; Gregoria, 17, and Carlos, jr., 19.

Carlos had volunteered, at 17, for the Philippine Army and following the fall of Bataan joined with guerrillas operating in a southern province of Luzon.

Evacuated Family.

Carlos shyly admitted he was responsible for the deaths of seven Japs. He also admitted he helped to evacuate his brothers and mother from behind the Japanese lines.

"It was necessary," he said, "for the guerrilla group, to which I belonged to build an emergency landing strip on a mountain top for Piper Cubs to land. This was done in short order, and my mother and two brothers were safely flown behind our lines in Central Luzon.

"My father's statement about the Fort Santiago dungeons are only too true. After we captured the fort we found the burned bodies of the Filipino men strewn around the building. Many of them still were clinging to the bars on the windows trying vainly to make an escape."

Romulo then took up the story of the horror of Manila's last days under Japanese domination to describe how they found "thousands of women and children, wantonly machine-gunned as they fled through a break in the Intramuros.

"The Imperial Marines told the people of Manila," Romulo continued. "'you love Americans—you no see. We no leave, you no leave'."

THREE SONS SERVING—Three sons of Mr. and Mrs. Michael A. Lettke of Annie Street, Albia Terrace, are serving in the armed forces. Private Michael T., who enlisted in the Army several years before the war, has been overseas 18 months, now stationed in Germany with the First Army. Sergeant George, in the Army two years, has been overseas in the European theater. Francis, fireman 1/c, in the Navy, enlisted 18 months ago, soon after his 17th birthday. He is stationed in Norfolk, Va.

TOO MANY COOKS MAY SPOIL BROTH FOR INDUSTRIALS

Chef at Y. M. C. A. Is to Help Club Leaders Will Prepare Dinner

Too many cooks may spoil the broth, but they'll be necessary to insure service at tonight's monthly meeting of the Troy Industrial Club in the Troy Y. M. C. A.

With 200 reservations on hand for the dinner session, William E. Stacey, Y. M. C. A. chef, was taken ill yesterday. A council of war yesterday afternoon decided the course of action.

A. James McCracken, industrial secretary and Harley G. Hodgkins, physical director, made a shopping foray this morning to purchase the articles on the dinner menu — a menu planned at the conference.

Mrs. Stacey will be on hand to supervise the cooking of the meat dish — after all preliminary work has been done by Messrs. McCracken and Hodgkins.

Robert W. Ames, membership secretary, has been promoted to salad chef. When the meal is ready Mr. McCracken will take his place at the head table. Mr. Hodgkins will assist in serving the portions and will supervise table service. Mr. Ames will dole out the salads and otherwise help about the kitchen.

Later, all three will help again. There are dishes to be washed.

ARMY ORDNANCE GETS CAPTURED JAP EQUIPMENT

150 Tons of Enemy Material Taken in Philippines Being Studied in Maryland

One hundred and fifty tons of Japanese equipment, captured in the Philippines, were shipped to the United States and are now being examined and tested at Aberdeen Proving Ground, Maryland.

This enemy material was collected in Philippine battlefields by six Army Ordnance members of an Army Service Forces Enemy Equipment Service team attached to the American Sixth Army.

Prize items included unused 8-inch rockets, a 3,000-pound bomb, seven uncrated 130-mm. dual-purpose field guns and ammunition, a 17-ton tank, and the ten-ton prime movers.

Brig. Gen. A. G. Gillespie, commanding Watervliet Arsenal, said today that a test received the Ordnance Headquarters in Washington showed that the American landing on Leyte caught the enemy off guard and resulted in a usual collection of Japanese weapons and equipment, some of it in original containers and in perfect condition.

This enemy material is now being carefully analysed and tested by ordnance technicians at Aberdeen in order to find out possible Japanese manufacturing improvements to keep the quality of our own equipment well out in front of the best that the Nips can produce.

Ordnance members of the service team reported that Army ordnance carbines were landed by submarine on Mindoro many months prior to the Philippine invasion. When the American task force passed near Mindoro on its way to Leyte, fierce Moro guerilla fighters swarmed down from the hills and kept the Japanese on the island fully occupied until the task force had passed safely by.

High praise was also given the Cargo Carrier M29, nicknamed the "Weasel," which proved invaluable on Leyte where, beyond the beach, many swamp areas were encountered.

HOOSICK.

Hoosac School closed Saturday for its spring vacation of two weeks.

Sgt. Frank Cipperly, who has been wounded in Germany, has returned to the United States.

Mrs. Frank Cipperly of Troy spent Sunday with Mr. and Mrs. Harry E. Cipperly in Breese Hollow.

Mr. and Mrs. George Rifenburg spent Sunday in Tamarac with their parents, Mr. and Mrs. Sanford Rifenburg.

Rt. Rev. George Ashton Oldham, D. D., bishop of Albany, will visit and preach at All Saints' Church Sunday, April 15.

All Saints' Parish Guild will sponsor a baked hash supper for the public today at 5:30 p.m. in the parish hall.

Sgt. Sylvester James of Camp Shanks and sister, Mrs. Arthur Guiden of Williamstown, called Saturday on Mrs. James D. Paddock.

Mr. and Mrs. Frank LeBarron of North Hoosick were Thursday dinner guests of their brother and family, Mr. and Mrs. Harrison J. Philpott.

At the Hoosick Baptist Church on Sunday Rev. J. J. Gould, the pastor, will preach at 9:30 a.m. on "Thy Will Be Done." Sunday School will be at 10:30 a.m.

Mr. and Mrs. Don Stevens of Troy were Sunday dinner guests of their grandparents, Mr. and Mrs. LeVern Prebble. Robert McCart spent Sunday at the Prebble home.

At All Saints' Episcopal Church Sunday Rev. William Garner will preach and celebrate communion at 11 a.m. He will have charge of the Mission of the Holy Name, Boyntonville, at 3 p.m.

At the Laf-A-Lot card party Saturday night awards went to Mrs. Harold C. Prebble and Forrest Sherman with consolation prizes to Mrs. Carl Stevens and Daniel Webster. Their next party will be held at the home of Mrs. Ellsworth Stevens, Potter Hill, March 24.

The next meeting of All Saints' Branch of the Girls' Friendly Society will be held at the home of Miss Caroline A. Lohnes with Mrs. Bernard Porter as assisting hostess Monday night. Miss Lohnes will take care of recreation and Mrs. Robert Engquist will have charge of worship service.

YOUTH DANCES SHOW PROFIT FOR SAGINAW

Saginaw, Mich. (UP)—"Solid" is the word for the Wednesday and Saturday night youth dances at Saginaw that have put the city auditorium back in the black again.

It seems that from 1937 until 1942 the books showed red until a group of young people, who liked dancing for the joy of it, suggested to the board of directors and the city manager that the city might capitalize on dances.

Now after two years the city manager reports that the dances have been chiefly responsible for wiping out the five years of operation in the red and building up a profit of $7,500. Every time the manager looks at a monthly statement of operations, he says it practically "sends him."

ON THE AIR

Radio Programs From Local Stations

TONIGHT

(Radio program listings)

TOMORROW

(Radio program listings)

Butter For Solons, Scribes Marmalade

BY FREDERICK C. OTHMAN
United Press Staff Correspondent.

Washington (UP)—We're hungry. Congress and me. We want meat in which a feller can sink his teeth. We also want fresh butter on our bread. OPA, you better have a care. Or as Sen. Albert W. Hawkes of New Jersey put it:

"We are getting plenty of rancid butter at the Senate restaurant right now. If you don't believe it, come on over and eat there."

He's a senator. He gets rancid butter. I'm no senator. I get marmalade in paper cups. 'V much for class distinction in the senatorial beanery; now we'll get on with the story of why there ain't no meat.

Rep. Frank L. Sundstrom of East Orange, N. J., who used to be a meat-eater before OPA, called a special hearing on the lack cf beef steak, to which he invited congressmen, senators, butchers and the hungry, like me. He said this country had more cows than ever and fewer steaks. "There must be something wrong," he said. He called as his first witness Morris Cohn, dapper, brown-suited counsel for most of the New Jersey meat packers.

Cohn said the OPA said that civilians were eating more meat than they ever did. He said he was prepared to prove that was a lie. He said housewives ought to be allowed to use their red ration

stamps for meat alone. He said they should have a special stamp for butter. "Incidentally, he continued, "I understand there is a large surplus of butter in New York now, but the housewife can't buy it. Soon it will be rancid."

It was here that Senator Hawkes revealed the sorry situation in the Senate luncheon.

Next witness: A. G. Williams, a New Jersey slaughterer in a black and yellow necktie with yellow socks to match.

"Our industry is being regimented into the red," he testified. How, he asked, can a meat packer pack meat when he has to sell it for less than he paid for it?

"You slaughterers are being thrown out of business," observed Rep. Gordon Canfield of Paterson, N. J.

"And the black market is getting the hogs in Pennsylvania," added Rep. Chester H. Gross of the Keystone State.

Came then Charles S. Winters, who identified himself as a justice of the peace representing the rural slaughterers near Lancaster, Pa. They're all lawbreakers, he said, in spite of themselves. "When they go into Philadelphia to buy steers, they are pushed aside by the black marketers with $10,000 cash in their pockets," he added.

Arthur Dennis, vice-president of the National Meat Council, said good American citizens were going to jail when faced by the choice of bankruptcy or of breaking the law. "You're damned if you do and you're damned if you don't," he said.

Rep. Emmanuel Celler of New York said his wife went from store to store, looking for meat. She always looked in vain in Brooklyn. "It's hopeless," he said.

The chairman said he'd give the government men a chance to answer. M. O. Cooper of the War Food Administration passed the buck to the OPA. A. E. Erickson of the OPA looked unhappy. He said the meat problem was difficult. He said he wanted to study the evidence.

End hearing. Luncheon special at the House of Representatives restaurant: Scrambled eggs with tomatoes. At the Senate restaurant: Omelette.

RUSSIAN INSTITUTE.

Stockholm (INS)—A Russian Institute, attached to the University of Stockholm, will soon open here. A library catalogue containing a list of about 10,000 volumes in Russian or on Russian conditions at present available in Sweden, has been compiled. A Russian and a Swedish-born teacher will be employed.

How Shall We Deal With a Defeated Japan?

Admiral H. E. Yarnell   Dr. Y. C. James Yen

Shall we punish all Japs . . . throttle their industry? Or allow the better elements in Japan to prosper? Permanent peace may depend on the answer. Hear both sides of this puzzling question discussed on America's Town Meeting tonight by four authorities: Admiral H. E. Yarnell (former Commander-in-Chief of Asiatic Fleet); Dr. Y. C. James Yen (Director of Chinese Mass Education Movement); Otto Tolischus (New York Times correspondent, author of "Tokyo Record") and Wilfrid Fleisher (author of "What to do with Japan"). Tune in tonight to the exciting program that gives you both sides of problems affecting your life. America's Town Meeting, sponsored by The Reader's Digest, 8:30, WTRY.

THE WEATHER
Tonight—Fair, warm.

THE TIMES RECORD

FINAL EDITION

SERIES 1945—NO. 88 (Entered as Second Class Matter at the Postoffice at Troy, N. Y., Under the Act of March 3, 1879.) TROY, N. Y.; FRIDAY EVENING, APRIL 13, 1945. (Published Daily Except Sunday) PRICE FOUR CENTS

Truman Proclaims Tomorrow Mourning Day For Roosevelt

ROOSEVELT TO BE PAID TRIBUTE AT SERVICES IN CITY

Various Churches and Municipal Officials Will Honor Dead President Tomorrow

Citizens of Troy prepared today to pay tribute to the memory of the dead President and to dedicate themselves to the continued well being of the nation.

School children, church worshippers, the Negro people of the city whom he had befriended, men of the armed forces home on furloughs united in the spontaneous tribute to President Roosevelt today as many other services were planned for tomorrow.

During the time of the funeral, which will be at 4 p.m. tomorrow, memorial services will be held in Barker Park, Mayor John J. Ahern has announced. All non-essential business places and industries will be asked to close during the services.

At 12:15 p.m. a short memorial service will be conducted by naval officers at R. P. I. for all students. The service will take place on the quadrangle in front of the freshman dormitories. Capt. Mark C. Bowman, commanding all Navy men on the hill, said that the service was being held early so that the students could then join in the church services which would be held in the city.

Prayers for the fulfilment of President Roosevelt's labors, his successor in office and for the nation will be offered in all Catholic Churches of the Albany Diocese Sunday morning, Rt. Rev. Edmund F. Gibbons, Bishop of the diocese, has announced.

The city awoke today to a shocked realization of the President's death. One of the most touching services took place early in the morning at Liberty Presbyterian Church in State Street where the Negro people, hastily called together by their pastor, Rev. D. Talmadge Murray, prayed for "the bereaved nation." The prayers were heard outside the church auditorium through the loud speaker system and people gathered quietly in State Street to listen.

Tribute of Pastor.

The pastor said:

"Trully a great man is fallen, a great statesman, a great Christian gentleman, a man to whom the world looked for leadership, and lasting peace. It is for us the living to carry on the unfinished task for which he so courageously lived and died."

The effect of the President's death on the young people of the city was noted by school teachers and parents. The children have never known any president but Franklin D. Roosevelt. They were shocked and saddened by his death but as Rev. T. Gerald Mulqueen principal of Catholic Central High School said this morning, "Our high school children, through their social studies, know that the death of our President does not mean the end of everything but that we must go forward with courage from this point."

At the school, the students joined in prayers for the late President and prayers for divine guidance of President Truman, this afternoon. A dance scheduled for tonight was cancelled by the pupils.

Students Gather.

At St. Mary's Church at 10 a. m. the entire student body of La Salle Institute and St. Mary's School gathered for prayers led by Rev. Joseph P. Kelly, D.D., the pastor. Prayers were offered, first for the successful completion

(Continued on Page 13.)

CONDOLENCES SENT TO MRS. ROOSEVELT BY ADMIRAL NIMITZ

Guam (AP)—Fleet Admr. Chester W. Nimitz sent the following message to Mrs. Franklin D. Roosevelt:

"The officers and men of the Pacific Fleet and the members of all armed services in the Pacific Ocean Areas join me in deepest sympathy to you in the lamentable loss of President Roosevelt.

"We in the Navy have lost an outstanding commander-in-chief and the American people a great leader.

"In your hour of sorrow, I know that your husband's great and historic achievements during his full life will give you comfort."

From Secretary of the Navy James V. Forrestal came the message announcing the death.

It said: "Colors should be displayed at halfmast for thirty days beginning April 13 at 8 a.m., in so far as war operations permit.

"Memorial services are to be held on the day of the funeral to be announced later at all yards, stations and on board all vessels of the Navy, war operations permitting. The wearing of mourning badges and the firing of salutes will be dispensed with in view of war conditions."

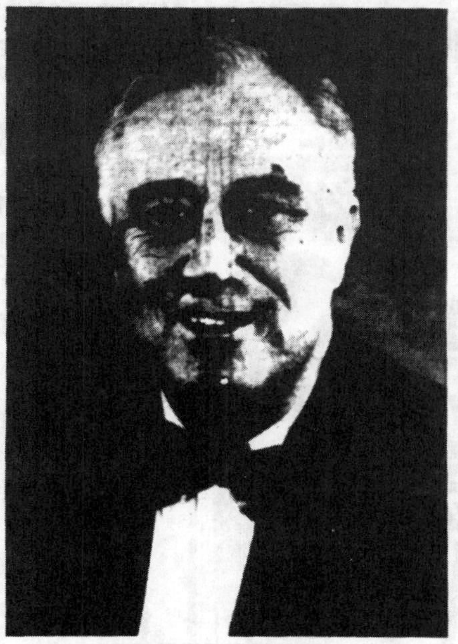

FRANKLIN D. ROOSEVELT

STALIN PLEDGES SOVIET TO FOLLOW F. D. R. POLICIES

All Russia Mourns American President as Their "Greatest Friend"

Moscow (AP)—Premier Marshal Stalin led the Russian people today in expressing deep personal grief at the death of Franklin D. Roosevelt and in making plain that the Russian nation desired continued Russian-American collaboration along the lines laid down by the late President.

All Russia mourned at the loss of a man regarded here as having been the Soviet Union's greatest friend in America.

The Soviet press printed two-column photographs of Roosevelt, bordered in black, on the front pages, along with Premier Stalin's condolences to Mrs. Roosevelt and his personal note to President Truman.

The Moscow radio broadcast an official memorial.

Every Russian credited Roosevelt with bringing about diplomatic relations with the Soviet Union, and the speed with which he dispatched aid when Germany attacked Russia while the United States was not yet at war with the reich endeared him to the people of this country.

The continuation of the President's policy toward Russia and in building a world security organization are of highest concern here was evidenced by Stalin's quick assurance to Truman of his desire for continued cooperation.

The Russians were firmly convinced by Roosevelt's election to a fourth term that the American people wished close relations with Russia in building peace and security after the war and will look for every sign that his program will be continued without interruption.

In a messages expressing condolences to Mrs. Roosevelt, Stalin said:

"The Soviet people highly valued President Roosevelt as a great or-

(Continued on Page 14.)

CHURCHILL CALLS ROOSEVELT 'DEAR, CHERISHED FRIEND'

Commons Adjourns in Respect to President's Memory; Press Eulogies

London (AP)—A solemnly hushed House of Commons adjourned five minutes after it had convened today in respect to the memory of President Roosevelt.

His shoulders bowed and face pale, Prime Minister Churchill informed the house of the death of "this great departed statesman and war leader," a "dear and cherished" friend.

Britain—king, prime minister and commoner—mourned that the President, their friend in the days of darkest despair, had been denied almost on the eve of victory the triumph of his war leadership.

The swelling chorus of tributes to the man who helped turn the tide of war by bracing Britain when she stood alone and under German bombs was mingled with widespread curiosity over the personality and policy of President Truman and expressions of satisfaction over his intention to carry on administration aims.

There was conjecture in the British press whether Churchill might fly to the funeral, but the British Press Association said Foreign Secretary Anthony Eden would attend as the British government representative.

Appearing tired and worn—there were reports he had been in lengthy conversation with Washington by telephone during the night—Churchill came before the house and asked that it adjourn out of respect to a man of "immortal renown."

Speaking with considerable emotion, he said, "It is not fitting that we should continue our work this day."

His few phrases were spoken in

(Continued on Page 14.)

Roosevelt Died After Stroke At Warm Springs, Ga.

"I Have a Terrific Headache," Last Words of President Before Fainting at Southern Resort; Cerebral Hemorrhage Ends Long and Colorful Career; Body Begins Northward Journey for Funeral Services at White House and Burial at Hyde Park.

Warm Springs, Ga. (AP)—Franklin Delano Roosevelt's long and colorful public career is at an end.

A tragic though painless death halted it abruptly yesterday as the nation's 31st president seemingly was about to see the truition of his plans for bringing lasting peace to a war-ridden world. He was 63 last January 30.

Death came unexpectedly at 4:35 p.m. (E. W. T.) in a simply furnished bedroom of his Pine Mountain cottage. The cause: A "massive" cerebral hemorrhage.

Mr. Roosevelt came here March 30 for one of his periodic visits to seek rest and to bask in the sun. He had planned to stay another week, then return to Washington, spend a day and start out again for a cross-country trip to San Francisco to open the world security conference April 25.

All this now is up to his successor, Harry S. Truman of Missouri, with the aid of a sympathetic Congress.

The President's body was en route to Washington today for funeral services in the White House and burial Sunday at Hyde Park, N. Y.

The ten-car special train, full of friends and associates, who hurried here when news of his death spread, got under way at 10:15 a.m., Central War Time.

The body was taken to the train on a motor hauled Army caisson through a lane of soldiers from Ft. Benning, Ga.

Two companies of Fort Benning troops lined both sides of the three-quarter-mile highway stretched from the Warm Springs Foundation to the railroad station. The cortege passed the administration building where polio patients sat and stood to watch their benefactor pass for the last time.

The train will reach the national capital at 10 a.m. (E. W. T.) Saturday.

Mrs. Roosevelt arrived last night from Washington. She flew in an Army plane to Fort Benning at nearby Columbus with Stephen T. Early, White House secretary, and Vice Admr. Ross T. McIntire, White House physician and Navy surgeon general.

Funeral services are to be held at 4 p.m. (E. W. T.) Saturday in the historic east room of the White House.

The body will not lie in state.

Burial will be at the family home at Hyde Park, N. Y., Sunday.

Presidential Secretary William D. Hassett said the funeral services would be of the same "utmost simplicity" the President decreed for his mother, who died in 1941.

Funeral Services.

Later—after midnight—Hassett gave out details for the funeral.

He said that six hours after the services in the East Room the body will be entrained for Hyde Park, to arrive at the family estate on the east bank of the Hudson at 9 a.m., Sunday.

Burial will be at 10 a.m. in the family garden between the rambling stone and stucco house and the Roosevelt library.

Members of the cabinet and Supreme Court, heads of federal agencies, a representative group of senators and representatives, members of the family and friends will accompany the funeral party from Washington.

The East Room services will be conducted by Bishop Angus Dun of the Washington Episcopal Cathedral, Rev. Howard S. Wilkinson, of St. Thomas' Episcopal Church, and Rev. John G. Magee, of St. John's Episcopal Church across Lafayette Park from the White House.

Mrs. Roosevelt Calm.

The President prayed each March 4 at St. John's until the inaugural date was changed to Jan. 20. In the last two years, however, he attended inaugural church services in the White House.

Conducting the burial service at the graveside in Hyde Park will be Rev. Dr. George W. Anthony, new rector of St. James' Episcopal Church where the President was senior deacon.

Mrs. Roosevelt, Early and McIntyre were driven immediately to the President's cottage after they arrived by car from Fort Benning shortly before midnight.

Mrs. Roosevelt was described by officials as bearing up "very nobly—heroically."

Warm Springs village and its nearby foundation for after-treatment of infantile paralysis—which Mr. Roosevelt helped found after he had been stricken and crippled by the disease—were stunned by the news of the passing of the nation's 31st president and its first chief executive to serve more than two terms.

He was elected to a fourth term a little more than five months ago and was inaugurated Jan. 20, ten days before his birthday.

Barbecue Planned.

Many had tears in their eyes as they passed the word of Mr. Roosevelt's demise among polio patients and foundation officials. The patients were looking forward to a visit from the President early last night. They were to put on a minstrel show for him.

Also cancelled, just as it was about to get underway, was an old-fashioned southern barbecue at the hilltop cabin of Mayor Frank W. Alcorn of Warm Springs. Mr. Roosevelt, who was to have been the honor guest, was due at the barbeque around 4:30 p.m. yesterday. When he was not there close to 5 o'clock inquiries were made by the three reporters who came here with the President from Washington.

"Come down to the Carver cottage (headquarters of Secretary

(Continued on Page 2.)

Roosevelt Knew He Was Ill, White House Reporters Think

Editor's Note: The author of the following special feature has been chief of the White House staff of the United Press since before Pearl Harbor. He has accompanied the late President on all of his domestic inspection trips, his visits to Quebec and Hawaii, all of his fourth-term campaign tours, and met him in North Africa after Yalta.

BY MERRIMAN SMITH
United Press White House Correspondent
(Copyright, 1945, by United Press)

Warm Springs, Ga. (UP)—Did President Roosevelt know that he was an ill man and that the time had come to husband his strength?

Many of us who saw him often and traveled with him believe he did.

There was nothing wrong with him organically. But the tremendous pressure of the toughest job on earth had begun to take its toll in nervous energy.

This was first noticeable last year after the Teheran conference. For two mnoths he suffered from sinus trouble and bronchitits, and it was then that he decided to go to Bernard M. Baruch's estate near Georgetown, S. C., and fight it out for himself.

He was fighting more than bronchitiss. He was, I think, trying to decide whether he was able to go through the rigors of another presidential campaign. He thought he had won. He took it easy in South Carolina for a month and came back to Washington, confident that he was in tip-top shape.

Voice Was Weaker.

But he did not snap back as he used to do. His voice was weaker, his tan faded faster and he began spending almost every week-end in the restful atmosphere of Hyde Park.

Then came the fourth-term campaign, a terrific physical beating. He spent hours touring cities in an open car, often in miserable weather. He delivered a speech at Ebbets Field in Brooklyn standing bare-handed in a cold driving rain. Next day at Hyde Park he laughed at those in his party who had the sniffles and told them he felt fine.

Yalta Trip Ordeal.

But the Yalta conference was ahead of him and that trip I think, was a serious drain on his vitality. It was probably the hardest ten days he ever went through in his life. On the ship coming back I saw more of him than I had ever seen in the same length of time. It seemed he had aged ten years in ten days. He sat all day in the sun on the boat trip back. He had lost weight, but he refused to take it seriously, said he would gain it back at Warm Springs.

On March 1 he made this report

(Continued on Page 26.)

"Lord God, Take Care of Him Now!"

Warm Sprngs, Ga. (UP)—The body of Franklin D. Roosevelt was borne from the "little white house" of Georgia today to the roll of muffled drums, starting the long, last journey to Washington.

The hot southern sun shone in a blue sky as the funeral cortege slowly moved down the winding mile-long road to Warm Springs station between lines of mourners that included hundreds of victims of the dread malady that struck Mr. Roosevelt years ago. They bared their heads and tears were shed as the cortege passed. Old Tom Logan, for 14 years Mr. Roosevelt's Negro waiter at Warm Springs, watched the body of his great friend pass by. With trembling chin he probably expressed the sentiment of the polio patients when he reverently said:

"Lord God, take care of him now."

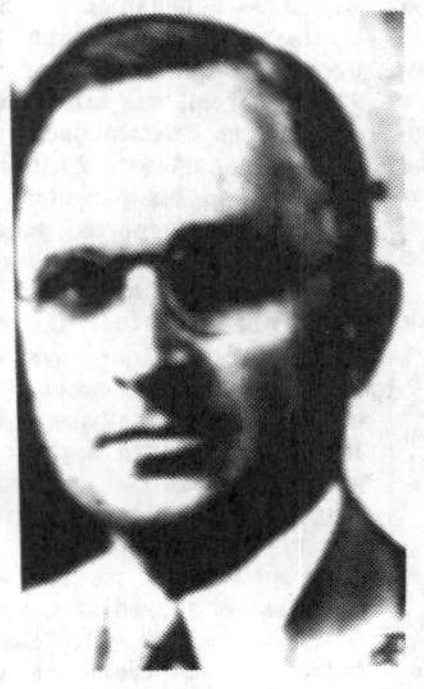

PRESIDENT TRUMAN

TRUMAN TOOK UP NATION'S REINS IN DRAMATIC SETTING

No Back-Slapping, No Smiles, Just Whispered Words of "Courage"

Washington (UP)—The gray-haired man with the gold-rimmed spectacles walked into the White House and into the most momentous hour of his life.

He came in as Vice President Harry S. Truman and he walked out as the 32nd President of the United States.

He stepped around reporters eager for more news of the death of Franklin D. Roosevelt. He walked past red-eyed secretaries and stenographers who couldn't believe the news.

He made his way into the apple-green cabinet room of the White House. Cabinet members were seated there, solemn-faced. Leaders of Congress were there, standing in groups, talking quietly.

Harry S. Truman sat down in an overstuffed leather chair. It was understandable that he was not completely at ease.

Up stepped Chief Justice Harlan F. Stone of the United States Supreme Court. The Vice President rose to his feet. Someone gave him a Bible from President Roosevelt's office.

He held it reverently on his left

(Continued on Page 26.)

THREE PUBLIC FIGURES DIE IN SIX MONTHS

New York (AP) Within a period of slightly more than six months, America has lost three of its most important public figures: Alfred E. Smith, former New York governor and 1928 Democratic presidential nominee, who died last Oct. 4; Wendell L. Willkie, Republican presidential candidate in 1940, who died last Oct. 8, and President Franklin D. Roosevelt, who died yesterday.

Milestones In Life Of President Truman

Washington (UP)—Milestones in the life of President Harry S. Truman:

1884, May 8—Born in Lamar, Mo., son of Mr. and Mrs. John Anderson Truman, farm folk.

1902—Just out of high school, took first job as drug store clerk at $3 a week.

1917-18 — In France with American troops first as captain of field artillery, later major.

1919—Married Miss Bess Wallace, childhood sweetheart.

1922—Elected judge of Jackson County (Mo.) Court.

1926—Elected presiding judge of Jackson County (Mo.) Court.

1934—Elected to U. S. Senate.

1940—Reelected to Senate.

1944—Won Democratic vice presidential nomination in contest with Henry A. Wallace; elected vice president on ticket with President Roosevelt.

1945, April 12—Took oath as President.

New President Holds Conference With U.S. Leaders

Army and Navy Chiefs and Secretary of State Attend White House Meeting; Truman Proclaims Tomorrow National Day of Mourning for Roosevelt; Washington Still Dazed by Sudden Death of President; Truman to "Carry On" Chief's Policies.

Washington (AP)—Harry S. Truman seized immediately on the grim problems of winning the war and securing the peace today as he shouldered the responsibilities of the presidency.

Leaving his modest Connecticut Avenue apartment early for the White House, the new President:

1. Held an emergency war council with his top military commanders.

2. Reviewed world political problems in a twenty-minute conference with Secretary of State Stettinius.

3. Issued a proclamation setting aside tomorrow as a national day of mourning for Franklin D. Roosevelt.

4. Conferred with a close lawyer friend, Hugh Fulton, who has been mentioned for a post if any cabinet changes are made.

5. Made an immediate and probably unprecedented trip to capitol hill where he lunched with congressional leaders.

6. Announced he will attend burial services at Hyde Park Sunday for Mr. Roosevelt, whose body was en route to Washington from Warm Springs.

Tears glistening in his eyes, President Truman today told a group of White House reporters:

"Last night the whole weight of the moon and stars fell on me. If you fellows pray, please pray for me. I mean that."

Secretary of State Stettinius, whose knowledge of the international situation was second only to that of the late President Roosevelt, arrived to join Mr. Truman at 10:15 a.m. (E. W. T.). Top military commanders were due minutes later.

The military chieftains summoned were Fleet Admr. William D. Leahy, the late President's military adviser; Fleet Admr. Ernest J. King, chief of the Navy; Gen. George C. Marshall, Army chief of staff; Secretary of War Stimson and Secretary of the Navy Forrestal.

These grave conferences dealt with a question mark raised throughout the world by the death of Franklin D. Roosevelt—intimate of Allied war leaders—and the intricacies of international relations. What of the new chief of state, Harry Truman of Missouri?

The new President announced at the outset that he would try to carry on the Roosevelt policies. He asked the cabinet to stay on, gave assurance that the United Nations' conference will open in San Francisco April 25 on schedule.

There were reports at the White House, not yet official, that Mr. Truman may address a joint session of Congress next week, possibly Tuesday.

To the 60-year-old, ruddy complexioned new President fell the immediate and sorrowful task of burying a chief executive for whom he had boundless admiration and unfaltering loyalty.

Mr. Roosevelt was struck down by a cerebral hemorrhage as he posed for a sketching artist in his cottage at the Warm Springs Infantile Paralysis Foundation where he had gone last month for a rest.

Carried into the bedroom of the little white cottage on pine mountain that was his vacation home, he died without regaining consciousness.

It was as simple as that, the blow that struck the nation to its heart as it read of climactic military successes in Germany and of a quickening of the war in the Pacific, and speculated on the success or failure of the forthcoming conference to form an organization Mr. Roosevelt hoped would prevent future wars.

Mrs. Roosevelt, at a charity benefit, received the news by telephone. Without a word, she went to the White House. The call went out for Mr. Truman. He rushed there with a hastily assembled secret service escort.

His first words to Mrs. Roosevelt were of her and the four Roosevelt sons. Mrs. Roosevelt had sent them a message that their father had slept away. He did his job to the end as he would have them do, she said.

"What can I do?" asked the new President.

"Tell us what we can do," Mrs. Roosevelt replied bravely. "Is there any way we can help you?"

Outside on the street, a quiet, unbelieving crowd gathered quickly. Confused and dazed, hundreds stood in Lafayette Park, across from the White House Square, far into the night.

Long since Mr. Truman had been sworn in by Chief Justice Stone in the cabinet room. Placing his hand on a red-edged Bible, the new President repeated the oath, reading from a small slip of paper.

He, his wife and their daughter, left from a rear entrance for their apartment home where they spent

(Continued on Page 16.)

NAZIS SHOCK EVEN JAPAN IN TIRADE AT MR. ROOSEVELT

Propagandists Gloat Over President's Death; "Great Man," Tokyo Admits

London (UP)—The Nazis burst the last bounds of decency today and continued a villification of President Roosevelt—even in death.

German propagandists gloated openly over the President's death. They poured out an abusive tirade that shocked the rest of the world even Japan.

While the Japanese joined with the Germans in accusing Mr Roosevelt of causing the present war, Tokyo conceded at least the President was a "great man."

But Berlin's commentators heaped abuse upon the President's memory.

One commentator, in a speech which apparently was written by Propaganda Minister Joseph Goebbels, said that the miracle which had saved Adolf Hitler had killed the "inventor of this war."

The commentator was Wilfred Vonofen, one of Berlin's best. But expert listeners said his remarks did not follow his usual tone and that they were termed much after the way Goebbels writes.

The broadcast was unusual in that Vonofen spoke in the first person. It broke all rules and it appeared obvious that Goebbels was directing the "hate" program against Roosevelt's name.

"It is for me, who believes in

(Continued on Page 16.)

Important Dates In Roosevelt's Career

Washington (AP)—Important dates in the career of Franklin D. Roosevelt

1882, Jan. 30—Born Hyde Park, N. Y., the son of James and Sara Delano Roosevelt.

1904—Graduated from Harvard.

1905 — Married Eleanor Anna Roosevelt.

1907—Admitted to New York State Bar

1910-13—Member of New York State Senate.

1913-20—Assistant Secretary of the Navy.

1920 — Unsuccessful Democratic nominee for vice president.

1921—Stricken with paralysis.

1928—Elected governor of New York

1930—Reelected governor.

1932—Elected President of the United States.

1936—Reelected President.

1940—Elected to unprecedented third term.

1941—Framed Atlantic Charter with Prime Minister Churchill.

1943—Enunciated "unconditional surrender" formula for Axis at Casablanca conference.

1943—Met at Tehran with Churchill and Stalin.

1944—Reelected to fourth term.

1945, Feb. 2-11—Met wth Stalin and Churchill.

1945—April 12—Died at Warm Springs, Ga.

The Index

SUFFERS HEAD INJURY.

Stanton Hussey, 5, 309 River Street, was treated at the Troy Hospital yesterday afternoon for a scalp laceration which, police reported, he received when struck by a stone. He was taken to the hospital in a police radio car by Sgt. Joseph Ormsby and Patrolman Edward S. Kirkpatrick. After being treated by Dr. Joseph Padalino the boy was returned to his home.

U.S. PLANNING TO MAKE SYNTHETIC GAS OUT OF COAL

Experiments Based on Investigation of Congress Committee

BY CHARLES G. HULL
United Press Staff Correspondent

St. Louis, Mo. (UP)—The U. S. Bureau of Mines has begun a survey of 105 areas in 39 coal-producing states to select two sites for experimental production of synthetic oil and gasoline from coal.

One possible location of such a research plant is reported to be in the St. Louis area, which embraces the Southern Illinois coal fields.

Motivating the bureau's investigation is the report of the nation's top oil men before a joint congressional committee that at the current or even peacetime rate of consumption the country's oil reserves will run out in 17 to 20 years.

Not only the fear of exhausting oil reserves, but also realization that other nations, especially Germany, were far ahead of the U. S. in developing liquid fuels from coal prompted a research program. England is said to produce one-fifth of her gasoline synthetically.

3,000 Years Supply.

Two Bureau of Mines engineers, Herschel M. Snead, of the bureau's office of synthetic fuels in Washington, and Joseph J. Curoe, Pittsburgh, Pa., recently surveyed potential plant sites in this district.

As a means of promoting greater employment, synthetic oil and gasoline production would mean much, Curoe said. He pointed out that all the miners in this country, and more, would be required to mine the coal needed if the nation were forced to depend entirely on synthetic liquid fuels.

United States coal reserves, the engineers explained, are practically inexhaustible — in contrast to dwindling oil. Experts estimate coal reserves at about 1,300 billion tons, enough to supply the nation for 3,000 years.

One experimental synthetic fuel plant now is being operated by the bureau, and another is building. That in operation, at Pittsburg, produces only ten gallons daily. Another going up at Bruceton, Pa., will turn out ten barrels a day.

Synthetic Cost High.

These are only experimental stations. Quantity production awaits private investment, now held up only by further necessary experimentation.

Presently, cost of producing synthetic oils and gasoline is thrice that of making gasoline from natural petroleum. The Bureau of Mines, however, believes that improved techniques will cut costs so the synthetic products can be made to sell within five cent a gallon of present rates.

Railroad facilities, electric power resources, proximity of coal fields yielding the proper type of coal, and adequate water supplies will determine location of the proposed new plants. Even a small plant, turning out only 200 barrels of synthetic fuels a day, must use 200,000 gallons of water daily for cooling purposes.

BUSKIRK.

Mr. and Mrs. John Beadle of Coila visited Mr. and Mrs. Harvey Bailey this week.

Peter Geelan, who has been ill for several weeks, is showing slight improvement.

Miss Mabel Lewis of Albany spent a few days this week with her mother Mrs. E. H. Roby.

Miss Corrine Eddy of Schenectady is spending the week with her parents, Mr. and Mrs. Guy Eddy.

Mr. and Mrs. Raymond O'Brien and family of Glens Falls visited Mr. and Mrs. Perry Kipp this week.

Mrs. Edward Goodrich has returned from Fayetteville where she was the guest of Mr. Foster Goodrich and family.

Mr. and Mrs. Francis Rogers and daughters, Ann and Barbara, visited Mr. and Mrs. William Spink, sr., this week at Schenectady.

Mrs. Alice Albergine and daughter, Roberta, have returned from Schenectady where they were guests of Mr. and Mrs. Maurice Amazon.

Mr. and Mrs. Kenneth Eldred and children, Kenneth Allen and Jean Marie, of Potter Hill, who visited Mr. and Mrs. Ralph Galloway, have returned.

KILLED—Sgt. James G. Chressanthis, son of Mr. and Mrs. George Chressanthis of 137 Fourth Street, was killed in action over England, according to War Department notification yesterday to his parents. The sergeant was reported missing in action March 17, according to word received April 5. His family believes that the flyer had been on a mission over Germany and that the bomber was unable to make the base in England on the return flight. Sergeant Chressanthis enlisted in August, 1943. He was a graduate of Troy High School and attended R. P. I. for one year, then was employed at the General Electric Co. at Schenectady. Two brothers are serving, Pfc. John Chressanthis with the field artillery and Pfc. Andrew in the Air Corps. A sister, Dorothy, also survives, and an uncle, James Triantafellou.

AMERICAN SOLDIER SAID TO HAVE BEST OF MEDICAL CARE

Maj. Lester Samuels, Army Medical Corps, Makes Observation

Camp Robinson, Ark (UP)—The American soldier goes into battle today with the assurance that, should he be wounded, he will be treated by the greatest medical machine the world has ever known—a machine which has kept alive 97 out of every 100 casualties reaching a forward hospital.

That is the observation of Maj. Lester Samuels, Army Medical Corps, now on the surgical staff of the regional hospital here, after service in the European theater.

The handsome, be-mustached native of England, came to the United States in 1927 as a lecturer of the British Empire Cancer Research Foundation, and remained here, becoming an American citizen. He returned to England during this war as a medical officer and accompanied Gen. George S. Patton's Third Army in the European invasion.

Unsurpassed by Any.

"From my observation as a soldier in the British Army during the last war, and an officer in American Army in this war, the Surgeon General of the United States Army has built up the greatest medical machine ever known," Major Samuels said. "No soldier in any army has a greater or more complete coverage of medical care than the United States soldier."

He said that in comparison, the difference between the medical service in World War I and World War II, notwithstanding all recent medical advances, is "unbelievable."

"The Surgeon General's methods in the movement of casualties from the battlelines to base hospitals have been so intricately worked out that not a moment is lost in caring for patients, even to complete operations," Samuels stated. "During no part of that journey—which is extremely rapid—is the patient without expert medical care."

The medical officer said that outstanding surgical achievements of this war—whereby 97 out of every 100 casualties reaching a forward hospital remain alive — are solely due to the "extreme care and sagacity shown in the medical department's preparations for evacuations."

Major Samuels said the Medical Corps should not receive all the credit for this achievement, and declared that a great share of the credit belongs to the Army nurses.

Outstanding Job.

"The greatest single item which struck me in my service overseas was the tremendous job done by the Army Nursing Corps," the major said. "These girls took all that came their way with a smile."

Major Samuels was first in the public limelight in January, 1944, when a presidential order recalled him while he was preparing to embark for overseas and sent him to the bedside of a young woman suffering from what threatened to be a fatal attack of hiccoughs.

The patient, Miss Anna Mayer, 21, New York City, had been hiccoughing at the rate of 120 per minute for 46 days. While practicing as a civilian two years before, Samuels had successfully cured the young woman of a similar attack and it was believed that he alone might be able to save her life.

The matter was brought to the attention of President Roosevelt, who ordered Major Samuels to Miss Mayer's bedside. The order halted the medical officer as he was proceeding on overseas orders.

Samuels found and removed a tumor on the patient's phrenic nerve, bringing about her complete recovery.

DEMONSTRATION STAGED.

Candling and grading of eggs were demonstrated recently by John Zweig recently at the Cackle and Crow 4-H Club of West Sand Lake. Eugene Rescott discussed the classes and breeds of poultry. The proper methods of handling chickens were shown by Walter Wehanau. Donald Stiles was accepted as a new member.

MAIL GROUP WILL MAKE LAP ROBES FOR MEN IN WAR VETERAN HOSPITALS

Lap robes for veterans at general hospitals throughout the state will be made by members of the Railway Mail Association, it was decided at last night's meeting at the Y. W. C. A., after the kind letter of acknowledgment for their afghan was received from Rhoads General Hospital in Utica.

Edward Wells of Troy reported on the recent minstrel show presented at Diamond Rock Hall and thanked the committee for their cooperation. Mrs. Richard Cassin presided in the absence of the president.

The report of the progress of the postal registration in Washington, D. C., was read by Mrs. H. E. Burton. The next meeting will be held May 16 at the home of Mrs. James Kieselbach on Cardinal Road in Albany.

After the business session games were played and winners were Mrs. Cassin, Mrs. E. P. Gero and Mrs. Reuben Graves.

WYNANTSKILL

Townsend Club No. 1 met Tuesday evening at the school with Rev. Leslie Moody, president, presiding. The meeting opened with the singing of "America" and salute to the Flag, followed by invocation. Mr. Moody spoke of the National Council and the work it is doing.

A meeting of the Ladies Auxiliary was announced by Mrs. Nellie Windover, president. The program will be for the benefit of the Ladies Auxiliary.

WORKMAN BURNED.

John Saekley, Grangerville, suffered burns on both legs when he fell into a heating machine at the United Paper Board mill at Thomson yesterday. Dr. M. D. Duby is attending him at his home.

Troy, Monday evening, May 7. The Men's Council meets at the home of Mr. and Mrs. George Wagner of Lansingburg, May 1. An entertainment will be presented at Firemen's Hall, May 15. Prof. Edwin Walsh and his pupils. Refreshments will be served. The program will be for the benefit of the Ladies Auxiliary.

THE WEATHER
Tonight—Cloudy, warmer.

THE TIMES RECORD

FINAL EDITION

SERIES 1945—NO. 108 (Entered as Second Class Matter at the Postoffice at Troy, N. Y., Under the Act of March 3, 1879.) TROY, N. Y., MONDAY EVENING, MAY 7, 1945. (Published Daily Except Sunday) PRICE FOUR CENTS

GERMANY QUITS

GERMAN PEOPLE FORMALLY TOLD OF NAZI SURRENDER

Reich Overwhelmed by Enemies After Six Years, Von Krosigk Says

London (UP)—All remaining German forces have surrendered, a German broadcast said today, and an official Allied proclamation of the end of the war in Europe was expected at 6 p.m. (12 noon E. W. T.)

A speaker identified as German Foreign Minister Count Ludwig Schwerin Von Krosigk announced over the Flensburg radio at 2:09 p.m. (8:09 a.m. E. W. T.) that the high command of the German armed forces had surrendered unconditionally all "fighting German troops" today.

The order for surrender was given by Fuehrer Grand Admr. Karl Doenitz, the broadcast said. It came on the 2,074th day of the European war.

Text of Announcement.

The text of Von Krosigk's announcement to the German people follows:

German men and women: The high command of the armed forces on orders of Grand Admiral Doenitz has today declared the unconditional surrender of all German fighting troops.

As leading minister of the Reich government which the admiral of the fleet has appointed for dealing with war tasks, I turn at this tragic moment of our history to the German nation.

After a heroic fight of almost six years of incomparable hardness, Germany has succumbed to the overwhelming power of her enemies.

To continue the war would only mean senseless bloodshed and futile disintegration.

The government which has a feeling of responsibility for the future of its nation was compelled to act on the collapse of all physical and material forces, and to demand of the enemy the cessation of hostilities.

Gave Maximum Lives.

It was the noblest task of the admiral of the fleet and of the government supporting him after the terrible sacrifices which the war demanded to save in the last phase of the war the lives of a maximum number of fellow countrymen.

That the war was not ended simultaneously in the west and in the east is to be explained by this reason alone. We end this gravest hour of the German nation and its Reich.

In this gravest hour of the German nation and its Reich we bow deep in reverence before the dead of this war. Their sacrifices place the highest obligations on us.

"We Must Face Our Fate."

It goes out above all to the wounded and bereaved and to all on whom this struggle has inflicted blows. No one must be under any illusions about the severity of terms to be imposed on the

(Continued on Page 18.)

HIGH COURT BACKS MINERS' PAY PLEA

Workers Ruled Entitled to Portal-to-Portal Wage

Washington (AP)—The Supreme Court ruled today that bituminous coal miners are entitled to portal-to-portal underground wages.

Justice Murphy delivered the court's 5-4 decision. Justice Jackson wrote a dissent in which Roberts and Frankfurter concurred.

The court on March 27, 1944 ruled that iron ore miners must be paid portal-to-portal wages—that is pay for the time spent traveling from the mine opening to the actual working place and back again.

Today's decision was given on an appeal by the Jewell Ridge Coal Corp., employer of 900 men in two mines in southwest Virginia. The concern protested a decision by the fourth federal circuit court that such travel time is time worked for which pay is required under the federal wage-hour law.

The bituminous industry has been operating on a portal-to-portal pay basis under a 1943 war-time agreement.

Justice Murphy said the majority agreed with the fourth federal circuit court that there was no substantial factual or legal difference between the case involving the bituminous coal miners and that involving the iron ore miners.

The Index

Surrender News Received Quietly By Troy People

YANKS, RUSSIANS MOPPING UP LAST RESISTING NAZIS

General Patton's Tanks Reported Only 15 Miles from Embattled Prague

Paris (AP) — American and Russian Armies beat through Czechoslovakia and Austria today in the final mopup of organized German resistance and embattled patriots in Prague said U. S. Third Army tanks were only 15 miles from that city, largest still in German hands.

General Patton threw nearly a quarter million Third Army troops into the closing campaign. In advances of up to 25 miles, his tanks and infantry advanced within fifty miles southwest and 52 miles south of the Czech capital.

The German-controlled Prague radio said Marshal Ivan S. Konev's First Ukrainian Army Group had driven into Bohemia from Saxony to a point about sixty or 65 miles north of Prague. Patriots engaged German Seventh Army troops in the capital, which the Germans declared "a hospital city" last week.

In Germany itself, only three cities remained under the swastika. These were encircled Breslau and the Saxony cities of Dresden and Chemnitz, both ripe for capture.

Alpine Groups Surrender.

Two more German Alpine groups not previously surrendered to the Sixth Army Group in the south, capitulated effective at 10 p.m. tonight. One was a corps commanded by General Von Henkle. The other was a division commanded by Colonel Buchner. Both commanders said they had just heard of the surrender in the South, so chaotic were German communications. The number of troops was not announced.

The Seventh and Fifth Armies made another contact in an Alpine pass 25 miles south of Landeck, the 44th and Tenth Mountain Divisions effecting the tie.

Two Russian Army Groups were pressing in from the east, fighting into the outskirts of the big rail junction of Olmuetz and the Hohenstadt region, 128 and 115 miles from Prague—largest city still in German hands.

The Fifth Army from Italy fought into southern Austria for the kill.

The German Seventh Army, believed commanded by Field Marshal Albert Kesselring, was the only really organized enemy force still fighting although a few hundred thousands of Germans still were unsurrendered in various scattered pockets in Europe.

Nearly 4,000,000 Prisoners.

Supreme headquarters noted that 398,630 Germans surrendered Saturday for a three-day total of 987,573 and an aggregate since D-Day of 3,874,771 for General Eisenhower's armies of the West.

With the great munitions and beer center of Pilsen captured, and Karlsbad behind Third Army lines, Patton's famous break-through (Fourth Armored) Division in twin stabs drove 25 miles to the northeast reaching Brez, fifty miles southwest of Prague, and Borochowitz, 52 miles south of the capital.

Brig. Gen. William M. Hoge's Division returned to action after a long layoff and encountered little or no resistance. Its drive carried through sectors held by the Red

(Continued on Page 18.)

WOMAN STAR PLUNGES TO DEATH AT CIRCUS IN NEW YORK GARDEN

New York (INS)—Another circus tragedy was recorded on police blotters today in the death of Victoria Torrance, 30, one of the featured aerial performers of Ringling Brothers and Barnum and Bailey Circus.

Mrs. Torrance fell 60 feet to her death last night before 10,000 spectators.

She and her husband, childhood sweethearts, were completing their act above the center ring and had started to descend. The finale of the act called for her to stretch out horizontally and lock her legs around her husband's right foot. He then lowered both himself and his wife to the tanbark by means of a rope.

It was considered one of the most dramatic and graceful conclusions in the circus.

Suddenly Victoria's grasp on her husband loosened and she fell face down to her death.

WAVES RECRUITING AGAIN.

New York (AP)—WAVE recruiting has been re-opened by the Navy, the Third Naval District announced today. About 2,000 WAVES a month will be sought for the rest of the year for general service and special duties with the Hospital

Business Proceeds as Usual with City Very Calm: Many Phone Calls

The middleaged man in the street stared at the "surrender bulletin" in the newspaper office window and whistled, softly, a few bars of "Over There."

The veteran of Pacific combat, the left hand pocket of his tunic covered with ribbons, said, "Wait until they announce the surrender of Japan. Then we'll celebrate."

The mother, on duty at the USO whose son had just called her from a far distant airfield, said, "I can't celebrate until he is right here where I can get my arms around him and know he is safe."

In that way were the hints that VE-Day may be just around the corner, received in Troy this morning.

Those who had feared there might be wild rejoicing, like that on Armistice Day in World War I, were encouraged by the calm acceptance of the early reports and the fact that the general public went about business as usual this morning.

Prayers of Gratitude.

A clergyman said, "I feel like ringing my church bell with all my might because we have made such great strides ahead in this war. No one can be blamed for feeling that way and yet I know that the war will not be over until we get every last boy home. This is a time for rejoicing through prayers of gratitude."

There were places in Troy where rumors of surrender brought noticeable excitement. At the Blood Bank in the First Baptist Church donors suddenly crowded in about 11 a.m. and the line stretched to the sidewalk. Bulletins on the situation were given by the Red Cross to those donating blood and there was a feeling of excitement among the group, most of whom had sons, husbands or brothers overseas. There were others, still in mourning for someone killed in action, who chose the day as most appropriate for the giving of blood.

The New York Telephone Co. office in Troy suddenly went crazy. Within a few minutes after the first rumors of surrender, telephone calls jumped 56 per cent above normal as families called sons in service, men at Navy bases and Army camps all over the country called their families here, and neighbor called neighbor to spread the good news.

Worked Like Beavers.

Telephone operators worked like beavers as calls jammed the wires. Later in the day Harvey Hoffsis, manager of the Troy office, said that the telephone company urged the public to cooperate by confining calls only to those absolutely necessary and by making the necessary calls brief. "Only in this way," Mr. Hoffsis said, " can we maintain normal service."

In the hospitals of the city, the early reports brought rejoicing from convalescent patients who were kept informed of the situation.

Watervliet Arsenal, where thousands are employed, was considered a good indication of how war workers felt this morning. Men and women stayed quietly at their machines and waited—and waited—for news. They showed no inclination to start the kind of celebration the government has urged against. "All of us are waiting for word from our Commander-in-Chief," officers at the gun plant said. "When that comes we hope for a thankful but thoughtful few minutes after which we will get on with the war in the Pacific."

FIVE LIVES LOST IN PROVIDENCE BLAZE

Mother and Two Children Among Victims

Providence, R. I. (INS)—Five persons, including a mother and two small children, were killed today when fire of mysterious origin swept a combination business and tenement block at Almy and Tell Streets.

Dead from suffocation: Mrs. Anna Cerbo, 27; her two sons, Joseph, 7, and Emelio, 2, and her brother, John Iacono, jr., 15. Burned to death: John Iacono, sr., 55, father of Mrs. Cerbo.

Camelio Cerbo, 30, husband of the dead woman, was removed to Rhode Island Hospital suffering from slight burns and smoke inhalation.

Mrs. Maria Annarino, 52, second floor tenant, jumped 15 feet to the ground. She suffered only slight bruises on her arm.

All the dead were trapped in their apartments on the third floor.

According to police, the fire started in a market on the ground floor. Flames swept to the roof trapping cutting off all exits and the Cerbo family. Damage was estimated at several thousand dollars.

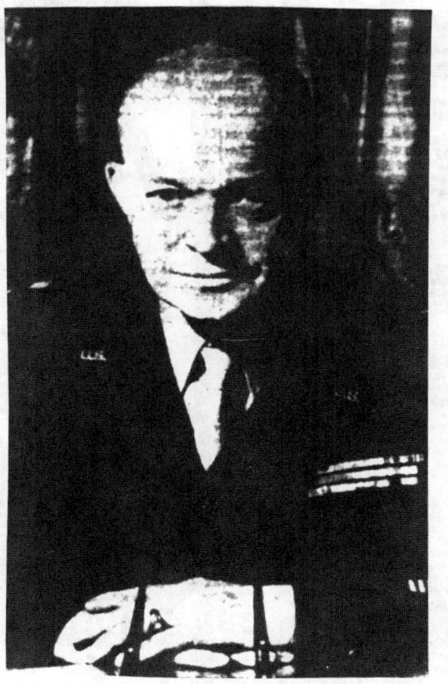

LED ALLIES TO VICTORY: The unswerving purpose that led the Allied powers to victory over the Axis nations in Europe is evident in this latest photo of General of the Armies Dwight D. Eisenhower.

The Day Dawns.

Five and a half years ago the sun went down on civilziation. Since that time the world has been making its way through darkness that could be felt. Human fiends have found themselves unhindered and have filled their hours with the most horrible sadistic crimes. Hitler and his men feared neither God nor men. Having created a powerful instrument of destruction, they felt themselves compelled to use it.

The first year or two of the conflict proved in many ways the most terrible of all time. Then time began to work in our favor. Decency gained the ascendancy in many quarters. The nations that had not sold themselves to the devil organized to resist this greatest of all attacks upon a peaceful world.

Since then, first with wavering footsteps but lately with firm tread, mankind has been marching toward the dawn. The end in Europe has come dramatically, the result of a sharp spring campaign from the East, the West, and the South. It was too much for the tired hosts of Hell. Everywhere they fell back, first slowly giving ground, later running like a pack of hunted wolves. Today they have finished their battle of destruction; they themselves have been destroyed.

And so the dark night comes to its end and the first bold rays of light streak the sky. The sun is up. The trained murderers of Germany have been driven back to their own dens; and they will be kept there. Those who have led them through this evil highway will meet their deserved fate; and, unless the victorious nations are governed by fools, the rest of Germany will be bound by such engagements as will make a repetition of this warfare impossible.

There is much to be done. Victory in Europe means more than the laying down of arms. It means assurance that the arms will never be taken up again. It implies the end of a terrible era, an era that has wearied its leaders beyond recovery. It calls for the concentrated effort of our young, unspoiled idealists to make a peace there which shall be more than a repetition of ancient words. We need a new spirit, an intent toward understanding and a curb on all the powers of darkness that might in combination again attempt to destroy the world.

Today we breathe the clear air of another morning. The sun has arisen and we must be at work again. That work must this time be the sort that persists, the creation of a world at peace, the arrival of maturity to mankind. It must end in a peace which shall encircle the world.

Hitler's Retreat Totally Wrecked

Berchtesgaden (AP)—Hitler's favorite retreat, Haus Wachenfeld on his Berghof estate at Oberslazberg eight miles from Berchtesgaden, is symbolic today of the Fuehrer's entire work—it is totally wrecked.

Allied bombers a fortnight ago blasted buildings all around it but, according to natives, did not hit Hitler's chalet itself. They said SS guards set fire to the chalet rather than have it fall into Allied hands.

At any rate gone is the celebrated 30 by 20 foot window of the huge parlor from which Hitler used to look across the deep valley at Bavaria's most famous mountain, the Watzmann.

Gone is the spacious dining room in which he entertained European bigwigs. Gone are the reception halls and private apartments for visiting friends.

Gone also are those costly paintings and sculptures which made Haus Wachenfeld a veritable art museum.

The art objects as well as quantities of food, materials and possibly doucments, may be hidden somewhere in the mountain recesses behind Hitler's estate.

Frau Therese Aaschauer Scheffau, a native of the nearby village of Schellenburg, says she saw hundreds of trucks rolling in the direction of Oberslazberg carrying supplies of all kinds.

Two days before the American seizure of Berchtesgaden last Thursday, she said; Nazi SS (Elite Guard) troops blew up and set fire to Haus Wachenfeld and sealed with thick stones many caches in the mountains which, on opening, may yield surprises.

"Nobody believes Hitler is dead," Frau Scheffau added. "We all believe that some day he'll try to reappear. Destruction of his home is God's just punishment for Hitler's misdeeds."

Hitler, she said, had not been in Berchtesgaden since the attempt on his life on July 20, 1944. Marshal Goering, she added, was a frequent visitor in this region until quite recently, while Himmler and Goebbels seldom were seen here even in Hitler's heyday.

Greatest War In History Ends With Unconditional Surrender Of Nazi Armies

Once Mighty Wehrmacht Of Adolf Hitler Gives Up Ghost In Dramatic Ceremony At General Eisenhower's Headquarters In Rheims, France; Official Announcements Of V-E Day Delayed Pending Simultaneous Action In Washington, London And Moscow; News Causes Rejoicing In Allied World; A. P. Correspondent Pictures Finale In Great Conflict As Germans Signed Capituation In Allied Headquarters At Rheims.

London (AP)—The war against Germany, the greatest in history, ended today with the unconditional surrender of the once mighty wehrmacht.

The surrender to the Western Allies and Russia was made at General Eisenhower's headquarters at Rheims, France, but official announcement by the Big Three was held up, pending simultaneous action by Washington, Moscow and London.

The British Ministry of Information announced this afternoon that tomorrow will be treated as V-E Day.

The ministry said officially that, "in accordance with arrangements between the three great powers, the prime minister will make an official announcement at 3 p.m., British Double Summer Time, (9 a.m., Eastern War Time), tomorrow, the 8th of May."

The annonucement said that the prime minister "will broadcast at 3 p.m. and his majesty, the King, will broadcast to the peoples of the British empire and the commonwealth tomorrow at 9 p.m., British Double Summer Time (3 p.m., E. W. T.)"

"In view of this fact," the announcement said, "tomorrow will be a public holiday and the day after, Wednesday, will also be regarded as a holiday."

President Truman said today he had agreed with the London and Moscow governments that he would make no announcement on the surrender of enemy forces "until a simultaneous announcement can be made by the three governments."

"I'm on my knees. What else can any good American say at this moment." That was the comment of Mrs. George S. Patton, wife of General Patton, when informed at Hamilton, Mass., this morning that Germany had surrendered."

News of the surrender came in an Associated Press dispatch from Rheims, at 9:35 a.m., Eastern War Time, and immediately set the church bells tolling in Rome and elsewhere.

In the hour before the news from Rheims, German broadcasts told the German people that Grand Admiral Karl Doenitz had ordered capitulation of all fighting forces, and called off U-boat warfare.

Joy at the news was tempered only by the realization that the war against Japan remains to be resolved, with many casualties still ahead.

The end of the European warfare, greatest, bloodiest and costliest war in human history—it has claimed at least 40,000,000 casualties on both sides in killed, wounded and captured—came after five years, eight months and six days of strife that overspread the glode.

Hitler's arrogant armies invaded Poland on Sept. 1, 1939, beginning the agony that convulsed the world for 2,319 days.

Unconditional surrender of the beaten remnants of his legions first was announced by the Germans.

Then the new German foreign minister, Ludwig Schwerin Von Krosigk, announced to the German people, shortly after 2 p.m. (8 a.m., Eastern War Time), that "after almost six years' struggle we have succumbed."

Von Krosigk announced Grand Admiral Karl Doenitz had "ordered the unconditional surrender of all fighting German troops."

Surrender In Schoolhouse.

The world waited tensely. Then at 9:35 a.m., E. W. T., came an Associated Press flash from Reims, France, telling of the signing at General Eisenhower's headquarters of the unconditional surrender at 2:41 a.m., French Time (8:41 a.m., E. W. T.) Germany had given up to the western Allies and to Russia.

The surrender took place at a little red schoolhouse which is the headquarters of General Eisenhower.

The surrender which brought the war in Europe to a formal end after five years, eight months and six days of bloodshed and destruction was signed for Germany by Col. Gen. Gustav Jodl. Jodl is the new chief of staff of the German army.

It was also signed by Gen. Ivan Susloparoff for Russia and by Gen. Francois Sevez for France.

General Eisenhower was not present at the signing, but immediately afterward Jodl and his fellow delegate, Gen. Admr. Hans Georg Friedeburg, were received by the supreme commander.

They were asked sternly if they understood the surrender terms imposed upon Germany and if they would be carried out by Germany.

They answered yes.

Germany, which began the war with a ruthless attack upon Poland followed by successive aggressions and brutality in internment camps, surrendered with an appeal to the victors for mercy toward the German people and armed forces.

After signing the full surrender, Jodl said he wanted to speak and was given leave to do so.

"With this signature," he said in soft-spoken German, "the German people and armed forces are for better or worse delivered into the victors' hands."

"In this war which has lasted more than five years both have achieved and suffered more than perhaps any other people in the world."

Sour Note From Prague.

London went wild at the news. Crowds jammed Piccadilly Circus. Smiling throngs poured out of subways and lined the streets.

A sour note came from the German-controlled radio at Prague. A broadcast monitored by the Czechoslovak government office in London said the German commander in Czechoslovakia did not recognize the surrender of Admiral Doenitz and would fight on until his forces "have secured free passage for German troops out of the country." But the Prague radio earlier announced the capitulation of Breslau, long besieged by Russian forces.

An announcement on the wavelength of the Flensburg radio, which has been carrying German communiques and orders for several days, said:

"German men and women! The high command of the armed forces has today, at the order of Grand Admiral Doenitz, declared the unconditional surrender of all fighting German troops."

The announcement was attributed to the new German foreign minister, Count Schwerin Von Krosigk.

U-boats Recalled.

Shortly after the broadcast attributed to Von Krosigk, the German communique was broadcast on the Flensburg wavelength.

This said "bitter fighting continues" in the area of Olmuetz in Moravia where the Germans have been opposing the Russians. This communique usually has related the events of the previous day.

An order of the day attributed to Doenitz ordered German U-boats to cease fire.

Delay V-E Day Announcement.

E. P. Stackpole, Press Association correspondent in the London Parliament lobbies, wrote today that "although the war

(Continued on Page 2)

DOENITZ ORDERS GERMAN SUBS TO END HOSTILITIES

Fuehrer's Edict Terminates Nearly Six Years of Destructive Sea Warfare

London (UP) — Fuehrer Grand Admr. Karl Doenitz today ordered Germany's U-boat fleet, most potent weapon left the shattered Reich, to cease hostilities and return to port.

The order, revealed by the German-controlled Flensburg radio, said continuation of submarine warfare was impossible from the bases that remained in German hands in Norway and France.

Vast Tonnage Sunk.

Doenitz' action ended nearly six years of what probably was the most destructive sea offensive ever waged.

Exact Allied tonnage sunk by U-boats has not yet been revealed but it probably was in eight figures. Victims ranged from tramp freighters to the British Royal Oak.

Many ships were sent to the bottom within sight of the east coast of the United States, but an intensified air and sea patrol finally drove the raiders back to mid-Atlantic.

The offensive reached its first peak just before the Allied invasion of North Africa and its second in the months preceding the Allied landing in Normandy.

A brief resurgence followed last winter with the introduction of a "floating lung" that enabled the U-boats to re-charge their batteries beneath the surface.

Ruthless Sea War.

Radio Flensburg said Doenitz order was dated last Friday. Doenitz, first as a submarine commander and later as commander in chief of the German navy, was the master-mind behind the U-boat campaign. He sent his crews out with orders to "kill! kill! kill!"

In an order of the day to U-boat crews, Radio Flensburg said, Doenitz told his men that they had "fought like lions."

"Crushing superiority has compressed us into a very narrow area," he said. "Continuation of the struggle is impossible from the base that remain.

"U-boat men, unbroken in your warlike courage, you are laying down your arms after a heroic fight that knows no equal. In reverent memory, we think of our comrades who have sealed their loyalty to the Fuehrer and the fatherland with their death.

"Comrades, maintain in the future your U-boat spirit with which you have fought at sea bravely and unflinchingly during long years for the welfare of our fatherland. Long live German

EGGS FORM BASIS FOR TWO DISHES DESCRIBED BELOW

Use While in Abundance to Replace Meat Due to Shortage

Eggs are plentiful and can take the place of meat in the menu. Here's a delicious main dish using eggs:

Curried Mushrooms and Eggs
(Serves 4-6)

Four tablespoons butter or fortified margarine, ¼ pound mushrooms, peeled and sliced, 2 tablespoons finely chopped onion, 2-3 cup diced celery, 1-3 cup diced green pepper, ½ teaspoon curry powder, 3 tablespoons flour, 1 teaspoon salt, 2 cups hot milk, 5 hard-cooked eggs, ¼ cup grated cheese 12 butter crackers, parsley.

Melt the butter; add sliced mushrooms, chopped onion, diced celery and diced green pepper. Cook slowly until the vegetables are almost tender. Mix curry powder, flour and salt together; then add to the vegetables and stir until all the ingredients are well blended. Add the hot milk slowly to the vegetable mixture, stirring constantly until thickened. Add the hard-cooked eggs, which have been cut into quarters, to the other ingredients. Pour into a well-greased round heat-resistant glass cake dish. Sprinkle grated cheese over the top of the curried mushrooms and eggs and place the butter crackers on top of the cheese. Bake in a moderate oven (350 degrees Fahrenheit) about 20 minutes. Garnish with parsley and serve with a crisp green salad.

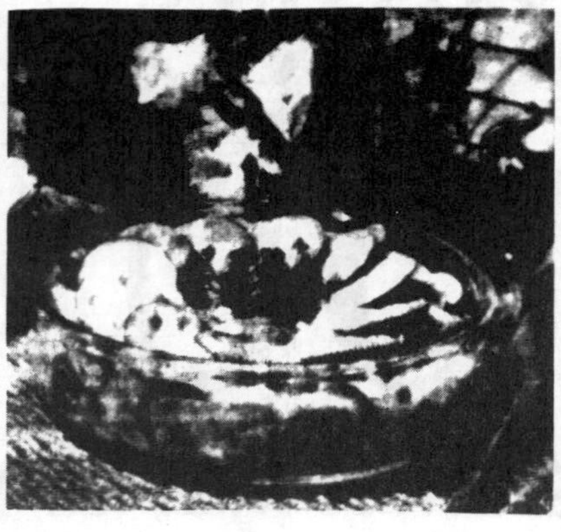

SPICY DISH: Curried eggs and mushrooms for main dish.

For a luncheon salad, try this recipe from Lily Haxworth Wallace's valuable new book "Egg Cookery."

Luncheon Egg Salad Bowl.

One-half cup shredded cooked ham or tongue; ½ cup diced celery, 1 cup orange or grapefruit sections, 3 hard-cooked eggs, salt and pepper, French dressing, radishes.

Combine ham, celery, salad greens (lettuce, romaine, watercress, heart leaves of spinach, chicory), orange or grapefruit sections and eggs, sliced or cut into eighths. Season, moisten with French dressing and arrange in a salad bowl, garnishing with thinly sliced crisp radishes.

VALUABLE HINTS FOR HOME CANNERS GIVEN IN ARTICLE BELOW

If you are wise and have access to fresh vegetables, better begin making definite plans for canning as much food as you can find room for this summer and fall. From present indications, there will be a shortage of many foods next year—that is next winter, so plan your Victory Garden to grow those foods your family likes. Remember that all vegetables except tomatoes, require processing in a steam pressure canner. Here are some hints that may save you many headaches later on!

1. Don't plan to can vegetables unless you can do so in a steam pressure canner.
2. Sort over empty glass jars now, discard any with nicked edges or cracks, and decide how many new ones you will need.
3. Be sure each jar has the right kind of a cap or closure. New ones will probably have to be bought, as well as new rubber rings.
4. Remember that for best results, food must be fresh, and young enough to be tender.
5. Don't waste time and jars canning foods your family does not like.
6. If you do not know much about canning, find out if there is a canning school or class in your neighborhood and plan to attend it.

Baked Fillet of Perch in Tomato Sauce.

In
1 tablespoon bacon drippings
Brown
2 tablespoons chopped onion.
Combine—
1 11-ounce can condensed cream of tomato soup, undiluted.
¼ cup lemon juice
2 tablespoons Worcestershire sauce
2 tablespoons brown sugar
¼ teaspoon salt
⅛ teaspoon pepper
In a shallow baking pan place—
6 fillets of perch (approximately 1¼ pounds.

Pour tomato sauce over the fillets, lifting each to allow sauce to flow underneath. Bake in a hot oven (425 degrees Fahrenheit) for 35 minutes. Serves 4.

Tomato Fish Sauce.

Combine, then simmer for 20 minutes, stirring occasionally—
1 11-ounce can condensed cream of tomato soup, undiluted
1 small onion, peeled
1 clove garlic, peeled
1½ tablespoons sugar
¼ cup cider vinegar
⅛ teaspoon ground cloves
¼ teaspoon allspice
¼ teaspoon cinnamon
¼ teaspoon prepared yellow mustard
⅛ teaspoon black pepper.

Run through fine sieve. Serve over fried fish. Yiels ¾ cup sauce.

GINGERBREAD

2¼ cups flour
⅓ teaspoon salt
1 teaspoon soda
1 teaspoon baking powder
1 teaspoon cinnamon
½ teaspoon ginger
⅛ teaspoon allspice
⅓ cup shortening
⅓ cup brown sugar
1 cup honey
1 egg
1 cup milk

Mix and sift dry ingredients Cream shortening. Add sugar and honey and beat well. Add and beat again. Add dry ingredients and milk alternately. Bake in well-greased pan at 350 degrees Fahrenheit about forty minutes. Cut in squares to serve.

LIME SOUFFLE.

4 egg yolks
2 tablespoons lime juice
Grated rind of 1 lime
¼ teaspoon salt
1 cup sugar.
4 egg whites

Beat egg yolks until thick. Add sugar slowly, beating constantly. Add lime juice and rind and salt. Beat egg whites until thick and cut into rest of mixture. Pile in buttered baking dish, set in a pan of hot water and bake 45 minutes at 350 degrees. Serve at once with

Rum Foamy Sauce.

3 egg yolks
¼ cup powdered sugar
3 egg whites
Pinch of salt
2 ounces rum

Beat yolks till thick and lemon colored. Stir in sugar and salt. Add rum. Stir in stiffly-beaten egg whites.

Fish Assumes Added Importance In Diet

With meat and poultry waning on civilian tables, fish assumes new importance in our meals. And if fish is going to be your steady eating for the year, you'd better give it a good build-up with the family. Fish can easily become a favorite if you present it well. What other food affords such variety . . . where can you find more subtle flavors . . . what textures so gratify the tongue . . . what dishes make such pleasing pictures on the table?

Be market-wise about the fish in your locality. Don't just stick to mackerel, halibut, and cod fish cakes. There are hundreds more fish in the sea than ever make most of our tables. In selecting fish, keep in mind the following facts. A fresh fish has firm flesh that leaves no pressure mask when touched. The eyes are bright, clear, and bulging; the gills should be moist, and red. Never buy a fish with dull scales that have dried. And be sure the flesh does not pull away too easily from the back bone. A fresh fish is practically odorless; it should smack only of a clear ocean breeze.

The best shopping practice is to buy for immediate use. Even so, it's likely your fish will spend a few hours in the refrigerator before cooking. So wrap it loosely and place in, or just below, the freezing compartment. If you are using an ice refrigerator, do the fish up lightly and place it right on the block of ice.

Praises Fish.

Nutritionally, fish is realy a bonanza. The editor of the "Journal of the American Medical Association," Dr. Morris Fishbein, gives fish plaudits when he says, "The proteins provided by the flesh of the fish include all those that are found to be necessary for growth and health in the human body." Put that is not fishes' whole service record. Fish oils are rich in vitamin D, and fish liver is an excellent source of vitamin A. The minerals of fish are similar to those of meat, even better in some cases; for fish supplies iodine, a mineral greatly needed by the body and present in few other foods. All of which add up to strong reasons why you should make fish popular with your people.

When it comes to cooking fish, use plenty of imagination. If your previous fish cookery has been confined to the frying pan, branch out. Try boiling, baking, steaming, broiling, stuffing. Add above all, use seasonings and sauces. You'll find the perfect fish sauce is made these days from soup. Yes, soup! The condensed kind that comes done up in cans condensed cream of tomato soup.

This tomato soup is thick, almost like a pure puree. But it is richer from the cream that was added in the making, and more pungent from the precious spice infusion. This sauce is easy to make, too, because condensed soup gives you a prepared base so that little else needs adding. Here it is with perch fillets, but you'll find it equally delicious with any fish that's suitable for baking.

BAKED BEEF HEART.

1 beef heart
1 cup dry bread crumbs
1 cup soft bread crumbs
¼ cup margarine
⅛ cup boiling water
Salt and pepper
1 teaspoon poultry stuffing
2 cups stock, or 2 bouillon cubes in 2 cups boiling water

Soak beef heart in cold water one hour. Dry, cut away muscle. Make stuffing by melting margarine in boiling water. Pour over mixed crumbs and add seasonings. Fill heart with crumb mixture and tie with string. Place in casserole and pour over two cups of stock. Cover tightly and bake in moderate oven until tender or approximately three hours.

LIFE SUIT SUBSTITUTES.

Japanese occupation of the Dutch East Indies cut off the only source of supply of kapok, from which life-saving suits are made. To make up for this loss of supply 4-H Club members in 1944 collected 600 carloads of milkweed floss, kapok substitute, enough to make a million suits.

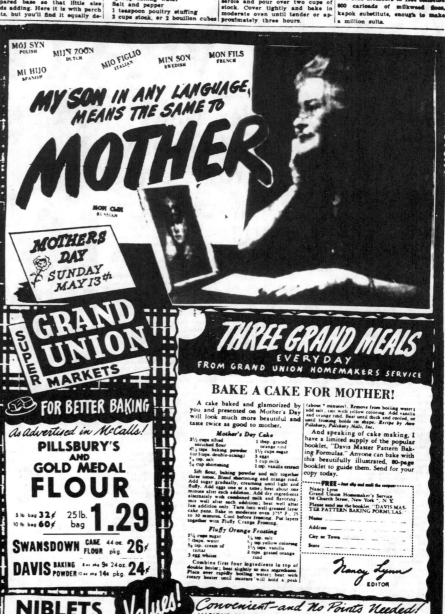

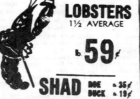

Jane H. Gillespie Bride of Sgt. R. W. Keeler

Miss Jane H. Gillespie, daughter of Mr. and Mrs. John C. Gillespie of 26 Winter Street, and Tech. Sgt. Richard W. Keeler, U. S. A., son of Farnam J. Keeler of 65 Brunswick Avenue, were married Saturday at the Woodside Presbyterian Church. Rev. Robert G. Mallery performed the ceremony.

Miss Mary Lee played the organ and sang "I Love You Truly" and "Because." The church was decorated with palms.

The matron of honor was Mrs. Donald F. Miller. William E. Gillespie, brother of the bride, was best man.

The bride's gown was of white chiffon designed with a fitted bodice and full skirt, three-quarter length sleeves and high neckline formed by a yoke of chiffon. She wore a bridal cap fashioned with clusters of white flowers at the sides, from which fell her shoulder veil of bridal illusion. She carried a colonial bouquet of white roses and sweet peas.

The matron of honor wore a similar gown in wing blue chiffon. She had a blue flowered tiara and carried a bouquet of pale, pink carnations.

A reception was held at the home of the bride for sixty persons.

The bride's mother wore a blue print dress with white accessories and a corsage of pink roses. The bridegroom's stepmother, Mrs. Farnam J. Keeler wore a grey ensemble with white accessories and a corsage of pink roses.

Mrs. Keeler is a graduate of Troy High School and is employed by the Berh-Manning Corp. The bridegroom is a graduate of Troy High School and just returned from three year's service in the European theater of war. He was awarded the Bronze Star.

The couple left on a trip to the coast of Maine. For traveling the bride wore a knit suit with matching accessories and an orchid corsage.

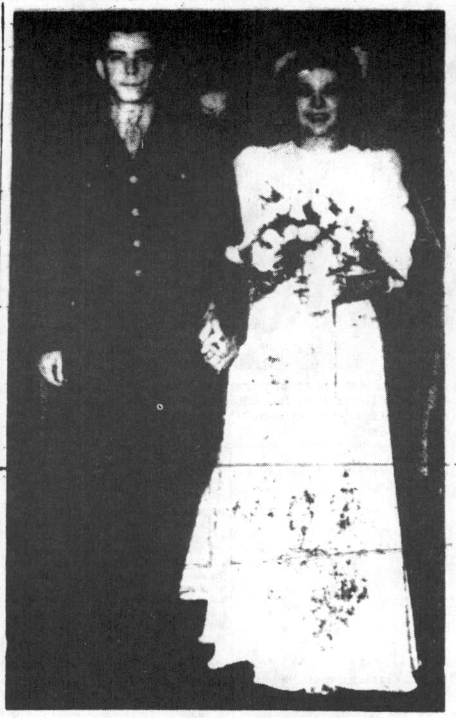

TECH. SGT. AND MRS. RICHARD W. KEELER

To Teach in Fall

Mrs. Marcia Schultz Pierce graduated June 4 from Houghton College and is spending the summer recess with her parents, Mr. and Mrs. Otto Schultz of Niskayuna, who attended the commencement exercises.

Mrs. Pierce will teach French and English at the Downsville Central School in the fall.

Birthday Party

Mr. and Mrs. Ernest Hall, R. D. 1, Troy, gave a birthday party Saturday evening in honor of James Quackenbush. Three tables of pinochle were in play with awards going to the honor guest, Mrs. Roland Shoemaker and Mr. and Mrs. Charles Brunelle.

Kansas Girl To Marry Lt. G. A. Oldham, jr.

Mr. and Mrs. Henry Slover Pegues of Hutchinson, Kan., have announced the engagement of their daughter, Miss Harriet Lee Pegues to Lt. George Ashton Oldham, jr., Naval Air Arm, son of Rt. Rev. G. Ashton Oldham, Bishop of the Episcopal Diocese of Albany, and Mrs. Oldham.

Miss Pegues is studying at Carelton College, Northfield, Minn. Her fiance is a graduate of Kent School and of Williams College. He is stationed in Hutchinson after serving for two years in the Pacific. The wedding will take place after Lieutenant Oldham serves another tour of duty in the Pacific.

Record Pattern

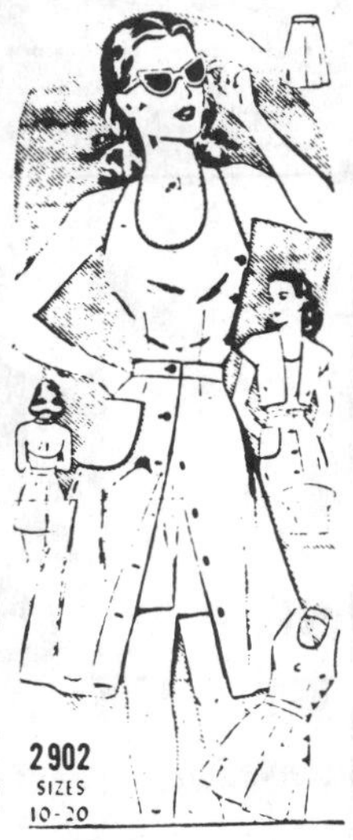

HALTER-NECK PLAY OUTFIT.

Wonderful complete, this outfit of play clothes with the air of smart simplicity. Halter-neck playsuit, skirt and bolero, all in one pattern. A not for a little sewing.

No 2902 is cut in sizes 10, 12, 14, 16, 18 and 20. Size 16 requires 2⅞ yds 35-in. fabric for playsuit; 1 yd. 35-in. fabric for bolero; 1⅞ yds 35-in. fabric for skirt.

Send 15c for pattern, which includes complete sewing guide. Print your name, address and style number plainly. Be sure to state size you wish. Include postal unit or zone number in your address.

Vacation clothes—clothes for all summer long you'll find wonderful suggestions in the Summer Fashion Book — easy-to-make pattern designs for all ages and occasions, many of them with the little cap sleeves that everybody wants. Illustrated in full color. Price 15 cents.

Address Pattern Department, The Times Record, 121 W. 19th St., New York 11, N. Y.

ABOUT TOWN

GUEST RETURNS

Mrs. John H. McCutcheon, who has been visiting at the home of Charles C. Freihofer for a few days, returned today to her home in Philadelphia.

LEAVES FOR VISIT

Mrs. J. C. Smyth of 148 Fifth Avenue left Saturday to spend the summer with her daughter, Mrs John A. Bacon, at Hermosa Beach, Cal. Mrs. Smyth was accompanied by her grandson, Robert Smyth Bacon, a student at Phillips Exter Academy, N. H.

Mrs. Schneider To Address Women's Club

The Women's Club of Valley Falls and vicinity will meet Wednesday, at the home of Mrs. Lora Stover in Valley Falls. Mrs. L. Burton Schneider will be the guest speaker and her subject will be "Flower Arrangements." The report of the recently held district meeting will be given by one of the attending delegates. The refreshment committee includes Mrs. Esther Betts, Mrs. Freda Stark, Mrs. Ellen Hack, Mrs. Josie Bryan and Mrs. Dorothy Becker.

Navy Man Honored

Mrs. Anna Matthews entertained last night at her home in Pleasantdale in honor of her nephew, John G. Kewley, signalman 3 c of the Navy, who is spending a leave with his parents, Mr. and Mrs. Edward C. Kewley also of Pleasantdale. The honor guest has been in the amphibious branch of the Navy for two years and has been stationed overseas for one and one-half years, having taken part in the invasion of Normandy and the crossing of the Rhine. He has a brother, George Kewley, seaman 1 c, who is with the Seabees in the Philippines. Both boys are graduates of Lansingburg High School.

Home from Visit

Mrs. Kenneth Teetsel of 5 Putnam Street has returned after spending a few days in South Glens Falls where she was the guest of her brother-in-law and sister, Mr. and Mrs. Edwin Smith.

Visitors in Town

Edwin Hussey, M M 3 C, with his wife and daughter, Diane, of Providence, R. I., are visiting Mrs. Lela Hussey of 228 Hoosick Street. Mrs Hussey and her daughter will remain for the week, while Mr. Hussey will report for duty.

Deodorant Haste Is Costly Waste

Save yourself grief and money—this tip is from the dry cleaners—by waiting five or ten minutes to allow anti-perspirants and beauty preparations to dry thoroughly before you climb into your clothes.

The safest procedure usually in using a cream type of anti-perspirant, is to apply only the amount which can be absorbed by the skin and to massage it on until there is no greasy excess. When a liquid type is used, allow time for it to dry on your skin—when you're in a hurry, fanning armpits helps—and wipe afterward with a wet washrag and dry with a towel.

Make-up preparations to be watched with a particularly wary eye to see that they are dry before you dress are tan-faking lotions or creams used on neck and legs.

You're warned by dry cleaners not to put perfume directly on garments but where it's nicer and much safer to use—on yourself.

WHEN FEET GET TIRED.

Like the infantryman in the song, the average civilian must now "march and march and march." Walking is good exercise, but it can make unaccustomed feet sore and weary. For a quick pick-me-up, take a foot bath. Plunge the feet in a basin of warm water, then in a basin of cold water. Repeat three or four times, then add a little soap to the warm water and wash the feet thoroughly with a cloth. Rinse and wipe them dry. Dust a little powder between the toes, rub a bit of cream across the heel, put on clean stockings or socks, slip into a different pair of shoes and your feet will feel fit as a fiddle.

Greenwich Couple United In Marriage

Miss Irene Elizabeth Gillis, daughter of Mrs. Emma Gillis of Greenwich, was married yesterday at 1 p.m. to Ralph Hillard Thomas, son of Mr. and Mrs. Charles Thomas, also of Greenwich, in a ceremony performed at Centenary Methodist Church in Greenwich. Rev. Charles Edington, pastor, was the officiating clergyman.

Mrs. Helen Styring, organist, provided a program of appropriate music and the church was decorated with flowering mountain laurel, mock orange blossoms and peonies.

Miss Jacqueline Barber of Greenwich was the maid of honor and best man was Robinson Thomas, brother of the bridegroom. Serving as ushers were cousins of the bride, Donald and Richard Gillis. Miss Helen Gillis, cousin of the bride, was a bridesmaid and Emalyn Ruth Davies was the flower girl.

The bride wore a white satin wedding gown with lace trimming on the fitted bodice and full skirt which ended in a long train. Her tulle veil was edged with lace and fell from a tiara of orange blossoms. She carried a cascade bouquet of white flowers. She also wore a double strand of pearls. She was given in marriage by her uncle, J. Edward Darlett.

The honor attendant was attired in a powder blue marquisette gown trimmed with white flowers and a matching flowered hat. She carried a powder puff bouquet of assorted carnations and delphiniums. The bridesmaid was also attired in powder blue marquisette and carried a similar bouquet. The flower girl was dressed in pink organza and carried pink roses.

The couple left on a wedding trip to New Haven, Conn., and New York. Mrs. Thomas traveled in a maize costume with white accents, an orchid hat and a corsage of white camellias. She attended Greenwich Central School and has been a member of the staff of staff of Davies' Florist in Greenwhich for the last two and one-half years. The bridegroom also attended Greenwich Central School and manages his own farm at North Cambridge where the couple will reside.

Hoosick Falls Couple Married

The marriage of Miss Jayne Lovell, daughter of Mr. and Mrs. William Lovell of Hoosick Falls, to T 3 Edward A. Hanselman, son of Mr. and Mrs. William Hanselman of that village, took place Saturday at 2 p.m. at the rectory of the Church of the Immaculate Conception, Hoosick Falls, Rev. Paul K. Lynch, O.S.A., performing the ceremony.

The attendants were Mrs. Andrew Djernes and Henry Hanselman, sister and brother of the bridegroom.

The bride wore a blue suit with black hat and accessories and a corsage of white orchids. Mrs. Djernes wore an old rose suit with black hat and accessories and a corsage of white flowers.

A reception was held at the home of the bride's parents, 72 High Street, Hoosick Falls, with about fifty relatives and friends present. The bride's mother wore a purple and white print dress and the bridegroom's mother, a blue dress. Each had a white and pink corsage.

The newlyweds left for Petersburg, Va., where the bridegroom is stationed at Camp Lee, and will reside there.

Mrs. Hanselman is a graduate of Hoosick Falls High School and has been employed by the W. and S. Machine and Assembly Co., Hoosick Falls. She is associate conductress of Hoosick Court of Amaranth. The bridegroom attended Hoosick Falls High School and was in his last year there when he entered the armed forces. He returned in April to this country after being in Greenland for two years.

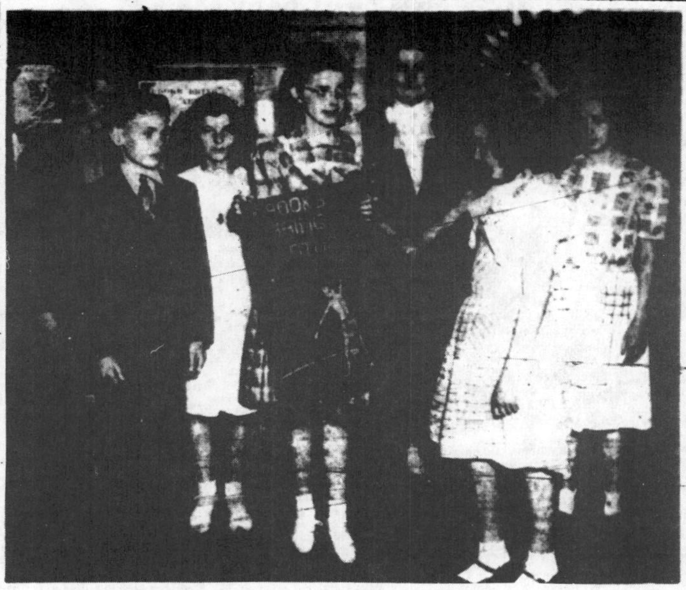

POSTER CONTEST WINNERS—Winners of the poster contest sponsored by the Junior League of Troy in conjunction with a series of children's programs were pictured Saturday at the Troy Public Library. In the front row, from left to right, are Dirk Van Zandt of School 16, who won second prize; Carol Collins, first prize winner of Emma Willard School, and Shirley Green, also of School 16, who won third prize. Fourth prize winners in the back row are Edith Mackey, Ruth Bird, Lillian Green and Mary Gundrum.

Junior League Conducts Poster Contest

Prizes were awarded to the winners of a poster contest sponsored by the Junior League of Troy on Saturday in the Children's Room at the Troy Public Library. The posters, made by children in Troy schools in the fourth, fifth and sixth grades, illustrated pictures from the "Books Bring Adventure" series of programs sponsored by the league.

Miss Sarah K. Flynn was in charge of the contest and judging the posters were Miss Flynn, Miss Ethel Knowlson of the library and Miss Ruth Folger of Russell Sage College.

Carol Collins won first prize. A student at Emma Willard School, she was awarded a book of her own selection. Dirk Van Zandt and Shirley Green, both students at School 16, won second and third prizes, respectively, which were defense stamps. Fourth prize winners included Edith Mackey, Ruth Bird, Lillian Green and Mary Gundrum.

Memorial Church Plans Activities

The Fidelity Bible Class of the Memorial Methodist Church will meet Tuesday at 6.30 p.m. for their annual covered dish picnic supper. The affair will be held in the church house and officers of the class will be in charge. Following the supper the election of officers will take place and the mystery sisters will be revealed at this meeting.

On Wednesday, the apron committee will have its monthly sewing day from 10 a.m. to 4 p.m. in the church house. At 6.30 p.m. on Wednesday the youth choir will rehearse and will be followed by the senior choir rehearsal at 7.30 p.m. The midweek service will be held in the Fidelity Room at 7.45 p.m.

Articles for the rummage sale to be held Saturday at 93 Congress Street may be left Friday in the church house. Miss Dorothy McCabe will call for articels for the the sale which is sponsored by the Business Girls.

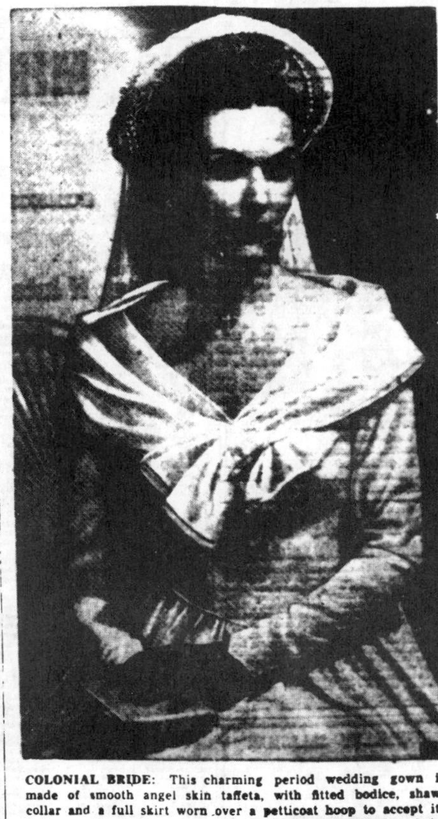

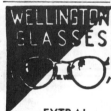

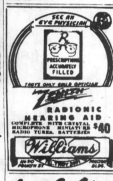

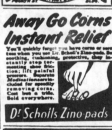

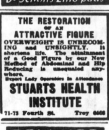

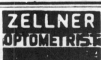

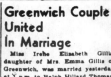

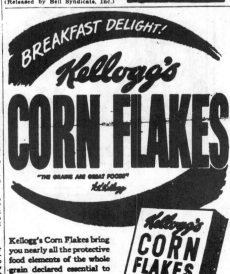

COLONIAL BRIDE: This charming period wedding gown is made of smooth angel skin taffeta, with fitted bodice, shawl collar and a full skirt worn over a petticoat hoop to accept its fullness. This bride wears a diamond cross on a slender chain, star-shaped ear clips and a narrow diamond circlet wedding rind.

Wise Girl Avoids Temptation, Walks Straight and Narrow Path

BY DOROTHY DIX

DEAR MISS DIX: I have been engaged to a young man with whom I am very much in love for several years, but it has not been feasible for us to marry.

Now he is about to be sent overseas and he wants me to live with him as his common law wife until he goes. That is against my principles and upbringing, but does it make sense for us not to take what happiness we can have while we can get it?

BEWILDERED GIRL.

Yes, doing right always makes sense, just as doing wrong is always folly in the long run. Look over the people you know. Especially consider the women you know. Who are the happy ones? Who are the contented ones? Who are the respected one? Aren't they, every one of them, the women who had sense enough not to be carried away by their passions or by the temptation of the minute, but who were wise enough to walk the straight and narrow path?

Plenty of girls nowadays are throwing their caps over the windmill. They are thinking that the men they are in love with may not come back from the war and that this might be the only chance they will have at a bite of romance and a bit of adventure. They are thinking that this little interlude of lovemaking may be the one bright spot in a darb existence and that they would be silly not to take it.

They're Wrong.

But that is where they are wrong. The foolishness comes in when they pay too high for their fun, when they gamble too recklessly with fate and when they stake a whole life's happiness on a few days' pleasure.

It makes sense to count the cost of what we do and take thought of the future. Before you go off on this premature honeymoon with your fiance, reflect on a number of things. One is that a man's mistress is never as glamorous to him as his sweetheart was and that many a husband throws up to his wife the indiscretion that he persuaded her into committing. Also, remember that the boy friend may fall in love with some other girl, marry her and leave you in the lurch, with your soiled reputation. And what if you should be left as that most unfortunate of women, one who has an illegitimate child clinging to her skirts?

It always makes sense for a girl to be good.

• • •

Dear Dorothy Dix: I am 17 years old and I wish to enlist in the Maritime Service, but my parents refuse to give their consent—perhaps because I already have two brothers in the service overseas. Two months have passed since they refused and I have completely changed and do all of the dreadful things I never thought of doing before. I know I am off to a bad start, but I don't care what becomes of me. I feel that I am being cheated out of my life's dreams and yearnings. What is your advice?

UNHAPPY.

Well, son, as you are so near the draft age, my advice to you is to have enough common sense and endurance to wait for it patiently instead of going off the deep end. You are acting like a spoiled little child and not showing the stuff of which sailors are made.

Be Fine Man.

Anyway, you must be animated by patriotism in being so anxious to enlist and the best way you can serve your country is by making a fine man of yourself. Character has to be behind every act of the sailor or the soldier to make him of value. So don't you see that you are being a traitor to your country when, because you can't do at once what you want to do, you take to evil courses? No army would ever win a battle if it were filled with drunken adolescents.

So brace up and behave yourself. Get hold of yourself while there is yet time.

• • •

Dear Miss Dix: Can you tell me what to talk about during a date? I get tongue-tied when I go out with a boy, but everybody else can think of snappy comebacks. All I can do is listen.

MARY ELLEN.

Well, you couldn't have a greater accomplishment than being an intelligent listener. The world is too full of talkers, but listeners are few and far between. All that you have to do is to ask a boy some question about himself and that will get him started. Then all that you will have to do will be just to lend him your ears and you will never lack for dates.

(Released by Bell Syndicate, Inc.)

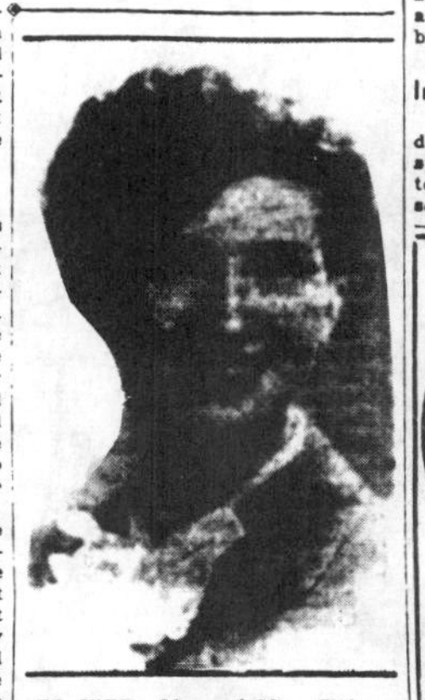

TO WED—Mr. and Mrs. Clifton Shuhart, Berlin, announce the engagement of their daughter, Miss Nona Shuhart, to Kenneth White, son of Mr. and Mrs. Herman White of Rensselaer. The wedding will take place in the near future.

Old Shoes Can Be Rejuvenated

Simplest rejuvenating trick to wipe the tired look off the face of shoes which must do until the August coupon is valid is achieved by renewing bows or buckles. You can also replace wornout or antiquated toe patterns with stylized ornaments, obtained from and put on by your shoe-repairman.

You can have winter shoes perforated or have toe-windows built in to give your feet cooler and more attractive summer homes. Dye baths to change light-colored shoes dark will also wipe out stains or faded tones and will make surface bruises or scratches much less noticable.

An expert "shoe doctor" can take battered suede shoes and bring the nap up to look velvety again, or shave off pile and turn leather into surfaces as lustrous as kid. He can also put his Midas touch of gold—or silver—on any kind of leather shoe that you want to turn into a Cinderella evening slipper.

Bernice Lester Wed To E. Duane Davis

Miss Bernice F. Lester, daughter of Mr. and Mrs. Bernard F. Lester of Hoosick Falls, and E. Duane Davis, son of Mr. and Mrs. Elbert G. Davis of Bennington, Vt., were married Saturday at 3:30 p.m. at the Baptist parsonage, Hoosick Falls, by Rev. Wallace E. McCoy. Miss Edith Lester, sister of the bride, and Lacy Pratt of Albany were the attendants.

The bride wore a white jersey street length dress with powder blue hat and accessories and a corsage of gardenias and forget-me-nots. Her sister wore a pink crepe street length dress with white hat and accessories and a corsage of white roses and sweet peas.

A reception for the immediate families was held at the home of the bride's parents, 15 River Street, Hoosick Falls. The bride's mother wore a fuschia dress and a corsage of white carnations, and the bridegroom's mother, an aqua dress with a corsage of deep pink carnations.

Mr. and Mrs. Davis left on a wedding trip to Hampton Beach, the bride wearing a pink dress with white accessories. They will reside at 214 North Street, Bennington.

Mrs. Davis attended Hoosick Falls High School and for the last two years has been employed by the Winthrop Chemical Co., Rensselaer. Mr. Davis is a graduate of Bennington High School, honorably discharged from the Navy, he is in the employ of the National Carbon Co., Bennington.

Emma Willard Graduate Married

Miss Jane Spaulding Martin, daughter of Mrs. Charles Wesley Martin of Woodmere, L. I., was married Saturday to James Garrett Hilton, Medical Corps, U. S. N. R., son of Mr. and Mrs. James Carroll Hilton, in Trinity Episcopal Church, Hewlett, with Rev. J. Reginald Moodey officiating.

The bride is a graduate of Emma Willard School and attended Wells College. Mr. Hilton, an alumnus of Princeton University, will be graduated from the College of Physicians and Surgeons this month and will be an intern at New York Hospital.

In Binghamton

Mrs. Harold Van Husen and children of 2214 Thirteenth Street are spending two weeks in Binghamton as the guests of Mrs. Van Husen's mother.

WELLINGTON GLASSES
EXTRA!
That Extra Pair of GLASSES may come in very handy. Why not have a pair made up with colored lenses. Fine for bright sunshine, to serve as a spare.
TINLEY-WELLINGTON CO. INC.
OPTOMETRISTS-OPTICIANS
45 3rd STREET

SPECIAL!
Raincoats: Dupont's Zelon. Water repellent, durable.
Were 10.95
White . . . now 5.00
Colors . . . now 8.95
KNITCRAFT
"DEBS TO STOUTS"
SHOPPE 9 Third St. Troy, N. Y.

TICKETS NOW FOR
TONITE At 8:30
"LA BOHEME"
TROY THEATRE

Know the Satisfaction of Tea at its Best
"SALADA" TEA
In Packages and Tea Bags at Your Grocer's

SEE AN EYE PHYSICIAN
Rx PRESCRIPTIONS ACCURATELY FILLED
TROY'S ONLY GUILD OPTICIAN
ZENITH RADIONIC HEARING AID
COMPLETE WITH CRYSTAL MICROPHONE MINIATURE RADIO TUBES, BATTERIES $40
Williams

Away Go Corns Instant Relief
You'll quickly forget you have corns or sore toes when you use Dr. Scholl's Zino-pads. So soothing, cushioning, protective, they instantly stop tormenting shoe friction; lift painful pressure. Separate Medications are included for speedily removing corns. Cost but a trifle. Sold everywhere.
Dr Scholls Zino-pads

THE RESTORATION OF AN ATTRACTIVE FIGURE
OVERWEIGHT IS UNBECOMING and UNSIGHTLY. It shortens life. The attainment of a Good Figure by our New Method of Abdominal and Hip Reducing is unequaled anywhere.
Expert Lady Operators in Attendance
STUARTS HEALTH INSTITUTE
71-73 Fourth St. Troy 6608

ZELLNER OPTOMETRIST

BREAKFAST DELIGHT!
Kellogg's CORN FLAKES
"THE GRAINS ARE GREAT FOODS" W.K. Kellogg
Kellogg's Corn Flakes bring you nearly all the protective food elements of the whole grain declared essential to human nutrition.
Kellogg's CORN FLAKES

The umbrella was invented by Jonas Hanway, an Englishman.

WE REPAIR ANY MAKE OF WASHING MACHINE
EXPERT REPAIRMEN
SOUTH END WASHER
173 4th St., Troy 4115

BUYS CATS IN SPARE TIME

Tell City, Ind. (UP)—Herman F. Wolf has a novel "sideline" after he finishes his days' work at a local chair company. He buys cats and sells them to the government for experimental purposes. A sign on his car says—"The Man Who Will Buy Your Cat."

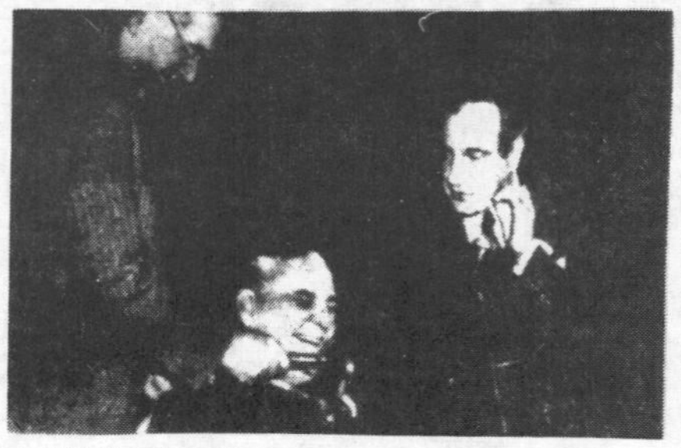

DUNNINGER, The Master Mentalist, sends a member of the audience into gales of laughter with his astonishing mind-reading act. This brand-new Variety Show—with the amazing Dunninger, plus MUSIC, SONGS, FUN and CASH PRIZES for listeners—and Bill Slater as MC—IS ON TONIGHT! Don't miss this new program—"The Dunninger Show!" You'll love it! Presented by Rinso TONIGHT AND EVERY FRIDAY—STATION WGY, 10 P.M. —Adv.

UNION WILL BACK TROY'S CAMPAIGN TO GET CEMETERY

Mine Worker Declares Veterans' Burial Place Should Be Located Here

Location of a proposed national cemetery in the Troy Area was unanimously endorsed last night at a meeting of the Instrument Makers' Union, affiliated with the United Mine Workers of America. Eighty-eight members, comprising employees of W. & L. E. Gurley, supported the measure at their election meeting held at 81 Fourth Street.

James Bulson, president of the local, stated that the group will give every possible aid to the Joint Veterans Committee backing the project. He stated: "It is altogether fitting and proper that one of the proposed national cemeteries for our heroic dead be located in this area. Our community is ideally situated for this purpose for many reasons. It is easily accessible by air, rail and highway travel, and because so many of our boys have fought and died for their country, in equal if not greater proportion to similar areas in other parts of the country. Again, the Troy Area is historically suitable because the early battles for American liberty were fought and won here

Members also unanimously voted to purchase three more $100 bonds, thus bringing their total bond purchases to $1,000.

The following officers for two years were named. James Bulson, incumbent, elected president; Walter Robinson, reelected vice president; A. John Snyder, reelected recording secretary; Walter Bentley, reelected financial secretary; Frank Lee, new treasurer; Leroy Schrauder, reelected sergeant at arms. George Faro was reelected trustee for three years.

Several district and national officers attended and spoke at the session. Robert Fohl, district director, was promoted to international director, it was announced. Wayne Brayfield was appointed in his place as district director. District representative Al Churney also addressed the meeting.

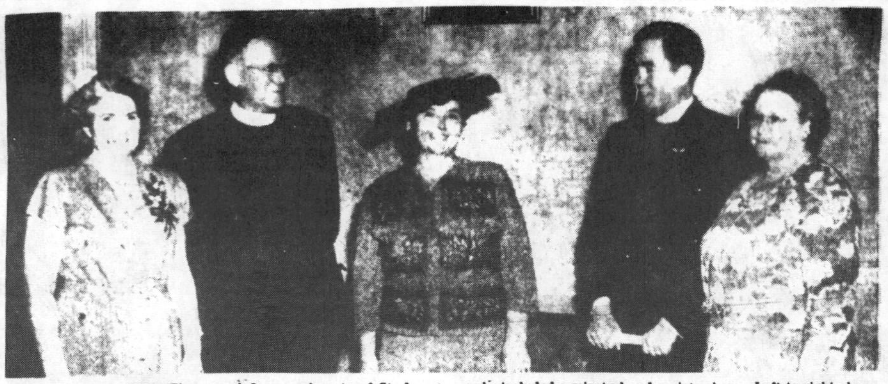

PARISH CARD PARTY—The annual June card party of St. Joseph's Church was conducted last night in the parish hall where attendance was excellent despite the heat. All societies of the church cooperate for the annual function which, in addition to cards, included a minstrel and variety show. Left to right above, are Miss Gertrude M. Ryan, Rev. James A. Nolan, pastor; Mrs. James F. Egan, Rev. Bernard J. Lannon, assistant pastor and Mrs. Mae E. Akin.

SEAMAN TRAVELS MANY MILES BUT NEVER SEES SEA

Has Spent Time Riding Back and Forth on Trains as Shore Patrolman

(AP) Special Washington Service.

Washington (AP)—Seaman Specialist Howard B. Whitescarver has traveled 400,000 miles, and has yet to see an ocean.

He's done all that traveling as a shore patrolman, most of the time as chaperon for sailors riding on trains.

That makes him the Navy's most traveled shore patrolman. And he did it all after joining the Navy in November, 1942.

But he hasn't yet seen the world, or been aboard a ship.

"In fact," the Detroit landlubber blushingly told a reporter today "I haven't yet even seen the ocean. The closest I have come to that is looking at the harbor in New York."

He came here to receive a special citation, along with a group of other shore patrolmen and military police, for their work in aiding the nation's transportation trains, from David A. Crawford, president of the Pullman Co.

Sgt. Albert Rose of Blue Hill, Neb., the Army's most traveled military policeman — with 341,000 miles to his credit—has yet to make his first arrest of a soldier for violence.

Both agreed that some of the servicemen on the trains want to "blow off a little steam," but "you just talk them out of going too far."

Whitescarver, 39 years old, spent 16 years as a Detroit policeman prior to his Navy duty. His run has been confined mainly to Chicago-Denver-Cheyenne and other northwest points. Rose, 30, has been primarily on West Coast trains from California to Washington.

RECORD NEWSPAPERS' VICTORY GARDEN CONTEST

ENTRY BLANK

Name ....

Address ....

Garden location ....

Backyard .... Community .... (Check type)

Contest open to all residents of Troy, Cohoes, Watervliet, Green Island and Waterford. Gardens must be at least 500 square feet; 25 by 20 or its equivalent. Community gardens must be marked for identification by judges.

Prizes—War Bonds and Stamps worth $330, face value.

SARATOGA COUNTY LEADS BOND DRIVE

Reneselsa Follows Closely in Second Place

Two of the 16 counties in District 5 have gone over the top in individual sales for the Seventh War Loan, Clinton County with 103 per cent of individual sales quota and Franklin County, 116.4 per cent. Among the five area counties, Albany ranks first with 82.9 per cent of quota of individual sales, Barnard Townsend, Rensselaer County War Finance Committee head, announced.

In the E Bond sales of quota, Saratoga County continues to lead Rensselaer by a small margin. The E Bond sales standings:

County	Per Cent
Saratoga	63.1
Rensselaer	62.2
Albany	61.3
Washington	61.2
Schenectady	55.3

TROY HIGH CHORAL CONDUCTS RECITAL

Informal Program of Music Presented at School

At the final meeting of the Choral Club of Troy High School an informal recital was conducted yesterday. This procedure was first inaugurated last year by Frank Catricala, school music director. The talent was selected voluntarily from the group.

The program included: "Valscis" by Morves, piano solo by Marilyn Brothwell; soprano solo, "Beguine The Beguine" by Adlene Martucci; Elizabeth Clayton, piano solo, "Military Palonaise" by Chopin; "American Prayer," vocal duet by Eleanor Barley and Helen Hogan.

A piano impromptu by Shubert was played by June Ott. Other selections included a soprano solo by Leona Sharples, "Just a Prayer Away;" Chopin's "Palonaise in A Flat" played by Carolyn Eycleshimer and "Claire De Lune," played by Dawn Y. Hall.

Mary Bailey was chairman of the program.

WHITEHALL.

Mrs. George LaCasse is ill at her home, Williams Street.

Lt. Gerald Douglas of the Army Air Force, who recently returned from overseas duty, is visiting his mother, Mrs. Horatio S. Douglas of Brooklyn Avenue.

Mrs. Melva McCann and daughter, Pamela, have returned from a five months' visit with her husband, Edward McCann, of the Army.

Mr. and Mrs. Joseph Santora and daughter Cynthia, have returned to their home in Woodstock, Vt., after visiting Mrs. Santora's parents, Mr. and Mrs. Bettina, Poultney Street.

The Eight Wizards Club met at the New Arlington Hotel Monday night. Cards were played and refreshments were served. Prize winners were Mrs. Vera Terry, first, and Mrs. Laverne Colomb, second.

The War Bond and Stamp sale in the schools Tuesday morning totalled $520.95. Bernard P. Murphy, principal of the high school, has announced. The rooms purchasing 100 per cent in Tuesday's sales were Miss Louise Waite, Miss Mary Hogan, Miss Isabelle Carrington, Mrs. Mildred Crotty. This will be the last sale until the opening of schools in September.

Word has been received here of the death Tuesday of Clifton Haskell, 53, employed in the Veterans' Hospital, Roxbury, Mass. A former resident of Whitehall he was the son of the late Frank Haskell, Whitehall. He served overseas during World War I. He is survived by a half-brother, Charles Haskell, and his stepmother, Mrs. Frank Haskell, Williams Street.

INJURES HAND IN FALL.

Edward Mallory, 10, of 420 Eighth Street, was removed to the Troy Hospital yesterday afternoon in a police car by Patrolmen Albert Prezio and John McClure after he received a laceration of the right hand in a fall at Ingalls and Sixth Avenues. He was attended by Dr. A. T. Purificato and held at the hospital.

GRAFTON.

Sgt. Merrill Warren visited Mr. and Mrs. Everett Lamphere Sunday.

Mrs. Glenford Simmons and daughter, Judith have returned home.

Mrs. Lydia Winard is visiting Miss E. H. Burdick at Camp Wildwood.

Lydia Seitz of Petersburg spent the week-end with Miss Marie Schermerhorn.

Charles Hayner and daughter of New York visited Mr. and Mrs. S. S. Barnhart Sunday.

The West Grafton school closed today with a picnic, the Quackenkill school joined them.

Mrs. Mattie Trumble has moved back from Troy after spending the last two winters there.

Miss Beulah Weeden, Miss Mabel Schermerhorn, and Miss Lydia Seitz spent Saturday in Troy.

Mr. and Mrs. Joseph Mahoney and sons of Watervliet were week-end guests of Mr. and Mrs. Elmer Jacobs.

LATHAM.

Rev. Daniel F. Cronin has announced that the summer schedule for masses at St. Ambrose's Church will be 7, 8, 9 and 10 a.m.

Mrs. Thomas Collins and son, Thomas, jr., of Cleveland, O., were recent guests of Mrs. Edward Foley of Stop 36, Troy-Schenectady Road.

Mrs. Lillian Holmes, chairman of the Red Cross organization at Newtonville, has made an appeal for more volunteers to help with Red Cross sewing.

The W. S. C. S. of Calvary Methodist Church will hold a food sale Saturday at 10 a.m. at Gaffer's store. Mrs. Nettie McCabe and Mrs. Frank Dupree will have charge of the sale.

A. M. M. 1/c James Kachedurian recently arrived home by plane from the Hawaiian Islands for a thirty-day leave with his wife, the former Ruth Hotchkiss. He has been overseas for 21 months and will later report to Chicago, where he will attend school.

Eugene W. Richards, jr., of Latham, has sent word from France of his promotion to staff sergeant. He is with the Troop Carrier Command and has been overseas 15 months. In December, he was awarded a Presidential Unit Citation and two battle stars. He is the son of Mr. and Mrs. Eu[illegible] W. Richards of Latham.

Pfc. Richard Simpkins son of Mr. and Mrs. George Simpkins of Latham, is home for a thirty-day furlough. Private Simpkins participated in the major engagements in the Pacific and was wounded on Saipan and Iwo Jima. After his furlough he will report to a convalescent hospital at Asbury Park, N. J., where he is stationed.

The newly organized Girl Scouts of Latham, under the direction of Miss Jean Ruhtz, met Tuesday at Calvary Hall. Mrs. Donald Weed, district nurse, was present and gave first aid instructions. Plans were discussed for a mother and daughter banquet to be held in the near future. The girls will meet Saturday for an all-day hike.

The Latham Home Bureau has completed two lessons in the making of lamp shades. This course was under the direction of Mrs. Alice Radigan and was held in St. Ambrose's Assembly Hall. The Home Bureau will hold its annual picnic at Calvary Hall Monday at 12:30 p.m. Everyone planning to attend is requested to bring a covered dish and her own table service.

Church School will begin at 9:30 a.m. at Calvary Methodist Church with William R. Williams superintendent in charge. At the morning worship service at 10:45 a.m., Rev. Herbert S. Roberts will speak on the topic, "Judge Not." Sunday at 8 p.m. "The Robert Allen Memorial" will be dedicated as the Sunday School Worship Center. A painting of Chr[illegible]

The service will interpret this new picture and [illegible] ship. Rev. Arthur Lanmesser of Troy will introduce the [illegible] tion. The public is invited to attend this service.

MAKE 10 BIG GLASSES DELICIOUS DRINKS 5¢ PAR-AID
ASSORTED FLAVORS
AT ALL DEALERS

SPOT CASH FOR RADIO COMBINATION
With Automatic Record Changer
BENSON'S
OPP. COURT HOUSE

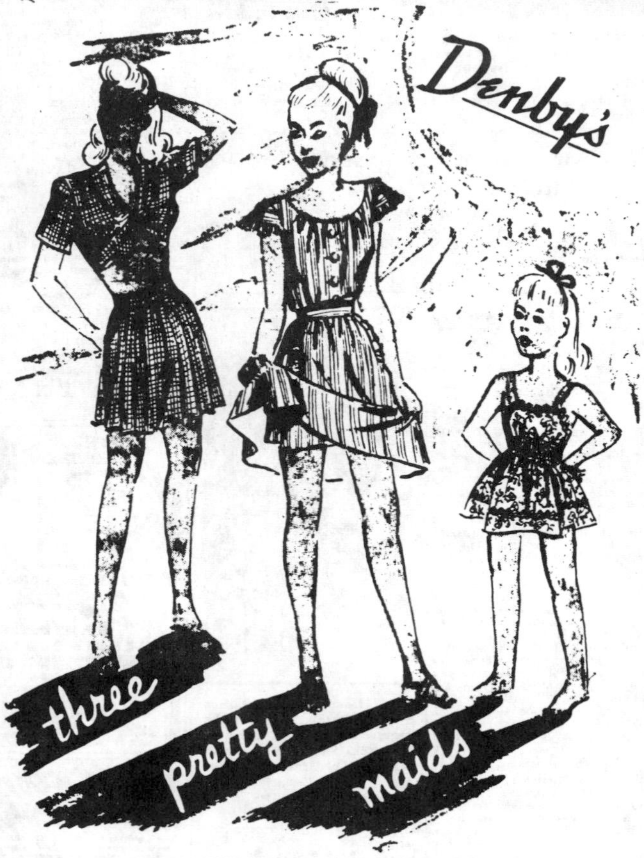

ALL OUT FOR SUN-FUN IN SUN DUDS FROM DENBY'S

Dare to be bare in a midrif sun suit that exposes you tactfully. Tiny checked seersucker with bow bodice and pleated shorts. Red, blue, and green. Sizes 12 to 18. 6.98

There's nothing like multi-colored stripes to express the spirit of youthful gayety. One piece playsuit with matching dirndle skirt. Victorian neck line and cap sleeves. Sizes 12 to 18 7.98

The small-fry can play and swim in this adorable cotton print sun suit lined with jersey. Shirred waistline, and full skirt, trimmed with lace ric-rac. Pink blue, yellow, and aqua. Sizes small, medium, and large. 2.98

YOU CAN SHOP IN COOL COMFORT AT AIR-CONDITIONED DENBY'S

Denby's

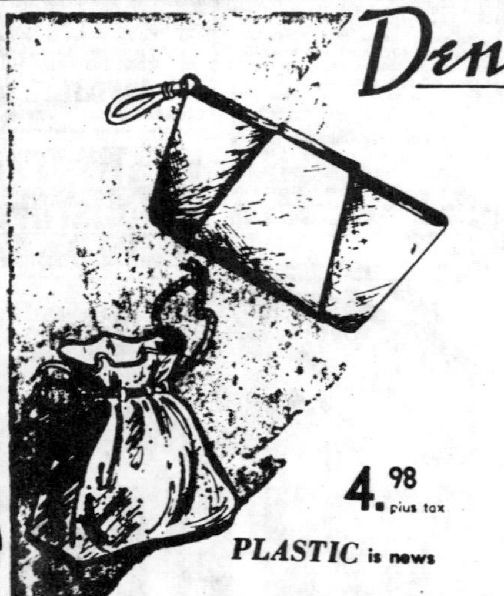

4.98 plus tax

PLASTIC is news

— KADAR is a name to remember—white plastic that looks like leather. Odorless, color-fast, scuff resistant and durable— So washable that even lipstick and ink stains can be removed. They're the answer to your summer handbag worries. Both roomy drawstring and underarm zipper styles.

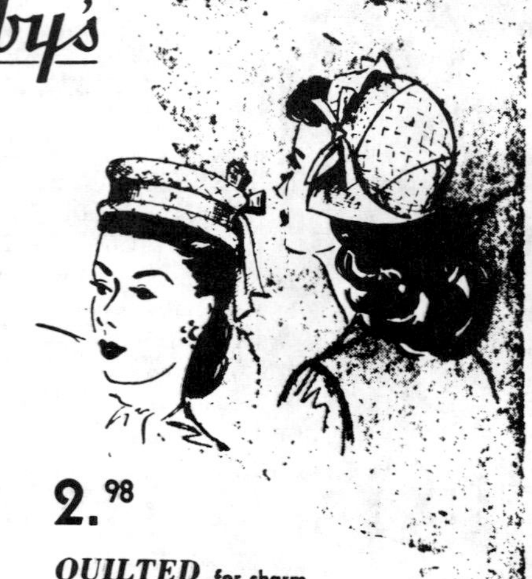

2.98

QUILTED for charm

So very young and becoming—these little quilted white rayon bonnets all crisped up with dainty bows. Perfect to wear all through summer with town cottons and sheers. Illustrated are the dashing spool pill box and lovable dutch cap.

WE'RE BEGINNING TO SEE THE WHITE!

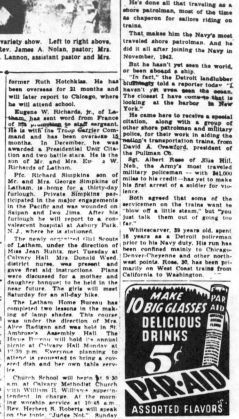

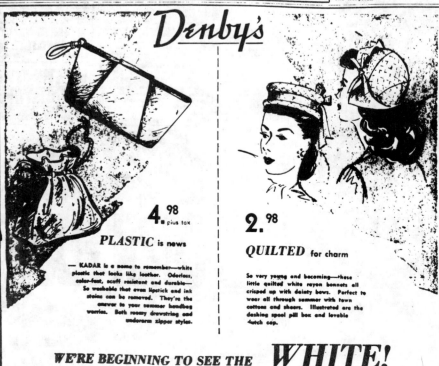

ON THE AIR

Radio Programs From Local Stations

TONIGHT

1,000—WTRY, Troy—980

P. M.

5:00—Terry and Pirates
5:15—Dick Tracy
5:30—Jack Armstrong
5:45—Capt. Midnight
6:00—Club Men
6:15—Roy Shudt—News
6:30—Servicemen Sing
6:40—U. S. Employment
6:45—Ask Washington
7:00—Headline Edition
7:15—Raym'd Gram Swing
7:30—Lone Ranger
8:00—Pages of Melody
8:30—This Is Your F.B.I.
9:00—Famous Jury Trials
9:30—Spotlight Bands
9:55—Coronet Story Teller
10:00—Swing time
10:30—Jim Healey
10:40—Paul Baron
10:45—Doctor Talks It Over
11:00—Music for Listening
12:00—News

370—WGY, Schenectady, 810

P. M.

5:00—When a Girl Marries
5:15—Portia Faces Life
5:30—Just Plain Bill
5:45—Front Page Farrell
6:00—News
6:05—News
6:15—Varieties
6:25—Sports
6:30—Dinner Dance
6:45—Lowell Thomas
7:00—Supper Club
7:15—John W. Vandercook
7:30—Music Builders
8:00—Highways in Melody
8:30—Farm Forum
9:00—Waltz Time
9:30—People are Funny
10:00—Dunninger
10:30—Bill Stern
10:45—To Be Announced
11:00—News Reporter
11:05—Melodic Moods
11:15—Harkness
11:30—World's Great Novels
12:00—News

300—WOKO—Albany, 1460

P. M.

5:00—Calling All Girls
5:15—Last of the Mohicans
5:30—Say It With Music
5:45—Jam Session
6:00—News
6:15—Jimmy Carroll Sings
6:30—Pleasure Parade
6:45—World Today
6:55—Meaning of News
7:00—Jack Kirkwood Show
7:15—L. W. Brockington
7:30—Friday on Broadway
8:00—Aldrich Family
8:30—Adventures Thin Man
8:55—Bill Henry—News
9:00—Pays to be Ignorant
9:30—Those Websters
10:00—Durante-Moore show
10:30—Harry James
11:00—News
11:15—Jean Brooks
11:30—Ben Ribble Orch.
12:00—News

TOMORROW

1,000—WTRY—Troy, 980

A. M.

6:45—Top of the Morning
6:50—Morning Newspaper
6:55—News
7:00—Rise 'n' Shine
7:15—Timekeeper
7:30—News
7:45—Timekeeper
7:55—News
8:00—Timekeeper
8:15—Morning Melodies
8:40—Timekeeper
8:55—News
9:00—Breakfast Club
9:30—Breakfast Club
9:45—Breakfast Club
10:00—What's Cookin!
10:25—News
10:30—Land of the Lost
11:00—It's Murder
11:15—Evelyn Johnson
11:30—To Be Announced
11:45—Lois Long and Sons
12:00—News

P. M.

12:15—Melody Time
12:20—Stars at Noon
12:30—Home and Garden
1:00—News Summary
1:02—Fun Canteen
1:30—Fight A. A. F.
2:00—News Summary
2:15—Hidden Valley Gang
2:30—It's a Hit
3:00—Senior Swing
3:30—Roseland Orchestra
4:00—News Summary
4:02—Saturday Symphony
5:00—News Summary
5:02—Duke Ellington
6:00—Treasury Salute

370—WGY, Schenectady, 810

A. M.

6:00—Farm News
6:05—Music
6:10—News
6:15—Song Service
6:30—Here Comes Band
6:45—Sports Special
6:50—Music
6:55—News
7:00—Yawn Chasers
7:15—Spotlight On Peace
7:20—Yawn Chasers
7:30—News Reporter
7:35—Music
7:45—News
8:00—Morning Devotions
8:15—Victory Garden
8:30—Market Basket
8:45—Morning Moods
9:00—Sam Adams
9:15—Catholic Radio Guild
9:30—Tell Me A Story
9:45—Health Hunters
10:00—Bob Armstrong
10:30—News
10:35—Better Business
10:40—Rhythm and Reason
10:45—Alex Dreier
11:00—First Piano Quartet
11:30—Smilin' Ed McConnell
12:00—News Reporter

P. M.

12:05—Noontime Melodies
12:15—News
12:30—Farm Paper
1:00—Veterans Advisor
1:15—N. Y. State College
1:30—Musical Matinee
1:45—War Telescope
2:00—Musicana
2:15—All American Band
2:30—Sky High
3:00—Father's Day
3:15—Music
3:30—Music On Display
4:00—Doctors Look Ahead
4:30—Bond Rally
5:00—Grand Hotel
5:30—News
5:45—Tin Pan Alley
6:00—News Reporter

300—WOKO—Albany, 1460

A. M.

6:45—Sacred Heart Pgm.
7:00—News
7:05—Sun Up Time
7:15—Minute Man
7:45—News
8:00—Musical Clock
9:00—Newsflash
9:05—Interlude
9:15—Garden Gate
9:30—Treasury Salute
9:45—Whitney Headliner
10:00—Youth On Parade
10:30—Mary Lee Taylor
11:00—Warren Sweeney
11:05—Let's Pretend
11:30—Billie Burke Show
12:00—Theater of Today

P. M.

12:30—Stars O'r Hollywood
1:00—Grand Central Sta.
1:30—Eliot Lawrence Orch.
2:00—Of Men and Books
2:15—Adventure in Science
2:30—Barnyard Follies
3:00—Land is Bright
3:30—World Reconstruction
3:45—Builders of Victory
4:00—Washington Report
4:15—Report from Overseas
4:30—Assignment Home
5:00—We Deliver the Goods
5:30—Timely Tunes
5:35—Viva America
6:00—News

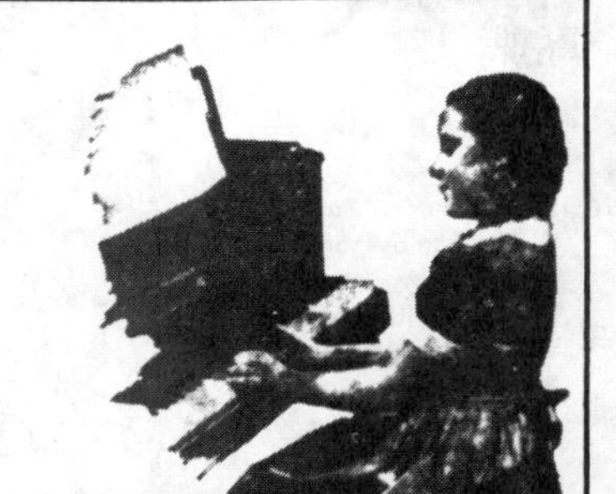

She PLAYS while she LEARNS!

LEARNING to play the piano nowadays is a very different matter from the *old* way, and a far better one. Your child learns *by playing!*

First she's shown how to play a very simple little tune—a tune that she enjoys playing. Then, step by step, she is willingly and happily led to learn more tunes, more songs, more "pieces"—things she loves and enjoys to play, more and more every day. She gets her practice *by playing!* And almost before you know it, she's playing like an old-timer!

That's the new method about which we want to tell you. Won't you come in and hear how easily, how inexpensively, you can give your child this joy of music? We'd love to tell you. And there is no obligation, of course!

UPRIGHTS Reconditioned, Tuned Delivered Locally $55.00 up
GRANDS Guaranteed $395.00

AS LITTLE AS $15 DOWN AND $5 MONTHLY

OR

MAYBE SHE WANTS TO PLAY

Accordion $40.00
Clarinet $50.00
Flute $90.00
Saxophone $29.50
Drums—Professional $209.50
Violins $10.00
Guitar $19.95
Banjo $20.00

FOR EVERY MUSICAL NEED VISIT
MUSIC HEADQUARTERS
OPEN SATURDAY TO 8:30

CLUETT & SONS

BROADWAY and 2ND ST. TROY, N. Y.

TOMATOES NEED NITROGEN AFTER HEAVY RAINFALL

First Aid Should Be Given Plants by Applying Fertilizer

By HENRY L. FREE
Written for NEA Service.

Tomato plants in the Victory Garden have taken an awful beating, judging by reports coming to this editor. Wet and cold weather, general throughout the country, following a rather early and warm spring, caused a leaching away of much of the available nitrogen from the area about the plant roots. This loss of plant food is indicated by the yellowing of the lower leaves on many tomato plants.

First aid should be given your plants by applying a small handful of Victory Garden 4-12-4 fertilizer about each plant, says H. D. Brown, Department of Horticulture, Ohio State University. Care should be taken not to get the fertilizer or the roots, which, due to the wet season, have formed very near the surface. Cultivation should be light and water should be applied if rain does not follow spreading of the fertilizer. Straw mulches are advised in conserving moisture and to eliminate the root injury which is frequently the cause of leaf curl. Top pruning also causes the lower leaves to curl.

Due to the wet season, tomato plants are bound to be infected with the two foliage diseases, Alternaria and Septoria leaf blight, which are already causing a great deal of damage. This disease can be partially controlled by use of fixed copper dusts or sprays. Dusts which contain 7 per cent insoluble copper are most generally used. The dusts should be applied in the morning while the dew is on and, if the wet weather persists, it will be necessary to make five or six applications to get reasonable control of the foliage diseases. The application should be made five to 10 days apart.

We can look for an unusual amount of mosaic, including the fern leaf and shoestring types, this year because of the early influx of aphids. At the present time the aphid population has been almost entirely eliminated by favorable temperatures, and by the attacks of many of the parasites which kill aphids.

Victory gardeners also can expect a great deal of blossom end rot this year. Blossom end rot is caused by a sudden withdrawal of moisture from the tip of tomato fruit. These sudden withdrawals come most frequently when the tomato plant is started with an abundant supply of moisture, which is suddenly cut off. With the roots formed near the surface of the soil, it is quite likely that the moisture supply will be sharply reduced when the surface soil dries out. As already indicated, this can be partially controlled by the use of straw or, better, clover hay mulches.

Many tomato diseases are easily recognized, but others may be hard to identify. When there is any question as to the diagnosis, it is best to consult your local garden expert or county agricultural agent, or send specimens to the state agricultural college.

Well-staked and cared-for tomatoes will bring a smile on your face as bright as this girl gardener wears in contemplating a rosy-cheeked product.

CHINESE CHASING JAPANESE TROOPS TOWARD LINGLING

Advance 23 Miles Beyond Kweilin in Hard-Hitting Drive on Nipe

Chungking (AP) — Hard-hitting Chinese troops, swiftly capitalizing on the liberation of Kweilin, have advanced 23 miles northeastward and are driving toward their next major objective, the old Flying Tigers' airfield at Lingling, the Chinese high command disclosed last night.

Pounding on the heels of the withdrawing Japanese who abandoned the triple-airfield city of Kweilin Friday, Chinese columns Saturday reached the walled town of Lingchwan in a 14-mile push from Kweilin, the capital of Kwangsi Province 360 miles southeast of Chungking.

While one force laid siege to Lingchwan, another by-passed the town of the Hunap-Kwangsi railroad and swept on another nine miles, reaching Tajungkiang, 85 miles southwest of Lingling, a communique said.

Lingling was abandoned by the U. S. 14th Air Force Sept. 7 last year. Its recapture by Chiang Kai-shek's troops would clear the way for a drive toward the key railroad hub of Hengyang, on Tokyo's transcontinental corridor from Korea to Hong Kong.

Chinese rearguards meanwhile were mopping up Japanese remnants still putting up a fight outside Kweilin. Front dispatches said that Kweilin, formerly the biggest American air base in south-central China, had been almost completely destroyed by the vengeful enemy. The Japanese blew up or set fire to practically every building in the rubbled provincial capital.

Japanese rearguards in the western and southern suburbs were cleared out while a few Japanese units offering sporadic resistance in the northern outskirts and on the east bank of the Li River were being wiped out, headquarters said.

The high command said that reports that all of Kweilin's three airfields had been recaptured were premature. Yang Tong airstrip, the last of the three blown up by American flyers last November, has been retaken, but fighting with a few enemy defenders still is going on for the other two.

WIFE APPEARS TO WRECK PLANS FOR WAC'S MARRIAGE

Prospective Bridegroom Claims Red Cross Reported Spouse Dead

Berlin (AP)—Acting on the plea of a Chicago woman that she was the wife of airborne Capt. Carl G. Schultz and the mother of his two children, Army authorities placed the Captain under detention and called off his planned church wedding last night to WAC Sgt. Kanella Koulouvaris of Brooklyn.

Sgt. Koulouvaris said she and Schultz were married at a civil ceremony in Berlin last Monday "but as far as the two of us were concerned we planned to make our home together only after the military ceremony today."

When news of the approaching wedding was published in the United States, Mrs. Ruth Priscilla Schultz, Chicago, the same address as given on the Captain's service records, said she was the wife of the officer and the mother of his two children.

Capt. Schultz said he had received information through the Red Cross that his wife had been killed in an automobile accident last May. The Army is checking the Red Cross for a copy of this message. Mrs. Schultz said:

"I've sent him a letter a week for the last six weeks and received a $100 check from him on the last week. I feel sorry for the WAC who has been taken in by the whole thing. He's gone on toots—but nothing like this."

PRISONERS OF GERMANS ATE MEAT ONLY ONCE IN PERIOD OF MONTH

Mt. Carroll, Ill. (UP)—Pvt. Kenneth Bro, 23, who visited his family here while en route to an Army hospital for rehabilitation treatment, said that he and 15 other war prisoners in a German camp near Waldbori ate meat only once during their month's imprisonment and then it was horse meat, cooked with grass.

The meat "treat" resulted, he said, when a horse was killed by artillery fire near the camp. One of the forced laborers confined at the camp ran outside and cut off a chunk of the horse's flesh with a pen knife. That night they boiled the meat in a helmet, adding some "nice new tender grass" for the greens.

The camp's regular fare for prisoners consisted, Bro said, of black bread and coffee substitute for breakfast; a half bowl of soup made of bread crumbs and water for dinner; and one slice of black bread for supper. Bro and his companions were liberated in about a month when their own division captured Waldbori.

NAZIS STILL HOLDING OCCUPIED AREA JOBS

Ploen, Germany (AP)—Some Nazi officials still hold positions in the British-occupied Hamburg and Schleswig-Holstein areas but Lt. Gen. E. H. Barker, Area commander, said yesterday they were being "eradicated as quickly as conditions permit."

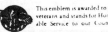

IWO JIMA HAVEN FOR B-29 BOMBERS SMASHING JAPAN

Planes from Marianas Find Refuge on Hard-Won Isle

Iwo Jima (AP)—Almost nightly now the air over Iwo throbs steadily, hour after hour, with the purposeful drumming of the big parade of Japan-bound B-29s from Marianas bases.

The giant sky-train rumbles in the blackness somewhere off the bulge of Mount Suribachi, wingtip lights forming a chain of points glowing in the dark. There's a rhythm in their drumming, the receding roar of one plane's engines blending with the approaching roar of another's to make a relentless, cosmic symphony. It is Japan's doom music.

Once the Superforts gave Iwo a wide berth, especially on the return trip where Japanese fighters could lie in wait like vultures for the crippled kings. Now Iwo is haven, coming or going. That is part of the fruits of the Marines' costly victory here.

The skies are dark up there and often turbulent with storm. The waters below lie deep, vast and hostile under the night, but here stands Iwo, the isle by the side of road. And long before daylight, long before the first wounded or fuel-thirsty planes return, Iwo is ready for them. The welcome mat is out.

Up long before dawn to meet them are flight surgeons, control tower men, ambulance drivers, fuel truck drivers, the Red Cross men who pass out coffee and doughnuts, the mechanics, the men in charge of billeting, the cooks and mess sergeants who must feed the arriving crews.

They're all there as the first of the weary planes, the long silver antennae of its headlights cutting the blackness and feeling the runway, swoops down for a landing.

Col. John G. Fowler of Newnan, Ga., is in charge of the Superfort base on Iwo, with Lt. Col. Max R. Fennell of Seattle, Wash., directing landing operations. Today Fennell's tower operators are S/Sgt. George Gagnon of Waterville, Me., T/Sgt. Kenneth B. Marshall of Johnstown, Pa., and Sgt. Theodore Kimelman of the Bronx, New York City.

Fennell, whether in the tower or about the field, is in constant touch by radio. Today his job is not too hard. Weather has been fair, enemy opposition light, and most of the planes are coming in merely for refueling.

But sometimes it is a grueling work, calling for quick—and heart-rending—decisions. When the B-29s had to land on the short, muddy Japanese runway in the early days, before the modern asphalted strip was ready, there was suspense, excitement and dread on Iwo. Sometimes the havening island was "socked in" by fog and there were distressed planes circling the island, all clamoring to be "let in."

Those days, and there have been several, Fennell had to limit Iwo's hospitality. One day all but seven planes, those in most serious trouble, had to be sent on to their home bases without landing. It was wild, nerve-wracking business, fighting to save those lost men of the air who could not even see the runway for the fog. There were bail-outs, some over the island, some over the sea, and there were crashes. But 75 of the 77 men were rescued. One wounded crewman fell, by lucky chance, in the hospital area. Others were fished from the ocean by persistently searching "ducks" of air sea rescue off shore.

But today is calm, routine. A few planes arrive with one or two engines gone bad. Most of them have landed for gasoline, or for minor engine repairs, playing it safe.

From the tower you can see them lined up, nose to tail, for a distance of two or three city blocks, wings shining in the rising sun. Not all, but at least some of them, would have been lost with their 11-man crews—but for Iwo Jima, the eyesore of the Pacific and—

"The most beautiful sight in the world to us," said a pilot, and his sleepy crewman yawned a fervent amen.

BOY HURT SWIMMING.

Robert Dissoway, 16, of 1 Glen Avenue, was treated at the Leonard Hospital yesterday afternoon for a cut on the sole of the right foot received while swimming at Pleasantdale. He was taken to the hospital in a police radio car by Sgt. Joseph Ormsby and Patrolman Peter Magnetto. After being treated he was taken to his home.

ANDREW DANISH TO INTRODUCE NEW BREED OF JERSEYS

County Farmer Obtains Canadian Bull to Sire New Herd Here

It's a far cry from chicken to cattle but Andrew K. Danish of Clums Corners who this year was designated as the outstanding poultry raiser in America and was honored as such by Gov. Thomas E. Dewey, has purchased a herd of cattle.

He will introduce into Rensselaer County a new breed of Jersey cattle obtained from the herd of B. H. Bull and Son at Brampton, Ontario, Canada.

The bull itself, "Brampton Danish Pinnacle Wizs," less than five months old, is valued at $1,000. The baby heifers, all born in March or April are "Brampton World Record Daisy," "Brampton Estel Clarissa," "Brampton Wren," and "Brampton Valley Pinn."

Mr. Danish plans to breed three so as to establish in the county a better breed of Jerseys. Mr. Bull, who signs himself "John Bull," obtained the nucleus of his herd direct from the Jersey Islands and has shipped prize cattle to establish herds in England, South Africa, New Zealand, Australia and Central America.

He is considered the largest importer of Jersey cattle and now has more than 1,000 on his farms in Ontario. The bull Mr. Danish bought was sired by "Imported Excellent Superior Gold Medal Herd Sire Pinnacle" and is half-brother to "Pinnacle Wizs" being shipped to Africa for $10,000.

The young cattle arrived here this week and were taken direct to the Danish Farm.

NEW VENTURE—Mr. and Mrs. Andrew Danish, operators of one of Rensselaer County's outstanding poultry farms at Clums Corners, yesterday embarked upon a new venture when they received five Jersey calves which will be the nucleus of a Jersey breeding station they will establish. Above are Mr. and Mrs. Danish, receiving the calves, valued at $3,500, from O. L. O'Brien of the American Railway Express Co., which transported them from Ontario, Canada.

HOME HONORS ROWAN.

Sweet Springs, W. Va. (UP)—A state home for the aged and infirm was opened this month at Old Sweet Springs, an ante-bellum resort, and was named for Andrew Summers Rowan, who carried the famed "Message to Garcia." Rowan was born in Monroe County, where the home is situated, a portrait of him, presented by the Spanish American War Veterans, hangs in the governor's suite at the statehouse in Charleston.

THE WEATHER
Tonight—Rain.

THE TIMES RECORD

FINAL EDITION

SERIES 1945—NO. 184

TROY, N. Y., MONDAY EVENING, AUGUST 6, 1945.

PRICE FOUR CENTS

JAPAN TREMBLES UNDER BLAST OF ATOMIC BOMB

U. S. Senator Hiram W. Johnson, Noted Isolationist, Dies At 78

CALIFORNIAN LED BATTLE AGAINST LEAGUE IN 1920

SEN. HIRAM W. JOHNSON

Also Opposed United Nations Charter; Review of Colorful Career

Washington (UP)—Sen. Hiram Warren Johnson, (R., Cal.) one of the few survivors of the "little band of wilful men" who kept the United States out of the League of Nations in 1920, died today a few weeks after he had reaffirmed his life-long isolationism by opposing the United Nations Charter.

The California elder statesman, dean of Senate Republicans, died in his sleep at Bethesda, Md., Naval Hospital at 6:45 a.m. E.W.T. He would have celebrated his 79th birthday on Sept. 2.

Johnson, who had been in ill health for several years, took little part in the charter debate. He telephoned his "no" vote, the first recorded, to the Senate Foreign Affairs Committee when it approved the charter. When the Senate itself voted, Johnson was unable to be on the floor, but was paired against the charter.

The other two survivors of the little isolationist group in the 1920 Senate credited with frustrating the dream of President Woodrow Wilson for U. S. leadership in the League of Nations both voted for the charter this time. They are Sen. Arthur Capper (R. Kan.) and Sen. David I. Walsh, (D., Mass.)

Entered Hospital July 18.

Johnson had been in the hospital since July 18, three days after he cast his committee vote on the charter. During the past several years, he had been absent from the Senate floor for long periods due to illness.

The immediate cause of death was given as cerebral thrombosis. He wife, the former Minnie L. McNeal, was with him when he died, and his only remaining son, Lt. Cpl. Hiram W. Johnson, jr., 55, was flying here from San Francisco.

Funeral arrangements were not announced immediately.

He was the second ranking member of the Senate in terms of continuous service. He had been a senator continuously since March 16, 1917, being outranked only by Sen. Kenneth McKellar (D., Tenn.)

His death leaves vacancies on five Senate committees. Most important was his position on the Foreign Relations Committee of which he was ranking Republican member and, in event of a change of administration, of which he would have been chairman.

Colorful Career.

Few men in public life had a more action-packed career than Johnson. From his election as governor of California in 1910 until his death, he played an important role in national affairs.

Perhaps the high point in his career was reached when he led a handful of other "irreconcilables" led a successful fight against the League of Nations in the Senate in 1920. He believed that the United States had no business in affairs outside the western hemisphere.

His feeling about the United States' role in world affairs was well demonstrated immediately after Pearl Harbor. A bill was pending in the Senate to remove the ban on sending American troops outside the western hemisphere. It required unanimous consent of the Senate to consider the bill immediately. When that request was made, Johnson arose slowly from the Senate seat he had occupied since 1916.

It was a tense moment. War had just been declared. That was a proposal to make it possible for American soldiers to fight again on European soil.

Objection Delayed Bill.

Johnson, in his deliberate way, looked from one senator to another.

"I object," he said.

That was all. But that was enough to delay the passage of the bill for one day.

His colleagues once regarded Johnson as the most powerful ora-

(Continued on Page 2.)

Mother Wrote 3,200 Letters To Troops

New York (INS)—If you think you don't want to write to the boys in uniform, consider Mrs. Theresa Danielle. This New York mother was revealed today to have written 3,200 letters in the last two and a half years to our five sons in the armed services and their friends in uniform. She devotes four hours every day writing 12 letters a week and only to her own boys but to others whose names and addresses they send her.

JAP WAR CENTERS AFIRE AFTER NEW BOMBER ATTACKS

Superforts and Mustangs Smash Nippon From Tokyo to Kyushu

Guam (UP)—Striking savagely for the second time in five days, 680 Superfortresses and Mustang fighters spread fire and destruction through six Japanese war centers stretching almost from the imperial palace in Tokyo to the southern home island of Kyushu yesterday and today.

Once again an all but helpless Japan—forewarned that the big bombers were coming on a mission of death—was unable to offer effective resistance while the industrial areas of Nishinomiya, Imabari, Maebashi and Saga and Ube Coal Liquefaction Co. burned and fell apart from 3,850 tons of incendiary and high explosive bombs dropped by a fleet of 580 Superforts.

Yesterday air raid sirens screamed throughout Tokyo in a warning that 100 P-51 Mustangs had returned to strike terror with rockets and machineguns against anything they could find in the Tokyo area.

Tokyo Bombed Again.

Radio Tokyo said 150 Mustangs carried the assault into the daylight today with an attack on the Tokyo area.

A single Japanese fighter watched them come yesterday and then fled from the skies.

The B-29s in two raids Aug. 2 and today have sown 10,500 tons of dreaded fire and demolition bombs on Japanese cities in warnings to the people of Japan to surrender unconditionally.

They have burned out approximately 160 square miles of war producing cities since the first fire raid on Tokyo March 9.

While the newest series of incendiary raids has always been preceded by warnings to civilians to flee to safety, their effectiveness was told bluntly in a single sentence in General Spaatz' communique which, reporting on the record raid Aug. 2, said:

"First photographs available on results of the B-29 strike in the early hours Aug. 2 show that the industrial area of Toyama was totally destroyed."

Toyama, with a population of 127,000, was the third largest city on Honshu fronting the Japan Sea, and had the empire's largest aluminum plant.

Japs Admit Loss.

The Japanese radio acknowledged the attacks as announced since July 18, about the number of dreaded air announced that 20-29s also bombed the Honshu cities of Asaka, Takasaki and Shibukawa.

Maebashi, Tokyo admitted, "suffered a considerable loss." It claimed eight B-29s were shot down.

Tokyo radio also reported extensive mine sowing "operations by B-29s in Wakasa Bay, off the west coast of Honshu; in the Harima Sea, between the Inland Sea and Osaka Bay, and the Sea of Japan.

The tremendous B-29 blow, in which one of the Marianas-based 20th Airforces planes was lost, was described by headquarters as merely a "normal effort" for the constantly-growing Superfortress forces.

Returning crewmen said they set towering fires in the pre-dawn darkness in the cities of Imabari and Saga, both of which had received their warning notices only yesterday; and Nishinomiya-Mikage and Maebashi, both of which were

(Continued on Page 2.)

Girl Says Goering "Burped" Like Tuba

Frankfurt (UP)—Hannalore Hinkel, pin-up girl of the defunct Wehrmacht, said that sitting down to breakfast with former Reichsmarshal Hermann Goering was like having a date with tuba. How that fat man burped!

Hannalore, who claims that she has always been anti-Nazi, spends most of her time in Frankfurt now. But she still can't forget those noises which used to rocket from the Goering stomach when she was visiting at Karin Hall.

Miss Hinkel, who is slim and lovely, said that bad news didn't keep Goering from eating—or burping. He would listen to a morning radio report of the previous night's Allied bombings with an egg stuffed in his throat. Then he would blast "My (burp) that's too bad."

Miss Hinkel a frequent guest at Karin Hall as the closest friend of Frau Emmy Goering, the Marshal's niece.

Miss Hinkel said Goering's day started about mid-morning when bulging in silk lavender or purple pajamas he would wander into the dining hall for breakfast. Once, she actually saw him in pajamas with medals across the chest.

Goering, himself, always carried the key to his food cellars which were jammed with such delicacies as caviar, sturgeon, frozen turkey or goose. If he liked someone real well, he would give him a box of caviar.

Goering had an elaborate and intricate set of electric trains.

"He would sit on the dais and press buttons as the trains scooted all about—with his adjutants squealing in joy," Miss Hinkel said. "He almost always closed the play period by arranging for two locomotives to crash by Buffalo police motives to crash the way it goes sometimes—and then order more."

MARSHAL PETAIN FRENCH PATRIOT, WITNESS ASSERTS

Weygand Ordered Troops to Hide Military Equipment From Nazis

Paris (UP)—Gen. Pico Andart testified at the treason trial of Marshal Petain today that French troops were ordered by Gen. Maxime Weygand at the end of the armistice to hide all military equipments. They concealed 18,000,000,000 francs of war material from the Germans and an equal amount of food and raw materials by the end of 1942, he asserted.

Andart said underground factories, at the order of Petain, started building machinegun carriers as early as 1941 and produced 270 of them in one year. The general said Petain congratulated him for his part in the activity and ordered him to continue his work.

"Pierre Laval knew of this but he did not appear to be interested," the witness said. Andart said the French hid and produced enough equipment for 24 divisions, except for heavy artillery and tanks. General Weygand, a previous witness, was French commander at the time of the armistice.

Pierre Merillon, French delegate to the United Nations conference at San Francisco, sent a cable to the trial from Santa Barbara, Cal., describing Petain as a man who served France with "perfect patriotism and loyalty" and "with all his power and energy."

The description was in a telegram from Pierre Merillon, former member of the French embassy in Madrid where Petain served.

It was read as the third week of the trial opened, just before Gen. Henri La Calle testified that Winston Churchill told a Vichy representative to Great Britain:

"We have been momentarily separated. Let us try not to damage each other any further."

The representative was a Colonel Groussard, whom the defense described as a former member of the pro-Fascist Cagoulard and as present representative of the de Gaulle government in Switzerland. The general said Groussard was sent by London to inquire if Great Britain could assist the French with military aid in North Africa. LaCalle did not say whether the British made commitments, most of his testimony was concerned with the material weakness of the French army in the years immediately preceding the war.

A heated argument developed when Prosecutor Andre Mornet asked Judge Paul Mongibeaux to order defense witnesses to be brief and specific in testimony.

(Continued on Page 2.)

FIRST CANADIAN TROOPS ARRIVE IN PACIFIC ZONE

Guam (UP)—Canadian troops, the vanguard of 30,000 men of the Canadian Army Pacific force, have arrived in advanced Pacific areas. They will be followed by Royal Canadian Air Force squadrons and sixty ships of the Canadian Navy, including two aircraft carriers, two cruisers, destroyers and frigates.

Col. Richard S. Malone, director of the Canadian Army public relations, said the Canadians will fight alongside Americans in the Pacific, using American weapons, organization, tactics and terms.

WOMAN ARRESTED FOR KIDNAPING BUFFALO BOY

Buffalo (UP)—Mrs. Venda Taylor Jones, 24, was committed to jail in default of $25,000 bail today after pleading innocent to a charge of kidnaping eight-year-old Peter Watson. She was arrested in Meridian, Miss., terminating a long man-and-Miss, terminating a week which sent the police on a frantic hunt from coast to coast. The mother was arrested by Buffalo police and at her arraignment her case was adjourned until Aug. 8.

BOMBERS BLAST JAP BATTLESHIP: U. S. and British carrier-based planes score direct hits on fantail of Jap battleship Haruna as she is moored in the Kure area July 28. Near misses send geysers of water towering above the enemy warship.

NOTED U. S. GUNNER MISSING IN ACTION

Hermann Fought Over Rome, Berlin and Tokyo

Guam (UP)—Tailgunner Kurt J. Hermann, who fought over two oceans and all three enemy capitals, is missing in action—just two trips short of his self-set 110-mission retirement goal.

The 26-year-old tech sergeant from Babylon, N. Y., passed up at least two chances to go home to stay. He wanted to complete 110 combat missions. On the 108th, over Kochi, Japan, on July 4, his Superfort was lost.

The 20th Air Force yesterday disclosed his amazing record, topping even the 107-mission record of T/Sgt. Lewis L. Coburn, Niagara Falls, N. Y.

Serving first in the Merchant Marine, Hermann survived a torpedoing, spent 26 days on a life raft, was rescued, and enlisted in the Air Force in August, 1942.

He bagged his first German Messerschmitt as a waist gunner aboard a 12th Air Force Fortress based in North Africa. Transferring to a Marauder force, he knocked down three more enemy fighters. Parachuting from a badly damaged B-26 after a strike at Sardinia, he landed unhurt beside an American field hospital. And in July, 1943, he participated in the first bombing of Rome.

Furloughed, he hitch-hiked home by air, was called to Washington by Gen. Henry H. Arnold, the Air Forces chief, and got his requested transfer to the Eighth Air Force in England. He participated in the first bombardment of Berlin—and in his nights off, used to fly with the R. A. F.

After 75 missions—a record, at that time—he was due to return home. He sought an interview with General Spaatz, and from it came his assignment to Superfort training.

On his first raid on Japan he added a Nipponese fighter to his Axis bag; and from his tailgunner's position he watched 32 demolition or fire raids on the enemy homeland before he set forth for his 108th mission on July 4, 1945.

He could have gone home when the Army inaugurated its point system.

Private Phone Was Not So Exclusive

Kansas City (UP)—After waiting patiently for three years Mr. and Mrs. Paul Fleming finally got a telephone installed at their home—and on a private line, too.

At least they thought for a few hours it was private.

The lineman had connected their phone to the Braniff Airways, Inc., line, and all the Flemings' conversations went out on the air via the Braniff radio transmitter to planes and stations everywhere—just everywhere.

LONG LOST ARMY TRANSPORT FOUND

Three Died in Crash on Adirondack Mountain

Rome (UP) Search continued today for a civilian plane, missing since July 18, after forest rangers last night reached a wrecked Army transport with three decomposed bodies inside on Snowy Mountain.

Authorities at the Rome Army Air Field said soldiers would attempt to reach the wrecked transport, tentatively identified as a C-46, sometime today.

A C-46 disappeared last fall on a routine flight from the Syracuse Army Air Base. Army officials said. Aboard it were Second Lt. William R. Farohn, Syracuse; Second Lt. C C Pate, Pine Bluff, Ark., and Tech. Sgt. Edward V. Paska, Hartford, Conn.

A civilian plane, searching for the civilian plane which disappeared on a flight from Lake Placid to Boomville, spotted the transport. Fred MacLane, Conservation Department pilot, directed the rangers to the scene from the air by walkie talkie.

The missing civilian plane was piloted by Ray Giles, Camden, and carried the Misses Shirley Whitey and Jeanne Adams of Rome.

Five Die In Fire At Detroit Orphanage

Detroit (UP)—Five persons, including two 7-year-old twin brothers, lost their lives and another inmate was in critical condition after a Sunday night explosion and fire at a Detroit orphanage and old people's home.

More than 130 other persons were led or carried to safety by orphanage employees and firemen. Police identified the dead as: Albert and Alfred Cade, 7; Christine Loath, 30; Elizabeth Berchtel, 52, and Ida Albrecht, 85.

Receiving hospital authorities listed the critically injured as Helene Kreutz, 90, who is suffering from shock and smoke inhalation.

Inspector George W. Smith of the Detroit Fire Department arson squad said the blaze broke out in the basement laundry of the Evangelical Home for Orphans and Old People, which is on West Grand Boulevard.

Firemen responding to three alarms joined in the rescue work and then confined the blaze to the basement of the home.

TYPHOON DAMAGED AIRCRAFT CARRIER

U.S.S. Hornet Arrives in California for Repairs

BY COURTENAY MOORE

Washington (UP—The aircraft carrier Hornet, which has sunk or damaged about 1,270,000 tons of Japanese shipping and destroyed 1,410 enemy planes, is back home for repair—but it took a typhoon to bring her back. The Japanese never touched her.

The 27,000-ton Essex class carrier, named in honor of the ship which took the first American flyers to Tokyo in 1942, put in 16 months of battle-packed action in the Pacific before arriving at San Francisco for a rest.

During that period, the Hornet and her flyers inflicted the following damage on the enemy: 668 planes shot down; 742 planes destroyed on the ground; one carrier, one cruiser, ten destroyers and 43 cargo ships sunk; and an "assist" in the sinking of the battleship Yamato.

The Hornet had been through one typhoon in the Philippines, but the typhoon on June 5—which damaged many other American warships—bounced her around like a chip. The 120-knot gale caught the Hornet 150 miles east of Okinawa at 3 a.m.

Suddenly her bow rose atop a tremendous wave and crashed downward with such force that the forward corners of the flight deck folded down along her sides. She was forced to retire from the battle area and head home.

PLANE CRASHES NEAR NEWBURG, TWO KILLED

Newburg (UP)—A Stewart field flying instructor and a West Point cadet were killed yesterday in the crash near here of an AT-6 plane, the Stewart field commanding officer said today.

Lt. William F. Hall of Sheffield, Ala., was fatally injured in the crash at Beaver Dam farm at 5:45 p.m. yesterday. The cadet's identity was not revealed pending notification of his next-of kin, Col. Gen. Jamin J. Webster said. The plane fell while engaged in a routine training mission.

U.S. Airmen Drop Death Missile On Hiroshima Base

Sensational Bomb Packs Explosive Force of 20,000 Tons of TNT; American and Allied Scientists Win Race for Control of Atom; President Truman Warns Japanese They Now Face Rain of Ruin from Skies; Stimson Reports Even More Deadly Bomb Due Shortly.

Washington (UP) — The United States has unleashed against Japan the terror of an atomic bomb, 2,000 times more powerful than the biggest blockbusters ever used in warfare.

President Truman revealed this great scientific achievement today and warned the Japanese that they now face "a rain of ruin from the air the like of which has never been seen on this earth."

More and more of these devastating bombs, unlocking the vast hidden energy that lies within the atom, will tumble on Japan if they continue to reject the Potsdam surrender ultimatum, he said.

The new atomic bomb was used for the first time yesterday. An American plane dropped one on the Japanese army base at Hiroshima.

Its use marked victory for the Allies in the greatest scientific race in history. We put $2,000,000,000 and the work of 125,000 persons into the project.

A single blast has more power than 20,000 tons of TNT, it has more than 2,000 times the blast powder of the British "grand slam" bomb, the largest ever used previously in the history of warfare.

Secretary of War Henry L. Stimson disclosed that an improved bomb would be forthcoming shortly that would increase "by several fold" the present effectiveness of the new weapon.

The War Department said it was not yet able to make an accurate report of the damage caused by the first bomb.

Uranium Essential Ore.

"Reconnaissance planes state that an impenetrable cloud of dust and smoke covered the target area," an announcement said. "As soon as accurate details of the result of the bombing become available, they will be released by the secretary of war."

Stimson revealed that uranium is the essential ore in the production of the bombs. He added that "steps have been taken and will continue to be taken to insure adequate supplies of this mineral."

Stimson said "we are convinced that Japan will not be in a position to use an atomic bomb in this war."

"It is abundantly clear that the possession of this weapon by the United States even in its present form should prove a tremendous aid in the shortening of the war against Japan," he said.

Stimson praised highly the scientists who had developed atomic power.

Development of the bomb, a victory of American scientists in a desperate race with Germany, is "the greatest achievement of organized science in history," Mr. Truman said in a statement released at the White House.

The United States, he added, is now prepared "to obliterate more rapidly and completely every productive enterprise the Japanese have above ground in any city."

He revealed that the July 26 ultimatum issued to Japan at Potsdam was made "to spare the Japanese people from utter destruction."

Closely Guarded Secret.

When the ultimatum was rejected, the atomic bomb was sent into action.

"If they (the Japanese leaders) do not now accept our terms, they may expect a rain of ruin from the air, the like of which has never been seen on this earth," he said.

Mr. Truman revealed that "two great plants and many lesser works" employing more than 65,000 workers are producing the new atomic bomb. Even more destructive bombs are being developed, he said.

Production centers are located at Oak Ridge, near Knoxville, Tenn., at Richland, near Pasco, Wash., and near Sante Fe, N. M.

Mr. Truman's statement, released while he was still en route home by cruiser from Potsdam, lifted the secrecy from one of the most closely-guarded secrets of the war. No mention of atomic power or any possible use of it in warfare has been allowed under the newspaper and radio code of the Office of Censorship.

Mr. Truman did not reveal the effects of the first bomb used against Japan. He said, however, that despite the vast multiplied potency of the bomb, "the physical size of the explosive charge is exceedingly small."

"It is an atomic bomb," he said. "It is harnessing of the basic power of the universe.

"The force from which the sun draws its power has been loosed against those who brought war to the Far East."

The first atomic bomb presumably was dropped from a B-29 Superfortress.

Reviewing the fearful potency of the new bomb, the President said he would recommend that Congress consider the establishment of an appropriate commission to control the production and use of atomic power within the United States.

"I shall give further consideration and make further recommendations to the Congress as to how atomic power can become a powerful forceful influence toward the maintenance of world peace," the President said.

Germans Failed.

Mr. Truman revealed that yesterday's use of the bomb signaled an American victory in a feverish race with German scientists to find some way to harness and release atomic energy.

Before 1939, he said, it was the accepted belief of scientists that it was "theoretically possible" to release atomic energy. But no one

then knew any practical method of doing it, he added.

By 1942, however, Mr. Truman continued, "we knew that the Germans were working feverishly to find a way to add atomic energy

(Continued on Page 2.)

The Index

	Page
Classified	14-15
Cohoes	7
Comics	12
Death Notices	7
Editorial	6
Obituary	7
Pulse of the People	6
Radio	12
Society	10
Sports	8-9
Theaters	11
Women's Features	10

THE WEATHER
Tonight—Clear, cool.

THE TIMES RECORD

SERIES 1945—NO. 192 · TROY, N. Y., WEDNESDAY EVENING, AUGUST 15, 1945.

WORLD PEACE DAWNING AFTER JAP SURRENDER

Japan's Cabinet Resigns, Sequel To War Defeat

One Member Commits Suicide; Others May Follow Suit

San Francisco (UP)—The Japanese cabinet resigned today and one member already has committed hari-kari in the first of what may become a wave of suicides among Japan's beaten war lords.

The official Japanese Domei News Agency said War Minister Gen. Korechika Anami, 56, took his life at his official residence to "atone for his failure in accomplishing his duties as his majesty's minister."

Domei said Premier Kantaro Suzuki tendered the resignation of his cabinet at 3:20 p.m. Tokyo time (2:20 a.m., E. W. T.) because of "the new situation created by Japanese acceptance of the Potsdam declaration."

Japan's surrender requires a new cabinet of men "with fresh ideas," Tokyo said. The cabinet's decision was reached at an extraordinary meeting at the Premier's official residence.

Others May End Lives.

Disclosure of Anami's suicide touched off speculation that other members of the Suzuki and past cabinets similarly would "atone for their failure" to win the war.

Next to carry out Japan's traditional "face saving" gesture of death by disembowelment might well be Suzuki himself or Navy Minister Admr. Mitsumasa Yonai, a former premier, whose ships and planes failed to halt the American march across the Philippines and Okinawa. Suzuki became Premier April 7, 1945.

Another former premier, Gen. Hideki Tojo, one of the chief instigators of the Pearl Harbor attack also may choose suicide. Tojo is expected to be named by the Allies among Japan's leading war criminals.

Domei gave no details of Anami's suicide, but there seemed little doubt that he followed the ancient custom of plunging a dagged into the left side of his stomach, drawing it to the right and turning it upward.

Military Careerist.

Tradition calls for an official second simultaneously to behead the victim with a sword.

Anami, a military careerist, became war minister when Suzuki installed his cabinet April 7, 1945. The former cabinet under Gen. Kuniaki Koiso resigned after the American invasion of Okinawa and Russia's denunciation of the Russo-Japanese friendship pact.

Anami was graduated from the Japanese Military Academy in 1907 and held a succession of minor posts before becoming director general of army aviation headquarters prior to joining the cabinet.

Yonai, Navy minister in the Suzuki cabinet, held the same post in the Koiso government and served briefly as premier in 1940. His predecessor, Admr. Shigetaro Shimada, another possible candidate for hara-kari was navy minister at the time of Pearl Harbor.

MILLIONS CHEER DAWN OF PEACE IN WILD CELEBRATION

America Flings Off Wartime Restraint to Hail Victory

BY THE ASSOCIATED PRESS.

Millions lifted their hearts and voices today to hail the dawn of peace.

There were tears, laughter, hysteria and prayers throughout the Allied world as Japan, last undefeated aggressor nation, announced it had surrendered.

"Thank God—Thank God it's over at last!" were words repeated again and again, in every language. The bloodiest, most destructive war in history was at an end.

America flung off its wartime restraint and exploded in the greatest, wildest, most ecstatic celebration of all time. Boisterous, happy crowds sang, danced and cheered into the early morning. Thousands prepared to continue the fiesta during the two-day holiday proclaimed for today and tomorrow by the United States and Britain.

Veterans Happy.

Everywhere, veterans of the war were in the forefront of the jubilation.

In the Pacific islands, in shattered Germany and bomb-scarred England, in Manila, in Paris, in ships at sea and in hospital wards—they cheered and cried and thumped each other on the back. 'Now we'll be home sooner," they said.

In America, they were toasted and kissed and praised and wept over.

All through Latin America and the West Indies there was wild rejoicing. Tiny Bermuda kicked over the traces in the most boisterous celebration ever seen there, aided by shouting, singing American servicemen.

Shooting, fireworks and some disorders were reported in Havana. In Buenos Aires there were violent demonstrations and frequent clashes between student and Nationalist groups, which were stopped by police.

Pearl Harbor, where the Pacific war began on Dec. 7, 1941, sounded its air raid sirens to proclaim peace, not war, and confetti, not shrapnel, littered the streets

Washington's traditional reserve vanished in the melee of hilarious celebrants.

In New York State.

Formal observances and grateful prayers of thanksgiving in churches and family groups today followed New York State's night of wild jubilation over the unconditional surrender of Japan.

There were still sporadic outbursts of horn blowing and cheering but the excitement that gripped every city and hamlet in the state—in some, after one or more false starts—had tired itself into quiet.

Factories, stores and offices were closed following Governor Dewey's proclamation last night setting aside today as "a day of thanksgiving and celebration." State offices also will be closed tomorrow "in recognition of the momentous services rendered" by state employes during the war.

Business places generally were expected to be closed for the two-

(Continued on Page 2.)

Celebrations Take Toll Of 12 Lives

BY THE ASSOCIATED PRESS.

Victory celebrations — gay and unrestrained in every hamlet and city throughout the nation—brought death to a dozen persons and injury to thousands last night.

A 66-year-old mother of two servicemen died in Scottdale, Pa., when she heard the announcement of Japan's surrender.

In New York City two celebrators were killed by automobiles, one by stabbing and one from a fall from a window. A Los Angeles woman dropped dead when she became caught in a milling throng.

A Marine, just returned from the Pacific, died after a fall down a San Francisco hotel stairway. In the same city a railroad switchman, confused by the noise, stepped in front of a moving locomotive.

Excitement over the war's end brought death to a Pittsburg man and a Norfolk, Va., clerk.

GIANT MUNITIONS CUT ANNOUNCED

War Department Reveals 23 Billion Reduction

Washington (AP)—A $23,500,000,000-a-year cut in procurement of munitions and supplies was announced today by the War Department.

The department said that as soon as President Truman announced the Japanese surrender last night, telegrams went out to prime contractors notifying them of cutbacks reducing Army procurement from $2,400,000,000 a month to $435,000,000 amonth.

Of the procurement which is continuing, the department announced, $368,000,000 monthly represents food purchases.

Production of most types of weapons and equipment has been halted entirely. Those which are still being manufactured on a "limited basis" are primarily experimental items.

Further reductions will be made as the Army is demobilized the department said.

The percentage cut-backs by items follow:

Aircraft, 94 per cent artillery and tanks 98; ammunition, all types, 98; construction equipment, including tractors, and bridging equipment, 100; medical supplies, including drugs, pharmaceuticals, hospital equipment and supplies, 50; food, 20; clothing and equipage, including shoes and textile items 75; locomotives and railroad cars, 100; telephone and telegraph equipment, 100; radio and radar equipment 80; tires, 100; and gasoline 44.

RUSSIAN FORCES CONTINUE DRIVE INTO MANCHURIA

Vasilevsky Announces Jap Surrender but Gives No Cease-Fire Order

London (UP)—Marshal Alexander M. Vasilevsky announced Japan's surrender in a broadcast to his Soviet Far Eastern armies today, but gave no "cease fire" order and hostilities apparently still continue.

London sources believed the Soviet armies would continue their advances in Manchuria, Korea and the Japanese half of Sakhalin Island at least until Japan formally signs the Allied surrender terms.

Russia's Trans-Baikal army already was threatening Manchuria's inner citadels of Harbin, Mukden and Changchun after caving in the enemy's western defenses with a 93-mile advance in the last 24 hours.

More than 8,000 Japanese prisoners were taken in the first six days of the Far Eastern campaign, a Moscow communique said.

"Smashed Aggressors."

Vasilevsky told his Red Banner armies over the Khabarovsk radio that they, together with their great allies, had smashed the "nest of imperialism and aggression in the Far East."

"At last, the peoples of the world can look forward to peace and peaceful toil," he said. "Having carried out the order of our fatherland and of our great leader Stalin, the heroic Red Army men have secured the safety of our Far Eastern frontiers.

"You have fought courageously. You went into battle with the name of our fatherland and of our Comrade Stalin on your lips and won.

"Today we are giving the solemn oath to vigilantly guard our frontiers and make certain that peaceful toil is again possible in our invincible country."

Taonan Captured.

Marshal Rodion Y. Malinovsky's Trans-Baikal army, bursting from the Outer Mongolian deserts, swept 62 to 93 miles across western Manchuria along a 300-mile front.

Overrun in the advance were Taonan, 185 miles west of Harbin; Chanyu, 135 miles northwest of Changchun, capital of Manchuria, and Linso, 200 miles north of the Chinese border and 263 miles north of Peiping, ancient capital of China.

Tokyo broadcast said another Soviet spearhead was near Tungliau, 140 miles northwest of the Manchurian industrial center of Mukden.

Marshal K. A. Meretskov's First Red Banner Army in eastern Manchuria crossed the Mutankiang River and captured a town of the same name 170 miles southeast of Harbin.

To the northeast, the Second Red Banner Army advanced 25 to 31 miles south along both banks of the Sungari River. It captured the railway junction of Hingshanchen, forty miles south of the Amur River and 211 miles north of Harbin.

In Korea, Soviet Pacific fleet marines captured the naval base of Seishin, 56 miles south of the Soviet border, after a two-day battle.

Moscow confirmed that Russian troops on Sakhalin Island had forced the entire frontier into the Japanese half of the island, known as Karafuto, and pushed nine to 13 miles south. The southern tip of Karafuto lies only twenty to thirty miles north of the Japanese home island of Hokkaido.

BANKER DIES UPSTATE.

Saranac Lake (AP)—Eric P. Swenson, 90, New York banker and industrialist, died yesterday at his summer home on upper Saranac Lake.

GAS, FUEL OIL RATIONING END

Washington (AP)—OPA today announced immediate termination of the rationing of gasoline, canned fruits and vegetables, fuel oil and oil stoves.

Price Administrator Chester Bowles said that meats, fats and oils, butter, sugar, shoes and tires will stay on the ration list "until military cutbacks and increased production brings civilian supplies more nearly in balance with civilian demand.

"Nobody is any happier than we in OPA," Bowles said, "that as far as gasoline is concerned, the day is finally here when we can drive our cars whenever we please, when we please and as much as we please."

The OPA chief said "right now it's impossible" to estimate when other commodities can be removed from rationing. He added:

"It certainly can't come too soon as far as we are concerned. You can be sure that the other items will go off the list the minute we hear that supplies are anywhere near big enough to go around."

Gasoline rationing began in the east May 15, 1942, and was extended throughout the nation Dec. 1, 1942.

The canned fruits and vegetables program began in March, 1943, while fuel oil rationing came to the east in October, 1942, and to the rest of the nation in March, 1943.

Hirohito Gives People Of Japan News Of Defeat

Emperor Says Atomic Bomb Threatened to Obliterate Nippon

BY THE ASSOCIATED PRESS.

The Japanese people heard from the lips of Emperor Hirohito today the news that Japan — a nation which has boasted it never lost a war—had been compelled to surrender to the Allies to escape "obliteration."

Hirohito's announcement, the first radio broadcast ever made by a Japanese emperor to his subjects, attributed Japan's plight to the invention of the atomic bomb, which he described as "a new and most cruel weapon, the power of which to do damage is incalculable."

"This is the reason we have ordered the acceptance of the joint declaration of the powers, "the Emperor declared.

Hirohito—in the face-saving tradition dear to the Japanese—maintained to the end that Japan had been battling only in self defense and that she had given up the fight "to strive for the common prosperity and happiness of all nations and the well-being of our subjects.

The bitter reaction of Japan's militarists to the ignominy of unconditional surrender, however, was reflected in the immediate suicide of War Minister Gen. Koreichika Anami and a broadcast address by Premier Baron Kantaro Suzuki in which he declared:

"This day has become the day that never, never will be forgotten by the Japanese people."

The same bitterness was reflected in a Tokyo broadcast in which Kusuo Oya, identified as chief of the Overseas Bureau of the Japan Broadcasting Corp., told troops on the fighting fronts of the surrender.

"We have come to a point where it is useless to resist the enemy further," Oya said. "We have bowed to the enemy's material and scientific power. x x x we have lost, but this is temporary."

Oya added, the FCC said, that Japan's mistake was the lack of "material strength, necessary scientific knowledge and equipment,"

(Continued on Page 2.)

WORKERS GETTING DOUBLE HOLIDAY

War Labor Board Rules on Pay Angles Involved

Washington (AP)—Who gets today and tomorrow off?

All government employees except skeleton forces.

Most war workers. Those who do work, President Truman has ruled, are entitled to premium pay.

Some banks. Comptroller of the Currency Preston Delano says the board of directors of each national bank must decide for itself.

Practically everyone else. Many governors have, or are expected to, come out with proclamations declaring legal holidays.

In connection with the President's two-day victory holiday directive, War Labor Board Chairman George W. Taylor reiterated in an interview that the pay angles involved won't conflict with the stabilization policy.

These two days—plus V-J Day if Mr. Truman proclaims that a holiday, too—may be considered as time worked for purposes of making up the payroll, says Taylor.

That means:

1. The worker may be paid for these two days at regular rates, just as though he had been on the job.

2. The two days may be considered as worked in figuring overtime or premium pay.

3. If required to work on these two days, he may be given premium rates, if that's the company's practice on holidays.

OKINAWA YANKS TONE DOWN VICTORY SALUTE

Okinawa (AP)—At least six men were killed in a spontaneous premature victory celebration last night on this island by a wild ack-ack display.

Today there was no such celebrating. Word had been spread to all personnel on the island that a stretch in the brig would be the penalty for any unauthorized use of firearms.

Cruiser Indianapolis Sunk In Pacific; 800 Of Crew Perish

Guam (UP)—Two tremendous torpedo explosions sank the heavy Cruiser Indianapolis July 30 and caused 1,196 casualties—every man aboard ship—while she was bound from Guam to Leyte, survivors reported today.

The Navy announced that 880 of the casualties were killed or missing in one of the worst U. S. naval disasters of war or peacetime history. The other 316 casualties were wounded.

The 9,950-ton cruiser was sunk shortly after delivering essential atomic bomb material to Guam.

Survivors said they watched some 200 of their shipmates perish after five days of helpless threshing in the sea. Many of the men went mad from drinking sea water before the group was sighted by search planes 280 miles north of Peleliu.

Capt. Charles Butler McVay III, Washington, D. C., commander of the, Indianapolis, said the cruiser, Vice Admr. Raymond A. Spruance's former flagship, was, torpedoed at 12:15 a.m. July 30.

In a matter of minutes the Indianapolis took on a 90 degree list and sank by the bow, carrying almost 700 of her crew to the bottom.

The first shock of the torpedo hurled men from their bunks, Lt. Cmdr. Lewis L. Haynes, Fairfield, Conn., said.

As the ship listed heavily, 800 men grabbed life jackets and rubber life rings and literally walked into the sea. In the water they locked arms and struggled to keep their heads above the oily surface.

Scores of the injured died before dawn. On the second day others slipped from their lifebelts from exhaustion and during hallucinations brought on by swallowing salt water.

Many of the men began to talk of home, food and water," Haynes said. "They were babbling of 'going to the galley for coffee,' or 'swimming over to that island where there is a beautiful native girl, seabees and tomato juice." Then they began swimming toward the 'island' that wasn't there. Twenty-five of them drowned. You could hear their ravings growing fainter and then silence."

"After the kapok life jackets had passed their normal water tolerance of 48 hours they became waterlogged and lost their buoyancy. They barely kept the men's heads above the surface, and waves were slapping them in the face."

Fifty-six of the group in life jackets were rescued by a Catalina flying boat, piloted by Lt. Radrain Marks, Ladoga, Ind., which loaded twenty men on the wings, McVay said.

McVay and 92 officers and men were brought to Peleliu by the destroyer escort Cecil J. Doyle. Other destroyers picked up the remainder from liferafts.

The Indianapolis was blacked out and traveling at 17 knots when she was hit, the skipper declared. At first he thought his ship had been struck by a suicide plane.

McVay was washed overboard as the ship went down. He grabbed floating debris and later found a craft.

JAP PLANES SHOT DOWN BY FLEET AFTER SURRENDER

Nipponese Made Abortive Attack on U. S. Warships Off Honshu

Guam (UP)—Japan sent planes against the U.S. Third Fleet today—as late as eight hours after her surrender was announced. At the same time, Tokyo warned Allied warships not to enter Japanese home waters pending an official Japanese "cease fire" order.

Adm. Chester W. Nimitz announced at 4 p.m. Tokyo time—eight hours after he had ordered his Pacific forces to cease offensive operations—that the Third Fleet had shot down five approaching Japanese planes off Honshu since noon.

The five planes—a bomber and four Zero fighters—were shot down during an "abortive enemy assault" that lasted 14 minutes, a fleet dispatch said.

The Third Fleet was 110 miles off the Japanese coast at the time and ready, in the words of its commander, Adm. William F. (Bull) Halsey, to take "prompt and profitable advantage of the surrender."

Nimitz said Gen. Douglas MacArthur, the new supreme Allied commander, had been asked to inform Japan that defense measures required American naval forces to destroy "any Japanese aircraft approaching our dispositions."

Yanks Take No Chances.

In any event, American anti-aircraft gun crews and carrier planes were taking no chances. Adm. William F. Halsey, commander of the Third Fleet, has radioed his pilots:

"It looks like the war is over, but if any enemy planes appear, shoot them down in friendly fashion."

Reports from the fleet said the first enemy planes approached the fleet even as Halsey hoisted a giant 30-foot American Flag over his flagship in triumphant acknowledgement of the Allied victory.

One enemy plane was shot down 14 minutes later. An air raid alert warned the fleet.

Nimits's orders to all forces under his command to cease offensive operations was flashed throughout his command at 8 a.m. Tokyo time—the very hour that President Truman in Washington was announcing Japan's surrender.

Radio word to "cease fire" interrupted the final carrier-based air attack of the war on the Tokyo area. One wave of planes already had completed their attack and a second was airborne when the dramatic order to return reached the pilots.

Eight Jap Planes Downed.

A dispatch from Vice Adm. John S. McCain's flagship said the last planes over Japan ran into some of the most intensive opposition of the summer. First reports said at least eight intercepting Japanese planes were shot down in flames.

"This task force is maintaining every precaution," the dispatch said. "We still do not know whether some Japanese may want to continue the fight despite the emperor's surrender rescript."

All combat planes later were ordered not to fly over Japan during the next 24 hours, presumably to give the Japanese time to promulgate their surrender orders.

Hours earlier, almost 400 Superfortresses had delivered their last blow of the war against Japan. They struck last night 12 hours after Tokyo had broadcast that Japan would surrender.

ROOSEVELT'S GRAVE DESERTED IN HOUR OF COMPLETE WAR VICTORY

Hyde Park (AP)—The Hudson Valley grave of Franklin D. Roosevelt lay in stillness punctuated only by footsteps of a lone sentry as the complete victory for which the late President worked so hard and long finally came.

There were no visitors at the grave, but, in the nearby village residents had not forgotten their neighbor who had led them through most of the war.

Supervisor Elmer Van Wagener said at a community church service, "We are all happy that it's all over, but we all regret that the late President Roosevelt couldn't have lived to be with us in this celebration."

How Long Have Wars Lasted?

Washington (AP) — How long have the wars lasted?

Our war with Japan lasted 1,346 days after the Pearl Harbor attack of Dec. 7, 1941.

The European was lasted 2,075 days after Hitler's legions struck Poland Sept. 1, 1939.

For the Chinese, peace came after 2,946 days of uninterrupted warfare with the Japanese, beginning with the Marco Polo Bridge incident of July 7, 1937.

Guns Silent On Bulk Of Great Pacific Front

President Announces Unconditional Capitulation Of Japanese Forces; Gen. Douglas MacArthur Named Allied Supreme Commander; Notifies Tokyo Government To Send Peace Envoy To Ie Island Friday; Truman Points Nation To Problems Of Reconversion.

Washington (AP)—Blasted and frightened into defeat, Japan has accepted unconditional surrender.

Thus the world entered a new era of peace today.

Along the enormous battlefronts of the Pacific and Asia the mightiest forces of destruction ever assembled rolled to a victorious halt around the prostrate, vanquished empire of Japan.

Throughout the Allied world, wracked by war or threat of war since Germany struck Poland on Sept. 1, 1939, it was a time for rejoicing and celebration. But already the problems of peace were beginning to pile up.

"We are faced with the greatest task we ever have been faced with," said President Truman. "The emergency is as great as it was on Dec. 7, 1941."

General MacArthur, Allied commander in Japan, ordered Emperor Hirohito to put a radio station at his disposal and told him to send his peace envoy in a white plane with green crosses to Ie Island off Okinawa Friday morning.

Accepting command of the Allied occupation forces of Japan, General MacArthur said at Manila:

"I thank a merciful God that this mighty struggle is about to end." His next sentence was "I shall at once take steps to stop hostilities and further bloodshed."

Truman Announces Surrender.

Mr. Truman announced Japan's capitulation at 7 o'clock, Eastern War Time, last night. The act marked the beginning of a truce that will last a few days until Gen. of the Army Douglas MacArthur, as supreme Allied commander, can accept formal Japanese surrender on the basis of the Potsdam declaration.

While promising the Japanese people free and decent lives, this declaration lays down a hard future for them. It is much like that imposed on Germany, except that the Japanese will have their own national government, including an emperor, under rigid Allied control.

All means ever to make war again are to be stripped from them. At advance Pacific bases military government officers stood ready to move in with occupation forces and carry out these terms.

More than four hours after Mr. Truman announced the surrender, the war was still on in the Pacific. A communique from Guam early today reported that units of the U. S. Third Fleet in the vicinity of Honshu were being approached by Japanese aircraft.

"Those that do so are being shot down," the war bulletin said, adding that five had been destroyed since noon Japanese time (11 p.m. E. W. T. Tuesday night.)

"Useless To Resist"

Radio Tokyo, however, waited another hour, until 1 p.m., Japanese time, to tell its troops of the surrender.

"We have come to a point where it is useless to resist the enemy any longer," the broadcast said. "We have lost, but this is temporary," it added.

A Domei dispatch broadcast by the Tokyo radio today said imperial headquarters is endeavoring to transmit the imperial order to every branch of the forces but before it took full effect a part of the Japanese air force is reported to have made an attack to the Allied base and fleet in the south.

Domei News Agency reported that Emperor Hirohito, addressing his nation for the first time by radio, blamed surrender on two main facts:

1. That the trend of the world was against Japan.

2. On the atomic bomb — which went into action only nine days ago and was used against only two cities.

Hirohito told his subjects, according to Domei, not to make trouble, to avoid fighting among themselves and to unite their strength "to be devoted to the construction of the future." Allied plans call for the victorious powers to control that future for a long time to come.

No Conditions Attached.

Mr. Truman announced the surrender at a two-minute news conference. He released at the same time the text of an acceptance note which the Japanese government had sent to Washington through neutral Switzerland yesterday afternoon.

"I deem this reply a full acceptance of the Potsdam declaration which specifies the unconditional surrender of Japan," Mr. Truman said.

There were no conditions, although the foe had sought last Friday to win guarantees that the emperor would remain a sovereign ruler.

The nation that set out at Pearl Harbor to defeat America and conquer the Pacific and lands beyond had caved in completely.

With the President's announcement came a flood of orders:

1. General MacArthur was designated formally as supreme commander for the Allied powers—the United States, Russia, Britain and China—to accept the formal Japanese surrender.

2. The Japanese government, in a message sent through Switzerland, was ordered by Mr. Truman to stop hostilities on all front and to send emissaries to MacArthur to arrange for the surrender.

3. Allied armed forces were ordered to suspend offensive action.

4. Today and tomorrow were proclaimed by the President as holidays, although V-J Day awaits the formal surrender.

At Guam Admr. Chester W. Nimitz followed through with an order to the Pacific fleet and other forces under his command to cease their attacks on the Japanese.

Admr. William F. Halsey radioed the death-dealing pilots of his Third Fleet carrier planes to cease firing "but if you see any enemy planes in the air shoot them down in friendly fashion."

At Manila MacArthur, who had been building up an invasion army that eventually would have struck the death blow had Japan not surrendered, declared "I shall at once take steps to stop hostilities and further bloodshed."

But no steps taken anywhere could make up for the losses of life and treasure already lost in mankind's most frightful conflict.

The United States alone could count nearly [illegible] dead and wounded and a [illegible] cost estimated at [illegible].

The nations of the world [illegible]

(Continued on Page 2.)

The Index

JAP BAN SUSPENDED.

Washington (AP)—The Army cancelled last night orders banning individuals of Japanese descent from the West Coast.

As of midnight, Pacific War Time, those in eight relocation centers are free to return to California, Arizona, Washington and Oregon. But some 6,700 who are in interment will stay there a while.

Hans Lippershey invented the refracting telescope in 1608. Perfected by Galileo, it came to be known as the Galilean Telescope.

Pal Pioneered, Perfected and Possessed the *Hollow Ground* blade—a different, modern blade. Shaves with just a "Feather Touch" because Pal is *flexible* in the razor—follows facial contours. No need to "bear down". Blades last longer, too. Try them.

PAL

Charge Purchases
MADE IN SEPT.
Not Payable Until
NOV. 10th
358 BROADWAY
Paula Shop

265 REGISTER AT ST. PAUL'S SCHOOL; CLASSES STARTED

Twenty-five Children in Newly-Formed Kindergarten Group; Other Notes

MECHANICVILLE

Providing for one of the largest student bodies in recent years, St. Paul's Parochial School reopened yesterday at 9 a.m. following mass in St. Paul's Church celebrated by Rev. Michael A. Hopkins, O.S.A., pastor.

The registration of 265 pupils, including a kindergarten class of 25, the first kindergarten class in the history of the school, provided a substantial increase in the enrollment over last year.

Following the mass Father Hopkins spoke briefly to the students on the reasons for a Catholic school and the Catholic system of education, stating that the system provides not only for the material needs of life but also for the spiritual.

This week only morning classes will be held at the school.

Board To Meet.

The War Price and Rationing Board will meet in School 1 today at 8 p.m., with Everett J. Norman, chairman, presiding.

Halfmoon Books Audited.

The State Comptroller has examined the fiscal affairs of School District 6, Town of Halfmoon, for the period July 1, 1943, to June 30, 1944. The report of the examination has been filed in the office of Curtis W. DuBois, clerk, and is available for inspection by any persons interested.

City Clamsteam.

The annual clamsteam for the local city officials and employees was held Saturday afternoon at Zurlo's Grove in the Town of Stillwater and was very largely attended. Softball and bocci ball were played. Angelo DeCrescente, commissioner of public works, assisted by James Fuschino and other department employees, was in charge of the affair.

Shower for Bride.

Mrs. George Butler of North Third Avenue recently entertained at a shower for Mrs. Charles Mellon. The home was decorated in pink and white. Games were played and refreshments served and the guest of honor received many gifts. Mrs. Mellon, the former Sheldon Noonan, daughter of Mrs. John Noonan, this city, was recently married to Cpl. Charles Mellon, now stationed at Camp Cook, Cal.

Bowling Notes.

The officials and captains of the City Bowling League will meet in the Masonic Club parlor today at 8 p.m., with James E. Phinney, president, presiding. The rosters of teams will be presented and the schedule prepared. The season will open on Wednesday, Sept. 12, at 8 p.m.

Arrangements were made at the meeting of the Women's Bowling League in the Masonic Temple last evening to open the season on Tuesday, Sept. 11. Another meeting will take place tomorrow night to organize the teams on a percentage basis and also to present the schedule for the season.

Church Notes.

The choir of the First Methodist Church will hold a rehearsal today at 7:30 p.m.

Arrangements for the forthcoming sessions of the Week-day School of Religion in the various churches will be made at a meeting in the First Methodist Church today at 7:30 p.m., Rev. Freeman S. Kline, pastor, has announced.

The Newman Circle of King's Daughters of the First Methodist Church will meet with Mrs. Elmer E. Woodin, lower South Main Street, tomorrow at 3 p.m., for a business meeting. The annual picnic for the members of the unit will be enjoyed.

Personal.

Miss Marilyn Thompson of this city is visiting friends at Baldwin, L. I.

Former Mayor and Mrs. Anson B. Collins have returned after a trip to Vermont.

Mrs. Beatrice Farrell, deputy commissioner of accounts, is enjoying her annual vacation.

Mr. and Mrs. Fred Bather of Union City, N. J., have returned after visiting Mrs. Margaret Beebe of this city.

Mr. and Mrs. Mitchell Bullis and daughter Margaret of Corinth, former residents, have returned after visiting relatives and friends in this city.

Mrs. George W. Tilly and daughter Marion have returned from Kingston, where they attended the funeral of Mrs. Tilly's sister, Mrs. Emma Jane Chipp.

Miss Gloria DeCasperis, daughter of Mr. and Mrs. Fred DeCasperis of Pruyn's Terrace, has entered Syracuse University. She is a graduate of the 1945 High School Class.

Brevities.

An important meeting of the Mothers' Club of Troop 39, Boy Scouts, will be held at the home of Mrs. Lloyd Hostetter, South Third Avenue, today at 7:30 p.m.

Mechanicville Lodge, B. P. O. E., will hold a clamsteam at Zurlo's Grove in the Town of Stillwater on Sunday afternoon. Plans have been made for a program of sports.

Ondawa Chapter, R. A. M., conducted its first convocation of the season in the Masonic Temple last evening with Percy G. Waller, high priest, presiding. Convocations will be held the first and third Tuesday nights of each month.

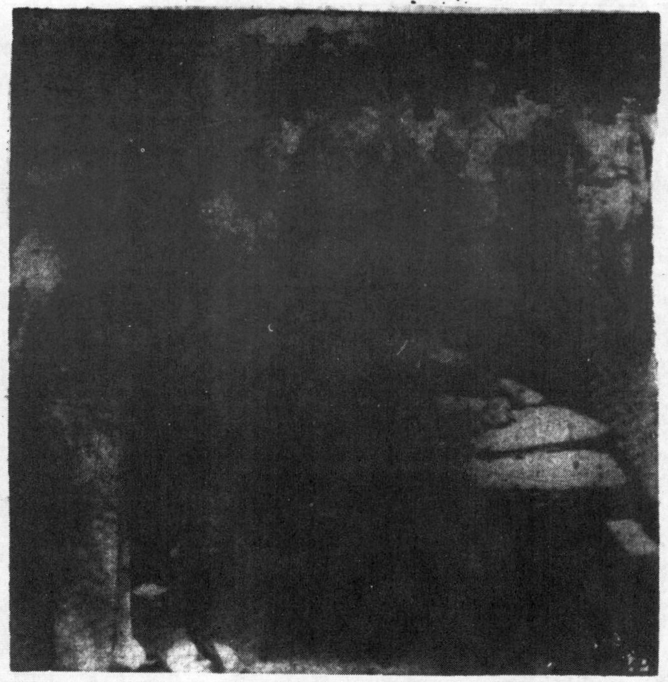

NIMITZ SIGNS SURRENDER PAPERS FOR U. S.—Fleet Adm. Chester W. Nimitz signs the Japanese surrender papers for the United States at ceremonies aboard the USS Missouri in Tokyo Bay. Watching are (left to right) Gen. Douglas MacArthur, Adm. William F. Halsey and Rear Adm. Forrest Sherman. Other U. S. Navy officers (background) look on.

NAME SARATOGA VOTE MACHINE CUSTODIANS

Names of custodians of Saratoga County voting machines have been filed in the office of the Board of Elections at Saratoga Springs. They are:

Floyd Timmerman, of Ballston; John Szurek, Charlton; Howard F. Young Clifton Park; William Allen, jr., of Day; Merrill Brownell, Edinburg; Arthur Follett, Galway; Glen E. Baugh, Greenfield; James Killough, Hadley; Leland DeVoe, Halfmoon; Frank S. Carpenter, Malta; James Corning, Milton; David W. Sexton, Moreau; Anson Purinton, Northumberland; Peter Zajaceskowski, Providence; Burtis K. Irish, Saratoga; Leo Duval, Saratoga Springs; Eben Holmwood, Saratoga Springs; Harold W. Tompkins, Stillwater; Robert Halpin, Waterford, and William Lohnes of Wilton.

POMONA GRANGE WILL MEET AT KINGSBURY

The annual fall meeting of Washington County Pomona Grange will take place Saturday, Sept. 15, at Kingsbury Grange Hall in Burgoyne Avenue. There will be three sessions, morning, afternoon and evening.

The election of officers will take place and delegates will be named to represent the organization at the state session in December. Annual reports will be given. An unusual lecturer's program is being arranged. Each person is asked to provide sugar for coffee.

FIRST TROOPSHIP FROM PACIFIC ARRIVES HOME

New York (AP)—The first American troops to come home from the Southwest Pacific arrived yesterday on the Dutch liner Bloemfontein, one of eight ships docking in three east ports with 10,000 veterans.

A huge banner reading "Noah's Ark—44 days and nights from Manila" hung from the ship's deck railing. Debarking were 699 U. S. Air Force personnel, 1,025 members of the Royal Air Force bound for England, and some civilians.

GRANGE OBSERVES 'NEIGHBORS NIGHT' AT BEMIS HEIGHTS

Interesting Program of Event Carried Out at Meeting Last Night

STILLWATER

"Neighbors Night" was observed last night Bemis Heights Grange. Stillwater Grange officers with Robert McOmber, master, opened the meeting. The meeting was turned over to the Bemis Heights Grange with Miss Ruth Cowin, matser, presiding. The lecturer's hour was in charge of Mrs. George Birdsinger, lecturer of Bemis Heights; Mrs. Emery Boucher, Stillwater Grange, and Ray Stevens, Saratoga Grange. The theme of the program was "Soldiers of the Soil," which opened with a song followed by a poem "A Guardian of the World," read by Mrs. Jacob Pratt. Tableau on "Soldiers of the Soil" was presented by Carl Schultz, William Eaton, Jack Pratt and Albert Barbolt. Mrs. Carl Schultz was the reader. A talk on the Grange and its benefits to the community was given by Spencer Kellogg; piano solo, Miss Margaret Fuller; vocal selection, Miss Mildred Clothier, "Just a Prayer Away," with Miss Margaret Fuller, accompanist. A talk on "Efficiency" was given by William Baker; vocal solo, "Billy Boy," Mrs. Lawrence Ferris, accompanied by Mrs. Carlton Abel; playlet with Miss Mildred Thomas, Miss Helen Robbins, Frances Robbins and Ray Stevens taking part; potato race, Lawrence Ferris, Albert Barbolt and Melvin Thomas. Lawrence Ferris was the winner. Closing song. Mr. and Mrs. Jacob Pratt, who observed their 31st anniversary yesterday were presented with flowers. Short talks were given by Eugene Chatfield, district deputy and Mrs. Chatfield, juvenile deputy. Mrs. Eleanor Wagar, lecturer of Pomona, also spoke. Four masters were present and spoke briefly, Cecil Barrett, Milton Grange; J. Mincher, Halfmoon Grange; Wallace Dodd, Saratoga Grange and Robert McOmber. The meeting closed with Saratoga Grange taking it over. Announcement was made that Pomona would be held tomorrow at Wilton. Jacob Pratt will be the guest speaker. Refreshments were served by Spencer Kellogg, Mrs. Clara Schultz, Mrs. Beulah Parker and Aubrey Perry. Regular meetings will now be resumed on the first and third Monday of the month.

Suffers Broken Arm.

Jay Van Vranken, son of Mr. and Mrs. Henry Van Vranken suffered a broken arm yesterday while wrestling with two other boys. The arm was broken between the wrist and the elbow. He was taken to the Leonard Hospital, where X-rays were taken and the fracture reduced.

Personal.

Joseph Brown is enjoying his vacation from the Wood-Flong Corp. in Hoosick Falls.

Mrs. Albert Wilson, of Hayward, Cal., is visiting her parents, Mr. and Mrs. John Whalen.

The Misses Grace Hall and Harriet Lane have returned from a week's vacation spent in Botson and Old Orchard Beach, Me.

NORTH COUNTY BAR TO HONOR JUSTICE RYAN

An informal testimonial dinner will be given in honor of Supreme Court Justice Andrew Ryan of Plattsburg at Hotel Cambridge at Cambridge Monday evening by members of the Washington County Bar Association.

The affair is occasioned by the first appearance of Justice Ryan at term of Supreme Court in Washington County. However he is well known througbout the county where he appeared on numerous occasions in Supreme Court before being elected to the bench. He will convene the Salem term on September 10.

Reservations for the dinner should be made with F. Arthur Howland, secretary of the association, on or before Thursday, Sept. 6.

Side Glances **By Galbraith**

"Mother used to get me to eat mashed carrots by calling them golden oats—it would help if she thought up some pretty names for these funny messes we're getting now!"

TROY COUNCIL, K. OF C., TO INSTALL TUESDAY

The installation of officers of Troy Council, Knights of Columbus, will take place Tuesday at 8 p.m. Charles A. Cassidy, district deputy of the 39th District, and his staff will be in charge.

A buffet lunch will be served under the direction of Lecturer Michael J. McElligott.

The annual clamsteam of the council will be held at Cassidy's Grove, Hoosick Road, and plans for the affair are now near completion. Reservations must be made before Saturday. Deputy Grand Knight John J. Alashey will be chairman.

Gas on Stomach

Relieved in 5 minutes or double your money back

—Adv.

U F SCHOOL-DAY SPECIAL

BIG 3 in One Combination For Your Child

NO DOWN PAYMENT 5.95

Desk, With Blackboard Top and Bench

Ideal for the youngster just starting school again. A sturdily built desk with compartment for books, etc. Blackboard top for hours of entertainment and a matching stool

BUDGET TERMS

Steel Desk With a Convertible Blackboard Top---Plus Tubular Steel Chair

29.95

Inspire your child to constructive, orderly work and play with his beautiful outfit! Steel desk has blue 28½-inch plywood top with convertible blackboard that automatically locks into place. Complete with chair—in baked-on red enamel and wood seat. For 3 to 9-year-olds.

UNION FERN

Canning Specials at your Grocer's

IVORY SALT

SALT SOME AWAY

PLAIN OR IODIZED

Whitney's IN ALBANY

TROY 5000

Store Open Daily 10 to 5:30
Open Thursday Evening 'Til 9

September Housewares To Streamline Your Work!

Renuzit liquid dry cleaner, nationally known and used. Just dip the garment and it's clean. Gal. 1.09

Toilet tissue in blue, green, yellow or white. 1,000 sheet rolls. 16 rolls for 1.00

Press Mitt makes shoulder pressing easy. Has a removable, washable cover. .69

Metal vegetable bins with 3 compartments. Painted ivory, red or green. 2.98

Air-Wick destroys unpleasant odors quickly and gives a fresh, pleasant fragrance. Just pull the wick, it does the trick. .69

Johnson's All Purpose Cleaner for rugs, draperies, furniture, painted sufaces. Johnson Products Co., Buffalo, N. Y. Per Gal. 1.50

Handy Andy Juice Extractor. Made of aluminum, complete with 16-oz. glass measuring cup. 1.79

Cold-Pac Canners save you work. Sturdy galvanized Cold-Pac Canners in big 44-quart size that holds 8 jars. Oblong oval shape fits over 2 burners. 4.49

Ash Trays of Fostoria glass. 1 blue, 1 crystal, 1 amber in fluted shape. Set 1.25

Swing-a-way, wall-type can opener for quick, smooth job. Folds away when not in use. 1.98

The big apple cookie jar with stem for handle. Keep 'em nice and fresh. 2.45

Tavern wax, for non-rub, non-skid type. Just apply and let it dry. ½ gal. with applier head. 1.59

Stainless Steel Knife Set. A limited number of these 7-piece knife sets. One for every kitchen purpose and all with sturdy stainless steel blades. 3.98

Cast iron chicken or deep fryer with Pyrex glass cover. For frying large quantities of food. Pre-seasoned and ready to use. 2.45

Lever-type "Juice -O- Mat." Gets the juice minus the seeds and pulp. Does the job quickly and easily. 3.95

Whitney's Housewares . . . Downstairs Store

Legion Parades

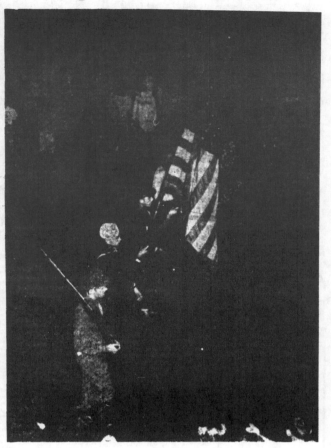

THE FLAG GOES BY—Hats come off along the line of march of last night's American Legion state convention parade as the massed colors, above, pass at the head of the marching line. Noble-Callahan Post colors, right, and color guard are well up in the column.

HONOR GUESTS—Mayor John J. Ahern, Brig. Gen. Ogden J. Ross and Col. E. C. Patridge, Arsenal commandant, left to right above, ride in the parade. A tumbling drum majorette from Cohoes, right, puts on her show while three more majorettes from Albany, far right, pass the reviewing stand at the Court House. The grand marshal's aids lead the parade, left below. Noble-Callahan Post members march by, right below.

THUMBNAIL VIEW OF SOME OTHER LENGTHY SERIES

By JOE REICHLER.

New York (AP)—Only eight previous World Series have gone to seven games, each producing fireworks in its own way.

Here are thumbnail sketches of those deciding seventh games of the past.

1909—Babe Adams, who won only 12 games for Pittsburg during the regular campaign, gained his third triumph of the Series with a six-hit, 8-0 shutout against Detroit.

1912—This finale between the Boston Red Sox and New York Giants had several heroes and goats. With the Giants ahead 2-1 as a result of a run in the top half of the 10th frame, Centerfielder Fred Snodgrass earned the right to the goat's horns by dropping an easy fly by Boston's Clyde Engle for a two-base muff. After Harry Hooper was retired, Steve Yerkes walked. Tris Speaker raised an easy pop foul that dropped untouched betweeen First Baseman Fred Merkle and Catcher Chief Meyers. Speaker then singled in Engle with the tying run and moved Yerkes to third whence he scored the winning run on a long fly by Larry Gardner.

1924—A tricky bounder, hit by Washington's Earl McNeely, hopped over the head of New York Giants third baseman Fred Lindstrom and brought in Muddy Ruel from second base with the 12th inning run that gave the Nats a 4-3 triumph.

1925—Kiki Cuyler's eighth inning double with the bases loaded scored three mates and put Pittsburg ahead for the first time in the game against Washington, the Pirates eventually winning 9-7. The blow climaxed a thrilling comeback by the Pirates who had lost three of the first four games.

1926—The big hero was Grover Alexander. Already the winner of the second and sixth games for the St. Louis Cardinals over the New York Yankees, the then 39-year-old Alexander came back to save the seventh. With St. Louis leading 3-2, Alex relieved Jesse Haines with the bases full in the seventh inning and proceeded to fan the dangerous Tony Lazerri for the third out. He retired the next six men in order.

1931—Pepper Martin, who was a one-man show in the first six games, was forced to yield the final honors to Burleigh Grimes, the Cardinals' grizzled spitball veteran, who humbled the Philadelphia Athletics 4-2.

1934—The game was marked by a fruit shower tendered Joe Medwick of the Cards by irate Detroit fans. Already feeling blue over Dizzy Dean's 11-0 shutout hurling against the Tigers, the 40,000 disappointed Tiger rooters became aroused when Medwick collided forcibly with Tiger third sacker Marv Owen while running out a three-base hit. When Medwick returned to his position he was bombarded by fruit, vegetables and lunch boxes and papers. Commissioner K. M. Landis removed Medwick from the game to stop the disturbance.

1940—Paul Derringer, then a Cincinnati pitcher but now a Cub, was the hero with a brilliant 2-1 victory over Detroit's Bobo Newsom who was trying for his third triumph of the series. Only the day before, Newsom's father had died. A two-run rally in the seventh featured by doubles by Frank McCormick and Jimmy Ripple and a long fly by Billy Myers won the game for the Reds.

FANS EAGER FOR SERIES TICKETS

By CHARLES DUNKLEY.

Chicago (AP)—Wild-eyed, hardy fans—many of them keeping an all night vigil—stormed Wrigley Field ticket booths for three and a half hours yesterday to gobble up a sell-out batch of 36,200 reserved seats for today's World Series finale between the Chicago Cubs and the Detroit Tigers.

It was the second time in baseball history that a seventh World Series contest produced a pre-game sellout, the others also involving the Tigers when they closed against the St. Louis Cardinals in the 1934 series at Detroit.

When the ticket windows opened at 8 a.m. (Chicago time), there was a shivering, but noisy queue of between 6,000 and 7,000 fans on hand. By 11:30, all the reserved ducats were gone, but at 2 p.m. there were still hundreds of hopeful fans still straggling around the ticket booths.

ALWAYS SMOKE
Q & Q
CIGARS
113-117 CONGRESS ST.

NICK BOON

WAYNE CALDWELL

COAST GUARD STALWARTS—R. P. I. gridders will have to keep a watchful eye on the pair above when they play the U. S. Coast Guard Academy here Saturday. "Nick" Boon, left above, captain of the team, was named a year ago on several all-eastern teams; Wayne Caldwell, at right, former Ohio State frosh center is the team's crack quarterback.

Bowling Notes

Industrial Class A.

Allegheny Ludlum won two games from Berk-Ray in the Industrial "A" League. Marchand with 231, 179 and 173 for a 583 total topped the winners. Other 500 scores were Terrible, 213-553, and Dabkowski with an even 500.

M. Hensell with 232-581 and D. Marro with 203-200-566 were high for the losers.

New York Power and Light took two from the Buchman's. J. Byer with 544 that included games of 194, 183 and 166 topped the winners. Other 500 scores were A. Lewandowski 527; Ring 536 and S. Byer 511. Barrett had 545 and DeThomas 516 for the vanquished.

Behr-Manning copped three from the Arsenal. Krause's 586 that included games of 189, 193 and 204 topped the victors. Tucker had 579 and Sokal 542.

Four of the five men hit over 500 for the Arsenal. They were Mooney, 194-536; Fleck, 191-545; Tetrault, 204-541 and Russell, 190-520.

The Mohawks took all three matches from the Diamond Rock with L. Roberts posting 586 to lead his team. Roberts had scores of 243, 189 and 154. Moore had a 203-556; E. Roberts 199-521 and Fero 204-520. Hensen with 235-551 and Anderson with 182-518 topped the losers.

Berk-Ray Women.

Alice Turpin cornered honors in the Berk-Ray Women's League with a 162 single and a 436 triple. Hazel Champine was next in line with 155 and 424.

This was the first night of competition and the pinners were slightly off form.

St. Mary's Waterford.

Mary Doud had 155-430 to lead the pinners in St. Mary's Women's League of Waterford. Clara Brundage had 151-405, L. Bertrand had a 160 single and B. McLeod 154.

Mary McGarry made the 6-7-10 split for the second time in two weeks. Team Four won three games from Team One and Team Three copped the odd game from Team Two.

Trojan Lodge.

The newly formed bowling team of Trojan Lodge No. 27, I.O.O.F., will start the season tomorrow at the Mayfair Bowling Alleys at 8:15 p.m. Member of the league will form inter-league bowling teams for this game.

Alpha Beta League.

Cote, with 196, and Wooster, with 504, were high in the Alpha Beta loop.

The high scores included the following: Wooster, 179, 504; Cote, 196, 480; Lorenson, 152 and 446; Frament, 156, 428; Goerld, 151 and 415, and Heath, 148 and 406.

The Framents took three games from the Wagers, the Woosters blanked the Woodworths, the Heaths took two from the Perrines and the Cotes defeated the Damons, two to one.

North Troy Masonic.

Harry Nielsen was the only one to hit over 400 in the North Troy Masonic League Duckpin League. He rolled games of 173, 180, 167 for a total of 520. Nice going Harry.

Troy Business.

Hallman with 604 that included games of 212, 195 and 197, paced the Norge Refrigerators to a 2-1 victory over the the Maytag Washers. Bear Beale had 574 to lead the losers. Bear put together games of 210, 187 and 177. S. Piche also contributed 550 to losers cause. He had single of 207.

Mutual Coal took the odd game from Bendix Home Laundry. Morrison had 523 for the winners. He had games of 205, 171 and 147. Simmons had 190, 193 and 164 for 547. Foley had 532 for the vanquished. His games were 181, 168 and 183.

Practical Shoe took two from Berners. Link with a triple of 577 that included games of 164, 201 and 212 paced the winners. Barna with 546 and a 212 single and Cocca with 520 and 180 single topped the losers.

Fowler Heating won two from Troy Camera. Harrington had 520 for the winners. He posed games of 163, 181 and 176. Barrett had 550 that included a 213 single for the losers. Lanni had 506. Fowler also had 511 for the winners.

DORP DRIVER IN ALTAMONT RACE

Two more district drivers were added to the field for Saturday's big car automobile races at the Altamont Fair Grounds when Eddie Gallione of Schenectady and Carl Boss of Scotia filed entries yesterday.

Henry Gritzbach of Schenectady, the veteran of big car drivers who recently placed third to Bill Holland and Joie Chitwood at Bloomsburg, Pa., previously was entered and Lee Wallard, a former Schenectadian who now lives in Lebanon, Pa., also agreed to race.

The district pilots will face stiff competition in the second speed program of the fall at Altamont because some of the East's crack drivers are slated to race.

Ted Horn of Paterson, N. J., has entered his three Offenhausers and will have Tommy Hinnershitz of Reading, Pa., and Walt Ader of Summerville, N. J., to help him, as drivers.

Holland, winner of the September 16 race at Altamont and Harold (Bumpy) Bumpus of Hartford who was second that day, both are signed to go Saturday.

Bob Sall, of Paterson, N. J., long favorite at Altamont, will be back again along with Bud Tatro of Danbury, the New England dirt track champion, and George Cavanna of Bridgeport who was a heat winner September 15, but was forced out of the feature event by engine trouble.

Saturday's program will include four heats and a final in addition to the time trials with a purse of $1,000 and an additional $100 posted as a prize for a new record to beat Chitwood's 26:02.

Racing Notes

By the Associated Press.

Tropical Park moguls anticipate a banner racing season in Miami this winter. Gerald Brady, director of racing at the Florida track, has sent word to horsemen that applications for stalls must be filed not later than Oct. 15 with Racing Secretary Francis P. Dunne.

William J. (Buddy) Hirsch and his brother Max, jr., showed up in civilian clothes at Jamaica eager to get back to saddling winners after long stretches in the Army. Buddy is getting together a string of horses which he'll train in Florida.

Apprentice Jockey Don Padgett, leading rider at the Laurel meeting, will be out of action for at least two months because of a fractured left arm. He was injured in an auto crash Monday night.

Saturday's national racing program will be topped by Jamaica's $50,000 added Gallant Fox Handicap and Laurel's $20,000 added Selima stakes.

Teddy Atkinson, one of the most successful riders at the current Jamaica meeting, booted in three winners yesterday. He connected with Helvetian, $16, Sun Lady $17.50 and Cantharis, $6.30.

Yesterday's feature winners included:

Jamaica—Greek Warrior, $9.90, in the $10,000 Interborough Handicap. Apache was second and Fighting Don third.

Hawthorne—K Don-Doe, $4.20, in the $2,500 Burgoo King purse. Sassy Patricia took second and Baby Gold third.

Rockingham—King Leroy, $7.20, in the Tamworth. Side Arm placed with Aboyne earning the show.

Laurel—Bright Argosy, $12.30 in the Lancegaye Handicap. One Only finished second with Salvo third.

Hollywood Park—Sirde, $7.4, in the $10,000 Crater Lake Handicap. Paperboy second and Challence Me third.

CORNELL POINTS FOR PRINCETON GAME

Ithaca (AP)—Defense against anticipated Tiger football plays was stressed yesterday as Coach Ed McKeever prepared his Cornell charges for the game against Princeton here Saturday.

Fullback Julius Woznicki, Erie, Pa., Marine, injured in the submarine base game Saturday, was back for light practice. He and right end Harold Devold, also hurt in the sub tilt, are expected to play Saturday.

NEW SONG OUT IN SEVENTH RACE AT SARATOGA TONIGHT

Saratoga Raceway — New Song, the 4-year-old trotter which came out here Friday night and won in 2:12 to pay $31.90, the record win payoff for the fall season, is entered in tonight's seventh race but it's a safe bet it will not be anywhere near that price if it wins tonight.

The field is much tougher. Among the entries in that race is Regardless, Joseph Kupic's gelding which Charley Peckham has put on top in three of its last five races, the last time being only Monday when Regardless paid $39.70.

Ernest B. Morris, the association secretary, who is putting together a stable for his Long Acre Farm in Albany, recently added Steve Braden and Kay Dreams, both of which are entered on tonight's program, Steve going in the first race and Kay Dreams in the fifth. Mr. Morris also owns Kay Hanover and Red Cross.

Horsemen may disagree, but fans attending the races here often have been heard to say that Ginger Hanover is the prettiest horse on the grounds. Ginger goes in tonight's fourth race.

The old time advice of the experts to bet the outsider in a three-horse race paid off at Saratoga Raceway last night when Miss Fixit, driven by John Porter, was the handy winner of the opening dash of the feature. It was the Poughkeepsie purse for pacers at a mile, four having been withdrawn because of the heavy going.

It was a procession from a few strides after the start with W. Ellis Gilmour's Propoganda the one to three choice racing second and Mighty Worthy, driven by Harry Bushway, third.

The winner paid $8.70, there being only straight betting.

There were heavy withdrawals throughout the program, trainers scratching the horses which had in the past shown a dislike for heavy footing.

It was the same story when the trio came back in the eighth, except that this time Miss Fixit was second choice to Propaganda. She was on top at every pole.

Propaganda trailed to the paddock turn on the way home, coming on in the stretch to be second.

First Race—Trot, 1 1-16 mile
Sky Cloud (Ed Jones) 3.50 2.70 2.40
Lady Might (S. Craig) 4.20 2.90
Cedar Direct (Peckham) 3.00
Time 2:30. Lone Rose, M. I. Car, Zorita Brooke also finished.

Second Race—Pace, 1 1-16 mile
Scotland Yard (Cross) 4.90 3.60 2.40
Daughter-in-Law (Bullis) 8.70 4.30
Tony Grattan (Masten) 2.60
Time 2:29¼. Powder Puff, Malcolm Peters, Major Smilevdale also finished.

Daily Double: Sky Cloud and Scotland Yard paid $11.00 for $2.00.

Third Race—Trot, 1 1-16 mile
Arlene Worthy (Hoyt) 2.70 2.10 out
Miss Van (Latham) 2.20 out
Profile Girl (Mrs. Tice) out
Time 2:29. Fricka V. V. also finished.

Fourth Race—Pace, one mile
Haine Henley (Dennis) 9.80 5.50 4.30
Springtime (Reynolds) 6.40 3.30
Lucky Day Tiberas (Peckham) 3.20
Time 2:17. Stoneridge Adam, Farmer Grattan, Blackie McKinney, Denise also finished.

Fifth Race—Pace, one mile
Mel Direct (Retzlaff) 5.50 3.10 out
Brown Derby (Garnsey) 7.30 out
High Axworthy (Peckham) out
Time 2:18. Eddy Scott also finished.

Sixth Race—Pace, One mile. The Poughkeepsier Purse $945. Div.
Miss Fixit (Porter) 8.70 out out
Propaganda (Gilmour) out out
Mighty Worthy (Bushway) out
Time 2:15. Only three starters.

Seventh Race—Trot, One mile.
Dana (Gray) 2.90 2.90 out
Alto Bella (Berry) 5.70 out
Louis Cobb (Hoyt) out
Time 2:17. Nelson Brewer also finished.

Eighth Race—Pace, 1 1-16 mile. Purse $955. Div.
Miss Fixit (Porter) 4.60 out out
Propaganda (Gilmour) out out
Mighty Worthy (Bushway) out
Time 2:23. Only three starters.

Raceway Entries

First Race—Purse $350. Trotting. One mile, for all ages. (1st div.)
1. Steve Braden (F. Wiswall)
2. Burma Bells (M. VanAuken)
3. Golden Hoof (A. Rodney)
4. Climatic Express (J. Hanafin)
5. Mike Walters (E. Dwyer)
6. Calumet McJay (F. Duel)
7. May Ebils (H. Bushway)
8. Lolie Stout (No driver)

Also eligible: Yahodi, Prince Druion, Kernel Brooke, Mollie D. and Frank Meehan.

Second Race—Purse $350. Pacing. One mile, for three-year-olds and upward.
1. Tilly Dale (S. Craig)
2. Betty Stanford (R. Allen)
3. Ben Stout (J. Somerville)
4. Charlotte W. (P. Losee)
5. Frisco Faro (H. Stout)
6. Mamie Hedgewood (W. Berry)
7. Joe Rea (W. Reynolds)

Also eligible: Josedale, Count Frisco.

Third Race—Purse $350. Trotting. One mile, for all ages. (2nd div. of 1st race)
1. Bunter Baine (J. Amato)
2. Wave Song (A. Williams)
3. Lincoln Hanover (C. Kerr)
4. Speculation (L. Latham)
5. Zorita Brooke (C. Knicrim)
6. Little Trouble (L. Shafer)
7. Lone Rose (E. Ashton)
8. Eben Scott (S. Craig)

Also eligibles in first race.

Fourth Race—Purse $400. Trotting. One mile, for three-year-olds and upward. (1st div.)
1. Captain Sidney (G. Munz)
2. Charles Ruffin (No driver)
3. Ginger Hanover (G. McLear)
4. Wye Boy (G. Garnsey)
5. Argo (S. Craig)
6. Margaret Song (L. Toole)
7. Moonbeam Hanover (A. Rodney)
8. Hollyrood Latimer (R. Allen)

Also eligible: Arlene Worthy and Jaffa.

Fifth Race—Purse $400. Trotting. One mile, for three-year-olds and upward. (2nd div. of fourth race).
1. Kay Dreams (A. Williams)
2. Lady Vibart (S. Craig)
3. Quite Sure Jr. 1st (No driver)
4. Calumet Forever (A. Tromper)
5. Commander Lee (C. Knicrim)
6. Lord Drew (No driver)
7. Dillon Shoot (E. Jones)
8. Everett Hanover (M. Akoury)

Also eligibles in fourth race.

Sixth Race—Purse $400. Pacing. One mile, for four-year-olds and upward.
1. Blackie McKinney (W. Berry)
2. Mc I. Direct (A. Retzlaff)
3. Obediah (W. Dennis)
4. Guy Nutonia (H. Stout)
5. Zam Zam (A. Howell)
6. Cheerful (E. Morgan)
7. Gypsy Scott (P. Losee)

Seventh Race—Purse $400. Trotting. One mile, for four-year-olds and upward.
1. Hank Thomson (A. Williams)
2. Regardless (C. Peckham)
3. Edna Hanover (No driver)
4. New Song (L. Toole)
5. Desperado (R. Cobb)
6. Cherokee (L. Bol, Jr.)
7. Leta Hanover (H. Bushway)
8. Red Day (S. Craig)

Also eligible: Frances Prologue and Louis Cobb.

Eighth Race—Purse $400. Pacing. One mile, for three-year-olds and upward.
1. High 'N' Mighty (G. Thompson)
2. Billy Clay (F. Sargent)
3. Lindy's Ace (M. Shank)
4. Miss Abbe Peters (F. Parks)
5. Mighty (H. Hotaliff)
6. Hester Scott (W. Dennis)
7. Burr Siskiyou (L. Latham)
8. Time's Scarce (A. Rodney)

Also eligible: Southland Miss, Prince Adam, Real One, Brown Derby and Doris Isle.

Horses listed according to post positions. First post 8:15 p.m.

GEORGE DANIANOR

WILLIAMS BRINGS FINE RING RECORD TO BOUT MONDAY

Danny Williams, Albany welterweight star, who meets Bernie Miller of Brooklyn in the ten-round, main event of the opening indoor pro-boxing show in LaSalle Institute gym, Monday night, has won six contests in a row since he was discharged from the United States Army after seeing service in Guadalcanal and New Hebrides.

Four of his six victories were scored via the knockout route. The victims were Jack Durham of Indianapolis; Dominick Callahan of Minneapolis; Dominick Fussa of New York and Willis Scott of Harlem.

He decisioned hard-punching Gene Gudgill of Detroit in ten rounds and also defeated Frankie Wills, well known welterweight of Washington, D. C.

Before entering the Army Williams won 27 bouts. Among the mittslingers he defeated were George (Red) Doty, Young Kid McCoy, Freddy Flores and Tommy Speigel.

Williams will be facing a tough foe, for Miller boasts an impressive record and has 16 knockouts to his credit.

Monday's semi-final argument also is attracting considerable attention. This will send George Danianor of Philadelphia against Oscar Pondexter of Newark, N. J.

Danianor recently was released from the U. S. Army after three years service with the paratroopers.

CATHOLIC CENTRAL WILL BE HOST TO SCHENECTADY '11'

Seeking to register its first victory of the season after dropping the 1945 opener to a powerful Christian Brothers Academy team last Sunday, the Catholic Central High School eleven will meet Nott Terrace High of Schenectady at Catholic High field, Friday afternoon.

The Eighth Streeters smoothed out some of the rough edges in tackling the tough assignment last Sunday and Coach Bill Carley expects his club to be a much improved outfit this week.

The CCHS squad is in the midst of a busy week of practice with emphasis on defense against Nott Terrace plays.

The Schenectady eleven, beaten by Troy High last week, also is expected to be a much improved club this week.

This is the first meeting between CCHS and Nott Terrace in several years.

Friday's game should help clarify the Troy city championship picture for it will give a line on the respective strength of Troy High and CCHS.

JOE KUNARICH TO REJOIN GRID CARDS

Chicago (AP)—Joe Kunarich, All National Fooball League guard in 1941, will rejoin his former teammates, the Chicago Cardinals for their battle with the Chicago Bears Sunday.

Recently discharged from the Navy with lieutenant ranking, Kunarich was signed by the Cardinals yesterday along with and John Durko of Albright College, who was cut loose by the Philadelphia Eagles. The Cardinals have dropped three league starts to date.

SPORTS MIRROR

By The Associated Press.

Today a Year Ago—The Baltimore Orioles defeated the Louisville Colonels 10-0 and took a 3-2 lead in the Little World Series.

Three Years Ago—Alsab beat Whirlaway in the New York Handicap at Belmont Park to boost his earnings to $332,815.

Five Years Ago—Cincinnati's world champion Reds reported their profits for the 1940 season were less than that of the year before when they were defeated in the World Series.

Ten Years Ago—Jimmy Wilson was signed to manage the Philadelphia Phillies in 1936.

TEAMS RESUME AFTER MOST ZANY SERIES IN YEARS

By WHITNEY MARTIN

Chicago (AP)—The Chicago Cubs and Detroit Tigers paused yesterday to catch their breath before plunging into the final game of the World Series, although there were some skeptical fans who had their doubt that the two teams could do even that without an error of some sort on the play.

After Monday's fantastic performance the current classic seemed destined to go down in Series history labeled "bound to win" or "the rocky road to victory," although if the Tigers were putting the tag on it they probably would call it "the ball done us wrong—the bounder."

It wasn't alone the dramatic climax which saw a hard-hit ball from Stan Hack's bat suddenly leap from the ground over the head of Hank Greenberg in left field that sent the shivering fans home reeling and groggy. It was the game in general, which ran the gamut from keystone cop shenanigans to a sparkling play.

For the most part is wasn't good baseball, yet it was the kind of baseball that brings the fans back, and also brings the teams back, as a killer is supposed to return to the scene of the crime and what some of those players did to baseball on occasion was nothing short of murder.

In how many games do you see a player round third base under full head of steam and fall flat on his face? In how many games do you see 38 men parade to the field? In how many games do you see a lead-off man come to bat twice with the bases full and two outs and register the third out? How many games do you see tied up so dramatically, with a tremendous home run?

How many games would you find erding as the result of the ball taking a freakish hop over an outfielder's head

It was the latter play which raised the tempest in the teapot, in that Greenberg at first officially was charged with an error on a ball he never touched. That in itself was a minor matter. Whether Hank Greenberg got an error or not was of no particular importance, except to Greenberg. It did not alter the outcome in the slightest.

It was the bad hop that told the story, and it is emphatically denied that the Cubs are cutting the groundskeeper in for a full series share. That the Tigers would have won even if the ball had continued its natural course and been stopped by Hank also is problematical. The Cubs would have had men on first and third, and although Dizzy Trout had flirted with similar trouble before and escaped unscathed a guy can press his luck too far.

It has been a weird series from the start, with the 9-0 score of the first game making it appear the Tigers never showed up, which they were sorry they did.

Anything that happens today must of necessity be in the nature of an anti-climax. Two ball clubs just couldn't put two games together like Monday's. It was one for the books, both literally and figuratively.

TIGERS FAVORITES.

St. Louis (AP)—James J. Carroll, betting commissioner, favors the Detroit Tigers to win today's final World Series game. Carroll announced yesterday that with Hal Newhouser pitching a $10 bet on the Tigers would net only $7, while with Hank Borowy starting for the Chicago Cubs a $5 bet on the Cubs would return $6.

A BIT OF THIS AND A BIT OF THAT

By JACK (Peerless) McGRATH

When the college football experts start casting around for the leading Eastern College players of 1945 they will do well to take more than a cursory glance at Edwin Heikkinen of Ramsey, Michigan, who has been sparking the Rensselaer Polytechnic attack.

Heikkinen has established himself as one of the best passers in the East and has been responsible for many long gains on the part of the Trojans.

Running the engineer team from the T formation, Heikkinen has passed for a total of 500 yards and has eight touchdown heaves to his credit in the first five games of the season.

His outstanding performances came against Rochester last Saturday and against Worcester a few weeks back.

A 70-yard touchdown toss from Heikkinen to Art Beard, R. P. I. halfback, gave R. P. I. one of its touchdowns last Saturday when it disposed of Rochester University.

Another long pass by Heikkinen accounted for a 60-yard gain against Worcester Tech. Keep tabs on Heikkinen. He has the stuff.

R. P. I. faces Coast Guard Saturday at '86 Field and if we don't outguess one of the largest crowds of the season will be out to look over a fine RPI team.

• • •

That much-discussed one-hitter Claude Passeau, Cubs' pitcher, hurled the other day in beating the Tigers, recalls a similar feat by Ed Reulbach, famous pitcher of the Cubs, in the 1906 triumph over the Chisox.

Johnny Evers, famous Trojan, was a member of that Cub team along with Frank Chance and Joe Tinker, members of that great double play combination that made baseball history.

We are reprinting this box score because of the discussion aroused by Passeau's recent feat.

Here is the score:

CUBS.

	A.B.	R.	H.	O.	A.
Hofman, cf.	4	0	1	2	0
Sheckard, lf.	4	0	0	3	1
Schulte, rf.	4	0	1	1	0
Chance, 1b.	5	2	1	12	0
Steinfeldt, 3b.	3	1	3	0	2
Tinker, ss.	3	3	2	0	3
Evers, 2b.	4	1	1	4	6
Kling, c.	2	0	1	5	1
Reulbach, p.	3	0	0	0	2
Totals	32	7	10	27	15

WHITE SOX.

	A.B.	R.	H.	O.	A.
Hahn, rf.	3	0	0	0	0
Jones, cf.	3	0	0	1	0
Isbel, 2b.	4	0	0	6	2
Rohe, 3b.	2	0	0	0	3
Donohue, 1b.	3	0	1	10	1
Dougherty, lf.	2	1	0	1	0
Sullivan, c.	4	0	0	8	2
Tannehill, ss.	3	0	0	0	3
White, p.	0	0	0	0	1
xTowne	1	0	0	0	0
Owen, p.	2	0	0	1	4
Totals	27	1	1	27	16

CUBS 031 001 020—7
WHITE SOX 000 010 000—1

Errors—Tinker, Evers, Isbel, Sullivan. Three base hit—Kling. Stolen bases—Hofman, Chance 2, Tinker and Evers. Sacrifices—Speckard, Steinfeldt, Reulbach. Double play—Evers to Chance. Left on bases—Cubs 5, White Sox 5. Bases on balls—Off Reulbach 6, White 1, Owen 3. Hits—Off White 4 in 3 innings, Owen 6 in 6. Hit by pitcher By Reulback (Rohe). Struck out—By Reulbach 3, White 1, Owen 2. Losing pitcher—White. Umpires—Johnstone and O'Loughlin. Time—1:58. Attendance—12,595.

• • •

Whichever way it goes, the 1945 World Series, weirdest in many a year, will come to an end today when the Detroit Tigers and Chicago Cubs square off for the seventh game on Wrigley Field, Chicago.

Sometime late this afternoon the current classic will be a matter of history.

EDWIN HEIKKINEN

Both teams will be "shooting the works" today in an effort to cop the lion's share of the player pool and under those conditions anything may happen.

It's the Tigers in our book, however. We picked them in four out of six games before the series started and we're sticking by our choice.

We think Hal Newhouser, who pitched a good game Sunday to put th Tigers ahead in the classic will be able to stop the Cubs today despite the fact he will be stacked up against a tough opponent in Hank Borowy. Borowy, who won the first game for the Cubs, was knocked out of the box Sunday but he received credit for Monday's victory in a relief role.

He'll be making every effort to gain revenge for that rough handling Sunday and he'll be hard to stop.

This corner thinks Newhouser will take care of that, however.

The tall left-hander made a grand comeback Sunday after being shelled from the mound in the third inning of the inaugural game.

After that setback, Newhouser said he would be ready for the Cub gunners when he faced them again and he certainly was Sunday.

• • •

James H. (Jim) Malloy, well known sportsman and an authoritty on old-timers, won't agree with us when we pick the Tigers to clinch the series today.

Malloy believes the Detroit team is a bunch of misfits and "there isn't a player in the regular lineup who is playing in the same position in which he started to play baseball."

Jim thinks the toughest baseball game ever lost in a World Series was played in 1912 when Fred Snodgrass, center fielder for the New York Giants, dropped a fly ball with two out costing the Giants the series with the Red Sox.

WOMAN HURT WHEN AUTO STRIKES POLE IN HOOSICK STREET

Mrs. Fannie Orunsten, 55, of 2522 Lewis Court, received an injury to the back and suffered nervous shock when an auto in which she was riding and driven by her husband, Charles Orunsten, 56, struck a pole at Hoosick and Tenth Streets about 10:15 p.m. Sunday, a report to police shows.

Orunsten said he was driving south in Tenth Street and turned east into Hoosick Street. The steering apparatus snapped and the machine went out of control and struck the pole, the report claims.

CATHOLIC LEAGUE HEARS ADDRESS ON TROY WAR CHEST

Rev. Elmer J. Donnelly Speaks Before Local Women's Group

Rev. Elmer J. Donnelly, Director of Catholic Charities in Troy, spoke on the spiritual and moral value of the "Philosophy of Giving" at the meeting of th. board of directors of the Catholic Women's Service League at The Hendrick Hudson last night.

Stressing the basic good to be derived in giving to organizations devoted to community uplift, Father Donnelly described the work of some of the organizations serviced by funds given to the Allied Communities War Chest Victory Drive.

Chairmen of standing committees also presented reports at the meeting at which Mrs. Edward W. Golden, presided. Plans for the year were discussed, to be more specifically formulated at subsequent meetings. It was announced the annual membership tea will be held Wednesday afternoon, Nov. 14, at The Hendrick Hudson. Mrs. Joseph J. Maloney and Mrs. John J. Noonan are chairman and cochairman, respectively.

Committee heads announced last night who will prepare for the event, include: Mrs. Edmund F. Herbert, chairman of the printing committee; Miss Rita Bennett, and Mrs. Augustus J. Hambrook, chairman and cochairman respectively of finance; Mrs. Walter Prediger and Mrs. Ferdinand Haverly, hotel arrangements; Mrs. John Stanton Mahony and Mrs. Wilbur H. Caney, table arrangements; Mrs. Eugene F. Connally and Mrs. John J Mackrell, accessories; Mrs. William Helm and Mrs. C. Carlton Carroll, servers committee.

SPEEDY NAZI JET PLANE—RAF fliers examine a German "Volksjaeger," a plane with maximum speed of 522 miles per hour, powered by a turbo-jet unit mounted above the fuselage.

OVERSEAS BOXES ONLY HALF LAST YEAR'S SHIPMENTS

Deadline Day Brings Rush at Postoffice; Third Window Opened

Until the final day, yesterday, packages to be mailed overseas to servicemen were few in number, Postmaster Frank M. Collins said last night, but yesterday afternoon a third window had to be staffed for the volume that poured in during a last minute rush.

During the month long mailing time, overseas packages numbered less than half those sent last year. Yesterday's rush probably topped this figure to about half, he said.

Extensive demobilization of troops is the answer. This year so many servicemen have returned or are expected to return from all theaters of war that there is no need for the volume of Christmas mail.

The Army postal authorities in Washington urged that the Christmas package for the serviceman be kept at home if there were any indication he would be home before the holiday.

"Last year we had to put on extra help and open additional windows to handle the packages," the postmaster said. "This year the package window hardly noticed any additional mail until late on deadline day when last minute gifts were being sent. Then we opened an extra window and were really rushed for about three hours."

The shortest railroad in the United States is the Valley Railroad, one mile long, at Westline, McKean County, Pa.

VICTORIOUS FLEET RETURNS TO AMERICA SCORING PLAUDITS

San Francisco (UP)—Admiral Halsey, like his dungareed seamen, scorned ceremonial dignity to wave an enthusiastic greeting to crowds high above as his homecoming Third Fleet flagship steamed beneath the Golden Gate Bridge yesterday at noon.

At the final day, yesterday, package Third-Fleet flagship steamed beneath Third Fleet column which brought in 10,000 Navy, Coast Guard and Marine personnel for discharge.

At first he stood rigid, silent and alone on the veranda deck of the battleship South Dakota. Planes and dirigibles wheeled overhead, and the bridge loomed nearer. The Admiral turned his head for a twinkling aside to his staff:

"They used to throw pop bottles off there . . ."

Then, as the cheers of the waiting throng became audible, his gold-braided arm swept aloft in reply. Down at the quarter-deck a seaman burst forth with: "The heck with this standing at attention!" And he and his shipmates waved, too.

California's Gov. Earl Warren was first up the white-roped gangway as the big flagship reached its anchorage inside the bay. "Welcome home, sir; it's great to see you," he told Halsey.

"How are you, Governor!" the Admiral grinned.

Steamers and small craft all over the harbor tied down whistle cords, and air raid sirens swelled the clamor as the South Dakota steamed in at the head of the

ON THE AIR
Radio Programs From Local Stations

TONIGHT

1000—WHRY, Troy—890.

[Radio program listings]

TOMORROW

1,000—WHRY, Troy, 880

A. M.

[Radio program listings]

370—WGY, Schenectady—810

[Radio program listings]

205—WOKO, Albany—1460.

[Radio program listings]

370—WGY, Schenectady, 810

[Radio program listings]

DRUM CORPS WILL PRESENT PROGRAM

Preparations for its fall and winter musical program will be made by Noble-Callahan Squadron, Sons of American Legion, Bugle and Drum Corps, at a meeting to be held at the Post home, 14 First Street, today at 7.30 p.m. The unit will participate in the city-wide celebration honoring returning servicemen and women Nov. 12, besides contributing its services to indoor community activities on the program this season. John E. Heenan, adjutant, is director of the group.

DEMOCRAT WOMEN MAKE PLANS FOR HALLOWEEN PARTY

Social Affair Will Be Conducted Here on Tuesday, Oct. 30

Arrangements for a Halloween cider and doughnut party of the Women's Democratic Club of Rensselaer County, to be conducted Oct. 30, at a meeting of the group held last night at Democratic Headquarters, in The Hotel Troy. The meeting was conducted by Mrs. Charles E. MCarthy, president.

Mrs. Edward T. Nehill was selected to head the general committee, assisted by Mrs. Loretta Foley Bird, Miss Sheryl Seigle, Mrs. Francis McCarthy, Mrs. Mary Casey, Miss Betty Kavanaugh, Mrs. Francis Rickey and Mrs. Matthew Rourke. The entertainment committee will be headed by Mrs. Edward Cronin. The refreshment committee head will be headed by Mrs. Alice Jackson.

The group will be addressed by Democratic candidates including: Judge John J. Sweeney, Thomas P. McLaughlin, James F. Cox and Joseph F. Purcell.

Speakers committee will be under the direction of Mrs. John J. Sweeney. Decorations will be in charge of Mrs. James Visk. Invitations will be sent out by Mrs. Ross Birkbeck of Brunswick. The party to be held at Democratic Headquarters begins at 8 p.m.

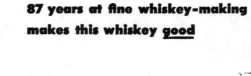
TRADE NAMES FILED WITH COUNTY CLERK

Papers filed in the County Clerk's office yesterday show that the Troy Storage Warehouse at 2332 Seventh Avenue, is now being operated by the Oviatt Plumbing & Heating Distributing Co., Inc., of 2312 Seventh Avenue.

The certificate, signed by G. Thomas Oviatt, president of the Oviatt firm, states that the corporation is successor to Henry A. Conway, who has operated the warehouse since April 25, 1919.

Edward Kacharian of 364 Tenth Street, will operate a business known as "Eddie's Place" at 2364 Sixth Avenue, according to a certificate filed by Leo R. Toomajian, attorney for Kacharian.

REBEKAH LODGE TO INSTALL

Public installation of officers will be conducted Thursday night by Bethlehem Rebekah Lodge at Diamond Rock Hall. A short business meeting will be conducted at 7.30 p.m., and the installation will start at 8 p.m. Miss Ruth C. Shaw, retiring noble grand, will preside at both sessions. Mrs. Cecil Brown, district deputy president, will be the installing officer.

Welcome to Heroes

REVIEWERS take their places in the stand at Barker Park for Troy's parade welcoming home Trojan servicemen and women. Colors of the Second Regiment, State Guard, are dipped, at left, on approaching the reviewing stand. Veterans of Troy's own regiment, the 105th Infantry, march behind this huge sign, below, borne by Boy Scouts. The Appleknockers were cheered all along the line of march. Military vehicles, at right, were among the attractions on display in the hour-and-a-half parade.

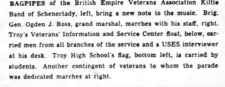

BAGPIPES of the British Empire Veterans Association Kiltie Band of Schenectady, left, bring a new note to the music. Brig. Gen. Ogden J. Ross, grand marshal, marches with his staff, right. Troy's Veterans' Information and Service Center float, below, carried men from all branches of the service and a USES interviewer at his desk. Troy High School's flag, bottom left, is carried by students. Another contingent of veterans to whom the parade was dedicated marches at right.

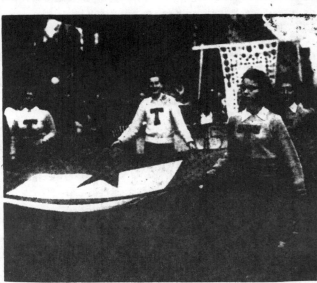

THE WEATHER
Tonight Fair Colder

THE TIMES RECORD

FINAL EDITION

SERIES 1945—NO 274 (Entered as Second Class Matter at the Postoffice at Troy N. Y., Under the Act of March 3, 1879) TROY, N. Y., TUESDAY EVENING, NOVEMBER 20, 1945. (Published Daily Except Sunday) PRICE FOUR CENTS

Nazi War Criminals Face Trial

Roosevelt Rejected Admiral's Protest On Pearl Harbor Base

UNION MAY CALL OUT WORKERS IN GENERAL MOTORS

Auto Firm Must Reply to Arbitration Offer by 4 P.M. Today

Detroit (AP)—General Motors Corp. today informed the C. I. O. United Automobile Workers Union that it will reply to the union proposal for arbitration of the 30 per cent wage increase "on or before Friday, Nov. 23."

The union proposal called for the appointment of a three-man board of arbitration with the right to examine the corporation's books as well as those of the union and that any wage increase resulting from the arbitration should not be tied in with higher prices for General Motors products.

BY THE ASSOCIATED PRESS

The long and bitter wage dispute between the C.I.O. United Automobile Workers and General Motors Corp., appeared headed for another showdown today. Strike action, which would affect some 300,000 of the nation's automobile workers, was regarded as possible by one union spokesman

The union's latest move in its drive to obtain a 30 per cent wage increase for auto workers was its proposal to submit the controversy to arbitration. General Motors had until 4 p.m., E.S.T. today to reply to the union's offer.

The action came in Detroit from delegates to the General Motors council of the C.I.O.U.A.W., representing more than 300,000 workers, and was termed by R. J. Thomas, C.I.O.-U.A.W. president as "not an ultimatum," but as "the last resort" to peaceful settlement.

One informed union spokesman said he believed rejection of the proposal by General Motors would prompt council delegates to recommend immediate strike action. Such authority is vested in the union's six-man strategy committee.

Walter P. Reuther, C.I.O.-U.A.W. vice president, said "we want to avert a strike," and added that the union proposes to G-M. that "we submit to immediate arbitration our controversy over 30 per cent increase in wage rates without price increases." G-M President C. E. Wilson in Washington declined comment on the merits of the offer.

The other main trouble spot along the nation's labor front was in Chicago while across the country some 150 labor disputes kept idle about 275,000 workers.

The strike of 8,700 telephone operators crippled long distance service in Chicago and paralyzed service in manual switchboards in 115 communities in Illinois and in two Indiana counties. A union official in New York said long lines operators throughout the country have refused to handle long distance calls to and from Chicago.

A conciliation conference, arranged by federal officials after the start of the strike Monday morning in a dispute over wages, failed when both company and union representatives were unable to reach agreement. The Illinois Telephone Traffic Union is asking a $6 week wage boost, having rejected a War Labor Board award boosting wages $4 a week.

Holiday Cheer

Is in every golden drop of dry Utica Pilsner Lager and XXX Cream Ale. Millions prefer them the year 'round. Adv.

To the People of this Community

For all clear-thinking Americans, reconversion from war to peacetime living spells V-i-c-t-o-r-y B-o-n-d-s. Industrial reconversion is racing along but it will be a long, long time according to competent observers, before industry can make a dent in the backlog of orders. Americans have amassed upward of 100 billion dollars of war savings.

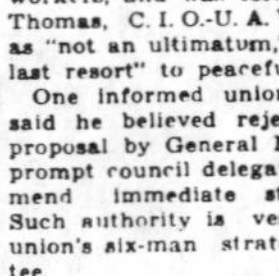

Farmers will have five billion dollars in cash left after paying all expenses and living costs this year. The best crop they can harvest is Victory Bonds. They can help their country and themselves while waiting for a plentiful supply of farm equipment and the other things which they crave for their property and family.

Here is a crop which can only grow taller than a Kansas sunflower with the passage of the years. Here is a crop in which not only farmers but every American can raise and enjoy for as many harvest moons as he or she wishes.

THE EDITOR

Superfort Sets New Non-Stop Distance Record

U. S. Bomber Flies 8,198 Miles from Guam to Washington

Washington (UP)—A U. S. Superfortress arrived here from Guam today, setting a new world's non stop distance flight record of an estimated 8,198 miles.

The flying time was 35 hours and five minutes.

The flight was the latest in a series designed, according to the War Department, to demonstrate (1) How easily U. S. long-range aircraft could bomb great distances away and (2) How vulnerable this country could be to "enemy attacks from vast distances."

The flights, the War Department said, demonstrate "the fundamental aeronautical smallness of the world" and prove that "only through constant experiment and trial can we maintain dominant air power."

The plane landed at National Airport at 1:35 p.m. E.S.T. It left Guam at 2:30 a.m. E.S.T. Monday.

Arnold Decorates Crew.

Manned by a double crew and stripped of excess equipment, the B-29 came on to Washington after exceeding the old record for non-stop distance flight as it passed over Lacrosse, Wis., at 9:30 a.m., E. S. T.

The former record was held by British flyers who flew 7,158 miles from Egypt to Australia in 1938. At Lacrosse, the B-29 had flown 7,368 miles.

Gen. Henry H. Arnold, commander of the Army Air Forces, was at the airport to meet the plane. He immediately awarded each member of the flight crew the Distinguished Flying Cross.

The crew was led by Col. Clarence S. Irvine of St. Paul, Neb., and Lt. Col. George R. Stanley of West Hartford, Conn, pilots.

Arnold greeted the recordmakers warmly. Addressing Irvine, he said:

"That was a grand flight—beating the world record by over a thousand miles. Did you have any trouble?"

"No trouble at all," Irvine replied.

The plane was stripped of excess weight and slightly modified to streamline it for the flight. It carried 11,110 gallons of gasoline at the takeoff. The fuel load constituted almost half of its gross weight of 141,000 pounds when it left Guam. The Superfort carried 13 auxiliary fuel tanks.

Stripped of Armament.

The craft was stripped of all armament, radar and other equipment not required for the flight. To insure safety, air-sea rescue stations on the route were alerted. Weather conditions were favorable at the takeoff.

The long-distance flight was the latest in a series by B-29's designed, the War Department said, "to demonstrate range and capabilities of our military aircraft as well as to show vulnerability of our country to enemy attacks from vast distances."

"Demonstrating again the fundamental aeronautical smallness of the world," the department said, "these flights all served to carry out General Arnold's dictum that only through constant experiment and trial can we maintain dominant air power."

Members of Crew

The crew members in the current flight:

Irvine and Stanley, pilots; Capt. W. J. Bennett, (no home address available), and First Lt W. S. O'Hare, Knoxville, Ia., flight engineers; Maj. Kenneth L. Royer, Madisonburg, Pa., and Capt. Francis S. O'Leary, Pittsburg navigators; M/Sgt. Dock West, (no home address available), crew chief and scanner; S/Sgt. J. A. Shinnault, (no home address available), radio operator; T/Sgt. G. F. Broughton, (no home address available), flight engineer and scanner; and Lt. Col. F. J. Shannon, (no home address available), radio operator

BARON GEN. HONGO COMMITS SUICIDE IN TOKYO OFFICE

Kwantung Army Chief Ordered Arrested Yesterday as War Criminal

Tokyo (AP)—Baron Gen. Shigeru Hongo, accused war criminal and reputed ringleader in the conquest of Manchuria, committeed hara-kiri today less than 24 hours after he was ordered arrested.

The baron was lying on his right side in a pool of blood in his office at the former Japanese war college when Allied reporters and photographers arrived.

Honjo performed the ceremonial disembowelment in the "regular and respectable" manner, said Maj. Gen. Matsutoshi Miyano of the demobilized soldiers' general bureau. "He knelt and died facing the imperial palace."

The old-line officer performed the Japanese hara-kiri ritual by slashing his stomach cross wise, then cutting his throat.

But instead of the ritualistic kimono, Honjo wore his army uniform. His upthrust boots were highly polished.

Arrest Ordered Yesterday.

Honjo, one of the 11 war leaders of the past imperialistic decade ordered imprisoned yesterday, died shortly after his secretary found his slashed body on his office floor

"I cannot endure as a soldier of our country to appear before a court of Allied powers," Honjo said in a letter written shortly before he killed himself.

"I find no way of apologizing to his majesty and the people for bringing my nation to such a miserable state of affairs.

"It grieves my heart when I think of the surviving families of our men who died on battlefields x x x

"I therefore have decided to seek death."

The letter, addressed to his secretary, Kawamura, said it was Honjo's desire that his eldest son, Kazou, not succeed to his title of baron.

Headed Kwantung Army.

Honjo's Tokyo home burned in a May 25 air raid. The general since had lived in an air raid shelter in his garden. His son quoted him as remarking "I'm old now and can do nothing for my country. It's up to the young fellows."

Most of Honjo's military career was devoted to the Kwantung Army push northward along the Asiatic continent. He served as captain in the Russo-Japanese war and later as regimental commander in the Siberian occupation.

Preceding the Manchurian imperialism, he was adviser to War Lord Chang Tso-Lin from 1921 to 1923. Subsequently he served in North China and other continental commands until he became commander of the Kwantung Army in 1931 with the rank of lieutenant general.

The Manchurian incident exploded under his command and he was considered the major planner and executioner of the entire imperialistic scheme which was conducted independent of Tokyo.

GENERAL EISENHOWER AWARDED D. S. M. AT LEGION CONVENTION

Chicago (UP) Gen. Dwight D. Eisenhower received the American Legion's Distinguished Service Medal today as more than 9,000 Legionnaires cheered wildly.

Smiling broadly, the general stood under the glare of floodlights and waved to the delegates at the Legion's 27th annual convention. Many of them were fighting men who had followed him in Africa and across Europe.

His brief acceptance speech was interrupted frequently by cheers. He said he accepted the medal for his 3,000,000 men and their Allies "who did their bit for their countries."

The crowded platform was the scene of a reunion between Eisenhower and Gen. Omar N. Bradley, chief of the Veterans' Affairs Bureau. Eisenhower hurried to Bradley's side, threw his arms about him and brought him to the front of the platform to share the ovation with him.

GREEK CABINET RESIGNS.

Athens (AP)—The cabinet of Greek Premier Panayotis Kanellopoulos resigned today.

NAVY RELEASES YOUTH WHO GREW TOO MUCH

Sampson (AP)—Donald (Shorty) Holler is out of the Navy because he grew too fast—and too much.

Holler, 18-year-old seaman second class from Jeanette, Pa., grew almost four inches in eight months to become 6 feet, 6¼ inches tall, or 2¼ inches over the maximum for Navy men, officials of Sampson Naval Center said today.

As a result, Holler, who entered the Navy last March, has been processed at the personnel separation center here and released, Sampson officials said.

INDICTED FOR THEFT.

New York (UP)—A federal grand jury late yesterday indicted Leroy Timmerman, former postmaster at Cairo, N. Y., on charges of embezzling $162.25 of federal funds in the period between July 1 and Aug. 6, 1945.

KNOX WARNED OF POSSIBLE ATTACK, LETTER REVEALS

Admiral Richardson Says F. D. R. Rejected Plea for More Men

Washington (UP)—Admr. J. O. Richardson said today that Admr. Harold R. Stark, chief of naval operations, agreed with his arguments against basing the fleet at Pearl Harbor in 1940 but that the late President Roosevelt overruled them.

Richardson was commander of the United States fleet from January, 1940, until he was relieved on Feb. 1, 1941, by Rear Admr. Husband E. Kimmel. He told the congressional Pearl Harbor investigating committee he strongly opposed keeping the fleet in Hawaiian waters because it could not be effectively defended or supplied there.

He also testified that he never heard until today of a letter sent in January, 1941, by the late Sec. of the Navy Frank Knox to former Sec. of War Henry L. Stimson in which Knox said it was "easily possible" that Japan might start hostilities with a surprise attack on Pearl Harbor.

The Knox letter was made public last August when results of the Army and Navy investigations were released by President Truman.

F. D. R. Rejected Protests.

Richardson told the committee that he made two trips to Washington in 1940 to talk with President Roosevelt. He said the President:

1. Rejected his protests against keeping the Pacific Fleet at Pearl Harbor, asserting that its presence there was a deterrent to Japanese aggression. (Former Secretary of State Cordell Hull also favored keeping the fleet at Pearl Harbor.)

2. Overruled his plea for additional personnel on the grounds that the needed men could be quickly inducted later.

Richardson said Stark agreed with his fears about keeping the fleet at Pearl Harbor where, the witness said. Army defense arrangements were wholly inadequate.

In the course of his testimony on defense preparations, Richardson told the committee that the Army in Hawaii was ordered on the alert for an air raid in the spring of 1940 but that he never was able to find out whether it was a drill or the real thing.

Knox Feared Attack.

His efforts to get an explanation from Washington were unavailing, Richardson said, and he assumed it was a drill.

The Knox letter was a summation of the defense situation at Pearl Harbor and was written as a result of Richardson's previous reports.

In the letter, Knox listed the dangers of a Japanese attack, in order of their probability, as follows: (1) Air bombing attack; (2) air torpedo plane attack; (3) sabotage; (4) submarine attack; (5) mining; (6) bombardment by gun fire."

"If war eventuates with Japan," the Knox letter said, "it is believed easily possible that hostilities would be initiated by a surprise attack on the fleet or the naval base at Pearl Harbor."

Stimson replied on Feb. 1, 1941, agreeing with Knox's views and promising that the Army would send additional fighter planes, anti-aircraft guns, and barrage balloons to Pearl Harbor.

Stimson's letter also had been made public in August.

Although Knox's letter was based in large part on reports Richardson had sent to Washington before leaving his fleet command, the Admiral told the committee that

(Continued on Page 14.)

HERMANN GOERING

WILHELM KEITEL

ALBERT KESSELRING

JULIUS STREICHER

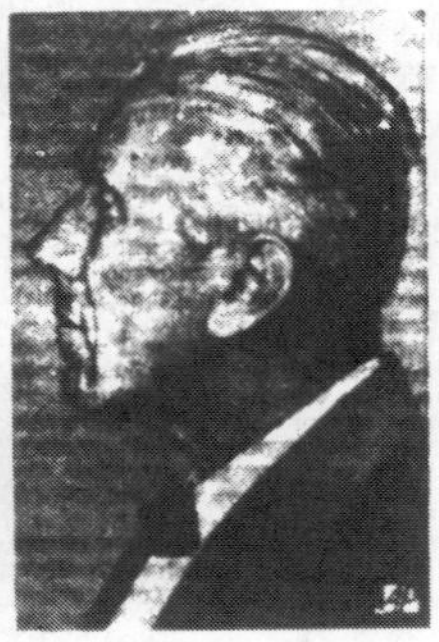

FRANZ VON PAPEN

JOACHIM RIBBENTROP

FEAR FOUR DEAD IN SUNKEN PLANE

Craft Plunged Into Hudson Near Jersey Shore

New York (AP)—A twin-engined airplane, carrying three passengers besides its pilot, according to its flight plan, plunged into the Hudson River near the New Jersey shore early last night, narrowly missing a crowded ferryboat.

Witnesses said the plane sank almost immediately.

Ralph Byrnes, air controller at La Guardia Field, said the craft was owned by Chester A. Bolles, chairman of the board of directors of Continental Industries, Inc., and was piloted by Jerome Casper, a former Army flyer, employed by Bolles.

The plane left Washington at 5:30 p.m. for La Guardia Field and crashed off Edgewater, N. J., about an hour later. The Civil Aeronautics Administration said the flight plan listed three passengers besides the pilot as scheduled to make the trip. Identity of the passengers was not revealed.

Hours after the accident, rescue crews from several New Jersey cities and New York City had found only splintered wood and twisted steel wreckage that had floated to the New Jersey shore.

The airways traffic control center of the C. A. A. at La Guardia Field reported the plane had been in contact with the center shortly before the crash and had requested "standard clearance" to land. The pilot was told, it was explained, that because of traffic congestion at the field, he should circle at a designated altitude and await his turn to come in.

Witnesses reported that the pilot of the plane had "gunned" the engines several times before the crash and that the motors had roared erratically, indicating engine trouble.

PRESIDENT TO ATTEND ARMY-NAVY GRID GAME

Washington (UP)—President Truman will attend the Army-Navy football game in Philadelphia on Dec. 1, the White House announced today.

The President's wife and daughter will accompany him.

Mr. Truman will sit during the first half on the Army side of the field, then switch to the Navy side for the second half.

He will leave Washington by train in the forenoon of Dec. 1, and return here immediately after the game.

State May Have White Thanksgiving

Albany (AP)—Snow flurries and gusty winds, sweeping over much of New York, brought the prediction today that the state's Thanksgiving probably will be white.

A low pressure area moving eastward from Iowa, the weather bureau explained, is likely to cause light snows generally throughout the state tomorrow night and Thanksgiving Day.

Temperatures on Thanksgiving probably will be somewhat lower than those expectd tomorrow, when the mercury should be in the 25-30 region, the bureau added.

POLISH ORPHAN, 10, "HOME" WITH YANK

Youngster Arrives in Chicago by Plane

Chicago (UP)—Bobby Sokolowski, 10-year-old Polish war orphan, was "home" today with the American buddy he met on the battlegrounds of Europe.

Bobby arrived in Chicago by plane last night with T/Sgt. Edward Klonowski, who immediately began making arrangements to adopt the curly-haired immigrant youngster.

Bobby first came to the U. S., by hitching a ride on a bomber in an effort to rejoin the American soldier who had befriended him in France. But immigration authorities turned him back because he had no relatives in the county.

Klonowski started legal procedure and the two were reunited Sunday when the little Polish orphan arrived aboard the transport James Swan at Portland, Me.

Bobby, who spent long dreary months in a German prison camp after his parents were killed by the Nazis, was so tired after the long trip that he couldn't eat the big dinner his new mother, Mrs. John A Klonowski, had prepared for him.

But he couldn't resist American ice cream.

Bobby still was wearing his cut-down GI uniform, but he'll change to civvies today when Sgt. Eddie takes him out to buy a new suit.

16 MICHIGAN HUNTERS KILLED IN SIX DAYS

Detroit (AP)—Michigan listed 16 hunters dead today as the state's 16-day deer hunting season went into its sixth day.

Gunshot wounds accounted for nine of the fatalities, heart attacks for five, while auto accidents and pneumonia claimed one victim apiece. There were 33 deaths during last year's season.

Parents Congratulate Golden Wedding Pair

Cleveland (INS) — Golden wedding anniversaries are not unusual these days, but when your own parents can felicitate you on the occasion — that is something for the books.

This was the happy experience yesterday of a Cleveland couple, Mr. and Mrs. Frank Wagner, both 72, who celebrated their fiftieth wedding anniversary yesterday. The couple was congratulated by Wagner's parents, Conrad, 95, and Margaret, 91, who have been married 73 years.

STORM-MAROONED HUNTERS RESCUED

Party of 58 Brought from Mountain Wilderness

Pomeroy, Wash. (AP)—Fifty-eight elk hunters, marooned for ten days in the snowbound wilderness of the Blue Mountains, were brought to safety today by rescue parties which at times had to fight their way through a seventy-mile an hour gale and snowstorm that reduced visibility to a few feet.

Hero of the ordeal was Lester Riley, Snake River cattle ranch owner who made his way to civilization on horseback to bring help to the group which was isolated by a sudden storm that buried the hunters' automobiles and their supplies.

After struggling through snowdrifts which sometimes were as much as 40 feet deep in places, Riley finally reached Pomeroy almost dead from exhaustion. It took a bulldozer three days to break a path back to the marooned hunters.

There were four casualties. Mrs. Minnie Boganne of Anatone, Wash., suffered a heart attack and was left at the Clearwater ranger station.

One man contracted pneumonia, another suffered a broken leg, and a third a ruptured kidney. They were not identified immediately.

When the blizzard closed in on the mountain top where several groups of the hunters were camping, they banded together and pooled their supplies.

After the bulldozer arrived Saturday, the hunters worked all day with shovels, digging out the cars. Food, running dangerously low, had to be rationed. The cars finally were assembled in a caravan and on Sunday morning started back toward Pomeroy with the bulldozer clearing a path ahead.

By Sunday night the party had made three miles. They slept that night in the snow, or huddled in the cars for warmth. Meanwhile, Governor Wallgren and Virgil Bennington, state game commissioner, had arranged with the Walla Walla air base for three Army rotary snowplows to start from Pomeroy in an attempt to clear the road for the party.

Late Monday, the caravan had traveled three more miles and met the snow plows and the Army rescue party.

During the last few miles of travel on Monday, screaming gales of seventy miles an hour velocity blew swirls of freezing snow so thick the party could see only a few feet ahead. Frequently they had to leave the cars to get out and dig with shovels as the bulldozer labored up ahead.

STATE MASONS HONOR KING AND MARSHALL

New York (INS) Admr. Ernest J. King, commander in chief of the United States Fleet, today wore the distinguished achievement medal of the New York State Grand Lodge of Free and Accepted Masons.

He was awarded the honor before more than 1,400 state Masonic leaders gathered in annual session. Justice Charles W. Froessel of the State Supreme Court presented the medal to King personally and to General of the Army George C. Marshall, who was not present to receive it. Hailed for "exceptionally meritorious service" during the war, King was principal speaker last night at the Masons' "victory dinner."

FALL PROVES FATAL.

Rochester (AP) — Clarence Peech, 43, died yesterday of head injuries suffered Sunday when he fell down the steps in his home.

HITLER HENCHMEN HEAR RECITAL OF ALLIED CHARGES

Lengthy Indictment Cites Story of Murders, Plunder and Torture

Nuernberg (AP) A strangely assorted score of gloomy Nazis sat dejectedly today before an international military tribunal and heard themselves formally accused of Nazi war crimes, the murder of 10,000,000 Europeans, plunder, horror and torture.

Throughout the opening session of the historic trial for their lives, Hitlerian followers such as corpulent Hermann Goering, vague Rudolf Hess and defiant Field Marshal Wilhelm Keitel listened through earphones while spokesmen of the nations which crushed their hierarchy recited crimes the world had never before witnessed.

By turns, prosecutors of the United States, Great Britain, France and Russia droned through the four counts of the 25,000-word indictment accusing the last of the leading Nazis of conspiracy to commit crimes against the peace, actual commission of crimes against the peace, war crimes and crimes against humanity.

Arraignment Tomorrow.

Even the appendices containing individual charges against the twenty defendants were read, meaning that the men who terrorized Europe only a year ago could not be arraigned until the Wednesday session.

The Nazis sometimes sat with earphones clasped on to hear translations in German piped to them as the prosecutors read in English, French and Russian. Robed attorneys sat beside them.

Of the 24 originally indicted, one is at large, two are too ill to attend and one has committed suicide. Martin Bormann, Hitler's deputy, was being tried in absentia. Robert Ley, the labor leader, took his own life. Ernst Kaltenbrunner of the Gestapo and Gustav Krupp were ill.

After the indictments are read in full, each defendant will plead either "guilty" or "not guilty." Then the prosecution will make its opening statement.

Hess' Status Uncertain.

Rudolf Hess, an almost impish grin playing about his sunken mouth, was lined up in the dock with the Nazi defendants—twenty in all. The 21st, Martin Bormann, Hitler's deputy, is being tried in absentia.

What disposition the tribunal would make of the reports of alienists on Hess' mental condition had yet to be announced. But the former Hitler deputy seemed at moments almost friovlous as the proceedings got under way.

After the recess, British Lord Justice Geoffrey Lawrence, presiding, announced the trial would continue without the presence of Ernst Kaltenbrunner, former Nazi security police chief, who has suffered a cranial hemmorhage.

The black gowned defense attorneys listened intently to every word that was spoken, but their clients, as strangely garbed as a cast of beggars in an opera, exhibited varying emotions.

Lawrence Presides.

From the paunchy prima donna of Nazism, Hermann Goering himself, to the quiet, relatively obscure propaganda ministry's handyman, Hans Fritzsche, the defendants listened with varying emotions as lurid deed after lurid deed of the Third Reich was reconstructed in English prose.

There were no legal furbelows at the start of the historic case in the small, oak-panelled courtroom whose windows overlook the onetime shrine city of Nazidom.

Lord Geoffrey Lawrence, British judge who is presiding, told the defendants Britain, the United States, the Soviet Union and France had been entrusted with the punishment of war criminals, adding "This trial which is about to begin is unique in the history of jurisprudence and in importance to people all over the world."

Goering Appears Bored.

Sidney S. Alderman, assistant to Chief U. S. Prosecutor Justice Robert H. Jackson, opened the proceedings by reading a condensed version of the indictment. His voice trembled with nervousness.

The defendants stared glumly during the lengthy reading of the indictment. Hess, Ribbentrop, Keitel, and Rosenberg listened without using the translators' earphones provided for each man on trial.

Goering, his fat countenance exhibiting bored composure, soon removed his headphones. Grand Admiral Erich Raeder and Walther Funk, former Reichsbank presi-

(Continued on Page 14.)

The Index

"Ike" Would Send GI Wives Abroad

Boone, Ia. (AP)—Gen. Dwight D. Eisenhower, who spent most of two days at the hospital bedside of his wife, recovering from bronchial pneumonia, says he favors taking the wives of occupation troops to Europe "after we have gotten down to occupation forces."

General Eisenhower, in a press conference prior to leaving for the American Legion convention in Chicago and after being advised by physicians that his wife was "on the road to recovery," said his policy "will give the wife of the lowliest GI the same right as any officer's wife, or my wife, for instance."

The general explained the great problem of getting military governments established in Germany and of getting large numbers of troops home made it difficult to estimate when a policy might be put into effect.

He asserted the German situation "might be classed as harsh and forbidding, but not black and tragic. The United States is not going to let people die of mass starvation. That won't be done."

Asked if he expected any trouble with Russia, the general remarked, "no, of course I don't expect any trouble with Russia. If I did, I'd want every soldier I could keep there."

Physicians attending Mrs. Eisenhower, who came here with the general Saturday to visit her parents and relatives, said she had shown "marked improvement" in the last 24 hours. They said she would remain in the hospital for several days.

General Eisenhower, who is to speak at the Legion's convention tonight, is scheduled to leave Washington Friday by plane on his return trip to Germany.

AUTO STRIKERS GET HELP BUT NO PAY FROM THEIR UNION

U. A. W. Takes Care of Hardship Cases; Some Get Unemployment Aid

BY JAMES MARLOW

Washington (AP)—Striking auto workers get help—but no pay—from their union.

How can they afford to strike against the General Motors? How do they live?

Officials of the United Auto Workers (U. A. W.) parent organization of about 100 local unions, give this answer:

Neither the parent nor the locals are able to give strikers any weekly pay.

The strikers have to live off their savings, try to extend their credit, and perhaps seek help from their friends.

The locals set up soup kitchens for strikers and their families, providing them with three meals a day.

And the union steps in with financial help for needy cases. For instance:

A striker about to be thrown out of his home because he can't pay his rent, or lose his gas, lights or heat because he can't pay, or who needs medical care and can't pay for that.

Strike Fund.

U. A. W. says it has approximately $4,000,000 in its so-called war chest. The locals have funds of their own, amount unknown, set aside for strike purposes.

If U. A. W. attempted to give weekly pay, say to 200,000 strikers, the $4,000,000 wouldn't last long. It would be used up in one week if each of the 200,000 strikers received $20 a week.

U. A. W. dues are $1 a month. Of that money the Local keeps 60 cents and turns over 40 cents to the parent U. A. W.

But can't strikers draw unemployment pay from the states in which they live? There's no single clear cut answer to this. The U. A. W. is striking against General Motors in a number of states.

Under the Social Security Act employers, but generally not employees, have to contribute to an unemployment fund to help workers who have lost jobs.

The money is turned over to the Federal Government. It's administered by the Social Security Board. But each state has a board or commission which decides individually who can or can't get unemployment pay.

Social Security Statement.

The Social Security Board makes this statement: with the exception of five states employees participating in strikes are not entitled to benefits.

The five exceptions are Tennessee, Louisiana, New York, Rhode Island, Pennsylvania. Strikers can get unemployment pay in those states but only after a longer waiting period than is necessary for workers who lose their jobs through no fault of their own.

But when it comes time for each state to decide the exact meaning of the phrase "employees participating in a strike," each state may differ.

A survey over the week-end showed that few, if any, of the current strikers are eligible for unemployment compensation.

The inability of U. A. W. to give its striking members weekly pay does not mean that all unions in this country are unable to do so.

Some American Federation of Labor Unions can give striking members weekly pay, but never more than 50 per cent of their pay while working. This explanation was given at A. F. L. headquarters here.

U. A. W. is a C. I. O. organization. It has no connection with the A. F. L.

VICTORY BOND ENTERTAINERS—The dance troupe which will provide one of the entertainment features for tonight's Victory Bond show at Proctors rehearses a number. The dancers are, first row, left to right, Marjorie Weaver, Shirley LeQue, Joan Geer, Merriam Saner, Sally Burke, Myrtle Beaupre, Carole Rogers; second row, Mary Church, Eugene Gordon, Sandra Rogers; third row, Marilyn Linen, Margaret Church, Eleanor Whalen, Herbert Hunt, Sally Warren, Geraldine Rudebush and Joan Blair.

Troop Arrivals At U. S. Ports Today

BY INTERNATIONAL NEWS

At New York—Carrier Enterprise, from Southampton, 4,658 troops; Lewiston Victory, from Marseille, 1,947; Hampden Sydney Victory, from Marseille, 1,941; Hilary Herbert, from Antwerp, 557; Lyman Abbott, from Havre, 531; Portland, from Havre, 1,245; Philadelphia, from Havre, 1,310; Chester Valley, 26; Duncan U. Fletcher, 15; hospital ship Slanger, Cape Palmas, 31.

At San Francisco—Battleship West Virginia, from Pearl Harbor, 2,115 Navy men, one Marine; Achilles, from Pearl Harbor, 165 Navy; Elwood Haynes, from Okinawa, 19 Army; Kochab, from Pearl Harbor, 117 Navy; Mobjack, from Pearl Harbor, 128 Navy; Oyster Bay, from Pearl Harbor, 207 Navy; Robert Morris, from Manila, eight Army; cruiser San Juan, from Honolulu, 449 Navy, one Marine, one Army; submarine Scabbard Fish, from Pearl Harbor, 20; Situla, from Saipan, 99 Army and Navy; Thomas F. Farrell, from Balboa, 34 Army; Triolus, from Okinawa, 522 Navy; Sepulgia, from Tinian, 51 Navy; Gantt, from Jinsen, 15 Army.

At Seattle—Ernie Pyle, from Yokohama, 3,280 Army; Shoshone, from Korea, 314 Army, 115 Navy.

At Tacoma—Jean La Fitte, from Okinawa, 1,097 Army.

At Portland, Ore—Troopship Diphda, from Okinawa, 222 Navy; troopship Bracken, from Okinawa, 978 Navy.

At Newport News—Ezra Meech, 27 troops; William Tilghmar, 29; W. W. Keene, 15.

At San Diego—LST 449, from Pearl Harbor, 580 Marines; destroyer Lamson, from Pearl Harbor, 35 Army.

At Boston—Howard Victory, from Havre, 1,540 including 3014th and 3027th Quartermaster Bakery Companies, 662nd Field Artillery; Bienville, from Marseille, 1,783; Smith Victory, from Antwerp, 1,530 including 443rd Medical Collecting Company, 753rd Clearing Company, 710th Engineers Base Company, 431st Ordnance Motor Vehicle Company; Kokomo Victory, from Havre, 1,693 troops.

GREENWICH.

Mr. and Mrs. Harry Wilson of St. Albans, Vt., have purchased the Hendricks farm on the Argyle road.

Jarvis Stevens, EM3/c, U. S. N. R., son of Mr. and Mrs. Raymond Stevens of Greenwich, is now stationed at Tokyo Bay.

Miss Pearl Townsend has returned from Proctor, Vt., where she spent the Thanksgiving weekend with her brother, J. Foster Townsend, and Mrs. Townsend.

Mr. and Mrs. Roscoe McEachron have closed their home on R. D. 3 and left for a motor trip to Salinas, Cal., where they plan to spend the winter.

Several members of the United Presbyterian Church attended the Bible study class held in the Coila United Presbyterian Church, recently.

Seven members of Ashlar Lodge, 584, F. and A. M. of Greenwich recently spent an evening in Amsterdam where they attended a communication of Welcome Lodge, 829, of that city. The Master Mason Degree was conferred upon a class of candidates at this meeting. The members of Ashlar Lodge who made the trip were John Kinnin, David Kinnin, Malcolm Gemmell, Malcolm Smith, Joseph Wever, Charles Perkins and Harry Perkins.

At a recent session of the Juvenile Grange in Easton the following officers were elected: Master, Raymond Lucey; overseer, Raymond Johnson; lecturer, Virginia Booth; steward, Liston Batty, jr.; assistant steward, Harold Delurey; chaplain, Esther Coffin; treasurer, Faith Booth; secretary, Marle Booth; Ceres, Helen Pratt; Pomona, Joan Batty; Flora, Marion Pratt; day assistant steward, Shirley Booth; pianist, Gretchen Booth; flag bearer, Carl Johnson.

A number of legionnaires and auxiliary members of Liberty Post, American Legion, from Greenwich, attended the welcoming of the state commander, Miles D. Kennedy, and the state auxiliary president, Betty Burdett, on their official visit to Washington County Monday evening. The event took place in Whitehall in the Elks' Club with the Whitehall Post, 83, and auxiliary units as hosts. Supper was served to 300 persons. The GI Bill of Rights was the theme of the business meeting which followed. At the close of the session George Neddo's rhythm orchestra provided music for dancing.

DISCLOSE PILSEN DAMAGE.

Prague (U.P.)—Air-raid damage to the beer and Skodka works town of Pilsen was roughly estimated at 4,500,000 crowns or approximately $140,000,000 at prewar rate of exchange, ministry of information officials disclosed recently. Officials said that 6,922 houses in the city, out of a prewar total of 11,120, had been destroyed or damaged.

EASTERN CAMPING ASSOCIATION UNIT ELECTS OFFICERS

Youth Organizations in City Represented at Annual Session

Plans for the 1946 camping season were discussed by the Northeastern New York Section of the American Camping Association, at an election meeting held at the Y. M. C. A. last night. Andrew F. Allen, director of camp sanitation, State Health Department, heads the list of new officers elected.

Janet Webb, executive director of Schenectady Girl Scouts, and Wallace MacBride, Boy Scout executive of Fort Orange Council, Albany, were elected vice presidents. Marion Evans, executive director of Albany Boy Scouts, was named secretary; Paul R. Long, executive director of Albany Y. M. C. A., treasurer.

Representatives from a score of youth organizations in the Troy Area attended the meeting at which discussions ranged from instituting a lecture program to educate youth leaders on the philosophy of camping to setting up workshops. In view of the expanding camping programs being sponsored by youth organizations in the area for this summer, leaders in the field will be invited to address the membership during the year, it was stated.

Mrs. Warren Quinn, retiring president, presided. Paul R. Long was chairman of the nominating committee comprising Florence Myers, ...

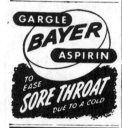

WILSON'S WEEKLY Bulletin

By George Rector
Food and Nutrition Consultant to Wilson & Co.

Soup for Lunch

Ever notice how sharp the appetites of your school youngsters are at noon? Fill their tummies but remember to keep the meal well-balanced. An easy way to get plenty of vegetables eaten is to serve a delicious cream soup literally filled with vegetables.

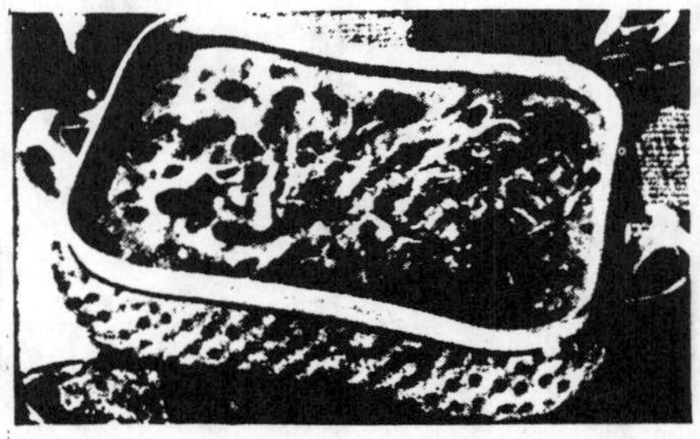

Cream of Vegetable Soup . . . nourishing and satisfying

To 2 cups boiling water
Add 1½ cups diced potatoes
1 cup sliced onion
½ cup sliced celery
½ cup diced carrot
¼ cup tomatoes
2 cups coarsely shredded cabbage
½ tsp. salt

Cover and simmer 45 min. or until all vegetables are very tender.
Add 2 cups rich milk
2 tbsp. CERTIFIED MARGARINE
2 tsp. WILSON'S B-V dissolved in the hot liquid.
Serves 6.

------------ Clip Recipe Here ------------

Cream Soup Simplifies Lunch

Cream of vegetable soup, brimming with a variety of vegetables, is a hearty, nutritious soup. Add a tart kidney bean salad, gingerbread with mixed fruit topping plus a beverage to complete the meal.

Meat flavor adds deliciousness to cream soups. A little B-V dissolved in the hot soup does the trick. Save steps to and from the kitchen by serving the soup from a tureen. Keeps the soup hot, handy for a second helpings.

Busy Day Finds

The vegetables for the vegetable cream soup may be cooked the day before. Reheat the last minute along with the milk and B-V. The kidney bean salad is one of the few salads that is really better if made the day before. Prepared gingerbread mix and canned fruit cocktail, drained and chilled, for the topping, save valuable minutes, too.

Did You Know That?

You can add eye and flavor appeal to creamed soups with pimiento strips; diced, crisp Certified Bacon; grated Certified American Cheese; croutons (squares of day-old bread, toasted)?

B-V adds valuable minerals and vitamins to soups as well as delicious meat flavor?

Yours for tastier soups,
George Rector

CHAPLAIN NAMED FOR SANITARIUM BY COUNTY BOARD

Rev. William E. Gaston Gets Appointment; Acts on Other Business

Rev. William E. Gaston was appointed chaplain of the Pawling Sanitarium by the Rensselaer County Board of Supervisors last night to fill the unexpired term of Rev. Nelson Van Raalte, pastor of the Wynantskill Reformed Church, who resigned when he accepted the call of a church in Schenectady County. The appointment of Mr. Gaston is effective Thursday.

The board approved a resolution to place on the assessment rolls of the 14 towns and also upon the nine wards of the City of Rensselaer the taxes for 1945-1946, which had previously been presented to the board. The chairman and the clerk of the board were authorized to execute and issue to each collector of the towns and the treasurer of the City of Rensselaer a warrant for the collection of taxes upon the rolls and books of his town or city.

The county treasurer was authorized to make available to the county extension services the sums of $9,000 to the Farm Bureau and $2,300 to the tuberculosis department of the Farm Bureau; $6,000 to the Home Bureau, and $11,000 to the 4-H Club organization, each in quarterly installments.

Authority was voted to the county treasurer to convey by quit claim deed four pieces of property in the Towns of Brunswick, East Greenbush, Stephentown and Schodack to new ownership for a total of $217.68. On one of the parcels, the delinquent taxes dated back to 1909. All will now be back on a tax paying basis.

The supervisors adjourned until Tuesday, Dec. 11, at 2 p.m.

TROY AREA OFFICERS AT SAGE—In photo above are officers, secretaries and chairmen at Van Der Heyden House, day students' house at Russell Sage College, now marking its 11th year and one of the first houses for the exclusive use of day students to be established on any college campus in the country. Jane Lane is president; Helen Howe, vice president; Rosemary Sheehy, treasurer, and Lois Ives, assistant treasurer. All reside in Troy. Those in photo are: First row, left to right—Sally Burgess, Elizabeth Sheridan, Ruth Dugan, Helen Howe, Jane Lane, Ruth Fagan, Rosemary Sheehy, all of Troy, Jane Pedlow, Albany, and Jeanne Vermilyea, Troy; second row—Joan McCarthy and Patricia Boyce, Troy, Ione Vetoich, Watervliet, Carolyn Lewis, Schenectady, Patricia Maloney, Troy, Ruth Callaghan, Cohoes, Rita Burke, Troy, Lois Brown, Rensselaer, Barbara Hawley, Troy, Jane Powers, Troy, and Lois Ives, Troy.

147 Persons To Seek Citizenship Rights In Court Here On Dec. 7

The names of 147 aliens who have applied for citizenship appear on the calendar for the term of Naturalization Court which will be convened here Friday, Dec. 7 by Supreme Court Justice Pierce H. Russell:

Of this number, 76 will be given the oath of allegiance in a bloc and they will not be required to have their witnesses present. This is a new procedure in Naturalization Court here. The applications for final papers by these 76 persons were processed since May 1, 1945, and passed by the Federal examiner.

Witnesses will not be required to be present in court in connection with the applications of the following persons:

Oskar P. Reinstrom, 11 Marion Avenue.
Thomas W. Fox, 2318 Fifteenth Street.
Winifred M. Casey, 181 Hill Street.
Stanley F. Peak, 216 Third Street.
Michael Suchecki, 654 First Avenue.
William Wadlar, Marshall Sanitarium.
Cristine Roberts, 892 First Avenue.
Albert D. Baker, 81 River Street.
Jonas Adamaitis, Hoosick Falls.
John R. Girken, Averill Park.
Margaret Winkler, 732 Fourth Avenue.
Ralph Isabella, 61 State Street.
Herman Monch, Averill Park.
Paul Rossi, 3223 Seventh Avenue.
Doris M. Deubel, Petersburg.
Bernice M. Banford, Rensselaer.
Margaret B. Saur, 84 Fourteenth Street.
Anahid Zekian, 1009 Second Avenue.
Mary I. Hodge, 92 Genesee Street.
Joseph Rogers, Averill Park.
Sumpad S. Charchian, 319 Fourth Street.
James K. Hermiston, Averill Park.
Margaret M. O'Rourke (Sister Mary Margaret), 1225 Peoples Avenue.
Bridget M. Kennedy (Sister Mary Clare), 1225 Peoples Avenue.
Bertha Geis (Sister Dietlinde), Rensselaer.
Amalia Nicklaus (Sister Procula), Rensselaer.
Anna Nirsberger, Hastings Lane.
Michael Nirsberger, Hastings Lane.
Giovanni A. Signorelli, 880 River Street.
Carmela Morano, 165 First Street.
Daniel Siegel, East Nassau.
Esther Genta, Castleton.
Mary Mulhall (Sister Mary Carmeletta), 1225 Peoples Avenue.
Bridget Healy (Sister Mary St. Michael), 1225 Peoples Avenue.
Mary Dennigan (Sister Mary Bernadine), 1225 Peoples Avenue.
Julia Leahy (Sister Mary St. Louis), 1225 Peoples Avenue.
Maria Reidy (Sister Mary Julian), 1225 Peoples Avenue.
Margaret E. D. Bickelhaupt, Averill Park.
Honorah M. O'Connor (Sister Mary Xystus), 1225 Peoples Avenue.
Mary Margaret Connolly (Sister Mary of St. Mel), 1225 Peoples Avenue.
Mary Galvin (Sister Mary Heart of Mary), 1225 Peoples Avenue.
Rose Kuen, 17-102nd Street.
Margaret Lawson, 5 Balsam Avenue.
Pauline P. Sud, 6 Gale Place.
Nora A O'Gara, 506 Grand Street.
Klara Siegel, East Nassau.
Cosimo Adamo, 2519 Fifth Avenue.
Ida K. Simon, Rensselaer.
Rizieri Ciccarone, 2314 Sixth Avenue.
Anna Lucrezio, 1451 Fifth Avenue.
Peter Futerko, Castleton.
Elizabeth V. Tennant, 115 Stow Avenue
George E. W. Taylor 140 Fifth Avenue.
Nellie V. Taylor, 140 Fifth avenue.
George V. Tooghlajian, 2314 11th Street.
David Dick, sr., Averill Park.
David Dick, Averill Park.
Alex Molga, 755 Broadway, Watervliet.
Andrew L. Rozum, 2003 Fifth Avenue
Florence Whittaker, North Greenbush.
Anthony Suen, 1486 Fifth Avenue.
Anastatia Murphy, 170 Fifth Avenue.
Catherine Starzyk (sister Zita), Castleton.
Peter Bogacz, 105 Monroe Street.
John Wrenowski, 107 Jackson Street.
Jessie Niczewicz, 23 Tyler Street.
Maryanna Zilka, 361 Second Street
Carrie Sopko, 4 Center Street.
William H. Roberts, 841 River Street.
Winifred M. Roberts, 841 River Street.
Armand C. Dauphinaid, 2912 Fifth Avenue.
Peter Ghienes, 2332 15th Street.
Mary E. O'Connell, 520 Second Street.
Anna Mlak, Rensselaer.
Sophie Wawroski, 14 Forbes Avenue.
Stefanja Tomaszeska, Hoosick Falls.

The applications of the following persons have been pending prior to May 1, 1945, and the witnesses in each of these cases are required to be present on Dec. 7.

Joseph Kruse, Rensselaer.
Wilhelm Duffner, 421 Ninth Street.
Amelia Wagar, 27 118th Street.
Evagalia Rallis, Bristol, Conn.
William Mack, South Schodack.
Albert Knapp, Hampton Manor.
Lucy DiValentino, Rensselaer.
Emanuel H. Dell, 55 Fourth Street.
Elizabeth A. Booch, Canaan.
Caroline Weber, Nassau.
Friedrich C. Hangst, Cropseyville.
Antoine LaPorte, Rensselaer.
Emalia Buttino, Rensselaer.
Theresa Siegal, East Nassau.
Herbert Heumann, Nassau.
Philip J. Roder, 83 Ford Avenue.
Alfred E. Krolow, Nassau.
Johanna M. Kuhn, Schenectady.
Martha S. Keppert, South Lake Avenue.
Katharine Eachmann, Nassau.
Franz C. Plath, Rensselaer.
Gustav Pallack, Nassau.
Antonio Rossetti, Rensselaer.
Michael McCarthy, 60 State Street.
Jakob Saur, Valley Falls.
Joseph A. Ziegler, 570 Second Avenue.
Anilla Tietz, Castleton.
Grace Borst, 637 Fifth Avenue.
Rubin Ryvkin, Berlin.
Martha Mausolf, East Nassau.
Mary DeFazio, 689 Hoosick Street.
Joseph DeFazio, 689 Hoosick Street.
Agostino Gatto, 604 Fourth Street.
John DiDio, 28 Eighth Street.
Sebastina Patania, 62 Havermans Avenue.
Adolf Lehmann, Nassau.
Elizabeth Pitzer, Rensselaer.
Otto Jesse, East Nassau.
Mary DiDio, 28 Eighth Street.
Lucie Jesse, East Nassau.
Henry Raquette, Johnsonville.
Michele Mischitelli, 35 Havermans Avenue.
Felicia Anthony, 176 Hoosick Street.
Louise Levonian, 22 Detroit Avenue.
Anna E. Schmitt, Rensselaer.
Josephine Ryvkin, Berlin.
Carl Fritzsche, 10 Kinloch Avenue.
Stefano Giancotti, 203 Church Street.
Maria C. Mantello, 2135 Seventh Avenue.
Waldemar C. Zwinge, Stephentown.
Jeanne Appel, 40 Fifth Avenue.
Gregers Kjelgaard, Hoosick Falls.
Joanna Budkowski, 513 First Street.
Eudoxie M. Gervais, Troy.
Frances Pappas, 2148 Seventh Avenue.
Concetta Martone, 250 Fourth Street.
Herta R. Leng, 1996 Fifteenth Street.
Berthold Preiss, Hoosick Falls.
Erna Preiss, Hoosick Falls.
Angeline Carelli, Hoosick Falls.
Francesco Marchione, 637 Sixth Avenue.
Anna Walsh, 25½ Eighth Street.
Justina Roeth (Sister Stilla) Rensselaer.
Frank A. Massaro, 8 Sampson Avenue.
Mary Krupinskaite (Sister Mary Albertina) Troy, R. D. 4.
Anna V. Gorski, 540 Second Street.
Susan Kaliski, 504 Fourth Street.
Anna Rutledge, 763 Pawling Avenue.
Sarah Dolan, 763 Pawling Avenue.
Bertha Kasper, 520 Fourth Street.
Jennie Budkowski, 513 First Street.

STATE COURT UPHOLDS LABOR BOARD ACTION

Albany (AP) — The Court of Appeals upheld yesterday in two unanimous decisions the right of the State Labor Relations Board to investigate disputes over collective bargaining in New York State industries and to demand company records during such investigations.

The cases, which had been decided in favor of the board in lower courts, arose out of bargaining disputes between the Foremen's Association of America and the Bethlehem Steel Corp. and the Alleghany Ludlum Steel Corp.

There were no written opinions. Associate Judge George Z. Medalie did not participate.

SUNKEN BUS HUNTED—Diver Spud O'Donnell comes up after searching 200 feet for school bus loaded with children that plunged into Lake Chelan near Chelan, Wash. Fifteen youngsters and driver were carried to death in the deep waters. Five children and a woman passenger escaped. (AP Wirephoto.)

ORIENTAL TEMPLE FALL CEREMONIAL HERE TOMORROW

Affair Opens at 4 P.M.; Dinner Slated During Evening

Gilbert C. Bindewald, of Cohoes, illustrious potentate, will preside at all sessions of the fall ceremonial of Oriental Temple, A.A.O. N.M.S., at Masonic Temple tomorrow afternoon and evening. Nobles from throughout the area will attend the sessions which will be highlighted by special events and ceremonies.

The ceremonial will open at 4 p.m. when novices will report to the recorder, Frank M. Ames, past potentate. At 4:30 p.m. a business session will be held in the temple, where balloting on various fraternal petitions will take place. The afternoon's sessions will be climaxed by a dinner to be served from 5 to 7:30 p.m. in The Hendrick Hudson, under the direction of Noble Elmer A. Hempstead, caravan steward.

A band concert, for which the Shrine orchestra has been rehearsing several weeks, will be given at Music Hall, under the direction of George H. Slater, jr., from 7:45 to 8:15 p.m. Following the concert, special visitors will be introduced.

The schedule of the Second Section will continue at 9 p.m. when Roy Brown and his assistants will entertain the guests and visitors. At 9:45 p.m. a floor show will be held at Music Hall. The day's festivities will conclude with a buffet lunch at the Masonic Temple at 10:45 p.m.

GILBERT C. BINDEWALD.

FREIGHT RATE REVIEW ASKED BY NINE STATES

New York (AP) — Atty. Gen. Nathaniel L. Goldstein said yesterday nine northern states had instituted action in the U. S. District Court at Utica, seeking review of Interstate Commerce Commission orders increasing freight rates 10 per cent throughout the northeast and reducing them in the south.

The nine states also asked that an injunction be granted to restrain enforcement of the I. C. C. orders, scheduled to take effect Jan. 1, pending final determination of the suit. Goldstein, New York State attorney general, said the injunctive relief asked also would affect six other New England states.

The nine joining in yesterday's action were New York, Delaware, Indiana, Maryland, Michigan, New Jersey, Ohio, Pennsylvania and Wisconsin.

They charged that the I.C.C., in ordering the rate changes, acted in an "arbitrary, biased and capricious" manner.

PEANUT REMOVED FROM BOY'S LUNG

Philadelphia (AP)—A peanut was successfully removed fro mthe lung of 27-month-old Ronald William DeRocher yesterday by physicians at Temple University's Jackson Bronchoscopic Clinic.

Ronald, who was flown here from Watertown Monday, after attempts to remove the peanut failed there, will be able to leave the hospital in about five days, physicians said.

He swallowed the peanut three weeks ago.

His parents are Mr. and Mrs. Carl W. DeRocher. The father is a Navy hospital corpsman on leave from Fort Eustis, Va.

STEEL UNION TO DECIDE STRIKE PLANS DEC. 10

Pittsburg (AP)—Given sanction by its members to take strike action, the C.I.O. United Steelworkers Union yesterday called a meeting of its wage policy committee for Dec. 10 to decide how to proceed with its demand for a $2-a-day wage increase affecting nearly 1,000,000 workers.

The union set the meeting date upon the strength of almost complete returns in which steel workers in 29 states declared themselves in favor of a strike by a majority of nearly five to one.

Latest returns totaled 394,969 for a strike and 81,857 against. The balloting Wednesday was the largest strike vote ever held under National Labor Relations Board auspices.

FORT EDWARD SEEKS FEDERAL HOUSING FUND FOR DWELLING UNITS

The village of Fort Edward has filed application for fifty housing units with total value of $275,000 with the Federal Public Housing Administration, it was announced yesterday at administration offices in Washington.

Data concerning various applications for a total of 24,450 units was presented to the Senate's banking and currency committee which is studying finances for the dwellings, according to the Associated Press.

BUS-TANK CRASH KILLS FOUR PERSONS

Lumberton, N. C. (AP)—At least four persons were killed and 22 were injured late last night in a bus-oil tanker collision on a highway about ten miles from this eastern North Carolina city.

Sheriff E. C. Wade said the bus, loaded with textile mill workers returning to their homes in or near Lumberton after work at the Bladenboro, N. C., cotton mills, caught fire after the collision.

RUSSIA THREATENS TO DISPATCH MORE TROOPS INTO IRAN

London (AP)—A spokesman of the Iranian embassy declared yesterday Russia had threatened to reinforce Red Army garrisons in Northern Iran if fresh Iranian troops moved up into that troubled area, where insurgent activities now are reported to have spread to a third province.

In Washington, Iranian Ambassador Hussein Ala quoted a Russian note to Iran as saying that bloodshed would result if more Iranian forces moved northward, and that this would necessitate Russia's sending more Soviet forces into Iran. Russia occupies the northern part of the country under a wartime agreement with Britain and Iran.

Both Ala and the spokesman here said Russia had rejected Iran's request to send reinforcements northward after disorders, blamed by the Iranian government on "separatists," broke out last week in Azerbaijan, the northwest province of Iran bordering Russia.

A Russian commander stopped four battalions of Iranians near Kasvin, northwest of Tehran, refusing to allow them to go further.

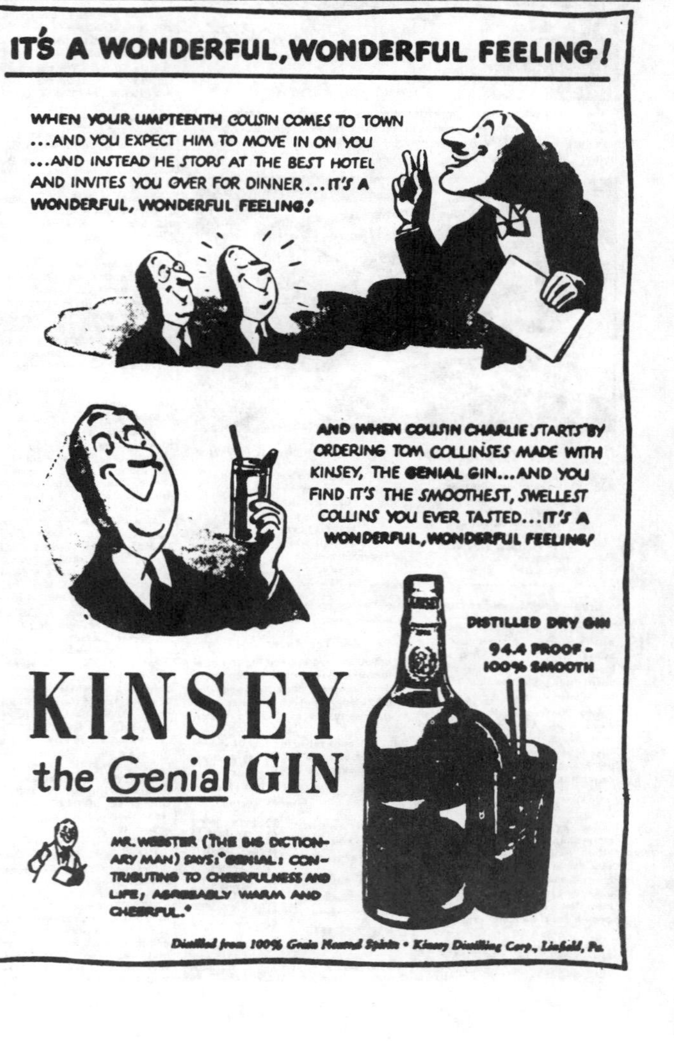

Annual Christmas Party, Sale Planned By St. Paul's Women

Plans have been completed for the annual Christmas party sponsored each year by the women of St. Paul's Episcopal Church.

The party this year will be held in the Guild House on State Street on Wednesday, Dec. 12, under the general chairmanship of Mrs. Eugene Warren.

A white elephant sale will be conducted in the morning starting at 11 a.m. and there will be appropriate gifts for Christmas such as children's dresses, hand knitted and sewn garments for sale.

Mrs. Warren is being assisted by the following at the white elephant table: Miss Marion C. Lally, Mrs. George H. Laskey, Mrs Guy Phelps, Mrs. J. C. Beatty, Mrs J. Lansing Van Schoonhoven, Mrs. Chauncey W. Cook, Mrs. Charles M. Connolly, Mrs. Mark C. Bowman, Mrs. C. Whitney Tillinghast, jr., Mrs. Leland W. Lane, Mrs John Ayres, Mrs. Sanford L. Cluett, Mrs. John Sarkis, Mrs. Frederick T. Weyburn and Mrs. George I. Miller.

In the afternoon there will be a food sale with the usual surprise Christmas tree and a silver tea will be held from 3 to 5:30 p.m. Mrs. A. E. Cluett heads the tea committee and will be assisted by Mrs. Thomas Vail, Mrs. David W. Houston, jr., Mrs. Leslie W. Rolfe and Mrs. Scott Mackay. Mrs. Louis H. Baker heads the reception committee and Mrs. Shelton S. Jackson and Mrs. Alexander L. Darby are in charge of decorations.

Other committee chairmen include Mrs. Cook, invitations; Mrs. R. Stanley Thomson, Christmas tree; Mrs. Connolly and Mrs. Lattimer W. Reeder, publicity; Mrs. A. R. Trego, waitresses and Mrs. James L. Ryan, Mrs. John Sarkis and Mrs. Arthur L. Collins, food.

Contributions for the white elephant sale may be left at any time at the Martha Memorial House on Third Street.

Lillian Reiter Bride Of Bernard W. Graham

Miss Lillian Lois Reiter, daughter of Mr. and Mrs. Paul H. Reiter of 147 President Street, became the bride of Bernard W. Graham, son of Mr. and Mrs. B. W. Graham of Stratford, Conn., in a double ring ceremony performed Wednesday at St. Patrick's Church. Rev. John G. O'Grady was the officiating clergyman. Palms and bouquets of white flowers decorated the church, and Mrs. Mary Woods Patrick rendered vocal selections, including "Ave Maria," "On This Day, O Beautiful Mother" and "O Lord, I am Not Worthy."

Miss Helen Graham, sister of the bridegroom, was the maid of honor and Charles E. Kelly served as best man. Serving as ushers were Kenneth Graham and Frank A. Greagan.

Given in marriage by her father, the bride wore a wedding gown of white satin and tulle designed with a fitted long-waisted bodice of Dutchess satin with a bouffant skirt and court train of double tulle, sweetheart neckline and three-quarter length sleeves. Her bridal cap was fashioned with clusters of white flowers at the sides and held in place her shoulder and fingertip length veils of bridal illusion. She carried a bouquet of white roses and white pompons.

Her attendant was attired in a pink lace and tulle gown with a fitted bodice of the lace and a bouffant skirt of tulle. Her headpiece was of pink flowers trimmed with a shoulder length veil and she carried a bouquet of copper and yellow pompons.

A reception followed in the Surf room of the Annex Restaurant. Mrs. Reiter received the guests wearing a print afternoon dress with a corsage of pink roses. The mother of the bridegroom, who also received the guests, was attired in an orchid afternoon dress with a shoulder bouquet of white roses.

The couple left on a wedding trip to an undisclosed destination, the bride traveling in a fuchsia suit with brown accessories and a corsage of orchids. They will reside in Bridgeport. The bride is a graduate of Troy High School and the Troy Business College. The bridegroom received his education at Stratford High School and Yale University.

Out of town guests included Miss Mary Graham of Farmington, Conn.; Mr. and Mrs. Steven McMahon, Sally and Mary Ann McMahon, Mr. and Mrs. John Crowley and Mrs. Frank J. Kelly all of Bridgeport.

MR. AND MRS. BERNARD W. GRAHAM —St. Odell photo

MR. AND MRS WILLIAM GRAY CLARK —St. Odell photo

—Lloyd studio

UNITED IN MARRIAGE—Mr. and Mrs. Daniel Joyes were married Nov. 25 in St. Nicholas' Church, Watervliet. The bride is the former Miss Rose Haitko, daughter of Mr. and Mrs. Panko Haitko of 2707 Second Avenue, Watervliet. The bridegroom is the son of Mr. and Mrs. Rock Joyes of 426 River Street.

—Lloyd studio

HAVE DOUBLE RING SERVICE—Cpl. and Mrs. Joseph Edward Hebert were married in a double ring ceremony performed Nov. 25 at the residence of Rev. Seth N. Genung, 702 Third Avenue. Mrs. Hebert is the former Marcella Arlene Peters, daughter of Mrs. Verna A. Peters of Pleasantdale and the bridegroom is the son of Mr. and Mrs. Fred Hebert of Schenectady.

Couple Married In Double Ring Ceremony

The wedding of Miss Ruth M. Wariex, daughter of Mr. and Mrs. Wilbert Wariex of 314 Seventh Street, Watervliet, and Henry J. Lawson, signalman 3/c of the Navy, son of Henry J. Lawson and the late Mrs. Lawson of 11 Amsterdam Avenue, Menands, was solemnized Wednesday at 2 p.m. in St. Bridget's rectory by Rev. John J. Bourke.

The double ring service was used. Mrs. Donald Caswell was the matron of honor and Frederick Martin acted as best man. The bride wore a white satin wedding gown with a sweetheart neckline and a long train. Her fingertip length veil fell from a wreath of orange blossoms and she carried a bouquet of white roses and pompons with streamers of white satin ribbons. Her attendant was dressed in yellow taffeta with shoulder veil of net fastened to a tiara of yellow flowers. Her bouquet was of lavender chrysanthemums.

A reception was held at the home of the bride's parents following a dinner served for the bridal party at Vandenburg Inn. The bride's mother was attired in an aquamarine crepe afternoon dress with a corsage of red roses.

The couple left on an extended wedding trip to an undisclosed destination. The bridegroom has just returned after three and a half years' service in the Pacific. He will report to New York for reassignment.

Returns to Base

Pvt. Thomas F. Powers, jr., of the Air Corps, returned recently to his base at Greensboro, N. C., after spending a 15-day furlough with his parents, Mr. and Mrs. Thomas Powers of 89 Hoosick Street. Private Powers expects to be assigned to overseas duty.

Tendered Shower

Miss Carolyn Butler, daughter of Mr. and Mrs. James E. Butler of 91 High Street, Green Island, was tendered a personal shower Thursday evening by Miss Betty Canavan of Upper Paine Street. There were 24 guests present. Refreshments were served from a table centered with a bride's cake. The honor guest who is a prospective bride, was the recipient of many gifts.

To Meet Tomorrow

The Women's Club of St. Paul the Apostle's Church will hold its regular monthly meeting tomorrow night in the school hall at 8 p.m. Mrs. Michael Flynn, president, will be the presiding officer.

--Goldstone studio

TO WED—Mr. and Mrs. George L. Grady of 429 Third Avenue, Watervliet, announce the engagement of their daughter, Miss Barbara Jane Grady, to John Gernon, son of Mr and Mrs. Edward Gernon of 86 Broad Street Waterford. Mr. Gernon has recently been discharged from the Army after serving with the Fifth Army in Italy.

Laura Xander Wed In Home Service

In a home ceremony performed Saturday at 10 a.m., Miss Laura A. Xander, daughter of Mr. and Mrs. Arthur E. Xander of 47 Fifth Avenue was married to Harmond T. Hafensteiner, son of Mr. and Mrs. Michael Hafensteiner of 369 Fifth Avenue. Rev. Eldon H. Martin, D.D., pastor of the Fifth Avenue-State Street Methodist Church, was the officiating clergyman.

The bride's father played the wedding marches and the house was decorated with bouquets of white pompons and palms. Mrs. George W. Cropsey was the matron of honor and Lee R. Hafensteiner, brother of the bridegroom, served as best man. The ushers were Edward W. Xander and George W. Cropsey.

Given in marriage by her father, the bride wore a maroon velvet suit with winter white accessories and a white feathered hat. Her corsage was of white roses. The honor attendant was attired in royal blue velvet suit with a black feathered hat and a shoulder bouquet of red roses. A reception followed for members of the immediate families and a wedding breakfast was served. Mrs. Xander was dressed in a navy blue print suit with a corsage of red roses and the mother of the bridegroom chose an orchid crepe dress with a corsage of white roses.

The bride is a graduate of Lansingburg High School and is employed at the Covert Manufacturing Co. in Watervliet. The bridegroom also graduated from Lansingburg High School and is now employed at the D. & H. Railroad Co. Recently discharged, Mr. Hafensteiner spent 29 months in the African theater of operations in the Army Air Corps.

Leaving on a wedding trip to New York, Mrs. Hafensteiner traveled in a brown gabardine suit with white accessories and a brown fur coat. They will reside in Watervliet. Out of town guests present for the wedding included Mr. and Mrs. Karl Bauer of Albany and Harold Bauer of the Navy.

Church Society To Hold Bazaar

The Woman's Missionary Society of the United Presbyterian Church will hold a bazaar and cafeteria luncheon and supper Wednesday from 11 a.m. to 7:30 p.m. Mrs. Henry Martin, general chairman, has announced the King's Daughters will have charge of the cafeteria with Mrs. Isabelle Bibb, Mrs. Adam Ross and Mrs. H. J. Scriram in charge of the food. Mrs. Arthur Leppard and Mrs Joseph Chambers have charge of the dining room.

The white elephant table and the fancy article table will be in charge of members of the Woman's Missionary Society.

Plan Christmas Meeting

The Farther Lights Society of the Second Baptist Church will hold its Christmas meeting and grabbag Tuesday evening at the home of Mrs. Marion Gibson on Highland Avenue. Mrs. William Pipping and Mrs. Arthur Chrestensen will be the assisting hostesses. Mrs. Chrestensen will also have the devotions and study period. Mrs. DeWitt Shaeffer will have charge of the business sessions.

The society will serve a chicken dinner Wednesday evening at the church in connection with the bazaar being held at the Second Baptist Church Wednesday afternoon and evening.

ABOUT TOWN

LEAVING TONIGHT

Mrs. Clark Cipperly will leave tonight for New York where she will spend a few day

IN NEW YORK

Dr. William E. McCarthy and Dr. Caleb H. Bird are spending a week in New York attending the Greater New York Dental meeting being held at the Pennsylvania Hotel.

TO VISIT RELATIVES

Mrs. Henry J. Speck of the Caldwell left today for Forest Hills, L. I., where she will visit with relatives until after the Christmas holidays.

Honored at Shower

The Misses Agnes and Grace Barton of Johnsonville were guests of honor at a miscellaneous shower given recently by Mrs. Paul Barton and Mrs. James Barton of Johnsonville at the latter's home. Games were played and a mock wedding performed. Two bridal cakes formed the centerpiece of the refreshment table and a pink and blue color scheme prevailed. The guests of honor were the recipients of many gifts.

Group To Meet

The senior Hadassah study group will meet tomorrow night at the home of Mrs. Morris E. Lasdon 25 Maple Avenue.

Record Pattern

2531
SIZES
10-20

SIDE CLOSING STYLE.

This becoming princess style, with its unusual side closing treatment, will just fill your need for a frock that can be worn almost anywhere, at anytime.

No. 2531 is cut in sizes 10, 12, 14, 16, 18 and 20. Size 16 requires 2⅞ yards 54-inch fabric; ¼ yard 39-inch for collar.

Send 15c for pattern, which includes complete sewing guide. Print your name, address, and style number plainly. Be sure to state size you wish. Include postal unit or zone number in your address.

Address Pattern Department, The Times Record, 121 W. 19th Street, New York 11, N. Y.

Miss Ranney Fetes Recent Bride At Tea

Miss Mary Aileen Ranney entertained yesterday afternoon at her home on Hoosick Street with a tea for members of the sophomore class at Vanderheyden House, Russell Sage College. The affair was in honor of Mrs. Starrett Clark Kennedy, the former Miss Joanne Woodhouse, a recent bride.

The hostess was assisted in receiving the guests by her mother, Mrs. Charles J. Ranney. Bronze and orchid chrysanthemums centered the tea table which was lighted by tall white candles. Mrs. Margaret Demers Woodhouse, mother of the honor guest, and Miss Margaret L. Lovell, housemother of Vanderheyden House, poured. Members of the class presented Mrs. Kennedy with two sterling silver place settings.

R. P. I. Group Holds Tea Dance

The Women's Student Organization of Rensselaer Polytechnic Institute conducted a tea dance and cocktail party yesterday at 4 p.m. at The Hendrick Hudson in honor of the women freshmen at R. P. I.

Miss Adrienne Gray, president of the group and Miss Joan Scanlon, secretary-treasurer of the club, headed the committee on arrangements and were assisted by a committee which includes Miss Helen Ketchum, Miss Trent Cluett and Miss Ethel Katz.

Dr. and Mrs. Warren Stoker and Mr. and Mrs. Paul Graham were chaperones at the event.

Sage Graduate To Wed Harold E. Campbell

Mr. and Mrs. G. Craig Wayman of Schenectady have announced the engagement of their daughter, Miss Ruth Alice Wayman, to Harold E. Campbell, also of Schenectady, son of Mr. and Mrs. Ellis W. Campbell of Lynchburg, Va.

The prospective bride is a graduate of Russell Sage College and is with the General Electric Co. Mr. Campbell graduated from Virginia Polytechnic Institute and is an engineer with the General Electric Co. He is a member of Tau Beta Pi and Phi Kappa Phi, honorary engineering fraternities. oN date has been set for the nuptials.

Mothers' Club To Meet

The Mothers' Club of St. Augustine's School will hold its regular monthly meeting Wednesday evening in Bradley Hall. Plans will be made for the annual Christmas party. Mrs. William Schubert, president, will preside. At the conclusion of the meeting, a social hour will be enjoyed during which refreshments will be served.

Guests in Town

Mrs. Fannie Rubenstein of Flushing, L. I., is the guest of her son and daughter-in-law, Mr. and Mrs. Irving Rubenstein of 43 South Lake Avenue. Mrs. Rubenstein was accompanied to Troy by her son, Michael Rubenstein who has just been discharged after four years' of overseas service. He has now returned to New York City.

Returns Home

Mrs. William F. Puncer has returned to New York after spending the week-end as the guest of her brother-in-law and sister, Mr. and Mrs. Dean H. Weller.

Social Situations

THE SITUATION: The husband of a friend returns from overseas and he seems nervous and restless to you.

WRONG WAY: Say as much to his wife, when her husband isn't around.

RIGHT WAY: Don't add to her worries by making any comment about the effect the war has had on him.

Memorial Church Names Bazaar Chairmen

Wednesday will be the final sewing session at the Memorial Methodist Church for this year. Many of the women are needed to help complete the work for the bazaar being held Thursday from 2:30 p.m. to 8:30 p.m.

From 5:30 p.m. to 7 p.m., a Virginia ham supper will be served. The sale chairmen are: Aprons, Mrs. Russell Cash; fancy articles, Miss Dorothy McCabe; children's articles, Mrs. Doris McEchron; county fair, Mrs. Wesley Griffith and Mrs. Thomas Tynan; marionette show, Richard Birkmeyer; candy, Mrs. Reid C. Simpson and supper, Mrs. C. N. Powers; tickets, Mrs. Henry Lawless.

Wednesday at 2:30 p.m., the School for Religious Instruction will be held and at 6:30 p.m. the joint choir rehearsal for the Christmas music is scheduled.

Moving Out of Town

Mr. and Mrs. Richard C. Rourke and daughter, Ann Marie, will leave this week for Hudson Falls where they will reside. Mr. Rourke is an employee of the New York State Department of Correction and has been transferred to the Great Meadow Prison at Comstock. He was recently discharged from the Coast Guard after 38 months' of service.

Home from New York

Mrs. Cecile Duncan of Lord Avenue, has returned from a week in New York.

—Deiso photo.

ENGAGED—Mr. and Mrs. Floyd Thurman of Portland, Ore., announce the engagement of their daughter, Miss Melba Gail Thurman, to Ensign W. Scott Nugent, U.S.N.R., son of Mr. and Mrs. William G. Nugent of 404 Seventh Avenue, Watervliet. Ensign Nugent was graduated from Watervliet High School and attended Rensselaer Polytechnic Institute. He just returned after a year's service in the Pacific.

Returning Soldier and Wife Must Become Reacquainted

BY DOROTHY DIX

Now that the soldiers are coming back from the war, a domestic problem has arisen to which no one knows the answer, and that is causing almost as many tears and heartbreak as the war itself.

For months and months, perhaps for years, GI Joe has kept up his morale by thinking of his wife and babies, or the girl he left behind him, and picturing the home he was going back to that would be filled with love and peace and contentment and from which he would never wish to stir.

And the wife and the sweetheart also lived in a castle of dreams. She was lonely, with no husband or boy friend to take her stepping. Often she had to live with uncongenial and critical inlaws. Life was a dull routine of hard work, of poor food and shabby clothes, of days when she toiled to exhaustion to keep from thinking and nights when she wet the pillow with her tears, and the only way she kept herself going was by picturing to herself the joy she would experience when Johnny came marching home.

Getting Re-acquainted.

Now Johnny is safely back and, oh, the pity of it, both he and the wife, or the sweetheart, are finding out one of life's bitterest truths, and that is that we cannot revive an old emotion or repeat an old thrill, or see things again from the same angle. We pass this way but once. We go on from where we are and we cannot retrace our steps.

The epidemic of divorces that is sweeping the country at the close of the war, as the epidemic of marriages swept it at the beginning of the war, is the result of the disappointment that men and women are finding in discovering that the husbands and wives they have been idealizing in their absence are just plain human beings in reality.

The husband sheds his romantic halo when he takes off his uniform. The wife is a tired, workworn woman instead of a glamour girl. The children are brats instead of little angels. The house isn't a mansion. It is just a shabby cottage.

Bitter Disillusion

So it is not surprising that the soldier's return is so often a bitter disillusion, and that he is bored and restless and irritable and that his wife complains that she doesn't know what to make of him, that he doesn't seem glad at all to be at home; that he criticizes the way she looks and shushes the children when they make any noise, and never seems to want to talk to anybody but the men who were in the Army with him.

Neither of them realize that it is the inevitable happening. It is the pain of a new birth that every husband and wife who have been separated long have to endure, for the old husband and the old wife are gone, never to return. They have to adjust themselves to new personalities, learn new charms to conjure with, new domestic pitfalls to avoid, and build up a new life together on a new foundation.

This will require a lot of intelligence. A lot of patience. But it will be far better than getting a divorce. What the postwar husband and wife are going to need more than anything else is to get acquainted with each other all over again.

(Released by Bell Syndicate, Inc.)

Clark-LaMarsh Nuptials Solemnized

The marriage of Miss Margaret Mary LaMarsh, daughter of Mr. and Mrs. George H. LaMarsh of this city to William Gray Clark, son of Mr. and Mrs. William S. Clark of Cohoes took place Nov. 24 in the rectory of St. Augustine's Church with Rev. Thomas J. Kelly, O. S. A., performing the ceremony.

Mrs. Frank J. Walker was the matron of honor and Joseph F. LaMarsh, brother of the bride, served as best man. The bride wore an afternoon dress of ice blue crepe with a black velvet hat and carried a Colonial bouquet of white flowers. Her attendant was attired in an afternoon dress of coral wool with a winter white hat and also carried a Colonial bouquet.

A reception for 100 guests followed at The Hendrick Hudson. The bride's mother was dressed in coral crepe and the mother of the bridegroom chose a light blue ensemble. During the reception, a program of music was furnished by Leon Nelson.

The bride is a graduate of Lansingburg High School and the Mildred Elley School in Albany. Prior to her marriage she was employed by the Covert Manufacturing Co., in Watervliet. The bridegroom, recently discharged from the service after serving with the 105th Infantry, is a graduate of Albany Academy. He is affiliated with the R. S. Clark & Son, printing firm in Cohoes.

The couple left on a wedding trip to Canada, Mrs. Clark traveling in a winter white suit with an Indian lamb fur coat with matching hat. Her corsage was of orchids.

Out-of-town guests were present from Saratoga, Schenectady, New Jersey and Endicott.

Green Island Girl To Wed Major DeCicco

Joseph H. Ingrato, of 40 George Street, Green Island, announces the engagement of his daughter, First Lt. Theresa Rita Ingrato, to Maj. Ralph E. De Cicco, Army Medical Corps, son of Mr. and Mrs. Ralph De Cicco of Des Moines, Ia.

The prospective bride, who is the daughter of the late Mrs. Angela Picarillo Ingrato, graduated from Troy High School, Pratt Institute, Brooklyn, and studied at the University of Maryland Hospital. She has served as administrative dietitian at Neoponset Hospital, L. I. She is now assigned as procurement officer in the station hospital of the Women's Army Corps at Des Moines, Ia.

Major De Cicco attended Drake University in Des Moines where he took his pre-medical course and graduated from Iowa University. He took a special course at the University of Michigan and interned at St. Elizabeth Hospital at Covington, Ky. He expects to resume his practice in Des Moines after the first of the year. Serving for four years in the Southwest Pacific, Major De Cicco is now on four months' terminal leave. The wedding will take place during December.

Elected to Societies

Miss Janet Hannon, daughter of Mr. and Mrs. Raymond J. Hannon of 9 Whitman Court and Miss Margaret L. Johnson, daughter of Mr. and Mrs. James F. Johnson of North Lake Avenue, students at Wellesley College, were recently elected to Tau Zeta Epsilon and Zeta Alpha respectively. These are two of Wellesley's six semi-social, semi-academic societies and the first is devoted to the study of art and music while the latter studies modern drama.

THE WEATHER
Tonight Fair cold

THE TIMES RECORD

FINAL
EDITION

SERIES 1945—NO. 300   (Entered as Second Class Matter at the Postoffice at Troy, N. Y., Under the Act of March 3, 1879.)   TROY, N. Y., FRIDAY EVENING, DECEMBER 21, 1945.   (Published Daily Except Sunday)   PRICE FOUR CENTS

GEN. GEORGE PATTON DIES

Boards May Inquire Into Company's Ability To Boost Wages

PANELS MAY NOT SUBPOENA BOOKS, DIRECTIVE SAYS

Decision in Oil Dispute Expected to Apply to Other Strikes

Washington (UP)—The administration today gave government fact-finding panels extensive authority to inquire into a company's ability to pay when recommending a wage increase for settlement of an industrial dispute.

The authority was granted in a directive to the oil industry fact-finding board for the Office of Price Administration and the Labor Department. The principles laid down will apply to other fact-finding boards.

The only limitation imposed was that a panel "ought not to recommend a wage increase which it believes will require the employer after six months to obtain price relief."

Under present government policy, employers may increase wages by any amount if they do not seek Office of Price Administration approval to raise prices. They are permitted, however, to make such application if, after six months trial, they find that such wage boosts have forced them into unprofitable operations.

No Power to Subpoena Books.

The directive gave the panels no power to subpoena books or to enforce their recommendations. It was drafted for the panel hearing the dispute over a demand by the Oil Workers Union (C.I.O.) for a 30 per cent wage rate increase from ten major oil refining companies.

It spelled out in detail the principles adopted by President Truman late yesterday. It was intended to apply to the panel in the General Motors Corp. strike and to the board to be appointed to hear the wage dispute between the U. S. Steel Corp. and United Steelworkers (C.I.O.)

After the statement was read and a recess taken, representatives of the oil companies and union agreed to an adjournment of the oil panel until Jan. 7 to permit resumption of collective bargaining between the companies and union at plant levels.

What Panel May Do.

The statement authorizes a panel:

1. To satisfy itself whether any increase it recommends is absorbable by an employer.

2. To inquire into profits and earnings position of the employer, and into the production and other costs, where relevant, as well as other data bearing on the issue of ability to pay.

3. To suggest to the administration administrator that existing standards for approval of wage or salary increases for price purposes be broadened. Under existing executive orders, the administrator is permitted to accept such recommendation and order it into effect as a government policy.

4. To consider wage increases permitted under existing executive orders as well as such other increases as the 30 per cent demanded by the oil workers and the United Automobile Workers.

If an employer fails to produce evidence on the ability to pay, the panel is free to draw such inferences as it may choose to draw from the employer's failure, the statement said.

General Motors Corp. and the United Automobile Workers (C. I. O.) agreed today to meet in Detroit next Wednesday to discuss local plant union demands.

(Continued on Page 18.)

THIRTY SEAMEN MISSING AFTER SHIP HITS MINES

Washington, (INS)—The United Nations Relief and Rehabilitation Administration disclosed today that thirty crewmen aboard the Liberty ship Nathaniel Bacon were reported missing after the vessel hit two mines off the Italian coast.

The ship, en route to Civitavecchia with UNRRA supplies from the United States, hit the mines after unloading cotton supplies at Genoa. Fire broke out and the crew abandoned ship.

PLAN SHOWS FOR JAPS.

Yokohama (UP)—The U. S. Eighth Army has taken over the Toho Theater and plans to inaugurate shows in January for morale purposes of the troops. The theater has a seating capacity of 2,730.

HOLIDAY SPECIAL

Ultra Clun Ale and Beer add to the festive board and produce hospitality. They're preferred by millions because of their champagne-like dry flavor.

3 Full Shopping Days
Before CHRISTMAS

Airborne Division to Parade in New York

New York. (INS)—Chairman Grover Whalen of the Mayor's Reception Committee announced today that 15,000 members of the 82nd (All-American) Airborne Division will march up Fifth Avenue Jan. 13 in the biggest victory parade since World War I.

Maj. Gen. James M. Gavin, 38, youngest division commander in the history of the Army, will lead the marchers. Discharged veterans of the division and wounded GIs will be given places of honor in a reviewing stand in front of the Metropolitan Museum.

DIXIE DEMOCRATS HINT OPEN BREAK WITH PRESIDENT

Truman's Stand on FEPC and Full Employment Causes Resentment

Washington. (AP)—President Truman's relations with Congress took on a new air of tension today, particularly among southern Democrats.

Some of the latter declared "an open break" now exists between the Chief Executive and themselves. They told a reporter they saw little hope for improvement in the situation when legislative work is resumed next year.

The note of discord was prompted by three White House developments yesterday as members began heading home for the holidays:

1. Mr. Truman's news conference assertion that he would express himself forcibly upon on legislation calling for returning of the U. S. Employment Service (USES) to the states within 100 days. Several congressmen interpreted this as meaning either a veto or another verbal blast at Congress is in the offing.

2. Release of letters to key lawmakers in which the President termed "unacceptable" a House substitute for the so-called "full employment" bill the Senate has passed.

After the statement was read and a recess taken, representatives of the oil companies and union agreed to an adjournment of the oil panel until Jan. 7 to permit resumption of collective bargaining.

(Continued on Page 18.)

U. S. MILITARY COURT DENIES PLEA TO FREE ACCUSED JAP GUARD

Yokohama. (AP)—A U. S. military commission trying "Little Glass Eye" Tatsuo Tsuchiya on charges of killing an American prisoner of war today denied a defense motion to acquit the former guard.

The commission refused also to dismiss the count on which the prosecution is basing its request for the death penalty.

Two other specifications filed against Tsuchiya were dismissed. They charged him with beating Lt. Col. Allan M. Cory of Tulsa, Okla., and of withholding and misusing Red Cross supplies. Hearsay evidence and lack of evidence brought the dismissals.

Allowed to stand was the charge that Tsuchiya beat to death Pfc. Robert Gordon Teas of Streator, Ill.

The defense moves followed completion of the prosecution's case earlier today.

GAS KILLS FAMILY OF FOUR AT PITTSBURG, PA.

Pittsburg, (INS)—A young father died today in a Pittsburg hospital of carbon monoxide poisoning only a few hours after his wife and two children succumbed in their gasfilled one-room apartment.

The dead were Harrison Woy, 30; Mrs. Alice Sutton Woy, 22; Judith, 30 months, and Harrison, jr., 8 months.

Woy died without learning of the deaths of his wife and children. Police said the monoxide gas apparently came from a small stove, the only source of heat in the apartment.

KILLED BY ICICLE

Buffalo (AP)—Edward Gamble, 50, Lackawanna, died last night shortly after his skull was fractured by a falling icicle near the Bethlehem Steel Co. plant where he was employed.

BIG THREE ENVOYS REPORTED MAKING SOME PROGRESS

Russia, Britain and U. S. Closer Together Due to Conferences

Moscow (AP)—The exploratory conversations of the foreign ministers of Britain, Russia and the United States appear to have brought the three countries closer together than they were before the meeting, informed foreign quarters said today.

Certain suspicions are believed to have a good chance of being dispelled, it was reported.

On the sixth day of the Big Three ministers' meeting and the 66th birthday of Generalissimo Stalin, this appeared to be the situation on the basis of reports from informed foreign quarters.

There is a strong feeling that some results will come from the meeting and these results may be better than originally expected, but every difference among the three is not likely to be settled at this meeting.

Byrnes and Bevin are believed anxious not to raise the hopes and expectations of the American and British people too much.

The foreign ministers of the Big Three have no desire or intention of dominating the United Nations organization or of bypassing it.

Four Peace Mediums.

However, Big Three collaboration was applauded during the war and considerable good can be accomplished through such collaboration. If the United Nations organization was expected to handle all matters there would be no need for the nations to have ambassadors and foreign ministers.

Four mediums exist for trying to settle the peace and build a world safe from war as well as for exchanging opinions among nations, it was pointed out. These are:

1. The United Nations Organization for long-range matters.

2. The Council of Foreign Ministers, whose job it is to draft the peace treaties. This is the council that met in London in September and October, but got nowhere.

3. The Big Three foreign ministers.

4. Diplomatic channels which are used daily.

It was suggested that no movement was afoot to dissolve the council of foreign ministers, which includes the foreign ministers of China and France as well as the Big Three. But it appeared that the United Nations Organization should commence to take over some of its functions before long.

May Meet in Washington.

This may mean that the council eventually will die out, while the Big Three foreign ministers may keep on handling problems of vital interest among the United States, Britain and Russia.

As a result of the current conference the Big Three foreign ministers probably will meet in Washington in the spring, as suggested by Secretary of State James F. Byrnes.

Stalin, tanned and rested after his long vacation, was reported to be spending the day at his desk.

(Continued on Page 18.)

MRS. CARLAN REUNITED WITH SON: Mrs. Rose Carlan, 23, embraces her 3-year-old son, James, jr., in her Chelsea, Mass., home after she was freed on bail following hearing on a murder charge in death of her 6 months' old son Ronald.

M'ARTHUR DENIES THREAT TO RESIGN

General Declares Tighe's Story Inaccurate

Tokyo (UP)—Gen. Douglas MacArthur denied today a radio report that he had threatened to resign if he was not "let alone" in Japan.

(An American Broadcasting Company broadcast from Tokyo yesterday reported that MacArthur had disagreed with the Soviets over which Japanese home island they should occupy and that he had notified the State Department he would quit if he was not let alone and if the Russians were allowed further participation in occupation affairs.)

He declared today that the question of Russian participation is "a matter for other decision than my own."

In a formal statement denying the radio broadcast report, he said: "The statement purported to have been made by Larry Tighe of the American Broadcasting Corporation has absolutely no basis in fact.

"For the second time in recent weeks, it becomes necessary for me to deny the allegation that I have threatened to resign.

"I am here to serve, not hinder or obstruct the American government in my full purpose to see the thing through. The question of Russian participation is a matter for other decision than my own.

"If Tighe made the statement he is alleged to have broadcast from Tokyo, someone must have been feeding him a funny type of 'hooch' being peddled around Tokyo on the black market."

(In a broadcast following MacArthur's denial, Tighe said:

("I received this information from a reliable and honest source, and I still consider it both reliable and honest.

("The word 'MacArthur' has come to be regarded as a word denoting authoritative statements from his headquarters rather than from him personally.

("I did not imply that the supreme commander, himself, indulged in name calling and recriminations with the Russians. However, I reaffirm the story which I previously broadcast that the express desire of the commander of this area is that Russian troops not be allowed to take over the Japanese island of Hokkaido.")

DIES IN CROSSING CRASH.

Canastota (AP)—George L. Wales, Canastota man, was killed yesterday when the New York Central's advance Empire struck his car at a crossing.

TIRE RATIONING TO END NEXT MONTH

Motorists Warned Supply Still Below Normal

Washington (AP)—Tire rationing ends Jan. 1 after four long years of thin treads, but it will be months before pent-up demand is met in full.

The decision of OPA and Civilian Production Administration to lift controls is based on their "considered option" that there no longer is any danger of a transportation breakdown.

Both agencies emphasized, however, that despite a big increase in tire production, all motorists will not be able to walk in and buy new casings for some time.

"A plentiful supply of tires is not in sight for several months, perhaps all of 1946," said CPA Administrator John D. Small.

OPA Chief Chester Bowles cautioned that "many motorists will have to wait for tires." He urged dealers not to sell complete sets to those who can get along with one or two tires during the next several months."

Sugar Alone on List.

Termination of tire rationing New Year's Day will leave only sugar on a ration list that once included meats, canned goods, gasoline, automobiles, shoes, fuel oil, coffee and several other commodities. No early end to sugar rationing is in sight.

All tire stocks were frozen the day after Pearl Harbor and rationing began Jan. 5, 1942, the first of the wartime controls on consumer purchases to go into effect. In announcing that tire output now warrants an end of the rationing program, Bowles said production currently is at the rate of about 4,000,000 casings a month and that approximately 1,000,000 will be made this quarter.

This means that production will total about 28,000,000 passenger tires, an increase of 64 per cent over 1944 output. Production next year is forecast at 66,000,000 passenger tires, or 13,000,000 more than ever were made before in this country in one year.

Truck Outlook Good.

The outlook for production of truck and bus tires was described as even brighter than for passenger tires.

The issuing certificates in the hands of motorists will continue to be honored by dealers through Dec. 31, but no new certificates will be issued after today except in emergency cases.

CPA announced that "in order to increase the number of tires available in the immediate future," several non-rationing restrictions will remain in effect.

New cars still will come from the factory without a spare tire and white sidewall tires will continue to be banned because "this is an added manufacturing job."

Tire export restrictions will be maintained, too.

KIMMEL FAILED TO OBEY ORDERS, TURNER DECLARES

Admiral Says Pearl Harbor Losses Could Have Been Cut Materially

Washington (AP)—Admr. R. K. Turner asserted today that Admr. Husband E. Kimmel did not comply with "entirely clear" orders and expressed the opinion that if Kimmel had done so losses at Pearl Harbor would have been cut "materially."

Turner also told a Senate-House committee investigating the Dec. 7, 1941, disaster that the Pacific Fleet under Kimmel had been prepared for "just such an attack" and was "ready for war."

The Navy Department, Turner said, had given Kimmel "perfectly specific and entirely clear" orders to take the necessary measures against a Japanese attack.

"Did Kimmel comply, in your opinion?" asked Vice Chairman Cooper (D.-Tenn.).

"He did not, in my opinion," said Turner.

Turner, as chief of the Navy War Plans Division had prepared a Nov. 27, 1941, "war warning" message for Pacific commanders.

If Kimmel had complied, pursued Cooper, "would the disastrous effects not have occurred or have been materially reduced?"

"I think they would have been materially reduced," Turner replied, "and there was a good chance that could have inflicted considerable damage on the Japanese fleet."

"We know now from experience," Turner added, "that a carrier based attack is difficult to stop, and a considerable portion of the attack might have gotten in. But it could have been broken up and we have had considerably less effect."

"Even if only a considerable portion of our fighters had been in the air x x x I believe the Japanese attack would have been much less in its results."

Also, Turner noted, there were some land-based bombers available to the defenders of Pearl Harbor.

Turner upheld his warning message of Nov. 27 as entirely adequate. He said it was not necessary to send anything additional to Kimmel.

Turner said he had had "the utmost respect for his (Kimmel's) ability" and added that he believed this estimate of Kimmel was shared throughout the Navy.

U. S. GOVERNMENT PLANS EGG PRICE SUPPORT PROGRAM

Agriculture Department Fears Market Will Be Glutted by Next Spring

Washington (UP)—The Agriculture Department soon will announce a 1946 egg price support program which may cost the government $200,000,000, it was learned today.

Even though eggs are scarce at the moment, the department fears production next year may be 600,000,000 more dozens than consumers will be willing to buy. The worst market glut is anticipated between early March and June.

If this large surplus materialized it could bring a price collapse worse than two years ago when eggs sold for as little as 12 cents a dozen.

The government will seek to prevent that. It is committed by law to support prices at the farm level at 90 per cent of parity, or about 29 cents, according to the department's latest estimate.

The price support program will be designed to give farmers this return of 29 cents a dozen—but as a national average, not individually. For instance, farmers in the Midwest will be guaranteed only an average of 27 cents a dozen, and then only if the eggs they offered meet department standards.

Eggs in the big city markets on the East and West Coasts are expected to bring higher prices to pull the national average up to support levels. The central states produce 60 per cent of the nation's supply and their prices historically lag about two cents behind coastal areas.

Price support will be carried out, chiefly, by channelling the surplus into egg-drying plants. To seal dried egg powder to the government, dryers must certify they have paid at least support prices. The department plans to sell most of the dried eggs overseas to the United Nations Relief and Rehabilitation Administration and to European governments with ready cash or United States loans.

The government plans to buy fresh eggs only to relieve any spot market glut.

The department does not expect to lose all of the $200,000,000 it may have to invest in support measures. Whatever it can get back in foreign sales will help offset the deficit.

PRESIDENT CALLS FOR MEETING ON TRAFFIC SAFETY NEXT SPRING

Washington (AP)—President Truman, expressing deep concern over an increase in traffic accidents, has asked Maj. Gen. Philip B. Fleming, Federal Works Administrator, to head a White House safety conference next spring.

Representatives of states, municipalities and national organizations interested in traffic safety will be invited.

The White House said today that information supplied the President shows that traffic fatalities in the nation totaled 2,510 in August, the month in which gasoline rationing ended. This was 30 per cent higher than the corresponding month a year ago.

The total was 2,839 deaths in September, a 40 per cent increase over September, 1944, and 3,440 in October, a 53 per cent increase over October, 1944.

November figures are not yet available, but it was said preliminary reports indicated the sharp upward trend in fatal accidents continued.

FIVE NAVY FLYERS SAFE AFTER SHANTUNG CRASH

Tsingtao, (INS)—Five Navy flyers whose planes crashed early in December in the Shantung area were safe in Tsingtao today with the report they were well-treated by Chinese Communists.

Three other flyers downed in the area are believed still alive while seven are believed dead.

FAMOUS LEADER OF U.S. THIRD ARMY EXPIRES IN REICH

Fighting Heart Weakened from Effect of Pulmonary Complications

Heidelberg, Germany (AP)—Gen. George S. Patton, jr., who led the victorious U. S. Third Army from the beaches of Normandy into Czechoslovakia, died at 5:50 p. m. (11:50 a. m. Eastern Standard Time) today a dozen days after his neck was broken in a traffic accident.

The general's stout old fighting heart weakened during the day from effects of pulmonary complications which had beset his apparent recovery from the broken neck and partial paralysis.

Mrs. Patton was with him.

The announcement of the General's death was made by Brig. Gen. John M. Willen of the U. S. Seventh Army.

The General was 60 last Nov. 11.

He was commander of the U. S. 15th Army at the time of his death. He had served briefly as acting commander of all American forces in the European theater a few days before his automobile and an Army truck collided near Mannheim on Sunday, Dec. 9.

The official announcement said:

"General Patton died at 5:50 tonight, it was announced by Brig. Gen John M. Willen, chief of staff of the Seventh Army. The General died peacefully."

Patton himself, when his condition was critical after the motor car accident, described it as "a hell of a way to die."

Heidelberg, an old university town, was one of the thousands of places which the Third Army captured in its rough ride over Germany.

By an ironic twist, Patton had gone unscratched through all his campaigns of the war. The peacetime accident left him paralyzed from the shoulders down.

Gen. Joseph T. McNarney, U. S. commander in the European theater, commented that it was his "painful duty to announce the death of a great fighter and a great man.

"His injuries were grave, but his fight to overcome them was gallant. He went down fighting. Patton could have died in no other way. And now, for us over here and all who applauded his bravery, there is a sudden empty feeling.

"He brought to us a large part of our magnificent victory and this, too, well known to need description, belongs to history."

The expert at armored warfare campaigned brilliantly in Africa, Sicily, France, Belgium, Germany, Austria and Czechoslovakia in Allied drives that staggered Germany to her knees last spring and has been making an amazing recovery until yesterday.

Heart Became Affected.

It was then that the respiratory condition developed. By morning today, doctors were gravely worried about the deterioration in his condition. As Patton's life ebbed away, his heart became affected.

Shortly before his death, Maj. Gen. A. W. Kenner, chief of Army surgeons in Europe, left European headquarters in Frankfurt for Patton's bedside.

Warrior For 30 Years.

Gen. George Smith Patton, jr., warrior for more than 30 years, poet with the tongue of a mule-skinner, elegant disciplinarian of the "spit-and-polish" school, was a legend long before his spectacular job done in Europe.

His job was war and he did it with a skill that often amazed his colleagues. But as a diplomat the hell-for-leather cavalryman who brought tank warfare to a peak of perfection failed completely. He was constantly in hot water.

The story of Patton in World War II is the story of a fighting series of Allied victories from Africa through France and Germany to Austria and Czechoslovakia.

The Patton legend flowered on the African campaign, when the strong, running tankman, the pearl-handled six-shooters swinging from his hips, led American forces to the conquest of Tunisia.

In showman Patton, danger was the privilege of an officer, and he was constantly at the front.

"Attack And Attack."

His doctrine was expressed pithily: "We shall attack and attack until we are exhausted, and then we shall attack again."

He carried out this doctrine with spectacular success in Europe.

(Continued on Page 18.)

GEN. GEORGE S. PATTON

FIVE NAVY FLYERS SAFE AFTER SHANTUNG CRASH

Plan Christmas Parties For U.S. Troops Stranded In West

San Francisco (AP)—"It's the same old Army," said Cpl. A. L. Holsman, of Long Island, N. Y. "Hurry up and wait."

Holsman was one of nearly 100,000 veterans from the Pacific who today appeared likely to be stranded at West Coast ports on Christmas Day because of lack of transportation.

Nearly 120,000 veterans were stymied at the ports today, and ships were scheduled to dump an additional 15,000 more daily on the harassed Army and Navy transportation officials, a far larger number than they expected to have transportation for.

"We had hopes of getting home by Christmas," said Pfc. Julius T. Brenner, of Hudson, N. Y. "Nobody promised us we would. I've been overseas only 25 months. Lots of these fellows have been over a lot longer."

Men required to stay aboard ship—there were four "floating barracks" here today—were given an information sheet explaining the reason for the delay. The paper also listed entertainment and sight-seeing opportunities in San Francisco.

"Sure, this is good," said Sgt. Louis Jaffe of New York City, a ship-bound veteran of twenty months in the Western Pacific. "No mud, no filth, no duties—but it isn't home."

"Our 'operation Santa Claus' (the name the Army gave its plan for handling returning veterans) has been too successful. We've brought back more than the railroads can handle."

At Los Angeles, a huge theater on the docks was being readied for a Christmas Day show for harbor-bound men. An estimated 15,000 men were still aboard ships last night. At Santa Ana staging areas mess sergeants were flown in from other bases to help feed the troops, and German prisoners of war used as kitchen police.

Portland, Tacoma and Seattle also had huge backlogs of servicemen.

Navy authorities at San Francisco were liberal with leave passes. Sight-seeing tours were organized, put port officers planned Christmas parties with Red Cross bags of gifts. A jitter-bugging Santa Claus was planned for the entertainment group aboard the port's welcoming vessel.

Two local papers (Examiner and Call-Bulletin) urged their readers to invite servicemen into their homes during the holidays.

With more than 81,000 unhappy servicemen on their hands, Army

90,000 Veterans Under Treatment

Washington (AP)—More veterans will spend this Christmas in hospital beds than ever before in American history and the capacity for caring for them has reached a near crisis.

Maj. Gen. Paul R. Hawley, chief surgeon general of the Veterans' Administration, told a reporter today there are approximately 90,000 veterans, of all wars, under treatment in hospitals or at home.

The peak of World War I veterans is expected within a year or two. The peak of World War II will not be reached until 1975, experts have predicted. They say as many as 250,000 veterans may become patients.

Meanwhile the influx of patients at veterans hospitals sets new records daily with barely enough doctors, nurses and other attendants available to attend them.

Administrator, said the Veterans Administration Medical Reorganization Bill, now awaiting the President's signature, may help in staffing an additional 4,500 beds in veteran hospitals.

The Veterans Administration soon will take over seven Army hospitals, five of them on a temporary basis, with 6,000 beds, but more doctors are needed.

Forty-eight new hospitals have been requested, in a long term expansion program.

Of the 90,000 veterans now being treated, about one-third are World War II soldiers. They are being admitted at the rate of about 1,000 per month, slightly more than one-half of all the veterans applying for care.

Veterans' Administration officials are attempting to obtain more space in hospitals, but the peak of patient load is yet to come. Gen. Omar N. Bradley, Veterans